HEALTH CARE STATE RANKINGS
2000

Health Care in the 50 United States

Kathleen O'Leary Morgan and Scott Morgan, Editors

MORGAN QUITNO

Morgan Quitno Press
© Copyright 2000, All Rights Reserved

512 East 9th Street, P.O. Box 1656
Lawrence, KS 66044-8656
USA
800-457-0742 or 785-841-3534
www.morganquitno.com
Eighth Edition

© Copyright 2000 by
Morgan Quitno Corporation
512 East 9th Street, P.O. Box 1656
Lawrence, Kansas 66044-8656

800-457-0742 or 785-841-3534
www.morganquitno.com

ISBN: 0-7401-0001-7
ISSN: 1065-1403

Health Care State Rankings 2000 sells for $52.95 ($5.00 shipping) and is only available in paper binding. For those who prefer ranking information tailored to a particular state, we also offer Health Care State Perspectives, state-specific reports for each of the 50 states. These individual guides provide information on a state's data and rank for each of the categories featured in the national Health Care State Rankings volume. Perspectives sell for $19.00 or $9.50 if ordered with Health Care State Rankings. If crime statistics are your interest, please ask about our annual Crime State Rankings ($52.95 paper). If you are interested in city and metropolitan crime data, we offer City Crime Rankings ($39.95 paper). For a general view of the states, please ask about our annual State Rankings reference book ($52.95 paper). All of our data sets are also available in machine readable format. Shipping and handling is $5.00 per order.

Eighth Edition
Printed in the United States of America
April 2000

PREFACE

Health care continues to be a hot topic in the United States. Health insurance coverage, access to primary care physicians, cancer and disease rates are topics that affect every American. This newly-revised edition of *Health Care State Rankings* provides a huge collection of state health care statistics on these and hundreds of other health care-related issues. This eighth edition compares states in births and reproductive health, deaths, disease, insurance and finance, health care providers, facilities and physical fitness. In all, more than 500 tables of state comparisons give you all the information you need for virtually every aspect of health care in the 50 United States.

Important Notes About *Health Care State Rankings 2000*

Health Care State Rankings 2000 is the annual product of our ongoing search for essential state health care data. Information from both government and private sector sources are featured in this user-friendly volume. The vast majority of tables have been updated from last year, a few are brand new, while others were deleted. However, in some cases updated information is not available and tables are repeated. Unfortunately, once again the finance chapter has a number of repeat tables. The Health Care Financing Administration has not yet issued updates of its state estimates of health care expenditures (1993 are the latest available). While we await the revised state numbers, we have provided a table showing national health care expenditures for 1998 (see page 245.)

While you may find several changes in this revised edition, we have made sure to retain many of the book's popular features. These include source information and other pertinent footnotes clearly shown at the bottom of each page and national totals, rates and percentages prominently displayed at the top of each table. Every other line is shaded in gray for easier reading. In addition, numerous information finding tools are provided: a thorough table of contents, table listings at the beginning of each chapter, a roster of sources with addresses and phone numbers, a detailed index and a chapter thumb index.

As in all of our reference books, the numbers shown in *Health Care State Rankings* require no additional calculations to convert them from millions, thousands, etc. All states are ranked on a high to low basis, with any ties among the states listed alphabetically for a given ranking. Negative numbers are shown in parentheses "( )." For tables with national totals (as opposed to rates, per capita's, etc.) a separate column is included showing what percent of the national total each individual state's total represents. This column is headed by "% of USA." This percentage figure is particularly interesting when compared with a state's share of the nation's population for a particular year (provided in an appendix).

If you need information for just one state, check out our *Health Care State Perspective* series of publications.

These 21-page comb bound reports feature data and ranking information for an individual state, as reported in *Health Care State Rankings 2000*. (For example *California Health Care in Perspective* features information about the state of California only.) They serve as handy, quick reference guides for those who do not want to page through the entire *Health Care State Rankings* volume searching for information for their particular state. When purchased by themselves, *Health Care State Perspectives* sell for $19. When purchased with a copy of *Health Care State Rankings*, these handy quick reference guides are just $9.50. For additional information, please call us toll-free at 1-800-457-0742.

Other Books From Morgan Quitno Press

In addition to *Health Care State Rankings*, our company offers three other rankings reference books. The first of these, *State Rankings*, provides a general view of the states. Statistics for a wide variety of categories are featured, including agriculture, transportation, government finance, health, population, crime, education, social welfare, energy and environment. Our annual compilation of state crime data is presented in *Crime State Rankings*. This reference volume offers a huge collection of user friendly statistics on law enforcement personnel and expenditures, corrections, arrests and offenses. If city and metro area crime are your interest, *City Crime Rankings* compares crime in all metropolitan areas and cities of 75,000 or more population (approx. 300 cities). Numbers of crimes, crime rates, changes in crime rates over one and five years are presented for all major crime categories reported by the FBI. Final 1998 crime data are featured.

City Crime Rankings sells for $39.95. The *State Rankings* and *Crime State Rankings* books each are available for $52.95. (paper; S/H $5 per order). For true data aficionados, the information in our books also is available on diskette (PC format dbf, ASCII or Excel). This electronic format allows you to import our data into your computer program for tailor-made analyses.

The newest member of the Morgan Quitno family of publications is *State Statistical Trends,* a monthly journal that examines changes in life and government for the 50 United States. Each 100-page monthly issue focuses on a different subject and provides a collection of tables, graphics and commentary showing state multi-year trends. For further information about *Trends* or any of our other publications, please call us toll-free at 1-800-457-0742 or check out our web site at www.morganquitno.com.

Finally, we would like to extend a "thank you" to the librarians, government and health care industry officials who help us each year with the development, design and production of this book. Your guidance is invaluable. Thanks also to you, our readers. Please don't hesitate to keep those comments and suggestions coming our way.

- THE EDITORS

WHICH STATE IS HEALTHIEST?

Waiting patiently in the top ten for the last several years, New Hampshire this year surged to number one as our 2000 Healthiest State. Having last won in 1995, New Hampshire put together a particularly strong showing to jump from fourth all the way to the top. Last year's winner, Minnesota, dropped to third. At the opposite end of the scale, Mississippi comes in as the least healthy state, pushing Louisiana back up to 49th.

Each year we take a step back from our objective reporting of health statistics, throw some basic figures into our computer and determine which is the Healthiest State. While we never claim our findings are indisputable, we do believe they provide an interesting statistical match-up of how the states are doing with regard to health care.

Methodology

The Healthiest State designation is awarded based on 21 factors chosen from the year 2000 edition of our annual reference book, *Health Care State Rankings*. These factors reflect access to health care

2000 HEALTHIEST STATE AWARD

RANK	STATE	SUM	'99	RANK	STATE	SUM	'99
1	New Hampshire	18.66	4	26	Illinois	2.17	30
2	Vermont	16.64	3	27	Arizona	1.26	35
3	Minnesota	15.85	1	28	Maryland	1.05	25
4	Hawaii	14.53	2	29	Oklahoma	0.94	31
5	Utah	13.52	10	30	Pennsylvania	(0.30)	22
6	Maine	12.84	7	31	Michigan	(0.40)	33
7	Washington	12.02	10	32	Montana	(1.15)	12
8	Massachusetts	10.44	8	33	Kentucky	(1.67)	37
9	Connecticut	9.34	20	34	North Carolina	(3.63)	32
10	Nebraska	9.17	5	35	West Virginia	(3.72)	36
11	Kansas	8.46	8	36	Missouri	(4.17)	38
12	Colorado	8.12	24	37	Delaware	(4.30)	40
13	Rhode Island	7.76	21	38	South Dakota	(5.25)	27
14	Oregon	7.75	17	39	New Mexico	(6.07)	44
15	Iowa	7.50	6	40	Tennessee	(6.72)	39
16	Virginia	6.64	16	41	Texas	(6.73)	41
17	New Jersey	6.44	23	42	New York	(7.19)	43
18	Alaska	5.57	28	43	Florida	(7.52)	42
19	California	5.53	19	44	Arkansas	(8.46)	45
20	Idaho	4.93	29	45	Georgia	(9.33)	34
21	Ohio	4.92	18	46	Nevada	(9.91)	47
22	Wisconsin	4.64	15	47	South Carolina	(14.42)	46
23	North Dakota	3.53	13	48	Alabama	(16.15)	48
23	Wyoming	3.53	14	49	Louisiana	(23.84)	50
25	Indiana	3.41	26	50	Mississippi	(26.42)	49

providers, affordability of health care and a generally healthy population (see box below.) The same 21 factors considered for last year's award were measured for this year. The 21 factors were divided into two groups: those that are "negative" for which a high ranking would be considered bad for a state, and those that are "positive" for which a high ranking would be considered good for a state. Rates for each of the 21 factors were processed through a formula that measures how a state compares to the national average for a given category. The positive and negative nature of each factor was taken into account as part of the formula. Once these computations were made, the factors then were weighted (factors were weighted equally.) These weighted scores were then added together to get a state's final score ("SUM" on the table above.) This way, states are assessed based on how they stack up against the national average. The end result is that the farther below the national average a state's health ranking is, the lower (and less healthy) it ranks. The farther above the national average, the higher (and healthier) a state ranks. This same methodology was used for our Dangerous State and Safest/Dangerous City Awards.

The table above shows how each state fared in the 2000 Healthiest State Award as well as its placement in 1999. Cheers and continued good health to the citizens of New Hampshire!

THE EDITORS

POSITIVE (+) AND NEGATIVE (-) FACTORS CONSIDERED:
1. Births of Low Birthweight as a Percent of All Births (Table 15) -
2. Births to Teenage Mothers as a Percent of Live Births (Table 30) -
3. Percent of Mothers Receiving Late or No Prenatal Care (Table 56) -
4. Age-Adjusted Death Rate (Table 79) -
5. Infant Mortality Rate (Table 86) -
6. Age-Adjusted Death Rate by Malignant Neoplasms (Table 154) -
7. Age-Adjusted Death Rate by Suicide (Table 178) -
8. Health Care Expenditures as a Percent of Gross State Product (Table 247) -
9. Per Capita Personal Health Expenditures (Table 248) -
10. Percent of Population Not Covered by Health Insurance (Table 293) -
11. Estimated Rate of New Cancer Cases (Table 354) -
12. AIDS Rate (Table 376) -
13. Sexually Transmitted Disease Rate (Table 409) -
14. Percent of Population Lacking Access to Primary Care (Table 438) -
15. Percent of Adults Who Are Binge Drinkers (Table 501) -
16. Percent of Adults Who Smoke (Table 502) -
17. Percent of Adults Overweight (Table 506) -
18. Number of Days in Past Month When Physical Health was "Not Good" (Table 507) -
19. Beds in Community Hospitals per 100,000 Population (Table 207) +
20. Percent of Children Aged 19-35 Months Fully Immunized (Table 407) +
21. Safety Belt Usage Rate (Table 511) +

TABLE OF CONTENTS

I. Births and Reproductive Health

TABLE OF CONTENTS (continued)

Abortions

II. Deaths

TABLE OF CONTENTS (continued)

TABLE OF CONTENTS (continued)

III. Facilities

TABLE OF CONTENTS (continued)

TABLE OF CONTENTS (continued)

TABLE OF CONTENTS (continued)

V. Incidence of Disease

TABLE OF CONTENTS (continued)

TABLE OF CONTENTS (continued)

VII. Physical Fitness

VIII. Appendix

IX. Sources

X. Index

I. BIRTHS AND REPRODUCTIVE HEALTH

1   Births in 1998
2   Birth Rate in 1998
3   Births in 1997
4   Birth Rate in 1997
5   Births in 1990
6   Birth Rate in 1990
7   Births in 1980
8   Birth Rate in 1980
9   Fertility Rate in 1998
10 Births to White Women in 1998
11 White Births as a Percent of All Births in 1998
12 Births to Black Women in 1998
13 Black Births as a Percent of All Births in 1998
14 Births of Low Birthweight in 1998
15 Births of Low Birthweight as a Percent of All Births in 1998
16 Births of Low Birthweight of White Women in 1998
17 Births of Low Birthweight to White Women as a Percent of All Births to White Women in 1998
18 Births of Low Birthweight to Black Women in 1998
19 Births of Low Birthweight to Black Women as a Percent of All Births to Black Women in 1998
20 Births to Unmarried Women in 1998
21 Births to Unmarried Women as a Percent of All Births in 1998
22 Births to Unmarried White Women in 1998
23 Births to Unmarried White Women as a Percent of All Births to White Women in 1998
24 Births to Unmarried Black Women in 1998
25 Births to Unmarried Black Women as a Percent of All Births to Black Women in 1998
26 Births to Teenage Mothers in 1998
27 Percent of Births to Teenage Mothers in 1998
28 Births to Teenage Mothers in 1997
29 Teenage Birth Rate in 1997
30 Births to Teenage Mothers as a Percent of Live Births in 1997
31 Births to White Teenage Mothers in 1997
32 Births to White Teenage Mothers as a Percent of White Births in 1997
33 Births to Black Teenage Mothers in 1997
34 Births to Black Teenage Mothers as a Percent of Black Births in 1997
35 Pregnancy Rate for 15 to 19 Year Old Women in 1996
36 Percent Change in Pregnancy Rate for 15 to 19 Year Old Women: 1992 to 1996
37 Births to Teenage Mothers in 1990
38 Teenage Birth Rate in 1990
39 Percent Change in Teenage Birth Rate: 1990 to 1997
40 Births to Teenage Mothers in 1980
41 Teenage Birth Rate in 1980
42 Births to Women 35 to 49 Years Old in 1997
43 Births to Women 35 to 49 Years Old as a Percent of All Births in 1997
44 Multiple Birth Rate in 1997
45 Percent Change in Multiple Birth Rate: 1993 to 1997
46 Births by Vaginal Delivery in 1997
47 Percent of Births by Vaginal Delivery in 1997
48 Births by Cesarean Delivery in 1997
49 Percent of Births by Cesarean Delivery in 1997
50 Percent Change in Rate of Cesarean Births: 1993 to 1997
51 Births by Vaginal Delivery After a Previous Cesarean Delivery (VBAC) in 1997
52 Percent of Vaginal Births After a Cesarean (VBAC) in 1997
53 Percent of Mothers Beginning Prenatal Care in First Trimester in 1998
54 Percent of White Mothers Beginning Prenatal Care in First Trimester in 1998
55 Percent of Black Mothers Beginning Prenatal Care in First Trimester in 1998
56 Percent of Mothers Receiving Latc or No Prenatal Care in 1997
57 Percent of White Mother Receiving Late or No Prenatal Care in 1997
58 Percent of Black Mothers Receiving Late or No Prenatal Care in 1997
59 Percent of Births Attended by Midwives in 1997

I. BIRTHS AND REPRODUCTIVE HEALTH (CONTINUED)

Abortions

Births in 1998

National Total = 3,946,000 Live Births*

ALPHA ORDER

RANK ORDER

RANK	STATE	BIRTHS	% of USA		RANK	STATE	BIRTHS	% of USA
23	Alabama	62,306	1.6%		1	California	542,476	13.7%
44	Alaska	10,898	0.3%		2	Texas	346,400	8.8%
18	Arizona	75,415	1.9%		3	New York	249,069	6.3%
33	Arkansas	37,099	0.9%		4	Florida	195,543	5.0%
1	California	542,476	13.7%		5	Illinois	181,464	4.6%
24	Colorado	59,789	1.5%		6	Ohio	151,289	3.8%
30	Connecticut	42,675	1.1%		7	Pennsylvania	144,959	3.7%
47	Delaware	10,298	0.3%		8	Michigan	133,262	3.4%
4	Florida	195,543	5.0%		9	Georgia	122,618	3.1%
9	Georgia	122,618	3.1%		10	New Jersey	116,860	3.0%
40	Hawaii	17,204	0.4%		11	North Carolina	108,166	2.7%
39	Idaho	19,464	0.5%		12	Virginia	95,641	2.4%
5	Illinois	181,464	4.6%		13	Massachusetts	88,719	2.2%
15	Indiana	78,525	2.0%		14	Washington	80,612	2.0%
34	Iowa	35,648	0.9%		15	Indiana	78,525	2.0%
32	Kansas	37,432	0.9%		16	Missouri	75,486	1.9%
25	Kentucky	54,976	1.4%		17	Tennessee	75,447	1.9%
21	Louisiana	66,172	1.7%		18	Arizona	75,415	1.9%
41	Maine	13,841	0.4%		19	Maryland	70,576	1.8%
19	Maryland	70,576	1.8%		20	Wisconsin	67,391	1.7%
13	Massachusetts	88,719	2.2%		21	Louisiana	66,172	1.7%
8	Michigan	133,262	3.4%		22	Minnesota	64,998	1.6%
22	Minnesota	64,998	1.6%		23	Alabama	62,306	1.6%
31	Mississippi	40,013	1.0%		24	Colorado	59,789	1.5%
16	Missouri	75,486	1.9%		25	Kentucky	54,976	1.4%
45	Montana	10,430	0.3%		26	South Carolina	53,442	1.4%
37	Nebraska	23,112	0.6%		27	Oklahoma	50,978	1.3%
36	Nevada	27,508	0.7%		28	Utah	45,744	1.2%
42	New Hampshire	13,472	0.3%		29	Oregon	44,362	1.1%
10	New Jersey	116,860	3.0%		30	Connecticut	42,675	1.1%
35	New Mexico	27,838	0.7%		31	Mississippi	40,013	1.0%
3	New York	249,069	6.3%		32	Kansas	37,432	0.9%
11	North Carolina	108,166	2.7%		33	Arkansas	37,099	0.9%
48	North Dakota	8,081	0.2%		34	Iowa	35,648	0.9%
6	Ohio	151,289	3.8%		35	New Mexico	27,838	0.7%
27	Oklahoma	50,978	1.3%		36	Nevada	27,508	0.7%
29	Oregon	44,362	1.1%		37	Nebraska	23,112	0.6%
7	Pennsylvania	144,959	3.7%		38	West Virginia	21,714	0.6%
43	Rhode Island	12,442	0.3%		39	Idaho	19,464	0.5%
26	South Carolina	53,442	1.4%		40	Hawaii	17,204	0.4%
46	South Dakota	10,299	0.3%		41	Maine	13,841	0.4%
17	Tennessee	75,447	1.9%		42	New Hampshire	13,472	0.3%
2	Texas	346,400	8.8%		43	Rhode Island	12,442	0.3%
28	Utah	45,744	1.2%		44	Alaska	10,898	0.3%
50	Vermont	6,286	0.2%		45	Montana	10,430	0.3%
12	Virginia	95,641	2.4%		46	South Dakota	10,299	0.3%
14	Washington	80,612	2.0%		47	Delaware	10,298	0.3%
38	West Virginia	21,714	0.6%		48	North Dakota	8,081	0.2%
20	Wisconsin	67,391	1.7%		49	Wyoming	6,363	0.2%
49	Wyoming	6,363	0.2%		50	Vermont	6,286	0.2%
						District of Columbia	8,373	0.2%

Source: U.S. Department of Health and Human Services, National Center for Health Statistics
    "National Vital Statistics Reports" (Vol. 47, No. 21, July 6, 1999)
*Data are preliminary estimates by state of residence.

Birth Rate in 1998

National Rate = 14.6 Live Births per 1,000 Population*

ALPHA ORDER

RANK	STATE	RATE
19	Alabama	14.3
2	Alaska	17.7
5	Arizona	16.2
14	Arkansas	14.6
4	California	16.6
11	Colorado	15.1
40	Connecticut	13.0
30	Delaware	13.8
39	Florida	13.1
6	Georgia	16.0
16	Hawaii	14.4
8	Idaho	15.8
11	Illinois	15.1
37	Indiana	13.3
44	Iowa	12.5
21	Kansas	14.2
24	Kentucky	14.0
11	Louisiana	15.1
49	Maine	11.1
32	Maryland	13.7
16	Massachusetts	14.4
34	Michigan	13.6
30	Minnesota	13.8
15	Mississippi	14.5
26	Missouri	13.9
47	Montana	11.8
26	Nebraska	13.9
9	Nevada	15.7
48	New Hampshire	11.4
16	New Jersey	14.4
6	New Mexico	16.0
32	New York	13.7
19	North Carolina	14.3
42	North Dakota	12.7
35	Ohio	13.5
10	Oklahoma	15.2
35	Oregon	13.5
45	Pennsylvania	12.1
43	Rhode Island	12.6
26	South Carolina	13.9
24	South Dakota	14.0
26	Tennessee	13.9
3	Texas	17.5
1	Utah	21.8
50	Vermont	10.6
23	Virginia	14.1
21	Washington	14.2
46	West Virginia	12.0
41	Wisconsin	12.9
38	Wyoming	13.2

RANK ORDER

RANK	STATE	RATE
1	Utah	21.8
2	Alaska	17.7
3	Texas	17.5
4	California	16.6
5	Arizona	16.2
6	Georgia	16.0
6	New Mexico	16.0
8	Idaho	15.8
9	Nevada	15.7
10	Oklahoma	15.2
11	Colorado	15.1
11	Illinois	15.1
11	Louisiana	15.1
14	Arkansas	14.6
15	Mississippi	14.5
16	Hawaii	14.4
16	Massachusetts	14.4
16	New Jersey	14.4
19	Alabama	14.3
19	North Carolina	14.3
21	Kansas	14.2
21	Washington	14.2
23	Virginia	14.1
24	Kentucky	14.0
24	South Dakota	14.0
26	Missouri	13.9
26	Nebraska	13.9
26	South Carolina	13.9
26	Tennessee	13.9
30	Delaware	13.8
30	Minnesota	13.8
32	Maryland	13.7
32	New York	13.7
34	Michigan	13.6
35	Ohio	13.5
35	Oregon	13.5
37	Indiana	13.3
38	Wyoming	13.2
39	Florida	13.1
40	Connecticut	13.0
41	Wisconsin	12.9
42	North Dakota	12.7
43	Rhode Island	12.6
44	Iowa	12.5
45	Pennsylvania	12.1
46	West Virginia	12.0
47	Montana	11.8
48	New Hampshire	11.4
49	Maine	11.1
50	Vermont	10.6
	District of Columbia	16.0

Source: Morgan Quitno Press using data from U.S. Dept. of Health and Human Services, Nat'l Center for Health Statistics "National Vital Statistics Reports" (Vol. 47, No. 21, July 6, 1999)
*Data are preliminary estimates by state of residence.

Births in 1997

National Total = 3,880,894 Live Births*

ALPHA ORDER

RANK	STATE	BIRTHS	% of USA
23	Alabama	60,914	1.6%
47	Alaska	9,947	0.3%
16	Arizona	75,699	2.0%
34	Arkansas	36,478	0.9%
1	California	524,840	13.5%
24	Colorado	56,533	1.5%
29	Connecticut	43,109	1.1%
45	Delaware	10,253	0.3%
4	Florida	192,383	5.0%
9	Georgia	118,221	3.0%
40	Hawaii	17,393	0.4%
39	Idaho	18,582	0.5%
5	Illinois	180,803	4.7%
13	Indiana	83,436	2.1%
33	Iowa	36,659	0.9%
32	Kansas	37,289	1.0%
25	Kentucky	53,203	1.4%
21	Louisiana	66,025	1.7%
42	Maine	13,669	0.4%
19	Maryland	70,215	1.8%
14	Massachusetts	80,364	2.1%
8	Michigan	133,714	3.4%
22	Minnesota	64,499	1.7%
31	Mississippi	41,533	1.1%
18	Missouri	74,037	1.9%
44	Montana	10,849	0.3%
37	Nebraska	23,319	0.6%
35	Nevada	26,911	0.7%
41	New Hampshire	14,313	0.4%
10	New Jersey	113,279	2.9%
36	New Mexico	26,871	0.7%
3	New York	257,238	6.6%
11	North Carolina	107,015	2.8%
48	North Dakota	8,353	0.2%
6	Ohio	152,033	3.9%
27	Oklahoma	48,269	1.2%
28	Oregon	43,809	1.1%
7	Pennsylvania	144,224	3.7%
43	Rhode Island	12,455	0.3%
26	South Carolina	52,214	1.3%
46	South Dakota	10,173	0.3%
17	Tennessee	74,478	1.9%
2	Texas	333,974	8.6%
30	Utah	43,059	1.1%
49	Vermont	6,607	0.2%
12	Virginia	91,862	2.4%
15	Washington	78,190	2.0%
38	West Virginia	20,730	0.5%
20	Wisconsin	66,557	1.7%
50	Wyoming	6,387	0.2%

RANK ORDER

RANK	STATE	BIRTHS	% of USA
1	California	524,840	13.5%
2	Texas	333,974	8.6%
3	New York	257,238	6.6%
4	Florida	192,383	5.0%
5	Illinois	180,803	4.7%
6	Ohio	152,033	3.9%
7	Pennsylvania	144,224	3.7%
8	Michigan	133,714	3.4%
9	Georgia	118,221	3.0%
10	New Jersey	113,279	2.9%
11	North Carolina	107,015	2.8%
12	Virginia	91,862	2.4%
13	Indiana	83,436	2.1%
14	Massachusetts	80,364	2.1%
15	Washington	78,190	2.0%
16	Arizona	75,699	2.0%
17	Tennessee	74,478	1.9%
18	Missouri	74,037	1.9%
19	Maryland	70,215	1.8%
20	Wisconsin	66,557	1.7%
21	Louisiana	66,025	1.7%
22	Minnesota	64,499	1.7%
23	Alabama	60,914	1.6%
24	Colorado	56,533	1.5%
25	Kentucky	53,203	1.4%
26	South Carolina	52,214	1.3%
27	Oklahoma	48,269	1.2%
28	Oregon	43,809	1.1%
29	Connecticut	43,109	1.1%
30	Utah	43,059	1.1%
31	Mississippi	41,533	1.1%
32	Kansas	37,289	1.0%
33	Iowa	36,659	0.9%
34	Arkansas	36,478	0.9%
35	Nevada	26,911	0.7%
36	New Mexico	26,871	0.7%
37	Nebraska	23,319	0.6%
38	West Virginia	20,730	0.5%
39	Idaho	18,582	0.5%
40	Hawaii	17,393	0.4%
41	New Hampshire	14,313	0.4%
42	Maine	13,669	0.4%
43	Rhode Island	12,455	0.3%
44	Montana	10,849	0.3%
45	Delaware	10,253	0.3%
46	South Dakota	10,173	0.3%
47	Alaska	9,947	0.3%
48	North Dakota	8,353	0.2%
49	Vermont	6,607	0.2%
50	Wyoming	6,387	0.2%
	District of Columbia	7,927	0.2%

Source: U.S. Department of Health and Human Services, National Center for Health Statistics
   "National Vital Statistics Reports" (Vol. 47, No. 18, April 29, 1999)
*Final data by state of residence.

Birth Rate in 1997

National Rate = 14.5 Live Births per 1,000 Population*

ALPHA ORDER			RANK ORDER		
RANK	STATE	RATE	RANK	STATE	RATE
21	Alabama	14.1	1	Utah	20.9
4	Alaska	16.3	2	Texas	17.2
3	Arizona	16.6	3	Arizona	16.6
15	Arkansas	14.5	4	Alaska	16.3
4	California	16.3	4	California	16.3
15	Colorado	14.5	6	Nevada	16.0
38	Connecticut	13.2	7	Georgia	15.8
24	Delaware	14.0	8	New Mexico	15.5
39	Florida	13.1	9	Idaho	15.4
7	Georgia	15.8	10	Illinois	15.2
13	Hawaii	14.7	10	Louisiana	15.2
9	Idaho	15.4	10	Mississippi	15.2
10	Illinois	15.2	13	Hawaii	14.7
19	Indiana	14.2	14	Oklahoma	14.6
42	Iowa	12.9	15	Arkansas	14.5
17	Kansas	14.4	15	Colorado	14.5
33	Kentucky	13.6	17	Kansas	14.4
10	Louisiana	15.2	17	North Carolina	14.4
50	Maine	11.0	19	Indiana	14.2
28	Maryland	13.8	19	New York	14.2
39	Massachusetts	13.1	21	Alabama	14.1
31	Michigan	13.7	21	Nebraska	14.1
28	Minnesota	13.8	21	New Jersey	14.1
10	Mississippi	15.2	24	Delaware	14.0
31	Missouri	13.7	25	South Carolina	13.9
45	Montana	12.3	25	Tennessee	13.9
21	Nebraska	14.1	25	Washington	13.9
6	Nevada	16.0	28	Maryland	13.8
46	New Hampshire	12.2	28	Minnesota	13.8
21	New Jersey	14.1	28	South Dakota	13.8
8	New Mexico	15.5	31	Michigan	13.7
19	New York	14.2	31	Missouri	13.7
17	North Carolina	14.4	33	Kentucky	13.6
41	North Dakota	13.0	33	Ohio	13.6
33	Ohio	13.6	33	Virginia	13.6
14	Oklahoma	14.6	36	Oregon	13.5
36	Oregon	13.5	37	Wyoming	13.3
47	Pennsylvania	12.0	38	Connecticut	13.2
44	Rhode Island	12.6	39	Florida	13.1
25	South Carolina	13.9	39	Massachusetts	13.1
28	South Dakota	13.8	41	North Dakota	13.0
25	Tennessee	13.9	42	Iowa	12.9
2	Texas	17.2	42	Wisconsin	12.9
1	Utah	20.9	44	Rhode Island	12.6
49	Vermont	11.2	45	Montana	12.3
33	Virginia	13.6	46	New Hampshire	12.2
25	Washington	13.9	47	Pennsylvania	12.0
48	West Virginia	11.4	48	West Virginia	11.4
42	Wisconsin	12.9	49	Vermont	11.2
37	Wyoming	13.3	50	Maine	11.0
				District of Columbia	15.0

Source: U.S. Department of Health and Human Services, National Center for Health Statistics
"National Vital Statistics Reports" (Vol. 47, No. 18, April 29, 1999)
*Final data by state of residence.

Births in 1990

National Total = 4,158,212 Live Births*

ALPHA ORDER

RANK	STATE	BIRTHS	% of USA
23	Alabama	63,487	1.5%
44	Alaska	11,902	0.3%
21	Arizona	68,995	1.7%
33	Arkansas	36,457	0.9%
1	California	612,628	14.7%
26	Colorado	53,525	1.3%
27	Connecticut	50,123	1.2%
46	Delaware	11,113	0.3%
4	Florida	199,339	4.8%
10	Georgia	112,666	2.7%
39	Hawaii	20,489	0.5%
42	Idaho	16,433	0.4%
5	Illinois	195,790	4.7%
14	Indiana	86,214	2.1%
31	Iowa	39,409	0.9%
32	Kansas	39,020	0.9%
25	Kentucky	54,362	1.3%
20	Louisiana	72,192	1.7%
41	Maine	17,359	0.4%
15	Maryland	80,245	1.9%
13	Massachusetts	92,654	2.2%
8	Michigan	153,700	3.7%
22	Minnesota	68,013	1.6%
29	Mississippi	43,563	1.0%
16	Missouri	79,260	1.9%
45	Montana	11,613	0.3%
36	Nebraska	24,380	0.6%
38	Nevada	21,599	0.5%
40	New Hampshire	17,569	0.4%
9	New Jersey	122,289	2.9%
35	New Mexico	27,402	0.7%
3	New York	297,576	7.2%
11	North Carolina	104,525	2.5%
48	North Dakota	9,250	0.2%
7	Ohio	166,913	4.0%
28	Oklahoma	47,649	1.1%
30	Oregon	42,891	1.0%
6	Pennsylvania	171,961	4.1%
43	Rhode Island	15,195	0.4%
24	South Carolina	58,610	1.4%
47	South Dakota	10,999	0.3%
18	Tennessee	74,962	1.8%
2	Texas	316,423	7.6%
34	Utah	36,277	0.9%
49	Vermont	8,273	0.2%
12	Virginia	99,352	2.4%
17	Washington	79,251	1.9%
37	West Virginia	22,585	0.5%
19	Wisconsin	72,895	1.8%
50	Wyoming	6,985	0.2%

RANK ORDER

RANK	STATE	BIRTHS	% of USA
1	California	612,628	14.7%
2	Texas	316,423	7.6%
3	New York	297,576	7.2%
4	Florida	199,339	4.8%
5	Illinois	195,790	4.7%
6	Pennsylvania	171,961	4.1%
7	Ohio	166,913	4.0%
8	Michigan	153,700	3.7%
9	New Jersey	122,289	2.9%
10	Georgia	112,666	2.7%
11	North Carolina	104,525	2.5%
12	Virginia	99,352	2.4%
13	Massachusetts	92,654	2.2%
14	Indiana	86,214	2.1%
15	Maryland	80,245	1.9%
16	Missouri	79,260	1.9%
17	Washington	79,251	1.9%
18	Tennessee	74,962	1.8%
19	Wisconsin	72,895	1.8%
20	Louisiana	72,192	1.7%
21	Arizona	68,995	1.7%
22	Minnesota	68,013	1.6%
23	Alabama	63,487	1.5%
24	South Carolina	58,610	1.4%
25	Kentucky	54,362	1.3%
26	Colorado	53,525	1.3%
27	Connecticut	50,123	1.2%
28	Oklahoma	47,649	1.1%
29	Mississippi	43,563	1.0%
30	Oregon	42,891	1.0%
31	Iowa	39,409	0.9%
32	Kansas	39,020	0.9%
33	Arkansas	36,457	0.9%
34	Utah	36,277	0.9%
35	New Mexico	27,402	0.7%
36	Nebraska	24,380	0.6%
37	West Virginia	22,585	0.5%
38	Nevada	21,599	0.5%
39	Hawaii	20,489	0.5%
40	New Hampshire	17,569	0.4%
41	Maine	17,359	0.4%
42	Idaho	16,433	0.4%
43	Rhode Island	15,195	0.4%
44	Alaska	11,902	0.3%
45	Montana	11,613	0.3%
46	Delaware	11,113	0.3%
47	South Dakota	10,999	0.3%
48	North Dakota	9,250	0.2%
49	Vermont	8,273	0.2%
50	Wyoming	6,985	0.2%
	District of Columbia	11,850	0.3%

Source: U.S. Department of Health and Human Services, National Center for Health Statistics
   "Monthly Vital Statistics Report" (Vol. 41, No. 9, Supplement, February 25, 1993)
*Final data by state of residence.

Birth Rate in 1990

National Rate = 16.7 Births per 1,000 Population*

ALPHA ORDER

RANK	STATE	RATE
26	Alabama	15.7
1	Alaska	21.6
4	Arizona	18.8
29	Arkansas	15.5
3	California	20.6
20	Colorado	16.2
38	Connecticut	15.2
15	Delaware	16.7
32	Florida	15.4
9	Georgia	17.4
6	Hawaii	18.5
18	Idaho	16.3
10	Illinois	17.1
28	Indiana	15.6
48	Iowa	14.2
26	Kansas	15.7
43	Kentucky	14.8
10	Louisiana	17.1
49	Maine	14.1
13	Maryland	16.8
32	Massachusetts	15.4
16	Michigan	16.5
29	Minnesota	15.5
12	Mississippi	16.9
29	Missouri	15.5
45	Montana	14.5
32	Nebraska	15.4
8	Nevada	18.0
22	New Hampshire	15.8
22	New Jersey	15.8
7	New Mexico	18.1
16	New York	16.5
22	North Carolina	15.8
45	North Dakota	14.5
32	Ohio	15.4
39	Oklahoma	15.1
39	Oregon	15.1
45	Pennsylvania	14.5
39	Rhode Island	15.1
13	South Carolina	16.8
22	South Dakota	15.8
32	Tennessee	15.4
5	Texas	18.6
2	Utah	21.1
44	Vermont	14.7
21	Virginia	16.1
18	Washington	16.3
50	West Virginia	12.6
42	Wisconsin	14.9
32	Wyoming	15.4

RANK ORDER

RANK	STATE	RATE
1	Alaska	21.6
2	Utah	21.1
3	California	20.6
4	Arizona	18.8
5	Texas	18.6
6	Hawaii	18.5
7	New Mexico	18.1
8	Nevada	18.0
9	Georgia	17.4
10	Illinois	17.1
10	Louisiana	17.1
12	Mississippi	16.9
13	Maryland	16.8
13	South Carolina	16.8
15	Delaware	16.7
16	Michigan	16.5
16	New York	16.5
18	Idaho	16.3
18	Washington	16.3
20	Colorado	16.2
21	Virginia	16.1
22	New Hampshire	15.8
22	New Jersey	15.8
22	North Carolina	15.8
22	South Dakota	15.8
26	Alabama	15.7
26	Kansas	15.7
28	Indiana	15.6
29	Arkansas	15.5
29	Minnesota	15.5
29	Missouri	15.5
32	Florida	15.4
32	Massachusetts	15.4
32	Nebraska	15.4
32	Ohio	15.4
32	Tennessee	15.4
32	Wyoming	15.4
38	Connecticut	15.2
39	Oklahoma	15.1
39	Oregon	15.1
39	Rhode Island	15.1
42	Wisconsin	14.9
43	Kentucky	14.8
44	Vermont	14.7
45	Montana	14.5
45	North Dakota	14.5
45	Pennsylvania	14.5
48	Iowa	14.2
49	Maine	14.1
50	West Virginia	12.6
	District of Columbia	19.5

Source: U.S. Department of Health and Human Services, National Center for Health Statistics
    "Monthly Vital Statistics Report" (Vol. 41, No. 9, Supplement, February 25, 1993)
*Final data by state of residence.

Births in 1980

National Total = 3,612,000 Births*

ALPHA ORDER					RANK ORDER			
RANK	STATE		BIRTHS	% of USA	RANK	STATE	BIRTHS	% of USA
21	Alabama		64,000	1.8%	1	California	403,000	11.2%
48	Alaska		10,000	0.3%	2	Texas	274,000	7.6%
26	Arizona		50,000	1.4%	3	New York	239,000	6.6%
34	Arkansas		37,000	1.0%	4	Illinois	190,000	5.3%
1	California		403,000	11.2%	5	Ohio	169,000	4.7%
26	Colorado		50,000	1.4%	6	Pennsylvania	159,000	4.4%
33	Connecticut		39,000	1.1%	7	Michigan	146,000	4.0%
49	Delaware		9,000	0.2%	8	Florida	132,000	3.7%
8	Florida		132,000	3.7%	9	New Jersey	97,000	2.7%
10	Georgia		92,000	2.5%	10	Georgia	92,000	2.5%
39	Hawaii		18,000	0.5%	11	Indiana	88,000	2.4%
38	Idaho		20,000	0.6%	12	North Carolina	84,000	2.3%
4	Illinois		190,000	5.3%	13	Louisiana	82,000	2.3%
11	Indiana		88,000	2.4%	14	Missouri	79,000	2.2%
28	Iowa		48,000	1.3%	15	Virginia	78,000	2.2%
32	Kansas		41,000	1.1%	16	Wisconsin	75,000	2.1%
22	Kentucky		60,000	1.7%	17	Massachusetts	73,000	2.0%
13	Louisiana		82,000	2.3%	18	Tennessee	69,000	1.9%
40	Maine		16,000	0.4%	19	Minnesota	68,000	1.9%
22	Maryland		60,000	1.7%	19	Washington	68,000	1.9%
17	Massachusetts		73,000	2.0%	21	Alabama	64,000	1.8%
7	Michigan		146,000	4.0%	22	Kentucky	60,000	1.7%
19	Minnesota		68,000	1.9%	22	Maryland	60,000	1.7%
28	Mississippi		48,000	1.3%	24	Oklahoma	52,000	1.4%
14	Missouri		79,000	2.2%	24	South Carolina	52,000	1.4%
41	Montana		14,000	0.4%	26	Arizona	50,000	1.4%
36	Nebraska		27,000	0.7%	26	Colorado	50,000	1.4%
43	Nevada		13,000	0.4%	28	Iowa	48,000	1.3%
41	New Hampshire		14,000	0.4%	28	Mississippi	48,000	1.3%
9	New Jersey		97,000	2.7%	30	Oregon	43,000	1.2%
37	New Mexico		26,000	0.7%	31	Utah	42,000	1.2%
3	New York		239,000	6.6%	32	Kansas	41,000	1.1%
12	North Carolina		84,000	2.3%	33	Connecticut	39,000	1.1%
45	North Dakota		12,000	0.3%	34	Arkansas	37,000	1.0%
5	Ohio		169,000	4.7%	35	West Virginia	29,000	0.8%
24	Oklahoma		52,000	1.4%	36	Nebraska	27,000	0.7%
30	Oregon		43,000	1.2%	37	New Mexico	26,000	0.7%
6	Pennsylvania		159,000	4.4%	38	Idaho	20,000	0.6%
45	Rhode Island		12,000	0.3%	39	Hawaii	18,000	0.5%
24	South Carolina		52,000	1.4%	40	Maine	16,000	0.4%
43	South Dakota		13,000	0.4%	41	Montana	14,000	0.4%
18	Tennessee		69,000	1.9%	41	New Hampshire	14,000	0.4%
2	Texas		274,000	7.6%	43	Nevada	13,000	0.4%
31	Utah		42,000	1.2%	43	South Dakota	13,000	0.4%
50	Vermont		8,000	0.2%	45	North Dakota	12,000	0.3%
15	Virginia		78,000	2.2%	45	Rhode Island	12,000	0.3%
19	Washington		68,000	1.9%	47	Wyoming	11,000	0.3%
35	West Virginia		29,000	0.8%	48	Alaska	10,000	0.3%
16	Wisconsin		75,000	2.1%	49	Delaware	9,000	0.2%
47	Wyoming		11,000	0.3%	50	Vermont	8,000	0.2%
						District of Columbia	9,000	0.2%

Source: U.S. Department of Health and Human Services, National Center for Health Statistics
"Vital Statistics of the United States, 1980" and "Monthly Vital Statistics Report"
*Live births by state of residence.

Birth Rate in 1980

National Rate = 15.9 Births per 1,000 Population*

ALPHA ORDER

RANK ORDER

RANK	STATE	RATE		RANK	STATE	RATE
27	Alabama	16.3		1	Utah	28.6
2	Alaska	23.7		2	Alaska	23.7
11	Arizona	18.4		3	Wyoming	22.5
27	Arkansas	16.3		4	Idaho	21.4
18	California	17.0		5	New Mexico	20.0
15	Colorado	17.2		6	Louisiana	19.5
50	Connecticut	12.5		7	South Dakota	19.2
33	Delaware	15.8		7	Texas	19.2
45	Florida	13.5		9	Mississippi	19.0
19	Georgia	16.9		10	Hawaii	18.8
10	Hawaii	18.8		11	Arizona	18.4
4	Idaho	21.4		11	North Dakota	18.4
20	Illinois	16.6		13	Montana	18.1
30	Indiana	16.1		14	Nebraska	17.4
24	Iowa	16.4		15	Colorado	17.2
15	Kansas	17.2		15	Kansas	17.2
27	Kentucky	16.3		15	Oklahoma	17.2
6	Louisiana	19.5		18	California	17.0
41	Maine	14.6		19	Georgia	16.9
43	Maryland	14.2		20	Illinois	16.6
49	Massachusetts	12.7		20	Minnesota	16.6
34	Michigan	15.7		20	Nevada	16.6
20	Minnesota	16.6		20	South Carolina	16.6
9	Mississippi	19.0		24	Iowa	16.4
30	Missouri	16.1		24	Oregon	16.4
13	Montana	18.1		24	Washington	16.4
14	Nebraska	17.4		27	Alabama	16.3
20	Nevada	16.6		27	Arkansas	16.3
39	New Hampshire	14.9		27	Kentucky	16.3
47	New Jersey	13.2		30	Indiana	16.1
5	New Mexico	20.0		30	Missouri	16.1
44	New York	13.6		32	Wisconsin	15.9
42	North Carolina	14.4		33	Delaware	15.8
11	North Dakota	18.4		34	Michigan	15.7
34	Ohio	15.7		34	Ohio	15.7
15	Oklahoma	17.2		36	Vermont	15.4
24	Oregon	16.4		37	Tennessee	15.1
46	Pennsylvania	13.4		37	West Virginia	15.1
48	Rhode Island	12.9		39	New Hampshire	14.9
20	South Carolina	16.6		40	Virginia	14.7
7	South Dakota	19.2		41	Maine	14.6
37	Tennessee	15.1		42	North Carolina	14.4
7	Texas	19.2		43	Maryland	14.2
1	Utah	28.6		44	New York	13.6
36	Vermont	15.4		45	Florida	13.5
40	Virginia	14.7		46	Pennsylvania	13.4
24	Washington	16.4		47	New Jersey	13.2
37	West Virginia	15.1		48	Rhode Island	12.9
32	Wisconsin	15.9		49	Massachusetts	12.7
3	Wyoming	22.5		50	Connecticut	12.5
					District of Columbia	14.7

Source: U.S. Department of Health and Human Services, National Center for Health Statistics
    "Vital Statistics of the United States, 1980" and "Monthly Vital Statistics Report"
Live births by state of residence.

Fertility Rate in 1998

National Rate = 65.6 Live Births per 1,000 Women 15 to 44 Years Old*

ALPHA ORDER

RANK ORDER

RANK	STATE	RATE	RANK	STATE	RATE
26	Alabama	63.3	1	Utah	91.4
6	Alaska	73.2	2	Arizona	78.3
2	Arizona	78.3	3	Nevada	77.8
13	Arkansas	67.6	4	Texas	76.2
8	California	70.7	5	New Mexico	73.4
14	Colorado	67.4	6	Alaska	73.2
33	Connecticut	61.3	7	Idaho	72.3
35	Delaware	61.2	8	California	70.7
21	Florida	65.1	9	Hawaii	69.7
15	Georgia	67.2	10	Oklahoma	69.0
9	Hawaii	69.7	11	Mississippi	68.3
7	Idaho	72.3	12	Illinois	68.2
12	Illinois	68.2	13	Arkansas	67.6
25	Indiana	63.5	14	Colorado	67.4
32	Iowa	61.4	15	Georgia	67.2
16	Kansas	67.1	16	Kansas	67.1
31	Kentucky	61.5	17	Louisiana	66.7
17	Louisiana	66.7	18	North Carolina	66.6
49	Maine	49.8	19	New Jersey	65.4
39	Maryland	60.2	20	Nebraska	65.2
41	Massachusetts	58.6	21	Florida	65.1
38	Michigan	60.4	21	South Dakota	65.1
30	Minnesota	61.8	23	Oregon	64.7
11	Mississippi	68.3	24	New York	63.9
28	Missouri	62.9	25	Indiana	63.5
43	Montana	58.4	26	Alabama	63.3
20	Nebraska	65.2	27	Tennessee	63.1
3	Nevada	77.8	28	Missouri	62.9
48	New Hampshire	53.0	29	Washington	62.3
19	New Jersey	65.4	30	Minnesota	61.8
5	New Mexico	73.4	31	Kentucky	61.5
24	New York	63.9	32	Iowa	61.4
18	North Carolina	66.6	33	Connecticut	61.3
44	North Dakota	58.3	33	South Carolina	61.3
35	Ohio	61.2	35	Delaware	61.2
10	Oklahoma	69.0	35	Ohio	61.2
23	Oregon	64.7	37	Wyoming	61.0
46	Pennsylvania	57.0	38	Michigan	60.4
45	Rhode Island	57.6	39	Maryland	60.2
33	South Carolina	61.3	40	Virginia	59.2
21	South Dakota	65.1	41	Massachusetts	58.6
27	Tennessee	63.1	42	Wisconsin	58.5
4	Texas	76.2	43	Montana	58.4
1	Utah	91.4	44	North Dakota	58.3
50	Vermont	49.1	45	Rhode Island	57.6
40	Virginia	59.2	46	Pennsylvania	57.0
29	Washington	62.3	47	West Virginia	53.7
47	West Virginia	53.7	48	New Hampshire	53.0
42	Wisconsin	58.5	49	Maine	49.8
37	Wyoming	61.0	50	Vermont	49.1
				District of Columbia	60.9

Source: U.S. Department of Health and Human Services, National Center for Health Statistics
   "National Vital Statistics Reports" (Vol. 47, No. 25, October 5, 1999)
*Data are preliminary estimates by state of residence.

Births to White Women in 1998

National Total = 3,122,391 Live Births to White Women*

ALPHA ORDER

RANK	STATE	BIRTHS	% of USA
26	Alabama	41,564	1.3%
47	Alaska	6,684	0.2%
16	Arizona	68,428	2.2%
33	Arkansas	28,311	0.9%
1	California	424,662	13.6%
21	Colorado	54,527	1.7%
29	Connecticut	36,938	1.2%
45	Delaware	7,703	0.2%
4	Florida	146,218	4.7%
11	Georgia	78,194	2.5%
50	Hawaii	4,175	0.1%
39	Idaho	18,774	0.6%
5	Illinois	140,144	4.5%
12	Indiana	73,884	2.4%
30	Iowa	35,229	1.1%
31	Kansas	34,288	1.1%
22	Kentucky	48,815	1.6%
28	Louisiana	38,124	1.2%
41	Maine	13,382	0.4%
23	Maryland	44,913	1.4%
13	Massachusetts	69,578	2.2%
8	Michigan	105,603	3.4%
20	Minnesota	57,290	1.8%
36	Mississippi	22,953	0.7%
17	Missouri	62,527	2.0%
43	Montana	9,389	0.3%
37	Nebraska	21,445	0.7%
34	Nevada	24,322	0.8%
40	New Hampshire	14,253	0.5%
9	New Jersey	86,486	2.8%
35	New Mexico	23,409	0.7%
3	New York	186,144	6.0%
10	North Carolina	79,336	2.5%
46	North Dakota	7,035	0.2%
6	Ohio	127,376	4.1%
27	Oklahoma	38,924	1.2%
25	Oregon	41,614	1.3%
7	Pennsylvania	121,830	3.9%
42	Rhode Island	11,030	0.4%
32	South Carolina	34,209	1.1%
44	South Dakota	8,392	0.3%
18	Tennessee	59,299	1.9%
2	Texas	291,831	9.3%
24	Utah	42,930	1.4%
48	Vermont	6,494	0.2%
15	Virginia	68,728	2.2%
14	Washington	69,018	2.2%
38	West Virginia	19,857	0.6%
19	Wisconsin	58,187	1.9%
49	Wyoming	5,888	0.2%

RANK ORDER

RANK	STATE	BIRTHS	% of USA
1	California	424,662	13.6%
2	Texas	291,831	9.3%
3	New York	186,144	6.0%
4	Florida	146,218	4.7%
5	Illinois	140,144	4.5%
6	Ohio	127,376	4.1%
7	Pennsylvania	121,830	3.9%
8	Michigan	105,603	3.4%
9	New Jersey	86,486	2.8%
10	North Carolina	79,336	2.5%
11	Georgia	78,194	2.5%
12	Indiana	73,884	2.4%
13	Massachusetts	69,578	2.2%
14	Washington	69,018	2.2%
15	Virginia	68,728	2.2%
16	Arizona	68,428	2.2%
17	Missouri	62,527	2.0%
18	Tennessee	59,299	1.9%
19	Wisconsin	58,187	1.9%
20	Minnesota	57,290	1.8%
21	Colorado	54,527	1.7%
22	Kentucky	48,815	1.6%
23	Maryland	44,913	1.4%
24	Utah	42,930	1.4%
25	Oregon	41,614	1.3%
26	Alabama	41,564	1.3%
27	Oklahoma	38,924	1.2%
28	Louisiana	38,124	1.2%
29	Connecticut	36,938	1.2%
30	Iowa	35,229	1.1%
31	Kansas	34,288	1.1%
32	South Carolina	34,209	1.1%
33	Arkansas	28,311	0.9%
34	Nevada	24,322	0.8%
35	New Mexico	23,409	0.7%
36	Mississippi	22,953	0.7%
37	Nebraska	21,445	0.7%
38	West Virginia	19,857	0.6%
39	Idaho	18,774	0.6%
40	New Hampshire	14,253	0.5%
41	Maine	13,382	0.4%
42	Rhode Island	11,030	0.4%
43	Montana	9,389	0.3%
44	South Dakota	8,392	0.3%
45	Delaware	7,703	0.2%
46	North Dakota	7,035	0.2%
47	Alaska	6,684	0.2%
48	Vermont	6,494	0.2%
49	Wyoming	5,888	0.2%
50	Hawaii	4,175	0.1%
	District of Columbia	2,054	0.1%

Source: U.S. Department of Health and Human Services, National Center for Health Statistics "National Vital Statistics Reports" (Vol. 47, No. 25, October 5, 1999)
Preliminary data by state of residence. By race of mother.

White Births as a Percent of All Births in 1998

National Percent = 79.2% of Live Births*

ALPHA ORDER

RANK	STATE	PERCENT
44	Alabama	66.9
43	Alaska	67.3
19	Arizona	87.4
35	Arkansas	76.7
31	California	81.4
10	Colorado	91.2
25	Connecticut	84.3
39	Delaware	72.8
37	Florida	74.7
45	Georgia	63.9
50	Hawaii	23.7
4	Idaho	96.8
34	Illinois	76.8
17	Indiana	87.8
7	Iowa	94.5
13	Kansas	89.3
12	Kentucky	89.9
48	Louisiana	57.0
3	Maine	97.3
47	Maryland	62.4
22	Massachusetts	85.3
32	Michigan	79.0
15	Minnesota	87.9
49	Mississippi	53.5
29	Missouri	82.9
15	Montana	87.9
11	Nebraska	91.1
24	Nevada	84.8
2	New Hampshire	97.5
38	New Jersey	74.2
26	New Mexico	84.2
41	New York	72.1
42	North Carolina	71.0
14	North Dakota	88.7
28	Ohio	83.3
33	Oklahoma	78.7
9	Oregon	91.9
27	Pennsylvania	83.4
18	Rhode Island	87.5
46	South Carolina	63.5
30	South Dakota	81.6
36	Tennessee	76.6
22	Texas	85.3
6	Utah	95.1
1	Vermont	98.7
40	Virginia	72.7
20	Washington	86.6
5	West Virginia	95.7
21	Wisconsin	86.3
8	Wyoming	94.1

RANK ORDER

RANK	STATE	PERCENT
1	Vermont	98.7
2	New Hampshire	97.5
3	Maine	97.3
4	Idaho	96.8
5	West Virginia	95.7
6	Utah	95.1
7	Iowa	94.5
8	Wyoming	94.1
9	Oregon	91.9
10	Colorado	91.2
11	Nebraska	91.1
12	Kentucky	89.9
13	Kansas	89.3
14	North Dakota	88.7
15	Minnesota	87.9
15	Montana	87.9
17	Indiana	87.8
18	Rhode Island	87.5
19	Arizona	87.4
20	Washington	86.6
21	Wisconsin	86.3
22	Massachusetts	85.3
22	Texas	85.3
24	Nevada	84.8
25	Connecticut	84.3
26	New Mexico	84.2
27	Pennsylvania	83.4
28	Ohio	83.3
29	Missouri	82.9
30	South Dakota	81.6
31	California	81.4
32	Michigan	79.0
33	Oklahoma	78.7
34	Illinois	76.8
35	Arkansas	76.7
36	Tennessee	76.6
37	Florida	74.7
38	New Jersey	74.2
39	Delaware	72.8
40	Virginia	72.7
41	New York	72.1
42	North Carolina	71.0
43	Alaska	67.3
44	Alabama	66.9
45	Georgia	63.9
46	South Carolina	63.5
47	Maryland	62.4
48	Louisiana	57.0
49	Mississippi	53.5
50	Hawaii	23.7
	District of Columbia	26.7

Source: Morgan Quitno Press using data from U.S. Dept. of Health and Human Services, Nat'l Center for Health Statistics "National Vital Statistics Reports" (Vol. 47, No. 25, October 5, 1999)
*Preliminary data by state of residence. By race of mother.

Births to Black Women in 1998

National Total = 610,203 Live Births to Black Women*

RANK	STATE	BIRTHS	% of USA
15	Alabama	20,041	3.3%
41	Alaska	405	0.1%
31	Arizona	2,663	0.4%
21	Arkansas	7,990	1.3%
5	California	36,738	6.0%
29	Colorado	2,880	0.5%
24	Connecticut	5,375	0.9%
32	Delaware	2,623	0.4%
2	Florida	44,386	7.3%
3	Georgia	41,252	6.8%
39	Hawaii	558	0.1%
47	Idaho	82	0.0%
6	Illinois	35,713	5.9%
20	Indiana	9,035	1.5%
35	Iowa	1,093	0.2%
30	Kansas	2,787	0.5%
25	Kentucky	4,862	0.8%
8	Louisiana	27,452	4.5%
44	Maine	91	0.0%
10	Maryland	24,176	4.0%
22	Massachusetts	7,907	1.3%
9	Michigan	24,277	4.0%
27	Minnesota	3,665	0.6%
16	Mississippi	19,359	3.2%
19	Missouri	11,406	1.9%
49	Montana	43	0.0%
34	Nebraska	1,236	0.2%
33	Nevada	2,253	0.4%
43	New Hampshire	137	0.0%
13	New Jersey	21,848	3.6%
40	New Mexico	519	0.1%
1	New York	54,497	8.9%
7	North Carolina	28,244	4.6%
45	North Dakota	87	0.0%
11	Ohio	22,813	3.7%
26	Oklahoma	4,804	0.8%
37	Oregon	966	0.2%
14	Pennsylvania	20,530	3.4%
36	Rhode Island	967	0.2%
17	South Carolina	18,839	3.1%
46	South Dakota	85	0.0%
18	Tennessee	16,883	2.8%
4	Texas	40,202	6.6%
42	Utah	281	0.0%
50	Vermont	27	0.0%
12	Virginia	22,190	3.6%
28	Washington	3,112	0.5%
38	West Virginia	762	0.1%
23	Wisconsin	6,541	1.1%
48	Wyoming	54	0.0%

RANK	STATE	BIRTHS	% of USA
1	New York	54,497	8.9%
2	Florida	44,386	7.3%
3	Georgia	41,252	6.8%
4	Texas	40,202	6.6%
5	California	36,738	6.0%
6	Illinois	35,713	5.9%
7	North Carolina	28,244	4.6%
8	Louisiana	27,452	4.5%
9	Michigan	24,277	4.0%
10	Maryland	24,176	4.0%
11	Ohio	22,813	3.7%
12	Virginia	22,190	3.6%
13	New Jersey	21,848	3.6%
14	Pennsylvania	20,530	3.4%
15	Alabama	20,041	3.3%
16	Mississippi	19,359	3.2%
17	South Carolina	18,839	3.1%
18	Tennessee	16,883	2.8%
19	Missouri	11,406	1.9%
20	Indiana	9,035	1.5%
21	Arkansas	7,990	1.3%
22	Massachusetts	7,907	1.3%
23	Wisconsin	6,541	1.1%
24	Connecticut	5,375	0.9%
25	Kentucky	4,862	0.8%
26	Oklahoma	4,804	0.8%
27	Minnesota	3,665	0.6%
28	Washington	3,112	0.5%
29	Colorado	2,880	0.5%
30	Kansas	2,787	0.5%
31	Arizona	2,663	0.4%
32	Delaware	2,623	0.4%
33	Nevada	2,253	0.4%
34	Nebraska	1,236	0.2%
35	Iowa	1,093	0.2%
36	Rhode Island	967	0.2%
37	Oregon	966	0.2%
38	West Virginia	762	0.1%
39	Hawaii	558	0.1%
40	New Mexico	519	0.1%
41	Alaska	405	0.1%
42	Utah	281	0.0%
43	New Hampshire	137	0.0%
44	Maine	91	0.0%
45	North Dakota	87	0.0%
46	South Dakota	85	0.0%
47	Idaho	82	0.0%
48	Wyoming	54	0.0%
49	Montana	43	0.0%
50	Vermont	27	0.0%
	District of Columbia	5,467	0.9%

*Source: U.S. Department of Health and Human Services, National Center for Health Statistics
"National Vital Statistics Reports" (Vol. 47, No. 25, October 5, 1999)*
*Preliminary data by state of residence. By race of mother.

Black Births as a Percent of All Births in 1998

National Percent = 15.5% of Live Births*

RANK	STATE (ALPHA ORDER)	PERCENT	RANK	STATE (RANK ORDER)	PERCENT
6	Alabama	32.3	1	Mississippi	45.1
34	Alaska	4.1	2	Louisiana	41.0
37	Arizona	3.4	3	South Carolina	35.0
12	Arkansas	21.7	4	Georgia	33.7
30	California	7.0	5	Maryland	33.6
33	Colorado	4.8	6	Alabama	32.3
20	Connecticut	12.3	7	North Carolina	25.3
8	Delaware	24.8	8	Delaware	24.8
10	Florida	22.7	9	Virginia	23.5
4	Georgia	33.7	10	Florida	22.7
38	Hawaii	3.2	11	Tennessee	21.8
48	Idaho	0.4	12	Arkansas	21.7
14	Illinois	19.6	13	New York	21.1
22	Indiana	10.7	14	Illinois	19.6
39	Iowa	2.9	15	New Jersey	18.8
29	Kansas	7.3	16	Michigan	18.2
26	Kentucky	9.0	17	Missouri	15.1
2	Louisiana	41.0	18	Ohio	14.9
46	Maine	0.7	19	Pennsylvania	14.1
5	Maryland	33.6	20	Connecticut	12.3
23	Massachusetts	9.7	21	Texas	11.7
16	Michigan	18.2	22	Indiana	10.7
31	Minnesota	5.6	23	Massachusetts	9.7
1	Mississippi	45.1	23	Oklahoma	9.7
17	Missouri	15.1	23	Wisconsin	9.7
48	Montana	0.4	26	Kentucky	9.0
32	Nebraska	5.3	27	Nevada	7.9
27	Nevada	7.9	28	Rhode Island	7.7
43	New Hampshire	0.9	29	Kansas	7.3
15	New Jersey	18.8	30	California	7.0
41	New Mexico	1.9	31	Minnesota	5.6
13	New York	21.1	32	Nebraska	5.3
7	North Carolina	25.3	33	Colorado	4.8
42	North Dakota	1.1	34	Alaska	4.1
18	Ohio	14.9	35	Washington	3.9
23	Oklahoma	9.7	36	West Virginia	3.7
40	Oregon	2.1	37	Arizona	3.4
19	Pennsylvania	14.1	38	Hawaii	3.2
28	Rhode Island	7.7	39	Iowa	2.9
3	South Carolina	35.0	40	Oregon	2.1
45	South Dakota	0.8	41	New Mexico	1.9
11	Tennessee	21.8	42	North Dakota	1.1
21	Texas	11.7	43	New Hampshire	0.9
47	Utah	0.6	43	Wyoming	0.9
48	Vermont	0.4	45	South Dakota	0.8
9	Virginia	23.5	46	Maine	0.7
35	Washington	3.9	47	Utah	0.6
36	West Virginia	3.7	48	Idaho	0.4
23	Wisconsin	9.7	48	Montana	0.4
43	Wyoming	0.9	48	Vermont	0.4
				District of Columbia	71.1

Source: Morgan Quitno Press using data from U.S. Dept. of Health and Human Services, Nat'l Center for Health Statistics "National Vital Statistics Reports" (Vol. 47, No. 25, October 5, 1999)
*Preliminary data by state of residence. By race of mother.

Births of Low Birthweight in 1998

National Total = 299,747 Live Births*

ALPHA ORDER

RANK	STATE	BIRTHS	% of USA
18	Alabama	5,778	1.9%
47	Alaska	586	0.2%
20	Arizona	5,324	1.8%
30	Arkansas	3,283	1.1%
1	California	32,352	10.8%
21	Colorado	5,143	1.7%
29	Connecticut	3,374	1.1%
42	Delaware	889	0.3%
4	Florida	15,847	5.3%
9	Georgia	10,402	3.5%
39	Hawaii	1,407	0.5%
40	Idaho	1,164	0.4%
5	Illinois	14,599	4.9%
15	Indiana	6,730	2.2%
34	Iowa	2,386	0.8%
32	Kansas	2,689	0.9%
24	Kentucky	4,453	1.5%
14	Louisiana	6,755	2.3%
44	Maine	797	0.3%
16	Maryland	6,267	2.1%
19	Massachusetts	5,627	1.9%
8	Michigan	10,427	3.5%
27	Minnesota	3,782	1.3%
26	Mississippi	4,336	1.4%
17	Missouri	5,880	2.0%
45	Montana	748	0.2%
38	Nebraska	1,530	0.5%
35	Nevada	2,179	0.7%
43	New Hampshire	833	0.3%
11	New Jersey	9,322	3.1%
36	New Mexico	2,113	0.7%
3	New York	20,134	6.7%
10	North Carolina	9,828	3.3%
49	North Dakota	516	0.2%
6	Ohio	11,773	3.9%
28	Oklahoma	3,562	1.2%
33	Oregon	2,445	0.8%
7	Pennsylvania	11,100	3.7%
41	Rhode Island	958	0.3%
22	South Carolina	5,119	1.7%
46	South Dakota	597	0.2%
13	Tennessee	7,042	2.3%
2	Texas	25,329	8.5%
31	Utah	3,026	1.0%
50	Vermont	441	0.1%
12	Virginia	7,466	2.5%
23	Washington	4,541	1.5%
37	West Virginia	1,681	0.6%
25	Wisconsin	4,385	1.5%
48	Wyoming	557	0.2%

RANK ORDER

RANK	STATE	BIRTHS	% of USA
1	California	32,352	10.8%
2	Texas	25,329	8.5%
3	New York	20,134	6.7%
4	Florida	15,847	5.3%
5	Illinois	14,599	4.9%
6	Ohio	11,773	3.9%
7	Pennsylvania	11,100	3.7%
8	Michigan	10,427	3.5%
9	Georgia	10,402	3.5%
10	North Carolina	9,828	3.3%
11	New Jersey	9,322	3.1%
12	Virginia	7,466	2.5%
13	Tennessee	7,042	2.3%
14	Louisiana	6,755	2.3%
15	Indiana	6,730	2.2%
16	Maryland	6,267	2.1%
17	Missouri	5,880	2.0%
18	Alabama	5,778	1.9%
19	Massachusetts	5,627	1.9%
20	Arizona	5,324	1.8%
21	Colorado	5,143	1.7%
22	South Carolina	5,119	1.7%
23	Washington	4,541	1.5%
24	Kentucky	4,453	1.5%
25	Wisconsin	4,385	1.5%
26	Mississippi	4,336	1.4%
27	Minnesota	3,782	1.3%
28	Oklahoma	3,562	1.2%
29	Connecticut	3,374	1.1%
30	Arkansas	3,283	1.1%
31	Utah	3,026	1.0%
32	Kansas	2,689	0.9%
33	Oregon	2,445	0.8%
34	Iowa	2,386	0.8%
35	Nevada	2,179	0.7%
36	New Mexico	2,113	0.7%
37	West Virginia	1,681	0.6%
38	Nebraska	1,530	0.5%
39	Hawaii	1,407	0.5%
40	Idaho	1,164	0.4%
41	Rhode Island	958	0.3%
42	Delaware	889	0.3%
43	New Hampshire	833	0.3%
44	Maine	797	0.3%
45	Montana	748	0.2%
46	South Dakota	597	0.2%
47	Alaska	586	0.2%
48	Wyoming	557	0.2%
49	North Dakota	516	0.2%
50	Vermont	441	0.1%
	District of Columbia	1,008	0.3%

Source: Morgan Quitno Press using data from U.S. Dept. of Health and Human Services, Nat'l Center for Health Statistics "National Vital Statistics Reports" (Vol. 47, No. 25, October 5, 1999)
*Estimates based on preliminary data by state of residence. Births of less than 2,500 grams (5 pounds 8 ounces).

Births of Low Birthweight as a Percent of All Births in 1998

National Percent = 7.6% of Live Births*

ALPHA ORDER			RANK ORDER		
RANK	STATE	PERCENT	RANK	STATE	PERCENT
4	Alabama	9.3	1	Louisiana	10.1
44	Alaska	5.9	1	Mississippi	10.1
35	Arizona	6.8	3	South Carolina	9.5
6	Arkansas	8.9	4	Alabama	9.3
42	California	6.2	5	Tennessee	9.1
10	Colorado	8.6	6	Arkansas	8.9
24	Connecticut	7.7	6	Wyoming	8.9
12	Delaware	8.4	8	North Carolina	8.8
14	Florida	8.1	9	Maryland	8.7
11	Georgia	8.5	10	Colorado	8.6
16	Hawaii	8.0	11	Georgia	8.5
43	Idaho	6.0	12	Delaware	8.4
16	Illinois	8.0	13	Kentucky	8.2
16	Indiana	8.0	14	Florida	8.1
41	Iowa	6.4	14	West Virginia	8.1
32	Kansas	7.0	16	Hawaii	8.0
13	Kentucky	8.2	16	Illinois	8.0
1	Louisiana	10.1	16	Indiana	8.0
45	Maine	5.8	16	New Jersey	8.0
9	Maryland	8.7	20	Virginia	7.9
34	Massachusetts	6.9	21	Michigan	7.8
21	Michigan	7.8	21	Missouri	7.8
45	Minnesota	5.8	21	New York	7.8
1	Mississippi	10.1	24	Connecticut	7.7
21	Missouri	7.8	24	Ohio	7.7
32	Montana	7.0	26	Nevada	7.6
38	Nebraska	6.5	26	New Mexico	7.6
26	Nevada	7.6	26	Pennsylvania	7.6
48	New Hampshire	5.7	26	Rhode Island	7.6
16	New Jersey	8.0	30	Texas	7.4
26	New Mexico	7.6	31	Oklahoma	7.2
21	New York	7.8	32	Kansas	7.0
8	North Carolina	8.8	32	Montana	7.0
38	North Dakota	6.5	34	Massachusetts	6.9
24	Ohio	7.7	35	Arizona	6.8
31	Oklahoma	7.2	36	Utah	6.7
50	Oregon	5.4	36	Vermont	6.7
26	Pennsylvania	7.6	38	Nebraska	6.5
26	Rhode Island	7.6	38	North Dakota	6.5
3	South Carolina	9.5	38	Wisconsin	6.5
45	South Dakota	5.8	41	Iowa	6.4
5	Tennessee	9.1	42	California	6.2
30	Texas	7.4	43	Idaho	6.0
36	Utah	6.7	44	Alaska	5.9
36	Vermont	6.7	45	Maine	5.8
20	Virginia	7.9	45	Minnesota	5.8
48	Washington	5.7	45	South Dakota	5.8
14	West Virginia	8.1	48	New Hampshire	5.7
38	Wisconsin	6.5	48	Washington	5.7
6	Wyoming	8.9	50	Oregon	5.4
				District of Columbia	13.1

Source: U.S. Department of Health and Human Services, National Center for Health Statistics
"National Vital Statistics Reports" (Vol. 47, No. 25, October 5, 1999)
*Estimates based on preliminary data by state of residence. Births of less than 2,500 grams (5 pounds 8 ounces).

Births of Low Birthweight of White Women in 1998

National Total = 202,955 Live Births*

ALPHA ORDER

RANK	STATE	BIRTHS	% of USA
23	Alabama	3,034	1.5%
49	Alaska	374	0.2%
15	Arizona	4,516	2.2%
33	Arkansas	2,123	1.0%
1	California	24,206	11.9%
13	Colorado	4,526	2.2%
28	Connecticut	2,586	1.3%
45	Delaware	485	0.2%
4	Florida	9,943	4.9%
12	Georgia	5,004	2.5%
50	Hawaii	263	0.1%
39	Idaho	1,126	0.6%
5	Illinois	8,969	4.4%
11	Indiana	5,394	2.7%
31	Iowa	2,184	1.1%
30	Kansas	2,229	1.1%
20	Kentucky	3,710	1.8%
26	Louisiana	2,669	1.3%
42	Maine	776	0.4%
24	Maryland	2,874	1.4%
14	Massachusetts	4,523	2.2%
8	Michigan	6,864	3.4%
22	Minnesota	3,094	1.5%
36	Mississippi	1,653	0.8%
18	Missouri	4,189	2.1%
43	Montana	648	0.3%
38	Nebraska	1,330	0.7%
35	Nevada	1,678	0.8%
40	New Hampshire	798	0.4%
9	New Jersey	5,795	2.9%
34	New Mexico	1,802	0.9%
3	New York	12,472	6.1%
10	North Carolina	5,554	2.7%
47	North Dakota	457	0.2%
6	Ohio	8,662	4.3%
27	Oklahoma	2,608	1.3%
32	Oregon	2,164	1.1%
7	Pennsylvania	8,041	4.0%
41	Rhode Island	783	0.4%
29	South Carolina	2,429	1.2%
46	South Dakota	478	0.2%
16	Tennessee	4,507	2.2%
2	Texas	19,553	9.6%
25	Utah	2,833	1.4%
48	Vermont	442	0.2%
17	Virginia	4,399	2.2%
19	Washington	3,727	1.8%
37	West Virginia	1,549	0.8%
21	Wisconsin	3,317	1.6%
44	Wyoming	518	0.3%

RANK ORDER

RANK	STATE	BIRTHS	% of USA
1	California	24,206	11.9%
2	Texas	19,553	9.6%
3	New York	12,472	6.1%
4	Florida	9,943	4.9%
5	Illinois	8,969	4.4%
6	Ohio	8,662	4.3%
7	Pennsylvania	8,041	4.0%
8	Michigan	6,864	3.4%
9	New Jersey	5,795	2.9%
10	North Carolina	5,554	2.7%
11	Indiana	5,394	2.7%
12	Georgia	5,004	2.5%
13	Colorado	4,526	2.2%
14	Massachusetts	4,523	2.2%
15	Arizona	4,516	2.2%
16	Tennessee	4,507	2.2%
17	Virginia	4,399	2.2%
18	Missouri	4,189	2.1%
19	Washington	3,727	1.8%
20	Kentucky	3,710	1.8%
21	Wisconsin	3,317	1.6%
22	Minnesota	3,094	1.5%
23	Alabama	3,034	1.5%
24	Maryland	2,874	1.4%
25	Utah	2,833	1.4%
26	Louisiana	2,669	1.3%
27	Oklahoma	2,608	1.3%
28	Connecticut	2,586	1.3%
29	South Carolina	2,429	1.2%
30	Kansas	2,229	1.1%
31	Iowa	2,184	1.1%
32	Oregon	2,164	1.1%
33	Arkansas	2,123	1.0%
34	New Mexico	1,802	0.9%
35	Nevada	1,678	0.8%
36	Mississippi	1,653	0.8%
37	West Virginia	1,549	0.8%
38	Nebraska	1,330	0.7%
39	Idaho	1,126	0.6%
40	New Hampshire	798	0.4%
41	Rhode Island	783	0.4%
42	Maine	776	0.4%
43	Montana	648	0.3%
44	Wyoming	518	0.3%
45	Delaware	485	0.2%
46	South Dakota	478	0.2%
47	North Dakota	457	0.2%
48	Vermont	442	0.2%
49	Alaska	374	0.2%
50	Hawaii	263	0.1%
	District of Columbia	123	0.1%

Source: Morgan Quitno Press using data from U.S. Dept. of Health and Human Services, Nat'l Center for Health Statistics "National Vital Statistics Reports" (Vol. 47, No. 25, October 5, 1999)

*Preliminary data by state of residence. Births of less than 2,500 grams (5 pounds 8 ounces). Calculated by the editors by multiplying total number of births to white women by percent of such births reported as being of low birthweight.

Births of Low Birthweight to White Women
As a Percent of All Births to White Women in 1998
National Percent = 6.5% of Live Births to White Women*

RANK	STATE	PERCENT
8	Alabama	7.3
46	Alaska	5.6
26	Arizona	6.6
7	Arkansas	7.5
43	California	5.7
2	Colorado	8.3
13	Connecticut	7.0
37	Delaware	6.3
18	Florida	6.8
33	Georgia	6.4
37	Hawaii	6.3
41	Idaho	6.0
33	Illinois	6.4
8	Indiana	7.3
39	Iowa	6.2
29	Kansas	6.5
5	Kentucky	7.6
13	Louisiana	7.0
42	Maine	5.8
33	Maryland	6.4
29	Massachusetts	6.5
29	Michigan	6.5
48	Minnesota	5.4
10	Mississippi	7.2
21	Missouri	6.7
16	Montana	6.9
39	Nebraska	6.2
16	Nevada	6.9
46	New Hampshire	5.6
21	New Jersey	6.7
4	New Mexico	7.7
21	New York	6.7
13	North Carolina	7.0
29	North Dakota	6.5
18	Ohio	6.8
21	Oklahoma	6.7
50	Oregon	5.2
26	Pennsylvania	6.6
11	Rhode Island	7.1
11	South Carolina	7.1
43	South Dakota	5.7
5	Tennessee	7.6
21	Texas	6.7
26	Utah	6.6
18	Vermont	6.8
33	Virginia	6.4
48	Washington	5.4
3	West Virginia	7.8
43	Wisconsin	5.7
1	Wyoming	8.8

RANK	STATE	PERCENT
1	Wyoming	8.8
2	Colorado	8.3
3	West Virginia	7.8
4	New Mexico	7.7
5	Kentucky	7.6
5	Tennessee	7.6
7	Arkansas	7.5
8	Alabama	7.3
8	Indiana	7.3
10	Mississippi	7.2
11	Rhode Island	7.1
11	South Carolina	7.1
13	Connecticut	7.0
13	Louisiana	7.0
13	North Carolina	7.0
16	Montana	6.9
16	Nevada	6.9
18	Florida	6.8
18	Ohio	6.8
18	Vermont	6.8
21	Missouri	6.7
21	New Jersey	6.7
21	New York	6.7
21	Oklahoma	6.7
21	Texas	6.7
26	Arizona	6.6
26	Pennsylvania	6.6
26	Utah	6.6
29	Kansas	6.5
29	Massachusetts	6.5
29	Michigan	6.5
29	North Dakota	6.5
33	Georgia	6.4
33	Illinois	6.4
33	Maryland	6.4
33	Virginia	6.4
37	Delaware	6.3
37	Hawaii	6.3
39	Iowa	6.2
39	Nebraska	6.2
41	Idaho	6.0
42	Maine	5.8
43	California	5.7
43	South Dakota	5.7
43	Wisconsin	5.7
46	Alaska	5.6
46	New Hampshire	5.6
48	Minnesota	5.4
48	Washington	5.4
50	Oregon	5.2
	District of Columbia	6.0

Source: U.S. Department of Health and Human Services, National Center for Health Statistics
"National Vital Statistics Reports" (Vol. 47, No. 25, October 5, 1999)
*Preliminary data by state of residence. Births of less than 2,500 grams (5 pounds 8 ounces).

Births of Low Birthweight to Black Women in 1998

National Total = 79,326 Live Births*

ALPHA ORDER

RANK	STATE	BIRTHS	% of USA
15	Alabama	2,665	3.4%
41	Alaska	42	0.1%
31	Arizona	322	0.4%
21	Arkansas	1,111	1.4%
6	California	4,262	5.4%
29	Colorado	383	0.5%
24	Connecticut	710	0.9%
28	Delaware	388	0.5%
2	Florida	5,415	6.8%
3	Georgia	5,239	6.6%
39	Hawaii	59	0.1%
NA	Idaho**	NA	NA
4	Illinois	5,071	6.4%
20	Indiana	1,229	1.5%
35	Iowa	140	0.2%
30	Kansas	362	0.5%
25	Kentucky	666	0.8%
7	Louisiana	4,008	5.1%
NA	Maine**	NA	NA
10	Maryland	3,119	3.9%
23	Massachusetts	799	1.0%
9	Michigan	3,350	4.2%
27	Minnesota	403	0.5%
16	Mississippi	2,652	3.3%
19	Missouri	1,597	2.0%
NA	Montana**	NA	NA
34	Nebraska	151	0.2%
33	Nevada	300	0.4%
NA	New Hampshire**	NA	NA
12	New Jersey	2,906	3.7%
39	New Mexico	59	0.1%
1	New York	6,485	8.2%
8	North Carolina	3,926	4.9%
NA	North Dakota**	NA	NA
11	Ohio	3,011	3.8%
26	Oklahoma	601	0.8%
38	Oregon	95	0.1%
14	Pennsylvania	2,772	3.5%
36	Rhode Island	110	0.1%
17	South Carolina	2,637	3.3%
NA	South Dakota**	NA	NA
18	Tennessee	2,414	3.0%
5	Texas	5,065	6.4%
41	Utah	42	0.1%
NA	Vermont**	NA	NA
13	Virginia	2,796	3.5%
32	Washington	311	0.4%
37	West Virginia	103	0.1%
22	Wisconsin	890	1.1%
NA	Wyoming**	NA	NA

RANK ORDER

RANK	STATE	BIRTHS	% of USA
1	New York	6,485	8.2%
2	Florida	5,415	6.8%
3	Georgia	5,239	6.6%
4	Illinois	5,071	6.4%
5	Texas	5,065	6.4%
6	California	4,262	5.4%
7	Louisiana	4,008	5.1%
8	North Carolina	3,926	4.9%
9	Michigan	3,350	4.2%
10	Maryland	3,119	3.9%
11	Ohio	3,011	3.8%
12	New Jersey	2,906	3.7%
13	Virginia	2,796	3.5%
14	Pennsylvania	2,772	3.5%
15	Alabama	2,665	3.4%
16	Mississippi	2,652	3.3%
17	South Carolina	2,637	3.3%
18	Tennessee	2,414	3.0%
19	Missouri	1,597	2.0%
20	Indiana	1,229	1.5%
21	Arkansas	1,111	1.4%
22	Wisconsin	890	1.1%
23	Massachusetts	799	1.0%
24	Connecticut	710	0.9%
25	Kentucky	666	0.8%
26	Oklahoma	601	0.8%
27	Minnesota	403	0.5%
28	Delaware	388	0.5%
29	Colorado	383	0.5%
30	Kansas	362	0.5%
31	Arizona	322	0.4%
32	Washington	311	0.4%
33	Nevada	300	0.4%
34	Nebraska	151	0.2%
35	Iowa	140	0.2%
36	Rhode Island	110	0.1%
37	West Virginia	103	0.1%
38	Oregon	95	0.1%
39	Hawaii	59	0.1%
39	New Mexico	59	0.1%
41	Alaska	42	0.1%
41	Utah	42	0.1%
NA	Idaho**	NA	NA
NA	Maine**	NA	NA
NA	Montana**	NA	NA
NA	New Hampshire**	NA	NA
NA	North Dakota**	NA	NA
NA	South Dakota**	NA	NA
NA	Vermont**	NA	NA
NA	Wyoming**	NA	NA

District of Columbia 864 1.1%

Source: Morgan Quitno Press using data from U.S. Dept. of Health and Human Services, Nat'l Center for Health Statistics
"National Vital Statistics Reports" (Vol. 47, No. 25, October 5, 1999)
*Preliminary data by state of residence. Births of less than 2,500 grams (5 pounds 8 ounces). Calculated by the
editors by multiplying total number of births to black women by percent of such births reported as being of low
birthweight.
**Not available.

Births of Low Birthweight to Black Women
As a Percent of All Births to Black Women in 1998
National Percent = 13.0% of Live Births to Black Women*

<table>
<tr><td colspan="3">ALPHA ORDER</td><td colspan="3">RANK ORDER</td></tr>
<tr><td>RANK</td><td>STATE</td><td>PERCENT</td><td>RANK</td><td>STATE</td><td>PERCENT</td></tr>
<tr><td>17</td><td>Alabama</td><td>13.3</td><td>1</td><td>Utah</td><td>15.0</td></tr>
<tr><td>39</td><td>Alaska</td><td>10.4</td><td>2</td><td>Delaware</td><td>14.8</td></tr>
<tr><td>32</td><td>Arizona</td><td>12.1</td><td>3</td><td>Louisiana</td><td>14.6</td></tr>
<tr><td>8</td><td>Arkansas</td><td>13.9</td><td>4</td><td>Tennessee</td><td>14.3</td></tr>
<tr><td>34</td><td>California</td><td>11.6</td><td>5</td><td>Illinois</td><td>14.2</td></tr>
<tr><td>17</td><td>Colorado</td><td>13.3</td><td>6</td><td>Missouri</td><td>14.0</td></tr>
<tr><td>21</td><td>Connecticut</td><td>13.2</td><td>6</td><td>South Carolina</td><td>14.0</td></tr>
<tr><td>2</td><td>Delaware</td><td>14.8</td><td>8</td><td>Arkansas</td><td>13.9</td></tr>
<tr><td>30</td><td>Florida</td><td>12.2</td><td>8</td><td>North Carolina</td><td>13.9</td></tr>
<tr><td>26</td><td>Georgia</td><td>12.7</td><td>10</td><td>Michigan</td><td>13.8</td></tr>
<tr><td>38</td><td>Hawaii</td><td>10.5</td><td>11</td><td>Kentucky</td><td>13.7</td></tr>
<tr><td>NA</td><td>Idaho**</td><td>NA</td><td>11</td><td>Mississippi</td><td>13.7</td></tr>
<tr><td>5</td><td>Illinois</td><td>14.2</td><td>13</td><td>Indiana</td><td>13.6</td></tr>
<tr><td>13</td><td>Indiana</td><td>13.6</td><td>13</td><td>Wisconsin</td><td>13.6</td></tr>
<tr><td>25</td><td>Iowa</td><td>12.8</td><td>15</td><td>Pennsylvania</td><td>13.5</td></tr>
<tr><td>23</td><td>Kansas</td><td>13.0</td><td>15</td><td>West Virginia</td><td>13.5</td></tr>
<tr><td>11</td><td>Kentucky</td><td>13.7</td><td>17</td><td>Alabama</td><td>13.3</td></tr>
<tr><td>3</td><td>Louisiana</td><td>14.6</td><td>17</td><td>Colorado</td><td>13.3</td></tr>
<tr><td>NA</td><td>Maine**</td><td>NA</td><td>17</td><td>Nevada</td><td>13.3</td></tr>
<tr><td>24</td><td>Maryland</td><td>12.9</td><td>17</td><td>New Jersey</td><td>13.3</td></tr>
<tr><td>40</td><td>Massachusetts</td><td>10.1</td><td>21</td><td>Connecticut</td><td>13.2</td></tr>
<tr><td>10</td><td>Michigan</td><td>13.8</td><td>21</td><td>Ohio</td><td>13.2</td></tr>
<tr><td>37</td><td>Minnesota</td><td>11.0</td><td>23</td><td>Kansas</td><td>13.0</td></tr>
<tr><td>11</td><td>Mississippi</td><td>13.7</td><td>24</td><td>Maryland</td><td>12.9</td></tr>
<tr><td>6</td><td>Missouri</td><td>14.0</td><td>25</td><td>Iowa</td><td>12.8</td></tr>
<tr><td>NA</td><td>Montana**</td><td>NA</td><td>26</td><td>Georgia</td><td>12.7</td></tr>
<tr><td>30</td><td>Nebraska</td><td>12.2</td><td>27</td><td>Texas</td><td>12.6</td></tr>
<tr><td>17</td><td>Nevada</td><td>13.3</td><td>27</td><td>Virginia</td><td>12.6</td></tr>
<tr><td>NA</td><td>New Hampshire**</td><td>NA</td><td>29</td><td>Oklahoma</td><td>12.5</td></tr>
<tr><td>17</td><td>New Jersey</td><td>13.3</td><td>30</td><td>Florida</td><td>12.2</td></tr>
<tr><td>35</td><td>New Mexico</td><td>11.4</td><td>30</td><td>Nebraska</td><td>12.2</td></tr>
<tr><td>33</td><td>New York</td><td>11.9</td><td>32</td><td>Arizona</td><td>12.1</td></tr>
<tr><td>8</td><td>North Carolina</td><td>13.9</td><td>33</td><td>New York</td><td>11.9</td></tr>
<tr><td>NA</td><td>North Dakota**</td><td>NA</td><td>34</td><td>California</td><td>11.6</td></tr>
<tr><td>21</td><td>Ohio</td><td>13.2</td><td>35</td><td>New Mexico</td><td>11.4</td></tr>
<tr><td>29</td><td>Oklahoma</td><td>12.5</td><td>35</td><td>Rhode Island</td><td>11.4</td></tr>
<tr><td>42</td><td>Oregon</td><td>9.8</td><td>37</td><td>Minnesota</td><td>11.0</td></tr>
<tr><td>15</td><td>Pennsylvania</td><td>13.5</td><td>38</td><td>Hawaii</td><td>10.5</td></tr>
<tr><td>35</td><td>Rhode Island</td><td>11.4</td><td>39</td><td>Alaska</td><td>10.4</td></tr>
<tr><td>6</td><td>South Carolina</td><td>14.0</td><td>40</td><td>Massachusetts</td><td>10.1</td></tr>
<tr><td>NA</td><td>South Dakota**</td><td>NA</td><td>41</td><td>Washington</td><td>10.0</td></tr>
<tr><td>4</td><td>Tennessee</td><td>14.3</td><td>42</td><td>Oregon</td><td>9.8</td></tr>
<tr><td>27</td><td>Texas</td><td>12.6</td><td>NA</td><td>Idaho**</td><td>NA</td></tr>
<tr><td>1</td><td>Utah</td><td>15.0</td><td>NA</td><td>Maine**</td><td>NA</td></tr>
<tr><td>NA</td><td>Vermont**</td><td>NA</td><td>NA</td><td>Montana**</td><td>NA</td></tr>
<tr><td>27</td><td>Virginia</td><td>12.6</td><td>NA</td><td>New Hampshire**</td><td>NA</td></tr>
<tr><td>41</td><td>Washington</td><td>10.0</td><td>NA</td><td>North Dakota**</td><td>NA</td></tr>
<tr><td>15</td><td>West Virginia</td><td>13.5</td><td>NA</td><td>South Dakota**</td><td>NA</td></tr>
<tr><td>13</td><td>Wisconsin</td><td>13.6</td><td>NA</td><td>Vermont**</td><td>NA</td></tr>
<tr><td>NA</td><td>Wyoming**</td><td>NA</td><td>NA</td><td>Wyoming**</td><td>NA</td></tr>
<tr><td></td><td></td><td></td><td></td><td>District of Columbia</td><td>15.8</td></tr>
</table>

Source: U.S. Department of Health and Human Services, National Center for Health Statistics
"National Vital Statistics Reports" (Vol. 47, No. 25, October 5, 1999)
*Preliminary data by state of residence. Births of less than 2,500 grams (5 pounds 8 ounces).
**Insufficient data.

Births to Unmarried Women in 1998

National Total = 1,293,647 Live Births*

ALPHA ORDER

RANK	STATE	BIRTHS	% of USA
21	Alabama	21,185	1.6%
47	Alaska	3,090	0.2%
12	Arizona	30,066	2.3%
31	Arkansas	12,949	1.0%
1	California	170,629	13.2%
28	Colorado	15,309	1.2%
29	Connecticut	13,713	1.1%
43	Delaware	3,926	0.3%
4	Florida	71,603	5.5%
8	Georgia	44,299	3.4%
39	Hawaii	5,522	0.4%
41	Idaho	4,266	0.3%
5	Illinois	62,229	4.8%
15	Indiana	28,100	2.2%
34	Iowa	10,141	0.8%
33	Kansas	10,679	0.8%
27	Kentucky	16,236	1.3%
13	Louisiana	30,031	2.3%
42	Maine	4,207	0.3%
18	Maryland	24,778	1.9%
20	Massachusetts	21,284	1.6%
9	Michigan	43,981	3.4%
25	Minnesota	16,692	1.3%
23	Mississippi	19,534	1.5%
17	Missouri	25,705	2.0%
46	Montana	3,193	0.2%
38	Nebraska	6,167	0.5%
35	Nevada	9,948	0.8%
44	New Hampshire	3,521	0.3%
11	New Jersey	32,975	2.5%
32	New Mexico	12,260	0.9%
3	New York	90,088	7.0%
10	North Carolina	36,632	2.8%
48	North Dakota	2,142	0.2%
6	Ohio	51,986	4.0%
26	Oklahoma	16,427	1.3%
30	Oregon	13,447	1.0%
7	Pennsylvania	47,907	3.7%
40	Rhode Island	4,271	0.3%
22	South Carolina	20,855	1.6%
45	South Dakota	3,292	0.3%
16	Tennessee	27,008	2.1%
2	Texas	107,818	8.3%
36	Utah	7,722	0.6%
50	Vermont	1,842	0.1%
14	Virginia	28,165	2.2%
19	Washington	22,225	1.7%
37	West Virginia	6,725	0.5%
24	Wisconsin	19,224	1.5%
49	Wyoming	1,853	0.1%

RANK ORDER

RANK	STATE	BIRTHS	% of USA
1	California	170,629	13.2%
2	Texas	107,818	8.3%
3	New York	90,088	7.0%
4	Florida	71,603	5.5%
5	Illinois	62,229	4.8%
6	Ohio	51,986	4.0%
7	Pennsylvania	47,907	3.7%
8	Georgia	44,299	3.4%
9	Michigan	43,981	3.4%
10	North Carolina	36,632	2.8%
11	New Jersey	32,975	2.5%
12	Arizona	30,066	2.3%
13	Louisiana	30,031	2.3%
14	Virginia	28,165	2.2%
15	Indiana	28,100	2.2%
16	Tennessee	27,008	2.1%
17	Missouri	25,705	2.0%
18	Maryland	24,778	1.9%
19	Washington	22,225	1.7%
20	Massachusetts	21,284	1.6%
21	Alabama	21,185	1.6%
22	South Carolina	20,855	1.6%
23	Mississippi	19,534	1.5%
24	Wisconsin	19,224	1.5%
25	Minnesota	16,692	1.3%
26	Oklahoma	16,427	1.3%
27	Kentucky	16,236	1.3%
28	Colorado	15,309	1.2%
29	Connecticut	13,713	1.1%
30	Oregon	13,447	1.0%
31	Arkansas	12,949	1.0%
32	New Mexico	12,260	0.9%
33	Kansas	10,679	0.8%
34	Iowa	10,141	0.8%
35	Nevada	9,948	0.8%
36	Utah	7,722	0.6%
37	West Virginia	6,725	0.5%
38	Nebraska	6,167	0.5%
39	Hawaii	5,522	0.4%
40	Rhode Island	4,271	0.3%
41	Idaho	4,266	0.3%
42	Maine	4,207	0.3%
43	Delaware	3,926	0.3%
44	New Hampshire	3,521	0.3%
45	South Dakota	3,292	0.3%
46	Montana	3,193	0.2%
47	Alaska	3,090	0.2%
48	North Dakota	2,142	0.2%
49	Wyoming	1,853	0.1%
50	Vermont	1,842	0.1%
	District of Columbia	4,832	0.4%

Source: Morgan Quitno Press using data from U.S. Dept. of Health and Human Services, Nat'l Center for Health Statistics
"National Vital Statistics Reports" (Vol. 47, No. 25, October 5, 1999)
*Preliminary data by state of residence. Calculated by the editors by multiplying total number of births by reported percent of births to unmarried women.

Births to Unmarried Women as a Percent of All Births in 1998

National Percent = 32.8% of Live Births*

RANK	STATE	PERCENT
14	Alabama	34.1
30	Alaska	31.1
5	Arizona	38.4
9	Arkansas	35.1
24	California	32.7
46	Colorado	25.6
29	Connecticut	31.3
6	Delaware	37.1
7	Florida	36.6
8	Georgia	36.2
28	Hawaii	31.4
49	Idaho	22.0
14	Illinois	34.1
19	Indiana	33.4
42	Iowa	27.2
41	Kansas	27.8
32	Kentucky	29.9
2	Louisiana	44.9
31	Maine	30.6
13	Maryland	34.4
45	Massachusetts	26.1
21	Michigan	32.9
46	Minnesota	25.6
1	Mississippi	45.5
14	Missouri	34.1
32	Montana	29.9
44	Nebraska	26.2
12	Nevada	34.7
48	New Hampshire	24.1
38	New Jersey	28.3
3	New Mexico	44.1
10	New York	34.9
22	North Carolina	32.8
43	North Dakota	27.0
17	Ohio	34.0
20	Oklahoma	33.2
35	Oregon	29.7
22	Pennsylvania	32.8
18	Rhode Island	33.9
4	South Carolina	38.7
26	South Dakota	32.0
10	Tennessee	34.9
27	Texas	31.5
50	Utah	17.1
39	Vermont	28.0
34	Virginia	29.8
40	Washington	27.9
25	West Virginia	32.4
37	Wisconsin	28.5
36	Wyoming	29.6

RANK	STATE	PERCENT
1	Mississippi	45.5
2	Louisiana	44.9
3	New Mexico	44.1
4	South Carolina	38.7
5	Arizona	38.4
6	Delaware	37.1
7	Florida	36.6
8	Georgia	36.2
9	Arkansas	35.1
10	New York	34.9
10	Tennessee	34.9
12	Nevada	34.7
13	Maryland	34.4
14	Alabama	34.1
14	Illinois	34.1
14	Missouri	34.1
17	Ohio	34.0
18	Rhode Island	33.9
19	Indiana	33.4
20	Oklahoma	33.2
21	Michigan	32.9
22	North Carolina	32.8
22	Pennsylvania	32.8
24	California	32.7
25	West Virginia	32.4
26	South Dakota	32.0
27	Texas	31.5
28	Hawaii	31.4
29	Connecticut	31.3
30	Alaska	31.1
31	Maine	30.6
32	Kentucky	29.9
32	Montana	29.9
34	Virginia	29.8
35	Oregon	29.7
36	Wyoming	29.6
37	Wisconsin	28.5
38	New Jersey	28.3
39	Vermont	28.0
40	Washington	27.9
41	Kansas	27.8
42	Iowa	27.2
43	North Dakota	27.0
44	Nebraska	26.2
45	Massachusetts	26.1
46	Colorado	25.6
46	Minnesota	25.6
48	New Hampshire	24.1
49	Idaho	22.0
50	Utah	17.1
	District of Columbia	62.8

Source: U.S. Department of Health and Human Services, National Center for Health Statistics
"National Vital Statistics Reports" (Vol. 47, No. 25, October 5, 1999)
*Preliminary data by state of residence.

Births to Unmarried White Women in 1998

National Total = 821,189 Live Births*

ALPHA ORDER

RANK	STATE	BIRTHS	% of USA
33	Alabama	7,191	0.9%
49	Alaska	1,457	0.2%
9	Arizona	24,429	3.0%
35	Arkansas	6,823	0.8%
1	California	138,015	16.8%
19	Colorado	13,141	1.6%
25	Connecticut	9,641	1.2%
44	Delaware	1,987	0.2%
4	Florida	40,795	5.0%
15	Georgia	16,264	2.0%
50	Hawaii	643	0.1%
40	Idaho	3,999	0.5%
6	Illinois	33,775	4.1%
10	Indiana	20,983	2.6%
29	Iowa	9,089	1.1%
30	Kansas	8,401	1.0%
21	Kentucky	12,692	1.5%
28	Louisiana	9,302	1.1%
39	Maine	4,068	0.5%
26	Maryland	9,566	1.2%
16	Massachusetts	15,933	1.9%
8	Michigan	25,556	3.1%
22	Minnesota	12,661	1.5%
38	Mississippi	4,682	0.6%
13	Missouri	16,570	2.0%
43	Montana	2,357	0.3%
37	Nebraska	4,975	0.6%
31	Nevada	7,832	1.0%
41	New Hampshire	3,421	0.4%
12	New Jersey	18,076	2.2%
27	New Mexico	9,364	1.1%
3	New York	51,190	6.2%
14	North Carolina	16,502	2.0%
48	North Dakota	1,576	0.2%
5	Ohio	34,137	4.2%
24	Oklahoma	10,587	1.3%
23	Oregon	12,026	1.5%
7	Pennsylvania	31,310	3.8%
42	Rhode Island	3,375	0.4%
32	South Carolina	7,526	0.9%
45	South Dakota	1,947	0.2%
17	Tennessee	14,291	1.7%
2	Texas	81,129	9.9%
34	Utah	6,998	0.9%
46	Vermont	1,812	0.2%
18	Virginia	13,746	1.7%
11	Washington	18,221	2.2%
36	West Virginia	6,116	0.7%
20	Wisconsin	13,034	1.6%
47	Wyoming	1,643	0.2%

RANK ORDER

RANK	STATE	BIRTHS	% of USA
1	California	138,015	16.8%
2	Texas	81,129	9.9%
3	New York	51,190	6.2%
4	Florida	40,795	5.0%
5	Ohio	34,137	4.2%
6	Illinois	33,775	4.1%
7	Pennsylvania	31,310	3.8%
8	Michigan	25,556	3.1%
9	Arizona	24,429	3.0%
10	Indiana	20,983	2.6%
11	Washington	18,221	2.2%
12	New Jersey	18,076	2.2%
13	Missouri	16,570	2.0%
14	North Carolina	16,502	2.0%
15	Georgia	16,264	2.0%
16	Massachusetts	15,933	1.9%
17	Tennessee	14,291	1.7%
18	Virginia	13,746	1.7%
19	Colorado	13,141	1.6%
20	Wisconsin	13,034	1.6%
21	Kentucky	12,692	1.5%
22	Minnesota	12,661	1.5%
23	Oregon	12,026	1.5%
24	Oklahoma	10,587	1.3%
25	Connecticut	9,641	1.2%
26	Maryland	9,566	1.2%
27	New Mexico	9,364	1.1%
28	Louisiana	9,302	1.1%
29	Iowa	9,089	1.1%
30	Kansas	8,401	1.0%
31	Nevada	7,832	1.0%
32	South Carolina	7,526	0.9%
33	Alabama	7,191	0.9%
34	Utah	6,998	0.9%
35	Arkansas	6,823	0.8%
36	West Virginia	6,116	0.7%
37	Nebraska	4,975	0.6%
38	Mississippi	4,682	0.6%
39	Maine	4,068	0.5%
40	Idaho	3,999	0.5%
41	New Hampshire	3,421	0.4%
42	Rhode Island	3,375	0.4%
43	Montana	2,357	0.3%
44	Delaware	1,987	0.2%
45	South Dakota	1,947	0.2%
46	Vermont	1,812	0.2%
47	Wyoming	1,643	0.2%
48	North Dakota	1,576	0.2%
49	Alaska	1,457	0.2%
50	Hawaii	643	0.1%
	District of Columbia	479	0.1%

Source: Morgan Quitno Press using data from U.S. Dept. of Health and Human Services, Nat'l Center for Health Statistics "National Vital Statistics Reports" (Vol. 47, No. 25, October 5, 1999)
*Preliminary data by state of residence. Calculated by the editors by multiplying total number of births to white women by percent of such births reported as being to unmarried white women.

Births to Unmarried White Women
As a Percent of All Births to White Women in 1998
National Percent = 26.3% of Live Births*

ALPHA ORDER

RANK	STATE	PERCENT
48	Alabama	17.3
40	Alaska	21.8
2	Arizona	35.7
28	Arkansas	24.1
3	California	32.5
28	Colorado	24.1
19	Connecticut	26.1
21	Delaware	25.8
10	Florida	27.9
44	Georgia	20.8
50	Hawaii	15.4
41	Idaho	21.3
28	Illinois	24.1
9	Indiana	28.4
21	Iowa	25.8
25	Kansas	24.5
20	Kentucky	26.0
26	Louisiana	24.4
7	Maine	30.4
41	Maryland	21.3
35	Massachusetts	22.9
27	Michigan	24.2
38	Minnesota	22.1
46	Mississippi	20.4
17	Missouri	26.5
24	Montana	25.1
33	Nebraska	23.2
4	Nevada	32.2
32	New Hampshire	24.0
43	New Jersey	20.9
1	New Mexico	40.0
14	New York	27.5
44	North Carolina	20.8
36	North Dakota	22.4
16	Ohio	26.8
15	Oklahoma	27.2
8	Oregon	28.9
23	Pennsylvania	25.7
6	Rhode Island	30.6
39	South Carolina	22.0
33	South Dakota	23.2
28	Tennessee	24.1
13	Texas	27.8
49	Utah	16.3
10	Vermont	27.9
47	Virginia	20.0
18	Washington	26.4
5	West Virginia	30.8
36	Wisconsin	22.4
10	Wyoming	27.9

RANK ORDER

RANK	STATE	PERCENT
1	New Mexico	40.0
2	Arizona	35.7
3	California	32.5
4	Nevada	32.2
5	West Virginia	30.8
6	Rhode Island	30.6
7	Maine	30.4
8	Oregon	28.9
9	Indiana	28.4
10	Florida	27.9
10	Vermont	27.9
10	Wyoming	27.9
13	Texas	27.8
14	New York	27.5
15	Oklahoma	27.2
16	Ohio	26.8
17	Missouri	26.5
18	Washington	26.4
19	Connecticut	26.1
20	Kentucky	26.0
21	Delaware	25.8
21	Iowa	25.8
23	Pennsylvania	25.7
24	Montana	25.1
25	Kansas	24.5
26	Louisiana	24.4
27	Michigan	24.2
28	Arkansas	24.1
28	Colorado	24.1
28	Illinois	24.1
28	Tennessee	24.1
32	New Hampshire	24.0
33	Nebraska	23.2
33	South Dakota	23.2
35	Massachusetts	22.9
36	North Dakota	22.4
36	Wisconsin	22.4
38	Minnesota	22.1
39	South Carolina	22.0
40	Alaska	21.8
41	Idaho	21.3
41	Maryland	21.3
43	New Jersey	20.9
44	Georgia	20.8
44	North Carolina	20.8
46	Mississippi	20.4
47	Virginia	20.0
48	Alabama	17.3
49	Utah	16.3
50	Hawaii	15.4
	District of Columbia	23.3

Source: U.S. Department of Health and Human Services, National Center for Health Statistics
    "National Vital Statistics Reports" (Vol. 47, No. 25, October 5, 1999)
*Preliminary data by state of residence. By race of mother.

Births to Unmarried Black Women in 1998

National Total = 421,040 Live Births*

ALPHA ORDER					RANK ORDER			
RANK	STATE	BIRTHS	% of USA		RANK	STATE	BIRTHS	% of USA
16	Alabama	13,888	3.3%		1	New York	36,132	8.6%
40	Alaska	163	0.0%		2	Florida	29,783	7.1%
31	Arizona	1,678	0.4%		3	Illinois	27,785	6.6%
21	Arkansas	5,945	1.4%		4	Georgia	27,680	6.6%
6	California	22,704	5.4%		5	Texas	25,327	6.0%
32	Colorado	1,572	0.4%		6	California	22,704	5.4%
24	Connecticut	3,703	0.9%		7	Louisiana	20,369	4.8%
29	Delaware	1,902	0.5%		8	North Carolina	18,839	4.5%
2	Florida	29,783	7.1%		9	Michigan	17,746	4.2%
4	Georgia	27,680	6.6%		10	Ohio	17,498	4.2%
42	Hawaii	121	0.0%		11	Pennsylvania	15,911	3.8%
45	Idaho	33	0.0%		12	Maryland	14,868	3.5%
3	Illinois	27,785	6.6%		13	Mississippi	14,616	3.5%
20	Indiana	6,930	1.6%		14	New Jersey	14,398	3.4%
35	Iowa	791	0.2%		15	Virginia	14,024	3.3%
28	Kansas	1,926	0.5%		16	Alabama	13,888	3.3%
25	Kentucky	3,467	0.8%		17	South Carolina	13,150	3.1%
7	Louisiana	20,369	4.8%		18	Tennessee	12,460	3.0%
44	Maine	45	0.0%		19	Missouri	8,783	2.1%
12	Maryland	14,868	3.5%		20	Indiana	6,930	1.6%
23	Massachusetts	4,618	1.1%		21	Arkansas	5,945	1.4%
9	Michigan	17,746	4.2%		22	Wisconsin	5,370	1.3%
27	Minnesota	2,412	0.6%		23	Massachusetts	4,618	1.1%
13	Mississippi	14,616	3.5%		24	Connecticut	3,703	0.9%
19	Missouri	8,783	2.1%		25	Kentucky	3,467	0.8%
49	Montana	21	0.0%		26	Oklahoma	3,320	0.8%
34	Nebraska	852	0.2%		27	Minnesota	2,412	0.6%
33	Nevada	1,489	0.4%		28	Kansas	1,926	0.5%
43	New Hampshire	60	0.0%		29	Delaware	1,902	0.5%
14	New Jersey	14,398	3.4%		30	Washington	1,693	0.4%
39	New Mexico	317	0.1%		31	Arizona	1,678	0.4%
1	New York	36,132	8.6%		32	Colorado	1,572	0.4%
8	North Carolina	18,839	4.5%		33	Nevada	1,489	0.4%
48	North Dakota	25	0.0%		34	Nebraska	852	0.2%
10	Ohio	17,498	4.2%		35	Iowa	791	0.2%
26	Oklahoma	3,320	0.8%		36	Rhode Island	642	0.2%
37	Oregon	632	0.2%		37	Oregon	632	0.2%
11	Pennsylvania	15,911	3.8%		38	West Virginia	585	0.1%
36	Rhode Island	642	0.2%		39	New Mexico	317	0.1%
17	South Carolina	13,150	3.1%		40	Alaska	163	0.0%
46	South Dakota	32	0.0%		41	Utah	139	0.0%
18	Tennessee	12,460	3.0%		42	Hawaii	121	0.0%
5	Texas	25,327	6.0%		43	New Hampshire	60	0.0%
41	Utah	139	0.0%		44	Maine	45	0.0%
NA	Vermont**	NA	NA		45	Idaho	33	0.0%
15	Virginia	14,024	3.3%		46	South Dakota	32	0.0%
30	Washington	1,693	0.4%		47	Wyoming	27	0.0%
38	West Virginia	585	0.1%		48	North Dakota	25	0.0%
22	Wisconsin	5,370	1.3%		49	Montana	21	0.0%
47	Wyoming	27	0.0%		NA	Vermont**	NA	NA
						District of Columbia	4,319	1.0%

Source: Morgan Quitno Press using data from U.S. Dept. of Health and Human Services, Nat'l Center for Health Statistics "National Vital Statistics Reports" (Vol. 47, No. 25, October 5, 1999)

Preliminary data by state of residence. Calculated by the editors by multiplying total number of births to black women by percent of such births reported as being to unmarried black women.

***Not available.*

Births to Unmarried Black Women
As a Percent of All Births to Black Women in 1998
National Percent = 69.0% of Live Births*

ALPHA ORDER

RANK	STATE	PERCENT
17	Alabama	69.3
45	Alaska	40.2
32	Arizona	63.0
9	Arkansas	74.4
34	California	61.8
38	Colorado	54.6
20	Connecticut	68.9
13	Delaware	72.5
22	Florida	67.1
22	Georgia	67.1
49	Hawaii	21.7
45	Idaho	40.2
2	Illinois	77.8
6	Indiana	76.7
14	Iowa	72.4
18	Kansas	69.1
15	Kentucky	71.3
10	Louisiana	74.2
42	Maine	49.4
35	Maryland	61.5
37	Massachusetts	58.4
12	Michigan	73.1
29	Minnesota	65.8
8	Mississippi	75.5
4	Missouri	77.0
43	Montana	48.8
20	Nebraska	68.9
27	Nevada	66.1
44	New Hampshire	44.1
28	New Jersey	65.9
36	New Mexico	61.0
26	New York	66.3
24	North Carolina	66.7
48	North Dakota	28.7
6	Ohio	76.7
18	Oklahoma	69.1
30	Oregon	65.4
3	Pennsylvania	77.5
25	Rhode Island	66.4
16	South Carolina	69.8
47	South Dakota	37.6
11	Tennessee	73.8
32	Texas	63.0
41	Utah	49.5
NA	Vermont**	NA
31	Virginia	63.2
39	Washington	54.4
5	West Virginia	76.8
1	Wisconsin	82.1
40	Wyoming	50.0

RANK ORDER

RANK	STATE	PERCENT
1	Wisconsin	82.1
2	Illinois	77.8
3	Pennsylvania	77.5
4	Missouri	77.0
5	West Virginia	76.8
6	Indiana	76.7
6	Ohio	76.7
8	Mississippi	75.5
9	Arkansas	74.4
10	Louisiana	74.2
11	Tennessee	73.8
12	Michigan	73.1
13	Delaware	72.5
14	Iowa	72.4
15	Kentucky	71.3
16	South Carolina	69.8
17	Alabama	69.3
18	Kansas	69.1
18	Oklahoma	69.1
20	Connecticut	68.9
20	Nebraska	68.9
22	Florida	67.1
22	Georgia	67.1
24	North Carolina	66.7
25	Rhode Island	66.4
26	New York	66.3
27	Nevada	66.1
28	New Jersey	65.9
29	Minnesota	65.8
30	Oregon	65.4
31	Virginia	63.2
32	Arizona	63.0
32	Texas	63.0
34	California	61.8
35	Maryland	61.5
36	New Mexico	61.0
37	Massachusetts	58.4
38	Colorado	54.6
39	Washington	54.4
40	Wyoming	50.0
41	Utah	49.5
42	Maine	49.4
43	Montana	48.8
44	New Hampshire	44.1
45	Alaska	40.2
45	Idaho	40.2
47	South Dakota	37.6
48	North Dakota	28.7
49	Hawaii	21.7
NA	Vermont**	NA
	District of Columbia	79.0

Source: U.S. Department of Health and Human Services, National Center for Health Statistics
   "National Vital Statistics Reports" (Vol. 47, No. 25, October 5, 1999)
*Data are preliminary estimates by state of residence. By race of mother.
**Too few births for a reliable figure.

Births to Teenage Mothers in 1998

National Total = 498,250 Live Births*

ALPHA ORDER

RANK	STATE	BIRTHS	% of USA
15	Alabama	10,654	2.2%
46	Alaska	1,221	0.2%
13	Arizona	11,388	2.3%
27	Arkansas	6,900	1.4%
1	California	61,300	12.4%
24	Colorado	7,234	1.5%
36	Connecticut	3,542	0.7%
42	Delaware	1,349	0.3%
3	Florida	25,812	5.2%
7	Georgia	18,393	3.7%
40	Hawaii	1,841	0.4%
38	Idaho	2,491	0.5%
4	Illinois	22,502	4.6%
14	Indiana	10,758	2.2%
34	Iowa	3,779	0.8%
32	Kansas	4,716	1.0%
21	Kentucky	8,466	1.7%
11	Louisiana	12,176	2.5%
41	Maine	1,356	0.3%
25	Maryland	7,199	1.5%
28	Massachusetts	6,388	1.3%
8	Michigan	15,458	3.1%
29	Minnesota	5,590	1.1%
23	Mississippi	8,003	1.6%
16	Missouri	10,417	2.1%
44	Montana	1,283	0.3%
39	Nebraska	2,450	0.5%
35	Nevada	3,604	0.7%
47	New Hampshire	1,037	0.2%
18	New Jersey	9,115	1.8%
31	New Mexico	5,067	1.0%
5	New York	21,918	4.4%
9	North Carolina	15,143	3.1%
49	North Dakota	792	0.2%
6	Ohio	19,668	4.0%
22	Oklahoma	8,309	1.7%
30	Oregon	5,545	1.1%
10	Pennsylvania	14,931	3.0%
43	Rhode Island	1,306	0.3%
20	South Carolina	8,551	1.7%
45	South Dakota	1,236	0.3%
12	Tennessee	11,996	2.4%
2	Texas	55,770	11.3%
33	Utah	4,483	0.9%
50	Vermont	497	0.1%
17	Virginia	10,329	2.1%
19	Washington	8,787	1.8%
37	West Virginia	3,409	0.7%
26	Wisconsin	7,076	1.4%
48	Wyoming	1,031	0.2%

RANK ORDER

RANK	STATE	BIRTHS	% of USA
1	California	61,300	12.4%
2	Texas	55,770	11.3%
3	Florida	25,812	5.2%
4	Illinois	22,502	4.6%
5	New York	21,918	4.4%
6	Ohio	19,668	4.0%
7	Georgia	18,393	3.7%
8	Michigan	15,458	3.1%
9	North Carolina	15,143	3.1%
10	Pennsylvania	14,931	3.0%
11	Louisiana	12,176	2.5%
12	Tennessee	11,996	2.4%
13	Arizona	11,388	2.3%
14	Indiana	10,758	2.2%
15	Alabama	10,654	2.2%
16	Missouri	10,417	2.1%
17	Virginia	10,329	2.1%
18	New Jersey	9,115	1.8%
19	Washington	8,787	1.8%
20	South Carolina	8,551	1.7%
21	Kentucky	8,466	1.7%
22	Oklahoma	8,309	1.7%
23	Mississippi	8,003	1.6%
24	Colorado	7,234	1.5%
25	Maryland	7,199	1.5%
26	Wisconsin	7,076	1.4%
27	Arkansas	6,900	1.4%
28	Massachusetts	6,388	1.3%
29	Minnesota	5,590	1.1%
30	Oregon	5,545	1.1%
31	New Mexico	5,067	1.0%
32	Kansas	4,716	1.0%
33	Utah	4,483	0.9%
34	Iowa	3,779	0.8%
35	Nevada	3,604	0.7%
36	Connecticut	3,542	0.7%
37	West Virginia	3,409	0.7%
38	Idaho	2,491	0.5%
39	Nebraska	2,450	0.5%
40	Hawaii	1,841	0.4%
41	Maine	1,356	0.3%
42	Delaware	1,349	0.3%
43	Rhode Island	1,306	0.3%
44	Montana	1,283	0.3%
45	South Dakota	1,236	0.3%
46	Alaska	1,221	0.2%
47	New Hampshire	1,037	0.2%
48	Wyoming	1,031	0.2%
49	North Dakota	792	0.2%
50	Vermont	497	0.1%
	District of Columbia	1,281	0.3%

Source: Morgan Quitno Press using data from U.S. Dept. of Health and Human Services, Nat'l Center for Health Statistics "National Vital Statistics Reports" (Vol. 47, No. 25, October 5, 1999)

*Preliminary data. Live births to women under the age of 20 years old. These numbers were calculated by the editors by multiplying the percent of live births to teenage women times total births. These are rough estimates and differ from other teenage birth numbers in this book in that they include births to women under the age of 15.

Percent of Births to Teenage Mothers in 1998

National Percent = 12.5% of Live Births*

ALPHA ORDER

RANK	STATE	PERCENT
5	Alabama	17.1
31	Alaska	11.2
13	Arizona	15.1
2	Arkansas	18.6
30	California	11.3
27	Colorado	12.1
46	Connecticut	8.3
19	Delaware	13.1
18	Florida	13.2
14	Georgia	15.0
34	Hawaii	10.7
22	Idaho	12.8
25	Illinois	12.4
17	Indiana	13.7
35	Iowa	10.6
23	Kansas	12.6
12	Kentucky	15.4
3	Louisiana	18.4
41	Maine	9.8
40	Maryland	10.2
50	Massachusetts	7.2
29	Michigan	11.6
45	Minnesota	8.6
1	Mississippi	20.0
16	Missouri	13.8
26	Montana	12.3
35	Nebraska	10.6
19	Nevada	13.1
49	New Hampshire	7.7
48	New Jersey	7.8
4	New Mexico	18.2
44	New York	8.8
15	North Carolina	14.0
41	North Dakota	9.8
21	Ohio	13.0
6	Oklahoma	16.3
24	Oregon	12.5
39	Pennsylvania	10.3
37	Rhode Island	10.5
9	South Carolina	16.0
28	South Dakota	12.0
10	Tennessee	15.9
8	Texas	16.1
41	Utah	9.8
47	Vermont	7.9
33	Virginia	10.8
32	Washington	10.9
11	West Virginia	15.7
37	Wisconsin	10.5
7	Wyoming	16.2

RANK ORDER

RANK	STATE	PERCENT
1	Mississippi	20.0
2	Arkansas	18.6
3	Louisiana	18.4
4	New Mexico	18.2
5	Alabama	17.1
6	Oklahoma	16.3
7	Wyoming	16.2
8	Texas	16.1
9	South Carolina	16.0
10	Tennessee	15.9
11	West Virginia	15.7
12	Kentucky	15.4
13	Arizona	15.1
14	Georgia	15.0
15	North Carolina	14.0
16	Missouri	13.8
17	Indiana	13.7
18	Florida	13.2
19	Delaware	13.1
19	Nevada	13.1
21	Ohio	13.0
22	Idaho	12.8
23	Kansas	12.6
24	Oregon	12.5
25	Illinois	12.4
26	Montana	12.3
27	Colorado	12.1
28	South Dakota	12.0
29	Michigan	11.6
30	California	11.3
31	Alaska	11.2
32	Washington	10.9
33	Virginia	10.8
34	Hawaii	10.7
35	Iowa	10.6
35	Nebraska	10.6
37	Rhode Island	10.5
37	Wisconsin	10.5
39	Pennsylvania	10.3
40	Maryland	10.2
41	Maine	9.8
41	North Dakota	9.8
41	Utah	9.8
44	New York	8.8
45	Minnesota	8.6
46	Connecticut	8.3
47	Vermont	7.9
48	New Jersey	7.8
49	New Hampshire	7.7
50	Massachusetts	7.2
	District of Columbia	15.3

Source: U.S. Department of Health and Human Services, National Center for Health Statistics "National Vital Statistics Reports" (Vol. 47, No. 25, October 5, 1999)
Births to women 19 years old and younger.

Births to Teenage Mothers in 1997

National Total = 483,220 Live Births*

ALPHA ORDER

RANK	STATE	BIRTHS	% of USA
15	Alabama	10,461	2.2%
47	Alaska	1,099	0.2%
14	Arizona	11,035	2.3%
26	Arkansas	6,835	1.4%
1	California	59,955	12.4%
27	Colorado	6,645	1.4%
36	Connecticut	3,498	0.7%
42	Delaware	1,343	0.3%
3	Florida	25,168	5.2%
7	Georgia	17,847	3.7%
40	Hawaii	1,733	0.4%
39	Idaho	2,330	0.5%
4	Illinois	22,201	4.6%
13	Indiana	11,577	2.4%
34	Iowa	3,888	0.8%
31	Kansas	4,758	1.0%
19	Kentucky	8,524	1.8%
11	Louisiana	11,963	2.5%
41	Maine	1,378	0.3%
24	Maryland	7,002	1.4%
28	Massachusetts	5,805	1.2%
8	Michigan	15,383	3.2%
29	Minnesota	5,583	1.2%
22	Mississippi	8,307	1.7%
16	Missouri	10,095	2.1%
44	Montana	1,311	0.3%
38	Nebraska	2,397	0.5%
35	Nevada	3,559	0.7%
46	New Hampshire	1,111	0.2%
18	New Jersey	8,643	1.8%
32	New Mexico	4,706	1.0%
5	New York	22,197	4.6%
9	North Carolina	15,032	3.1%
49	North Dakota	751	0.2%
6	Ohio	19,894	4.1%
23	Oklahoma	8,058	1.7%
30	Oregon	5,356	1.1%
10	Pennsylvania	14,691	3.0%
43	Rhode Island	1,313	0.3%
21	South Carolina	8,341	1.7%
45	South Dakota	1,224	0.3%
12	Tennessee	11,889	2.5%
2	Texas	52,728	10.9%
33	Utah	4,503	0.9%
50	Vermont	551	0.1%
17	Virginia	9,850	2.0%
20	Washington	8,421	1.7%
37	West Virginia	3,268	0.7%
25	Wisconsin	6,933	1.4%
48	Wyoming	896	0.2%

RANK ORDER

RANK	STATE	BIRTHS	% of USA
1	California	59,955	12.4%
2	Texas	52,728	10.9%
3	Florida	25,168	5.2%
4	Illinois	22,201	4.6%
5	New York	22,197	4.6%
6	Ohio	19,894	4.1%
7	Georgia	17,847	3.7%
8	Michigan	15,383	3.2%
9	North Carolina	15,032	3.1%
10	Pennsylvania	14,691	3.0%
11	Louisiana	11,963	2.5%
12	Tennessee	11,889	2.5%
13	Indiana	11,577	2.4%
14	Arizona	11,035	2.3%
15	Alabama	10,461	2.2%
16	Missouri	10,095	2.1%
17	Virginia	9,850	2.0%
18	New Jersey	8,643	1.8%
19	Kentucky	8,524	1.8%
20	Washington	8,421	1.7%
21	South Carolina	8,341	1.7%
22	Mississippi	8,307	1.7%
23	Oklahoma	8,058	1.7%
24	Maryland	7,002	1.4%
25	Wisconsin	6,933	1.4%
26	Arkansas	6,835	1.4%
27	Colorado	6,645	1.4%
28	Massachusetts	5,805	1.2%
29	Minnesota	5,583	1.2%
30	Oregon	5,356	1.1%
31	Kansas	4,758	1.0%
32	New Mexico	4,706	1.0%
33	Utah	4,503	0.9%
34	Iowa	3,888	0.8%
35	Nevada	3,559	0.7%
36	Connecticut	3,498	0.7%
37	West Virginia	3,268	0.7%
38	Nebraska	2,397	0.5%
39	Idaho	2,330	0.5%
40	Hawaii	1,733	0.4%
41	Maine	1,378	0.3%
42	Delaware	1,343	0.3%
43	Rhode Island	1,313	0.3%
44	Montana	1,311	0.3%
45	South Dakota	1,224	0.3%
46	New Hampshire	1,111	0.2%
47	Alaska	1,099	0.2%
48	Wyoming	896	0.2%
49	North Dakota	751	0.2%
50	Vermont	551	0.1%
	District of Columbia	1,184	0.2%

Source: U.S. Dept of Health & Human Services, National Center for Health Statistics
    (unpublished data)
*Live births to women age 15 to 19 years old by state of residence.

Teenage Birth Rate in 1997

National Rate = 52.3 Births per 1,000 Teenage Women*

<table>
<tr><td colspan="3">ALPHA ORDER</td><td colspan="3">RANK ORDER</td></tr>
<tr><td>RANK</td><td>STATE</td><td>RATE</td><td>RANK</td><td>STATE</td><td>RATE</td></tr>
<tr><td>8</td><td>Alabama</td><td>66.6</td><td>1</td><td>Mississippi</td><td>73.7</td></tr>
<tr><td>26</td><td>Alaska</td><td>44.6</td><td>2</td><td>Arkansas</td><td>72.9</td></tr>
<tr><td>4</td><td>Arizona</td><td>69.7</td><td>3</td><td>Texas</td><td>71.7</td></tr>
<tr><td>2</td><td>Arkansas</td><td>72.9</td><td>4</td><td>Arizona</td><td>69.7</td></tr>
<tr><td>16</td><td>California</td><td>57.3</td><td>5</td><td>New Mexico</td><td>68.4</td></tr>
<tr><td>24</td><td>Colorado</td><td>48.2</td><td>6</td><td>Nevada</td><td>67.7</td></tr>
<tr><td>41</td><td>Connecticut</td><td>36.1</td><td>7</td><td>Georgia</td><td>67.2</td></tr>
<tr><td>17</td><td>Delaware</td><td>55.8</td><td>8</td><td>Alabama</td><td>66.6</td></tr>
<tr><td>15</td><td>Florida</td><td>57.7</td><td>9</td><td>Louisiana</td><td>66.3</td></tr>
<tr><td>7</td><td>Georgia</td><td>67.2</td><td>10</td><td>Tennessee</td><td>64.5</td></tr>
<tr><td>30</td><td>Hawaii</td><td>43.8</td><td>11</td><td>Oklahoma</td><td>64.3</td></tr>
<tr><td>31</td><td>Idaho</td><td>43.3</td><td>12</td><td>South Carolina</td><td>61.4</td></tr>
<tr><td>18</td><td>Illinois</td><td>54.7</td><td>13</td><td>North Carolina</td><td>61.3</td></tr>
<tr><td>19</td><td>Indiana</td><td>54.2</td><td>14</td><td>Kentucky</td><td>59.6</td></tr>
<tr><td>43</td><td>Iowa</td><td>35.7</td><td>15</td><td>Florida</td><td>57.7</td></tr>
<tr><td>23</td><td>Kansas</td><td>48.5</td><td>16</td><td>California</td><td>57.3</td></tr>
<tr><td>14</td><td>Kentucky</td><td>59.6</td><td>17</td><td>Delaware</td><td>55.8</td></tr>
<tr><td>9</td><td>Louisiana</td><td>66.3</td><td>18</td><td>Illinois</td><td>54.7</td></tr>
<tr><td>45</td><td>Maine</td><td>32.0</td><td>19</td><td>Indiana</td><td>54.2</td></tr>
<tr><td>28</td><td>Maryland</td><td>43.9</td><td>20</td><td>Missouri</td><td>51.5</td></tr>
<tr><td>47</td><td>Massachusetts</td><td>31.7</td><td>21</td><td>Ohio</td><td>49.8</td></tr>
<tr><td>28</td><td>Michigan</td><td>43.9</td><td>22</td><td>West Virginia</td><td>49.1</td></tr>
<tr><td>45</td><td>Minnesota</td><td>32.0</td><td>23</td><td>Kansas</td><td>48.5</td></tr>
<tr><td>1</td><td>Mississippi</td><td>73.7</td><td>24</td><td>Colorado</td><td>48.2</td></tr>
<tr><td>20</td><td>Missouri</td><td>51.5</td><td>25</td><td>Oregon</td><td>46.9</td></tr>
<tr><td>38</td><td>Montana</td><td>37.6</td><td>26</td><td>Alaska</td><td>44.6</td></tr>
<tr><td>40</td><td>Nebraska</td><td>37.2</td><td>27</td><td>Virginia</td><td>44.2</td></tr>
<tr><td>6</td><td>Nevada</td><td>67.7</td><td>28</td><td>Maryland</td><td>43.9</td></tr>
<tr><td>49</td><td>New Hampshire</td><td>28.6</td><td>28</td><td>Michigan</td><td>43.9</td></tr>
<tr><td>44</td><td>New Jersey</td><td>35.0</td><td>30</td><td>Hawaii</td><td>43.8</td></tr>
<tr><td>5</td><td>New Mexico</td><td>68.4</td><td>31</td><td>Idaho</td><td>43.3</td></tr>
<tr><td>37</td><td>New York</td><td>38.8</td><td>31</td><td>Wyoming</td><td>43.3</td></tr>
<tr><td>13</td><td>North Carolina</td><td>61.3</td><td>33</td><td>Rhode Island</td><td>42.7</td></tr>
<tr><td>48</td><td>North Dakota</td><td>30.1</td><td>34</td><td>Utah</td><td>42.6</td></tr>
<tr><td>21</td><td>Ohio</td><td>49.8</td><td>35</td><td>Washington</td><td>42.5</td></tr>
<tr><td>11</td><td>Oklahoma</td><td>64.3</td><td>36</td><td>South Dakota</td><td>39.7</td></tr>
<tr><td>25</td><td>Oregon</td><td>46.9</td><td>37</td><td>New York</td><td>38.8</td></tr>
<tr><td>39</td><td>Pennsylvania</td><td>37.3</td><td>38</td><td>Montana</td><td>37.6</td></tr>
<tr><td>33</td><td>Rhode Island</td><td>42.7</td><td>39</td><td>Pennsylvania</td><td>37.3</td></tr>
<tr><td>12</td><td>South Carolina</td><td>61.4</td><td>40</td><td>Nebraska</td><td>37.2</td></tr>
<tr><td>36</td><td>South Dakota</td><td>39.7</td><td>41</td><td>Connecticut</td><td>36.1</td></tr>
<tr><td>10</td><td>Tennessee</td><td>64.5</td><td>42</td><td>Wisconsin</td><td>35.9</td></tr>
<tr><td>3</td><td>Texas</td><td>71.7</td><td>43</td><td>Iowa</td><td>35.7</td></tr>
<tr><td>34</td><td>Utah</td><td>42.6</td><td>44</td><td>New Jersey</td><td>35.0</td></tr>
<tr><td>50</td><td>Vermont</td><td>26.9</td><td>45</td><td>Maine</td><td>32.0</td></tr>
<tr><td>27</td><td>Virginia</td><td>44.2</td><td>45</td><td>Minnesota</td><td>32.0</td></tr>
<tr><td>35</td><td>Washington</td><td>42.5</td><td>47</td><td>Massachusetts</td><td>31.7</td></tr>
<tr><td>22</td><td>West Virginia</td><td>49.1</td><td>48</td><td>North Dakota</td><td>30.1</td></tr>
<tr><td>42</td><td>Wisconsin</td><td>35.9</td><td>49</td><td>New Hampshire</td><td>28.6</td></tr>
<tr><td>31</td><td>Wyoming</td><td>43.3</td><td>50</td><td>Vermont</td><td>26.9</td></tr>
<tr><td></td><td></td><td></td><td></td><td>District of Columbia</td><td>91.0</td></tr>
</table>

Source: U.S. Department of Health and Human Services, National Center for Health Statistics
    "National Vital Statistics Reports" (Vol. 47, No. 18, April 29, 1999)
*Women aged 15 to 19 years old.

Births to Teenage Mothers as a Percent of Live Births in 1997

National Percent = 12.5% of Live Births*

ALPHA ORDER			RANK ORDER		
RANK	STATE	PERCENT	RANK	STATE	PERCENT
5	Alabama	17.2	1	Mississippi	20.0
31	Alaska	11.0	2	Arkansas	18.7
13	Arizona	14.6	3	Louisiana	18.1
2	Arkansas	18.7	4	New Mexico	17.5
30	California	11.4	5	Alabama	17.2
28	Colorado	11.8	6	Oklahoma	16.7
47	Connecticut	8.1	7	Kentucky	16.0
19	Delaware	13.1	7	South Carolina	16.0
19	Florida	13.1	7	Tennessee	16.0
12	Georgia	15.1	10	Texas	15.8
41	Hawaii	10.0	10	West Virginia	15.8
23	Idaho	12.5	12	Georgia	15.1
24	Illinois	12.3	13	Arizona	14.6
16	Indiana	13.9	14	North Carolina	14.0
34	Iowa	10.6	14	Wyoming	14.0
22	Kansas	12.8	16	Indiana	13.9
7	Kentucky	16.0	17	Missouri	13.6
3	Louisiana	18.1	18	Nevada	13.2
40	Maine	10.1	19	Delaware	13.1
41	Maryland	10.0	19	Florida	13.1
50	Massachusetts	7.2	19	Ohio	13.1
29	Michigan	11.5	22	Kansas	12.8
44	Minnesota	8.7	23	Idaho	12.5
1	Mississippi	20.0	24	Illinois	12.3
17	Missouri	13.6	25	Oregon	12.2
26	Montana	12.1	26	Montana	12.1
38	Nebraska	10.3	27	South Dakota	12.0
18	Nevada	13.2	28	Colorado	11.8
48	New Hampshire	7.8	29	Michigan	11.5
49	New Jersey	7.6	30	California	11.4
4	New Mexico	17.5	31	Alaska	11.0
45	New York	8.6	32	Washington	10.8
14	North Carolina	14.0	33	Virginia	10.7
43	North Dakota	9.0	34	Iowa	10.6
19	Ohio	13.1	35	Rhode Island	10.5
6	Oklahoma	16.7	35	Utah	10.5
25	Oregon	12.2	37	Wisconsin	10.4
39	Pennsylvania	10.2	38	Nebraska	10.3
35	Rhode Island	10.5	39	Pennsylvania	10.2
7	South Carolina	16.0	40	Maine	10.1
27	South Dakota	12.0	41	Hawaii	10.0
7	Tennessee	16.0	41	Maryland	10.0
10	Texas	15.8	43	North Dakota	9.0
35	Utah	10.5	44	Minnesota	8.7
46	Vermont	8.3	45	New York	8.6
33	Virginia	10.7	46	Vermont	8.3
32	Washington	10.8	47	Connecticut	8.1
10	West Virginia	15.8	48	New Hampshire	7.8
37	Wisconsin	10.4	49	New Jersey	7.6
14	Wyoming	14.0	50	Massachusetts	7.2
				District of Columbia	14.9

Source: Morgan Quitno Press using data from U.S. Dept of Health & Human Services, National Center for Health Statistics
(unpublished data)
*Live births to women age 15 to 19 years old by state of residence.

Births to White Teenage Mothers in 1997

National Total = 338,272 Live Births*

ALPHA ORDER					RANK ORDER			
RANK	STATE	BIRTHS	% of USA		RANK	STATE	BIRTHS	% of USA
20	Alabama	5,495	1.6%		1	California	49,814	14.7%
47	Alaska	593	0.2%		2	Texas	43,292	12.8%
9	Arizona	9,464	2.8%		3	Florida	15,513	4.6%
25	Arkansas	4,527	1.3%		4	Ohio	14,278	4.2%
1	California	49,814	14.7%		5	New York	13,723	4.1%
17	Colorado	5,926	1.8%		6	Illinois	13,180	3.9%
37	Connecticut	2,504	0.7%		7	Michigan	10,027	3.0%
46	Delaware	714	0.2%		8	Pennsylvania	10,011	3.0%
3	Florida	15,513	4.6%		9	Arizona	9,464	2.8%
11	Georgia	8,908	2.6%		10	Indiana	9,357	2.8%
50	Hawaii	258	0.1%		11	Georgia	8,908	2.6%
38	Idaho	2,250	0.7%		12	North Carolina	8,547	2.5%
6	Illinois	13,180	3.9%		13	Tennessee	7,815	2.3%
10	Indiana	9,357	2.8%		14	Missouri	7,374	2.2%
32	Iowa	3,491	1.0%		15	Kentucky	7,314	2.2%
31	Kansas	3,928	1.2%		16	Washington	7,129	2.1%
15	Kentucky	7,314	2.2%		17	Colorado	5,926	1.8%
21	Louisiana	5,033	1.5%		18	Oklahoma	5,688	1.7%
40	Maine	1,341	0.4%		19	Virginia	5,574	1.6%
35	Maryland	3,003	0.9%		20	Alabama	5,495	1.6%
26	Massachusetts	4,471	1.3%		21	Louisiana	5,033	1.5%
7	Michigan	10,027	3.0%		22	Oregon	4,866	1.4%
28	Minnesota	4,168	1.2%		23	New Jersey	4,800	1.4%
34	Mississippi	3,050	0.9%		24	Wisconsin	4,718	1.4%
14	Missouri	7,374	2.2%		25	Arkansas	4,527	1.3%
43	Montana	979	0.3%		26	Massachusetts	4,471	1.3%
39	Nebraska	1,985	0.6%		27	Utah	4,237	1.3%
36	Nevada	2,874	0.8%		28	Minnesota	4,168	1.2%
41	New Hampshire	1,085	0.3%		29	New Mexico	4,004	1.2%
23	New Jersey	4,800	1.4%		30	South Carolina	3,952	1.2%
29	New Mexico	4,004	1.2%		31	Kansas	3,928	1.2%
5	New York	13,723	4.1%		32	Iowa	3,491	1.0%
12	North Carolina	8,547	2.5%		33	West Virginia	3,076	0.9%
48	North Dakota	572	0.2%		34	Mississippi	3,050	0.9%
4	Ohio	14,278	4.2%		35	Maryland	3,003	0.9%
18	Oklahoma	5,688	1.7%		36	Nevada	2,874	0.8%
22	Oregon	4,866	1.4%		37	Connecticut	2,504	0.7%
8	Pennsylvania	10,011	3.0%		38	Idaho	2,250	0.7%
42	Rhode Island	1,050	0.3%		39	Nebraska	1,985	0.6%
30	South Carolina	3,952	1.2%		40	Maine	1,341	0.4%
45	South Dakota	819	0.2%		41	New Hampshire	1,085	0.3%
13	Tennessee	7,815	2.3%		42	Rhode Island	1,050	0.3%
2	Texas	43,292	12.8%		43	Montana	979	0.3%
27	Utah	4,237	1.3%		44	Wyoming	840	0.2%
49	Vermont	547	0.2%		45	South Dakota	819	0.2%
19	Virginia	5,574	1.6%		46	Delaware	714	0.2%
16	Washington	7,129	2.1%		47	Alaska	593	0.2%
33	West Virginia	3,076	0.9%		48	North Dakota	572	0.2%
24	Wisconsin	4,718	1.4%		49	Vermont	547	0.2%
44	Wyoming	840	0.2%		50	Hawaii	258	0.1%
						District of Columbia	108	0.0%

Source: U.S. Dept of Health & Human Services, National Center for Health Statistics
    (unpublished data)
*Live births to women age 15 to 19 years old by state of residence.

Births to White Teenage Mothers as a Percent of White Births in 1997

National Percent = 11.0% of White Live Births*

ALPHA ORDER

RANK	STATE	PERCENT
10	Alabama	13.6
37	Alaska	9.2
7	Arizona	14.3
2	Arkansas	16.0
21	California	11.7
22	Colorado	11.5
46	Connecticut	6.9
33	Delaware	9.5
25	Florida	10.8
19	Georgia	11.8
49	Hawaii	5.8
13	Idaho	12.5
33	Illinois	9.5
13	Indiana	12.5
30	Iowa	10.0
19	Kansas	11.8
4	Kentucky	15.3
12	Louisiana	13.4
29	Maine	10.1
47	Maryland	6.8
48	Massachusetts	6.4
33	Michigan	9.5
44	Minnesota	7.3
11	Mississippi	13.5
18	Missouri	11.9
26	Montana	10.4
36	Nebraska	9.3
13	Nevada	12.5
42	New Hampshire	7.7
50	New Jersey	5.7
1	New Mexico	17.6
44	New York	7.3
23	North Carolina	11.3
42	North Dakota	7.7
24	Ohio	11.2
6	Oklahoma	15.0
16	Oregon	12.1
38	Pennsylvania	8.3
31	Rhode Island	9.7
17	South Carolina	12.0
31	South Dakota	9.7
9	Tennessee	13.7
5	Texas	15.2
28	Utah	10.2
38	Vermont	8.3
38	Virginia	8.3
26	Washington	10.4
3	West Virginia	15.5
41	Wisconsin	8.2
8	Wyoming	13.8

RANK ORDER

RANK	STATE	PERCENT
1	New Mexico	17.6
2	Arkansas	16.0
3	West Virginia	15.5
4	Kentucky	15.3
5	Texas	15.2
6	Oklahoma	15.0
7	Arizona	14.3
8	Wyoming	13.8
9	Tennessee	13.7
10	Alabama	13.6
11	Mississippi	13.5
12	Louisiana	13.4
13	Idaho	12.5
13	Indiana	12.5
13	Nevada	12.5
16	Oregon	12.1
17	South Carolina	12.0
18	Missouri	11.9
19	Georgia	11.8
19	Kansas	11.8
21	California	11.7
22	Colorado	11.5
23	North Carolina	11.3
24	Ohio	11.2
25	Florida	10.8
26	Montana	10.4
26	Washington	10.4
28	Utah	10.2
29	Maine	10.1
30	Iowa	10.0
31	Rhode Island	9.7
31	South Dakota	9.7
33	Delaware	9.5
33	Illinois	9.5
33	Michigan	9.5
36	Nebraska	9.3
37	Alaska	9.2
38	Pennsylvania	8.3
38	Vermont	8.3
38	Virginia	8.3
41	Wisconsin	8.2
42	New Hampshire	7.7
42	North Dakota	7.7
44	Minnesota	7.3
44	New York	7.3
46	Connecticut	6.9
47	Maryland	6.8
48	Massachusetts	6.4
49	Hawaii	5.8
50	New Jersey	5.7

District of Columbia — 5.5

Source: Morgan Quitno Press using data from U.S. Dept of Health & Human Services, National Center for Health Statistics (unpublished data)

*Live births to women age 15 to 19 years old by state of residence.

Births to Black Teenage Mothers in 1997

National Total = 128,539 Live Births*

ALPHA ORDER

ALPHA ORDER

RANK	STATE	BIRTHS	% of USA
12	Alabama	4,902	3.8%
40	Alaska	68	0.1%
31	Arizona	513	0.4%
20	Arkansas	2,241	1.7%
7	California	6,575	5.1%
32	Colorado	492	0.4%
26	Connecticut	938	0.7%
29	Delaware	621	0.5%
1	Florida	9,366	7.3%
4	Georgia	8,804	6.8%
42	Hawaii	53	0.0%
43	Idaho	17	0.0%
3	Illinois	8,828	6.9%
21	Indiana	2,170	1.7%
35	Iowa	292	0.2%
28	Kansas	721	0.6%
24	Kentucky	1,162	0.9%
6	Louisiana	6,796	5.3%
48	Maine	7	0.0%
17	Maryland	3,911	3.0%
25	Massachusetts	1,115	0.9%
11	Michigan	5,111	4.0%
27	Minnesota	726	0.6%
10	Mississippi	5,197	4.0%
19	Missouri	2,603	2.0%
49	Montana	6	0.0%
34	Nebraska	316	0.2%
33	Nevada	486	0.4%
45	New Hampshire	14	0.0%
18	New Jersey	3,718	2.9%
39	New Mexico	107	0.1%
5	New York	8,018	6.2%
8	North Carolina	5,981	4.7%
47	North Dakota	8	0.0%
9	Ohio	5,467	4.3%
23	Oklahoma	1,185	0.9%
36	Oregon	197	0.2%
13	Pennsylvania	4,526	3.5%
38	Rhode Island	172	0.1%
14	South Carolina	4,324	3.4%
44	South Dakota	16	0.0%
16	Tennessee	3,986	3.1%
2	Texas	8,975	7.0%
41	Utah	60	0.0%
50	Vermont	2	0.0%
15	Virginia	4,141	3.2%
30	Washington	572	0.4%
37	West Virginia	187	0.1%
22	Wisconsin	1,761	1.4%
45	Wyoming	14	0.0%

RANK ORDER

RANK	STATE	BIRTHS	% of USA
1	Florida	9,366	7.3%
2	Texas	8,975	7.0%
3	Illinois	8,828	6.9%
4	Georgia	8,804	6.8%
5	New York	8,018	6.2%
6	Louisiana	6,796	5.3%
7	California	6,575	5.1%
8	North Carolina	5,981	4.7%
9	Ohio	5,467	4.3%
10	Mississippi	5,197	4.0%
11	Michigan	5,111	4.0%
12	Alabama	4,902	3.8%
13	Pennsylvania	4,526	3.5%
14	South Carolina	4,324	3.4%
15	Virginia	4,141	3.2%
16	Tennessee	3,986	3.1%
17	Maryland	3,911	3.0%
18	New Jersey	3,718	2.9%
19	Missouri	2,603	2.0%
20	Arkansas	2,241	1.7%
21	Indiana	2,170	1.7%
22	Wisconsin	1,761	1.4%
23	Oklahoma	1,185	0.9%
24	Kentucky	1,162	0.9%
25	Massachusetts	1,115	0.9%
26	Connecticut	938	0.7%
27	Minnesota	726	0.6%
28	Kansas	721	0.6%
29	Delaware	621	0.5%
30	Washington	572	0.4%
31	Arizona	513	0.4%
32	Colorado	492	0.4%
33	Nevada	486	0.4%
34	Nebraska	316	0.2%
35	Iowa	292	0.2%
36	Oregon	197	0.2%
37	West Virginia	187	0.1%
38	Rhode Island	172	0.1%
39	New Mexico	107	0.1%
40	Alaska	68	0.1%
41	Utah	60	0.0%
42	Hawaii	53	0.0%
43	Idaho	17	0.0%
44	South Dakota	16	0.0%
45	New Hampshire	14	0.0%
45	Wyoming	14	0.0%
47	North Dakota	8	0.0%
48	Maine	7	0.0%
49	Montana	6	0.0%
50	Vermont	2	0.0%
	District of Columbia	1,071	0.8%

Source: U.S. Dept of Health & Human Services, National Center for Health Statistics
(unpublished data)
*Live births to women age 15 to 19 years old by state of residence.

Births to Black Teenage Mothers as a Percent of Black Births in 1997

National Percent = 21.4% of Black Live Births*

ALPHA ORDER

RANK	STATE	PERCENT
14	Alabama	24.7
43	Alaska	15.0
32	Arizona	20.5
2	Arkansas	28.3
41	California	17.5
35	Colorado	19.0
37	Connecticut	17.9
14	Delaware	24.7
28	Florida	21.5
26	Georgia	22.1
48	Hawaii	9.2
11	Idaho	25.0
13	Illinois	24.9
1	Indiana	28.4
5	Iowa	26.3
6	Kansas	25.6
11	Kentucky	25.0
8	Louisiana	25.1
49	Maine	8.6
42	Maryland	17.0
45	Massachusetts	14.1
29	Michigan	21.1
22	Minnesota	22.3
4	Mississippi	26.6
19	Missouri	23.4
34	Montana	19.4
7	Nebraska	25.2
20	Nevada	22.7
46	New Hampshire	13.3
38	New Jersey	17.8
29	New Mexico	21.1
44	New York	14.2
27	North Carolina	21.8
47	North Dakota	9.5
17	Ohio	24.1
8	Oklahoma	25.1
31	Oregon	21.0
24	Pennsylvania	22.2
36	Rhode Island	18.5
18	South Carolina	23.7
40	South Dakota	17.6
16	Tennessee	24.4
20	Texas	22.7
22	Utah	22.3
50	Vermont	8.3
33	Virginia	19.6
38	Washington	17.8
8	West Virginia	25.1
3	Wisconsin	27.4
24	Wyoming	22.2

RANK ORDER

RANK	STATE	PERCENT
1	Indiana	28.4
2	Arkansas	28.3
3	Wisconsin	27.4
4	Mississippi	26.6
5	Iowa	26.3
6	Kansas	25.6
7	Nebraska	25.2
8	Louisiana	25.1
8	Oklahoma	25.1
8	West Virginia	25.1
11	Idaho	25.0
11	Kentucky	25.0
13	Illinois	24.9
14	Alabama	24.7
14	Delaware	24.7
16	Tennessee	24.4
17	Ohio	24.1
18	South Carolina	23.7
19	Missouri	23.4
20	Nevada	22.7
20	Texas	22.7
22	Minnesota	22.3
22	Utah	22.3
24	Pennsylvania	22.2
24	Wyoming	22.2
26	Georgia	22.1
27	North Carolina	21.8
28	Florida	21.5
29	Michigan	21.1
29	New Mexico	21.1
31	Oregon	21.0
32	Arizona	20.5
33	Virginia	19.6
34	Montana	19.4
35	Colorado	19.0
36	Rhode Island	18.5
37	Connecticut	17.9
38	New Jersey	17.8
38	Washington	17.8
40	South Dakota	17.6
41	California	17.5
42	Maryland	17.0
43	Alaska	15.0
44	New York	14.2
45	Massachusetts	14.1
46	New Hampshire	13.3
47	North Dakota	9.5
48	Hawaii	9.2
49	Maine	8.6
50	Vermont	8.3
	District of Columbia	18.5

Source: Morgan Quitno Press using data from U.S. Dept of Health & Human Services, National Center for Health Statistics (unpublished data)
*Live births to women age 15 to 19 years old by state of residence.

Pregnancy Rate for 15 to 19 Year Old Women in 1996

National Rate = 74.0 Births and Abortions per 1,000 Women 15-19 Years Old*

ALPHA ORDER

RANK	STATE	RATE
8	Alabama	87.3
27	Alaska	62.0
9	Arizona	86.7
6	Arkansas	89.4
NA	California**	NA
24	Colorado	66.1
21	Connecticut	69.0
NA	Delaware**	NA
NA	Florida**	NA
2	Georgia	94.2
16	Hawaii	75.5
36	Idaho	52.2
NA	Illinois**	NA
20	Indiana	69.4
NA	Iowa**	NA
17	Kansas	75.2
19	Kentucky	71.7
12	Louisiana	80.5
42	Maine	45.7
28	Maryland	61.5
33	Massachusetts	56.9
26	Michigan	63.5
39	Minnesota	47.6
11	Mississippi	82.5
25	Missouri	64.6
31	Montana	57.8
34	Nebraska	56.7
3	Nevada	93.7
NA	New Hampshire**	NA
29	New Jersey	59.7
7	New Mexico	87.8
5	New York	90.5
4	North Carolina	90.6
43	North Dakota	45.6
23	Ohio	66.3
NA	Oklahoma**	NA
13	Oregon	77.8
32	Pennsylvania	57.4
14	Rhode Island	76.7
15	South Carolina	76.3
40	South Dakota	47.4
10	Tennessee	85.2
1	Texas	96.6
38	Utah	49.3
35	Vermont	54.7
22	Virginia	68.9
18	Washington	72.5
30	West Virginia	59.2
37	Wisconsin	50.2
41	Wyoming	46.1

RANK ORDER

RANK	STATE	RATE
1	Texas	96.6
2	Georgia	94.2
3	Nevada	93.7
4	North Carolina	90.6
5	New York	90.5
6	Arkansas	89.4
7	New Mexico	87.8
8	Alabama	87.3
9	Arizona	86.7
10	Tennessee	85.2
11	Mississippi	82.5
12	Louisiana	80.5
13	Oregon	77.8
14	Rhode Island	76.7
15	South Carolina	76.3
16	Hawaii	75.5
17	Kansas	75.2
18	Washington	72.5
19	Kentucky	71.7
20	Indiana	69.4
21	Connecticut	69.0
22	Virginia	68.9
23	Ohio	66.3
24	Colorado	66.1
25	Missouri	64.6
26	Michigan	63.5
27	Alaska	62.0
28	Maryland	61.5
29	New Jersey	59.7
30	West Virginia	59.2
31	Montana	57.8
32	Pennsylvania	57.4
33	Massachusetts	56.9
34	Nebraska	56.7
35	Vermont	54.7
36	Idaho	52.2
37	Wisconsin	50.2
38	Utah	49.3
39	Minnesota	47.6
40	South Dakota	47.4
41	Wyoming	46.1
42	Maine	45.7
43	North Dakota	45.6
NA	California**	NA
NA	Delaware**	NA
NA	Florida**	NA
NA	Illinois**	NA
NA	Iowa**	NA
NA	New Hampshire**	NA
NA	Oklahoma**	NA
	District of Columbia**	NA

Source: Morgan Quitno Press using data from US Dept of Health & Human Serv's, Centers for Disease Control-Prevention "Abortion Surveillance-United States, 1996" (Morbidity Mortality Weekly Report, Vol. 48, No. SS-4, July 30, 1999)
*The sum of live births and legal induced abortions per 1,000 women aged 15-19 years old. Births by state of residence, abortions by state of occurrence. National rate includes only states reporting abortions and births.
**Not available.

Percent Change in Pregnancy Rate for 15 to 19 Year Old Women: 1992 to 1996

National Percent Change = 7.4% Decrease*

ALPHA ORDER				RANK ORDER		
RANK	STATE	PERCENT CHANGE		RANK	STATE	PERCENT CHANGE
4	Alabama	(6.3)		1	Arkansas	(1.4)
NA	Alaska**	NA		2	Indiana	(3.9)
29	Arizona	(16.2)		3	Oregon	(4.0)
1	Arkansas	(1.4)		4	Alabama	(6.3)
NA	California**	NA		4	New York	(6.3)
30	Colorado	(17.2)		6	Texas	(6.8)
NA	Connecticut**	NA		7	Tennessee	(9.4)
NA	Delaware**	NA		8	West Virginia	(10.4)
NA	Florida**	NA		9	Nebraska	(10.6)
13	Georgia	(11.9)		10	Ohio	(11.1)
15	Hawaii	(12.6)		11	Utah	(11.3)
15	Idaho	(12.6)		12	Nevada	(11.6)
NA	Illinois**	NA		13	Georgia	(11.9)
2	Indiana	(3.9)		14	Kentucky	(12.2)
NA	Iowa**	NA		15	Hawaii	(12.6)
22	Kansas	(13.6)		15	Idaho	(12.6)
14	Kentucky	(12.2)		17	Virginia	(12.8)
19	Louisiana	(13.1)		18	Rhode Island	(12.9)
30	Maine	(17.2)		19	Louisiana	(13.1)
38	Maryland	(20.0)		20	South Carolina	(13.3)
35	Massachusetts	(18.1)		21	North Carolina	(13.4)
40	Michigan	(20.3)		22	Kansas	(13.6)
23	Minnesota	(13.8)		23	Minnesota	(13.8)
36	Mississippi	(18.2)		23	New Mexico	(13.8)
30	Missouri	(17.2)		25	Wyoming	(14.2)
34	Montana	(17.7)		26	New Jersey	(14.3)
9	Nebraska	(10.6)		27	Washington	(14.8)
12	Nevada	(11.6)		28	North Dakota	(15.9)
NA	New Hampshire**	NA		29	Arizona	(16.2)
26	New Jersey	(14.3)		30	Colorado	(17.2)
23	New Mexico	(13.8)		30	Maine	(17.2)
4	New York	(6.3)		30	Missouri	(17.2)
21	North Carolina	(13.4)		33	Wisconsin	(17.4)
28	North Dakota	(15.9)		34	Montana	(17.7)
10	Ohio	(11.1)		35	Massachusetts	(18.1)
NA	Oklahoma**	NA		36	Mississippi	(18.2)
3	Oregon	(4.0)		37	Pennsylvania	(19.9)
37	Pennsylvania	(19.9)		38	Maryland	(20.0)
18	Rhode Island	(12.9)		39	South Dakota	(20.2)
20	South Carolina	(13.3)		40	Michigan	(20.3)
39	South Dakota	(20.2)		41	Vermont	(20.4)
7	Tennessee	(9.4)		NA	Alaska**	NA
6	Texas	(6.8)		NA	California**	NA
11	Utah	(11.3)		NA	Connecticut**	NA
41	Vermont	(20.4)		NA	Delaware**	NA
17	Virginia	(12.8)		NA	Florida**	NA
27	Washington	(14.8)		NA	Illinois**	NA
8	West Virginia	(10.4)		NA	Iowa**	NA
33	Wisconsin	(17.4)		NA	New Hampshire**	NA
25	Wyoming	(14.2)		NA	Oklahoma**	NA
					District of Columbia**	NA

Source: Morgan Quitno Press using data from US Dept of Health & Human Serv's, Centers for Disease Control-Prevention "Abortion Surveillance-United States, 1996" (Morbidity Mortality Weekly Report, Vol. 48, No. SS-4, July 30, 1999)
*The sum of live births and legal induced abortions per 1,000 women aged 15-19 years old. Births by state of residence, abortions by state of occurrence. National rate includes only states reporting abortions and births.
**Not available.

Births to Teenage Mothers in 1990

National Total = 521,826 Live Births*

ALPHA ORDER

RANK	STATE	BIRTHS	% of USA
15	Alabama	11,252	2.2%
47	Alaska	1,142	0.2%
19	Arizona	9,612	1.8%
27	Arkansas	7,011	1.3%
1	California	69,712	13.4%
28	Colorado	5,975	1.1%
33	Connecticut	4,038	0.8%
44	Delaware	1,277	0.2%
3	Florida	27,017	5.2%
8	Georgia	18,369	3.5%
39	Hawaii	2,122	0.4%
40	Idaho	2,009	0.4%
5	Illinois	24,967	4.8%
12	Indiana	12,335	2.4%
34	Iowa	3,989	0.8%
31	Kansas	4,722	0.9%
20	Kentucky	9,349	1.8%
13	Louisiana	12,270	2.4%
41	Maine	1,857	0.4%
23	Maryland	8,143	1.6%
26	Massachusetts	7,266	1.4%
7	Michigan	20,312	3.9%
29	Minnesota	5,342	1.0%
21	Mississippi	8,909	1.7%
16	Missouri	11,227	2.2%
43	Montana	1,331	0.3%
38	Nebraska	2,352	0.5%
37	Nevada	2,663	0.5%
45	New Hampshire	1,258	0.2%
17	New Jersey	10,068	1.9%
32	New Mexico	4,367	0.8%
4	New York	26,608	5.1%
10	North Carolina	16,506	3.2%
49	North Dakota	793	0.2%
6	Ohio	22,690	4.3%
24	Oklahoma	7,590	1.5%
30	Oregon	5,084	1.0%
9	Pennsylvania	18,216	3.5%
42	Rhode Island	1,564	0.3%
18	South Carolina	9,721	1.9%
46	South Dakota	1,172	0.2%
11	Tennessee	12,928	2.5%
2	Texas	48,302	9.3%
36	Utah	3,707	0.7%
50	Vermont	702	0.1%
14	Virginia	11,353	2.2%
22	Washington	8,397	1.6%
35	West Virginia	3,976	0.8%
25	Wisconsin	7,281	1.4%
48	Wyoming	943	0.2%

RANK ORDER

RANK	STATE	BIRTHS	% of USA
1	California	69,712	13.4%
2	Texas	48,302	9.3%
3	Florida	27,017	5.2%
4	New York	26,608	5.1%
5	Illinois	24,967	4.8%
6	Ohio	22,690	4.3%
7	Michigan	20,312	3.9%
8	Georgia	18,369	3.5%
9	Pennsylvania	18,216	3.5%
10	North Carolina	16,506	3.2%
11	Tennessee	12,928	2.5%
12	Indiana	12,335	2.4%
13	Louisiana	12,270	2.4%
14	Virginia	11,353	2.2%
15	Alabama	11,252	2.2%
16	Missouri	11,227	2.2%
17	New Jersey	10,068	1.9%
18	South Carolina	9,721	1.9%
19	Arizona	9,612	1.8%
20	Kentucky	9,349	1.8%
21	Mississippi	8,909	1.7%
22	Washington	8,397	1.6%
23	Maryland	8,143	1.6%
24	Oklahoma	7,590	1.5%
25	Wisconsin	7,281	1.4%
26	Massachusetts	7,266	1.4%
27	Arkansas	7,011	1.3%
28	Colorado	5,975	1.1%
29	Minnesota	5,342	1.0%
30	Oregon	5,084	1.0%
31	Kansas	4,722	0.9%
32	New Mexico	4,367	0.8%
33	Connecticut	4,038	0.8%
34	Iowa	3,989	0.8%
35	West Virginia	3,976	0.8%
36	Utah	3,707	0.7%
37	Nevada	2,663	0.5%
38	Nebraska	2,352	0.5%
39	Hawaii	2,122	0.4%
40	Idaho	2,009	0.4%
41	Maine	1,857	0.4%
42	Rhode Island	1,564	0.3%
43	Montana	1,331	0.3%
44	Delaware	1,277	0.2%
45	New Hampshire	1,258	0.2%
46	South Dakota	1,172	0.2%
47	Alaska	1,142	0.2%
48	Wyoming	943	0.2%
49	North Dakota	793	0.2%
50	Vermont	702	0.1%
	District of Columbia	2,030	0.4%

Source: U.S. Department of Health and Human Services, Centers for Disease Control and Prevention
 "Surveillance for Pregnancy and Birth Rates Among Teenagers" (MMWR, Vol. 42, No. SS-6, 12/17/93)
*Women aged 15 to 19 years old.

Teenage Birth Rate in 1990

National Rate = 59.9 Live Births per 1,000 Teenage Women*

ALPHA ORDER		
RANK	STATE	RATE
11	Alabama	71.0
17	Alaska	65.3
4	Arizona	75.5
2	Arkansas	80.1
12	California	70.6
28	Colorado	54.5
45	Connecticut	38.8
28	Delaware	54.5
13	Florida	69.1
4	Georgia	75.5
20	Hawaii	61.2
33	Idaho	50.6
18	Illinois	62.9
22	Indiana	58.6
43	Iowa	40.5
26	Kansas	56.1
14	Kentucky	67.6
7	Louisiana	74.2
40	Maine	43.0
30	Maryland	53.2
48	Massachusetts	35.1
21	Michigan	59.0
46	Minnesota	36.3
1	Mississippi	81.0
19	Missouri	62.8
35	Montana	48.4
42	Nebraska	42.3
8	Nevada	73.3
50	New Hampshire	33.0
43	New Jersey	40.5
3	New Mexico	78.2
39	New York	43.6
14	North Carolina	67.6
47	North Dakota	35.4
23	Ohio	57.9
16	Oklahoma	66.8
27	Oregon	54.6
37	Pennsylvania	44.9
38	Rhode Island	43.9
10	South Carolina	71.3
36	South Dakota	46.8
9	Tennessee	72.3
6	Texas	75.3
34	Utah	48.5
49	Vermont	34.0
32	Virginia	52.9
31	Washington	53.1
24	West Virginia	57.3
41	Wisconsin	42.6
25	Wyoming	56.3

RANK ORDER		
RANK	STATE	RATE
1	Mississippi	81.0
2	Arkansas	80.1
3	New Mexico	78.2
4	Arizona	75.5
4	Georgia	75.5
6	Texas	75.3
7	Louisiana	74.2
8	Nevada	73.3
9	Tennessee	72.3
10	South Carolina	71.3
11	Alabama	71.0
12	California	70.6
13	Florida	69.1
14	Kentucky	67.6
14	North Carolina	67.6
16	Oklahoma	66.8
17	Alaska	65.3
18	Illinois	62.9
19	Missouri	62.8
20	Hawaii	61.2
21	Michigan	59.0
22	Indiana	58.6
23	Ohio	57.9
24	West Virginia	57.3
25	Wyoming	56.3
26	Kansas	56.1
27	Oregon	54.6
28	Colorado	54.5
28	Delaware	54.5
30	Maryland	53.2
31	Washington	53.1
32	Virginia	52.9
33	Idaho	50.6
34	Utah	48.5
35	Montana	48.4
36	South Dakota	46.8
37	Pennsylvania	44.9
38	Rhode Island	43.9
39	New York	43.6
40	Maine	43.0
41	Wisconsin	42.6
42	Nebraska	42.3
43	Iowa	40.5
43	New Jersey	40.5
45	Connecticut	38.8
46	Minnesota	36.3
47	North Dakota	35.4
48	Massachusetts	35.1
49	Vermont	34.0
50	New Hampshire	33.0
	District of Columbia	93.1

Source: U.S. Department of Health and Human Services, Centers for Disease Control and Prevention
   "Surveillance for Pregnancy and Birth Rates Among Teenagers" (MMWR, Vol. 42, No. SS-6, 12/17/93)
*Women aged 15 to 19 years old.

Percent Change in Teenage Birth Rate: 1990 to 1997

National Percent Change = 12.7% Decrease*

ALPHA ORDER

RANK	STATE	PERCENT CHANGE
5	Alabama	(6.2)
50	Alaska	(31.7)
9	Arizona	(7.7)
10	Arkansas	(9.0)
42	California	(18.8)
18	Colorado	(11.6)
6	Connecticut	(7.0)
1	Delaware	2.4
38	Florida	(16.5)
16	Georgia	(11.0)
49	Hawaii	(28.4)
33	Idaho	(14.4)
25	Illinois	(13.0)
7	Indiana	(7.5)
21	Iowa	(11.9)
27	Kansas	(13.5)
19	Kentucky	(11.8)
14	Louisiana	(10.6)
47	Maine	(25.6)
40	Maryland	(17.5)
13	Massachusetts	(9.7)
47	Michigan	(25.6)
19	Minnesota	(11.8)
10	Mississippi	(9.0)
41	Missouri	(18.0)
45	Montana	(22.3)
22	Nebraska	(12.1)
8	Nevada	(7.6)
26	New Hampshire	(13.3)
28	New Jersey	(13.6)
24	New Mexico	(12.5)
16	New York	(11.0)
12	North Carolina	(9.3)
34	North Dakota	(15.0)
30	Ohio	(14.0)
3	Oklahoma	(3.7)
31	Oregon	(14.1)
39	Pennsylvania	(16.9)
2	Rhode Island	(2.7)
29	South Carolina	(13.9)
35	South Dakota	(15.2)
15	Tennessee	(10.8)
4	Texas	(4.8)
23	Utah	(12.2)
44	Vermont	(20.9)
37	Virginia	(16.4)
43	Washington	(20.0)
32	West Virginia	(14.3)
36	Wisconsin	(15.7)
46	Wyoming	(23.1)

RANK ORDER

RANK	STATE	PERCENT CHANGE
1	Delaware	2.4
2	Rhode Island	(2.7)
3	Oklahoma	(3.7)
4	Texas	(4.8)
5	Alabama	(6.2)
6	Connecticut	(7.0)
7	Indiana	(7.5)
8	Nevada	(7.6)
9	Arizona	(7.7)
10	Arkansas	(9.0)
10	Mississippi	(9.0)
12	North Carolina	(9.3)
13	Massachusetts	(9.7)
14	Louisiana	(10.6)
15	Tennessee	(10.8)
16	Georgia	(11.0)
16	New York	(11.0)
18	Colorado	(11.6)
19	Kentucky	(11.8)
19	Minnesota	(11.8)
21	Iowa	(11.9)
22	Nebraska	(12.1)
23	Utah	(12.2)
24	New Mexico	(12.5)
25	Illinois	(13.0)
26	New Hampshire	(13.3)
27	Kansas	(13.5)
28	New Jersey	(13.6)
29	South Carolina	(13.9)
30	Ohio	(14.0)
31	Oregon	(14.1)
32	West Virginia	(14.3)
33	Idaho	(14.4)
34	North Dakota	(15.0)
35	South Dakota	(15.2)
36	Wisconsin	(15.7)
37	Virginia	(16.4)
38	Florida	(16.5)
39	Pennsylvania	(16.9)
40	Maryland	(17.5)
41	Missouri	(18.0)
42	California	(18.8)
43	Washington	(20.0)
44	Vermont	(20.9)
45	Montana	(22.3)
46	Wyoming	(23.1)
47	Maine	(25.6)
47	Michigan	(25.6)
49	Hawaii	(28.4)
50	Alaska	(31.7)
	District of Columbia	(2.3)

Source: Morgan Quitno Press using data from U.S. Department of Health and Human Services
   "National Vital Statistics Reports" (Vol. 47, No. 18, April 29, 1999)
   "Surveillance for Pregnancy and Birth Rates Among Teenagers" (MMWR, Vol. 42, No. SS-6, 12/17/93)
*Women aged 15 to 19 years old.

Births to Teenage Mothers in 1980

National Total = 562,330 Live Births*

ALPHA ORDER

RANK	STATE	BIRTHS	% of USA
15	Alabama	13,096	2.3%
49	Alaska	1,123	0.2%
25	Arizona	8,235	1.5%
26	Arkansas	8,060	1.4%
1	California	56,138	10.0%
29	Colorado	6,592	1.2%
36	Connecticut	4,408	0.8%
45	Delaware	1,572	0.3%
6	Florida	24,042	4.3%
9	Georgia	19,137	3.4%
40	Hawaii	2,085	0.4%
38	Idaho	2,645	0.5%
3	Illinois	29,798	5.3%
12	Indiana	15,331	2.7%
31	Iowa	5,962	1.1%
30	Kansas	6,090	1.1%
16	Kentucky	12,559	2.2%
10	Louisiana	16,504	2.9%
39	Maine	2,522	0.4%
23	Maryland	8,885	1.6%
27	Massachusetts	7,765	1.4%
8	Michigan	20,401	3.6%
28	Minnesota	7,048	1.3%
19	Mississippi	11,079	2.0%
14	Missouri	13,312	2.4%
43	Montana	1,761	0.3%
37	Nebraska	3,313	0.6%
41	Nevada	2,048	0.4%
47	New Hampshire	1,475	0.3%
18	New Jersey	11,904	2.1%
34	New Mexico	4,758	0.8%
4	New York	28,206	5.0%
11	North Carolina	16,192	2.9%
48	North Dakota	1,304	0.2%
5	Ohio	26,567	4.7%
21	Oklahoma	10,206	1.8%
33	Oregon	5,731	1.0%
7	Pennsylvania	22,029	3.9%
46	Rhode Island	1,502	0.3%
20	South Carolina	10,282	1.8%
42	South Dakota	1,797	0.3%
13	Tennessee	13,792	2.5%
2	Texas	50,125	8.9%
35	Utah	4,594	0.8%
50	Vermont	1,024	0.2%
17	Virginia	12,138	2.2%
24	Washington	8,495	1.5%
32	West Virginia	5,911	1.1%
22	Wisconsin	9,220	1.6%
44	Wyoming	1,634	0.3%

RANK ORDER

RANK	STATE	BIRTHS	% of USA
1	California	56,138	10.0%
2	Texas	50,125	8.9%
3	Illinois	29,798	5.3%
4	New York	28,206	5.0%
5	Ohio	26,567	4.7%
6	Florida	24,042	4.3%
7	Pennsylvania	22,029	3.9%
8	Michigan	20,401	3.6%
9	Georgia	19,137	3.4%
10	Louisiana	16,504	2.9%
11	North Carolina	16,192	2.9%
12	Indiana	15,331	2.7%
13	Tennessee	13,792	2.5%
14	Missouri	13,312	2.4%
15	Alabama	13,096	2.3%
16	Kentucky	12,559	2.2%
17	Virginia	12,138	2.2%
18	New Jersey	11,904	2.1%
19	Mississippi	11,079	2.0%
20	South Carolina	10,282	1.8%
21	Oklahoma	10,206	1.8%
22	Wisconsin	9,220	1.6%
23	Maryland	8,885	1.6%
24	Washington	8,495	1.5%
25	Arizona	8,235	1.5%
26	Arkansas	8,060	1.4%
27	Massachusetts	7,765	1.4%
28	Minnesota	7,048	1.3%
29	Colorado	6,592	1.2%
30	Kansas	6,090	1.1%
31	Iowa	5,962	1.1%
32	West Virginia	5,911	1.1%
33	Oregon	5,731	1.0%
34	New Mexico	4,758	0.8%
35	Utah	4,594	0.8%
36	Connecticut	4,408	0.8%
37	Nebraska	3,313	0.6%
38	Idaho	2,645	0.5%
39	Maine	2,522	0.4%
40	Hawaii	2,085	0.4%
41	Nevada	2,048	0.4%
42	South Dakota	1,797	0.3%
43	Montana	1,761	0.3%
44	Wyoming	1,634	0.3%
45	Delaware	1,572	0.3%
46	Rhode Island	1,502	0.3%
47	New Hampshire	1,475	0.3%
48	North Dakota	1,304	0.2%
49	Alaska	1,123	0.2%
50	Vermont	1,024	0.2%
	District of Columbia	1,933	0.3%

Source: U.S. Department of Health and Human Services, National Center for Health Statistics
"Vital Statistics of the United States, 1980" (Vol. I-Natality, issued 1984)
*Births to women age 15 to 19 years old.

Teenage Birth Rate in 1980

National Rate = 53.0 Live Births per 1,000 Teenage Women*

ALPHA ORDER			RANK ORDER		
RANK	STATE	RATE	RANK	STATE	RATE
10	Alabama	68.3	1	Mississippi	83.7
15	Alaska	64.4	2	Wyoming	78.7
12	Arizona	65.5	3	Louisiana	76.0
5	Arkansas	74.5	4	Oklahoma	74.6
25	California	53.3	5	Arkansas	74.5
31	Colorado	49.9	6	Texas	74.3
49	Connecticut	30.5	7	Kentucky	72.3
28	Delaware	51.2	8	Georgia	71.9
18	Florida	58.5	9	New Mexico	71.8
8	Georgia	71.9	10	Alabama	68.3
30	Hawaii	50.7	11	West Virginia	67.8
17	Idaho	59.5	12	Arizona	65.5
24	Illinois	55.8	13	Utah	65.2
21	Indiana	57.5	14	South Carolina	64.8
39	Iowa	43.0	15	Alaska	64.4
23	Kansas	56.8	16	Tennessee	64.1
7	Kentucky	72.3	17	Idaho	59.5
3	Louisiana	76.0	18	Florida	58.5
34	Maine	47.4	18	Nevada	58.5
38	Maryland	43.4	20	Missouri	57.8
50	Massachusetts	28.1	21	Indiana	57.5
37	Michigan	45.0	21	North Carolina	57.5
44	Minnesota	35.4	23	Kansas	56.8
1	Mississippi	83.7	24	Illinois	55.8
20	Missouri	57.8	25	California	53.3
32	Montana	48.5	26	South Dakota	52.6
36	Nebraska	45.1	27	Ohio	52.5
18	Nevada	58.5	28	Delaware	51.2
47	New Hampshire	33.6	29	Oregon	50.9
45	New Jersey	35.2	30	Hawaii	50.7
9	New Mexico	71.8	31	Colorado	49.9
46	New York	34.8	32	Montana	48.5
21	North Carolina	57.5	33	Virginia	48.3
40	North Dakota	41.7	34	Maine	47.4
27	Ohio	52.5	35	Washington	46.7
4	Oklahoma	74.6	36	Nebraska	45.1
29	Oregon	50.9	37	Michigan	45.0
41	Pennsylvania	40.5	38	Maryland	43.4
48	Rhode Island	33.0	39	Iowa	43.0
14	South Carolina	64.8	40	North Dakota	41.7
26	South Dakota	52.6	41	Pennsylvania	40.5
16	Tennessee	64.1	42	Vermont	39.5
6	Texas	74.3	42	Wisconsin	39.5
13	Utah	65.2	44	Minnesota	35.4
42	Vermont	39.5	45	New Jersey	35.2
33	Virginia	48.3	46	New York	34.8
35	Washington	46.7	47	New Hampshire	33.6
11	West Virginia	67.8	48	Rhode Island	33.0
42	Wisconsin	39.5	49	Connecticut	30.5
2	Wyoming	78.7	50	Massachusetts	28.1
				District of Columbia	62.4

Source: U.S. Department of Health and Human Services, Centers for Disease Control and Prevention
   "Surveillance for Pregnancy and Birth Rates Among Teenagers" (MMWR, Vol. 42, No. SS-6, 12/17/93)
*Women aged 15 to 19 years old.

Births to Women 35 to 49 Years Old in 1997

National Total = 489,127 Live Births*

ALPHA ORDER					RANK ORDER			
RANK	STATE	BIRTHS	% of USA		RANK	STATE	BIRTHS	% of USA
27	Alabama	4,957	1.0%		1	California	76,991	15.7%
45	Alaska	1,339	0.3%		2	New York	43,212	8.8%
18	Arizona	8,130	1.7%		3	Texas	33,157	6.8%
38	Arkansas	2,501	0.5%		4	Florida	24,877	5.1%
1	California	76,991	15.7%		5	Illinois	23,769	4.9%
19	Colorado	8,083	1.7%		6	New Jersey	20,832	4.3%
20	Connecticut	8,012	1.6%		7	Pennsylvania	20,245	4.1%
46	Delaware	1,256	0.3%		8	Ohio	16,769	3.4%
4	Florida	24,877	5.1%		9	Michigan	15,677	3.2%
12	Georgia	12,591	2.6%		10	Massachusetts	15,605	3.2%
37	Hawaii	2,640	0.5%		11	Virginia	13,056	2.7%
40	Idaho	1,836	0.4%		12	Georgia	12,591	2.6%
5	Illinois	23,769	4.9%		13	Maryland	11,458	2.3%
22	Indiana	7,771	1.6%		14	North Carolina	10,968	2.2%
32	Iowa	3,847	0.8%		15	Washington	10,442	2.1%
29	Kansas	4,092	0.8%		16	Minnesota	9,026	1.8%
28	Kentucky	4,380	0.9%		17	Wisconsin	8,240	1.7%
24	Louisiana	5,651	1.2%		18	Arizona	8,130	1.7%
42	Maine	1,708	0.3%		19	Colorado	8,083	1.7%
13	Maryland	11,458	2.3%		20	Connecticut	8,012	1.6%
10	Massachusetts	15,605	3.2%		21	Missouri	7,881	1.6%
9	Michigan	15,677	3.2%		22	Indiana	7,771	1.6%
16	Minnesota	9,026	1.8%		23	Tennessee	6,565	1.3%
34	Mississippi	3,011	0.6%		24	Louisiana	5,651	1.2%
21	Missouri	7,881	1.6%		25	Oregon	5,338	1.1%
44	Montana	1,383	0.3%		26	South Carolina	5,041	1.0%
36	Nebraska	2,734	0.6%		27	Alabama	4,957	1.0%
33	Nevada	3,032	0.6%		28	Kentucky	4,380	0.9%
39	New Hampshire	2,155	0.4%		29	Kansas	4,092	0.8%
6	New Jersey	20,832	4.3%		30	Utah	3,919	0.8%
35	New Mexico	2,750	0.6%		31	Oklahoma	3,866	0.8%
2	New York	43,212	8.8%		32	Iowa	3,847	0.8%
14	North Carolina	10,968	2.2%		33	Nevada	3,032	0.6%
49	North Dakota	907	0.2%		34	Mississippi	3,011	0.6%
8	Ohio	16,769	3.4%		35	New Mexico	2,750	0.6%
31	Oklahoma	3,866	0.8%		36	Nebraska	2,734	0.6%
25	Oregon	5,338	1.1%		37	Hawaii	2,640	0.5%
7	Pennsylvania	20,245	4.1%		38	Arkansas	2,501	0.5%
41	Rhode Island	1,811	0.4%		39	New Hampshire	2,155	0.4%
26	South Carolina	5,041	1.0%		40	Idaho	1,836	0.4%
47	South Dakota	1,095	0.2%		41	Rhode Island	1,811	0.4%
23	Tennessee	6,565	1.3%		42	Maine	1,708	0.3%
3	Texas	33,157	6.8%		43	West Virginia	1,592	0.3%
30	Utah	3,919	0.8%		44	Montana	1,383	0.3%
48	Vermont	1,029	0.2%		45	Alaska	1,339	0.3%
11	Virginia	13,056	2.7%		46	Delaware	1,256	0.3%
15	Washington	10,442	2.1%		47	South Dakota	1,095	0.2%
43	West Virginia	1,592	0.3%		48	Vermont	1,029	0.2%
17	Wisconsin	8,240	1.7%		49	North Dakota	907	0.2%
50	Wyoming	615	0.1%		50	Wyoming	615	0.1%
						District of Columbia	1,285	0.3%

Source: Morgan Quitno Press using data from U.S. Dept of Health & Human Services, National Center for Health Statistics
   (unpublished data)
*By state of residence.

Births to Women 35 to 49 Years Old as a Percent of All Births in 1997

National Percent = 12.6% of Live Births*

ALPHA ORDER				RANK ORDER		
RANK	STATE	PERCENT		RANK	STATE	PERCENT
46	Alabama	8.1		1	Massachusetts	19.4
15	Alaska	13.5		2	Connecticut	18.6
31	Arizona	10.7		3	New Jersey	18.4
50	Arkansas	6.9		4	New York	16.8
9	California	14.7		5	Maryland	16.3
11	Colorado	14.3		6	Vermont	15.6
2	Connecticut	18.6		7	Hawaii	15.2
22	Delaware	12.3		8	New Hampshire	15.1
18	Florida	12.9		9	California	14.7
31	Georgia	10.7		10	Rhode Island	14.5
7	Hawaii	15.2		11	Colorado	14.3
37	Idaho	9.9		12	Virginia	14.2
17	Illinois	13.1		13	Minnesota	14.0
41	Indiana	9.3		13	Pennsylvania	14.0
34	Iowa	10.5		15	Alaska	13.5
27	Kansas	11.0		16	Washington	13.4
45	Kentucky	8.2		17	Illinois	13.1
44	Louisiana	8.6		18	Florida	12.9
20	Maine	12.5		19	Montana	12.7
5	Maryland	16.3		20	Maine	12.5
1	Massachusetts	19.4		21	Wisconsin	12.4
24	Michigan	11.7		22	Delaware	12.3
13	Minnesota	14.0		23	Oregon	12.2
49	Mississippi	7.2		24	Michigan	11.7
33	Missouri	10.6		24	Nebraska	11.7
19	Montana	12.7		26	Nevada	11.3
24	Nebraska	11.7		27	Kansas	11.0
26	Nevada	11.3		27	Ohio	11.0
8	New Hampshire	15.1		29	North Dakota	10.9
3	New Jersey	18.4		30	South Dakota	10.8
35	New Mexico	10.2		31	Arizona	10.7
4	New York	16.8		31	Georgia	10.7
35	North Carolina	10.2		33	Missouri	10.6
29	North Dakota	10.9		34	Iowa	10.5
27	Ohio	11.0		35	New Mexico	10.2
47	Oklahoma	8.0		35	North Carolina	10.2
23	Oregon	12.2		37	Idaho	9.9
13	Pennsylvania	14.0		37	Texas	9.9
10	Rhode Island	14.5		39	South Carolina	9.7
39	South Carolina	9.7		40	Wyoming	9.6
30	South Dakota	10.8		41	Indiana	9.3
43	Tennessee	8.8		42	Utah	9.1
37	Texas	9.9		43	Tennessee	8.8
42	Utah	9.1		44	Louisiana	8.6
6	Vermont	15.6		45	Kentucky	8.2
12	Virginia	14.2		46	Alabama	8.1
16	Washington	13.4		47	Oklahoma	8.0
48	West Virginia	7.7		48	West Virginia	7.7
21	Wisconsin	12.4		49	Mississippi	7.2
40	Wyoming	9.6		50	Arkansas	6.9
					District of Columbia	16.2

Source: Morgan Quitno Press using data from U.S. Dept of Health & Human Services, National Center for Health Statistics (unpublished data)
*By state of residence.

Multiple Birth Rate in 1997

National Rate = 27.3 Multiple Births per 1,000 Live Births*

ALPHA ORDER

RANK	STATE	RATE
25	Alabama	27.0
35	Alaska	24.8
38	Arizona	24.5
34	Arkansas	25.0
38	California	24.5
8	Colorado	30.6
2	Connecticut	35.0
5	Delaware	31.5
32	Florida	26.2
26	Georgia	26.9
50	Hawaii	19.1
47	Idaho	22.3
9	Illinois	30.2
27	Indiana	26.8
13	Iowa	29.2
20	Kansas	27.4
33	Kentucky	25.6
20	Louisiana	27.4
16	Maine	28.4
6	Maryland	31.0
1	Massachusetts	35.3
12	Michigan	29.4
9	Minnesota	30.2
42	Mississippi	24.2
19	Missouri	27.6
44	Montana	24.0
4	Nebraska	33.5
45	Nevada	23.9
18	New Hampshire	28.0
3	New Jersey	34.3
49	New Mexico	21.4
7	New York	30.7
23	North Carolina	27.2
9	North Dakota	30.2
17	Ohio	28.3
46	Oklahoma	23.1
37	Oregon	24.6
14	Pennsylvania	29.0
15	Rhode Island	28.6
30	South Carolina	26.4
27	South Dakota	26.8
30	Tennessee	26.4
40	Texas	24.4
43	Utah	24.1
48	Vermont	22.1
20	Virginia	27.4
36	Washington	24.7
40	West Virginia	24.4
23	Wisconsin	27.2
29	Wyoming	26.6

RANK ORDER

RANK	STATE	RATE
1	Massachusetts	35.3
2	Connecticut	35.0
3	New Jersey	34.3
4	Nebraska	33.5
5	Delaware	31.5
6	Maryland	31.0
7	New York	30.7
8	Colorado	30.6
9	Illinois	30.2
9	Minnesota	30.2
9	North Dakota	30.2
12	Michigan	29.4
13	Iowa	29.2
14	Pennsylvania	29.0
15	Rhode Island	28.6
16	Maine	28.4
17	Ohio	28.3
18	New Hampshire	28.0
19	Missouri	27.6
20	Kansas	27.4
20	Louisiana	27.4
20	Virginia	27.4
23	North Carolina	27.2
23	Wisconsin	27.2
25	Alabama	27.0
26	Georgia	26.9
27	Indiana	26.8
27	South Dakota	26.8
29	Wyoming	26.6
30	South Carolina	26.4
30	Tennessee	26.4
32	Florida	26.2
33	Kentucky	25.6
34	Arkansas	25.0
35	Alaska	24.8
36	Washington	24.7
37	Oregon	24.6
38	Arizona	24.5
38	California	24.5
40	Texas	24.4
40	West Virginia	24.4
42	Mississippi	24.2
43	Utah	24.1
44	Montana	24.0
45	Nevada	23.9
46	Oklahoma	23.1
47	Idaho	22.3
48	Vermont	22.1
49	New Mexico	21.4
50	Hawaii	19.1
	District of Columbia	29.5

Source: Morgan Quitno Press using data from U.S. Dept. of Health and Human Services, Nat'l Center for Health Statistics "National Vital Statistics Reports" (Vol. 47, No. 24, September 14, 1999)

*By state of residence of mother. Multiple births include all births of twins, triplets or more. Rate is based on a three-year average of rates for 1995 through 1997.

Percent Change in Multiple Birth Rate: 1993 to 1997

National Percent Change = 11.4% Increase*

ALPHA ORDER

RANK	STATE	PERCENT CHANGE
25	Alabama	10.4
18	Alaska	12.2
22	Arizona	11.4
32	Arkansas	9.0
29	California	9.7
5	Colorado	27.1
7	Connecticut	24.0
9	Delaware	22.3
17	Florida	13.1
27	Georgia	10.1
50	Hawaii	(11.8)
30	Idaho	9.5
19	Illinois	12.1
36	Indiana	8.6
11	Iowa	15.1
15	Kansas	14.0
24	Kentucky	10.7
34	Louisiana	8.9
16	Maine	13.8
10	Maryland	17.1
8	Massachusetts	23.4
25	Michigan	10.4
6	Minnesota	24.1
48	Mississippi	(6.0)
39	Missouri	7.3
41	Montana	7.1
1	Nebraska	32.9
45	Nevada	3.3
34	New Hampshire	8.9
4	New Jersey	28.3
32	New Mexico	9.0
12	New York	14.8
38	North Carolina	7.7
2	North Dakota	29.6
42	Ohio	6.7
47	Oklahoma	(1.0)
46	Oregon	0.0
20	Pennsylvania	12.0
13	Rhode Island	14.4
44	South Carolina	4.6
28	South Dakota	10.0
31	Tennessee	9.2
23	Texas	11.2
43	Utah	6.2
49	Vermont	(11.2)
20	Virginia	12.0
14	Washington	14.2
39	West Virginia	7.3
37	Wisconsin	7.8
3	Wyoming	28.7

RANK ORDER

RANK	STATE	PERCENT CHANGE
1	Nebraska	32.9
2	North Dakota	29.6
3	Wyoming	28.7
4	New Jersey	28.3
5	Colorado	27.1
6	Minnesota	24.1
7	Connecticut	24.0
8	Massachusetts	23.4
9	Delaware	22.3
10	Maryland	17.1
11	Iowa	15.1
12	New York	14.8
13	Rhode Island	14.4
14	Washington	14.2
15	Kansas	14.0
16	Maine	13.8
17	Florida	13.1
18	Alaska	12.2
19	Illinois	12.1
20	Pennsylvania	12.0
20	Virginia	12.0
22	Arizona	11.4
23	Texas	11.2
24	Kentucky	10.7
25	Alabama	10.4
25	Michigan	10.4
27	Georgia	10.1
28	South Dakota	10.0
29	California	9.7
30	Idaho	9.5
31	Tennessee	9.2
32	Arkansas	9.0
32	New Mexico	9.0
34	Louisiana	8.9
34	New Hampshire	8.9
36	Indiana	8.6
37	Wisconsin	7.8
38	North Carolina	7.7
39	Missouri	7.3
39	West Virginia	7.3
41	Montana	7.1
42	Ohio	6.7
43	Utah	6.2
44	South Carolina	4.6
45	Nevada	3.3
46	Oregon	0.0
47	Oklahoma	(1.0)
48	Mississippi	(6.0)
49	Vermont	(11.2)
50	Hawaii	(11.8)

District of Columbia	15.8

Source: Morgan Quitno Press using data from U.S. Dept. of Health and Human Services, Nat'l Center for Health Statistics
"National Vital Statistics Report" (Vol. 47, No. 24, September 14, 1999) and
"Vital Statistics of the United States: Volume I-Natality" (various years)
*By state of residence of mother. Multiple births include all births of twins, triplets or more. Rate is based on a three-year average of rates for 1991-1993 and 1995-1997.

Births by Vaginal Delivery in 1997

National Total = 3,081,861 Live Births*

ALPHA ORDER

RANK	STATE	BIRTHS	% of USA
24	Alabama	46,408	1.5%
45	Alaska	8,264	0.3%
16	Arizona	63,038	2.0%
34	Arkansas	27,593	0.9%
1	California	414,709	13.5%
23	Colorado	47,889	1.6%
30	Connecticut	35,210	1.1%
47	Delaware	8,101	0.3%
4	Florida	149,979	4.9%
9	Georgia	93,763	3.0%
40	Hawaii	15,059	0.5%
39	Idaho	15,536	0.5%
5	Illinois	146,353	4.7%
13	Indiana	67,103	2.2%
33	Iowa	29,770	1.0%
31	Kansas	30,567	1.0%
25	Kentucky	41,886	1.4%
22	Louisiana	49,239	1.6%
42	Maine	10,833	0.4%
20	Maryland	55,506	1.8%
15	Massachusetts	64,639	2.1%
8	Michigan	106,947	3.5%
21	Minnesota	53,927	1.7%
32	Mississippi	30,462	1.0%
17	Missouri	59,259	1.9%
44	Montana	8,798	0.3%
37	Nebraska	18,620	0.6%
36	Nevada	21,551	0.7%
41	New Hampshire	11,555	0.4%
10	New Jersey	85,189	2.8%
35	New Mexico	22,432	0.7%
3	New York	198,406	6.4%
11	North Carolina	84,409	2.7%
48	North Dakota	6,828	0.2%
6	Ohio	123,229	4.0%
27	Oklahoma	39,806	1.3%
28	Oregon	36,405	1.2%
7	Pennsylvania	116,321	3.8%
43	Rhode Island	10,142	0.3%
26	South Carolina	40,381	1.3%
46	South Dakota	8,143	0.3%
18	Tennessee	58,274	1.9%
2	Texas	257,221	8.3%
29	Utah	36,272	1.2%
49	Vermont	5,576	0.2%
12	Virginia	72,183	2.3%
14	Washington	64,851	2.1%
38	West Virginia	15,689	0.5%
19	Wisconsin	56,085	1.8%
50	Wyoming	5,200	0.2%

RANK ORDER

RANK	STATE	BIRTHS	% of USA
1	California	414,709	13.5%
2	Texas	257,221	8.3%
3	New York	198,406	6.4%
4	Florida	149,979	4.9%
5	Illinois	146,353	4.7%
6	Ohio	123,229	4.0%
7	Pennsylvania	116,321	3.8%
8	Michigan	106,947	3.5%
9	Georgia	93,763	3.0%
10	New Jersey	85,189	2.8%
11	North Carolina	84,409	2.7%
12	Virginia	72,183	2.3%
13	Indiana	67,103	2.2%
14	Washington	64,851	2.1%
15	Massachusetts	64,639	2.1%
16	Arizona	63,038	2.0%
17	Missouri	59,259	1.9%
18	Tennessee	58,274	1.9%
19	Wisconsin	56,085	1.8%
20	Maryland	55,506	1.8%
21	Minnesota	53,927	1.7%
22	Louisiana	49,239	1.6%
23	Colorado	47,889	1.6%
24	Alabama	46,408	1.5%
25	Kentucky	41,886	1.4%
26	South Carolina	40,381	1.3%
27	Oklahoma	39,806	1.3%
28	Oregon	36,405	1.2%
29	Utah	36,272	1.2%
30	Connecticut	35,210	1.1%
31	Kansas	30,567	1.0%
32	Mississippi	30,462	1.0%
33	Iowa	29,770	1.0%
34	Arkansas	27,593	0.9%
35	New Mexico	22,432	0.7%
36	Nevada	21,551	0.7%
37	Nebraska	18,620	0.6%
38	West Virginia	15,689	0.5%
39	Idaho	15,536	0.5%
40	Hawaii	15,059	0.5%
41	New Hampshire	11,555	0.4%
42	Maine	10,833	0.4%
43	Rhode Island	10,142	0.3%
44	Montana	8,798	0.3%
45	Alaska	8,264	0.3%
46	South Dakota	8,143	0.3%
47	Delaware	8,101	0.3%
48	North Dakota	6,828	0.2%
49	Vermont	5,576	0.2%
50	Wyoming	5,200	0.2%
	District of Columbia	6,245	0.2%

Source: Morgan Quitno Press using data from U.S. Dept of Health & Human Services, National Center for Health Statistics unpublished data

By state of residence. Includes VBACs (vaginal births after cesarean).

Percent of Births by Vaginal Delivery in 1997

National Percent = 79.4% of Live Births*

ALPHA ORDER

RANK	STATE	PERCENT
45	Alabama	76.2
10	Alaska	83.1
9	Arizona	83.3
47	Arkansas	75.6
35	California	79.0
2	Colorado	84.7
15	Connecticut	81.7
35	Delaware	79.0
41	Florida	78.0
32	Georgia	79.3
1	Hawaii	86.6
6	Idaho	83.6
22	Illinois	80.9
25	Indiana	80.4
19	Iowa	81.2
14	Kansas	82.0
38	Kentucky	78.7
49	Louisiana	74.6
32	Maine	79.3
34	Maryland	79.1
25	Massachusetts	80.4
28	Michigan	80.0
6	Minnesota	83.6
50	Mississippi	73.3
28	Missouri	80.0
20	Montana	81.1
31	Nebraska	79.8
27	Nevada	80.1
23	New Hampshire	80.7
48	New Jersey	75.2
8	New Mexico	83.5
43	New York	77.1
37	North Carolina	78.9
15	North Dakota	81.7
20	Ohio	81.1
13	Oklahoma	82.5
10	Oregon	83.1
23	Pennsylvania	80.7
17	Rhode Island	81.4
42	South Carolina	77.3
28	South Dakota	80.0
40	Tennessee	78.2
44	Texas	77.0
5	Utah	84.2
3	Vermont	84.4
39	Virginia	78.6
12	Washington	82.9
46	West Virginia	75.7
4	Wisconsin	84.3
17	Wyoming	81.4

RANK ORDER

RANK	STATE	PERCENT
1	Hawaii	86.6
2	Colorado	84.7
3	Vermont	84.4
4	Wisconsin	84.3
5	Utah	84.2
6	Idaho	83.6
6	Minnesota	83.6
8	New Mexico	83.5
9	Arizona	83.3
10	Alaska	83.1
10	Oregon	83.1
12	Washington	82.9
13	Oklahoma	82.5
14	Kansas	82.0
15	Connecticut	81.7
15	North Dakota	81.7
17	Rhode Island	81.4
17	Wyoming	81.4
19	Iowa	81.2
20	Montana	81.1
20	Ohio	81.1
22	Illinois	80.9
23	New Hampshire	80.7
23	Pennsylvania	80.7
25	Indiana	80.4
25	Massachusetts	80.4
27	Nevada	80.1
28	Michigan	80.0
28	Missouri	80.0
28	South Dakota	80.0
31	Nebraska	79.8
32	Georgia	79.3
32	Maine	79.3
34	Maryland	79.1
35	California	79.0
35	Delaware	79.0
37	North Carolina	78.9
38	Kentucky	78.7
39	Virginia	78.6
40	Tennessee	78.2
41	Florida	78.0
42	South Carolina	77.3
43	New York	77.1
44	Texas	77.0
45	Alabama	76.2
46	West Virginia	75.7
47	Arkansas	75.6
48	New Jersey	75.2
49	Louisiana	74.6
50	Mississippi	73.3

District of Columbia — 78.8

Source: Morgan Quitno Press using data from U.S. Dept of Health & Human Services, National Center for Health Statistics
    unpublished data
*By state of residence. Includes VBACs (vaginal births after cesarean).

Births by Cesarean Delivery in 1997

National Total = 799,033 Live Cesarean Births*

ALPHA ORDER					RANK ORDER			
RANK	STATE		BIRTHS	% of USA	RANK	STATE	BIRTHS	% of USA
19	Alabama		14,506	1.8%	1	California	110,131	13.8%
47	Alaska		1,683	0.2%	2	Texas	76,753	9.6%
21	Arizona		12,661	1.6%	3	New York	58,832	7.4%
27	Arkansas		8,885	1.1%	4	Florida	42,404	5.3%
1	California		110,131	13.8%	5	Illinois	34,450	4.3%
28	Colorado		8,644	1.1%	6	Ohio	28,804	3.6%
30	Connecticut		7,899	1.0%	7	New Jersey	28,090	3.5%
44	Delaware		2,152	0.3%	8	Pennsylvania	27,903	3.5%
4	Florida		42,404	5.3%	9	Michigan	26,767	3.3%
10	Georgia		24,458	3.1%	10	Georgia	24,458	3.1%
42	Hawaii		2,334	0.3%	11	North Carolina	22,606	2.8%
39	Idaho		3,046	0.4%	12	Virginia	19,679	2.5%
5	Illinois		34,450	4.3%	13	Louisiana	16,786	2.1%
14	Indiana		16,333	2.0%	14	Indiana	16,333	2.0%
32	Iowa		6,889	0.9%	15	Tennessee	16,204	2.0%
34	Kansas		6,722	0.8%	16	Massachusetts	15,725	2.0%
23	Kentucky		11,317	1.4%	17	Missouri	14,778	1.8%
13	Louisiana		16,786	2.1%	18	Maryland	14,709	1.8%
40	Maine		2,836	0.4%	19	Alabama	14,506	1.8%
18	Maryland		14,709	1.8%	20	Washington	13,339	1.7%
16	Massachusetts		15,725	2.0%	21	Arizona	12,661	1.6%
9	Michigan		26,767	3.3%	22	South Carolina	11,833	1.5%
25	Minnesota		10,572	1.3%	23	Kentucky	11,317	1.4%
24	Mississippi		11,071	1.4%	24	Mississippi	11,071	1.4%
17	Missouri		14,778	1.8%	25	Minnesota	10,572	1.3%
45	Montana		2,051	0.3%	26	Wisconsin	10,472	1.3%
37	Nebraska		4,699	0.6%	27	Arkansas	8,885	1.1%
35	Nevada		5,360	0.7%	28	Colorado	8,644	1.1%
41	New Hampshire		2,758	0.3%	29	Oklahoma	8,463	1.1%
7	New Jersey		28,090	3.5%	30	Connecticut	7,899	1.0%
38	New Mexico		4,439	0.6%	31	Oregon	7,404	0.9%
3	New York		58,832	7.4%	32	Iowa	6,889	0.9%
11	North Carolina		22,606	2.8%	33	Utah	6,787	0.8%
48	North Dakota		1,525	0.2%	34	Kansas	6,722	0.8%
6	Ohio		28,804	3.6%	35	Nevada	5,360	0.7%
29	Oklahoma		8,463	1.1%	36	West Virginia	5,041	0.6%
31	Oregon		7,404	0.9%	37	Nebraska	4,699	0.6%
8	Pennsylvania		27,903	3.5%	38	New Mexico	4,439	0.6%
43	Rhode Island		2,313	0.3%	39	Idaho	3,046	0.4%
22	South Carolina		11,833	1.5%	40	Maine	2,836	0.4%
46	South Dakota		2,030	0.3%	41	New Hampshire	2,758	0.3%
15	Tennessee		16,204	2.0%	42	Hawaii	2,334	0.3%
2	Texas		76,753	9.6%	43	Rhode Island	2,313	0.3%
33	Utah		6,787	0.8%	44	Delaware	2,152	0.3%
50	Vermont		1,031	0.1%	45	Montana	2,051	0.3%
12	Virginia		19,679	2.5%	46	South Dakota	2,030	0.3%
20	Washington		13,339	1.7%	47	Alaska	1,683	0.2%
36	West Virginia		5,041	0.6%	48	North Dakota	1,525	0.2%
26	Wisconsin		10,472	1.3%	49	Wyoming	1,187	0.1%
49	Wyoming		1,187	0.1%	50	Vermont	1,031	0.1%
						District of Columbia	1,682	0.2%

Source: U.S. Department of Health and Human Services, National Center for Health Statistics
unpublished data
*By state of residence.

Percent of Births by Cesarean Delivery in 1997

National Percent = 20.8% of Live Births*

ALPHA ORDER

RANK	STATE	PERCENT
6	Alabama	23.9
42	Alaska	16.8
42	Arizona	16.8
4	Arkansas	24.5
16	California	21.0
50	Colorado	15.3
26	Connecticut	19.8
16	Delaware	21.0
12	Florida	22.2
19	Georgia	20.8
44	Hawaii	16.7
46	Idaho	16.4
31	Illinois	19.1
27	Indiana	19.7
34	Iowa	18.9
37	Kansas	18.5
10	Kentucky	22.4
2	Louisiana	25.4
19	Maine	20.8
16	Maryland	21.0
27	Massachusetts	19.7
22	Michigan	20.1
40	Minnesota	17.1
1	Mississippi	26.7
22	Missouri	20.1
32	Montana	19.0
21	Nebraska	20.2
22	Nevada	20.1
30	New Hampshire	19.3
3	New Jersey	24.9
45	New Mexico	16.6
8	New York	23.0
15	North Carolina	21.2
38	North Dakota	18.4
32	Ohio	19.0
11	Oklahoma	22.3
41	Oregon	16.9
29	Pennsylvania	19.4
35	Rhode Island	18.6
9	South Carolina	22.8
25	South Dakota	20.0
13	Tennessee	21.9
7	Texas	23.1
47	Utah	15.8
49	Vermont	15.6
14	Virginia	21.5
39	Washington	17.2
5	West Virginia	24.4
48	Wisconsin	15.7
35	Wyoming	18.6

RANK ORDER

RANK	STATE	PERCENT
1	Mississippi	26.7
2	Louisiana	25.4
3	New Jersey	24.9
4	Arkansas	24.5
5	West Virginia	24.4
6	Alabama	23.9
7	Texas	23.1
8	New York	23.0
9	South Carolina	22.8
10	Kentucky	22.4
11	Oklahoma	22.3
12	Florida	22.2
13	Tennessee	21.9
14	Virginia	21.5
15	North Carolina	21.2
16	California	21.0
16	Delaware	21.0
16	Maryland	21.0
19	Georgia	20.8
19	Maine	20.8
21	Nebraska	20.2
22	Michigan	20.1
22	Missouri	20.1
22	Nevada	20.1
25	South Dakota	20.0
26	Connecticut	19.8
27	Indiana	19.7
27	Massachusetts	19.7
29	Pennsylvania	19.4
30	New Hampshire	19.3
31	Illinois	19.1
32	Montana	19.0
32	Ohio	19.0
34	Iowa	18.9
35	Rhode Island	18.6
35	Wyoming	18.6
37	Kansas	18.5
38	North Dakota	18.4
39	Washington	17.2
40	Minnesota	17.1
41	Oregon	16.9
42	Alaska	16.8
42	Arizona	16.8
44	Hawaii	16.7
45	New Mexico	16.6
46	Idaho	16.4
47	Utah	15.8
48	Wisconsin	15.7
49	Vermont	15.6
50	Colorado	15.3
	District of Columbia	21.2

Source: U.S. Department of Health and Human Services, National Center for Health Statistics
"National Vital Statistics Reports" (Vol. 47, No. 27, December 2, 1999)
*By state of residence.

Percent Change in Rate of Cesarean Births: 1993 to 1997

National Percent Change = 4.6% Decrease*

RANK	STATE (ALPHA ORDER)	PERCENT CHANGE	RANK	STATE (RANK ORDER)	PERCENT CHANGE
27	Alabama	(3.6)	1	Alaska	10.5
1	Alaska	10.5	2	Minnesota	3.0
6	Arizona	0.0	3	Rhode Island	1.6
46	Arkansas	(9.3)	4	Idaho	1.2
18	California	(1.4)	5	New Jersey	0.8
14	Colorado	(0.6)	6	Arizona	0.0
24	Connecticut	(3.4)	6	Mississippi	0.0
35	Delaware	(6.7)	6	Wisconsin	0.0
23	Florida	(3.1)	9	Iowa	(0.5)
22	Georgia	(2.3)	9	Maine	(0.5)
45	Hawaii	(9.2)	9	Montana	(0.5)
4	Idaho	1.2	9	South Dakota	(0.5)
44	Illinois	(9.0)	9	Tennessee	(0.5)
37	Indiana	(7.5)	14	Colorado	(0.6)
9	Iowa	(0.5)	15	South Carolina	(0.9)
48	Kansas	(12.3)	16	Nevada	(1.0)
39	Kentucky	(7.8)	17	Washington	(1.1)
41	Louisiana	(8.3)	18	California	(1.4)
9	Maine	(0.5)	19	New York	(1.7)
47	Maryland	(9.5)	20	Nebraska	(1.9)
40	Massachusetts	(7.9)	21	West Virginia	(2.0)
33	Michigan	(4.3)	22	Georgia	(2.3)
2	Minnesota	3.0	23	Florida	(3.1)
6	Mississippi	0.0	24	Connecticut	(3.4)
36	Missouri	(6.9)	24	Oregon	(3.4)
9	Montana	(0.5)	26	Oklahoma	(3.5)
20	Nebraska	(1.9)	27	Alabama	(3.6)
16	Nevada	(1.0)	27	Wyoming	(3.6)
30	New Hampshire	(4.0)	29	North Dakota	(3.7)
5	New Jersey	0.8	30	New Hampshire	(4.0)
34	New Mexico	(4.6)	30	Virginia	(4.0)
19	New York	(1.7)	32	North Carolina	(4.1)
32	North Carolina	(4.1)	33	Michigan	(4.3)
29	North Dakota	(3.7)	34	New Mexico	(4.6)
49	Ohio	(13.2)	35	Delaware	(6.7)
26	Oklahoma	(3.5)	36	Missouri	(6.9)
24	Oregon	(3.4)	37	Indiana	(7.5)
42	Pennsylvania	(8.5)	38	Texas	(7.6)
3	Rhode Island	1.6	39	Kentucky	(7.8)
15	South Carolina	(0.9)	40	Massachusetts	(7.9)
9	South Dakota	(0.5)	41	Louisiana	(8.3)
9	Tennessee	(0.5)	42	Pennsylvania	(8.5)
38	Texas	(7.6)	43	Utah	(8.7)
43	Utah	(8.7)	44	Illinois	(9.0)
50	Vermont	(15.7)	45	Hawaii	(9.2)
30	Virginia	(4.0)	46	Arkansas	(9.3)
17	Washington	(1.1)	47	Maryland	(9.5)
21	West Virginia	(2.0)	48	Kansas	(12.3)
6	Wisconsin	0.0	49	Ohio	(13.2)
27	Wyoming	(3.6)	50	Vermont	(15.7)
				District of Columbia	(4.9)

Source: Morgan Quitno Press using data from US Dept of Health & Human Services, National Center for Health Statistics unpublished data

*Of those births for which delivery data are available.

Births by Vaginal Delivery After a Previous Cesarean Delivery (VBAC) in 1997

National Total = 112,145 Live VBAC Births

RANK	STATE	BIRTHS	% of USA	RANK	STATE	BIRTHS	% of USA
23	Alabama	1,505	1.3%	1	California	11,111	9.9%
47	Alaska	291	0.3%	2	New York	10,173	9.1%
21	Arizona	1,655	1.5%	3	Texas	7,495	6.7%
35	Arkansas	837	0.7%	4	Illinois	6,272	5.6%
1	California	11,111	9.9%	5	Ohio	5,798	5.2%
24	Colorado	1,399	1.2%	6	Pennsylvania	5,602	5.0%
26	Connecticut	1,381	1.2%	7	New Jersey	5,382	4.8%
44	Delaware	363	0.3%	8	Florida	4,864	4.3%
8	Florida	4,864	4.3%	9	Michigan	3,720	3.3%
13	Georgia	2,660	2.4%	10	Virginia	3,040	2.7%
36	Hawaii	698	0.6%	11	North Carolina	2,960	2.6%
39	Idaho	595	0.5%	12	Massachusetts	2,703	2.4%
4	Illinois	6,272	5.6%	13	Georgia	2,660	2.4%
15	Indiana	2,439	2.2%	14	Washington	2,440	2.2%
28	Iowa	1,334	1.2%	15	Indiana	2,439	2.2%
30	Kansas	1,075	1.0%	16	Missouri	2,344	2.1%
27	Kentucky	1,362	1.2%	17	Maryland	2,255	2.0%
31	Louisiana	976	0.9%	18	Minnesota	1,955	1.7%
42	Maine	440	0.4%	19	Wisconsin	1,922	1.7%
17	Maryland	2,255	2.0%	20	Tennessee	1,896	1.7%
12	Massachusetts	2,703	2.4%	21	Arizona	1,655	1.5%
9	Michigan	3,720	3.3%	22	Oregon	1,506	1.3%
18	Minnesota	1,955	1.7%	23	Alabama	1,505	1.3%
34	Mississippi	850	0.8%	24	Colorado	1,399	1.2%
16	Missouri	2,344	2.1%	25	Utah	1,385	1.2%
43	Montana	386	0.3%	26	Connecticut	1,381	1.2%
38	Nebraska	653	0.6%	27	Kentucky	1,362	1.2%
37	Nevada	687	0.6%	28	Iowa	1,334	1.2%
40	New Hampshire	569	0.5%	29	South Carolina	1,262	1.1%
7	New Jersey	5,382	4.8%	30	Kansas	1,075	1.0%
32	New Mexico	974	0.9%	31	Louisiana	976	0.9%
2	New York	10,173	9.1%	32	New Mexico	974	0.9%
11	North Carolina	2,960	2.6%	33	Oklahoma	902	0.8%
46	North Dakota	300	0.3%	34	Mississippi	850	0.8%
5	Ohio	5,798	5.2%	35	Arkansas	837	0.7%
33	Oklahoma	902	0.8%	36	Hawaii	698	0.6%
22	Oregon	1,506	1.3%	37	Nevada	687	0.6%
6	Pennsylvania	5,602	5.0%	38	Nebraska	653	0.6%
45	Rhode Island	357	0.3%	39	Idaho	595	0.5%
29	South Carolina	1,262	1.1%	40	New Hampshire	569	0.5%
48	South Dakota	258	0.2%	41	West Virginia	494	0.4%
20	Tennessee	1,896	1.7%	42	Maine	440	0.4%
3	Texas	7,495	6.7%	43	Montana	386	0.3%
25	Utah	1,385	1.2%	44	Delaware	363	0.3%
49	Vermont	249	0.2%	45	Rhode Island	357	0.3%
10	Virginia	3,040	2.7%	46	North Dakota	300	0.3%
14	Washington	2,440	2.2%	47	Alaska	291	0.3%
41	West Virginia	494	0.4%	48	South Dakota	258	0.2%
19	Wisconsin	1,922	1.7%	49	Vermont	249	0.2%
50	Wyoming	201	0.2%	50	Wyoming	201	0.2%
					District of Columbia	170	0.2%

Source: U.S. Department of Health and Human Services, National Center for Health Statistics
    unpublished data

Percent of Vaginal Births After a Cesarean (VBAC) in 1997

National Percent = 27.4% of Live Births to Women Who Have Had a Cesarean*

<table>
<tr><td colspan="3">ALPHA ORDER</td><td colspan="3">RANK ORDER</td></tr>
<tr><th>RANK</th><th>STATE</th><th>PERCENT</th><th>RANK</th><th>STATE</th><th>PERCENT</th></tr>
<tr><td>43</td><td>Alabama</td><td>22.3</td><td>1</td><td>Hawaii</td><td>44.7</td></tr>
<tr><td>16</td><td>Alaska</td><td>33.4</td><td>2</td><td>New Mexico</td><td>39.3</td></tr>
<tr><td>36</td><td>Arizona</td><td>26.4</td><td>2</td><td>Vermont</td><td>39.3</td></tr>
<tr><td>48</td><td>Arkansas</td><td>19.3</td><td>4</td><td>Oregon</td><td>37.6</td></tr>
<tr><td>46</td><td>California</td><td>20.6</td><td>5</td><td>New Hampshire</td><td>36.3</td></tr>
<tr><td>6</td><td>Colorado</td><td>35.7</td><td>6</td><td>Colorado</td><td>35.7</td></tr>
<tr><td>17</td><td>Connecticut</td><td>33.2</td><td>7</td><td>Ohio</td><td>35.5</td></tr>
<tr><td>27</td><td>Delaware</td><td>31.0</td><td>8</td><td>Pennsylvania</td><td>35.0</td></tr>
<tr><td>38</td><td>Florida</td><td>24.2</td><td>9</td><td>Minnesota</td><td>34.7</td></tr>
<tr><td>40</td><td>Georgia</td><td>23.7</td><td>10</td><td>Washington</td><td>34.3</td></tr>
<tr><td>1</td><td>Hawaii</td><td>44.7</td><td>11</td><td>New Jersey</td><td>34.1</td></tr>
<tr><td>15</td><td>Idaho</td><td>33.5</td><td>12</td><td>Massachusetts</td><td>33.7</td></tr>
<tr><td>19</td><td>Illinois</td><td>32.7</td><td>13</td><td>Iowa</td><td>33.6</td></tr>
<tr><td>31</td><td>Indiana</td><td>27.7</td><td>13</td><td>Wisconsin</td><td>33.6</td></tr>
<tr><td>13</td><td>Iowa</td><td>33.6</td><td>15</td><td>Idaho</td><td>33.5</td></tr>
<tr><td>33</td><td>Kansas</td><td>27.1</td><td>16</td><td>Alaska</td><td>33.4</td></tr>
<tr><td>39</td><td>Kentucky</td><td>24.1</td><td>17</td><td>Connecticut</td><td>33.2</td></tr>
<tr><td>50</td><td>Louisiana</td><td>13.0</td><td>18</td><td>Utah</td><td>32.9</td></tr>
<tr><td>29</td><td>Maine</td><td>29.3</td><td>19</td><td>Illinois</td><td>32.7</td></tr>
<tr><td>26</td><td>Maryland</td><td>31.1</td><td>20</td><td>Montana</td><td>32.5</td></tr>
<tr><td>12</td><td>Massachusetts</td><td>33.7</td><td>21</td><td>North Dakota</td><td>32.3</td></tr>
<tr><td>33</td><td>Michigan</td><td>27.1</td><td>22</td><td>Rhode Island</td><td>31.8</td></tr>
<tr><td>9</td><td>Minnesota</td><td>34.7</td><td>23</td><td>New York</td><td>31.7</td></tr>
<tr><td>49</td><td>Mississippi</td><td>15.6</td><td>24</td><td>Virginia</td><td>31.6</td></tr>
<tr><td>28</td><td>Missouri</td><td>30.8</td><td>24</td><td>Wyoming</td><td>31.6</td></tr>
<tr><td>20</td><td>Montana</td><td>32.5</td><td>26</td><td>Maryland</td><td>31.1</td></tr>
<tr><td>32</td><td>Nebraska</td><td>27.6</td><td>27</td><td>Delaware</td><td>31.0</td></tr>
<tr><td>35</td><td>Nevada</td><td>26.6</td><td>28</td><td>Missouri</td><td>30.8</td></tr>
<tr><td>5</td><td>New Hampshire</td><td>36.3</td><td>29</td><td>Maine</td><td>29.3</td></tr>
<tr><td>11</td><td>New Jersey</td><td>34.1</td><td>30</td><td>North Carolina</td><td>28.2</td></tr>
<tr><td>2</td><td>New Mexico</td><td>39.3</td><td>31</td><td>Indiana</td><td>27.7</td></tr>
<tr><td>23</td><td>New York</td><td>31.7</td><td>32</td><td>Nebraska</td><td>27.6</td></tr>
<tr><td>30</td><td>North Carolina</td><td>28.2</td><td>33</td><td>Kansas</td><td>27.1</td></tr>
<tr><td>21</td><td>North Dakota</td><td>32.3</td><td>33</td><td>Michigan</td><td>27.1</td></tr>
<tr><td>7</td><td>Ohio</td><td>35.5</td><td>35</td><td>Nevada</td><td>26.6</td></tr>
<tr><td>44</td><td>Oklahoma</td><td>21.6</td><td>36</td><td>Arizona</td><td>26.4</td></tr>
<tr><td>4</td><td>Oregon</td><td>37.6</td><td>37</td><td>Tennessee</td><td>25.6</td></tr>
<tr><td>8</td><td>Pennsylvania</td><td>35.0</td><td>38</td><td>Florida</td><td>24.2</td></tr>
<tr><td>22</td><td>Rhode Island</td><td>31.8</td><td>39</td><td>Kentucky</td><td>24.1</td></tr>
<tr><td>42</td><td>South Carolina</td><td>23.3</td><td>40</td><td>Georgia</td><td>23.7</td></tr>
<tr><td>41</td><td>South Dakota</td><td>23.6</td><td>41</td><td>South Dakota</td><td>23.6</td></tr>
<tr><td>37</td><td>Tennessee</td><td>25.6</td><td>42</td><td>South Carolina</td><td>23.3</td></tr>
<tr><td>47</td><td>Texas</td><td>19.5</td><td>43</td><td>Alabama</td><td>22.3</td></tr>
<tr><td>18</td><td>Utah</td><td>32.9</td><td>44</td><td>Oklahoma</td><td>21.6</td></tr>
<tr><td>2</td><td>Vermont</td><td>39.3</td><td>45</td><td>West Virginia</td><td>21.2</td></tr>
<tr><td>24</td><td>Virginia</td><td>31.6</td><td>46</td><td>California</td><td>20.6</td></tr>
<tr><td>10</td><td>Washington</td><td>34.3</td><td>47</td><td>Texas</td><td>19.5</td></tr>
<tr><td>45</td><td>West Virginia</td><td>21.2</td><td>48</td><td>Arkansas</td><td>19.3</td></tr>
<tr><td>13</td><td>Wisconsin</td><td>33.6</td><td>49</td><td>Mississippi</td><td>15.6</td></tr>
<tr><td>24</td><td>Wyoming</td><td>31.6</td><td>50</td><td>Louisiana</td><td>13.0</td></tr>
<tr><td></td><td></td><td></td><td></td><td>District of Columbia</td><td>23.4</td></tr>
</table>

Source: U.S. Department of Health and Human Services, National Center for Health Statistics
    "National Vital Statistics Reports" (Vol. 47, No. 27, December 2, 1999)
*Vaginal births after a cesarean delivery as a percent of all births to women with a previous cesarean delivery
giving birth in 1997.

Percent of Mothers Beginning Prenatal Care in First Trimester in 1998

National Percent = 82.8% of Mothers*

<u>ALPHA ORDER</u>

RANK	STATE	PERCENT
30	Alabama	82.4
38	Alaska	81.4
48	Arizona	75.2
47	Arkansas	77.8
32	California	82.3
33	Colorado	82.2
5	Connecticut	88.0
26	Delaware	83.4
24	Florida	83.7
10	Georgia	86.4
15	Hawaii	85.4
45	Idaho	78.7
28	Illinois	82.7
43	Indiana	79.4
7	Iowa	87.4
12	Kansas	85.8
9	Kentucky	86.5
33	Louisiana	82.2
4	Maine	88.9
6	Maryland	87.8
3	Massachusetts	89.5
20	Michigan	84.3
18	Minnesota	84.5
41	Mississippi	80.6
11	Missouri	86.1
30	Montana	82.4
23	Nebraska	83.9
49	Nevada	74.6
1	New Hampshire	89.7
36	New Jersey	81.6
50	New Mexico	67.6
40	New York	81.2
18	North Carolina	84.5
13	North Dakota	85.6
14	Ohio	85.5
46	Oklahoma	78.6
42	Oregon	80.2
17	Pennsylvania	84.8
1	Rhode Island	89.7
37	South Carolina	81.5
28	South Dakota	82.7
22	Tennessee	84.1
44	Texas	79.3
35	Utah	82.1
7	Vermont	87.4
16	Virginia	85.2
27	Washington	83.0
24	West Virginia	83.7
20	Wisconsin	84.3
39	Wyoming	81.3

<u>RANK ORDER</u>

RANK	STATE	PERCENT
1	New Hampshire	89.7
1	Rhode Island	89.7
3	Massachusetts	89.5
4	Maine	88.9
5	Connecticut	88.0
6	Maryland	87.8
7	Iowa	87.4
7	Vermont	87.4
9	Kentucky	86.5
10	Georgia	86.4
11	Missouri	86.1
12	Kansas	85.8
13	North Dakota	85.6
14	Ohio	85.5
15	Hawaii	85.4
16	Virginia	85.2
17	Pennsylvania	84.8
18	Minnesota	84.5
18	North Carolina	84.5
20	Michigan	84.3
20	Wisconsin	84.3
22	Tennessee	84.1
23	Nebraska	83.9
24	Florida	83.7
24	West Virginia	83.7
26	Delaware	83.4
27	Washington	83.0
28	Illinois	82.7
28	South Dakota	82.7
30	Alabama	82.4
30	Montana	82.4
32	California	82.3
33	Colorado	82.2
33	Louisiana	82.2
35	Utah	82.1
36	New Jersey	81.6
37	South Carolina	81.5
38	Alaska	81.4
39	Wyoming	81.3
40	New York	81.2
41	Mississippi	80.6
42	Oregon	80.2
43	Indiana	79.4
44	Texas	79.3
45	Idaho	78.7
46	Oklahoma	78.6
47	Arkansas	77.8
48	Arizona	75.2
49	Nevada	74.6
50	New Mexico	67.6
	District of Columbia	71.9

Source: U.S. Department of Health and Human Services, National Center for Health Statistics
   "National Vital Statistics Reports" (Vol. 47, No. 25, October 5, 1999)
*Preliminary data by state of residence.

Percent of White Mothers Beginning Prenatal Care in First Trimester in 1998

National Percent = 84.8% of White Mothers*

ALPHA ORDER

RANK	STATE	PERCENT
12	Alabama	88.3
37	Alaska	83.5
48	Arizona	76.0
43	Arkansas	80.8
40	California	82.3
39	Colorado	82.7
8	Connecticut	89.3
29	Delaware	86.5
26	Florida	86.9
5	Georgia	90.0
4	Hawaii	90.1
47	Idaho	79.1
30	Illinois	85.7
42	Indiana	81.1
15	Iowa	87.9
27	Kansas	86.7
18	Kentucky	87.4
7	Louisiana	89.4
10	Maine	89.1
1	Maryland	91.5
2	Massachusetts	90.9
23	Michigan	87.1
23	Minnesota	87.1
8	Mississippi	89.3
13	Missouri	88.2
33	Montana	84.8
32	Nebraska	84.9
49	Nevada	75.3
6	New Hampshire	89.9
31	New Jersey	85.5
50	New Mexico	69.1
34	New York	84.5
14	North Carolina	88.1
19	North Dakota	87.3
16	Ohio	87.6
44	Oklahoma	80.7
45	Oregon	80.4
19	Pennsylvania	87.3
2	Rhode Island	90.9
22	South Carolina	87.2
28	South Dakota	86.6
19	Tennessee	87.3
46	Texas	79.6
38	Utah	82.9
17	Vermont	87.5
11	Virginia	88.8
36	Washington	83.6
35	West Virginia	84.2
25	Wisconsin	87.0
41	Wyoming	82.2

RANK ORDER

RANK	STATE	PERCENT
1	Maryland	91.5
2	Massachusetts	90.9
2	Rhode Island	90.9
4	Hawaii	90.1
5	Georgia	90.0
6	New Hampshire	89.9
7	Louisiana	89.4
8	Connecticut	89.3
8	Mississippi	89.3
10	Maine	89.1
11	Virginia	88.8
12	Alabama	88.3
13	Missouri	88.2
14	North Carolina	88.1
15	Iowa	87.9
16	Ohio	87.6
17	Vermont	87.5
18	Kentucky	87.4
19	North Dakota	87.3
19	Pennsylvania	87.3
19	Tennessee	87.3
22	South Carolina	87.2
23	Michigan	87.1
23	Minnesota	87.1
25	Wisconsin	87.0
26	Florida	86.9
27	Kansas	86.7
28	South Dakota	86.6
29	Delaware	86.5
30	Illinois	85.7
31	New Jersey	85.5
32	Nebraska	84.9
33	Montana	84.8
34	New York	84.5
35	West Virginia	84.2
36	Washington	83.6
37	Alaska	83.5
38	Utah	82.9
39	Colorado	82.7
40	California	82.3
41	Wyoming	82.2
42	Indiana	81.1
43	Arkansas	80.8
44	Oklahoma	80.7
45	Oregon	80.4
46	Texas	79.6
47	Idaho	79.1
48	Arizona	76.0
49	Nevada	75.3
50	New Mexico	69.1
	District of Columbia	84.5

Source: U.S. Department of Health and Human Services, National Center for Health Statistics
   "National Vital Statistics Reports" (Vol. 47, No. 25, October 5, 1999)
*Preliminary data by state of residence.

Percent of Black Mothers Beginning Prenatal Care in First Trimester in 1998

National Percent = 73.3% of Black Mothers*

ALPHA ORDER				RANK ORDER		
RANK	STATE	PERCENT		RANK	STATE	PERCENT
37	Alabama	70.1		1	Hawaii	91.7
3	Alaska	82.6		2	Maine	85.6
25	Arizona	73.5		3	Alaska	82.6
41	Arkansas	67.6		4	Maryland	80.4
6	California	79.5		5	Massachusetts	80.0
17	Colorado	75.9		6	California	79.5
11	Connecticut	79.0		7	Georgia	79.4
24	Delaware	74.2		7	Oregon	79.4
27	Florida	72.8		9	Rhode Island	79.3
7	Georgia	79.4		10	Montana	79.1
1	Hawaii	91.7		11	Connecticut	79.0
40	Idaho	69.1		12	North Dakota	78.8
37	Illinois	70.1		13	Kentucky	78.1
47	Indiana	64.6		14	Washington	77.1
21	Iowa	74.8		15	New Hampshire	76.5
16	Kansas	76.0		16	Kansas	76.0
13	Kentucky	78.1		17	Colorado	75.9
29	Louisiana	72.1		18	Texas	75.7
2	Maine	85.6		19	South Dakota	75.3
4	Maryland	80.4		20	North Carolina	75.2
5	Massachusetts	80.0		21	Iowa	74.8
30	Michigan	71.1		22	Missouri	74.5
44	Minnesota	66.7		22	Virginia	74.5
35	Mississippi	70.3		24	Delaware	74.2
22	Missouri	74.5		25	Arizona	73.5
10	Montana	79.1		26	Ohio	73.2
32	Nebraska	71.0		27	Florida	72.8
45	Nevada	66.3		28	Tennessee	72.7
15	New Hampshire	76.5		29	Louisiana	72.1
46	New Jersey	65.1		30	Michigan	71.1
49	New Mexico	58.4		30	South Carolina	71.1
33	New York	70.9		32	Nebraska	71.0
20	North Carolina	75.2		33	New York	70.9
12	North Dakota	78.8		33	Pennsylvania	70.9
26	Ohio	73.2		35	Mississippi	70.3
39	Oklahoma	69.6		36	West Virginia	70.2
7	Oregon	79.4		37	Alabama	70.1
33	Pennsylvania	70.9		37	Illinois	70.1
9	Rhode Island	79.3		39	Oklahoma	69.6
30	South Carolina	71.1		40	Idaho	69.1
19	South Dakota	75.3		41	Arkansas	67.6
28	Tennessee	72.7		42	Wisconsin	67.5
18	Texas	75.7		43	Wyoming	67.3
47	Utah	64.6		44	Minnesota	66.7
NA	Vermont**	NA		45	Nevada	66.3
22	Virginia	74.5		46	New Jersey	65.1
14	Washington	77.1		47	Indiana	64.6
36	West Virginia	70.2		47	Utah	64.6
42	Wisconsin	67.5		49	New Mexico	58.4
43	Wyoming	67.3		NA	Vermont**	NA
					District of Columbia	66.9

Source: U.S. Department of Health and Human Services, National Center for Health Statistics
   "National Vital Statistics Reports" (Vol. 47, No. 25, October 5, 1999)
*Preliminary data by state of residence.
**Insufficient data.

Percent of Mothers Receiving Late or No Prenatal Care in 1997

National Percent = 3.9% of Mothers*

ALPHA ORDER				RANK ORDER		
RANK	STATE	PERCENT		RANK	STATE	PERCENT
21	Alabama	3.7		1	New Mexico	7.6
11	Alaska	4.4		2	Arizona	6.6
2	Arizona	6.6		3	Nevada	6.3
4	Arkansas	5.8		4	Arkansas	5.8
21	California	3.7		5	Texas	5.1
18	Colorado	3.9		6	New York	5.0
47	Connecticut	1.9		7	Oklahoma	4.8
29	Delaware	3.3		8	New Jersey	4.7
30	Florida	3.2		8	South Carolina	4.7
34	Georgia	3.1		10	Hawaii	4.6
10	Hawaii	4.6		11	Alaska	4.4
14	Idaho	4.2		11	Pennsylvania	4.4
17	Illinois	4.0		13	Ohio	4.3
18	Indiana	3.9		14	Idaho	4.2
44	Iowa	2.5		15	Louisiana	4.1
40	Kansas	2.7		15	Mississippi	4.1
42	Kentucky	2.6		17	Illinois	4.0
15	Louisiana	4.1		18	Colorado	3.9
49	Maine	1.7		18	Indiana	3.9
42	Maryland	2.6		18	Tennessee	3.9
40	Massachusetts	2.7		21	Alabama	3.7
37	Michigan	3.0		21	California	3.7
34	Minnesota	3.1		21	Wyoming	3.7
15	Mississippi	4.1		24	Montana	3.6
39	Missouri	2.8		24	Oregon	3.6
24	Montana	3.6		26	Utah	3.5
38	Nebraska	2.9		27	South Dakota	3.4
3	Nevada	6.3		27	Washington	3.4
48	New Hampshire	1.8		29	Delaware	3.3
8	New Jersey	4.7		30	Florida	3.2
1	New Mexico	7.6		30	North Carolina	3.2
6	New York	5.0		30	Virginia	3.2
30	North Carolina	3.2		30	Wisconsin	3.2
45	North Dakota	2.2		34	Georgia	3.1
13	Ohio	4.3		34	Minnesota	3.1
7	Oklahoma	4.8		34	West Virginia	3.1
24	Oregon	3.6		37	Michigan	3.0
11	Pennsylvania	4.4		38	Nebraska	2.9
49	Rhode Island	1.7		39	Missouri	2.8
8	South Carolina	4.7		40	Kansas	2.7
27	South Dakota	3.4		40	Massachusetts	2.7
18	Tennessee	3.9		42	Kentucky	2.6
5	Texas	5.1		42	Maryland	2.6
26	Utah	3.5		44	Iowa	2.5
46	Vermont	2.0		45	North Dakota	2.2
30	Virginia	3.2		46	Vermont	2.0
27	Washington	3.4		47	Connecticut	1.9
34	West Virginia	3.1		48	New Hampshire	1.8
30	Wisconsin	3.2		49	Maine	1.7
21	Wyoming	3.7		49	Rhode Island	1.7
					District of Columbia	12.3

Source: U.S. Department of Health and Human Services, National Center for Health Statistics
    "National Vital Statistics Reports" (Vol. 47, No. 18, April 29, 1999)
*Final data by state of residence. "Late" means care begun in third trimester.

Percent of White Mother Receiving Late or No Prenatal Care in 1997

National Rate = 3.2% of White Mothers*

ALPHA ORDER

RANK	STATE	PERCENT
30	Alabama	2.3
12	Alaska	3.5
2	Arizona	6.2
5	Arkansas	4.4
10	California	3.7
8	Colorado	3.8
47	Connecticut	1.5
34	Delaware	2.2
30	Florida	2.3
38	Georgia	2.1
17	Hawaii	3.1
6	Idaho	4.0
22	Illinois	2.8
14	Indiana	3.4
28	Iowa	2.4
28	Kansas	2.4
30	Kentucky	2.3
42	Louisiana	2.0
46	Maine	1.6
47	Maryland	1.5
34	Massachusetts	2.2
34	Michigan	2.2
30	Minnesota	2.3
44	Mississippi	1.8
38	Missouri	2.1
22	Montana	2.8
25	Nebraska	2.6
3	Nevada	6.1
45	New Hampshire	1.7
20	New Jersey	3.0
1	New Mexico	6.9
8	New York	3.8
34	North Carolina	2.2
47	North Dakota	1.5
16	Ohio	3.3
7	Oklahoma	3.9
11	Oregon	3.6
14	Pennsylvania	3.4
50	Rhode Island	1.3
24	South Carolina	2.7
38	South Dakota	2.1
25	Tennessee	2.6
4	Texas	5.1
17	Utah	3.1
43	Vermont	1.9
38	Virginia	2.1
17	Washington	3.1
21	West Virginia	2.9
27	Wisconsin	2.5
12	Wyoming	3.5

RANK ORDER

RANK	STATE	PERCENT
1	New Mexico	6.9
2	Arizona	6.2
3	Nevada	6.1
4	Texas	5.1
5	Arkansas	4.4
6	Idaho	4.0
7	Oklahoma	3.9
8	Colorado	3.8
8	New York	3.8
10	California	3.7
11	Oregon	3.6
12	Alaska	3.5
12	Wyoming	3.5
14	Indiana	3.4
14	Pennsylvania	3.4
16	Ohio	3.3
17	Hawaii	3.1
17	Utah	3.1
17	Washington	3.1
20	New Jersey	3.0
21	West Virginia	2.9
22	Illinois	2.8
22	Montana	2.8
24	South Carolina	2.7
25	Nebraska	2.6
25	Tennessee	2.6
27	Wisconsin	2.5
28	Iowa	2.4
28	Kansas	2.4
30	Alabama	2.3
30	Florida	2.3
30	Kentucky	2.3
30	Minnesota	2.3
34	Delaware	2.2
34	Massachusetts	2.2
34	Michigan	2.2
34	North Carolina	2.2
38	Georgia	2.1
38	Missouri	2.1
38	South Dakota	2.1
38	Virginia	2.1
42	Louisiana	2.0
43	Vermont	1.9
44	Mississippi	1.8
45	New Hampshire	1.7
46	Maine	1.6
47	Connecticut	1.5
47	Maryland	1.5
47	North Dakota	1.5
50	Rhode Island	1.3
	District of Columbia	7.2

Source: U.S. Department of Health and Human Services, National Center for Health Statistics
"National Vital Statistics Reports" (Vol. 47, No. 18, April 29, 1999)
*Final data by state of residence. "Late" means care begun in third trimester.

Percent of Black Mothers Receiving Late or No Prenatal Care in 1997

National Rate = 7.3% of Black Mothers*

RANK	STATE	PERCENT
23	Alabama	6.6
31	Alaska	5.8
8	Arizona	9.2
3	Arkansas	10.7
39	California	4.6
29	Colorado	6.0
41	Connecticut	4.0
25	Delaware	6.4
30	Florida	5.9
38	Georgia	5.0
NA	Hawaii**	NA
NA	Idaho**	NA
11	Illinois	8.8
17	Indiana	7.9
34	Iowa	5.5
32	Kansas	5.6
32	Kentucky	5.6
18	Louisiana	7.0
NA	Maine**	NA
36	Maryland	5.2
25	Massachusetts	6.4
20	Michigan	6.9
6	Minnesota	10.3
21	Mississippi	6.8
18	Missouri	7.0
NA	Montana**	NA
21	Nebraska	6.8
9	Nevada	9.1
NA	New Hampshire**	NA
1	New Jersey	12.1
2	New Mexico	10.8
12	New York	8.7
27	North Carolina	6.1
NA	North Dakota**	NA
7	Ohio	9.9
13	Oklahoma	8.3
40	Oregon	4.1
5	Pennsylvania	10.5
34	Rhode Island	5.5
13	South Carolina	8.3
NA	South Dakota**	NA
13	Tennessee	8.3
27	Texas	6.1
4	Utah	10.6
NA	Vermont**	NA
24	Virginia	6.5
37	Washington	5.1
10	West Virginia	8.9
16	Wisconsin	8.0
NA	Wyoming**	NA

RANK	STATE	PERCENT
1	New Jersey	12.1
2	New Mexico	10.8
3	Arkansas	10.7
4	Utah	10.6
5	Pennsylvania	10.5
6	Minnesota	10.3
7	Ohio	9.9
8	Arizona	9.2
9	Nevada	9.1
10	West Virginia	8.9
11	Illinois	8.8
12	New York	8.7
13	Oklahoma	8.3
13	South Carolina	8.3
13	Tennessee	8.3
16	Wisconsin	8.0
17	Indiana	7.9
18	Louisiana	7.0
18	Missouri	7.0
20	Michigan	6.9
21	Mississippi	6.8
21	Nebraska	6.8
23	Alabama	6.6
24	Virginia	6.5
25	Delaware	6.4
25	Massachusetts	6.4
27	North Carolina	6.1
27	Texas	6.1
29	Colorado	6.0
30	Florida	5.9
31	Alaska	5.8
32	Kansas	5.6
32	Kentucky	5.6
34	Iowa	5.5
34	Rhode Island	5.5
36	Maryland	5.2
37	Washington	5.1
38	Georgia	5.0
39	California	4.6
40	Oregon	4.1
41	Connecticut	4.0
NA	Hawaii**	NA
NA	Idaho**	NA
NA	Maine**	NA
NA	Montana**	NA
NA	New Hampshire**	NA
NA	North Dakota**	NA
NA	South Dakota**	NA
NA	Vermont**	NA
NA	Wyoming**	NA

District of Columbia 14.2

Source: U.S. Department of Health and Human Services, National Center for Health Statistics
  "National Vital Statistics Reports" (Vol. 47, No. 18, April 29, 1999)
*Final data by state of residence. "Late" means care begun in third trimester.
**Insufficient data.

Percent of Births Attended by Midwives in 1997

National Percent = 7.0% of Live Births*

RANK	STATE	PERCENT
42	Alabama	2.9
2	Alaska	16.8
13	Arizona	9.6
46	Arkansas	1.8
18	California	8.2
19	Colorado	7.7
20	Connecticut	7.6
10	Delaware	11.6
9	Florida	11.8
3	Georgia	15.2
33	Hawaii	4.5
38	Idaho	4.0
41	Illinois	3.0
43	Indiana	2.7
44	Iowa	2.4
47	Kansas	1.5
40	Kentucky	3.2
49	Louisiana	1.2
11	Maine	11.1
15	Maryland	8.8
7	Massachusetts	13.2
26	Michigan	6.5
17	Minnesota	8.3
47	Mississippi	1.5
50	Missouri	0.8
14	Montana	9.5
45	Nebraska	2.0
20	Nevada	7.6
5	New Hampshire	14.4
29	New Jersey	5.1
1	New Mexico	20.0
12	New York	10.9
23	North Carolina	7.1
28	North Dakota	5.8
34	Ohio	4.3
34	Oklahoma	4.3
6	Oregon	13.4
25	Pennsylvania	6.6
8	Rhode Island	11.9
27	South Carolina	6.1
39	South Dakota	3.3
37	Tennessee	4.1
31	Texas	4.8
22	Utah	7.2
4	Vermont	14.6
31	Virginia	4.8
15	Washington	8.8
23	West Virginia	7.1
30	Wisconsin	4.9
36	Wyoming	4.2

RANK	STATE	PERCENT
1	New Mexico	20.0
2	Alaska	16.8
3	Georgia	15.2
4	Vermont	14.6
5	New Hampshire	14.4
6	Oregon	13.4
7	Massachusetts	13.2
8	Rhode Island	11.9
9	Florida	11.8
10	Delaware	11.6
11	Maine	11.1
12	New York	10.9
13	Arizona	9.6
14	Montana	9.5
15	Maryland	8.8
15	Washington	8.8
17	Minnesota	8.3
18	California	8.2
19	Colorado	7.7
20	Connecticut	7.6
20	Nevada	7.6
22	Utah	7.2
23	North Carolina	7.1
23	West Virginia	7.1
25	Pennsylvania	6.6
26	Michigan	6.5
27	South Carolina	6.1
28	North Dakota	5.8
29	New Jersey	5.1
30	Wisconsin	4.9
31	Texas	4.8
31	Virginia	4.8
33	Hawaii	4.5
34	Ohio	4.3
34	Oklahoma	4.3
36	Wyoming	4.2
37	Tennessee	4.1
38	Idaho	4.0
39	South Dakota	3.3
40	Kentucky	3.2
41	Illinois	3.0
42	Alabama	2.9
43	Indiana	2.7
44	Iowa	2.4
45	Nebraska	2.0
46	Arkansas	1.8
47	Kansas	1.5
47	Mississippi	1.5
49	Louisiana	1.2
50	Missouri	0.8
	District of Columbia	4.7

*Source: U.S. Department of Health and Human Services, National Center for Health Statistics
"National Vital Statistics Reports" (Vol. 47, No. 27, December 2, 1999)
Includes certified nurse midwives and other midwives.

Reported Legal Abortions in 1996

National Total = 1,221,585 Abortions*

ALPHA ORDER

RANK	STATE	ABORTIONS	% of USA
18	Alabama	13,826	1.1%
45	Alaska	2,139	0.2%
25	Arizona	11,016	0.9%
33	Arkansas	5,882	0.5%
1	California	280,180	22.9%
27	Colorado	9,710	0.8%
17	Connecticut	14,094	1.2%
38	Delaware	4,482	0.4%
4	Florida	80,040	6.6%
8	Georgia	35,790	2.9%
37	Hawaii	4,916	0.4%
48	Idaho	1,022	0.1%
5	Illinois	53,613	4.4%
21	Indiana	13,341	1.1%
29	Iowa	7,602	0.6%
26	Kansas	10,685	0.9%
30	Kentucky	7,000	0.6%
23	Louisiana	11,865	1.0%
42	Maine	2,615	0.2%
22	Maryland	12,363	1.0%
12	Massachusetts	29,293	2.4%
11	Michigan	30,208	2.5%
16	Minnesota	14,193	1.2%
39	Mississippi	4,206	0.3%
24	Missouri	11,629	1.0%
41	Montana	2,763	0.2%
35	Nebraska	5,214	0.4%
31	Nevada	6,965	0.6%
44	New Hampshire	2,300	0.2%
10	New Jersey	31,860	2.6%
36	New Mexico	5,033	0.4%
2	New York	152,991	12.5%
9	North Carolina	33,554	2.7%
47	North Dakota	1,291	0.1%
7	Ohio	36,530	3.0%
32	Oklahoma	6,769	0.6%
19	Oregon	13,767	1.1%
6	Pennsylvania	38,004	3.1%
34	Rhode Island	5,437	0.4%
28	South Carolina	9,326	0.8%
49	South Dakota	901	0.1%
15	Tennessee	17,989	1.5%
3	Texas	91,470	7.5%
40	Utah	3,639	0.3%
45	Vermont	2,139	0.2%
14	Virginia	25,770	2.1%
13	Washington	26,138	2.1%
43	West Virginia	2,470	0.2%
20	Wisconsin	13,673	1.1%
50	Wyoming	208	0.0%

RANK ORDER

RANK	STATE	ABORTIONS	% of USA
1	California	280,180	22.9%
2	New York	152,991	12.5%
3	Texas	91,470	7.5%
4	Florida	80,040	6.6%
5	Illinois	53,613	4.4%
6	Pennsylvania	38,004	3.1%
7	Ohio	36,530	3.0%
8	Georgia	35,790	2.9%
9	North Carolina	33,554	2.7%
10	New Jersey	31,860	2.6%
11	Michigan	30,208	2.5%
12	Massachusetts	29,293	2.4%
13	Washington	26,138	2.1%
14	Virginia	25,770	2.1%
15	Tennessee	17,989	1.5%
16	Minnesota	14,193	1.2%
17	Connecticut	14,094	1.2%
18	Alabama	13,826	1.1%
19	Oregon	13,767	1.1%
20	Wisconsin	13,673	1.1%
21	Indiana	13,341	1.1%
22	Maryland	12,363	1.0%
23	Louisiana	11,865	1.0%
24	Missouri	11,629	1.0%
25	Arizona	11,016	0.9%
26	Kansas	10,685	0.9%
27	Colorado	9,710	0.8%
28	South Carolina	9,326	0.8%
29	Iowa	7,602	0.6%
30	Kentucky	7,000	0.6%
31	Nevada	6,965	0.6%
32	Oklahoma	6,769	0.6%
33	Arkansas	5,882	0.5%
34	Rhode Island	5,437	0.4%
35	Nebraska	5,214	0.4%
36	New Mexico	5,033	0.4%
37	Hawaii	4,916	0.4%
38	Delaware	4,482	0.4%
39	Mississippi	4,206	0.3%
40	Utah	3,639	0.3%
41	Montana	2,763	0.2%
42	Maine	2,615	0.2%
43	West Virginia	2,470	0.2%
44	New Hampshire	2,300	0.2%
45	Alaska	2,139	0.2%
45	Vermont	2,139	0.2%
47	North Dakota	1,291	0.1%
48	Idaho	1,022	0.1%
49	South Dakota	901	0.1%
50	Wyoming	208	0.0%
	District of Columbia	13,674	1.1%

Source: U.S. Department of Health and Human Services, Centers for Disease Control and Prevention
   "Abortion Surveillance-United States, 1996" (Morbidity Mortality Weekly Report, Vol. 48, No. SS-4, July 30, 1999)
By state of occurrence.

Reported Legal Abortions per 1,000 Live Births in 1996

National Rate = 314 Abortions per 1,000 Live Births*

ALPHA ORDER

RANK	STATE	RATE
24	Alabama	229
28	Alaska	213
43	Arizona	146
37	Arkansas	162
2	California	519
35	Colorado	174
9	Connecticut	317
3	Delaware	441
5	Florida	423
12	Georgia	314
18	Hawaii	267
49	Idaho	55
13	Illinois	293
38	Indiana	160
29	Iowa	205
14	Kansas	292
44	Kentucky	133
33	Louisiana	182
31	Maine	190
36	Maryland	173
6	Massachusetts	365
25	Michigan	226
27	Minnesota	223
46	Mississippi	103
39	Missouri	158
21	Montana	255
26	Nebraska	224
18	Nevada	267
39	New Hampshire	158
15	New Jersey	279
32	New Mexico	185
1	New York	580
8	North Carolina	321
41	North Dakota	155
23	Ohio	241
42	Oklahoma	147
11	Oregon	315
20	Pennsylvania	256
4	Rhode Island	430
33	South Carolina	182
47	South Dakota	86
22	Tennessee	244
17	Texas	277
47	Utah	86
10	Vermont	316
15	Virginia	279
7	Washington	335
45	West Virginia	119
30	Wisconsin	204
50	Wyoming	33

RANK ORDER

RANK	STATE	RATE
1	New York	580
2	California	519
3	Delaware	441
4	Rhode Island	430
5	Florida	423
6	Massachusetts	365
7	Washington	335
8	North Carolina	321
9	Connecticut	317
10	Vermont	316
11	Oregon	315
12	Georgia	314
13	Illinois	293
14	Kansas	292
15	New Jersey	279
15	Virginia	279
17	Texas	277
18	Hawaii	267
18	Nevada	267
20	Pennsylvania	256
21	Montana	255
22	Tennessee	244
23	Ohio	241
24	Alabama	229
25	Michigan	226
26	Nebraska	224
27	Minnesota	223
28	Alaska	213
29	Iowa	205
30	Wisconsin	204
31	Maine	190
32	New Mexico	185
33	Louisiana	182
33	South Carolina	182
35	Colorado	174
36	Maryland	173
37	Arkansas	162
38	Indiana	160
39	Missouri	158
39	New Hampshire	158
41	North Dakota	155
42	Oklahoma	147
43	Arizona	146
44	Kentucky	133
45	West Virginia	119
46	Mississippi	103
47	South Dakota	86
47	Utah	86
49	Idaho	55
50	Wyoming	33
	District of Columbia**	NA

Source: U.S. Department of Health and Human Services, Centers for Disease Control and Prevention
   "Abortion Surveillance-United States, 1996" (Morbidity Mortality Weekly Report, Vol. 48, No. SS-4, July 30, 1999)
*By state of occurrence.
**The District of Columbia's ratio was not listed but was noted as being greater than 1,000 abortions per 1,000 live births.

Reported Legal Abortions per 1,000 Women Ages 15 to 44 in 1996

National Rate = 20 Reported Legal Abortions per 1,000 Women Ages 15 to 44*

ALPHA ORDER

RANK	STATE	RATE
25	Alabama	14
20	Alaska	15
33	Arizona	11
33	Arkansas	11
1	California	39
33	Colorado	11
9	Connecticut	20
4	Delaware	26
3	Florida	27
9	Georgia	20
15	Hawaii	19
49	Idaho	4
9	Illinois	20
37	Indiana	10
30	Iowa	12
15	Kansas	19
43	Kentucky	8
30	Louisiana	12
41	Maine	9
37	Maryland	10
6	Massachusetts	21
25	Michigan	14
28	Minnesota	13
46	Mississippi	7
37	Missouri	10
20	Montana	15
25	Nebraska	14
9	Nevada	20
43	New Hampshire	8
17	New Jersey	18
28	New Mexico	13
2	New York	37
9	North Carolina	20
41	North Dakota	9
20	Ohio	15
37	Oklahoma	10
9	Oregon	20
20	Pennsylvania	15
5	Rhode Island	24
33	South Carolina	11
47	South Dakota	6
20	Tennessee	15
6	Texas	21
43	Utah	8
18	Vermont	16
18	Virginia	16
6	Washington	21
47	West Virginia	6
30	Wisconsin	12
50	Wyoming	2

RANK ORDER

RANK	STATE	RATE
1	California	39
2	New York	37
3	Florida	27
4	Delaware	26
5	Rhode Island	24
6	Massachusetts	21
6	Texas	21
6	Washington	21
9	Connecticut	20
9	Georgia	20
9	Illinois	20
9	Nevada	20
9	North Carolina	20
9	Oregon	20
15	Hawaii	19
15	Kansas	19
17	New Jersey	18
18	Vermont	16
18	Virginia	16
20	Alaska	15
20	Montana	15
20	Ohio	15
20	Pennsylvania	15
20	Tennessee	15
25	Alabama	14
25	Michigan	14
25	Nebraska	14
28	Minnesota	13
28	New Mexico	13
30	Iowa	12
30	Louisiana	12
30	Wisconsin	12
33	Arizona	11
33	Arkansas	11
33	Colorado	11
33	South Carolina	11
37	Indiana	10
37	Maryland	10
37	Missouri	10
37	Oklahoma	10
41	Maine	9
41	North Dakota	9
43	Kentucky	8
43	New Hampshire	8
43	Utah	8
46	Mississippi	7
47	South Dakota	6
47	West Virginia	6
49	Idaho	4
50	Wyoming	2
	District of Columbia**	NA

Source: U.S. Department of Health and Human Services, Centers for Disease Control and Prevention
    "Abortion Surveillance-United States, 1996" (Morbidity Mortality Weekly Report, Vol. 48, No. SS-4, July 30, 1999)
*By state of occurrence.
**The District of Columbia's rate was not listed but was noted as being greater than 100 abortions per 1,000 women ages 15 to 44 years.

Percent of Legal Abortions Obtained by Out-Of-State Residents in 1996

National Percent = 8.1% Reported Legal Abortions*

ALPHA ORDER

ALPHA ORDER

RANK	STATE	PERCENT
10	Alabama	14.6
41	Alaska	0.8
40	Arizona	1.3
19	Arkansas	9.3
NA	California**	NA
16	Colorado	10.2
36	Connecticut	3.7
NA	Delaware**	NA
NA	Florida**	NA
18	Georgia	9.4
42	Hawaii	0.3
25	Idaho	5.9
22	Illinois	7.2
37	Indiana	3.5
NA	Iowa**	NA
1	Kansas	40.9
5	Kentucky	20.6
NA	Louisiana**	NA
38	Maine	2.9
28	Maryland	5.6
25	Massachusetts	5.9
32	Michigan	4.3
20	Minnesota	9.2
29	Mississippi	5.3
14	Missouri	10.9
9	Montana	16.7
6	Nebraska	19.8
13	Nevada	11.4
NA	New Hampshire**	NA
39	New Jersey	2.2
32	New Mexico	4.3
NA	New York**	NA
15	North Carolina	10.8
2	North Dakota	33.2
21	Ohio	7.4
NA	Oklahoma**	NA
12	Oregon	12.2
30	Pennsylvania	4.9
8	Rhode Island	18.5
24	South Carolina	6.2
3	South Dakota	22.8
7	Tennessee	18.9
32	Texas	4.3
17	Utah	9.8
4	Vermont	20.9
27	Virginia	5.8
31	Washington	4.7
11	West Virginia	12.8
35	Wisconsin	4.1
23	Wyoming	6.3

RANK ORDER

RANK	STATE	PERCENT
1	Kansas	40.9
2	North Dakota	33.2
3	South Dakota	22.8
4	Vermont	20.9
5	Kentucky	20.6
6	Nebraska	19.8
7	Tennessee	18.9
8	Rhode Island	18.5
9	Montana	16.7
10	Alabama	14.6
11	West Virginia	12.8
12	Oregon	12.2
13	Nevada	11.4
14	Missouri	10.9
15	North Carolina	10.8
16	Colorado	10.2
17	Utah	9.8
18	Georgia	9.4
19	Arkansas	9.3
20	Minnesota	9.2
21	Ohio	7.4
22	Illinois	7.2
23	Wyoming	6.3
24	South Carolina	6.2
25	Idaho	5.9
25	Massachusetts	5.9
27	Virginia	5.8
28	Maryland	5.6
29	Mississippi	5.3
30	Pennsylvania	4.9
31	Washington	4.7
32	Michigan	4.3
32	New Mexico	4.3
32	Texas	4.3
35	Wisconsin	4.1
36	Connecticut	3.7
37	Indiana	3.5
38	Maine	2.9
39	New Jersey	2.2
40	Arizona	1.3
41	Alaska	0.8
42	Hawaii	0.3
NA	California**	NA
NA	Delaware**	NA
NA	Florida**	NA
NA	Iowa**	NA
NA	Louisiana**	NA
NA	New Hampshire**	NA
NA	New York**	NA
NA	Oklahoma**	NA
	District of Columbia	49.9

Source: U.S. Department of Health and Human Services, Centers for Disease Control and Prevention
    "Abortion Surveillance-United States, 1996" (Morbidity Mortality Weekly Report, Vol. 48, No. SS-4, July 30, 1999)
*By state of occurrence.
**Not reported.

Percent of Reported Legal Abortions Obtained by White Women in 1996

Reporting States' Percent = 57.0% of Reported Legal Abortions*

ALPHA ORDER

RANK	STATE	PERCENT
27	Alabama	52.1
NA	Alaska**	NA
13	Arizona	76.9
20	Arkansas	63.7
NA	California**	NA
NA	Colorado**	NA
NA	Connecticut**	NA
NA	Delaware**	NA
NA	Florida**	NA
30	Georgia	44.0
35	Hawaii	26.7
2	Idaho	95.0
NA	Illinois**	NA
19	Indiana	65.8
NA	Iowa**	NA
13	Kansas	76.9
16	Kentucky	74.0
29	Louisiana	47.7
3	Maine	92.5
31	Maryland	40.7
NA	Massachusetts**	NA
NA	Michigan**	NA
15	Minnesota	74.9
34	Mississippi	31.9
21	Missouri	62.5
8	Montana	86.0
NA	Nebraska**	NA
10	Nevada	82.2
NA	New Hampshire**	NA
33	New Jersey	35.3
9	New Mexico	85.7
32	New York**	38.7
28	North Carolina	51.3
4	North Dakota	90.0
22	Ohio	61.4
NA	Oklahoma**	NA
7	Oregon	86.5
23	Pennsylvania	58.2
12	Rhode Island	79.2
26	South Carolina	54.5
6	South Dakota	88.3
24	Tennessee	58.0
18	Texas	70.0
11	Utah	80.7
1	Vermont	97.0
25	Virginia	55.1
NA	Washington**	NA
5	West Virginia	89.1
17	Wisconsin	72.9
NA	Wyoming**	NA

RANK ORDER

RANK	STATE	PERCENT
1	Vermont	97.0
2	Idaho	95.0
3	Maine	92.5
4	North Dakota	90.0
5	West Virginia	89.1
6	South Dakota	88.3
7	Oregon	86.5
8	Montana	86.0
9	New Mexico	85.7
10	Nevada	82.2
11	Utah	80.7
12	Rhode Island	79.2
13	Arizona	76.9
13	Kansas	76.9
15	Minnesota	74.9
16	Kentucky	74.0
17	Wisconsin	72.9
18	Texas	70.0
19	Indiana	65.8
20	Arkansas	63.7
21	Missouri	62.5
22	Ohio	61.4
23	Pennsylvania	58.2
24	Tennessee	58.0
25	Virginia	55.1
26	South Carolina	54.5
27	Alabama	52.1
28	North Carolina	51.3
29	Louisiana	47.7
30	Georgia	44.0
31	Maryland	40.7
32	New York**	38.7
33	New Jersey	35.3
34	Mississippi	31.9
35	Hawaii	26.7
NA	Alaska**	NA
NA	California**	NA
NA	Colorado**	NA
NA	Connecticut**	NA
NA	Delaware**	NA
NA	Florida**	NA
NA	Illinois**	NA
NA	Iowa**	NA
NA	Massachusetts**	NA
NA	Michigan**	NA
NA	Nebraska**	NA
NA	New Hampshire**	NA
NA	Oklahoma**	NA
NA	Washington**	NA
NA	Wyoming**	NA
	District of Columbia**	NA

Source: U.S. Department of Health and Human Services, Centers for Disease Control and Prevention
    "Abortion Surveillance-United States, 1996" (Morbidity Mortality Weekly Report, Vol. 48, No. SS-4, July 30, 1999)
*By state of occurrence. Includes those of Hispanic ethnicity. National percent is for reporting states only.
**Not reported. New York's number is for New York City only.

Percent of Reported Legal Abortions Obtained by Black Women in 1996

Reporting States' Percent = 34.0% of Reported Legal Abortions*

ALPHA ORDER				RANK ORDER		
RANK	STATE	PERCENT		RANK	STATE	PERCENT
6	Alabama	45.7		1	Mississippi	66.7
NA	Alaska**	NA		2	Maryland	51.6
26	Arizona	5.0		3	Georgia	50.7
13	Arkansas	33.9		4	Louisiana	49.9
NA	California**	NA		5	New York**	48.8
NA	Colorado**	NA		6	Alabama	45.7
NA	Connecticut**	NA		7	New Jersey	44.7
NA	Delaware**	NA		8	South Carolina	43.3
NA	Florida**	NA		9	North Carolina	40.9
3	Georgia	50.7		10	Tennessee	39.0
28	Hawaii	2.7		11	Pennsylvania	38.8
34	Idaho	0.9		12	Virginia	37.6
NA	Illinois**	NA		13	Arkansas	33.9
16	Indiana	25.2		14	Missouri	33.0
NA	Iowa**	NA		15	Ohio	31.7
20	Kansas	17.0		16	Indiana	25.2
19	Kentucky	20.0		17	Wisconsin	21.6
4	Louisiana	49.9		18	Texas	21.4
32	Maine	1.1		19	Kentucky	20.0
2	Maryland	51.6		20	Kansas	17.0
NA	Massachusetts**	NA		21	Rhode Island	13.4
NA	Michigan**	NA		22	Minnesota	12.9
22	Minnesota	12.9		23	West Virginia	9.5
1	Mississippi	66.7		24	Nevada	7.6
14	Missouri	33.0		25	Oregon	5.4
35	Montana	0.4		26	Arizona	5.0
NA	Nebraska**	NA		27	New Mexico	3.3
24	Nevada	7.6		28	Hawaii	2.7
NA	New Hampshire**	NA		29	South Dakota	2.2
7	New Jersey	44.7		30	Utah	1.8
27	New Mexico	3.3		31	North Dakota	1.5
5	New York**	48.8		32	Maine	1.1
9	North Carolina	40.9		33	Vermont	1.0
31	North Dakota	1.5		34	Idaho	0.9
15	Ohio	31.7		35	Montana	0.4
NA	Oklahoma**	NA		NA	Alaska**	NA
25	Oregon	5.4		NA	California**	NA
11	Pennsylvania	38.8		NA	Colorado**	NA
21	Rhode Island	13.4		NA	Connecticut**	NA
8	South Carolina	43.3		NA	Delaware**	NA
29	South Dakota	2.2		NA	Florida**	NA
10	Tennessee	39.0		NA	Illinois**	NA
18	Texas	21.4		NA	Iowa**	NA
30	Utah	1.8		NA	Massachusetts**	NA
33	Vermont	1.0		NA	Michigan**	NA
12	Virginia	37.6		NA	Nebraska**	NA
NA	Washington**	NA		NA	New Hampshire**	NA
23	West Virginia	9.5		NA	Oklahoma**	NA
17	Wisconsin	21.6		NA	Washington**	NA
NA	Wyoming**	NA		NA	Wyoming**	NA
					District of Columbia**	NA

Source: U.S. Department of Health and Human Services, Centers for Disease Control and Prevention
   "Abortion Surveillance-United States, 1996" (Morbidity Mortality Weekly Report, Vol. 48, No. SS-4, July 30, 1999)
*By state of occurrence. National percent is for reporting states only.
**Not reported. New York's number is for New York City only.

Percent of Reported Legal Abortions Obtained by Married Women in 1996

Reporting States' Percent = 19.0% of Reported Legal Abortions*

ALPHA ORDER

RANK	STATE	PERCENT
31	Alabama	16.0
NA	Alaska**	NA
13	Arizona	19.7
NA	Arkansas**	NA
14	California	19.4
NA	Colorado**	NA
NA	Connecticut**	NA
NA	Delaware**	NA
20	Florida	18.4
11	Georgia	19.9
8	Hawaii	20.7
NA	Idaho**	NA
27	Illinois	17.1
33	Indiana	14.7
NA	Iowa**	NA
6	Kansas	21.1
30	Kentucky	16.5
NA	Louisiana**	NA
NA	Maine**	NA
22	Maryland	17.6
NA	Massachusetts**	NA
28	Michigan	16.6
17	Minnesota	19.3
34	Mississippi	14.5
5	Missouri	21.2
23	Montana	17.5
NA	Nebraska**	NA
2	Nevada	24.3
NA	New Hampshire**	NA
21	New Jersey	18.2
28	New Mexico	16.6
11	New York**	19.9
NA	North Carolina**	NA
14	North Dakota	19.4
25	Ohio	17.4
NA	Oklahoma**	NA
3	Oregon	22.8
25	Pennsylvania	17.4
9	Rhode Island	20.2
19	South Carolina	18.7
14	South Dakota	19.4
18	Tennessee	19.2
7	Texas	21.0
1	Utah	39.8
4	Vermont	21.4
NA	Virginia**	NA
NA	Washington**	NA
23	West Virginia	17.5
10	Wisconsin	20.1
32	Wyoming	14.9

RANK ORDER

RANK	STATE	PERCENT
1	Utah	39.8
2	Nevada	24.3
3	Oregon	22.8
4	Vermont	21.4
5	Missouri	21.2
6	Kansas	21.1
7	Texas	21.0
8	Hawaii	20.7
9	Rhode Island	20.2
10	Wisconsin	20.1
11	Georgia	19.9
11	New York**	19.9
13	Arizona	19.7
14	California	19.4
14	North Dakota	19.4
14	South Dakota	19.4
17	Minnesota	19.3
18	Tennessee	19.2
19	South Carolina	18.7
20	Florida	18.4
21	New Jersey	18.2
22	Maryland	17.6
23	Montana	17.5
23	West Virginia	17.5
25	Ohio	17.4
25	Pennsylvania	17.4
27	Illinois	17.1
28	Michigan	16.6
28	New Mexico	16.6
30	Kentucky	16.5
31	Alabama	16.0
32	Wyoming	14.9
33	Indiana	14.7
34	Mississippi	14.5
NA	Alaska**	NA
NA	Arkansas**	NA
NA	Colorado**	NA
NA	Connecticut**	NA
NA	Delaware**	NA
NA	Idaho**	NA
NA	Iowa**	NA
NA	Louisiana**	NA
NA	Maine**	NA
NA	Massachusetts**	NA
NA	Nebraska**	NA
NA	New Hampshire**	NA
NA	North Carolina**	NA
NA	Oklahoma**	NA
NA	Virginia**	NA
NA	Washington**	NA
	District of Columbia**	NA

Source: U.S. Department of Health and Human Services, Centers for Disease Control and Prevention
       "Abortion Surveillance-United States, 1996" (Morbidity Mortality Weekly Report, Vol. 48, No. SS-4, July 30, 1999)
*By state of occurrence. National percent is for reporting states only.
**Not reported. New York's percentage is for New York City only.

Percent of Reported Legal Abortions Obtained by Unmarried Women in 1996

Reporting States' Percent = 78.1% of Reported Legal Abortions*

ALPHA ORDER

RANK ORDER

RANK	STATE	PERCENT		RANK	STATE	PERCENT
3	Alabama	83.5		1	Mississippi	85.1
NA	Alaska**	NA		1	Wyoming	85.1
24	Arizona	77.7		3	Alabama	83.5
NA	Arkansas**	NA		4	Michigan	82.9
21	California	79.0		5	New Mexico	82.7
NA	Colorado**	NA		6	Pennsylvania	82.5
NA	Connecticut**	NA		6	West Virginia	82.5
NA	Delaware**	NA		8	New Jersey	81.4
10	Florida	80.9		9	South Carolina	81.1
18	Georgia	79.3		10	Florida	80.9
20	Hawaii	79.1		11	Kentucky	80.7
NA	Idaho**	NA		12	South Dakota	80.6
15	Illinois	80.2		13	North Dakota	80.5
29	Indiana	74.8		14	Tennessee	80.3
NA	Iowa**	NA		15	Illinois	80.2
23	Kansas	78.4		16	Ohio	79.9
11	Kentucky	80.7		17	Wisconsin	79.8
NA	Louisiana**	NA		18	Georgia	79.3
NA	Maine**	NA		18	Maryland	79.3
18	Maryland	79.3		20	Hawaii	79.1
NA	Massachusetts**	NA		21	California	79.0
4	Michigan	82.9		22	Minnesota	78.5
22	Minnesota	78.5		23	Kansas	78.4
1	Mississippi	85.1		24	Arizona	77.7
26	Missouri	77.0		24	Rhode Island	77.7
27	Montana	76.8		26	Missouri	77.0
NA	Nebraska**	NA		27	Montana	76.8
30	Nevada	74.4		28	Oregon	75.7
NA	New Hampshire**	NA		29	Indiana	74.8
8	New Jersey	81.4		30	Nevada	74.4
5	New Mexico	82.7		30	New York**	74.4
30	New York**	74.4		32	Texas	74.1
NA	North Carolina**	NA		33	Vermont	72.8
13	North Dakota	80.5		34	Utah	60.2
16	Ohio	79.9		NA	Alaska**	NA
NA	Oklahoma**	NA		NA	Arkansas**	NA
28	Oregon	75.7		NA	Colorado**	NA
6	Pennsylvania	82.5		NA	Connecticut**	NA
24	Rhode Island	77.7		NA	Delaware**	NA
9	South Carolina	81.1		NA	Idaho**	NA
12	South Dakota	80.6		NA	Iowa**	NA
14	Tennessee	80.3		NA	Louisiana**	NA
32	Texas	74.1		NA	Maine**	NA
34	Utah	60.2		NA	Massachusetts**	NA
33	Vermont	72.8		NA	Nebraska**	NA
NA	Virginia**	NA		NA	New Hampshire**	NA
NA	Washington**	NA		NA	North Carolina**	NA
6	West Virginia	82.5		NA	Oklahoma**	NA
17	Wisconsin	79.8		NA	Virginia**	NA
1	Wyoming	85.1		NA	Washington**	NA
					District of Columbia**	NA

Source: U.S. Department of Health and Human Services, Centers for Disease Control and Prevention
   "Abortion Surveillance-United States, 1996" (Morbidity Mortality Weekly Report, Vol. 48, No. SS-4, July 30, 1999)
By state of occurrence. National percent is for reporting states only.
**Not reported. New York's percentage is for New York City only.*

Reported Legal Abortions Obtained by Teenagers in 1996

Reporting States' Total = 154,303 Legal Abortions Obtained by Teenagers*

ALPHA ORDER

RANK	STATE	ABORTIONS	% of USA
14	Alabama	3,131	2.0%
39	Alaska	386	0.3%
24	Arizona	2,206	1.4%
27	Arkansas	1,427	0.9%
NA	California**	NA	NA
22	Colorado	2,285	1.5%
13	Connecticut	3,145	2.0%
NA	Delaware**	NA	NA
NA	Florida**	NA	NA
4	Georgia	7,186	4.7%
31	Hawaii	1,131	0.7%
41	Idaho	280	0.2%
NA	Illinois**	NA	NA
16	Indiana	2,957	1.9%
NA	Iowa**	NA	NA
20	Kansas	2,594	1.7%
26	Kentucky	1,579	1.0%
19	Louisiana	2,630	1.7%
37	Maine	628	0.4%
21	Maryland	2,534	1.6%
11	Massachusetts	4,613	3.0%
7	Michigan	6,406	4.2%
17	Minnesota	2,711	1.8%
33	Mississippi	866	0.6%
23	Missouri	2,284	1.5%
35	Montana	683	0.4%
30	Nebraska	1,163	0.8%
28	Nevada	1,253	0.8%
NA	New Hampshire**	NA	NA
8	New Jersey	6,239	4.0%
29	New Mexico	1,194	0.8%
1	New York	29,061	18.8%
5	North Carolina	6,868	4.5%
40	North Dakota	334	0.2%
6	Ohio	6,582	4.3%
NA	Oklahoma**	NA	NA
15	Oregon	3,108	2.0%
3	Pennsylvania	7,436	4.8%
32	Rhode Island	1,073	0.7%
25	South Carolina	2,044	1.3%
42	South Dakota	259	0.2%
12	Tennessee	3,689	2.4%
2	Texas	16,981	11.0%
34	Utah	766	0.5%
38	Vermont	503	0.3%
10	Virginia	5,274	3.4%
9	Washington	5,440	3.5%
36	West Virginia	644	0.4%
18	Wisconsin	2,683	1.7%
43	Wyoming	47	0.0%

RANK ORDER

RANK	STATE	ABORTIONS	% of USA
1	New York	29,061	18.8%
2	Texas	16,981	11.0%
3	Pennsylvania	7,436	4.8%
4	Georgia	7,186	4.7%
5	North Carolina	6,868	4.5%
6	Ohio	6,582	4.3%
7	Michigan	6,406	4.2%
8	New Jersey	6,239	4.0%
9	Washington	5,440	3.5%
10	Virginia	5,274	3.4%
11	Massachusetts	4,613	3.0%
12	Tennessee	3,689	2.4%
13	Connecticut	3,145	2.0%
14	Alabama	3,131	2.0%
15	Oregon	3,108	2.0%
16	Indiana	2,957	1.9%
17	Minnesota	2,711	1.8%
18	Wisconsin	2,683	1.7%
19	Louisiana	2,630	1.7%
20	Kansas	2,594	1.7%
21	Maryland	2,534	1.6%
22	Colorado	2,285	1.5%
23	Missouri	2,284	1.5%
24	Arizona	2,206	1.4%
25	South Carolina	2,044	1.3%
26	Kentucky	1,579	1.0%
27	Arkansas	1,427	0.9%
28	Nevada	1,253	0.8%
29	New Mexico	1,194	0.8%
30	Nebraska	1,163	0.8%
31	Hawaii	1,131	0.7%
32	Rhode Island	1,073	0.7%
33	Mississippi	866	0.6%
34	Utah	766	0.5%
35	Montana	683	0.4%
36	West Virginia	644	0.4%
37	Maine	628	0.4%
38	Vermont	503	0.3%
39	Alaska	386	0.3%
40	North Dakota	334	0.2%
41	Idaho	280	0.2%
42	South Dakota	259	0.2%
43	Wyoming	47	0.0%
NA	California**	NA	NA
NA	Delaware**	NA	NA
NA	Florida**	NA	NA
NA	Illinois**	NA	NA
NA	Iowa**	NA	NA
NA	New Hampshire**	NA	NA
NA	Oklahoma**	NA	NA
	District of Columbia**	NA	NA

Source: U.S. Department of Health and Human Services, Centers for Disease Control and Prevention
    "Abortion Surveillance-United States, 1996" (Morbidity Mortality Weekly Report, Vol. 48, No. SS-4, July 30, 1999)
*Nineteen years old and younger by state of occurrence. National total is for reporting states only.
**Not reported.

Percent of Reported Legal Abortions Obtained by Teenagers in 1996

Reporting States' Percent = 20.0% of Legal Abortions*

ALPHA ORDER			RANK ORDER		
RANK	STATE	PERCENT	RANK	STATE	PERCENT
13	Alabama	22.6	1	South Dakota	28.7
40	Alaska	18.0	2	Idaho	27.4
31	Arizona	20.0	3	West Virginia	26.1
6	Arkansas	24.3	4	North Dakota	25.9
NA	California**	NA	5	Montana	24.7
10	Colorado	23.5	6	Arkansas	24.3
17	Connecticut	22.3	6	Kansas	24.3
NA	Delaware**	NA	8	Maine	24.0
NA	Florida**	NA	9	New Mexico	23.7
30	Georgia	20.1	10	Colorado	23.5
12	Hawaii	23.0	10	Vermont	23.5
2	Idaho	27.4	12	Hawaii	23.0
NA	Illinois**	NA	13	Alabama	22.6
19	Indiana	22.2	13	Kentucky	22.6
NA	Iowa**	NA	13	Oregon	22.6
6	Kansas	24.3	13	Wyoming	22.6
13	Kentucky	22.6	17	Connecticut	22.3
19	Louisiana	22.2	17	Nebraska	22.3
8	Maine	24.0	19	Indiana	22.2
26	Maryland	20.5	19	Louisiana	22.2
43	Massachusetts	15.7	21	South Carolina	21.9
22	Michigan	21.2	22	Michigan	21.2
37	Minnesota	19.1	23	Utah	21.0
25	Mississippi	20.6	24	Washington	20.8
33	Missouri	19.6	25	Mississippi	20.6
5	Montana	24.7	26	Maryland	20.5
17	Nebraska	22.3	26	North Carolina	20.5
40	Nevada	18.0	26	Tennessee	20.5
NA	New Hampshire**	NA	26	Virginia	20.5
33	New Jersey	19.6	30	Georgia	20.1
9	New Mexico	23.7	31	Arizona	20.0
38	New York	19.0	32	Rhode Island	19.7
26	North Carolina	20.5	33	Missouri	19.6
4	North Dakota	25.9	33	New Jersey	19.6
40	Ohio	18.0	33	Pennsylvania	19.6
NA	Oklahoma**	NA	33	Wisconsin	19.6
13	Oregon	22.6	37	Minnesota	19.1
33	Pennsylvania	19.6	38	New York	19.0
32	Rhode Island	19.7	39	Texas	18.6
21	South Carolina	21.9	40	Alaska	18.0
1	South Dakota	28.7	40	Nevada	18.0
26	Tennessee	20.5	40	Ohio	18.0
39	Texas	18.6	43	Massachusetts	15.7
23	Utah	21.0	NA	California**	NA
10	Vermont	23.5	NA	Delaware**	NA
26	Virginia	20.5	NA	Florida**	NA
24	Washington	20.8	NA	Illinois**	NA
3	West Virginia	26.1	NA	Iowa**	NA
33	Wisconsin	19.6	NA	New Hampshire**	NA
13	Wyoming	22.6	NA	Oklahoma**	NA
				District of Columbia**	NA

Source: Morgan Quitno Press using data from US Dept of Health & Human Serv's, Centers for Disease Control-Prevention "Abortion Surveillance-United States, 1996" (Morbidity Mortality Weekly Report, Vol. 48, No. SS-4, July 30, 1999)
Nineteen and younger by state of occurrence. National percent is for reporting states only.
***Not reported.*

Reported Legal Abortions Obtained by Teenagers 17 Years and Younger in 1996

Reporting States' Total = 63,883 Reported Legal Abortions*

ALPHA ORDER

RANK	STATE	ABORTIONS	% of USA
15	Alabama	1,284	2.0%
39	Alaska	163	0.3%
23	Arizona	969	1.5%
27	Arkansas	616	1.0%
NA	California**	NA	NA
22	Colorado	1,033	1.6%
13	Connecticut	1,431	2.2%
NA	Delaware**	NA	NA
NA	Florida**	NA	NA
3	Georgia	3,115	4.9%
30	Hawaii	519	0.8%
42	Idaho	114	0.2%
NA	Illinois**	NA	NA
17	Indiana	1,125	1.8%
NA	Iowa**	NA	NA
16	Kansas	1,180	1.8%
26	Kentucky	651	1.0%
18	Louisiana	1,114	1.7%
37	Maine	261	0.4%
19	Maryland	1,103	1.7%
11	Massachusetts	1,756	2.7%
6	Michigan	2,648	4.1%
20	Minnesota	1,100	1.7%
32	Mississippi	339	0.5%
24	Missouri	941	1.5%
34	Montana	296	0.5%
31	Nebraska	437	0.7%
29	Nevada	562	0.9%
NA	New Hampshire**	NA	NA
8	New Jersey	2,618	4.1%
28	New Mexico	580	0.9%
1	New York	12,492	19.6%
5	North Carolina	2,761	4.3%
40	North Dakota	143	0.2%
7	Ohio	2,624	4.1%
NA	Oklahoma**	NA	NA
14	Oregon	1,317	2.1%
4	Pennsylvania	2,795	4.4%
33	Rhode Island	319	0.5%
25	South Carolina	912	1.4%
41	South Dakota	129	0.2%
12	Tennessee	1,543	2.4%
2	Texas	6,475	10.1%
36	Utah	265	0.4%
38	Vermont	210	0.3%
10	Virginia	2,117	3.3%
9	Washington	2,427	3.8%
35	West Virginia	280	0.4%
21	Wisconsin	1,090	1.7%
43	Wyoming	29	0.0%

RANK ORDER

RANK	STATE	ABORTIONS	% of USA
1	New York	12,492	19.6%
2	Texas	6,475	10.1%
3	Georgia	3,115	4.9%
4	Pennsylvania	2,795	4.4%
5	North Carolina	2,761	4.3%
6	Michigan	2,648	4.1%
7	Ohio	2,624	4.1%
8	New Jersey	2,618	4.1%
9	Washington	2,427	3.8%
10	Virginia	2,117	3.3%
11	Massachusetts	1,756	2.7%
12	Tennessee	1,543	2.4%
13	Connecticut	1,431	2.2%
14	Oregon	1,317	2.1%
15	Alabama	1,284	2.0%
16	Kansas	1,180	1.8%
17	Indiana	1,125	1.8%
18	Louisiana	1,114	1.7%
19	Maryland	1,103	1.7%
20	Minnesota	1,100	1.7%
21	Wisconsin	1,090	1.7%
22	Colorado	1,033	1.6%
23	Arizona	969	1.5%
24	Missouri	941	1.5%
25	South Carolina	912	1.4%
26	Kentucky	651	1.0%
27	Arkansas	616	1.0%
28	New Mexico	580	0.9%
29	Nevada	562	0.9%
30	Hawaii	519	0.8%
31	Nebraska	437	0.7%
32	Mississippi	339	0.5%
33	Rhode Island	319	0.5%
34	Montana	296	0.5%
35	West Virginia	280	0.4%
36	Utah	265	0.4%
37	Maine	261	0.4%
38	Vermont	210	0.3%
39	Alaska	163	0.3%
40	North Dakota	143	0.2%
41	South Dakota	129	0.2%
42	Idaho	114	0.2%
43	Wyoming	29	0.0%
NA	California**	NA	NA
NA	Delaware**	NA	NA
NA	Florida**	NA	NA
NA	Illinois**	NA	NA
NA	Iowa**	NA	NA
NA	New Hampshire**	NA	NA
NA	Oklahoma**	NA	NA
	District of Columbia**	NA	NA

Source: Morgan Quitno Press using data from US Dept of Health & Human Serv's, Centers for Disease Control-Prevention "Abortion Surveillance-United States, 1996" (Morbidity Mortality Weekly Report, Vol. 48, No. SS-4, July 30, 1999)
*By state of occurrence. National total is for reporting states only.
**Not reported.

Percent of Reported Legal Abortions Obtained
By Teenagers 17 Years and Younger in 1996
Reporting States' Percent = 8.3% of Reported Legal Abortions*

ALPHA ORDER

RANK	STATE	PERCENT
18	Alabama	9.3
37	Alaska	7.6
22	Arizona	8.8
11	Arkansas	10.5
NA	California**	NA
9	Colorado	10.6
12	Connecticut	10.2
NA	Delaware**	NA
NA	Florida**	NA
24	Georgia	8.7
9	Hawaii	10.6
5	Idaho	11.2
NA	Illinois**	NA
26	Indiana	8.4
NA	Iowa**	NA
7	Kansas	11.0
18	Kentucky	9.3
17	Louisiana	9.4
13	Maine	10.0
21	Maryland	8.9
42	Massachusetts	6.0
22	Michigan	8.8
36	Minnesota	7.8
32	Mississippi	8.1
32	Missouri	8.1
8	Montana	10.7
26	Nebraska	8.4
32	Nevada	8.1
NA	New Hampshire**	NA
28	New Jersey	8.2
3	New Mexico	11.5
28	New York	8.2
28	North Carolina	8.2
6	North Dakota	11.1
40	Ohio	7.2
NA	Oklahoma**	NA
16	Oregon	9.6
38	Pennsylvania	7.4
43	Rhode Island	5.9
14	South Carolina	9.8
1	South Dakota	14.3
25	Tennessee	8.6
41	Texas	7.1
39	Utah	7.3
14	Vermont	9.8
28	Virginia	8.2
18	Washington	9.3
4	West Virginia	11.3
35	Wisconsin	8.0
2	Wyoming	13.9

RANK ORDER

RANK	STATE	PERCENT
1	South Dakota	14.3
2	Wyoming	13.9
3	New Mexico	11.5
4	West Virginia	11.3
5	Idaho	11.2
6	North Dakota	11.1
7	Kansas	11.0
8	Montana	10.7
9	Colorado	10.6
9	Hawaii	10.6
11	Arkansas	10.5
12	Connecticut	10.2
13	Maine	10.0
14	South Carolina	9.8
14	Vermont	9.8
16	Oregon	9.6
17	Louisiana	9.4
18	Alabama	9.3
18	Kentucky	9.3
18	Washington	9.3
21	Maryland	8.9
22	Arizona	8.8
22	Michigan	8.8
24	Georgia	8.7
25	Tennessee	8.6
26	Indiana	8.4
26	Nebraska	8.4
28	New Jersey	8.2
28	New York	8.2
28	North Carolina	8.2
28	Virginia	8.2
32	Mississippi	8.1
32	Missouri	8.1
32	Nevada	8.1
35	Wisconsin	8.0
36	Minnesota	7.8
37	Alaska	7.6
38	Pennsylvania	7.4
39	Utah	7.3
40	Ohio	7.2
41	Texas	7.1
42	Massachusetts	6.0
43	Rhode Island	5.9
NA	California**	NA
NA	Delaware**	NA
NA	Florida**	NA
NA	Illinois**	NA
NA	Iowa**	NA
NA	New Hampshire**	NA
NA	Oklahoma**	NA
	District of Columbia**	NA

Source: Morgan Quitno Press using data from US Dept of Health & Human Serv's, Centers for Disease Control-Prevention
"Abortion Surveillance-United States, 1996" (Morbidity Mortality Weekly Report, Vol. 48, No. SS-4, July 30, 1999)
*By state of occurrence. National percent is for reporting states only.
**Not reported.

Percent of Teenage Abortions Obtained
By Teenagers 17 Years and Younger in 1996
Reporting States' Percent = 41.0% of Teenage Abortions*

ALPHA ORDER

RANK	STATE	PERCENT
29	Alabama	41.0
21	Alaska	42.2
11	Arizona	43.9
16	Arkansas	43.2
NA	California**	NA
7	Colorado	45.2
5	Connecticut	45.5
NA	Delaware**	NA
NA	Florida**	NA
14	Georgia	43.3
4	Hawaii	45.9
30	Idaho	40.7
NA	Illinois**	NA
39	Indiana	38.0
NA	Iowa**	NA
5	Kansas	45.5
27	Kentucky	41.2
19	Louisiana	42.4
25	Maine	41.6
12	Maryland	43.5
37	Massachusetts	38.1
26	Michigan	41.3
31	Minnesota	40.6
36	Mississippi	39.1
27	Missouri	41.2
14	Montana	43.3
40	Nebraska	37.6
8	Nevada	44.9
NA	New Hampshire**	NA
22	New Jersey	42.0
3	New Mexico	48.6
17	New York	43.0
33	North Carolina	40.2
18	North Dakota	42.8
35	Ohio	39.9
NA	Oklahoma**	NA
19	Oregon	42.4
40	Pennsylvania	37.6
43	Rhode Island	29.7
9	South Carolina	44.6
2	South Dakota	49.8
23	Tennessee	41.8
37	Texas	38.1
42	Utah	34.6
24	Vermont	41.7
34	Virginia	40.1
9	Washington	44.6
12	West Virginia	43.5
31	Wisconsin	40.6
1	Wyoming	61.7

RANK ORDER

RANK	STATE	PERCENT
1	Wyoming	61.7
2	South Dakota	49.8
3	New Mexico	48.6
4	Hawaii	45.9
5	Connecticut	45.5
5	Kansas	45.5
7	Colorado	45.2
8	Nevada	44.9
9	South Carolina	44.6
9	Washington	44.6
11	Arizona	43.9
12	Maryland	43.5
12	West Virginia	43.5
14	Georgia	43.3
14	Montana	43.3
16	Arkansas	43.2
17	New York	43.0
18	North Dakota	42.8
19	Louisiana	42.4
19	Oregon	42.4
21	Alaska	42.2
22	New Jersey	42.0
23	Tennessee	41.8
24	Vermont	41.7
25	Maine	41.6
26	Michigan	41.3
27	Kentucky	41.2
27	Missouri	41.2
29	Alabama	41.0
30	Idaho	40.7
31	Minnesota	40.6
31	Wisconsin	40.6
33	North Carolina	40.2
34	Virginia	40.1
35	Ohio	39.9
36	Mississippi	39.1
37	Massachusetts	38.1
37	Texas	38.1
39	Indiana	38.0
40	Nebraska	37.6
40	Pennsylvania	37.6
42	Utah	34.6
43	Rhode Island	29.7
NA	California**	NA
NA	Delaware**	NA
NA	Florida**	NA
NA	Illinois**	NA
NA	Iowa**	NA
NA	New Hampshire**	NA
NA	Oklahoma**	NA
	District of Columbia**	NA

Source: Morgan Quitno Press using data from US Dept of Health & Human Serv's, Centers for Disease Control-Prevention "Abortion Surveillance-United States, 1996" (Morbidity Mortality Weekly Report, Vol. 48, No. SS-4, July 30, 1999)
By state of occurrence. National percent is for reporting states only.
**Not reported.*

Reported Legal Abortions Performed at 12 Weeks or Less of Gestation in 1996

Reporting States' Total = 579,161 Abortions*

ALPHA ORDER

RANK	STATE	ABORTIONS	% of USA
14	Alabama	11,883	2.1%
34	Alaska	1,886	0.3%
19	Arizona	9,332	1.6%
26	Arkansas	4,790	0.8%
NA	California**	NA	NA
22	Colorado	8,219	1.4%
12	Connecticut	12,386	2.1%
NA	Delaware**	NA	NA
NA	Florida**	NA	NA
4	Georgia	29,789	5.1%
27	Hawaii	4,155	0.7%
36	Idaho	970	0.2%
NA	Illinois**	NA	NA
10	Indiana	12,731	2.2%
NA	Iowa**	NA	NA
21	Kansas	8,602	1.5%
24	Kentucky	5,832	1.0%
18	Louisiana	9,653	1.7%
30	Maine	2,587	0.4%
15	Maryland	11,643	2.0%
NA	Massachusetts**	NA	NA
5	Michigan	26,693	4.6%
11	Minnesota	12,438	2.1%
28	Mississippi	3,759	0.6%
17	Missouri	10,435	1.8%
31	Montana	2,477	0.4%
NA	Nebraska**	NA	NA
23	Nevada	6,107	1.1%
NA	New Hampshire**	NA	NA
7	New Jersey	24,458	4.2%
NA	New Mexico**	NA	NA
1	New York	127,984	22.1%
NA	North Carolina**	NA	NA
35	North Dakota	1,161	0.2%
NA	Ohio**	NA	NA
NA	Oklahoma**	NA	NA
13	Oregon	12,150	2.1%
3	Pennsylvania	33,445	5.8%
25	Rhode Island	4,903	0.8%
20	South Carolina	9,201	1.6%
37	South Dakota	901	0.2%
9	Tennessee	17,069	2.9%
2	Texas	79,321	13.7%
29	Utah	3,270	0.6%
33	Vermont	2,054	0.4%
6	Virginia	24,846	4.3%
8	Washington	22,363	3.9%
32	West Virginia	2,124	0.4%
16	Wisconsin	11,636	2.0%
38	Wyoming	203	0.0%

RANK ORDER

RANK	STATE	ABORTIONS	% of USA
1	New York	127,984	22.1%
2	Texas	79,321	13.7%
3	Pennsylvania	33,445	5.8%
4	Georgia	29,789	5.1%
5	Michigan	26,693	4.6%
6	Virginia	24,846	4.3%
7	New Jersey	24,458	4.2%
8	Washington	22,363	3.9%
9	Tennessee	17,069	2.9%
10	Indiana	12,731	2.2%
11	Minnesota	12,438	2.1%
12	Connecticut	12,386	2.1%
13	Oregon	12,150	2.1%
14	Alabama	11,883	2.1%
15	Maryland	11,643	2.0%
16	Wisconsin	11,636	2.0%
17	Missouri	10,435	1.8%
18	Louisiana	9,653	1.7%
19	Arizona	9,332	1.6%
20	South Carolina	9,201	1.6%
21	Kansas	8,602	1.5%
22	Colorado	8,219	1.4%
23	Nevada	6,107	1.1%
24	Kentucky	5,832	1.0%
25	Rhode Island	4,903	0.8%
26	Arkansas	4,790	0.8%
27	Hawaii	4,155	0.7%
28	Mississippi	3,759	0.6%
29	Utah	3,270	0.6%
30	Maine	2,587	0.4%
31	Montana	2,477	0.4%
32	West Virginia	2,124	0.4%
33	Vermont	2,054	0.4%
34	Alaska	1,886	0.3%
35	North Dakota	1,161	0.2%
36	Idaho	970	0.2%
37	South Dakota	901	0.2%
38	Wyoming	203	0.0%
NA	California**	NA	NA
NA	Delaware**	NA	NA
NA	Florida**	NA	NA
NA	Illinois**	NA	NA
NA	Iowa**	NA	NA
NA	Massachusetts**	NA	NA
NA	Nebraska**	NA	NA
NA	New Hampshire**	NA	NA
NA	New Mexico**	NA	NA
NA	North Carolina**	NA	NA
NA	Ohio**	NA	NA
NA	Oklahoma**	NA	NA
	District of Columbia	5,705	1.0%

Source: Morgan Quitno Press using data from US Dept of Health & Human Serv's, Centers for Disease Control-Prevention
"Abortion Surveillance-United States, 1996" (Morbidity Mortality Weekly Report, Vol. 48, No. SS-4, July 30, 1999)
*By state of occurrence. National total is for reporting states only.
**Not reported.

Percent of Reported Legal Abortions Performed
At 12 Weeks or Less of Gestation in 1996
Reporting States' Percent = 86.6% of Reported Legal Abortions*

ALPHA ORDER

RANK ORDER

RANK	STATE	PERCENT	RANK	STATE	PERCENT
26	Alabama	86.0	1	South Dakota	100.0
20	Alaska	88.2	2	Maine	98.9
29	Arizona	84.7	3	South Carolina	98.7
35	Arkansas	81.4	4	Wyoming	97.6
NA	California**	NA	5	Virginia	96.4
30	Colorado	84.6	6	Vermont	96.0
22	Connecticut	87.8	7	Indiana	95.4
NA	Delaware**	NA	8	Idaho	94.9
NA	Florida**	NA	8	Tennessee	94.9
34	Georgia	83.2	10	Maryland	94.2
31	Hawaii	84.5	11	Rhode Island	90.2
8	Idaho	94.9	12	North Dakota	90.0
NA	Illinois**	NA	13	Missouri	89.8
7	Indiana	95.4	13	Utah	89.8
NA	Iowa**	NA	15	Montana	89.7
37	Kansas	80.4	16	Mississippi	89.3
33	Kentucky	83.3	17	Wisconsin	88.7
36	Louisiana	81.3	18	Michigan	88.4
2	Maine	98.9	19	Oregon	88.3
10	Maryland	94.2	20	Alaska	88.2
NA	Massachusetts**	NA	21	Pennsylvania	88.0
18	Michigan	88.4	22	Connecticut	87.8
24	Minnesota	87.6	23	Nevada	87.7
16	Mississippi	89.3	24	Minnesota	87.6
13	Missouri	89.8	25	Texas	86.7
15	Montana	89.7	26	Alabama	86.0
NA	Nebraska**	NA	26	West Virginia	86.0
23	Nevada	87.7	28	Washington	85.5
NA	New Hampshire**	NA	29	Arizona	84.7
38	New Jersey	76.7	30	Colorado	84.6
NA	New Mexico**	NA	31	Hawaii	84.5
32	New York	83.7	32	New York	83.7
NA	North Carolina**	NA	33	Kentucky	83.3
12	North Dakota	90.0	34	Georgia	83.2
NA	Ohio**	NA	35	Arkansas	81.4
NA	Oklahoma**	NA	36	Louisiana	81.3
19	Oregon	88.3	37	Kansas	80.4
21	Pennsylvania	88.0	38	New Jersey	76.7
11	Rhode Island	90.2	NA	California**	NA
3	South Carolina	98.7	NA	Delaware**	NA
1	South Dakota	100.0	NA	Florida**	NA
8	Tennessee	94.9	NA	Illinois**	NA
25	Texas	86.7	NA	Iowa**	NA
13	Utah	89.8	NA	Massachusetts**	NA
6	Vermont	96.0	NA	Nebraska**	NA
5	Virginia	96.4	NA	New Hampshire**	NA
28	Washington	85.5	NA	New Mexico**	NA
26	West Virginia	86.0	NA	North Carolina**	NA
17	Wisconsin	88.7	NA	Ohio**	NA
4	Wyoming	97.6	NA	Oklahoma**	NA

District of Columbia   84.8

Source: Morgan Quitno Press using data from US Dept of Health & Human Serv's, Centers for Disease Control-Prevention
"Abortion Surveillance-United States, 1996" (Morbidity Mortality Weekly Report, Vol. 48, No. SS-4, July 30, 1999)
*By state of occurrence. National percent is for reporting states only.
**Not reported.

Reported Legal Abortions Performed At or After 21 Weeks of Gestation in 1996

Reporting States' Total = 10,132 Abortions*

ALPHA ORDER

RANK	STATE	ABORTIONS	% of USA
15	Alabama	91	0.9%
27	Alaska	9	0.1%
21	Arizona	34	0.3%
25	Arkansas	15	0.1%
NA	California**	NA	NA
12	Colorado	147	1.5%
29	Connecticut	6	0.1%
NA	Delaware**	NA	NA
NA	Florida**	NA	NA
3	Georgia	1,290	12.7%
20	Hawaii	39	0.4%
31	Idaho	5	0.0%
NA	Illinois**	NA	NA
36	Indiana	0	0.0%
NA	Iowa**	NA	NA
4	Kansas	895	8.8%
13	Kentucky	123	1.2%
7	Louisiana	335	3.3%
34	Maine	1	0.0%
28	Maryland	8	0.1%
NA	Massachusetts**	NA	NA
10	Michigan	213	2.1%
14	Minnesota	105	1.0%
26	Mississippi	13	0.1%
16	Missouri	87	0.9%
18	Montana	42	0.4%
NA	Nebraska**	NA	NA
19	Nevada	41	0.4%
NA	New Hampshire**	NA	NA
5	New Jersey	798	7.9%
NA	New Mexico**	NA	NA
1	New York	2,917	28.8%
NA	North Carolina**	NA	NA
34	North Dakota	1	0.0%
NA	Ohio**	NA	NA
NA	Oklahoma**	NA	NA
9	Oregon	242	2.4%
8	Pennsylvania	280	2.8%
24	Rhode Island	16	0.2%
23	South Carolina	26	0.3%
36	South Dakota	0	0.0%
22	Tennessee	30	0.3%
2	Texas	1,559	15.4%
31	Utah	5	0.0%
29	Vermont	6	0.1%
17	Virginia	80	0.8%
6	Washington	500	4.9%
33	West Virginia	2	0.0%
11	Wisconsin	168	1.7%
36	Wyoming	0	0.0%

RANK ORDER

RANK	STATE	ABORTIONS	% of USA
1	New York	2,917	28.8%
2	Texas	1,559	15.4%
3	Georgia	1,290	12.7%
4	Kansas	895	8.8%
5	New Jersey	798	7.9%
6	Washington	500	4.9%
7	Louisiana	335	3.3%
8	Pennsylvania	280	2.8%
9	Oregon	242	2.4%
10	Michigan	213	2.1%
11	Wisconsin	168	1.7%
12	Colorado	147	1.5%
13	Kentucky	123	1.2%
14	Minnesota	105	1.0%
15	Alabama	91	0.9%
16	Missouri	87	0.9%
17	Virginia	80	0.8%
18	Montana	42	0.4%
19	Nevada	41	0.4%
20	Hawaii	39	0.4%
21	Arizona	34	0.3%
22	Tennessee	30	0.3%
23	South Carolina	26	0.3%
24	Rhode Island	16	0.2%
25	Arkansas	15	0.1%
26	Mississippi	13	0.1%
27	Alaska	9	0.1%
28	Maryland	8	0.1%
29	Connecticut	6	0.1%
29	Vermont	6	0.1%
31	Idaho	5	0.0%
31	Utah	5	0.0%
33	West Virginia	2	0.0%
34	Maine	1	0.0%
34	North Dakota	1	0.0%
36	Indiana	0	0.0%
36	South Dakota	0	0.0%
36	Wyoming	0	0.0%
NA	California**	NA	NA
NA	Delaware**	NA	NA
NA	Florida**	NA	NA
NA	Illinois**	NA	NA
NA	Iowa**	NA	NA
NA	Massachusetts**	NA	NA
NA	Nebraska**	NA	NA
NA	New Hampshire**	NA	NA
NA	New Mexico**	NA	NA
NA	North Carolina**	NA	NA
NA	Ohio**	NA	NA
NA	Oklahoma**	NA	NA
	District of Columbia	3	0.0%

Source: U.S. Department of Health and Human Services, Centers for Disease Control and Prevention
     "Abortion Surveillance-United States, 1996" (Morbidity Mortality Weekly Report, Vol. 48, No. SS-4, July 30, 1999)
*By state of occurrence. National total is for reporting states only.
**Not reported.

Percent of Reported Legal Abortions Performed At or After
21 Weeks of Gestation in 1996
Reporting States' Percent = 1.5% of Reported Legal Abortions*

ALPHA ORDER

RANK	STATE	PERCENT
14	Alabama	0.7
21	Alaska	0.4
22	Arizona	0.3
22	Arkansas	0.3
NA	California**	NA
10	Colorado	1.5
34	Connecticut	0.0
NA	Delaware**	NA
NA	Florida**	NA
2	Georgia	3.6
13	Hawaii	0.8
20	Idaho	0.5
NA	Illinois**	NA
34	Indiana	0.0
NA	Iowa**	NA
1	Kansas	8.4
7	Kentucky	1.8
3	Louisiana	2.8
34	Maine	0.0
30	Maryland	0.1
NA	Massachusetts**	NA
14	Michigan	0.7
14	Minnesota	0.7
22	Mississippi	0.3
14	Missouri	0.7
10	Montana	1.5
NA	Nebraska**	NA
19	Nevada	0.6
NA	New Hampshire**	NA
4	New Jersey	2.5
NA	New Mexico**	NA
5	New York	1.9
NA	North Carolina**	NA
30	North Dakota	0.1
NA	Ohio**	NA
NA	Oklahoma**	NA
7	Oregon	1.8
14	Pennsylvania	0.7
22	Rhode Island	0.3
22	South Carolina	0.3
34	South Dakota	0.0
29	Tennessee	0.2
9	Texas	1.7
30	Utah	0.1
22	Vermont	0.3
22	Virginia	0.3
5	Washington	1.9
30	West Virginia	0.1
12	Wisconsin	1.3
34	Wyoming	0.0

RANK ORDER

RANK	STATE	PERCENT
1	Kansas	8.4
2	Georgia	3.6
3	Louisiana	2.8
4	New Jersey	2.5
5	New York	1.9
5	Washington	1.9
7	Kentucky	1.8
7	Oregon	1.8
9	Texas	1.7
10	Colorado	1.5
10	Montana	1.5
12	Wisconsin	1.3
13	Hawaii	0.8
14	Alabama	0.7
14	Michigan	0.7
14	Minnesota	0.7
14	Missouri	0.7
14	Pennsylvania	0.7
19	Nevada	0.6
20	Idaho	0.5
21	Alaska	0.4
22	Arizona	0.3
22	Arkansas	0.3
22	Mississippi	0.3
22	Rhode Island	0.3
22	South Carolina	0.3
22	Vermont	0.3
22	Virginia	0.3
29	Tennessee	0.2
30	Maryland	0.1
30	North Dakota	0.1
30	Utah	0.1
30	West Virginia	0.1
34	Connecticut	0.0
34	Indiana	0.0
34	Maine	0.0
34	South Dakota	0.0
34	Wyoming	0.0
NA	California**	NA
NA	Delaware**	NA
NA	Florida**	NA
NA	Illinois**	NA
NA	Iowa**	NA
NA	Massachusetts**	NA
NA	Nebraska**	NA
NA	New Hampshire**	NA
NA	New Mexico**	NA
NA	North Carolina**	NA
NA	Ohio**	NA
NA	Oklahoma**	NA

District of Columbia	0.0

Source: Morgan Quitno Press using data from US Dept of Health & Human Serv's, Centers for Disease Control-Prevention "Abortion Surveillance-United States, 1996" (Morbidity Mortality Weekly Report, Vol. 48, No. SS-4, July 30, 1999)
*By state of occurrence. National percent is for reporting states only.
**Not reported.

II. DEATHS

II. DEATHS (Continued)

Deaths in 1998

National Total = 2,338,070 Deaths*

ALPHA ORDER

RANK	STATE	DEATHS	% of USA
18	Alabama	43,930	1.9%
50	Alaska	2,559	0.1%
22	Arizona	38,329	1.6%
31	Arkansas	27,528	1.2%
1	California**	226,845	9.7%
32	Colorado	26,695	1.1%
27	Connecticut	29,736	1.3%
46	Delaware	6,587	0.3%
2	Florida	158,224	6.8%
11	Georgia	60,485	2.6%
43	Hawaii	8,096	0.3%
42	Idaho	9,167	0.4%
7	Illinois	104,501	4.5%
16	Indiana	52,774	2.3%
29	Iowa	28,359	1.2%
33	Kansas	24,192	1.0%
23	Kentucky	37,861	1.6%
21	Louisiana	40,390	1.7%
38	Maine	12,155	0.5%
20	Maryland	42,068	1.8%
12	Massachusetts	55,235	2.4%
8	Michigan	85,222	3.6%
24	Minnesota	37,233	1.6%
30	Mississippi	27,858	1.2%
13	Missouri	55,110	2.4%
44	Montana	7,911	0.3%
35	Nebraska	15,194	0.6%
36	Nevada	14,499	0.6%
41	New Hampshire	9,550	0.4%
9	New Jersey	71,127	3.0%
37	New Mexico	13,412	0.6%
3	New York	156,517	6.7%
10	North Carolina	67,976	2.9%
47	North Dakota	5,928	0.3%
6	Ohio	106,077	4.5%
26	Oklahoma	33,983	1.5%
28	Oregon	29,392	1.3%
5	Pennsylvania	126,765	5.4%
40	Rhode Island	9,618	0.4%
25	South Carolina	34,826	1.5%
45	South Dakota	6,872	0.3%
15	Tennessee	54,122	2.3%
4	Texas	142,494	6.1%
39	Utah	11,849	0.5%
48	Vermont	4,951	0.2%
14	Virginia	54,546	2.3%
19	Washington	42,731	1.8%
34	West Virginia	20,760	0.9%
17	Wisconsin	46,007	2.0%
49	Wyoming	3,856	0.2%

RANK ORDER

RANK	STATE	DEATHS	% of USA
1	California**	226,845	9.7%
2	Florida	158,224	6.8%
3	New York	156,517	6.7%
4	Texas	142,494	6.1%
5	Pennsylvania	126,765	5.4%
6	Ohio	106,077	4.5%
7	Illinois	104,501	4.5%
8	Michigan	85,222	3.6%
9	New Jersey	71,127	3.0%
10	North Carolina	67,976	2.9%
11	Georgia	60,485	2.6%
12	Massachusetts	55,235	2.4%
13	Missouri	55,110	2.4%
14	Virginia	54,546	2.3%
15	Tennessee	54,122	2.3%
16	Indiana	52,774	2.3%
17	Wisconsin	46,007	2.0%
18	Alabama	43,930	1.9%
19	Washington	42,731	1.8%
20	Maryland	42,068	1.8%
21	Louisiana	40,390	1.7%
22	Arizona	38,329	1.6%
23	Kentucky	37,861	1.6%
24	Minnesota	37,233	1.6%
25	South Carolina	34,826	1.5%
26	Oklahoma	33,983	1.5%
27	Connecticut	29,736	1.3%
28	Oregon	29,392	1.3%
29	Iowa	28,359	1.2%
30	Mississippi	27,858	1.2%
31	Arkansas	27,528	1.2%
32	Colorado	26,695	1.1%
33	Kansas	24,192	1.0%
34	West Virginia	20,760	0.9%
35	Nebraska	15,194	0.6%
36	Nevada	14,499	0.6%
37	New Mexico	13,412	0.6%
38	Maine	12,155	0.5%
39	Utah	11,849	0.5%
40	Rhode Island	9,618	0.4%
41	New Hampshire	9,550	0.4%
42	Idaho	9,167	0.4%
43	Hawaii	8,096	0.3%
44	Montana	7,911	0.3%
45	South Dakota	6,872	0.3%
46	Delaware	6,587	0.3%
47	North Dakota	5,928	0.3%
48	Vermont	4,951	0.2%
49	Wyoming	3,856	0.2%
50	Alaska	2,559	0.1%
	District of Columbia	5,968	0.3%

Source: U.S. Department of Health and Human Services, National Center for Health Statistics
"National Vital Statistics Reports" (Vol. 47, No. 25, October 5, 1999)
*Preliminary data by state of residence.
**Due to data processing problems, California's figure is an estimate.

Death Rate in 1998

National Rate = 865.0 Deaths per 100,000 Population*

ALPHA ORDER

RANK	STATE	RATE
8	Alabama	1,009.4
50	Alaska	416.8
35	Arizona	821.0
2	Arkansas	1,084.5
46	California**	704.1
48	Colorado	672.3
20	Connecticut	908.2
27	Delaware	885.8
3	Florida	1,060.8
40	Georgia	791.5
47	Hawaii	678.6
44	Idaho	746.1
31	Illinois	867.6
26	Indiana	894.6
10	Iowa	990.7
18	Kansas	920.2
13	Kentucky	961.8
17	Louisiana	924.5
11	Maine	976.9
36	Maryland	819.3
23	Massachusetts	898.5
30	Michigan	868.1
41	Minnesota	787.9
7	Mississippi	1,012.2
6	Missouri	1,013.3
23	Montana	898.5
19	Nebraska	913.8
34	Nevada	830.0
37	New Hampshire	805.9
29	New Jersey	876.5
42	New Mexico	772.2
32	New York	861.2
22	North Carolina	900.8
16	North Dakota	928.8
14	Ohio	946.3
5	Oklahoma	1,015.4
25	Oregon	895.6
4	Pennsylvania	1,056.2
12	Rhode Island	973.0
21	South Carolina	907.9
15	South Dakota	930.9
9	Tennessee	996.6
45	Texas	721.1
49	Utah	564.3
33	Vermont	837.9
38	Virginia	803.2
43	Washington	751.1
1	West Virginia	1,146.2
28	Wisconsin	880.8
39	Wyoming	801.8

RANK ORDER

RANK	STATE	RATE
1	West Virginia	1,146.2
2	Arkansas	1,084.5
3	Florida	1,060.8
4	Pennsylvania	1,056.2
5	Oklahoma	1,015.4
6	Missouri	1,013.3
7	Mississippi	1,012.2
8	Alabama	1,009.4
9	Tennessee	996.6
10	Iowa	990.7
11	Maine	976.9
12	Rhode Island	973.0
13	Kentucky	961.8
14	Ohio	946.3
15	South Dakota	930.9
16	North Dakota	928.8
17	Louisiana	924.5
18	Kansas	920.2
19	Nebraska	913.8
20	Connecticut	908.2
21	South Carolina	907.9
22	North Carolina	900.8
23	Massachusetts	898.5
23	Montana	898.5
25	Oregon	895.6
26	Indiana	894.6
27	Delaware	885.8
28	Wisconsin	880.8
29	New Jersey	876.5
30	Michigan	868.1
31	Illinois	867.6
32	New York	861.2
33	Vermont	837.9
34	Nevada	830.0
35	Arizona	821.0
36	Maryland	819.3
37	New Hampshire	805.9
38	Virginia	803.2
39	Wyoming	801.8
40	Georgia	791.5
41	Minnesota	787.9
42	New Mexico	772.2
43	Washington	751.1
44	Idaho	746.1
45	Texas	721.1
46	California**	704.1
47	Hawaii	678.6
48	Colorado	672.3
49	Utah	564.3
50	Alaska	416.8
	District of Columbia	1,140.8

Source: U.S. Department of Health and Human Services, National Center for Health Statistics
    "National Vital Statistics Reports" (Vol. 47, No. 25, October 5, 1999)
*Preliminary data by state of residence.
**Due to data processing problems, California's figure is an estimate.

Age-Adjusted Death Rate in 1998

National Rate = 470.8 Deaths per 100,000 Population*

ALPHA ORDER

RANK	STATE	RATE
3	Alabama	565.7
35	Alaska	440.0
26	Arizona	461.9
5	Arkansas	551.4
NA	California**	NA
45	Colorado	420.2
40	Connecticut	426.0
14	Delaware	496.7
27	Florida	458.8
8	Georgia	540.2
49	Hawaii	370.1
41	Idaho	424.8
19	Illinois	480.9
17	Indiana	489.5
43	Iowa	421.3
29	Kansas	450.6
10	Kentucky	532.9
2	Louisiana	576.3
25	Maine	463.5
15	Maryland	495.0
44	Massachusetts	421.0
18	Michigan	484.9
48	Minnesota	395.1
1	Mississippi	606.9
13	Missouri	511.4
30	Montana	445.1
39	Nebraska	431.4
8	Nevada	540.2
34	New Hampshire	440.4
33	New Jersey	442.2
21	New Mexico	475.1
31	New York	443.2
12	North Carolina	518.1
46	North Dakota	415.6
16	Ohio	489.8
11	Oklahoma	530.2
28	Oregon	452.1
22	Pennsylvania	474.6
37	Rhode Island	434.1
6	South Carolina	550.7
32	South Dakota	443.1
4	Tennessee	564.9
22	Texas	474.6
47	Utah	405.5
38	Vermont	433.2
19	Virginia	480.9
42	Washington	423.4
7	West Virginia	547.4
36	Wisconsin	434.6
24	Wyoming	465.3

RANK ORDER

RANK	STATE	RATE
1	Mississippi	606.9
2	Louisiana	576.3
3	Alabama	565.7
4	Tennessee	564.9
5	Arkansas	551.4
6	South Carolina	550.7
7	West Virginia	547.4
8	Georgia	540.2
8	Nevada	540.2
10	Kentucky	532.9
11	Oklahoma	530.2
12	North Carolina	518.1
13	Missouri	511.4
14	Delaware	496.7
15	Maryland	495.0
16	Ohio	489.8
17	Indiana	489.5
18	Michigan	484.9
19	Illinois	480.9
19	Virginia	480.9
21	New Mexico	475.1
22	Pennsylvania	474.6
22	Texas	474.6
24	Wyoming	465.3
25	Maine	463.5
26	Arizona	461.9
27	Florida	458.8
28	Oregon	452.1
29	Kansas	450.6
30	Montana	445.1
31	New York	443.2
32	South Dakota	443.1
33	New Jersey	442.2
34	New Hampshire	440.4
35	Alaska	440.0
36	Wisconsin	434.6
37	Rhode Island	434.1
38	Vermont	433.2
39	Nebraska	431.4
40	Connecticut	426.0
41	Idaho	424.8
42	Washington	423.4
43	Iowa	421.3
44	Massachusetts	421.0
45	Colorado	420.2
46	North Dakota	415.6
47	Utah	405.5
48	Minnesota	395.1
49	Hawaii	370.1
NA	California**	NA
	District of Columbia	672.5

Source: U.S. Department of Health and Human Services, National Center for Health Statistics
"National Vital Statistics Reports" (Vol. 47, No. 25, October 5, 1999)
*Preliminary data by state of residence. Age-adjusted rates eliminate the distorting effects of the aging of the population.
**Not available.

Births to Deaths Ratio in 1998

National Ratio = 1.69 Births for Every Death in 1998*

ALPHA ORDER

RANK	STATE	RATIO
37	Alabama	1.42
1	Alaska	4.26
10	Arizona	1.97
42	Arkansas	1.35
4	California	2.39
5	Colorado	2.24
34	Connecticut	1.44
23	Delaware	1.56
47	Florida	1.24
9	Georgia	2.03
6	Hawaii	2.13
7	Idaho	2.12
15	Illinois	1.74
31	Indiana	1.49
46	Iowa	1.26
25	Kansas	1.55
33	Kentucky	1.45
18	Louisiana	1.64
48	Maine	1.14
16	Maryland	1.68
20	Massachusetts	1.61
23	Michigan	1.56
13	Minnesota	1.75
34	Mississippi	1.44
40	Missouri	1.37
43	Montana	1.32
27	Nebraska	1.52
11	Nevada	1.90
38	New Hampshire	1.41
18	New Jersey	1.64
8	New Mexico	2.08
21	New York	1.59
21	North Carolina	1.59
41	North Dakota	1.36
36	Ohio	1.43
29	Oklahoma	1.50
28	Oregon	1.51
48	Pennsylvania	1.14
44	Rhode Island	1.29
26	South Carolina	1.53
29	South Dakota	1.50
39	Tennessee	1.39
3	Texas	2.43
2	Utah	3.86
45	Vermont	1.27
13	Virginia	1.75
12	Washington	1.89
50	West Virginia	1.05
32	Wisconsin	1.46
17	Wyoming	1.65

RANK ORDER

RANK	STATE	RATIO
1	Alaska	4.26
2	Utah	3.86
3	Texas	2.43
4	California	2.39
5	Colorado	2.24
6	Hawaii	2.13
7	Idaho	2.12
8	New Mexico	2.08
9	Georgia	2.03
10	Arizona	1.97
11	Nevada	1.90
12	Washington	1.89
13	Minnesota	1.75
13	Virginia	1.75
15	Illinois	1.74
16	Maryland	1.68
17	Wyoming	1.65
18	Louisiana	1.64
18	New Jersey	1.64
20	Massachusetts	1.61
21	New York	1.59
21	North Carolina	1.59
23	Delaware	1.56
23	Michigan	1.56
25	Kansas	1.55
26	South Carolina	1.53
27	Nebraska	1.52
28	Oregon	1.51
29	Oklahoma	1.50
29	South Dakota	1.50
31	Indiana	1.49
32	Wisconsin	1.46
33	Kentucky	1.45
34	Connecticut	1.44
34	Mississippi	1.44
36	Ohio	1.43
37	Alabama	1.42
38	New Hampshire	1.41
39	Tennessee	1.39
40	Missouri	1.37
41	North Dakota	1.36
42	Arkansas	1.35
43	Montana	1.32
44	Rhode Island	1.29
45	Vermont	1.27
46	Iowa	1.26
47	Florida	1.24
48	Maine	1.14
48	Pennsylvania	1.14
50	West Virginia	1.05

District of Columbia 1.40

Source: Morgan Quitno Press using data from U.S. Dept. of Health & Human Services, National Center for Health Statistics
"National Vital Statistics Reports" (Vol. 47, No. 25, October 5, 1999)
*Preliminary data by state of residence.

Deaths in 1990

National Total = 2,148,463 Deaths*

ALPHA ORDER				RANK ORDER			
RANK	STATE	DEATHS	% of USA	RANK	STATE	DEATHS	% of USA
18	Alabama	39,381	1.8%	1	California	214,369	10.0%
50	Alaska	2,188	0.1%	2	New York	168,936	7.9%
26	Arizona	28,789	1.3%	3	Florida	134,385	6.3%
31	Arkansas	24,652	1.1%	4	Texas	125,479	5.8%
1	California	214,369	10.0%	5	Pennsylvania	121,951	5.7%
33	Colorado	21,583	1.0%	6	Illinois	103,006	4.8%
27	Connecticut	27,607	1.3%	7	Ohio	98,822	4.6%
46	Delaware	5,764	0.3%	8	Michigan	78,744	3.7%
3	Florida	134,385	6.3%	9	New Jersey	70,383	3.3%
12	Georgia	51,810	2.4%	10	North Carolina	57,315	2.7%
44	Hawaii	6,782	0.3%	11	Massachusetts	53,179	2.5%
42	Idaho	7,452	0.3%	12	Georgia	51,810	2.4%
6	Illinois	103,006	4.8%	13	Missouri	50,377	2.3%
14	Indiana	49,569	2.3%	14	Indiana	49,569	2.3%
28	Iowa	26,884	1.3%	15	Virginia	48,013	2.2%
32	Kansas	22,279	1.0%	16	Tennessee	46,315	2.2%
22	Kentucky	35,078	1.6%	17	Wisconsin	42,733	2.0%
20	Louisiana	37,571	1.7%	18	Alabama	39,381	1.8%
36	Maine	11,106	0.5%	19	Maryland	38,413	1.8%
19	Maryland	38,413	1.8%	20	Louisiana	37,571	1.7%
11	Massachusetts	53,179	2.5%	21	Washington	37,087	1.7%
8	Michigan	78,744	3.7%	22	Kentucky	35,078	1.6%
23	Minnesota	34,776	1.6%	23	Minnesota	34,776	1.6%
30	Mississippi	25,127	1.2%	24	Oklahoma	30,378	1.4%
13	Missouri	50,377	2.3%	25	South Carolina	29,715	1.4%
43	Montana	6,861	0.3%	26	Arizona	28,789	1.3%
35	Nebraska	14,769	0.7%	27	Connecticut	27,607	1.3%
39	Nevada	9,318	0.4%	28	Iowa	26,884	1.3%
41	New Hampshire	8,488	0.4%	29	Oregon	25,136	1.2%
9	New Jersey	70,383	3.3%	30	Mississippi	25,127	1.2%
37	New Mexico	10,625	0.5%	31	Arkansas	24,652	1.1%
2	New York	168,936	7.9%	32	Kansas	22,279	1.0%
10	North Carolina	57,315	2.7%	33	Colorado	21,583	1.0%
47	North Dakota	5,678	0.3%	34	West Virginia	19,385	0.9%
7	Ohio	98,822	4.6%	35	Nebraska	14,769	0.7%
24	Oklahoma	30,378	1.4%	36	Maine	11,106	0.5%
29	Oregon	25,136	1.2%	37	New Mexico	10,625	0.5%
5	Pennsylvania	121,951	5.7%	38	Rhode Island	9,576	0.4%
38	Rhode Island	9,576	0.4%	39	Nevada	9,318	0.4%
25	South Carolina	29,715	1.4%	40	Utah	9,192	0.4%
45	South Dakota	6,326	0.3%	41	New Hampshire	8,488	0.4%
16	Tennessee	46,315	2.2%	42	Idaho	7,452	0.3%
4	Texas	125,479	5.8%	43	Montana	6,861	0.3%
40	Utah	9,192	0.4%	44	Hawaii	6,782	0.3%
48	Vermont	4,595	0.2%	45	South Dakota	6,326	0.3%
15	Virginia	48,013	2.2%	46	Delaware	5,764	0.3%
21	Washington	37,087	1.7%	47	North Dakota	5,678	0.3%
34	West Virginia	19,385	0.9%	48	Vermont	4,595	0.2%
17	Wisconsin	42,733	2.0%	49	Wyoming	3,203	0.1%
49	Wyoming	3,203	0.1%	50	Alaska	2,188	0.1%
					District of Columbia	7,313	0.3%

Source: U.S. Department of Health and Human Services, National Center for Health Statistics
  "Monthly Vital Statistics Report" (Vol. 41, No. 7(S), January 7, 1993)
*Final data by state of residence.

Death Rate in 1990

National Rate = 863 Deaths per 100,000 Population*

<table>
<tr><td colspan="3">ALPHA ORDER</td><td colspan="3">RANK ORDER</td></tr>
<tr><th>RANK</th><th>STATE</th><th>RATE</th><th>RANK</th><th>STATE</th><th>RATE</th></tr>
<tr><td>7</td><td>Alabama</td><td>974</td><td>1</td><td>West Virginia</td><td>1,080</td></tr>
<tr><td>50</td><td>Alaska</td><td>398</td><td>2</td><td>Arkansas</td><td>1,048</td></tr>
<tr><td>37</td><td>Arizona</td><td>784</td><td>3</td><td>Florida</td><td>1,038</td></tr>
<tr><td>2</td><td>Arkansas</td><td>1,048</td><td>4</td><td>Pennsylvania</td><td>1,026</td></tr>
<tr><td>44</td><td>California</td><td>719</td><td>5</td><td>Missouri</td><td>984</td></tr>
<tr><td>47</td><td>Colorado</td><td>655</td><td>6</td><td>Mississippi</td><td>976</td></tr>
<tr><td>32</td><td>Connecticut</td><td>840</td><td>7</td><td>Alabama</td><td>974</td></tr>
<tr><td>27</td><td>Delaware</td><td>864</td><td>8</td><td>Iowa</td><td>968</td></tr>
<tr><td>3</td><td>Florida</td><td>1,038</td><td>9</td><td>Oklahoma</td><td>966</td></tr>
<tr><td>35</td><td>Georgia</td><td>799</td><td>10</td><td>Rhode Island</td><td>954</td></tr>
<tr><td>48</td><td>Hawaii</td><td>611</td><td>11</td><td>Kentucky</td><td>951</td></tr>
<tr><td>42</td><td>Idaho</td><td>740</td><td>12</td><td>Tennessee</td><td>949</td></tr>
<tr><td>19</td><td>Illinois</td><td>900</td><td>13</td><td>New York</td><td>938</td></tr>
<tr><td>21</td><td>Indiana</td><td>894</td><td>14</td><td>Nebraska</td><td>936</td></tr>
<tr><td>8</td><td>Iowa</td><td>968</td><td>15</td><td>Ohio</td><td>911</td></tr>
<tr><td>20</td><td>Kansas</td><td>899</td><td>16</td><td>New Jersey</td><td>910</td></tr>
<tr><td>11</td><td>Kentucky</td><td>951</td><td>17</td><td>South Dakota</td><td>909</td></tr>
<tr><td>22</td><td>Louisiana</td><td>890</td><td>18</td><td>Maine</td><td>905</td></tr>
<tr><td>18</td><td>Maine</td><td>905</td><td>19</td><td>Illinois</td><td>900</td></tr>
<tr><td>34</td><td>Maryland</td><td>803</td><td>20</td><td>Kansas</td><td>899</td></tr>
<tr><td>24</td><td>Massachusetts</td><td>884</td><td>21</td><td>Indiana</td><td>894</td></tr>
<tr><td>31</td><td>Michigan</td><td>847</td><td>22</td><td>Louisiana</td><td>890</td></tr>
<tr><td>36</td><td>Minnesota</td><td>795</td><td>22</td><td>North Dakota</td><td>890</td></tr>
<tr><td>6</td><td>Mississippi</td><td>976</td><td>24</td><td>Massachusetts</td><td>884</td></tr>
<tr><td>5</td><td>Missouri</td><td>984</td><td>24</td><td>Oregon</td><td>884</td></tr>
<tr><td>29</td><td>Montana</td><td>859</td><td>26</td><td>Wisconsin</td><td>874</td></tr>
<tr><td>14</td><td>Nebraska</td><td>936</td><td>27</td><td>Delaware</td><td>864</td></tr>
<tr><td>38</td><td>Nevada</td><td>775</td><td>27</td><td>North Carolina</td><td>864</td></tr>
<tr><td>40</td><td>New Hampshire</td><td>765</td><td>29</td><td>Montana</td><td>859</td></tr>
<tr><td>16</td><td>New Jersey</td><td>910</td><td>30</td><td>South Carolina</td><td>852</td></tr>
<tr><td>46</td><td>New Mexico</td><td>701</td><td>31</td><td>Michigan</td><td>847</td></tr>
<tr><td>13</td><td>New York</td><td>938</td><td>32</td><td>Connecticut</td><td>840</td></tr>
<tr><td>27</td><td>North Carolina</td><td>864</td><td>33</td><td>Vermont</td><td>817</td></tr>
<tr><td>22</td><td>North Dakota</td><td>890</td><td>34</td><td>Maryland</td><td>803</td></tr>
<tr><td>15</td><td>Ohio</td><td>911</td><td>35</td><td>Georgia</td><td>799</td></tr>
<tr><td>9</td><td>Oklahoma</td><td>966</td><td>36</td><td>Minnesota</td><td>795</td></tr>
<tr><td>24</td><td>Oregon</td><td>884</td><td>37</td><td>Arizona</td><td>784</td></tr>
<tr><td>4</td><td>Pennsylvania</td><td>1,026</td><td>38</td><td>Nevada</td><td>775</td></tr>
<tr><td>10</td><td>Rhode Island</td><td>954</td><td>38</td><td>Virginia</td><td>775</td></tr>
<tr><td>30</td><td>South Carolina</td><td>852</td><td>40</td><td>New Hampshire</td><td>765</td></tr>
<tr><td>17</td><td>South Dakota</td><td>909</td><td>41</td><td>Washington</td><td>762</td></tr>
<tr><td>12</td><td>Tennessee</td><td>949</td><td>42</td><td>Idaho</td><td>740</td></tr>
<tr><td>43</td><td>Texas</td><td>738</td><td>43</td><td>Texas</td><td>738</td></tr>
<tr><td>49</td><td>Utah</td><td>533</td><td>44</td><td>California</td><td>719</td></tr>
<tr><td>33</td><td>Vermont</td><td>817</td><td>45</td><td>Wyoming</td><td>706</td></tr>
<tr><td>38</td><td>Virginia</td><td>775</td><td>46</td><td>New Mexico</td><td>701</td></tr>
<tr><td>41</td><td>Washington</td><td>762</td><td>47</td><td>Colorado</td><td>655</td></tr>
<tr><td>1</td><td>West Virginia</td><td>1,080</td><td>48</td><td>Hawaii</td><td>611</td></tr>
<tr><td>26</td><td>Wisconsin</td><td>874</td><td>49</td><td>Utah</td><td>533</td></tr>
<tr><td>45</td><td>Wyoming</td><td>706</td><td>50</td><td>Alaska</td><td>398</td></tr>
<tr><td></td><td></td><td></td><td></td><td>District of Columbia</td><td>1,200</td></tr>
</table>

Source: U.S. Department of Health and Human Services, National Center for Health Statistics
"Monthly Vital Statistics Report" (Vol. 41, No. 7(S), January 7, 1993)
*Final data by state of residence. Not age adjusted.

Deaths in 1980

National Total = 1,989,841 Deaths*

ALPHA ORDER

RANK	STATE	DEATHS	% of USA
19	Alabama	35,542	1.8%
50	Alaska	1,714	0.1%
32	Arizona	21,367	1.1%
29	Arkansas	22,744	1.1%
1	California	186,624	9.4%
34	Colorado	18,956	1.0%
25	Connecticut	27,275	1.4%
46	Delaware	5,044	0.3%
5	Florida	104,670	5.3%
14	Georgia	44,262	2.2%
47	Hawaii	4,981	0.3%
41	Idaho	6,763	0.3%
6	Illinois	102,935	5.2%
13	Indiana	47,345	2.4%
26	Iowa	27,120	1.4%
30	Kansas	22,034	1.1%
21	Kentucky	33,796	1.7%
18	Louisiana	35,651	1.8%
36	Maine	10,800	0.5%
20	Maryland	34,016	1.7%
10	Massachusetts	55,070	2.8%
8	Michigan	75,187	3.8%
22	Minnesota	33,366	1.7%
28	Mississippi	23,656	1.2%
11	Missouri	49,660	2.5%
42	Montana	6,666	0.3%
35	Nebraska	14,474	0.7%
44	Nevada	5,896	0.3%
40	New Hampshire	7,647	0.4%
9	New Jersey	68,943	3.5%
38	New Mexico	9,093	0.5%
2	New York	172,853	8.7%
12	North Carolina	48,440	2.4%
45	North Dakota	5,596	0.3%
7	Ohio	98,421	4.9%
24	Oklahoma	28,234	1.4%
31	Oregon	21,798	1.1%
3	Pennsylvania	123,594	6.2%
37	Rhode Island	9,325	0.5%
27	South Carolina	25,154	1.3%
43	South Dakota	6,556	0.3%
17	Tennessee	40,774	2.0%
4	Texas	108,180	5.4%
39	Utah	8,120	0.4%
48	Vermont	4,582	0.2%
15	Virginia	42,506	2.1%
23	Washington	32,007	1.6%
33	West Virginia	19,237	1.0%
16	Wisconsin	40,838	2.1%
49	Wyoming	3,221	0.2%

RANK ORDER

RANK	STATE	DEATHS	% of USA
1	California	186,624	9.4%
2	New York	172,853	8.7%
3	Pennsylvania	123,594	6.2%
4	Texas	108,180	5.4%
5	Florida	104,670	5.3%
6	Illinois	102,935	5.2%
7	Ohio	98,421	4.9%
8	Michigan	75,187	3.8%
9	New Jersey	68,943	3.5%
10	Massachusetts	55,070	2.8%
11	Missouri	49,660	2.5%
12	North Carolina	48,440	2.4%
13	Indiana	47,345	2.4%
14	Georgia	44,262	2.2%
15	Virginia	42,506	2.1%
16	Wisconsin	40,838	2.1%
17	Tennessee	40,774	2.0%
18	Louisiana	35,651	1.8%
19	Alabama	35,542	1.8%
20	Maryland	34,016	1.7%
21	Kentucky	33,796	1.7%
22	Minnesota	33,366	1.7%
23	Washington	32,007	1.6%
24	Oklahoma	28,234	1.4%
25	Connecticut	27,275	1.4%
26	Iowa	27,120	1.4%
27	South Carolina	25,154	1.3%
28	Mississippi	23,656	1.2%
29	Arkansas	22,744	1.1%
30	Kansas	22,034	1.1%
31	Oregon	21,798	1.1%
32	Arizona	21,367	1.1%
33	West Virginia	19,237	1.0%
34	Colorado	18,956	1.0%
35	Nebraska	14,474	0.7%
36	Maine	10,800	0.5%
37	Rhode Island	9,325	0.5%
38	New Mexico	9,093	0.5%
39	Utah	8,120	0.4%
40	New Hampshire	7,647	0.4%
41	Idaho	6,763	0.3%
42	Montana	6,666	0.3%
43	South Dakota	6,556	0.3%
44	Nevada	5,896	0.3%
45	North Dakota	5,596	0.3%
46	Delaware	5,044	0.3%
47	Hawaii	4,981	0.3%
48	Vermont	4,582	0.2%
49	Wyoming	3,221	0.2%
50	Alaska	1,714	0.1%
	District of Columbia	7,108	0.4%

Source: U.S. Department of Health and Human Services, National Center for Health Statistics
    "Vital Statistics of the United States 1980" and "Monthly Vital Statistics Report"
*Final data by state of residence.

Death Rate in 1980

National Rate = 877 Deaths per 100,000 Population*

ALPHA ORDER				RANK ORDER		
RANK	STATE	RATE		RANK	STATE	RATE
18	Alabama	912		1	Florida	1,072
50	Alaska	425		2	Pennsylvania	1,041
40	Arizona	784		3	Missouri	1,008
4	Arkansas	994		4	Arkansas	994
39	California	786		5	West Virginia	987
47	Colorado	654		6	New York	984
23	Connecticut	877		6	Rhode Island	984
27	Delaware	847		8	Maine	960
1	Florida	1,072		9	Massachusetts	959
35	Georgia	809		10	South Dakota	947
49	Hawaii	515		11	Mississippi	937
44	Idaho	715		12	New Jersey	936
20	Illinois	899		13	Oklahoma	932
25	Indiana	862		14	Iowa	930
14	Iowa	930		14	Kansas	930
14	Kansas	930		16	Kentucky	922
16	Kentucky	922		17	Nebraska	920
28	Louisiana	846		18	Alabama	912
8	Maine	960		19	Ohio	911
36	Maryland	806		20	Illinois	899
9	Massachusetts	959		21	Vermont	895
34	Michigan	811		22	Tennessee	887
33	Minnesota	817		23	Connecticut	877
11	Mississippi	937		24	Wisconsin	867
3	Missouri	1,008		25	Indiana	862
28	Montana	846		26	North Dakota	856
17	Nebraska	920		27	Delaware	847
43	Nevada	735		28	Louisiana	846
30	New Hampshire	830		28	Montana	846
12	New Jersey	936		30	New Hampshire	830
45	New Mexico	696		31	Oregon	827
6	New York	984		32	North Carolina	823
32	North Carolina	823		33	Minnesota	817
26	North Dakota	856		34	Michigan	811
19	Ohio	911		35	Georgia	809
13	Oklahoma	932		36	Maryland	806
31	Oregon	827		37	South Carolina	805
2	Pennsylvania	1,041		38	Virginia	794
6	Rhode Island	984		39	California	786
37	South Carolina	805		40	Arizona	784
10	South Dakota	947		41	Washington	773
22	Tennessee	887		42	Texas	758
42	Texas	758		43	Nevada	735
48	Utah	554		44	Idaho	715
21	Vermont	895		45	New Mexico	696
38	Virginia	794		46	Wyoming	684
41	Washington	773		47	Colorado	654
5	West Virginia	987		48	Utah	554
24	Wisconsin	867		49	Hawaii	515
46	Wyoming	684		50	Alaska	425
				District of Columbia		1,109

Source: U.S. Department of Health and Human Services, National Center for Health Statistics
"Vital Statistics of the United States 1980" and "Monthly Vital Statistics Report"
*Final data by state of residence. Not age adjusted.

Infant Deaths in 1999

National Total = 27,500 Infant Deaths*

ALPHA ORDER

RANK	STATE	DEATHS	% of USA
15	Alabama	604	2.2%
47	Alaska	56	0.2%
13	Arizona	609	2.2%
28	Arkansas	295	1.1%
NA	California**	NA	NA
23	Colorado	412	1.5%
29	Connecticut	294	1.1%
40	Delaware	106	0.4%
3	Florida	1,439	5.2%
7	Georgia	1,061	3.9%
39	Hawaii	112	0.4%
38	Idaho	131	0.5%
2	Illinois	1,506	5.5%
25	Indiana	396	1.4%
33	Iowa	246	0.9%
31	Kansas	257	0.9%
24	Kentucky	409	1.5%
14	Louisiana	607	2.2%
44	Maine	71	0.3%
17	Maryland	542	2.0%
21	Massachusetts	424	1.5%
6	Michigan	1,121	4.1%
27	Minnesota	330	1.2%
20	Mississippi	428	1.6%
16	Missouri	597	2.2%
43	Montana	79	0.3%
36	Nebraska	170	0.6%
34	Nevada	208	0.8%
45	New Hampshire	64	0.2%
11	New Jersey	694	2.5%
35	New Mexico	175	0.6%
4	New York	1,394	5.1%
8	North Carolina	1,036	3.8%
46	North Dakota	60	0.2%
5	Ohio	1,130	4.1%
26	Oklahoma	333	1.2%
32	Oregon	250	0.9%
9	Pennsylvania	941	3.4%
42	Rhode Island	84	0.3%
18	South Carolina	480	1.7%
41	South Dakota	87	0.3%
12	Tennessee	676	2.5%
1	Texas	2,219	8.1%
30	Utah	272	1.0%
48	Vermont	40	0.1%
10	Virginia	720	2.6%
22	Washington	420	1.5%
37	West Virginia	146	0.5%
19	Wisconsin	479	1.7%
49	Wyoming	28	0.1%

RANK ORDER

RANK	STATE	DEATHS	% of USA
1	Texas	2,219	8.1%
2	Illinois	1,506	5.5%
3	Florida	1,439	5.2%
4	New York	1,394	5.1%
5	Ohio	1,130	4.1%
6	Michigan	1,121	4.1%
7	Georgia	1,061	3.9%
8	North Carolina	1,036	3.8%
9	Pennsylvania	941	3.4%
10	Virginia	720	2.6%
11	New Jersey	694	2.5%
12	Tennessee	676	2.5%
13	Arizona	609	2.2%
14	Louisiana	607	2.2%
15	Alabama	604	2.2%
16	Missouri	597	2.2%
17	Maryland	542	2.0%
18	South Carolina	480	1.7%
19	Wisconsin	479	1.7%
20	Mississippi	428	1.6%
21	Massachusetts	424	1.5%
22	Washington	420	1.5%
23	Colorado	412	1.5%
24	Kentucky	409	1.5%
25	Indiana	396	1.4%
26	Oklahoma	333	1.2%
27	Minnesota	330	1.2%
28	Arkansas	295	1.1%
29	Connecticut	294	1.1%
30	Utah	272	1.0%
31	Kansas	257	0.9%
32	Oregon	250	0.9%
33	Iowa	246	0.9%
34	Nevada	208	0.8%
35	New Mexico	175	0.6%
36	Nebraska	170	0.6%
37	West Virginia	146	0.5%
38	Idaho	131	0.5%
39	Hawaii	112	0.4%
40	Delaware	106	0.4%
41	South Dakota	87	0.3%
42	Rhode Island	84	0.3%
43	Montana	79	0.3%
44	Maine	71	0.3%
45	New Hampshire	64	0.2%
46	North Dakota	60	0.2%
47	Alaska	56	0.2%
48	Vermont	40	0.1%
49	Wyoming	28	0.1%
NA	California**	NA	NA
	District of Columbia	84	0.3%

Source: U.S. Department of Health and Human Services, National Center for Health Statistics
   "National Vital Statistics Reports" (Vol. 48, No. 1, January 25, 2000)
*For 12 months ending January 1999. Provisional data. Deaths under 1 year old by state of residence.
**Not available.

Infant Mortality Rate in 1999

National Rate = 6.9 Infant Deaths per 1,000 Live Births*

ALPHA ORDER

RANK	STATE	RATE
3	Alabama	9.7
44	Alaska	5.1
14	Arizona	7.6
12	Arkansas	8.0
NA	California**	NA
27	Colorado	6.9
26	Connecticut	7.0
1	Delaware	10.2
21	Florida	7.4
7	Georgia	8.6
34	Hawaii	6.5
30	Idaho	6.7
11	Illinois	8.3
46	Indiana	5.0
30	Iowa	6.7
30	Kansas	6.7
15	Kentucky	7.5
5	Louisiana	9.1
43	Maine	5.2
15	Maryland	7.5
47	Massachusetts	4.8
9	Michigan	8.4
44	Minnesota	5.1
2	Mississippi	10.1
13	Missouri	7.8
15	Montana	7.5
21	Nebraska	7.4
21	Nevada	7.4
48	New Hampshire	4.7
38	New Jersey	5.9
35	New Mexico	6.3
39	New York	5.8
4	North Carolina	9.3
15	North Dakota	7.5
15	Ohio	7.5
33	Oklahoma	6.6
40	Oregon	5.7
28	Pennsylvania	6.8
28	Rhode Island	6.8
6	South Carolina	9.0
8	South Dakota	8.5
9	Tennessee	8.4
35	Texas	6.3
41	Utah	5.6
37	Vermont	6.2
15	Virginia	7.5
42	Washington	5.4
24	West Virginia	7.1
24	Wisconsin	7.1
49	Wyoming	4.4

RANK ORDER

RANK	STATE	RATE
1	Delaware	10.2
2	Mississippi	10.1
3	Alabama	9.7
4	North Carolina	9.3
5	Louisiana	9.1
6	South Carolina	9.0
7	Georgia	8.6
8	South Dakota	8.5
9	Michigan	8.4
9	Tennessee	8.4
11	Illinois	8.3
12	Arkansas	8.0
13	Missouri	7.8
14	Arizona	7.6
15	Kentucky	7.5
15	Maryland	7.5
15	Montana	7.5
15	North Dakota	7.5
15	Ohio	7.5
15	Virginia	7.5
21	Florida	7.4
21	Nebraska	7.4
21	Nevada	7.4
24	West Virginia	7.1
24	Wisconsin	7.1
26	Connecticut	7.0
27	Colorado	6.9
28	Pennsylvania	6.8
28	Rhode Island	6.8
30	Idaho	6.7
30	Iowa	6.7
30	Kansas	6.7
33	Oklahoma	6.6
34	Hawaii	6.5
35	New Mexico	6.3
35	Texas	6.3
37	Vermont	6.2
38	New Jersey	5.9
39	New York	5.8
40	Oregon	5.7
41	Utah	5.6
42	Washington	5.4
43	Maine	5.2
44	Alaska	5.1
44	Minnesota	5.1
46	Indiana	5.0
47	Massachusetts	4.8
48	New Hampshire	4.7
49	Wyoming	4.4
NA	California**	NA
	District of Columbia	10.1

Source: U.S. Department of Health and Human Services, National Center for Health Statistics
    "National Vital Statistics Reports" (Vol. 48, No. 1, January 25, 2000)
*For 12 months ending January 1999. Provisional data. Deaths under 1 year old by state of residence.
**Not available.

Infant Deaths in 1997

National Total = 28,045 Infant Deaths*

ALPHA ORDER

RANK	STATE	DEATHS	% of USA
17	Alabama	581	2.1%
44	Alaska	75	0.3%
19	Arizona	536	1.9%
29	Arkansas	316	1.1%
1	California	3,104	11.1%
25	Colorado	397	1.4%
30	Connecticut	310	1.1%
42	Delaware	80	0.3%
5	Florida	1,366	4.9%
9	Georgia	1,022	3.6%
40	Hawaii	114	0.4%
39	Idaho	127	0.5%
4	Illinois	1,523	5.4%
13	Indiana	682	2.4%
34	Iowa	229	0.8%
31	Kansas	276	1.0%
26	Kentucky	387	1.4%
15	Louisiana	630	2.2%
46	Maine	70	0.2%
16	Maryland	616	2.2%
24	Massachusetts	421	1.5%
8	Michigan	1,092	3.9%
27	Minnesota	382	1.4%
21	Mississippi	442	1.6%
18	Missouri	564	2.0%
44	Montana	75	0.3%
37	Nebraska	173	0.6%
36	Nevada	175	0.6%
47	New Hampshire	62	0.2%
11	New Jersey	719	2.6%
38	New Mexico	164	0.6%
3	New York	1,727	6.2%
10	North Carolina	985	3.5%
48	North Dakota	52	0.2%
6	Ohio	1,189	4.2%
28	Oklahoma	361	1.3%
32	Oregon	256	0.9%
7	Pennsylvania	1,098	3.9%
41	Rhode Island	87	0.3%
20	South Carolina	501	1.8%
43	South Dakota	78	0.3%
14	Tennessee	637	2.3%
2	Texas	2,150	7.7%
33	Utah	249	0.9%
49	Vermont	40	0.1%
12	Virginia	714	2.5%
22	Washington	440	1.6%
35	West Virginia	198	0.7%
23	Wisconsin	431	1.5%
50	Wyoming	37	0.1%

RANK ORDER

RANK	STATE	DEATHS	% of USA
1	California	3,104	11.1%
2	Texas	2,150	7.7%
3	New York	1,727	6.2%
4	Illinois	1,523	5.4%
5	Florida	1,366	4.9%
6	Ohio	1,189	4.2%
7	Pennsylvania	1,098	3.9%
8	Michigan	1,092	3.9%
9	Georgia	1,022	3.6%
10	North Carolina	985	3.5%
11	New Jersey	719	2.6%
12	Virginia	714	2.5%
13	Indiana	682	2.4%
14	Tennessee	637	2.3%
15	Louisiana	630	2.2%
16	Maryland	616	2.2%
17	Alabama	581	2.1%
18	Missouri	564	2.0%
19	Arizona	536	1.9%
20	South Carolina	501	1.8%
21	Mississippi	442	1.6%
22	Washington	440	1.6%
23	Wisconsin	431	1.5%
24	Massachusetts	421	1.5%
25	Colorado	397	1.4%
26	Kentucky	387	1.4%
27	Minnesota	382	1.4%
28	Oklahoma	361	1.3%
29	Arkansas	316	1.1%
30	Connecticut	310	1.1%
31	Kansas	276	1.0%
32	Oregon	256	0.9%
33	Utah	249	0.9%
34	Iowa	229	0.8%
35	West Virginia	198	0.7%
36	Nevada	175	0.6%
37	Nebraska	173	0.6%
38	New Mexico	164	0.6%
39	Idaho	127	0.5%
40	Hawaii	114	0.4%
41	Rhode Island	87	0.3%
42	Delaware	80	0.3%
43	South Dakota	78	0.3%
44	Alaska	75	0.3%
44	Montana	75	0.3%
46	Maine	70	0.2%
47	New Hampshire	62	0.2%
48	North Dakota	52	0.2%
49	Vermont	40	0.1%
50	Wyoming	37	0.1%
	District of Columbia	105	0.4%

Source: U.S. Department of Health and Human Services, National Center for Health Statistics
"National Vital Statistics Reports" (Vol. 47, No. 19, June 30, 1999)
*Final data. Deaths under 1 year old by state of residence.

Infant Mortality Rate in 1997

National Rate = 7.2 Infant Deaths per 1,000 Live Births*

ALPHA ORDER

RANK	STATE	RATE
4	Alabama	9.5
20	Alaska	7.5
26	Arizona	7.1
8	Arkansas	8.7
42	California	5.9
28	Colorado	7.0
25	Connecticut	7.2
14	Delaware	7.8
26	Florida	7.1
9	Georgia	8.6
33	Hawaii	6.6
31	Idaho	6.8
11	Illinois	8.4
12	Indiana	8.2
38	Iowa	6.2
22	Kansas	7.4
24	Kentucky	7.3
4	Louisiana	9.5
49	Maine	5.1
7	Maryland	8.8
48	Massachusetts	5.2
12	Michigan	8.2
42	Minnesota	5.9
1	Mississippi	10.6
18	Missouri	7.6
30	Montana	6.9
22	Nebraska	7.4
34	Nevada	6.5
50	New Hampshire	4.3
37	New Jersey	6.3
40	New Mexico	6.1
32	New York	6.7
6	North Carolina	9.2
38	North Dakota	6.2
14	Ohio	7.8
20	Oklahoma	7.5
44	Oregon	5.8
18	Pennsylvania	7.6
28	Rhode Island	7.0
2	South Carolina	9.6
17	South Dakota	7.7
9	Tennessee	8.6
36	Texas	6.4
44	Utah	5.8
40	Vermont	6.1
14	Virginia	7.8
47	Washington	5.6
2	West Virginia	9.6
34	Wisconsin	6.5
44	Wyoming	5.8

RANK ORDER

RANK	STATE	RATE
1	Mississippi	10.6
2	South Carolina	9.6
2	West Virginia	9.6
4	Alabama	9.5
4	Louisiana	9.5
6	North Carolina	9.2
7	Maryland	8.8
8	Arkansas	8.7
9	Georgia	8.6
9	Tennessee	8.6
11	Illinois	8.4
12	Indiana	8.2
12	Michigan	8.2
14	Delaware	7.8
14	Ohio	7.8
14	Virginia	7.8
17	South Dakota	7.7
18	Missouri	7.6
18	Pennsylvania	7.6
20	Alaska	7.5
20	Oklahoma	7.5
22	Kansas	7.4
22	Nebraska	7.4
24	Kentucky	7.3
25	Connecticut	7.2
26	Arizona	7.1
26	Florida	7.1
28	Colorado	7.0
28	Rhode Island	7.0
30	Montana	6.9
31	Idaho	6.8
32	New York	6.7
33	Hawaii	6.6
34	Nevada	6.5
34	Wisconsin	6.5
36	Texas	6.4
37	New Jersey	6.3
38	Iowa	6.2
38	North Dakota	6.2
40	New Mexico	6.1
40	Vermont	6.1
42	California	5.9
42	Minnesota	5.9
44	Oregon	5.8
44	Utah	5.8
44	Wyoming	5.8
47	Washington	5.6
48	Massachusetts	5.2
49	Maine	5.1
50	New Hampshire	4.3
	District of Columbia	13.2

Source: U.S. Department of Health and Human Services, National Center for Health Statistics
    "National Vital Statistics Reports" (Vol. 47, No. 19, June 30, 1999)
*Final data. Deaths under 1 year old by state of residence.

Infant Mortality Rate in 1990

National Rate = 9.22 Infant Deaths per 1,000 Live Births*

ALPHA ORDER

RANK ORDER

RANK	STATE	RATE	RANK	STATE	RATE
5	Alabama	10.84	1	Georgia	12.36
9	Alaska	10.50	2	Mississippi	12.14
27	Arizona	8.84	3	South Carolina	11.65
22	Arkansas	9.22	4	Louisiana	11.07
42	California	7.91	5	Alabama	10.84
28	Colorado	8.82	6	Illinois	10.75
41	Connecticut	7.94	7	Michigan	10.68
13	Delaware	10.08	8	North Carolina	10.61
17	Florida	9.62	9	Alaska	10.50
1	Georgia	12.36	10	Tennessee	10.29
48	Hawaii	6.74	11	Virginia	10.20
29	Idaho	8.70	12	South Dakota	10.09
6	Illinois	10.75	13	Delaware	10.08
16	Indiana	9.64	14	West Virginia	9.87
37	Iowa	8.09	15	Ohio	9.83
32	Kansas	8.43	16	Indiana	9.64
31	Kentucky	8.48	17	Florida	9.62
4	Louisiana	11.07	18	New York	9.58
50	Maine	6.22	19	Maryland	9.55
19	Maryland	9.55	19	Pennsylvania	9.55
47	Massachusetts	7.02	21	Missouri	9.44
7	Michigan	10.68	22	Arkansas	9.22
45	Minnesota	7.29	23	Oklahoma	9.19
2	Mississippi	12.14	24	Montana	9.04
21	Missouri	9.44	25	New Jersey	9.01
24	Montana	9.04	26	New Mexico	8.98
34	Nebraska	8.29	27	Arizona	8.84
33	Nevada	8.38	28	Colorado	8.82
46	New Hampshire	7.11	29	Idaho	8.70
25	New Jersey	9.01	30	Wyoming	8.59
26	New Mexico	8.98	31	Kentucky	8.48
18	New York	9.58	32	Kansas	8.43
8	North Carolina	10.61	33	Nevada	8.38
40	North Dakota	8.00	34	Nebraska	8.29
15	Ohio	9.83	35	Oregon	8.25
23	Oklahoma	9.19	36	Wisconsin	8.20
35	Oregon	8.25	37	Iowa	8.09
19	Pennsylvania	9.55	37	Rhode Island	8.09
37	Rhode Island	8.09	39	Texas	8.07
3	South Carolina	11.65	40	North Dakota	8.00
12	South Dakota	10.09	41	Connecticut	7.94
10	Tennessee	10.29	42	California	7.91
39	Texas	8.07	43	Washington	7.84
44	Utah	7.47	44	Utah	7.47
49	Vermont	6.41	45	Minnesota	7.29
11	Virginia	10.20	46	New Hampshire	7.11
43	Washington	7.84	47	Massachusetts	7.02
14	West Virginia	9.87	48	Hawaii	6.74
36	Wisconsin	8.20	49	Vermont	6.41
30	Wyoming	8.59	50	Maine	6.22

District of Columbia   20.68

Source: U.S. Department of Health and Human Services, National Center for Health Statistics
"Monthly Vital Statistics Report" (Vol. 41, No. 7(S), January 7, 1993)
*Final data by state of residence. Infant deaths are those under 1 year old.

Infant Mortality Rate in 1980

National Rate = 12.60 Infant Deaths per 1,000 Live Births*

ALPHA ORDER

RANK	STATE	RATE
3	Alabama	15.15
24	Alaska	12.28
22	Arizona	12.39
18	Arkansas	12.66
35	California	11.05
46	Colorado	10.07
34	Connecticut	11.17
10	Delaware	13.92
5	Florida	14.58
7	Georgia	14.48
44	Hawaii	10.30
39	Idaho	10.71
4	Illinois	14.80
28	Indiana	11.87
29	Iowa	11.82
43	Kansas	10.41
14	Kentucky	12.86
8	Louisiana	14.34
50	Maine	9.23
9	Maryland	14.05
41	Massachusetts	10.51
15	Michigan	12.80
47	Minnesota	10.00
1	Mississippi	17.01
21	Missouri	12.42
22	Montana	12.39
33	Nebraska	11.48
38	Nevada	10.74
48	New Hampshire	9.89
19	New Jersey	12.54
32	New Mexico	11.53
20	New York	12.53
6	North Carolina	14.49
27	North Dakota	12.10
16	Ohio	12.77
17	Oklahoma	12.72
25	Oregon	12.17
13	Pennsylvania	13.23
36	Rhode Island	10.99
2	South Carolina	15.62
37	South Dakota	10.92
12	Tennessee	13.51
26	Texas	12.16
42	Utah	10.43
40	Vermont	10.65
11	Virginia	13.60
31	Washington	11.76
30	West Virginia	11.81
45	Wisconsin	10.29
49	Wyoming	9.75

RANK ORDER

RANK	STATE	RATE
1	Mississippi	17.01
2	South Carolina	15.62
3	Alabama	15.15
4	Illinois	14.80
5	Florida	14.58
6	North Carolina	14.49
7	Georgia	14.48
8	Louisiana	14.34
9	Maryland	14.05
10	Delaware	13.92
11	Virginia	13.60
12	Tennessee	13.51
13	Pennsylvania	13.23
14	Kentucky	12.86
15	Michigan	12.80
16	Ohio	12.77
17	Oklahoma	12.72
18	Arkansas	12.66
19	New Jersey	12.54
20	New York	12.53
21	Missouri	12.42
22	Arizona	12.39
22	Montana	12.39
24	Alaska	12.28
25	Oregon	12.17
26	Texas	12.16
27	North Dakota	12.10
28	Indiana	11.87
29	Iowa	11.82
30	West Virginia	11.81
31	Washington	11.76
32	New Mexico	11.53
33	Nebraska	11.48
34	Connecticut	11.17
35	California	11.05
36	Rhode Island	10.99
37	South Dakota	10.92
38	Nevada	10.74
39	Idaho	10.71
40	Vermont	10.65
41	Massachusetts	10.51
42	Utah	10.43
43	Kansas	10.41
44	Hawaii	10.30
45	Wisconsin	10.29
46	Colorado	10.07
47	Minnesota	10.00
48	New Hampshire	9.89
49	Wyoming	9.75
50	Maine	9.23
	District of Columbia	25.00

Source: U.S. Department of Health and Human Services, National Center for Health Statistics
      "Monthly Vital Statistics Report"
*Final data by state of residence. Deaths under 1 year old, exclusive of fetal deaths.

Percent Change in Infant Mortality Rate: 1990 to 1997

National Percent Change = 21.9% Decrease*

ALPHA ORDER

RANK	STATE	PERCENT CHANGE
9	Alabama	(12.4)
42	Alaska	(28.6)
22	Arizona	(19.7)
4	Arkansas	(5.6)
39	California	(25.4)
24	Colorado	(20.6)
6	Connecticut	(9.3)
33	Delaware	(22.6)
41	Florida	(26.2)
47	Georgia	(30.4)
1	Hawaii	(2.1)
28	Idaho	(21.8)
29	Illinois	(21.9)
15	Indiana	(14.9)
35	Iowa	(23.4)
8	Kansas	(12.2)
13	Kentucky	(13.9)
14	Louisiana	(14.2)
18	Maine	(18.0)
5	Maryland	(7.9)
40	Massachusetts	(25.9)
34	Michigan	(23.2)
20	Minnesota	(19.1)
10	Mississippi	(12.7)
21	Missouri	(19.5)
37	Montana	(23.7)
7	Nebraska	(10.7)
30	Nevada	(22.4)
50	New Hampshire	(39.5)
45	New Jersey	(30.1)
48	New Mexico	(32.1)
45	New York	(30.1)
11	North Carolina	(13.3)
32	North Dakota	(22.5)
25	Ohio	(20.7)
19	Oklahoma	(18.4)
44	Oregon	(29.7)
23	Pennsylvania	(20.4)
12	Rhode Island	(13.5)
17	South Carolina	(17.6)
37	South Dakota	(23.7)
16	Tennessee	(16.4)
25	Texas	(20.7)
30	Utah	(22.4)
3	Vermont	(4.8)
36	Virginia	(23.5)
42	Washington	(28.6)
2	West Virginia	(2.7)
25	Wisconsin	(20.7)
49	Wyoming	(32.5)

RANK ORDER

RANK	STATE	PERCENT CHANGE
1	Hawaii	(2.1)
2	West Virginia	(2.7)
3	Vermont	(4.8)
4	Arkansas	(5.6)
5	Maryland	(7.9)
6	Connecticut	(9.3)
7	Nebraska	(10.7)
8	Kansas	(12.2)
9	Alabama	(12.4)
10	Mississippi	(12.7)
11	North Carolina	(13.3)
12	Rhode Island	(13.5)
13	Kentucky	(13.9)
14	Louisiana	(14.2)
15	Indiana	(14.9)
16	Tennessee	(16.4)
17	South Carolina	(17.6)
18	Maine	(18.0)
19	Oklahoma	(18.4)
20	Minnesota	(19.1)
21	Missouri	(19.5)
22	Arizona	(19.7)
23	Pennsylvania	(20.4)
24	Colorado	(20.6)
25	Ohio	(20.7)
25	Texas	(20.7)
25	Wisconsin	(20.7)
28	Idaho	(21.8)
29	Illinois	(21.9)
30	Nevada	(22.4)
30	Utah	(22.4)
32	North Dakota	(22.5)
33	Delaware	(22.6)
34	Michigan	(23.2)
35	Iowa	(23.4)
36	Virginia	(23.5)
37	Montana	(23.7)
37	South Dakota	(23.7)
39	California	(25.4)
40	Massachusetts	(25.9)
41	Florida	(26.2)
42	Alaska	(28.6)
42	Washington	(28.6)
44	Oregon	(29.7)
45	New Jersey	(30.1)
45	New York	(30.1)
47	Georgia	(30.4)
48	New Mexico	(32.1)
49	Wyoming	(32.5)
50	New Hampshire	(39.5)
	District of Columbia	(36.2)

Source: Morgan Quitno Press using data from US Dept of Health & Human Services, National Center for Health Statistics "Monthly Vital Statistics Report" (Vol. 41, No. 7(S), January 7, 1993) and "National Vital Statistics Reports" (Vol. 47, No. 19, June 30, 1999)

*By state of residence. Infant deaths are those under 1 year old.

Percent Change in Infant Mortality Rate: 1980 to 1997

National Percent Change = 42.9% Decrease*

<table>
<tr><td colspan="3">ALPHA ORDER</td><td colspan="3">RANK ORDER</td></tr>
<tr><td>RANK</td><td>STATE</td><td>PERCENT CHANGE</td><td>RANK</td><td>STATE</td><td>PERCENT CHANGE</td></tr>
<tr><td>17</td><td>Alabama</td><td>(37.3)</td><td>1</td><td>West Virginia</td><td>(18.7)</td></tr>
<tr><td>22</td><td>Alaska</td><td>(38.9)</td><td>2</td><td>Kansas</td><td>(28.9)</td></tr>
<tr><td>31</td><td>Arizona</td><td>(42.7)</td><td>3</td><td>South Dakota</td><td>(29.5)</td></tr>
<tr><td>6</td><td>Arkansas</td><td>(31.3)</td><td>4</td><td>Colorado</td><td>(30.5)</td></tr>
<tr><td>40</td><td>California</td><td>(46.6)</td><td>5</td><td>Indiana</td><td>(30.9)</td></tr>
<tr><td>4</td><td>Colorado</td><td>(30.5)</td><td>6</td><td>Arkansas</td><td>(31.3)</td></tr>
<tr><td>8</td><td>Connecticut</td><td>(35.5)</td><td>7</td><td>Louisiana</td><td>(33.8)</td></tr>
<tr><td>35</td><td>Delaware</td><td>(44.0)</td><td>8</td><td>Connecticut</td><td>(35.5)</td></tr>
<tr><td>47</td><td>Florida</td><td>(51.3)</td><td>8</td><td>Nebraska</td><td>(35.5)</td></tr>
<tr><td>26</td><td>Georgia</td><td>(40.6)</td><td>10</td><td>Hawaii</td><td>(35.9)</td></tr>
<tr><td>10</td><td>Hawaii</td><td>(35.9)</td><td>10</td><td>Michigan</td><td>(35.9)</td></tr>
<tr><td>14</td><td>Idaho</td><td>(36.5)</td><td>12</td><td>Rhode Island</td><td>(36.3)</td></tr>
<tr><td>33</td><td>Illinois</td><td>(43.2)</td><td>12</td><td>Tennessee</td><td>(36.3)</td></tr>
<tr><td>5</td><td>Indiana</td><td>(30.9)</td><td>14</td><td>Idaho</td><td>(36.5)</td></tr>
<tr><td>43</td><td>Iowa</td><td>(47.5)</td><td>14</td><td>North Carolina</td><td>(36.5)</td></tr>
<tr><td>2</td><td>Kansas</td><td>(28.9)</td><td>16</td><td>Wisconsin</td><td>(36.8)</td></tr>
<tr><td>33</td><td>Kentucky</td><td>(43.2)</td><td>17</td><td>Alabama</td><td>(37.3)</td></tr>
<tr><td>7</td><td>Louisiana</td><td>(33.8)</td><td>18</td><td>Maryland</td><td>(37.4)</td></tr>
<tr><td>38</td><td>Maine</td><td>(44.7)</td><td>19</td><td>Mississippi</td><td>(37.7)</td></tr>
<tr><td>18</td><td>Maryland</td><td>(37.4)</td><td>20</td><td>South Carolina</td><td>(38.5)</td></tr>
<tr><td>46</td><td>Massachusetts</td><td>(50.5)</td><td>21</td><td>Missouri</td><td>(38.8)</td></tr>
<tr><td>10</td><td>Michigan</td><td>(35.9)</td><td>22</td><td>Alaska</td><td>(38.9)</td></tr>
<tr><td>27</td><td>Minnesota</td><td>(41.0)</td><td>22</td><td>Ohio</td><td>(38.9)</td></tr>
<tr><td>19</td><td>Mississippi</td><td>(37.7)</td><td>24</td><td>Nevada</td><td>(39.5)</td></tr>
<tr><td>21</td><td>Missouri</td><td>(38.8)</td><td>25</td><td>Wyoming</td><td>(40.5)</td></tr>
<tr><td>36</td><td>Montana</td><td>(44.3)</td><td>26</td><td>Georgia</td><td>(40.6)</td></tr>
<tr><td>8</td><td>Nebraska</td><td>(35.5)</td><td>27</td><td>Minnesota</td><td>(41.0)</td></tr>
<tr><td>24</td><td>Nevada</td><td>(39.5)</td><td>27</td><td>Oklahoma</td><td>(41.0)</td></tr>
<tr><td>50</td><td>New Hampshire</td><td>(56.5)</td><td>29</td><td>Pennsylvania</td><td>(42.6)</td></tr>
<tr><td>45</td><td>New Jersey</td><td>(49.8)</td><td>29</td><td>Virginia</td><td>(42.6)</td></tr>
<tr><td>41</td><td>New Mexico</td><td>(47.1)</td><td>31</td><td>Arizona</td><td>(42.7)</td></tr>
<tr><td>39</td><td>New York</td><td>(46.5)</td><td>31</td><td>Vermont</td><td>(42.7)</td></tr>
<tr><td>14</td><td>North Carolina</td><td>(36.5)</td><td>33</td><td>Illinois</td><td>(43.2)</td></tr>
<tr><td>44</td><td>North Dakota</td><td>(48.8)</td><td>33</td><td>Kentucky</td><td>(43.2)</td></tr>
<tr><td>22</td><td>Ohio</td><td>(38.9)</td><td>35</td><td>Delaware</td><td>(44.0)</td></tr>
<tr><td>27</td><td>Oklahoma</td><td>(41.0)</td><td>36</td><td>Montana</td><td>(44.3)</td></tr>
<tr><td>48</td><td>Oregon</td><td>(52.3)</td><td>37</td><td>Utah</td><td>(44.4)</td></tr>
<tr><td>29</td><td>Pennsylvania</td><td>(42.6)</td><td>38</td><td>Maine</td><td>(44.7)</td></tr>
<tr><td>12</td><td>Rhode Island</td><td>(36.3)</td><td>39</td><td>New York</td><td>(46.5)</td></tr>
<tr><td>20</td><td>South Carolina</td><td>(38.5)</td><td>40</td><td>California</td><td>(46.6)</td></tr>
<tr><td>3</td><td>South Dakota</td><td>(29.5)</td><td>41</td><td>New Mexico</td><td>(47.1)</td></tr>
<tr><td>12</td><td>Tennessee</td><td>(36.3)</td><td>42</td><td>Texas</td><td>(47.4)</td></tr>
<tr><td>42</td><td>Texas</td><td>(47.4)</td><td>43</td><td>Iowa</td><td>(47.5)</td></tr>
<tr><td>37</td><td>Utah</td><td>(44.4)</td><td>44</td><td>North Dakota</td><td>(48.8)</td></tr>
<tr><td>31</td><td>Vermont</td><td>(42.7)</td><td>45</td><td>New Jersey</td><td>(49.8)</td></tr>
<tr><td>29</td><td>Virginia</td><td>(42.6)</td><td>46</td><td>Massachusetts</td><td>(50.5)</td></tr>
<tr><td>49</td><td>Washington</td><td>(52.4)</td><td>47</td><td>Florida</td><td>(51.3)</td></tr>
<tr><td>1</td><td>West Virginia</td><td>(18.7)</td><td>48</td><td>Oregon</td><td>(52.3)</td></tr>
<tr><td>16</td><td>Wisconsin</td><td>(36.8)</td><td>49</td><td>Washington</td><td>(52.4)</td></tr>
<tr><td>25</td><td>Wyoming</td><td>(40.5)</td><td>50</td><td>New Hampshire</td><td>(56.5)</td></tr>
</table>

District of Columbia   (47.2)

Source: Morgan Quitno Press using data from US Dept of Health & Human Services, National Center for Health Statistics
"National Vital Statistics Reports" (Vol. 47, No. 19, June 30, 1999)
"Vital Statistics of the United States, 1980" (Vol. I-Natality, issued 1984) and unpublished data
*Final data by state of residence. Infant deaths are those occurring under 1 year, exclusive of fetal deaths.

White Infant Deaths in 1997

National Total = 18,539 Deaths*

<u>ALPHA ORDER</u>

RANK	STATE	DEATHS	% of USA
22	Alabama	302	1.6%
44	Alaska	45	0.2%
12	Arizona	450	2.4%
32	Arkansas	208	1.1%
1	California	2,370	12.8%
18	Colorado	348	1.9%
29	Connecticut	227	1.2%
47	Delaware	43	0.2%
6	Florida	815	4.4%
11	Georgia	464	2.5%
50	Hawaii	14	0.1%
39	Idaho	125	0.7%
4	Illinois	885	4.8%
9	Indiana	538	2.9%
33	Iowa	204	1.1%
30	Kansas	221	1.2%
20	Kentucky	334	1.8%
25	Louisiana	250	1.3%
41	Maine	70	0.4%
28	Maryland	228	1.2%
19	Massachusetts	342	1.8%
8	Michigan	650	3.5%
23	Minnesota	294	1.6%
35	Mississippi	157	0.8%
15	Missouri	377	2.0%
43	Montana	57	0.3%
36	Nebraska	144	0.8%
37	Nevada	141	0.8%
42	New Hampshire	60	0.3%
13	New Jersey	418	2.3%
38	New Mexico	127	0.7%
3	New York	1,056	5.7%
10	North Carolina	520	2.8%
46	North Dakota	44	0.2%
5	Ohio	830	4.5%
24	Oklahoma	254	1.4%
27	Oregon	231	1.2%
7	Pennsylvania	724	3.9%
40	Rhode Island	76	0.4%
31	South Carolina	213	1.1%
44	South Dakota	45	0.2%
16	Tennessee	368	2.0%
2	Texas	1,682	9.1%
26	Utah	236	1.3%
48	Vermont	40	0.2%
14	Virginia	401	2.2%
17	Washington	359	1.9%
34	West Virginia	181	1.0%
21	Wisconsin	330	1.8%
49	Wyoming	34	0.2%

<u>RANK ORDER</u>

RANK	STATE	DEATHS	% of USA
1	California	2,370	12.8%
2	Texas	1,682	9.1%
3	New York	1,056	5.7%
4	Illinois	885	4.8%
5	Ohio	830	4.5%
6	Florida	815	4.4%
7	Pennsylvania	724	3.9%
8	Michigan	650	3.5%
9	Indiana	538	2.9%
10	North Carolina	520	2.8%
11	Georgia	464	2.5%
12	Arizona	450	2.4%
13	New Jersey	418	2.3%
14	Virginia	401	2.2%
15	Missouri	377	2.0%
16	Tennessee	368	2.0%
17	Washington	359	1.9%
18	Colorado	348	1.9%
19	Massachusetts	342	1.8%
20	Kentucky	334	1.8%
21	Wisconsin	330	1.8%
22	Alabama	302	1.6%
23	Minnesota	294	1.6%
24	Oklahoma	254	1.4%
25	Louisiana	250	1.3%
26	Utah	236	1.3%
27	Oregon	231	1.2%
28	Maryland	228	1.2%
29	Connecticut	227	1.2%
30	Kansas	221	1.2%
31	South Carolina	213	1.1%
32	Arkansas	208	1.1%
33	Iowa	204	1.1%
34	West Virginia	181	1.0%
35	Mississippi	157	0.8%
36	Nebraska	144	0.8%
37	Nevada	141	0.8%
38	New Mexico	127	0.7%
39	Idaho	125	0.7%
40	Rhode Island	76	0.4%
41	Maine	70	0.4%
42	New Hampshire	60	0.3%
43	Montana	57	0.3%
44	Alaska	45	0.2%
44	South Dakota	45	0.2%
46	North Dakota	44	0.2%
47	Delaware	43	0.2%
48	Vermont	40	0.2%
49	Wyoming	34	0.2%
50	Hawaii	14	0.1%
	District of Columbia	7	0.0%

Source. U.S. Department of Health and Human Services, National Center for Health Statistics
  "National Vital Statistics Reports" (Vol. 47, No. 19, June 30, 1999)
*Final data. Deaths of infants under 1 year old, exclusive of fetal deaths. Based on race of the mother.

White Infant Mortality Rate in 1997

National Rate = 6.0 White Infant Deaths per 1,000 White Live Births*

ALPHA ORDER

RANK ORDER

RANK	STATE	RATE		RANK	STATE	RATE
2	Alabama	7.5		1	West Virginia	9.1
10	Alaska	6.8		2	Alabama	7.5
10	Arizona	6.8		3	Arkansas	7.4
3	Arkansas	7.4		4	Indiana	7.3
39	California	5.6		5	Mississippi	7.1
13	Colorado	6.7		6	Kentucky	7.0
21	Connecticut	6.3		6	Rhode Island	7.0
34	Delaware	5.7		8	Idaho	6.9
34	Florida	5.7		8	North Carolina	6.9
23	Georgia	6.1		10	Alaska	6.8
NA	Hawaii**	NA		10	Arizona	6.8
8	Idaho	6.9		10	Nebraska	6.8
19	Illinois	6.4		13	Colorado	6.7
4	Indiana	7.3		13	Oklahoma	6.7
30	Iowa	5.9		15	Kansas	6.6
15	Kansas	6.6		15	Louisiana	6.6
6	Kentucky	7.0		17	Ohio	6.5
15	Louisiana	6.6		17	Tennessee	6.5
42	Maine	5.3		19	Illinois	6.4
45	Maryland	5.1		19	South Carolina	6.4
47	Massachusetts	5.0		21	Connecticut	6.3
23	Michigan	6.1		22	Nevada	6.2
45	Minnesota	5.1		23	Georgia	6.1
5	Mississippi	7.1		23	Michigan	6.1
23	Missouri	6.1		23	Missouri	6.1
27	Montana	6.0		23	Vermont	6.1
10	Nebraska	6.8		27	Montana	6.0
22	Nevada	6.2		27	Pennsylvania	6.0
49	New Hampshire	4.3		27	Virginia	6.0
48	New Jersey	4.9		30	Iowa	5.9
39	New Mexico	5.6		30	North Dakota	5.9
34	New York	5.7		30	Texas	5.9
8	North Carolina	6.9		33	Utah	5.8
30	North Dakota	5.9		34	Delaware	5.7
17	Ohio	6.5		34	Florida	5.7
13	Oklahoma	6.7		34	New York	5.7
34	Oregon	5.7		34	Oregon	5.7
27	Pennsylvania	6.0		34	Wisconsin	5.7
6	Rhode Island	7.0		39	California	5.6
19	South Carolina	6.4		39	New Mexico	5.6
42	South Dakota	5.3		39	Wyoming	5.6
17	Tennessee	6.5		42	Maine	5.3
30	Texas	5.9		42	South Dakota	5.3
33	Utah	5.8		42	Washington	5.3
23	Vermont	6.1		45	Maryland	5.1
27	Virginia	6.0		45	Minnesota	5.1
42	Washington	5.3		47	Massachusetts	5.0
1	West Virginia	9.1		48	New Jersey	4.9
34	Wisconsin	5.7		49	New Hampshire	4.3
39	Wyoming	5.6		NA	Hawaii**	NA
					District of Columbia**	NA

Source: U.S. Department of Health and Human Services, National Center for Health Statistics
    "National Vital Statistics Reports" (Vol. 47, No. 19, June 30, 1999)
*Final data. Deaths of infants under 1 year old, exclusive of fetal deaths. Based on race of the mother.
**Not available, fewer than 20 white infant deaths.

Black Infant Deaths in 1997

National Total = 8,496 Deaths*

<table>
<tr><td colspan="4">ALPHA ORDER</td><td colspan="4">RANK ORDER</td></tr>
<tr><td>RANK</td><td>STATE</td><td>DEATHS</td><td>% of USA</td><td>RANK</td><td>STATE</td><td>DEATHS</td><td>% of USA</td></tr>
<tr><td>17</td><td>Alabama</td><td>275</td><td>3.2%</td><td>1</td><td>Illinois</td><td>607</td><td>7.1%</td></tr>
<tr><td>40</td><td>Alaska</td><td>4</td><td>0.0%</td><td>2</td><td>New York</td><td>604</td><td>7.1%</td></tr>
<tr><td>31</td><td>Arizona</td><td>36</td><td>0.4%</td><td>3</td><td>Georgia</td><td>548</td><td>6.5%</td></tr>
<tr><td>21</td><td>Arkansas</td><td>108</td><td>1.3%</td><td>4</td><td>Florida</td><td>536</td><td>6.3%</td></tr>
<tr><td>5</td><td>California</td><td>489</td><td>5.8%</td><td>5</td><td>California</td><td>489</td><td>5.8%</td></tr>
<tr><td>30</td><td>Colorado</td><td>42</td><td>0.5%</td><td>6</td><td>Texas</td><td>432</td><td>5.1%</td></tr>
<tr><td>23</td><td>Connecticut</td><td>77</td><td>0.9%</td><td>7</td><td>North Carolina</td><td>431</td><td>5.1%</td></tr>
<tr><td>31</td><td>Delaware</td><td>36</td><td>0.4%</td><td>8</td><td>Michigan</td><td>425</td><td>5.0%</td></tr>
<tr><td>4</td><td>Florida</td><td>536</td><td>6.3%</td><td>9</td><td>Louisiana</td><td>375</td><td>4.4%</td></tr>
<tr><td>3</td><td>Georgia</td><td>548</td><td>6.5%</td><td>10</td><td>Maryland</td><td>371</td><td>4.4%</td></tr>
<tr><td>41</td><td>Hawaii</td><td>3</td><td>0.0%</td><td>11</td><td>Pennsylvania</td><td>359</td><td>4.2%</td></tr>
<tr><td>48</td><td>Idaho</td><td>0</td><td>0.0%</td><td>12</td><td>Ohio</td><td>352</td><td>4.1%</td></tr>
<tr><td>1</td><td>Illinois</td><td>607</td><td>7.1%</td><td>13</td><td>Virginia</td><td>299</td><td>3.5%</td></tr>
<tr><td>20</td><td>Indiana</td><td>139</td><td>1.6%</td><td>14</td><td>South Carolina</td><td>283</td><td>3.3%</td></tr>
<tr><td>35</td><td>Iowa</td><td>20</td><td>0.2%</td><td>15</td><td>Mississippi</td><td>282</td><td>3.3%</td></tr>
<tr><td>29</td><td>Kansas</td><td>48</td><td>0.6%</td><td>15</td><td>New Jersey</td><td>282</td><td>3.3%</td></tr>
<tr><td>27</td><td>Kentucky</td><td>51</td><td>0.6%</td><td>17</td><td>Alabama</td><td>275</td><td>3.2%</td></tr>
<tr><td>9</td><td>Louisiana</td><td>375</td><td>4.4%</td><td>18</td><td>Tennessee</td><td>266</td><td>3.1%</td></tr>
<tr><td>48</td><td>Maine</td><td>0</td><td>0.0%</td><td>19</td><td>Missouri</td><td>180</td><td>2.1%</td></tr>
<tr><td>10</td><td>Maryland</td><td>371</td><td>4.4%</td><td>20</td><td>Indiana</td><td>139</td><td>1.6%</td></tr>
<tr><td>25</td><td>Massachusetts</td><td>68</td><td>0.8%</td><td>21</td><td>Arkansas</td><td>108</td><td>1.3%</td></tr>
<tr><td>8</td><td>Michigan</td><td>425</td><td>5.0%</td><td>22</td><td>Wisconsin</td><td>89</td><td>1.0%</td></tr>
<tr><td>26</td><td>Minnesota</td><td>55</td><td>0.6%</td><td>23</td><td>Connecticut</td><td>77</td><td>0.9%</td></tr>
<tr><td>15</td><td>Mississippi</td><td>282</td><td>3.3%</td><td>24</td><td>Oklahoma</td><td>71</td><td>0.8%</td></tr>
<tr><td>19</td><td>Missouri</td><td>180</td><td>2.1%</td><td>25</td><td>Massachusetts</td><td>68</td><td>0.8%</td></tr>
<tr><td>43</td><td>Montana</td><td>1</td><td>0.0%</td><td>26</td><td>Minnesota</td><td>55</td><td>0.6%</td></tr>
<tr><td>34</td><td>Nebraska</td><td>24</td><td>0.3%</td><td>27</td><td>Kentucky</td><td>51</td><td>0.6%</td></tr>
<tr><td>33</td><td>Nevada</td><td>29</td><td>0.3%</td><td>28</td><td>Washington</td><td>49</td><td>0.6%</td></tr>
<tr><td>43</td><td>New Hampshire</td><td>1</td><td>0.0%</td><td>29</td><td>Kansas</td><td>48</td><td>0.6%</td></tr>
<tr><td>15</td><td>New Jersey</td><td>282</td><td>3.3%</td><td>30</td><td>Colorado</td><td>42</td><td>0.5%</td></tr>
<tr><td>39</td><td>New Mexico</td><td>8</td><td>0.1%</td><td>31</td><td>Arizona</td><td>36</td><td>0.4%</td></tr>
<tr><td>2</td><td>New York</td><td>604</td><td>7.1%</td><td>31</td><td>Delaware</td><td>36</td><td>0.4%</td></tr>
<tr><td>7</td><td>North Carolina</td><td>431</td><td>5.1%</td><td>33</td><td>Nevada</td><td>29</td><td>0.3%</td></tr>
<tr><td>43</td><td>North Dakota</td><td>1</td><td>0.0%</td><td>34</td><td>Nebraska</td><td>24</td><td>0.3%</td></tr>
<tr><td>12</td><td>Ohio</td><td>352</td><td>4.1%</td><td>35</td><td>Iowa</td><td>20</td><td>0.2%</td></tr>
<tr><td>24</td><td>Oklahoma</td><td>71</td><td>0.8%</td><td>36</td><td>West Virginia</td><td>15</td><td>0.2%</td></tr>
<tr><td>37</td><td>Oregon</td><td>14</td><td>0.2%</td><td>37</td><td>Oregon</td><td>14</td><td>0.2%</td></tr>
<tr><td>11</td><td>Pennsylvania</td><td>359</td><td>4.2%</td><td>38</td><td>Rhode Island</td><td>9</td><td>0.1%</td></tr>
<tr><td>38</td><td>Rhode Island</td><td>9</td><td>0.1%</td><td>39</td><td>New Mexico</td><td>8</td><td>0.1%</td></tr>
<tr><td>14</td><td>South Carolina</td><td>283</td><td>3.3%</td><td>40</td><td>Alaska</td><td>4</td><td>0.0%</td></tr>
<tr><td>41</td><td>South Dakota</td><td>3</td><td>0.0%</td><td>41</td><td>Hawaii</td><td>3</td><td>0.0%</td></tr>
<tr><td>18</td><td>Tennessee</td><td>266</td><td>3.1%</td><td>41</td><td>South Dakota</td><td>3</td><td>0.0%</td></tr>
<tr><td>6</td><td>Texas</td><td>432</td><td>5.1%</td><td>43</td><td>Montana</td><td>1</td><td>0.0%</td></tr>
<tr><td>43</td><td>Utah</td><td>1</td><td>0.0%</td><td>43</td><td>New Hampshire</td><td>1</td><td>0.0%</td></tr>
<tr><td>48</td><td>Vermont</td><td>0</td><td>0.0%</td><td>43</td><td>North Dakota</td><td>1</td><td>0.0%</td></tr>
<tr><td>13</td><td>Virginia</td><td>299</td><td>3.5%</td><td>43</td><td>Utah</td><td>1</td><td>0.0%</td></tr>
<tr><td>28</td><td>Washington</td><td>49</td><td>0.6%</td><td>43</td><td>Wyoming</td><td>1</td><td>0.0%</td></tr>
<tr><td>36</td><td>West Virginia</td><td>15</td><td>0.2%</td><td>48</td><td>Idaho</td><td>0</td><td>0.0%</td></tr>
<tr><td>22</td><td>Wisconsin</td><td>89</td><td>1.0%</td><td>48</td><td>Maine</td><td>0</td><td>0.0%</td></tr>
<tr><td>43</td><td>Wyoming</td><td>1</td><td>0.0%</td><td>48</td><td>Vermont</td><td>0</td><td>0.0%</td></tr>
<tr><td></td><td></td><td></td><td></td><td></td><td>District of Columbia</td><td>97</td><td>1.1%</td></tr>
</table>

Source: U.S. Department of Health and Human Services, National Center for Health Statistics
   "National Vital Statistics Reports" (Vol. 47, No. 19, June 30, 1999)
*Final data. Deaths of infants under 1 year old, exclusive of fetal deaths. Based on race of the mother.

Black Infant Mortality Rate in 1997

National Rate = 14.2 Black Infant Deaths per 1,000 Black Live Births*

ALPHA ORDER

RANK	STATE	RATE
23	Alabama	13.9
NA	Alaska**	NA
20	Arizona	14.4
25	Arkansas	13.8
30	California	13.1
8	Colorado	16.3
21	Connecticut	14.3
19	Delaware	14.5
31	Florida	12.3
25	Georgia	13.8
NA	Hawaii**	NA
NA	Idaho**	NA
5	Illinois	17.1
12	Indiana	15.8
2	Iowa	18.2
5	Kansas	17.1
32	Kentucky	11.0
25	Louisiana	13.8
NA	Maine**	NA
11	Maryland	16.2
35	Massachusetts	8.8
4	Michigan	17.5
7	Minnesota	16.5
18	Mississippi	14.9
8	Missouri	16.3
NA	Montana**	NA
1	Nebraska	19.2
28	Nevada	13.6
NA	New Hampshire**	NA
29	New Jersey	13.4
NA	New Mexico**	NA
33	New York	10.9
13	North Carolina	15.7
NA	North Dakota**	NA
14	Ohio	15.6
17	Oklahoma	15.0
NA	Oregon**	NA
3	Pennsylvania	17.6
NA	Rhode Island**	NA
15	South Carolina	15.4
NA	South Dakota**	NA
8	Tennessee	16.3
33	Texas	10.9
NA	Utah**	NA
NA	Vermont**	NA
22	Virginia	14.2
15	Washington	15.4
NA	West Virginia**	NA
23	Wisconsin	13.9
NA	Wyoming**	NA

RANK ORDER

RANK	STATE	RATE
1	Nebraska	19.2
2	Iowa	18.2
3	Pennsylvania	17.6
4	Michigan	17.5
5	Illinois	17.1
5	Kansas	17.1
7	Minnesota	16.5
8	Colorado	16.3
8	Missouri	16.3
8	Tennessee	16.3
11	Maryland	16.2
12	Indiana	15.8
13	North Carolina	15.7
14	Ohio	15.6
15	South Carolina	15.4
15	Washington	15.4
17	Oklahoma	15.0
18	Mississippi	14.9
19	Delaware	14.5
20	Arizona	14.4
21	Connecticut	14.3
22	Virginia	14.2
23	Alabama	13.9
23	Wisconsin	13.9
25	Arkansas	13.8
25	Georgia	13.8
25	Louisiana	13.8
28	Nevada	13.6
29	New Jersey	13.4
30	California	13.1
31	Florida	12.3
32	Kentucky	11.0
33	New York	10.9
33	Texas	10.9
35	Massachusetts	8.8
NA	Alaska**	NA
NA	Hawaii**	NA
NA	Idaho**	NA
NA	Maine**	NA
NA	Montana**	NA
NA	New Hampshire**	NA
NA	New Mexico**	NA
NA	North Dakota**	NA
NA	Oregon**	NA
NA	Rhode Island**	NA
NA	South Dakota**	NA
NA	Utah**	NA
NA	Vermont**	NA
NA	West Virginia**	NA
NA	Wyoming**	NA

District of Columbia	16.7

Source: U.S. Department of Health and Human Services, National Center for Health Statistics
"National Vital Statistics Reports" (Vol. 47, No. 19, June 30, 1999)
*Final data. Deaths of infants under 1 year old, exclusive of fetal deaths. Based on race of the mother.
**Not available, fewer than 20 black infant deaths.

Percent Change in White Infant Mortality Rate: 1990 to 1997

National Percent Change = 22.1% Decrease*

ALPHA ORDER

RANK	STATE	PERCENT CHANGE		RANK	STATE	PERCENT CHANGE
6	Alabama	(9.6)		1	Connecticut	(4.5)
19	Alaska	(20.0)		2	West Virginia	(5.2)
16	Arizona	(17.1)		3	Nebraska	(5.6)
5	Arkansas	(7.5)		4	Vermont	(6.2)
39	California	(26.3)		5	Arkansas	(7.5)
21	Colorado	(20.2)		6	Alabama	(9.6)
1	Connecticut	(4.5)		6	Louisiana	(9.6)
28	Delaware	(21.9)		8	Kentucky	(12.5)
35	Florida	(25.0)		9	Kansas	(14.3)
45	Georgia	(33.0)		10	Maine	(14.5)
NA	Hawaii**	NA		11	Rhode Island	(15.7)
22	Idaho	(20.7)		12	Mississippi	(16.5)
13	Illinois	(16.9)		13	Illinois	(16.9)
17	Indiana	(18.0)		13	North Carolina	(16.9)
34	Iowa	(24.4)		13	Texas	(16.9)
9	Kansas	(14.3)		16	Arizona	(17.1)
8	Kentucky	(12.5)		17	Indiana	(18.0)
6	Louisiana	(9.6)		18	Tennessee	(18.8)
10	Maine	(14.5)		19	Alaska	(20.0)
25	Maryland	(21.5)		19	Virginia	(20.0)
37	Massachusetts	(25.4)		21	Colorado	(20.2)
29	Michigan	(22.8)		22	Idaho	(20.7)
33	Minnesota	(23.9)		22	Ohio	(20.7)
12	Mississippi	(16.5)		24	Wisconsin	(20.8)
27	Missouri	(21.8)		25	Maryland	(21.5)
43	Montana	(30.2)		26	Utah	(21.6)
3	Nebraska	(5.6)		27	Missouri	(21.8)
32	Nevada	(23.5)		28	Delaware	(21.9)
49	New Hampshire	(40.3)		29	Michigan	(22.8)
40	New Jersey	(27.9)		30	South Carolina	(22.9)
48	New Mexico	(39.8)		31	Pennsylvania	(23.1)
38	New York	(26.0)		32	Nevada	(23.5)
13	North Carolina	(16.9)		33	Minnesota	(23.9)
36	North Dakota	(25.3)		34	Iowa	(24.4)
22	Ohio	(20.7)		35	Florida	(25.0)
41	Oklahoma	(28.7)		36	North Dakota	(25.3)
42	Oregon	(29.6)		37	Massachusetts	(25.4)
31	Pennsylvania	(23.1)		38	New York	(26.0)
11	Rhode Island	(15.7)		39	California	(26.3)
30	South Carolina	(22.9)		40	New Jersey	(27.9)
47	South Dakota	(38.4)		41	Oklahoma	(28.7)
18	Tennessee	(18.8)		42	Oregon	(29.6)
13	Texas	(16.9)		43	Montana	(30.2)
26	Utah	(21.6)		44	Washington	(30.3)
4	Vermont	(6.2)		45	Georgia	(33.0)
19	Virginia	(20.0)		46	Wyoming	(36.4)
44	Washington	(30.3)		47	South Dakota	(38.4)
2	West Virginia	(5.2)		48	New Mexico	(39.8)
24	Wisconsin	(20.8)		49	New Hampshire	(40.3)
46	Wyoming	(36.4)		NA	Hawaii**	NA
					District of Columbia**	NA

Source: Morgan Quitno Press using data from US Dept of Health & Human Services, National Center for Health Statistics "National Vital Statistics Reports" (Vol. 47, No. 19, June 30, 1999) and "Vital Statistics of the United States"
Final data. Deaths of infants under 1 year old, exclusive of fetal deaths. Based on race of the mother.
**Not available, fewer than 20 white infant deaths.*

Percent Change in Black Infant Mortality Rate: 1990 to 1997

National Percent Change = 16.5% Decrease*

RANK	STATE	PERCENT CHANGE
19	Alabama	(12.6)
NA	Alaska**	NA
20	Arizona	(13.8)
6	Arkansas	1.5
16	California	(7.7)
9	Colorado	(1.2)
18	Connecticut	(10.6)
34	Delaware	(25.3)
32	Florida	(24.1)
31	Georgia	(23.3)
NA	Hawaii**	NA
NA	Idaho**	NA
27	Illinois	(20.5)
9	Indiana	(1.2)
7	Iowa	1.1
3	Kansas	11.0
26	Kentucky	(19.1)
24	Louisiana	(16.4)
NA	Maine**	NA
8	Maryland	(0.6)
22	Massachusetts	(15.4)
25	Michigan	(16.7)
23	Minnesota	(16.2)
15	Mississippi	(7.5)
13	Missouri	(6.9)
NA	Montana**	NA
1	Nebraska	14.3
4	Nevada	8.8
NA	New Hampshire**	NA
29	New Jersey	(22.5)
NA	New Mexico**	NA
35	New York	(37.0)
11	North Carolina	(1.9)
NA	North Dakota**	NA
21	Ohio	(14.8)
2	Oklahoma	13.6
NA	Oregon**	NA
12	Pennsylvania	(6.4)
NA	Rhode Island**	NA
17	South Carolina	(9.9)
NA	South Dakota**	NA
13	Tennessee	(6.9)
28	Texas	(21.6)
NA	Utah**	NA
NA	Vermont**	NA
33	Virginia	(24.5)
5	Washington	6.2
NA	West Virginia**	NA
30	Wisconsin	(23.2)
NA	Wyoming**	NA

RANK	STATE	PERCENT CHANGE
1	Nebraska	14.3
2	Oklahoma	13.6
3	Kansas	11.0
4	Nevada	8.8
5	Washington	6.2
6	Arkansas	1.5
7	Iowa	1.1
8	Maryland	(0.6)
9	Colorado	(1.2)
9	Indiana	(1.2)
11	North Carolina	(1.9)
12	Pennsylvania	(6.4)
13	Missouri	(6.9)
13	Tennessee	(6.9)
15	Mississippi	(7.5)
16	California	(7.7)
17	South Carolina	(9.9)
18	Connecticut	(10.6)
19	Alabama	(12.6)
20	Arizona	(13.8)
21	Ohio	(14.8)
22	Massachusetts	(15.4)
23	Minnesota	(16.2)
24	Louisiana	(16.4)
25	Michigan	(16.7)
26	Kentucky	(19.1)
27	Illinois	(20.5)
28	Texas	(21.6)
29	New Jersey	(22.5)
30	Wisconsin	(23.2)
31	Georgia	(23.3)
32	Florida	(24.1)
33	Virginia	(24.5)
34	Delaware	(25.3)
35	New York	(37.0)
NA	Alaska**	NA
NA	Hawaii**	NA
NA	Idaho**	NA
NA	Maine**	NA
NA	Montana**	NA
NA	New Hampshire**	NA
NA	New Mexico**	NA
NA	North Dakota**	NA
NA	Oregon**	NA
NA	Rhode Island**	NA
NA	South Dakota**	NA
NA	Utah**	NA
NA	Vermont**	NA
NA	West Virginia**	NA
NA	Wyoming**	NA

District of Columbia (31.6)

Source: Morgan Quitno Press using data from US Dept of Health & Human Services, National Center for Health Statistics "National Vital Statistics Reports" (Vol. 47, No. 19, June 30, 1999) and "Vital Statistics of the United States"
Final data. Deaths of infants under 1 year old, exclusive of fetal deaths. Based on race of the mother.
***Not available, fewer than 20 black infant deaths.*

Neonatal Deaths in 1997

National Total = 18,524 Deaths*

ALPHA ORDER

RANK	STATE	DEATHS	% of USA
17	Alabama	375	2.0%
47	Alaska	35	0.2%
20	Arizona	343	1.9%
30	Arkansas	189	1.0%
1	California	2,063	11.1%
24	Colorado	265	1.4%
27	Connecticut	241	1.3%
42	Delaware	53	0.3%
5	Florida	894	4.8%
9	Georgia	706	3.8%
40	Hawaii	73	0.4%
39	Idaho	79	0.4%
4	Illinois	1,017	5.5%
14	Indiana	439	2.4%
34	Iowa	148	0.8%
31	Kansas	176	1.0%
28	Kentucky	240	1.3%
15	Louisiana	409	2.2%
43	Maine	46	0.2%
13	Maryland	442	2.4%
21	Massachusetts	323	1.7%
8	Michigan	754	4.1%
26	Minnesota	242	1.3%
23	Mississippi	271	1.5%
19	Missouri	352	1.9%
45	Montana	41	0.2%
36	Nebraska	124	0.7%
37	Nevada	105	0.6%
43	New Hampshire	46	0.2%
11	New Jersey	511	2.8%
38	New Mexico	88	0.5%
3	New York	1,204	6.5%
10	North Carolina	692	3.7%
48	North Dakota	30	0.2%
6	Ohio	794	4.3%
29	Oklahoma	220	1.2%
32	Oregon	157	0.8%
7	Pennsylvania	763	4.1%
41	Rhode Island	69	0.4%
18	South Carolina	359	1.9%
46	South Dakota	39	0.2%
16	Tennessee	380	2.1%
2	Texas	1,257	6.8%
33	Utah	153	0.8%
49	Vermont	28	0.2%
12	Virginia	505	2.7%
25	Washington	263	1.4%
35	West Virginia	133	0.7%
22	Wisconsin	291	1.6%
50	Wyoming	20	0.1%

RANK ORDER

RANK	STATE	DEATHS	% of USA
1	California	2,063	11.1%
2	Texas	1,257	6.8%
3	New York	1,204	6.5%
4	Illinois	1,017	5.5%
5	Florida	894	4.8%
6	Ohio	794	4.3%
7	Pennsylvania	763	4.1%
8	Michigan	754	4.1%
9	Georgia	706	3.8%
10	North Carolina	692	3.7%
11	New Jersey	511	2.8%
12	Virginia	505	2.7%
13	Maryland	442	2.4%
14	Indiana	439	2.4%
15	Louisiana	409	2.2%
16	Tennessee	380	2.1%
17	Alabama	375	2.0%
18	South Carolina	359	1.9%
19	Missouri	352	1.9%
20	Arizona	343	1.9%
21	Massachusetts	323	1.7%
22	Wisconsin	291	1.6%
23	Mississippi	271	1.5%
24	Colorado	265	1.4%
25	Washington	263	1.4%
26	Minnesota	242	1.3%
27	Connecticut	241	1.3%
28	Kentucky	240	1.3%
29	Oklahoma	220	1.2%
30	Arkansas	189	1.0%
31	Kansas	176	1.0%
32	Oregon	157	0.8%
33	Utah	153	0.8%
34	Iowa	148	0.8%
35	West Virginia	133	0.7%
36	Nebraska	124	0.7%
37	Nevada	105	0.6%
38	New Mexico	88	0.5%
39	Idaho	79	0.4%
40	Hawaii	73	0.4%
41	Rhode Island	69	0.4%
42	Delaware	53	0.3%
43	Maine	46	0.2%
43	New Hampshire	46	0.2%
45	Montana	41	0.2%
46	South Dakota	39	0.2%
47	Alaska	35	0.2%
48	North Dakota	30	0.2%
49	Vermont	28	0.2%
50	Wyoming	20	0.1%
	District of Columbia	77	0.4%

Source: U.S. Department of Health and Human Services, National Center for Health Statistics
"National Vital Statistics Reports" (Vol. 47, No. 19, June 30, 1999)
*Final data. Deaths of infants under 28 days, exclusive of fetal deaths.

Neonatal Death Rate in 1997

National Rate = 4.8 Deaths per 1,000 Live Births*

RANK	STATE	RATE		RANK	STATE	RATE
6	Alabama	6.2		1	South Carolina	6.9
45	Alaska	3.5		2	Mississippi	6.5
27	Arizona	4.5		2	North Carolina	6.5
17	Arkansas	5.2		4	West Virginia	6.4
36	California	3.9		5	Maryland	6.3
22	Colorado	4.7		6	Alabama	6.2
9	Connecticut	5.6		6	Louisiana	6.2
17	Delaware	5.2		8	Georgia	6.0
25	Florida	4.6		9	Connecticut	5.6
8	Georgia	6.0		9	Illinois	5.6
32	Hawaii	4.2		9	Michigan	5.6
31	Idaho	4.3		12	Rhode Island	5.5
9	Illinois	5.6		12	Virginia	5.5
14	Indiana	5.3		14	Indiana	5.3
34	Iowa	4.0		14	Nebraska	5.3
22	Kansas	4.7		14	Pennsylvania	5.3
27	Kentucky	4.5		17	Arkansas	5.2
6	Louisiana	6.2		17	Delaware	5.2
46	Maine	3.4		17	Ohio	5.2
5	Maryland	6.3		20	Tennessee	5.1
34	Massachusetts	4.0		21	Missouri	4.8
9	Michigan	5.6		22	Colorado	4.7
38	Minnesota	3.8		22	Kansas	4.7
2	Mississippi	6.5		22	New York	4.7
21	Missouri	4.8		25	Florida	4.6
38	Montana	3.8		25	Oklahoma	4.6
14	Nebraska	5.3		27	Arizona	4.5
36	Nevada	3.9		27	Kentucky	4.5
49	New Hampshire	3.2		27	New Jersey	4.5
27	New Jersey	4.5		30	Wisconsin	4.4
48	New Mexico	3.3		31	Idaho	4.3
22	New York	4.7		32	Hawaii	4.2
2	North Carolina	6.5		32	Vermont	4.2
42	North Dakota	3.6		34	Iowa	4.0
17	Ohio	5.2		34	Massachusetts	4.0
25	Oklahoma	4.6		36	California	3.9
42	Oregon	3.6		36	Nevada	3.9
14	Pennsylvania	5.3		38	Minnesota	3.8
12	Rhode Island	5.5		38	Montana	3.8
1	South Carolina	6.9		38	South Dakota	3.8
38	South Dakota	3.8		38	Texas	3.8
20	Tennessee	5.1		42	North Dakota	3.6
38	Texas	3.8		42	Oregon	3.6
42	Utah	3.6		42	Utah	3.6
32	Vermont	4.2		45	Alaska	3.5
12	Virginia	5.5		46	Maine	3.4
46	Washington	3.4		46	Washington	3.4
4	West Virginia	6.4		48	New Mexico	3.3
30	Wisconsin	4.4		49	New Hampshire	3.2
50	Wyoming	3.1		50	Wyoming	3.1
					District of Columbia	9.7

Source: U.S. Department of Health and Human Services, National Center for Health Statistics
   "National Vital Statistics Reports" (Vol. 47, No. 19, June 30, 1999)
Final data. Deaths of infants under 28 days, exclusive of fetal deaths.

White Neonatal Deaths in 1997

National Total = 12,269 Deaths*

<u>ALPHA ORDER</u>

RANK	STATE	DEATHS	% of USA
22	Alabama	193	1.6%
48	Alaska	20	0.2%
13	Arizona	295	2.4%
34	Arkansas	117	1.0%
1	California	1,584	12.9%
16	Colorado	234	1.9%
24	Connecticut	176	1.4%
46	Delaware	27	0.2%
6	Florida	525	4.3%
11	Georgia	317	2.6%
50	Hawaii	9	0.1%
38	Idaho	78	0.6%
4	Illinois	607	4.9%
10	Indiana	350	2.9%
32	Iowa	133	1.1%
31	Kansas	139	1.1%
21	Kentucky	206	1.7%
25	Louisiana	159	1.3%
41	Maine	46	0.4%
27	Maryland	156	1.3%
15	Massachusetts	268	2.2%
8	Michigan	461	3.8%
23	Minnesota	189	1.5%
36	Mississippi	97	0.8%
17	Missouri	233	1.9%
43	Montana	36	0.3%
35	Nebraska	103	0.8%
37	Nevada	83	0.7%
42	New Hampshire	45	0.4%
12	New Jersey	313	2.6%
39	New Mexico	70	0.6%
3	New York	748	6.1%
9	North Carolina	363	3.0%
44	North Dakota	29	0.2%
5	Ohio	567	4.6%
26	Oklahoma	158	1.3%
29	Oregon	147	1.2%
7	Pennsylvania	496	4.0%
40	Rhode Island	60	0.5%
27	South Carolina	156	1.3%
46	South Dakota	27	0.2%
20	Tennessee	219	1.8%
2	Texas	985	8.0%
29	Utah	147	1.2%
45	Vermont	28	0.2%
14	Virginia	279	2.3%
19	Washington	220	1.8%
33	West Virginia	122	1.0%
18	Wisconsin	227	1.9%
49	Wyoming	17	0.1%

<u>RANK ORDER</u>

RANK	STATE	DEATHS	% of USA
1	California	1,584	12.9%
2	Texas	985	8.0%
3	New York	748	6.1%
4	Illinois	607	4.9%
5	Ohio	567	4.6%
6	Florida	525	4.3%
7	Pennsylvania	496	4.0%
8	Michigan	461	3.8%
9	North Carolina	363	3.0%
10	Indiana	350	2.9%
11	Georgia	317	2.6%
12	New Jersey	313	2.6%
13	Arizona	295	2.4%
14	Virginia	279	2.3%
15	Massachusetts	268	2.2%
16	Colorado	234	1.9%
17	Missouri	233	1.9%
18	Wisconsin	227	1.9%
19	Washington	220	1.8%
20	Tennessee	219	1.8%
21	Kentucky	206	1.7%
22	Alabama	193	1.6%
23	Minnesota	189	1.5%
24	Connecticut	176	1.4%
25	Louisiana	159	1.3%
26	Oklahoma	158	1.3%
27	Maryland	156	1.3%
27	South Carolina	156	1.3%
29	Oregon	147	1.2%
29	Utah	147	1.2%
31	Kansas	139	1.1%
32	Iowa	133	1.1%
33	West Virginia	122	1.0%
34	Arkansas	117	1.0%
35	Nebraska	103	0.8%
36	Mississippi	97	0.8%
37	Nevada	83	0.7%
38	Idaho	78	0.6%
39	New Mexico	70	0.6%
40	Rhode Island	60	0.5%
41	Maine	46	0.4%
42	New Hampshire	45	0.4%
43	Montana	36	0.3%
44	North Dakota	29	0.2%
45	Vermont	28	0.2%
46	Delaware	27	0.2%
46	South Dakota	27	0.2%
48	Alaska	20	0.2%
49	Wyoming	17	0.1%
50	Hawaii	9	0.1%
	District of Columbia	5	0.0%

Source: U.S. Department of Health and Human Services, National Center for Health Statistics
"National Vital Statistics Reports" (Vol. 47, No. 19, June 30, 1999)
*Final data. Deaths of infants under 28 days, exclusive of fetal deaths. Based on race of the mother.

White Neonatal Death Rate in 1997

National Rate = 4.0 White Neonatal Deaths per 1,000 White Live Births*

ALPHA ORDER

RANK	STATE	RATE
4	Alabama	4.8
48	Alaska	3.0
9	Arizona	4.5
18	Arkansas	4.2
33	California	3.7
9	Colorado	4.5
3	Connecticut	4.9
36	Delaware	3.6
36	Florida	3.6
18	Georgia	4.2
NA	Hawaii**	NA
15	Idaho	4.3
12	Illinois	4.4
4	Indiana	4.8
29	Iowa	3.8
18	Kansas	4.2
15	Kentucky	4.3
18	Louisiana	4.2
40	Maine	3.5
40	Maryland	3.5
27	Massachusetts	3.9
12	Michigan	4.4
43	Minnesota	3.3
12	Mississippi	4.4
29	Missouri	3.8
29	Montana	3.8
4	Nebraska	4.8
36	Nevada	3.6
45	New Hampshire	3.2
33	New Jersey	3.7
47	New Mexico	3.1
24	New York	4.1
4	North Carolina	4.8
27	North Dakota	3.9
9	Ohio	4.5
18	Oklahoma	4.2
33	Oregon	3.7
24	Pennsylvania	4.1
2	Rhode Island	5.5
8	South Carolina	4.7
45	South Dakota	3.2
29	Tennessee	3.8
40	Texas	3.5
36	Utah	3.6
15	Vermont	4.3
18	Virginia	4.2
43	Washington	3.3
1	West Virginia	6.1
26	Wisconsin	4.0
NA	Wyoming**	NA

RANK ORDER

RANK	STATE	RATE
1	West Virginia	6.1
2	Rhode Island	5.5
3	Connecticut	4.9
4	Alabama	4.8
4	Indiana	4.8
4	Nebraska	4.8
4	North Carolina	4.8
8	South Carolina	4.7
9	Arizona	4.5
9	Colorado	4.5
9	Ohio	4.5
12	Illinois	4.4
12	Michigan	4.4
12	Mississippi	4.4
15	Idaho	4.3
15	Kentucky	4.3
15	Vermont	4.3
18	Arkansas	4.2
18	Georgia	4.2
18	Kansas	4.2
18	Louisiana	4.2
18	Oklahoma	4.2
18	Virginia	4.2
24	New York	4.1
24	Pennsylvania	4.1
26	Wisconsin	4.0
27	Massachusetts	3.9
27	North Dakota	3.9
29	Iowa	3.8
29	Missouri	3.8
29	Montana	3.8
29	Tennessee	3.8
33	California	3.7
33	New Jersey	3.7
33	Oregon	3.7
36	Delaware	3.6
36	Florida	3.6
36	Nevada	3.6
36	Utah	3.6
40	Maine	3.5
40	Maryland	3.5
40	Texas	3.5
43	Minnesota	3.3
43	Washington	3.3
45	New Hampshire	3.2
45	South Dakota	3.2
47	New Mexico	3.1
48	Alaska	3.0
NA	Hawaii**	NA
NA	Wyoming**	NA
	District of Columbia**	NA

Source: U.S. Department of Health and Human Services, National Center for Health Statistics
     "National Vital Statistics Reports" (Vol. 47, No. 19, June 30, 1999)
*Final data. Deaths of infants under 28 days, exclusive of fetal deaths. Based on race of the mother.
**Not available. Fewer than 20 white neonatal deaths.

Black Neonatal Deaths in 1997

National Total = 5,637 Deaths*

RANK	STATE	DEATHS	% of USA		RANK	STATE	DEATHS	% of USA
16	Alabama	179	3.2%		1	New York	407	7.2%
40	Alaska	3	0.1%		2	Illinois	386	6.8%
31	Arizona	24	0.4%		3	Georgia	385	6.8%
21	Arkansas	72	1.3%		4	Florida	363	6.4%
5	California	329	5.8%		5	California	329	5.8%
30	Colorado	25	0.4%		6	North Carolina	302	5.4%
22	Connecticut	61	1.1%		7	Michigan	282	5.0%
29	Delaware	26	0.5%		8	Maryland	270	4.8%
4	Florida	363	6.4%		9	Pennsylvania	258	4.6%
3	Georgia	385	6.8%		10	Louisiana	246	4.4%
41	Hawaii	2	0.0%		11	Texas	244	4.3%
44	Idaho	0	0.0%		12	Ohio	222	3.9%
2	Illinois	386	6.8%		13	Virginia	215	3.8%
20	Indiana	87	1.5%		14	South Carolina	200	3.5%
35	Iowa	12	0.2%		15	New Jersey	191	3.4%
28	Kansas	30	0.5%		16	Alabama	179	3.2%
26	Kentucky	33	0.6%		17	Mississippi	171	3.0%
10	Louisiana	246	4.4%		18	Tennessee	160	2.8%
44	Maine	0	0.0%		19	Missouri	115	2.0%
8	Maryland	270	4.8%		20	Indiana	87	1.5%
24	Massachusetts	48	0.9%		21	Arkansas	72	1.3%
7	Michigan	282	5.0%		22	Connecticut	61	1.1%
26	Minnesota	33	0.6%		23	Wisconsin	56	1.0%
17	Mississippi	171	3.0%		24	Massachusetts	48	0.9%
19	Missouri	115	2.0%		25	Oklahoma	41	0.7%
44	Montana	0	0.0%		26	Kentucky	33	0.6%
34	Nebraska	17	0.3%		26	Minnesota	33	0.6%
33	Nevada	18	0.3%		28	Kansas	30	0.5%
44	New Hampshire	0	0.0%		29	Delaware	26	0.5%
15	New Jersey	191	3.4%		30	Colorado	25	0.4%
38	New Mexico	6	0.1%		31	Arizona	24	0.4%
1	New York	407	7.2%		32	Washington	23	0.4%
6	North Carolina	302	5.4%		33	Nevada	18	0.3%
44	North Dakota	0	0.0%		34	Nebraska	17	0.3%
12	Ohio	222	3.9%		35	Iowa	12	0.2%
25	Oklahoma	41	0.7%		36	West Virginia	9	0.2%
39	Oregon	4	0.1%		37	Rhode Island	7	0.1%
9	Pennsylvania	258	4.6%		38	New Mexico	6	0.1%
37	Rhode Island	7	0.1%		39	Oregon	4	0.1%
14	South Carolina	200	3.5%		40	Alaska	3	0.1%
41	South Dakota	2	0.0%		41	Hawaii	2	0.0%
18	Tennessee	160	2.8%		41	South Dakota	2	0.0%
11	Texas	244	4.3%		43	Wyoming	1	0.0%
44	Utah	0	0.0%		44	Idaho	0	0.0%
44	Vermont	0	0.0%		44	Maine	0	0.0%
13	Virginia	215	3.8%		44	Montana	0	0.0%
32	Washington	23	0.4%		44	New Hampshire	0	0.0%
36	West Virginia	9	0.2%		44	North Dakota	0	0.0%
23	Wisconsin	56	1.0%		44	Utah	0	0.0%
43	Wyoming	1	0.0%		44	Vermont	0	0.0%
						District of Columbia	72	1.3%

Source: U.S. Department of Health and Human Services, National Center for Health Statistics
"National Vital Statistics Reports" (Vol. 47, No. 19, June 30, 1999)
*Final data. Deaths of infants under 28 days, exclusive of fetal deaths. Based on race of the mother.

Black Neonatal Death Rate in 1997

National Rate = 9.4 Black Neonatal Deaths per 1,000 Black Live Births*

ALPHA ORDER

RANK	STATE	RATE
22	Alabama	9.0
NA	Alaska**	NA
18	Arizona	9.6
19	Arkansas	9.2
24	California	8.8
16	Colorado	9.7
4	Connecticut	11.4
9	Delaware	10.4
27	Florida	8.3
16	Georgia	9.7
NA	Hawaii**	NA
NA	Idaho**	NA
6	Illinois	10.9
12	Indiana	9.9
NA	Iowa**	NA
8	Kansas	10.7
30	Kentucky	7.1
20	Louisiana	9.1
NA	Maine**	NA
2	Maryland	11.8
31	Massachusetts	6.2
3	Michigan	11.6
12	Minnesota	9.9
22	Mississippi	9.0
9	Missouri	10.4
NA	Montana**	NA
NA	Nebraska**	NA
NA	Nevada**	NA
NA	New Hampshire**	NA
20	New Jersey	9.1
NA	New Mexico**	NA
28	New York	7.4
5	North Carolina	11.0
NA	North Dakota**	NA
14	Ohio	9.8
26	Oklahoma	8.6
NA	Oregon**	NA
1	Pennsylvania	12.6
NA	Rhode Island**	NA
6	South Carolina	10.9
NA	South Dakota**	NA
14	Tennessee	9.8
31	Texas	6.2
NA	Utah**	NA
NA	Vermont**	NA
11	Virginia	10.2
29	Washington	7.2
NA	West Virginia**	NA
25	Wisconsin	8.7
NA	Wyoming**	NA

RANK ORDER

RANK	STATE	RATE
1	Pennsylvania	12.6
2	Maryland	11.8
3	Michigan	11.6
4	Connecticut	11.4
5	North Carolina	11.0
6	Illinois	10.9
6	South Carolina	10.9
8	Kansas	10.7
9	Delaware	10.4
9	Missouri	10.4
11	Virginia	10.2
12	Indiana	9.9
12	Minnesota	9.9
14	Ohio	9.8
14	Tennessee	9.8
16	Colorado	9.7
16	Georgia	9.7
18	Arizona	9.6
19	Arkansas	9.2
20	Louisiana	9.1
20	New Jersey	9.1
22	Alabama	9.0
22	Mississippi	9.0
24	California	8.8
25	Wisconsin	8.7
26	Oklahoma	8.6
27	Florida	8.3
28	New York	7.4
29	Washington	7.2
30	Kentucky	7.1
31	Massachusetts	6.2
31	Texas	6.2
NA	Alaska**	NA
NA	Hawaii**	NA
NA	Idaho**	NA
NA	Iowa**	NA
NA	Maine**	NA
NA	Montana**	NA
NA	Nebraska**	NA
NA	Nevada**	NA
NA	New Hampshire**	NA
NA	New Mexico**	NA
NA	North Dakota**	NA
NA	Oregon**	NA
NA	Rhode Island**	NA
NA	South Dakota**	NA
NA	Utah**	NA
NA	Vermont**	NA
NA	West Virginia**	NA
NA	Wyoming**	NA
	District of Columbia	12.4

Source: U.S. Department of Health and Human Services, National Center for Health Statistics
"National Vital Statistics Reports" (Vol. 47, No. 19, June 30, 1999)
*Final data. Deaths of infants under 28 days, exclusive of fetal deaths. Based on race of the mother.
**Not available. Fewer than 20 black neonatal deaths.

Deaths by AIDS Through 1997

National Total = 310,603 Deaths*

ALPHA ORDER

RANK	STATE	DEATHS	% of USA
23	Alabama	2,573	0.8%
46	Alaska	170	0.1%
20	Arizona	3,138	1.0%
32	Arkansas	1,025	0.3%
2	California	52,393	16.9%
21	Colorado	3,102	1.0%
17	Connecticut	3,919	1.3%
36	Delaware	860	0.3%
3	Florida	29,673	9.6%
6	Georgia	10,702	3.4%
34	Hawaii	940	0.3%
44	Idaho	240	0.1%
7	Illinois	10,192	3.3%
24	Indiana	2,378	0.8%
39	Iowa	603	0.2%
33	Kansas	1,003	0.3%
31	Kentucky	1,247	0.4%
15	Louisiana	5,179	1.7%
42	Maine	478	0.2%
9	Maryland	7,902	2.5%
11	Massachusetts	6,267	2.0%
14	Michigan	5,213	1.7%
27	Minnesota	1,728	0.6%
26	Mississippi	1,755	0.6%
19	Missouri	3,398	1.1%
47	Montana	156	0.1%
41	Nebraska	479	0.2%
30	Nevada	1,369	0.4%
43	New Hampshire	328	0.1%
5	New Jersey	18,817	6.1%
35	New Mexico	924	0.3%
1	New York	60,867	19.6%
10	North Carolina	6,398	2.1%
50	North Dakota	61	0.0%
12	Ohio	5,657	1.8%
28	Oklahoma	1,720	0.6%
25	Oregon	2,039	0.7%
8	Pennsylvania	9,517	3.1%
37	Rhode Island	776	0.2%
18	South Carolina	3,753	1.2%
48	South Dakota	88	0.0%
22	Tennessee	3,049	1.0%
4	Texas	21,262	6.8%
38	Utah	610	0.2%
45	Vermont	181	0.1%
13	Virginia	5,353	1.7%
16	Washington	4,132	1.3%
40	West Virginia	480	0.2%
29	Wisconsin	1,602	0.5%
49	Wyoming	78	0.0%

RANK ORDER

RANK	STATE	DEATHS	% of USA
1	New York	60,867	19.6%
2	California	52,393	16.9%
3	Florida	29,673	9.6%
4	Texas	21,262	6.8%
5	New Jersey	18,817	6.1%
6	Georgia	10,702	3.4%
7	Illinois	10,192	3.3%
8	Pennsylvania	9,517	3.1%
9	Maryland	7,902	2.5%
10	North Carolina	6,398	2.1%
11	Massachusetts	6,267	2.0%
12	Ohio	5,657	1.8%
13	Virginia	5,353	1.7%
14	Michigan	5,213	1.7%
15	Louisiana	5,179	1.7%
16	Washington	4,132	1.3%
17	Connecticut	3,919	1.3%
18	South Carolina	3,753	1.2%
19	Missouri	3,398	1.1%
20	Arizona	3,138	1.0%
21	Colorado	3,102	1.0%
22	Tennessee	3,049	1.0%
23	Alabama	2,573	0.8%
24	Indiana	2,378	0.8%
25	Oregon	2,039	0.7%
26	Mississippi	1,755	0.6%
27	Minnesota	1,728	0.6%
28	Oklahoma	1,720	0.6%
29	Wisconsin	1,602	0.5%
30	Nevada	1,369	0.4%
31	Kentucky	1,247	0.4%
32	Arkansas	1,025	0.3%
33	Kansas	1,003	0.3%
34	Hawaii	940	0.3%
35	New Mexico	924	0.3%
36	Delaware	860	0.3%
37	Rhode Island	776	0.2%
38	Utah	610	0.2%
39	Iowa	603	0.2%
40	West Virginia	480	0.2%
41	Nebraska	479	0.2%
42	Maine	478	0.2%
43	New Hampshire	328	0.1%
44	Idaho	240	0.1%
45	Vermont	181	0.1%
46	Alaska	170	0.1%
47	Montana	156	0.1%
48	South Dakota	88	0.0%
49	Wyoming	78	0.0%
50	North Dakota	61	0.0%
	District of Columbia	4,829	1.6%

Source: U.S. Department of Health and Human Services, National Center for Health Statistics
   (http://wonder.cdc.gov/WONDER/)
*Cumulative deaths through 1997. However, due to reporting delays, these totals should increase. AIDS is Acquired Immunodeficiency Syndrome. The definition of what is AIDS was expanded in 1985, 1987 and 1993. Of these deaths, 266,267 were male and 44,336 were female.

Deaths by AIDS in 1997

National Total = 16,516 Deaths*

RANK	STATE	DEATHS	% of USA
19	Alabama	195	1.2%
45	Alaska	10	0.1%
21	Arizona	162	1.0%
32	Arkansas	66	0.4%
3	California	1,864	11.3%
25	Colorado	125	0.8%
18	Connecticut	201	1.2%
33	Delaware	60	0.4%
2	Florida	1,881	11.4%
6	Georgia	740	4.5%
37	Hawaii	36	0.2%
44	Idaho	12	0.1%
9	Illinois	517	3.1%
23	Indiana	155	0.9%
41	Iowa	26	0.2%
34	Kansas	45	0.3%
30	Kentucky	74	0.4%
11	Louisiana	401	2.4%
40	Maine	27	0.2%
7	Maryland	589	3.6%
49	Massachusetts	4	0.0%
13	Michigan	316	1.9%
31	Minnesota	68	0.4%
22	Mississippi	156	0.9%
24	Missouri	147	0.9%
45	Montana	10	0.1%
38	Nebraska	31	0.2%
27	Nevada	88	0.5%
43	New Hampshire	14	0.1%
5	New Jersey	1,003	6.1%
35	New Mexico	44	0.3%
1	New York	2,910	17.6%
10	North Carolina	488	3.0%
48	North Dakota	5	0.0%
15	Ohio	286	1.7%
26	Oklahoma	110	0.7%
28	Oregon	80	0.5%
8	Pennsylvania	574	3.5%
36	Rhode Island	41	0.2%
14	South Carolina	315	1.9%
47	South Dakota	7	0.0%
16	Tennessee	277	1.7%
4	Texas	1,199	7.3%
42	Utah	25	0.2%
17	Vermont	244	1.5%
12	Virginia	331	2.0%
20	Washington	174	1.1%
38	West Virginia	31	0.2%
28	Wisconsin	80	0.5%
50	Wyoming	1	0.0%

RANK	STATE	DEATHS	% of USA
1	New York	2,910	17.6%
2	Florida	1,881	11.4%
3	California	1,864	11.3%
4	Texas	1,199	7.3%
5	New Jersey	1,003	6.1%
6	Georgia	740	4.5%
7	Maryland	589	3.6%
8	Pennsylvania	574	3.5%
9	Illinois	517	3.1%
10	North Carolina	488	3.0%
11	Louisiana	401	2.4%
12	Virginia	331	2.0%
13	Michigan	316	1.9%
14	South Carolina	315	1.9%
15	Ohio	286	1.7%
16	Tennessee	277	1.7%
17	Vermont	244	1.5%
18	Connecticut	201	1.2%
19	Alabama	195	1.2%
20	Washington	174	1.1%
21	Arizona	162	1.0%
22	Mississippi	156	0.9%
23	Indiana	155	0.9%
24	Missouri	147	0.9%
25	Colorado	125	0.8%
26	Oklahoma	110	0.7%
27	Nevada	88	0.5%
28	Oregon	80	0.5%
28	Wisconsin	80	0.5%
30	Kentucky	74	0.4%
31	Minnesota	68	0.4%
32	Arkansas	66	0.4%
33	Delaware	60	0.4%
34	Kansas	45	0.3%
35	New Mexico	44	0.3%
36	Rhode Island	41	0.2%
37	Hawaii	36	0.2%
38	Nebraska	31	0.2%
38	West Virginia	31	0.2%
40	Maine	27	0.2%
41	Iowa	26	0.2%
42	Utah	25	0.2%
43	New Hampshire	14	0.1%
44	Idaho	12	0.1%
45	Alaska	10	0.1%
45	Montana	10	0.1%
47	South Dakota	7	0.0%
48	North Dakota	5	0.0%
49	Massachusetts	4	0.0%
50	Wyoming	1	0.0%
	District of Columbia	271	1.6%

Source: U.S. Department of Health and Human Services, National Center for Health Statistics
"National Vital Statistics Reports" (Vol. 47, No. 19, June 30, 1999)
*AIDS is Acquired Immunodeficiency Syndrome. It is a specific group of diseases or conditions which are indicative of severe immunosuppression related to infection with the Human Immunodeficiency Virus (HIV).

Death Rate by AIDS in 1997

National Rate = 6.2 Deaths per 100,000 Population*

ALPHA ORDER					RANK ORDER			
RANK	STATE		RATE	% of USA	RANK	STATE	RATE	% of USA
18	Alabama		4.5	0.0%	1	New York	16.0	0.0%
NA	Alaska**		NA	0.0%	2	Florida	12.8	0.0%
22	Arizona		3.6	0.0%	3	New Jersey	12.5	0.0%
29	Arkansas		2.6	0.0%	4	Maryland	11.6	0.0%
12	California		5.8	0.0%	5	Georgia	9.9	0.0%
24	Colorado		3.2	0.0%	6	Louisiana	9.2	0.0%
11	Connecticut		6.1	0.0%	7	South Carolina	8.4	0.0%
8	Delaware		8.2	0.0%	8	Delaware	8.2	0.0%
2	Florida		12.8	0.0%	9	North Carolina	6.6	0.0%
5	Georgia		9.9	0.0%	10	Texas	6.2	0.0%
27	Hawaii		3.0	0.0%	11	Connecticut	6.1	0.0%
NA	Idaho**		NA	0.0%	12	California	5.8	0.0%
19	Illinois		4.3	0.0%	13	Mississippi	5.7	0.0%
29	Indiana		2.6	0.0%	14	Nevada	5.2	0.0%
42	Iowa		0.9	0.0%	14	Tennessee	5.2	0.0%
37	Kansas		1.7	0.0%	16	Virginia	4.9	0.0%
35	Kentucky		1.9	0.0%	17	Pennsylvania	4.8	0.0%
6	Louisiana		9.2	0.0%	18	Alabama	4.5	0.0%
34	Maine		2.2	0.0%	19	Illinois	4.3	0.0%
4	Maryland		11.6	0.0%	20	Rhode Island	4.2	0.0%
21	Massachusetts		4.0	0.0%	21	Massachusetts	4.0	0.0%
24	Michigan		3.2	0.0%	22	Arizona	3.6	0.0%
39	Minnesota		1.5	0.0%	23	Oklahoma	3.3	0.0%
13	Mississippi		5.7	0.0%	24	Colorado	3.2	0.0%
28	Missouri		2.7	0.0%	24	Michigan	3.2	0.0%
NA	Montana**		NA	0.0%	26	Washington	3.1	0.0%
35	Nebraska		1.9	0.0%	27	Hawaii	3.0	0.0%
14	Nevada		5.2	0.0%	28	Missouri	2.7	0.0%
NA	New Hampshire**		NA	0.0%	29	Arkansas	2.6	0.0%
3	New Jersey		12.5	0.0%	29	Indiana	2.6	0.0%
32	New Mexico		2.5	0.0%	29	Ohio	2.6	0.0%
1	New York		16.0	0.0%	32	New Mexico	2.5	0.0%
9	North Carolina		6.6	0.0%	32	Oregon	2.5	0.0%
NA	North Dakota**		NA	0.0%	34	Maine	2.2	0.0%
29	Ohio		2.6	0.0%	35	Kentucky	1.9	0.0%
23	Oklahoma		3.3	0.0%	35	Nebraska	1.9	0.0%
32	Oregon		2.5	0.0%	37	Kansas	1.7	0.0%
17	Pennsylvania		4.8	0.0%	37	West Virginia	1.7	0.0%
20	Rhode Island		4.2	0.0%	39	Minnesota	1.5	0.0%
7	South Carolina		8.4	0.0%	39	Wisconsin	1.5	0.0%
NA	South Dakota**		NA	0.0%	41	Utah	1.2	0.0%
14	Tennessee		5.2	0.0%	42	Iowa	0.9	0.0%
10	Texas		6.2	0.0%	NA	Alaska**	NA	0.0%
41	Utah		1.2	0.0%	NA	Idaho**	NA	0.0%
NA	Vermont**		NA	0.0%	NA	Montana**	NA	0.0%
16	Virginia		4.9	0.0%	NA	New Hampshire**	NA	0.0%
26	Washington		3.1	0.0%	NA	North Dakota**	NA	0.0%
37	West Virginia		1.7	0.0%	NA	South Dakota**	NA	0.0%
39	Wisconsin		1.5	0.0%	NA	Vermont**	NA	0.0%
NA	Wyoming**		NA	0.0%	NA	Wyoming**	NA	0.0%
						District of Columbia	51.2	0.0%

Source: U.S. Department of Health and Human Services, National Center for Health Statistics
    "National Vital Statistics Reports" (Vol. 47, No. 19, June 30, 1999)
*AIDS is Acquired Immunodeficiency Syndrome. It is a specific group of diseases or conditions which are indicative
of severe immunosuppression related to infection with the Human Immunodeficiency Virus (HIV). Not age-adjusted.
**Insufficient data to determine a reliable rate.

Age-Adjusted Death Rate by AIDS in 1997

National Rate = 5.8 Deaths per 100,000 Population*

ALPHA ORDER			RANK ORDER		
RANK	STATE	RATE	RANK	STATE	RATE
17	Alabama	4.4	1	New York	14.8
NA	Alaska**	NA	2	Florida	12.8
21	Arizona	3.6	3	New Jersey	11.4
28	Arkansas	2.7	4	Maryland	10.1
13	California	5.4	5	Louisiana	9.2
25	Colorado	2.9	6	Georgia	9.0
11	Connecticut	5.7	7	South Carolina	7.9
8	Delaware	7.2	8	Delaware	7.2
2	Florida	12.8	9	North Carolina	6.2
6	Georgia	9.0	10	Texas	6.0
27	Hawaii	2.8	11	Connecticut	5.7
NA	Idaho**	NA	11	Mississippi	5.7
19	Illinois	4.1	13	California	5.4
30	Indiana	2.5	14	Nevada	4.9
42	Iowa	1.0	14	Tennessee	4.9
37	Kansas	1.7	16	Pennsylvania	4.5
36	Kentucky	1.8	17	Alabama	4.4
5	Louisiana	9.2	17	Virginia	4.4
34	Maine	2.1	19	Illinois	4.1
4	Maryland	10.1	20	Rhode Island	4.0
22	Massachusetts	3.5	21	Arizona	3.6
24	Michigan	3.0	22	Massachusetts	3.5
41	Minnesota	1.3	23	Oklahoma	3.3
11	Mississippi	5.7	24	Michigan	3.0
28	Missouri	2.7	25	Colorado	2.9
NA	Montana**	NA	25	Washington	2.9
35	Nebraska	1.9	27	Hawaii	2.8
14	Nevada	4.9	28	Arkansas	2.7
NA	New Hampshire**	NA	28	Missouri	2.7
3	New Jersey	11.4	30	Indiana	2.5
30	New Mexico	2.5	30	New Mexico	2.5
1	New York	14.8	30	Ohio	2.5
9	North Carolina	6.2	33	Oregon	2.3
NA	North Dakota**	NA	34	Maine	2.1
30	Ohio	2.5	35	Nebraska	1.9
23	Oklahoma	3.3	36	Kentucky	1.8
33	Oregon	2.3	37	Kansas	1.7
16	Pennsylvania	4.5	37	West Virginia	1.7
20	Rhode Island	4.0	39	Wisconsin	1.5
7	South Carolina	7.9	40	Utah	1.4
NA	South Dakota**	NA	41	Minnesota	1.3
14	Tennessee	4.9	42	Iowa	1.0
10	Texas	6.0	NA	Alaska**	NA
40	Utah	1.4	NA	Idaho**	NA
NA	Vermont**	NA	NA	Montana**	NA
17	Virginia	4.4	NA	New Hampshire**	NA
25	Washington	2.9	NA	North Dakota**	NA
37	West Virginia	1.7	NA	South Dakota**	NA
39	Wisconsin	1.5	NA	Vermont**	NA
NA	Wyoming**	NA	NA	Wyoming**	NA
				District of Columbia	45.0

Source: U.S. Department of Health and Human Services, National Center for Health Statistics
"National Vital Statistics Reports" (Vol. 47, No. 19, June 30, 1999)

*AIDS is Acquired Immunodeficiency Syndrome. It is a specific group of diseases or conditions which are indicative of severe immunosuppression related to infection with the Human Immunodeficiency Virus (HIV).

**Insufficient data to determine a reliable rate.

Estimated Deaths by Cancer in 2000

National Total = 552,200 Deaths

ALPHA ORDER

RANK	STATE	DEATHS	% of USA
20	Alabama	9,700	1.8%
50	Alaska	700	0.1%
23	Arizona	9,200	1.7%
30	Arkansas	6,200	1.1%
1	California	51,200	9.3%
31	Colorado	6,100	1.1%
28	Connecticut	7,000	1.3%
45	Delaware	1,800	0.3%
2	Florida	39,900	7.2%
12	Georgia	13,300	2.4%
43	Hawaii	2,000	0.4%
42	Idaho	2,100	0.4%
7	Illinois	24,900	4.5%
14	Indiana	12,600	2.3%
29	Iowa	6,400	1.2%
33	Kansas	5,400	1.0%
22	Kentucky	9,300	1.7%
21	Louisiana	9,400	1.7%
37	Maine	3,100	0.6%
19	Maryland	10,200	1.8%
11	Massachusetts	13,600	2.5%
8	Michigan	20,000	3.6%
24	Minnesota	9,000	1.6%
32	Mississippi	6,000	1.1%
16	Missouri	12,200	2.2%
44	Montana	1,900	0.3%
36	Nebraska	3,300	0.6%
35	Nevada	3,800	0.7%
39	New Hampshire	2,500	0.5%
9	New Jersey	18,100	3.3%
38	New Mexico	3,000	0.5%
3	New York	36,900	6.7%
10	North Carolina	16,200	2.9%
47	North Dakota	1,300	0.2%
6	Ohio	25,400	4.6%
26	Oklahoma	7,300	1.3%
27	Oregon	7,100	1.3%
5	Pennsylvania	30,100	5.5%
40	Rhode Island	2,400	0.4%
25	South Carolina	8,200	1.5%
46	South Dakota	1,600	0.3%
15	Tennessee	12,400	2.2%
4	Texas	34,400	6.2%
41	Utah	2,300	0.4%
48	Vermont	1,200	0.2%
12	Virginia	13,300	2.4%
17	Washington	10,700	1.9%
34	West Virginia	4,800	0.9%
17	Wisconsin	10,700	1.9%
49	Wyoming	900	0.2%

RANK ORDER

RANK	STATE	DEATHS	% of USA
1	California	51,200	9.3%
2	Florida	39,900	7.2%
3	New York	36,900	6.7%
4	Texas	34,400	6.2%
5	Pennsylvania	30,100	5.5%
6	Ohio	25,400	4.6%
7	Illinois	24,900	4.5%
8	Michigan	20,000	3.6%
9	New Jersey	18,100	3.3%
10	North Carolina	16,200	2.9%
11	Massachusetts	13,600	2.5%
12	Georgia	13,300	2.4%
12	Virginia	13,300	2.4%
14	Indiana	12,600	2.3%
15	Tennessee	12,400	2.2%
16	Missouri	12,200	2.2%
17	Washington	10,700	1.9%
17	Wisconsin	10,700	1.9%
19	Maryland	10,200	1.8%
20	Alabama	9,700	1.8%
21	Louisiana	9,400	1.7%
22	Kentucky	9,300	1.7%
23	Arizona	9,200	1.7%
24	Minnesota	9,000	1.6%
25	South Carolina	8,200	1.5%
26	Oklahoma	7,300	1.3%
27	Oregon	7,100	1.3%
28	Connecticut	7,000	1.3%
29	Iowa	6,400	1.2%
30	Arkansas	6,200	1.1%
31	Colorado	6,100	1.1%
32	Mississippi	6,000	1.1%
33	Kansas	5,400	1.0%
34	West Virginia	4,800	0.9%
35	Nevada	3,800	0.7%
36	Nebraska	3,300	0.6%
37	Maine	3,100	0.6%
38	New Mexico	3,000	0.5%
39	New Hampshire	2,500	0.5%
40	Rhode Island	2,400	0.4%
41	Utah	2,300	0.4%
42	Idaho	2,100	0.4%
43	Hawaii	2,000	0.4%
44	Montana	1,900	0.3%
45	Delaware	1,800	0.3%
46	South Dakota	1,600	0.3%
47	North Dakota	1,300	0.2%
48	Vermont	1,200	0.2%
49	Wyoming	900	0.2%
50	Alaska	700	0.1%
	District of Columbia	1,200	0.2%

Source: American Cancer Society
"Cancer Facts & Figures 2000" (Copyright 2000, Reprinted with permission from the American Cancer Society)

Estimated Death Rate by Cancer in 2000

National Estimated Rate = 202.5 Deaths per 100,000 Population*

ALPHA ORDER			RANK ORDER		
RANK	STATE	RATE	RANK	STATE	RATE
14	Alabama	222.0	1	West Virginia	265.6
49	Alaska	113.0	2	Florida	264.0
38	Arizona	192.5	3	Pennsylvania	251.0
5	Arkansas	243.0	4	Maine	247.4
47	California	154.5	5	Arkansas	243.0
48	Colorado	150.4	6	Rhode Island	242.2
22	Connecticut	213.3	7	Delaware	238.9
7	Delaware	238.9	8	Kentucky	234.8
2	Florida	264.0	9	Tennessee	226.1
44	Georgia	170.8	10	Ohio	225.6
45	Hawaii	168.7	11	Missouri	223.1
46	Idaho	167.8	12	Iowa	223.0
28	Illinois	205.3	13	New Jersey	222.3
23	Indiana	212.0	14	Alabama	222.0
12	Iowa	223.0	15	Massachusetts	220.2
31	Kansas	203.5	16	South Dakota	218.2
8	Kentucky	234.8	17	Oklahoma	217.4
20	Louisiana	215.0	18	Mississippi	216.7
4	Maine	247.4	19	Montana	215.2
36	Maryland	197.2	20	Louisiana	215.0
15	Massachusetts	220.2	21	Oregon	214.1
32	Michigan	202.8	22	Connecticut	213.3
39	Minnesota	188.5	23	Indiana	212.0
18	Mississippi	216.7	24	North Carolina	211.7
11	Missouri	223.1	25	South Carolina	211.0
19	Montana	215.2	26	Nevada	210.0
35	Nebraska	198.1	27	New Hampshire	208.1
26	Nevada	210.0	28	Illinois	205.3
27	New Hampshire	208.1	29	North Dakota	205.2
13	New Jersey	222.3	30	Wisconsin	203.8
42	New Mexico	172.4	31	Kansas	203.5
32	New York	202.8	32	Michigan	202.8
24	North Carolina	211.7	32	New York	202.8
29	North Dakota	205.2	34	Vermont	202.1
10	Ohio	225.6	35	Nebraska	198.1
17	Oklahoma	217.4	36	Maryland	197.2
21	Oregon	214.1	37	Virginia	193.5
3	Pennsylvania	251.0	38	Arizona	192.5
6	Rhode Island	242.2	39	Minnesota	188.5
25	South Carolina	211.0	40	Wyoming	187.7
16	South Dakota	218.2	41	Washington	185.9
9	Tennessee	226.1	42	New Mexico	172.4
43	Texas	171.6	43	Texas	171.6
50	Utah	108.0	44	Georgia	170.8
34	Vermont	202.1	45	Hawaii	168.7
37	Virginia	193.5	46	Idaho	167.8
41	Washington	185.9	47	California	154.5
1	West Virginia	265.6	48	Colorado	150.4
30	Wisconsin	203.8	49	Alaska	113.0
40	Wyoming	187.7	50	Utah	108.0
				District of Columbia	231.2

Source: Morgan Quitno Press using data from American Cancer Society
        "Cancer Facts & Figures 2000" (Copyright 2000, Reprinted with permission from the American Cancer Society)
*Rates calculated using 1999 Census resident population estimates. Not age-adjusted.

Estimated Deaths by Female Breast Cancer in 2000

National Estimated Total = 40,800 Deaths

ALPHA ORDER

RANK	STATE	DEATHS	% of USA
21	Alabama	600	1.5%
43	Alaska	100	0.2%
21	Arizona	600	1.5%
30	Arkansas	400	1.0%
1	California	4,000	9.8%
30	Colorado	400	1.0%
26	Connecticut	500	1.2%
43	Delaware	100	0.2%
3	Florida	2,700	6.6%
11	Georgia	1,000	2.5%
43	Hawaii	100	0.2%
36	Idaho	200	0.5%
6	Illinois	2,000	4.9%
14	Indiana	900	2.2%
26	Iowa	500	1.2%
30	Kansas	400	1.0%
21	Kentucky	600	1.5%
19	Louisiana	700	1.7%
36	Maine	200	0.5%
16	Maryland	800	2.0%
11	Massachusetts	1,000	2.5%
8	Michigan	1,500	3.7%
21	Minnesota	600	1.5%
30	Mississippi	400	1.0%
16	Missouri	800	2.0%
43	Montana	100	0.2%
34	Nebraska	300	0.7%
36	Nevada	200	0.5%
36	New Hampshire	200	0.5%
9	New Jersey	1,400	3.4%
36	New Mexico	200	0.5%
2	New York	3,100	7.6%
10	North Carolina	1,200	2.9%
43	North Dakota	100	0.2%
7	Ohio	1,900	4.7%
26	Oklahoma	500	1.2%
26	Oregon	500	1.2%
5	Pennsylvania	2,300	5.6%
36	Rhode Island	200	0.5%
21	South Carolina	600	1.5%
43	South Dakota	100	0.2%
14	Tennessee	900	2.2%
4	Texas	2,600	6.4%
36	Utah	200	0.5%
43	Vermont	100	0.2%
11	Virginia	1,000	2.5%
16	Washington	800	2.0%
34	West Virginia	300	0.7%
19	Wisconsin	700	1.7%
43	Wyoming	100	0.2%

RANK ORDER

RANK	STATE	DEATHS	% of USA
1	California	4,000	9.8%
2	New York	3,100	7.6%
3	Florida	2,700	6.6%
4	Texas	2,600	6.4%
5	Pennsylvania	2,300	5.6%
6	Illinois	2,000	4.9%
7	Ohio	1,900	4.7%
8	Michigan	1,500	3.7%
9	New Jersey	1,400	3.4%
10	North Carolina	1,200	2.9%
11	Georgia	1,000	2.5%
11	Massachusetts	1,000	2.5%
11	Virginia	1,000	2.5%
14	Indiana	900	2.2%
14	Tennessee	900	2.2%
16	Maryland	800	2.0%
16	Missouri	800	2.0%
16	Washington	800	2.0%
19	Louisiana	700	1.7%
19	Wisconsin	700	1.7%
21	Alabama	600	1.5%
21	Arizona	600	1.5%
21	Kentucky	600	1.5%
21	Minnesota	600	1.5%
21	South Carolina	600	1.5%
26	Connecticut	500	1.2%
26	Iowa	500	1.2%
26	Oklahoma	500	1.2%
26	Oregon	500	1.2%
30	Arkansas	400	1.0%
30	Colorado	400	1.0%
30	Kansas	400	1.0%
30	Mississippi	400	1.0%
34	Nebraska	300	0.7%
34	West Virginia	300	0.7%
36	Idaho	200	0.5%
36	Maine	200	0.5%
36	Nevada	200	0.5%
36	New Hampshire	200	0.5%
36	New Mexico	200	0.5%
36	Rhode Island	200	0.5%
36	Utah	200	0.5%
43	Alaska	100	0.2%
43	Delaware	100	0.2%
43	Hawaii	100	0.2%
43	Montana	100	0.2%
43	North Dakota	100	0.2%
43	South Dakota	100	0.2%
43	Vermont	100	0.2%
43	Wyoming	100	0.2%
	District of Columbia	100	0.2%

Source: American Cancer Society
"Cancer Facts & Figures 2000" (Copyright 2000, Reprinted with permission from the American Cancer Society)

Estimated Death Rate by Female Breast Cancer in 2000

National Estimated Rate = 29.5 Deaths per 100,000 Female Population*

ALPHA ORDER				RANK ORDER		
RANK	STATE	RATE		RANK	STATE	RATE
37	Alabama	26.5		1	Wyoming	41.8
6	Alaska	34.3		2	Rhode Island	39.0
42	Arizona	25.4		3	Pennsylvania	36.9
22	Arkansas	30.5		4	Nebraska	35.3
44	California	24.5		5	Florida	35.2
48	Colorado	20.0		6	Alaska	34.3
28	Connecticut	29.7		7	Iowa	34.0
39	Delaware	26.2		8	New Jersey	33.5
5	Florida	35.2		9	Vermont	33.3
41	Georgia	25.5		10	New Hampshire	33.2
50	Hawaii	16.8		11	New York	32.9
13	Idaho	32.5		12	Ohio	32.8
14	Illinois	32.4		13	Idaho	32.5
28	Indiana	29.7		14	Illinois	32.4
7	Iowa	34.0		15	Tennessee	32.0
26	Kansas	29.9		15	West Virginia	32.0
30	Kentucky	29.6		17	Maine	31.4
20	Louisiana	30.9		17	Massachusetts	31.4
17	Maine	31.4		19	North Dakota	31.2
23	Maryland	30.3		20	Louisiana	30.9
17	Massachusetts	31.4		20	North Carolina	30.9
27	Michigan	29.8		22	Arkansas	30.5
43	Minnesota	25.0		23	Maryland	30.3
35	Mississippi	27.9		24	South Carolina	30.2
33	Missouri	28.5		25	Oregon	30.1
47	Montana	22.6		26	Kansas	29.9
4	Nebraska	35.3		27	Michigan	29.8
45	Nevada	23.3		28	Connecticut	29.7
10	New Hampshire	33.2		28	Indiana	29.7
8	New Jersey	33.5		30	Kentucky	29.6
46	New Mexico	22.7		31	Oklahoma	29.2
11	New York	32.9		32	Virginia	28.8
20	North Carolina	30.9		33	Missouri	28.5
19	North Dakota	31.2		34	Washington	28.0
12	Ohio	32.8		35	Mississippi	27.9
31	Oklahoma	29.2		36	South Dakota	26.7
25	Oregon	30.1		37	Alabama	26.5
3	Pennsylvania	36.9		38	Wisconsin	26.3
2	Rhode Island	39.0		39	Delaware	26.2
24	South Carolina	30.2		40	Texas	26.0
36	South Dakota	26.7		41	Georgia	25.5
15	Tennessee	32.0		42	Arizona	25.4
40	Texas	26.0		43	Minnesota	25.0
49	Utah	18.9		44	California	24.5
9	Vermont	33.3		45	Nevada	23.3
32	Virginia	28.8		46	New Mexico	22.7
34	Washington	28.0		47	Montana	22.6
15	West Virginia	32.0		48	Colorado	20.0
38	Wisconsin	26.3		49	Utah	18.9
1	Wyoming	41.8		50	Hawaii	16.8
					District of Columbia	36.0

Source: Morgan Quitno Press using data from American Cancer Society
"Cancer Facts & Figures 2000" (Copyright 2000, Reprinted with permission from the American Cancer Society)
*Rates calculated using 1998 Census resident female population estimates. Not age-adjusted.

Estimated Deaths by Colon and Rectum Cancer in 2000

National Estimated Total = 56,300 Deaths

ALPHA ORDER

RANK	STATE	DEATHS	% of USA
24	Alabama	800	1.4%
49	Alaska	100	0.2%
21	Arizona	900	1.6%
29	Arkansas	600	1.1%
1	California	4,900	8.7%
29	Colorado	600	1.1%
29	Connecticut	600	1.1%
41	Delaware	200	0.4%
3	Florida	3,900	6.9%
15	Georgia	1,200	2.1%
41	Hawaii	200	0.4%
41	Idaho	200	0.4%
7	Illinois	2,600	4.6%
12	Indiana	1,300	2.3%
24	Iowa	800	1.4%
33	Kansas	500	0.9%
21	Kentucky	900	1.6%
19	Louisiana	1,000	1.8%
37	Maine	300	0.5%
17	Maryland	1,100	2.0%
11	Massachusetts	1,500	2.7%
8	Michigan	2,100	3.7%
21	Minnesota	900	1.6%
29	Mississippi	600	1.1%
12	Missouri	1,300	2.3%
41	Montana	200	0.4%
35	Nebraska	400	0.7%
35	Nevada	400	0.7%
37	New Hampshire	300	0.5%
9	New Jersey	2,000	3.6%
37	New Mexico	300	0.5%
2	New York	4,000	7.1%
10	North Carolina	1,600	2.8%
41	North Dakota	200	0.4%
6	Ohio	2,700	4.8%
27	Oklahoma	700	1.2%
27	Oregon	700	1.2%
5	Pennsylvania	3,400	6.0%
37	Rhode Island	300	0.5%
24	South Carolina	800	1.4%
41	South Dakota	200	0.4%
15	Tennessee	1,200	2.1%
4	Texas	3,600	6.4%
41	Utah	200	0.4%
41	Vermont	200	0.4%
12	Virginia	1,300	2.3%
19	Washington	1,000	1.8%
33	West Virginia	500	0.9%
17	Wisconsin	1,100	2.0%
49	Wyoming	100	0.2%

RANK ORDER

RANK	STATE	DEATHS	% of USA
1	California	4,900	8.7%
2	New York	4,000	7.1%
3	Florida	3,900	6.9%
4	Texas	3,600	6.4%
5	Pennsylvania	3,400	6.0%
6	Ohio	2,700	4.8%
7	Illinois	2,600	4.6%
8	Michigan	2,100	3.7%
9	New Jersey	2,000	3.6%
10	North Carolina	1,600	2.8%
11	Massachusetts	1,500	2.7%
12	Indiana	1,300	2.3%
12	Missouri	1,300	2.3%
12	Virginia	1,300	2.3%
15	Georgia	1,200	2.1%
15	Tennessee	1,200	2.1%
17	Maryland	1,100	2.0%
17	Wisconsin	1,100	2.0%
19	Louisiana	1,000	1.8%
19	Washington	1,000	1.8%
21	Arizona	900	1.6%
21	Kentucky	900	1.6%
21	Minnesota	900	1.6%
24	Alabama	800	1.4%
24	Iowa	800	1.4%
24	South Carolina	800	1.4%
27	Oklahoma	700	1.2%
27	Oregon	700	1.2%
29	Arkansas	600	1.1%
29	Colorado	600	1.1%
29	Connecticut	600	1.1%
29	Mississippi	600	1.1%
33	Kansas	500	0.9%
33	West Virginia	500	0.9%
35	Nebraska	400	0.7%
35	Nevada	400	0.7%
37	Maine	300	0.5%
37	New Hampshire	300	0.5%
37	New Mexico	300	0.5%
37	Rhode Island	300	0.5%
41	Delaware	200	0.4%
41	Hawaii	200	0.4%
41	Idaho	200	0.4%
41	Montana	200	0.4%
41	North Dakota	200	0.4%
41	South Dakota	200	0.4%
41	Utah	200	0.4%
41	Vermont	200	0.4%
49	Alaska	100	0.2%
49	Wyoming	100	0.2%
	District of Columbia	100	0.2%

Source: American Cancer Society
"Cancer Facts & Figures 2000" (Copyright 2000, Reprinted with permission from the American Cancer Society)

Estimated Death Rate by Colon and Rectum Cancer in 2000

National Estimated Rate = 20.6 Deaths per 100,000 Population*

ALPHA ORDER

RANK	STATE	RATE
39	Alabama	18.3
45	Alaska	16.1
36	Arizona	18.8
17	Arkansas	23.5
48	California	14.8
48	Colorado	14.8
39	Connecticut	18.3
8	Delaware	26.5
9	Florida	25.8
47	Georgia	15.4
44	Hawaii	16.9
46	Idaho	16.0
26	Illinois	21.4
23	Indiana	21.9
5	Iowa	27.9
36	Kansas	18.8
19	Kentucky	22.7
18	Louisiana	22.9
15	Maine	23.9
27	Maryland	21.3
12	Massachusetts	24.3
27	Michigan	21.3
36	Minnesota	18.8
25	Mississippi	21.7
16	Missouri	23.8
19	Montana	22.7
13	Nebraska	24.0
21	Nevada	22.1
10	New Hampshire	25.0
11	New Jersey	24.6
43	New Mexico	17.2
22	New York	22.0
31	North Carolina	20.9
2	North Dakota	31.6
13	Ohio	24.0
33	Oklahoma	20.8
29	Oregon	21.1
4	Pennsylvania	28.3
3	Rhode Island	30.3
34	South Carolina	20.6
7	South Dakota	27.3
23	Tennessee	21.9
41	Texas	18.0
50	Utah	9.4
1	Vermont	33.7
35	Virginia	18.9
42	Washington	17.4
6	West Virginia	27.7
30	Wisconsin	21.0
31	Wyoming	20.9

RANK ORDER

RANK	STATE	RATE
1	Vermont	33.7
2	North Dakota	31.6
3	Rhode Island	30.3
4	Pennsylvania	28.3
5	Iowa	27.9
6	West Virginia	27.7
7	South Dakota	27.3
8	Delaware	26.5
9	Florida	25.8
10	New Hampshire	25.0
11	New Jersey	24.6
12	Massachusetts	24.3
13	Nebraska	24.0
13	Ohio	24.0
15	Maine	23.9
16	Missouri	23.8
17	Arkansas	23.5
18	Louisiana	22.9
19	Kentucky	22.7
19	Montana	22.7
21	Nevada	22.1
22	New York	22.0
23	Indiana	21.9
23	Tennessee	21.9
25	Mississippi	21.7
26	Illinois	21.4
27	Maryland	21.3
27	Michigan	21.3
29	Oregon	21.1
30	Wisconsin	21.0
31	North Carolina	20.9
31	Wyoming	20.9
33	Oklahoma	20.8
34	South Carolina	20.6
35	Virginia	18.9
36	Arizona	18.8
36	Kansas	18.8
36	Minnesota	18.8
39	Alabama	18.3
39	Connecticut	18.3
41	Texas	18.0
42	Washington	17.4
43	New Mexico	17.2
44	Hawaii	16.9
45	Alaska	16.1
46	Idaho	16.0
47	Georgia	15.4
48	California	14.8
48	Colorado	14.8
50	Utah	9.4
	District of Columbia	19.3

Source: Morgan Quitno Press using data from American Cancer Society
"Cancer Facts & Figures 2000" (Copyright 2000, Reprinted with permission from the American Cancer Society)
Rates calculated using 1999 Census resident population estimates. Not age-adjusted.

Estimated Deaths by Leukemia in 2000

National Estimated Total = 21,700 Deaths

ALPHA ORDER

RANK	STATE	DEATHS	% of USA
22	Alabama	300	1.4%
NA	Alaska*	NA	NA
22	Arizona	300	1.4%
31	Arkansas	200	0.9%
1	California	2,100	9.7%
22	Colorado	300	1.4%
22	Connecticut	300	1.4%
36	Delaware	100	0.5%
2	Florida	1,500	6.9%
11	Georgia	500	2.3%
36	Hawaii	100	0.5%
36	Idaho	100	0.5%
6	Illinois	1,000	4.6%
11	Indiana	500	2.3%
22	Iowa	300	1.4%
31	Kansas	200	0.9%
22	Kentucky	300	1.4%
18	Louisiana	400	1.8%
36	Maine	100	0.5%
18	Maryland	400	1.8%
11	Massachusetts	500	2.3%
9	Michigan	700	3.2%
18	Minnesota	400	1.8%
31	Mississippi	200	0.9%
11	Missouri	500	2.3%
36	Montana	100	0.5%
31	Nebraska	200	0.9%
36	Nevada	100	0.5%
36	New Hampshire	100	0.5%
8	New Jersey	800	3.7%
36	New Mexico	100	0.5%
3	New York	1,400	6.5%
10	North Carolina	600	2.8%
36	North Dakota	100	0.5%
6	Ohio	1,000	4.6%
22	Oklahoma	300	1.4%
22	Oregon	300	1.4%
5	Pennsylvania	1,200	5.5%
36	Rhode Island	100	0.5%
22	South Carolina	300	1.4%
36	South Dakota	100	0.5%
18	Tennessee	400	1.8%
3	Texas	1,400	6.5%
36	Utah	100	0.5%
NA	Vermont*	NA	NA
11	Virginia	500	2.3%
11	Washington	500	2.3%
31	West Virginia	200	0.9%
11	Wisconsin	500	2.3%
NA	Wyoming*	NA	NA

RANK ORDER

RANK	STATE	DEATHS	% of USA
1	California	2,100	9.7%
2	Florida	1,500	6.9%
3	New York	1,400	6.5%
3	Texas	1,400	6.5%
5	Pennsylvania	1,200	5.5%
6	Illinois	1,000	4.6%
6	Ohio	1,000	4.6%
8	New Jersey	800	3.7%
9	Michigan	700	3.2%
10	North Carolina	600	2.8%
11	Georgia	500	2.3%
11	Indiana	500	2.3%
11	Massachusetts	500	2.3%
11	Missouri	500	2.3%
11	Virginia	500	2.3%
11	Washington	500	2.3%
11	Wisconsin	500	2.3%
18	Louisiana	400	1.8%
18	Maryland	400	1.8%
18	Minnesota	400	1.8%
18	Tennessee	400	1.8%
22	Alabama	300	1.4%
22	Arizona	300	1.4%
22	Colorado	300	1.4%
22	Connecticut	300	1.4%
22	Iowa	300	1.4%
22	Kentucky	300	1.4%
22	Oklahoma	300	1.4%
22	Oregon	300	1.4%
22	South Carolina	300	1.4%
31	Arkansas	200	0.9%
31	Kansas	200	0.9%
31	Mississippi	200	0.9%
31	Nebraska	200	0.9%
31	West Virginia	200	0.9%
36	Delaware	100	0.5%
36	Hawaii	100	0.5%
36	Idaho	100	0.5%
36	Maine	100	0.5%
36	Montana	100	0.5%
36	Nevada	100	0.5%
36	New Hampshire	100	0.5%
36	New Mexico	100	0.5%
36	North Dakota	100	0.5%
36	Rhode Island	100	0.5%
36	South Dakota	100	0.5%
36	Utah	100	0.5%
NA	Alaska*	NA	NA
NA	Vermont*	NA	NA
NA	Wyoming*	NA	NA
	District of Columbia*	NA	NA

Source: American Cancer Society
   "Cancer Facts & Figures 2000" (Copyright 2000, Reprinted with permission from the American Cancer Society)
Fewer than 50 deaths.

Estimated Death Rate by Leukemia in 2000

National Estimated Rate = 8.0 Deaths per 100,000 Population*

ALPHA ORDER

RANK	STATE	RATE
41	Alabama	6.9
NA	Alaska**	NA
43	Arizona	6.3
28	Arkansas	7.8
43	California	6.3
35	Colorado	7.4
13	Connecticut	9.1
3	Delaware	13.3
10	Florida	9.9
42	Georgia	6.4
20	Hawaii	8.4
26	Idaho	8.0
24	Illinois	8.2
20	Indiana	8.4
7	Iowa	10.5
34	Kansas	7.5
33	Kentucky	7.6
13	Louisiana	9.1
26	Maine	8.0
30	Maryland	7.7
25	Massachusetts	8.1
39	Michigan	7.1
20	Minnesota	8.4
38	Mississippi	7.2
13	Missouri	9.1
5	Montana	11.3
4	Nebraska	12.0
46	Nevada	5.5
23	New Hampshire	8.3
11	New Jersey	9.8
45	New Mexico	5.7
30	New York	7.7
28	North Carolina	7.8
1	North Dakota	15.8
17	Ohio	8.9
17	Oklahoma	8.9
16	Oregon	9.0
9	Pennsylvania	10.0
8	Rhode Island	10.1
30	South Carolina	7.7
2	South Dakota	13.6
36	Tennessee	7.3
40	Texas	7.0
47	Utah	4.7
NA	Vermont**	NA
36	Virginia	7.3
19	Washington	8.7
6	West Virginia	11.1
12	Wisconsin	9.5
NA	Wyoming**	NA

RANK ORDER

RANK	STATE	RATE
1	North Dakota	15.8
2	South Dakota	13.6
3	Delaware	13.3
4	Nebraska	12.0
5	Montana	11.3
6	West Virginia	11.1
7	Iowa	10.5
8	Rhode Island	10.1
9	Pennsylvania	10.0
10	Florida	9.9
11	New Jersey	9.8
12	Wisconsin	9.5
13	Connecticut	9.1
13	Louisiana	9.1
13	Missouri	9.1
16	Oregon	9.0
17	Ohio	8.9
17	Oklahoma	8.9
19	Washington	8.7
20	Hawaii	8.4
20	Indiana	8.4
20	Minnesota	8.4
23	New Hampshire	8.3
24	Illinois	8.2
25	Massachusetts	8.1
26	Idaho	8.0
26	Maine	8.0
28	Arkansas	7.8
28	North Carolina	7.8
30	Maryland	7.7
30	New York	7.7
30	South Carolina	7.7
33	Kentucky	7.6
34	Kansas	7.5
35	Colorado	7.4
36	Tennessee	7.3
36	Virginia	7.3
38	Mississippi	7.2
39	Michigan	7.1
40	Texas	7.0
41	Alabama	6.9
42	Georgia	6.4
43	Arizona	6.3
43	California	6.3
45	New Mexico	5.7
46	Nevada	5.5
47	Utah	4.7
NA	Alaska**	NA
NA	Vermont**	NA
NA	Wyoming**	NA
	District of Columbia**	NA

Source: Morgan Quitno Press using data from American Cancer Society
    "Cancer Facts & Figures 2000" (Copyright 2000, Reprinted with permission from the American Cancer Society)
*Rates calculated using 1999 Census resident population estimates. Not age-adjusted.
**Fewer than 50 deaths.

Estimated Deaths by Liver Cancer in 2000

National Estimated Total = 13,800 Deaths

ALPHA ORDER

RANK ORDER

RANK	STATE	DEATHS	% of USA		RANK	STATE	DEATHS	% of USA
10	Alabama	300	2.2%		1	California	1,700	12.3%
NA	Alaska*	NA	NA		2	Texas	1,100	8.0%
20	Arizona	200	1.4%		3	Florida	1,000	7.2%
20	Arkansas	200	1.4%		4	New York	900	6.5%
1	California	1,700	12.3%		5	Illinois	700	5.1%
30	Colorado	100	0.7%		5	Pennsylvania	700	5.1%
20	Connecticut	200	1.4%		7	Michigan	500	3.6%
NA	Delaware*	NA	NA		7	New Jersey	500	3.6%
3	Florida	1,000	7.2%		7	Ohio	500	3.6%
10	Georgia	300	2.2%		10	Alabama	300	2.2%
30	Hawaii	100	0.7%		10	Georgia	300	2.2%
NA	Idaho*	NA	NA		10	Indiana	300	2.2%
5	Illinois	700	5.1%		10	Louisiana	300	2.2%
10	Indiana	300	2.2%		10	Massachusetts	300	2.2%
30	Iowa	100	0.7%		10	Missouri	300	2.2%
30	Kansas	100	0.7%		10	North Carolina	300	2.2%
20	Kentucky	200	1.4%		10	Tennessee	300	2.2%
10	Louisiana	300	2.2%		10	Virginia	300	2.2%
NA	Maine*	NA	NA		10	Washington	300	2.2%
20	Maryland	200	1.4%		20	Arizona	200	1.4%
10	Massachusetts	300	2.2%		20	Arkansas	200	1.4%
7	Michigan	500	3.6%		20	Connecticut	200	1.4%
20	Minnesota	200	1.4%		20	Kentucky	200	1.4%
20	Mississippi	200	1.4%		20	Maryland	200	1.4%
10	Missouri	300	2.2%		20	Minnesota	200	1.4%
30	Montana	100	0.7%		20	Mississippi	200	1.4%
30	Nebraska	100	0.7%		20	Oklahoma	200	1.4%
30	Nevada	100	0.7%		20	South Carolina	200	1.4%
30	New Hampshire	100	0.7%		20	Wisconsin	200	1.4%
7	New Jersey	500	3.6%		30	Colorado	100	0.7%
30	New Mexico	100	0.7%		30	Hawaii	100	0.7%
4	New York	900	6.5%		30	Iowa	100	0.7%
10	North Carolina	300	2.2%		30	Kansas	100	0.7%
NA	North Dakota*	NA	NA		30	Montana	100	0.7%
7	Ohio	500	3.6%		30	Nebraska	100	0.7%
20	Oklahoma	200	1.4%		30	Nevada	100	0.7%
30	Oregon	100	0.7%		30	New Hampshire	100	0.7%
5	Pennsylvania	700	5.1%		30	New Mexico	100	0.7%
30	Rhode Island	100	0.7%		30	Oregon	100	0.7%
20	South Carolina	200	1.4%		30	Rhode Island	100	0.7%
NA	South Dakota*	NA	NA		30	Utah	100	0.7%
10	Tennessee	300	2.2%		30	West Virginia	100	0.7%
2	Texas	1,100	8.0%		NA	Alaska*	NA	NA
30	Utah	100	0.7%		NA	Delaware*	NA	NA
NA	Vermont*	NA	NA		NA	Idaho*	NA	NA
10	Virginia	300	2.2%		NA	Maine*	NA	NA
10	Washington	300	2.2%		NA	North Dakota*	NA	NA
30	West Virginia	100	0.7%		NA	South Dakota*	NA	NA
20	Wisconsin	200	1.4%		NA	Vermont*	NA	NA
NA	Wyoming*	NA	NA		NA	Wyoming*	NA	NA
						District of Columbia*	NA	NA

Source: American Cancer Society
   "Cancer Facts & Figures 2000" (Copyright 2000, Reprinted with permission from the American Cancer Society)
*Fewer than 50 deaths.

Estimated Death Rate by Liver Cancer in 2000

National Estimated Rate = 5.1 Deaths per 100,000 Population*

ALPHA ORDER				RANK ORDER		
RANK	STATE	RATE		RANK	STATE	RATE
7	Alabama	6.9		1	Montana	11.3
NA	Alaska**	NA		2	Rhode Island	10.1
33	Arizona	4.2		3	Hawaii	8.4
5	Arkansas	7.8		4	New Hampshire	8.3
23	California	5.1		5	Arkansas	7.8
42	Colorado	2.5		6	Mississippi	7.2
10	Connecticut	6.1		7	Alabama	6.9
NA	Delaware**	NA		7	Louisiana	6.9
9	Florida	6.6		9	Florida	6.6
35	Georgia	3.9		10	Connecticut	6.1
3	Hawaii	8.4		10	New Jersey	6.1
NA	Idaho**	NA		12	Nebraska	6.0
14	Illinois	5.8		12	Oklahoma	6.0
26	Indiana	5.0		14	Illinois	5.8
40	Iowa	3.5		14	Pennsylvania	5.8
38	Kansas	3.8		16	New Mexico	5.7
26	Kentucky	5.0		17	Missouri	5.5
7	Louisiana	6.9		17	Nevada	5.5
NA	Maine**	NA		17	Tennessee	5.5
35	Maryland	3.9		17	Texas	5.5
28	Massachusetts	4.9		17	West Virginia	5.5
23	Michigan	5.1		22	Washington	5.2
33	Minnesota	4.2		23	California	5.1
6	Mississippi	7.2		23	Michigan	5.1
17	Missouri	5.5		23	South Carolina	5.1
1	Montana	11.3		26	Indiana	5.0
12	Nebraska	6.0		26	Kentucky	5.0
17	Nevada	5.5		28	Massachusetts	4.9
4	New Hampshire	8.3		28	New York	4.9
10	New Jersey	6.1		30	Utah	4.7
16	New Mexico	5.7		31	Ohio	4.4
28	New York	4.9		31	Virginia	4.4
35	North Carolina	3.9		33	Arizona	4.2
NA	North Dakota**	NA		33	Minnesota	4.2
31	Ohio	4.4		35	Georgia	3.9
12	Oklahoma	6.0		35	Maryland	3.9
41	Oregon	3.0		35	North Carolina	3.9
14	Pennsylvania	5.8		38	Kansas	3.8
2	Rhode Island	10.1		38	Wisconsin	3.8
23	South Carolina	5.1		40	Iowa	3.5
NA	South Dakota**	NA		41	Oregon	3.0
17	Tennessee	5.5		42	Colorado	2.5
17	Texas	5.5		NA	Alaska**	NA
30	Utah	4.7		NA	Delaware**	NA
NA	Vermont**	NA		NA	Idaho**	NA
31	Virginia	4.4		NA	Maine**	NA
22	Washington	5.2		NA	North Dakota**	NA
17	West Virginia	5.5		NA	South Dakota**	NA
38	Wisconsin	3.8		NA	Vermont**	NA
NA	Wyoming**	NA		NA	Wyoming**	NA
					District of Columbia**	NA

Source: Morgan Quitno Press using data from American Cancer Society
   "Cancer Facts & Figures 2000" (Copyright 2000, Reprinted with permission from the American Cancer Society)
*Rates calculated using 1999 Census resident population estimates. Not age-adjusted.
**Fewer than 50 deaths.

Estimated Deaths by Lung Cancer in 2000

National Estimated Total = 156,900 Deaths

ALPHA ORDER

RANK	STATE	DEATHS	% of USA
20	Alabama	2,800	1.8%
49	Alaska	200	0.1%
23	Arizona	2,600	1.7%
27	Arkansas	2,100	1.3%
1	California	13,400	8.5%
34	Colorado	1,400	0.9%
29	Connecticut	1,900	1.2%
41	Delaware	500	0.3%
2	Florida	12,000	7.6%
11	Georgia	4,000	2.5%
41	Hawaii	500	0.3%
41	Idaho	500	0.3%
7	Illinois	6,900	4.4%
13	Indiana	3,900	2.5%
30	Iowa	1,800	1.1%
32	Kansas	1,600	1.0%
17	Kentucky	3,200	2.0%
21	Louisiana	2,700	1.7%
36	Maine	900	0.6%
19	Maryland	2,900	1.8%
16	Massachusetts	3,700	2.4%
8	Michigan	5,800	3.7%
26	Minnesota	2,200	1.4%
30	Mississippi	1,800	1.1%
14	Missouri	3,800	2.4%
41	Montana	500	0.3%
36	Nebraska	900	0.6%
35	Nevada	1,200	0.8%
39	New Hampshire	700	0.4%
10	New Jersey	4,600	2.9%
39	New Mexico	700	0.4%
4	New York	9,400	6.0%
9	North Carolina	5,000	3.2%
48	North Dakota	300	0.2%
6	Ohio	7,400	4.7%
24	Oklahoma	2,400	1.5%
27	Oregon	2,100	1.3%
5	Pennsylvania	8,200	5.2%
38	Rhode Island	800	0.5%
24	South Carolina	2,400	1.5%
45	South Dakota	400	0.3%
11	Tennessee	4,000	2.5%
3	Texas	10,300	6.6%
45	Utah	400	0.3%
45	Vermont	400	0.3%
14	Virginia	3,800	2.4%
18	Washington	3,000	1.9%
33	West Virginia	1,500	1.0%
21	Wisconsin	2,700	1.7%
49	Wyoming	200	0.1%

RANK ORDER

RANK	STATE	DEATHS	% of USA
1	California	13,400	8.5%
2	Florida	12,000	7.6%
3	Texas	10,300	6.6%
4	New York	9,400	6.0%
5	Pennsylvania	8,200	5.2%
6	Ohio	7,400	4.7%
7	Illinois	6,900	4.4%
8	Michigan	5,800	3.7%
9	North Carolina	5,000	3.2%
10	New Jersey	4,600	2.9%
11	Georgia	4,000	2.5%
11	Tennessee	4,000	2.5%
13	Indiana	3,900	2.5%
14	Missouri	3,800	2.4%
14	Virginia	3,800	2.4%
16	Massachusetts	3,700	2.4%
17	Kentucky	3,200	2.0%
18	Washington	3,000	1.9%
19	Maryland	2,900	1.8%
20	Alabama	2,800	1.8%
21	Louisiana	2,700	1.7%
21	Wisconsin	2,700	1.7%
23	Arizona	2,600	1.7%
24	Oklahoma	2,400	1.5%
24	South Carolina	2,400	1.5%
26	Minnesota	2,200	1.4%
27	Arkansas	2,100	1.3%
27	Oregon	2,100	1.3%
29	Connecticut	1,900	1.2%
30	Iowa	1,800	1.1%
30	Mississippi	1,800	1.1%
32	Kansas	1,600	1.0%
33	West Virginia	1,500	1.0%
34	Colorado	1,400	0.9%
35	Nevada	1,200	0.8%
36	Maine	900	0.6%
36	Nebraska	900	0.6%
38	Rhode Island	800	0.5%
39	New Hampshire	700	0.4%
39	New Mexico	700	0.4%
41	Delaware	500	0.3%
41	Hawaii	500	0.3%
41	Idaho	500	0.3%
41	Montana	500	0.3%
45	South Dakota	400	0.3%
45	Utah	400	0.3%
45	Vermont	400	0.3%
48	North Dakota	300	0.2%
49	Alaska	200	0.1%
49	Wyoming	200	0.1%
	District of Columbia	300	0.2%

Source: American Cancer Society
"Cancer Facts & Figures 2000" (Copyright 2000, Reprinted with permission from the American Cancer Society)

Estimated Death Rate by Lung Cancer in 2000

National Estimated Rate = 57.5 Deaths per 100,000 Population*

ALPHA ORDER			RANK ORDER		
RANK	STATE	RATE	RANK	STATE	RATE
18	Alabama	64.1	1	West Virginia	83.0
49	Alaska	32.3	2	Arkansas	82.3
34	Arizona	54.4	3	Kentucky	80.8
2	Arkansas	82.3	4	Rhode Island	80.7
45	California	40.4	5	Florida	79.4
48	Colorado	34.5	6	Tennessee	72.9
27	Connecticut	57.9	7	Maine	71.8
12	Delaware	66.4	8	Oklahoma	71.5
5	Florida	79.4	9	Missouri	69.5
38	Georgia	51.4	10	Pennsylvania	68.4
43	Hawaii	42.2	11	Vermont	67.4
47	Idaho	39.9	12	Delaware	66.4
28	Illinois	56.9	13	Nevada	66.3
15	Indiana	65.6	14	Ohio	65.7
20	Iowa	62.7	15	Indiana	65.6
23	Kansas	60.3	16	North Carolina	65.4
3	Kentucky	80.8	17	Mississippi	65.0
21	Louisiana	61.8	18	Alabama	64.1
7	Maine	71.8	19	Oregon	63.3
31	Maryland	56.1	20	Iowa	62.7
24	Massachusetts	59.9	21	Louisiana	61.8
25	Michigan	58.8	21	South Carolina	61.8
42	Minnesota	46.1	23	Kansas	60.3
17	Mississippi	65.0	24	Massachusetts	59.9
9	Missouri	69.5	25	Michigan	58.8
29	Montana	56.6	26	New Hampshire	58.3
35	Nebraska	54.0	27	Connecticut	57.9
13	Nevada	66.3	28	Illinois	56.9
26	New Hampshire	58.3	29	Montana	56.6
30	New Jersey	56.5	30	New Jersey	56.5
46	New Mexico	40.2	31	Maryland	56.1
37	New York	51.7	32	Virginia	55.3
16	North Carolina	65.4	33	South Dakota	54.6
41	North Dakota	47.3	34	Arizona	54.4
14	Ohio	65.7	35	Nebraska	54.0
8	Oklahoma	71.5	36	Washington	52.1
19	Oregon	63.3	37	New York	51.7
10	Pennsylvania	68.4	38	Georgia	51.4
4	Rhode Island	80.7	38	Texas	51.4
21	South Carolina	61.8	38	Wisconsin	51.4
33	South Dakota	54.6	41	North Dakota	47.3
6	Tennessee	72.9	42	Minnesota	46.1
38	Texas	51.4	43	Hawaii	42.2
50	Utah	18.8	44	Wyoming	41.7
11	Vermont	67.4	45	California	40.4
32	Virginia	55.3	46	New Mexico	40.2
36	Washington	52.1	47	Idaho	39.9
1	West Virginia	83.0	48	Colorado	34.5
38	Wisconsin	51.4	49	Alaska	32.3
44	Wyoming	41.7	50	Utah	18.8
				District of Columbia	57.8

Source: Morgan Quitno Press using data from American Cancer Society
"Cancer Facts & Figures 2000" (Copyright 2000, Reprinted with permission from the American Cancer Society)
*Rates calculated using 1999 Census resident population estimates. Not age-adjusted.

Estimated Deaths by Non-Hodgkin's Lymphoma in 2000

National Estimated Total = 26,100 Deaths

ALPHA ORDER

RANK	STATE	DEATHS	% of USA
20	Alabama	400	1.5%
NA	Alaska*	NA	NA
20	Arizona	400	1.5%
25	Arkansas	300	1.1%
1	California	2,500	9.6%
25	Colorado	300	1.1%
25	Connecticut	300	1.1%
38	Delaware	100	0.4%
2	Florida	1,900	7.3%
16	Georgia	500	1.9%
38	Hawaii	100	0.4%
38	Idaho	100	0.4%
7	Illinois	1,200	4.6%
12	Indiana	600	2.3%
25	Iowa	300	1.1%
32	Kansas	200	0.8%
20	Kentucky	400	1.5%
20	Louisiana	400	1.5%
32	Maine	200	0.8%
20	Maryland	400	1.5%
10	Massachusetts	700	2.7%
8	Michigan	1,000	3.8%
16	Minnesota	500	1.9%
32	Mississippi	200	0.8%
16	Missouri	500	1.9%
38	Montana	100	0.4%
32	Nebraska	200	0.8%
32	Nevada	200	0.8%
38	New Hampshire	100	0.4%
9	New Jersey	900	3.4%
38	New Mexico	100	0.4%
3	New York	1,800	6.9%
10	North Carolina	700	2.7%
38	North Dakota	100	0.4%
6	Ohio	1,300	5.0%
25	Oklahoma	300	1.1%
25	Oregon	300	1.1%
5	Pennsylvania	1,400	5.4%
38	Rhode Island	100	0.4%
25	South Carolina	300	1.1%
38	South Dakota	100	0.4%
12	Tennessee	600	2.3%
4	Texas	1,700	6.5%
38	Utah	100	0.4%
38	Vermont	100	0.4%
12	Virginia	600	2.3%
16	Washington	500	1.9%
32	West Virginia	200	0.8%
12	Wisconsin	600	2.3%
NA	Wyoming*	NA	NA

RANK ORDER

RANK	STATE	DEATHS	% of USA
1	California	2,500	9.6%
2	Florida	1,900	7.3%
3	New York	1,800	6.9%
4	Texas	1,700	6.5%
5	Pennsylvania	1,400	5.4%
6	Ohio	1,300	5.0%
7	Illinois	1,200	4.6%
8	Michigan	1,000	3.8%
9	New Jersey	900	3.4%
10	Massachusetts	700	2.7%
10	North Carolina	700	2.7%
12	Indiana	600	2.3%
12	Tennessee	600	2.3%
12	Virginia	600	2.3%
12	Wisconsin	600	2.3%
16	Georgia	500	1.9%
16	Minnesota	500	1.9%
16	Missouri	500	1.9%
16	Washington	500	1.9%
20	Alabama	400	1.5%
20	Arizona	400	1.5%
20	Kentucky	400	1.5%
20	Louisiana	400	1.5%
20	Maryland	400	1.5%
25	Arkansas	300	1.1%
25	Colorado	300	1.1%
25	Connecticut	300	1.1%
25	Iowa	300	1.1%
25	Oklahoma	300	1.1%
25	Oregon	300	1.1%
25	South Carolina	300	1.1%
32	Kansas	200	0.8%
32	Maine	200	0.8%
32	Mississippi	200	0.8%
32	Nebraska	200	0.8%
32	Nevada	200	0.8%
32	West Virginia	200	0.8%
38	Delaware	100	0.4%
38	Hawaii	100	0.4%
38	Idaho	100	0.4%
38	Montana	100	0.4%
38	New Hampshire	100	0.4%
38	New Mexico	100	0.4%
38	North Dakota	100	0.4%
38	Rhode Island	100	0.4%
38	South Dakota	100	0.4%
38	Utah	100	0.4%
38	Vermont	100	0.4%
NA	Alaska*	NA	NA
NA	Wyoming*	NA	NA
	District of Columbia*	NA	NA

Source: American Cancer Society
   "Cancer Facts & Figures 2000" (Copyright 2000, Reprinted with permission from the American Cancer Society)
*Fewer than 50 deaths.

Estimated Death Rate by Non-Hodgkin's Lymphoma in 2000

National Estimated Rate = 9.6 Deaths per 100,000 Population*

ALPHA ORDER				RANK ORDER		
RANK	STATE	RATE		RANK	STATE	RATE
26	Alabama	9.2		1	Vermont	16.8
NA	Alaska**	NA		2	Maine	16.0
36	Arizona	8.4		3	North Dakota	15.8
8	Arkansas	11.8		4	South Dakota	13.6
42	California	7.5		5	Delaware	13.3
44	Colorado	7.4		6	Florida	12.6
27	Connecticut	9.1		7	Nebraska	12.0
5	Delaware	13.3		8	Arkansas	11.8
6	Florida	12.6		9	Pennsylvania	11.7
46	Georgia	6.4		10	Ohio	11.5
36	Hawaii	8.4		11	Wisconsin	11.4
39	Idaho	8.0		12	Massachusetts	11.3
24	Illinois	9.9		12	Montana	11.3
20	Indiana	10.1		14	Nevada	11.1
18	Iowa	10.5		14	New Jersey	11.1
42	Kansas	7.5		14	West Virginia	11.1
20	Kentucky	10.1		17	Tennessee	10.9
27	Louisiana	9.1		18	Iowa	10.5
2	Maine	16.0		18	Minnesota	10.5
40	Maryland	7.7		20	Indiana	10.1
12	Massachusetts	11.3		20	Kentucky	10.1
20	Michigan	10.1		20	Michigan	10.1
18	Minnesota	10.5		20	Rhode Island	10.1
45	Mississippi	7.2		24	Illinois	9.9
27	Missouri	9.1		24	New York	9.9
12	Montana	11.3		26	Alabama	9.2
7	Nebraska	12.0		27	Connecticut	9.1
14	Nevada	11.1		27	Louisiana	9.1
38	New Hampshire	8.3		27	Missouri	9.1
14	New Jersey	11.1		27	North Carolina	9.1
47	New Mexico	5.7		31	Oregon	9.0
24	New York	9.9		32	Oklahoma	8.9
27	North Carolina	9.1		33	Virginia	8.7
3	North Dakota	15.8		33	Washington	8.7
10	Ohio	11.5		35	Texas	8.5
32	Oklahoma	8.9		36	Arizona	8.4
31	Oregon	9.0		36	Hawaii	8.4
9	Pennsylvania	11.7		38	New Hampshire	8.3
20	Rhode Island	10.1		39	Idaho	8.0
40	South Carolina	7.7		40	Maryland	7.7
4	South Dakota	13.6		40	South Carolina	7.7
17	Tennessee	10.9		42	California	7.5
35	Texas	8.5		42	Kansas	7.5
48	Utah	4.7		44	Colorado	7.4
1	Vermont	16.8		45	Mississippi	7.2
33	Virginia	8.7		46	Georgia	6.4
33	Washington	8.7		47	New Mexico	5.7
14	West Virginia	11.1		48	Utah	4.7
11	Wisconsin	11.4		NA	Alaska**	NA
NA	Wyoming**	NA		NA	Wyoming**	NA
					District of Columbia**	NA

Source: Morgan Quitno Press using data from American Cancer Society
"Cancer Facts & Figures 2000" (Copyright 2000, Reprinted with permission from the American Cancer Society)
*Rates calculated using 1999 Census resident population estimates. Not age-adjusted.
**Fewer than 50 deaths.

Estimated Deaths by Pancreatic Cancer in 2000

National Estimated Total = 28,200 Deaths

ALPHA ORDER

RANK	STATE	DEATHS	% of USA
17	Alabama	500	1.8%
NA	Alaska*	NA	NA
17	Arizona	500	1.8%
28	Arkansas	300	1.1%
1	California	2,700	9.6%
28	Colorado	300	1.1%
24	Connecticut	400	1.4%
37	Delaware	100	0.4%
3	Florida	2,100	7.4%
12	Georgia	600	2.1%
37	Hawaii	100	0.4%
37	Idaho	100	0.4%
6	Illinois	1,300	4.6%
12	Indiana	600	2.1%
28	Iowa	300	1.1%
28	Kansas	300	1.1%
24	Kentucky	400	1.4%
17	Louisiana	500	1.8%
34	Maine	200	0.7%
17	Maryland	500	1.8%
11	Massachusetts	700	2.5%
8	Michigan	1,000	3.5%
17	Minnesota	500	1.8%
28	Mississippi	300	1.1%
17	Missouri	500	1.8%
37	Montana	100	0.4%
37	Nebraska	100	0.4%
34	Nevada	200	0.7%
37	New Hampshire	100	0.4%
8	New Jersey	1,000	3.5%
37	New Mexico	100	0.4%
2	New York	2,200	7.8%
10	North Carolina	800	2.8%
37	North Dakota	100	0.4%
6	Ohio	1,300	4.6%
28	Oklahoma	300	1.1%
24	Oregon	400	1.4%
5	Pennsylvania	1,500	5.3%
37	Rhode Island	100	0.4%
24	South Carolina	400	1.4%
37	South Dakota	100	0.4%
12	Tennessee	600	2.1%
4	Texas	1,700	6.0%
37	Utah	100	0.4%
NA	Vermont*	NA	NA
12	Virginia	600	2.1%
17	Washington	500	1.8%
34	West Virginia	200	0.7%
12	Wisconsin	600	2.1%
NA	Wyoming*	NA	NA

RANK ORDER

RANK	STATE	DEATHS	% of USA
1	California	2,700	9.6%
2	New York	2,200	7.8%
3	Florida	2,100	7.4%
4	Texas	1,700	6.0%
5	Pennsylvania	1,500	5.3%
6	Illinois	1,300	4.6%
6	Ohio	1,300	4.6%
8	Michigan	1,000	3.5%
8	New Jersey	1,000	3.5%
10	North Carolina	800	2.8%
11	Massachusetts	700	2.5%
12	Georgia	600	2.1%
12	Indiana	600	2.1%
12	Tennessee	600	2.1%
12	Virginia	600	2.1%
12	Wisconsin	600	2.1%
17	Alabama	500	1.8%
17	Arizona	500	1.8%
17	Louisiana	500	1.8%
17	Maryland	500	1.8%
17	Minnesota	500	1.8%
17	Missouri	500	1.8%
17	Washington	500	1.8%
24	Connecticut	400	1.4%
24	Kentucky	400	1.4%
24	Oregon	400	1.4%
24	South Carolina	400	1.4%
28	Arkansas	300	1.1%
28	Colorado	300	1.1%
28	Iowa	300	1.1%
28	Kansas	300	1.1%
28	Mississippi	300	1.1%
28	Oklahoma	300	1.1%
34	Maine	200	0.7%
34	Nevada	200	0.7%
34	West Virginia	200	0.7%
37	Delaware	100	0.4%
37	Hawaii	100	0.4%
37	Idaho	100	0.4%
37	Montana	100	0.4%
37	Nebraska	100	0.4%
37	New Hampshire	100	0.4%
37	New Mexico	100	0.4%
37	North Dakota	100	0.4%
37	Rhode Island	100	0.4%
37	South Dakota	100	0.4%
37	Utah	100	0.4%
NA	Alaska*	NA	NA
NA	Vermont*	NA	NA
NA	Wyoming*	NA	NA
	District of Columbia	100	0.4%

Source: American Cancer Society
"Cancer Facts & Figures 2000" (Copyright 2000, Reprinted with permission from the American Cancer Society)
*Fewer than 50 deaths.

Estimated Death Rate by Pancreatic Cancer in 2000

National Estimated Rate = 10.3 Deaths per 100,000 Population*

ALPHA ORDER

RANK	STATE	RATE
13	Alabama	11.4
NA	Alaska**	NA
24	Arizona	10.5
11	Arkansas	11.8
41	California	8.1
44	Colorado	7.4
8	Connecticut	12.2
5	Delaware	13.3
3	Florida	13.9
43	Georgia	7.7
39	Hawaii	8.4
42	Idaho	8.0
23	Illinois	10.7
29	Indiana	10.1
24	Iowa	10.5
16	Kansas	11.3
29	Kentucky	10.1
13	Louisiana	11.4
1	Maine	16.0
33	Maryland	9.7
16	Massachusetts	11.3
29	Michigan	10.1
24	Minnesota	10.5
22	Mississippi	10.8
34	Missouri	9.1
16	Montana	11.3
45	Nebraska	6.0
19	Nevada	11.1
40	New Hampshire	8.3
7	New Jersey	12.3
46	New Mexico	5.7
9	New York	12.1
24	North Carolina	10.5
2	North Dakota	15.8
12	Ohio	11.5
35	Oklahoma	8.9
9	Oregon	12.1
6	Pennsylvania	12.5
29	Rhode Island	10.1
28	South Carolina	10.3
4	South Dakota	13.6
21	Tennessee	10.9
38	Texas	8.5
47	Utah	4.7
NA	Vermont**	NA
36	Virginia	8.7
36	Washington	8.7
19	West Virginia	11.1
13	Wisconsin	11.4
NA	Wyoming**	NA

RANK ORDER

RANK	STATE	RATE
1	Maine	16.0
2	North Dakota	15.8
3	Florida	13.9
4	South Dakota	13.6
5	Delaware	13.3
6	Pennsylvania	12.5
7	New Jersey	12.3
8	Connecticut	12.2
9	New York	12.1
9	Oregon	12.1
11	Arkansas	11.8
12	Ohio	11.5
13	Alabama	11.4
13	Louisiana	11.4
13	Wisconsin	11.4
16	Kansas	11.3
16	Massachusetts	11.3
16	Montana	11.3
19	Nevada	11.1
19	West Virginia	11.1
21	Tennessee	10.9
22	Mississippi	10.8
23	Illinois	10.7
24	Arizona	10.5
24	Iowa	10.5
24	Minnesota	10.5
24	North Carolina	10.5
28	South Carolina	10.3
29	Indiana	10.1
29	Kentucky	10.1
29	Michigan	10.1
29	Rhode Island	10.1
33	Maryland	9.7
34	Missouri	9.1
35	Oklahoma	8.9
36	Virginia	8.7
36	Washington	8.7
38	Texas	8.5
39	Hawaii	8.4
40	New Hampshire	8.3
41	California	8.1
42	Idaho	8.0
43	Georgia	7.7
44	Colorado	7.4
45	Nebraska	6.0
46	New Mexico	5.7
47	Utah	4.7
NA	Alaska**	NA
NA	Vermont**	NA
NA	Wyoming**	NA

District of Columbia   19.3

Source: Morgan Quitno Press using data from American Cancer Society
"Cancer Facts & Figures 2000" (Copyright 2000, Reprinted with permission from the American Cancer Society)
Rates calculated using 1999 Census resident population estimates. Not age-adjusted.
***Fewer than 50 deaths.*

Estimated Deaths by Prostate Cancer in 2000

National Estimated Total = 31,900 Deaths

ALPHA ORDER

RANK ORDER

RANK	STATE	DEATHS	% of USA		RANK	STATE	DEATHS	% of USA
16	Alabama	600	1.9%		1	California	2,900	9.1%
NA	Alaska*	NA	NA		2	Florida	2,400	7.5%
16	Arizona	600	1.9%		3	New York	2,100	6.6%
27	Arkansas	400	1.3%		4	Texas	2,000	6.3%
1	California	2,900	9.1%		5	Pennsylvania	1,800	5.6%
32	Colorado	300	0.9%		6	Illinois	1,400	4.4%
27	Connecticut	400	1.3%		6	Ohio	1,400	4.4%
40	Delaware	100	0.3%		8	Michigan	1,200	3.8%
2	Florida	2,400	7.5%		9	New Jersey	1,000	3.1%
11	Georgia	800	2.5%		10	North Carolina	900	2.8%
40	Hawaii	100	0.3%		11	Georgia	800	2.5%
40	Idaho	100	0.3%		11	Virginia	800	2.5%
6	Illinois	1,400	4.4%		13	Indiana	700	2.2%
13	Indiana	700	2.2%		13	Massachusetts	700	2.2%
27	Iowa	400	1.3%		13	Wisconsin	700	2.2%
32	Kansas	300	0.9%		16	Alabama	600	1.9%
24	Kentucky	500	1.6%		16	Arizona	600	1.9%
16	Louisiana	600	1.9%		16	Louisiana	600	1.9%
34	Maine	200	0.6%		16	Maryland	600	1.9%
16	Maryland	600	1.9%		16	Minnesota	600	1.9%
13	Massachusetts	700	2.2%		16	Missouri	600	1.9%
8	Michigan	1,200	3.8%		16	Tennessee	600	1.9%
16	Minnesota	600	1.9%		16	Washington	600	1.9%
27	Mississippi	400	1.3%		24	Kentucky	500	1.6%
16	Missouri	600	1.9%		24	Oregon	500	1.6%
40	Montana	100	0.3%		24	South Carolina	500	1.6%
34	Nebraska	200	0.6%		27	Arkansas	400	1.3%
34	Nevada	200	0.6%		27	Connecticut	400	1.3%
40	New Hampshire	100	0.3%		27	Iowa	400	1.3%
9	New Jersey	1,000	3.1%		27	Mississippi	400	1.3%
34	New Mexico	200	0.6%		27	Oklahoma	400	1.3%
3	New York	2,100	6.6%		32	Colorado	300	0.9%
10	North Carolina	900	2.8%		32	Kansas	300	0.9%
40	North Dakota	100	0.3%		34	Maine	200	0.6%
6	Ohio	1,400	4.4%		34	Nebraska	200	0.6%
27	Oklahoma	400	1.3%		34	Nevada	200	0.6%
24	Oregon	500	1.6%		34	New Mexico	200	0.6%
5	Pennsylvania	1,800	5.6%		34	Utah	200	0.6%
40	Rhode Island	100	0.3%		34	West Virginia	200	0.6%
24	South Carolina	500	1.6%		40	Delaware	100	0.3%
40	South Dakota	100	0.3%		40	Hawaii	100	0.3%
16	Tennessee	600	1.9%		40	Idaho	100	0.3%
4	Texas	2,000	6.3%		40	Montana	100	0.3%
34	Utah	200	0.6%		40	New Hampshire	100	0.3%
40	Vermont	100	0.3%		40	North Dakota	100	0.3%
11	Virginia	800	2.5%		40	Rhode Island	100	0.3%
16	Washington	600	1.9%		40	South Dakota	100	0.3%
34	West Virginia	200	0.6%		40	Vermont	100	0.3%
13	Wisconsin	700	2.2%		40	Wyoming	100	0.3%
40	Wyoming	100	0.3%		NA	Alaska*	NA	NA
						District of Columbia	100	0.3%

Source: American Cancer Society
"Cancer Facts & Figures 2000" (Copyright 2000, Reprinted with permission from the American Cancer Society)
*Fewer than 50 deaths.

125

Estimated Death Rate by Prostate Cancer in 2000

National Estimated Rate = 24.2 Deaths per 100,000 Male Population*

ALPHA ORDER

RANK	STATE	RATE
10	Alabama	28.7
NA	Alaska**	NA
18	Arizona	26.0
5	Arkansas	32.6
45	California	17.8
49	Colorado	15.2
22	Connecticut	25.2
13	Delaware	27.7
3	Florida	33.2
40	Georgia	21.5
47	Hawaii	16.7
48	Idaho	16.3
31	Illinois	23.8
27	Indiana	24.4
10	Iowa	28.7
34	Kansas	23.2
17	Kentucky	26.2
12	Louisiana	28.6
4	Maine	33.0
28	Maryland	24.1
32	Massachusetts	23.6
23	Michigan	25.1
19	Minnesota	25.8
9	Mississippi	30.3
37	Missouri	22.8
37	Montana	22.8
24	Nebraska	24.6
39	Nevada	22.5
46	New Hampshire	17.2
21	New Jersey	25.4
33	New Mexico	23.4
30	New York	24.0
24	North Carolina	24.6
6	North Dakota	31.5
19	Ohio	25.8
26	Oklahoma	24.5
8	Oregon	30.8
7	Pennsylvania	31.2
42	Rhode Island	21.0
16	South Carolina	27.0
14	South Dakota	27.5
35	Tennessee	22.9
43	Texas	20.5
44	Utah	19.2
2	Vermont	34.4
28	Virginia	24.1
41	Washington	21.2
35	West Virginia	22.9
15	Wisconsin	27.3
1	Wyoming	41.4

RANK ORDER

RANK	STATE	RATE
1	Wyoming	41.4
2	Vermont	34.4
3	Florida	33.2
4	Maine	33.0
5	Arkansas	32.6
6	North Dakota	31.5
7	Pennsylvania	31.2
8	Oregon	30.8
9	Mississippi	30.3
10	Alabama	28.7
10	Iowa	28.7
12	Louisiana	28.6
13	Delaware	27.7
14	South Dakota	27.5
15	Wisconsin	27.3
16	South Carolina	27.0
17	Kentucky	26.2
18	Arizona	26.0
19	Minnesota	25.8
19	Ohio	25.8
21	New Jersey	25.4
22	Connecticut	25.2
23	Michigan	25.1
24	Nebraska	24.6
24	North Carolina	24.6
26	Oklahoma	24.5
27	Indiana	24.4
28	Maryland	24.1
28	Virginia	24.1
30	New York	24.0
31	Illinois	23.8
32	Massachusetts	23.6
33	New Mexico	23.4
34	Kansas	23.2
35	Tennessee	22.9
35	West Virginia	22.9
37	Missouri	22.8
37	Montana	22.8
39	Nevada	22.5
40	Georgia	21.5
41	Washington	21.2
42	Rhode Island	21.0
43	Texas	20.5
44	Utah	19.2
45	California	17.8
46	New Hampshire	17.2
47	Hawaii	16.7
48	Idaho	16.3
49	Colorado	15.2
NA	Alaska**	NA
	District of Columbia	40.8

Source: Morgan Quitno Press using data from American Cancer Society
    "Cancer Facts & Figures 2000" (Copyright 2000, Reprinted with permission from the American Cancer Society)
*Rates calculated using 1998 Census resident male population estimates. Not age-adjusted.
**Fewer than 50 deaths.

Estimated Deaths by Ovarian Cancer in 2000

National Estimated Total = 14,000 Deaths

ALPHA ORDER

RANK	STATE	DEATHS	% of USA
19	Alabama	200	1.4%
NA	Alaska*	NA	NA
19	Arizona	200	1.4%
19	Arkansas	200	1.4%
1	California	1,400	10.0%
31	Colorado	100	0.7%
19	Connecticut	200	1.4%
NA	Delaware*	NA	NA
3	Florida	900	6.4%
10	Georgia	400	2.9%
NA	Hawaii*	NA	NA
31	Idaho	100	0.7%
6	Illinois	700	5.0%
12	Indiana	300	2.1%
19	Iowa	200	1.4%
31	Kansas	100	0.7%
19	Kentucky	200	1.4%
19	Louisiana	200	1.4%
31	Maine	100	0.7%
19	Maryland	200	1.4%
12	Massachusetts	300	2.1%
8	Michigan	500	3.6%
19	Minnesota	200	1.4%
31	Mississippi	100	0.7%
12	Missouri	300	2.1%
31	Montana	100	0.7%
31	Nebraska	100	0.7%
31	Nevada	100	0.7%
31	New Hampshire	100	0.7%
8	New Jersey	500	3.6%
31	New Mexico	100	0.7%
2	New York	1,000	7.1%
10	North Carolina	400	2.9%
NA	North Dakota*	NA	NA
7	Ohio	600	4.3%
19	Oklahoma	200	1.4%
19	Oregon	200	1.4%
5	Pennsylvania	800	5.7%
31	Rhode Island	100	0.7%
19	South Carolina	200	1.4%
NA	South Dakota*	NA	NA
12	Tennessee	300	2.1%
3	Texas	900	6.4%
31	Utah	100	0.7%
NA	Vermont*	NA	NA
12	Virginia	300	2.1%
12	Washington	300	2.1%
31	West Virginia	100	0.7%
12	Wisconsin	300	2.1%
NA	Wyoming*	NA	NA

RANK ORDER

RANK	STATE	DEATHS	% of USA
1	California	1,400	10.0%
2	New York	1,000	7.1%
3	Florida	900	6.4%
3	Texas	900	6.4%
5	Pennsylvania	800	5.7%
6	Illinois	700	5.0%
7	Ohio	600	4.3%
8	Michigan	500	3.6%
8	New Jersey	500	3.6%
10	Georgia	400	2.9%
10	North Carolina	400	2.9%
12	Indiana	300	2.1%
12	Massachusetts	300	2.1%
12	Missouri	300	2.1%
12	Tennessee	300	2.1%
12	Virginia	300	2.1%
12	Washington	300	2.1%
12	Wisconsin	300	2.1%
19	Alabama	200	1.4%
19	Arizona	200	1.4%
19	Arkansas	200	1.4%
19	Connecticut	200	1.4%
19	Iowa	200	1.4%
19	Kentucky	200	1.4%
19	Louisiana	200	1.4%
19	Maryland	200	1.4%
19	Minnesota	200	1.4%
19	Oklahoma	200	1.4%
19	Oregon	200	1.4%
19	South Carolina	200	1.4%
31	Colorado	100	0.7%
31	Idaho	100	0.7%
31	Kansas	100	0.7%
31	Maine	100	0.7%
31	Mississippi	100	0.7%
31	Montana	100	0.7%
31	Nebraska	100	0.7%
31	Nevada	100	0.7%
31	New Hampshire	100	0.7%
31	New Mexico	100	0.7%
31	Rhode Island	100	0.7%
31	Utah	100	0.7%
31	West Virginia	100	0.7%
NA	Alaska*	NA	NA
NA	Delaware*	NA	NA
NA	Hawaii*	NA	NA
NA	North Dakota*	NA	NA
NA	South Dakota*	NA	NA
NA	Vermont*	NA	NA
NA	Wyoming*	NA	NA
	District of Columbia*	NA	NA

Source: American Cancer Society
"Cancer Facts & Figures 2000" (Copyright 2000, Reprinted with permission from the American Cancer Society)
*Fewer than 50 deaths.

Estimated Death Rate by Ovarian Cancer in 2000

National Estimated Rate = 10.1 Deaths per 100,000 Female Population*

ALPHA ORDER

RANK	STATE	RATE
34	Alabama	8.8
NA	Alaska**	NA
38	Arizona	8.5
6	Arkansas	15.2
36	California	8.6
43	Colorado	5.0
10	Connecticut	11.9
NA	Delaware**	NA
13	Florida	11.7
26	Georgia	10.2
NA	Hawaii**	NA
4	Idaho	16.2
16	Illinois	11.3
28	Indiana	9.9
7	Iowa	13.6
41	Kansas	7.5
28	Kentucky	9.9
34	Louisiana	8.8
5	Maine	15.7
40	Maryland	7.6
32	Massachusetts	9.4
28	Michigan	9.9
39	Minnesota	8.3
42	Mississippi	7.0
19	Missouri	10.7
1	Montana	22.6
12	Nebraska	11.8
13	Nevada	11.7
3	New Hampshire	16.6
10	New Jersey	11.9
16	New Mexico	11.3
22	New York	10.6
25	North Carolina	10.3
NA	North Dakota**	NA
24	Ohio	10.4
13	Oklahoma	11.7
9	Oregon	12.0
8	Pennsylvania	12.8
2	Rhode Island	19.5
27	South Carolina	10.1
NA	South Dakota**	NA
19	Tennessee	10.7
33	Texas	9.0
31	Utah	9.5
NA	Vermont**	NA
36	Virginia	8.6
23	Washington	10.5
19	West Virginia	10.7
16	Wisconsin	11.3
NA	Wyoming**	NA

RANK ORDER

RANK	STATE	RATE
1	Montana	22.6
2	Rhode Island	19.5
3	New Hampshire	16.6
4	Idaho	16.2
5	Maine	15.7
6	Arkansas	15.2
7	Iowa	13.6
8	Pennsylvania	12.8
9	Oregon	12.0
10	Connecticut	11.9
10	New Jersey	11.9
12	Nebraska	11.8
13	Florida	11.7
13	Nevada	11.7
13	Oklahoma	11.7
16	Illinois	11.3
16	New Mexico	11.3
16	Wisconsin	11.3
19	Missouri	10.7
19	Tennessee	10.7
19	West Virginia	10.7
22	New York	10.6
23	Washington	10.5
24	Ohio	10.4
25	North Carolina	10.3
26	Georgia	10.2
27	South Carolina	10.1
28	Indiana	9.9
28	Kentucky	9.9
28	Michigan	9.9
31	Utah	9.5
32	Massachusetts	9.4
33	Texas	9.0
34	Alabama	8.8
34	Louisiana	8.8
36	California	8.6
36	Virginia	8.6
38	Arizona	8.5
39	Minnesota	8.3
40	Maryland	7.6
41	Kansas	7.5
42	Mississippi	7.0
43	Colorado	5.0
NA	Alaska**	NA
NA	Delaware**	NA
NA	Hawaii**	NA
NA	North Dakota**	NA
NA	South Dakota**	NA
NA	Vermont**	NA
NA	Wyoming**	NA
	District of Columbia**	NA

Source: Morgan Quitno Press using data from American Cancer Society
    "Cancer Facts & Figures 2000" (Copyright 2000, Reprinted with permission from the American Cancer Society)
*Rates calculated using 1998 Census resident female population estimates. Not age-adjusted.
**Fewer than 50 deaths.

Estimated Deaths by Stomach Cancer in 2000

National Estimated Total = 13,000 Deaths

ALPHA ORDER

RANK	STATE	DEATHS	% of USA
18	Alabama	200	1.5%
NA	Alaska*	NA	NA
18	Arizona	200	1.5%
27	Arkansas	100	0.8%
1	California	1,500	11.5%
27	Colorado	100	0.8%
18	Connecticut	200	1.5%
NA	Delaware*	NA	NA
3	Florida	900	6.9%
10	Georgia	300	2.3%
27	Hawaii	100	0.8%
NA	Idaho*	NA	NA
5	Illinois	600	4.6%
18	Indiana	200	1.5%
27	Iowa	100	0.8%
27	Kansas	100	0.8%
18	Kentucky	200	1.5%
10	Louisiana	300	2.3%
27	Maine	100	0.8%
10	Maryland	300	2.3%
10	Massachusetts	300	2.3%
9	Michigan	400	3.1%
18	Minnesota	200	1.5%
27	Mississippi	100	0.8%
10	Missouri	300	2.3%
NA	Montana*	NA	NA
27	Nebraska	100	0.8%
27	Nevada	100	0.8%
NA	New Hampshire*	NA	NA
7	New Jersey	500	3.8%
27	New Mexico	100	0.8%
2	New York	1,100	8.5%
10	North Carolina	300	2.3%
NA	North Dakota*	NA	NA
7	Ohio	500	3.8%
27	Oklahoma	100	0.8%
27	Oregon	100	0.8%
5	Pennsylvania	600	4.6%
27	Rhode Island	100	0.8%
18	South Carolina	200	1.5%
NA	South Dakota*	NA	NA
10	Tennessee	300	2.3%
3	Texas	900	6.9%
NA	Utah*	NA	NA
NA	Vermont*	NA	NA
10	Virginia	300	2.3%
18	Washington	200	1.5%
27	West Virginia	100	0.8%
18	Wisconsin	200	1.5%
NA	Wyoming*	NA	NA

RANK ORDER

RANK	STATE	DEATHS	% of USA
1	California	1,500	11.5%
2	New York	1,100	8.5%
3	Florida	900	6.9%
3	Texas	900	6.9%
5	Illinois	600	4.6%
5	Pennsylvania	600	4.6%
7	New Jersey	500	3.8%
7	Ohio	500	3.8%
9	Michigan	400	3.1%
10	Georgia	300	2.3%
10	Louisiana	300	2.3%
10	Maryland	300	2.3%
10	Massachusetts	300	2.3%
10	Missouri	300	2.3%
10	North Carolina	300	2.3%
10	Tennessee	300	2.3%
10	Virginia	300	2.3%
18	Alabama	200	1.5%
18	Arizona	200	1.5%
18	Connecticut	200	1.5%
18	Indiana	200	1.5%
18	Kentucky	200	1.5%
18	Minnesota	200	1.5%
18	South Carolina	200	1.5%
18	Washington	200	1.5%
18	Wisconsin	200	1.5%
27	Arkansas	100	0.8%
27	Colorado	100	0.8%
27	Hawaii	100	0.8%
27	Iowa	100	0.8%
27	Kansas	100	0.8%
27	Maine	100	0.8%
27	Mississippi	100	0.8%
27	Nebraska	100	0.8%
27	Nevada	100	0.8%
27	New Mexico	100	0.8%
27	Oklahoma	100	0.8%
27	Oregon	100	0.8%
27	Rhode Island	100	0.8%
27	West Virginia	100	0.8%
NA	Alaska*	NA	NA
NA	Delaware*	NA	NA
NA	Idaho*	NA	NA
NA	Montana*	NA	NA
NA	New Hampshire*	NA	NA
NA	North Dakota*	NA	NA
NA	South Dakota*	NA	NA
NA	Utah*	NA	NA
NA	Vermont*	NA	NA
NA	Wyoming*	NA	NA
	District of Columbia	100	0.8%

Source: American Cancer Society
"Cancer Facts & Figures 2000" (Copyright 2000, Reprinted with permission from the American Cancer Society)
*Fewer than 50 deaths.

Estimated Death Rate by Stomach Cancer in 2000

National Estimated Rate = 4.8 Deaths per 100,000 Population*

ALPHA ORDER

RANK	STATE	RATE
21	Alabama	4.6
NA	Alaska**	NA
26	Arizona	4.2
29	Arkansas	3.9
22	California	4.5
40	Colorado	2.5
5	Connecticut	6.1
NA	Delaware**	NA
7	Florida	6.0
29	Georgia	3.9
2	Hawaii	8.4
NA	Idaho**	NA
19	Illinois	4.9
37	Indiana	3.4
35	Iowa	3.5
32	Kansas	3.8
17	Kentucky	5.0
4	Louisiana	6.9
3	Maine	8.0
10	Maryland	5.8
19	Massachusetts	4.9
28	Michigan	4.1
26	Minnesota	4.2
34	Mississippi	3.6
12	Missouri	5.5
NA	Montana**	NA
7	Nebraska	6.0
12	Nevada	5.5
NA	New Hampshire**	NA
5	New Jersey	6.1
11	New Mexico	5.7
7	New York	6.0
29	North Carolina	3.9
NA	North Dakota**	NA
24	Ohio	4.4
38	Oklahoma	3.0
38	Oregon	3.0
17	Pennsylvania	5.0
1	Rhode Island	10.1
16	South Carolina	5.1
NA	South Dakota**	NA
12	Tennessee	5.5
22	Texas	4.5
NA	Utah**	NA
NA	Vermont**	NA
24	Virginia	4.4
35	Washington	3.5
12	West Virginia	5.5
32	Wisconsin	3.8
NA	Wyoming**	NA

RANK ORDER

RANK	STATE	RATE
1	Rhode Island	10.1
2	Hawaii	8.4
3	Maine	8.0
4	Louisiana	6.9
5	Connecticut	6.1
5	New Jersey	6.1
7	Florida	6.0
7	Nebraska	6.0
7	New York	6.0
10	Maryland	5.8
11	New Mexico	5.7
12	Missouri	5.5
12	Nevada	5.5
12	Tennessee	5.5
12	West Virginia	5.5
16	South Carolina	5.1
17	Kentucky	5.0
17	Pennsylvania	5.0
19	Illinois	4.9
19	Massachusetts	4.9
21	Alabama	4.6
22	California	4.5
22	Texas	4.5
24	Ohio	4.4
24	Virginia	4.4
26	Arizona	4.2
26	Minnesota	4.2
28	Michigan	4.1
29	Arkansas	3.9
29	Georgia	3.9
29	North Carolina	3.9
32	Kansas	3.8
32	Wisconsin	3.8
34	Mississippi	3.6
35	Iowa	3.5
35	Washington	3.5
37	Indiana	3.4
38	Oklahoma	3.0
38	Oregon	3.0
40	Colorado	2.5
NA	Alaska**	NA
NA	Delaware**	NA
NA	Idaho**	NA
NA	Montana**	NA
NA	New Hampshire**	NA
NA	North Dakota**	NA
NA	South Dakota**	NA
NA	Utah**	NA
NA	Vermont**	NA
NA	Wyoming**	NA
	District of Columbia	19.3

Source: Morgan Quitno Press using data from American Cancer Society
   "Cancer Facts & Figures 2000" (Copyright 2000, Reprinted with permission from the American Cancer Society)
*Rates calculated using 1999 Census resident population estimates. Not age-adjusted.
**Fewer than 50 deaths.

Deaths by Alzheimer's Disease in 1997

National Total = 22,475 Deaths*

ALPHA ORDER

RANK	STATE	DEATHS	% of USA
19	Alabama	464	2.1%
50	Alaska	11	0.0%
22	Arizona	438	1.9%
32	Arkansas	252	1.1%
1	California	2,054	9.1%
26	Colorado	357	1.6%
30	Connecticut	262	1.2%
47	Delaware	57	0.3%
3	Florida	1,598	7.1%
12	Georgia	618	2.7%
49	Hawaii	50	0.2%
39	Idaho	116	0.5%
4	Illinois	1,054	4.7%
13	Indiana	570	2.5%
27	Iowa	334	1.5%
31	Kansas	261	1.2%
24	Kentucky	381	1.7%
21	Louisiana	440	2.0%
36	Maine	152	0.7%
25	Maryland	372	1.7%
8	Massachusetts	677	3.0%
9	Michigan	672	3.0%
18	Minnesota	468	2.1%
35	Mississippi	182	0.8%
17	Missouri	479	2.1%
43	Montana	82	0.4%
33	Nebraska	218	1.0%
42	Nevada	103	0.5%
37	New Hampshire	146	0.6%
11	New Jersey	623	2.8%
41	New Mexico	108	0.5%
10	New York	661	2.9%
7	North Carolina	726	3.2%
46	North Dakota	64	0.3%
5	Ohio	1,016	4.5%
28	Oklahoma	304	1.4%
23	Oregon	416	1.9%
6	Pennsylvania	994	4.4%
40	Rhode Island	113	0.5%
29	South Carolina	303	1.3%
44	South Dakota	71	0.3%
20	Tennessee	447	2.0%
2	Texas	1,611	7.2%
38	Utah	144	0.6%
45	Vermont	69	0.3%
15	Virginia	544	2.4%
13	Washington	570	2.5%
34	West Virginia	210	0.9%
16	Wisconsin	524	2.3%
48	Wyoming	56	0.2%

RANK ORDER

RANK	STATE	DEATHS	% of USA
1	California	2,054	9.1%
2	Texas	1,611	7.2%
3	Florida	1,598	7.1%
4	Illinois	1,054	4.7%
5	Ohio	1,016	4.5%
6	Pennsylvania	994	4.4%
7	North Carolina	726	3.2%
8	Massachusetts	677	3.0%
9	Michigan	672	3.0%
10	New York	661	2.9%
11	New Jersey	623	2.8%
12	Georgia	618	2.7%
13	Indiana	570	2.5%
13	Washington	570	2.5%
15	Virginia	544	2.4%
16	Wisconsin	524	2.3%
17	Missouri	479	2.1%
18	Minnesota	468	2.1%
19	Alabama	464	2.1%
20	Tennessee	447	2.0%
21	Louisiana	440	2.0%
22	Arizona	438	1.9%
23	Oregon	416	1.9%
24	Kentucky	381	1.7%
25	Maryland	372	1.7%
26	Colorado	357	1.6%
27	Iowa	334	1.5%
28	Oklahoma	304	1.4%
29	South Carolina	303	1.3%
30	Connecticut	262	1.2%
31	Kansas	261	1.2%
32	Arkansas	252	1.1%
33	Nebraska	218	1.0%
34	West Virginia	210	0.9%
35	Mississippi	182	0.8%
36	Maine	152	0.7%
37	New Hampshire	146	0.6%
38	Utah	144	0.6%
39	Idaho	116	0.5%
40	Rhode Island	113	0.5%
41	New Mexico	108	0.5%
42	Nevada	103	0.5%
43	Montana	82	0.4%
44	South Dakota	71	0.3%
45	Vermont	69	0.3%
46	North Dakota	64	0.3%
47	Delaware	57	0.3%
48	Wyoming	56	0.2%
49	Hawaii	50	0.2%
50	Alaska	11	0.0%
	District of Columbia	33	0.1%

Source: U.S. Department of Health and Human Services, National Center for Health Statistics
    "National Vital Statistics Reports" (Vol. 47, No. 19, June 30, 1999)
*Final data by state of residence. A degenerative disease of the brain cells producing loss of memory and general intellectual impairment. It usually affects people over age 65. As the disease progresses, a variety of symptoms may become apparent, including confusion, irritability, and restlessness, as well as disorientation and impaired judgment and concentration.

Death Rate by Alzheimer's Disease in 1997

National Rate = 8.4 Deaths per 100,000 Population*

ALPHA ORDER

RANK	STATE	RATE
12	Alabama	10.7
NA	Alaska**	NA
23	Arizona	9.6
17	Arkansas	10.0
45	California	6.4
27	Colorado	9.2
38	Connecticut	8.0
39	Delaware	7.8
11	Florida	10.9
32	Georgia	8.3
48	Hawaii	4.2
23	Idaho	9.6
30	Illinois	8.9
21	Indiana	9.7
5	Iowa	11.7
14	Kansas	10.1
21	Kentucky	9.7
14	Louisiana	10.1
4	Maine	12.2
41	Maryland	7.3
10	Massachusetts	11.1
43	Michigan	6.9
17	Minnesota	10.0
44	Mississippi	6.7
30	Missouri	8.9
26	Montana	9.3
1	Nebraska	13.2
47	Nevada	6.1
3	New Hampshire	12.4
40	New Jersey	7.7
46	New Mexico	6.2
49	New York	3.6
20	North Carolina	9.8
17	North Dakota	10.0
29	Ohio	9.1
27	Oklahoma	9.2
2	Oregon	12.8
32	Pennsylvania	8.3
9	Rhode Island	11.4
36	South Carolina	8.1
23	South Dakota	9.6
32	Tennessee	8.3
32	Texas	8.3
42	Utah	7.0
5	Vermont	11.7
36	Virginia	8.1
13	Washington	10.2
8	West Virginia	11.6
14	Wisconsin	10.1
5	Wyoming	11.7

RANK ORDER

RANK	STATE	RATE
1	Nebraska	13.2
2	Oregon	12.8
3	New Hampshire	12.4
4	Maine	12.2
5	Iowa	11.7
5	Vermont	11.7
5	Wyoming	11.7
8	West Virginia	11.6
9	Rhode Island	11.4
10	Massachusetts	11.1
11	Florida	10.9
12	Alabama	10.7
13	Washington	10.2
14	Kansas	10.1
14	Louisiana	10.1
14	Wisconsin	10.1
17	Arkansas	10.0
17	Minnesota	10.0
17	North Dakota	10.0
20	North Carolina	9.8
21	Indiana	9.7
21	Kentucky	9.7
23	Arizona	9.6
23	Idaho	9.6
23	South Dakota	9.6
26	Montana	9.3
27	Colorado	9.2
27	Oklahoma	9.2
29	Ohio	9.1
30	Illinois	8.9
30	Missouri	8.9
32	Georgia	8.3
32	Pennsylvania	8.3
32	Tennessee	8.3
32	Texas	8.3
36	South Carolina	8.1
36	Virginia	8.1
38	Connecticut	8.0
39	Delaware	7.8
40	New Jersey	7.7
41	Maryland	7.3
42	Utah	7.0
43	Michigan	6.9
44	Mississippi	6.7
45	California	6.4
46	New Mexico	6.2
47	Nevada	6.1
48	Hawaii	4.2
49	New York	3.6
NA	Alaska**	NA
	District of Columbia	6.2

Source: U.S. Department of Health and Human Services, National Center for Health Statistics
    "National Vital Statistics Reports" (Vol. 47, No. 19, June 30, 1999)
Final data by state of residence. A degenerative disease of the brain cells producing loss of memory and general intellectual impairment. It usually affects people over age 65. As the disease progresses, a variety of symptoms may become apparent, including confusion, irritability, and restlessness, as well as disorientation and impaired judgment and concentration. Not age-adjusted.

Age-Adjusted Death Rate by Alzheimer's Disease in 1997

National Rate = 2.7 Deaths per 100,000 Population*

ALPHA ORDER

RANK	STATE	RATE
5	Alabama	3.7
NA	Alaska**	NA
21	Arizona	3.1
21	Arkansas	3.1
41	California	2.4
5	Colorado	3.7
45	Connecticut	2.2
33	Delaware	2.7
41	Florida	2.4
7	Georgia	3.6
48	Hawaii	1.4
15	Idaho	3.3
29	Illinois	2.8
18	Indiana	3.2
33	Iowa	2.7
25	Kansas	2.9
18	Kentucky	3.2
2	Louisiana	3.9
12	Maine	3.4
29	Maryland	2.8
21	Massachusetts	3.1
39	Michigan	2.5
25	Minnesota	2.9
39	Mississippi	2.5
33	Missouri	2.7
33	Montana	2.7
12	Nebraska	3.4
29	Nevada	2.8
2	New Hampshire	3.9
44	New Jersey	2.3
41	New Mexico	2.4
49	New York	1.1
10	North Carolina	3.5
33	North Dakota	2.7
25	Ohio	2.9
24	Oklahoma	3.0
7	Oregon	3.6
45	Pennsylvania	2.2
38	Rhode Island	2.6
18	South Carolina	3.2
47	South Dakota	2.0
29	Tennessee	2.8
7	Texas	3.6
15	Utah	3.3
4	Vermont	3.8
15	Virginia	3.3
10	Washington	3.5
12	West Virginia	3.4
25	Wisconsin	2.9
1	Wyoming	4.1

RANK ORDER

RANK	STATE	RATE
1	Wyoming	4.1
2	Louisiana	3.9
2	New Hampshire	3.9
4	Vermont	3.8
5	Alabama	3.7
5	Colorado	3.7
7	Georgia	3.6
7	Oregon	3.6
7	Texas	3.6
10	North Carolina	3.5
10	Washington	3.5
12	Maine	3.4
12	Nebraska	3.4
12	West Virginia	3.4
15	Idaho	3.3
15	Utah	3.3
15	Virginia	3.3
18	Indiana	3.2
18	Kentucky	3.2
18	South Carolina	3.2
21	Arizona	3.1
21	Arkansas	3.1
21	Massachusetts	3.1
24	Oklahoma	3.0
25	Kansas	2.9
25	Minnesota	2.9
25	Ohio	2.9
25	Wisconsin	2.9
29	Illinois	2.8
29	Maryland	2.8
29	Nevada	2.8
29	Tennessee	2.8
33	Delaware	2.7
33	Iowa	2.7
33	Missouri	2.7
33	Montana	2.7
33	North Dakota	2.7
38	Rhode Island	2.6
39	Michigan	2.5
39	Mississippi	2.5
41	California	2.4
41	Florida	2.4
41	New Mexico	2.4
44	New Jersey	2.3
45	Connecticut	2.2
45	Pennsylvania	2.2
47	South Dakota	2.0
48	Hawaii	1.4
49	New York	1.1
NA	Alaska**	NA
	District of Columbia	1.7

Source: U.S. Department of Health and Human Services, National Center for Health Statistics
    "National Vital Statistics Reports" (Vol. 47, No. 19, June 30, 1999)
*Final data by state of residence. A degenerative disease of the brain cells producing loss of memory and general intellectual impairment. It usually affects people over age 65. As the disease progresses, a variety of symptoms may become apparent, including confusion, irritability, and restlessness, as well as disorientation and impaired judgment and concentration. **Not available.

Deaths by Atherosclerosis in 1997

National Total = 16,057 Deaths*

ALPHA ORDER

RANK	STATE	DEATHS	% of USA
27	Alabama	213	1.3%
50	Alaska	9	0.1%
23	Arizona	269	1.7%
32	Arkansas	165	1.0%
1	California	1,984	12.4%
13	Colorado	392	2.4%
33	Connecticut	157	1.0%
47	Delaware	21	0.1%
2	Florida	1,070	6.7%
9	Georgia	543	3.4%
49	Hawaii	11	0.1%
45	Idaho	49	0.3%
7	Illinois	648	4.0%
11	Indiana	469	2.9%
16	Iowa	360	2.2%
26	Kansas	233	1.5%
28	Kentucky	197	1.2%
20	Louisiana	309	1.9%
39	Maine	72	0.4%
31	Maryland	175	1.1%
19	Massachusetts	320	2.0%
6	Michigan	700	4.4%
24	Minnesota	245	1.5%
35	Mississippi	103	0.6%
21	Missouri	291	1.8%
41	Montana	69	0.4%
29	Nebraska	192	1.2%
36	Nevada	88	0.5%
38	New Hampshire	79	0.5%
10	New Jersey	522	3.3%
37	New Mexico	82	0.5%
4	New York	793	4.9%
12	North Carolina	414	2.6%
39	North Dakota	72	0.4%
8	Ohio	624	3.9%
15	Oklahoma	386	2.4%
25	Oregon	234	1.5%
5	Pennsylvania	721	4.5%
43	Rhode Island	64	0.4%
34	South Carolina	118	0.7%
44	South Dakota	56	0.3%
14	Tennessee	388	2.4%
3	Texas	877	5.5%
42	Utah	66	0.4%
46	Vermont	24	0.1%
17	Virginia	336	2.1%
17	Washington	336	2.1%
30	West Virginia	188	1.2%
22	Wisconsin	273	1.7%
48	Wyoming	19	0.1%

RANK ORDER

RANK	STATE	DEATHS	% of USA
1	California	1,984	12.4%
2	Florida	1,070	6.7%
3	Texas	877	5.5%
4	New York	793	4.9%
5	Pennsylvania	721	4.5%
6	Michigan	700	4.4%
7	Illinois	648	4.0%
8	Ohio	624	3.9%
9	Georgia	543	3.4%
10	New Jersey	522	3.3%
11	Indiana	469	2.9%
12	North Carolina	414	2.6%
13	Colorado	392	2.4%
14	Tennessee	388	2.4%
15	Oklahoma	386	2.4%
16	Iowa	360	2.2%
17	Virginia	336	2.1%
17	Washington	336	2.1%
19	Massachusetts	320	2.0%
20	Louisiana	309	1.9%
21	Missouri	291	1.8%
22	Wisconsin	273	1.7%
23	Arizona	269	1.7%
24	Minnesota	245	1.5%
25	Oregon	234	1.5%
26	Kansas	233	1.5%
27	Alabama	213	1.3%
28	Kentucky	197	1.2%
29	Nebraska	192	1.2%
30	West Virginia	188	1.2%
31	Maryland	175	1.1%
32	Arkansas	165	1.0%
33	Connecticut	157	1.0%
34	South Carolina	118	0.7%
35	Mississippi	103	0.6%
36	Nevada	88	0.5%
37	New Mexico	82	0.5%
38	New Hampshire	79	0.5%
39	Maine	72	0.4%
39	North Dakota	72	0.4%
41	Montana	69	0.4%
42	Utah	66	0.4%
43	Rhode Island	64	0.4%
44	South Dakota	56	0.3%
45	Idaho	49	0.3%
46	Vermont	24	0.1%
47	Delaware	21	0.1%
48	Wyoming	19	0.1%
49	Hawaii	11	0.1%
50	Alaska	9	0.1%
	District of Columbia	31	0.2%

Source: U.S. Department of Health and Human Services, National Center for Health Statistics
    (http://wonder.cdc.gov/WONDER/)
*Final data by state of residence. Atherosclerosis is a form of hardening of the arteries.

Death Rate by Atherosclerosis in 1997

National Rate = 6.0 Deaths per 100,000 Population*

ALPHA ORDER

RANK STATE

RANK	STATE	RATE
36	Alabama	4.9
49	Alaska**	1.5
24	Arizona	5.9
18	Arkansas	6.5
21	California	6.1
6	Colorado	10.1
37	Connecticut	4.8
48	Delaware	2.9
11	Florida	7.3
12	Georgia	7.2
50	Hawaii**	0.9
42	Idaho	4.0
28	Illinois	5.4
8	Indiana	8.0
1	Iowa	12.6
7	Kansas	9.0
34	Kentucky	5.0
16	Louisiana	7.1
25	Maine	5.8
45	Maryland	3.4
31	Massachusetts	5.2
12	Michigan	7.2
31	Minnesota	5.2
44	Mississippi	3.8
28	Missouri	5.4
9	Montana	7.8
2	Nebraska	11.6
31	Nevada	5.2
17	New Hampshire	6.7
18	New Jersey	6.5
38	New Mexico	4.7
40	New York	4.4
26	North Carolina	5.6
4	North Dakota	11.2
26	Ohio	5.6
2	Oklahoma	11.6
12	Oregon	7.2
22	Pennsylvania	6.0
18	Rhode Island	6.5
47	South Carolina	3.1
10	South Dakota	7.6
12	Tennessee	7.2
39	Texas	4.5
46	Utah	3.2
41	Vermont	4.1
34	Virginia	5.0
22	Washington	6.0
5	West Virginia	10.4
30	Wisconsin	5.3
42	Wyoming**	4.0

RANK ORDER

RANK STATE

RANK	STATE	RATE
1	Iowa	12.6
2	Nebraska	11.6
2	Oklahoma	11.6
4	North Dakota	11.2
5	West Virginia	10.4
6	Colorado	10.1
7	Kansas	9.0
8	Indiana	8.0
9	Montana	7.8
10	South Dakota	7.6
11	Florida	7.3
12	Georgia	7.2
12	Michigan	7.2
12	Oregon	7.2
12	Tennessee	7.2
16	Louisiana	7.1
17	New Hampshire	6.7
18	Arkansas	6.5
18	New Jersey	6.5
18	Rhode Island	6.5
21	California	6.1
22	Pennsylvania	6.0
22	Washington	6.0
24	Arizona	5.9
25	Maine	5.8
26	North Carolina	5.6
26	Ohio	5.6
28	Illinois	5.4
28	Missouri	5.4
30	Wisconsin	5.3
31	Massachusetts	5.2
31	Minnesota	5.2
31	Nevada	5.2
34	Kentucky	5.0
34	Virginia	5.0
36	Alabama	4.9
37	Connecticut	4.8
38	New Mexico	4.7
39	Texas	4.5
40	New York	4.4
41	Vermont	4.1
42	Idaho	4.0
42	Wyoming**	4.0
44	Mississippi	3.8
45	Maryland	3.4
46	Utah	3.2
47	South Carolina	3.1
48	Delaware	2.9
49	Alaska**	1.5
50	Hawaii**	0.9

District of Columbia 5.8

Source: U.S. Department of Health and Human Services, National Center for Health Statistics
(http://wonder.cdc.gov/WONDER/)
*Final data by state of residence. Atherosclerosis is a form of hardening of the arteries. Not age-adjusted.
**Due to low numbers of deaths, rates for these states should be interpreted with caution.

Age-Adjusted Death Rate by Atherosclerosis in 1997

National Rate = 2.1 Deaths per 100,000 Population*

ALPHA ORDER

RANK	STATE	RATE
17	Alabama	2.2
39	Alaska**	1.5
23	Arizona	2.0
23	Arkansas	2.0
13	California	2.5
1	Colorado	3.9
39	Connecticut	1.5
48	Delaware	1.1
31	Florida	1.7
3	Georgia	3.5
50	Hawaii**	0.3
39	Idaho	1.5
35	Illinois	1.6
8	Indiana	2.8
6	Iowa	3.1
16	Kansas	2.3
31	Kentucky	1.7
8	Louisiana	2.8
27	Maine	1.9
48	Maryland	1.1
35	Massachusetts	1.6
13	Michigan	2.5
35	Minnesota	1.6
45	Mississippi	1.4
31	Missouri	1.7
4	Montana	3.2
7	Nebraska	3.0
11	Nevada	2.6
11	New Hampshire	2.6
17	New Jersey	2.2
27	New Mexico	1.9
47	New York	1.3
21	North Carolina	2.1
17	North Dakota	2.2
23	Ohio	2.0
1	Oklahoma	3.9
15	Oregon	2.4
31	Pennsylvania	1.7
35	Rhode Island	1.6
39	South Carolina	1.5
27	South Dakota	1.9
10	Tennessee	2.7
23	Texas	2.0
30	Utah	1.8
39	Vermont	1.5
17	Virginia	2.2
21	Washington	2.1
4	West Virginia	3.2
39	Wisconsin	1.5
45	Wyoming**	1.4

RANK ORDER

RANK	STATE	RATE
1	Colorado	3.9
1	Oklahoma	3.9
3	Georgia	3.5
4	Montana	3.2
4	West Virginia	3.2
6	Iowa	3.1
7	Nebraska	3.0
8	Indiana	2.8
8	Louisiana	2.8
10	Tennessee	2.7
11	Nevada	2.6
11	New Hampshire	2.6
13	California	2.5
13	Michigan	2.5
15	Oregon	2.4
16	Kansas	2.3
17	Alabama	2.2
17	New Jersey	2.2
17	North Dakota	2.2
17	Virginia	2.2
21	North Carolina	2.1
21	Washington	2.1
23	Arizona	2.0
23	Arkansas	2.0
23	Ohio	2.0
23	Texas	2.0
27	Maine	1.9
27	New Mexico	1.9
27	South Dakota	1.9
30	Utah	1.8
31	Florida	1.7
31	Kentucky	1.7
31	Missouri	1.7
31	Pennsylvania	1.7
35	Illinois	1.6
35	Massachusetts	1.6
35	Minnesota	1.6
35	Rhode Island	1.6
39	Alaska**	1.5
39	Connecticut	1.5
39	Idaho	1.5
39	South Carolina	1.5
39	Vermont	1.5
39	Wisconsin	1.5
45	Mississippi	1.4
45	Wyoming**	1.4
47	New York	1.3
48	Delaware	1.1
48	Maryland	1.1
50	Hawaii**	0.3
	District of Columbia	1.7

Source: U.S. Department of Health and Human Services, National Center for Health Statistics
        (http://wonder.cdc.gov/WONDER/)
*Final data by state of residence. Atherosclerosis is a form of hardening of the arteries.
**Due to low numbers of deaths, rates for these states should be interpreted with caution.

Deaths by Cerebrovascular Diseases in 1997

National Total = 159,791 Deaths*

ALPHA ORDER

RANK	STATE	DEATHS	% of USA
20	Alabama	2,885	1.8%
50	Alaska	132	0.1%
26	Arizona	2,483	1.6%
27	Arkansas	2,461	1.5%
1	California	16,727	10.5%
33	Colorado	1,708	1.1%
30	Connecticut	1,904	1.2%
47	Delaware	347	0.2%
3	Florida	10,026	6.3%
10	Georgia	4,267	2.7%
41	Hawaii	710	0.4%
40	Idaho	711	0.4%
6	Illinois	7,222	4.5%
14	Indiana	3,832	2.4%
29	Iowa	2,158	1.4%
32	Kansas	1,717	1.1%
25	Kentucky	2,502	1.6%
24	Louisiana	2,528	1.6%
38	Maine	789	0.5%
22	Maryland	2,607	1.6%
17	Massachusetts	3,410	2.1%
8	Michigan	5,757	3.6%
19	Minnesota	2,997	1.9%
31	Mississippi	1,858	1.2%
15	Missouri	3,708	2.3%
45	Montana	544	0.3%
35	Nebraska	1,102	0.7%
37	Nevada	798	0.5%
42	New Hampshire	689	0.4%
11	New Jersey	4,129	2.6%
39	New Mexico	768	0.5%
5	New York	8,009	5.0%
9	North Carolina	5,227	3.3%
46	North Dakota	482	0.3%
7	Ohio	6,878	4.3%
28	Oklahoma	2,393	1.5%
23	Oregon	2,569	1.6%
4	Pennsylvania	8,371	5.2%
43	Rhode Island	684	0.4%
21	South Carolina	2,845	1.8%
44	South Dakota	571	0.4%
13	Tennessee	4,021	2.5%
2	Texas	10,150	6.4%
36	Utah	875	0.5%
47	Vermont	347	0.2%
12	Virginia	4,041	2.5%
18	Washington	3,365	2.1%
34	West Virginia	1,237	0.8%
16	Wisconsin	3,681	2.3%
49	Wyoming	233	0.1%

RANK ORDER

RANK	STATE	DEATHS	% of USA
1	California	16,727	10.5%
2	Texas	10,150	6.4%
3	Florida	10,026	6.3%
4	Pennsylvania	8,371	5.2%
5	New York	8,009	5.0%
6	Illinois	7,222	4.5%
7	Ohio	6,878	4.3%
8	Michigan	5,757	3.6%
9	North Carolina	5,227	3.3%
10	Georgia	4,267	2.7%
11	New Jersey	4,129	2.6%
12	Virginia	4,041	2.5%
13	Tennessee	4,021	2.5%
14	Indiana	3,832	2.4%
15	Missouri	3,708	2.3%
16	Wisconsin	3,681	2.3%
17	Massachusetts	3,410	2.1%
18	Washington	3,365	2.1%
19	Minnesota	2,997	1.9%
20	Alabama	2,885	1.8%
21	South Carolina	2,845	1.8%
22	Maryland	2,607	1.6%
23	Oregon	2,569	1.6%
24	Louisiana	2,528	1.6%
25	Kentucky	2,502	1.6%
26	Arizona	2,483	1.6%
27	Arkansas	2,461	1.5%
28	Oklahoma	2,393	1.5%
29	Iowa	2,158	1.4%
30	Connecticut	1,904	1.2%
31	Mississippi	1,858	1.2%
32	Kansas	1,717	1.1%
33	Colorado	1,708	1.1%
34	West Virginia	1,237	0.8%
35	Nebraska	1,102	0.7%
36	Utah	875	0.5%
37	Nevada	798	0.5%
38	Maine	789	0.5%
39	New Mexico	768	0.5%
40	Idaho	711	0.4%
41	Hawaii	710	0.4%
42	New Hampshire	689	0.4%
43	Rhode Island	684	0.4%
44	South Dakota	571	0.4%
45	Montana	544	0.3%
46	North Dakota	482	0.3%
47	Delaware	347	0.2%
47	Vermont	347	0.2%
49	Wyoming	233	0.1%
50	Alaska	132	0.1%
	District of Columbia	336	0.2%

Source: U.S. Department of Health and Human Services, National Center for Health Statistics
   "National Vital Statistics Reports" (Vol. 47, No. 19, June 30, 1999)
*Final data by state of residence. Cerebrovascular diseases include stroke and other disorders of the blood vessels of the brain.

Death Rate by Cerebrovascular Diseases in 1997

National Rate = 59.7 Deaths per 100,000 Population*

ALPHA ORDER

RANK	STATE	RATE
17	Alabama	66.8
50	Alaska	21.7
38	Arizona	54.5
1	Arkansas	97.5
40	California	51.8
48	Colorado	43.9
34	Connecticut	58.2
45	Delaware	47.4
14	Florida	68.4
36	Georgia	57.0
29	Hawaii	59.8
33	Idaho	58.7
26	Illinois	60.7
20	Indiana	65.3
4	Iowa	75.7
19	Kansas	66.2
21	Kentucky	64.0
35	Louisiana	58.1
23	Maine	63.5
42	Maryland	51.2
37	Massachusetts	55.7
30	Michigan	58.9
21	Minnesota	64.0
16	Mississippi	68.0
13	Missouri	68.6
24	Montana	61.9
18	Nebraska	66.5
44	Nevada	47.6
32	New Hampshire	58.8
41	New Jersey	51.3
46	New Mexico	44.4
47	New York	44.2
10	North Carolina	70.4
6	North Dakota	75.2
25	Ohio	61.5
8	Oklahoma	72.1
2	Oregon	79.2
11	Pennsylvania	69.6
12	Rhode Island	69.3
4	South Carolina	75.7
3	South Dakota	77.4
7	Tennessee	74.9
39	Texas	52.2
49	Utah	42.5
30	Vermont	58.9
27	Virginia	60.0
27	Washington	60.0
15	West Virginia	68.1
9	Wisconsin	71.2
43	Wyoming	48.6

RANK ORDER

RANK	STATE	RATE
1	Arkansas	97.5
2	Oregon	79.2
3	South Dakota	77.4
4	Iowa	75.7
4	South Carolina	75.7
6	North Dakota	75.2
7	Tennessee	74.9
8	Oklahoma	72.1
9	Wisconsin	71.2
10	North Carolina	70.4
11	Pennsylvania	69.6
12	Rhode Island	69.3
13	Missouri	68.6
14	Florida	68.4
15	West Virginia	68.1
16	Mississippi	68.0
17	Alabama	66.8
18	Nebraska	66.5
19	Kansas	66.2
20	Indiana	65.3
21	Kentucky	64.0
21	Minnesota	64.0
23	Maine	63.5
24	Montana	61.9
25	Ohio	61.5
26	Illinois	60.7
27	Virginia	60.0
27	Washington	60.0
29	Hawaii	59.8
30	Michigan	58.9
30	Vermont	58.9
32	New Hampshire	58.8
33	Idaho	58.7
34	Connecticut	58.2
35	Louisiana	58.1
36	Georgia	57.0
37	Massachusetts	55.7
38	Arizona	54.5
39	Texas	52.2
40	California	51.8
41	New Jersey	51.3
42	Maryland	51.2
43	Wyoming	48.6
44	Nevada	47.6
45	Delaware	47.4
46	New Mexico	44.4
47	New York	44.2
48	Colorado	43.9
49	Utah	42.5
50	Alaska	21.7
	District of Columbia	63.5

Source: U.S. Department of Health and Human Services, National Center for Health Statistics
"National Vital Statistics Reports" (Vol. 47, No. 19, June 30, 1999)
*Final data by state of residence. Cerebrovascular diseases include stroke and other disorders of the blood vessels of the brain. Not age-adjusted.

Age-Adjusted Death Rate by Cerebrovascular Diseases in 1997

National Rate = 25.9 Deaths per 100,000 Population*

ALPHA ORDER

RANK	STATE	RATE
7	Alabama	31.2
40	Alaska	23.0
35	Arizona	23.4
2	Arkansas	38.5
21	California	25.9
42	Colorado	22.3
48	Connecticut	20.5
44	Delaware	22.1
42	Florida	22.3
4	Georgia	34.2
12	Hawaii	28.3
23	Idaho	25.7
17	Illinois	26.5
13	Indiana	28.0
37	Iowa	23.3
35	Kansas	23.4
14	Kentucky	27.9
8	Louisiana	30.1
38	Maine	23.1
26	Maryland	25.3
49	Massachusetts	19.8
19	Michigan	26.2
28	Minnesota	24.5
3	Mississippi	35.2
18	Missouri	26.4
32	Montana	23.8
38	Nebraska	23.1
20	Nevada	26.0
29	New Hampshire	24.4
47	New Jersey	21.2
45	New Mexico	21.6
50	New York	19.2
6	North Carolina	32.2
34	North Dakota	23.6
22	Ohio	25.8
11	Oklahoma	28.7
10	Oregon	29.0
29	Pennsylvania	24.4
40	Rhode Island	23.0
1	South Carolina	39.3
24	South Dakota	25.5
5	Tennessee	33.7
14	Texas	27.9
29	Utah	24.4
33	Vermont	23.7
9	Virginia	29.8
24	Washington	25.5
27	West Virginia	25.1
16	Wisconsin	26.6
45	Wyoming	21.6

RANK ORDER

RANK	STATE	RATE
1	South Carolina	39.3
2	Arkansas	38.5
3	Mississippi	35.2
4	Georgia	34.2
5	Tennessee	33.7
6	North Carolina	32.2
7	Alabama	31.2
8	Louisiana	30.1
9	Virginia	29.8
10	Oregon	29.0
11	Oklahoma	28.7
12	Hawaii	28.3
13	Indiana	28.0
14	Kentucky	27.9
14	Texas	27.9
16	Wisconsin	26.6
17	Illinois	26.5
18	Missouri	26.4
19	Michigan	26.2
20	Nevada	26.0
21	California	25.9
22	Ohio	25.8
23	Idaho	25.7
24	South Dakota	25.5
24	Washington	25.5
26	Maryland	25.3
27	West Virginia	25.1
28	Minnesota	24.5
29	New Hampshire	24.4
29	Pennsylvania	24.4
29	Utah	24.4
32	Montana	23.8
33	Vermont	23.7
34	North Dakota	23.6
35	Arizona	23.4
35	Kansas	23.4
37	Iowa	23.3
38	Maine	23.1
38	Nebraska	23.1
40	Alaska	23.0
40	Rhode Island	23.0
42	Colorado	22.3
42	Florida	22.3
44	Delaware	22.1
45	New Mexico	21.6
45	Wyoming	21.6
47	New Jersey	21.2
48	Connecticut	20.5
49	Massachusetts	19.8
50	New York	19.2
	District of Columbia	31.4

Source: U.S. Department of Health and Human Services, National Center for Health Statistics
    "National Vital Statistics Reports" (Vol. 47, No. 19, June 30, 1999)
*Final data by state of residence. Cerebrovascular diseases include stroke and other disorders of the blood vessels of the brain.

Deaths by Chronic Liver Disease and Cirrhosis in 1997

National Total = 25,175 Deaths*

ALPHA ORDER

RANK	STATE	DEATHS	% of USA
20	Alabama	389	1.5%
47	Alaska	48	0.2%
11	Arizona	606	2.4%
34	Arkansas	182	0.7%
1	California	3,510	13.9%
26	Colorado	338	1.3%
28	Connecticut	291	1.2%
44	Delaware	65	0.3%
3	Florida	1,942	7.7%
12	Georgia	599	2.4%
45	Hawaii	60	0.2%
41	Idaho	98	0.4%
5	Illinois	1,082	4.3%
17	Indiana	428	1.7%
35	Iowa	177	0.7%
36	Kansas	173	0.7%
24	Kentucky	367	1.5%
22	Louisiana	378	1.5%
38	Maine	116	0.5%
18	Maryland	413	1.6%
14	Massachusetts	520	2.1%
7	Michigan	969	3.8%
29	Minnesota	286	1.1%
31	Mississippi	255	1.0%
19	Missouri	410	1.6%
43	Montana	77	0.3%
42	Nebraska	86	0.3%
31	Nevada	255	1.0%
40	New Hampshire	105	0.4%
9	New Jersey	745	3.0%
30	New Mexico	257	1.0%
4	New York	1,579	6.3%
10	North Carolina	666	2.6%
46	North Dakota	56	0.2%
8	Ohio	958	3.8%
25	Oklahoma	343	1.4%
27	Oregon	297	1.2%
6	Pennsylvania	1,074	4.3%
37	Rhode Island	118	0.5%
21	South Carolina	379	1.5%
49	South Dakota	42	0.2%
13	Tennessee	562	2.2%
2	Texas	2,027	8.1%
39	Utah	115	0.5%
48	Vermont	45	0.2%
16	Virginia	499	2.0%
15	Washington	507	2.0%
33	West Virginia	194	0.8%
23	Wisconsin	375	1.5%
50	Wyoming	35	0.1%

RANK ORDER

RANK	STATE	DEATHS	% of USA
1	California	3,510	13.9%
2	Texas	2,027	8.1%
3	Florida	1,942	7.7%
4	New York	1,579	6.3%
5	Illinois	1,082	4.3%
6	Pennsylvania	1,074	4.3%
7	Michigan	969	3.8%
8	Ohio	958	3.8%
9	New Jersey	745	3.0%
10	North Carolina	666	2.6%
11	Arizona	606	2.4%
12	Georgia	599	2.4%
13	Tennessee	562	2.2%
14	Massachusetts	520	2.1%
15	Washington	507	2.0%
16	Virginia	499	2.0%
17	Indiana	428	1.7%
18	Maryland	413	1.6%
19	Missouri	410	1.6%
20	Alabama	389	1.5%
21	South Carolina	379	1.5%
22	Louisiana	378	1.5%
23	Wisconsin	375	1.5%
24	Kentucky	367	1.5%
25	Oklahoma	343	1.4%
26	Colorado	338	1.3%
27	Oregon	297	1.2%
28	Connecticut	291	1.2%
29	Minnesota	286	1.1%
30	New Mexico	257	1.0%
31	Mississippi	255	1.0%
31	Nevada	255	1.0%
33	West Virginia	194	0.8%
34	Arkansas	182	0.7%
35	Iowa	177	0.7%
36	Kansas	173	0.7%
37	Rhode Island	118	0.5%
38	Maine	116	0.5%
39	Utah	115	0.5%
40	New Hampshire	105	0.4%
41	Idaho	98	0.4%
42	Nebraska	86	0.3%
43	Montana	77	0.3%
44	Delaware	65	0.3%
45	Hawaii	60	0.2%
46	North Dakota	56	0.2%
47	Alaska	48	0.2%
48	Vermont	45	0.2%
49	South Dakota	42	0.2%
50	Wyoming	35	0.1%
	District of Columbia	77	0.3%

Source: U.S. Department of Health and Human Services, National Center for Health Statistics
"National Vital Statistics Reports" (Vol. 47, No. 19, June 30, 1999)
Final data by state of residence. Cirrhosis of the liver is characterized by the replacement of normal tissue with fibrous tissue and the loss of functional liver cells. It can result from alcohol abuse, nutritional deprivation, or infection especially by the hepatitis virus.

Death Rate by Chronic Liver Disease and Cirrhosis in 1997

National Rate = 9.4 Deaths per 100,000 Population*

<table>
<tr><td colspan="3">ALPHA ORDER</td><td colspan="3">RANK ORDER</td></tr>
<tr><td>RANK</td><td>STATE</td><td>RATE</td><td>RANK</td><td>STATE</td><td>RATE</td></tr>
<tr><td>19</td><td>Alabama</td><td>9.0</td><td>1</td><td>Nevada</td><td>15.2</td></tr>
<tr><td>36</td><td>Alaska</td><td>7.9</td><td>2</td><td>New Mexico</td><td>14.9</td></tr>
<tr><td>3</td><td>Arizona</td><td>13.3</td><td>3</td><td>Arizona</td><td>13.3</td></tr>
<tr><td>43</td><td>Arkansas</td><td>7.2</td><td>3</td><td>Florida</td><td>13.3</td></tr>
<tr><td>6</td><td>California</td><td>10.9</td><td>5</td><td>Rhode Island</td><td>12.0</td></tr>
<tr><td>27</td><td>Colorado</td><td>8.7</td><td>6</td><td>California</td><td>10.9</td></tr>
<tr><td>23</td><td>Connecticut</td><td>8.9</td><td>7</td><td>West Virginia</td><td>10.7</td></tr>
<tr><td>23</td><td>Delaware</td><td>8.9</td><td>8</td><td>Tennessee</td><td>10.5</td></tr>
<tr><td>3</td><td>Florida</td><td>13.3</td><td>9</td><td>Texas</td><td>10.4</td></tr>
<tr><td>35</td><td>Georgia</td><td>8.0</td><td>10</td><td>Oklahoma</td><td>10.3</td></tr>
<tr><td>50</td><td>Hawaii</td><td>5.1</td><td>11</td><td>South Carolina</td><td>10.1</td></tr>
<tr><td>33</td><td>Idaho</td><td>8.1</td><td>12</td><td>Michigan</td><td>9.9</td></tr>
<tr><td>18</td><td>Illinois</td><td>9.1</td><td>13</td><td>Kentucky</td><td>9.4</td></tr>
<tr><td>40</td><td>Indiana</td><td>7.3</td><td>14</td><td>Maine</td><td>9.3</td></tr>
<tr><td>45</td><td>Iowa</td><td>6.2</td><td>14</td><td>Mississippi</td><td>9.3</td></tr>
<tr><td>44</td><td>Kansas</td><td>6.7</td><td>14</td><td>New Jersey</td><td>9.3</td></tr>
<tr><td>13</td><td>Kentucky</td><td>9.4</td><td>17</td><td>Oregon</td><td>9.2</td></tr>
<tr><td>27</td><td>Louisiana</td><td>8.7</td><td>18</td><td>Illinois</td><td>9.1</td></tr>
<tr><td>14</td><td>Maine</td><td>9.3</td><td>19</td><td>Alabama</td><td>9.0</td></tr>
<tr><td>33</td><td>Maryland</td><td>8.1</td><td>19</td><td>New Hampshire</td><td>9.0</td></tr>
<tr><td>32</td><td>Massachusetts</td><td>8.5</td><td>19</td><td>North Carolina</td><td>9.0</td></tr>
<tr><td>12</td><td>Michigan</td><td>9.9</td><td>19</td><td>Washington</td><td>9.0</td></tr>
<tr><td>46</td><td>Minnesota</td><td>6.1</td><td>23</td><td>Connecticut</td><td>8.9</td></tr>
<tr><td>14</td><td>Mississippi</td><td>9.3</td><td>23</td><td>Delaware</td><td>8.9</td></tr>
<tr><td>37</td><td>Missouri</td><td>7.6</td><td>23</td><td>Pennsylvania</td><td>8.9</td></tr>
<tr><td>26</td><td>Montana</td><td>8.8</td><td>26</td><td>Montana</td><td>8.8</td></tr>
<tr><td>49</td><td>Nebraska</td><td>5.2</td><td>27</td><td>Colorado</td><td>8.7</td></tr>
<tr><td>1</td><td>Nevada</td><td>15.2</td><td>27</td><td>Louisiana</td><td>8.7</td></tr>
<tr><td>19</td><td>New Hampshire</td><td>9.0</td><td>27</td><td>New York</td><td>8.7</td></tr>
<tr><td>14</td><td>New Jersey</td><td>9.3</td><td>27</td><td>North Dakota</td><td>8.7</td></tr>
<tr><td>2</td><td>New Mexico</td><td>14.9</td><td>31</td><td>Ohio</td><td>8.6</td></tr>
<tr><td>27</td><td>New York</td><td>8.7</td><td>32</td><td>Massachusetts</td><td>8.5</td></tr>
<tr><td>19</td><td>North Carolina</td><td>9.0</td><td>33</td><td>Idaho</td><td>8.1</td></tr>
<tr><td>27</td><td>North Dakota</td><td>8.7</td><td>33</td><td>Maryland</td><td>8.1</td></tr>
<tr><td>31</td><td>Ohio</td><td>8.6</td><td>35</td><td>Georgia</td><td>8.0</td></tr>
<tr><td>10</td><td>Oklahoma</td><td>10.3</td><td>36</td><td>Alaska</td><td>7.9</td></tr>
<tr><td>17</td><td>Oregon</td><td>9.2</td><td>37</td><td>Missouri</td><td>7.6</td></tr>
<tr><td>23</td><td>Pennsylvania</td><td>8.9</td><td>37</td><td>Vermont</td><td>7.6</td></tr>
<tr><td>5</td><td>Rhode Island</td><td>12.0</td><td>39</td><td>Virginia</td><td>7.4</td></tr>
<tr><td>11</td><td>South Carolina</td><td>10.1</td><td>40</td><td>Indiana</td><td>7.3</td></tr>
<tr><td>47</td><td>South Dakota</td><td>5.7</td><td>40</td><td>Wisconsin</td><td>7.3</td></tr>
<tr><td>8</td><td>Tennessee</td><td>10.5</td><td>40</td><td>Wyoming</td><td>7.3</td></tr>
<tr><td>9</td><td>Texas</td><td>10.4</td><td>43</td><td>Arkansas</td><td>7.2</td></tr>
<tr><td>48</td><td>Utah</td><td>5.6</td><td>44</td><td>Kansas</td><td>6.7</td></tr>
<tr><td>37</td><td>Vermont</td><td>7.6</td><td>45</td><td>Iowa</td><td>6.2</td></tr>
<tr><td>39</td><td>Virginia</td><td>7.4</td><td>46</td><td>Minnesota</td><td>6.1</td></tr>
<tr><td>19</td><td>Washington</td><td>9.0</td><td>47</td><td>South Dakota</td><td>5.7</td></tr>
<tr><td>7</td><td>West Virginia</td><td>10.7</td><td>48</td><td>Utah</td><td>5.6</td></tr>
<tr><td>40</td><td>Wisconsin</td><td>7.3</td><td>49</td><td>Nebraska</td><td>5.2</td></tr>
<tr><td>40</td><td>Wyoming</td><td>7.3</td><td>50</td><td>Hawaii</td><td>5.1</td></tr>
<tr><td></td><td></td><td></td><td></td><td>District of Columbia</td><td>14.6</td></tr>
</table>

Source: U.S. Department of Health and Human Services, National Center for Health Statistics
    "National Vital Statistics Reports" (Vol. 47, No. 19, June 30, 1999)
*Final data by state of residence. Cirrhosis of the liver is characterized by the replacement of normal tissue with fibrous tissue and the loss of functional liver cells. It can result from alcohol abuse, nutritional deprivation, or infection especially by the hepatitis virus. Not age-adjusted.

Age-Adjusted Death Rate by Chronic Liver Disease and Cirrhosis in 1997

National Rate = 7.4 Deaths per 100,000 Population*

<table>
<tr><td colspan="3">ALPHA ORDER</td><td colspan="3">RANK ORDER</td></tr>
<tr><td>RANK</td><td>STATE</td><td>RATE</td><td>RANK</td><td>STATE</td><td>RATE</td></tr>
<tr><td>22</td><td>Alabama</td><td>6.9</td><td>1</td><td>New Mexico</td><td>13.1</td></tr>
<tr><td>11</td><td>Alaska</td><td>7.8</td><td>2</td><td>Nevada</td><td>12.6</td></tr>
<tr><td>3</td><td>Arizona</td><td>10.8</td><td>3</td><td>Arizona</td><td>10.8</td></tr>
<tr><td>41</td><td>Arkansas</td><td>5.5</td><td>4</td><td>California</td><td>9.6</td></tr>
<tr><td>4</td><td>California</td><td>9.6</td><td>5</td><td>Florida</td><td>9.1</td></tr>
<tr><td>18</td><td>Colorado</td><td>7.1</td><td>5</td><td>Texas</td><td>9.1</td></tr>
<tr><td>33</td><td>Connecticut</td><td>6.3</td><td>7</td><td>Tennessee</td><td>8.2</td></tr>
<tr><td>30</td><td>Delaware</td><td>6.5</td><td>8</td><td>Rhode Island</td><td>8.1</td></tr>
<tr><td>5</td><td>Florida</td><td>9.1</td><td>9</td><td>Oklahoma</td><td>7.9</td></tr>
<tr><td>24</td><td>Georgia</td><td>6.8</td><td>9</td><td>South Carolina</td><td>7.9</td></tr>
<tr><td>50</td><td>Hawaii</td><td>3.7</td><td>11</td><td>Alaska</td><td>7.8</td></tr>
<tr><td>27</td><td>Idaho</td><td>6.6</td><td>11</td><td>Michigan</td><td>7.8</td></tr>
<tr><td>17</td><td>Illinois</td><td>7.2</td><td>13</td><td>Mississippi</td><td>7.6</td></tr>
<tr><td>39</td><td>Indiana</td><td>5.7</td><td>14</td><td>Washington</td><td>7.4</td></tr>
<tr><td>48</td><td>Iowa</td><td>4.1</td><td>15</td><td>New Hampshire</td><td>7.3</td></tr>
<tr><td>45</td><td>Kansas</td><td>4.9</td><td>15</td><td>West Virginia</td><td>7.3</td></tr>
<tr><td>18</td><td>Kentucky</td><td>7.1</td><td>17</td><td>Illinois</td><td>7.2</td></tr>
<tr><td>18</td><td>Louisiana</td><td>7.1</td><td>18</td><td>Colorado</td><td>7.1</td></tr>
<tr><td>34</td><td>Maine</td><td>6.1</td><td>18</td><td>Kentucky</td><td>7.1</td></tr>
<tr><td>31</td><td>Maryland</td><td>6.4</td><td>18</td><td>Louisiana</td><td>7.1</td></tr>
<tr><td>34</td><td>Massachusetts</td><td>6.1</td><td>21</td><td>North Dakota</td><td>7.0</td></tr>
<tr><td>11</td><td>Michigan</td><td>7.8</td><td>22</td><td>Alabama</td><td>6.9</td></tr>
<tr><td>46</td><td>Minnesota</td><td>4.8</td><td>22</td><td>Oregon</td><td>6.9</td></tr>
<tr><td>13</td><td>Mississippi</td><td>7.6</td><td>24</td><td>Georgia</td><td>6.8</td></tr>
<tr><td>39</td><td>Missouri</td><td>5.7</td><td>24</td><td>New Jersey</td><td>6.8</td></tr>
<tr><td>27</td><td>Montana</td><td>6.6</td><td>24</td><td>North Carolina</td><td>6.8</td></tr>
<tr><td>49</td><td>Nebraska</td><td>4.0</td><td>27</td><td>Idaho</td><td>6.6</td></tr>
<tr><td>2</td><td>Nevada</td><td>12.6</td><td>27</td><td>Montana</td><td>6.6</td></tr>
<tr><td>15</td><td>New Hampshire</td><td>7.3</td><td>27</td><td>New York</td><td>6.6</td></tr>
<tr><td>24</td><td>New Jersey</td><td>6.8</td><td>30</td><td>Delaware</td><td>6.5</td></tr>
<tr><td>1</td><td>New Mexico</td><td>13.1</td><td>31</td><td>Maryland</td><td>6.4</td></tr>
<tr><td>27</td><td>New York</td><td>6.6</td><td>31</td><td>Ohio</td><td>6.4</td></tr>
<tr><td>24</td><td>North Carolina</td><td>6.8</td><td>33</td><td>Connecticut</td><td>6.3</td></tr>
<tr><td>21</td><td>North Dakota</td><td>7.0</td><td>34</td><td>Maine</td><td>6.1</td></tr>
<tr><td>31</td><td>Ohio</td><td>6.4</td><td>34</td><td>Massachusetts</td><td>6.1</td></tr>
<tr><td>9</td><td>Oklahoma</td><td>7.9</td><td>36</td><td>Virginia</td><td>6.0</td></tr>
<tr><td>22</td><td>Oregon</td><td>6.9</td><td>36</td><td>Wyoming</td><td>6.0</td></tr>
<tr><td>38</td><td>Pennsylvania</td><td>5.9</td><td>38</td><td>Pennsylvania</td><td>5.9</td></tr>
<tr><td>8</td><td>Rhode Island</td><td>8.1</td><td>39</td><td>Indiana</td><td>5.7</td></tr>
<tr><td>9</td><td>South Carolina</td><td>7.9</td><td>39</td><td>Missouri</td><td>5.7</td></tr>
<tr><td>47</td><td>South Dakota</td><td>4.5</td><td>41</td><td>Arkansas</td><td>5.5</td></tr>
<tr><td>7</td><td>Tennessee</td><td>8.2</td><td>41</td><td>Utah</td><td>5.5</td></tr>
<tr><td>5</td><td>Texas</td><td>9.1</td><td>43</td><td>Wisconsin</td><td>5.4</td></tr>
<tr><td>41</td><td>Utah</td><td>5.5</td><td>44</td><td>Vermont</td><td>5.1</td></tr>
<tr><td>44</td><td>Vermont</td><td>5.1</td><td>45</td><td>Kansas</td><td>4.9</td></tr>
<tr><td>36</td><td>Virginia</td><td>6.0</td><td>46</td><td>Minnesota</td><td>4.8</td></tr>
<tr><td>14</td><td>Washington</td><td>7.4</td><td>47</td><td>South Dakota</td><td>4.5</td></tr>
<tr><td>15</td><td>West Virginia</td><td>7.3</td><td>48</td><td>Iowa</td><td>4.1</td></tr>
<tr><td>43</td><td>Wisconsin</td><td>5.4</td><td>49</td><td>Nebraska</td><td>4.0</td></tr>
<tr><td>36</td><td>Wyoming</td><td>6.0</td><td>50</td><td>Hawaii</td><td>3.7</td></tr>
<tr><td></td><td></td><td></td><td></td><td>District of Columbia</td><td>11.5</td></tr>
</table>

Source: U.S. Department of Health and Human Services, National Center for Health Statistics
    "National Vital Statistics Reports" (Vol. 47, No. 19, June 30, 1999)
Final data by state of residence. Cirrhosis of the liver is characterized by the replacement of normal tissue with fibrous tissue and the loss of functional liver cells. It can result from alcohol abuse, nutritional deprivation, or infection especially by the hepatitis virus.

Deaths by Chronic Obstructive Pulmonary Diseases in 1997

National Total = 109,029 Deaths*

ALPHA ORDER

RANK	STATE	DEATHS	% of USA
21	Alabama	1,852	1.7%
50	Alaska	119	0.1%
17	Arizona	2,377	2.2%
32	Arkansas	1,254	1.2%
1	California	11,777	10.8%
24	Colorado	1,657	1.5%
31	Connecticut	1,265	1.2%
45	Delaware	296	0.3%
2	Florida	8,089	7.4%
13	Georgia	2,507	2.3%
48	Hawaii	256	0.2%
41	Idaho	523	0.5%
7	Illinois	4,260	3.9%
11	Indiana	2,674	2.5%
29	Iowa	1,290	1.2%
30	Kansas	1,271	1.2%
20	Kentucky	1,948	1.8%
28	Louisiana	1,477	1.4%
38	Maine	695	0.6%
22	Maryland	1,815	1.7%
15	Massachusetts	2,437	2.2%
8	Michigan	3,634	3.3%
26	Minnesota	1,630	1.5%
34	Mississippi	1,111	1.0%
12	Missouri	2,579	2.4%
40	Montana	534	0.5%
36	Nebraska	792	0.7%
35	Nevada	868	0.8%
39	New Hampshire	548	0.5%
10	New Jersey	2,853	2.6%
37	New Mexico	739	0.7%
4	New York	6,091	5.6%
9	North Carolina	3,195	2.9%
49	North Dakota	235	0.2%
6	Ohio	5,182	4.8%
23	Oklahoma	1,728	1.6%
25	Oregon	1,639	1.5%
5	Pennsylvania	5,329	4.9%
43	Rhode Island	431	0.4%
27	South Carolina	1,497	1.4%
44	South Dakota	336	0.3%
14	Tennessee	2,468	2.3%
3	Texas	6,702	6.1%
42	Utah	442	0.4%
46	Vermont	287	0.3%
16	Virginia	2,408	2.2%
18	Washington	2,345	2.2%
33	West Virginia	1,139	1.0%
19	Wisconsin	2,017	1.8%
47	Wyoming	270	0.2%

RANK ORDER

RANK	STATE	DEATHS	% of USA
1	California	11,777	10.8%
2	Florida	8,089	7.4%
3	Texas	6,702	6.1%
4	New York	6,091	5.6%
5	Pennsylvania	5,329	4.9%
6	Ohio	5,182	4.8%
7	Illinois	4,260	3.9%
8	Michigan	3,634	3.3%
9	North Carolina	3,195	2.9%
10	New Jersey	2,853	2.6%
11	Indiana	2,674	2.5%
12	Missouri	2,579	2.4%
13	Georgia	2,507	2.3%
14	Tennessee	2,468	2.3%
15	Massachusetts	2,437	2.2%
16	Virginia	2,408	2.2%
17	Arizona	2,377	2.2%
18	Washington	2,345	2.2%
19	Wisconsin	2,017	1.8%
20	Kentucky	1,948	1.8%
21	Alabama	1,852	1.7%
22	Maryland	1,815	1.7%
23	Oklahoma	1,728	1.6%
24	Colorado	1,657	1.5%
25	Oregon	1,639	1.5%
26	Minnesota	1,630	1.5%
27	South Carolina	1,497	1.4%
28	Louisiana	1,477	1.4%
29	Iowa	1,290	1.2%
30	Kansas	1,271	1.2%
31	Connecticut	1,265	1.2%
32	Arkansas	1,254	1.2%
33	West Virginia	1,139	1.0%
34	Mississippi	1,111	1.0%
35	Nevada	868	0.8%
36	Nebraska	792	0.7%
37	New Mexico	739	0.7%
38	Maine	695	0.6%
39	New Hampshire	548	0.5%
40	Montana	534	0.5%
41	Idaho	523	0.5%
42	Utah	442	0.4%
43	Rhode Island	431	0.4%
44	South Dakota	336	0.3%
45	Delaware	296	0.3%
46	Vermont	287	0.3%
47	Wyoming	270	0.2%
48	Hawaii	256	0.2%
49	North Dakota	235	0.2%
50	Alaska	119	0.1%
	District of Columbia	161	0.1%

Source: U.S. Department of Health and Human Services, National Center for Health Statistics
    "National Vital Statistics Reports" (Vol. 47, No. 19, June 30, 1999)
*Final data by state of residence. Chronic obstructive pulmonary diseases are diseases of the lungs including bronchitis, emphysema and asthma. Includes allied conditions.

Death Rate by Chronic Obstructive Pulmonary Diseases in 1997

National Rate = 40.7 Deaths per 100,000 Population*

ALPHA ORDER

RANK	STATE	RATE
26	Alabama	42.9
50	Alaska	19.5
6	Arizona	52.2
11	Arkansas	49.7
38	California	36.5
28	Colorado	42.6
35	Connecticut	38.7
31	Delaware	40.5
5	Florida	55.2
47	Georgia	33.5
48	Hawaii	21.6
24	Idaho	43.2
39	Illinois	35.8
19	Indiana	45.6
21	Iowa	45.2
12	Kansas	49.0
10	Kentucky	49.8
45	Louisiana	33.9
4	Maine	56.0
41	Maryland	35.6
32	Massachusetts	39.8
36	Michigan	37.2
43	Minnesota	34.8
30	Mississippi	40.7
15	Missouri	47.7
2	Montana	60.8
14	Nebraska	47.8
8	Nevada	51.8
16	New Hampshire	46.7
42	New Jersey	35.4
27	New Mexico	42.7
46	New York	33.6
25	North Carolina	43.0
37	North Dakota	36.7
17	Ohio	46.3
7	Oklahoma	52.1
9	Oregon	50.5
22	Pennsylvania	44.3
23	Rhode Island	43.6
32	South Carolina	39.8
20	South Dakota	45.5
18	Tennessee	46.0
44	Texas	34.5
49	Utah	21.5
13	Vermont	48.7
39	Virginia	35.8
29	Washington	41.8
1	West Virginia	62.7
34	Wisconsin	39.0
3	Wyoming	56.3

RANK ORDER

RANK	STATE	RATE
1	West Virginia	62.7
2	Montana	60.8
3	Wyoming	56.3
4	Maine	56.0
5	Florida	55.2
6	Arizona	52.2
7	Oklahoma	52.1
8	Nevada	51.8
9	Oregon	50.5
10	Kentucky	49.8
11	Arkansas	49.7
12	Kansas	49.0
13	Vermont	48.7
14	Nebraska	47.8
15	Missouri	47.7
16	New Hampshire	46.7
17	Ohio	46.3
18	Tennessee	46.0
19	Indiana	45.6
20	South Dakota	45.5
21	Iowa	45.2
22	Pennsylvania	44.3
23	Rhode Island	43.6
24	Idaho	43.2
25	North Carolina	43.0
26	Alabama	42.9
27	New Mexico	42.7
28	Colorado	42.6
29	Washington	41.8
30	Mississippi	40.7
31	Delaware	40.5
32	Massachusetts	39.8
32	South Carolina	39.8
34	Wisconsin	39.0
35	Connecticut	38.7
36	Michigan	37.2
37	North Dakota	36.7
38	California	36.5
39	Illinois	35.8
39	Virginia	35.8
41	Maryland	35.6
42	New Jersey	35.4
43	Minnesota	34.8
44	Texas	34.5
45	Louisiana	33.9
46	New York	33.6
47	Georgia	33.5
48	Hawaii	21.6
49	Utah	21.5
50	Alaska	19.5
	District of Columbia	30.4

Source: U.S. Department of Health and Human Services, National Center for Health Statistics
"National Vital Statistics Reports" (Vol. 47, No. 19, June 30, 1999)
*Final data by state of residence. Chronic obstructive pulmonary diseases are diseases of the lungs including bronchitis, emphysema and asthma. Includes allied conditions. Not age-adjusted.

Age-Adjusted Death Rate by Chronic Obstructive Pulmonary Diseases in 1997

National Rate = 21.1 Deaths per 100,000 Population*

ALPHA ORDER

RANK	STATE	RATE
27	Alabama	22.5
24	Alaska	22.7
6	Arizona	27.0
11	Arkansas	24.9
31	California	21.1
8	Colorado	26.2
45	Connecticut	16.9
30	Delaware	21.3
33	Florida	20.4
24	Georgia	22.7
50	Hawaii	10.9
18	Idaho	24.0
39	Illinois	19.1
14	Indiana	24.6
38	Iowa	19.5
17	Kansas	24.2
5	Kentucky	27.1
35	Louisiana	19.9
10	Maine	25.2
34	Maryland	20.0
42	Massachusetts	17.7
35	Michigan	19.9
44	Minnesota	17.0
24	Mississippi	22.7
20	Missouri	23.6
3	Montana	29.2
29	Nebraska	22.0
2	Nevada	31.0
15	New Hampshire	24.5
46	New Jersey	16.5
12	New Mexico	24.8
47	New York	16.4
19	North Carolina	23.9
48	North Dakota	16.1
23	Ohio	22.9
7	Oklahoma	26.7
15	Oregon	24.5
40	Pennsylvania	18.6
42	Rhode Island	17.7
20	South Carolina	23.6
35	South Dakota	19.9
9	Tennessee	25.6
28	Texas	22.1
49	Utah	15.6
13	Vermont	24.7
32	Virginia	20.7
22	Washington	23.2
4	West Virginia	28.3
41	Wisconsin	18.4
1	Wyoming	32.2

RANK ORDER

RANK	STATE	RATE
1	Wyoming	32.2
2	Nevada	31.0
3	Montana	29.2
4	West Virginia	28.3
5	Kentucky	27.1
6	Arizona	27.0
7	Oklahoma	26.7
8	Colorado	26.2
9	Tennessee	25.6
10	Maine	25.2
11	Arkansas	24.9
12	New Mexico	24.8
13	Vermont	24.7
14	Indiana	24.6
15	New Hampshire	24.5
15	Oregon	24.5
17	Kansas	24.2
18	Idaho	24.0
19	North Carolina	23.9
20	Missouri	23.6
20	South Carolina	23.6
22	Washington	23.2
23	Ohio	22.9
24	Alaska	22.7
24	Georgia	22.7
24	Mississippi	22.7
27	Alabama	22.5
28	Texas	22.1
29	Nebraska	22.0
30	Delaware	21.3
31	California	21.1
32	Virginia	20.7
33	Florida	20.4
34	Maryland	20.0
35	Louisiana	19.9
35	Michigan	19.9
35	South Dakota	19.9
38	Iowa	19.5
39	Illinois	19.1
40	Pennsylvania	18.6
41	Wisconsin	18.4
42	Massachusetts	17.7
42	Rhode Island	17.7
44	Minnesota	17.0
45	Connecticut	16.9
46	New Jersey	16.5
47	New York	16.4
48	North Dakota	16.1
49	Utah	15.6
50	Hawaii	10.9
	District of Columbia	16.2

Source: U.S. Department of Health and Human Services, National Center for Health Statistics
   "National Vital Statistics Reports" (Vol. 47, No. 19, June 30, 1999)
*Final data by state of residence. Chronic obstructive pulmonary diseases are diseases of the lungs including bronchitis, emphysema and asthma. Includes allied conditions.

Deaths by Diabetes Mellitus in 1997

National Total = 62,636 Deaths*

ALPHA ORDER

ALPHA ORDER

RANK	STATE	DEATHS	% of USA
20	Alabama	1,173	1.9%
49	Alaska	81	0.1%
25	Arizona	947	1.5%
30	Arkansas	639	1.0%
1	California	5,625	9.0%
34	Colorado	522	0.8%
31	Connecticut	620	1.0%
43	Delaware	204	0.3%
3	Florida	3,844	6.1%
17	Georgia	1,276	2.0%
44	Hawaii	202	0.3%
42	Idaho	242	0.4%
7	Illinois	2,734	4.4%
12	Indiana	1,481	2.4%
29	Iowa	677	1.1%
32	Kansas	578	0.9%
24	Kentucky	1,011	1.6%
11	Louisiana	1,685	2.7%
38	Maine	303	0.5%
13	Maryland	1,394	2.2%
14	Massachusetts	1,359	2.2%
8	Michigan	2,435	3.9%
22	Minnesota	1,051	1.7%
33	Mississippi	571	0.9%
16	Missouri	1,300	2.1%
47	Montana	169	0.3%
37	Nebraska	315	0.5%
41	Nevada	243	0.4%
39	New Hampshire	277	0.4%
9	New Jersey	2,340	3.7%
36	New Mexico	399	0.6%
4	New York	3,649	5.8%
10	North Carolina	1,834	2.9%
46	North Dakota	183	0.3%
6	Ohio	3,349	5.3%
26	Oklahoma	931	1.5%
27	Oregon	811	1.3%
5	Pennsylvania	3,550	5.7%
40	Rhode Island	274	0.4%
23	South Carolina	1,029	1.6%
45	South Dakota	196	0.3%
15	Tennessee	1,316	2.1%
2	Texas	4,760	7.6%
35	Utah	432	0.7%
48	Vermont	143	0.2%
18	Virginia	1,244	2.0%
21	Washington	1,094	1.7%
28	West Virginia	682	1.1%
19	Wisconsin	1,176	1.9%
50	Wyoming	80	0.1%

RANK ORDER

RANK	STATE	DEATHS	% of USA
1	California	5,625	9.0%
2	Texas	4,760	7.6%
3	Florida	3,844	6.1%
4	New York	3,649	5.8%
5	Pennsylvania	3,550	5.7%
6	Ohio	3,349	5.3%
7	Illinois	2,734	4.4%
8	Michigan	2,435	3.9%
9	New Jersey	2,340	3.7%
10	North Carolina	1,834	2.9%
11	Louisiana	1,685	2.7%
12	Indiana	1,481	2.4%
13	Maryland	1,394	2.2%
14	Massachusetts	1,359	2.2%
15	Tennessee	1,316	2.1%
16	Missouri	1,300	2.1%
17	Georgia	1,276	2.0%
18	Virginia	1,244	2.0%
19	Wisconsin	1,176	1.9%
20	Alabama	1,173	1.9%
21	Washington	1,094	1.7%
22	Minnesota	1,051	1.7%
23	South Carolina	1,029	1.6%
24	Kentucky	1,011	1.6%
25	Arizona	947	1.5%
26	Oklahoma	931	1.5%
27	Oregon	811	1.3%
28	West Virginia	682	1.1%
29	Iowa	677	1.1%
30	Arkansas	639	1.0%
31	Connecticut	620	1.0%
32	Kansas	578	0.9%
33	Mississippi	571	0.9%
34	Colorado	522	0.8%
35	Utah	432	0.7%
36	New Mexico	399	0.6%
37	Nebraska	315	0.5%
38	Maine	303	0.5%
39	New Hampshire	277	0.4%
40	Rhode Island	274	0.4%
41	Nevada	243	0.4%
42	Idaho	242	0.4%
43	Delaware	204	0.3%
44	Hawaii	202	0.3%
45	South Dakota	196	0.3%
46	North Dakota	183	0.3%
47	Montana	169	0.3%
48	Vermont	143	0.2%
49	Alaska	81	0.1%
50	Wyoming	80	0.1%
	District of Columbia	206	0.3%

Source: U.S. Department of Health and Human Services, National Center for Health Statistics
"National Vital Statistics Reports" (Vol. 47, No. 19, June 30, 1999)
*Final data by state of residence. A severe, chronic form of diabetes caused by insufficient production of insulin and resulting in abnormal metabolism of carbohydrates, fats, and proteins. The disease, which typically appears in childhood or adolescence, is characterized by increased sugar levels in the blood and urine, excessive thirst and frequent urination.

Death Rate by Diabetes Mellitus in 1997

National Rate = 23.4 Deaths per 100,000 Population*

ALPHA ORDER

RANK	STATE	RATE
12	Alabama	27.2
50	Alaska	13.3
36	Arizona	20.8
16	Arkansas	25.3
44	California	17.4
49	Colorado	13.4
41	Connecticut	19.0
8	Delaware	27.9
14	Florida	26.2
45	Georgia	17.0
45	Hawaii	17.0
38	Idaho	20.0
29	Illinois	23.0
16	Indiana	25.3
26	Iowa	23.7
32	Kansas	22.3
15	Kentucky	25.9
1	Louisiana	38.7
23	Maine	24.4
10	Maryland	27.4
33	Massachusetts	22.2
19	Michigan	24.9
31	Minnesota	22.4
35	Mississippi	20.9
25	Missouri	24.1
40	Montana	19.2
41	Nebraska	19.0
48	Nevada	14.5
27	New Hampshire	23.6
5	New Jersey	29.1
28	New Mexico	23.1
37	New York	20.1
20	North Carolina	24.7
6	North Dakota	28.6
3	Ohio	29.9
7	Oklahoma	28.1
18	Oregon	25.0
4	Pennsylvania	29.5
9	Rhode Island	27.7
10	South Carolina	27.4
13	South Dakota	26.6
21	Tennessee	24.5
21	Texas	24.5
34	Utah	21.0
24	Vermont	24.3
43	Virginia	18.5
39	Washington	19.5
2	West Virginia	37.6
30	Wisconsin	22.7
47	Wyoming	16.7

RANK ORDER

RANK	STATE	RATE
1	Louisiana	38.7
2	West Virginia	37.6
3	Ohio	29.9
4	Pennsylvania	29.5
5	New Jersey	29.1
6	North Dakota	28.6
7	Oklahoma	28.1
8	Delaware	27.9
9	Rhode Island	27.7
10	Maryland	27.4
10	South Carolina	27.4
12	Alabama	27.2
13	South Dakota	26.6
14	Florida	26.2
15	Kentucky	25.9
16	Arkansas	25.3
16	Indiana	25.3
18	Oregon	25.0
19	Michigan	24.9
20	North Carolina	24.7
21	Tennessee	24.5
21	Texas	24.5
23	Maine	24.4
24	Vermont	24.3
25	Missouri	24.1
26	Iowa	23.7
27	New Hampshire	23.6
28	New Mexico	23.1
29	Illinois	23.0
30	Wisconsin	22.7
31	Minnesota	22.4
32	Kansas	22.3
33	Massachusetts	22.2
34	Utah	21.0
35	Mississippi	20.9
36	Arizona	20.8
37	New York	20.1
38	Idaho	20.0
39	Washington	19.5
40	Montana	19.2
41	Connecticut	19.0
41	Nebraska	19.0
43	Virginia	18.5
44	California	17.4
45	Georgia	17.0
45	Hawaii	17.0
47	Wyoming	16.7
48	Nevada	14.5
49	Colorado	13.4
50	Alaska	13.3
	District of Columbia	38.9

Source: U.S. Department of Health and Human Services, National Center for Health Statistics
"National Vital Statistics Reports" (Vol. 47, No. 19, June 30, 1999)
*Final data by state of residence. A severe, chronic form of diabetes caused by insufficient production of insulin and resulting in abnormal metabolism of carbohydrates, fats, and proteins. The disease, which typically appears in childhood or adolescence, is characterized by increased sugar levels in the blood and urine, excessive thirst and frequent urination. Not age-adjusted.

Age-Adjusted Death Rate by Diabetes Mellitus in 1997

National Rate = 13.5 Deaths per 100,000 Population*

ALPHA ORDER			RANK ORDER		
RANK	STATE	RATE	RANK	STATE	RATE
12	Alabama	15.3	1	Louisiana	24.4
8	Alaska	16.0	2	West Virginia	18.0
29	Arizona	12.6	3	South Carolina	17.3
18	Arkansas	14.2	4	Texas	17.2
35	California	11.8	5	Maryland	17.1
50	Colorado	8.8	6	Ohio	16.3
46	Connecticut	9.6	7	Delaware	16.1
7	Delaware	16.1	8	Alaska	16.0
38	Florida	11.7	9	New Jersey	15.7
32	Georgia	12.1	10	Oklahoma	15.6
44	Hawaii	10.2	11	Utah	15.5
34	Idaho	11.9	12	Alabama	15.3
23	Illinois	13.3	13	North Carolina	15.0
17	Indiana	14.4	14	Kentucky	14.7
43	Iowa	10.8	15	New Mexico	14.6
38	Kansas	11.7	16	Michigan	14.5
14	Kentucky	14.7	17	Indiana	14.4
1	Louisiana	24.4	18	Arkansas	14.2
28	Maine	12.7	19	Pennsylvania	14.1
5	Maryland	17.1	19	Tennessee	14.1
41	Massachusetts	11.4	21	Rhode Island	13.7
16	Michigan	14.5	22	New Hampshire	13.6
38	Minnesota	11.7	23	Illinois	13.3
26	Mississippi	13.0	23	Vermont	13.3
26	Missouri	13.0	25	Oregon	13.2
46	Montana	9.6	26	Mississippi	13.0
49	Nebraska	9.4	26	Missouri	13.0
46	Nevada	9.6	28	Maine	12.7
22	New Hampshire	13.6	29	Arizona	12.6
9	New Jersey	15.7	30	South Dakota	12.2
15	New Mexico	14.6	30	Wisconsin	12.2
42	New York	11.2	32	Georgia	12.1
13	North Carolina	15.0	32	Washington	12.1
35	North Dakota	11.8	34	Idaho	11.9
6	Ohio	16.3	35	California	11.8
10	Oklahoma	15.6	35	North Dakota	11.8
25	Oregon	13.2	35	Virginia	11.8
19	Pennsylvania	14.1	38	Florida	11.7
21	Rhode Island	13.7	38	Kansas	11.7
3	South Carolina	17.3	38	Minnesota	11.7
30	South Dakota	12.2	41	Massachusetts	11.4
19	Tennessee	14.1	42	New York	11.2
4	Texas	17.2	43	Iowa	10.8
11	Utah	15.5	44	Hawaii	10.2
23	Vermont	13.3	45	Wyoming	10.1
35	Virginia	11.8	46	Connecticut	9.6
32	Washington	12.1	46	Montana	9.6
2	West Virginia	18.0	46	Nevada	9.6
30	Wisconsin	12.2	49	Nebraska	9.4
45	Wyoming	10.1	50	Colorado	8.8
				District of Columbia	20.7

Source: U.S. Department of Health and Human Services, National Center for Health Statistics
    "National Vital Statistics Reports" (Vol. 47, No. 19, June 30, 1999)

*Final data by state of residence. A severe, chronic form of diabetes caused by insufficient production of insulin and resulting in abnormal metabolism of carbohydrates, fats, and proteins. The disease, which typically appears in childhood or adolescence, is characterized by increased sugar levels in the blood and urine, excessive thirst and frequent urination.

Deaths by Diseases of the Heart in 1997

National Total = 726,974 Deaths*

ALPHA ORDER

RANK ORDER

RANK	STATE	DEATHS	% of USA		RANK	STATE	DEATHS	% of USA
18	Alabama	13,570	1.9%		1	California	68,657	9.4%
50	Alaska	557	0.1%		2	New York	60,914	8.4%
24	Arizona	10,174	1.4%		3	Florida	49,795	6.8%
30	Arkansas	8,464	1.2%		4	Texas	43,618	6.0%
1	California	68,657	9.4%		5	Pennsylvania	42,127	5.8%
34	Colorado	6,485	0.9%		6	Ohio	34,322	4.7%
26	Connecticut	9,737	1.3%		7	Illinois	32,631	4.5%
46	Delaware	1,992	0.3%		8	Michigan	27,250	3.7%
3	Florida	49,795	6.8%		9	New Jersey	23,392	3.2%
12	Georgia	17,665	2.4%		10	North Carolina	19,303	2.7%
43	Hawaii	2,380	0.3%		11	Missouri	18,460	2.5%
42	Idaho	2,518	0.3%		12	Georgia	17,665	2.4%
7	Illinois	32,631	4.5%		13	Indiana	16,661	2.3%
13	Indiana	16,661	2.3%		14	Tennessee	16,660	2.3%
29	Iowa	9,111	1.3%		15	Massachusetts	16,505	2.3%
32	Kansas	7,275	1.0%		16	Virginia	15,632	2.2%
19	Kentucky	12,458	1.7%		17	Wisconsin	13,697	1.9%
21	Louisiana	11,868	1.6%		18	Alabama	13,570	1.9%
37	Maine	3,637	0.5%		19	Kentucky	12,458	1.7%
20	Maryland	12,009	1.7%		20	Maryland	12,009	1.7%
15	Massachusetts	16,505	2.3%		21	Louisiana	11,868	1.6%
8	Michigan	27,250	3.7%		22	Oklahoma	11,273	1.6%
28	Minnesota	9,612	1.3%		23	Washington	11,116	1.5%
27	Mississippi	9,702	1.3%		24	Arizona	10,174	1.4%
11	Missouri	18,460	2.5%		25	South Carolina	9,896	1.4%
45	Montana	2,108	0.3%		26	Connecticut	9,737	1.3%
35	Nebraska	4,937	0.7%		27	Mississippi	9,702	1.3%
36	Nevada	3,897	0.5%		28	Minnesota	9,612	1.3%
41	New Hampshire	2,802	0.4%		29	Iowa	9,111	1.3%
9	New Jersey	23,392	3.2%		30	Arkansas	8,464	1.2%
38	New Mexico	3,274	0.5%		31	Oregon	7,518	1.0%
2	New York	60,914	8.4%		32	Kansas	7,275	1.0%
10	North Carolina	19,303	2.7%		33	West Virginia	6,924	1.0%
47	North Dakota	1,827	0.3%		34	Colorado	6,485	0.9%
6	Ohio	34,322	4.7%		35	Nebraska	4,937	0.7%
22	Oklahoma	11,273	1.6%		36	Nevada	3,897	0.5%
31	Oregon	7,518	1.0%		37	Maine	3,637	0.5%
5	Pennsylvania	42,127	5.8%		38	New Mexico	3,274	0.5%
39	Rhode Island	3,265	0.4%		39	Rhode Island	3,265	0.4%
25	South Carolina	9,896	1.4%		40	Utah	3,007	0.4%
44	South Dakota	2,130	0.3%		41	New Hampshire	2,802	0.4%
14	Tennessee	16,660	2.3%		42	Idaho	2,518	0.3%
4	Texas	43,618	6.0%		43	Hawaii	2,380	0.3%
40	Utah	3,007	0.4%		44	South Dakota	2,130	0.3%
48	Vermont	1,506	0.2%		45	Montana	2,108	0.3%
16	Virginia	15,632	2.2%		46	Delaware	1,992	0.3%
23	Washington	11,116	1.5%		47	North Dakota	1,827	0.3%
33	West Virginia	6,924	1.0%		48	Vermont	1,506	0.2%
17	Wisconsin	13,697	1.9%		49	Wyoming	1,040	0.1%
49	Wyoming	1,040	0.1%		50	Alaska	557	0.1%
						District of Columbia	1,616	0.2%

Source: U.S. Department of Health and Human Services, National Center tor Health Statistics
"National Vital Statistics Reports" (Vol. 47, No. 19, June 30, 1999)
*Final data by state of residence.

Death Rate by Diseases of the Heart in 1997

National Rate = 271.6 Deaths per 100,000 Population*

ALPHA ORDER

RANK	STATE	RATE
12	Alabama	314.2
50	Alaska	91.4
40	Arizona	223.4
8	Arkansas	335.5
42	California	212.8
48	Colorado	166.6
16	Connecticut	297.8
26	Delaware	272.3
5	Florida	339.8
34	Georgia	236.0
45	Hawaii	200.6
43	Idaho	208.1
24	Illinois	274.3
21	Indiana	284.1
10	Iowa	319.4
22	Kansas	280.4
11	Kentucky	318.8
25	Louisiana	272.7
17	Maine	292.8
35	Maryland	235.7
27	Massachusetts	269.8
23	Michigan	278.8
44	Minnesota	205.1
2	Mississippi	355.3
4	Missouri	341.7
32	Montana	239.9
15	Nebraska	298.0
36	Nevada	232.4
33	New Hampshire	238.9
18	New Jersey	290.5
47	New Mexico	189.3
7	New York	335.9
30	North Carolina	260.0
20	North Dakota	285.1
14	Ohio	306.8
5	Oklahoma	339.8
38	Oregon	231.8
3	Pennsylvania	350.5
9	Rhode Island	330.7
29	South Carolina	263.2
19	South Dakota	288.6
13	Tennessee	310.3
39	Texas	224.4
49	Utah	146.0
31	Vermont	255.7
37	Virginia	232.1
46	Washington	198.1
1	West Virginia	381.3
28	Wisconsin	264.9
41	Wyoming	216.8

RANK ORDER

RANK	STATE	RATE
1	West Virginia	381.3
2	Mississippi	355.3
3	Pennsylvania	350.5
4	Missouri	341.7
5	Florida	339.8
5	Oklahoma	339.8
7	New York	335.9
8	Arkansas	335.5
9	Rhode Island	330.7
10	Iowa	319.4
11	Kentucky	318.8
12	Alabama	314.2
13	Tennessee	310.3
14	Ohio	306.8
15	Nebraska	298.0
16	Connecticut	297.8
17	Maine	292.8
18	New Jersey	290.5
19	South Dakota	288.6
20	North Dakota	285.1
21	Indiana	284.1
22	Kansas	280.4
23	Michigan	278.8
24	Illinois	274.3
25	Louisiana	272.7
26	Delaware	272.3
27	Massachusetts	269.8
28	Wisconsin	264.9
29	South Carolina	263.2
30	North Carolina	260.0
31	Vermont	255.7
32	Montana	239.9
33	New Hampshire	238.9
34	Georgia	236.0
35	Maryland	235.7
36	Nevada	232.4
37	Virginia	232.1
38	Oregon	231.8
39	Texas	224.4
40	Arizona	223.4
41	Wyoming	216.8
42	California	212.8
43	Idaho	208.1
44	Minnesota	205.1
45	Hawaii	200.6
46	Washington	198.1
47	New Mexico	189.3
48	Colorado	166.6
49	Utah	146.0
50	Alaska	91.4
	District of Columbia	305.5

Source: U.S. Department of Health and Human Services, National Center for Health Statistics
    "National Vital Statistics Reports" (Vol. 47, No. 19, June 30, 1999)
*Final data by state of residence. Not age-adjusted.

Age-Adjusted Death Rate by Diseases of the Heart in 1997

National Rate = 130.5 Deaths per 100,000 Population*

<u>ALPHA ORDER</u>

RANK	STATE	RATE
5	Alabama	157.0
47	Alaska	100.5
40	Arizona	110.3
9	Arkansas	149.7
35	California	114.1
49	Colorado	94.0
28	Connecticut	119.7
18	Delaware	138.3
31	Florida	118.6
10	Georgia	148.9
44	Hawaii	101.9
42	Idaho	105.2
21	Illinois	134.0
14	Indiana	139.1
29	Iowa	119.5
32	Kansas	117.2
3	Kentucky	159.5
7	Louisiana	153.8
24	Maine	126.0
23	Maryland	128.3
39	Massachusetts	112.1
17	Michigan	138.5
50	Minnesota	93.2
1	Mississippi	188.1
8	Missouri	149.9
41	Montana	106.4
27	Nebraska	120.8
15	Nevada	138.6
36	New Hampshire	113.7
25	New Jersey	124.7
43	New Mexico	102.2
12	New York	146.0
19	North Carolina	136.5
37	North Dakota	113.4
13	Ohio	143.3
6	Oklahoma	156.8
45	Oregon	101.4
15	Pennsylvania	138.6
26	Rhode Island	122.3
11	South Carolina	148.2
33	South Dakota	117.1
4	Tennessee	157.8
20	Texas	135.2
48	Utah	95.2
30	Vermont	119.0
22	Virginia	129.4
46	Washington	100.6
2	West Virginia	160.7
34	Wisconsin	115.3
38	Wyoming	113.3

<u>RANK ORDER</u>

RANK	STATE	RATE
1	Mississippi	188.1
2	West Virginia	160.7
3	Kentucky	159.5
4	Tennessee	157.8
5	Alabama	157.0
6	Oklahoma	156.8
7	Louisiana	153.8
8	Missouri	149.9
9	Arkansas	149.7
10	Georgia	148.9
11	South Carolina	148.2
12	New York	146.0
13	Ohio	143.3
14	Indiana	139.1
15	Nevada	138.6
15	Pennsylvania	138.6
17	Michigan	138.5
18	Delaware	138.3
19	North Carolina	136.5
20	Texas	135.2
21	Illinois	134.0
22	Virginia	129.4
23	Maryland	128.3
24	Maine	126.0
25	New Jersey	124.7
26	Rhode Island	122.3
27	Nebraska	120.8
28	Connecticut	119.7
29	Iowa	119.5
30	Vermont	119.0
31	Florida	118.6
32	Kansas	117.2
33	South Dakota	117.1
34	Wisconsin	115.3
35	California	114.1
36	New Hampshire	113.7
37	North Dakota	113.4
38	Wyoming	113.3
39	Massachusetts	112.1
40	Arizona	110.3
41	Montana	106.4
42	Idaho	105.2
43	New Mexico	102.2
44	Hawaii	101.9
45	Oregon	101.4
46	Washington	100.6
47	Alaska	100.5
48	Utah	95.2
49	Colorado	94.0
50	Minnesota	93.2
	District of Columbia	157.2

Source: U.S. Department of Health and Human Services, National Center for Health Statistics
  "National Vital Statistics Reports" (Vol. 47, No. 19, June 30, 1999)
Final data by state of residence.

Death by Malignant Neoplasms in 1997

National Total = 539,577 Deaths*

ALPHA ORDER					RANK ORDER			
RANK	**STATE**	**DEATHS**	**% of USA**		**RANK**	**STATE**	**DEATHS**	**% of USA**
20	Alabama	9,577	1.8%		1	California	51,990	9.6%
50	Alaska	622	0.1%		2	Florida	38,100	7.1%
24	Arizona	8,448	1.6%		3	New York	37,360	6.9%
30	Arkansas	6,063	1.1%		4	Texas	32,193	6.0%
1	California	51,990	9.6%		5	Pennsylvania	30,181	5.6%
32	Colorado	5,647	1.0%		6	Ohio	24,693	4.6%
27	Connecticut	7,137	1.3%		7	Illinois	24,479	4.5%
45	Delaware	1,669	0.3%		8	Michigan	19,610	3.6%
2	Florida	38,100	7.1%		9	New Jersey	18,157	3.4%
12	Georgia	13,025	2.4%		10	North Carolina	15,171	2.8%
43	Hawaii	1,846	0.3%		11	Massachusetts	13,687	2.5%
42	Idaho	1,947	0.4%		12	Georgia	13,025	2.4%
7	Illinois	24,479	4.5%		13	Virginia	12,928	2.4%
14	Indiana	12,332	2.3%		14	Indiana	12,332	2.3%
29	Iowa	6,331	1.2%		15	Missouri	11,959	2.2%
33	Kansas	5,219	1.0%		16	Tennessee	11,861	2.2%
22	Kentucky	8,970	1.7%		17	Wisconsin	10,577	2.0%
21	Louisiana	9,352	1.7%		18	Maryland	10,129	1.9%
37	Maine	2,980	0.6%		19	Washington	10,035	1.9%
18	Maryland	10,129	1.9%		20	Alabama	9,577	1.8%
11	Massachusetts	13,687	2.5%		21	Louisiana	9,352	1.7%
8	Michigan	19,610	3.6%		22	Kentucky	8,970	1.7%
23	Minnesota	8,777	1.6%		23	Minnesota	8,777	1.6%
31	Mississippi	5,849	1.1%		24	Arizona	8,448	1.6%
15	Missouri	11,959	2.2%		25	South Carolina	7,640	1.4%
44	Montana	1,788	0.3%		26	Oklahoma	7,235	1.3%
35	Nebraska	3,238	0.6%		27	Connecticut	7,137	1.3%
36	Nevada	3,179	0.6%		28	Oregon	6,768	1.3%
40	New Hampshire	2,414	0.4%		29	Iowa	6,331	1.2%
9	New Jersey	18,157	3.4%		30	Arkansas	6,063	1.1%
38	New Mexico	2,766	0.5%		31	Mississippi	5,849	1.1%
3	New York	37,360	6.9%		32	Colorado	5,647	1.0%
10	North Carolina	15,171	2.8%		33	Kansas	5,219	1.0%
47	North Dakota	1,322	0.2%		34	West Virginia	4,757	0.9%
6	Ohio	24,693	4.6%		35	Nebraska	3,238	0.6%
26	Oklahoma	7,235	1.3%		36	Nevada	3,179	0.6%
28	Oregon	6,768	1.3%		37	Maine	2,980	0.6%
5	Pennsylvania	30,181	5.6%		38	New Mexico	2,766	0.5%
39	Rhode Island	2,466	0.5%		39	Rhode Island	2,466	0.5%
25	South Carolina	7,640	1.4%		40	New Hampshire	2,414	0.4%
46	South Dakota	1,548	0.3%		41	Utah	2,133	0.4%
16	Tennessee	11,861	2.2%		42	Idaho	1,947	0.4%
4	Texas	32,193	6.0%		43	Hawaii	1,846	0.3%
41	Utah	2,133	0.4%		44	Montana	1,788	0.3%
48	Vermont	1,230	0.2%		45	Delaware	1,669	0.3%
13	Virginia	12,928	2.4%		46	South Dakota	1,548	0.3%
19	Washington	10,035	1.9%		47	North Dakota	1,322	0.2%
34	West Virginia	4,757	0.9%		48	Vermont	1,230	0.2%
17	Wisconsin	10,577	2.0%		49	Wyoming	844	0.2%
49	Wyoming	844	0.2%		50	Alaska	622	0.1%
						District of Columbia	1,348	0.2%

Source: U.S. Department of Health and Human Services, National Center for Health Statistics
"National Vital Statistics Reports" (Vol. 47, No. 19, June 30, 1999)
*Final data by state of residence. Neoplasms are abnormal tissue, tumors. Includes many cancers.

Death Rate by Malignant Neoplasms in 1997

National Rate = 201.6 Deaths per 100,000 Population*

ALPHA ORDER

RANK	STATE	RATE
12	Alabama	221.7
50	Alaska	102.1
39	Arizona	185.5
5	Arkansas	240.3
44	California	161.1
48	Colorado	145.1
16	Connecticut	218.3
8	Delaware	228.1
2	Florida	260.0
42	Georgia	174.0
47	Hawaii	155.6
45	Idaho	160.9
26	Illinois	205.8
20	Indiana	210.3
11	Iowa	222.0
32	Kansas	201.1
7	Kentucky	229.5
18	Louisiana	214.9
6	Maine	239.9
34	Maryland	198.8
10	Massachusetts	223.7
33	Michigan	200.6
38	Minnesota	187.3
19	Mississippi	214.2
13	Missouri	221.4
30	Montana	203.5
35	Nebraska	195.4
37	Nevada	189.6
26	New Hampshire	205.8
9	New Jersey	225.5
46	New Mexico	159.9
25	New York	206.0
29	North Carolina	204.3
24	North Dakota	206.3
15	Ohio	220.7
17	Oklahoma	218.1
23	Oregon	208.7
3	Pennsylvania	251.1
4	Rhode Island	249.7
31	South Carolina	203.2
21	South Dakota	209.8
14	Tennessee	220.9
43	Texas	165.6
49	Utah	103.6
22	Vermont	208.8
36	Virginia	192.0
40	Washington	178.9
1	West Virginia	262.0
28	Wisconsin	204.6
41	Wyoming	175.9

RANK ORDER

RANK	STATE	RATE
1	West Virginia	262.0
2	Florida	260.0
3	Pennsylvania	251.1
4	Rhode Island	249.7
5	Arkansas	240.3
6	Maine	239.9
7	Kentucky	229.5
8	Delaware	228.1
9	New Jersey	225.5
10	Massachusetts	223.7
11	Iowa	222.0
12	Alabama	221.7
13	Missouri	221.4
14	Tennessee	220.9
15	Ohio	220.7
16	Connecticut	218.3
17	Oklahoma	218.1
18	Louisiana	214.9
19	Mississippi	214.2
20	Indiana	210.3
21	South Dakota	209.8
22	Vermont	208.8
23	Oregon	208.7
24	North Dakota	206.3
25	New York	206.0
26	Illinois	205.8
26	New Hampshire	205.8
28	Wisconsin	204.6
29	North Carolina	204.3
30	Montana	203.5
31	South Carolina	203.2
32	Kansas	201.1
33	Michigan	200.6
34	Maryland	198.8
35	Nebraska	195.4
36	Virginia	192.0
37	Nevada	189.6
38	Minnesota	187.3
39	Arizona	185.5
40	Washington	178.9
41	Wyoming	175.9
42	Georgia	174.0
43	Texas	165.6
44	California	161.1
45	Idaho	160.9
46	New Mexico	159.9
47	Hawaii	155.6
48	Colorado	145.1
49	Utah	103.6
50	Alaska	102.1
	District of Columbia	254.8

Source: U.S. Department of Health and Human Services, National Center for Health Statistics
"National Vital Statistics Reports" (Vol. 47, No. 19, June 30, 1999)
*Final data by state of residence. Neoplasms are abnormal tissue, tumors. Includes many cancers. Not age-adjusted.

Age-Adjusted Death Rate by Malignant Neoplasms in 1997

National Rate = 125.6 Deaths per 100,000 Population*

ALPHA ORDER

RANK	STATE	RATE
9	Alabama	136.2
37	Alaska	116.9
43	Arizona	114.0
7	Arkansas	139.4
41	California	114.1
48	Colorado	101.4
33	Connecticut	120.2
3	Delaware	142.2
28	Florida	125.7
14	Georgia	132.3
49	Hawaii	95.5
46	Idaho	107.6
20	Illinois	130.9
21	Indiana	130.6
36	Iowa	117.0
34	Kansas	118.5
2	Kentucky	145.7
1	Louisiana	146.6
8	Maine	136.4
13	Maryland	133.9
27	Massachusetts	126.4
26	Michigan	127.1
39	Minnesota	115.6
4	Mississippi	141.4
16	Missouri	131.7
40	Montana	114.5
44	Nebraska	112.7
25	Nevada	128.6
12	New Hampshire	134.6
24	New Jersey	130.2
45	New Mexico	107.9
30	New York	122.5
19	North Carolina	131.0
47	North Dakota	107.4
15	Ohio	132.1
21	Oklahoma	130.6
31	Oregon	121.3
18	Pennsylvania	131.5
10	Rhode Island	135.6
11	South Carolina	135.0
38	South Dakota	116.1
6	Tennessee	140.4
29	Texas	122.8
50	Utah	84.9
17	Vermont	131.6
21	Virginia	130.6
35	Washington	117.9
5	West Virginia	140.5
32	Wisconsin	120.4
41	Wyoming	114.1

RANK ORDER

RANK	STATE	RATE
1	Louisiana	146.6
2	Kentucky	145.7
3	Delaware	142.2
4	Mississippi	141.4
5	West Virginia	140.5
6	Tennessee	140.4
7	Arkansas	139.4
8	Maine	136.4
9	Alabama	136.2
10	Rhode Island	135.6
11	South Carolina	135.0
12	New Hampshire	134.6
13	Maryland	133.9
14	Georgia	132.3
15	Ohio	132.1
16	Missouri	131.7
17	Vermont	131.6
18	Pennsylvania	131.5
19	North Carolina	131.0
20	Illinois	130.9
21	Indiana	130.6
21	Oklahoma	130.6
21	Virginia	130.6
24	New Jersey	130.2
25	Nevada	128.6
26	Michigan	127.1
27	Massachusetts	126.4
28	Florida	125.7
29	Texas	122.8
30	New York	122.5
31	Oregon	121.3
32	Wisconsin	120.4
33	Connecticut	120.2
34	Kansas	118.5
35	Washington	117.9
36	Iowa	117.0
37	Alaska	116.9
38	South Dakota	116.1
39	Minnesota	115.6
40	Montana	114.5
41	California	114.1
41	Wyoming	114.1
43	Arizona	114.0
44	Nebraska	112.7
45	New Mexico	107.9
46	Idaho	107.6
47	North Dakota	107.4
48	Colorado	101.4
49	Hawaii	95.5
50	Utah	84.9
	District of Columbia	155.8

Source: U.S. Department of Health and Human Services, National Center for Health Statistics
"National Vital Statistics Reports" (Vol. 47, No. 19, June 30, 1999)
*Final data by state of residence. Neoplasms are abnormal tissue, tumors. Includes many cancers.

Deaths by Pneumonia and Influenza in 1997

National Total = 86,449 Deaths*

ALPHA ORDER

RANK	STATE	DEATHS	% of USA
20	Alabama	1,438	1.7%
50	Alaska	48	0.1%
24	Arizona	1,274	1.5%
28	Arkansas	1,051	1.2%
1	California	12,305	14.2%
33	Colorado	850	1.0%
25	Connecticut	1,230	1.4%
46	Delaware	227	0.3%
5	Florida	3,895	4.5%
13	Georgia	2,154	2.5%
41	Hawaii	351	0.4%
40	Idaho	353	0.4%
6	Illinois	3,759	4.3%
16	Indiana	1,778	2.1%
26	Iowa	1,210	1.4%
30	Kansas	984	1.1%
21	Kentucky	1,339	1.5%
27	Louisiana	1,112	1.3%
38	Maine	430	0.5%
19	Maryland	1,452	1.7%
9	Massachusetts	2,666	3.1%
8	Michigan	2,826	3.3%
22	Minnesota	1,322	1.5%
29	Mississippi	1,036	1.2%
12	Missouri	2,241	2.6%
43	Montana	300	0.3%
35	Nebraska	566	0.7%
39	Nevada	412	0.5%
45	New Hampshire	251	0.3%
11	New Jersey	2,360	2.7%
37	New Mexico	454	0.5%
2	New York	6,578	7.6%
10	North Carolina	2,459	2.8%
47	North Dakota	222	0.3%
7	Ohio	3,467	4.0%
23	Oklahoma	1,304	1.5%
32	Oregon	920	1.1%
4	Pennsylvania	4,379	5.1%
42	Rhode Island	325	0.4%
31	South Carolina	962	1.1%
44	South Dakota	268	0.3%
14	Tennessee	2,047	2.4%
3	Texas	4,621	5.3%
36	Utah	531	0.6%
48	Vermont	195	0.2%
14	Virginia	2,047	2.4%
18	Washington	1,651	1.9%
34	West Virginia	706	0.8%
17	Wisconsin	1,768	2.0%
49	Wyoming	138	0.2%

RANK ORDER

RANK	STATE	DEATHS	% of USA
1	California	12,305	14.2%
2	New York	6,578	7.6%
3	Texas	4,621	5.3%
4	Pennsylvania	4,379	5.1%
5	Florida	3,895	4.5%
6	Illinois	3,759	4.3%
7	Ohio	3,467	4.0%
8	Michigan	2,826	3.3%
9	Massachusetts	2,666	3.1%
10	North Carolina	2,459	2.8%
11	New Jersey	2,360	2.7%
12	Missouri	2,241	2.6%
13	Georgia	2,154	2.5%
14	Tennessee	2,047	2.4%
14	Virginia	2,047	2.4%
16	Indiana	1,778	2.1%
17	Wisconsin	1,768	2.0%
18	Washington	1,651	1.9%
19	Maryland	1,452	1.7%
20	Alabama	1,438	1.7%
21	Kentucky	1,339	1.5%
22	Minnesota	1,322	1.5%
23	Oklahoma	1,304	1.5%
24	Arizona	1,274	1.5%
25	Connecticut	1,230	1.4%
26	Iowa	1,210	1.4%
27	Louisiana	1,112	1.3%
28	Arkansas	1,051	1.2%
29	Mississippi	1,036	1.2%
30	Kansas	984	1.1%
31	South Carolina	962	1.1%
32	Oregon	920	1.1%
33	Colorado	850	1.0%
34	West Virginia	706	0.8%
35	Nebraska	566	0.7%
36	Utah	531	0.6%
37	New Mexico	454	0.5%
38	Maine	430	0.5%
39	Nevada	412	0.5%
40	Idaho	353	0.4%
41	Hawaii	351	0.4%
42	Rhode Island	325	0.4%
43	Montana	300	0.3%
44	South Dakota	268	0.3%
45	New Hampshire	251	0.3%
46	Delaware	227	0.3%
47	North Dakota	222	0.3%
48	Vermont	195	0.2%
49	Wyoming	138	0.2%
50	Alaska	48	0.1%
	District of Columbia	187	0.2%

Source: U.S. Department of Health and Human Services, National Center for Health Statistics
     "National Vital Statistics Reports" (Vol. 47, No. 19, June 30, 1999)
*Final data by state of residence.

Death Rate by Pneumonia and Influenza in 1997

National Rate = 32.3 Deaths per 100,000 Population*

ALPHA ORDER

RANK	STATE	RATE
21	Alabama	33.3
50	Alaska	7.9
40	Arizona	28.0
3	Arkansas	41.7
7	California	38.1
48	Colorado	21.8
11	Connecticut	37.6
26	Delaware	31.0
41	Florida	26.6
35	Georgia	28.8
30	Hawaii	29.6
33	Idaho	29.2
25	Illinois	31.6
29	Indiana	30.3
2	Iowa	42.4
9	Kansas	37.9
17	Kentucky	34.3
44	Louisiana	25.6
15	Maine	34.6
37	Maryland	28.5
1	Massachusetts	43.6
34	Michigan	28.9
39	Minnesota	28.2
9	Mississippi	37.9
4	Missouri	41.5
20	Montana	34.1
18	Nebraska	34.2
46	Nevada	24.6
49	New Hampshire	21.4
32	New Jersey	29.3
42	New Mexico	26.2
13	New York	36.3
22	North Carolina	33.1
15	North Dakota	34.6
26	Ohio	31.0
5	Oklahoma	39.3
38	Oregon	28.4
12	Pennsylvania	36.4
24	Rhode Island	32.9
44	South Carolina	25.6
13	South Dakota	36.3
7	Tennessee	38.1
47	Texas	23.8
43	Utah	25.8
22	Vermont	33.1
28	Virginia	30.4
31	Washington	29.4
6	West Virginia	38.9
18	Wisconsin	34.2
35	Wyoming	28.8

RANK ORDER

RANK	STATE	RATE
1	Massachusetts	43.6
2	Iowa	42.4
3	Arkansas	41.7
4	Missouri	41.5
5	Oklahoma	39.3
6	West Virginia	38.9
7	California	38.1
7	Tennessee	38.1
9	Kansas	37.9
9	Mississippi	37.9
11	Connecticut	37.6
12	Pennsylvania	36.4
13	New York	36.3
13	South Dakota	36.3
15	Maine	34.6
15	North Dakota	34.6
17	Kentucky	34.3
18	Nebraska	34.2
18	Wisconsin	34.2
20	Montana	34.1
21	Alabama	33.3
22	North Carolina	33.1
22	Vermont	33.1
24	Rhode Island	32.9
25	Illinois	31.6
26	Delaware	31.0
26	Ohio	31.0
28	Virginia	30.4
29	Indiana	30.3
30	Hawaii	29.6
31	Washington	29.4
32	New Jersey	29.3
33	Idaho	29.2
34	Michigan	28.9
35	Georgia	28.8
35	Wyoming	28.8
37	Maryland	28.5
38	Oregon	28.4
39	Minnesota	28.2
40	Arizona	28.0
41	Florida	26.6
42	New Mexico	26.2
43	Utah	25.8
44	Louisiana	25.6
44	South Carolina	25.6
46	Nevada	24.6
47	Texas	23.8
48	Colorado	21.8
49	New Hampshire	21.4
50	Alaska	7.9
	District of Columbia	35.4

Source: U.S. Department of Health and Human Services, National Center for Health Statistics
   "National Vital Statistics Reports" (Vol. 47, No. 19, June 30, 1999)
*Final data by state of residence. Not age-adjusted.

Age-Adjusted Death Rate by Pneumonia and Influenza in 1997

National Rate = 12.9 Deaths per 100,000 Population*

ALPHA ORDER

RANK	STATE	RATE
15	Alabama	13.5
49	Alaska	8.5
20	Arizona	12.5
5	Arkansas	15.4
2	California	16.8
43	Colorado	10.0
21	Connecticut	12.4
17	Delaware	13.1
48	Florida	8.8
3	Georgia	16.0
30	Hawaii	12.1
37	Idaho	11.4
19	Illinois	12.7
26	Indiana	12.2
21	Iowa	12.4
34	Kansas	11.8
14	Kentucky	13.6
26	Louisiana	12.2
41	Maine	10.6
16	Maryland	13.2
11	Massachusetts	13.8
21	Michigan	12.4
47	Minnesota	8.9
1	Mississippi	17.3
6	Missouri	14.8
32	Montana	12.0
40	Nebraska	10.8
10	Nevada	13.9
50	New Hampshire	8.2
39	New Jersey	11.0
25	New Mexico	12.3
11	New York	13.8
7	North Carolina	14.5
42	North Dakota	10.5
34	Ohio	11.8
8	Oklahoma	14.4
45	Oregon	9.9
32	Pennsylvania	12.0
43	Rhode Island	10.0
21	South Carolina	12.4
45	South Dakota	9.9
3	Tennessee	16.0
26	Texas	12.2
9	Utah	14.0
37	Vermont	11.4
11	Virginia	13.8
26	Washington	12.2
17	West Virginia	13.1
36	Wisconsin	11.5
30	Wyoming	12.1

RANK ORDER

RANK	STATE	RATE
1	Mississippi	17.3
2	California	16.8
3	Georgia	16.0
3	Tennessee	16.0
5	Arkansas	15.4
6	Missouri	14.8
7	North Carolina	14.5
8	Oklahoma	14.4
9	Utah	14.0
10	Nevada	13.9
11	Massachusetts	13.8
11	New York	13.8
11	Virginia	13.8
14	Kentucky	13.6
15	Alabama	13.5
16	Maryland	13.2
17	Delaware	13.1
17	West Virginia	13.1
19	Illinois	12.7
20	Arizona	12.5
21	Connecticut	12.4
21	Iowa	12.4
21	Michigan	12.4
21	South Carolina	12.4
25	New Mexico	12.3
26	Indiana	12.2
26	Louisiana	12.2
26	Texas	12.2
26	Washington	12.2
30	Hawaii	12.1
30	Wyoming	12.1
32	Montana	12.0
32	Pennsylvania	12.0
34	Kansas	11.8
34	Ohio	11.8
36	Wisconsin	11.5
37	Idaho	11.4
37	Vermont	11.4
39	New Jersey	11.0
40	Nebraska	10.8
41	Maine	10.6
42	North Dakota	10.5
43	Colorado	10.0
43	Rhode Island	10.0
45	Oregon	9.9
45	South Dakota	9.9
47	Minnesota	8.9
48	Florida	8.8
49	Alaska	8.5
50	New Hampshire	8.2
	District of Columbia	17.0

Source: U.S. Department of Health and Human Services, National Center for Health Statistics
"National Vital Statistics Reports" (Vol. 47, No. 19, June 30, 1999)
*Final data by state of residence.

Deaths by Complications of Pregnancy and Childbirth in 1997

National Total = 327 Deaths*

RANK	STATE	DEATHS	% of USA
15	Alabama	6	1.8%
36	Alaska	1	0.3%
9	Arizona	11	3.4%
22	Arkansas	4	1.2%
1	California	45	13.8%
17	Colorado	5	1.5%
45	Connecticut	0	0.0%
36	Delaware	1	0.3%
4	Florida	21	6.4%
5	Georgia	13	4.0%
36	Hawaii	1	0.3%
30	Idaho	2	0.6%
7	Illinois	12	3.7%
27	Indiana	3	0.9%
36	Iowa	1	0.3%
17	Kansas	5	1.5%
27	Kentucky	3	0.9%
22	Louisiana	4	1.2%
36	Maine	1	0.3%
13	Maryland	8	2.4%
36	Massachusetts	1	0.3%
7	Michigan	12	3.7%
22	Minnesota	4	1.2%
11	Mississippi	10	3.1%
12	Missouri	9	2.8%
45	Montana	0	0.0%
36	Nebraska	1	0.3%
22	Nevada	4	1.2%
36	New Hampshire	1	0.3%
5	New Jersey	13	4.0%
36	New Mexico	1	0.3%
3	New York	30	9.2%
9	North Carolina	11	3.4%
45	North Dakota	0	0.0%
17	Ohio	5	1.5%
30	Oklahoma	2	0.6%
17	Oregon	5	1.5%
13	Pennsylvania	8	2.4%
30	Rhode Island	2	0.6%
17	South Carolina	5	1.5%
45	South Dakota	0	0.0%
15	Tennessee	6	1.8%
2	Texas	36	11.0%
30	Utah	2	0.6%
45	Vermont	0	0.0%
22	Virginia	4	1.2%
27	Washington	3	0.9%
30	West Virginia	2	0.6%
30	Wisconsin	2	0.6%
45	Wyoming	0	0.0%

RANK	STATE	DEATHS	% of USA
1	California	45	13.8%
2	Texas	36	11.0%
3	New York	30	9.2%
4	Florida	21	6.4%
5	Georgia	13	4.0%
5	New Jersey	13	4.0%
7	Illinois	12	3.7%
7	Michigan	12	3.7%
9	Arizona	11	3.4%
9	North Carolina	11	3.4%
11	Mississippi	10	3.1%
12	Missouri	9	2.8%
13	Maryland	8	2.4%
13	Pennsylvania	8	2.4%
15	Alabama	6	1.8%
15	Tennessee	6	1.8%
17	Colorado	5	1.5%
17	Kansas	5	1.5%
17	Ohio	5	1.5%
17	Oregon	5	1.5%
17	South Carolina	5	1.5%
22	Arkansas	4	1.2%
22	Louisiana	4	1.2%
22	Minnesota	4	1.2%
22	Nevada	4	1.2%
22	Virginia	4	1.2%
27	Indiana	3	0.9%
27	Kentucky	3	0.9%
27	Washington	3	0.9%
30	Idaho	2	0.6%
30	Oklahoma	2	0.6%
30	Rhode Island	2	0.6%
30	Utah	2	0.6%
30	West Virginia	2	0.6%
30	Wisconsin	2	0.6%
36	Alaska	1	0.3%
36	Delaware	1	0.3%
36	Hawaii	1	0.3%
36	Iowa	1	0.3%
36	Maine	1	0.3%
36	Massachusetts	1	0.3%
36	Nebraska	1	0.3%
36	New Hampshire	1	0.3%
36	New Mexico	1	0.3%
45	Connecticut	0	0.0%
45	Montana	0	0.0%
45	North Dakota	0	0.0%
45	South Dakota	0	0.0%
45	Vermont	0	0.0%
45	Wyoming	0	0.0%
	District of Columbia	1	0.3%

Source: U.S. Department of Health and Human Services, National Center for Health Statistics
(http://wonder.cdc.gov/WONDER/)
*By state of residence.

Death Rate by Complications of Pregnancy and Childbirth in 1997

National Rate = 0.24 Deaths per 100,000 Female Population*

ALPHA ORDER

RANK	STATE	RATE
19	Alabama	0.27
7	Alaska	0.35
3	Arizona	0.48
12	Arkansas	0.31
17	California	0.28
22	Colorado	0.25
45	Connecticut	0.00
19	Delaware	0.27
17	Florida	0.28
8	Georgia	0.34
29	Hawaii	0.17
9	Idaho	0.33
26	Illinois	0.20
40	Indiana	0.10
43	Iowa	0.07
5	Kansas	0.38
33	Kentucky	0.15
28	Louisiana	0.18
32	Maine	0.16
12	Maryland	0.31
44	Massachusetts	0.03
23	Michigan	0.24
29	Minnesota	0.17
1	Mississippi	0.70
10	Missouri	0.32
45	Montana	0.00
35	Nebraska	0.12
2	Nevada	0.49
29	New Hampshire	0.17
12	New Jersey	0.31
38	New Mexico	0.11
10	New York	0.32
16	North Carolina	0.29
45	North Dakota	0.00
41	Ohio	0.09
35	Oklahoma	0.12
12	Oregon	0.31
34	Pennsylvania	0.13
4	Rhode Island	0.39
21	South Carolina	0.26
45	South Dakota	0.00
24	Tennessee	0.22
6	Texas	0.37
27	Utah	0.19
45	Vermont	0.00
35	Virginia	0.12
38	Washington	0.11
25	West Virginia	0.21
42	Wisconsin	0.08
45	Wyoming	0.00

RANK ORDER

RANK	STATE	RATE
1	Mississippi	0.70
2	Nevada	0.49
3	Arizona	0.48
4	Rhode Island	0.39
5	Kansas	0.38
6	Texas	0.37
7	Alaska	0.35
8	Georgia	0.34
9	Idaho	0.33
10	Missouri	0.32
10	New York	0.32
12	Arkansas	0.31
12	Maryland	0.31
12	New Jersey	0.31
12	Oregon	0.31
16	North Carolina	0.29
17	California	0.28
17	Florida	0.28
19	Alabama	0.27
19	Delaware	0.27
21	South Carolina	0.26
22	Colorado	0.25
23	Michigan	0.24
24	Tennessee	0.22
25	West Virginia	0.21
26	Illinois	0.20
27	Utah	0.19
28	Louisiana	0.18
29	Hawaii	0.17
29	Minnesota	0.17
29	New Hampshire	0.17
32	Maine	0.16
33	Kentucky	0.15
34	Pennsylvania	0.13
35	Nebraska	0.12
35	Oklahoma	0.12
35	Virginia	0.12
38	New Mexico	0.11
38	Washington	0.11
40	Indiana	0.10
41	Ohio	0.09
42	Wisconsin	0.08
43	Iowa	0.07
44	Massachusetts	0.03
45	Connecticut	0.00
45	Montana	0.00
45	North Dakota	0.00
45	South Dakota	0.00
45	Vermont	0.00
45	Wyoming	0.00

District of Columbia 0.36

Source: Morgan Quitno Press using data from U.S. Dept of Health & Human Serv's, Nat'l Center for Health Statistics
(http://wonder.cdc.gov/WONDER/)
*By state of residence. Not-age adjusted. Due to low numbers of deaths, rates for all states should be interpreted
with caution.

Age-Adjusted Death Rate by Complications of Pregnancy and Childbirth in 1997

National Rate = 0.2 Deaths per 100,000 Population*

ALPHA ORDER

RANK	STATE	RATE
9	Alabama	0.1
3	Alaska	0.2
3	Arizona	0.2
9	Arkansas	0.1
27	California	0.0
9	Colorado	0.1
27	Connecticut	0.0
3	Delaware	0.2
9	Florida	0.1
9	Georgia	0.1
9	Hawaii	0.1
3	Idaho	0.2
27	Illinois	0.0
27	Indiana	0.0
27	Iowa	0.0
9	Kansas	0.1
27	Kentucky	0.0
27	Louisiana	0.0
9	Maine	0.1
9	Maryland	0.1
27	Massachusetts	0.0
27	Michigan	0.0
27	Minnesota	0.0
1	Mississippi	0.4
9	Missouri	0.1
27	Montana	0.0
9	Nebraska	0.1
2	Nevada	0.3
9	New Hampshire	0.1
9	New Jersey	0.1
9	New Mexico	0.1
9	New York	0.1
27	North Carolina	0.0
27	North Dakota	0.0
27	Ohio	0.0
27	Oklahoma	0.0
3	Oregon	0.2
27	Pennsylvania	0.0
9	Rhode Island	0.1
3	South Carolina	0.2
27	South Dakota	0.0
27	Tennessee	0.0
9	Texas	0.1
9	Utah	0.1
27	Vermont	0.0
27	Virginia	0.0
27	Washington	0.0
27	West Virginia	0.0
27	Wisconsin	0.0
27	Wyoming	0.0

RANK ORDER

RANK	STATE	RATE
1	Mississippi	0.4
2	Nevada	0.3
3	Alaska	0.2
3	Arizona	0.2
3	Delaware	0.2
3	Idaho	0.2
3	Oregon	0.2
3	South Carolina	0.2
9	Alabama	0.1
9	Arkansas	0.1
9	Colorado	0.1
9	Florida	0.1
9	Georgia	0.1
9	Hawaii	0.1
9	Kansas	0.1
9	Maine	0.1
9	Maryland	0.1
9	Missouri	0.1
9	Nebraska	0.1
9	New Hampshire	0.1
9	New Jersey	0.1
9	New Mexico	0.1
9	New York	0.1
9	Rhode Island	0.1
9	Texas	0.1
9	Utah	0.1
27	California	0.0
27	Connecticut	0.0
27	Illinois	0.0
27	Indiana	0.0
27	Iowa	0.0
27	Kentucky	0.0
27	Louisiana	0.0
27	Massachusetts	0.0
27	Michigan	0.0
27	Minnesota	0.0
27	Montana	0.0
27	North Carolina	0.0
27	North Dakota	0.0
27	Ohio	0.0
27	Oklahoma	0.0
27	Pennsylvania	0.0
27	South Dakota	0.0
27	Tennessee	0.0
27	Vermont	0.0
27	Virginia	0.0
27	Washington	0.0
27	West Virginia	0.0
27	Wisconsin	0.0
27	Wyoming	0.0
	District of Columbia	0.1

Source: U.S. Department of Health and Human Services, National Center for Health Statistics
(http://wonder.cdc.gov/WONDER/)
*By state of residence. Due to low numbers of deaths, rates for all states should be interpreted with caution.

Deaths by Tuberculosis in 1997

National Total = 1,166 Deaths*

ALPHA ORDER

ALPHA ORDER

RANK	STATE	DEATHS	% of USA
15	Alabama	23	2.0%
45	Alaska	1	0.1%
14	Arizona	24	2.1%
21	Arkansas	18	1.5%
1	California	190	16.3%
29	Colorado	9	0.8%
35	Connecticut	6	0.5%
32	Delaware	7	0.6%
4	Florida	79	6.8%
7	Georgia	42	3.6%
25	Hawaii	12	1.0%
47	Idaho	0	0.0%
5	Illinois	57	4.9%
22	Indiana	16	1.4%
31	Iowa	8	0.7%
38	Kansas	5	0.4%
10	Kentucky	29	2.5%
16	Louisiana	22	1.9%
41	Maine	3	0.3%
17	Maryland	20	1.7%
25	Massachusetts	12	1.0%
9	Michigan	34	2.9%
35	Minnesota	6	0.5%
24	Mississippi	14	1.2%
23	Missouri	15	1.3%
44	Montana	2	0.2%
41	Nebraska	3	0.3%
32	Nevada	7	0.6%
41	New Hampshire	3	0.3%
11	New Jersey	28	2.4%
32	New Mexico	7	0.6%
3	New York	89	7.6%
13	North Carolina	26	2.2%
38	North Dakota	5	0.4%
11	Ohio	28	2.4%
17	Oklahoma	20	1.7%
29	Oregon	9	0.8%
8	Pennsylvania	40	3.4%
45	Rhode Island	1	0.1%
20	South Carolina	19	1.6%
47	South Dakota	0	0.0%
6	Tennessee	47	4.0%
2	Texas	121	10.4%
40	Utah	4	0.3%
47	Vermont	0	0.0%
25	Virginia	12	1.0%
17	Washington	20	1.7%
35	West Virginia	6	0.5%
28	Wisconsin	11	0.9%
47	Wyoming	0	0.0%

RANK ORDER

RANK	STATE	DEATHS	% of USA
1	California	190	16.3%
2	Texas	121	10.4%
3	New York	89	7.6%
4	Florida	79	6.8%
5	Illinois	57	4.9%
6	Tennessee	47	4.0%
7	Georgia	42	3.6%
8	Pennsylvania	40	3.4%
9	Michigan	34	2.9%
10	Kentucky	29	2.5%
11	New Jersey	28	2.4%
11	Ohio	28	2.4%
13	North Carolina	26	2.2%
14	Arizona	24	2.1%
15	Alabama	23	2.0%
16	Louisiana	22	1.9%
17	Maryland	20	1.7%
17	Oklahoma	20	1.7%
17	Washington	20	1.7%
20	South Carolina	19	1.6%
21	Arkansas	18	1.5%
22	Indiana	16	1.4%
23	Missouri	15	1.3%
24	Mississippi	14	1.2%
25	Hawaii	12	1.0%
25	Massachusetts	12	1.0%
25	Virginia	12	1.0%
28	Wisconsin	11	0.9%
29	Colorado	9	0.8%
29	Oregon	9	0.8%
31	Iowa	8	0.7%
32	Delaware	7	0.6%
32	Nevada	7	0.6%
32	New Mexico	7	0.6%
35	Connecticut	6	0.5%
35	Minnesota	6	0.5%
35	West Virginia	6	0.5%
38	Kansas	5	0.4%
38	North Dakota	5	0.4%
40	Utah	4	0.3%
41	Maine	3	0.3%
41	Nebraska	3	0.3%
41	New Hampshire	3	0.3%
44	Montana	2	0.2%
45	Alaska	1	0.1%
45	Rhode Island	1	0.1%
47	Idaho	0	0.0%
47	South Dakota	0	0.0%
47	Vermont	0	0.0%
47	Wyoming	0	0.0%
	District of Columbia	6	0.5%

Source: U.S. Department of Health and Human Services, National Center for Health Statistics
(http://wonder.cdc.gov/WONDER/)
*By state of residence.

Death Rate by Tuberculosis in 1997

National Rate = 0.44 Deaths per 100,000 Population*

ALPHA ORDER

RANK	STATE	RATE
12	Alabama	0.53
44	Alaska	0.16
12	Arizona	0.53
6	Arkansas	0.71
9	California	0.59
35	Colorado	0.23
41	Connecticut	0.18
2	Delaware	0.95
11	Florida	0.54
10	Georgia	0.56
1	Hawaii	1.01
47	Idaho	0.00
18	Illinois	0.47
31	Indiana	0.27
28	Iowa	0.28
39	Kansas	0.19
5	Kentucky	0.74
14	Louisiana	0.51
34	Maine	0.24
21	Maryland	0.39
38	Massachusetts	0.20
23	Michigan	0.35
45	Minnesota	0.13
14	Mississippi	0.51
28	Missouri	0.28
35	Montana	0.23
41	Nebraska	0.18
19	Nevada	0.42
32	New Hampshire	0.26
23	New Jersey	0.35
20	New Mexico	0.41
17	New York	0.49
23	North Carolina	0.35
4	North Dakota	0.78
33	Ohio	0.25
8	Oklahoma	0.60
28	Oregon	0.28
26	Pennsylvania	0.33
46	Rhode Island	0.10
16	South Carolina	0.50
47	South Dakota	0.00
3	Tennessee	0.87
7	Texas	0.63
39	Utah	0.19
47	Vermont	0.00
41	Virginia	0.18
22	Washington	0.36
26	West Virginia	0.33
37	Wisconsin	0.21
47	Wyoming	0.00

RANK ORDER

RANK	STATE	RATE
1	Hawaii	1.01
2	Delaware	0.95
3	Tennessee	0.87
4	North Dakota	0.78
5	Kentucky	0.74
6	Arkansas	0.71
7	Texas	0.63
8	Oklahoma	0.60
9	California	0.59
10	Georgia	0.56
11	Florida	0.54
12	Alabama	0.53
12	Arizona	0.53
14	Louisiana	0.51
14	Mississippi	0.51
16	South Carolina	0.50
17	New York	0.49
18	Illinois	0.47
19	Nevada	0.42
20	New Mexico	0.41
21	Maryland	0.39
22	Washington	0.36
23	Michigan	0.35
23	New Jersey	0.35
23	North Carolina	0.35
26	Pennsylvania	0.33
26	West Virginia	0.33
28	Iowa	0.28
28	Missouri	0.28
28	Oregon	0.28
31	Indiana	0.27
32	New Hampshire	0.26
33	Ohio	0.25
34	Maine	0.24
35	Colorado	0.23
35	Montana	0.23
37	Wisconsin	0.21
38	Massachusetts	0.20
39	Kansas	0.19
39	Utah	0.19
41	Connecticut	0.18
41	Nebraska	0.18
41	Virginia	0.18
44	Alaska	0.16
45	Minnesota	0.13
46	Rhode Island	0.10
47	Idaho	0.00
47	South Dakota	0.00
47	Vermont	0.00
47	Wyoming	0.00

District of Columbia	1.13

Source: Morgan Quitno Press using data from U.S. Dept of Health & Human Serv's, Nat'l Center for Health Statistics
    (http://wonder.cdc.gov/WONDER/)
*By state of residence. Not age-adjusted. Due to low numbers of deaths, rates for all states should be interpreted
with caution.

Age-Adjusted Death Rate by Tuberculosis in 1997

National Rate = 0.3 Deaths per 100,000 Population*

ALPHA ORDER

RANK	STATE	RATE
18	Alabama	0.2
18	Alaska	0.2
18	Arizona	0.2
18	Arkansas	0.2
6	California	0.4
37	Colorado	0.0
25	Connecticut	0.1
1	Delaware	0.7
18	Florida	0.2
3	Georgia	0.5
2	Hawaii	0.6
37	Idaho	0.0
11	Illinois	0.3
37	Indiana	0.0
37	Iowa	0.0
37	Kansas	0.0
6	Kentucky	0.4
3	Louisiana	0.5
25	Maine	0.1
18	Maryland	0.2
37	Massachusetts	0.0
11	Michigan	0.3
37	Minnesota	0.0
11	Mississippi	0.3
37	Missouri	0.0
25	Montana	0.1
25	Nebraska	0.1
11	Nevada	0.3
25	New Hampshire	0.1
37	New Jersey	0.0
6	New Mexico	0.4
6	New York	0.4
25	North Carolina	0.1
11	North Dakota	0.3
37	Ohio	0.0
11	Oklahoma	0.3
25	Oregon	0.1
25	Pennsylvania	0.1
37	Rhode Island	0.0
11	South Carolina	0.3
37	South Dakota	0.0
3	Tennessee	0.5
6	Texas	0.4
18	Utah	0.2
37	Vermont	0.0
25	Virginia	0.1
25	Washington	0.1
25	West Virginia	0.1
25	Wisconsin	0.1
37	Wyoming	0.0

RANK ORDER

RANK	STATE	RATE
1	Delaware	0.7
2	Hawaii	0.6
3	Georgia	0.5
3	Louisiana	0.5
3	Tennessee	0.5
6	California	0.4
6	Kentucky	0.4
6	New Mexico	0.4
6	New York	0.4
6	Texas	0.4
11	Illinois	0.3
11	Michigan	0.3
11	Mississippi	0.3
11	Nevada	0.3
11	North Dakota	0.3
11	Oklahoma	0.3
11	South Carolina	0.3
18	Alabama	0.2
18	Alaska	0.2
18	Arizona	0.2
18	Arkansas	0.2
18	Florida	0.2
18	Maryland	0.2
18	Utah	0.2
25	Connecticut	0.1
25	Maine	0.1
25	Montana	0.1
25	Nebraska	0.1
25	New Hampshire	0.1
25	North Carolina	0.1
25	Oregon	0.1
25	Pennsylvania	0.1
25	Virginia	0.1
25	Washington	0.1
25	West Virginia	0.1
25	Wisconsin	0.1
37	Colorado	0.0
37	Idaho	0.0
37	Indiana	0.0
37	Iowa	0.0
37	Kansas	0.0
37	Massachusetts	0.0
37	Minnesota	0.0
37	Missouri	0.0
37	New Jersey	0.0
37	Ohio	0.0
37	Rhode Island	0.0
37	South Dakota	0.0
37	Vermont	0.0
37	Wyoming	0.0
	District of Columbia	0.8

Source: U.S. Department of Health and Human Services, National Center for Health Statistics
   (http://wonder.cdc.gov/WONDER/)
*By state of residence. Due to low numbers of deaths, rates for all states should be interpreted with caution.

Deaths by Injury in 1997

National Total = 149,691 Deaths*

ALPHA ORDER				RANK ORDER			
RANK	STATE	DEATHS	% of USA	RANK	STATE	DEATHS	% of USA
16	Alabama	3,382	2.3%	1	California	15,490	10.3%
44	Alaska	459	0.3%	2	Texas	10,986	7.3%
15	Arizona	3,414	2.3%	3	Florida	8,885	5.9%
29	Arkansas	2,058	1.4%	4	New York	7,642	5.1%
1	California	15,490	10.3%	5	Pennsylvania	7,182	4.8%
28	Colorado	2,293	1.5%	6	Illinois	5,629	3.8%
34	Connecticut	1,422	0.9%	7	Ohio	5,132	3.4%
46	Delaware	424	0.3%	8	Michigan	5,110	3.4%
3	Florida	8,885	5.9%	9	Georgia	4,710	3.1%
9	Georgia	4,710	3.1%	10	North Carolina	4,684	3.1%
42	Hawaii	575	0.4%	11	Tennessee	3,880	2.6%
39	Idaho	807	0.5%	12	Virginia	3,609	2.4%
6	Illinois	5,629	3.8%	13	Missouri	3,568	2.4%
17	Indiana	3,333	2.2%	14	New Jersey	3,426	2.3%
31	Iowa	1,519	1.0%	15	Arizona	3,414	2.3%
32	Kansas	1,512	1.0%	16	Alabama	3,382	2.3%
22	Kentucky	2,574	1.7%	17	Indiana	3,333	2.2%
18	Louisiana	3,204	2.1%	18	Louisiana	3,204	2.1%
41	Maine	592	0.4%	19	Washington	3,008	2.0%
20	Maryland	2,939	2.0%	20	Maryland	2,939	2.0%
27	Massachusetts	2,330	1.6%	21	Wisconsin	2,673	1.8%
8	Michigan	5,110	3.4%	22	Kentucky	2,574	1.7%
26	Minnesota	2,336	1.6%	23	South Carolina	2,519	1.7%
25	Mississippi	2,347	1.6%	24	Oklahoma	2,433	1.6%
13	Missouri	3,568	2.4%	25	Mississippi	2,347	1.6%
40	Montana	679	0.5%	26	Minnesota	2,336	1.6%
38	Nebraska	923	0.6%	27	Massachusetts	2,330	1.6%
35	Nevada	1,314	0.9%	28	Colorado	2,293	1.5%
43	New Hampshire	496	0.3%	29	Arkansas	2,058	1.4%
14	New Jersey	3,426	2.3%	30	Oregon	2,015	1.3%
33	New Mexico	1,470	1.0%	31	Iowa	1,519	1.0%
4	New York	7,642	5.1%	32	Kansas	1,512	1.0%
10	North Carolina	4,684	3.1%	33	New Mexico	1,470	1.0%
49	North Dakota	345	0.2%	34	Connecticut	1,422	0.9%
7	Ohio	5,132	3.4%	35	Nevada	1,314	0.9%
24	Oklahoma	2,433	1.6%	36	West Virginia	1,187	0.8%
30	Oregon	2,015	1.3%	37	Utah	1,177	0.8%
5	Pennsylvania	7,182	4.8%	38	Nebraska	923	0.6%
47	Rhode Island	396	0.3%	39	Idaho	807	0.5%
23	South Carolina	2,519	1.7%	40	Montana	679	0.5%
44	South Dakota	459	0.3%	41	Maine	592	0.4%
11	Tennessee	3,880	2.6%	42	Hawaii	575	0.4%
2	Texas	10,986	7.3%	43	New Hampshire	496	0.3%
37	Utah	1,177	0.8%	44	Alaska	459	0.3%
50	Vermont	293	0.2%	44	South Dakota	459	0.3%
12	Virginia	3,609	2.4%	46	Delaware	424	0.3%
19	Washington	3,008	2.0%	47	Rhode Island	396	0.3%
36	West Virginia	1,187	0.8%	48	Wyoming	365	0.2%
21	Wisconsin	2,673	1.8%	49	North Dakota	345	0.2%
48	Wyoming	365	0.2%	50	Vermont	293	0.2%
					District of Columbia	486	0.3%

Source: U.S. Department of Health and Human Services, National Center for Health Statistics
   (http://wonder.cdc.gov/WONDER/)
*By state of residence. Injury as used here includes Accidents (including motor vehicle), Suicides, Homicides and "Other" undetermined.

Death Rate by Injury in 1997

National Rate = 55.9 Deaths per 100,000 Population*

RANK	STATE	RATE
4	Alabama	78.3
8	Alaska	75.3
9	Arizona	74.9
3	Arkansas	81.5
41	California	48.0
24	Colorado	58.9
45	Connecticut	43.5
26	Delaware	57.9
22	Florida	60.6
19	Georgia	62.9
40	Hawaii	48.5
14	Idaho	66.7
43	Illinois	47.3
29	Indiana	56.8
35	Iowa	53.2
25	Kansas	58.2
16	Kentucky	65.8
10	Louisiana	73.6
42	Maine	47.7
27	Maryland	57.7
50	Massachusetts	38.1
36	Michigan	52.3
38	Minnesota	49.8
1	Mississippi	85.9
15	Missouri	66.0
6	Montana	77.2
31	Nebraska	55.7
4	Nevada	78.3
47	New Hampshire	42.3
46	New Jersey	42.5
2	New Mexico	85.0
48	New York	42.1
18	North Carolina	63.0
32	North Dakota	53.8
44	Ohio	45.9
11	Oklahoma	73.3
21	Oregon	62.1
23	Pennsylvania	59.8
49	Rhode Island	40.1
13	South Carolina	66.9
20	South Dakota	62.2
12	Tennessee	72.2
30	Texas	56.5
28	Utah	57.1
39	Vermont	49.7
33	Virginia	53.6
33	Washington	53.6
17	West Virginia	65.4
37	Wisconsin	51.7
7	Wyoming	76.0

RANK ORDER

RANK	STATE	RATE
1	Mississippi	85.9
2	New Mexico	85.0
3	Arkansas	81.5
4	Alabama	78.3
4	Nevada	78.3
6	Montana	77.2
7	Wyoming	76.0
8	Alaska	75.3
9	Arizona	74.9
10	Louisiana	73.6
11	Oklahoma	73.3
12	Tennessee	72.2
13	South Carolina	66.9
14	Idaho	66.7
15	Missouri	66.0
16	Kentucky	65.8
17	West Virginia	65.4
18	North Carolina	63.0
19	Georgia	62.9
20	South Dakota	62.2
21	Oregon	62.1
22	Florida	60.6
23	Pennsylvania	59.8
24	Colorado	58.9
25	Kansas	58.2
26	Delaware	57.9
27	Maryland	57.7
28	Utah	57.1
29	Indiana	56.8
30	Texas	56.5
31	Nebraska	55.7
32	North Dakota	53.8
33	Virginia	53.6
33	Washington	53.6
35	Iowa	53.2
36	Michigan	52.3
37	Wisconsin	51.7
38	Minnesota	49.8
39	Vermont	49.7
40	Hawaii	48.5
41	California	48.0
42	Maine	47.7
43	Illinois	47.3
44	Ohio	45.9
45	Connecticut	43.5
46	New Jersey	42.5
47	New Hampshire	42.3
48	New York	42.1
49	Rhode Island	40.1
50	Massachusetts	38.1
	District of Columbia	91.6

Source: U.S. Department of Health and Human Services, National Center for Health Statistics
        (http://wonder.cdc.gov/WONDER/)
*By state of residence. Injury as used here includes Accidents (including motor vehicle), Suicides, Homicides and
"Other" undetermined. Not age-adjusted.

Age-Adjusted Death Rate by Injury in 1997

National Rate = 49.8 Deaths per 100,000 Population*

ALPHA ORDER

RANK	STATE	RATE
7	Alabama	70.1
3	Alaska	77.0
10	Arizona	68.7
4	Arkansas	74.0
35	California	44.9
25	Colorado	52.7
47	Connecticut	36.3
29	Delaware	50.5
22	Florida	54.0
16	Georgia	57.4
40	Hawaii	42.0
13	Idaho	61.4
37	Illinois	43.6
29	Indiana	50.5
39	Iowa	42.7
28	Kansas	51.0
17	Kentucky	57.1
8	Louisiana	69.2
43	Maine	38.5
26	Maryland	51.8
50	Massachusetts	31.1
33	Michigan	46.7
42	Minnesota	39.2
2	Mississippi	78.4
15	Missouri	57.9
6	Montana	70.7
34	Nebraska	46.0
5	Nevada	72.9
48	New Hampshire	35.2
46	New Jersey	37.0
1	New Mexico	79.2
45	New York	37.3
18	North Carolina	56.5
36	North Dakota	44.8
41	Ohio	39.3
11	Oklahoma	65.6
23	Oregon	53.8
27	Pennsylvania	51.2
49	Rhode Island	34.7
14	South Carolina	61.3
21	South Dakota	54.5
12	Tennessee	64.4
24	Texas	52.9
20	Utah	54.9
43	Vermont	38.5
32	Virginia	47.0
31	Washington	47.3
19	West Virginia	55.0
38	Wisconsin	42.9
9	Wyoming	68.9

RANK ORDER

RANK	STATE	RATE
1	New Mexico	79.2
2	Mississippi	78.4
3	Alaska	77.0
4	Arkansas	74.0
5	Nevada	72.9
6	Montana	70.7
7	Alabama	70.1
8	Louisiana	69.2
9	Wyoming	68.9
10	Arizona	68.7
11	Oklahoma	65.6
12	Tennessee	64.4
13	Idaho	61.4
14	South Carolina	61.3
15	Missouri	57.9
16	Georgia	57.4
17	Kentucky	57.1
18	North Carolina	56.5
19	West Virginia	55.0
20	Utah	54.9
21	South Dakota	54.5
22	Florida	54.0
23	Oregon	53.8
24	Texas	52.9
25	Colorado	52.7
26	Maryland	51.8
27	Pennsylvania	51.2
28	Kansas	51.0
29	Delaware	50.5
29	Indiana	50.5
31	Washington	47.3
32	Virginia	47.0
33	Michigan	46.7
34	Nebraska	46.0
35	California	44.9
36	North Dakota	44.8
37	Illinois	43.6
38	Wisconsin	42.9
39	Iowa	42.7
40	Hawaii	42.0
41	Ohio	39.3
42	Minnesota	39.2
43	Maine	38.5
43	Vermont	38.5
45	New York	37.3
46	New Jersey	37.0
47	Connecticut	36.3
48	New Hampshire	35.2
49	Rhode Island	34.7
50	Massachusetts	31.1

| | District of Columbia | 96.8 |

Source: U.S. Department of Health and Human Services, National Center for Health Statistics
    (http://wonder.cdc.gov/WONDER/)
By state of residence. Injury as used here includes Accidents (including motor vehicle), Suicides, Homicides and "Other" undetermined.

Deaths by Accidents in 1997

National Total = 95,644 Deaths*

ALPHA ORDER					RANK ORDER			
RANK	STATE	DEATHS	% of USA		RANK	STATE	DEATHS	% of USA
15	Alabama	2,298	2.4%		1	California	9,020	9.4%
46	Alaska	269	0.3%		2	Texas	7,175	7.5%
16	Arizona	2,147	2.2%		3	Florida	5,547	5.8%
28	Arkansas	1,345	1.4%		4	New York	4,946	5.2%
1	California	9,020	9.4%		5	Pennsylvania	4,779	5.0%
26	Colorado	1,431	1.5%		6	Illinois	3,470	3.6%
32	Connecticut	1,011	1.1%		7	Ohio	3,450	3.6%
45	Delaware	290	0.3%		8	Michigan	3,170	3.3%
3	Florida	5,547	5.8%		9	Georgia	3,081	3.2%
9	Georgia	3,081	3.2%		10	North Carolina	3,056	3.2%
42	Hawaii	355	0.4%		11	Tennessee	2,525	2.6%
39	Idaho	546	0.6%		12	Missouri	2,383	2.5%
6	Illinois	3,470	3.6%		13	New Jersey	2,372	2.5%
17	Indiana	2,093	2.2%		14	Virginia	2,307	2.4%
31	Iowa	1,087	1.1%		15	Alabama	2,298	2.4%
32	Kansas	1,011	1.1%		16	Arizona	2,147	2.2%
21	Kentucky	1,800	1.9%		17	Indiana	2,093	2.2%
19	Louisiana	1,908	2.0%		18	Washington	1,920	2.0%
41	Maine	428	0.4%		19	Louisiana	1,908	2.0%
27	Maryland	1,372	1.4%		20	Wisconsin	1,841	1.9%
30	Massachusetts	1,287	1.3%		21	Kentucky	1,800	1.9%
8	Michigan	3,170	3.3%		22	South Carolina	1,716	1.8%
23	Minnesota	1,704	1.8%		23	Minnesota	1,704	1.8%
25	Mississippi	1,588	1.7%		24	Oklahoma	1,604	1.7%
12	Missouri	2,383	2.5%		25	Mississippi	1,588	1.7%
40	Montana	450	0.5%		26	Colorado	1,431	1.5%
37	Nebraska	666	0.7%		27	Maryland	1,372	1.4%
38	Nevada	663	0.7%		28	Arkansas	1,345	1.4%
43	New Hampshire	321	0.3%		29	Oregon	1,305	1.4%
13	New Jersey	2,372	2.5%		30	Massachusetts	1,287	1.3%
34	New Mexico	1,002	1.0%		31	Iowa	1,087	1.1%
4	New York	4,946	5.2%		32	Connecticut	1,011	1.1%
10	North Carolina	3,056	3.2%		32	Kansas	1,011	1.1%
48	North Dakota	245	0.3%		34	New Mexico	1,002	1.0%
7	Ohio	3,450	3.6%		35	West Virginia	802	0.8%
24	Oklahoma	1,604	1.7%		36	Utah	686	0.7%
29	Oregon	1,305	1.4%		37	Nebraska	666	0.7%
5	Pennsylvania	4,779	5.0%		38	Nevada	663	0.7%
49	Rhode Island	242	0.3%		39	Idaho	546	0.6%
22	South Carolina	1,716	1.8%		40	Montana	450	0.5%
44	South Dakota	306	0.3%		41	Maine	428	0.4%
11	Tennessee	2,525	2.6%		42	Hawaii	355	0.4%
2	Texas	7,175	7.5%		43	New Hampshire	321	0.3%
36	Utah	686	0.7%		44	South Dakota	306	0.3%
50	Vermont	201	0.2%		45	Delaware	290	0.3%
14	Virginia	2,307	2.4%		46	Alaska	269	0.3%
18	Washington	1,920	2.0%		47	Wyoming	246	0.3%
35	West Virginia	802	0.8%		48	North Dakota	245	0.3%
20	Wisconsin	1,841	1.9%		49	Rhode Island	242	0.3%
47	Wyoming	246	0.3%		50	Vermont	201	0.2%
						District of Columbia	177	0.2%

Source: U.S. Department of Health and Human Services, National Center for Health Statistics
    "National Vital Statistics Reports" (Vol. 47, No. 19, June 30, 1999)
*Final data by state of residence. Includes motor vehicle deaths, poisoning, falls, drowning and other accidents.

Death Rate by Accidents in 1997

National Rate = 35.7 Deaths per 100,000 Population*

RANK	STATE (ALPHA ORDER)	RATE		RANK	STATE (RANK ORDER)	RATE
4	Alabama	53.2		1	Mississippi	58.2
14	Alaska	44.1		2	New Mexico	57.9
8	Arizona	47.1		3	Arkansas	53.3
3	Arkansas	53.3		4	Alabama	53.2
45	California	28.0		5	Wyoming	51.3
30	Colorado	36.8		6	Montana	51.2
40	Connecticut	30.9		7	Oklahoma	48.4
23	Delaware	39.6		8	Arizona	47.1
28	Florida	37.9		9	Tennessee	47.0
18	Georgia	41.2		10	Kentucky	46.1
42	Hawaii	29.9		11	South Carolina	45.6
12	Idaho	45.1		12	Idaho	45.1
44	Illinois	29.2		13	West Virginia	44.2
32	Indiana	35.7		14	Alaska	44.1
27	Iowa	38.1		14	Missouri	44.1
25	Kansas	39.0		16	Louisiana	43.8
10	Kentucky	46.1		17	South Dakota	41.5
16	Louisiana	43.8		18	Georgia	41.2
34	Maine	34.5		18	North Carolina	41.2
48	Maryland	26.9		20	Nebraska	40.2
50	Massachusetts	21.0		20	Oregon	40.2
39	Michigan	32.4		22	Pennsylvania	39.8
31	Minnesota	36.4		23	Delaware	39.6
1	Mississippi	58.2		24	Nevada	39.5
14	Missouri	44.1		25	Kansas	39.0
6	Montana	51.2		26	North Dakota	38.2
20	Nebraska	40.2		27	Iowa	38.1
24	Nevada	39.5		28	Florida	37.9
46	New Hampshire	27.4		29	Texas	36.9
43	New Jersey	29.5		30	Colorado	36.8
2	New Mexico	57.9		31	Minnesota	36.4
47	New York	27.3		32	Indiana	35.7
18	North Carolina	41.2		33	Wisconsin	35.6
26	North Dakota	38.2		34	Maine	34.5
41	Ohio	30.8		35	Virginia	34.3
7	Oklahoma	48.4		36	Washington	34.2
20	Oregon	40.2		37	Vermont	34.1
22	Pennsylvania	39.8		38	Utah	33.3
49	Rhode Island	24.5		39	Michigan	32.4
11	South Carolina	45.6		40	Connecticut	30.9
17	South Dakota	41.5		41	Ohio	30.8
9	Tennessee	47.0		42	Hawaii	29.9
29	Texas	36.9		43	New Jersey	29.5
38	Utah	33.3		44	Illinois	29.2
37	Vermont	34.1		45	California	28.0
35	Virginia	34.3		46	New Hampshire	27.4
36	Washington	34.2		47	New York	27.3
13	West Virginia	44.2		48	Maryland	26.9
33	Wisconsin	35.6		49	Rhode Island	24.5
5	Wyoming	51.3		50	Massachusetts	21.0
					District of Columbia	33.5

*Source: U.S. Department of Health and Human Services, National Center for Health Statistics
"National Vital Statistics Reports" (Vol. 47, No. 19, June 30, 1999)*
*Final data by state of residence. Includes motor vehicle deaths, poisoning, falls, drowning and other accidents.
Not age-adjusted.*

Age-Adjusted Death Rate by Accidents in 1997

National Rate = 30.1 Deaths per 100,000 Population*

ALPHA ORDER

RANK	STATE	RATE
5	Alabama	45.9
3	Alaska	46.0
8	Arizona	40.8
3	Arkansas	46.0
39	California	25.0
26	Colorado	31.6
45	Connecticut	23.8
23	Delaware	33.2
24	Florida	32.2
15	Georgia	36.6
43	Hawaii	24.1
11	Idaho	40.2
40	Illinois	24.7
31	Indiana	29.8
34	Iowa	27.7
25	Kansas	32.0
14	Kentucky	38.4
13	Louisiana	39.3
38	Maine	25.9
47	Maryland	21.9
50	Massachusetts	15.0
36	Michigan	27.2
37	Minnesota	26.3
2	Mississippi	50.8
16	Missouri	36.5
6	Montana	45.4
28	Nebraska	31.0
16	Nevada	36.5
48	New Hampshire	21.1
44	New Jersey	24.0
1	New Mexico	52.1
46	New York	22.3
19	North Carolina	35.2
30	North Dakota	30.1
40	Ohio	24.7
9	Oklahoma	40.7
21	Oregon	33.6
27	Pennsylvania	31.2
49	Rhode Island	19.0
10	South Carolina	40.6
20	South Dakota	34.3
12	Tennessee	39.9
22	Texas	33.4
29	Utah	30.5
42	Vermont	24.6
33	Virginia	28.3
32	Washington	28.6
18	West Virginia	35.4
35	Wisconsin	27.5
7	Wyoming	45.2

RANK ORDER

RANK	STATE	RATE
1	New Mexico	52.1
2	Mississippi	50.8
3	Alaska	46.0
3	Arkansas	46.0
5	Alabama	45.9
6	Montana	45.4
7	Wyoming	45.2
8	Arizona	40.8
9	Oklahoma	40.7
10	South Carolina	40.6
11	Idaho	40.2
12	Tennessee	39.9
13	Louisiana	39.3
14	Kentucky	38.4
15	Georgia	36.6
16	Missouri	36.5
16	Nevada	36.5
18	West Virginia	35.4
19	North Carolina	35.2
20	South Dakota	34.3
21	Oregon	33.6
22	Texas	33.4
23	Delaware	33.2
24	Florida	32.2
25	Kansas	32.0
26	Colorado	31.6
27	Pennsylvania	31.2
28	Nebraska	31.0
29	Utah	30.5
30	North Dakota	30.1
31	Indiana	29.8
32	Washington	28.6
33	Virginia	28.3
34	Iowa	27.7
35	Wisconsin	27.5
36	Michigan	27.2
37	Minnesota	26.3
38	Maine	25.9
39	California	25.0
40	Illinois	24.7
40	Ohio	24.7
42	Vermont	24.6
43	Hawaii	24.1
44	New Jersey	24.0
45	Connecticut	23.8
46	New York	22.3
47	Maryland	21.9
48	New Hampshire	21.1
49	Rhode Island	19.0
50	Massachusetts	15.0
	District of Columbia	24.6

Source: U.S. Department of Health and Human Services, National Center for Health Statistics
    "National Vital Statistics Reports" (Vol. 47, No. 19, June 30, 1999)
*Final data by state of residence. Includes motor vehicle deaths, poisoning, falls, drowning and other accidents.

Deaths by Motor Vehicle Accidents in 1997

National Total = 43,458 Deaths*

ALPHA ORDER

RANK	STATE	DEATHS	% of USA
12	Alabama	1,245	2.9%
49	Alaska	84	0.2%
16	Arizona	954	2.2%
25	Arkansas	729	1.7%
1	California	3,852	8.9%
27	Colorado	632	1.5%
36	Connecticut	367	0.8%
44	Delaware	138	0.3%
3	Florida	2,768	6.4%
6	Georgia	1,606	3.7%
43	Hawaii	141	0.3%
39	Idaho	249	0.6%
10	Illinois	1,434	3.3%
14	Indiana	978	2.3%
32	Iowa	492	1.1%
30	Kansas	523	1.2%
21	Kentucky	853	2.0%
17	Louisiana	926	2.1%
41	Maine	189	0.4%
26	Maryland	649	1.5%
31	Massachusetts	503	1.2%
8	Michigan	1,545	3.6%
28	Minnesota	600	1.4%
19	Mississippi	873	2.0%
13	Missouri	1,171	2.7%
40	Montana	234	0.5%
38	Nebraska	306	0.7%
37	Nevada	359	0.8%
45	New Hampshire	133	0.3%
22	New Jersey	835	1.9%
33	New Mexico	427	1.0%
4	New York	1,840	4.2%
7	North Carolina	1,558	3.6%
47	North Dakota	106	0.2%
9	Ohio	1,447	3.3%
20	Oklahoma	855	2.0%
29	Oregon	548	1.3%
5	Pennsylvania	1,653	3.8%
48	Rhode Island	100	0.2%
18	South Carolina	904	2.1%
42	South Dakota	151	0.3%
11	Tennessee	1,255	2.9%
2	Texas	3,759	8.6%
35	Utah	377	0.9%
50	Vermont	77	0.2%
15	Virginia	962	2.2%
23	Washington	761	1.8%
34	West Virginia	387	0.9%
24	Wisconsin	750	1.7%
46	Wyoming	120	0.3%

RANK ORDER

RANK	STATE	DEATHS	% of USA
1	California	3,852	8.9%
2	Texas	3,759	8.6%
3	Florida	2,768	6.4%
4	New York	1,840	4.2%
5	Pennsylvania	1,653	3.8%
6	Georgia	1,606	3.7%
7	North Carolina	1,558	3.6%
8	Michigan	1,545	3.6%
9	Ohio	1,447	3.3%
10	Illinois	1,434	3.3%
11	Tennessee	1,255	2.9%
12	Alabama	1,245	2.9%
13	Missouri	1,171	2.7%
14	Indiana	978	2.3%
15	Virginia	962	2.2%
16	Arizona	954	2.2%
17	Louisiana	926	2.1%
18	South Carolina	904	2.1%
19	Mississippi	873	2.0%
20	Oklahoma	855	2.0%
21	Kentucky	853	2.0%
22	New Jersey	835	1.9%
23	Washington	761	1.8%
24	Wisconsin	750	1.7%
25	Arkansas	729	1.7%
26	Maryland	649	1.5%
27	Colorado	632	1.5%
28	Minnesota	600	1.4%
29	Oregon	548	1.3%
30	Kansas	523	1.2%
31	Massachusetts	503	1.2%
32	Iowa	492	1.1%
33	New Mexico	427	1.0%
34	West Virginia	387	0.9%
35	Utah	377	0.9%
36	Connecticut	367	0.8%
37	Nevada	359	0.8%
38	Nebraska	306	0.7%
39	Idaho	249	0.6%
40	Montana	234	0.5%
41	Maine	189	0.4%
42	South Dakota	151	0.3%
43	Hawaii	141	0.3%
44	Delaware	138	0.3%
45	New Hampshire	133	0.3%
46	Wyoming	120	0.3%
47	North Dakota	106	0.2%
48	Rhode Island	100	0.2%
49	Alaska	84	0.2%
50	Vermont	77	0.2%
	District of Columbia	53	0.1%

Source: U.S. Department of Health and Human Services, National Center for Health Statistics
"National Vital Statistics Reports" (Vol. 47, No. 19, June 30, 1999)

Final data by state of residence. These numbers are compiled from death certificates by the Centers for Disease Control and Prevention. They may differ from motor vehicle deaths collected by the U.S. Department of Transportation from other sources.

Death Rate by Motor Vehicle Accidents in 1997

National Rate = 16.2 Deaths per 100,000 Population*

ALPHA ORDER | | | RANK ORDER | |
--- | --- | --- | --- | --- | ---

RANK	STATE	RATE	RANK	STATE	RATE
3	Alabama	28.8	1	Mississippi	32.0
35	Alaska	13.8	2	Arkansas	28.9
17	Arizona	20.9	3	Alabama	28.8
2	Arkansas	28.9	4	Montana	26.6
43	California	11.9	5	Oklahoma	25.8
30	Colorado	16.2	6	Wyoming	25.0
46	Connecticut	11.2	7	New Mexico	24.7
22	Delaware	18.9	8	South Carolina	24.0
22	Florida	18.9	9	Tennessee	23.4
12	Georgia	21.5	10	Kentucky	21.8
43	Hawaii	11.9	11	Missouri	21.7
18	Idaho	20.6	12	Georgia	21.5
42	Illinois	12.1	13	Nevada	21.4
28	Indiana	16.7	14	Louisiana	21.3
26	Iowa	17.2	14	West Virginia	21.3
20	Kansas	20.2	16	North Carolina	21.0
10	Kentucky	21.8	17	Arizona	20.9
14	Louisiana	21.3	18	Idaho	20.6
32	Maine	15.2	19	South Dakota	20.5
41	Maryland	12.7	20	Kansas	20.2
50	Massachusetts	8.2	21	Texas	19.3
31	Michigan	15.8	22	Delaware	18.9
40	Minnesota	12.8	22	Florida	18.9
1	Mississippi	32.0	24	Nebraska	18.5
11	Missouri	21.7	25	Utah	18.3
4	Montana	26.6	26	Iowa	17.2
24	Nebraska	18.5	27	Oregon	16.9
13	Nevada	21.4	28	Indiana	16.7
45	New Hampshire	11.3	29	North Dakota	16.5
47	New Jersey	10.4	30	Colorado	16.2
7	New Mexico	24.7	31	Michigan	15.8
48	New York	10.1	32	Maine	15.2
16	North Carolina	21.0	33	Wisconsin	14.5
29	North Dakota	16.5	34	Virginia	14.3
39	Ohio	12.9	35	Alaska	13.8
5	Oklahoma	25.8	35	Pennsylvania	13.8
27	Oregon	16.9	37	Washington	13.6
35	Pennsylvania	13.8	38	Vermont	13.1
48	Rhode Island	10.1	39	Ohio	12.9
8	South Carolina	24.0	40	Minnesota	12.8
19	South Dakota	20.5	41	Maryland	12.7
9	Tennessee	23.4	42	Illinois	12.1
21	Texas	19.3	43	California	11.9
25	Utah	18.3	43	Hawaii	11.9
38	Vermont	13.1	45	New Hampshire	11.3
34	Virginia	14.3	46	Connecticut	11.2
37	Washington	13.6	47	New Jersey	10.4
14	West Virginia	21.3	48	New York	10.1
33	Wisconsin	14.5	48	Rhode Island	10.1
6	Wyoming	25.0	50	Massachusetts	8.2
				District of Columbia	10.0

Source: U.S. Department of Health and Human Services, National Center for Health Statistics
"National Vital Statistics Reports" (Vol. 47, No. 19, June 30, 1999)
*Final data by state of residence. These numbers are compiled from death certificates by the Centers for Disease Control and Prevention. They may differ from motor vehicle deaths collected by the U.S. Department of Transportation from other sources. Not age-adjusted.

Age-Adjusted Death Rate by Motor Vehicle Accidents in 1997

National Rate = 15.9 Deaths per 100,000 Population*

ALPHA ORDER

RANK	STATE	RATE
3	Alabama	27.8
32	Alaska	14.3
15	Arizona	20.6
2	Arkansas	28.7
43	California	11.6
30	Colorado	16.1
45	Connecticut	11.1
23	Delaware	18.3
22	Florida	18.4
12	Georgia	21.2
44	Hawaii	11.4
18	Idaho	20.2
42	Illinois	12.0
27	Indiana	16.8
28	Iowa	16.5
20	Kansas	19.5
11	Kentucky	21.4
12	Louisiana	21.2
35	Maine	13.7
40	Maryland	12.3
50	Massachusetts	8.0
31	Michigan	15.2
41	Minnesota	12.1
1	Mississippi	31.3
12	Missouri	21.2
4	Montana	27.0
25	Nebraska	17.8
10	Nevada	21.6
47	New Hampshire	10.7
48	New Jersey	9.8
7	New Mexico	24.9
49	New York	9.6
15	North Carolina	20.6
29	North Dakota	16.2
38	Ohio	12.8
5	Oklahoma	25.3
26	Oregon	17.0
35	Pennsylvania	13.7
46	Rhode Island	10.8
8	South Carolina	23.6
18	South Dakota	20.2
9	Tennessee	22.7
21	Texas	19.1
24	Utah	18.0
39	Vermont	12.4
34	Virginia	13.8
37	Washington	13.4
17	West Virginia	20.4
33	Wisconsin	14.0
6	Wyoming	25.2

RANK ORDER

RANK	STATE	RATE
1	Mississippi	31.3
2	Arkansas	28.7
3	Alabama	27.8
4	Montana	27.0
5	Oklahoma	25.3
6	Wyoming	25.2
7	New Mexico	24.9
8	South Carolina	23.6
9	Tennessee	22.7
10	Nevada	21.6
11	Kentucky	21.4
12	Georgia	21.2
12	Louisiana	21.2
12	Missouri	21.2
15	Arizona	20.6
15	North Carolina	20.6
17	West Virginia	20.4
18	Idaho	20.2
18	South Dakota	20.2
20	Kansas	19.5
21	Texas	19.1
22	Florida	18.4
23	Delaware	18.3
24	Utah	18.0
25	Nebraska	17.8
26	Oregon	17.0
27	Indiana	16.8
28	Iowa	16.5
29	North Dakota	16.2
30	Colorado	16.1
31	Michigan	15.2
32	Alaska	14.3
33	Wisconsin	14.0
34	Virginia	13.8
35	Maine	13.7
35	Pennsylvania	13.7
37	Washington	13.4
38	Ohio	12.8
39	Vermont	12.4
40	Maryland	12.3
41	Minnesota	12.1
42	Illinois	12.0
43	California	11.6
44	Hawaii	11.4
45	Connecticut	11.1
46	Rhode Island	10.8
47	New Hampshire	10.7
48	New Jersey	9.8
49	New York	9.6
50	Massachusetts	8.0
	District of Columbia	8.9

Source: U.S. Department of Health and Human Services, National Center for Health Statistics
    "National Vital Statistics Reports" (Vol. 47, No. 19, June 30, 1999)
*Final data by state of residence. These numbers are compiled from death certificates by the Centers for Disease Control and Prevention. They may differ from motor vehicle deaths collected by the U.S. Department of Transportation from other sources.

Deaths by Homicide in 1997

National Total = 19,846 Homicides*

ALPHA ORDER

ALPHA ORDER

RANK	STATE	HOMICIDES	% of USA
13	Alabama	520	2.6%
39	Alaska	55	0.3%
18	Arizona	431	2.2%
22	Arkansas	298	1.5%
1	California	2,838	14.3%
27	Colorado	183	0.9%
34	Connecticut	129	0.7%
43	Delaware	32	0.2%
5	Florida	1,128	5.7%
10	Georgia	655	3.3%
40	Hawaii	48	0.2%
41	Idaho	44	0.2%
3	Illinois	1,161	5.9%
17	Indiana	432	2.2%
36	Iowa	70	0.4%
30	Kansas	159	0.8%
25	Kentucky	256	1.3%
8	Louisiana	702	3.5%
46	Maine	22	0.1%
12	Maryland	554	2.8%
31	Massachusetts	142	0.7%
6	Michigan	787	4.0%
32	Minnesota	133	0.7%
19	Mississippi	387	2.0%
16	Missouri	434	2.2%
42	Montana	37	0.2%
37	Nebraska	65	0.3%
28	Nevada	176	0.9%
45	New Hampshire	26	0.1%
20	New Jersey	365	1.8%
29	New Mexico	164	0.8%
4	New York	1,143	5.8%
9	North Carolina	681	3.4%
49	North Dakota	11	0.1%
15	Ohio	487	2.5%
23	Oklahoma	289	1.5%
32	Oregon	133	0.7%
7	Pennsylvania	786	4.0%
44	Rhode Island	28	0.1%
21	South Carolina	358	1.8%
46	South Dakota	22	0.1%
11	Tennessee	556	2.8%
2	Texas	1,487	7.5%
38	Utah	63	0.3%
49	Vermont	11	0.1%
14	Virginia	510	2.6%
24	Washington	261	1.3%
35	West Virginia	97	0.5%
26	Wisconsin	214	1.1%
48	Wyoming	21	0.1%

RANK ORDER

RANK	STATE	HOMICIDES	% of USA
1	California	2,838	14.3%
2	Texas	1,487	7.5%
3	Illinois	1,161	5.9%
4	New York	1,143	5.8%
5	Florida	1,128	5.7%
6	Michigan	787	4.0%
7	Pennsylvania	786	4.0%
8	Louisiana	702	3.5%
9	North Carolina	681	3.4%
10	Georgia	655	3.3%
11	Tennessee	556	2.8%
12	Maryland	554	2.8%
13	Alabama	520	2.6%
14	Virginia	510	2.6%
15	Ohio	487	2.5%
16	Missouri	434	2.2%
17	Indiana	432	2.2%
18	Arizona	431	2.2%
19	Mississippi	387	2.0%
20	New Jersey	365	1.8%
21	South Carolina	358	1.8%
22	Arkansas	298	1.5%
23	Oklahoma	289	1.5%
24	Washington	261	1.3%
25	Kentucky	256	1.3%
26	Wisconsin	214	1.1%
27	Colorado	183	0.9%
28	Nevada	176	0.9%
29	New Mexico	164	0.8%
30	Kansas	159	0.8%
31	Massachusetts	142	0.7%
32	Minnesota	133	0.7%
32	Oregon	133	0.7%
34	Connecticut	129	0.7%
35	West Virginia	97	0.5%
36	Iowa	70	0.4%
37	Nebraska	65	0.3%
38	Utah	63	0.3%
39	Alaska	55	0.3%
40	Hawaii	48	0.2%
41	Idaho	44	0.2%
42	Montana	37	0.2%
43	Delaware	32	0.2%
44	Rhode Island	28	0.1%
45	New Hampshire	26	0.1%
46	Maine	22	0.1%
46	South Dakota	22	0.1%
48	Wyoming	21	0.1%
49	North Dakota	11	0.1%
49	Vermont	11	0.1%
	District of Columbia	255	1.3%

Source: U.S. Department of Health and Human Services, National Center for Health Statistics
     "National Vital Statistics Reports" (Vol. 47, No. 19, June 30, 1999)
By state of residence. Includes legal intervention. Homicide data shown here are collected by the Centers for Disease Control and Prevention based on death certificates and differ from murder data collected by the F.B.I. from other sources.

Death Rate by Homicide in 1997

National Rate = 7.4 Deaths per 100,000 Population*

ALPHA ORDER

RANK	STATE	RATE
3	Alabama	12.0
13	Alaska	9.0
9	Arizona	9.5
4	Arkansas	11.8
14	California	8.8
28	Colorado	4.7
38	Connecticut	3.9
31	Delaware	4.4
19	Florida	7.7
15	Georgia	8.7
37	Hawaii	4.0
40	Idaho	3.6
8	Illinois	9.8
22	Indiana	7.4
45	Iowa	2.5
26	Kansas	6.1
23	Kentucky	6.6
1	Louisiana	16.1
48	Maine	1.8
5	Maryland	10.9
46	Massachusetts	2.3
17	Michigan	8.1
43	Minnesota	2.8
2	Mississippi	14.2
18	Missouri	8.0
34	Montana	4.2
38	Nebraska	3.9
6	Nevada	10.5
47	New Hampshire	2.2
30	New Jersey	4.5
9	New Mexico	9.5
25	New York	6.3
12	North Carolina	9.2
NA	North Dakota**	NA
31	Ohio	4.4
15	Oklahoma	8.7
35	Oregon	4.1
24	Pennsylvania	6.5
43	Rhode Island	2.8
9	South Carolina	9.5
42	South Dakota	3.0
7	Tennessee	10.4
20	Texas	7.6
41	Utah	3.1
NA	Vermont**	NA
20	Virginia	7.6
28	Washington	4.7
27	West Virginia	5.3
35	Wisconsin	4.1
31	Wyoming	4.4

RANK ORDER

RANK	STATE	RATE
1	Louisiana	16.1
2	Mississippi	14.2
3	Alabama	12.0
4	Arkansas	11.8
5	Maryland	10.9
6	Nevada	10.5
7	Tennessee	10.4
8	Illinois	9.8
9	Arizona	9.5
9	New Mexico	9.5
9	South Carolina	9.5
12	North Carolina	9.2
13	Alaska	9.0
14	California	8.8
15	Georgia	8.7
15	Oklahoma	8.7
17	Michigan	8.1
18	Missouri	8.0
19	Florida	7.7
20	Texas	7.6
20	Virginia	7.6
22	Indiana	7.4
23	Kentucky	6.6
24	Pennsylvania	6.5
25	New York	6.3
26	Kansas	6.1
27	West Virginia	5.3
28	Colorado	4.7
28	Washington	4.7
30	New Jersey	4.5
31	Delaware	4.4
31	Ohio	4.4
31	Wyoming	4.4
34	Montana	4.2
35	Oregon	4.1
35	Wisconsin	4.1
37	Hawaii	4.0
38	Connecticut	3.9
38	Nebraska	3.9
40	Idaho	3.6
41	Utah	3.1
42	South Dakota	3.0
43	Minnesota	2.8
43	Rhode Island	2.8
45	Iowa	2.5
46	Massachusetts	2.3
47	New Hampshire	2.2
48	Maine	1.8
NA	North Dakota**	NA
NA	Vermont**	NA

	District of Columbia	48.2

Source: U.S. Department of Health and Human Services, National Center for Health Statistics
    "National Vital Statistics Reports" (Vol. 47, No. 19, June 30, 1999)
By state of residence. Includes legal intervention. Homicide data shown here are collected by the Centers for Disease Control and Prevention based on death certificates and differ from murder data collected by the F.B.I. from other sources. Not age-adjusted.

Age-Adjusted Death Rate by Homicide in 1997

National Rate = 8.0 Deaths per 100,000 Population*

ALPHA ORDER

RANK ORDER

RANK	STATE	RATE	RANK	STATE	RATE
3	Alabama	12.3	1	Louisiana	17.0
16	Alaska	8.6	2	Mississippi	14.7
9	Arizona	10.4	3	Alabama	12.3
3	Arkansas	12.3	3	Arkansas	12.3
12	California	9.5	5	Maryland	12.1
29	Colorado	4.9	6	Illinois	10.9
31	Connecticut	4.7	6	Nevada	10.9
34	Delaware	4.6	8	Tennessee	10.8
19	Florida	8.5	9	Arizona	10.4
15	Georgia	8.8	10	New Mexico	9.9
38	Hawaii	4.2	11	South Carolina	9.7
40	Idaho	3.7	12	California	9.5
6	Illinois	10.9	13	North Carolina	9.4
21	Indiana	7.9	14	Oklahoma	9.3
45	Iowa	2.7	15	Georgia	8.8
26	Kansas	6.7	16	Alaska	8.6
25	Kentucky	6.8	16	Michigan	8.6
1	Louisiana	17.0	16	Missouri	8.6
48	Maine	2.2	19	Florida	8.5
5	Maryland	12.1	20	Virginia	8.0
46	Massachusetts	2.6	21	Indiana	7.9
16	Michigan	8.6	21	Texas	7.9
43	Minnesota	3.0	23	Pennsylvania	7.5
2	Mississippi	14.7	24	New York	6.9
16	Missouri	8.6	25	Kentucky	6.8
31	Montana	4.7	26	Kansas	6.7
39	Nebraska	4.1	27	West Virginia	5.6
6	Nevada	10.9	28	New Jersey	5.2
47	New Hampshire	2.5	29	Colorado	4.9
28	New Jersey	5.2	29	Washington	4.9
10	New Mexico	9.9	31	Connecticut	4.7
24	New York	6.9	31	Montana	4.7
13	North Carolina	9.4	31	Wyoming	4.7
NA	North Dakota**	NA	34	Delaware	4.6
34	Ohio	4.6	34	Ohio	4.6
14	Oklahoma	9.3	36	Wisconsin	4.4
37	Oregon	4.3	37	Oregon	4.3
23	Pennsylvania	7.5	38	Hawaii	4.2
41	Rhode Island	3.4	39	Nebraska	4.1
11	South Carolina	9.7	40	Idaho	3.7
42	South Dakota	3.2	41	Rhode Island	3.4
8	Tennessee	10.8	42	South Dakota	3.2
21	Texas	7.9	43	Minnesota	3.0
43	Utah	3.0	43	Utah	3.0
NA	Vermont**	NA	45	Iowa	2.7
20	Virginia	8.0	46	Massachusetts	2.6
29	Washington	4.9	47	New Hampshire	2.5
27	West Virginia	5.6	48	Maine	2.2
36	Wisconsin	4.4	NA	North Dakota**	NA
31	Wyoming	4.7	NA	Vermont**	NA
				District of Columbia	61.8

Source: U.S. Department of Health and Human Services, National Center for Health Statistics
   "National Vital Statistics Reports" (Vol. 47, No. 19, June 30, 1999)
*By state of residence. Includes legal intervention. Homicide data shown here are collected by the Centers for Disease Control and Prevention based on death certificates and differ from murder data collected by the F.B.I. from other sources.
**Insufficient number for a valid rate.

Deaths by Suicide in 1997

National Total = 30,535 Suicides*

ALPHA ORDER

RANK	STATE	SUICIDES	% of USA
23	Alabama	512	1.7%
44	Alaska	128	0.4%
12	Arizona	757	2.5%
30	Arkansas	356	1.2%
1	California	3,430	11.2%
17	Colorado	611	2.0%
37	Connecticut	259	0.8%
47	Delaware	87	0.3%
3	Florida	2,098	6.9%
9	Georgia	903	3.0%
41	Hawaii	138	0.5%
38	Idaho	209	0.7%
10	Illinois	901	3.0%
13	Indiana	729	2.4%
31	Iowa	345	1.1%
33	Kansas	320	1.0%
26	Kentucky	488	1.6%
21	Louisiana	528	1.7%
42	Maine	137	0.4%
22	Maryland	519	1.7%
25	Massachusetts	492	1.6%
7	Michigan	1,010	3.3%
27	Minnesota	472	1.5%
32	Mississippi	339	1.1%
16	Missouri	710	2.3%
39	Montana	183	0.6%
40	Nebraska	176	0.6%
29	Nevada	411	1.3%
43	New Hampshire	136	0.4%
18	New Jersey	586	1.9%
35	New Mexico	300	1.0%
5	New York	1,372	4.5%
8	North Carolina	906	3.0%
48	North Dakota	80	0.3%
6	Ohio	1,126	3.7%
24	Oklahoma	497	1.6%
20	Oregon	534	1.7%
4	Pennsylvania	1,412	4.6%
50	Rhode Island	72	0.2%
28	South Carolina	432	1.4%
45	South Dakota	127	0.4%
13	Tennessee	729	2.4%
2	Texas	2,146	7.0%
34	Utah	301	1.0%
49	Vermont	73	0.2%
11	Virginia	762	2.5%
15	Washington	728	2.4%
36	West Virginia	262	0.9%
19	Wisconsin	576	1.9%
46	Wyoming	95	0.3%

RANK ORDER

RANK	STATE	SUICIDES	% of USA
1	California	3,430	11.2%
2	Texas	2,146	7.0%
3	Florida	2,098	6.9%
4	Pennsylvania	1,412	4.6%
5	New York	1,372	4.5%
6	Ohio	1,126	3.7%
7	Michigan	1,010	3.3%
8	North Carolina	906	3.0%
9	Georgia	903	3.0%
10	Illinois	901	3.0%
11	Virginia	762	2.5%
12	Arizona	757	2.5%
13	Indiana	729	2.4%
13	Tennessee	729	2.4%
15	Washington	728	2.4%
16	Missouri	710	2.3%
17	Colorado	611	2.0%
18	New Jersey	586	1.9%
19	Wisconsin	576	1.9%
20	Oregon	534	1.7%
21	Louisiana	528	1.7%
22	Maryland	519	1.7%
23	Alabama	512	1.7%
24	Oklahoma	497	1.6%
25	Massachusetts	492	1.6%
26	Kentucky	488	1.6%
27	Minnesota	472	1.5%
28	South Carolina	432	1.4%
29	Nevada	411	1.3%
30	Arkansas	356	1.2%
31	Iowa	345	1.1%
32	Mississippi	339	1.1%
33	Kansas	320	1.0%
34	Utah	301	1.0%
35	New Mexico	300	1.0%
36	West Virginia	262	0.9%
37	Connecticut	259	0.8%
38	Idaho	209	0.7%
39	Montana	183	0.6%
40	Nebraska	176	0.6%
41	Hawaii	138	0.5%
42	Maine	137	0.4%
43	New Hampshire	136	0.4%
44	Alaska	128	0.4%
45	South Dakota	127	0.4%
46	Wyoming	95	0.3%
47	Delaware	87	0.3%
48	North Dakota	80	0.3%
49	Vermont	73	0.2%
50	Rhode Island	72	0.2%
	District of Columbia	35	0.1%

Source: U.S. Department of Health and Human Services, National Center for Health Statistics
    "National Vital Statistics Reports" (Vol. 47, No. 19, June 30, 1999)
*Final data by state of residence.

Death Rate by Suicide in 1997

National Rate = 11.4 Suicides per 100,000 Population*

ALPHA ORDER

RANK ORDER

RANK	STATE	RATE	RANK	STATE	RATE
29	Alabama	11.9	1	Nevada	24.5
2	Alaska	21.0	2	Alaska	21.0
8	Arizona	16.6	3	Montana	20.8
15	Arkansas	14.1	4	Wyoming	19.8
39	California	10.6	5	Idaho	17.3
10	Colorado	15.7	5	New Mexico	17.3
46	Connecticut	7.9	7	South Dakota	17.2
29	Delaware	11.9	8	Arizona	16.6
14	Florida	14.3	9	Oregon	16.5
26	Georgia	12.1	10	Colorado	15.7
32	Hawaii	11.6	11	Oklahoma	15.0
5	Idaho	17.3	12	Utah	14.6
47	Illinois	7.6	13	West Virginia	14.4
21	Indiana	12.4	14	Florida	14.3
26	Iowa	12.1	15	Arkansas	14.1
24	Kansas	12.3	16	Tennessee	13.6
19	Kentucky	12.5	17	Missouri	13.1
26	Louisiana	12.1	18	Washington	13.0
37	Maine	11.0	19	Kentucky	12.5
42	Maryland	10.2	19	North Dakota	12.5
45	Massachusetts	8.0	21	Indiana	12.4
41	Michigan	10.3	21	Mississippi	12.4
43	Minnesota	10.1	21	Vermont	12.4
21	Mississippi	12.4	24	Kansas	12.3
17	Missouri	13.1	25	North Carolina	12.2
3	Montana	20.8	26	Georgia	12.1
39	Nebraska	10.6	26	Iowa	12.1
1	Nevada	24.5	26	Louisiana	12.1
32	New Hampshire	11.6	29	Alabama	11.9
49	New Jersey	7.3	29	Delaware	11.9
5	New Mexico	17.3	31	Pennsylvania	11.7
47	New York	7.6	32	Hawaii	11.6
25	North Carolina	12.2	32	New Hampshire	11.6
19	North Dakota	12.5	34	South Carolina	11.5
43	Ohio	10.1	35	Virginia	11.3
11	Oklahoma	15.0	36	Wisconsin	11.1
9	Oregon	16.5	37	Maine	11.0
31	Pennsylvania	11.7	37	Texas	11.0
49	Rhode Island	7.3	39	California	10.6
34	South Carolina	11.5	39	Nebraska	10.6
7	South Dakota	17.2	41	Michigan	10.3
16	Tennessee	13.6	42	Maryland	10.2
37	Texas	11.0	43	Minnesota	10.1
12	Utah	14.6	43	Ohio	10.1
21	Vermont	12.4	45	Massachusetts	8.0
35	Virginia	11.3	46	Connecticut	7.9
18	Washington	13.0	47	Illinois	7.6
13	West Virginia	14.4	47	New York	7.6
36	Wisconsin	11.1	49	New Jersey	7.3
4	Wyoming	19.8	49	Rhode Island	7.3
				District of Columbia	6.6

Source: U.S. Department of Health and Human Services, National Center for Health Statistics
"National Vital Statistics Reports" (Vol. 47, No. 19, June 30, 1999)
*Final data by state of residence. Not age-adjusted.

Age-Adjusted Death Rate by Suicide in 1997

National Rate = 10.6 Suicides per 100,000 Population*

ALPHA ORDER			RANK ORDER		
RANK	STATE	RATE	RANK	STATE	RATE
34	Alabama	10.6	1	Nevada	22.0
2	Alaska	21.3	2	Alaska	21.3
8	Arizona	15.8	3	Montana	19.8
13	Arkansas	13.4	4	Wyoming	18.5
40	California	9.8	5	New Mexico	17.1
10	Colorado	14.9	6	Idaho	16.7
46	Connecticut	7.1	7	South Dakota	16.4
30	Delaware	10.8	8	Arizona	15.8
15	Florida	12.4	9	Utah	15.0
26	Georgia	11.2	10	Colorado	14.9
28	Hawaii	11.1	11	Oregon	14.7
6	Idaho	16.7	12	Oklahoma	14.3
46	Illinois	7.1	13	Arkansas	13.4
23	Indiana	11.5	14	West Virginia	12.8
21	Iowa	11.6	15	Florida	12.4
20	Kansas	11.7	15	Tennessee	12.4
26	Kentucky	11.2	17	North Dakota	12.3
23	Louisiana	11.5	18	Missouri	12.1
38	Maine	10.1	18	Washington	12.1
43	Maryland	9.3	20	Kansas	11.7
45	Massachusetts	7.4	21	Iowa	11.6
41	Michigan	9.5	21	Mississippi	11.6
42	Minnesota	9.4	23	Indiana	11.5
21	Mississippi	11.6	23	Louisiana	11.5
18	Missouri	12.1	25	North Carolina	11.4
3	Montana	19.8	26	Georgia	11.2
39	Nebraska	10.0	26	Kentucky	11.2
1	Nevada	22.0	28	Hawaii	11.1
34	New Hampshire	10.6	29	Vermont	11.0
50	New Jersey	6.6	30	Delaware	10.8
5	New Mexico	17.1	30	Pennsylvania	10.8
46	New York	7.1	30	South Carolina	10.8
25	North Carolina	11.4	33	Texas	10.7
17	North Dakota	12.3	34	Alabama	10.6
43	Ohio	9.3	34	New Hampshire	10.6
12	Oklahoma	14.3	36	Virginia	10.4
11	Oregon	14.7	36	Wisconsin	10.4
30	Pennsylvania	10.8	38	Maine	10.1
46	Rhode Island	7.1	39	Nebraska	10.0
30	South Carolina	10.8	40	California	9.8
7	South Dakota	16.4	41	Michigan	9.5
15	Tennessee	12.4	42	Minnesota	9.4
33	Texas	10.7	43	Maryland	9.3
9	Utah	15.0	43	Ohio	9.3
29	Vermont	11.0	45	Massachusetts	7.4
36	Virginia	10.4	46	Connecticut	7.1
18	Washington	12.1	46	Illinois	7.1
14	West Virginia	12.8	46	New York	7.1
36	Wisconsin	10.4	46	Rhode Island	7.1
4	Wyoming	18.5	50	New Jersey	6.6
				District of Columbia	7.0

Source: U.S. Department of Health and Human Services, National Center for Health Statistics
   "National Vital Statistics Reports" (Vol. 47, No. 19, June 30, 1999)
*Final data by state of residence.

Years Lost by Premature Death in 1997

National Average = 7,398 Years Lost per 100,000 Population*

ALPHA ORDER

RANK	STATE	YEARS
4	Alabama	9,473
19	Alaska	7,722
16	Arizona	7,900
3	Arkansas	9,476
36	California	6,567
39	Colorado	6,359
38	Connecticut	6,371
18	Delaware	7,779
15	Florida	7,961
8	Georgia	8,580
45	Hawaii	5,991
33	Idaho	6,637
20	Illinois	7,635
21	Indiana	7,518
44	Iowa	6,002
30	Kansas	6,933
12	Kentucky	8,140
2	Louisiana	9,827
43	Maine	6,062
13	Maryland	8,005
47	Massachusetts	5,763
24	Michigan	7,427
50	Minnesota	5,461
1	Mississippi	10,554
14	Missouri	8,000
25	Montana	7,320
37	Nebraska	6,486
9	Nevada	8,459
49	New Hampshire	5,639
31	New Jersey	6,924
17	New Mexico	7,853
29	New York	7,029
10	North Carolina	8,365
46	North Dakota	5,921
27	Ohio	7,150
7	Oklahoma	8,678
34	Oregon	6,610
22	Pennsylvania	7,499
35	Rhode Island	6,602
5	South Carolina	9,274
32	South Dakota	6,862
6	Tennessee	9,000
23	Texas	7,446
42	Utah	6,117
48	Vermont	5,753
26	Virginia	7,193
40	Washington	6,191
11	West Virginia	8,248
41	Wisconsin	6,140
28	Wyoming	7,083

RANK ORDER

RANK	STATE	YEARS
1	Mississippi	10,554
2	Louisiana	9,827
3	Arkansas	9,476
4	Alabama	9,473
5	South Carolina	9,274
6	Tennessee	9,000
7	Oklahoma	8,678
8	Georgia	8,580
9	Nevada	8,459
10	North Carolina	8,365
11	West Virginia	8,248
12	Kentucky	8,140
13	Maryland	8,005
14	Missouri	8,000
15	Florida	7,961
16	Arizona	7,900
17	New Mexico	7,853
18	Delaware	7,779
19	Alaska	7,722
20	Illinois	7,635
21	Indiana	7,518
22	Pennsylvania	7,499
23	Texas	7,446
24	Michigan	7,427
25	Montana	7,320
26	Virginia	7,193
27	Ohio	7,150
28	Wyoming	7,083
29	New York	7,029
30	Kansas	6,933
31	New Jersey	6,924
32	South Dakota	6,862
33	Idaho	6,637
34	Oregon	6,610
35	Rhode Island	6,602
36	California	6,567
37	Nebraska	6,486
38	Connecticut	6,371
39	Colorado	6,359
40	Washington	6,191
41	Wisconsin	6,140
42	Utah	6,117
43	Maine	6,062
44	Iowa	6,002
45	Hawaii	5,991
46	North Dakota	5,921
47	Massachusetts	5,763
48	Vermont	5,753
49	New Hampshire	5,639
50	Minnesota	5,461

| | District of Columbia | 15,654 |

Source: U.S. Department of Health and Human Services, National Center for Health Statistics
unpublished data

*Age-adjusted years of potential life lost due to death before age 75.

Years Lost by Premature Death from Cancer in 1997

National Average = 1,524 Years Lost per 100,000 Population*

ALPHA ORDER			RANK ORDER		
RANK	STATE	YEARS	RANK	STATE	YEARS
10	Alabama	1,681	1	Mississippi	1,819
39	Alaska	1,360	2	Louisiana	1,797
37	Arizona	1,368	3	Kentucky	1,792
5	Arkansas	1,744	4	Tennessee	1,769
35	California	1,397	5	Arkansas	1,744
48	Colorado	1,159	6	Rhode Island	1,724
32	Connecticut	1,432	7	West Virginia	1,717
9	Delaware	1,711	8	South Carolina	1,713
11	Florida	1,661	9	Delaware	1,711
19	Georgia	1,594	10	Alabama	1,681
46	Hawaii	1,220	11	Florida	1,661
46	Idaho	1,220	12	Oklahoma	1,635
18	Illinois	1,600	13	North Carolina	1,624
24	Indiana	1,522	14	Missouri	1,622
38	Iowa	1,361	15	Maryland	1,612
31	Kansas	1,451	15	New Hampshire	1,612
3	Kentucky	1,792	17	Pennsylvania	1,606
2	Louisiana	1,797	18	Illinois	1,600
21	Maine	1,564	19	Georgia	1,594
15	Maryland	1,612	20	Ohio	1,570
29	Massachusetts	1,457	21	Maine	1,564
25	Michigan	1,520	22	New Jersey	1,555
41	Minnesota	1,332	23	Virginia	1,545
1	Mississippi	1,819	24	Indiana	1,522
14	Missouri	1,622	25	Michigan	1,520
45	Montana	1,239	26	Nevada	1,514
40	Nebraska	1,350	27	New York	1,503
26	Nevada	1,514	28	Vermont	1,481
15	New Hampshire	1,612	29	Massachusetts	1,457
22	New Jersey	1,555	29	Texas	1,457
44	New Mexico	1,278	31	Kansas	1,451
27	New York	1,503	32	Connecticut	1,432
13	North Carolina	1,624	33	Oregon	1,409
48	North Dakota	1,159	34	Washington	1,405
20	Ohio	1,570	35	California	1,397
12	Oklahoma	1,635	35	Wisconsin	1,397
33	Oregon	1,409	37	Arizona	1,368
17	Pennsylvania	1,606	38	Iowa	1,361
6	Rhode Island	1,724	39	Alaska	1,360
8	South Carolina	1,713	40	Nebraska	1,350
42	South Dakota	1,326	41	Minnesota	1,332
4	Tennessee	1,769	42	South Dakota	1,326
29	Texas	1,457	43	Wyoming	1,300
50	Utah	991	44	New Mexico	1,278
28	Vermont	1,481	45	Montana	1,239
23	Virginia	1,545	46	Hawaii	1,220
34	Washington	1,405	46	Idaho	1,220
7	West Virginia	1,717	48	Colorado	1,159
35	Wisconsin	1,397	48	North Dakota	1,159
43	Wyoming	1,300	50	Utah	991
				District of Columbia	2,146

Source: U.S. Department of Health and Human Services, National Center for Health Statistics
  unpublished data
*Age-adjusted years of potential life lost due to death before age 75.

Years Lost by Premature Death from Heart Disease in 1997

National Average = 1,190 Years Lost per 100,000 Population*

ALPHA ORDER

RANK	STATE	YEARS
2	Alabama	1,646
43	Alaska	887
30	Arizona	1,042
9	Arkansas	1,471
39	California	971
50	Colorado	773
34	Connecticut	1,017
15	Delaware	1,282
24	Florida	1,141
10	Georgia	1,438
26	Hawaii	1,093
44	Idaho	875
17	Illinois	1,249
16	Indiana	1,262
32	Iowa	1,032
32	Kansas	1,032
6	Kentucky	1,529
4	Louisiana	1,557
25	Maine	1,103
22	Maryland	1,210
38	Massachusetts	976
17	Michigan	1,249
48	Minnesota	805
1	Mississippi	1,987
11	Missouri	1,418
40	Montana	936
27	Nebraska	1,059
14	Nevada	1,285
42	New Hampshire	912
30	New Jersey	1,042
45	New Mexico	866
20	New York	1,236
12	North Carolina	1,348
28	North Dakota	1,058
13	Ohio	1,289
7	Oklahoma	1,520
46	Oregon	860
19	Pennsylvania	1,247
35	Rhode Island	1,009
4	South Carolina	1,557
29	South Dakota	1,043
3	Tennessee	1,583
21	Texas	1,229
49	Utah	804
41	Vermont	923
23	Virginia	1,208
47	Washington	856
8	West Virginia	1,481
37	Wisconsin	978
36	Wyoming	984

RANK ORDER

RANK	STATE	YEARS
1	Mississippi	1,987
2	Alabama	1,646
3	Tennessee	1,583
4	Louisiana	1,557
4	South Carolina	1,557
6	Kentucky	1,529
7	Oklahoma	1,520
8	West Virginia	1,481
9	Arkansas	1,471
10	Georgia	1,438
11	Missouri	1,418
12	North Carolina	1,348
13	Ohio	1,289
14	Nevada	1,285
15	Delaware	1,282
16	Indiana	1,262
17	Illinois	1,249
17	Michigan	1,249
19	Pennsylvania	1,247
20	New York	1,236
21	Texas	1,229
22	Maryland	1,210
23	Virginia	1,208
24	Florida	1,141
25	Maine	1,103
26	Hawaii	1,093
27	Nebraska	1,059
28	North Dakota	1,058
29	South Dakota	1,043
30	Arizona	1,042
30	New Jersey	1,042
32	Iowa	1,032
32	Kansas	1,032
34	Connecticut	1,017
35	Rhode Island	1,009
36	Wyoming	984
37	Wisconsin	978
38	Massachusetts	976
39	California	971
40	Montana	936
41	Vermont	923
42	New Hampshire	912
43	Alaska	887
44	Idaho	875
45	New Mexico	866
46	Oregon	860
47	Washington	856
48	Minnesota	805
49	Utah	804
50	Colorado	773
	District of Columbia	1,842

Source: U.S. Department of Health and Human Services, National Center for Health Statistics
unpublished data
*Age-adjusted years of potential life lost due to death before age 75.

Years Lost by Premature Death from Homicide in 1997

National Average = 363 Years Lost per 100,000 Population*

<table>
<tr><td colspan="3">ALPHA ORDER</td><td colspan="3">RANK ORDER</td></tr>
<tr><td>RANK</td><td>STATE</td><td>YEARS</td><td>RANK</td><td>STATE</td><td>YEARS</td></tr>
<tr><td>4</td><td>Alabama</td><td>542</td><td>1</td><td>Louisiana</td><td>786</td></tr>
<tr><td>17</td><td>Alaska</td><td>386</td><td>2</td><td>Mississippi</td><td>644</td></tr>
<tr><td>9</td><td>Arizona</td><td>458</td><td>3</td><td>Maryland</td><td>576</td></tr>
<tr><td>6</td><td>Arkansas</td><td>520</td><td>4</td><td>Alabama</td><td>542</td></tr>
<tr><td>10</td><td>California</td><td>441</td><td>5</td><td>Illinois</td><td>531</td></tr>
<tr><td>32</td><td>Colorado</td><td>214</td><td>6</td><td>Arkansas</td><td>520</td></tr>
<tr><td>29</td><td>Connecticut</td><td>229</td><td>7</td><td>Tennessee</td><td>476</td></tr>
<tr><td>31</td><td>Delaware</td><td>215</td><td>8</td><td>Nevada</td><td>475</td></tr>
<tr><td>19</td><td>Florida</td><td>377</td><td>9</td><td>Arizona</td><td>458</td></tr>
<tr><td>18</td><td>Georgia</td><td>382</td><td>10</td><td>California</td><td>441</td></tr>
<tr><td>39</td><td>Hawaii</td><td>185</td><td>11</td><td>New Mexico</td><td>434</td></tr>
<tr><td>42</td><td>Idaho</td><td>145</td><td>12</td><td>Oklahoma</td><td>424</td></tr>
<tr><td>5</td><td>Illinois</td><td>531</td><td>13</td><td>North Carolina</td><td>418</td></tr>
<tr><td>21</td><td>Indiana</td><td>359</td><td>14</td><td>South Carolina</td><td>413</td></tr>
<tr><td>45</td><td>Iowa</td><td>123</td><td>15</td><td>Michigan</td><td>397</td></tr>
<tr><td>25</td><td>Kansas</td><td>312</td><td>16</td><td>Missouri</td><td>387</td></tr>
<tr><td>26</td><td>Kentucky</td><td>300</td><td>17</td><td>Alaska</td><td>386</td></tr>
<tr><td>1</td><td>Louisiana</td><td>786</td><td>18</td><td>Georgia</td><td>382</td></tr>
<tr><td>47</td><td>Maine</td><td>104</td><td>19</td><td>Florida</td><td>377</td></tr>
<tr><td>3</td><td>Maryland</td><td>576</td><td>20</td><td>Virginia</td><td>370</td></tr>
<tr><td>46</td><td>Massachusetts</td><td>117</td><td>21</td><td>Indiana</td><td>359</td></tr>
<tr><td>15</td><td>Michigan</td><td>397</td><td>22</td><td>Pennsylvania</td><td>355</td></tr>
<tr><td>43</td><td>Minnesota</td><td>140</td><td>23</td><td>Texas</td><td>350</td></tr>
<tr><td>2</td><td>Mississippi</td><td>644</td><td>24</td><td>New York</td><td>320</td></tr>
<tr><td>16</td><td>Missouri</td><td>387</td><td>25</td><td>Kansas</td><td>312</td></tr>
<tr><td>36</td><td>Montana</td><td>199</td><td>26</td><td>Kentucky</td><td>300</td></tr>
<tr><td>38</td><td>Nebraska</td><td>187</td><td>27</td><td>New Jersey</td><td>251</td></tr>
<tr><td>8</td><td>Nevada</td><td>475</td><td>28</td><td>West Virginia</td><td>247</td></tr>
<tr><td>48</td><td>New Hampshire</td><td>100</td><td>29</td><td>Connecticut</td><td>229</td></tr>
<tr><td>27</td><td>New Jersey</td><td>251</td><td>30</td><td>Washington</td><td>223</td></tr>
<tr><td>11</td><td>New Mexico</td><td>434</td><td>31</td><td>Delaware</td><td>215</td></tr>
<tr><td>24</td><td>New York</td><td>320</td><td>32</td><td>Colorado</td><td>214</td></tr>
<tr><td>13</td><td>North Carolina</td><td>418</td><td>32</td><td>Ohio</td><td>214</td></tr>
<tr><td>NA</td><td>North Dakota**</td><td>NA</td><td>34</td><td>Wisconsin</td><td>208</td></tr>
<tr><td>32</td><td>Ohio</td><td>214</td><td>35</td><td>Wyoming</td><td>206</td></tr>
<tr><td>12</td><td>Oklahoma</td><td>424</td><td>36</td><td>Montana</td><td>199</td></tr>
<tr><td>37</td><td>Oregon</td><td>189</td><td>37</td><td>Oregon</td><td>189</td></tr>
<tr><td>22</td><td>Pennsylvania</td><td>355</td><td>38</td><td>Nebraska</td><td>187</td></tr>
<tr><td>41</td><td>Rhode Island</td><td>154</td><td>39</td><td>Hawaii</td><td>185</td></tr>
<tr><td>14</td><td>South Carolina</td><td>413</td><td>40</td><td>South Dakota</td><td>159</td></tr>
<tr><td>40</td><td>South Dakota</td><td>159</td><td>41</td><td>Rhode Island</td><td>154</td></tr>
<tr><td>7</td><td>Tennessee</td><td>476</td><td>42</td><td>Idaho</td><td>145</td></tr>
<tr><td>23</td><td>Texas</td><td>350</td><td>43</td><td>Minnesota</td><td>140</td></tr>
<tr><td>44</td><td>Utah</td><td>128</td><td>44</td><td>Utah</td><td>128</td></tr>
<tr><td>NA</td><td>Vermont**</td><td>NA</td><td>45</td><td>Iowa</td><td>123</td></tr>
<tr><td>20</td><td>Virginia</td><td>370</td><td>46</td><td>Massachusetts</td><td>117</td></tr>
<tr><td>30</td><td>Washington</td><td>223</td><td>47</td><td>Maine</td><td>104</td></tr>
<tr><td>28</td><td>West Virginia</td><td>247</td><td>48</td><td>New Hampshire</td><td>100</td></tr>
<tr><td>34</td><td>Wisconsin</td><td>208</td><td>NA</td><td>North Dakota**</td><td>NA</td></tr>
<tr><td>35</td><td>Wyoming</td><td>206</td><td>NA</td><td>Vermont**</td><td>NA</td></tr>
<tr><td></td><td></td><td></td><td></td><td>District of Columbia</td><td>3,198</td></tr>
</table>

Source: U.S. Department of Health and Human Services, National Center for Health Statistics
unpublished data

*Age-adjusted years of potential life lost due to death before age 75.

**Data for states with fewer than 20 deaths from homicide for persons under 75 years of age are considered unreliable and are not shown.

Years Lost by Premature Death from Suicide in 1997

National Average = 378 Years Lost per 100,000 Population*

ALPHA ORDER

RANK	STATE	YEARS
36	Alabama	368
1	Alaska	817
8	Arizona	589
13	Arkansas	495
44	California	327
10	Colorado	550
49	Connecticut	254
31	Delaware	384
21	Florida	425
35	Georgia	380
28	Hawaii	392
7	Idaho	620
48	Illinois	259
23	Indiana	420
16	Iowa	447
16	Kansas	447
30	Kentucky	389
21	Louisiana	425
39	Maine	347
43	Maryland	329
46	Massachusetts	268
42	Michigan	342
40	Minnesota	345
24	Mississippi	415
18	Missouri	446
3	Montana	714
36	Nebraska	368
2	Nevada	729
33	New Hampshire	381
50	New Jersey	228
5	New Mexico	644
47	New York	260
25	North Carolina	411
14	North Dakota	491
40	Ohio	345
11	Oklahoma	534
12	Oregon	505
27	Pennsylvania	395
45	Rhode Island	276
32	South Carolina	382
6	South Dakota	643
20	Tennessee	438
33	Texas	381
9	Utah	559
26	Vermont	405
38	Virginia	366
19	Washington	445
15	West Virginia	454
29	Wisconsin	390
4	Wyoming	664

RANK ORDER

RANK	STATE	YEARS
1	Alaska	817
2	Nevada	729
3	Montana	714
4	Wyoming	664
5	New Mexico	644
6	South Dakota	643
7	Idaho	620
8	Arizona	589
9	Utah	559
10	Colorado	550
11	Oklahoma	534
12	Oregon	505
13	Arkansas	495
14	North Dakota	491
15	West Virginia	454
16	Iowa	447
16	Kansas	447
18	Missouri	446
19	Washington	445
20	Tennessee	438
21	Florida	425
21	Louisiana	425
23	Indiana	420
24	Mississippi	415
25	North Carolina	411
26	Vermont	405
27	Pennsylvania	395
28	Hawaii	392
29	Wisconsin	390
30	Kentucky	389
31	Delaware	384
32	South Carolina	382
33	New Hampshire	381
33	Texas	381
35	Georgia	380
36	Alabama	368
36	Nebraska	368
38	Virginia	366
39	Maine	347
40	Minnesota	345
40	Ohio	345
42	Michigan	342
43	Maryland	329
44	California	327
45	Rhode Island	276
46	Massachusetts	268
47	New York	260
48	Illinois	259
49	Connecticut	254
50	New Jersey	228
	District of Columbia	300

Source: U.S. Department of Health and Human Services, National Center for Health Statistics
   unpublished data

*Age-adjusted years of potential life lost due to death before age 75.

Years Lost by Premature Death from Unintentional Injuries in 1997

National Average = 1,115 Years Lost per 100,000 Population*

<table>
<tr><td colspan="3">ALPHA ORDER</td><td colspan="3">RANK ORDER</td></tr>
<tr><td>RANK</td><td>STATE</td><td>YEARS</td><td>RANK</td><td>STATE</td><td>YEARS</td></tr>
<tr><td>6</td><td>Alabama</td><td>1,739</td><td>1</td><td>Mississippi</td><td>1,934</td></tr>
<tr><td>4</td><td>Alaska</td><td>1,803</td><td>2</td><td>New Mexico</td><td>1,919</td></tr>
<tr><td>11</td><td>Arizona</td><td>1,525</td><td>3</td><td>Arkansas</td><td>1,842</td></tr>
<tr><td>3</td><td>Arkansas</td><td>1,842</td><td>4</td><td>Alaska</td><td>1,803</td></tr>
<tr><td>37</td><td>California</td><td>905</td><td>5</td><td>Montana</td><td>1,799</td></tr>
<tr><td>27</td><td>Colorado</td><td>1,142</td><td>6</td><td>Alabama</td><td>1,739</td></tr>
<tr><td>43</td><td>Connecticut</td><td>846</td><td>7</td><td>Wyoming</td><td>1,722</td></tr>
<tr><td>24</td><td>Delaware</td><td>1,232</td><td>8</td><td>Oklahoma</td><td>1,563</td></tr>
<tr><td>22</td><td>Florida</td><td>1,260</td><td>9</td><td>South Carolina</td><td>1,537</td></tr>
<tr><td>18</td><td>Georgia</td><td>1,346</td><td>10</td><td>Idaho</td><td>1,536</td></tr>
<tr><td>44</td><td>Hawaii</td><td>842</td><td>11</td><td>Arizona</td><td>1,525</td></tr>
<tr><td>10</td><td>Idaho</td><td>1,536</td><td>12</td><td>Louisiana</td><td>1,506</td></tr>
<tr><td>37</td><td>Illinois</td><td>905</td><td>13</td><td>Tennessee</td><td>1,492</td></tr>
<tr><td>29</td><td>Indiana</td><td>1,119</td><td>14</td><td>Kentucky</td><td>1,463</td></tr>
<tr><td>34</td><td>Iowa</td><td>997</td><td>15</td><td>Nevada</td><td>1,402</td></tr>
<tr><td>25</td><td>Kansas</td><td>1,213</td><td>16</td><td>Missouri</td><td>1,377</td></tr>
<tr><td>14</td><td>Kentucky</td><td>1,463</td><td>17</td><td>South Dakota</td><td>1,364</td></tr>
<tr><td>12</td><td>Louisiana</td><td>1,506</td><td>18</td><td>Georgia</td><td>1,346</td></tr>
<tr><td>39</td><td>Maine</td><td>900</td><td>19</td><td>North Carolina</td><td>1,311</td></tr>
<tr><td>47</td><td>Maryland</td><td>745</td><td>20</td><td>West Virginia</td><td>1,306</td></tr>
<tr><td>50</td><td>Massachusetts</td><td>526</td><td>21</td><td>Oregon</td><td>1,292</td></tr>
<tr><td>33</td><td>Michigan</td><td>1,006</td><td>22</td><td>Florida</td><td>1,260</td></tr>
<tr><td>42</td><td>Minnesota</td><td>875</td><td>23</td><td>Texas</td><td>1,258</td></tr>
<tr><td>1</td><td>Mississippi</td><td>1,934</td><td>24</td><td>Delaware</td><td>1,232</td></tr>
<tr><td>16</td><td>Missouri</td><td>1,377</td><td>25</td><td>Kansas</td><td>1,213</td></tr>
<tr><td>5</td><td>Montana</td><td>1,799</td><td>26</td><td>Pennsylvania</td><td>1,149</td></tr>
<tr><td>28</td><td>Nebraska</td><td>1,126</td><td>27</td><td>Colorado</td><td>1,142</td></tr>
<tr><td>15</td><td>Nevada</td><td>1,402</td><td>28</td><td>Nebraska</td><td>1,126</td></tr>
<tr><td>48</td><td>New Hampshire</td><td>706</td><td>29</td><td>Indiana</td><td>1,119</td></tr>
<tr><td>41</td><td>New Jersey</td><td>878</td><td>30</td><td>Utah</td><td>1,113</td></tr>
<tr><td>2</td><td>New Mexico</td><td>1,919</td><td>31</td><td>North Dakota</td><td>1,094</td></tr>
<tr><td>46</td><td>New York</td><td>797</td><td>32</td><td>Washington</td><td>1,044</td></tr>
<tr><td>19</td><td>North Carolina</td><td>1,311</td><td>33</td><td>Michigan</td><td>1,006</td></tr>
<tr><td>31</td><td>North Dakota</td><td>1,094</td><td>34</td><td>Iowa</td><td>997</td></tr>
<tr><td>40</td><td>Ohio</td><td>899</td><td>35</td><td>Wisconsin</td><td>993</td></tr>
<tr><td>8</td><td>Oklahoma</td><td>1,563</td><td>36</td><td>Virginia</td><td>979</td></tr>
<tr><td>21</td><td>Oregon</td><td>1,292</td><td>37</td><td>California</td><td>905</td></tr>
<tr><td>26</td><td>Pennsylvania</td><td>1,149</td><td>37</td><td>Illinois</td><td>905</td></tr>
<tr><td>49</td><td>Rhode Island</td><td>645</td><td>39</td><td>Maine</td><td>900</td></tr>
<tr><td>9</td><td>South Carolina</td><td>1,537</td><td>40</td><td>Ohio</td><td>899</td></tr>
<tr><td>17</td><td>South Dakota</td><td>1,364</td><td>41</td><td>New Jersey</td><td>878</td></tr>
<tr><td>13</td><td>Tennessee</td><td>1,492</td><td>42</td><td>Minnesota</td><td>875</td></tr>
<tr><td>23</td><td>Texas</td><td>1,258</td><td>43</td><td>Connecticut</td><td>846</td></tr>
<tr><td>30</td><td>Utah</td><td>1,113</td><td>44</td><td>Hawaii</td><td>842</td></tr>
<tr><td>45</td><td>Vermont</td><td>830</td><td>45</td><td>Vermont</td><td>830</td></tr>
<tr><td>36</td><td>Virginia</td><td>979</td><td>46</td><td>New York</td><td>797</td></tr>
<tr><td>32</td><td>Washington</td><td>1,044</td><td>47</td><td>Maryland</td><td>745</td></tr>
<tr><td>20</td><td>West Virginia</td><td>1,306</td><td>48</td><td>New Hampshire</td><td>706</td></tr>
<tr><td>35</td><td>Wisconsin</td><td>993</td><td>49</td><td>Rhode Island</td><td>645</td></tr>
<tr><td>7</td><td>Wyoming</td><td>1,722</td><td>50</td><td>Massachusetts</td><td>526</td></tr>
<tr><td></td><td></td><td></td><td></td><td>District of Columbia</td><td>791</td></tr>
</table>

Source: U.S. Department of Health and Human Services, National Center for Health Statistics
unpublished data

*Age-adjusted years of potential life lost due to death before age 75. Includes such subcategories as falls, drowning, fires/burns, poisonings and motor vehicle injuries.

Average Annual Years of Potential Life Lost Due to Smoking: 1990-94

National Total = 5,721,206 Years*

ALPHA ORDER

RANK	STATE	YEARS	% of USA
21	Alabama	101,953	1.8%
50	Alaska	7,228	0.1%
25	Arizona	77,939	1.4%
27	Arkansas	71,690	1.3%
1	California	554,042	9.7%
32	Colorado	58,838	1.0%
29	Connecticut	67,551	1.2%
43	Delaware	17,669	0.3%
3	Florida	376,988	6.6%
11	Georgia	146,318	2.6%
44	Hawaii	16,545	0.3%
42	Idaho	17,993	0.3%
7	Illinois	265,561	4.6%
12	Indiana	141,056	2.5%
31	Iowa	61,275	1.1%
34	Kansas	52,749	0.9%
17	Kentucky	112,695	2.0%
18	Louisiana	104,813	1.8%
37	Maine	30,556	0.5%
20	Maryland	102,119	1.8%
16	Massachusetts	132,751	2.3%
8	Michigan	223,229	3.9%
26	Minnesota	77,654	1.4%
28	Mississippi	68,818	1.2%
15	Missouri	134,994	2.4%
41	Montana	18,025	0.3%
36	Nebraska	32,866	0.6%
35	Nevada	38,269	0.7%
40	New Hampshire	23,416	0.4%
9	New Jersey	172,539	3.0%
38	New Mexico	24,569	0.4%
2	New York	417,206	7.3%
10	North Carolina	170,621	3.0%
47	North Dakota	12,032	0.2%
6	Ohio	270,475	4.7%
24	Oklahoma	85,650	1.5%
30	Oregon	67,351	1.2%
5	Pennsylvania	307,829	5.4%
39	Rhode Island	24,067	0.4%
23	South Carolina	90,122	1.6%
46	South Dakota	14,705	0.3%
14	Tennessee	135,175	2.4%
4	Texas	347,215	6.1%
45	Utah	15,158	0.3%
48	Vermont	12,019	0.2%
13	Virginia	135,385	2.4%
19	Washington	102,769	1.8%
33	West Virginia	57,678	1.0%
22	Wisconsin	100,624	1.8%
49	Wyoming	9,271	0.2%

RANK ORDER

RANK	STATE	YEARS	% of USA
1	California	554,042	9.7%
2	New York	417,206	7.3%
3	Florida	376,988	6.6%
4	Texas	347,215	6.1%
5	Pennsylvania	307,829	5.4%
6	Ohio	270,475	4.7%
7	Illinois	265,561	4.6%
8	Michigan	223,229	3.9%
9	New Jersey	172,539	3.0%
10	North Carolina	170,621	3.0%
11	Georgia	146,318	2.6%
12	Indiana	141,056	2.5%
13	Virginia	135,385	2.4%
14	Tennessee	135,175	2.4%
15	Missouri	134,994	2.4%
16	Massachusetts	132,751	2.3%
17	Kentucky	112,695	2.0%
18	Louisiana	104,813	1.8%
19	Washington	102,769	1.8%
20	Maryland	102,119	1.8%
21	Alabama	101,953	1.8%
22	Wisconsin	100,624	1.8%
23	South Carolina	90,122	1.6%
24	Oklahoma	85,650	1.5%
25	Arizona	77,939	1.4%
26	Minnesota	77,654	1.4%
27	Arkansas	71,690	1.3%
28	Mississippi	68,818	1.2%
29	Connecticut	67,551	1.2%
30	Oregon	67,351	1.2%
31	Iowa	61,275	1.1%
32	Colorado	58,838	1.0%
33	West Virginia	57,678	1.0%
34	Kansas	52,749	0.9%
35	Nevada	38,269	0.7%
36	Nebraska	32,866	0.6%
37	Maine	30,556	0.5%
38	New Mexico	24,569	0.4%
39	Rhode Island	24,067	0.4%
40	New Hampshire	23,416	0.4%
41	Montana	18,025	0.3%
42	Idaho	17,993	0.3%
43	Delaware	17,669	0.3%
44	Hawaii	16,545	0.3%
45	Utah	15,158	0.3%
46	South Dakota	14,705	0.3%
47	North Dakota	12,032	0.2%
48	Vermont	12,019	0.2%
49	Wyoming	9,271	0.2%
50	Alaska	7,228	0.1%
	District of Columbia	15,184	0.3%

Source: Centers for Disease Control and Prevention, Office on Smoking and Health
    "State and National Tobacco Control Highlights" (http://www.cdc.gov/nccdphp/osh/statehi/statehi.htm)
*Estimates. Calculated by using life expectancy at age of death.

Average Annual Deaths Due to Smoking: 1990-1994

National Estimated Total = 430,741 Deaths*

ALPHA ORDER

RANK	STATE	DEATHS	% of USA
22	Alabama	7,055	1.6%
50	Alaska	421	0.1%
25	Arizona	5,912	1.4%
27	Arkansas	5,271	1.2%
1	California	41,883	9.7%
32	Colorado	4,467	1.0%
28	Connecticut	5,251	1.2%
43	Delaware	1,248	0.3%
3	Florida	29,060	6.7%
14	Georgia	9,666	2.2%
45	Hawaii	1,163	0.3%
42	Idaho	1,404	0.3%
7	Illinois	19,016	4.4%
11	Indiana	10,373	2.4%
30	Iowa	4,962	1.2%
34	Kansas	4,215	1.0%
17	Kentucky	7,953	1.8%
21	Louisiana	7,075	1.6%
37	Maine	2,326	0.5%
20	Maryland	7,180	1.7%
12	Massachusetts	10,242	2.4%
8	Michigan	15,786	3.7%
24	Minnesota	6,150	1.4%
31	Mississippi	4,762	1.1%
13	Missouri	9,960	2.3%
41	Montana	1,434	0.3%
36	Nebraska	2,623	0.6%
35	Nevada	2,665	0.6%
40	New Hampshire	1,777	0.4%
9	New Jersey	12,831	3.0%
38	New Mexico	1,871	0.4%
2	New York	30,741	7.1%
10	North Carolina	11,642	2.7%
47	North Dakota	968	0.2%
6	Ohio	19,527	4.5%
23	Oklahoma	6,255	1.5%
29	Oregon	5,210	1.2%
5	Pennsylvania	23,170	5.4%
39	Rhode Island	1,849	0.4%
26	South Carolina	5,887	1.4%
44	South Dakota	1,198	0.3%
16	Tennessee	9,359	2.2%
4	Texas	24,789	5.8%
46	Utah	1,133	0.3%
48	Vermont	914	0.2%
15	Virginia	9,530	2.2%
18	Washington	7,892	1.8%
33	West Virginia	4,229	1.0%
19	Wisconsin	7,853	1.8%
49	Wyoming	712	0.2%

RANK ORDER

RANK	STATE	DEATHS	% of USA
1	California	41,883	9.7%
2	New York	30,741	7.1%
3	Florida	29,060	6.7%
4	Texas	24,789	5.8%
5	Pennsylvania	23,170	5.4%
6	Ohio	19,527	4.5%
7	Illinois	19,016	4.4%
8	Michigan	15,786	3.7%
9	New Jersey	12,831	3.0%
10	North Carolina	11,642	2.7%
11	Indiana	10,373	2.4%
12	Massachusetts	10,242	2.4%
13	Missouri	9,960	2.3%
14	Georgia	9,666	2.2%
15	Virginia	9,530	2.2%
16	Tennessee	9,359	2.2%
17	Kentucky	7,953	1.8%
18	Washington	7,892	1.8%
19	Wisconsin	7,853	1.8%
20	Maryland	7,180	1.7%
21	Louisiana	7,075	1.6%
22	Alabama	7,055	1.6%
23	Oklahoma	6,255	1.5%
24	Minnesota	6,150	1.4%
25	Arizona	5,912	1.4%
26	South Carolina	5,887	1.4%
27	Arkansas	5,271	1.2%
28	Connecticut	5,251	1.2%
29	Oregon	5,210	1.2%
30	Iowa	4,962	1.2%
31	Mississippi	4,762	1.1%
32	Colorado	4,467	1.0%
33	West Virginia	4,229	1.0%
34	Kansas	4,215	1.0%
35	Nevada	2,665	0.6%
36	Nebraska	2,623	0.6%
37	Maine	2,326	0.5%
38	New Mexico	1,871	0.4%
39	Rhode Island	1,849	0.4%
40	New Hampshire	1,777	0.4%
41	Montana	1,434	0.3%
42	Idaho	1,404	0.3%
43	Delaware	1,248	0.3%
44	South Dakota	1,198	0.3%
45	Hawaii	1,163	0.3%
46	Utah	1,133	0.3%
47	North Dakota	968	0.2%
48	Vermont	914	0.2%
49	Wyoming	712	0.2%
50	Alaska	421	0.1%
	District of Columbia	929	0.2%

*Source: Centers for Disease Control and Prevention, Office on Smoking and Health
"State and National Tobacco Control Highlights" (http://www.cdc.gov/nccdphp/osh/statehi/statehi.htm)*
Estimates.

Average Annual Death Rate Due to Smoking: 1990-1994

National Rate = 358 Deaths per 100,000 Population*

ALPHA ORDER

RANK	STATE	RATE
23	Alabama	353
15	Alaska	367
38	Arizona	325
4	Arkansas	405
32	California	343
35	Colorado	331
41	Connecticut	310
5	Delaware	400
27	Florida	350
17	Georgia	364
49	Hawaii	237
45	Idaho	296
30	Illinois	347
9	Indiana	387
43	Iowa	308
39	Kansas	319
2	Kentucky	444
8	Louisiana	388
12	Maine	371
24	Maryland	351
35	Massachusetts	331
13	Michigan	368
47	Minnesota	287
6	Mississippi	392
15	Missouri	367
28	Montana	348
43	Nebraska	308
1	Nevada	469
19	New Hampshire	361
37	New Jersey	327
46	New Mexico	289
32	New York	343
13	North Carolina	368
48	North Dakota	280
17	Ohio	364
9	Oklahoma	387
28	Oregon	348
31	Pennsylvania	346
34	Rhode Island	340
11	South Carolina	378
42	South Dakota	309
7	Tennessee	390
21	Texas	358
50	Utah	188
24	Vermont	351
20	Virginia	360
24	Washington	351
3	West Virginia	424
40	Wisconsin	313
22	Wyoming	357

RANK ORDER

RANK	STATE	RATE
1	Nevada	469
2	Kentucky	444
3	West Virginia	424
4	Arkansas	405
5	Delaware	400
6	Mississippi	392
7	Tennessee	390
8	Louisiana	388
9	Indiana	387
9	Oklahoma	387
11	South Carolina	378
12	Maine	371
13	Michigan	368
13	North Carolina	368
15	Alaska	367
15	Missouri	367
17	Georgia	364
17	Ohio	364
19	New Hampshire	361
20	Virginia	360
21	Texas	358
22	Wyoming	357
23	Alabama	353
24	Maryland	351
24	Vermont	351
24	Washington	351
27	Florida	350
28	Montana	348
28	Oregon	348
30	Illinois	347
31	Pennsylvania	346
32	California	343
32	New York	343
34	Rhode Island	340
35	Colorado	331
35	Massachusetts	331
37	New Jersey	327
38	Arizona	325
39	Kansas	319
40	Wisconsin	313
41	Connecticut	310
42	South Dakota	309
43	Iowa	308
43	Nebraska	308
45	Idaho	296
46	New Mexico	289
47	Minnesota	287
48	North Dakota	280
49	Hawaii	237
50	Utah	188

District of Columbia	327

Source: Centers for Disease Control and Prevention, Office on Smoking and Health
    "State and National Tobacco Control Highlights" (http://www.cdc.gov/nccdphp/osh/statehi/statehi.htm)
*Estimates.

Alcohol-Induced Deaths in 1997

National Total = 19,576 Deaths*

ALPHA ORDER

RANK	STATE	DEATHS	% of USA
27	Alabama	271	1.4%
40	Alaska	92	0.5%
11	Arizona	473	2.4%
36	Arkansas	119	0.6%
1	California	3,322	17.0%
18	Colorado	365	1.9%
34	Connecticut	129	0.7%
49	Delaware	40	0.2%
3	Florida	1,302	6.7%
10	Georgia	545	2.8%
48	Hawaii	41	0.2%
41	Idaho	86	0.4%
7	Illinois	642	3.3%
23	Indiana	294	1.5%
32	Iowa	146	0.7%
35	Kansas	125	0.6%
28	Kentucky	261	1.3%
28	Louisiana	261	1.3%
38	Maine	104	0.5%
26	Maryland	290	1.5%
21	Massachusetts	323	1.6%
5	Michigan	688	3.5%
22	Minnesota	302	1.5%
31	Mississippi	172	0.9%
20	Missouri	347	1.8%
42	Montana	77	0.4%
43	Nebraska	75	0.4%
30	Nevada	243	1.2%
39	New Hampshire	96	0.5%
12	New Jersey	467	2.4%
23	New Mexico	294	1.5%
2	New York	1,388	7.1%
6	North Carolina	660	3.4%
45	North Dakota	59	0.3%
8	Ohio	568	2.9%
25	Oklahoma	293	1.5%
16	Oregon	374	1.9%
13	Pennsylvania	464	2.4%
44	Rhode Island	70	0.4%
15	South Carolina	419	2.1%
46	South Dakota	54	0.3%
14	Tennessee	423	2.2%
4	Texas	1,170	6.0%
37	Utah	113	0.6%
50	Vermont	26	0.1%
16	Virginia	374	1.9%
9	Washington	551	2.8%
33	West Virginia	130	0.7%
19	Wisconsin	351	1.8%
47	Wyoming	45	0.2%

RANK ORDER

RANK	STATE	DEATHS	% of USA
1	California	3,322	17.0%
2	New York	1,388	7.1%
3	Florida	1,302	6.7%
4	Texas	1,170	6.0%
5	Michigan	688	3.5%
6	North Carolina	660	3.4%
7	Illinois	642	3.3%
8	Ohio	568	2.9%
9	Washington	551	2.8%
10	Georgia	545	2.8%
11	Arizona	473	2.4%
12	New Jersey	467	2.4%
13	Pennsylvania	464	2.4%
14	Tennessee	423	2.2%
15	South Carolina	419	2.1%
16	Oregon	374	1.9%
16	Virginia	374	1.9%
18	Colorado	365	1.9%
19	Wisconsin	351	1.8%
20	Missouri	347	1.8%
21	Massachusetts	323	1.6%
22	Minnesota	302	1.5%
23	Indiana	294	1.5%
23	New Mexico	294	1.5%
25	Oklahoma	293	1.5%
26	Maryland	290	1.5%
27	Alabama	271	1.4%
28	Kentucky	261	1.3%
28	Louisiana	261	1.3%
30	Nevada	243	1.2%
31	Mississippi	172	0.9%
32	Iowa	146	0.7%
33	West Virginia	130	0.7%
34	Connecticut	129	0.7%
35	Kansas	125	0.6%
36	Arkansas	119	0.6%
37	Utah	113	0.6%
38	Maine	104	0.5%
39	New Hampshire	96	0.5%
40	Alaska	92	0.5%
41	Idaho	86	0.4%
42	Montana	77	0.4%
43	Nebraska	75	0.4%
44	Rhode Island	70	0.4%
45	North Dakota	59	0.3%
46	South Dakota	54	0.3%
47	Wyoming	45	0.2%
48	Hawaii	41	0.2%
49	Delaware	40	0.2%
50	Vermont	26	0.1%
	District of Columbia	52	0.3%

Source: U.S. Department of Health and Human Services, National Center for Health Statistics
    (http://wonder.cdc.gov/WONDER/)
*By state of residence. Includes excessive blood level of alcohol, accidental poisoning by alcohol and the
following alcohol-related causes: psychoses, dependence syndrome, polyneuropathy, cardiomyopathy, gastritis,
chronic liver disease and cirrhosis. Excludes accidents, homicides and other causes indirectly related to alcohol use.

Death Rate from Alcohol-Induced Deaths in 1997

National Rate = 7.3 Deaths per 100,000 Population*

ALPHA ORDER

RANK ORDER

RANK	STATE	RATE
32	Alabama	5.4
2	Alaska	15.5
7	Arizona	9.0
45	Arkansas	4.1
4	California	9.4
10	Colorado	7.8
48	Connecticut	3.1
35	Delaware	4.9
16	Florida	7.0
18	Georgia	6.5
50	Hawaii	2.9
22	Idaho	6.2
35	Illinois	4.9
42	Indiana	4.3
44	Iowa	4.2
41	Kansas	4.4
32	Kentucky	5.4
32	Louisiana	5.4
20	Maine	6.4
38	Maryland	4.7
40	Massachusetts	4.5
24	Michigan	6.0
29	Minnesota	5.6
27	Mississippi	5.7
29	Missouri	5.6
14	Montana	7.2
46	Nebraska	3.8
3	Nevada	12.2
15	New Hampshire	7.1
38	New Jersey	4.7
1	New Mexico	15.7
18	New York	6.5
12	North Carolina	7.6
10	North Dakota	7.8
42	Ohio	4.3
13	Oklahoma	7.3
5	Oregon	9.3
48	Pennsylvania	3.1
25	Rhode Island	5.9
6	South Carolina	9.2
21	South Dakota	6.3
17	Tennessee	6.7
27	Texas	5.7
23	Utah	6.1
47	Vermont	3.2
37	Virginia	4.8
9	Washington	8.3
29	West Virginia	5.6
26	Wisconsin	5.8
8	Wyoming	8.4

RANK	STATE	RATE
1	New Mexico	15.7
2	Alaska	15.5
3	Nevada	12.2
4	California	9.4
5	Oregon	9.3
6	South Carolina	9.2
7	Arizona	9.0
8	Wyoming	8.4
9	Washington	8.3
10	Colorado	7.8
10	North Dakota	7.8
12	North Carolina	7.6
13	Oklahoma	7.3
14	Montana	7.2
15	New Hampshire	7.1
16	Florida	7.0
17	Tennessee	6.7
18	Georgia	6.5
18	New York	6.5
20	Maine	6.4
21	South Dakota	6.3
22	Idaho	6.2
23	Utah	6.1
24	Michigan	6.0
25	Rhode Island	5.9
26	Wisconsin	5.8
27	Mississippi	5.7
27	Texas	5.7
29	Minnesota	5.6
29	Missouri	5.6
29	West Virginia	5.6
32	Alabama	5.4
32	Kentucky	5.4
32	Louisiana	5.4
35	Delaware	4.9
35	Illinois	4.9
37	Virginia	4.8
38	Maryland	4.7
38	New Jersey	4.7
40	Massachusetts	4.5
41	Kansas	4.4
42	Indiana	4.3
42	Ohio	4.3
44	Iowa	4.2
45	Arkansas	4.1
46	Nebraska	3.8
47	Vermont	3.2
48	Connecticut	3.1
48	Pennsylvania	3.1
50	Hawaii	2.9

	District of Columbia	8.3

Source: U.S. Department of Health and Human Services, National Center for Health Statistics
    (http://wonder.cdc.gov/WONDER/)
*By state of residence. Includes excessive blood level of alcohol, accidental poisoning by alcohol and the following alcohol-related causes: psychoses, dependence syndrome, polyneuropathy, cardiomyopathy, gastritis, chronic liver disease and cirrhosis. Excludes accidents, homicides and other causes indirectly related to alcohol use. Not age-adjusted.

Age-Adjusted Death Rate from Alcohol-Induced Deaths in 1997

National Rate = 6.3 Deaths per 100,000 Population*

ALPHA ORDER

RANK	STATE	RATE
30	Alabama	6.3
2	Alaska	15.1
6	Arizona	10.4
45	Arkansas	4.7
7	California	10.3
9	Colorado	9.4
48	Connecticut	3.9
37	Delaware	5.5
12	Florida	8.9
20	Georgia	7.3
50	Hawaii	3.5
23	Idaho	7.1
39	Illinois	5.4
43	Indiana	5.0
41	Iowa	5.1
44	Kansas	4.8
27	Kentucky	6.7
32	Louisiana	6.0
16	Maine	8.4
35	Maryland	5.7
40	Massachusetts	5.3
25	Michigan	7.0
28	Minnesota	6.4
30	Mississippi	6.3
28	Missouri	6.4
14	Montana	8.8
46	Nebraska	4.5
3	Nevada	14.5
17	New Hampshire	8.2
34	New Jersey	5.8
1	New Mexico	17.0
19	New York	7.7
12	North Carolina	8.9
11	North Dakota	9.2
41	Ohio	5.1
14	Oklahoma	8.8
4	Oregon	11.5
48	Pennsylvania	3.9
23	Rhode Island	7.1
5	South Carolina	11.1
20	South Dakota	7.3
18	Tennessee	7.9
32	Texas	6.0
37	Utah	5.5
47	Vermont	4.4
36	Virginia	5.6
8	Washington	9.8
22	West Virginia	7.2
26	Wisconsin	6.8
9	Wyoming	9.4

RANK ORDER

RANK	STATE	RATE
1	New Mexico	17.0
2	Alaska	15.1
3	Nevada	14.5
4	Oregon	11.5
5	South Carolina	11.1
6	Arizona	10.4
7	California	10.3
8	Washington	9.8
9	Colorado	9.4
9	Wyoming	9.4
11	North Dakota	9.2
12	Florida	8.9
12	North Carolina	8.9
14	Montana	8.8
14	Oklahoma	8.8
16	Maine	8.4
17	New Hampshire	8.2
18	Tennessee	7.9
19	New York	7.7
20	Georgia	7.3
20	South Dakota	7.3
22	West Virginia	7.2
23	Idaho	7.1
23	Rhode Island	7.1
25	Michigan	7.0
26	Wisconsin	6.8
27	Kentucky	6.7
28	Minnesota	6.4
28	Missouri	6.4
30	Alabama	6.3
30	Mississippi	6.3
32	Louisiana	6.0
32	Texas	6.0
34	New Jersey	5.8
35	Maryland	5.7
36	Virginia	5.6
37	Delaware	5.5
37	Utah	5.5
39	Illinois	5.4
40	Massachusetts	5.3
41	Iowa	5.1
41	Ohio	5.1
43	Indiana	5.0
44	Kansas	4.8
45	Arkansas	4.7
46	Nebraska	4.5
47	Vermont	4.4
48	Connecticut	3.9
48	Pennsylvania	3.9
50	Hawaii	3.5
	District of Columbia	9.8

Source: U.S. Department of Health and Human Services, National Center for Health Statistics
(http://wonder.cdc.gov/WONDER/)

*By state of residence. Includes excessive blood level of alcohol, accidental poisoning by alcohol and the following alcohol-related causes: psychoses, dependence syndrome, polyneuropathy, cardiomyopathy, gastritis, chronic liver disease and cirrhosis. Excludes accidents, homicides and other causes indirectly related to alcohol use.

Drug-Induced Deaths in 1997

National Total = 16,004 Deaths*

ALPHA ORDER

RANK	STATE	DEATHS	% of USA
31	Alabama	136	0.8%
45	Alaska	37	0.2%
12	Arizona	403	2.5%
33	Arkansas	92	0.6%
1	California	2,635	16.5%
22	Colorado	210	1.3%
23	Connecticut	200	1.2%
38	Delaware	69	0.4%
5	Florida	870	5.4%
15	Georgia	316	2.0%
35	Hawaii	76	0.5%
42	Idaho	51	0.3%
9	Illinois	506	3.2%
25	Indiana	181	1.1%
37	Iowa	72	0.4%
36	Kansas	74	0.5%
29	Kentucky	146	0.9%
20	Louisiana	231	1.4%
44	Maine	39	0.2%
7	Maryland	602	3.8%
10	Massachusetts	469	2.9%
8	Michigan	580	3.6%
32	Minnesota	116	0.7%
40	Mississippi	66	0.4%
19	Missouri	234	1.5%
46	Montana	34	0.2%
43	Nebraska	47	0.3%
24	Nevada	186	1.2%
41	New Hampshire	54	0.3%
6	New Jersey	806	5.0%
21	New Mexico	211	1.3%
2	New York	1,252	7.8%
14	North Carolina	318	2.0%
50	North Dakota	10	0.1%
13	Ohio	375	2.3%
28	Oklahoma	156	1.0%
16	Oregon	295	1.8%
3	Pennsylvania	1,088	6.8%
38	Rhode Island	69	0.4%
29	South Carolina	146	0.9%
47	South Dakota	21	0.1%
18	Tennessee	250	1.6%
4	Texas	1,060	6.6%
26	Utah	170	1.1%
48	Vermont	20	0.1%
17	Virginia	266	1.7%
11	Washington	452	2.8%
34	West Virginia	78	0.5%
27	Wisconsin	163	1.0%
49	Wyoming	17	0.1%

RANK ORDER

RANK	STATE	DEATHS	% of USA
1	California	2,635	16.5%
2	New York	1,252	7.8%
3	Pennsylvania	1,088	6.8%
4	Texas	1,060	6.6%
5	Florida	870	5.4%
6	New Jersey	806	5.0%
7	Maryland	602	3.8%
8	Michigan	580	3.6%
9	Illinois	506	3.2%
10	Massachusetts	469	2.9%
11	Washington	452	2.8%
12	Arizona	403	2.5%
13	Ohio	375	2.3%
14	North Carolina	318	2.0%
15	Georgia	316	2.0%
16	Oregon	295	1.8%
17	Virginia	266	1.7%
18	Tennessee	250	1.6%
19	Missouri	234	1.5%
20	Louisiana	231	1.4%
21	New Mexico	211	1.3%
22	Colorado	210	1.3%
23	Connecticut	200	1.2%
24	Nevada	186	1.2%
25	Indiana	181	1.1%
26	Utah	170	1.1%
27	Wisconsin	163	1.0%
28	Oklahoma	156	1.0%
29	Kentucky	146	0.9%
29	South Carolina	146	0.9%
31	Alabama	136	0.8%
32	Minnesota	116	0.7%
33	Arkansas	92	0.6%
34	West Virginia	78	0.5%
35	Hawaii	76	0.5%
36	Kansas	74	0.5%
37	Iowa	72	0.4%
38	Delaware	69	0.4%
38	Rhode Island	69	0.4%
40	Mississippi	66	0.4%
41	New Hampshire	54	0.3%
42	Idaho	51	0.3%
43	Nebraska	47	0.3%
44	Maine	39	0.2%
45	Alaska	37	0.2%
46	Montana	34	0.2%
47	South Dakota	21	0.1%
48	Vermont	20	0.1%
49	Wyoming	17	0.1%
50	North Dakota	10	0.1%
	District of Columbia	49	0.3%

Source: U.S. Department of Health and Human Services, National Center for Health Statistics
   (http://wonder.cdc.gov/WONDER/)
By state of residence. Includes drug psychoses, drug dependence, nondependent use excluding alcohol and tobacco, accidental poisoning or suicide by drugs, medicaments and biologicals. Excludes accidents, homicides and other causes indirectly related to drug use.

Death Rate from Drug-Induced Deaths in 1997

National Rate = 6.0 Deaths per 100,000 Population*

ALPHA ORDER				RANK ORDER		
RANK	STATE	RATE		RANK	STATE	RATE
41	Alabama	3.1		1	New Mexico	12.2
16	Alaska	6.1		2	Maryland	11.8
8	Arizona	8.8		3	Nevada	11.1
36	Arkansas	3.6		4	New Jersey	10.0
9	California	8.2		5	Delaware	9.4
20	Colorado	5.4		6	Oregon	9.1
16	Connecticut	6.1		6	Pennsylvania	9.1
5	Delaware	9.4		8	Arizona	8.8
18	Florida	5.9		9	California	8.2
30	Georgia	4.2		9	Utah	8.2
15	Hawaii	6.4		11	Washington	8.1
30	Idaho	4.2		12	Massachusetts	7.7
26	Illinois	4.3		13	Rhode Island	7.0
41	Indiana	3.1		14	New York	6.9
47	Iowa	2.5		15	Hawaii	6.4
44	Kansas	2.9		16	Alaska	6.1
35	Kentucky	3.7		16	Connecticut	6.1
22	Louisiana	5.3		18	Florida	5.9
41	Maine	3.1		18	Michigan	5.9
2	Maryland	11.8		20	Colorado	5.4
12	Massachusetts	7.7		20	Texas	5.4
18	Michigan	5.9		22	Louisiana	5.3
47	Minnesota	2.5		23	Oklahoma	4.7
49	Mississippi	2.4		23	Tennessee	4.7
26	Missouri	4.3		25	New Hampshire	4.6
32	Montana	3.9		26	Illinois	4.3
45	Nebraska	2.8		26	Missouri	4.3
3	Nevada	11.1		26	North Carolina	4.3
25	New Hampshire	4.6		26	West Virginia	4.3
4	New Jersey	10.0		30	Georgia	4.2
1	New Mexico	12.2		30	Idaho	4.2
14	New York	6.9		32	Montana	3.9
26	North Carolina	4.3		32	South Carolina	3.9
50	North Dakota	1.6		32	Virginia	3.9
38	Ohio	3.4		35	Kentucky	3.7
23	Oklahoma	4.7		36	Arkansas	3.6
6	Oregon	9.1		37	Wyoming	3.5
6	Pennsylvania	9.1		38	Ohio	3.4
13	Rhode Island	7.0		38	Vermont	3.4
32	South Carolina	3.9		40	Wisconsin	3.2
45	South Dakota	2.8		41	Alabama	3.1
23	Tennessee	4.7		41	Indiana	3.1
20	Texas	5.4		41	Maine	3.1
9	Utah	8.2		44	Kansas	2.9
38	Vermont	3.4		45	Nebraska	2.8
32	Virginia	3.9		45	South Dakota	2.8
11	Washington	8.1		47	Iowa	2.5
26	West Virginia	4.3		47	Minnesota	2.5
40	Wisconsin	3.2		49	Mississippi	2.4
37	Wyoming	3.5		50	North Dakota	1.6
					District of Columbia	9.2

Source: U.S. Department of Health and Human Services, National Center for Health Statistics
   (http://wonder.cdc.gov/WONDER/)
*By state of residence. Includes drug psychoses, drug dependence, nondependent use excluding alcohol and
tobacco, accidental poisoning or suicide by drugs, medicaments and biologicals. Excludes accidents, homicides
and other causes indirectly related to drug use. Not age-adjusted.

Age-Adjusted Death Rate from Drug-Induced Deaths in 1997

National Rate = 5.6 Deaths per 100,000 Population*

ALPHA ORDER

RANK ORDER

RANK	STATE	RATE	RANK	STATE	RATE
45	Alabama	2.7	1	New Mexico	12.2
15	Alaska	6.0	2	Maryland	10.4
7	Arizona	8.6	3	Nevada	9.9
35	Arkansas	3.4	4	New Jersey	9.6
10	California	7.7	5	Utah	8.9
22	Colorado	4.8	6	Pennsylvania	8.7
18	Connecticut	5.6	7	Arizona	8.6
7	Delaware	8.6	7	Delaware	8.6
17	Florida	5.7	9	Oregon	8.5
31	Georgia	3.8	10	California	7.7
15	Hawaii	6.0	11	Washington	7.4
24	Idaho	4.3	12	Massachusetts	7.0
28	Illinois	4.0	13	New York	6.5
42	Indiana	2.8	13	Rhode Island	6.5
49	Iowa	2.1	15	Alaska	6.0
42	Kansas	2.8	15	Hawaii	6.0
37	Kentucky	3.3	17	Florida	5.7
21	Louisiana	5.1	18	Connecticut	5.6
40	Maine	2.9	19	Michigan	5.3
2	Maryland	10.4	20	Texas	5.2
12	Massachusetts	7.0	21	Louisiana	5.1
19	Michigan	5.3	22	Colorado	4.8
47	Minnesota	2.4	23	Oklahoma	4.5
48	Mississippi	2.2	24	Idaho	4.3
28	Missouri	4.0	25	New Hampshire	4.2
31	Montana	3.8	26	Tennessee	4.1
42	Nebraska	2.8	26	West Virginia	4.1
3	Nevada	9.9	28	Illinois	4.0
25	New Hampshire	4.2	28	Missouri	4.0
4	New Jersey	9.6	30	North Carolina	3.9
1	New Mexico	12.2	31	Georgia	3.8
13	New York	6.5	31	Montana	3.8
30	North Carolina	3.9	33	South Carolina	3.6
50	North Dakota**	1.7	33	Virginia	3.6
38	Ohio	3.0	35	Arkansas	3.4
23	Oklahoma	4.5	35	Wyoming**	3.4
9	Oregon	8.5	37	Kentucky	3.3
6	Pennsylvania	8.7	38	Ohio	3.0
13	Rhode Island	6.5	38	Vermont	3.0
33	South Carolina	3.6	40	Maine	2.9
46	South Dakota	2.5	40	Wisconsin	2.9
26	Tennessee	4.1	42	Indiana	2.8
20	Texas	5.2	42	Kansas	2.8
5	Utah	8.9	42	Nebraska	2.8
38	Vermont	3.0	45	Alabama	2.7
33	Virginia	3.6	46	South Dakota	2.5
11	Washington	7.4	47	Minnesota	2.4
26	West Virginia	4.1	48	Mississippi	2.2
40	Wisconsin	2.9	49	Iowa	2.1
35	Wyoming**	3.4	50	North Dakota**	1.7

District of Columbia   8.7

Source: U.S. Department of Health and Human Services, National Center for Health Statistics
  (http://wonder.cdc.gov/WONDER/)
*By state of residence. Includes drug psychoses, drug dependence, nondependent use excluding alcohol and
tobacco, accidental poisoning or suicide by drugs, medicaments and biologicals. Excludes accidents, homicides
and other causes indirectly related to drug use.
**Due to low numbers of deaths, rates for these states should be interpreted with caution.

Occupational Fatalities in 1998

National Total = 6,026 Deaths*

ALPHA ORDER

RANK	STATE	DEATHS	% of USA
16	Alabama	135	2.2%
41	Alaska	43	0.7%
30	Arizona	71	1.2%
24	Arkansas	86	1.4%
1	California	617	10.2%
27	Colorado	77	1.3%
37	Connecticut	55	0.9%
50	Delaware	11	0.2%
3	Florida	384	6.4%
8	Georgia	195	3.2%
48	Hawaii	12	0.2%
38	Idaho	51	0.8%
7	Illinois	216	3.6%
13	Indiana	154	2.6%
31	Iowa	68	1.1%
22	Kansas	98	1.6%
17	Kentucky	117	1.9%
12	Louisiana	159	2.6%
44	Maine	26	0.4%
26	Maryland	78	1.3%
40	Massachusetts	44	0.7%
10	Michigan	179	3.0%
25	Minnesota	84	1.4%
18	Mississippi	113	1.9%
15	Missouri	145	2.4%
34	Montana	58	1.0%
36	Nebraska	56	0.9%
33	Nevada	60	1.0%
46	New Hampshire	23	0.4%
21	New Jersey	103	1.7%
39	New Mexico	48	0.8%
4	New York	243	4.0%
6	North Carolina	228	3.8%
45	North Dakota	24	0.4%
9	Ohio	186	3.1%
28	Oklahoma	75	1.2%
29	Oregon	72	1.2%
5	Pennsylvania	235	3.9%
48	Rhode Island	12	0.2%
20	South Carolina	110	1.8%
43	South Dakota	28	0.5%
14	Tennessee	150	2.5%
2	Texas	523	8.7%
32	Utah	67	1.1%
47	Vermont	16	0.3%
11	Virginia	176	2.9%
19	Washington	112	1.9%
35	West Virginia	57	0.9%
23	Wisconsin	97	1.6%
42	Wyoming	33	0.5%

RANK ORDER

RANK	STATE	DEATHS	% of USA
1	California	617	10.2%
2	Texas	523	8.7%
3	Florida	384	6.4%
4	New York	243	4.0%
5	Pennsylvania	235	3.9%
6	North Carolina	228	3.8%
7	Illinois	216	3.6%
8	Georgia	195	3.2%
9	Ohio	186	3.1%
10	Michigan	179	3.0%
11	Virginia	176	2.9%
12	Louisiana	159	2.6%
13	Indiana	154	2.6%
14	Tennessee	150	2.5%
15	Missouri	145	2.4%
16	Alabama	135	2.2%
17	Kentucky	117	1.9%
18	Mississippi	113	1.9%
19	Washington	112	1.9%
20	South Carolina	110	1.8%
21	New Jersey	103	1.7%
22	Kansas	98	1.6%
23	Wisconsin	97	1.6%
24	Arkansas	86	1.4%
25	Minnesota	84	1.4%
26	Maryland	78	1.3%
27	Colorado	77	1.3%
28	Oklahoma	75	1.2%
29	Oregon	72	1.2%
30	Arizona	71	1.2%
31	Iowa	68	1.1%
32	Utah	67	1.1%
33	Nevada	60	1.0%
34	Montana	58	1.0%
35	West Virginia	57	0.9%
36	Nebraska	56	0.9%
37	Connecticut	55	0.9%
38	Idaho	51	0.8%
39	New Mexico	48	0.8%
40	Massachusetts	44	0.7%
41	Alaska	43	0.7%
42	Wyoming	33	0.5%
43	South Dakota	28	0.5%
44	Maine	26	0.4%
45	North Dakota	24	0.4%
46	New Hampshire	23	0.4%
47	Vermont	16	0.3%
48	Hawaii	12	0.2%
48	Rhode Island	12	0.2%
50	Delaware	11	0.2%
	District of Columbia	13	0.2%

Source: U.S. Department of Labor, Bureau of Labor Statistics
"National Census of Fatal Occupational Injuries, 1998" (press release, August 4, 1999)
Includes three fatalities that occurred outside the 50 states.

Occupational Fatalities per 100,000 Workers in 1998

National Rate = 4.6 Deaths per 100,000 Workers*

ALPHA ORDER

RANK	STATE	RATE
13	Alabama	6.5
1	Alaska	14.4
41	Arizona	3.3
8	Arkansas	7.5
33	California	4.0
36	Colorado	3.6
41	Connecticut	3.3
45	Delaware	2.9
21	Florida	5.6
25	Georgia	5.1
49	Hawaii	2.1
5	Idaho	8.2
36	Illinois	3.6
25	Indiana	5.1
29	Iowa	4.5
10	Kansas	7.2
15	Kentucky	6.4
5	Louisiana	8.2
31	Maine	4.2
44	Maryland	3.0
50	Massachusetts	1.4
35	Michigan	3.7
43	Minnesota	3.2
4	Mississippi	9.4
23	Missouri	5.3
3	Montana	13.1
16	Nebraska	6.3
12	Nevada	6.8
36	New Hampshire	3.6
47	New Jersey	2.6
17	New Mexico	6.2
45	New York	2.9
17	North Carolina	6.2
11	North Dakota	7.1
39	Ohio	3.4
28	Oklahoma	4.8
30	Oregon	4.3
31	Pennsylvania	4.2
48	Rhode Island	2.5
19	South Carolina	5.8
9	South Dakota	7.3
20	Tennessee	5.7
22	Texas	5.4
13	Utah	6.5
27	Vermont	5.0
24	Virginia	5.2
34	Washington	3.9
7	West Virginia	7.6
39	Wisconsin	3.4
2	Wyoming	13.4

RANK ORDER

RANK	STATE	RATE
1	Alaska	14.4
2	Wyoming	13.4
3	Montana	13.1
4	Mississippi	9.4
5	Idaho	8.2
5	Louisiana	8.2
7	West Virginia	7.6
8	Arkansas	7.5
9	South Dakota	7.3
10	Kansas	7.2
11	North Dakota	7.1
12	Nevada	6.8
13	Alabama	6.5
13	Utah	6.5
15	Kentucky	6.4
16	Nebraska	6.3
17	New Mexico	6.2
17	North Carolina	6.2
19	South Carolina	5.8
20	Tennessee	5.7
21	Florida	5.6
22	Texas	5.4
23	Missouri	5.3
24	Virginia	5.2
25	Georgia	5.1
25	Indiana	5.1
27	Vermont	5.0
28	Oklahoma	4.8
29	Iowa	4.5
30	Oregon	4.3
31	Maine	4.2
31	Pennsylvania	4.2
33	California	4.0
34	Washington	3.9
35	Michigan	3.7
36	Colorado	3.6
36	Illinois	3.6
36	New Hampshire	3.6
39	Ohio	3.4
39	Wisconsin	3.4
41	Arizona	3.3
41	Connecticut	3.3
43	Minnesota	3.2
44	Maryland	3.0
45	Delaware	2.9
45	New York	2.9
47	New Jersey	2.6
48	Rhode Island	2.5
49	Hawaii	2.1
50	Massachusetts	1.4

District of Columbia	5.3

Source: Morgan Quitno Press using data from U.S. Department of Labor, Bureau of Labor Statistics
"National Census of Fatal Occupational Injuries, 1998" (press release, August 4, 1999)
*Includes three fatalities that occurred outside the 50 states.

III. FACILITIES

Community Hospitals in 1998

National Total = 5,015 Hospitals*

ALPHA ORDER					RANK ORDER			

RANK	STATE	HOSPITALS	% of USA		RANK	STATE	HOSPITALS	% of USA
19	Alabama	110	2.2%		1	California	405	8.1%
47	Alaska	17	0.3%		2	Texas	400	8.0%
31	Arizona	64	1.3%		3	New York	222	4.4%
27	Arkansas	82	1.6%		4	Pennsylvania	212	4.2%
1	California	405	8.1%		5	Florida	204	4.1%
29	Colorado	69	1.4%		6	Illinois	203	4.0%
42	Connecticut	33	0.7%		7	Ohio	172	3.4%
50	Delaware	6	0.1%		8	Georgia	156	3.1%
5	Florida	204	4.1%		9	Michigan	151	3.0%
8	Georgia	156	3.1%		10	Minnesota	136	2.7%
45	Hawaii	20	0.4%		11	Kansas	129	2.6%
38	Idaho	42	0.8%		12	Louisiana	126	2.5%
6	Illinois	203	4.0%		13	Wisconsin	123	2.5%
18	Indiana	111	2.2%		14	Missouri	122	2.4%
16	Iowa	116	2.3%		14	Tennessee	122	2.4%
11	Kansas	129	2.6%		16	Iowa	116	2.3%
21	Kentucky	106	2.1%		16	North Carolina	116	2.3%
12	Louisiana	126	2.5%		18	Indiana	111	2.2%
40	Maine	38	0.8%		19	Alabama	110	2.2%
35	Maryland	51	1.0%		20	Oklahoma	109	2.2%
27	Massachusetts	82	1.6%		21	Kentucky	106	2.1%
9	Michigan	151	3.0%		22	Mississippi	96	1.9%
10	Minnesota	136	2.7%		23	Virginia	93	1.9%
22	Mississippi	96	1.9%		24	Nebraska	86	1.7%
14	Missouri	122	2.4%		24	Washington	86	1.7%
34	Montana	53	1.1%		26	New Jersey	83	1.7%
24	Nebraska	86	1.7%		27	Arkansas	82	1.6%
45	Nevada	20	0.4%		27	Massachusetts	82	1.6%
43	New Hampshire	28	0.6%		29	Colorado	69	1.4%
26	New Jersey	83	1.7%		30	South Carolina	65	1.3%
41	New Mexico	36	0.7%		31	Arizona	64	1.3%
3	New York	222	4.4%		32	Oregon	60	1.2%
16	North Carolina	116	2.3%		33	West Virginia	58	1.2%
37	North Dakota	43	0.9%		34	Montana	53	1.1%
7	Ohio	172	3.4%		35	Maryland	51	1.0%
20	Oklahoma	109	2.2%		36	South Dakota	49	1.0%
32	Oregon	60	1.2%		37	North Dakota	43	0.9%
4	Pennsylvania	212	4.2%		38	Idaho	42	0.8%
49	Rhode Island	12	0.2%		39	Utah	41	0.8%
30	South Carolina	65	1.3%		40	Maine	38	0.8%
36	South Dakota	49	1.0%		41	New Mexico	36	0.7%
14	Tennessee	122	2.4%		42	Connecticut	33	0.7%
2	Texas	400	8.0%		43	New Hampshire	28	0.6%
39	Utah	41	0.8%		44	Wyoming	25	0.5%
48	Vermont	14	0.3%		45	Hawaii	20	0.4%
23	Virginia	93	1.9%		45	Nevada	20	0.4%
24	Washington	86	1.7%		47	Alaska	17	0.3%
33	West Virginia	58	1.2%		48	Vermont	14	0.3%
13	Wisconsin	123	2.5%		49	Rhode Island	12	0.2%
44	Wyoming	25	0.5%		50	Delaware	6	0.1%
						District of Columbia	12	0.2%

Source: American Hospital Association (Chicago, IL)
   "Hospital Statistics" (2000 edition)
*Community hospitals are all nonfederal, short-term, general and special hospitals whose facilities and services are available to the public.

Rate of Community Hospitals in 1998

National Rate = 1.9 Community Hospitals per 100,000 Population*

ALPHA ORDER

RANK	STATE	RATE
18	Alabama	2.5
16	Alaska	2.8
39	Arizona	1.4
11	Arkansas	3.2
43	California	1.2
31	Colorado	1.7
47	Connecticut	1.0
50	Delaware	0.8
39	Florida	1.4
25	Georgia	2.0
31	Hawaii	1.7
9	Idaho	3.4
31	Illinois	1.7
28	Indiana	1.9
7	Iowa	4.1
6	Kansas	4.9
17	Kentucky	2.7
14	Louisiana	2.9
13	Maine	3.0
47	Maryland	1.0
42	Massachusetts	1.3
35	Michigan	1.5
14	Minnesota	2.9
8	Mississippi	3.5
22	Missouri	2.2
3	Montana	6.0
4	Nebraska	5.2
46	Nevada	1.1
19	New Hampshire	2.4
47	New Jersey	1.0
24	New Mexico	2.1
43	New York	1.2
35	North Carolina	1.5
1	North Dakota	6.7
35	Ohio	1.5
10	Oklahoma	3.3
29	Oregon	1.8
29	Pennsylvania	1.8
43	Rhode Island	1.2
31	South Carolina	1.7
1	South Dakota	6.7
22	Tennessee	2.2
25	Texas	2.0
25	Utah	2.0
19	Vermont	2.4
39	Virginia	1.4
35	Washington	1.5
11	West Virginia	3.2
19	Wisconsin	2.4
4	Wyoming	5.2

RANK ORDER

RANK	STATE	RATE
1	North Dakota	6.7
1	South Dakota	6.7
3	Montana	6.0
4	Nebraska	5.2
4	Wyoming	5.2
6	Kansas	4.9
7	Iowa	4.1
8	Mississippi	3.5
9	Idaho	3.4
10	Oklahoma	3.3
11	Arkansas	3.2
11	West Virginia	3.2
13	Maine	3.0
14	Louisiana	2.9
14	Minnesota	2.9
16	Alaska	2.8
17	Kentucky	2.7
18	Alabama	2.5
19	New Hampshire	2.4
19	Vermont	2.4
19	Wisconsin	2.4
22	Missouri	2.2
22	Tennessee	2.2
24	New Mexico	2.1
25	Georgia	2.0
25	Texas	2.0
25	Utah	2.0
28	Indiana	1.9
29	Oregon	1.8
29	Pennsylvania	1.8
31	Colorado	1.7
31	Hawaii	1.7
31	Illinois	1.7
31	South Carolina	1.7
35	Michigan	1.5
35	North Carolina	1.5
35	Ohio	1.5
35	Washington	1.5
39	Arizona	1.4
39	Florida	1.4
39	Virginia	1.4
42	Massachusetts	1.3
43	California	1.2
43	New York	1.2
43	Rhode Island	1.2
46	Nevada	1.1
47	Connecticut	1.0
47	Maryland	1.0
47	New Jersey	1.0
50	Delaware	0.8
	District of Columbia	2.3

Source: Morgan Quitno Press using data from American Hospital Association (Chicago, IL)
    "Hospital Statistics" (2000 edition)
*Community hospitals are all nonfederal, short-term, general and special hospitals whose facilities and services are available to the public.

Community Hospitals per 1,000 Square Miles in 1998

National Rate = 1.3 Community Hospitals*

ALPHA ORDER

RANK	STATE	RATE
23	Alabama	2.1
50	Alaska**	0.0
40	Arizona	0.6
33	Arkansas	1.5
17	California	2.5
39	Colorado	0.7
4	Connecticut	6.0
17	Delaware	2.5
10	Florida	3.4
15	Georgia	2.6
11	Hawaii	3.1
44	Idaho	0.5
9	Illinois	3.5
12	Indiana	3.0
23	Iowa	2.1
29	Kansas	1.6
15	Kentucky	2.6
17	Louisiana	2.5
37	Maine	1.1
6	Maryland	4.1
3	Massachusetts	8.9
29	Michigan	1.6
29	Minnesota	1.6
26	Mississippi	2.0
28	Missouri	1.8
46	Montana	0.4
37	Nebraska	1.1
49	Nevada	0.2
12	New Hampshire	3.0
1	New Jersey	10.1
47	New Mexico	0.3
6	New York	4.1
21	North Carolina	2.2
40	North Dakota	0.6
8	Ohio	3.8
29	Oklahoma	1.6
40	Oregon	0.6
5	Pennsylvania	4.6
2	Rhode Island	9.7
23	South Carolina	2.1
40	South Dakota	0.6
14	Tennessee	2.9
33	Texas	1.5
44	Utah	0.5
33	Vermont	1.5
21	Virginia	2.2
36	Washington	1.2
20	West Virginia	2.4
27	Wisconsin	1.9
47	Wyoming	0.3

RANK ORDER

RANK	STATE	RATE
1	New Jersey	10.1
2	Rhode Island	9.7
3	Massachusetts	8.9
4	Connecticut	6.0
5	Pennsylvania	4.6
6	Maryland	4.1
6	New York	4.1
8	Ohio	3.8
9	Illinois	3.5
10	Florida	3.4
11	Hawaii	3.1
12	Indiana	3.0
12	New Hampshire	3.0
14	Tennessee	2.9
15	Georgia	2.6
15	Kentucky	2.6
17	California	2.5
17	Delaware	2.5
17	Louisiana	2.5
20	West Virginia	2.4
21	North Carolina	2.2
21	Virginia	2.2
23	Alabama	2.1
23	Iowa	2.1
23	South Carolina	2.1
26	Mississippi	2.0
27	Wisconsin	1.9
28	Missouri	1.8
29	Kansas	1.6
29	Michigan	1.6
29	Minnesota	1.6
29	Oklahoma	1.6
33	Arkansas	1.5
33	Texas	1.5
33	Vermont	1.5
36	Washington	1.2
37	Maine	1.1
37	Nebraska	1.1
39	Colorado	0.7
40	Arizona	0.6
40	North Dakota	0.6
40	Oregon	0.6
40	South Dakota	0.6
44	Idaho	0.5
44	Utah	0.5
46	Montana	0.4
47	New Mexico	0.3
47	Wyoming	0.3
49	Nevada	0.2
50	Alaska**	0.0
	District of Columbia***	NA

Source: Morgan Quitno Press using data from American Hospital Association (Chicago, IL)
       "Hospital Statistics" (2000 edition)
*Based on 1990 Census land and water area figures. Community hospitals are nonfederal short-term general and other special hospitals, whose facilities and services are available to the public.
**Alaska has 17 community hospitals for its 615,230 square miles.
***The District of Columbia has 12 community hospitals for its 68 square miles.

Community Hospitals in Urban Areas in 1998

National Total = 2,816 Hospitals*

RANK	STATE	HOSPITALS	% of USA
17	Alabama	57	2.0%
48	Alaska	2	0.1%
20	Arizona	48	1.7%
28	Arkansas	27	1.0%
1	California	364	12.9%
27	Colorado	33	1.2%
28	Connecticut	27	1.0%
46	Delaware	4	0.1%
4	Florida	173	6.1%
12	Georgia	68	2.4%
38	Hawaii	12	0.4%
43	Idaho	7	0.2%
6	Illinois	131	4.7%
13	Indiana	65	2.3%
32	Iowa	21	0.7%
31	Kansas	24	0.9%
26	Kentucky	34	1.2%
10	Louisiana	78	2.8%
42	Maine	9	0.3%
23	Maryland	42	1.5%
11	Massachusetts	71	2.5%
8	Michigan	92	3.3%
22	Minnesota	45	1.6%
33	Mississippi	19	0.7%
14	Missouri	64	2.3%
47	Montana	3	0.1%
36	Nebraska	13	0.5%
38	Nevada	12	0.4%
41	New Hampshire	10	0.4%
9	New Jersey	83	2.9%
36	New Mexico	13	0.5%
3	New York	186	6.6%
19	North Carolina	54	1.9%
44	North Dakota	6	0.2%
7	Ohio	120	4.3%
24	Oklahoma	41	1.5%
28	Oregon	27	1.0%
5	Pennsylvania	167	5.9%
40	Rhode Island	11	0.4%
25	South Carolina	37	1.3%
45	South Dakota	5	0.2%
15	Tennessee	59	2.1%
2	Texas	238	8.5%
33	Utah	19	0.7%
48	Vermont	2	0.1%
16	Virginia	58	2.1%
21	Washington	46	1.6%
35	West Virginia	18	0.6%
17	Wisconsin	57	2.0%
48	Wyoming	2	0.1%

RANK	STATE	HOSPITALS	% of USA
1	California	364	12.9%
2	Texas	238	8.5%
3	New York	186	6.6%
4	Florida	173	6.1%
5	Pennsylvania	167	5.9%
6	Illinois	131	4.7%
7	Ohio	120	4.3%
8	Michigan	92	3.3%
9	New Jersey	83	2.9%
10	Louisiana	78	2.8%
11	Massachusetts	71	2.5%
12	Georgia	68	2.4%
13	Indiana	65	2.3%
14	Missouri	64	2.3%
15	Tennessee	59	2.1%
16	Virginia	58	2.1%
17	Alabama	57	2.0%
17	Wisconsin	57	2.0%
19	North Carolina	54	1.9%
20	Arizona	48	1.7%
21	Washington	46	1.6%
22	Minnesota	45	1.6%
23	Maryland	42	1.5%
24	Oklahoma	41	1.5%
25	South Carolina	37	1.3%
26	Kentucky	34	1.2%
27	Colorado	33	1.2%
28	Arkansas	27	1.0%
28	Connecticut	27	1.0%
28	Oregon	27	1.0%
31	Kansas	24	0.9%
32	Iowa	21	0.7%
33	Mississippi	19	0.7%
33	Utah	19	0.7%
35	West Virginia	18	0.6%
36	Nebraska	13	0.5%
36	New Mexico	13	0.5%
38	Hawaii	12	0.4%
38	Nevada	12	0.4%
40	Rhode Island	11	0.4%
41	New Hampshire	10	0.4%
42	Maine	9	0.3%
43	Idaho	7	0.2%
44	North Dakota	6	0.2%
45	South Dakota	5	0.2%
46	Delaware	4	0.1%
47	Montana	3	0.1%
48	Alaska	2	0.1%
48	Vermont	2	0.1%
48	Wyoming	2	0.1%
	District of Columbia	12	0.4%

Source: American Hospital Association (Chicago, IL)
    "Hospital Statistics" (2000 edition)
Community hospitals are all nonfederal, short-term, general and special hospitals whose facilities and services are available to the public. Urban is defined as any area inside a metropolitan statistical area as defined by the U.S. Office of Management and Budget.

Percent of Community Hospitals in Urban Areas in 1998

National Percent = 56.2% of Community Hospitals*

ALPHA ORDER

RANK	STATE	PERCENT
24	Alabama	51.8
47	Alaska	11.8
10	Arizona	75.0
36	Arkansas	32.9
3	California	89.9
26	Colorado	47.8
8	Connecticut	81.8
12	Delaware	66.7
5	Florida	84.8
31	Georgia	43.6
17	Hawaii	60.0
43	Idaho	16.7
13	Illinois	64.5
20	Indiana	58.6
42	Iowa	18.1
41	Kansas	18.6
37	Kentucky	32.1
15	Louisiana	61.9
39	Maine	23.7
7	Maryland	82.4
4	Massachusetts	86.6
16	Michigan	60.9
35	Minnesota	33.1
40	Mississippi	19.8
23	Missouri	52.5
50	Montana	5.7
44	Nebraska	15.1
17	Nevada	60.0
34	New Hampshire	35.7
1	New Jersey	100.0
33	New Mexico	36.1
6	New York	83.8
27	North Carolina	46.6
46	North Dakota	14.0
11	Ohio	69.8
32	Oklahoma	37.6
30	Oregon	45.0
9	Pennsylvania	78.8
2	Rhode Island	91.7
21	South Carolina	56.9
48	South Dakota	10.2
25	Tennessee	48.4
19	Texas	59.5
28	Utah	46.3
45	Vermont	14.3
14	Virginia	62.4
22	Washington	53.5
38	West Virginia	31.0
28	Wisconsin	46.3
49	Wyoming	8.0

RANK ORDER

RANK	STATE	PERCENT
1	New Jersey	100.0
2	Rhode Island	91.7
3	California	89.9
4	Massachusetts	86.6
5	Florida	84.8
6	New York	83.8
7	Maryland	82.4
8	Connecticut	81.8
9	Pennsylvania	78.8
10	Arizona	75.0
11	Ohio	69.8
12	Delaware	66.7
13	Illinois	64.5
14	Virginia	62.4
15	Louisiana	61.9
16	Michigan	60.9
17	Hawaii	60.0
17	Nevada	60.0
19	Texas	59.5
20	Indiana	58.6
21	South Carolina	56.9
22	Washington	53.5
23	Missouri	52.5
24	Alabama	51.8
25	Tennessee	48.4
26	Colorado	47.8
27	North Carolina	46.6
28	Utah	46.3
28	Wisconsin	46.3
30	Oregon	45.0
31	Georgia	43.6
32	Oklahoma	37.6
33	New Mexico	36.1
34	New Hampshire	35.7
35	Minnesota	33.1
36	Arkansas	32.9
37	Kentucky	32.1
38	West Virginia	31.0
39	Maine	23.7
40	Mississippi	19.8
41	Kansas	18.6
42	Iowa	18.1
43	Idaho	16.7
44	Nebraska	15.1
45	Vermont	14.3
46	North Dakota	14.0
47	Alaska	11.8
48	South Dakota	10.2
49	Wyoming	8.0
50	Montana	5.7

| | District of Columbia | 100.0 |

Source: Morgan Quitno Press using data from American Hospital Association (Chicago, IL)
    "Hospital Statistics" (2000 edition)

*Community hospitals are all nonfederal, short-term, general and special hospitals whose facilities and services are available to the public. Urban is defined as any area inside a metropolitan statistical area as defined by the U.S. Office of Management and Budget.

Community Hospitals in Rural Areas in 1998

National Total = 2,199 Hospitals*

ALPHA ORDER

RANK	STATE	HOSPITALS	% of USA
17	Alabama	53	2.4%
41	Alaska	15	0.7%
40	Arizona	16	0.7%
16	Arkansas	55	2.5%
24	California	41	1.9%
28	Colorado	36	1.6%
47	Connecticut	6	0.3%
48	Delaware	2	0.1%
33	Florida	31	1.4%
5	Georgia	88	4.0%
45	Hawaii	8	0.4%
30	Idaho	35	1.6%
8	Illinois	72	3.3%
21	Indiana	46	2.1%
3	Iowa	95	4.3%
2	Kansas	105	4.8%
8	Kentucky	72	3.3%
20	Louisiana	48	2.2%
34	Maine	29	1.3%
44	Maryland	9	0.4%
43	Massachusetts	11	0.5%
14	Michigan	59	2.7%
4	Minnesota	91	4.1%
6	Mississippi	77	3.5%
15	Missouri	58	2.6%
19	Montana	50	2.3%
7	Nebraska	73	3.3%
45	Nevada	8	0.4%
39	New Hampshire	18	0.8%
50	New Jersey	0	0.0%
36	New Mexico	23	1.0%
28	New York	36	1.6%
13	North Carolina	62	2.8%
27	North Dakota	37	1.7%
18	Ohio	52	2.4%
10	Oklahoma	68	3.1%
32	Oregon	33	1.5%
22	Pennsylvania	45	2.0%
49	Rhode Island	1	0.0%
35	South Carolina	28	1.3%
23	South Dakota	44	2.0%
12	Tennessee	63	2.9%
1	Texas	162	7.4%
38	Utah	22	1.0%
42	Vermont	12	0.5%
30	Virginia	35	1.6%
25	Washington	40	1.8%
25	West Virginia	40	1.8%
11	Wisconsin	66	3.0%
36	Wyoming	23	1.0%

RANK ORDER

RANK	STATE	HOSPITALS	% of USA
1	Texas	162	7.4%
2	Kansas	105	4.8%
3	Iowa	95	4.3%
4	Minnesota	91	4.1%
5	Georgia	88	4.0%
6	Mississippi	77	3.5%
7	Nebraska	73	3.3%
8	Illinois	72	3.3%
8	Kentucky	72	3.3%
10	Oklahoma	68	3.1%
11	Wisconsin	66	3.0%
12	Tennessee	63	2.9%
13	North Carolina	62	2.8%
14	Michigan	59	2.7%
15	Missouri	58	2.6%
16	Arkansas	55	2.5%
17	Alabama	53	2.4%
18	Ohio	52	2.4%
19	Montana	50	2.3%
20	Louisiana	48	2.2%
21	Indiana	46	2.1%
22	Pennsylvania	45	2.0%
23	South Dakota	44	2.0%
24	California	41	1.9%
25	Washington	40	1.8%
25	West Virginia	40	1.8%
27	North Dakota	37	1.7%
28	Colorado	36	1.6%
28	New York	36	1.6%
30	Idaho	35	1.6%
30	Virginia	35	1.6%
32	Oregon	33	1.5%
33	Florida	31	1.4%
34	Maine	29	1.3%
35	South Carolina	28	1.3%
36	New Mexico	23	1.0%
36	Wyoming	23	1.0%
38	Utah	22	1.0%
39	New Hampshire	18	0.8%
40	Arizona	16	0.7%
41	Alaska	15	0.7%
42	Vermont	12	0.5%
43	Massachusetts	11	0.5%
44	Maryland	9	0.4%
45	Hawaii	8	0.4%
45	Nevada	8	0.4%
47	Connecticut	6	0.3%
48	Delaware	2	0.1%
49	Rhode Island	1	0.0%
50	New Jersey	0	0.0%
	District of Columbia	0	0.0%

Source: American Hospital Association (Chicago, IL)
"Hospital Statistics" (2000 edition)

Community hospitals are all nonfederal, short-term, general and special hospitals whose facilities and services are available to the public. Rural is defined as any area outside a metropolitan statistical area as defined by the U.S. Office of Management and Budget.

Percent of Community Hospitals in Rural Areas in 1998

National Percent = 43.8% of Community Hospitals*

ALPHA ORDER				RANK ORDER		
RANK	STATE	PERCENT		RANK	STATE	PERCENT
27	Alabama	48.2		1	Montana	94.3
4	Alaska	88.2		2	Wyoming	92.0
41	Arizona	25.0		3	South Dakota	89.8
15	Arkansas	67.1		4	Alaska	88.2
48	California	10.1		5	North Dakota	86.0
25	Colorado	52.2		6	Vermont	85.7
43	Connecticut	18.2		7	Nebraska	84.9
39	Delaware	33.3		8	Idaho	83.3
46	Florida	15.2		9	Iowa	81.9
20	Georgia	56.4		10	Kansas	81.4
33	Hawaii	40.0		11	Mississippi	80.2
8	Idaho	83.3		12	Maine	76.3
38	Illinois	35.5		13	West Virginia	69.0
31	Indiana	41.4		14	Kentucky	67.9
9	Iowa	81.9		15	Arkansas	67.1
10	Kansas	81.4		16	Minnesota	66.9
14	Kentucky	67.9		17	New Hampshire	64.3
36	Louisiana	38.1		18	New Mexico	63.9
12	Maine	76.3		19	Oklahoma	62.4
44	Maryland	17.6		20	Georgia	56.4
47	Massachusetts	13.4		21	Oregon	55.0
35	Michigan	39.1		22	Utah	53.7
16	Minnesota	66.9		22	Wisconsin	53.7
11	Mississippi	80.2		24	North Carolina	53.4
28	Missouri	47.5		25	Colorado	52.2
1	Montana	94.3		26	Tennessee	51.6
7	Nebraska	84.9		27	Alabama	48.2
33	Nevada	40.0		28	Missouri	47.5
17	New Hampshire	64.3		29	Washington	46.5
50	New Jersey	0.0		30	South Carolina	43.1
18	New Mexico	63.9		31	Indiana	41.4
45	New York	16.2		32	Texas	40.5
24	North Carolina	53.4		33	Hawaii	40.0
5	North Dakota	86.0		33	Nevada	40.0
40	Ohio	30.2		35	Michigan	39.1
19	Oklahoma	62.4		36	Louisiana	38.1
21	Oregon	55.0		37	Virginia	37.6
42	Pennsylvania	21.2		38	Illinois	35.5
49	Rhode Island	8.3		39	Delaware	33.3
30	South Carolina	43.1		40	Ohio	30.2
3	South Dakota	89.8		41	Arizona	25.0
26	Tennessee	51.6		42	Pennsylvania	21.2
32	Texas	40.5		43	Connecticut	18.2
22	Utah	53.7		44	Maryland	17.6
6	Vermont	85.7		45	New York	16.2
37	Virginia	37.6		46	Florida	15.2
29	Washington	46.5		47	Massachusetts	13.4
13	West Virginia	69.0		48	California	10.1
22	Wisconsin	53.7		49	Rhode Island	8.3
2	Wyoming	92.0		50	New Jersey	0.0
					District of Columbia	0.0

Source: Morgan Quitno Press using data from American Hospital Association (Chicago, IL)
    "Hospital Statistics" (2000 edition)
*Community hospitals are all nonfederal, short-term, general and special hospitals whose facilities and services are available to the public. Rural is defined as any area outside a metropolitan statistical area as defined by the U.S. Office of Management and Budget.

Nongovernment Not-For-Profit Hospitals in 1998

National Total = 3,026 Hospitals*

ALPHA ORDER

RANK	STATE	HOSPITALS	% of USA
32	Alabama	38	1.3%
47	Alaska	8	0.3%
24	Arizona	43	1.4%
23	Arkansas	48	1.6%
1	California	226	7.5%
35	Colorado	32	1.1%
36	Connecticut	31	1.0%
48	Delaware	6	0.2%
9	Florida	90	3.0%
17	Georgia	58	1.9%
44	Hawaii	13	0.4%
44	Idaho	13	0.4%
4	Illinois	158	5.2%
20	Indiana	55	1.8%
21	Iowa	54	1.8%
19	Kansas	57	1.9%
12	Kentucky	73	2.4%
37	Louisiana	30	1.0%
33	Maine	34	1.1%
22	Maryland	49	1.6%
13	Massachusetts	72	2.4%
7	Michigan	128	4.2%
10	Minnesota	88	2.9%
38	Mississippi	29	1.0%
15	Missouri	71	2.3%
24	Montana	43	1.4%
24	Nebraska	43	1.4%
48	Nevada	6	0.2%
39	New Hampshire	24	0.8%
11	New Jersey	78	2.6%
42	New Mexico	18	0.6%
3	New York	189	6.2%
13	North Carolina	72	2.4%
29	North Dakota	41	1.4%
5	Ohio	139	4.6%
29	Oklahoma	41	1.4%
29	Oregon	41	1.4%
2	Pennsylvania	203	6.7%
46	Rhode Island	12	0.4%
40	South Carolina	20	0.7%
27	South Dakota	42	1.4%
17	Tennessee	58	1.9%
6	Texas	138	4.6%
40	Utah	20	0.7%
43	Vermont	14	0.5%
16	Virginia	70	2.3%
27	Washington	42	1.4%
34	West Virginia	33	1.1%
8	Wisconsin	120	4.0%
48	Wyoming	6	0.2%

RANK ORDER

RANK	STATE	HOSPITALS	% of USA
1	California	226	7.5%
2	Pennsylvania	203	6.7%
3	New York	189	6.2%
4	Illinois	158	5.2%
5	Ohio	139	4.6%
6	Texas	138	4.6%
7	Michigan	128	4.2%
8	Wisconsin	120	4.0%
9	Florida	90	3.0%
10	Minnesota	88	2.9%
11	New Jersey	78	2.6%
12	Kentucky	73	2.4%
13	Massachusetts	72	2.4%
13	North Carolina	72	2.4%
15	Missouri	71	2.3%
16	Virginia	70	2.3%
17	Georgia	58	1.9%
17	Tennessee	58	1.9%
19	Kansas	57	1.9%
20	Indiana	55	1.8%
21	Iowa	54	1.8%
22	Maryland	49	1.6%
23	Arkansas	48	1.6%
24	Arizona	43	1.4%
24	Montana	43	1.4%
24	Nebraska	43	1.4%
27	South Dakota	42	1.4%
27	Washington	42	1.4%
29	North Dakota	41	1.4%
29	Oklahoma	41	1.4%
29	Oregon	41	1.4%
32	Alabama	38	1.3%
33	Maine	34	1.1%
34	West Virginia	33	1.1%
35	Colorado	32	1.1%
36	Connecticut	31	1.0%
37	Louisiana	30	1.0%
38	Mississippi	29	1.0%
39	New Hampshire	24	0.8%
40	South Carolina	20	0.7%
40	Utah	20	0.7%
42	New Mexico	18	0.6%
43	Vermont	14	0.5%
44	Hawaii	13	0.4%
44	Idaho	13	0.4%
46	Rhode Island	12	0.4%
47	Alaska	8	0.3%
48	Delaware	6	0.2%
48	Nevada	6	0.2%
48	Wyoming	6	0.2%
	District of Columbia	9	0.3%

Source: American Hospital Association (Chicago, IL)
     "Hospital Statistics" (2000 edition)
*Nongovernment not-for-profit hospitals are a subset of community hospitals.

Investor-Owned (For-Profit) Hospitals in 1998

National Total = 771 Hospitals*

ALPHA ORDER

RANK	STATE	HOSPITALS	% of USA
7	Alabama	28	3.6%
39	Alaska	1	0.1%
14	Arizona	16	2.1%
11	Arkansas	19	2.5%
2	California	103	13.4%
21	Colorado	10	1.3%
44	Connecticut	0	0.0%
44	Delaware	0	0.0%
3	Florida	93	12.1%
5	Georgia	38	4.9%
39	Hawaii	1	0.1%
31	Idaho	3	0.4%
17	Illinois	14	1.8%
19	Indiana	11	1.4%
39	Iowa	1	0.1%
25	Kansas	7	0.9%
9	Kentucky	20	2.6%
4	Louisiana	39	5.1%
39	Maine	1	0.1%
33	Maryland	2	0.3%
27	Massachusetts	6	0.8%
33	Michigan	2	0.3%
44	Minnesota	0	0.0%
9	Mississippi	20	2.6%
15	Missouri	15	1.9%
44	Montana	0	0.0%
33	Nebraska	2	0.3%
25	Nevada	7	0.9%
29	New Hampshire	4	0.5%
33	New Jersey	2	0.3%
27	New Mexico	6	0.8%
23	New York	9	1.2%
19	North Carolina	11	1.4%
33	North Dakota	2	0.3%
21	Ohio	10	1.3%
11	Oklahoma	19	2.5%
29	Oregon	4	0.5%
24	Pennsylvania	8	1.0%
44	Rhode Island	0	0.0%
8	South Carolina	21	2.7%
44	South Dakota	0	0.0%
6	Tennessee	34	4.4%
1	Texas	129	16.7%
18	Utah	12	1.6%
44	Vermont	0	0.0%
13	Virginia	18	2.3%
31	Washington	3	0.4%
15	West Virginia	15	1.9%
39	Wisconsin	1	0.1%
33	Wyoming	2	0.3%

RANK ORDER

RANK	STATE	HOSPITALS	% of USA
1	Texas	129	16.7%
2	California	103	13.4%
3	Florida	93	12.1%
4	Louisiana	39	5.1%
5	Georgia	38	4.9%
6	Tennessee	34	4.4%
7	Alabama	28	3.6%
8	South Carolina	21	2.7%
9	Kentucky	20	2.6%
9	Mississippi	20	2.6%
11	Arkansas	19	2.5%
11	Oklahoma	19	2.5%
13	Virginia	18	2.3%
14	Arizona	16	2.1%
15	Missouri	15	1.9%
15	West Virginia	15	1.9%
17	Illinois	14	1.8%
18	Utah	12	1.6%
19	Indiana	11	1.4%
19	North Carolina	11	1.4%
21	Colorado	10	1.3%
21	Ohio	10	1.3%
23	New York	9	1.2%
24	Pennsylvania	8	1.0%
25	Kansas	7	0.9%
25	Nevada	7	0.9%
27	Massachusetts	6	0.8%
27	New Mexico	6	0.8%
29	New Hampshire	4	0.5%
29	Oregon	4	0.5%
31	Idaho	3	0.4%
31	Washington	3	0.4%
33	Maryland	2	0.3%
33	Michigan	2	0.3%
33	Nebraska	2	0.3%
33	New Jersey	2	0.3%
33	North Dakota	2	0.3%
33	Wyoming	2	0.3%
39	Alaska	1	0.1%
39	Hawaii	1	0.1%
39	Iowa	1	0.1%
39	Maine	1	0.1%
39	Wisconsin	1	0.1%
44	Connecticut	0	0.0%
44	Delaware	0	0.0%
44	Minnesota	0	0.0%
44	Montana	0	0.0%
44	Rhode Island	0	0.0%
44	South Dakota	0	0.0%
44	Vermont	0	0.0%
	District of Columbia	2	0.3%

Source: American Hospital Association (Chicago, IL)
    "Hospital Statistics" (2000 edition)
*Investor-owned (for-profit) hospitals are a subset of community hospitals.

State and Local Government-Owned Hospitals in 1998

National Total = 1,218 Hospitals*

ALPHA ORDER

RANK	STATE	HOSPITALS	% of USA
11	Alabama	44	3.6%
33	Alaska	8	0.7%
37	Arizona	5	0.4%
26	Arkansas	15	1.2%
2	California	76	6.2%
18	Colorado	27	2.2%
42	Connecticut	2	0.2%
45	Delaware	0	0.0%
23	Florida	21	1.7%
5	Georgia	60	4.9%
36	Hawaii	6	0.5%
19	Idaho	26	2.1%
16	Illinois	31	2.5%
10	Indiana	45	3.7%
4	Iowa	61	5.0%
3	Kansas	65	5.3%
28	Kentucky	13	1.1%
6	Louisiana	57	4.7%
40	Maine	3	0.2%
45	Maryland	0	0.0%
39	Massachusetts	4	0.3%
23	Michigan	21	1.7%
8	Minnesota	48	3.9%
9	Mississippi	47	3.9%
14	Missouri	36	3.0%
30	Montana	10	0.8%
12	Nebraska	41	3.4%
34	Nevada	7	0.6%
45	New Hampshire	0	0.0%
40	New Jersey	3	0.2%
29	New Mexico	12	1.0%
20	New York	24	2.0%
15	North Carolina	33	2.7%
45	North Dakota	0	0.0%
22	Ohio	23	1.9%
7	Oklahoma	49	4.0%
26	Oregon	15	1.2%
44	Pennsylvania	1	0.1%
45	Rhode Island	0	0.0%
20	South Carolina	24	2.0%
34	South Dakota	7	0.6%
17	Tennessee	30	2.5%
1	Texas	133	10.9%
32	Utah	9	0.7%
45	Vermont	0	0.0%
37	Virginia	5	0.4%
12	Washington	41	3.4%
30	West Virginia	10	0.8%
42	Wisconsin	2	0.2%
25	Wyoming	17	1.4%

RANK ORDER

RANK	STATE	HOSPITALS	% of USA
1	Texas	133	10.9%
2	California	76	6.2%
3	Kansas	65	5.3%
4	Iowa	61	5.0%
5	Georgia	60	4.9%
6	Louisiana	57	4.7%
7	Oklahoma	49	4.0%
8	Minnesota	48	3.9%
9	Mississippi	47	3.9%
10	Indiana	45	3.7%
11	Alabama	44	3.6%
12	Nebraska	41	3.4%
12	Washington	41	3.4%
14	Missouri	36	3.0%
15	North Carolina	33	2.7%
16	Illinois	31	2.5%
17	Tennessee	30	2.5%
18	Colorado	27	2.2%
19	Idaho	26	2.1%
20	New York	24	2.0%
20	South Carolina	24	2.0%
22	Ohio	23	1.9%
23	Florida	21	1.7%
23	Michigan	21	1.7%
25	Wyoming	17	1.4%
26	Arkansas	15	1.2%
26	Oregon	15	1.2%
28	Kentucky	13	1.1%
29	New Mexico	12	1.0%
30	Montana	10	0.8%
30	West Virginia	10	0.8%
32	Utah	9	0.7%
33	Alaska	8	0.7%
34	Nevada	7	0.6%
34	South Dakota	7	0.6%
36	Hawaii	6	0.5%
37	Arizona	5	0.4%
37	Virginia	5	0.4%
39	Massachusetts	4	0.3%
40	Maine	3	0.2%
40	New Jersey	3	0.2%
42	Connecticut	2	0.2%
42	Wisconsin	2	0.2%
44	Pennsylvania	1	0.1%
45	Delaware	0	0.0%
45	Maryland	0	0.0%
45	New Hampshire	0	0.0%
45	North Dakota	0	0.0%
45	Rhode Island	0	0.0%
45	Vermont	0	0.0%
	District of Columbia	1	0.1%

Source: American Hospital Association (Chicago, IL)
     "Hospital Statistics" (2000 edition)
*State and local government-owned hospitals are a subset of community hospitals.

Beds in Community Hospitals in 1998

National Total = 839,988 Beds*

RANK	STATE	BEDS	% of USA
17	Alabama	16,998	2.0%
50	Alaska	1,240	0.1%
28	Arizona	10,857	1.3%
30	Arkansas	9,876	1.2%
1	California	74,482	8.9%
31	Colorado	9,179	1.1%
34	Connecticut	6,949	0.8%
47	Delaware	1,977	0.2%
4	Florida	49,231	5.9%
10	Georgia	25,236	3.0%
45	Hawaii	2,791	0.3%
43	Idaho	3,414	0.4%
6	Illinois	39,218	4.7%
14	Indiana	19,401	2.3%
24	Iowa	12,219	1.5%
27	Kansas	10,923	1.3%
21	Kentucky	15,240	1.8%
16	Louisiana	17,820	2.1%
40	Maine	3,768	0.4%
23	Maryland	12,670	1.5%
19	Massachusetts	16,493	2.0%
8	Michigan	27,168	3.2%
20	Minnesota	16,486	2.0%
22	Mississippi	13,005	1.5%
12	Missouri	20,685	2.5%
36	Montana	4,413	0.5%
32	Nebraska	8,133	1.0%
41	Nevada	3,528	0.4%
44	New Hampshire	2,841	0.3%
9	New Jersey	26,353	3.1%
42	New Mexico	3,489	0.4%
2	New York	68,511	8.2%
11	North Carolina	23,297	2.8%
39	North Dakota	3,978	0.5%
7	Ohio	35,187	4.2%
26	Oklahoma	11,022	1.3%
35	Oregon	6,809	0.8%
5	Pennsylvania	44,739	5.3%
46	Rhode Island	2,581	0.3%
25	South Carolina	11,518	1.4%
37	South Dakota	4,401	0.5%
13	Tennessee	20,682	2.5%
3	Texas	56,573	6.7%
38	Utah	4,010	0.5%
49	Vermont	1,671	0.2%
15	Virginia	17,890	2.1%
29	Washington	10,739	1.3%
33	West Virginia	8,117	1.0%
18	Wisconsin	16,693	2.0%
48	Wyoming	1,935	0.2%

RANK ORDER

RANK	STATE	BEDS	% of USA
1	California	74,482	8.9%
2	New York	68,511	8.2%
3	Texas	56,573	6.7%
4	Florida	49,231	5.9%
5	Pennsylvania	44,739	5.3%
6	Illinois	39,218	4.7%
7	Ohio	35,187	4.2%
8	Michigan	27,168	3.2%
9	New Jersey	26,353	3.1%
10	Georgia	25,236	3.0%
11	North Carolina	23,297	2.8%
12	Missouri	20,685	2.5%
13	Tennessee	20,682	2.5%
14	Indiana	19,401	2.3%
15	Virginia	17,890	2.1%
16	Louisiana	17,820	2.1%
17	Alabama	16,998	2.0%
18	Wisconsin	16,693	2.0%
19	Massachusetts	16,493	2.0%
20	Minnesota	16,486	2.0%
21	Kentucky	15,240	1.8%
22	Mississippi	13,005	1.5%
23	Maryland	12,670	1.5%
24	Iowa	12,219	1.5%
25	South Carolina	11,518	1.4%
26	Oklahoma	11,022	1.3%
27	Kansas	10,923	1.3%
28	Arizona	10,857	1.3%
29	Washington	10,739	1.3%
30	Arkansas	9,876	1.2%
31	Colorado	9,179	1.1%
32	Nebraska	8,133	1.0%
33	West Virginia	8,117	1.0%
34	Connecticut	6,949	0.8%
35	Oregon	6,809	0.8%
36	Montana	4,413	0.5%
37	South Dakota	4,401	0.5%
38	Utah	4,010	0.5%
39	North Dakota	3,978	0.5%
40	Maine	3,768	0.4%
41	Nevada	3,528	0.4%
42	New Mexico	3,489	0.4%
43	Idaho	3,414	0.4%
44	New Hampshire	2,841	0.3%
45	Hawaii	2,791	0.3%
46	Rhode Island	2,581	0.3%
47	Delaware	1,977	0.2%
48	Wyoming	1,935	0.2%
49	Vermont	1,671	0.2%
50	Alaska	1,240	0.1%
	District of Columbia	3,552	0.4%

ALPHA ORDER

Source: American Hospital Association (Chicago, IL)
"Hospital Statistics" (2000 edition)
*All nonfederal short-term general and other special hospitals, whose facilities and services are available to the public. Includes beds in hospital and nursing home units.

Rate of Beds in Community Hospitals in 1998

National Rate = 311 Beds per 100,000 Population*

<table>
<tr><td colspan="3">ALPHA ORDER</td><td colspan="3">RANK ORDER</td></tr>
<tr><th>RANK</th><th>STATE</th><th>RATE</th><th>RANK</th><th>STATE</th><th>RATE</th></tr>
<tr><td>11</td><td>Alabama</td><td>391</td><td>1</td><td>North Dakota</td><td>624</td></tr>
<tr><td>46</td><td>Alaska</td><td>202</td><td>2</td><td>South Dakota</td><td>602</td></tr>
<tr><td>41</td><td>Arizona</td><td>233</td><td>3</td><td>Montana</td><td>502</td></tr>
<tr><td>12</td><td>Arkansas</td><td>389</td><td>4</td><td>Nebraska</td><td>490</td></tr>
<tr><td>43</td><td>California</td><td>228</td><td>5</td><td>Mississippi</td><td>473</td></tr>
<tr><td>42</td><td>Colorado</td><td>231</td><td>6</td><td>West Virginia</td><td>448</td></tr>
<tr><td>44</td><td>Connecticut</td><td>212</td><td>7</td><td>Iowa</td><td>427</td></tr>
<tr><td>35</td><td>Delaware</td><td>266</td><td>8</td><td>Kansas</td><td>414</td></tr>
<tr><td>19</td><td>Florida</td><td>330</td><td>9</td><td>Louisiana</td><td>408</td></tr>
<tr><td>19</td><td>Georgia</td><td>330</td><td>10</td><td>Wyoming</td><td>403</td></tr>
<tr><td>40</td><td>Hawaii</td><td>234</td><td>11</td><td>Alabama</td><td>391</td></tr>
<tr><td>32</td><td>Idaho</td><td>277</td><td>12</td><td>Arkansas</td><td>389</td></tr>
<tr><td>24</td><td>Illinois</td><td>325</td><td>13</td><td>Kentucky</td><td>387</td></tr>
<tr><td>22</td><td>Indiana</td><td>328</td><td>14</td><td>Tennessee</td><td>381</td></tr>
<tr><td>7</td><td>Iowa</td><td>427</td><td>15</td><td>Missouri</td><td>380</td></tr>
<tr><td>8</td><td>Kansas</td><td>414</td><td>16</td><td>New York</td><td>377</td></tr>
<tr><td>13</td><td>Kentucky</td><td>387</td><td>17</td><td>Pennsylvania</td><td>373</td></tr>
<tr><td>9</td><td>Louisiana</td><td>408</td><td>18</td><td>Minnesota</td><td>349</td></tr>
<tr><td>28</td><td>Maine</td><td>302</td><td>19</td><td>Florida</td><td>330</td></tr>
<tr><td>38</td><td>Maryland</td><td>247</td><td>19</td><td>Georgia</td><td>330</td></tr>
<tr><td>34</td><td>Massachusetts</td><td>268</td><td>19</td><td>Oklahoma</td><td>330</td></tr>
<tr><td>32</td><td>Michigan</td><td>277</td><td>22</td><td>Indiana</td><td>328</td></tr>
<tr><td>18</td><td>Minnesota</td><td>349</td><td>23</td><td>New Jersey</td><td>326</td></tr>
<tr><td>5</td><td>Mississippi</td><td>473</td><td>24</td><td>Illinois</td><td>325</td></tr>
<tr><td>15</td><td>Missouri</td><td>380</td><td>25</td><td>Wisconsin</td><td>320</td></tr>
<tr><td>3</td><td>Montana</td><td>502</td><td>26</td><td>Ohio</td><td>313</td></tr>
<tr><td>4</td><td>Nebraska</td><td>490</td><td>27</td><td>North Carolina</td><td>309</td></tr>
<tr><td>46</td><td>Nevada</td><td>202</td><td>28</td><td>Maine</td><td>302</td></tr>
<tr><td>39</td><td>New Hampshire</td><td>240</td><td>29</td><td>South Carolina</td><td>300</td></tr>
<tr><td>23</td><td>New Jersey</td><td>326</td><td>30</td><td>Texas</td><td>287</td></tr>
<tr><td>48</td><td>New Mexico</td><td>201</td><td>31</td><td>Vermont</td><td>283</td></tr>
<tr><td>16</td><td>New York</td><td>377</td><td>32</td><td>Idaho</td><td>277</td></tr>
<tr><td>27</td><td>North Carolina</td><td>309</td><td>32</td><td>Michigan</td><td>277</td></tr>
<tr><td>1</td><td>North Dakota</td><td>624</td><td>34</td><td>Massachusetts</td><td>268</td></tr>
<tr><td>26</td><td>Ohio</td><td>313</td><td>35</td><td>Delaware</td><td>266</td></tr>
<tr><td>19</td><td>Oklahoma</td><td>330</td><td>36</td><td>Virginia</td><td>264</td></tr>
<tr><td>45</td><td>Oregon</td><td>207</td><td>37</td><td>Rhode Island</td><td>261</td></tr>
<tr><td>17</td><td>Pennsylvania</td><td>373</td><td>38</td><td>Maryland</td><td>247</td></tr>
<tr><td>37</td><td>Rhode Island</td><td>261</td><td>39</td><td>New Hampshire</td><td>240</td></tr>
<tr><td>29</td><td>South Carolina</td><td>300</td><td>40</td><td>Hawaii</td><td>234</td></tr>
<tr><td>2</td><td>South Dakota</td><td>602</td><td>41</td><td>Arizona</td><td>233</td></tr>
<tr><td>14</td><td>Tennessee</td><td>381</td><td>42</td><td>Colorado</td><td>231</td></tr>
<tr><td>30</td><td>Texas</td><td>287</td><td>43</td><td>California</td><td>228</td></tr>
<tr><td>49</td><td>Utah</td><td>191</td><td>44</td><td>Connecticut</td><td>212</td></tr>
<tr><td>31</td><td>Vermont</td><td>283</td><td>45</td><td>Oregon</td><td>207</td></tr>
<tr><td>36</td><td>Virginia</td><td>264</td><td>46</td><td>Alaska</td><td>202</td></tr>
<tr><td>50</td><td>Washington</td><td>189</td><td>46</td><td>Nevada</td><td>202</td></tr>
<tr><td>6</td><td>West Virginia</td><td>448</td><td>48</td><td>New Mexico</td><td>201</td></tr>
<tr><td>25</td><td>Wisconsin</td><td>320</td><td>49</td><td>Utah</td><td>191</td></tr>
<tr><td>10</td><td>Wyoming</td><td>403</td><td>50</td><td>Washington</td><td>189</td></tr>
<tr><td></td><td></td><td></td><td></td><td>District of Columbia</td><td>681</td></tr>
</table>

Source: Morgan Quitno Press using data from American Hospital Association (Chicago, IL)
    "Hospital Statistics" (2000 edition)
*All nonfederal short-term general and other special hospitals, whose facilities and services are available to the public. Includes beds in hospital and nursing home units.

Average Number of Beds per Community Hospital in 1998

National Average = 167 Beds per Community Hospital*

ALPHA ORDER

RANK	STATE	BEDS
23	Alabama	155
50	Alaska	73
19	Arizona	170
34	Arkansas	120
14	California	184
31	Colorado	133
7	Connecticut	211
1	Delaware	330
5	Florida	241
22	Georgia	162
27	Hawaii	140
48	Idaho	81
12	Illinois	193
18	Indiana	175
37	Iowa	105
46	Kansas	85
24	Kentucky	144
25	Louisiana	141
40	Maine	99
4	Maryland	248
10	Massachusetts	201
15	Michigan	180
33	Minnesota	121
30	Mississippi	135
19	Missouri	170
47	Montana	83
43	Nebraska	95
17	Nevada	176
38	New Hampshire	101
2	New Jersey	318
42	New Mexico	97
3	New York	309
10	North Carolina	201
44	North Dakota	93
9	Ohio	205
38	Oklahoma	101
36	Oregon	113
7	Pennsylvania	211
6	Rhode Island	215
16	South Carolina	177
45	South Dakota	90
19	Tennessee	170
25	Texas	141
41	Utah	98
35	Vermont	119
13	Virginia	192
32	Washington	125
27	West Virginia	140
29	Wisconsin	136
49	Wyoming	77

RANK ORDER

RANK	STATE	BEDS
1	Delaware	330
2	New Jersey	318
3	New York	309
4	Maryland	248
5	Florida	241
6	Rhode Island	215
7	Connecticut	211
7	Pennsylvania	211
9	Ohio	205
10	Massachusetts	201
10	North Carolina	201
12	Illinois	193
13	Virginia	192
14	California	184
15	Michigan	180
16	South Carolina	177
17	Nevada	176
18	Indiana	175
19	Arizona	170
19	Missouri	170
19	Tennessee	170
22	Georgia	162
23	Alabama	155
24	Kentucky	144
25	Louisiana	141
25	Texas	141
27	Hawaii	140
27	West Virginia	140
29	Wisconsin	136
30	Mississippi	135
31	Colorado	133
32	Washington	125
33	Minnesota	121
34	Arkansas	120
35	Vermont	119
36	Oregon	113
37	Iowa	105
38	New Hampshire	101
38	Oklahoma	101
40	Maine	99
41	Utah	98
42	New Mexico	97
43	Nebraska	95
44	North Dakota	93
45	South Dakota	90
46	Kansas	85
47	Montana	83
48	Idaho	81
49	Wyoming	77
50	Alaska	73
	District of Columbia	296

*Source: Morgan Quitno Press using data from American Hospital Association (Chicago, IL)
"Hospital Statistics" (2000 edition)*

All nonfederal short-term general and other special hospitals, whose facilities and services are available to the public. Includes beds in hospital and nursing home units.

Admissions to Community Hospitals in 1998

National Total = 31,811,673 Admissions*

ALPHA ORDER

RANK	STATE	ADMISSIONS	% of USA
17	Alabama	644,283	2.0%
50	Alaska	41,294	0.1%
23	Arizona	495,155	1.6%
30	Arkansas	358,068	1.1%
1	California	3,170,435	10.0%
29	Colorado	373,257	1.2%
31	Connecticut	330,091	1.0%
47	Delaware	84,319	0.3%
4	Florida	1,947,024	6.1%
11	Georgia	821,895	2.6%
43	Hawaii	97,717	0.3%
41	Idaho	115,248	0.4%
6	Illinois	1,466,273	4.6%
16	Indiana	704,396	2.2%
28	Iowa	374,245	1.2%
33	Kansas	299,701	0.9%
21	Kentucky	551,325	1.7%
18	Louisiana	637,892	2.0%
39	Maine	144,363	0.5%
19	Maryland	564,913	1.8%
14	Massachusetts	738,018	2.3%
8	Michigan	1,104,883	3.5%
22	Minnesota	515,813	1.6%
26	Mississippi	413,907	1.3%
13	Missouri	741,816	2.3%
44	Montana	97,345	0.3%
36	Nebraska	192,313	0.6%
37	Nevada	171,158	0.5%
42	New Hampshire	108,942	0.3%
9	New Jersey	1,082,668	3.4%
38	New Mexico	157,875	0.5%
2	New York	2,364,608	7.4%
10	North Carolina	907,911	2.9%
46	North Dakota	85,176	0.3%
7	Ohio	1,355,186	4.3%
27	Oklahoma	391,243	1.2%
32	Oregon	313,350	1.0%
5	Pennsylvania	1,752,298	5.5%
40	Rhode Island	117,320	0.4%
25	South Carolina	457,347	1.4%
45	South Dakota	96,055	0.3%
12	Tennessee	744,913	2.3%
3	Texas	2,227,166	7.0%
35	Utah	192,357	0.6%
48	Vermont	50,076	0.2%
15	Virginia	716,976	2.3%
24	Washington	474,394	1.5%
34	West Virginia	280,729	0.9%
20	Wisconsin	553,810	1.7%
49	Wyoming	43,833	0.1%

RANK ORDER

RANK	STATE	ADMISSIONS	% of USA
1	California	3,170,435	10.0%
2	New York	2,364,608	7.4%
3	Texas	2,227,166	7.0%
4	Florida	1,947,024	6.1%
5	Pennsylvania	1,752,298	5.5%
6	Illinois	1,466,273	4.6%
7	Ohio	1,355,186	4.3%
8	Michigan	1,104,883	3.5%
9	New Jersey	1,082,668	3.4%
10	North Carolina	907,911	2.9%
11	Georgia	821,895	2.6%
12	Tennessee	744,913	2.3%
13	Missouri	741,816	2.3%
14	Massachusetts	738,018	2.3%
15	Virginia	716,976	2.3%
16	Indiana	704,396	2.2%
17	Alabama	644,283	2.0%
18	Louisiana	637,892	2.0%
19	Maryland	564,913	1.8%
20	Wisconsin	553,810	1.7%
21	Kentucky	551,325	1.7%
22	Minnesota	515,813	1.6%
23	Arizona	495,155	1.6%
24	Washington	474,394	1.5%
25	South Carolina	457,347	1.4%
26	Mississippi	413,907	1.3%
27	Oklahoma	391,243	1.2%
28	Iowa	374,245	1.2%
29	Colorado	373,257	1.2%
30	Arkansas	358,068	1.1%
31	Connecticut	330,091	1.0%
32	Oregon	313,350	1.0%
33	Kansas	299,701	0.9%
34	West Virginia	280,729	0.9%
35	Utah	192,357	0.6%
36	Nebraska	192,313	0.6%
37	Nevada	171,158	0.5%
38	New Mexico	157,875	0.5%
39	Maine	144,363	0.5%
40	Rhode Island	117,320	0.4%
41	Idaho	115,248	0.4%
42	New Hampshire	108,942	0.3%
43	Hawaii	97,717	0.3%
44	Montana	97,345	0.3%
45	South Dakota	96,055	0.3%
46	North Dakota	85,176	0.3%
47	Delaware	84,319	0.3%
48	Vermont	50,076	0.2%
49	Wyoming	43,833	0.1%
50	Alaska	41,294	0.1%
	District of Columbia	140,293	0.4%

Source: American Hospital Association (Chicago, IL)
"Hospital Statistics" (2000 edition)
*Admissions to all nonfederal short-term general and other special hospitals, whose facilities and services are available to the public. Includes admissions to hospital and nursing home units.

Inpatient Days in Community Hospitals in 1998

National Total = 191,430,450 Inpatient Days*

ALPHA ORDER					RANK ORDER			
RANK	STATE	DAYS	% of USA		RANK	STATE	DAYS	% of USA
18	Alabama	3,639,125	1.9%		1	New York	19,176,323	10.0%
50	Alaska	378,357	0.2%		2	California	16,658,170	8.7%
26	Arizona	2,407,367	1.3%		3	Texas	11,732,621	6.1%
30	Arkansas	2,108,469	1.1%		4	Pennsylvania	10,927,224	5.7%
2	California	16,658,170	8.7%		5	Florida	10,839,718	5.7%
31	Colorado	1,875,297	1.0%		6	Illinois	8,640,319	4.5%
34	Connecticut	1,758,052	0.9%		7	Ohio	7,289,259	3.8%
47	Delaware	508,870	0.3%		8	New Jersey	6,790,222	3.5%
5	Florida	10,839,718	5.7%		9	Michigan	6,380,260	3.3%
11	Georgia	5,471,839	2.9%		10	North Carolina	5,813,321	3.0%
42	Hawaii	776,392	0.4%		11	Georgia	5,471,839	2.9%
44	Idaho	697,744	0.4%		12	Missouri	4,325,879	2.3%
6	Illinois	8,640,319	4.5%		13	Tennessee	4,292,500	2.2%
17	Indiana	4,076,111	2.1%		14	Massachusetts	4,186,012	2.2%
25	Iowa	2,528,052	1.3%		15	Minnesota	4,110,360	2.1%
29	Kansas	2,148,493	1.1%		16	Virginia	4,090,018	2.1%
21	Kentucky	3,173,476	1.7%		17	Indiana	4,076,111	2.1%
19	Louisiana	3,564,901	1.9%		18	Alabama	3,639,125	1.9%
40	Maine	843,811	0.4%		19	Louisiana	3,564,901	1.9%
22	Maryland	3,144,315	1.6%		20	Wisconsin	3,442,860	1.8%
14	Massachusetts	4,186,012	2.2%		21	Kentucky	3,173,476	1.7%
9	Michigan	6,380,260	3.3%		22	Maryland	3,144,315	1.6%
15	Minnesota	4,110,360	2.1%		23	Mississippi	2,949,682	1.5%
23	Mississippi	2,949,682	1.5%		24	South Carolina	2,763,146	1.4%
12	Missouri	4,325,879	2.3%		25	Iowa	2,528,052	1.3%
36	Montana	1,090,989	0.6%		26	Arizona	2,407,367	1.3%
32	Nebraska	1,779,579	0.9%		27	Washington	2,295,333	1.2%
41	Nevada	837,270	0.4%		28	Oklahoma	2,169,379	1.1%
46	New Hampshire	658,884	0.3%		29	Kansas	2,148,493	1.1%
8	New Jersey	6,790,222	3.5%		30	Arkansas	2,108,469	1.1%
43	New Mexico	707,418	0.4%		31	Colorado	1,875,297	1.0%
1	New York	19,176,323	10.0%		32	Nebraska	1,779,579	0.9%
10	North Carolina	5,813,321	3.0%		33	West Virginia	1,778,264	0.9%
39	North Dakota	873,623	0.5%		34	Connecticut	1,758,052	0.9%
7	Ohio	7,289,259	3.8%		35	Oregon	1,401,720	0.7%
28	Oklahoma	2,169,379	1.1%		36	Montana	1,090,989	0.6%
35	Oregon	1,401,720	0.7%		37	South Dakota	1,032,566	0.5%
4	Pennsylvania	10,927,224	5.7%		38	Utah	885,746	0.5%
45	Rhode Island	659,966	0.3%		39	North Dakota	873,623	0.5%
24	South Carolina	2,763,146	1.4%		40	Maine	843,811	0.4%
37	South Dakota	1,032,566	0.5%		41	Nevada	837,270	0.4%
13	Tennessee	4,292,500	2.2%		42	Hawaii	776,392	0.4%
3	Texas	11,732,621	6.1%		43	New Mexico	707,418	0.4%
38	Utah	885,746	0.5%		44	Idaho	697,744	0.4%
48	Vermont	393,539	0.2%		45	Rhode Island	659,966	0.3%
16	Virginia	4,090,018	2.1%		46	New Hampshire	658,884	0.3%
27	Washington	2,295,333	1.2%		47	Delaware	508,870	0.3%
33	West Virginia	1,778,264	0.9%		48	Vermont	393,539	0.2%
20	Wisconsin	3,442,860	1.8%		49	Wyoming	380,351	0.2%
49	Wyoming	380,351	0.2%		50	Alaska	378,357	0.2%
						District of Columbia	977,258	0.5%

Source: American Hospital Association (Chicago, IL)
      "Hospital Statistics" (2000 edition)
Inpatient days in all nonfederal short-term general and other special hospitals, whose facilities and services are available to the public. Includes days in hospital and nursing home units.

Average Daily Census in Community Hospitals in 1998

National Average = 524,467 Inpatients*

ALPHA ORDER

RANK	STATE	INPATIENTS	% of USA
18	Alabama	9,970	1.9%
50	Alaska	1,037	0.2%
26	Arizona	6,596	1.3%
30	Arkansas	5,777	1.1%
2	California	45,639	8.7%
31	Colorado	5,138	1.0%
34	Connecticut	4,817	0.9%
47	Delaware	1,394	0.3%
5	Florida	29,698	5.7%
11	Georgia	14,991	2.9%
42	Hawaii	2,127	0.4%
44	Idaho	1,912	0.4%
6	Illinois	23,672	4.5%
17	Indiana	11,167	2.1%
25	Iowa	6,926	1.3%
29	Kansas	5,886	1.1%
21	Kentucky	8,694	1.7%
19	Louisiana	9,767	1.9%
40	Maine	2,312	0.4%
22	Maryland	8,615	1.6%
14	Massachusetts	11,469	2.2%
9	Michigan	17,480	3.3%
15	Minnesota	11,261	2.1%
23	Mississippi	8,081	1.5%
12	Missouri	11,852	2.3%
36	Montana	2,989	0.6%
32	Nebraska	4,876	0.9%
41	Nevada	2,294	0.4%
46	New Hampshire	1,805	0.3%
8	New Jersey	18,603	3.5%
43	New Mexico	1,938	0.4%
1	New York	52,538	10.0%
10	North Carolina	15,927	3.0%
39	North Dakota	2,393	0.5%
7	Ohio	19,971	3.8%
28	Oklahoma	5,944	1.1%
35	Oregon	3,840	0.7%
4	Pennsylvania	29,938	5.7%
45	Rhode Island	1,808	0.3%
24	South Carolina	7,570	1.4%
37	South Dakota	2,829	0.5%
13	Tennessee	11,760	2.2%
3	Texas	32,144	6.1%
38	Utah	2,427	0.5%
48	Vermont	1,078	0.2%
16	Virginia	11,206	2.1%
27	Washington	6,289	1.2%
33	West Virginia	4,872	0.9%
20	Wisconsin	9,432	1.8%
49	Wyoming	1,042	0.2%

RANK ORDER

RANK	STATE	INPATIENTS	% of USA
1	New York	52,538	10.0%
2	California	45,639	8.7%
3	Texas	32,144	6.1%
4	Pennsylvania	29,938	5.7%
5	Florida	29,698	5.7%
6	Illinois	23,672	4.5%
7	Ohio	19,971	3.8%
8	New Jersey	18,603	3.5%
9	Michigan	17,480	3.3%
10	North Carolina	15,927	3.0%
11	Georgia	14,991	2.9%
12	Missouri	11,852	2.3%
13	Tennessee	11,760	2.2%
14	Massachusetts	11,469	2.2%
15	Minnesota	11,261	2.1%
16	Virginia	11,206	2.1%
17	Indiana	11,167	2.1%
18	Alabama	9,970	1.9%
19	Louisiana	9,767	1.9%
20	Wisconsin	9,432	1.8%
21	Kentucky	8,694	1.7%
22	Maryland	8,615	1.6%
23	Mississippi	8,081	1.5%
24	South Carolina	7,570	1.4%
25	Iowa	6,926	1.3%
26	Arizona	6,596	1.3%
27	Washington	6,289	1.2%
28	Oklahoma	5,944	1.1%
29	Kansas	5,886	1.1%
30	Arkansas	5,777	1.1%
31	Colorado	5,138	1.0%
32	Nebraska	4,876	0.9%
33	West Virginia	4,872	0.9%
34	Connecticut	4,817	0.9%
35	Oregon	3,840	0.7%
36	Montana	2,989	0.6%
37	South Dakota	2,829	0.5%
38	Utah	2,427	0.5%
39	North Dakota	2,393	0.5%
40	Maine	2,312	0.4%
41	Nevada	2,294	0.4%
42	Hawaii	2,127	0.4%
43	New Mexico	1,938	0.4%
44	Idaho	1,912	0.4%
45	Rhode Island	1,808	0.3%
46	New Hampshire	1,805	0.3%
47	Delaware	1,394	0.3%
48	Vermont	1,078	0.2%
49	Wyoming	1,042	0.2%
50	Alaska	1,037	0.2%
	District of Columbia	2,677	0.5%

Source: Morgan Quitno Press using data from American Hospital Association (Chicago, IL)
"Hospital Statistics" (2000 edition)

*Average total of inpatients receiving care in all nonfederal short-term general and other special hospitals, whose facilities and services are available to the public. Excludes newborns.

Average Stay in Community Hospitals in 1998

National Average = 6.0 Days*

ALPHA ORDER				RANK ORDER		
RANK	STATE	DAYS		RANK	STATE	DAYS
34	Alabama	5.6		1	Montana	11.2
5	Alaska	9.2		2	South Dakota	10.7
45	Arizona	4.9		3	North Dakota	10.3
24	Arkansas	5.9		4	Nebraska	9.3
41	California	5.3		5	Alaska	9.2
44	Colorado	5.0		6	Wyoming	8.7
41	Connecticut	5.3		7	New York	8.1
21	Delaware	6.0		8	Minnesota	8.0
34	Florida	5.6		9	Hawaii	7.9
14	Georgia	6.7		9	Vermont	7.9
9	Hawaii	7.9		11	Kansas	7.2
20	Idaho	6.1		12	Mississippi	7.1
24	Illinois	5.9		13	Iowa	6.8
26	Indiana	5.8		14	Georgia	6.7
13	Iowa	6.8		15	North Carolina	6.4
11	Kansas	7.2		16	New Jersey	6.3
26	Kentucky	5.8		16	West Virginia	6.3
34	Louisiana	5.6		18	Pennsylvania	6.2
26	Maine	5.8		18	Wisconsin	6.2
34	Maryland	5.6		20	Idaho	6.1
32	Massachusetts	5.7		21	Delaware	6.0
26	Michigan	5.8		21	New Hampshire	6.0
8	Minnesota	8.0		21	South Carolina	6.0
12	Mississippi	7.1		24	Arkansas	5.9
26	Missouri	5.8		24	Illinois	5.9
1	Montana	11.2		26	Indiana	5.8
4	Nebraska	9.3		26	Kentucky	5.8
45	Nevada	4.9		26	Maine	5.8
21	New Hampshire	6.0		26	Michigan	5.8
16	New Jersey	6.3		26	Missouri	5.8
49	New Mexico	4.5		26	Tennessee	5.8
7	New York	8.1		32	Massachusetts	5.7
15	North Carolina	6.4		32	Virginia	5.7
3	North Dakota	10.3		34	Alabama	5.6
40	Ohio	5.4		34	Florida	5.6
39	Oklahoma	5.5		34	Louisiana	5.6
49	Oregon	4.5		34	Maryland	5.6
18	Pennsylvania	6.2		34	Rhode Island	5.6
34	Rhode Island	5.6		39	Oklahoma	5.5
21	South Carolina	6.0		40	Ohio	5.4
2	South Dakota	10.7		41	California	5.3
26	Tennessee	5.8		41	Connecticut	5.3
41	Texas	5.3		41	Texas	5.3
48	Utah	4.6		44	Colorado	5.0
9	Vermont	7.9		45	Arizona	4.9
32	Virginia	5.7		45	Nevada	4.9
47	Washington	4.8		47	Washington	4.8
16	West Virginia	6.3		48	Utah	4.6
18	Wisconsin	6.2		49	New Mexico	4.5
6	Wyoming	8.7		49	Oregon	4.5
					District of Columbia	7.0

Source: American Hospital Association (Chicago, IL)
   "Hospital Statistics" (2000 edition)
*All nonfederal short-term general and other special hospitals, whose facilities and services are available to the public.

Occupancy Rate in Community Hospitals in 1998

National Rate = 62.4% of Community Hospital Beds Occupied*

RANK	STATE	PERCENT
32	Alabama	58.7
1	Alaska	83.6
24	Arizona	60.8
34	Arkansas	58.5
23	California	61.3
44	Colorado	56.0
8	Connecticut	69.3
5	Delaware	70.5
27	Florida	60.3
31	Georgia	59.4
3	Hawaii	76.2
44	Idaho	56.0
26	Illinois	60.4
35	Indiana	57.6
41	Iowa	56.7
48	Kansas	53.9
37	Kentucky	57.0
47	Louisiana	54.8
22	Maine	61.4
11	Maryland	68.0
7	Massachusetts	69.5
17	Michigan	64.3
10	Minnesota	68.3
21	Mississippi	62.1
36	Missouri	57.3
12	Montana	67.7
29	Nebraska	60.0
15	Nevada	65.0
19	New Hampshire	63.5
4	New Jersey	70.6
46	New Mexico	55.5
2	New York	76.7
9	North Carolina	68.4
28	North Dakota	60.2
39	Ohio	56.8
48	Oklahoma	53.9
43	Oregon	56.4
13	Pennsylvania	66.9
6	Rhode Island	70.1
14	South Carolina	65.7
17	South Dakota	64.3
38	Tennessee	56.9
39	Texas	56.8
25	Utah	60.5
16	Vermont	64.5
20	Virginia	62.6
33	Washington	58.6
29	West Virginia	60.0
42	Wisconsin	56.5
48	Wyoming	53.9

RANK	STATE	PERCENT
1	Alaska	83.6
2	New York	76.7
3	Hawaii	76.2
4	New Jersey	70.6
5	Delaware	70.5
6	Rhode Island	70.1
7	Massachusetts	69.5
8	Connecticut	69.3
9	North Carolina	68.4
10	Minnesota	68.3
11	Maryland	68.0
12	Montana	67.7
13	Pennsylvania	66.9
14	South Carolina	65.7
15	Nevada	65.0
16	Vermont	64.5
17	Michigan	64.3
17	South Dakota	64.3
19	New Hampshire	63.5
20	Virginia	62.6
21	Mississippi	62.1
22	Maine	61.4
23	California	61.3
24	Arizona	60.8
25	Utah	60.5
26	Illinois	60.4
27	Florida	60.3
28	North Dakota	60.2
29	Nebraska	60.0
29	West Virginia	60.0
31	Georgia	59.4
32	Alabama	58.7
33	Washington	58.6
34	Arkansas	58.5
35	Indiana	57.6
36	Missouri	57.3
37	Kentucky	57.0
38	Tennessee	56.9
39	Ohio	56.8
39	Texas	56.8
41	Iowa	56.7
42	Wisconsin	56.5
43	Oregon	56.4
44	Colorado	56.0
44	Idaho	56.0
46	New Mexico	55.5
47	Louisiana	54.8
48	Kansas	53.9
48	Oklahoma	53.9
48	Wyoming	53.9
	District of Columbia	75.4

Source: Morgan Quitno Press using data from American Hospital Association (Chicago, IL)
   "Hospital Statistics" (2000 edition)
*Average daily census compared to number of community hospital beds.

Outpatient Visits to Community Hospitals in 1998

National Total = 474,193,468 Visits*

<u>ALPHA ORDER</u>

RANK	STATE	VISITS	% of USA
22	Alabama	6,763,322	1.4%
49	Alaska	1,038,611	0.2%
31	Arizona	4,583,900	1.0%
34	Arkansas	4,168,183	0.9%
1	California	45,030,334	9.5%
24	Colorado	6,045,715	1.3%
23	Connecticut	6,498,420	1.4%
47	Delaware	1,295,850	0.3%
8	Florida	19,446,242	4.1%
13	Georgia	10,306,058	2.2%
39	Hawaii	2,460,093	0.5%
42	Idaho	2,175,900	0.5%
6	Illinois	22,774,904	4.8%
11	Indiana	12,734,612	2.7%
20	Iowa	7,751,362	1.6%
30	Kansas	4,704,139	1.0%
21	Kentucky	7,392,711	1.6%
14	Louisiana	10,207,145	2.2%
38	Maine	2,674,240	0.6%
28	Maryland	5,020,323	1.1%
9	Massachusetts	15,425,713	3.3%
7	Michigan	21,772,334	4.6%
27	Minnesota	5,515,211	1.2%
35	Mississippi	3,429,968	0.7%
15	Missouri	10,161,072	2.1%
41	Montana	2,288,485	0.5%
37	Nebraska	2,849,124	0.6%
44	Nevada	1,592,643	0.3%
40	New Hampshire	2,335,274	0.5%
10	New Jersey	15,296,914	3.2%
36	New Mexico	3,264,571	0.7%
2	New York	43,673,425	9.2%
12	North Carolina	11,067,033	2.3%
46	North Dakota	1,421,937	0.3%
5	Ohio	24,798,222	5.2%
32	Oklahoma	4,387,002	0.9%
26	Oregon	5,788,748	1.2%
3	Pennsylvania	30,579,987	6.4%
43	Rhode Island	2,169,947	0.5%
25	South Carolina	5,858,641	1.2%
45	South Dakota	1,508,464	0.3%
17	Tennessee	9,230,560	1.9%
4	Texas	27,338,983	5.8%
33	Utah	4,224,291	0.9%
48	Vermont	1,151,627	0.2%
19	Virginia	8,323,995	1.8%
18	Washington	8,721,062	1.8%
29	West Virginia	5,007,361	1.1%
16	Wisconsin	9,633,522	2.0%
50	Wyoming	849,528	0.2%

<u>RANK ORDER</u>

RANK	STATE	VISITS	% of USA
1	California	45,030,334	9.5%
2	New York	43,673,425	9.2%
3	Pennsylvania	30,579,987	6.4%
4	Texas	27,338,983	5.8%
5	Ohio	24,798,222	5.2%
6	Illinois	22,774,904	4.8%
7	Michigan	21,772,334	4.6%
8	Florida	19,446,242	4.1%
9	Massachusetts	15,425,713	3.3%
10	New Jersey	15,296,914	3.2%
11	Indiana	12,734,612	2.7%
12	North Carolina	11,067,033	2.3%
13	Georgia	10,306,058	2.2%
14	Louisiana	10,207,145	2.2%
15	Missouri	10,161,072	2.1%
16	Wisconsin	9,633,522	2.0%
17	Tennessee	9,230,560	1.9%
18	Washington	8,721,062	1.8%
19	Virginia	8,323,995	1.8%
20	Iowa	7,751,362	1.6%
21	Kentucky	7,392,711	1.6%
22	Alabama	6,763,322	1.4%
23	Connecticut	6,498,420	1.4%
24	Colorado	6,045,715	1.3%
25	South Carolina	5,858,641	1.2%
26	Oregon	5,788,748	1.2%
27	Minnesota	5,515,211	1.2%
28	Maryland	5,020,323	1.1%
29	West Virginia	5,007,361	1.1%
30	Kansas	4,704,139	1.0%
31	Arizona	4,583,900	1.0%
32	Oklahoma	4,387,002	0.9%
33	Utah	4,224,291	0.9%
34	Arkansas	4,168,183	0.9%
35	Mississippi	3,429,968	0.7%
36	New Mexico	3,264,571	0.7%
37	Nebraska	2,849,124	0.6%
38	Maine	2,674,240	0.6%
39	Hawaii	2,460,093	0.5%
40	New Hampshire	2,335,274	0.5%
41	Montana	2,288,485	0.5%
42	Idaho	2,175,900	0.5%
43	Rhode Island	2,169,947	0.5%
44	Nevada	1,592,643	0.3%
45	South Dakota	1,508,464	0.3%
46	North Dakota	1,421,937	0.3%
47	Delaware	1,295,850	0.3%
48	Vermont	1,151,627	0.2%
49	Alaska	1,038,611	0.2%
50	Wyoming	849,528	0.2%
	District of Columbia	1,455,760	0.3%

Source: American Hospital Association (Chicago, IL)
    "Hospital Statistics" (2000 edition)
*All nonfederal short-term general and other special hospitals, whose facilities and services are available to the public. Includes emergency and other visits.

Emergency Outpatient Visits to Community Hospitals in 1998

National Total = 94,771,405 Visits*

ALPHA ORDER

RANK	STATE	VISITS	% of USA
18	Alabama	1,905,603	2.0%
50	Alaska	160,519	0.2%
25	Arizona	1,179,377	1.2%
33	Arkansas	931,213	1.0%
1	California	8,717,395	9.2%
26	Colorado	1,176,404	1.2%
27	Connecticut	1,164,247	1.2%
44	Delaware	267,369	0.3%
4	Florida	5,285,638	5.6%
10	Georgia	2,731,084	2.9%
43	Hawaii	306,804	0.3%
42	Idaho	380,805	0.4%
7	Illinois	4,325,178	4.6%
16	Indiana	2,154,402	2.3%
31	Iowa	982,497	1.0%
34	Kansas	809,296	0.9%
19	Kentucky	1,761,831	1.9%
15	Louisiana	2,254,789	2.4%
35	Maine	636,973	0.7%
23	Maryland	1,505,744	1.6%
12	Massachusetts	2,473,668	2.6%
8	Michigan	3,462,575	3.7%
28	Minnesota	1,143,117	1.2%
24	Mississippi	1,425,892	1.5%
17	Missouri	2,115,060	2.2%
45	Montana	259,462	0.3%
40	Nebraska	455,953	0.5%
39	Nevada	463,706	0.5%
37	New Hampshire	476,050	0.5%
11	New Jersey	2,675,241	2.8%
38	New Mexico	466,049	0.5%
2	New York	6,785,222	7.2%
9	North Carolina	2,885,802	3.0%
46	North Dakota	221,797	0.2%
5	Ohio	5,003,406	5.3%
29	Oklahoma	1,101,327	1.2%
32	Oregon	958,415	1.0%
6	Pennsylvania	4,620,945	4.9%
41	Rhode Island	407,366	0.4%
22	South Carolina	1,531,231	1.6%
48	South Dakota	183,556	0.2%
13	Tennessee	2,443,232	2.6%
3	Texas	6,722,059	7.1%
36	Utah	625,879	0.7%
47	Vermont	213,367	0.2%
14	Virginia	2,255,094	2.4%
21	Washington	1,602,826	1.7%
30	West Virginia	1,020,060	1.1%
20	Wisconsin	1,608,391	1.7%
49	Wyoming	173,155	0.2%

RANK ORDER

RANK	STATE	VISITS	% of USA
1	California	8,717,395	9.2%
2	New York	6,785,222	7.2%
3	Texas	6,722,059	7.1%
4	Florida	5,285,638	5.6%
5	Ohio	5,003,406	5.3%
6	Pennsylvania	4,620,945	4.9%
7	Illinois	4,325,178	4.6%
8	Michigan	3,462,575	3.7%
9	North Carolina	2,885,802	3.0%
10	Georgia	2,731,084	2.9%
11	New Jersey	2,675,241	2.8%
12	Massachusetts	2,473,668	2.6%
13	Tennessee	2,443,232	2.6%
14	Virginia	2,255,094	2.4%
15	Louisiana	2,254,789	2.4%
16	Indiana	2,154,402	2.3%
17	Missouri	2,115,060	2.2%
18	Alabama	1,905,603	2.0%
19	Kentucky	1,761,831	1.9%
20	Wisconsin	1,608,391	1.7%
21	Washington	1,602,826	1.7%
22	South Carolina	1,531,231	1.6%
23	Maryland	1,505,744	1.6%
24	Mississippi	1,425,892	1.5%
25	Arizona	1,179,377	1.2%
26	Colorado	1,176,404	1.2%
27	Connecticut	1,164,247	1.2%
28	Minnesota	1,143,117	1.2%
29	Oklahoma	1,101,327	1.2%
30	West Virginia	1,020,060	1.1%
31	Iowa	982,497	1.0%
32	Oregon	958,415	1.0%
33	Arkansas	931,213	1.0%
34	Kansas	809,296	0.9%
35	Maine	636,973	0.7%
36	Utah	625,879	0.7%
37	New Hampshire	476,050	0.5%
38	New Mexico	466,049	0.5%
39	Nevada	463,706	0.5%
40	Nebraska	455,953	0.5%
41	Rhode Island	407,366	0.4%
42	Idaho	380,805	0.4%
43	Hawaii	306,804	0.3%
44	Delaware	267,369	0.3%
45	Montana	259,462	0.3%
46	North Dakota	221,797	0.2%
47	Vermont	213,367	0.2%
48	South Dakota	183,556	0.2%
49	Wyoming	173,155	0.2%
50	Alaska	160,519	0.2%
	District of Columbia	354,334	0.4%

Source: American Hospital Association (Chicago, IL)
"Hospital Statistics" (2000 edition)
*All nonfederal short-term general and other special hospitals, whose facilities and services are available to the public.

Surgical Operations in Community Hospitals in 1998

National Total = 25,329,319 Surgical Operations*

ALPHA ORDER

RANK	STATE	OPERATIONS	% of USA
20	Alabama	489,895	1.9%
50	Alaska	30,984	0.1%
27	Arizona	305,143	1.2%
32	Arkansas	245,771	1.0%
1	California	2,338,201	9.2%
26	Colorado	325,167	1.3%
28	Connecticut	284,725	1.1%
43	Delaware	88,795	0.4%
5	Florida	1,423,138	5.6%
10	Georgia	687,989	2.7%
44	Hawaii	81,339	0.3%
41	Idaho	101,661	0.4%
7	Illinois	1,026,230	4.1%
15	Indiana	589,452	2.3%
24	Iowa	377,057	1.5%
34	Kansas	240,929	1.0%
17	Kentucky	492,747	1.9%
21	Louisiana	440,651	1.7%
38	Maine	133,452	0.5%
18	Maryland	490,446	1.9%
12	Massachusetts	643,088	2.5%
8	Michigan	973,680	3.8%
22	Minnesota	400,888	1.6%
33	Mississippi	245,360	1.0%
16	Missouri	573,870	2.3%
47	Montana	71,502	0.3%
36	Nebraska	186,617	0.7%
40	Nevada	115,234	0.5%
42	New Hampshire	92,454	0.4%
9	New Jersey	702,129	2.8%
37	New Mexico	139,392	0.6%
2	New York	1,949,791	7.7%
11	North Carolina	666,312	2.6%
46	North Dakota	75,082	0.3%
6	Ohio	1,200,049	4.7%
29	Oklahoma	272,778	1.1%
30	Oregon	268,792	1.1%
4	Pennsylvania	1,561,307	6.2%
39	Rhode Island	115,778	0.5%
25	South Carolina	359,457	1.4%
45	South Dakota	76,057	0.3%
13	Tennessee	601,559	2.4%
3	Texas	1,696,226	6.7%
35	Utah	188,526	0.7%
48	Vermont	47,961	0.2%
14	Virginia	593,747	2.3%
23	Washington	383,811	1.5%
31	West Virginia	267,366	1.1%
19	Wisconsin	490,242	1.9%
49	Wyoming	36,467	0.1%

RANK ORDER

RANK	STATE	OPERATIONS	% of USA
1	California	2,338,201	9.2%
2	New York	1,949,791	7.7%
3	Texas	1,696,226	6.7%
4	Pennsylvania	1,561,307	6.2%
5	Florida	1,423,138	5.6%
6	Ohio	1,200,049	4.7%
7	Illinois	1,026,230	4.1%
8	Michigan	973,680	3.8%
9	New Jersey	702,129	2.8%
10	Georgia	687,989	2.7%
11	North Carolina	666,312	2.6%
12	Massachusetts	643,088	2.5%
13	Tennessee	601,559	2.4%
14	Virginia	593,747	2.3%
15	Indiana	589,452	2.3%
16	Missouri	573,870	2.3%
17	Kentucky	492,747	1.9%
18	Maryland	490,446	1.9%
19	Wisconsin	490,242	1.9%
20	Alabama	489,895	1.9%
21	Louisiana	440,651	1.7%
22	Minnesota	400,888	1.6%
23	Washington	383,811	1.5%
24	Iowa	377,057	1.5%
25	South Carolina	359,457	1.4%
26	Colorado	325,167	1.3%
27	Arizona	305,143	1.2%
28	Connecticut	284,725	1.1%
29	Oklahoma	272,778	1.1%
30	Oregon	268,792	1.1%
31	West Virginia	267,366	1.1%
32	Arkansas	245,771	1.0%
33	Mississippi	245,360	1.0%
34	Kansas	240,929	1.0%
35	Utah	188,526	0.7%
36	Nebraska	186,617	0.7%
37	New Mexico	139,392	0.6%
38	Maine	133,452	0.5%
39	Rhode Island	115,778	0.5%
40	Nevada	115,234	0.5%
41	Idaho	101,661	0.4%
42	New Hampshire	92,454	0.4%
43	Delaware	88,795	0.4%
44	Hawaii	81,339	0.3%
45	South Dakota	76,057	0.3%
46	North Dakota	75,082	0.3%
47	Montana	71,502	0.3%
48	Vermont	47,961	0.2%
49	Wyoming	36,467	0.1%
50	Alaska	30,984	0.1%
	District of Columbia	110,025	0.4%

Source: American Hospital Association (Chicago, IL)
"Hospital Statistics" (2000 edition)
*Includes inpatient and outpatient surgeries.

Medicare and Medicaid Certified Facilities in 2000

National Total = 227,318 Facilities*

ALPHA ORDER					RANK ORDER			
RANK	STATE		FACILITIES	% of USA	RANK	STATE	FACILITIES	% of USA
19	Alabama		3,917	1.7%	1	California	22,288	9.8%
49	Alaska		502	0.2%	2	Texas	19,003	8.4%
29	Arizona		3,157	1.4%	3	Florida	13,714	6.0%
31	Arkansas		2,716	1.2%	4	New York	12,482	5.5%
1	California		22,288	9.8%	5	Ohio	11,062	4.9%
30	Colorado		2,973	1.3%	6	Illinois	9,824	4.3%
27	Connecticut		3,190	1.4%	7	Pennsylvania	9,529	4.2%
47	Delaware		661	0.3%	8	Michigan	7,433	3.3%
3	Florida		13,714	6.0%	9	Georgia	6,523	2.9%
9	Georgia		6,523	2.9%	10	North Carolina	6,395	2.8%
45	Hawaii		912	0.4%	11	Indiana	6,106	2.7%
40	Idaho		1,066	0.5%	12	New Jersey	5,735	2.5%
6	Illinois		9,824	4.3%	13	Missouri	5,653	2.5%
11	Indiana		6,106	2.7%	14	Louisiana	5,138	2.3%
24	Iowa		3,480	1.5%	15	Virginia	5,091	2.2%
28	Kansas		3,177	1.4%	16	Tennessee	4,991	2.2%
25	Kentucky		3,418	1.5%	17	Massachusetts	4,718	2.1%
14	Louisiana		5,138	2.3%	18	Maryland	4,098	1.8%
38	Maine		1,310	0.6%	19	Alabama	3,917	1.7%
18	Maryland		4,098	1.8%	20	Oklahoma	3,865	1.7%
17	Massachusetts		4,718	2.1%	21	Minnesota	3,625	1.6%
8	Michigan		7,433	3.3%	22	Washington	3,563	1.6%
21	Minnesota		3,625	1.6%	23	Wisconsin	3,542	1.6%
32	Mississippi		2,537	1.1%	24	Iowa	3,480	1.5%
13	Missouri		5,653	2.5%	25	Kentucky	3,418	1.5%
43	Montana		941	0.4%	26	South Carolina	3,413	1.5%
35	Nebraska		1,761	0.8%	27	Connecticut	3,190	1.4%
39	Nevada		1,133	0.5%	28	Kansas	3,177	1.4%
41	New Hampshire		1,040	0.5%	29	Arizona	3,157	1.4%
12	New Jersey		5,735	2.5%	30	Colorado	2,973	1.3%
36	New Mexico		1,472	0.6%	31	Arkansas	2,716	1.2%
4	New York		12,482	5.5%	32	Mississippi	2,537	1.1%
10	North Carolina		6,395	2.8%	33	Oregon	2,358	1.0%
46	North Dakota		842	0.4%	34	West Virginia	2,043	0.9%
5	Ohio		11,062	4.9%	35	Nebraska	1,761	0.8%
20	Oklahoma		3,865	1.7%	36	New Mexico	1,472	0.6%
33	Oregon		2,358	1.0%	37	Utah	1,322	0.6%
7	Pennsylvania		9,529	4.2%	38	Maine	1,310	0.6%
42	Rhode Island		952	0.4%	39	Nevada	1,133	0.5%
26	South Carolina		3,413	1.5%	40	Idaho	1,066	0.5%
44	South Dakota		915	0.4%	41	New Hampshire	1,040	0.5%
16	Tennessee		4,991	2.2%	42	Rhode Island	952	0.4%
2	Texas		19,003	8.4%	43	Montana	941	0.4%
37	Utah		1,322	0.6%	44	South Dakota	915	0.4%
48	Vermont		524	0.2%	45	Hawaii	912	0.4%
15	Virginia		5,091	2.2%	46	North Dakota	842	0.4%
22	Washington		3,563	1.6%	47	Delaware	661	0.3%
34	West Virginia		2,043	0.9%	48	Vermont	524	0.2%
23	Wisconsin		3,542	1.6%	49	Alaska	502	0.2%
50	Wyoming		499	0.2%	50	Wyoming	499	0.2%
						District of Columbia	709	0.3%

Source: U.S. Department of Health and Human Services, Health Care Financing Administration
   OSCAR Report 10 (February 1, 2000)
*Certified by HCFA to participate in the Medicare/Medicaid programs. All provider groups including hospitals, home health agencies, rural health centers, community mental health centers, nursing facilities, outpatient physical therapy facilities and hospices. Also includes 171,335 laboratories. National total does not include 1,229 certified facilities in U.S. territories.

Medicare and Medicaid Certified Hospitals in 2000

National Total = 6,039 Hospitals*

ALPHA ORDER

RANK	STATE	HOSPITALS	% of USA
19	Alabama	124	2.1%
47	Alaska	24	0.4%
29	Arizona	85	1.4%
26	Arkansas	99	1.6%
2	California	475	7.9%
30	Colorado	82	1.4%
39	Connecticut	48	0.8%
50	Delaware	11	0.2%
5	Florida	248	4.1%
8	Georgia	188	3.1%
46	Hawaii	27	0.4%
39	Idaho	48	0.8%
6	Illinois	225	3.7%
11	Indiana	155	2.6%
20	Iowa	121	2.0%
14	Kansas	147	2.4%
21	Kentucky	120	2.0%
10	Louisiana	171	2.8%
42	Maine	42	0.7%
32	Maryland	68	1.1%
21	Massachusetts	120	2.0%
9	Michigan	178	2.9%
12	Minnesota	151	2.5%
25	Mississippi	106	1.8%
17	Missouri	140	2.3%
36	Montana	60	1.0%
28	Nebraska	96	1.6%
43	Nevada	41	0.7%
44	New Hampshire	31	0.5%
24	New Jersey	107	1.8%
37	New Mexico	53	0.9%
3	New York	266	4.4%
17	North Carolina	140	2.3%
38	North Dakota	50	0.8%
7	Ohio	206	3.4%
13	Oklahoma	150	2.5%
34	Oregon	63	1.0%
4	Pennsylvania	252	4.2%
48	Rhode Island	17	0.3%
31	South Carolina	76	1.3%
34	South Dakota	63	1.0%
15	Tennessee	145	2.4%
1	Texas	488	8.1%
39	Utah	48	0.8%
49	Vermont	16	0.3%
23	Virginia	119	2.0%
27	Washington	98	1.6%
33	West Virginia	65	1.1%
16	Wisconsin	142	2.4%
45	Wyoming	28	0.5%

RANK ORDER

RANK	STATE	HOSPITALS	% of USA
1	Texas	488	8.1%
2	California	475	7.9%
3	New York	266	4.4%
4	Pennsylvania	252	4.2%
5	Florida	248	4.1%
6	Illinois	225	3.7%
7	Ohio	206	3.4%
8	Georgia	188	3.1%
9	Michigan	178	2.9%
10	Louisiana	171	2.8%
11	Indiana	155	2.6%
12	Minnesota	151	2.5%
13	Oklahoma	150	2.5%
14	Kansas	147	2.4%
15	Tennessee	145	2.4%
16	Wisconsin	142	2.4%
17	Missouri	140	2.3%
17	North Carolina	140	2.3%
19	Alabama	124	2.1%
20	Iowa	121	2.0%
21	Kentucky	120	2.0%
21	Massachusetts	120	2.0%
23	Virginia	119	2.0%
24	New Jersey	107	1.8%
25	Mississippi	106	1.8%
26	Arkansas	99	1.6%
27	Washington	98	1.6%
28	Nebraska	96	1.6%
29	Arizona	85	1.4%
30	Colorado	82	1.4%
31	South Carolina	76	1.3%
32	Maryland	68	1.1%
33	West Virginia	65	1.1%
34	Oregon	63	1.0%
34	South Dakota	63	1.0%
36	Montana	60	1.0%
37	New Mexico	53	0.9%
38	North Dakota	50	0.8%
39	Connecticut	48	0.8%
39	Idaho	48	0.8%
39	Utah	48	0.8%
42	Maine	42	0.7%
43	Nevada	41	0.7%
44	New Hampshire	31	0.5%
45	Wyoming	28	0.5%
46	Hawaii	27	0.4%
47	Alaska	24	0.4%
48	Rhode Island	17	0.3%
49	Vermont	16	0.3%
50	Delaware	11	0.2%
	District of Columbia	16	0.3%

Source: U.S. Department of Health and Human Services, Health Care Financing Administration
OSCAR Report 10 (February 1, 2000)

*Certified by HCFA to participate in the Medicare/Medicaid programs. Excludes licensed facilities that do not accept federal funding and facilities managed by the Department of Veterans Affairs. National total does not include 63 certified hospitals in U.S. territories.

Beds in Medicare and Medicaid Certified Hospitals in 2000

National Total = 984,509 Beds*

ALPHA ORDER

ALPHA ORDER

RANK ORDER

RANK	STATE	BEDS	% of USA		RANK	STATE	BEDS	% of USA
17	Alabama	20,631	2.1%		1	California	85,547	8.7%
50	Alaska	1,565	0.2%		2	New York	82,113	8.3%
31	Arizona	11,207	1.1%		3	Texas	58,645	6.0%
29	Arkansas	12,254	1.2%		4	Florida	54,776	5.6%
1	California	85,547	8.7%		5	Illinois	51,283	5.2%
30	Colorado	11,573	1.2%		6	Ohio	49,145	5.0%
32	Connecticut	11,201	1.1%		7	Pennsylvania	44,989	4.6%
47	Delaware	2,325	0.2%		8	New Jersey	32,046	3.3%
4	Florida	54,776	5.6%		9	Michigan	31,895	3.2%
10	Georgia	27,076	2.8%		10	Georgia	27,076	2.8%
46	Hawaii	2,831	0.3%		11	North Carolina	26,969	2.7%
44	Idaho	2,948	0.3%		12	Missouri	26,430	2.7%
5	Illinois	51,283	5.2%		13	Tennessee	25,960	2.6%
16	Indiana	22,106	2.2%		14	Virginia	22,470	2.3%
27	Iowa	12,469	1.3%		15	Louisiana	22,437	2.3%
28	Kansas	12,372	1.3%		16	Indiana	22,106	2.2%
20	Kentucky	18,016	1.8%		17	Alabama	20,631	2.1%
15	Louisiana	22,437	2.3%		18	Massachusetts	20,618	2.1%
39	Maine	4,276	0.4%		19	Wisconsin	20,570	2.1%
22	Maryland	16,879	1.7%		20	Kentucky	18,016	1.8%
18	Massachusetts	20,618	2.1%		21	Minnesota	17,483	1.8%
9	Michigan	31,895	3.2%		22	Maryland	16,879	1.7%
21	Minnesota	17,483	1.8%		23	Oklahoma	15,441	1.6%
25	Mississippi	12,597	1.3%		24	Washington	14,211	1.4%
12	Missouri	26,430	2.7%		25	Mississippi	12,597	1.3%
45	Montana	2,891	0.3%		26	South Carolina	12,564	1.3%
35	Nebraska	7,176	0.7%		27	Iowa	12,469	1.3%
38	Nevada	4,710	0.5%		28	Kansas	12,372	1.3%
42	New Hampshire	3,550	0.4%		29	Arkansas	12,254	1.2%
8	New Jersey	32,046	3.3%		30	Colorado	11,573	1.2%
37	New Mexico	5,071	0.5%		31	Arizona	11,207	1.1%
2	New York	82,113	8.3%		32	Connecticut	11,201	1.1%
11	North Carolina	26,969	2.7%		33	West Virginia	9,660	1.0%
41	North Dakota	3,652	0.4%		34	Oregon	8,189	0.8%
6	Ohio	49,145	5.0%		35	Nebraska	7,176	0.7%
23	Oklahoma	15,441	1.6%		36	Utah	5,215	0.5%
34	Oregon	8,189	0.8%		37	New Mexico	5,071	0.5%
7	Pennsylvania	44,989	4.6%		38	Nevada	4,710	0.5%
40	Rhode Island	4,220	0.4%		39	Maine	4,276	0.4%
26	South Carolina	12,564	1.3%		40	Rhode Island	4,220	0.4%
43	South Dakota	3,388	0.3%		41	North Dakota	3,652	0.4%
13	Tennessee	25,960	2.6%		42	New Hampshire	3,550	0.4%
3	Texas	58,645	6.0%		43	South Dakota	3,388	0.3%
36	Utah	5,215	0.5%		44	Idaho	2,948	0.3%
48	Vermont	2,101	0.2%		45	Montana	2,891	0.3%
14	Virginia	22,470	2.3%		46	Hawaii	2,831	0.3%
24	Washington	14,211	1.4%		47	Delaware	2,325	0.2%
33	West Virginia	9,660	1.0%		48	Vermont	2,101	0.2%
19	Wisconsin	20,570	2.1%		49	Wyoming	1,663	0.2%
49	Wyoming	1,663	0.2%		50	Alaska	1,565	0.2%
						District of Columbia	5,105	0.5%

Source: U.S. Department of Health and Human Services, Health Care Financing Administration
    OSCAR Report 10 (February 1, 2000)
*Beds in hospitals certified by HCFA to participate in the Medicare/Medicaid programs. Excludes licensed facilities that do not accept federal funding and facilities managed by the Department of Veterans Affairs. National total does not include 11,446 beds in U.S. territories.

Medicare and Medicaid Certified Children's Hospitals in 2000

National Total = 71 Hospitals*

ALPHA ORDER				RANK ORDER			
RANK	STATE	HOSPITALS	% of USA	RANK	STATE	HOSPITALS	% of USA
17	Alabama	1	1.4%	1	California	8	11.3%
33	Alaska	0	0.0%	1	Ohio	8	11.3%
17	Arizona	1	1.4%	1	Texas	8	11.3%
17	Arkansas	1	1.4%	4	Pennsylvania	5	7.0%
1	California	8	11.3%	5	Minnesota	3	4.2%
17	Colorado	1	1.4%	6	Florida	2	2.8%
17	Connecticut	1	1.4%	6	Georgia	2	2.8%
17	Delaware	1	1.4%	6	Illinois	2	2.8%
6	Florida	2	2.8%	6	Maryland	2	2.8%
6	Georgia	2	2.8%	6	Massachusetts	2	2.8%
17	Hawaii	1	1.4%	6	Missouri	2	2.8%
33	Idaho	0	0.0%	6	Nebraska	2	2.8%
6	Illinois	2	2.8%	6	Oklahoma	2	2.8%
17	Indiana	1	1.4%	6	Tennessee	2	2.8%
33	Iowa	0	0.0%	6	Virginia	2	2.8%
17	Kansas	1	1.4%	6	Washington	2	2.8%
33	Kentucky	0	0.0%	17	Alabama	1	1.4%
17	Louisiana	1	1.4%	17	Arizona	1	1.4%
33	Maine	0	0.0%	17	Arkansas	1	1.4%
6	Maryland	2	2.8%	17	Colorado	1	1.4%
6	Massachusetts	2	2.8%	17	Connecticut	1	1.4%
17	Michigan	1	1.4%	17	Delaware	1	1.4%
5	Minnesota	3	4.2%	17	Hawaii	1	1.4%
33	Mississippi	0	0.0%	17	Indiana	1	1.4%
6	Missouri	2	2.8%	17	Kansas	1	1.4%
33	Montana	0	0.0%	17	Louisiana	1	1.4%
6	Nebraska	2	2.8%	17	Michigan	1	1.4%
33	Nevada	0	0.0%	17	New Jersey	1	1.4%
33	New Hampshire	0	0.0%	17	New Mexico	1	1.4%
17	New Jersey	1	1.4%	17	New York	1	1.4%
17	New Mexico	1	1.4%	17	Utah	1	1.4%
17	New York	1	1.4%	17	Wisconsin	1	1.4%
33	North Carolina	0	0.0%	33	Alaska	0	0.0%
33	North Dakota	0	0.0%	33	Idaho	0	0.0%
1	Ohio	8	11.3%	33	Iowa	0	0.0%
6	Oklahoma	2	2.8%	33	Kentucky	0	0.0%
33	Oregon	0	0.0%	33	Maine	0	0.0%
4	Pennsylvania	5	7.0%	33	Mississippi	0	0.0%
33	Rhode Island	0	0.0%	33	Montana	0	0.0%
33	South Carolina	0	0.0%	33	Nevada	0	0.0%
33	South Dakota	0	0.0%	33	New Hampshire	0	0.0%
6	Tennessee	2	2.8%	33	North Carolina	0	0.0%
1	Texas	8	11.3%	33	North Dakota	0	0.0%
17	Utah	1	1.4%	33	Oregon	0	0.0%
33	Vermont	0	0.0%	33	Rhode Island	0	0.0%
6	Virginia	2	2.8%	33	South Carolina	0	0.0%
6	Washington	2	2.8%	33	South Dakota	0	0.0%
33	West Virginia	0	0.0%	33	Vermont	0	0.0%
17	Wisconsin	1	1.4%	33	West Virginia	0	0.0%
33	Wyoming	0	0.0%	33	Wyoming	0	0.0%
					District of Columbia	1	1.4%

Source: U.S. Department of Health and Human Services, Health Care Financing Administration
OSCAR Report 10 (February 1, 2000)

Certified by HCFA to participate in the Medicare/Medicaid programs. National total does not include one facility in U.S. territories. Excludes licensed facilities that do not accept federal funding and facilities managed by the Department of Veterans Affairs.

Beds in Medicare and Medicaid Certified Children's Hospitals in 2000

National Total = 11,211 Beds*

<table>
<tr><td colspan="4">ALPHA ORDER</td><td colspan="4">RANK ORDER</td></tr>
<tr><td>RANK</td><td>STATE</td><td>BEDS</td><td>% of USA</td><td>RANK</td><td>STATE</td><td>BEDS</td><td>% of USA</td></tr>
<tr><td>18</td><td>Alabama</td><td>225</td><td>2.0%</td><td>1</td><td>Ohio</td><td>1,809</td><td>16.1%</td></tr>
<tr><td>33</td><td>Alaska</td><td>0</td><td>0.0%</td><td>2</td><td>California</td><td>1,318</td><td>11.8%</td></tr>
<tr><td>32</td><td>Arizona</td><td>15</td><td>0.1%</td><td>3</td><td>Texas</td><td>1,277</td><td>11.4%</td></tr>
<tr><td>12</td><td>Arkansas</td><td>280</td><td>2.5%</td><td>4</td><td>Pennsylvania</td><td>641</td><td>5.7%</td></tr>
<tr><td>2</td><td>California</td><td>1,318</td><td>11.8%</td><td>5</td><td>Massachusetts</td><td>425</td><td>3.8%</td></tr>
<tr><td>14</td><td>Colorado</td><td>253</td><td>2.3%</td><td>6</td><td>New York</td><td>405</td><td>3.6%</td></tr>
<tr><td>25</td><td>Connecticut</td><td>97</td><td>0.9%</td><td>7</td><td>Missouri</td><td>402</td><td>3.6%</td></tr>
<tr><td>25</td><td>Delaware</td><td>97</td><td>0.9%</td><td>8</td><td>Georgia</td><td>400</td><td>3.6%</td></tr>
<tr><td>9</td><td>Florida</td><td>376</td><td>3.4%</td><td>9</td><td>Florida</td><td>376</td><td>3.4%</td></tr>
<tr><td>8</td><td>Georgia</td><td>400</td><td>3.6%</td><td>10</td><td>Illinois</td><td>351</td><td>3.1%</td></tr>
<tr><td>16</td><td>Hawaii</td><td>232</td><td>2.1%</td><td>11</td><td>Minnesota</td><td>329</td><td>2.9%</td></tr>
<tr><td>33</td><td>Idaho</td><td>0</td><td>0.0%</td><td>12</td><td>Arkansas</td><td>280</td><td>2.5%</td></tr>
<tr><td>10</td><td>Illinois</td><td>351</td><td>3.1%</td><td>13</td><td>Washington</td><td>276</td><td>2.5%</td></tr>
<tr><td>31</td><td>Indiana</td><td>20</td><td>0.2%</td><td>14</td><td>Colorado</td><td>253</td><td>2.3%</td></tr>
<tr><td>33</td><td>Iowa</td><td>0</td><td>0.0%</td><td>15</td><td>Virginia</td><td>250</td><td>2.2%</td></tr>
<tr><td>30</td><td>Kansas</td><td>34</td><td>0.3%</td><td>16</td><td>Hawaii</td><td>232</td><td>2.1%</td></tr>
<tr><td>33</td><td>Kentucky</td><td>0</td><td>0.0%</td><td>17</td><td>Michigan</td><td>228</td><td>2.0%</td></tr>
<tr><td>20</td><td>Louisiana</td><td>188</td><td>1.7%</td><td>18</td><td>Alabama</td><td>225</td><td>2.0%</td></tr>
<tr><td>33</td><td>Maine</td><td>0</td><td>0.0%</td><td>19</td><td>Utah</td><td>194</td><td>1.7%</td></tr>
<tr><td>23</td><td>Maryland</td><td>165</td><td>1.5%</td><td>20</td><td>Louisiana</td><td>188</td><td>1.7%</td></tr>
<tr><td>5</td><td>Massachusetts</td><td>425</td><td>3.8%</td><td>21</td><td>Wisconsin</td><td>186</td><td>1.7%</td></tr>
<tr><td>17</td><td>Michigan</td><td>228</td><td>2.0%</td><td>22</td><td>Tennessee</td><td>175</td><td>1.6%</td></tr>
<tr><td>11</td><td>Minnesota</td><td>329</td><td>2.9%</td><td>23</td><td>Maryland</td><td>165</td><td>1.5%</td></tr>
<tr><td>33</td><td>Mississippi</td><td>0</td><td>0.0%</td><td>24</td><td>Nebraska</td><td>142</td><td>1.3%</td></tr>
<tr><td>7</td><td>Missouri</td><td>402</td><td>3.6%</td><td>25</td><td>Connecticut</td><td>97</td><td>0.9%</td></tr>
<tr><td>33</td><td>Montana</td><td>0</td><td>0.0%</td><td>25</td><td>Delaware</td><td>97</td><td>0.9%</td></tr>
<tr><td>24</td><td>Nebraska</td><td>142</td><td>1.3%</td><td>27</td><td>New Jersey</td><td>73</td><td>0.7%</td></tr>
<tr><td>33</td><td>Nevada</td><td>0</td><td>0.0%</td><td>28</td><td>Oklahoma</td><td>68</td><td>0.6%</td></tr>
<tr><td>33</td><td>New Hampshire</td><td>0</td><td>0.0%</td><td>29</td><td>New Mexico</td><td>37</td><td>0.3%</td></tr>
<tr><td>27</td><td>New Jersey</td><td>73</td><td>0.7%</td><td>30</td><td>Kansas</td><td>34</td><td>0.3%</td></tr>
<tr><td>29</td><td>New Mexico</td><td>37</td><td>0.3%</td><td>31</td><td>Indiana</td><td>20</td><td>0.2%</td></tr>
<tr><td>6</td><td>New York</td><td>405</td><td>3.6%</td><td>32</td><td>Arizona</td><td>15</td><td>0.1%</td></tr>
<tr><td>33</td><td>North Carolina</td><td>0</td><td>0.0%</td><td>33</td><td>Alaska</td><td>0</td><td>0.0%</td></tr>
<tr><td>33</td><td>North Dakota</td><td>0</td><td>0.0%</td><td>33</td><td>Idaho</td><td>0</td><td>0.0%</td></tr>
<tr><td>1</td><td>Ohio</td><td>1,809</td><td>16.1%</td><td>33</td><td>Iowa</td><td>0</td><td>0.0%</td></tr>
<tr><td>28</td><td>Oklahoma</td><td>68</td><td>0.6%</td><td>33</td><td>Kentucky</td><td>0</td><td>0.0%</td></tr>
<tr><td>33</td><td>Oregon</td><td>0</td><td>0.0%</td><td>33</td><td>Maine</td><td>0</td><td>0.0%</td></tr>
<tr><td>4</td><td>Pennsylvania</td><td>641</td><td>5.7%</td><td>33</td><td>Mississippi</td><td>0</td><td>0.0%</td></tr>
<tr><td>33</td><td>Rhode Island</td><td>0</td><td>0.0%</td><td>33</td><td>Montana</td><td>0</td><td>0.0%</td></tr>
<tr><td>33</td><td>South Carolina</td><td>0</td><td>0.0%</td><td>33</td><td>Nevada</td><td>0</td><td>0.0%</td></tr>
<tr><td>33</td><td>South Dakota</td><td>0</td><td>0.0%</td><td>33</td><td>New Hampshire</td><td>0</td><td>0.0%</td></tr>
<tr><td>22</td><td>Tennessee</td><td>175</td><td>1.6%</td><td>33</td><td>North Carolina</td><td>0</td><td>0.0%</td></tr>
<tr><td>3</td><td>Texas</td><td>1,277</td><td>11.4%</td><td>33</td><td>North Dakota</td><td>0</td><td>0.0%</td></tr>
<tr><td>19</td><td>Utah</td><td>194</td><td>1.7%</td><td>33</td><td>Oregon</td><td>0</td><td>0.0%</td></tr>
<tr><td>33</td><td>Vermont</td><td>0</td><td>0.0%</td><td>33</td><td>Rhode Island</td><td>0</td><td>0.0%</td></tr>
<tr><td>15</td><td>Virginia</td><td>250</td><td>2.2%</td><td>33</td><td>South Carolina</td><td>0</td><td>0.0%</td></tr>
<tr><td>13</td><td>Washington</td><td>276</td><td>2.5%</td><td>33</td><td>South Dakota</td><td>0</td><td>0.0%</td></tr>
<tr><td>33</td><td>West Virginia</td><td>0</td><td>0.0%</td><td>33</td><td>Vermont</td><td>0</td><td>0.0%</td></tr>
<tr><td>21</td><td>Wisconsin</td><td>186</td><td>1.7%</td><td>33</td><td>West Virginia</td><td>0</td><td>0.0%</td></tr>
<tr><td>33</td><td>Wyoming</td><td>0</td><td>0.0%</td><td>33</td><td>Wyoming</td><td>0</td><td>0.0%</td></tr>
<tr><td></td><td></td><td></td><td></td><td></td><td>District of Columbia</td><td>243</td><td>2.2%</td></tr>
</table>

Source: U.S. Department of Health and Human Services, Health Care Financing Administration
OSCAR Report 10 (February 1, 2000)
*Beds in hospitals certified by HCFA to participate in the Medicare/Medicaid programs. Excludes licensed facilities that do not accept federal funding and facilities managed by the Department of Veterans Affairs. National total does not include 215 beds in U.S. territories.

Medicare and Medicaid Certified Rehabilitation Hospitals in 2000

National Total = 196 Hospitals*

ALPHA ORDER

RANK	STATE	HOSPITALS	% of USA
10	Alabama	5	2.6%
43	Alaska	0	0.0%
14	Arizona	4	2.0%
8	Arkansas	6	3.1%
5	California	10	5.1%
25	Colorado	2	1.0%
25	Connecticut	2	1.0%
32	Delaware	1	0.5%
3	Florida	13	6.6%
25	Georgia	2	1.0%
32	Hawaii	1	0.5%
32	Idaho	1	0.5%
21	Illinois	3	1.5%
10	Indiana	5	2.6%
43	Iowa	0	0.0%
14	Kansas	4	2.0%
14	Kentucky	4	2.0%
3	Louisiana	13	6.6%
32	Maine	1	0.5%
25	Maryland	2	1.0%
6	Massachusetts	7	3.6%
10	Michigan	5	2.6%
32	Minnesota	1	0.5%
32	Mississippi	1	0.5%
21	Missouri	3	1.5%
43	Montana	0	0.0%
32	Nebraska	1	0.5%
14	Nevada	4	2.0%
25	New Hampshire	2	1.0%
6	New Jersey	7	3.6%
14	New Mexico	4	2.0%
14	New York	4	2.0%
25	North Carolina	2	1.0%
43	North Dakota	0	0.0%
25	Ohio	2	1.0%
21	Oklahoma	3	1.5%
43	Oregon	0	0.0%
2	Pennsylvania	18	9.2%
32	Rhode Island	1	0.5%
21	South Carolina	3	1.5%
43	South Dakota	0	0.0%
14	Tennessee	4	2.0%
1	Texas	30	15.3%
32	Utah	1	0.5%
43	Vermont	0	0.0%
10	Virginia	5	2.6%
32	Washington	1	0.5%
8	West Virginia	6	3.1%
32	Wisconsin	1	0.5%
43	Wyoming	0	0.0%

RANK ORDER

RANK	STATE	HOSPITALS	% of USA
1	Texas	30	15.3%
2	Pennsylvania	18	9.2%
3	Florida	13	6.6%
3	Louisiana	13	6.6%
5	California	10	5.1%
6	Massachusetts	7	3.6%
6	New Jersey	7	3.6%
8	Arkansas	6	3.1%
8	West Virginia	6	3.1%
10	Alabama	5	2.6%
10	Indiana	5	2.6%
10	Michigan	5	2.6%
10	Virginia	5	2.6%
14	Arizona	4	2.0%
14	Kansas	4	2.0%
14	Kentucky	4	2.0%
14	Nevada	4	2.0%
14	New Mexico	4	2.0%
14	New York	4	2.0%
14	Tennessee	4	2.0%
21	Illinois	3	1.5%
21	Missouri	3	1.5%
21	Oklahoma	3	1.5%
21	South Carolina	3	1.5%
25	Colorado	2	1.0%
25	Connecticut	2	1.0%
25	Georgia	2	1.0%
25	Maryland	2	1.0%
25	New Hampshire	2	1.0%
25	North Carolina	2	1.0%
25	Ohio	2	1.0%
32	Delaware	1	0.5%
32	Hawaii	1	0.5%
32	Idaho	1	0.5%
32	Maine	1	0.5%
32	Minnesota	1	0.5%
32	Mississippi	1	0.5%
32	Nebraska	1	0.5%
32	Rhode Island	1	0.5%
32	Utah	1	0.5%
32	Washington	1	0.5%
32	Wisconsin	1	0.5%
43	Alaska	0	0.0%
43	Iowa	0	0.0%
43	Montana	0	0.0%
43	North Dakota	0	0.0%
43	Oregon	0	0.0%
43	South Dakota	0	0.0%
43	Vermont	0	0.0%
43	Wyoming	0	0.0%
	District of Columbia	1	0.5%

*Source: U.S. Department of Health and Human Services, Health Care Financing Administration
OSCAR Report 10 (February 1, 2000)*
Certified by HCFA to participate in the Medicare/Medicaid programs. Excludes licensed facilities that do not accept federal funding and facilities managed by the Department of Veterans Affairs.

Beds in Medicare and Medicaid Certified Rehabilitation Hospitals in 2000

National Total = 13,249 Beds*

ALPHA ORDER

RANK	STATE	BEDS	% of USA
13	Alabama	296	2.2%
43	Alaska	0	0.0%
20	Arizona	225	1.7%
8	Arkansas	452	3.4%
6	California	499	3.8%
23	Colorado	187	1.4%
34	Connecticut	84	0.6%
38	Delaware	60	0.5%
3	Florida	823	6.2%
30	Georgia	108	0.8%
32	Hawaii	100	0.8%
40	Idaho	52	0.4%
10	Illinois	371	2.8%
11	Indiana	349	2.6%
43	Iowa	0	0.0%
17	Kansas	257	1.9%
19	Kentucky	240	1.8%
7	Louisiana	484	3.7%
32	Maine	100	0.8%
37	Maryland	66	0.5%
4	Massachusetts	739	5.6%
12	Michigan	315	2.4%
42	Minnesota	12	0.1%
29	Mississippi	124	0.9%
24	Missouri	180	1.4%
43	Montana	0	0.0%
38	Nebraska	60	0.5%
16	Nevada	264	2.0%
26	New Hampshire	152	1.1%
5	New Jersey	680	5.1%
27	New Mexico	149	1.1%
9	New York	428	3.2%
21	North Carolina	223	1.7%
43	North Dakota	0	0.0%
28	Ohio	132	1.0%
25	Oklahoma	167	1.3%
43	Oregon	0	0.0%
2	Pennsylvania	1,666	12.6%
35	Rhode Island	82	0.6%
22	South Carolina	216	1.6%
43	South Dakota	0	0.0%
14	Tennessee	290	2.2%
1	Texas	1,697	12.8%
41	Utah	50	0.4%
43	Vermont	0	0.0%
15	Virginia	281	2.1%
31	Washington	102	0.8%
18	West Virginia	246	1.9%
36	Wisconsin	81	0.6%
43	Wyoming	0	0.0%

RANK ORDER

RANK	STATE	BEDS	% of USA
1	Texas	1,697	12.8%
2	Pennsylvania	1,666	12.6%
3	Florida	823	6.2%
4	Massachusetts	739	5.6%
5	New Jersey	680	5.1%
6	California	499	3.8%
7	Louisiana	484	3.7%
8	Arkansas	452	3.4%
9	New York	428	3.2%
10	Illinois	371	2.8%
11	Indiana	349	2.6%
12	Michigan	315	2.4%
13	Alabama	296	2.2%
14	Tennessee	290	2.2%
15	Virginia	281	2.1%
16	Nevada	264	2.0%
17	Kansas	257	1.9%
18	West Virginia	246	1.9%
19	Kentucky	240	1.8%
20	Arizona	225	1.7%
21	North Carolina	223	1.7%
22	South Carolina	216	1.6%
23	Colorado	187	1.4%
24	Missouri	180	1.4%
25	Oklahoma	167	1.3%
26	New Hampshire	152	1.1%
27	New Mexico	149	1.1%
28	Ohio	132	1.0%
29	Mississippi	124	0.9%
30	Georgia	108	0.8%
31	Washington	102	0.8%
32	Hawaii	100	0.8%
32	Maine	100	0.8%
34	Connecticut	84	0.6%
35	Rhode Island	82	0.6%
36	Wisconsin	81	0.6%
37	Maryland	66	0.5%
38	Delaware	60	0.5%
38	Nebraska	60	0.5%
40	Idaho	52	0.4%
41	Utah	50	0.4%
42	Minnesota	12	0.1%
43	Alaska	0	0.0%
43	Iowa	0	0.0%
43	Montana	0	0.0%
43	North Dakota	0	0.0%
43	Oregon	0	0.0%
43	South Dakota	0	0.0%
43	Vermont	0	0.0%
43	Wyoming	0	0.0%
	District of Columbia	160	1.2%

Source: U.S. Department of Health and Human Services, Health Care Financing Administration
OSCAR Report 10 (February 1, 2000)
*Beds in hospitals certified by HCFA to participate in the Medicare/Medicaid programs. Excludes licensed facilities that do not accept federal funding and facilities managed by the Department of Veterans Affairs.

Medicare and Medicaid Certified Psychiatric Hospitals in 2000

National Total = 560 Psychiatric Hospitals*

ALPHA ORDER

RANK ORDER

RANK	STATE	HOSPITALS	% of USA	RANK	STATE	HOSPITALS	% of USA
22	Alabama	10	1.8%	1	California	42	7.5%
44	Alaska	2	0.4%	2	Texas	39	7.0%
26	Arizona	7	1.3%	3	New York	35	6.3%
23	Arkansas	9	1.6%	4	Florida	32	5.7%
1	California	42	7.5%	5	Pennsylvania	26	4.6%
29	Colorado	6	1.1%	6	Indiana	25	4.5%
23	Connecticut	9	1.6%	7	Georgia	20	3.6%
41	Delaware	3	0.5%	8	Illinois	18	3.2%
4	Florida	32	5.7%	8	Louisiana	18	3.2%
7	Georgia	20	3.6%	10	Massachusetts	17	3.0%
49	Hawaii	1	0.2%	10	Virginia	17	3.0%
30	Idaho	5	0.9%	12	Missouri	16	2.9%
8	Illinois	18	3.2%	12	New Jersey	16	2.9%
6	Indiana	25	4.5%	12	Ohio	16	2.9%
33	Iowa	4	0.7%	15	Wisconsin	14	2.5%
26	Kansas	7	1.3%	16	Kentucky	13	2.3%
16	Kentucky	13	2.3%	16	North Carolina	13	2.3%
8	Louisiana	18	3.2%	16	Oklahoma	13	2.3%
33	Maine	4	0.7%	19	Maryland	12	2.1%
19	Maryland	12	2.1%	19	Michigan	12	2.1%
10	Massachusetts	17	3.0%	19	Tennessee	12	2.1%
19	Michigan	12	2.1%	22	Alabama	10	1.8%
26	Minnesota	7	1.3%	23	Arkansas	9	1.6%
33	Mississippi	4	0.7%	23	Connecticut	9	1.6%
12	Missouri	16	2.9%	25	South Carolina	8	1.4%
44	Montana	2	0.4%	26	Arizona	7	1.3%
33	Nebraska	4	0.7%	26	Kansas	7	1.3%
30	Nevada	5	0.9%	26	Minnesota	7	1.3%
41	New Hampshire	3	0.5%	29	Colorado	6	1.1%
12	New Jersey	16	2.9%	30	Idaho	5	0.9%
33	New Mexico	4	0.7%	30	Nevada	5	0.9%
3	New York	35	6.3%	30	Washington	5	0.9%
16	North Carolina	13	2.3%	33	Iowa	4	0.7%
44	North Dakota	2	0.4%	33	Maine	4	0.7%
12	Ohio	16	2.9%	33	Mississippi	4	0.7%
16	Oklahoma	13	2.3%	33	Nebraska	4	0.7%
33	Oregon	4	0.7%	33	New Mexico	4	0.7%
5	Pennsylvania	26	4.6%	33	Oregon	4	0.7%
41	Rhode Island	3	0.5%	33	Utah	4	0.7%
25	South Carolina	8	1.4%	33	West Virginia	4	0.7%
49	South Dakota	1	0.2%	41	Delaware	3	0.5%
19	Tennessee	12	2.1%	41	New Hampshire	3	0.5%
2	Texas	39	7.0%	41	Rhode Island	3	0.5%
33	Utah	4	0.7%	44	Alaska	2	0.4%
44	Vermont	2	0.4%	44	Montana	2	0.4%
10	Virginia	17	3.0%	44	North Dakota	2	0.4%
30	Washington	5	0.9%	44	Vermont	2	0.4%
33	West Virginia	4	0.7%	44	Wyoming	2	0.4%
15	Wisconsin	14	2.5%	49	Hawaii	1	0.2%
44	Wyoming	2	0.4%	49	South Dakota	1	0.2%
					District of Columbia	3	0.5%

Source: U.S. Department of Health and Human Services, Health Care Financing Administration OSCAR Report 10 (February 1, 2000)

Certified by HCFA to participate in the Medicare/Medicaid programs. Excludes licensed facilities that do not accept federal funding and facilities managed by the Department of Veterans Affairs. National total does not include four certified psychiatric hospitals in U.S. territories.

Beds in Medicare and Medicaid Certified Psychiatric Hospitals in 2000

National Total = 71,879 Beds*

ALPHA ORDER

RANK	STATE	BEDS	% of USA
28	Alabama	763	1.1%
45	Alaska	188	0.3%
39	Arizona	340	0.5%
29	Arkansas	711	1.0%
4	California	3,025	4.2%
22	Colorado	1,163	1.6%
21	Connecticut	1,197	1.7%
42	Delaware	241	0.3%
8	Florida	2,549	3.5%
10	Georgia	2,378	3.3%
48	Hawaii	88	0.1%
46	Idaho	159	0.2%
12	Illinois	1,910	2.7%
20	Indiana	1,276	1.8%
36	Iowa	363	0.5%
26	Kansas	906	1.3%
13	Kentucky	1,715	2.4%
11	Louisiana	1,963	2.7%
38	Maine	344	0.5%
5	Maryland	2,954	4.1%
18	Massachusetts	1,362	1.9%
9	Michigan	2,547	3.5%
17	Minnesota	1,446	2.0%
40	Mississippi	316	0.4%
25	Missouri	1,064	1.5%
50	Montana	30	0.0%
30	Nebraska	626	0.9%
33	Nevada	437	0.6%
34	New Hampshire	431	0.6%
6	New Jersey	2,917	4.1%
41	New Mexico	313	0.4%
1	New York	12,570	17.5%
3	North Carolina	3,213	4.5%
35	North Dakota	369	0.5%
16	Ohio	1,510	2.1%
24	Oklahoma	1,140	1.6%
37	Oregon	362	0.5%
2	Pennsylvania	5,376	7.5%
43	Rhode Island	219	0.3%
27	South Carolina	884	1.2%
47	South Dakota	133	0.2%
19	Tennessee	1,293	1.8%
7	Texas	2,751	3.8%
32	Utah	465	0.6%
44	Vermont	211	0.3%
14	Virginia	1,624	2.3%
23	Washington	1,142	1.6%
31	West Virginia	494	0.7%
15	Wisconsin	1,588	2.2%
49	Wyoming	80	0.1%

RANK ORDER

RANK	STATE	BEDS	% of USA
1	New York	12,570	17.5%
2	Pennsylvania	5,376	7.5%
3	North Carolina	3,213	4.5%
4	California	3,025	4.2%
5	Maryland	2,954	4.1%
6	New Jersey	2,917	4.1%
7	Texas	2,751	3.8%
8	Florida	2,549	3.5%
9	Michigan	2,547	3.5%
10	Georgia	2,378	3.3%
11	Louisiana	1,963	2.7%
12	Illinois	1,910	2.7%
13	Kentucky	1,715	2.4%
14	Virginia	1,624	2.3%
15	Wisconsin	1,588	2.2%
16	Ohio	1,510	2.1%
17	Minnesota	1,446	2.0%
18	Massachusetts	1,362	1.9%
19	Tennessee	1,293	1.8%
20	Indiana	1,276	1.8%
21	Connecticut	1,197	1.7%
22	Colorado	1,163	1.6%
23	Washington	1,142	1.6%
24	Oklahoma	1,140	1.6%
25	Missouri	1,064	1.5%
26	Kansas	906	1.3%
27	South Carolina	884	1.2%
28	Alabama	763	1.1%
29	Arkansas	711	1.0%
30	Nebraska	626	0.9%
31	West Virginia	494	0.7%
32	Utah	465	0.6%
33	Nevada	437	0.6%
34	New Hampshire	431	0.6%
35	North Dakota	369	0.5%
36	Iowa	363	0.5%
37	Oregon	362	0.5%
38	Maine	344	0.5%
39	Arizona	340	0.5%
40	Mississippi	316	0.4%
41	New Mexico	313	0.4%
42	Delaware	241	0.3%
43	Rhode Island	219	0.3%
44	Vermont	211	0.3%
45	Alaska	188	0.3%
46	Idaho	159	0.2%
47	South Dakota	133	0.2%
48	Hawaii	88	0.1%
49	Wyoming	80	0.1%
50	Montana	30	0.0%
	District of Columbia	733	1.0%

Source: U.S. Department of Health and Human Services, Health Care Financing Administration
    OSCAR Report 10 (February 1, 2000)
*Beds in hospitals certified by HCFA to participate in the Medicare/Medicaid programs. Excludes licensed facilities that do not accept federal funding and facilities managed by the Department of Veterans Affairs. National total does not include 903 beds in U.S. territories.

Medicare and Medicaid Certified Community Mental Health Centers in 2000

National Total = 860 Centers*

ALPHA ORDER					RANK ORDER			
RANK	STATE		CENTERS	% of USA	RANK	STATE	CENTERS	% of USA
3	Alabama		84	9.8%	1	Florida	140	16.3%
44	Alaska		0	0.0%	2	Texas	87	10.1%
30	Arizona		6	0.7%	3	Alabama	84	9.8%
18	Arkansas		14	1.6%	4	Louisiana	47	5.5%
10	California		23	2.7%	5	New Jersey	38	4.4%
18	Colorado		14	1.6%	6	Pennsylvania	33	3.8%
31	Connecticut		5	0.6%	7	North Carolina	32	3.7%
44	Delaware		0	0.0%	8	Washington	30	3.5%
1	Florida		140	16.3%	9	Ohio	29	3.4%
28	Georgia		8	0.9%	10	California	23	2.7%
44	Hawaii		0	0.0%	10	Missouri	23	2.7%
44	Idaho		0	0.0%	10	Tennessee	23	2.7%
13	Illinois		20	2.3%	13	Illinois	20	2.3%
23	Indiana		11	1.3%	14	Kansas	19	2.2%
26	Iowa		10	1.2%	15	Massachusetts	17	2.0%
14	Kansas		19	2.2%	16	Minnesota	16	1.9%
18	Kentucky		14	1.6%	16	New Mexico	16	1.9%
4	Louisiana		47	5.5%	18	Arkansas	14	1.6%
35	Maine		3	0.3%	18	Colorado	14	1.6%
28	Maryland		8	0.9%	18	Kentucky	14	1.6%
15	Massachusetts		17	2.0%	21	Oregon	12	1.4%
23	Michigan		11	1.3%	21	South Carolina	12	1.4%
16	Minnesota		16	1.9%	23	Indiana	11	1.3%
31	Mississippi		5	0.6%	23	Michigan	11	1.3%
10	Missouri		23	2.7%	23	New York	11	1.3%
35	Montana		3	0.3%	26	Iowa	10	1.2%
42	Nebraska		1	0.1%	26	Oklahoma	10	1.2%
41	Nevada		2	0.2%	28	Georgia	8	0.9%
31	New Hampshire		5	0.6%	28	Maryland	8	0.9%
5	New Jersey		38	4.4%	30	Arizona	6	0.7%
16	New Mexico		16	1.9%	31	Connecticut	5	0.6%
23	New York		11	1.3%	31	Mississippi	5	0.6%
7	North Carolina		32	3.7%	31	New Hampshire	5	0.6%
44	North Dakota		0	0.0%	31	Virginia	5	0.6%
9	Ohio		29	3.4%	35	Maine	3	0.3%
26	Oklahoma		10	1.2%	35	Montana	3	0.3%
21	Oregon		12	1.4%	35	South Dakota	3	0.3%
6	Pennsylvania		33	3.8%	35	Utah	3	0.3%
44	Rhode Island		0	0.0%	35	West Virginia	3	0.3%
21	South Carolina		12	1.4%	35	Wyoming	3	0.3%
35	South Dakota		3	0.3%	41	Nevada	2	0.2%
10	Tennessee		23	2.7%	42	Nebraska	1	0.1%
2	Texas		87	10.1%	42	Wisconsin	1	0.1%
35	Utah		3	0.3%	44	Alaska	0	0.0%
44	Vermont		0	0.0%	44	Delaware	0	0.0%
31	Virginia		5	0.6%	44	Hawaii	0	0.0%
8	Washington		30	3.5%	44	Idaho	0	0.0%
35	West Virginia		3	0.3%	44	North Dakota	0	0.0%
42	Wisconsin		1	0.1%	44	Rhode Island	0	0.0%
35	Wyoming		3	0.3%	44	Vermont	0	0.0%
						District of Columbia	0	0.0%

Source: U.S. Department of Health and Human Services, Health Care Financing Administration
OSCAR Report 10 (February 1, 2000)
*Certified by HCFA to participate in the Medicare/Medicaid programs. Excludes licensed facilities that do not accept federal funding and facilities managed by the Department of Veterans Affairs. National total does not include 10 certified mental health centers in U.S. territories.

Medicare and Medicaid Certified Outpatient Physical Therapy Facilities in 2000

National Total = 2,930 Facilities*

RANK	STATE	FACILITIES	% of USA
35	Alabama	21	0.7%
37	Alaska	18	0.6%
25	Arizona	38	1.3%
29	Arkansas	30	1.0%
2	California	241	8.2%
18	Colorado	56	1.9%
24	Connecticut	40	1.4%
33	Delaware	22	0.8%
1	Florida	280	9.6%
7	Georgia	126	4.3%
41	Hawaii	11	0.4%
38	Idaho	16	0.5%
12	Illinois	81	2.8%
16	Indiana	58	2.0%
26	Iowa	35	1.2%
31	Kansas	26	0.9%
14	Kentucky	62	2.1%
20	Louisiana	53	1.8%
32	Maine	23	0.8%
11	Maryland	88	3.0%
36	Massachusetts	19	0.6%
4	Michigan	197	6.7%
17	Minnesota	57	1.9%
23	Mississippi	45	1.5%
15	Missouri	61	2.1%
43	Montana	10	0.3%
39	Nebraska	12	0.4%
41	Nevada	11	0.4%
39	New Hampshire	12	0.4%
9	New Jersey	108	3.7%
27	New Mexico	34	1.2%
30	New York	27	0.9%
21	North Carolina	49	1.7%
45	North Dakota	6	0.2%
6	Ohio	127	4.3%
21	Oklahoma	49	1.7%
33	Oregon	22	0.8%
5	Pennsylvania	136	4.6%
49	Rhode Island	3	0.1%
19	South Carolina	54	1.8%
46	South Dakota	5	0.2%
10	Tennessee	97	3.3%
3	Texas	220	7.5%
43	Utah	10	0.3%
50	Vermont	2	0.1%
8	Virginia	121	4.1%
28	Washington	33	1.1%
46	West Virginia	5	0.2%
13	Wisconsin	67	2.3%
46	Wyoming	5	0.2%

RANK	STATE	FACILITIES	% of USA
1	Florida	280	9.6%
2	California	241	8.2%
3	Texas	220	7.5%
4	Michigan	197	6.7%
5	Pennsylvania	136	4.6%
6	Ohio	127	4.3%
7	Georgia	126	4.3%
8	Virginia	121	4.1%
9	New Jersey	108	3.7%
10	Tennessee	97	3.3%
11	Maryland	88	3.0%
12	Illinois	81	2.8%
13	Wisconsin	67	2.3%
14	Kentucky	62	2.1%
15	Missouri	61	2.1%
16	Indiana	58	2.0%
17	Minnesota	57	1.9%
18	Colorado	56	1.9%
19	South Carolina	54	1.8%
20	Louisiana	53	1.8%
21	North Carolina	49	1.7%
21	Oklahoma	49	1.7%
23	Mississippi	45	1.5%
24	Connecticut	40	1.4%
25	Arizona	38	1.3%
26	Iowa	35	1.2%
27	New Mexico	34	1.2%
28	Washington	33	1.1%
29	Arkansas	30	1.0%
30	New York	27	0.9%
31	Kansas	26	0.9%
32	Maine	23	0.8%
33	Delaware	22	0.8%
33	Oregon	22	0.8%
35	Alabama	21	0.7%
36	Massachusetts	19	0.6%
37	Alaska	18	0.6%
38	Idaho	16	0.5%
39	Nebraska	12	0.4%
39	New Hampshire	12	0.4%
41	Hawaii	11	0.4%
41	Nevada	11	0.4%
43	Montana	10	0.3%
43	Utah	10	0.3%
45	North Dakota	6	0.2%
46	South Dakota	5	0.2%
46	West Virginia	5	0.2%
46	Wyoming	5	0.2%
49	Rhode Island	3	0.1%
50	Vermont	2	0.1%
	District of Columbia	1	0.0%

*Source: U.S. Department of Health and Human Services, Health Care Financing Administration
OSCAR Report 10 (February 1, 2000)*

Certified by HCFA to participate in the Medicare/Medicaid programs. Excludes licensed facilities that do not accept federal funding and facilities managed by the Department of Veterans Affairs. National total does not include three certified outpatient physical therapy facilities in U.S. territories.

Medicare and Medicaid Certified Rural Health Clinics in 2000

National Total = 3,448 Rural Health Clinics*

ALPHA ORDER

RANK	STATE	CLINICS	% of USA
19	Alabama	64	1.9%
40	Alaska	11	0.3%
42	Arizona	9	0.3%
13	Arkansas	95	2.8%
2	California	216	6.3%
29	Colorado	40	1.2%
46	Connecticut	0	0.0%
46	Delaware	0	0.0%
10	Florida	128	3.7%
9	Georgia	133	3.9%
44	Hawaii	1	0.0%
31	Idaho	35	1.0%
3	Illinois	202	5.9%
27	Indiana	51	1.5%
8	Iowa	135	3.9%
5	Kansas	165	4.8%
16	Kentucky	74	2.1%
25	Louisiana	53	1.5%
28	Maine	50	1.5%
46	Maryland	0	0.0%
46	Massachusetts	0	0.0%
5	Michigan	165	4.8%
21	Minnesota	62	1.8%
7	Mississippi	142	4.1%
4	Missouri	173	5.0%
32	Montana	29	0.8%
15	Nebraska	78	2.3%
43	Nevada	2	0.1%
35	New Hampshire	21	0.6%
46	New Jersey	0	0.0%
37	New Mexico	16	0.5%
41	New York	10	0.3%
10	North Carolina	128	3.7%
14	North Dakota	81	2.3%
38	Ohio	15	0.4%
17	Oklahoma	73	2.1%
33	Oregon	26	0.8%
26	Pennsylvania	52	1.5%
44	Rhode Island	1	0.0%
12	South Carolina	96	2.8%
23	South Dakota	57	1.7%
30	Tennessee	38	1.1%
1	Texas	416	12.1%
39	Utah	14	0.4%
34	Vermont	23	0.7%
22	Virginia	61	1.8%
23	Washington	57	1.7%
18	West Virginia	69	2.0%
20	Wisconsin	63	1.8%
36	Wyoming	18	0.5%

RANK ORDER

RANK	STATE	CLINICS	% of USA
1	Texas	416	12.1%
2	California	216	6.3%
3	Illinois	202	5.9%
4	Missouri	173	5.0%
5	Kansas	165	4.8%
5	Michigan	165	4.8%
7	Mississippi	142	4.1%
8	Iowa	135	3.9%
9	Georgia	133	3.9%
10	Florida	128	3.7%
10	North Carolina	128	3.7%
12	South Carolina	96	2.8%
13	Arkansas	95	2.8%
14	North Dakota	81	2.3%
15	Nebraska	78	2.3%
16	Kentucky	74	2.1%
17	Oklahoma	73	2.1%
18	West Virginia	69	2.0%
19	Alabama	64	1.9%
20	Wisconsin	63	1.8%
21	Minnesota	62	1.8%
22	Virginia	61	1.8%
23	South Dakota	57	1.7%
23	Washington	57	1.7%
25	Louisiana	53	1.5%
26	Pennsylvania	52	1.5%
27	Indiana	51	1.5%
28	Maine	50	1.5%
29	Colorado	40	1.2%
30	Tennessee	38	1.1%
31	Idaho	35	1.0%
32	Montana	29	0.8%
33	Oregon	26	0.8%
34	Vermont	23	0.7%
35	New Hampshire	21	0.6%
36	Wyoming	18	0.5%
37	New Mexico	16	0.5%
38	Ohio	15	0.4%
39	Utah	14	0.4%
40	Alaska	11	0.3%
41	New York	10	0.3%
42	Arizona	9	0.3%
43	Nevada	2	0.1%
44	Hawaii	1	0.0%
44	Rhode Island	1	0.0%
46	Connecticut	0	0.0%
46	Delaware	0	0.0%
46	Maryland	0	0.0%
46	Massachusetts	0	0.0%
46	New Jersey	0	0.0%
	District of Columbia	0	0.0%

Source: U.S. Department of Health and Human Services, Health Care Financing Administration
 OSCAR Report 10 (February 1, 2000)
*Certified by HCFA to participate in the Medicare/Medicaid programs. Excludes licensed facilities that do not accept federal funding and facilities managed by the Department of Veterans Affairs. There are no certified rural health centers in U.S. territories.

Medicare and Medicaid Certified Home Health Agencies in 2000

National Total = 7,735 Home Health Agencies*

ALPHA ORDER

RANK	STATE	AGENCIES	% of USA
23	Alabama	140	1.8%
48	Alaska	18	0.2%
28	Arizona	77	1.0%
15	Arkansas	189	2.4%
2	California	617	8.0%
22	Colorado	144	1.9%
26	Connecticut	93	1.2%
49	Delaware	15	0.2%
5	Florida	333	4.3%
25	Georgia	100	1.3%
47	Hawaii	21	0.3%
35	Idaho	60	0.8%
6	Illinois	311	4.0%
11	Indiana	199	2.6%
13	Iowa	192	2.5%
18	Kansas	163	2.1%
24	Kentucky	114	1.5%
7	Louisiana	290	3.7%
44	Maine	36	0.5%
37	Maryland	56	0.7%
20	Massachusetts	156	2.0%
12	Michigan	197	2.5%
8	Minnesota	254	3.3%
32	Mississippi	64	0.8%
13	Missouri	192	2.5%
36	Montana	59	0.8%
30	Nebraska	75	1.0%
42	Nevada	42	0.5%
43	New Hampshire	41	0.5%
38	New Jersey	54	0.7%
31	New Mexico	74	1.0%
9	New York	222	2.9%
17	North Carolina	168	2.2%
45	North Dakota	35	0.5%
3	Ohio	385	5.0%
10	Oklahoma	206	2.7%
34	Oregon	61	0.8%
4	Pennsylvania	338	4.4%
46	Rhode Island	25	0.3%
27	South Carolina	79	1.0%
39	South Dakota	50	0.6%
16	Tennessee	169	2.2%
1	Texas	1,049	13.6%
40	Utah	48	0.6%
50	Vermont	13	0.2%
19	Virginia	159	2.1%
32	Washington	64	0.8%
29	West Virginia	76	1.0%
21	Wisconsin	151	2.0%
41	Wyoming	44	0.6%

RANK ORDER

RANK	STATE	AGENCIES	% of USA
1	Texas	1,049	13.6%
2	California	617	8.0%
3	Ohio	385	5.0%
4	Pennsylvania	338	4.4%
5	Florida	333	4.3%
6	Illinois	311	4.0%
7	Louisiana	290	3.7%
8	Minnesota	254	3.3%
9	New York	222	2.9%
10	Oklahoma	206	2.7%
11	Indiana	199	2.6%
12	Michigan	197	2.5%
13	Iowa	192	2.5%
13	Missouri	192	2.5%
15	Arkansas	189	2.4%
16	Tennessee	169	2.2%
17	North Carolina	168	2.2%
18	Kansas	163	2.1%
19	Virginia	159	2.1%
20	Massachusetts	156	2.0%
21	Wisconsin	151	2.0%
22	Colorado	144	1.9%
23	Alabama	140	1.8%
24	Kentucky	114	1.5%
25	Georgia	100	1.3%
26	Connecticut	93	1.2%
27	South Carolina	79	1.0%
28	Arizona	77	1.0%
29	West Virginia	76	1.0%
30	Nebraska	75	1.0%
31	New Mexico	74	1.0%
32	Mississippi	64	0.8%
32	Washington	64	0.8%
34	Oregon	61	0.8%
35	Idaho	60	0.8%
36	Montana	59	0.8%
37	Maryland	56	0.7%
38	New Jersey	54	0.7%
39	South Dakota	50	0.6%
40	Utah	48	0.6%
41	Wyoming	44	0.6%
42	Nevada	42	0.5%
43	New Hampshire	41	0.5%
44	Maine	36	0.5%
45	North Dakota	35	0.5%
46	Rhode Island	25	0.3%
47	Hawaii	21	0.3%
48	Alaska	18	0.2%
49	Delaware	15	0.2%
50	Vermont	13	0.2%
	District of Columbia	17	0.2%

Source: U.S. Department of Health and Human Services, Health Care Financing Administration
   OSCAR Report 10 (February 1, 2000)

*Certified by HCFA to participate in the Medicare/Medicaid programs. Excludes agencies that do not accept federal funding. National total does not include 50 certified home health agencies in U.S. territories. A home health agency provides health services to individuals in their homes for the purpose of promoting, maintaining or restoring health or maximizing the level of independence, while minimizing the effects of disability and illness.

Medicare and Medicaid Certified Hospices in 2000

National Total = 2,249 Hospices*

<u>ALPHA ORDER</u>

RANK	STATE	HOSPICES	% of USA
10	Alabama	66	2.9%
50	Alaska	2	0.1%
27	Arizona	36	1.6%
17	Arkansas	53	2.4%
1	California	184	8.2%
25	Colorado	39	1.7%
33	Connecticut	28	1.2%
49	Delaware	5	0.2%
23	Florida	40	1.8%
7	Georgia	71	3.2%
46	Hawaii	7	0.3%
36	Idaho	26	1.2%
5	Illinois	86	3.8%
14	Indiana	60	2.7%
15	Iowa	59	2.6%
28	Kansas	35	1.6%
31	Kentucky	29	1.3%
25	Louisiana	39	1.7%
41	Maine	16	0.7%
29	Maryland	31	1.4%
21	Massachusetts	41	1.8%
6	Michigan	80	3.6%
12	Minnesota	63	2.8%
23	Mississippi	40	1.8%
10	Missouri	66	2.9%
40	Montana	18	0.8%
31	Nebraska	29	1.3%
46	Nevada	7	0.3%
38	New Hampshire	20	0.9%
20	New Jersey	42	1.9%
35	New Mexico	27	1.2%
16	New York	54	2.4%
7	North Carolina	71	3.2%
42	North Dakota	15	0.7%
4	Ohio	94	4.2%
9	Oklahoma	67	3.0%
21	Oregon	41	1.8%
3	Pennsylvania	117	5.2%
46	Rhode Island	7	0.3%
29	South Carolina	31	1.4%
44	South Dakota	14	0.6%
13	Tennessee	61	2.7%
2	Texas	138	6.1%
37	Utah	21	0.9%
45	Vermont	9	0.4%
19	Virginia	46	2.0%
33	Washington	28	1.2%
38	West Virginia	20	0.9%
18	Wisconsin	51	2.3%
42	Wyoming	15	0.7%

<u>RANK ORDER</u>

RANK	STATE	HOSPICES	% of USA
1	California	184	8.2%
2	Texas	138	6.1%
3	Pennsylvania	117	5.2%
4	Ohio	94	4.2%
5	Illinois	86	3.8%
6	Michigan	80	3.6%
7	Georgia	71	3.2%
7	North Carolina	71	3.2%
9	Oklahoma	67	3.0%
10	Alabama	66	2.9%
10	Missouri	66	2.9%
12	Minnesota	63	2.8%
13	Tennessee	61	2.7%
14	Indiana	60	2.7%
15	Iowa	59	2.6%
16	New York	54	2.4%
17	Arkansas	53	2.4%
18	Wisconsin	51	2.3%
19	Virginia	46	2.0%
20	New Jersey	42	1.9%
21	Massachusetts	41	1.8%
21	Oregon	41	1.8%
23	Florida	40	1.8%
23	Mississippi	40	1.8%
25	Colorado	39	1.7%
25	Louisiana	39	1.7%
27	Arizona	36	1.6%
28	Kansas	35	1.6%
29	Maryland	31	1.4%
29	South Carolina	31	1.4%
31	Kentucky	29	1.3%
31	Nebraska	29	1.3%
33	Connecticut	28	1.2%
33	Washington	28	1.2%
35	New Mexico	27	1.2%
36	Idaho	26	1.2%
37	Utah	21	0.9%
38	New Hampshire	20	0.9%
38	West Virginia	20	0.9%
40	Montana	18	0.8%
41	Maine	16	0.7%
42	North Dakota	15	0.7%
42	Wyoming	15	0.7%
44	South Dakota	14	0.6%
45	Vermont	9	0.4%
46	Hawaii	7	0.3%
46	Nevada	7	0.3%
46	Rhode Island	7	0.3%
49	Delaware	5	0.2%
50	Alaska	2	0.1%
	District of Columbia	4	0.2%

Source: U.S. Department of Health and Human Services, Health Care Financing Administration
OSCAR Report 10 (February 1, 2000)

*Certified by HCFA to participate in the Medicare/Medicaid programs. Excludes licensed facilities that do not accept federal funding and facilities managed by the Department of Veterans Affairs. National total does not include 33 certified hospices in U.S. territories. An hospice provides specialized services for terminally ill people and their families.

Hospice Patients in Residential Facilities in 2000

National Total = 13,743 Patients*

ALPHA ORDER

RANK	STATE	PATIENTS	% of USA
26	Alabama	133	1.0%
47	Alaska	0	0.0%
19	Arizona	212	1.5%
29	Arkansas	96	0.7%
4	California	887	6.5%
18	Colorado	215	1.6%
30	Connecticut	68	0.5%
43	Delaware	7	0.1%
1	Florida	2,477	18.0%
16	Georgia	224	1.6%
45	Hawaii	3	0.0%
36	Idaho	24	0.2%
5	Illinois	873	6.4%
12	Indiana	313	2.3%
21	Iowa	194	1.4%
28	Kansas	100	0.7%
14	Kentucky	284	2.1%
34	Louisiana	36	0.3%
40	Maine	12	0.1%
22	Maryland	175	1.3%
20	Massachusetts	211	1.5%
13	Michigan	302	2.2%
23	Minnesota	146	1.1%
47	Mississippi	0	0.0%
10	Missouri	374	2.7%
35	Montana	33	0.2%
24	Nebraska	139	1.0%
31	Nevada	55	0.4%
47	New Hampshire	0	0.0%
15	New Jersey	262	1.9%
40	New Mexico	12	0.1%
8	New York	444	3.2%
17	North Carolina	217	1.6%
33	North Dakota	39	0.3%
7	Ohio	552	4.0%
6	Oklahoma	675	4.9%
11	Oregon	352	2.6%
2	Pennsylvania	1,695	12.3%
47	Rhode Island	0	0.0%
27	South Carolina	101	0.7%
44	South Dakota	4	0.0%
32	Tennessee	51	0.4%
3	Texas	1,072	7.8%
40	Utah	12	0.1%
39	Vermont	13	0.1%
37	Virginia	22	0.2%
9	Washington	427	3.1%
38	West Virginia	17	0.1%
25	Wisconsin	135	1.0%
46	Wyoming	2	0.0%

RANK ORDER

RANK	STATE	PATIENTS	% of USA
1	Florida	2,477	18.0%
2	Pennsylvania	1,695	12.3%
3	Texas	1,072	7.8%
4	California	887	6.5%
5	Illinois	873	6.4%
6	Oklahoma	675	4.9%
7	Ohio	552	4.0%
8	New York	444	3.2%
9	Washington	427	3.1%
10	Missouri	374	2.7%
11	Oregon	352	2.6%
12	Indiana	313	2.3%
13	Michigan	302	2.2%
14	Kentucky	284	2.1%
15	New Jersey	262	1.9%
16	Georgia	224	1.6%
17	North Carolina	217	1.6%
18	Colorado	215	1.6%
19	Arizona	212	1.5%
20	Massachusetts	211	1.5%
21	Iowa	194	1.4%
22	Maryland	175	1.3%
23	Minnesota	146	1.1%
24	Nebraska	139	1.0%
25	Wisconsin	135	1.0%
26	Alabama	133	1.0%
27	South Carolina	101	0.7%
28	Kansas	100	0.7%
29	Arkansas	96	0.7%
30	Connecticut	68	0.5%
31	Nevada	55	0.4%
32	Tennessee	51	0.4%
33	North Dakota	39	0.3%
34	Louisiana	36	0.3%
35	Montana	33	0.2%
36	Idaho	24	0.2%
37	Virginia	22	0.2%
38	West Virginia	17	0.1%
39	Vermont	13	0.1%
40	Maine	12	0.1%
40	New Mexico	12	0.1%
40	Utah	12	0.1%
43	Delaware	7	0.1%
44	South Dakota	4	0.0%
45	Hawaii	3	0.0%
46	Wyoming	2	0.0%
47	Alaska	0	0.0%
47	Mississippi	0	0.0%
47	New Hampshire	0	0.0%
47	Rhode Island	0	0.0%
	District of Columbia	46	0.3%

Source: U.S. Department of Health and Human Services, Health Care Financing Administration
OSCAR Report 10 (February 1, 2000)

*Patients in facilities certified by HCFA to participate in the Medicare/Medicaid programs. Excludes licensed facilities that do not accept federal funding and facilities managed by the Department of Veterans Affairs. National total does not include five patients in U.S. territories. An hospice provides specialized services for terminally ill people and their families.

Medicare and Medicaid Certified Nursing Care Facilities in 2000

National Total = 17,122 Nursing Care Facilities*

<u>ALPHA ORDER</u>

RANK	STATE	FACILITIES	% of USA
30	Alabama	225	1.3%
50	Alaska	15	0.1%
33	Arizona	160	0.9%
25	Arkansas	270	1.6%
1	California	1,395	8.1%
29	Colorado	227	1.3%
26	Connecticut	257	1.5%
48	Delaware	43	0.3%
6	Florida	741	4.3%
18	Georgia	363	2.1%
47	Hawaii	44	0.3%
43	Idaho	82	0.5%
4	Illinois	880	5.1%
8	Indiana	571	3.3%
11	Iowa	472	2.8%
17	Kansas	400	2.3%
22	Kentucky	311	1.8%
21	Louisiana	340	2.0%
36	Maine	126	0.7%
27	Maryland	252	1.5%
10	Massachusetts	545	3.2%
13	Michigan	440	2.6%
12	Minnesota	446	2.6%
31	Mississippi	198	1.2%
9	Missouri	557	3.3%
38	Montana	105	0.6%
28	Nebraska	241	1.4%
45	Nevada	51	0.3%
42	New Hampshire	84	0.5%
18	New Jersey	363	2.1%
43	New Mexico	82	0.5%
7	New York	660	3.9%
15	North Carolina	408	2.4%
41	North Dakota	89	0.5%
3	Ohio	1,010	5.9%
15	Oklahoma	408	2.4%
34	Oregon	156	0.9%
5	Pennsylvania	786	4.6%
39	Rhode Island	101	0.6%
32	South Carolina	176	1.0%
37	South Dakota	114	0.7%
20	Tennessee	356	2.1%
2	Texas	1,254	7.3%
40	Utah	92	0.5%
46	Vermont	45	0.3%
24	Virginia	277	1.6%
23	Washington	278	1.6%
35	West Virginia	139	0.8%
14	Wisconsin	426	2.5%
49	Wyoming	41	0.2%

<u>RANK ORDER</u>

RANK	STATE	FACILITIES	% of USA
1	California	1,395	8.1%
2	Texas	1,254	7.3%
3	Ohio	1,010	5.9%
4	Illinois	880	5.1%
5	Pennsylvania	786	4.6%
6	Florida	741	4.3%
7	New York	660	3.9%
8	Indiana	571	3.3%
9	Missouri	557	3.3%
10	Massachusetts	545	3.2%
11	Iowa	472	2.8%
12	Minnesota	446	2.6%
13	Michigan	440	2.6%
14	Wisconsin	426	2.5%
15	North Carolina	408	2.4%
15	Oklahoma	408	2.4%
17	Kansas	400	2.3%
18	Georgia	363	2.1%
18	New Jersey	363	2.1%
20	Tennessee	356	2.1%
21	Louisiana	340	2.0%
22	Kentucky	311	1.8%
23	Washington	278	1.6%
24	Virginia	277	1.6%
25	Arkansas	270	1.6%
26	Connecticut	257	1.5%
27	Maryland	252	1.5%
28	Nebraska	241	1.4%
29	Colorado	227	1.3%
30	Alabama	225	1.3%
31	Mississippi	198	1.2%
32	South Carolina	176	1.0%
33	Arizona	160	0.9%
34	Oregon	156	0.9%
35	West Virginia	139	0.8%
36	Maine	126	0.7%
37	South Dakota	114	0.7%
38	Montana	105	0.6%
39	Rhode Island	101	0.6%
40	Utah	92	0.5%
41	North Dakota	89	0.5%
42	New Hampshire	84	0.5%
43	Idaho	82	0.5%
43	New Mexico	82	0.5%
45	Nevada	51	0.3%
46	Vermont	45	0.3%
47	Hawaii	44	0.3%
48	Delaware	43	0.3%
49	Wyoming	41	0.2%
50	Alaska	15	0.1%
	District of Columbia	20	0.1%

Source: U.S. Department of Health and Human Services, Health Care Financing Administration
   OSCAR Report 10 (February 1, 2000)
Certified by HCFA to participate in the Medicare/Medicaid programs. Excludes licensed facilities that do not accept federal funding and facilities managed by the Department of Veterans Affairs. National total does not include nine certified nursing facilities in U.S. territories.

Beds in Medicare and Medicaid Certified Nursing Care Facilities in 2000

National Total = 1,731,359 Beds*

ALPHA ORDER

RANK	STATE	BEDS	% of USA
27	Alabama	24,924	1.4%
50	Alaska	726	0.0%
32	Arizona	17,092	1.0%
24	Arkansas	25,846	1.5%
1	California	127,608	7.4%
29	Colorado	19,197	1.1%
21	Connecticut	31,549	1.8%
46	Delaware	4,590	0.3%
7	Florida	79,830	4.6%
16	Georgia	39,519	2.3%
47	Hawaii	3,804	0.2%
44	Idaho	5,871	0.3%
4	Illinois	101,340	5.9%
9	Indiana	55,267	3.2%
19	Iowa	34,816	2.0%
25	Kansas	25,660	1.5%
28	Kentucky	24,440	1.4%
18	Louisiana	37,321	2.2%
37	Maine	8,363	0.5%
23	Maryland	28,613	1.7%
8	Massachusetts	56,316	3.3%
12	Michigan	48,521	2.8%
14	Minnesota	44,038	2.5%
31	Mississippi	17,166	1.0%
11	Missouri	50,105	2.9%
40	Montana	7,646	0.4%
30	Nebraska	17,513	1.0%
45	Nevada	5,133	0.3%
39	New Hampshire	7,849	0.5%
10	New Jersey	50,411	2.9%
42	New Mexico	7,168	0.4%
2	New York	119,866	6.9%
15	North Carolina	40,388	2.3%
43	North Dakota	7,043	0.4%
6	Ohio	95,154	5.5%
20	Oklahoma	33,476	1.9%
34	Oregon	13,238	0.8%
5	Pennsylvania	95,556	5.5%
36	Rhode Island	10,149	0.6%
33	South Carolina	16,802	1.0%
38	South Dakota	7,879	0.5%
17	Tennessee	38,795	2.2%
3	Texas	114,141	6.6%
41	Utah	7,389	0.4%
48	Vermont	3,728	0.2%
22	Virginia	29,781	1.7%
26	Washington	25,204	1.5%
35	West Virginia	11,142	0.6%
13	Wisconsin	47,201	2.7%
49	Wyoming	3,156	0.2%

RANK ORDER

RANK	STATE	BEDS	% of USA
1	California	127,608	7.4%
2	New York	119,866	6.9%
3	Texas	114,141	6.6%
4	Illinois	101,340	5.9%
5	Pennsylvania	95,556	5.5%
6	Ohio	95,154	5.5%
7	Florida	79,830	4.6%
8	Massachusetts	56,316	3.3%
9	Indiana	55,267	3.2%
10	New Jersey	50,411	2.9%
11	Missouri	50,105	2.9%
12	Michigan	48,521	2.8%
13	Wisconsin	47,201	2.7%
14	Minnesota	44,038	2.5%
15	North Carolina	40,388	2.3%
16	Georgia	39,519	2.3%
17	Tennessee	38,795	2.2%
18	Louisiana	37,321	2.2%
19	Iowa	34,816	2.0%
20	Oklahoma	33,476	1.9%
21	Connecticut	31,549	1.8%
22	Virginia	29,781	1.7%
23	Maryland	28,613	1.7%
24	Arkansas	25,846	1.5%
25	Kansas	25,660	1.5%
26	Washington	25,204	1.5%
27	Alabama	24,924	1.4%
28	Kentucky	24,440	1.4%
29	Colorado	19,197	1.1%
30	Nebraska	17,513	1.0%
31	Mississippi	17,166	1.0%
32	Arizona	17,092	1.0%
33	South Carolina	16,802	1.0%
34	Oregon	13,238	0.8%
35	West Virginia	11,142	0.6%
36	Rhode Island	10,149	0.6%
37	Maine	8,363	0.5%
38	South Dakota	7,879	0.5%
39	New Hampshire	7,849	0.5%
40	Montana	7,646	0.4%
41	Utah	7,389	0.4%
42	New Mexico	7,168	0.4%
43	North Dakota	7,043	0.4%
44	Idaho	5,871	0.3%
45	Nevada	5,133	0.3%
46	Delaware	4,590	0.3%
47	Hawaii	3,804	0.2%
48	Vermont	3,728	0.2%
49	Wyoming	3,156	0.2%
50	Alaska	726	0.0%
	District of Columbia	3,029	0.2%

*Source: U.S. Department of Health and Human Services, Health Care Financing Administration
OSCAR Report 10 (February 1, 2000)*
Beds in nursing care facilities certified by HCFA to participate in the Medicare/Medicaid programs. National total does not include 343 beds in U.S. territories.

Rate of Beds in Medicare and Medicaid Certified Nursing Care Facilities in 2000

National Rate = 427 Beds per 1,000 Population 85 Years and Older*

ALPHA ORDER

RANK	STATE	RATE
34	Alabama	387
45	Alaska	314
47	Arizona	273
4	Arkansas	582
46	California	310
29	Colorado	420
11	Connecticut	513
22	Delaware	479
48	Florida	257
22	Georgia	479
50	Hawaii	232
41	Idaho	343
6	Illinois	545
2	Indiana	628
6	Iowa	545
13	Kansas	508
28	Kentucky	428
1	Louisiana	670
35	Maine	381
24	Maryland	450
19	Massachusetts	499
40	Michigan	349
8	Minnesota	530
27	Mississippi	429
12	Missouri	511
10	Montana	519
9	Nebraska	520
42	Nevada	340
25	New Hampshire	448
33	New Jersey	392
43	New Mexico	332
30	New York	399
32	North Carolina	398
21	North Dakota	496
5	Ohio	558
3	Oklahoma	592
49	Oregon	249
26	Pennsylvania	432
16	Rhode Island	505
37	South Carolina	363
20	South Dakota	498
18	Tennessee	502
17	Texas	504
39	Utah	353
30	Vermont	399
36	Virginia	365
44	Washington	321
38	West Virginia	358
14	Wisconsin	507
15	Wyoming	506

RANK ORDER

RANK	STATE	RATE
1	Louisiana	670
2	Indiana	628
3	Oklahoma	592
4	Arkansas	582
5	Ohio	558
6	Illinois	545
6	Iowa	545
8	Minnesota	530
9	Nebraska	520
10	Montana	519
11	Connecticut	513
12	Missouri	511
13	Kansas	508
14	Wisconsin	507
15	Wyoming	506
16	Rhode Island	505
17	Texas	504
18	Tennessee	502
19	Massachusetts	499
20	South Dakota	498
21	North Dakota	496
22	Delaware	479
22	Georgia	479
24	Maryland	450
25	New Hampshire	448
26	Pennsylvania	432
27	Mississippi	429
28	Kentucky	428
29	Colorado	420
30	New York	399
30	Vermont	399
32	North Carolina	398
33	New Jersey	392
34	Alabama	387
35	Maine	381
36	Virginia	365
37	South Carolina	363
38	West Virginia	358
39	Utah	353
40	Michigan	349
41	Idaho	343
42	Nevada	340
43	New Mexico	332
44	Washington	321
45	Alaska	314
46	California	310
47	Arizona	273
48	Florida	257
49	Oregon	249
50	Hawaii	232

District of Columbia	335

Source: Morgan Quitno Press using data from U.S. Dept. of Health & Human Services, Health Care Financing Admin. OSCAR Report 10 (February 1, 2000)

*Beds in nursing care facilities certified by HCFA to participate in the Medicare/Medicaid programs. National rate does not include beds or population in U.S. territories. Calculated using 1998 Census population estimates.

Nursing Home Occupancy Rate in 1997

National Rate = 82.0% of Beds in Nursing Homes Occupied

ALPHA ORDER

RANK	STATE	RATE
6	Alabama	93.0
42	Alaska	73.6
38	Arizona	75.3
50	Arkansas	63.5
37	California	77.1
28	Colorado	83.1
11	Connecticut	92.2
39	Delaware	75.0
27	Florida	83.5
10	Georgia	92.5
13	Hawaii	91.4
41	Idaho	74.0
36	Illinois	78.2
45	Indiana	71.9
49	Iowa	66.4
33	Kansas	80.6
19	Kentucky	88.7
32	Louisiana	81.1
21	Maine	87.9
31	Maryland	82.1
18	Massachusetts	89.3
23	Michigan	86.4
8	Minnesota	92.6
8	Mississippi	92.6
43	Missouri	73.3
28	Montana	83.1
24	Nebraska	85.4
40	Nevada	74.4
7	New Hampshire	92.8
12	New Jersey	91.9
25	New Mexico	84.0
1	New York	95.2
5	North Carolina	93.7
4	North Dakota	93.9
48	Ohio	69.1
44	Oklahoma	72.4
34	Oregon	79.7
17	Pennsylvania	90.1
14	Rhode Island	91.3
22	South Carolina	86.6
2	South Dakota	94.2
16	Tennessee	90.3
46	Texas	69.8
35	Utah	78.3
3	Vermont	94.0
15	Virginia	90.8
30	Washington	82.3
47	West Virginia	69.5
20	Wisconsin	88.3
25	Wyoming	84.0

RANK ORDER

RANK	STATE	RATE
1	New York	95.2
2	South Dakota	94.2
3	Vermont	94.0
4	North Dakota	93.9
5	North Carolina	93.7
6	Alabama	93.0
7	New Hampshire	92.8
8	Minnesota	92.6
8	Mississippi	92.6
10	Georgia	92.5
11	Connecticut	92.2
12	New Jersey	91.9
13	Hawaii	91.4
14	Rhode Island	91.3
15	Virginia	90.8
16	Tennessee	90.3
17	Pennsylvania	90.1
18	Massachusetts	89.3
19	Kentucky	88.7
20	Wisconsin	88.3
21	Maine	87.9
22	South Carolina	86.6
23	Michigan	86.4
24	Nebraska	85.4
25	New Mexico	84.0
25	Wyoming	84.0
27	Florida	83.5
28	Colorado	83.1
28	Montana	83.1
30	Washington	82.3
31	Maryland	82.1
32	Louisiana	81.1
33	Kansas	80.6
34	Oregon	79.7
35	Utah	78.3
36	Illinois	78.2
37	California	77.1
38	Arizona	75.3
39	Delaware	75.0
40	Nevada	74.4
41	Idaho	74.0
42	Alaska	73.6
43	Missouri	73.3
44	Oklahoma	72.4
45	Indiana	71.9
46	Texas	69.8
47	West Virginia	69.5
48	Ohio	69.1
49	Iowa	66.4
50	Arkansas	63.5
	District of Columbia	94.9

*Source: U.S. Department of Health and Human Services, Health Care Financing Administration
"Health, United States, 1999" (October 1999)*

Nursing Home Resident Rate in 1997

National Rate = 363.2 Residents per 1,000 Population Age 85 and Older*

ALPHA ORDER

RANK ORDER

RANK	STATE	RATE		RANK	STATE	RATE
35	Alabama	328.8		1	Louisiana	573.9
43	Alaska	261.2		2	Indiana	504.4
50	Arizona	165.6		3	Connecticut	498.2
4	Arkansas	472.2		4	Arkansas	472.2
44	California	255.4		5	Kansas	470.8
29	Colorado	369.9		6	Ohio	466.2
3	Connecticut	498.2		7	Minnesota	465.5
22	Delaware	406.3		8	Nebraska	464.8
48	Florida	200.8		9	Illinois	463.8
10	Georgia	462.0		10	Georgia	462.0
46	Hawaii	220.1		11	Tennessee	454.6
42	Idaho	270.4		12	Wisconsin	454.5
9	Illinois	463.8		13	Iowa	449.7
2	Indiana	504.4		14	Massachusetts	449.3
13	Iowa	449.7		15	North Dakota	443.7
5	Kansas	470.8		16	South Dakota	441.6
33	Kentucky	343.9		17	Oklahoma	439.6
1	Louisiana	573.9		18	Rhode Island	436.1
30	Maine	365.0		19	Wyoming	428.0
26	Maryland	389.9		20	New Hampshire	424.4
14	Massachusetts	449.3		21	Missouri	416.1
38	Michigan	312.9		22	Delaware	406.3
7	Minnesota	465.5		23	Pennsylvania	404.7
25	Mississippi	390.6		24	Montana	398.3
21	Missouri	416.1		25	Mississippi	390.6
24	Montana	398.3		26	Maryland	389.9
8	Nebraska	464.8		27	Texas	383.7
45	Nevada	230.2		28	North Carolina	375.0
20	New Hampshire	424.4		29	Colorado	369.9
34	New Jersey	341.0		30	Maine	365.0
41	New Mexico	276.5		31	South Carolina	355.8
36	New York	325.1		32	Vermont	344.4
28	North Carolina	375.0		33	Kentucky	343.9
15	North Dakota	443.7		34	New Jersey	341.0
6	Ohio	466.2		35	Alabama	328.8
17	Oklahoma	439.6		36	New York	325.1
47	Oregon	206.1		37	Virginia	317.7
23	Pennsylvania	404.7		38	Michigan	312.9
18	Rhode Island	436.1		39	Utah	292.8
31	South Carolina	355.8		40	Washington	284.7
16	South Dakota	441.6		41	New Mexico	276.5
11	Tennessee	454.6		42	Idaho	270.4
27	Texas	383.7		43	Alaska	261.2
39	Utah	292.8		44	California	255.4
32	Vermont	344.4		45	Nevada	230.2
37	Virginia	317.7		46	Hawaii	220.1
40	Washington	284.7		47	Oregon	206.1
49	West Virginia	184.8		48	Florida	200.8
12	Wisconsin	454.5		49	West Virginia	184.8
19	Wyoming	428.0		50	Arizona	165.6
					District of Columbia	338.2

Source: U.S. Department of Health and Human Services, Health Care Financing Administration
   "Health, United States, 1999" (October 1999)
*Number of nursing home residents (all ages) per 1,000 resident population 85 years of age and over.

Nursing Home Population 85 Years Old and Older in 1997

National Total = 1,472,000*

ALPHA ORDER

RANK	STATE	POPULATION	% of USA
26	Alabama	21,000	1.4%
50	Alaska	1,000	0.1%
34	Arizona	10,000	0.7%
26	Arkansas	21,000	1.4%
1	California	105,000	7.1%
29	Colorado	17,000	1.2%
19	Connecticut	31,000	2.1%
45	Delaware	4,000	0.3%
7	Florida	62,000	4.2%
15	Georgia	38,000	2.6%
45	Hawaii	4,000	0.3%
44	Idaho	5,000	0.3%
5	Illinois	86,000	5.8%
9	Indiana	44,000	3.0%
20	Iowa	29,000	2.0%
24	Kansas	24,000	1.6%
28	Kentucky	20,000	1.4%
18	Louisiana	32,000	2.2%
36	Maine	8,000	0.5%
22	Maryland	25,000	1.7%
8	Massachusetts	51,000	3.5%
9	Michigan	44,000	3.0%
14	Minnesota	39,000	2.6%
30	Mississippi	16,000	1.1%
13	Missouri	41,000	2.8%
39	Montana	6,000	0.4%
30	Nebraska	16,000	1.1%
47	Nevada	3,000	0.2%
37	New Hampshire	7,000	0.5%
9	New Jersey	44,000	3.0%
39	New Mexico	6,000	0.4%
2	New York	98,000	6.7%
15	North Carolina	38,000	2.6%
39	North Dakota	6,000	0.4%
6	Ohio	80,000	5.4%
22	Oklahoma	25,000	1.7%
33	Oregon	11,000	0.7%
3	Pennsylvania	90,000	6.1%
35	Rhode Island	9,000	0.6%
30	South Carolina	16,000	1.1%
37	South Dakota	7,000	0.5%
17	Tennessee	35,000	2.4%
4	Texas	87,000	5.9%
39	Utah	6,000	0.4%
47	Vermont	3,000	0.2%
21	Virginia	26,000	1.8%
25	Washington	22,000	1.5%
39	West Virginia	6,000	0.4%
12	Wisconsin	42,000	2.9%
47	Wyoming	3,000	0.2%

RANK ORDER

RANK	STATE	POPULATION	% of USA
1	California	105,000	7.1%
2	New York	98,000	6.7%
3	Pennsylvania	90,000	6.1%
4	Texas	87,000	5.9%
5	Illinois	86,000	5.8%
6	Ohio	80,000	5.4%
7	Florida	62,000	4.2%
8	Massachusetts	51,000	3.5%
9	Indiana	44,000	3.0%
9	Michigan	44,000	3.0%
9	New Jersey	44,000	3.0%
12	Wisconsin	42,000	2.9%
13	Missouri	41,000	2.8%
14	Minnesota	39,000	2.6%
15	Georgia	38,000	2.6%
15	North Carolina	38,000	2.6%
17	Tennessee	35,000	2.4%
18	Louisiana	32,000	2.2%
19	Connecticut	31,000	2.1%
20	Iowa	29,000	2.0%
21	Virginia	26,000	1.8%
22	Maryland	25,000	1.7%
22	Oklahoma	25,000	1.7%
24	Kansas	24,000	1.6%
25	Washington	22,000	1.5%
26	Alabama	21,000	1.4%
26	Arkansas	21,000	1.4%
28	Kentucky	20,000	1.4%
29	Colorado	17,000	1.2%
30	Mississippi	16,000	1.1%
30	Nebraska	16,000	1.1%
30	South Carolina	16,000	1.1%
33	Oregon	11,000	0.7%
34	Arizona	10,000	0.7%
35	Rhode Island	9,000	0.6%
36	Maine	8,000	0.5%
37	New Hampshire	7,000	0.5%
37	South Dakota	7,000	0.5%
39	Montana	6,000	0.4%
39	New Mexico	6,000	0.4%
39	North Dakota	6,000	0.4%
39	Utah	6,000	0.4%
39	West Virginia	6,000	0.4%
44	Idaho	5,000	0.3%
45	Delaware	4,000	0.3%
45	Hawaii	4,000	0.3%
47	Nevada	3,000	0.2%
47	Vermont	3,000	0.2%
47	Wyoming	3,000	0.2%
50	Alaska	1,000	0.1%
	District of Columbia	3,000	0.2%

Source: Morgan Quitno Press using data from U.S. Dept. of Health & Human Services, Health Care Financing Admin.
   "Health, United States, 1999" (October 1999)
*Estimated using nursing home resident rate and population 85 years old and older.

Health Service Establishments in 1997

National Total = 645,853 Establishments*

ALPHA ORDER				RANK ORDER			
RANK	STATE	ESTABLISH'S	% of USA	RANK	STATE	ESTABLISH'S	% of USA
26	Alabama	8,496	1.3%	1	California	80,572	12.5%
48	Alaska	1,570	0.2%	2	New York	45,934	7.1%
21	Arizona	10,521	1.6%	3	Texas	43,520	6.7%
32	Arkansas	5,776	0.9%	4	Florida	39,738	6.2%
1	California	80,572	12.5%	5	Pennsylvania	31,512	4.9%
22	Colorado	10,320	1.6%	6	Illinois	26,042	4.0%
24	Connecticut	9,343	1.4%	7	Ohio	25,178	3.9%
47	Delaware	1,830	0.3%	8	Michigan	23,627	3.7%
4	Florida	39,738	6.2%	9	New Jersey	21,647	3.4%
11	Georgia	15,988	2.5%	10	Massachusetts	16,424	2.5%
42	Hawaii	2,941	0.5%	11	Georgia	15,988	2.5%
41	Idaho	3,070	0.5%	12	North Carolina	15,376	2.4%
6	Illinois	26,042	4.0%	13	Washington	14,885	2.3%
16	Indiana	12,801	2.0%	14	Virginia	14,157	2.2%
30	Iowa	7,195	1.1%	15	Maryland	13,022	2.0%
31	Kansas	6,414	1.0%	16	Indiana	12,801	2.0%
28	Kentucky	8,384	1.3%	17	Missouri	12,793	2.0%
23	Louisiana	10,086	1.6%	18	Tennessee	12,293	1.9%
37	Maine	3,801	0.6%	19	Wisconsin	12,247	1.9%
15	Maryland	13,022	2.0%	20	Minnesota	10,962	1.7%
10	Massachusetts	16,424	2.5%	21	Arizona	10,521	1.6%
8	Michigan	23,627	3.7%	22	Colorado	10,320	1.6%
20	Minnesota	10,962	1.7%	23	Louisiana	10,086	1.6%
33	Mississippi	4,986	0.8%	24	Connecticut	9,343	1.4%
17	Missouri	12,793	2.0%	25	Oregon	9,116	1.4%
43	Montana	2,725	0.4%	26	Alabama	8,496	1.3%
36	Nebraska	3,971	0.6%	27	Oklahoma	8,454	1.3%
39	Nevada	3,587	0.6%	28	Kentucky	8,384	1.3%
40	New Hampshire	3,207	0.5%	29	South Carolina	7,532	1.2%
9	New Jersey	21,647	3.4%	30	Iowa	7,195	1.1%
38	New Mexico	3,701	0.6%	31	Kansas	6,414	1.0%
2	New York	45,934	7.1%	32	Arkansas	5,776	0.9%
12	North Carolina	15,376	2.4%	33	Mississippi	4,986	0.8%
49	North Dakota	1,552	0.2%	34	Utah	4,372	0.7%
7	Ohio	25,178	3.9%	35	West Virginia	4,239	0.7%
27	Oklahoma	8,454	1.3%	36	Nebraska	3,971	0.6%
25	Oregon	9,116	1.4%	37	Maine	3,801	0.6%
5	Pennsylvania	31,512	4.9%	38	New Mexico	3,701	0.6%
44	Rhode Island	2,680	0.4%	39	Nevada	3,587	0.6%
29	South Carolina	7,532	1.2%	40	New Hampshire	3,207	0.5%
45	South Dakota	1,937	0.3%	41	Idaho	3,070	0.5%
18	Tennessee	12,293	1.9%	42	Hawaii	2,941	0.5%
3	Texas	43,520	6.7%	43	Montana	2,725	0.4%
34	Utah	4,372	0.7%	44	Rhode Island	2,680	0.4%
46	Vermont	1,854	0.3%	45	South Dakota	1,937	0.3%
14	Virginia	14,157	2.2%	46	Vermont	1,854	0.3%
13	Washington	14,885	2.3%	47	Delaware	1,830	0.3%
35	West Virginia	4,239	0.7%	48	Alaska	1,570	0.2%
19	Wisconsin	12,247	1.9%	49	North Dakota	1,552	0.2%
50	Wyoming	1,356	0.2%	50	Wyoming	1,356	0.2%
					District of Columbia	2,119	0.3%

Source: U.S. Bureau of the Census
    "1997 Economic Census, Health Care and Social Assistance" (EC97562A, October 1999)
*Includes establishments exempt from, as well as subject to, the federal income tax. These include those primarily engaged in furnishing medical, surgical and other health services to persons.

Offices and Clinics of Doctors of Medicine in 1997

National Total = 185,094 Establishments*

ALPHA ORDER

RANK	STATE	ESTABLISH'S	% of USA
21	Alabama	2,694	1.5%
47	Alaska	356	0.2%
17	Arizona	3,269	1.8%
29	Arkansas	1,645	0.9%
1	California	24,079	13.0%
23	Colorado	2,586	1.4%
22	Connecticut	2,661	1.4%
45	Delaware	572	0.3%
4	Florida	13,784	7.4%
10	Georgia	5,081	2.7%
37	Hawaii	1,022	0.6%
42	Idaho	752	0.4%
8	Illinois	7,440	4.0%
16	Indiana	3,387	1.8%
34	Iowa	1,283	0.7%
32	Kansas	1,368	0.7%
24	Kentucky	2,474	1.3%
20	Louisiana	3,051	1.6%
39	Maine	838	0.5%
11	Maryland	4,343	2.3%
14	Massachusetts	3,844	2.1%
9	Michigan	6,234	3.4%
36	Minnesota	1,217	0.7%
30	Mississippi	1,520	0.8%
18	Missouri	3,160	1.7%
44	Montana	586	0.3%
40	Nebraska	774	0.4%
33	Nevada	1,335	0.7%
43	New Hampshire	656	0.4%
6	New Jersey	7,644	4.1%
38	New Mexico	941	0.5%
2	New York	15,137	8.2%
13	North Carolina	3,858	2.1%
50	North Dakota	191	0.1%
7	Ohio	7,573	4.1%
27	Oklahoma	2,189	1.2%
28	Oregon	2,040	1.1%
5	Pennsylvania	9,078	4.9%
41	Rhode Island	764	0.4%
25	South Carolina	2,216	1.2%
49	South Dakota	332	0.2%
15	Tennessee	3,620	2.0%
3	Texas	14,041	7.6%
35	Utah	1,219	0.7%
46	Vermont	360	0.2%
12	Virginia	4,277	2.3%
19	Washington	3,058	1.7%
31	West Virginia	1,415	0.8%
26	Wisconsin	2,198	1.2%
48	Wyoming	345	0.2%

RANK ORDER

RANK	STATE	ESTABLISH'S	% of USA
1	California	24,079	13.0%
2	New York	15,137	8.2%
3	Texas	14,041	7.6%
4	Florida	13,784	7.4%
5	Pennsylvania	9,078	4.9%
6	New Jersey	7,644	4.1%
7	Ohio	7,573	4.1%
8	Illinois	7,440	4.0%
9	Michigan	6,234	3.4%
10	Georgia	5,081	2.7%
11	Maryland	4,343	2.3%
12	Virginia	4,277	2.3%
13	North Carolina	3,858	2.1%
14	Massachusetts	3,844	2.1%
15	Tennessee	3,620	2.0%
16	Indiana	3,387	1.8%
17	Arizona	3,269	1.8%
18	Missouri	3,160	1.7%
19	Washington	3,058	1.7%
20	Louisiana	3,051	1.6%
21	Alabama	2,694	1.5%
22	Connecticut	2,661	1.4%
23	Colorado	2,586	1.4%
24	Kentucky	2,474	1.3%
25	South Carolina	2,216	1.2%
26	Wisconsin	2,198	1.2%
27	Oklahoma	2,189	1.2%
28	Oregon	2,040	1.1%
29	Arkansas	1,645	0.9%
30	Mississippi	1,520	0.8%
31	West Virginia	1,415	0.8%
32	Kansas	1,368	0.7%
33	Nevada	1,335	0.7%
34	Iowa	1,283	0.7%
35	Utah	1,219	0.7%
36	Minnesota	1,217	0.7%
37	Hawaii	1,022	0.6%
38	New Mexico	941	0.5%
39	Maine	838	0.5%
40	Nebraska	774	0.4%
41	Rhode Island	764	0.4%
42	Idaho	752	0.4%
43	New Hampshire	656	0.4%
44	Montana	586	0.3%
45	Delaware	572	0.3%
46	Vermont	360	0.2%
47	Alaska	356	0.2%
48	Wyoming	345	0.2%
49	South Dakota	332	0.2%
50	North Dakota	191	0.1%
	District of Columbia	587	0.3%

Source: U.S. Bureau of the Census
"1997 Economic Census, Health Care and Social Assistance" (EC97562A, October 1999)
*Includes only establishments subject to the federal income tax.

Offices and Clinics of Dentists in 1997

National Total = 114,178 Establishments*

ALPHA ORDER

RANK	STATE	ESTABLISH'S	% of USA
27	Alabama	1,356	1.2%
45	Alaska	292	0.3%
24	Arizona	1,641	1.4%
33	Arkansas	898	0.8%
1	California	16,269	14.2%
20	Colorado	2,042	1.8%
22	Connecticut	1,774	1.6%
49	Delaware	218	0.2%
4	Florida	6,182	5.4%
13	Georgia	2,547	2.3%
36	Hawaii	657	0.6%
41	Idaho	502	0.4%
6	Illinois	5,383	4.7%
16	Indiana	2,208	1.9%
30	Iowa	1,113	1.0%
32	Kansas	1,012	0.9%
26	Kentucky	1,516	1.3%
25	Louisiana	1,541	1.3%
42	Maine	462	0.4%
14	Maryland	2,371	2.1%
10	Massachusetts	2,929	2.6%
8	Michigan	4,352	3.8%
21	Minnesota	2,002	1.8%
34	Mississippi	780	0.7%
18	Missouri	2,052	1.8%
43	Montana	419	0.4%
35	Nebraska	754	0.7%
38	Nevada	575	0.5%
40	New Hampshire	533	0.5%
9	New Jersey	4,272	3.7%
39	New Mexico	557	0.5%
2	New York	8,694	7.6%
15	North Carolina	2,323	2.0%
48	North Dakota	246	0.2%
7	Ohio	4,519	4.0%
28	Oklahoma	1,268	1.1%
23	Oregon	1,680	1.5%
5	Pennsylvania	5,433	4.8%
44	Rhode Island	410	0.4%
29	South Carolina	1,216	1.1%
46	South Dakota	267	0.2%
19	Tennessee	2,050	1.8%
3	Texas	6,691	5.9%
31	Utah	1,088	1.0%
47	Vermont	256	0.2%
12	Virginia	2,645	2.3%
11	Washington	2,827	2.5%
37	West Virginia	588	0.5%
17	Wisconsin	2,203	1.9%
50	Wyoming	209	0.2%

RANK ORDER

RANK	STATE	ESTABLISH'S	% of USA
1	California	16,269	14.2%
2	New York	8,694	7.6%
3	Texas	6,691	5.9%
4	Florida	6,182	5.4%
5	Pennsylvania	5,433	4.8%
6	Illinois	5,383	4.7%
7	Ohio	4,519	4.0%
8	Michigan	4,352	3.8%
9	New Jersey	4,272	3.7%
10	Massachusetts	2,929	2.6%
11	Washington	2,827	2.5%
12	Virginia	2,645	2.3%
13	Georgia	2,574	2.3%
14	Maryland	2,371	2.1%
15	North Carolina	2,323	2.0%
16	Indiana	2,208	1.9%
17	Wisconsin	2,203	1.9%
18	Missouri	2,052	1.8%
19	Tennessee	2,050	1.8%
20	Colorado	2,042	1.8%
21	Minnesota	2,002	1.8%
22	Connecticut	1,774	1.6%
23	Oregon	1,680	1.5%
24	Arizona	1,641	1.4%
25	Louisiana	1,541	1.3%
26	Kentucky	1,516	1.3%
27	Alabama	1,356	1.2%
28	Oklahoma	1,268	1.1%
29	South Carolina	1,216	1.1%
30	Iowa	1,113	1.0%
31	Utah	1,088	1.0%
32	Kansas	1,012	0.9%
33	Arkansas	898	0.8%
34	Mississippi	780	0.7%
35	Nebraska	754	0.7%
36	Hawaii	657	0.6%
37	West Virginia	588	0.5%
38	Nevada	575	0.5%
39	New Mexico	557	0.5%
40	New Hampshire	533	0.5%
41	Idaho	502	0.4%
42	Maine	462	0.4%
43	Montana	419	0.4%
44	Rhode Island	410	0.4%
45	Alaska	292	0.3%
46	South Dakota	267	0.2%
47	Vermont	256	0.2%
48	North Dakota	246	0.2%
49	Delaware	218	0.2%
50	Wyoming	209	0.2%
	District of Columbia	329	0.3%

Source: U.S. Bureau of the Census
"1997 Economic Census, Health Care and Social Assistance" (EC97562A, October 1999)
*Includes only establishments subject to the federal income tax.

Offices and Clinics of Doctors of Osteopathy in 1997

National Total = 10,355 Establishments*

ALPHA ORDER

RANK	STATE	ESTABLISH'S	% of USA
28	Alabama	103	1.0%
47	Alaska	13	0.1%
21	Arizona	143	1.4%
32	Arkansas	67	0.6%
1	California	1,456	14.1%
17	Colorado	195	1.9%
15	Connecticut	204	2.0%
44	Delaware	32	0.3%
3	Florida	793	7.7%
10	Georgia	317	3.1%
35	Hawaii	54	0.5%
39	Idaho	41	0.4%
5	Illinois	487	4.7%
23	Indiana	131	1.3%
33	Iowa	65	0.6%
30	Kansas	78	0.8%
24	Kentucky	121	1.2%
20	Louisiana	161	1.6%
43	Maine	34	0.3%
11	Maryland	296	2.9%
13	Massachusetts	260	2.5%
8	Michigan	346	3.3%
29	Minnesota	100	1.0%
31	Mississippi	76	0.7%
16	Missouri	197	1.9%
46	Montana	18	0.2%
38	Nebraska	44	0.4%
42	Nevada	37	0.4%
41	New Hampshire	38	0.4%
8	New Jersey	346	3.3%
36	New Mexico	51	0.5%
2	New York	876	8.5%
14	North Carolina	213	2.1%
50	North Dakota	8	0.1%
7	Ohio	358	3.5%
27	Oklahoma	106	1.0%
25	Oregon	112	1.1%
6	Pennsylvania	417	4.0%
39	Rhode Island	41	0.4%
26	South Carolina	110	1.1%
48	South Dakota	10	0.1%
19	Tennessee	183	1.8%
4	Texas	785	7.6%
34	Utah	56	0.5%
45	Vermont	21	0.2%
12	Virginia	292	2.8%
18	Washington	185	1.8%
37	West Virginia	47	0.5%
22	Wisconsin	141	1.4%
48	Wyoming	10	0.1%

RANK ORDER

RANK	STATE	ESTABLISH'S	% of USA
1	California	1,456	14.1%
2	New York	876	8.5%
3	Florida	793	7.7%
4	Texas	785	7.6%
5	Illinois	487	4.7%
6	Pennsylvania	417	4.0%
7	Ohio	358	3.5%
8	Michigan	346	3.3%
8	New Jersey	346	3.3%
10	Georgia	317	3.1%
11	Maryland	296	2.9%
12	Virginia	292	2.8%
13	Massachusetts	260	2.5%
14	North Carolina	213	2.1%
15	Connecticut	204	2.0%
16	Missouri	197	1.9%
17	Colorado	195	1.9%
18	Washington	185	1.8%
19	Tennessee	183	1.8%
20	Louisiana	161	1.6%
21	Arizona	143	1.4%
22	Wisconsin	141	1.4%
23	Indiana	131	1.3%
24	Kentucky	121	1.2%
25	Oregon	112	1.1%
26	South Carolina	110	1.1%
27	Oklahoma	106	1.0%
28	Alabama	103	1.0%
29	Minnesota	100	1.0%
30	Kansas	78	0.8%
31	Mississippi	76	0.7%
32	Arkansas	67	0.6%
33	Iowa	65	0.6%
34	Utah	56	0.5%
35	Hawaii	54	0.5%
36	New Mexico	51	0.5%
37	West Virginia	47	0.5%
38	Nebraska	44	0.4%
39	Idaho	41	0.4%
39	Rhode Island	41	0.4%
41	New Hampshire	38	0.4%
42	Nevada	37	0.4%
43	Maine	34	0.3%
44	Delaware	32	0.3%
45	Vermont	21	0.2%
46	Montana	18	0.2%
47	Alaska	13	0.1%
48	South Dakota	10	0.1%
48	Wyoming	10	0.1%
50	North Dakota	8	0.1%
	District of Columbia	80	0.8%

Source: U.S. Bureau of the Census
"1997 Economic Census, Health Care and Social Assistance" (EC97562A, October 1999)
*Includes only establishments subject to the federal income tax.

Offices and Clinics of Chiropractors in 1997

National Total = 30,487 Establishments*

ALPHA ORDER

RANK	STATE	ESTABLISH'S	% of USA
29	Alabama	319	1.0%
47	Alaska	81	0.3%
14	Arizona	742	2.4%
32	Arkansas	247	0.8%
1	California	4,111	13.5%
17	Colorado	634	2.1%
25	Connecticut	384	1.3%
49	Delaware	60	0.2%
2	Florida	1,963	6.4%
12	Georgia	829	2.7%
45	Hawaii	95	0.3%
37	Idaho	160	0.5%
7	Illinois	1,275	4.2%
20	Indiana	519	1.7%
19	Iowa	545	1.8%
26	Kansas	369	1.2%
27	Kentucky	343	1.1%
30	Louisiana	294	1.0%
38	Maine	143	0.5%
31	Maryland	273	0.9%
15	Massachusetts	642	2.1%
9	Michigan	1,015	3.3%
11	Minnesota	885	2.9%
41	Mississippi	131	0.4%
15	Missouri	642	2.1%
39	Montana	136	0.4%
34	Nebraska	201	0.7%
33	Nevada	205	0.7%
41	New Hampshire	131	0.4%
6	New Jersey	1,415	4.6%
36	New Mexico	182	0.6%
3	New York	1,915	6.3%
18	North Carolina	597	2.0%
44	North Dakota	104	0.3%
8	Ohio	1,070	3.5%
28	Oklahoma	341	1.1%
22	Oregon	478	1.6%
5	Pennsylvania	1,582	5.2%
46	Rhode Island	90	0.3%
24	South Carolina	392	1.3%
40	South Dakota	133	0.4%
23	Tennessee	437	1.4%
4	Texas	1,705	5.6%
35	Utah	197	0.6%
48	Vermont	73	0.2%
21	Virginia	491	1.6%
10	Washington	921	3.0%
43	West Virginia	125	0.4%
13	Wisconsin	802	2.6%
50	Wyoming	51	0.2%

RANK ORDER

RANK	STATE	ESTABLISH'S	% of USA
1	California	4,111	13.5%
2	Florida	1,963	6.4%
3	New York	1,915	6.3%
4	Texas	1,705	5.6%
5	Pennsylvania	1,582	5.2%
6	New Jersey	1,415	4.6%
7	Illinois	1,275	4.2%
8	Ohio	1,070	3.5%
9	Michigan	1,015	3.3%
10	Washington	921	3.0%
11	Minnesota	885	2.9%
12	Georgia	829	2.7%
13	Wisconsin	802	2.6%
14	Arizona	742	2.4%
15	Massachusetts	642	2.1%
15	Missouri	642	2.1%
17	Colorado	634	2.1%
18	North Carolina	597	2.0%
19	Iowa	545	1.8%
20	Indiana	519	1.7%
21	Virginia	491	1.6%
22	Oregon	478	1.6%
23	Tennessee	437	1.4%
24	South Carolina	392	1.3%
25	Connecticut	384	1.3%
26	Kansas	369	1.2%
27	Kentucky	343	1.1%
28	Oklahoma	341	1.1%
29	Alabama	319	1.0%
30	Louisiana	294	1.0%
31	Maryland	273	0.9%
32	Arkansas	247	0.8%
33	Nevada	205	0.7%
34	Nebraska	201	0.7%
35	Utah	197	0.6%
36	New Mexico	182	0.6%
37	Idaho	160	0.5%
38	Maine	143	0.5%
39	Montana	136	0.4%
40	South Dakota	133	0.4%
41	Mississippi	131	0.4%
41	New Hampshire	131	0.4%
43	West Virginia	125	0.4%
44	North Dakota	104	0.3%
45	Hawaii	95	0.3%
46	Rhode Island	90	0.3%
47	Alaska	81	0.3%
48	Vermont	73	0.2%
49	Delaware	60	0.2%
50	Wyoming	51	0.2%
	District of Columbia	12	0.0%

Source: U.S. Bureau of the Census
"1997 Economic Census, Health Care and Social Assistance" (EC97562A, October 1999)
*Includes only establishments subject to the federal income tax.

Offices and Clinics of Optometrists in 1997

National Total = 17,875 Establishments*

ALPHA ORDER

RANK	STATE	ESTABLISH'S	% of USA
26	Alabama	244	1.4%
49	Alaska	46	0.3%
29	Arizona	212	1.2%
31	Arkansas	203	1.1%
1	California	2,448	13.7%
20	Colorado	285	1.6%
28	Connecticut	221	1.2%
48	Delaware	48	0.3%
4	Florida	898	5.0%
14	Georgia	384	2.1%
40	Hawaii	111	0.6%
36	Idaho	124	0.7%
7	Illinois	699	3.9%
11	Indiana	510	2.9%
21	Iowa	277	1.5%
24	Kansas	257	1.4%
23	Kentucky	262	1.5%
32	Louisiana	188	1.1%
38	Maine	120	0.7%
25	Maryland	255	1.4%
15	Massachusetts	381	2.1%
10	Michigan	585	3.3%
22	Minnesota	267	1.5%
34	Mississippi	150	0.8%
19	Missouri	297	1.7%
41	Montana	91	0.5%
35	Nebraska	135	0.8%
36	Nevada	124	0.7%
44	New Hampshire	77	0.4%
9	New Jersey	589	3.3%
39	New Mexico	116	0.6%
6	New York	750	4.2%
8	North Carolina	590	3.3%
46	North Dakota	65	0.4%
5	Ohio	861	4.8%
17	Oklahoma	342	1.9%
27	Oregon	239	1.3%
3	Pennsylvania	928	5.2%
42	Rhode Island	90	0.5%
30	South Carolina	205	1.1%
45	South Dakota	74	0.4%
13	Tennessee	392	2.2%
2	Texas	1,225	6.9%
42	Utah	90	0.5%
49	Vermont	46	0.3%
12	Virginia	426	2.4%
16	Washington	379	2.1%
33	West Virginia	161	0.9%
18	Wisconsin	332	1.9%
47	Wyoming	60	0.3%

RANK ORDER

RANK	STATE	ESTABLISH'S	% of USA
1	California	2,448	13.7%
2	Texas	1,225	6.9%
3	Pennsylvania	928	5.2%
4	Florida	898	5.0%
5	Ohio	861	4.8%
6	New York	750	4.2%
7	Illinois	699	3.9%
8	North Carolina	590	3.3%
9	New Jersey	589	3.3%
10	Michigan	585	3.3%
11	Indiana	510	2.9%
12	Virginia	426	2.4%
13	Tennessee	392	2.2%
14	Georgia	384	2.1%
15	Massachusetts	381	2.1%
16	Washington	379	2.1%
17	Oklahoma	342	1.9%
18	Wisconsin	332	1.9%
19	Missouri	297	1.7%
20	Colorado	285	1.6%
21	Iowa	277	1.5%
22	Minnesota	267	1.5%
23	Kentucky	262	1.5%
24	Kansas	257	1.4%
25	Maryland	255	1.4%
26	Alabama	244	1.4%
27	Oregon	239	1.3%
28	Connecticut	221	1.2%
29	Arizona	212	1.2%
30	South Carolina	205	1.1%
31	Arkansas	203	1.1%
32	Louisiana	188	1.1%
33	West Virginia	161	0.9%
34	Mississippi	150	0.8%
35	Nebraska	135	0.8%
36	Idaho	124	0.7%
36	Nevada	124	0.7%
38	Maine	120	0.7%
39	New Mexico	116	0.6%
40	Hawaii	111	0.6%
41	Montana	91	0.5%
42	Rhode Island	90	0.5%
42	Utah	90	0.5%
44	New Hampshire	77	0.4%
45	South Dakota	74	0.4%
46	North Dakota	65	0.4%
47	Wyoming	60	0.3%
48	Delaware	48	0.3%
49	Alaska	46	0.3%
49	Vermont	46	0.3%
	District of Columbia	16	0.1%

Source: U.S. Bureau of the Census
"1997 Economic Census, Health Care and Social Assistance" (EC97562A, October 1999)
*Includes only establishments subject to the federal income tax.

Offices and Clinics of Podiatrists in 1997

National Total = 8,662 Establishments*

ALPHA ORDER

RANK	STATE	ESTABLISH'S	% of USA
26	Alabama	61	0.7%
48	Alaska	8	0.1%
19	Arizona	118	1.4%
40	Arkansas	29	0.3%
2	California	825	9.5%
22	Colorado	93	1.1%
16	Connecticut	158	1.8%
43	Delaware	21	0.2%
4	Florida	613	7.1%
13	Georgia	175	2.0%
45	Hawaii	13	0.2%
44	Idaho	20	0.2%
7	Illinois	489	5.6%
14	Indiana	174	2.0%
23	Iowa	81	0.9%
30	Kansas	54	0.6%
25	Kentucky	62	0.7%
31	Louisiana	53	0.6%
35	Maine	42	0.5%
11	Maryland	222	2.6%
10	Massachusetts	230	2.7%
9	Michigan	421	4.9%
27	Minnesota	59	0.7%
41	Mississippi	27	0.3%
20	Missouri	117	1.4%
42	Montana	25	0.3%
35	Nebraska	42	0.5%
38	Nevada	34	0.4%
39	New Hampshire	31	0.4%
5	New Jersey	531	6.1%
34	New Mexico	45	0.5%
1	New York	1,087	12.5%
17	North Carolina	141	1.6%
50	North Dakota	6	0.1%
6	Ohio	495	5.7%
29	Oklahoma	57	0.7%
24	Oregon	63	0.7%
3	Pennsylvania	663	7.7%
32	Rhode Island	48	0.6%
33	South Carolina	47	0.5%
45	South Dakota	13	0.2%
21	Tennessee	109	1.3%
8	Texas	427	4.9%
28	Utah	58	0.7%
47	Vermont	10	0.1%
12	Virginia	200	2.3%
15	Washington	169	2.0%
37	West Virginia	36	0.4%
18	Wisconsin	121	1.4%
48	Wyoming	8	0.1%

RANK ORDER

RANK	STATE	ESTABLISH'S	% of USA
1	New York	1,087	12.5%
2	California	825	9.5%
3	Pennsylvania	663	7.7%
4	Florida	613	7.1%
5	New Jersey	531	6.1%
6	Ohio	495	5.7%
7	Illinois	489	5.6%
8	Texas	427	4.9%
9	Michigan	421	4.9%
10	Massachusetts	230	2.7%
11	Maryland	222	2.6%
12	Virginia	200	2.3%
13	Georgia	175	2.0%
14	Indiana	174	2.0%
15	Washington	169	2.0%
16	Connecticut	158	1.8%
17	North Carolina	141	1.6%
18	Wisconsin	121	1.4%
19	Arizona	118	1.4%
20	Missouri	117	1.4%
21	Tennessee	109	1.3%
22	Colorado	93	1.1%
23	Iowa	81	0.9%
24	Oregon	63	0.7%
25	Kentucky	62	0.7%
26	Alabama	61	0.7%
27	Minnesota	59	0.7%
28	Utah	58	0.7%
29	Oklahoma	57	0.7%
30	Kansas	54	0.6%
31	Louisiana	53	0.6%
32	Rhode Island	48	0.6%
33	South Carolina	47	0.5%
34	New Mexico	45	0.5%
35	Maine	42	0.5%
35	Nebraska	42	0.5%
37	West Virginia	36	0.4%
38	Nevada	34	0.4%
39	New Hampshire	31	0.4%
40	Arkansas	29	0.3%
41	Mississippi	27	0.3%
42	Montana	25	0.3%
43	Delaware	21	0.2%
44	Idaho	20	0.2%
45	Hawaii	13	0.2%
45	South Dakota	13	0.2%
47	Vermont	10	0.1%
48	Alaska	8	0.1%
48	Wyoming	8	0.1%
50	North Dakota	6	0.1%
	District of Columbia	31	0.4%

Source: U.S. Bureau of the Census
   "1997 Economic Census, Health Care and Social Assistance" (EC97562A, October 1999)
*Includes only establishments subject to the federal income tax.

IV. FINANCE

IV. FINANCE (Continued)

National Health Care Expenditures in 1998

Total Health Care Expenditures = $1,149,100,000,000*

The 1993 health care expenditures broken down to the state level and shown in this book were released in the fall of 1995. The Health Care Financing Administration (HCFA) is committed to updating these numbers. Updates were expected in the summer of 1997 but difficulties inherent in allocating more than one trillion dollars in expenditures among the states have delayed the release of any updates a number of times. As we went to press in March of 2000, we were told that updates may be available in this summer of 2000. Let's keep our collective fingers crossed. We apologize for the inconvenience.

Given the high level of interest in health care finance data, we have assembled a table showing the most recent national level health care expenditure data. We will continue to monitor HCFA data releases and will include the state expenditure updates in forthcoming editions. The percent change numbers are based on updated 1997 figures.

	EXPENDITURES IN 1998	PERCENT CHANGE: 1997 TO 1998
Total Health Care Expenditures	$1,149,100,000,000	5.6
Per Capita Total Health Care Expenditures	$4,252	4.6
Personal Health Care Expenditures	$1,019,300,000,000	5.2
Per Capita Personal Health Care Expenditures	$3,772	4.3
Hospital Care Expenditures	$382,800,000,000	3.4
Per Capita Hospital Care Expenditures	$1,416	2.5
Physician Services Expenditures	$229,500,000,000	5.4
Per Capita Physician Services Expenditures	$849	4.4
Dental Services Expenditures	$53,800,000,000	5.3
Per Capita Dental Services Expenditures	$199	4.2
Other Professional Services	$66,600,000,000	8.3
Per Capita Other Professional Services	$246	7.0
Home Health Care Expenditures	$29,300,000,000	-3.9
Per Capita Home Health Care Expenditures	$108	-5.3
Drugs and Other Medical Nondurables	$121,900,000,000	12.2
Per Capita Drugs and Other Medical Nondurables	$451	11.1
Vision Products and Other Medical Durables	$15,500,000,000	2.6
Per Capita Vision Products and Other Medical Durables	$57	1.8
Nursing Home Care	$87,800,000,000	3.7
Per Capita Nursing Home Care	$325	2.8
Other Personal Care Expenditures	$32,100,000,000	9.9
Per Capita Other Personal Care Expenditures	$119	9.2

Source: U.S. Department of Health and Human Services, Health Care Financing Administration
"National Health Expenditures Aggregate Amounts and Average Annual Percent Change, by Type of Expenditure" (www.hcfa.gov/stats/nhe-oact/tables/t3.htm)
*Per Capita figures calculated by Morgan Quitno Press. For definitions see the corresponding 1993 state tables in this chapter.

Personal Health Care Expenditures in 1993

National Total = $778,510,000,000*

RANK	STATE	EXPENDITURES	% of USA
23	Alabama	$12,060,000,000	1.6%
48	Alaska	1,573,000,000	0.2%
24	Arizona	10,635,000,000	1.4%
33	Arkansas	6,111,000,000	0.8%
1	California	94,178,000,000	12.1%
26	Colorado	10,066,000,000	1.3%
22	Connecticut	12,216,000,000	1.6%
44	Delaware	2,260,000,000	0.3%
4	Florida	44,811,000,000	5.8%
11	Georgia	20,104,000,000	2.6%
39	Hawaii	3,485,000,000	0.5%
43	Idaho	2,277,000,000	0.3%
6	Illinois	34,747,000,000	4.5%
14	Indiana	16,401,000,000	2.1%
30	Iowa	7,341,000,000	0.9%
31	Kansas	6,903,000,000	0.9%
25	Kentucky	10,384,000,000	1.3%
21	Louisiana	13,014,000,000	1.7%
41	Maine	3,433,000,000	0.4%
17	Maryland	15,154,000,000	2.0%
10	Massachusetts	23,421,000,000	3.0%
8	Michigan	27,136,000,000	3.5%
20	Minnesota	14,194,000,000	1.8%
32	Mississippi	6,187,000,000	0.8%
16	Missouri	15,949,000,000	2.1%
45	Montana	2,103,000,000	0.3%
35	Nebraska	4,400,000,000	0.6%
38	Nevada	3,747,000,000	0.5%
40	New Hampshire	3,452,000,000	0.4%
9	New Jersey	25,741,000,000	3.3%
37	New Mexico	3,878,000,000	0.5%
2	New York	67,033,000,000	8.6%
12	North Carolina	18,241,000,000	2.3%
46	North Dakota	2,021,000,000	0.3%
7	Ohio	33,456,000,000	4.3%
28	Oklahoma	8,041,000,000	1.0%
29	Oregon	7,999,000,000	1.0%
5	Pennsylvania	41,521,000,000	5.3%
42	Rhode Island	3,428,000,000	0.4%
27	South Carolina	9,029,000,000	1.2%
47	South Dakota	1,953,000,000	0.3%
15	Tennessee	16,203,000,000	2.1%
3	Texas	49,816,000,000	6.4%
36	Utah	4,118,000,000	0.5%
49	Vermont	1,499,000,000	0.2%
13	Virginia	16,682,000,000	2.1%
18	Washington	15,129,000,000	1.9%
34	West Virginia	5,197,000,000	0.7%
19	Wisconsin	14,502,000,000	1.9%
50	Wyoming	998,000,000	0.1%

RANK	STATE	EXPENDITURES	% of USA
1	California	$94,178,000,000	12.1%
2	New York	67,033,000,000	8.6%
3	Texas	49,816,000,000	6.4%
4	Florida	44,811,000,000	5.8%
5	Pennsylvania	41,521,000,000	5.3%
6	Illinois	34,747,000,000	4.5%
7	Ohio	33,456,000,000	4.3%
8	Michigan	27,136,000,000	3.5%
9	New Jersey	25,741,000,000	3.3%
10	Massachusetts	23,421,000,000	3.0%
11	Georgia	20,104,000,000	2.6%
12	North Carolina	18,241,000,000	2.3%
13	Virginia	16,682,000,000	2.1%
14	Indiana	16,401,000,000	2.1%
15	Tennessee	16,203,000,000	2.1%
16	Missouri	15,949,000,000	2.1%
17	Maryland	15,154,000,000	2.0%
18	Washington	15,129,000,000	1.9%
19	Wisconsin	14,502,000,000	1.9%
20	Minnesota	14,194,000,000	1.8%
21	Louisiana	13,014,000,000	1.7%
22	Connecticut	12,216,000,000	1.6%
23	Alabama	12,060,000,000	1.6%
24	Arizona	10,635,000,000	1.4%
25	Kentucky	10,384,000,000	1.3%
26	Colorado	10,066,000,000	1.3%
27	South Carolina	9,029,000,000	1.2%
28	Oklahoma	8,041,000,000	1.0%
29	Oregon	7,999,000,000	1.0%
30	Iowa	7,341,000,000	0.9%
31	Kansas	6,903,000,000	0.9%
32	Mississippi	6,187,000,000	0.8%
33	Arkansas	6,111,000,000	0.8%
34	West Virginia	5,197,000,000	0.7%
35	Nebraska	4,400,000,000	0.6%
36	Utah	4,118,000,000	0.5%
37	New Mexico	3,878,000,000	0.5%
38	Nevada	3,747,000,000	0.5%
39	Hawaii	3,485,000,000	0.5%
40	New Hampshire	3,452,000,000	0.4%
41	Maine	3,433,000,000	0.4%
42	Rhode Island	3,428,000,000	0.4%
43	Idaho	2,277,000,000	0.3%
44	Delaware	2,260,000,000	0.3%
45	Montana	2,103,000,000	0.3%
46	North Dakota	2,021,000,000	0.3%
47	South Dakota	1,953,000,000	0.3%
48	Alaska	1,573,000,000	0.2%
49	Vermont	1,499,000,000	0.2%
50	Wyoming	998,000,000	0.1%
	District of Columbia	4,285,000,000	0.6%

Source: U.S. Department of Health and Human Services, Health Care Financing Administration
"State Health Expenditure Accounts" (Health Care Financing Review, Fall 1995, Volume 17, Number 1)
By state of provider. Includes hospital care, physician services, dental services, home health care, drugs, vision products and other personal health care services and products.

Health Care Expenditures as a Percent of Gross State Product in 1993

National Percent = 12.1% of Total Gross State Product*

<table>
<tr><td colspan="3">ALPHA ORDER</td><td colspan="3">RANK ORDER</td></tr>
<tr><td>RANK</td><td>STATE</td><td>PERCENT</td><td>RANK</td><td>STATE</td><td>PERCENT</td></tr>
<tr><td>6</td><td>Alabama</td><td>14.6</td><td>1</td><td>West Virginia</td><td>16.2</td></tr>
<tr><td>50</td><td>Alaska</td><td>6.3</td><td>2</td><td>North Dakota</td><td>16.0</td></tr>
<tr><td>19</td><td>Arizona</td><td>12.6</td><td>3</td><td>Florida</td><td>15.0</td></tr>
<tr><td>13</td><td>Arkansas</td><td>13.1</td><td>4</td><td>Pennsylvania</td><td>14.7</td></tr>
<tr><td>36</td><td>California</td><td>11.2</td><td>4</td><td>Rhode Island</td><td>14.7</td></tr>
<tr><td>40</td><td>Colorado</td><td>10.8</td><td>6</td><td>Alabama</td><td>14.6</td></tr>
<tr><td>33</td><td>Connecticut</td><td>11.5</td><td>7</td><td>Tennessee</td><td>14.0</td></tr>
<tr><td>48</td><td>Delaware</td><td>9.3</td><td>8</td><td>Louisiana</td><td>13.8</td></tr>
<tr><td>3</td><td>Florida</td><td>15.0</td><td>9</td><td>Maine</td><td>13.7</td></tr>
<tr><td>30</td><td>Georgia</td><td>11.8</td><td>10</td><td>Massachusetts</td><td>13.4</td></tr>
<tr><td>46</td><td>Hawaii</td><td>9.6</td><td>10</td><td>Mississippi</td><td>13.4</td></tr>
<tr><td>44</td><td>Idaho</td><td>10.2</td><td>10</td><td>Missouri</td><td>13.4</td></tr>
<tr><td>37</td><td>Illinois</td><td>11.1</td><td>13</td><td>Arkansas</td><td>13.1</td></tr>
<tr><td>16</td><td>Indiana</td><td>12.9</td><td>13</td><td>Ohio</td><td>13.1</td></tr>
<tr><td>28</td><td>Iowa</td><td>11.9</td><td>15</td><td>Montana</td><td>13.0</td></tr>
<tr><td>28</td><td>Kansas</td><td>11.9</td><td>16</td><td>Indiana</td><td>12.9</td></tr>
<tr><td>16</td><td>Kentucky</td><td>12.9</td><td>16</td><td>Kentucky</td><td>12.9</td></tr>
<tr><td>8</td><td>Louisiana</td><td>13.8</td><td>18</td><td>New Hampshire</td><td>12.7</td></tr>
<tr><td>9</td><td>Maine</td><td>13.7</td><td>19</td><td>Arizona</td><td>12.6</td></tr>
<tr><td>25</td><td>Maryland</td><td>12.2</td><td>19</td><td>Oklahoma</td><td>12.6</td></tr>
<tr><td>10</td><td>Massachusetts</td><td>13.4</td><td>21</td><td>Michigan</td><td>12.5</td></tr>
<tr><td>21</td><td>Michigan</td><td>12.5</td><td>22</td><td>Minnesota</td><td>12.3</td></tr>
<tr><td>22</td><td>Minnesota</td><td>12.3</td><td>22</td><td>New York</td><td>12.3</td></tr>
<tr><td>10</td><td>Mississippi</td><td>13.4</td><td>22</td><td>Wisconsin</td><td>12.3</td></tr>
<tr><td>10</td><td>Missouri</td><td>13.4</td><td>25</td><td>Maryland</td><td>12.2</td></tr>
<tr><td>15</td><td>Montana</td><td>13.0</td><td>26</td><td>South Dakota</td><td>12.1</td></tr>
<tr><td>33</td><td>Nebraska</td><td>11.5</td><td>27</td><td>South Carolina</td><td>12.0</td></tr>
<tr><td>47</td><td>Nevada</td><td>9.5</td><td>28</td><td>Iowa</td><td>11.9</td></tr>
<tr><td>18</td><td>New Hampshire</td><td>12.7</td><td>28</td><td>Kansas</td><td>11.9</td></tr>
<tr><td>43</td><td>New Jersey</td><td>10.5</td><td>30</td><td>Georgia</td><td>11.8</td></tr>
<tr><td>35</td><td>New Mexico</td><td>11.3</td><td>30</td><td>Vermont</td><td>11.8</td></tr>
<tr><td>22</td><td>New York</td><td>12.3</td><td>32</td><td>Oregon</td><td>11.6</td></tr>
<tr><td>40</td><td>North Carolina</td><td>10.8</td><td>33</td><td>Connecticut</td><td>11.5</td></tr>
<tr><td>2</td><td>North Dakota</td><td>16.0</td><td>33</td><td>Nebraska</td><td>11.5</td></tr>
<tr><td>13</td><td>Ohio</td><td>13.1</td><td>35</td><td>New Mexico</td><td>11.3</td></tr>
<tr><td>19</td><td>Oklahoma</td><td>12.6</td><td>36</td><td>California</td><td>11.2</td></tr>
<tr><td>32</td><td>Oregon</td><td>11.6</td><td>37</td><td>Illinois</td><td>11.1</td></tr>
<tr><td>4</td><td>Pennsylvania</td><td>14.7</td><td>37</td><td>Texas</td><td>11.1</td></tr>
<tr><td>4</td><td>Rhode Island</td><td>14.7</td><td>37</td><td>Washington</td><td>11.1</td></tr>
<tr><td>27</td><td>South Carolina</td><td>12.0</td><td>40</td><td>Colorado</td><td>10.8</td></tr>
<tr><td>26</td><td>South Dakota</td><td>12.1</td><td>40</td><td>North Carolina</td><td>10.8</td></tr>
<tr><td>7</td><td>Tennessee</td><td>14.0</td><td>40</td><td>Utah</td><td>10.8</td></tr>
<tr><td>37</td><td>Texas</td><td>11.1</td><td>43</td><td>New Jersey</td><td>10.5</td></tr>
<tr><td>40</td><td>Utah</td><td>10.8</td><td>44</td><td>Idaho</td><td>10.2</td></tr>
<tr><td>30</td><td>Vermont</td><td>11.8</td><td>45</td><td>Virginia</td><td>9.8</td></tr>
<tr><td>45</td><td>Virginia</td><td>9.8</td><td>46</td><td>Hawaii</td><td>9.6</td></tr>
<tr><td>37</td><td>Washington</td><td>11.1</td><td>47</td><td>Nevada</td><td>9.5</td></tr>
<tr><td>1</td><td>West Virginia</td><td>16.2</td><td>48</td><td>Delaware</td><td>9.3</td></tr>
<tr><td>22</td><td>Wisconsin</td><td>12.3</td><td>49</td><td>Wyoming</td><td>6.7</td></tr>
<tr><td>49</td><td>Wyoming</td><td>6.7</td><td>50</td><td>Alaska</td><td>6.3</td></tr>
<tr><td></td><td></td><td></td><td></td><td>District of Columbia</td><td>9.1</td></tr>
</table>

Source: Morgan Quitno Press using data from U.S. Dept of Health & Human Services, Health Care Financing Admin.
"State Health Expenditure Accounts" (Health Care Financing Review, Fall 1995, Volume 17, Number 1)
*By state of provider. Includes hospital care, physician services, dental services, home health care, drugs, vision products and other personal health care services and products.

Per Capita Personal Health Care Expenditures in 1993

National Per Capita = $3,020*

ALPHA ORDER				RANK ORDER		
RANK	STATE	PER CAPITA		RANK	STATE	PER CAPITA
21	Alabama	$2,884		1	Massachusetts	$3,892
37	Alaska	2,630		2	Connecticut	3,727
35	Arizona	2,697		3	New York	3,693
42	Arkansas	2,520		4	Pennsylvania	3,451
17	California	3,017		5	Rhode Island	3,431
27	Colorado	2,821		6	New Jersey	3,275
2	Connecticut	3,727		7	Florida	3,266
8	Delaware	3,233		8	Delaware	3,233
7	Florida	3,266		9	Tennessee	3,181
20	Georgia	2,913		10	North Dakota	3,173
18	Hawaii	2,989		11	Minnesota	3,137
50	Idaho	2,068		12	New Hampshire	3,074
19	Illinois	2,972		13	Maryland	3,060
24	Indiana	2,874		14	Missouri	3,047
40	Iowa	2,601		15	Louisiana	3,034
31	Kansas	2,726		16	Ohio	3,025
30	Kentucky	2,738		17	California	3,017
15	Louisiana	3,034		18	Hawaii	2,989
28	Maine	2,771		19	Illinois	2,972
13	Maryland	3,060		20	Georgia	2,913
1	Massachusetts	3,892		21	Alabama	2,884
25	Michigan	2,869		22	Washington	2,879
11	Minnesota	3,137		23	Wisconsin	2,875
47	Mississippi	2,344		24	Indiana	2,874
14	Missouri	3,047		25	Michigan	2,869
43	Montana	2,501		26	West Virginia	2,859
31	Nebraska	2,726		27	Colorado	2,821
34	Nevada	2,705		28	Maine	2,771
12	New Hampshire	3,074		29	Texas	2,760
6	New Jersey	3,275		30	Kentucky	2,738
46	New Mexico	2,400		31	Kansas	2,726
3	New York	3,693		31	Nebraska	2,726
38	North Carolina	2,623		33	South Dakota	2,724
10	North Dakota	3,173		34	Nevada	2,705
16	Ohio	3,025		35	Arizona	2,697
45	Oklahoma	2,488		36	Oregon	2,636
36	Oregon	2,636		37	Alaska	2,630
4	Pennsylvania	3,451		38	North Carolina	2,623
5	Rhode Island	3,431		39	Vermont	2,602
44	South Carolina	2,489		40	Iowa	2,601
33	South Dakota	2,724		41	Virginia	2,576
9	Tennessee	3,181		42	Arkansas	2,520
29	Texas	2,760		43	Montana	2,501
48	Utah	2,214		44	South Carolina	2,489
39	Vermont	2,602		45	Oklahoma	2,488
41	Virginia	2,576		46	New Mexico	2,400
22	Washington	2,879		47	Mississippi	2,344
26	West Virginia	2,859		48	Utah	2,214
23	Wisconsin	2,875		49	Wyoming	2,123
49	Wyoming	2,123		50	Idaho	2,068
					District of Columbia	7,413

Source: Morgan Quitno Press using data from U.S. Dept of Health & Human Services, Health Care Financing Admin. "State Health Expenditure Accounts" (Health Care Financing Review, Fall 1995, Volume 17, Number 1)
*By state of provider. Includes hospital care, physician services, dental services, home health care, drugs, vision products and other personal health care services and products.

Percent Change in Personal Health Care Expenditures: 1990 to 1993

National Percent Change = 28.0% Increase*

ALPHA ORDER				RANK ORDER		
RANK	STATE	PERCENT CHANGE		RANK	STATE	PERCENT CHANGE
13	Alabama	31.7		1	Idaho	37.4
32	Alaska	27.0		2	New Hampshire	36.9
41	Arizona	25.4		3	Nevada	35.4
37	Arkansas	26.1		3	Washington	35.4
30	California	27.1		5	South Carolina	34.8
20	Colorado	30.3		6	New Mexico	34.0
48	Connecticut	22.5		7	Texas	33.7
12	Delaware	32.2		8	North Carolina	33.1
28	Florida	27.6		8	Tennessee	33.1
15	Georgia	31.5		8	West Virginia	33.1
29	Hawaii	27.5		11	Kentucky	32.7
1	Idaho	37.4		12	Delaware	32.2
34	Illinois	26.7		13	Alabama	31.7
19	Indiana	30.7		14	Louisiana	31.6
50	Iowa	21.9		15	Georgia	31.5
43	Kansas	25.3		16	Mississippi	31.2
11	Kentucky	32.7		17	Montana	30.9
14	Louisiana	31.6		18	South Dakota	30.8
30	Maine	27.1		19	Indiana	30.7
27	Maryland	28.0		20	Colorado	30.3
49	Massachusetts	22.2		20	Oregon	30.3
46	Michigan	23.5		22	Utah	29.9
47	Minnesota	23.3		23	New Jersey	29.0
16	Mississippi	31.2		24	Oklahoma	28.1
34	Missouri	26.7		24	Pennsylvania	28.1
17	Montana	30.9		24	Wisconsin	28.1
36	Nebraska	26.5		27	Maryland	28.0
3	Nevada	35.4		28	Florida	27.6
2	New Hampshire	36.9		29	Hawaii	27.5
23	New Jersey	29.0		30	California	27.1
6	New Mexico	34.0		30	Maine	27.1
44	New York	24.8		32	Alaska	27.0
8	North Carolina	33.1		33	Vermont	26.8
44	North Dakota	24.8		34	Illinois	26.7
41	Ohio	25.4		34	Missouri	26.7
24	Oklahoma	28.1		36	Nebraska	26.5
20	Oregon	30.3		37	Arkansas	26.1
24	Pennsylvania	28.1		38	Virginia	25.9
40	Rhode Island	25.5		39	Wyoming	25.7
5	South Carolina	34.8		40	Rhode Island	25.5
18	South Dakota	30.8		41	Arizona	25.4
8	Tennessee	33.1		41	Ohio	25.4
7	Texas	33.7		43	Kansas	25.3
22	Utah	29.9		44	New York	24.8
33	Vermont	26.8		44	North Dakota	24.8
38	Virginia	25.9		46	Michigan	23.5
3	Washington	35.4		47	Minnesota	23.3
8	West Virginia	33.1		48	Connecticut	22.5
24	Wisconsin	28.1		49	Massachusetts	22.2
39	Wyoming	25.7		50	Iowa	21.9
					District of Columbia	21.2

Source: Morgan Quitno Press using data from U.S. Dept of Health & Human Services, Health Care Financing Admin.
"State Health Expenditure Accounts" (Health Care Financing Review, Fall 1995, Volume 17, Number 1)
*By state of provider. Includes hospital care, physician services, dental services, home health care, drugs, vision products and other personal health care services and products.

Percent Change in Per Capita Expenditures for
Personal Health Care: 1990 to 1993
National Percent Change = 23.5% Increase*

ALPHA ORDER

RANK	STATE	PERCENT CHANGE
8	Alabama	27.2
49	Alaska	16.7
50	Arizona	16.6
35	Arkansas	22.2
41	California	21.1
42	Colorado	20.3
33	Connecticut	22.8
16	Delaware	25.9
42	Florida	20.3
31	Georgia	23.4
40	Hawaii	21.2
18	Idaho	25.7
26	Illinois	23.9
11	Indiana	26.9
46	Iowa	20.0
34	Kansas	22.6
5	Kentucky	29.0
3	Louisiana	29.5
14	Maine	26.0
30	Maryland	23.6
36	Massachusetts	22.1
38	Michigan	21.4
47	Minnesota	19.3
6	Mississippi	28.0
27	Missouri	23.8
23	Montana	24.4
28	Nebraska	23.7
48	Nevada	17.5
1	New Hampshire	35.2
11	New Jersey	26.9
19	New Mexico	25.6
28	New York	23.7
9	North Carolina	27.0
21	North Dakota	25.2
32	Ohio	23.0
22	Oklahoma	24.6
36	Oregon	22.1
13	Pennsylvania	26.5
14	Rhode Island	26.0
3	South Carolina	29.5
9	South Dakota	27.0
7	Tennessee	27.4
17	Texas	25.8
42	Utah	20.3
25	Vermont	24.0
42	Virginia	20.3
20	Washington	25.4
2	West Virginia	31.3
24	Wisconsin	24.2
38	Wyoming	21.4

RANK ORDER

RANK	STATE	PERCENT CHANGE
1	New Hampshire	35.2
2	West Virginia	31.3
3	Louisiana	29.5
3	South Carolina	29.5
5	Kentucky	29.0
6	Mississippi	28.0
7	Tennessee	27.4
8	Alabama	27.2
9	North Carolina	27.0
9	South Dakota	27.0
11	Indiana	26.9
11	New Jersey	26.9
13	Pennsylvania	26.5
14	Maine	26.0
14	Rhode Island	26.0
16	Delaware	25.9
17	Texas	25.8
18	Idaho	25.7
19	New Mexico	25.6
20	Washington	25.4
21	North Dakota	25.2
22	Oklahoma	24.6
23	Montana	24.4
24	Wisconsin	24.2
25	Vermont	24.0
26	Illinois	23.9
27	Missouri	23.8
28	Nebraska	23.7
28	New York	23.7
30	Maryland	23.6
31	Georgia	23.4
32	Ohio	23.0
33	Connecticut	22.8
34	Kansas	22.6
35	Arkansas	22.2
36	Massachusetts	22.1
36	Oregon	22.1
38	Michigan	21.4
38	Wyoming	21.4
40	Hawaii	21.2
41	California	21.1
42	Colorado	20.3
42	Florida	20.3
42	Utah	20.3
42	Virginia	20.3
46	Iowa	20.0
47	Minnesota	19.3
48	Nevada	17.5
49	Alaska	16.7
50	Arizona	16.6
	District of Columbia	27.3

Source: Morgan Quitno Press using data from U.S. Dept of Health & Human Services, Health Care Financing Admin. "State Health Expenditure Accounts" (Health Care Financing Review, Fall 1995, Volume 17, Number 1)
*By state of provider. Includes hospital care, physician services, dental services, home health care, drugs, vision products and other personal health care services and products.

Average Annual Change in Expenditures for Personal Health Care: 1980 to 1993
National Percent = 10.3% Average Annual Growth*

ALPHA ORDER

RANK ORDER

RANK	STATE	PERCENT	RANK	STATE	PERCENT
16	Alabama	10.9	1	New Hampshire	13.0
27	Alaska	10.2	2	Florida	12.4
5	Arizona	11.9	3	Nevada	12.2
32	Arkansas	10.1	4	Georgia	12.1
27	California	10.2	5	Arizona	11.9
23	Colorado	10.5	5	North Carolina	11.9
15	Connecticut	11.0	5	South Carolina	11.9
9	Delaware	11.3	8	New Mexico	11.7
2	Florida	12.4	9	Delaware	11.3
4	Georgia	12.1	10	New Jersey	11.2
19	Hawaii	10.8	10	Tennessee	11.2
24	Idaho	10.4	12	Texas	11.1
47	Illinois	8.7	12	Utah	11.1
26	Indiana	10.3	12	Washington	11.1
50	Iowa	8.3	15	Connecticut	11.0
45	Kansas	9.0	16	Alabama	10.9
16	Kentucky	10.9	16	Kentucky	10.9
24	Louisiana	10.4	16	Virginia	10.9
21	Maine	10.6	19	Hawaii	10.8
21	Maryland	10.6	19	Vermont	10.8
27	Massachusetts	10.2	21	Maine	10.6
49	Michigan	8.5	21	Maryland	10.6
37	Minnesota	9.7	23	Colorado	10.5
32	Mississippi	10.1	24	Idaho	10.4
39	Missouri	9.6	24	Louisiana	10.4
35	Montana	9.8	26	Indiana	10.3
46	Nebraska	8.9	27	Alaska	10.2
3	Nevada	12.2	27	California	10.2
1	New Hampshire	13.0	27	Massachusetts	10.2
10	New Jersey	11.2	27	Pennsylvania	10.2
8	New Mexico	11.7	27	Rhode Island	10.2
37	New York	9.7	32	Arkansas	10.1
5	North Carolina	11.9	32	Mississippi	10.1
43	North Dakota	9.4	34	Oregon	9.9
39	Ohio	9.6	35	Montana	9.8
44	Oklahoma	9.1	35	South Dakota	9.8
34	Oregon	9.9	37	Minnesota	9.7
27	Pennsylvania	10.2	37	New York	9.7
27	Rhode Island	10.2	39	Missouri	9.6
5	South Carolina	11.9	39	Ohio	9.6
35	South Dakota	9.8	39	West Virginia	9.6
10	Tennessee	11.2	42	Wisconsin	9.5
12	Texas	11.1	43	North Dakota	9.4
12	Utah	11.1	44	Oklahoma	9.1
19	Vermont	10.8	45	Kansas	9.0
16	Virginia	10.9	46	Nebraska	8.9
12	Washington	11.1	47	Illinois	8.7
39	West Virginia	9.6	47	Wyoming	8.7
42	Wisconsin	9.5	49	Michigan	8.5
47	Wyoming	8.7	50	Iowa	8.3
				District of Columbia	9.1

Source: U.S. Department of Health and Human Services, Health Care Financing Administration
   "State Health Expenditure Accounts" (Health Care Financing Review, Fall 1995, Volume 17, Number 1)
*By state of provider. Includes hospital care, physician services, dental services, home health care, drugs, vision products and other personal health care services and products.

Average Annual Change in Per Capita Expenditures
For Personal Health Care: 1980 to 1993
National Percent = 9.3% Average Annual Increase*

ALPHA ORDER

RANK	STATE	PERCENT
7	Alabama	10.3
50	Alaska	6.8
38	Arizona	8.8
21	Arkansas	9.6
48	California	7.9
38	Colorado	8.8
5	Connecticut	10.5
13	Delaware	10.0
23	Florida	9.5
11	Georgia	10.1
30	Hawaii	9.2
31	Idaho	9.1
45	Illinois	8.5
13	Indiana	10.0
42	Iowa	8.6
46	Kansas	8.4
3	Kentucky	10.6
7	Louisiana	10.3
16	Maine	9.8
27	Maryland	9.3
16	Massachusetts	9.8
46	Michigan	8.4
37	Minnesota	8.9
19	Mississippi	9.7
31	Missouri	9.1
27	Montana	9.3
42	Nebraska	8.6
49	Nevada	7.6
1	New Hampshire	11.3
2	New Jersey	10.7
15	New Mexico	9.9
25	New York	9.4
5	North Carolina	10.5
21	North Dakota	9.6
25	Ohio	9.4
42	Oklahoma	8.6
40	Oregon	8.7
11	Pennsylvania	10.1
19	Rhode Island	9.7
3	South Carolina	10.6
23	South Dakota	9.5
7	Tennessee	10.3
31	Texas	9.1
35	Utah	9.0
16	Vermont	9.8
27	Virginia	9.3
31	Washington	9.1
10	West Virginia	10.2
35	Wisconsin	9.0
40	Wyoming	8.7

RANK ORDER

RANK	STATE	PERCENT
1	New Hampshire	11.3
2	New Jersey	10.7
3	Kentucky	10.6
3	South Carolina	10.6
5	Connecticut	10.5
5	North Carolina	10.5
7	Alabama	10.3
7	Louisiana	10.3
7	Tennessee	10.3
10	West Virginia	10.2
11	Georgia	10.1
11	Pennsylvania	10.1
13	Delaware	10.0
13	Indiana	10.0
15	New Mexico	9.9
16	Maine	9.8
16	Massachusetts	9.8
16	Vermont	9.8
19	Mississippi	9.7
19	Rhode Island	9.7
21	Arkansas	9.6
21	North Dakota	9.6
23	Florida	9.5
23	South Dakota	9.5
25	New York	9.4
25	Ohio	9.4
27	Maryland	9.3
27	Montana	9.3
27	Virginia	9.3
30	Hawaii	9.2
31	Idaho	9.1
31	Missouri	9.1
31	Texas	9.1
31	Washington	9.1
35	Utah	9.0
35	Wisconsin	9.0
37	Minnesota	8.9
38	Arizona	8.8
38	Colorado	8.8
40	Oregon	8.7
40	Wyoming	8.7
42	Iowa	8.6
42	Nebraska	8.6
42	Oklahoma	8.6
45	Illinois	8.5
46	Kansas	8.4
46	Michigan	8.4
48	California	7.9
49	Nevada	7.6
50	Alaska	6.8

District of Columbia	9.9

Source: Morgan Quitno Press using data from U.S. Dept of Health & Human Services, Health Care Financing Admin.
"State Health Expenditure Accounts" (Health Care Financing Review, Fall 1995, Volume 17, Number 1)
By state of provider. Includes hospital care, physician services, dental services, home health care, drugs, vision products and other personal health care services and products.

Expenditures for Hospital Care in 1993

National Total = $323,919,000,000*

ALPHA ORDER

RANK	STATE	EXPENDITURES	% of USA
21	Alabama	$5,301,000,000	1.6%
48	Alaska	701,000,000	0.2%
26	Arizona	3,999,000,000	1.2%
33	Arkansas	2,723,000,000	0.8%
1	California	34,827,000,000	10.8%
27	Colorado	3,932,000,000	1.2%
24	Connecticut	4,380,000,000	1.4%
43	Delaware	937,000,000	0.3%
5	Florida	17,131,000,000	5.3%
11	Georgia	8,704,000,000	2.7%
38	Hawaii	1,460,000,000	0.5%
46	Idaho	900,000,000	0.3%
6	Illinois	15,621,000,000	4.8%
16	Indiana	6,998,000,000	2.2%
29	Iowa	3,111,000,000	1.0%
32	Kansas	2,868,000,000	0.9%
23	Kentucky	4,515,000,000	1.4%
17	Louisiana	5,956,000,000	1.8%
40	Maine	1,376,000,000	0.4%
18	Maryland	5,926,000,000	1.8%
10	Massachusetts	10,034,000,000	3.1%
8	Michigan	11,711,000,000	3.6%
22	Minnesota	4,796,000,000	1.5%
31	Mississippi	2,897,000,000	0.9%
13	Missouri	7,652,000,000	2.4%
47	Montana	894,000,000	0.3%
35	Nebraska	2,003,000,000	0.6%
41	Nevada	1,362,000,000	0.4%
39	New Hampshire	1,388,000,000	0.4%
9	New Jersey	10,312,000,000	3.2%
36	New Mexico	1,848,000,000	0.6%
2	New York	28,001,000,000	8.7%
12	North Carolina	7,801,000,000	2.4%
45	North Dakota	903,000,000	0.3%
7	Ohio	14,305,000,000	4.4%
28	Oklahoma	3,329,000,000	1.0%
30	Oregon	2,966,000,000	0.9%
4	Pennsylvania	19,540,000,000	6.0%
42	Rhode Island	1,314,000,000	0.4%
25	South Carolina	4,221,000,000	1.3%
44	South Dakota	920,000,000	0.3%
14	Tennessee	7,208,000,000	2.2%
3	Texas	21,592,000,000	6.7%
37	Utah	1,743,000,000	0.5%
49	Vermont	562,000,000	0.2%
15	Virginia	7,031,000,000	2.2%
20	Washington	5,305,000,000	1.6%
34	West Virginia	2,346,000,000	0.7%
19	Wisconsin	5,537,000,000	1.7%
50	Wyoming	417,000,000	0.1%

RANK ORDER

RANK	STATE	EXPENDITURES	% of USA
1	California	$34,827,000,000	10.8%
2	New York	28,001,000,000	8.7%
3	Texas	21,592,000,000	6.7%
4	Pennsylvania	19,540,000,000	6.0%
5	Florida	17,131,000,000	5.3%
6	Illinois	15,621,000,000	4.8%
7	Ohio	14,305,000,000	4.4%
8	Michigan	11,711,000,000	3.6%
9	New Jersey	10,312,000,000	3.2%
10	Massachusetts	10,034,000,000	3.1%
11	Georgia	8,704,000,000	2.7%
12	North Carolina	7,801,000,000	2.4%
13	Missouri	7,652,000,000	2.4%
14	Tennessee	7,208,000,000	2.2%
15	Virginia	7,031,000,000	2.2%
16	Indiana	6,998,000,000	2.2%
17	Louisiana	5,956,000,000	1.8%
18	Maryland	5,926,000,000	1.8%
19	Wisconsin	5,537,000,000	1.7%
20	Washington	5,305,000,000	1.6%
21	Alabama	5,301,000,000	1.6%
22	Minnesota	4,796,000,000	1.5%
23	Kentucky	4,515,000,000	1.4%
24	Connecticut	4,380,000,000	1.4%
25	South Carolina	4,221,000,000	1.3%
26	Arizona	3,999,000,000	1.2%
27	Colorado	3,932,000,000	1.2%
28	Oklahoma	3,329,000,000	1.0%
29	Iowa	3,111,000,000	1.0%
30	Oregon	2,966,000,000	0.9%
31	Mississippi	2,897,000,000	0.9%
32	Kansas	2,868,000,000	0.9%
33	Arkansas	2,723,000,000	0.8%
34	West Virginia	2,346,000,000	0.7%
35	Nebraska	2,003,000,000	0.6%
36	New Mexico	1,848,000,000	0.6%
37	Utah	1,743,000,000	0.5%
38	Hawaii	1,460,000,000	0.5%
39	New Hampshire	1,388,000,000	0.4%
40	Maine	1,376,000,000	0.4%
41	Nevada	1,362,000,000	0.4%
42	Rhode Island	1,314,000,000	0.4%
43	Delaware	937,000,000	0.3%
44	South Dakota	920,000,000	0.3%
45	North Dakota	903,000,000	0.3%
46	Idaho	900,000,000	0.3%
47	Montana	894,000,000	0.3%
48	Alaska	701,000,000	0.2%
49	Vermont	562,000,000	0.2%
50	Wyoming	417,000,000	0.1%
	District of Columbia	2,612,000,000	0.8%

Source: U.S. Department of Health and Human Services, Health Care Financing Administration
     "State Health Expenditure Accounts" (Health Care Financing Review, Fall 1995, Volume 17, Number 1)
*By state of provider.

Percent of Total Personal Health Care Expenditures
Spent on Hospital Care in 1993
National Percent = 41.6%*

ALPHA ORDER

RANK	STATE	PERCENT
15	Alabama	44.0
12	Alaska	44.6
43	Arizona	37.6
12	Arkansas	44.6
46	California	37.0
38	Colorado	39.1
48	Connecticut	35.9
31	Delaware	41.5
41	Florida	38.2
17	Georgia	43.3
28	Hawaii	41.9
37	Idaho	39.5
10	Illinois	45.0
23	Indiana	42.7
25	Iowa	42.4
31	Kansas	41.5
16	Kentucky	43.5
7	Louisiana	45.8
35	Maine	40.1
38	Maryland	39.1
20	Massachusetts	42.8
19	Michigan	43.2
50	Minnesota	33.8
5	Mississippi	46.8
1	Missouri	48.0
24	Montana	42.5
8	Nebraska	45.5
47	Nevada	36.3
34	New Hampshire	40.2
35	New Jersey	40.1
2	New Mexico	47.7
29	New York	41.8
20	North Carolina	42.8
11	North Dakota	44.7
20	Ohio	42.8
33	Oklahoma	41.4
45	Oregon	37.1
3	Pennsylvania	47.1
40	Rhode Island	38.3
6	South Carolina	46.7
3	South Dakota	47.1
14	Tennessee	44.5
17	Texas	43.3
26	Utah	42.3
44	Vermont	37.5
27	Virginia	42.1
49	Washington	35.1
9	West Virginia	45.1
41	Wisconsin	38.2
29	Wyoming	41.8

RANK ORDER

RANK	STATE	PERCENT
1	Missouri	48.0
2	New Mexico	47.7
3	Pennsylvania	47.1
3	South Dakota	47.1
5	Mississippi	46.8
6	South Carolina	46.7
7	Louisiana	45.8
8	Nebraska	45.5
9	West Virginia	45.1
10	Illinois	45.0
11	North Dakota	44.7
12	Alaska	44.6
12	Arkansas	44.6
14	Tennessee	44.5
15	Alabama	44.0
16	Kentucky	43.5
17	Georgia	43.3
17	Texas	43.3
19	Michigan	43.2
20	Massachusetts	42.8
20	North Carolina	42.8
20	Ohio	42.8
23	Indiana	42.7
24	Montana	42.5
25	Iowa	42.4
26	Utah	42.3
27	Virginia	42.1
28	Hawaii	41.9
29	New York	41.8
29	Wyoming	41.8
31	Delaware	41.5
31	Kansas	41.5
33	Oklahoma	41.4
34	New Hampshire	40.2
35	Maine	40.1
35	New Jersey	40.1
37	Idaho	39.5
38	Colorado	39.1
38	Maryland	39.1
40	Rhode Island	38.3
41	Florida	38.2
41	Wisconsin	38.2
43	Arizona	37.6
44	Vermont	37.5
45	Oregon	37.1
46	California	37.0
47	Nevada	36.3
48	Connecticut	35.9
49	Washington	35.1
50	Minnesota	33.8

District of Columbia 61.0

Source: Morgan Quitno Press using data from U.S. Dept of Health & Human Services, Health Care Financing Admin. "State Health Expenditure Accounts" (Health Care Financing Review, Fall 1995, Volume 17, Number 1)
By state of provider.

Per Capita Expenditures for Hospital Care in 1993

National Per Capita = $1,256*

ALPHA ORDER

RANK	STATE	PER CAPITA
16	Alabama	$1,268
27	Alaska	1,172
43	Arizona	1,014
31	Arkansas	1,123
33	California	1,116
35	Colorado	1,102
9	Connecticut	1,336
8	Delaware	1,340
19	Florida	1,248
17	Georgia	1,261
18	Hawaii	1,252
50	Idaho	817
9	Illinois	1,336
23	Indiana	1,226
35	Iowa	1,102
30	Kansas	1,133
26	Kentucky	1,190
7	Louisiana	1,389
34	Maine	1,111
24	Maryland	1,197
1	Massachusetts	1,667
21	Michigan	1,238
41	Minnesota	1,060
37	Mississippi	1,098
4	Missouri	1,462
40	Montana	1,063
20	Nebraska	1,241
45	Nevada	983
22	New Hampshire	1,236
12	New Jersey	1,312
29	New Mexico	1,144
3	New York	1,542
32	North Carolina	1,122
5	North Dakota	1,418
13	Ohio	1,293
42	Oklahoma	1,030
46	Oregon	977
2	Pennsylvania	1,624
11	Rhode Island	1,315
28	South Carolina	1,164
15	South Dakota	1,283
6	Tennessee	1,415
25	Texas	1,196
48	Utah	937
47	Vermont	976
39	Virginia	1,086
44	Washington	1,010
14	West Virginia	1,290
37	Wisconsin	1,098
49	Wyoming	887

RANK ORDER

RANK	STATE	PER CAPITA
1	Massachusetts	$1,667
2	Pennsylvania	1,624
3	New York	1,542
4	Missouri	1,462
5	North Dakota	1,418
6	Tennessee	1,415
7	Louisiana	1,389
8	Delaware	1,340
9	Connecticut	1,336
9	Illinois	1,336
11	Rhode Island	1,315
12	New Jersey	1,312
13	Ohio	1,293
14	West Virginia	1,290
15	South Dakota	1,283
16	Alabama	1,268
17	Georgia	1,261
18	Hawaii	1,252
19	Florida	1,248
20	Nebraska	1,241
21	Michigan	1,238
22	New Hampshire	1,236
23	Indiana	1,226
24	Maryland	1,197
25	Texas	1,196
26	Kentucky	1,190
27	Alaska	1,172
28	South Carolina	1,164
29	New Mexico	1,144
30	Kansas	1,133
31	Arkansas	1,123
32	North Carolina	1,122
33	California	1,116
34	Maine	1,111
35	Colorado	1,102
35	Iowa	1,102
37	Mississippi	1,098
37	Wisconsin	1,098
39	Virginia	1,086
40	Montana	1,063
41	Minnesota	1,060
42	Oklahoma	1,030
43	Arizona	1,014
44	Washington	1,010
45	Nevada	983
46	Oregon	977
47	Vermont	976
48	Utah	937
49	Wyoming	887
50	Idaho	817

District of Columbia**   4,519

Source: Morgan Quitno Press using data from U.S. Dept of Health & Human Services, Health Care Financing Admin.
"State Health Expenditure Accounts" (Health Care Financing Review, Fall 1995, Volume 17, Number 1)
*By state of provider.
**The District of Columbia's per capita is greatly affected by residents of Maryland and Virginia receiving services.

Percent Change in Expenditures for Hospital Care: 1990 to 1993

National Percent Change = 27.4% Increase*

ALPHA ORDER				RANK ORDER		
RANK	STATE	PERCENT		RANK	STATE	PERCENT
12	Alabama	32.0		1	South Carolina	35.8
33	Alaska	25.9		2	New Mexico	35.5
40	Arizona	24.3		2	Texas	35.5
22	Arkansas	29.1		4	Idaho	35.3
38	California	24.6		5	Washington	33.9
29	Colorado	26.8		6	West Virginia	33.1
47	Connecticut	19.5		7	South Dakota	32.6
10	Delaware	32.2		8	Mississippi	32.5
26	Florida	27.3		9	Indiana	32.3
21	Georgia	30.2		10	Delaware	32.2
28	Hawaii	27.2		10	North Carolina	32.2
4	Idaho	35.3		12	Alabama	32.0
32	Illinois	26.0		13	Montana	31.7
9	Indiana	32.3		14	Utah	31.5
48	Iowa	18.1		15	Kentucky	31.4
37	Kansas	24.7		15	New Hampshire	31.4
15	Kentucky	31.4		15	Pennsylvania	31.4
24	Louisiana	28.7		18	New Jersey	31.2
44	Maine	23.0		19	Tennessee	30.8
26	Maryland	27.3		20	Nevada	30.6
44	Massachusetts	23.0		21	Georgia	30.2
42	Michigan	23.3		22	Arkansas	29.1
50	Minnesota	17.1		22	Oregon	29.1
8	Mississippi	32.5		24	Louisiana	28.7
25	Missouri	27.8		25	Missouri	27.8
13	Montana	31.7		26	Florida	27.3
31	Nebraska	26.2		26	Maryland	27.3
20	Nevada	30.6		28	Hawaii	27.2
15	New Hampshire	31.4		29	Colorado	26.8
18	New Jersey	31.2		30	Wisconsin	26.5
2	New Mexico	35.5		31	Nebraska	26.2
43	New York	23.1		32	Illinois	26.0
10	North Carolina	32.2		33	Alaska	25.9
33	North Dakota	25.9		33	North Dakota	25.9
36	Ohio	25.3		35	Vermont	25.7
39	Oklahoma	24.5		36	Ohio	25.3
22	Oregon	29.1		37	Kansas	24.7
15	Pennsylvania	31.4		38	California	24.6
46	Rhode Island	20.0		39	Oklahoma	24.5
1	South Carolina	35.8		40	Arizona	24.3
7	South Dakota	32.6		41	Virginia	24.2
19	Tennessee	30.8		42	Michigan	23.3
2	Texas	35.5		43	New York	23.1
14	Utah	31.5		44	Maine	23.0
35	Vermont	25.7		44	Massachusetts	23.0
41	Virginia	24.2		46	Rhode Island	20.0
5	Washington	33.9		47	Connecticut	19.5
6	West Virginia	33.1		48	Iowa	18.1
30	Wisconsin	26.5		48	Wyoming	18.1
48	Wyoming	18.1		50	Minnesota	17.1
					District of Columbia	22.5

Source: Morgan Quitno Press using data from U.S. Dept of Health & Human Services, Health Care Financing Admin.
"State Health Expenditure Accounts" (Health Care Financing Review, Fall 1995, Volume 17, Number 1)
*By state of provider.

Percent Change in Per Capita Expenditures for Hospital Care: 1990 to 1993

National Percent Change = 22.9% Increase*

ALPHA ORDER

RANK ORDER

RANK	STATE	PERCENT CHANGE	RANK	STATE	PERCENT CHANGE
10	Alabama	27.6	1	West Virginia	31.2
46	Alaska	15.7	2	South Carolina	30.5
47	Arizona	15.5	3	New Hampshire	29.8
17	Arkansas	25.2	4	Pennsylvania	29.7
42	California	18.8	5	Mississippi	29.3
44	Colorado	17.1	6	New Jersey	29.1
41	Connecticut	19.8	7	South Dakota	28.7
16	Delaware	25.8	8	Indiana	28.5
40	Florida	19.9	9	Kentucky	27.7
30	Georgia	22.2	10	Alabama	27.6
38	Hawaii	20.8	11	Texas	27.5
22	Idaho	23.8	12	New Mexico	27.1
24	Illinois	23.1	13	Louisiana	26.7
8	Indiana	28.5	14	North Dakota	26.4
45	Iowa	16.1	15	North Carolina	26.1
31	Kansas	22.1	16	Delaware	25.8
9	Kentucky	27.7	17	Arkansas	25.2
13	Louisiana	26.7	17	Tennessee	25.2
32	Maine	22.0	19	Montana	25.1
25	Maryland	22.9	20	Missouri	25.0
25	Massachusetts	22.9	21	Washington	24.1
36	Michigan	21.1	22	Idaho	23.8
49	Minnesota	13.2	23	Nebraska	23.4
5	Mississippi	29.3	24	Illinois	23.1
20	Missouri	25.0	25	Maryland	22.9
19	Montana	25.1	25	Massachusetts	22.9
23	Nebraska	23.4	25	Vermont	22.9
49	Nevada	13.2	28	Ohio	22.8
3	New Hampshire	29.8	29	Wisconsin	22.7
6	New Jersey	29.1	30	Georgia	22.2
12	New Mexico	27.1	31	Kansas	22.1
32	New York	22.0	32	Maine	22.0
15	North Carolina	26.1	32	New York	22.0
14	North Dakota	26.4	34	Utah	21.8
28	Ohio	22.8	35	Oklahoma	21.2
35	Oklahoma	21.2	36	Michigan	21.1
37	Oregon	20.9	37	Oregon	20.9
4	Pennsylvania	29.7	38	Hawaii	20.8
39	Rhode Island	20.4	39	Rhode Island	20.4
2	South Carolina	30.5	40	Florida	19.9
7	South Dakota	28.7	41	Connecticut	19.8
17	Tennessee	25.2	42	California	18.8
11	Texas	27.5	43	Virginia	18.7
34	Utah	21.8	44	Colorado	17.1
25	Vermont	22.9	45	Iowa	16.1
43	Virginia	18.7	46	Alaska	15.7
21	Washington	24.1	47	Arizona	15.5
1	West Virginia	31.2	48	Wyoming	14.0
29	Wisconsin	22.7	49	Minnesota	13.2
48	Wyoming	14.0	49	Nevada	13.2
				District of Columbia	28.6

Source: Morgan Quitno Press using data from U.S. Dept of Health & Human Services, Health Care Financing Admin.
    "State Health Expenditure Accounts" (Health Care Financing Review, Fall 1995, Volume 17, Number 1)
*By state of provider.

Average Annual Change in Expenditures for Hospital Care: 1980 to 1993

National Percent = 9.4% Average Annual Growth*

ALPHA ORDER				RANK ORDER		
RANK	STATE	PERCENT		RANK	STATE	PERCENT
23	Alabama	9.8		1	New Hampshire	12.2
19	Alaska	10.2		2	South Carolina	12.0
15	Arizona	10.5		3	Hawaii	11.5
13	Arkansas	10.6		3	New Mexico	11.5
33	California	8.8		5	Georgia	11.4
27	Colorado	9.5		6	North Carolina	11.3
31	Connecticut	9.2		7	Florida	11.1
16	Delaware	10.4		7	Texas	11.1
7	Florida	11.1		9	Utah	11.0
5	Georgia	11.4		10	Washington	10.9
3	Hawaii	11.5		11	Idaho	10.7
11	Idaho	10.7		11	New Jersey	10.7
50	Illinois	7.4		13	Arkansas	10.6
26	Indiana	9.7		13	Kentucky	10.6
47	Iowa	7.8		15	Arizona	10.5
47	Kansas	7.8		16	Delaware	10.4
13	Kentucky	10.6		17	Nevada	10.3
20	Louisiana	10.0		17	Tennessee	10.3
33	Maine	8.8		19	Alaska	10.2
37	Maryland	8.6		20	Louisiana	10.0
45	Massachusetts	8.1		21	Montana	9.9
49	Michigan	7.7		21	Virginia	9.9
44	Minnesota	8.2		23	Alabama	9.8
23	Mississippi	9.8		23	Mississippi	9.8
32	Missouri	8.9		23	South Dakota	9.8
21	Montana	9.9		26	Indiana	9.7
33	Nebraska	8.8		27	Colorado	9.5
17	Nevada	10.3		27	Pennsylvania	9.5
1	New Hampshire	12.2		27	Vermont	9.5
11	New Jersey	10.7		30	Oregon	9.4
3	New Mexico	11.5		31	Connecticut	9.2
37	New York	8.6		32	Missouri	8.9
6	North Carolina	11.3		33	California	8.8
39	North Dakota	8.5		33	Maine	8.8
33	Ohio	8.8		33	Nebraska	8.8
39	Oklahoma	8.5		33	Ohio	8.8
30	Oregon	9.4		37	Maryland	8.6
27	Pennsylvania	9.5		37	New York	8.6
45	Rhode Island	8.1		39	North Dakota	8.5
2	South Carolina	12.0		39	Oklahoma	8.5
23	South Dakota	9.8		39	Wyoming	8.5
17	Tennessee	10.3		42	West Virginia	8.4
7	Texas	11.1		42	Wisconsin	8.4
9	Utah	11.0		44	Minnesota	8.2
27	Vermont	9.5		45	Massachusetts	8.1
21	Virginia	9.9		45	Rhode Island	8.1
10	Washington	10.9		47	Iowa	7.8
42	West Virginia	8.4		47	Kansas	7.8
42	Wisconsin	8.4		49	Michigan	7.7
39	Wyoming	8.5		50	Illinois	7.4
					District of Columbia	8.4

Source: U.S. Department of Health and Human Services, Health Care Financing Administration
   "State Health Expenditure Accounts" (Health Care Financing Review, Fall 1995, Volume 17, Number 1)
By state of provider.

Average Annual Change in Per Capita Expenditures
For Hospital Care: 1980 to 1993
National Percent = 8.3% Average Annual Increase*

<table>
<tr><td colspan="3">ALPHA ORDER</td><td colspan="3">RANK ORDER</td></tr>
<tr><td>RANK</td><td>STATE</td><td>PERCENT</td><td>RANK</td><td>STATE</td><td>PERCENT</td></tr>
<tr><td>18</td><td>Alabama</td><td>9.1</td><td>1</td><td>South Carolina</td><td>10.6</td></tr>
<tr><td>48</td><td>Alaska</td><td>6.9</td><td>2</td><td>New Hampshire</td><td>10.4</td></tr>
<tr><td>43</td><td>Arizona</td><td>7.4</td><td>3</td><td>Kentucky</td><td>10.2</td></tr>
<tr><td>5</td><td>Arkansas</td><td>10.0</td><td>4</td><td>New Jersey</td><td>10.1</td></tr>
<tr><td>49</td><td>California</td><td>6.5</td><td>5</td><td>Arkansas</td><td>10.0</td></tr>
<tr><td>39</td><td>Colorado</td><td>7.7</td><td>6</td><td>Hawaii</td><td>9.8</td></tr>
<tr><td>24</td><td>Connecticut</td><td>8.7</td><td>6</td><td>North Carolina</td><td>9.8</td></tr>
<tr><td>19</td><td>Delaware</td><td>9.0</td><td>8</td><td>Louisiana</td><td>9.7</td></tr>
<tr><td>32</td><td>Florida</td><td>8.2</td><td>9</td><td>New Mexico</td><td>9.6</td></tr>
<tr><td>10</td><td>Georgia</td><td>9.4</td><td>10</td><td>Georgia</td><td>9.4</td></tr>
<tr><td>6</td><td>Hawaii</td><td>9.8</td><td>10</td><td>Pennsylvania</td><td>9.4</td></tr>
<tr><td>14</td><td>Idaho</td><td>9.3</td><td>10</td><td>South Dakota</td><td>9.4</td></tr>
<tr><td>44</td><td>Illinois</td><td>7.2</td><td>10</td><td>Tennessee</td><td>9.4</td></tr>
<tr><td>14</td><td>Indiana</td><td>9.3</td><td>14</td><td>Idaho</td><td>9.3</td></tr>
<tr><td>35</td><td>Iowa</td><td>8.0</td><td>14</td><td>Indiana</td><td>9.3</td></tr>
<tr><td>44</td><td>Kansas</td><td>7.2</td><td>14</td><td>Mississippi</td><td>9.3</td></tr>
<tr><td>3</td><td>Kentucky</td><td>10.2</td><td>14</td><td>Montana</td><td>9.3</td></tr>
<tr><td>8</td><td>Louisiana</td><td>9.7</td><td>18</td><td>Alabama</td><td>9.1</td></tr>
<tr><td>35</td><td>Maine</td><td>8.0</td><td>19</td><td>Delaware</td><td>9.0</td></tr>
<tr><td>44</td><td>Maryland</td><td>7.2</td><td>19</td><td>Texas</td><td>9.0</td></tr>
<tr><td>39</td><td>Massachusetts</td><td>7.7</td><td>21</td><td>Utah</td><td>8.9</td></tr>
<tr><td>42</td><td>Michigan</td><td>7.5</td><td>21</td><td>West Virginia</td><td>8.9</td></tr>
<tr><td>44</td><td>Minnesota</td><td>7.2</td><td>23</td><td>Washington</td><td>8.8</td></tr>
<tr><td>14</td><td>Mississippi</td><td>9.3</td><td>24</td><td>Connecticut</td><td>8.7</td></tr>
<tr><td>27</td><td>Missouri</td><td>8.4</td><td>24</td><td>North Dakota</td><td>8.7</td></tr>
<tr><td>14</td><td>Montana</td><td>9.3</td><td>26</td><td>Ohio</td><td>8.6</td></tr>
<tr><td>27</td><td>Nebraska</td><td>8.4</td><td>27</td><td>Missouri</td><td>8.4</td></tr>
<tr><td>50</td><td>Nevada</td><td>5.6</td><td>27</td><td>Nebraska</td><td>8.4</td></tr>
<tr><td>2</td><td>New Hampshire</td><td>10.4</td><td>27</td><td>Vermont</td><td>8.4</td></tr>
<tr><td>4</td><td>New Jersey</td><td>10.1</td><td>27</td><td>Wyoming</td><td>8.4</td></tr>
<tr><td>9</td><td>New Mexico</td><td>9.6</td><td>31</td><td>New York</td><td>8.3</td></tr>
<tr><td>31</td><td>New York</td><td>8.3</td><td>32</td><td>Florida</td><td>8.2</td></tr>
<tr><td>6</td><td>North Carolina</td><td>9.8</td><td>32</td><td>Oregon</td><td>8.2</td></tr>
<tr><td>24</td><td>North Dakota</td><td>8.7</td><td>32</td><td>Virginia</td><td>8.2</td></tr>
<tr><td>26</td><td>Ohio</td><td>8.6</td><td>35</td><td>Iowa</td><td>8.0</td></tr>
<tr><td>37</td><td>Oklahoma</td><td>7.8</td><td>35</td><td>Maine</td><td>8.0</td></tr>
<tr><td>32</td><td>Oregon</td><td>8.2</td><td>37</td><td>Oklahoma</td><td>7.8</td></tr>
<tr><td>10</td><td>Pennsylvania</td><td>9.4</td><td>37</td><td>Wisconsin</td><td>7.8</td></tr>
<tr><td>41</td><td>Rhode Island</td><td>7.6</td><td>39</td><td>Colorado</td><td>7.7</td></tr>
<tr><td>1</td><td>South Carolina</td><td>10.6</td><td>39</td><td>Massachusetts</td><td>7.7</td></tr>
<tr><td>10</td><td>South Dakota</td><td>9.4</td><td>41</td><td>Rhode Island</td><td>7.6</td></tr>
<tr><td>10</td><td>Tennessee</td><td>9.4</td><td>42</td><td>Michigan</td><td>7.5</td></tr>
<tr><td>19</td><td>Texas</td><td>9.0</td><td>43</td><td>Arizona</td><td>7.4</td></tr>
<tr><td>21</td><td>Utah</td><td>8.9</td><td>44</td><td>Illinois</td><td>7.2</td></tr>
<tr><td>27</td><td>Vermont</td><td>8.4</td><td>44</td><td>Kansas</td><td>7.2</td></tr>
<tr><td>32</td><td>Virginia</td><td>8.2</td><td>44</td><td>Maryland</td><td>7.2</td></tr>
<tr><td>23</td><td>Washington</td><td>8.8</td><td>44</td><td>Minnesota</td><td>7.2</td></tr>
<tr><td>21</td><td>West Virginia</td><td>8.9</td><td>48</td><td>Alaska</td><td>6.9</td></tr>
<tr><td>37</td><td>Wisconsin</td><td>7.8</td><td>49</td><td>California</td><td>6.5</td></tr>
<tr><td>27</td><td>Wyoming</td><td>8.4</td><td>50</td><td>Nevada</td><td>5.6</td></tr>
<tr><td></td><td></td><td></td><td></td><td>District of Columbia</td><td>9.3</td></tr>
</table>

Source: Morgan Quitno Press using data from U.S. Dept of Health & Human Services, Health Care Financing Admin.
"State Health Expenditure Accounts" (Health Care Financing Review, Fall 1995, Volume 17, Number 1)
*By state of provider.

Expenditures for Physician Services in 1993

National Total = $171,226,000,000*

ALPHA ORDER

RANK	STATE	EXPENDITURES	% of USA
22	Alabama	$2,631,000,000	1.5%
48	Alaska	301,000,000	0.2%
21	Arizona	2,799,000,000	1.6%
32	Arkansas	1,244,000,000	0.7%
1	California	28,981,000,000	16.9%
25	Colorado	2,452,000,000	1.4%
23	Connecticut	2,587,000,000	1.5%
44	Delaware	466,000,000	0.3%
4	Florida	10,498,000,000	6.1%
10	Georgia	4,543,000,000	2.7%
39	Hawaii	771,000,000	0.5%
43	Idaho	486,000,000	0.3%
7	Illinois	6,970,000,000	4.1%
18	Indiana	3,263,000,000	1.9%
31	Iowa	1,376,000,000	0.8%
30	Kansas	1,425,000,000	0.8%
26	Kentucky	2,038,000,000	1.2%
24	Louisiana	2,537,000,000	1.5%
41	Maine	601,000,000	0.4%
15	Maryland	3,704,000,000	2.2%
11	Massachusetts	4,442,000,000	2.6%
9	Michigan	5,562,000,000	3.3%
16	Minnesota	3,617,000,000	2.1%
33	Mississippi	1,107,000,000	0.7%
20	Missouri	2,958,000,000	1.7%
46	Montana	392,000,000	0.2%
37	Nebraska	825,000,000	0.5%
34	Nevada	1,029,000,000	0.6%
38	New Hampshire	780,000,000	0.5%
8	New Jersey	5,776,000,000	3.4%
40	New Mexico	716,000,000	0.4%
2	New York	12,003,000,000	7.0%
14	North Carolina	3,717,000,000	2.2%
45	North Dakota	445,000,000	0.3%
6	Ohio	7,118,000,000	4.2%
29	Oklahoma	1,640,000,000	1.0%
27	Oregon	1,904,000,000	1.1%
5	Pennsylvania	7,460,000,000	4.4%
42	Rhode Island	575,000,000	0.3%
28	South Carolina	1,685,000,000	1.0%
47	South Dakota	342,000,000	0.2%
19	Tennessee	3,137,000,000	1.8%
3	Texas	10,526,000,000	6.2%
36	Utah	864,000,000	0.5%
49	Vermont	265,000,000	0.2%
12	Virginia	3,769,000,000	2.2%
13	Washington	3,720,000,000	2.2%
35	West Virginia	988,000,000	0.6%
17	Wisconsin	3,362,000,000	2.0%
50	Wyoming	160,000,000	0.1%

RANK ORDER

RANK	STATE	EXPENDITURES	% of USA
1	California	$28,981,000,000	16.9%
2	New York	12,003,000,000	7.0%
3	Texas	10,526,000,000	6.2%
4	Florida	10,498,000,000	6.1%
5	Pennsylvania	7,460,000,000	4.4%
6	Ohio	7,118,000,000	4.2%
7	Illinois	6,970,000,000	4.1%
8	New Jersey	5,776,000,000	3.4%
9	Michigan	5,562,000,000	3.3%
10	Georgia	4,543,000,000	2.7%
11	Massachusetts	4,442,000,000	2.6%
12	Virginia	3,769,000,000	2.2%
13	Washington	3,720,000,000	2.2%
14	North Carolina	3,717,000,000	2.2%
15	Maryland	3,704,000,000	2.2%
16	Minnesota	3,617,000,000	2.1%
17	Wisconsin	3,362,000,000	2.0%
18	Indiana	3,263,000,000	1.9%
19	Tennessee	3,137,000,000	1.8%
20	Missouri	2,958,000,000	1.7%
21	Arizona	2,799,000,000	1.6%
22	Alabama	2,631,000,000	1.5%
23	Connecticut	2,587,000,000	1.5%
24	Louisiana	2,537,000,000	1.5%
25	Colorado	2,452,000,000	1.4%
26	Kentucky	2,038,000,000	1.2%
27	Oregon	1,904,000,000	1.1%
28	South Carolina	1,685,000,000	1.0%
29	Oklahoma	1,640,000,000	1.0%
30	Kansas	1,425,000,000	0.8%
31	Iowa	1,376,000,000	0.8%
32	Arkansas	1,244,000,000	0.7%
33	Mississippi	1,107,000,000	0.7%
34	Nevada	1,029,000,000	0.6%
35	West Virginia	988,000,000	0.6%
36	Utah	864,000,000	0.5%
37	Nebraska	825,000,000	0.5%
38	New Hampshire	780,000,000	0.5%
39	Hawaii	771,000,000	0.5%
40	New Mexico	716,000,000	0.4%
41	Maine	601,000,000	0.4%
42	Rhode Island	575,000,000	0.3%
43	Idaho	486,000,000	0.3%
44	Delaware	466,000,000	0.3%
45	North Dakota	445,000,000	0.3%
46	Montana	392,000,000	0.2%
47	South Dakota	342,000,000	0.2%
48	Alaska	301,000,000	0.2%
49	Vermont	265,000,000	0.2%
50	Wyoming	160,000,000	0.1%
	District of Columbia	672,000,000	0.4%

Source: U.S. Department of Health and Human Services, Health Care Financing Administration
"State Health Expenditure Accounts" (Health Care Financing Review, Fall 1995, Volume 17, Number 1)
*By state of provider.

Percent of Total Personal Health Care Expenditures
Spent on Physician Services in 1993
National Percent = 22.0%*

ALPHA ORDER

RANK	STATE	PERCENT
17	Alabama	21.8
34	Alaska	19.1
3	Arizona	26.3
26	Arkansas	20.4
1	California	30.8
6	Colorado	24.4
20	Connecticut	21.2
23	Delaware	20.6
9	Florida	23.4
11	Georgia	22.6
15	Hawaii	22.1
18	Idaho	21.3
29	Illinois	20.1
30	Indiana	19.9
38	Iowa	18.7
23	Kansas	20.6
31	Kentucky	19.6
32	Louisiana	19.5
47	Maine	17.5
6	Maryland	24.4
35	Massachusetts	19.0
25	Michigan	20.5
4	Minnesota	25.5
44	Mississippi	17.9
41	Missouri	18.5
40	Montana	18.6
37	Nebraska	18.8
2	Nevada	27.5
11	New Hampshire	22.6
14	New Jersey	22.4
41	New Mexico	18.5
44	New York	17.9
26	North Carolina	20.4
16	North Dakota	22.0
18	Ohio	21.3
26	Oklahoma	20.4
8	Oregon	23.8
43	Pennsylvania	18.0
49	Rhode Island	16.8
38	South Carolina	18.7
47	South Dakota	17.5
33	Tennessee	19.4
21	Texas	21.1
22	Utah	21.0
46	Vermont	17.7
11	Virginia	22.6
5	Washington	24.6
35	West Virginia	19.0
10	Wisconsin	23.2
50	Wyoming	16.0

RANK ORDER

RANK	STATE	PERCENT
1	California	30.8
2	Nevada	27.5
3	Arizona	26.3
4	Minnesota	25.5
5	Washington	24.6
6	Colorado	24.4
6	Maryland	24.4
8	Oregon	23.8
9	Florida	23.4
10	Wisconsin	23.2
11	Georgia	22.6
11	New Hampshire	22.6
11	Virginia	22.6
14	New Jersey	22.4
15	Hawaii	22.1
16	North Dakota	22.0
17	Alabama	21.8
18	Idaho	21.3
18	Ohio	21.3
20	Connecticut	21.2
21	Texas	21.1
22	Utah	21.0
23	Delaware	20.6
23	Kansas	20.6
25	Michigan	20.5
26	Arkansas	20.4
26	North Carolina	20.4
26	Oklahoma	20.4
29	Illinois	20.1
30	Indiana	19.9
31	Kentucky	19.6
32	Louisiana	19.5
33	Tennessee	19.4
34	Alaska	19.1
35	Massachusetts	19.0
35	West Virginia	19.0
37	Nebraska	18.8
38	Iowa	18.7
38	South Carolina	18.7
40	Montana	18.6
41	Missouri	18.5
41	New Mexico	18.5
43	Pennsylvania	18.0
44	Mississippi	17.9
44	New York	17.9
46	Vermont	17.7
47	Maine	17.5
47	South Dakota	17.5
49	Rhode Island	16.8
50	Wyoming	16.0
	District of Columbia	15.7

Source: Morgan Quitno Press using data from U.S. Dept of Health & Human Services, Health Care Financing Admin. "State Health Expenditure Accounts" (Health Care Financing Review, Fall 1995, Volume 17, Number 1)
*By state of provider.

Per Capita Expenditures for Physician Services in 1993

National Per Capita = $664*

ALPHA ORDER

RANK	STATE	PER CAPITA
20	Alabama	$629
39	Alaska	503
9	Arizona	710
36	Arkansas	513
1	California	928
13	Colorado	687
3	Connecticut	789
14	Delaware	667
4	Florida	765
18	Georgia	658
16	Hawaii	661
48	Idaho	441
24	Illinois	596
30	Indiana	572
40	Iowa	488
32	Kansas	563
34	Kentucky	537
25	Louisiana	592
41	Maine	485
5	Maryland	748
7	Massachusetts	738
26	Michigan	588
2	Minnesota	800
49	Mississippi	419
31	Missouri	565
43	Montana	466
37	Nebraska	511
6	Nevada	743
12	New Hampshire	695
8	New Jersey	735
47	New Mexico	443
16	New York	661
35	North Carolina	535
11	North Dakota	699
19	Ohio	644
38	Oklahoma	507
21	Oregon	627
22	Pennsylvania	620
29	Rhode Island	576
44	South Carolina	465
42	South Dakota	477
23	Tennessee	616
27	Texas	583
44	Utah	465
46	Vermont	460
28	Virginia	582
10	Washington	708
33	West Virginia	543
14	Wisconsin	667
50	Wyoming	340

RANK ORDER

RANK	STATE	PER CAPITA
1	California	$928
2	Minnesota	800
3	Connecticut	789
4	Florida	765
5	Maryland	748
6	Nevada	743
7	Massachusetts	738
8	New Jersey	735
9	Arizona	710
10	Washington	708
11	North Dakota	699
12	New Hampshire	695
13	Colorado	687
14	Delaware	667
14	Wisconsin	667
16	Hawaii	661
16	New York	661
18	Georgia	658
19	Ohio	644
20	Alabama	629
21	Oregon	627
22	Pennsylvania	620
23	Tennessee	616
24	Illinois	596
25	Louisiana	592
26	Michigan	588
27	Texas	583
28	Virginia	582
29	Rhode Island	576
30	Indiana	572
31	Missouri	565
32	Kansas	563
33	West Virginia	543
34	Kentucky	537
35	North Carolina	535
36	Arkansas	513
37	Nebraska	511
38	Oklahoma	507
39	Alaska	503
40	Iowa	488
41	Maine	485
42	South Dakota	477
43	Montana	466
44	South Carolina	465
44	Utah	465
46	Vermont	460
47	New Mexico	443
48	Idaho	441
49	Mississippi	419
50	Wyoming	340

District of Columbia**   1,163

Source: Morgan Quitno Press using data from U.S. Dept of Health & Human Services, Health Care Financing Admin.
"State Health Expenditure Accounts" (Health Care Financing Review, Fall 1995, Volume 17, Number 1)
*By state of provider.
**The District of Columbia's per capita is greatly affected by residents of Maryland and Virginia receiving services.

Percent Change in Expenditures for Physician Services: 1990 to 1993

National Percent Change = 21.9% Increase*

ALPHA ORDER

RANK	STATE	PERCENT CHANGE
42	Alabama	17.1
44	Alaska	16.7
46	Arizona	12.0
49	Arkansas	9.7
6	California	29.6
5	Colorado	29.7
37	Connecticut	18.4
19	Delaware	23.6
48	Florida	11.2
15	Georgia	24.6
20	Hawaii	22.6
4	Idaho	29.9
34	Illinois	18.9
23	Indiana	21.8
25	Iowa	20.5
40	Kansas	17.7
16	Kentucky	24.3
30	Louisiana	19.2
11	Maine	25.2
12	Maryland	24.8
38	Massachusetts	18.0
30	Michigan	19.2
21	Minnesota	22.3
28	Mississippi	19.7
33	Missouri	19.0
10	Montana	26.0
26	Nebraska	19.9
9	Nevada	26.7
1	New Hampshire	58.9
7	New Jersey	27.8
14	New Mexico	24.7
17	New York	23.8
18	North Carolina	23.7
24	North Dakota	20.9
40	Ohio	17.7
36	Oklahoma	18.7
30	Oregon	19.2
29	Pennsylvania	19.3
47	Rhode Island	11.9
8	South Carolina	27.2
12	South Dakota	24.8
22	Tennessee	22.1
38	Texas	18.0
43	Utah	16.9
26	Vermont	19.9
35	Virginia	18.8
2	Washington	31.3
45	West Virginia	15.4
3	Wisconsin	31.1
50	Wyoming	9.6

RANK ORDER

RANK	STATE	PERCENT CHANGE
1	New Hampshire	58.9
2	Washington	31.3
3	Wisconsin	31.1
4	Idaho	29.9
5	Colorado	29.7
6	California	29.6
7	New Jersey	27.8
8	South Carolina	27.2
9	Nevada	26.7
10	Montana	26.0
11	Maine	25.2
12	Maryland	24.8
12	South Dakota	24.8
14	New Mexico	24.7
15	Georgia	24.6
16	Kentucky	24.3
17	New York	23.8
18	North Carolina	23.7
19	Delaware	23.6
20	Hawaii	22.6
21	Minnesota	22.3
22	Tennessee	22.1
23	Indiana	21.8
24	North Dakota	20.9
25	Iowa	20.5
26	Nebraska	19.9
26	Vermont	19.9
28	Mississippi	19.7
29	Pennsylvania	19.3
30	Louisiana	19.2
30	Michigan	19.2
30	Oregon	19.2
33	Missouri	19.0
34	Illinois	18.9
35	Virginia	18.8
36	Oklahoma	18.7
37	Connecticut	18.4
38	Massachusetts	18.0
38	Texas	18.0
40	Kansas	17.7
40	Ohio	17.7
42	Alabama	17.1
43	Utah	16.9
44	Alaska	16.7
45	West Virginia	15.4
46	Arizona	12.0
47	Rhode Island	11.9
48	Florida	11.2
49	Arkansas	9.7
50	Wyoming	9.6

District of Columbia   2.3

Source: Morgan Quitno Press using data from U.S. Dept of Health & Human Services, Health Care Financing Admin. "State Health Expenditure Accounts" (Health Care Financing Review, Fall 1995, Volume 17, Number 1)
*By state of provider.

Percent Change in Per Capita Expenditures for Physician Services: 1990 to 1993

National Percent Change = 17.5% Increase*

ALPHA ORDER				RANK ORDER		
RANK	STATE	PERCENT CHANGE		RANK	STATE	PERCENT CHANGE
40	Alabama	13.1		1	New Hampshire	56.9
46	Alaska	7.2		2	Wisconsin	27.3
50	Arizona	4.1		3	New Jersey	25.6
47	Arkansas	6.4		4	Maine	24.0
5	California	23.4		5	California	23.4
14	Colorado	19.7		6	New York	22.6
17	Connecticut	18.6		7	South Carolina	22.4
23	Delaware	17.8		8	Washington	21.6
49	Florida	4.8		9	North Dakota	21.4
28	Georgia	16.9		10	South Dakota	21.1
32	Hawaii	16.4		11	Kentucky	20.7
15	Idaho	18.9		12	Maryland	20.5
34	Illinois	16.2		13	Montana	19.8
18	Indiana	18.4		14	Colorado	19.7
16	Iowa	18.7		15	Idaho	18.9
37	Kansas	15.1		16	Iowa	18.7
11	Kentucky	20.7		17	Connecticut	18.6
24	Louisiana	17.2		18	Indiana	18.4
4	Maine	24.0		19	Minnesota	18.3
12	Maryland	20.5		20	North Carolina	18.1
21	Massachusetts	17.9		21	Massachusetts	17.9
26	Michigan	17.1		21	Pennsylvania	17.9
19	Minnesota	18.3		23	Delaware	17.8
31	Mississippi	16.7		24	Louisiana	17.2
33	Missouri	16.3		24	Nebraska	17.2
13	Montana	19.8		26	Michigan	17.1
24	Nebraska	17.2		27	Vermont	17.0
44	Nevada	9.9		28	Georgia	16.9
1	New Hampshire	56.9		28	New Mexico	16.9
3	New Jersey	25.6		28	Tennessee	16.9
28	New Mexico	16.9		31	Mississippi	16.7
6	New York	22.6		32	Hawaii	16.4
20	North Carolina	18.1		33	Missouri	16.3
9	North Dakota	21.4		34	Illinois	16.2
36	Ohio	15.4		35	Oklahoma	15.5
35	Oklahoma	15.5		36	Ohio	15.4
42	Oregon	11.6		37	Kansas	15.1
21	Pennsylvania	17.9		38	West Virginia	13.8
41	Rhode Island	12.5		39	Virginia	13.5
7	South Carolina	22.4		40	Alabama	13.1
10	South Dakota	21.1		41	Rhode Island	12.5
28	Tennessee	16.9		42	Oregon	11.6
43	Texas	11.0		43	Texas	11.0
45	Utah	8.4		44	Nevada	9.9
27	Vermont	17.0		45	Utah	8.4
39	Virginia	13.5		46	Alaska	7.2
8	Washington	21.6		47	Arkansas	6.4
38	West Virginia	13.8		48	Wyoming	5.6
2	Wisconsin	27.3		49	Florida	4.8
48	Wyoming	5.6		50	Arizona	4.1
					District of Columbia	7.5

Source: Morgan Quitno Press using data from U.S. Dept of Health & Human Services, Health Care Financing Admin.
"State Health Expenditure Accounts" (Health Care Financing Review, Fall 1995, Volume 17, Number 1)
*By state of provider.

Average Annual Change in Expenditures for Physician Services: 1980 to 1993

National Percent = 10.8% Average Annual Increase*

ALPHA ORDER			RANK ORDER		
RANK	STATE	PERCENT CHANGE	RANK	STATE	PERCENT CHANGE
14	Alabama	11.6	1	New Hampshire	14.8
41	Alaska	9.1	2	Nevada	13.1
5	Arizona	12.1	3	Georgia	12.5
36	Arkansas	9.7	4	Massachusetts	12.3
14	California	11.6	5	Arizona	12.1
16	Colorado	11.4	5	Connecticut	12.1
5	Connecticut	12.1	5	Maryland	12.1
20	Delaware	11.0	8	North Carolina	11.9
11	Florida	11.7	9	New Jersey	11.8
3	Georgia	12.5	9	Virginia	11.8
41	Hawaii	9.1	11	Florida	11.7
29	Idaho	10.1	11	Maine	11.7
38	Illinois	9.6	11	South Carolina	11.7
24	Indiana	10.5	14	Alabama	11.6
48	Iowa	8.3	14	California	11.6
41	Kansas	9.1	16	Colorado	11.4
25	Kentucky	10.4	16	Washington	11.4
32	Louisiana	9.9	18	New Mexico	11.1
11	Maine	11.7	18	Vermont	11.1
5	Maryland	12.1	20	Delaware	11.0
4	Massachusetts	12.3	21	Minnesota	10.9
49	Michigan	8.2	21	Pennsylvania	10.9
21	Minnesota	10.9	23	Tennessee	10.7
33	Mississippi	9.8	24	Indiana	10.5
33	Missouri	9.8	25	Kentucky	10.4
47	Montana	8.4	25	New York	10.4
45	Nebraska	8.8	27	Wisconsin	10.3
2	Nevada	13.1	28	Utah	10.2
1	New Hampshire	14.8	29	Idaho	10.1
9	New Jersey	11.8	29	Texas	10.1
18	New Mexico	11.1	31	Rhode Island	10.0
25	New York	10.4	32	Louisiana	9.9
8	North Carolina	11.9	33	Mississippi	9.8
39	North Dakota	9.4	33	Missouri	9.8
36	Ohio	9.7	33	South Dakota	9.8
44	Oklahoma	9.0	36	Arkansas	9.7
40	Oregon	9.3	36	Ohio	9.7
21	Pennsylvania	10.9	38	Illinois	9.6
31	Rhode Island	10.0	39	North Dakota	9.4
11	South Carolina	11.7	40	Oregon	9.3
33	South Dakota	9.8	41	Alaska	9.1
23	Tennessee	10.7	41	Hawaii	9.1
29	Texas	10.1	41	Kansas	9.1
28	Utah	10.2	44	Oklahoma	9.0
18	Vermont	11.1	45	Nebraska	8.8
9	Virginia	11.8	45	West Virginia	8.8
16	Washington	11.4	47	Montana	8.4
45	West Virginia	8.8	48	Iowa	8.3
27	Wisconsin	10.3	49	Michigan	8.2
50	Wyoming	7.3	50	Wyoming	7.3
				District of Columbia	8.4

Source: U.S. Department of Health and Human Services, Health Care Financing Administration
   "State Health Expenditure Accounts" (Health Care Financing Review, Fall 1995, Volume 17, Number 1)
*By state of provider.

Average Annual Change in Per Capita Expenditures
For Physician Services: 1980 to 1993
National Percent = 9.7% Average Annual Increase*

ALPHA ORDER

RANK	STATE	PERCENT
5	Alabama	11.0
50	Alaska	5.8
35	Arizona	8.9
33	Arkansas	9.2
33	California	9.2
21	Colorado	9.6
3	Connecticut	11.6
21	Delaware	9.6
36	Florida	8.8
9	Georgia	10.4
48	Hawaii	7.5
36	Idaho	8.8
26	Illinois	9.4
12	Indiana	10.2
38	Iowa	8.6
39	Kansas	8.5
13	Kentucky	10.1
20	Louisiana	9.7
6	Maine	10.9
7	Maryland	10.8
2	Massachusetts	12.0
46	Michigan	8.0
16	Minnesota	10.0
26	Mississippi	9.4
31	Missouri	9.3
47	Montana	7.8
39	Nebraska	8.5
41	Nevada	8.4
1	New Hampshire	13.1
4	New Jersey	11.2
31	New Mexico	9.3
13	New York	10.1
9	North Carolina	10.4
21	North Dakota	9.6
25	Ohio	9.5
41	Oklahoma	8.4
43	Oregon	8.2
7	Pennsylvania	10.8
21	Rhode Island	9.6
9	South Carolina	10.4
26	South Dakota	9.4
18	Tennessee	9.8
45	Texas	8.1
43	Utah	8.2
16	Vermont	10.0
13	Virginia	10.1
26	Washington	9.4
26	West Virginia	9.4
18	Wisconsin	9.8
49	Wyoming	7.3

RANK ORDER

RANK	STATE	PERCENT
1	New Hampshire	13.1
2	Massachusetts	12.0
3	Connecticut	11.6
4	New Jersey	11.2
5	Alabama	11.0
6	Maine	10.9
7	Maryland	10.8
7	Pennsylvania	10.8
9	Georgia	10.4
9	North Carolina	10.4
9	South Carolina	10.4
12	Indiana	10.2
13	Kentucky	10.1
13	New York	10.1
13	Virginia	10.1
16	Minnesota	10.0
16	Vermont	10.0
18	Tennessee	9.8
18	Wisconsin	9.8
20	Louisiana	9.7
21	Colorado	9.6
21	Delaware	9.6
21	North Dakota	9.6
21	Rhode Island	9.6
25	Ohio	9.5
26	Illinois	9.4
26	Mississippi	9.4
26	South Dakota	9.4
26	Washington	9.4
26	West Virginia	9.4
31	Missouri	9.3
31	New Mexico	9.3
33	Arkansas	9.2
33	California	9.2
35	Arizona	8.9
36	Florida	8.8
36	Idaho	8.8
38	Iowa	8.6
39	Kansas	8.5
39	Nebraska	8.5
41	Nevada	8.4
41	Oklahoma	8.4
43	Oregon	8.2
43	Utah	8.2
45	Texas	8.1
46	Michigan	8.0
47	Montana	7.8
48	Hawaii	7.5
49	Wyoming	7.3
50	Alaska	5.8

District of Columbia 9.2

*Source: Morgan Quitno Press using data from U.S. Dept of Health & Human Services, Health Care Financing Admin.
"State Health Expenditure Accounts" (Health Care Financing Review, Fall 1995, Volume 17, Number 1)*
By state of provider.

Need Additional Copies? Order Today!

Use this easy, postage-paid order form to purchase copies of *State Rankings*, *Health Care State Rankings*, *Crime State Rankings* or *State Statistical Trends*.

State Rankings 2000. A huge collection of state facts. Taxes, transportation, housing, education, economy, social welfare, environment and more are featured.

"There's GREAT stuff in here!"
Andy Rooney, CBS News

ISBN: 0-7401-0003-3
Paper; 11th ed., 608 pgs. $52.95

Health Care State Rankings 2000. Learn about health in the U.S. Included are statistics on heath care facilities, providers, insurance, disease, births, reproductive health and deaths.

"Recommended!"
Library Journal

ISBN: 0-7401-0001-7
Paper; 8th ed., 540 pgs., $52.95

Crime State Rankings 2000. How safe is your state? Juvenile crime, arrests, corrections, courts, offenses and more are covered in this huge book of crime facts.

"Highly recommended!"
Library Journal

ISBN: 0-7401-0002-5
Paper; 7th ed., 540 pgs., $52.95

City Crime Rankings, 6th Ed. Check out crime in your community. Ninety tables report rates, numbers and trends for all major crime categories. Final 1998 FBI data are featured.

"Recommended!"
Library Journal

ISBN: 0-7401-0003-3
Paper; 6th ed., 540 pgs., $52.95

State Statistical Trends. This monthly journal monitors changes in life and government in the 50 states. Each 100-pg issue examines trends for a major topic. Free sample issues available. (see order form.)

"Excellent!"
Eddie Weeks
Legislative Librarian
TN General Assembly

ISSN: 1099-6486
$299/12 issues

Qty.	$Total	Title and Information
_____	$_____	**State Rankings 2000** (0-7401-0003-3; $52.95)
_____	$_____	**Health Care State Rankings 2000** (0-7401-0001-7; $52.95)
_____	$_____	**Crime State Rankings 2000** (0-7401-0002-5; $52.95)
_____	$_____	**City Crime Rankings 6th Edition** (0-7401-0003-3; $39.95)
_____	$_____	**State Statistical Trends** Journal — $299/12 issues (See below to receive a FREE sample issue)
	$_____	**Book Total**
	-$_____	**Standing Order Discount (Subtract 10%)** *(see below)
	$_____	**Subtotal**
	+$_____	**Shipping $5.00 per order** (overnight and international available at extra cost)
	+$_____	**Sales Tax (6.9% for Kansas Residents only)**
	$_____	**Order Total.** *Thank you! We appreciate your business.*

Ship to:

Organization:_____

ATTN:_____

Street Address:_____

City/State/Zip:_____

Telephone:_____

Purchase Order # (Optional): _____

Payment Method:

_____Please bill me.

_____Please charge my American Express, Visa or MasterCard:
Account no.:_____
Expiration date:_____
Signature:_____

Morgan Quitno Federal ID: 48-1078716

*When you sign up for a standing order, you'll automatically receive our reference books as soon as they are available each year at a 10% discount. You won't be billed until the book is shipped and you may cancel at any time.

100% No-Risk Guarantee!

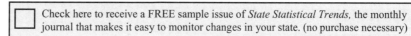

□ Check here to receive a FREE sample issue of *State Statistical Trends*, the monthly journal that makes it easy to monitor changes in your state. (no purchase necessary)

MORGAN QUITNO

Need Additional Copies? Order Today!

Use this easy, postage-paid order form to purchase copies of *State Rankings, Health Care State Rankings, Crime State Rankings* or *State Statistical Trends.*

Fold in half along this line

Detach order form, fold in half and secure with tape to mail

State Rankings 2000. A huge collection of state facts. Taxes, transportation, housing, education, economy, social welfare, environment and more are featured.

"There's GREAT stuff in here!"
Andy Rooney, CBS News

ISBN: 0-7401-0003-3
Paper; 11th ed., 608 pgs. $52.95

Health Care State Rankings 2000 Learn about health in the U.S. Included are statistics on heath care facilities, providers, insurance, disease, births, reproductive health and deaths.

"Recommended!"
Library Journal

ISBN: 0-7401-0001-7
Paper; 8th ed., 540 pgs., $52.95

Crime State Rankings 2000. How safe is your state? Juvenile crime, arrests, corrections, courts, offenses and more are covered in this huge book of crime facts.

"Highly recommended!"
Library Journal

ISBN: 0-7401-0002-5
Paper; 7th ed., 540 pgs., $52.95

City Crime Rankings, 6th Ed. Check out crime in your community. Ninety tables report numbers, rates and trends for major crime categories. Final 1998 FBI data are featured.

"Recommended!"
Library Journal

ISBN: 0-7401-0003-3
Paper; 6th ed., 540 pgs., $52.95

State Statistical Trends. This monthly journal monitors changes in life and government in the 50 states. Each 100-pg issue examines trends for a major topic. Free sample issues available. (see order form.)

"Excellent!"
Eddie Weeks
Legislative Librarian
TN General Assembly

ISSN: 1099-6486
$299/12 issues

Expenditures for Prescription Drugs in 1993

National Total = $48,840,000,000*

ALPHA ORDER

RANK	STATE	EXPENDITURES	% of USA
18	Alabama	$904,000,000	1.9%
49	Alaska	85,000,000	0.2%
24	Arizona	728,000,000	1.5%
31	Arkansas	484,000,000	1.0%
1	California	5,501,000,000	11.3%
28	Colorado	534,000,000	1.1%
26	Connecticut	650,000,000	1.3%
44	Delaware	129,000,000	0.3%
4	Florida	2,832,000,000	5.8%
10	Georgia	1,397,000,000	2.9%
41	Hawaii	197,000,000	0.4%
43	Idaho	182,000,000	0.4%
6	Illinois	2,206,000,000	4.5%
16	Indiana	1,106,000,000	2.3%
29	Iowa	516,000,000	1.1%
32	Kansas	465,000,000	1.0%
21	Kentucky	846,000,000	1.7%
22	Louisiana	832,000,000	1.7%
39	Maine	213,000,000	0.4%
15	Maryland	1,140,000,000	2.3%
13	Massachusetts	1,337,000,000	2.7%
8	Michigan	2,054,000,000	4.2%
23	Minnesota	739,000,000	1.5%
30	Mississippi	499,000,000	1.0%
17	Missouri	975,000,000	2.0%
45	Montana	120,000,000	0.3%
36	Nebraska	293,000,000	0.6%
38	Nevada	246,000,000	0.5%
41	New Hampshire	197,000,000	0.4%
9	New Jersey	1,601,000,000	3.3%
37	New Mexico	259,000,000	0.5%
2	New York	3,232,000,000	6.6%
11	North Carolina	1,392,000,000	2.9%
48	North Dakota	103,000,000	0.2%
7	Ohio	2,095,000,000	4.3%
27	Oklahoma	569,000,000	1.2%
33	Oregon	431,000,000	0.9%
5	Pennsylvania	2,386,000,000	4.9%
40	Rhode Island	206,000,000	0.4%
25	South Carolina	665,000,000	1.4%
47	South Dakota	104,000,000	0.2%
14	Tennessee	1,153,000,000	2.4%
3	Texas	3,153,000,000	6.5%
35	Utah	302,000,000	0.6%
46	Vermont	108,000,000	0.2%
12	Virginia	1,343,000,000	2.8%
20	Washington	853,000,000	1.8%
34	West Virginia	412,000,000	0.8%
19	Wisconsin	899,000,000	1.8%
50	Wyoming	64,000,000	0.1%

RANK ORDER

RANK	STATE	EXPENDITURES	% of USA
1	California	$5,501,000,000	11.3%
2	New York	3,232,000,000	6.6%
3	Texas	3,153,000,000	6.5%
4	Florida	2,832,000,000	5.8%
5	Pennsylvania	2,386,000,000	4.9%
6	Illinois	2,206,000,000	4.5%
7	Ohio	2,095,000,000	4.3%
8	Michigan	2,054,000,000	4.2%
9	New Jersey	1,601,000,000	3.3%
10	Georgia	1,397,000,000	2.9%
11	North Carolina	1,392,000,000	2.9%
12	Virginia	1,343,000,000	2.8%
13	Massachusetts	1,337,000,000	2.7%
14	Tennessee	1,153,000,000	2.4%
15	Maryland	1,140,000,000	2.3%
16	Indiana	1,106,000,000	2.3%
17	Missouri	975,000,000	2.0%
18	Alabama	904,000,000	1.9%
19	Wisconsin	899,000,000	1.8%
20	Washington	853,000,000	1.8%
21	Kentucky	846,000,000	1.7%
22	Louisiana	832,000,000	1.7%
23	Minnesota	739,000,000	1.5%
24	Arizona	728,000,000	1.5%
25	South Carolina	665,000,000	1.4%
26	Connecticut	650,000,000	1.3%
27	Oklahoma	569,000,000	1.2%
28	Colorado	534,000,000	1.1%
29	Iowa	516,000,000	1.1%
30	Mississippi	499,000,000	1.0%
31	Arkansas	484,000,000	1.0%
32	Kansas	465,000,000	1.0%
33	Oregon	431,000,000	0.9%
34	West Virginia	412,000,000	0.8%
35	Utah	302,000,000	0.6%
36	Nebraska	293,000,000	0.6%
37	New Mexico	259,000,000	0.5%
38	Nevada	246,000,000	0.5%
39	Maine	213,000,000	0.4%
40	Rhode Island	206,000,000	0.4%
41	Hawaii	197,000,000	0.4%
41	New Hampshire	197,000,000	0.4%
43	Idaho	182,000,000	0.4%
44	Delaware	129,000,000	0.3%
45	Montana	120,000,000	0.3%
46	Vermont	108,000,000	0.2%
47	South Dakota	104,000,000	0.2%
48	North Dakota	103,000,000	0.2%
49	Alaska	85,000,000	0.2%
50	Wyoming	64,000,000	0.1%
	District of Columbia	103,000,000	0.2%

Source: U.S. Department of Health and Human Services, Health Care Financing Administration
  "State Health Expenditure Accounts" (Health Care Financing Review, Fall 1995, Volume 17, Number 1)
*Purchases in retail outlets. By state of outlet. This is a subset of overall "Drug and Other Medical Non-Durable Expenditures" shown elsewhere in this book.

Percent of Total Personal Health Care Expenditures
Spent on Prescription Drugs in 1993
National Percent = 6.3%*

ALPHA ORDER

RANK	STATE	PERCENT
9	Alabama	7.5
43	Alaska	5.4
18	Arizona	6.8
5	Arkansas	7.9
35	California	5.8
45	Colorado	5.3
45	Connecticut	5.3
36	Delaware	5.7
26	Florida	6.3
17	Georgia	6.9
36	Hawaii	5.7
4	Idaho	8.0
26	Illinois	6.3
19	Indiana	6.7
16	Iowa	7.0
19	Kansas	6.7
1	Kentucky	8.1
24	Louisiana	6.4
30	Maine	6.2
9	Maryland	7.5
36	Massachusetts	5.7
7	Michigan	7.6
48	Minnesota	5.2
1	Mississippi	8.1
33	Missouri	6.1
36	Montana	5.7
19	Nebraska	6.7
23	Nevada	6.6
36	New Hampshire	5.7
30	New Jersey	6.2
19	New Mexico	6.7
50	New York	4.8
7	North Carolina	7.6
49	North Dakota	5.1
26	Ohio	6.3
14	Oklahoma	7.1
43	Oregon	5.4
36	Pennsylvania	5.7
34	Rhode Island	6.0
11	South Carolina	7.4
45	South Dakota	5.3
14	Tennessee	7.1
26	Texas	6.3
12	Utah	7.3
13	Vermont	7.2
1	Virginia	8.1
42	Washington	5.6
5	West Virginia	7.9
30	Wisconsin	6.2
24	Wyoming	6.4

RANK ORDER

RANK	STATE	PERCENT
1	Kentucky	8.1
1	Mississippi	8.1
1	Virginia	8.1
4	Idaho	8.0
5	Arkansas	7.9
5	West Virginia	7.9
7	Michigan	7.6
7	North Carolina	7.6
9	Alabama	7.5
9	Maryland	7.5
11	South Carolina	7.4
12	Utah	7.3
13	Vermont	7.2
14	Oklahoma	7.1
14	Tennessee	7.1
16	Iowa	7.0
17	Georgia	6.9
18	Arizona	6.8
19	Indiana	6.7
19	Kansas	6.7
19	Nebraska	6.7
19	New Mexico	6.7
23	Nevada	6.6
24	Louisiana	6.4
24	Wyoming	6.4
26	Florida	6.3
26	Illinois	6.3
26	Ohio	6.3
26	Texas	6.3
30	Maine	6.2
30	New Jersey	6.2
30	Wisconsin	6.2
33	Missouri	6.1
34	Rhode Island	6.0
35	California	5.8
36	Delaware	5.7
36	Hawaii	5.7
36	Massachusetts	5.7
36	Montana	5.7
36	New Hampshire	5.7
36	Pennsylvania	5.7
42	Washington	5.6
43	Alaska	5.4
43	Oregon	5.4
45	Colorado	5.3
45	Connecticut	5.3
45	South Dakota	5.3
48	Minnesota	5.2
49	North Dakota	5.1
50	New York	4.8

| | District of Columbia | 2.4 |

Source: Morgan Quitno Press using data from U.S. Dept of Health & Human Services, Health Care Financing Admin. "State Health Expenditure Accounts" (Health Care Financing Review, Fall 1995, Volume 17, Number 1)
*Purchases in retail outlets. By state of outlet. This is a subset of overall "Drug and Other Medical Non-Durable Expenditures" shown elsewhere in this book.

Per Capita Expenditures for Prescription Drugs in 1993

National Per Capita = $189*

ALPHA ORDER

RANK	STATE	PER CAPITA
7	Alabama	$216
48	Alaska	142
24	Arizona	185
13	Arkansas	200
33	California	176
45	Colorado	150
15	Connecticut	198
24	Delaware	185
9	Florida	206
12	Georgia	202
38	Hawaii	169
39	Idaho	165
19	Illinois	189
17	Indiana	194
27	Iowa	183
26	Kansas	184
4	Kentucky	223
17	Louisiana	194
37	Maine	172
1	Maryland	230
5	Massachusetts	222
6	Michigan	217
40	Minnesota	163
19	Mississippi	189
23	Missouri	186
47	Montana	143
29	Nebraska	182
30	Nevada	178
35	New Hampshire	175
11	New Jersey	204
44	New Mexico	160
30	New York	178
13	North Carolina	200
41	North Dakota	162
19	Ohio	189
33	Oklahoma	176
48	Oregon	142
15	Pennsylvania	198
9	Rhode Island	206
27	South Carolina	183
46	South Dakota	145
3	Tennessee	226
35	Texas	175
41	Utah	162
22	Vermont	188
8	Virginia	207
41	Washington	162
2	West Virginia	227
30	Wisconsin	178
50	Wyoming	136

RANK ORDER

RANK	STATE	PER CAPITA
1	Maryland	$230
2	West Virginia	227
3	Tennessee	226
4	Kentucky	223
5	Massachusetts	222
6	Michigan	217
7	Alabama	216
8	Virginia	207
9	Florida	206
9	Rhode Island	206
11	New Jersey	204
12	Georgia	202
13	Arkansas	200
13	North Carolina	200
15	Connecticut	198
15	Pennsylvania	198
17	Indiana	194
17	Louisiana	194
19	Illinois	189
19	Mississippi	189
19	Ohio	189
22	Vermont	188
23	Missouri	186
24	Arizona	185
24	Delaware	185
26	Kansas	184
27	Iowa	183
27	South Carolina	183
29	Nebraska	182
30	Nevada	178
30	New York	178
30	Wisconsin	178
33	California	176
33	Oklahoma	176
35	New Hampshire	175
35	Texas	175
37	Maine	172
38	Hawaii	169
39	Idaho	165
40	Minnesota	163
41	North Dakota	162
41	Utah	162
41	Washington	162
44	New Mexico	160
45	Colorado	150
46	South Dakota	145
47	Montana	143
48	Alaska	142
48	Oregon	142
50	Wyoming	136

District of Columbia 178

Source: Morgan Quitno Press using data from U.S. Dept of Health & Human Services, Health Care Financing Admin.
"State Health Expenditure Accounts" (Health Care Financing Review, Fall 1995, Volume 17, Number 1)
*Purchases in retail outlets. By state of outlet. This is a subset of overall "Drug and Other Medical Non-Durable
Expenditures" shown elsewhere in this book.

Percent Change in Expenditures for Prescription Drugs: 1990 to 1993

National Percent Change = 27.9% Increase*

ALPHA ORDER			RANK ORDER		
RANK	STATE	PERCENT CHANGE	RANK	STATE	PERCENT CHANGE
23	Alabama	27.9	1	Nevada	55.7
2	Alaska	46.6	2	Alaska	46.6
6	Arizona	38.4	3	Idaho	41.1
28	Arkansas	26.7	4	Colorado	40.9
19	California	30.3	5	Utah	38.5
4	Colorado	40.9	6	Arizona	38.4
49	Connecticut	19.5	7	Washington	38.0
15	Delaware	31.6	8	New Mexico	36.3
14	Florida	32.6	9	Oregon	35.5
10	Georgia	35.0	10	Georgia	35.0
13	Hawaii	33.1	11	Texas	34.4
3	Idaho	41.1	12	Montana	33.3
35	Illinois	24.6	13	Hawaii	33.1
29	Indiana	26.5	14	Florida	32.6
42	Iowa	23.2	15	Delaware	31.6
33	Kansas	24.7	16	North Carolina	31.2
26	Kentucky	26.8	17	Virginia	30.9
35	Louisiana	24.6	18	Wyoming	30.6
45	Maine	22.4	19	California	30.3
22	Maryland	28.4	20	South Carolina	30.1
47	Massachusetts	20.1	20	Tennessee	30.1
39	Michigan	24.2	22	Maryland	28.4
24	Minnesota	27.4	23	Alabama	27.9
32	Mississippi	25.1	24	Minnesota	27.4
37	Missouri	24.5	25	Wisconsin	27.0
12	Montana	33.3	26	Kentucky	26.8
33	Nebraska	24.7	26	South Dakota	26.8
1	Nevada	55.7	28	Arkansas	26.7
43	New Hampshire	23.1	29	Indiana	26.5
41	New Jersey	23.3	30	Oklahoma	26.4
8	New Mexico	36.3	31	Vermont	25.6
46	New York	21.3	32	Mississippi	25.1
16	North Carolina	31.2	33	Kansas	24.7
48	North Dakota	19.8	33	Nebraska	24.7
38	Ohio	24.4	35	Illinois	24.6
30	Oklahoma	26.4	35	Louisiana	24.6
9	Oregon	35.5	37	Missouri	24.5
44	Pennsylvania	22.5	38	Ohio	24.4
50	Rhode Island	18.4	39	Michigan	24.2
20	South Carolina	30.1	40	West Virginia	23.7
26	South Dakota	26.8	41	New Jersey	23.3
20	Tennessee	30.1	42	Iowa	23.2
11	Texas	34.4	43	New Hampshire	23.1
5	Utah	38.5	44	Pennsylvania	22.5
31	Vermont	25.6	45	Maine	22.4
17	Virginia	30.9	46	New York	21.3
7	Washington	38.0	47	Massachusetts	20.1
40	West Virginia	23.7	48	North Dakota	19.8
25	Wisconsin	27.0	49	Connecticut	19.5
18	Wyoming	30.6	50	Rhode Island	18.4
				District of Columbia	10.8

Source: Morgan Quitno Press using data from U.S. Dept of Health & Human Services, Health Care Financing Admin. "State Health Expenditure Accounts" (Health Care Financing Review, Fall 1995, Volume 17, Number 1) *Purchases in retail outlets. By state of outlet. This is a subset of overall "Drug and Other Medical Non-Durable Expenditures" shown elsewhere in this book.

Percent Change in Per Capita Expenditures for Prescription Drugs: 1990 to 1993

National Percent Change = 22.7% Increase*

ALPHA ORDER

RANK	STATE	PERCENT CHANGE
24	Alabama	23.4
2	Alaska	35.2
5	Arizona	28.5
23	Arkansas	23.5
21	California	23.9
3	Colorado	30.4
49	Connecticut	19.3
14	Delaware	25.9
17	Florida	24.8
12	Georgia	26.3
13	Hawaii	26.1
4	Idaho	28.9
35	Illinois	21.9
29	Indiana	22.8
43	Iowa	21.2
35	Kansas	21.9
25	Kentucky	23.2
29	Louisiana	22.8
44	Maine	21.1
22	Maryland	23.7
47	Massachusetts	20.0
35	Michigan	21.9
32	Minnesota	22.6
35	Mississippi	21.9
40	Missouri	21.6
11	Montana	26.5
33	Nebraska	22.1
1	Nevada	35.9
41	New Hampshire	21.5
42	New Jersey	21.4
6	New Mexico	28.0
46	New York	20.3
16	North Carolina	25.0
47	North Dakota	20.0
35	Ohio	21.9
26	Oklahoma	23.1
9	Oregon	26.8
45	Pennsylvania	20.7
50	Rhode Island	19.1
19	South Carolina	24.5
27	South Dakota	22.9
20	Tennessee	24.2
9	Texas	26.8
7	Utah	27.6
27	Vermont	22.9
18	Virginia	24.7
7	Washington	27.6
34	West Virginia	22.0
29	Wisconsin	22.8
14	Wyoming	25.9

RANK ORDER

RANK	STATE	PERCENT CHANGE
1	Nevada	35.9
2	Alaska	35.2
3	Colorado	30.4
4	Idaho	28.9
5	Arizona	28.5
6	New Mexico	28.0
7	Utah	27.6
7	Washington	27.6
9	Oregon	26.8
9	Texas	26.8
11	Montana	26.5
12	Georgia	26.3
13	Hawaii	26.1
14	Delaware	25.9
14	Wyoming	25.9
16	North Carolina	25.0
17	Florida	24.8
18	Virginia	24.7
19	South Carolina	24.5
20	Tennessee	24.2
21	California	23.9
22	Maryland	23.7
23	Arkansas	23.5
24	Alabama	23.4
25	Kentucky	23.2
26	Oklahoma	23.1
27	South Dakota	22.9
27	Vermont	22.9
29	Indiana	22.8
29	Louisiana	22.8
29	Wisconsin	22.8
32	Minnesota	22.6
33	Nebraska	22.1
34	West Virginia	22.0
35	Illinois	21.9
35	Kansas	21.9
35	Michigan	21.9
35	Mississippi	21.9
35	Ohio	21.9
40	Missouri	21.6
41	New Hampshire	21.5
42	New Jersey	21.4
43	Iowa	21.2
44	Maine	21.1
45	Pennsylvania	20.7
46	New York	20.3
47	Massachusetts	20.0
47	North Dakota	20.0
49	Connecticut	19.3
50	Rhode Island	19.1

District of Columbia   16.3

Source: Morgan Quitno Press using data from U.S. Dept of Health & Human Services, Health Care Financing Admin. "State Health Expenditure Accounts" (Health Care Financing Review, Fall 1995, Volume 17, Number 1)
*Purchases in retail outlets. By state of outlet. This is a subset of overall "Drug and Other Medical Non-Durable Expenditures" shown elsewhere in this book.

Average Annual Change in Expenditures for Prescription Drugs: 1980 to 1993

National Percent = 11.4% Average Annual Increase*

<table>
<tr><td colspan="3">ALPHA ORDER</td><td colspan="3">RANK ORDER</td></tr>
<tr><td>RANK</td><td>STATE</td><td>PERCENT</td><td>RANK</td><td>STATE</td><td>PERCENT</td></tr>
<tr><td>32</td><td>Alabama</td><td>10.9</td><td>1</td><td>Nevada</td><td>15.8</td></tr>
<tr><td>4</td><td>Alaska</td><td>13.7</td><td>2</td><td>Arizona</td><td>14.7</td></tr>
<tr><td>2</td><td>Arizona</td><td>14.7</td><td>3</td><td>Utah</td><td>14.2</td></tr>
<tr><td>49</td><td>Arkansas</td><td>9.3</td><td>4</td><td>Alaska</td><td>13.7</td></tr>
<tr><td>16</td><td>California</td><td>11.8</td><td>4</td><td>Florida</td><td>13.7</td></tr>
<tr><td>18</td><td>Colorado</td><td>11.7</td><td>6</td><td>Delaware</td><td>13.3</td></tr>
<tr><td>33</td><td>Connecticut</td><td>10.7</td><td>6</td><td>Maryland</td><td>13.3</td></tr>
<tr><td>6</td><td>Delaware</td><td>13.3</td><td>6</td><td>New Hampshire</td><td>13.3</td></tr>
<tr><td>4</td><td>Florida</td><td>13.7</td><td>9</td><td>New Mexico</td><td>13.2</td></tr>
<tr><td>12</td><td>Georgia</td><td>12.7</td><td>10</td><td>Vermont</td><td>13.0</td></tr>
<tr><td>14</td><td>Hawaii</td><td>12.2</td><td>10</td><td>Virginia</td><td>13.0</td></tr>
<tr><td>20</td><td>Idaho</td><td>11.6</td><td>12</td><td>Georgia</td><td>12.7</td></tr>
<tr><td>26</td><td>Illinois</td><td>11.1</td><td>13</td><td>Massachusetts</td><td>12.5</td></tr>
<tr><td>39</td><td>Indiana</td><td>10.4</td><td>14</td><td>Hawaii</td><td>12.2</td></tr>
<tr><td>46</td><td>Iowa</td><td>9.6</td><td>15</td><td>South Carolina</td><td>11.9</td></tr>
<tr><td>37</td><td>Kansas</td><td>10.5</td><td>16</td><td>California</td><td>11.8</td></tr>
<tr><td>33</td><td>Kentucky</td><td>10.7</td><td>16</td><td>Rhode Island</td><td>11.8</td></tr>
<tr><td>47</td><td>Louisiana</td><td>9.5</td><td>18</td><td>Colorado</td><td>11.7</td></tr>
<tr><td>20</td><td>Maine</td><td>11.6</td><td>18</td><td>New Jersey</td><td>11.7</td></tr>
<tr><td>6</td><td>Maryland</td><td>13.3</td><td>20</td><td>Idaho</td><td>11.6</td></tr>
<tr><td>13</td><td>Massachusetts</td><td>12.5</td><td>20</td><td>Maine</td><td>11.6</td></tr>
<tr><td>28</td><td>Michigan</td><td>11.0</td><td>22</td><td>North Carolina</td><td>11.5</td></tr>
<tr><td>28</td><td>Minnesota</td><td>11.0</td><td>22</td><td>Wisconsin</td><td>11.5</td></tr>
<tr><td>42</td><td>Mississippi</td><td>10.1</td><td>24</td><td>Washington</td><td>11.3</td></tr>
<tr><td>41</td><td>Missouri</td><td>10.2</td><td>25</td><td>Tennessee</td><td>11.2</td></tr>
<tr><td>28</td><td>Montana</td><td>11.0</td><td>26</td><td>Illinois</td><td>11.1</td></tr>
<tr><td>37</td><td>Nebraska</td><td>10.5</td><td>26</td><td>New York</td><td>11.1</td></tr>
<tr><td>1</td><td>Nevada</td><td>15.8</td><td>28</td><td>Michigan</td><td>11.0</td></tr>
<tr><td>6</td><td>New Hampshire</td><td>13.3</td><td>28</td><td>Minnesota</td><td>11.0</td></tr>
<tr><td>18</td><td>New Jersey</td><td>11.7</td><td>28</td><td>Montana</td><td>11.0</td></tr>
<tr><td>9</td><td>New Mexico</td><td>13.2</td><td>28</td><td>Pennsylvania</td><td>11.0</td></tr>
<tr><td>26</td><td>New York</td><td>11.1</td><td>32</td><td>Alabama</td><td>10.9</td></tr>
<tr><td>22</td><td>North Carolina</td><td>11.5</td><td>33</td><td>Connecticut</td><td>10.7</td></tr>
<tr><td>35</td><td>North Dakota</td><td>10.6</td><td>33</td><td>Kentucky</td><td>10.7</td></tr>
<tr><td>43</td><td>Ohio</td><td>10.0</td><td>35</td><td>North Dakota</td><td>10.6</td></tr>
<tr><td>47</td><td>Oklahoma</td><td>9.5</td><td>35</td><td>Texas</td><td>10.6</td></tr>
<tr><td>43</td><td>Oregon</td><td>10.0</td><td>37</td><td>Kansas</td><td>10.5</td></tr>
<tr><td>28</td><td>Pennsylvania</td><td>11.0</td><td>37</td><td>Nebraska</td><td>10.5</td></tr>
<tr><td>16</td><td>Rhode Island</td><td>11.8</td><td>39</td><td>Indiana</td><td>10.4</td></tr>
<tr><td>15</td><td>South Carolina</td><td>11.9</td><td>40</td><td>West Virginia</td><td>10.3</td></tr>
<tr><td>43</td><td>South Dakota</td><td>10.0</td><td>41</td><td>Missouri</td><td>10.2</td></tr>
<tr><td>25</td><td>Tennessee</td><td>11.2</td><td>42</td><td>Mississippi</td><td>10.1</td></tr>
<tr><td>35</td><td>Texas</td><td>10.6</td><td>43</td><td>Ohio</td><td>10.0</td></tr>
<tr><td>3</td><td>Utah</td><td>14.2</td><td>43</td><td>Oregon</td><td>10.0</td></tr>
<tr><td>10</td><td>Vermont</td><td>13.0</td><td>43</td><td>South Dakota</td><td>10.0</td></tr>
<tr><td>10</td><td>Virginia</td><td>13.0</td><td>46</td><td>Iowa</td><td>9.6</td></tr>
<tr><td>24</td><td>Washington</td><td>11.3</td><td>47</td><td>Louisiana</td><td>9.5</td></tr>
<tr><td>40</td><td>West Virginia</td><td>10.3</td><td>47</td><td>Oklahoma</td><td>9.5</td></tr>
<tr><td>22</td><td>Wisconsin</td><td>11.5</td><td>49</td><td>Arkansas</td><td>9.3</td></tr>
<tr><td>50</td><td>Wyoming</td><td>8.2</td><td>50</td><td>Wyoming</td><td>8.2</td></tr>
<tr><td></td><td></td><td></td><td></td><td>District of Columbia</td><td>9.5</td></tr>
</table>

Source: U.S. Department of Health and Human Services, Health Care Financing Administration
"State Health Expenditure Accounts" (Health Care Financing Review, Fall 1995, Volume 17, Number 1)
*Purchases in retail outlets. By state of outlet. This is a subset of overall "Drug and Other Medical Non-Durable Expenditures" shown elsewhere in this book.

Average Annual Change in Per Capita Expenditures
For Prescription Drugs: 1980 to 1993
National Percent = 10.3% Average Annual Increase*

ALPHA ORDER

RANK	STATE	PERCENT
27	Alabama	10.4
30	Alaska	10.2
7	Arizona	11.5
48	Arkansas	8.8
43	California	9.4
36	Colorado	9.9
30	Connecticut	10.2
1	Delaware	12.1
20	Florida	10.7
20	Georgia	10.7
24	Hawaii	10.5
32	Idaho	10.1
14	Illinois	10.9
33	Indiana	10.0
38	Iowa	9.8
36	Kansas	9.9
24	Kentucky	10.5
43	Louisiana	9.4
14	Maine	10.9
5	Maryland	11.8
2	Massachusetts	12.0
17	Michigan	10.8
33	Minnesota	10.0
38	Mississippi	9.8
42	Missouri	9.7
24	Montana	10.5
28	Nebraska	10.3
11	Nevada	11.2
6	New Hampshire	11.6
12	New Jersey	11.1
9	New Mexico	11.3
17	New York	10.8
33	North Carolina	10.0
20	North Dakota	10.7
38	Ohio	9.8
46	Oklahoma	8.9
46	Oregon	8.9
17	Pennsylvania	10.8
9	Rhode Island	11.3
20	South Carolina	10.7
38	South Dakota	9.8
28	Tennessee	10.3
49	Texas	8.6
2	Utah	12.0
2	Vermont	12.0
8	Virginia	11.4
45	Washington	9.3
14	West Virginia	10.9
13	Wisconsin	11.0
50	Wyoming	8.2

RANK ORDER

RANK	STATE	PERCENT
1	Delaware	12.1
2	Massachusetts	12.0
2	Utah	12.0
2	Vermont	12.0
5	Maryland	11.8
6	New Hampshire	11.6
7	Arizona	11.5
8	Virginia	11.4
9	New Mexico	11.3
9	Rhode Island	11.3
11	Nevada	11.2
12	New Jersey	11.1
13	Wisconsin	11.0
14	Illinois	10.9
14	Maine	10.9
14	West Virginia	10.9
17	Michigan	10.8
17	New York	10.8
17	Pennsylvania	10.8
20	Florida	10.7
20	Georgia	10.7
20	North Dakota	10.7
20	South Carolina	10.7
24	Hawaii	10.5
24	Kentucky	10.5
24	Montana	10.5
27	Alabama	10.4
28	Nebraska	10.3
28	Tennessee	10.3
30	Alaska	10.2
30	Connecticut	10.2
32	Idaho	10.1
33	Indiana	10.0
33	Minnesota	10.0
33	North Carolina	10.0
36	Colorado	9.9
36	Kansas	9.9
38	Iowa	9.8
38	Mississippi	9.8
38	Ohio	9.8
38	South Dakota	9.8
42	Missouri	9.7
43	California	9.4
43	Louisiana	9.4
45	Washington	9.3
46	Oklahoma	8.9
46	Oregon	8.9
48	Arkansas	8.8
49	Texas	8.6
50	Wyoming	8.2

District of Columbia 10.3

*Source: Morgan Quitno Press using data from U.S. Dept of Health & Human Services, Health Care Financing Admin. "State Health Expenditure Accounts" (Health Care Financing Review, Fall 1995, Volume 17, Number 1) *Purchases in retail outlets. By state of outlet. This is a subset of overall "Drug and Other Medical Non-Durable Expenditures" shown elsewhere in this book.*

Expenditures for Dental Service in 1993

National Total = $37,383,000,000*

ALPHA ORDER					RANK ORDER			

RANK	STATE	EXPENDITURES	% of USA		RANK	STATE	EXPENDITURES	% of USA
25	Alabama	$456,000,000	1.2%		1	California	$5,664,000,000	15.2%
44	Alaska	124,000,000	0.3%		2	New York	2,837,000,000	7.6%
24	Arizona	551,000,000	1.5%		3	Texas	2,081,000,000	5.6%
33	Arkansas	242,000,000	0.7%		4	Florida	2,029,000,000	5.4%
1	California	5,664,000,000	15.2%		5	Pennsylvania	1,634,000,000	4.4%
21	Colorado	605,000,000	1.6%		6	Illinois	1,588,000,000	4.3%
19	Connecticut	685,000,000	1.8%		7	Michigan	1,531,000,000	4.1%
45	Delaware	104,000,000	0.3%		8	New Jersey	1,460,000,000	3.9%
4	Florida	2,029,000,000	5.4%		9	Ohio	1,398,000,000	3.7%
12	Georgia	898,000,000	2.4%		10	Washington	1,189,000,000	3.2%
34	Hawaii	235,000,000	0.6%		11	Massachusetts	1,022,000,000	2.7%
41	Idaho	163,000,000	0.4%		12	Georgia	898,000,000	2.4%
6	Illinois	1,588,000,000	4.3%		13	Virginia	863,000,000	2.3%
18	Indiana	692,000,000	1.9%		14	North Carolina	810,000,000	2.2%
30	Iowa	341,000,000	0.9%		15	Wisconsin	765,000,000	2.1%
31	Kansas	325,000,000	0.9%		16	Maryland	749,000,000	2.0%
28	Kentucky	369,000,000	1.0%		17	Minnesota	741,000,000	2.0%
26	Louisiana	432,000,000	1.2%		18	Indiana	692,000,000	1.9%
42	Maine	157,000,000	0.4%		19	Connecticut	685,000,000	1.8%
16	Maryland	749,000,000	2.0%		20	Tennessee	609,000,000	1.6%
11	Massachusetts	1,022,000,000	2.7%		21	Colorado	605,000,000	1.6%
7	Michigan	1,531,000,000	4.1%		22	Missouri	602,000,000	1.6%
17	Minnesota	741,000,000	2.0%		23	Oregon	578,000,000	1.6%
36	Mississippi	214,000,000	0.6%		24	Arizona	551,000,000	1.5%
22	Missouri	602,000,000	1.6%		25	Alabama	456,000,000	1.2%
46	Montana	103,000,000	0.3%		26	Louisiana	432,000,000	1.2%
37	Nebraska	191,000,000	0.5%		27	South Carolina	387,000,000	1.0%
35	Nevada	215,000,000	0.6%		28	Kentucky	369,000,000	1.0%
39	New Hampshire	177,000,000	0.5%		29	Oklahoma	356,000,000	1.0%
8	New Jersey	1,460,000,000	3.9%		30	Iowa	341,000,000	0.9%
40	New Mexico	175,000,000	0.5%		31	Kansas	325,000,000	0.9%
2	New York	2,837,000,000	7.6%		32	Utah	276,000,000	0.7%
14	North Carolina	810,000,000	2.2%		33	Arkansas	242,000,000	0.7%
49	North Dakota	78,000,000	0.2%		34	Hawaii	235,000,000	0.6%
9	Ohio	1,398,000,000	3.7%		35	Nevada	215,000,000	0.6%
29	Oklahoma	356,000,000	1.0%		36	Mississippi	214,000,000	0.6%
23	Oregon	578,000,000	1.6%		37	Nebraska	191,000,000	0.5%
5	Pennsylvania	1,634,000,000	4.4%		38	West Virginia	182,000,000	0.5%
43	Rhode Island	150,000,000	0.4%		39	New Hampshire	177,000,000	0.5%
27	South Carolina	387,000,000	1.0%		40	New Mexico	175,000,000	0.5%
47	South Dakota	87,000,000	0.2%		41	Idaho	163,000,000	0.4%
20	Tennessee	609,000,000	1.6%		42	Maine	157,000,000	0.4%
3	Texas	2,081,000,000	5.6%		43	Rhode Island	150,000,000	0.4%
32	Utah	276,000,000	0.7%		44	Alaska	124,000,000	0.3%
48	Vermont	84,000,000	0.2%		45	Delaware	104,000,000	0.3%
13	Virginia	863,000,000	2.3%		46	Montana	103,000,000	0.3%
10	Washington	1,189,000,000	3.2%		47	South Dakota	87,000,000	0.2%
38	West Virginia	182,000,000	0.5%		48	Vermont	84,000,000	0.2%
15	Wisconsin	765,000,000	2.1%		49	North Dakota	78,000,000	0.2%
50	Wyoming	57,000,000	0.2%		50	Wyoming	57,000,000	0.2%
						District of Columbia	119,000,000	0.3%

Source: U.S. Department of Health and Human Services, Health Care Financing Administration
  "State Health Expenditure Accounts" (Health Care Financing Review, Fall 1995, Volume 17, Number 1)
*By state of provider.

Percent of Total Personal Health Care Expenditures
Spent on Dental Service in 1993
National Percent = 4.8%*

ALPHA ORDER

RANK	STATE	PERCENT
44	Alabama	3.8
1	Alaska	7.9
16	Arizona	5.2
41	Arkansas	4.0
7	California	6.0
7	Colorado	6.0
12	Connecticut	5.6
23	Delaware	4.6
27	Florida	4.5
27	Georgia	4.5
5	Hawaii	6.7
3	Idaho	7.2
23	Illinois	4.6
37	Indiana	4.2
23	Iowa	4.6
22	Kansas	4.7
47	Kentucky	3.6
50	Louisiana	3.3
23	Maine	4.6
20	Maryland	4.9
31	Massachusetts	4.4
12	Michigan	5.6
16	Minnesota	5.2
48	Mississippi	3.5
44	Missouri	3.8
20	Montana	4.9
35	Nebraska	4.3
9	Nevada	5.7
19	New Hampshire	5.1
9	New Jersey	5.7
27	New Mexico	4.5
37	New York	4.2
31	North Carolina	4.4
42	North Dakota	3.9
37	Ohio	4.2
31	Oklahoma	4.4
3	Oregon	7.2
42	Pennsylvania	3.9
31	Rhode Island	4.4
35	South Carolina	4.3
27	South Dakota	4.5
44	Tennessee	3.8
37	Texas	4.2
5	Utah	6.7
12	Vermont	5.6
16	Virginia	5.2
1	Washington	7.9
48	West Virginia	3.5
15	Wisconsin	5.3
9	Wyoming	5.7

RANK ORDER

RANK	STATE	PERCENT
1	Alaska	7.9
1	Washington	7.9
3	Idaho	7.2
3	Oregon	7.2
5	Hawaii	6.7
5	Utah	6.7
7	California	6.0
7	Colorado	6.0
9	Nevada	5.7
9	New Jersey	5.7
9	Wyoming	5.7
12	Connecticut	5.6
12	Michigan	5.6
12	Vermont	5.6
15	Wisconsin	5.3
16	Arizona	5.2
16	Minnesota	5.2
16	Virginia	5.2
19	New Hampshire	5.1
20	Maryland	4.9
20	Montana	4.9
22	Kansas	4.7
23	Delaware	4.6
23	Illinois	4.6
23	Iowa	4.6
23	Maine	4.6
27	Florida	4.5
27	Georgia	4.5
27	New Mexico	4.5
27	South Dakota	4.5
31	Massachusetts	4.4
31	North Carolina	4.4
31	Oklahoma	4.4
31	Rhode Island	4.4
35	Nebraska	4.3
35	South Carolina	4.3
37	Indiana	4.2
37	New York	4.2
37	Ohio	4.2
37	Texas	4.2
41	Arkansas	4.0
42	North Dakota	3.9
42	Pennsylvania	3.9
44	Alabama	3.8
44	Missouri	3.8
44	Tennessee	3.8
47	Kentucky	3.6
48	Mississippi	3.5
48	West Virginia	3.5
50	Louisiana	3.3
	District of Columbia	2.8

Source: Morgan Quitno Press using data from U.S. Dept of Health & Human Services, Health Care Financing Admin.
"State Health Expenditure Accounts" (Health Care Financing Review, Fall 1995, Volume 17, Number 1)
*By state of provider.

Per Capita Expenditures for Dental Service in 1993

National Per Capita = $145*

<table>
<tr><td colspan="3">ALPHA ORDER</td><td colspan="3">RANK ORDER</td></tr>
<tr><td>RANK</td><td>STATE</td><td>PER CAPITA</td><td>RANK</td><td>STATE</td><td>PER CAPITA</td></tr>
<tr><td>43</td><td>Alabama</td><td>$109</td><td>1</td><td>Washington</td><td>$226</td></tr>
<tr><td>3</td><td>Alaska</td><td>207</td><td>2</td><td>Connecticut</td><td>209</td></tr>
<tr><td>23</td><td>Arizona</td><td>140</td><td>3</td><td>Alaska</td><td>207</td></tr>
<tr><td>47</td><td>Arkansas</td><td>100</td><td>4</td><td>Hawaii</td><td>202</td></tr>
<tr><td>7</td><td>California</td><td>181</td><td>5</td><td>Oregon</td><td>190</td></tr>
<tr><td>8</td><td>Colorado</td><td>170</td><td>6</td><td>New Jersey</td><td>186</td></tr>
<tr><td>2</td><td>Connecticut</td><td>209</td><td>7</td><td>California</td><td>181</td></tr>
<tr><td>18</td><td>Delaware</td><td>149</td><td>8</td><td>Colorado</td><td>170</td></tr>
<tr><td>19</td><td>Florida</td><td>148</td><td>8</td><td>Massachusetts</td><td>170</td></tr>
<tr><td>27</td><td>Georgia</td><td>130</td><td>10</td><td>Minnesota</td><td>164</td></tr>
<tr><td>4</td><td>Hawaii</td><td>202</td><td>11</td><td>Michigan</td><td>162</td></tr>
<tr><td>19</td><td>Idaho</td><td>148</td><td>12</td><td>New Hampshire</td><td>158</td></tr>
<tr><td>24</td><td>Illinois</td><td>136</td><td>13</td><td>New York</td><td>156</td></tr>
<tr><td>33</td><td>Indiana</td><td>121</td><td>14</td><td>Nevada</td><td>155</td></tr>
<tr><td>33</td><td>Iowa</td><td>121</td><td>15</td><td>Wisconsin</td><td>152</td></tr>
<tr><td>28</td><td>Kansas</td><td>128</td><td>16</td><td>Maryland</td><td>151</td></tr>
<tr><td>49</td><td>Kentucky</td><td>97</td><td>17</td><td>Rhode Island</td><td>150</td></tr>
<tr><td>46</td><td>Louisiana</td><td>101</td><td>18</td><td>Delaware</td><td>149</td></tr>
<tr><td>29</td><td>Maine</td><td>127</td><td>19</td><td>Florida</td><td>148</td></tr>
<tr><td>16</td><td>Maryland</td><td>151</td><td>19</td><td>Idaho</td><td>148</td></tr>
<tr><td>8</td><td>Massachusetts</td><td>170</td><td>19</td><td>Utah</td><td>148</td></tr>
<tr><td>11</td><td>Michigan</td><td>162</td><td>22</td><td>Vermont</td><td>146</td></tr>
<tr><td>10</td><td>Minnesota</td><td>164</td><td>23</td><td>Arizona</td><td>140</td></tr>
<tr><td>50</td><td>Mississippi</td><td>81</td><td>24</td><td>Illinois</td><td>136</td></tr>
<tr><td>40</td><td>Missouri</td><td>115</td><td>24</td><td>Pennsylvania</td><td>136</td></tr>
<tr><td>31</td><td>Montana</td><td>122</td><td>26</td><td>Virginia</td><td>133</td></tr>
<tr><td>38</td><td>Nebraska</td><td>118</td><td>27</td><td>Georgia</td><td>130</td></tr>
<tr><td>14</td><td>Nevada</td><td>155</td><td>28</td><td>Kansas</td><td>128</td></tr>
<tr><td>12</td><td>New Hampshire</td><td>158</td><td>29</td><td>Maine</td><td>127</td></tr>
<tr><td>6</td><td>New Jersey</td><td>186</td><td>30</td><td>Ohio</td><td>126</td></tr>
<tr><td>44</td><td>New Mexico</td><td>108</td><td>31</td><td>Montana</td><td>122</td></tr>
<tr><td>13</td><td>New York</td><td>156</td><td>31</td><td>North Dakota</td><td>122</td></tr>
<tr><td>39</td><td>North Carolina</td><td>116</td><td>33</td><td>Indiana</td><td>121</td></tr>
<tr><td>31</td><td>North Dakota</td><td>122</td><td>33</td><td>Iowa</td><td>121</td></tr>
<tr><td>30</td><td>Ohio</td><td>126</td><td>33</td><td>South Dakota</td><td>121</td></tr>
<tr><td>42</td><td>Oklahoma</td><td>110</td><td>33</td><td>Wyoming</td><td>121</td></tr>
<tr><td>5</td><td>Oregon</td><td>190</td><td>37</td><td>Tennessee</td><td>120</td></tr>
<tr><td>24</td><td>Pennsylvania</td><td>136</td><td>38</td><td>Nebraska</td><td>118</td></tr>
<tr><td>17</td><td>Rhode Island</td><td>150</td><td>39</td><td>North Carolina</td><td>116</td></tr>
<tr><td>45</td><td>South Carolina</td><td>107</td><td>40</td><td>Missouri</td><td>115</td></tr>
<tr><td>33</td><td>South Dakota</td><td>121</td><td>40</td><td>Texas</td><td>115</td></tr>
<tr><td>37</td><td>Tennessee</td><td>120</td><td>42</td><td>Oklahoma</td><td>110</td></tr>
<tr><td>40</td><td>Texas</td><td>115</td><td>43</td><td>Alabama</td><td>109</td></tr>
<tr><td>19</td><td>Utah</td><td>148</td><td>44</td><td>New Mexico</td><td>108</td></tr>
<tr><td>22</td><td>Vermont</td><td>146</td><td>45</td><td>South Carolina</td><td>107</td></tr>
<tr><td>26</td><td>Virginia</td><td>133</td><td>46</td><td>Louisiana</td><td>101</td></tr>
<tr><td>1</td><td>Washington</td><td>226</td><td>47</td><td>Arkansas</td><td>100</td></tr>
<tr><td>47</td><td>West Virginia</td><td>100</td><td>47</td><td>West Virginia</td><td>100</td></tr>
<tr><td>15</td><td>Wisconsin</td><td>152</td><td>49</td><td>Kentucky</td><td>97</td></tr>
<tr><td>33</td><td>Wyoming</td><td>121</td><td>50</td><td>Mississippi</td><td>81</td></tr>
<tr><td></td><td></td><td></td><td></td><td>District of Columbia</td><td>206</td></tr>
</table>

Source: Morgan Quitno Press using data from U.S. Dept of Health & Human Services, Health Care Financing Admin.
"State Health Expenditure Accounts" (Health Care Financing Review, Fall 1995, Volume 17, Number 1)
*By state of provider.

Expenditures for Other Professional Health Care Services in 1993

National Total = $51,200,000,000*

ALPHA ORDER

RANK	STATE	EXPENDITURES	% of USA
26	Alabama	$641,000,000	1.3%
45	Alaska	127,000,000	0.3%
21	Arizona	821,000,000	1.6%
32	Arkansas	332,000,000	0.7%
1	California	6,859,000,000	13.4%
23	Colorado	751,000,000	1.5%
22	Connecticut	769,000,000	1.5%
44	Delaware	156,000,000	0.3%
4	Florida	3,505,000,000	6.8%
11	Georgia	1,226,000,000	2.4%
40	Hawaii	222,000,000	0.4%
46	Idaho	126,000,000	0.3%
6	Illinois	2,063,000,000	4.0%
16	Indiana	993,000,000	1.9%
31	Iowa	431,000,000	0.8%
30	Kansas	470,000,000	0.9%
25	Kentucky	691,000,000	1.4%
24	Louisiana	736,000,000	1.4%
42	Maine	210,000,000	0.4%
18	Maryland	942,000,000	1.8%
10	Massachusetts	1,524,000,000	3.0%
9	Michigan	1,844,000,000	3.6%
19	Minnesota	933,000,000	1.8%
35	Mississippi	288,000,000	0.6%
15	Missouri	1,013,000,000	2.0%
43	Montana	166,000,000	0.3%
39	Nebraska	225,000,000	0.4%
34	Nevada	307,000,000	0.6%
36	New Hampshire	269,000,000	0.5%
8	New Jersey	1,870,000,000	3.7%
37	New Mexico	254,000,000	0.5%
2	New York	3,717,000,000	7.3%
13	North Carolina	1,102,000,000	2.2%
49	North Dakota	93,000,000	0.2%
7	Ohio	1,969,000,000	3.8%
28	Oklahoma	504,000,000	1.0%
27	Oregon	530,000,000	1.0%
5	Pennsylvania	3,005,000,000	5.9%
38	Rhode Island	239,000,000	0.5%
29	South Carolina	472,000,000	0.9%
48	South Dakota	117,000,000	0.2%
12	Tennessee	1,166,000,000	2.3%
3	Texas	3,591,000,000	7.0%
41	Utah	220,000,000	0.4%
47	Vermont	122,000,000	0.2%
17	Virginia	970,000,000	1.9%
13	Washington	1,102,000,000	2.2%
33	West Virginia	326,000,000	0.6%
20	Wisconsin	875,000,000	1.7%
50	Wyoming	68,000,000	0.1%

RANK ORDER

RANK	STATE	EXPENDITURES	% of USA
1	California	$6,859,000,000	13.4%
2	New York	3,717,000,000	7.3%
3	Texas	3,591,000,000	7.0%
4	Florida	3,505,000,000	6.8%
5	Pennsylvania	3,005,000,000	5.9%
6	Illinois	2,063,000,000	4.0%
7	Ohio	1,969,000,000	3.8%
8	New Jersey	1,870,000,000	3.7%
9	Michigan	1,844,000,000	3.6%
10	Massachusetts	1,524,000,000	3.0%
11	Georgia	1,226,000,000	2.4%
12	Tennessee	1,166,000,000	2.3%
13	North Carolina	1,102,000,000	2.2%
13	Washington	1,102,000,000	2.2%
15	Missouri	1,013,000,000	2.0%
16	Indiana	993,000,000	1.9%
17	Virginia	970,000,000	1.9%
18	Maryland	942,000,000	1.8%
19	Minnesota	933,000,000	1.8%
20	Wisconsin	875,000,000	1.7%
21	Arizona	821,000,000	1.6%
22	Connecticut	769,000,000	1.5%
23	Colorado	751,000,000	1.5%
24	Louisiana	736,000,000	1.4%
25	Kentucky	691,000,000	1.4%
26	Alabama	641,000,000	1.3%
27	Oregon	530,000,000	1.0%
28	Oklahoma	504,000,000	1.0%
29	South Carolina	472,000,000	0.9%
30	Kansas	470,000,000	0.9%
31	Iowa	431,000,000	0.8%
32	Arkansas	332,000,000	0.7%
33	West Virginia	326,000,000	0.6%
34	Nevada	307,000,000	0.6%
35	Mississippi	288,000,000	0.6%
36	New Hampshire	269,000,000	0.5%
37	New Mexico	254,000,000	0.5%
38	Rhode Island	239,000,000	0.5%
39	Nebraska	225,000,000	0.4%
40	Hawaii	222,000,000	0.4%
41	Utah	220,000,000	0.4%
42	Maine	210,000,000	0.4%
43	Montana	166,000,000	0.3%
44	Delaware	156,000,000	0.3%
45	Alaska	127,000,000	0.3%
46	Idaho	126,000,000	0.3%
47	Vermont	122,000,000	0.2%
48	South Dakota	117,000,000	0.2%
49	North Dakota	93,000,000	0.2%
50	Wyoming	68,000,000	0.1%
	District of Columbia	267,000,000	0.5%

Source: U.S. Department of Health and Human Services, Health Care Financing Administration
"State Health Expenditure Accounts" (Health Care Financing Review, Fall 1995, Volume 17, Number 1)
*By state of provider. Includes services by chiropractors, optometrists and podiatrists. Also includes spending in kidney dialysis clinics, alcohol treatment centers, rehabilitation clinics and other health care establishments not elsewhere classified. Medicare ambulance expenditures are also included.

Percent of Total Personal Health Care Expenditures
Spent on Other Professional Services in 1993
National Percent = 6.6%*

<table>
<tr><td colspan="3">ALPHA ORDER</td><td colspan="3">RANK ORDER</td></tr>
<tr><td>RANK</td><td>STATE</td><td>PERCENT</td><td>RANK</td><td>STATE</td><td>PERCENT</td></tr>
<tr><td>45</td><td>Alabama</td><td>5.3</td><td>1</td><td>Nevada</td><td>8.2</td></tr>
<tr><td>2</td><td>Alaska</td><td>8.1</td><td>2</td><td>Alaska</td><td>8.1</td></tr>
<tr><td>7</td><td>Arizona</td><td>7.7</td><td>2</td><td>Vermont</td><td>8.1</td></tr>
<tr><td>44</td><td>Arkansas</td><td>5.4</td><td>4</td><td>Montana</td><td>7.9</td></tr>
<tr><td>9</td><td>California</td><td>7.3</td><td>5</td><td>Florida</td><td>7.8</td></tr>
<tr><td>8</td><td>Colorado</td><td>7.5</td><td>5</td><td>New Hampshire</td><td>7.8</td></tr>
<tr><td>27</td><td>Connecticut</td><td>6.3</td><td>7</td><td>Arizona</td><td>7.7</td></tr>
<tr><td>16</td><td>Delaware</td><td>6.9</td><td>8</td><td>Colorado</td><td>7.5</td></tr>
<tr><td>5</td><td>Florida</td><td>7.8</td><td>9</td><td>California</td><td>7.3</td></tr>
<tr><td>31</td><td>Georgia</td><td>6.1</td><td>9</td><td>New Jersey</td><td>7.3</td></tr>
<tr><td>25</td><td>Hawaii</td><td>6.4</td><td>9</td><td>Washington</td><td>7.3</td></tr>
<tr><td>42</td><td>Idaho</td><td>5.5</td><td>12</td><td>Pennsylvania</td><td>7.2</td></tr>
<tr><td>37</td><td>Illinois</td><td>5.9</td><td>12</td><td>Tennessee</td><td>7.2</td></tr>
<tr><td>31</td><td>Indiana</td><td>6.1</td><td>12</td><td>Texas</td><td>7.2</td></tr>
<tr><td>37</td><td>Iowa</td><td>5.9</td><td>15</td><td>Rhode Island</td><td>7.0</td></tr>
<tr><td>17</td><td>Kansas</td><td>6.8</td><td>16</td><td>Delaware</td><td>6.9</td></tr>
<tr><td>20</td><td>Kentucky</td><td>6.7</td><td>17</td><td>Kansas</td><td>6.8</td></tr>
<tr><td>41</td><td>Louisiana</td><td>5.7</td><td>17</td><td>Michigan</td><td>6.8</td></tr>
<tr><td>31</td><td>Maine</td><td>6.1</td><td>17</td><td>Wyoming</td><td>6.8</td></tr>
<tr><td>30</td><td>Maryland</td><td>6.2</td><td>20</td><td>Kentucky</td><td>6.7</td></tr>
<tr><td>23</td><td>Massachusetts</td><td>6.5</td><td>21</td><td>Minnesota</td><td>6.6</td></tr>
<tr><td>17</td><td>Michigan</td><td>6.8</td><td>21</td><td>Oregon</td><td>6.6</td></tr>
<tr><td>21</td><td>Minnesota</td><td>6.6</td><td>23</td><td>Massachusetts</td><td>6.5</td></tr>
<tr><td>49</td><td>Mississippi</td><td>4.7</td><td>23</td><td>New Mexico</td><td>6.5</td></tr>
<tr><td>25</td><td>Missouri</td><td>6.4</td><td>25</td><td>Hawaii</td><td>6.4</td></tr>
<tr><td>4</td><td>Montana</td><td>7.9</td><td>25</td><td>Missouri</td><td>6.4</td></tr>
<tr><td>48</td><td>Nebraska</td><td>5.1</td><td>27</td><td>Connecticut</td><td>6.3</td></tr>
<tr><td>1</td><td>Nevada</td><td>8.2</td><td>27</td><td>Oklahoma</td><td>6.3</td></tr>
<tr><td>5</td><td>New Hampshire</td><td>7.8</td><td>27</td><td>West Virginia</td><td>6.3</td></tr>
<tr><td>9</td><td>New Jersey</td><td>7.3</td><td>30</td><td>Maryland</td><td>6.2</td></tr>
<tr><td>23</td><td>New Mexico</td><td>6.5</td><td>31</td><td>Georgia</td><td>6.1</td></tr>
<tr><td>42</td><td>New York</td><td>5.5</td><td>31</td><td>Indiana</td><td>6.1</td></tr>
<tr><td>34</td><td>North Carolina</td><td>6.0</td><td>31</td><td>Maine</td><td>6.1</td></tr>
<tr><td>50</td><td>North Dakota</td><td>4.6</td><td>34</td><td>North Carolina</td><td>6.0</td></tr>
<tr><td>37</td><td>Ohio</td><td>5.9</td><td>34</td><td>South Dakota</td><td>6.0</td></tr>
<tr><td>27</td><td>Oklahoma</td><td>6.3</td><td>34</td><td>Wisconsin</td><td>6.0</td></tr>
<tr><td>21</td><td>Oregon</td><td>6.6</td><td>37</td><td>Illinois</td><td>5.9</td></tr>
<tr><td>12</td><td>Pennsylvania</td><td>7.2</td><td>37</td><td>Iowa</td><td>5.9</td></tr>
<tr><td>15</td><td>Rhode Island</td><td>7.0</td><td>37</td><td>Ohio</td><td>5.9</td></tr>
<tr><td>47</td><td>South Carolina</td><td>5.2</td><td>40</td><td>Virginia</td><td>5.8</td></tr>
<tr><td>34</td><td>South Dakota</td><td>6.0</td><td>41</td><td>Louisiana</td><td>5.7</td></tr>
<tr><td>12</td><td>Tennessee</td><td>7.2</td><td>42</td><td>Idaho</td><td>5.5</td></tr>
<tr><td>12</td><td>Texas</td><td>7.2</td><td>42</td><td>New York</td><td>5.5</td></tr>
<tr><td>45</td><td>Utah</td><td>5.3</td><td>44</td><td>Arkansas</td><td>5.4</td></tr>
<tr><td>2</td><td>Vermont</td><td>8.1</td><td>45</td><td>Alabama</td><td>5.3</td></tr>
<tr><td>40</td><td>Virginia</td><td>5.8</td><td>45</td><td>Utah</td><td>5.3</td></tr>
<tr><td>9</td><td>Washington</td><td>7.3</td><td>47</td><td>South Carolina</td><td>5.2</td></tr>
<tr><td>27</td><td>West Virginia</td><td>6.3</td><td>48</td><td>Nebraska</td><td>5.1</td></tr>
<tr><td>34</td><td>Wisconsin</td><td>6.0</td><td>49</td><td>Mississippi</td><td>4.7</td></tr>
<tr><td>17</td><td>Wyoming</td><td>6.8</td><td>50</td><td>North Dakota</td><td>4.6</td></tr>
<tr><td></td><td></td><td></td><td></td><td>District of Columbia</td><td>6.2</td></tr>
</table>

Source: Morgan Quitno Press using data from U.S. Dept of Health & Human Services, Health Care Financing Admin.
"State Health Expenditure Accounts" (Health Care Financing Review, Fall 1995, Volume 17, Number 1)
*By state of provider. Includes services by chiropractors, optometrists and podiatrists. Also includes spending in
kidney dialysis clinics, alcohol treatment centers, rehabilitation clinics and other health care establishments not
elsewhere classified. Medicare ambulance expenditures are also included.

Per Capita Expenditures for Other Professional Health Care Services in 1993

National Per Capita = $199*

ALPHA ORDER			RANK ORDER		
RANK	STATE	PER CAPITA	RANK	STATE	PER CAPITA
40	Alabama	$153	1	Florida	$255
12	Alaska	212	2	Massachusetts	253
16	Arizona	208	3	Pennsylvania	250
46	Arkansas	137	4	New Hampshire	240
11	California	220	5	Rhode Island	239
14	Colorado	210	6	New Jersey	238
7	Connecticut	235	7	Connecticut	235
9	Delaware	223	8	Tennessee	229
1	Florida	255	9	Delaware	223
28	Georgia	178	10	Nevada	222
23	Hawaii	190	11	California	220
49	Idaho	114	12	Alaska	212
30	Illinois	176	12	Vermont	212
32	Indiana	174	14	Colorado	210
40	Iowa	153	14	Washington	210
25	Kansas	186	16	Arizona	208
26	Kentucky	182	17	Minnesota	206
34	Louisiana	172	18	New York	205
35	Maine	169	19	Texas	199
23	Maryland	190	20	Montana	197
2	Massachusetts	253	21	Michigan	195
21	Michigan	195	22	Missouri	194
17	Minnesota	206	23	Hawaii	190
50	Mississippi	109	23	Maryland	190
22	Missouri	194	25	Kansas	186
20	Montana	197	26	Kentucky	182
45	Nebraska	139	27	West Virginia	179
10	Nevada	222	28	Georgia	178
4	New Hampshire	240	28	Ohio	178
6	New Jersey	238	30	Illinois	176
38	New Mexico	157	31	Oregon	175
18	New York	205	32	Indiana	174
37	North Carolina	158	33	Wisconsin	173
43	North Dakota	146	34	Louisiana	172
28	Ohio	178	35	Maine	169
39	Oklahoma	156	36	South Dakota	163
31	Oregon	175	37	North Carolina	158
3	Pennsylvania	250	38	New Mexico	157
5	Rhode Island	239	39	Oklahoma	156
47	South Carolina	130	40	Alabama	153
36	South Dakota	163	40	Iowa	153
8	Tennessee	229	42	Virginia	150
19	Texas	199	43	North Dakota	146
48	Utah	118	44	Wyoming	145
12	Vermont	212	45	Nebraska	139
42	Virginia	150	46	Arkansas	137
14	Washington	210	47	South Carolina	130
27	West Virginia	179	48	Utah	118
33	Wisconsin	173	49	Idaho	114
44	Wyoming	145	50	Mississippi	109

District of Columbia 462

Source: Morgan Quitno Press using data from U.S. Dept of Health & Human Services, Health Care Financing Admin.
"State Health Expenditure Accounts" (Health Care Financing Review, Fall 1995, Volume 17, Number 1)
*By state of provider. Includes services by chiropractors, optometrists and podiatrists. Also includes spending in kidney dialysis clinics, alcohol treatment centers, rehabilitation clinics and other health care establishments not elsewhere classified. Medicare ambulance expenditures are also included.

Expenditures for Home Health Care in 1993

National Total = $22,982,000,000*

ALPHA ORDER

RANK	STATE	EXPENDITURES	% of USA
13	Alabama	$602,000,000	2.6%
50	Alaska	5,000,000	0.0%
22	Arizona	317,000,000	1.4%
32	Arkansas	145,000,000	0.6%
3	California	1,640,000,000	7.1%
29	Colorado	195,000,000	0.9%
17	Connecticut	391,000,000	1.7%
43	Delaware	51,000,000	0.2%
2	Florida	2,323,000,000	10.1%
9	Georgia	729,000,000	3.2%
46	Hawaii	32,000,000	0.1%
45	Idaho	49,000,000	0.2%
6	Illinois	853,000,000	3.7%
24	Indiana	308,000,000	1.3%
33	Iowa	137,000,000	0.6%
30	Kansas	152,000,000	0.7%
20	Kentucky	357,000,000	1.6%
16	Louisiana	410,000,000	1.8%
36	Maine	104,000,000	0.5%
23	Maryland	314,000,000	1.4%
7	Massachusetts	835,000,000	3.6%
11	Michigan	714,000,000	3.1%
15	Minnesota	414,000,000	1.8%
25	Mississippi	300,000,000	1.3%
21	Missouri	347,000,000	1.5%
44	Montana	50,000,000	0.2%
39	Nebraska	74,000,000	0.3%
35	Nevada	120,000,000	0.5%
40	New Hampshire	71,000,000	0.3%
10	New Jersey	718,000,000	3.1%
41	New Mexico	62,000,000	0.3%
1	New York	3,562,000,000	15.5%
14	North Carolina	541,000,000	2.4%
48	North Dakota	16,000,000	0.1%
12	Ohio	649,000,000	2.8%
26	Oklahoma	273,000,000	1.2%
34	Oregon	122,000,000	0.5%
8	Pennsylvania	796,000,000	3.5%
37	Rhode Island	103,000,000	0.5%
28	South Carolina	216,000,000	0.9%
48	South Dakota	16,000,000	0.1%
5	Tennessee	899,000,000	3.9%
4	Texas	1,583,000,000	6.9%
38	Utah	100,000,000	0.4%
42	Vermont	52,000,000	0.2%
19	Virginia	368,000,000	1.6%
18	Washington	380,000,000	1.7%
31	West Virginia	150,000,000	0.7%
27	Wisconsin	265,000,000	1.2%
47	Wyoming	29,000,000	0.1%

RANK ORDER

RANK	STATE	EXPENDITURES	% of USA
1	New York	$3,562,000,000	15.5%
2	Florida	2,323,000,000	10.1%
3	California	1,640,000,000	7.1%
4	Texas	1,583,000,000	6.9%
5	Tennessee	899,000,000	3.9%
6	Illinois	853,000,000	3.7%
7	Massachusetts	835,000,000	3.6%
8	Pennsylvania	796,000,000	3.5%
9	Georgia	729,000,000	3.2%
10	New Jersey	718,000,000	3.1%
11	Michigan	714,000,000	3.1%
12	Ohio	649,000,000	2.8%
13	Alabama	602,000,000	2.6%
14	North Carolina	541,000,000	2.4%
15	Minnesota	414,000,000	1.8%
16	Louisiana	410,000,000	1.8%
17	Connecticut	391,000,000	1.7%
18	Washington	380,000,000	1.7%
19	Virginia	368,000,000	1.6%
20	Kentucky	357,000,000	1.6%
21	Missouri	347,000,000	1.5%
22	Arizona	317,000,000	1.4%
23	Maryland	314,000,000	1.4%
24	Indiana	308,000,000	1.3%
25	Mississippi	300,000,000	1.3%
26	Oklahoma	273,000,000	1.2%
27	Wisconsin	265,000,000	1.2%
28	South Carolina	216,000,000	0.9%
29	Colorado	195,000,000	0.9%
30	Kansas	152,000,000	0.7%
31	West Virginia	150,000,000	0.7%
32	Arkansas	145,000,000	0.6%
33	Iowa	137,000,000	0.6%
34	Oregon	122,000,000	0.5%
35	Nevada	120,000,000	0.5%
36	Maine	104,000,000	0.5%
37	Rhode Island	103,000,000	0.5%
38	Utah	100,000,000	0.4%
39	Nebraska	74,000,000	0.3%
40	New Hampshire	71,000,000	0.3%
41	New Mexico	62,000,000	0.3%
42	Vermont	52,000,000	0.2%
43	Delaware	51,000,000	0.2%
44	Montana	50,000,000	0.2%
45	Idaho	49,000,000	0.2%
46	Hawaii	32,000,000	0.1%
47	Wyoming	29,000,000	0.1%
48	North Dakota	16,000,000	0.1%
48	South Dakota	16,000,000	0.1%
50	Alaska	5,000,000	0.0%
	District of Columbia	45,000,000	0.2%

Source: U.S. Department of Health and Human Services, Health Care Financing Administration
"State Health Expenditure Accounts" (Health Care Financing Review, Fall 1995, Volume 17, Number 1)
By state of provider. Includes spending for services and products by public and private freestanding home health agencies. Excludes home health care services provided by hospital-based agencies which are included in hospital expenditures.

Percent of Total Personal Health Care Expenditures
Spent on Home Health Care in 1993
National Percent = 3.0%*

ALPHA ORDER

RANK	STATE	PERCENT
4	Alabama	5.0
50	Alaska	0.3
15	Arizona	3.0
26	Arkansas	2.4
43	California	1.7
37	Colorado	1.9
11	Connecticut	3.2
30	Delaware	2.3
3	Florida	5.2
6	Georgia	3.6
47	Hawaii	0.9
31	Idaho	2.2
24	Illinois	2.5
37	Indiana	1.9
37	Iowa	1.9
31	Kansas	2.2
9	Kentucky	3.4
11	Louisiana	3.2
15	Maine	3.0
35	Maryland	2.1
6	Massachusetts	3.6
23	Michigan	2.6
19	Minnesota	2.9
5	Mississippi	4.8
31	Missouri	2.2
26	Montana	2.4
43	Nebraska	1.7
11	Nevada	3.2
35	New Hampshire	2.1
22	New Jersey	2.8
45	New Mexico	1.6
2	New York	5.3
15	North Carolina	3.0
48	North Dakota	0.8
37	Ohio	1.9
9	Oklahoma	3.4
46	Oregon	1.5
37	Pennsylvania	1.9
15	Rhode Island	3.0
26	South Carolina	2.4
48	South Dakota	0.8
1	Tennessee	5.5
11	Texas	3.2
26	Utah	2.4
8	Vermont	3.5
31	Virginia	2.2
24	Washington	2.5
19	West Virginia	2.9
42	Wisconsin	1.8
19	Wyoming	2.9

RANK ORDER

RANK	STATE	PERCENT
1	Tennessee	5.5
2	New York	5.3
3	Florida	5.2
4	Alabama	5.0
5	Mississippi	4.8
6	Georgia	3.6
6	Massachusetts	3.6
8	Vermont	3.5
9	Kentucky	3.4
9	Oklahoma	3.4
11	Connecticut	3.2
11	Louisiana	3.2
11	Nevada	3.2
11	Texas	3.2
15	Arizona	3.0
15	Maine	3.0
15	North Carolina	3.0
15	Rhode Island	3.0
19	Minnesota	2.9
19	West Virginia	2.9
19	Wyoming	2.9
22	New Jersey	2.8
23	Michigan	2.6
24	Illinois	2.5
24	Washington	2.5
26	Arkansas	2.4
26	Montana	2.4
26	South Carolina	2.4
26	Utah	2.4
30	Delaware	2.3
31	Idaho	2.2
31	Kansas	2.2
31	Missouri	2.2
31	Virginia	2.2
35	Maryland	2.1
35	New Hampshire	2.1
37	Colorado	1.9
37	Indiana	1.9
37	Iowa	1.9
37	Ohio	1.9
37	Pennsylvania	1.9
42	Wisconsin	1.8
43	California	1.7
43	Nebraska	1.7
45	New Mexico	1.6
46	Oregon	1.5
47	Hawaii	0.9
48	North Dakota	0.8
48	South Dakota	0.8
50	Alaska	0.3

District of Columbia 1.1

Source: Morgan Quitno Press using data from U.S. Dept of Health & Human Services, Health Care Financing Admin. "State Health Expenditure Accounts" (Health Care Financing Review, Fall 1995, Volume 17, Number 1)
By state of provider. Includes spending for services and products by public and private freestanding home health agencies. Excludes home health care services provided by hospital-based agencies which are included in hospital expenditures.

Per Capita Expenditures for Home Health Care in 1993

National Per Capita = $89*

ALPHA ORDER

RANK	STATE	PER CAPITA
4	Alabama	$144
50	Alaska	8
20	Arizona	80
31	Arkansas	60
40	California	53
37	Colorado	55
6	Connecticut	119
23	Delaware	73
3	Florida	169
8	Georgia	106
47	Hawaii	27
44	Idaho	45
23	Illinois	73
38	Indiana	54
42	Iowa	49
31	Kansas	60
11	Kentucky	94
10	Louisiana	96
17	Maine	84
28	Maryland	63
5	Massachusetts	139
22	Michigan	75
12	Minnesota	92
7	Mississippi	114
26	Missouri	66
34	Montana	59
43	Nebraska	46
16	Nevada	87
28	New Hampshire	63
13	New Jersey	91
46	New Mexico	38
1	New York	196
21	North Carolina	78
48	North Dakota	25
34	Ohio	59
17	Oklahoma	84
45	Oregon	40
26	Pennsylvania	66
9	Rhode Island	103
31	South Carolina	60
49	South Dakota	22
2	Tennessee	177
15	Texas	88
38	Utah	54
14	Vermont	90
36	Virginia	57
25	Washington	72
19	West Virginia	83
40	Wisconsin	53
30	Wyoming	62

RANK ORDER

RANK	STATE	PER CAPITA
1	New York	$196
2	Tennessee	177
3	Florida	169
4	Alabama	144
5	Massachusetts	139
6	Connecticut	119
7	Mississippi	114
8	Georgia	106
9	Rhode Island	103
10	Louisiana	96
11	Kentucky	94
12	Minnesota	92
13	New Jersey	91
14	Vermont	90
15	Texas	88
16	Nevada	87
17	Maine	84
17	Oklahoma	84
19	West Virginia	83
20	Arizona	80
21	North Carolina	78
22	Michigan	75
23	Delaware	73
23	Illinois	73
25	Washington	72
26	Missouri	66
26	Pennsylvania	66
28	Maryland	63
28	New Hampshire	63
30	Wyoming	62
31	Arkansas	60
31	Kansas	60
31	South Carolina	60
34	Montana	59
34	Ohio	59
36	Virginia	57
37	Colorado	55
38	Indiana	54
38	Utah	54
40	California	53
40	Wisconsin	53
42	Iowa	49
43	Nebraska	46
44	Idaho	45
45	Oregon	40
46	New Mexico	38
47	Hawaii	27
48	North Dakota	25
49	South Dakota	22
50	Alaska	8

District of Columbia 78

Source: Morgan Quitno Press using data from U.S. Dept of Health & Human Services, Health Care Financing Admin. "State Health Expenditure Accounts" (Health Care Financing Review, Fall 1995, Volume 17, Number 1)
By state of provider. Includes spending for services and products by public and private freestanding home health agencies. Excludes home health care services provided by hospital-based agencies which are included in hospital expenditures.

Expenditures for Drugs and Other Medical Non-Durables in 1993

National Total = $74,956,000,000*

ALPHA ORDER

RANK	STATE	EXPENDITURES	% of USA
21	Alabama	$1,247,000,000	1.7%
46	Alaska	165,000,000	0.2%
24	Arizona	1,124,000,000	1.5%
33	Arkansas	684,000,000	0.9%
1	California	9,017,000,000	12.0%
27	Colorado	919,000,000	1.2%
25	Connecticut	996,000,000	1.3%
44	Delaware	214,000,000	0.3%
4	Florida	4,450,000,000	5.9%
10	Georgia	2,117,000,000	2.8%
37	Hawaii	416,000,000	0.6%
43	Idaho	265,000,000	0.4%
6	Illinois	3,263,000,000	4.4%
16	Indiana	1,594,000,000	2.1%
30	Iowa	743,000,000	1.0%
32	Kansas	695,000,000	0.9%
22	Kentucky	1,196,000,000	1.6%
20	Louisiana	1,269,000,000	1.7%
40	Maine	333,000,000	0.4%
14	Maryland	1,749,000,000	2.3%
13	Massachusetts	1,961,000,000	2.6%
8	Michigan	2,937,000,000	3.9%
23	Minnesota	1,146,000,000	1.5%
31	Mississippi	720,000,000	1.0%
18	Missouri	1,420,000,000	1.9%
45	Montana	209,000,000	0.3%
36	Nebraska	421,000,000	0.6%
39	Nevada	408,000,000	0.5%
41	New Hampshire	319,000,000	0.4%
9	New Jersey	2,452,000,000	3.3%
38	New Mexico	409,000,000	0.6%
3	New York	5,081,000,000	6.8%
11	North Carolina	2,027,000,000	2.7%
49	North Dakota	160,000,000	0.2%
7	Ohio	3,218,000,000	4.3%
28	Oklahoma	874,000,000	1.2%
29	Oregon	762,000,000	1.0%
5	Pennsylvania	3,519,000,000	4.7%
42	Rhode Island	310,000,000	0.4%
26	South Carolina	978,000,000	1.3%
47	South Dakota	163,000,000	0.2%
15	Tennessee	1,635,000,000	2.2%
2	Texas	5,131,000,000	6.9%
35	Utah	439,000,000	0.6%
48	Vermont	161,000,000	0.2%
12	Virginia	2,015,000,000	2.7%
17	Washington	1,474,000,000	2.0%
34	West Virginia	574,000,000	0.8%
19	Wisconsin	1,290,000,000	1.7%
50	Wyoming	113,000,000	0.2%

RANK ORDER

RANK	STATE	EXPENDITURES	% of USA
1	California	$9,017,000,000	12.0%
2	Texas	5,131,000,000	6.9%
3	New York	5,081,000,000	6.8%
4	Florida	4,450,000,000	5.9%
5	Pennsylvania	3,519,000,000	4.7%
6	Illinois	3,263,000,000	4.4%
7	Ohio	3,218,000,000	4.3%
8	Michigan	2,937,000,000	3.9%
9	New Jersey	2,452,000,000	3.3%
10	Georgia	2,117,000,000	2.8%
11	North Carolina	2,027,000,000	2.7%
12	Virginia	2,015,000,000	2.7%
13	Massachusetts	1,961,000,000	2.6%
14	Maryland	1,749,000,000	2.3%
15	Tennessee	1,635,000,000	2.2%
16	Indiana	1,594,000,000	2.1%
17	Washington	1,474,000,000	2.0%
18	Missouri	1,420,000,000	1.9%
19	Wisconsin	1,290,000,000	1.7%
20	Louisiana	1,269,000,000	1.7%
21	Alabama	1,247,000,000	1.7%
22	Kentucky	1,196,000,000	1.6%
23	Minnesota	1,146,000,000	1.5%
24	Arizona	1,124,000,000	1.5%
25	Connecticut	996,000,000	1.3%
26	South Carolina	978,000,000	1.3%
27	Colorado	919,000,000	1.2%
28	Oklahoma	874,000,000	1.2%
29	Oregon	762,000,000	1.0%
30	Iowa	743,000,000	1.0%
31	Mississippi	720,000,000	1.0%
32	Kansas	695,000,000	0.9%
33	Arkansas	684,000,000	0.9%
34	West Virginia	574,000,000	0.8%
35	Utah	439,000,000	0.6%
36	Nebraska	421,000,000	0.6%
37	Hawaii	416,000,000	0.6%
38	New Mexico	409,000,000	0.6%
39	Nevada	408,000,000	0.5%
40	Maine	333,000,000	0.4%
41	New Hampshire	319,000,000	0.4%
42	Rhode Island	310,000,000	0.4%
43	Idaho	265,000,000	0.4%
44	Delaware	214,000,000	0.3%
45	Montana	209,000,000	0.3%
46	Alaska	165,000,000	0.2%
47	South Dakota	163,000,000	0.2%
48	Vermont	161,000,000	0.2%
49	North Dakota	160,000,000	0.2%
50	Wyoming	113,000,000	0.2%
	District of Columbia	175,000,000	0.2%

Source: U.S. Department of Health and Human Services, Health Care Financing Administration
"State Health Expenditure Accounts" (Health Care Financing Review, Fall 1995, Volume 17, Number 1)
*By state of provider. Includes prescription and over-the-counter drugs and sundries. Limited to spending that occurs in retail outlets such as food stores, drug stores, HMO pharmacies or through mail-order pharmacies.

Percent of Total Personal Health Care Expenditures
Spent on Drugs and Other Medical Non-Durables in 1993
National Percent = 9.6%*

ALPHA ORDER

RANK	STATE	PERCENT
21	Alabama	10.3
18	Alaska	10.5
17	Arizona	10.6
8	Arkansas	11.2
32	California	9.6
40	Colorado	9.1
47	Connecticut	8.2
35	Delaware	9.5
26	Florida	9.9
18	Georgia	10.5
2	Hawaii	11.9
3	Idaho	11.6
38	Illinois	9.4
29	Indiana	9.7
23	Iowa	10.1
23	Kansas	10.1
5	Kentucky	11.5
28	Louisiana	9.8
29	Maine	9.7
5	Maryland	11.5
45	Massachusetts	8.4
13	Michigan	10.8
48	Minnesota	8.1
3	Mississippi	11.6
42	Missouri	8.9
26	Montana	9.9
32	Nebraska	9.6
11	Nevada	10.9
39	New Hampshire	9.2
35	New Jersey	9.5
18	New Mexico	10.5
50	New York	7.6
9	North Carolina	11.1
49	North Dakota	7.9
32	Ohio	9.6
11	Oklahoma	10.9
35	Oregon	9.5
44	Pennsylvania	8.5
41	Rhode Island	9.0
13	South Carolina	10.8
46	South Dakota	8.3
23	Tennessee	10.1
21	Texas	10.3
15	Utah	10.7
15	Vermont	10.7
1	Virginia	12.1
29	Washington	9.7
10	West Virginia	11.0
42	Wisconsin	8.9
7	Wyoming	11.3

RANK ORDER

RANK	STATE	PERCENT
1	Virginia	12.1
2	Hawaii	11.9
3	Idaho	11.6
3	Mississippi	11.6
5	Kentucky	11.5
5	Maryland	11.5
7	Wyoming	11.3
8	Arkansas	11.2
9	North Carolina	11.1
10	West Virginia	11.0
11	Nevada	10.9
11	Oklahoma	10.9
13	Michigan	10.8
13	South Carolina	10.8
15	Utah	10.7
15	Vermont	10.7
17	Arizona	10.6
18	Alaska	10.5
18	Georgia	10.5
18	New Mexico	10.5
21	Alabama	10.3
21	Texas	10.3
23	Iowa	10.1
23	Kansas	10.1
23	Tennessee	10.1
26	Florida	9.9
26	Montana	9.9
28	Louisiana	9.8
29	Indiana	9.7
29	Maine	9.7
29	Washington	9.7
32	California	9.6
32	Nebraska	9.6
32	Ohio	9.6
35	Delaware	9.5
35	New Jersey	9.5
35	Oregon	9.5
38	Illinois	9.4
39	New Hampshire	9.2
40	Colorado	9.1
41	Rhode Island	9.0
42	Missouri	8.9
42	Wisconsin	8.9
44	Pennsylvania	8.5
45	Massachusetts	8.4
46	South Dakota	8.3
47	Connecticut	8.2
48	Minnesota	8.1
49	North Dakota	7.9
50	New York	7.6

| | District of Columbia | 4.1 |

Source: Morgan Quitno Press using data from U.S. Dept of Health & Human Services, Health Care Financing Admin. "State Health Expenditure Accounts" (Health Care Financing Review, Fall 1995, Volume 17, Number 1)
By state of provider. Includes prescription and over-the-counter drugs and sundries. Limited to spending that occurs in retail outlets such as food stores, drug stores, HMO pharmacies or through mail-order pharmacies.

Expenditures for Other Professional Health Care Services in 1993

National Total = $51,200,000,000*

ALPHA ORDER

RANK	STATE	EXPENDITURES	% of USA
26	Alabama	$641,000,000	1.3%
45	Alaska	127,000,000	0.3%
21	Arizona	821,000,000	1.6%
32	Arkansas	332,000,000	0.7%
1	California	6,859,000,000	13.4%
23	Colorado	751,000,000	1.5%
22	Connecticut	769,000,000	1.5%
44	Delaware	156,000,000	0.3%
4	Florida	3,505,000,000	6.8%
11	Georgia	1,226,000,000	2.4%
40	Hawaii	222,000,000	0.4%
46	Idaho	126,000,000	0.3%
6	Illinois	2,063,000,000	4.0%
16	Indiana	993,000,000	1.9%
31	Iowa	431,000,000	0.8%
30	Kansas	470,000,000	0.9%
25	Kentucky	691,000,000	1.4%
24	Louisiana	736,000,000	1.4%
42	Maine	210,000,000	0.4%
18	Maryland	942,000,000	1.8%
10	Massachusetts	1,524,000,000	3.0%
9	Michigan	1,844,000,000	3.6%
19	Minnesota	933,000,000	1.8%
35	Mississippi	288,000,000	0.6%
15	Missouri	1,013,000,000	2.0%
43	Montana	166,000,000	0.3%
39	Nebraska	225,000,000	0.4%
34	Nevada	307,000,000	0.6%
36	New Hampshire	269,000,000	0.5%
8	New Jersey	1,870,000,000	3.7%
37	New Mexico	254,000,000	0.5%
2	New York	3,717,000,000	7.3%
13	North Carolina	1,102,000,000	2.2%
49	North Dakota	93,000,000	0.2%
7	Ohio	1,969,000,000	3.8%
28	Oklahoma	504,000,000	1.0%
27	Oregon	530,000,000	1.0%
5	Pennsylvania	3,005,000,000	5.9%
38	Rhode Island	239,000,000	0.5%
29	South Carolina	472,000,000	0.9%
48	South Dakota	117,000,000	0.2%
12	Tennessee	1,166,000,000	2.3%
3	Texas	3,591,000,000	7.0%
41	Utah	220,000,000	0.4%
47	Vermont	122,000,000	0.2%
17	Virginia	970,000,000	1.9%
13	Washington	1,102,000,000	2.2%
33	West Virginia	326,000,000	0.6%
20	Wisconsin	875,000,000	1.7%
50	Wyoming	68,000,000	0.1%

RANK ORDER

RANK	STATE	EXPENDITURES	% of USA
1	California	$6,859,000,000	13.4%
2	New York	3,717,000,000	7.3%
3	Texas	3,591,000,000	7.0%
4	Florida	3,505,000,000	6.8%
5	Pennsylvania	3,005,000,000	5.9%
6	Illinois	2,063,000,000	4.0%
7	Ohio	1,969,000,000	3.8%
8	New Jersey	1,870,000,000	3.7%
9	Michigan	1,844,000,000	3.6%
10	Massachusetts	1,524,000,000	3.0%
11	Georgia	1,226,000,000	2.4%
12	Tennessee	1,166,000,000	2.3%
13	North Carolina	1,102,000,000	2.2%
13	Washington	1,102,000,000	2.2%
15	Missouri	1,013,000,000	2.0%
16	Indiana	993,000,000	1.9%
17	Virginia	970,000,000	1.9%
18	Maryland	942,000,000	1.8%
19	Minnesota	933,000,000	1.8%
20	Wisconsin	875,000,000	1.7%
21	Arizona	821,000,000	1.6%
22	Connecticut	769,000,000	1.5%
23	Colorado	751,000,000	1.5%
24	Louisiana	736,000,000	1.4%
25	Kentucky	691,000,000	1.4%
26	Alabama	641,000,000	1.3%
27	Oregon	530,000,000	1.0%
28	Oklahoma	504,000,000	1.0%
29	South Carolina	472,000,000	0.9%
30	Kansas	470,000,000	0.9%
31	Iowa	431,000,000	0.8%
32	Arkansas	332,000,000	0.7%
33	West Virginia	326,000,000	0.6%
34	Nevada	307,000,000	0.6%
35	Mississippi	288,000,000	0.6%
36	New Hampshire	269,000,000	0.5%
37	New Mexico	254,000,000	0.5%
38	Rhode Island	239,000,000	0.5%
39	Nebraska	225,000,000	0.4%
40	Hawaii	222,000,000	0.4%
41	Utah	220,000,000	0.4%
42	Maine	210,000,000	0.4%
43	Montana	166,000,000	0.3%
44	Delaware	156,000,000	0.3%
45	Alaska	127,000,000	0.3%
46	Idaho	126,000,000	0.3%
47	Vermont	122,000,000	0.2%
48	South Dakota	117,000,000	0.2%
49	North Dakota	93,000,000	0.2%
50	Wyoming	68,000,000	0.1%
	District of Columbia	267,000,000	0.5%

Source: U.S. Department of Health and Human Services, Health Care Financing Administration
"State Health Expenditure Accounts" (Health Care Financing Review, Fall 1995, Volume 17, Number 1)
*By state of provider. Includes services by chiropractors, optometrists and podiatrists. Also includes spending in kidney dialysis clinics, alcohol treatment centers, rehabilitation clinics and other health care establishments not elsewhere classified. Medicare ambulance expenditures are also included.

Expenditures for Vision Products and Other Medical Durables in 1993

National Total = $12,636,000,000*

ALPHA ORDER

RANK	STATE	EXPENDITURES	% of USA
25	Alabama	$155,000,000	1.2%
48	Alaska	26,000,000	0.2%
21	Arizona	227,000,000	1.8%
39	Arkansas	56,000,000	0.4%
1	California	1,522,000,000	12.0%
22	Colorado	226,000,000	1.8%
23	Connecticut	192,000,000	1.5%
43	Delaware	35,000,000	0.3%
4	Florida	872,000,000	6.9%
10	Georgia	331,000,000	2.6%
37	Hawaii	64,000,000	0.5%
43	Idaho	35,000,000	0.3%
6	Illinois	604,000,000	4.8%
14	Indiana	270,000,000	2.1%
26	Iowa	148,000,000	1.2%
31	Kansas	107,000,000	0.9%
27	Kentucky	141,000,000	1.1%
24	Louisiana	160,000,000	1.3%
40	Maine	46,000,000	0.4%
13	Maryland	272,000,000	2.2%
15	Massachusetts	269,000,000	2.1%
8	Michigan	457,000,000	3.6%
12	Minnesota	277,000,000	2.2%
38	Mississippi	60,000,000	0.5%
17	Missouri	244,000,000	1.9%
42	Montana	36,000,000	0.3%
33	Nebraska	80,000,000	0.6%
34	Nevada	76,000,000	0.6%
41	New Hampshire	43,000,000	0.3%
8	New Jersey	457,000,000	3.6%
36	New Mexico	69,000,000	0.6%
2	New York	1,090,000,000	8.6%
16	North Carolina	268,000,000	2.1%
47	North Dakota	28,000,000	0.2%
7	Ohio	531,000,000	4.2%
28	Oklahoma	121,000,000	1.0%
32	Oregon	91,000,000	0.7%
5	Pennsylvania	617,000,000	4.9%
45	Rhode Island	33,000,000	0.3%
30	South Carolina	115,000,000	0.9%
46	South Dakota	30,000,000	0.2%
20	Tennessee	228,000,000	1.8%
3	Texas	883,000,000	7.0%
29	Utah	117,000,000	0.9%
49	Vermont	24,000,000	0.2%
11	Virginia	295,000,000	2.3%
18	Washington	242,000,000	1.9%
35	West Virginia	74,000,000	0.6%
19	Wisconsin	240,000,000	1.9%
50	Wyoming	17,000,000	0.1%

RANK ORDER

RANK	STATE	EXPENDITURES	% of USA
1	California	$1,522,000,000	12.0%
2	New York	1,090,000,000	8.6%
3	Texas	883,000,000	7.0%
4	Florida	872,000,000	6.9%
5	Pennsylvania	617,000,000	4.9%
6	Illinois	604,000,000	4.8%
7	Ohio	531,000,000	4.2%
8	Michigan	457,000,000	3.6%
8	New Jersey	457,000,000	3.6%
10	Georgia	331,000,000	2.6%
11	Virginia	295,000,000	2.3%
12	Minnesota	277,000,000	2.2%
13	Maryland	272,000,000	2.2%
14	Indiana	270,000,000	2.1%
15	Massachusetts	269,000,000	2.1%
16	North Carolina	268,000,000	2.1%
17	Missouri	244,000,000	1.9%
18	Washington	242,000,000	1.9%
19	Wisconsin	240,000,000	1.9%
20	Tennessee	228,000,000	1.8%
21	Arizona	227,000,000	1.8%
22	Colorado	226,000,000	1.8%
23	Connecticut	192,000,000	1.5%
24	Louisiana	160,000,000	1.3%
25	Alabama	155,000,000	1.2%
26	Iowa	148,000,000	1.2%
27	Kentucky	141,000,000	1.1%
28	Oklahoma	121,000,000	1.0%
29	Utah	117,000,000	0.9%
30	South Carolina	115,000,000	0.9%
31	Kansas	107,000,000	0.9%
32	Oregon	91,000,000	0.7%
33	Nebraska	80,000,000	0.6%
34	Nevada	76,000,000	0.6%
35	West Virginia	74,000,000	0.6%
36	New Mexico	69,000,000	0.6%
37	Hawaii	64,000,000	0.5%
38	Mississippi	60,000,000	0.5%
39	Arkansas	56,000,000	0.4%
40	Maine	46,000,000	0.4%
41	New Hampshire	43,000,000	0.3%
42	Montana	36,000,000	0.3%
43	Delaware	35,000,000	0.3%
43	Idaho	35,000,000	0.3%
45	Rhode Island	33,000,000	0.3%
46	South Dakota	30,000,000	0.2%
47	North Dakota	28,000,000	0.2%
48	Alaska	26,000,000	0.2%
49	Vermont	24,000,000	0.2%
50	Wyoming	17,000,000	0.1%
	District of Columbia	34,000,000	0.3%

Source: U.S. Department of Health and Human Services, Health Care Financing Administration
"State Health Expenditure Accounts" (Health Care Financing Review, Fall 1995, Volume 17, Number 1)
*By state of provider. Includes eyeglasses, hearing aids, surgical appliances and supplies, bulk and cylinder oxygen and medical equipment rentals.

Percent of Total Personal Health Care Expenditures
Spent on Vision Products and Other Medical Durables in 1993
National Percent = 1.6%*

ALPHA ORDER

RANK	STATE	PERCENT
41	Alabama	1.3
15	Alaska	1.7
3	Arizona	2.1
50	Arkansas	0.9
21	California	1.6
2	Colorado	2.2
21	Connecticut	1.6
30	Delaware	1.5
7	Florida	1.9
21	Georgia	1.6
8	Hawaii	1.8
30	Idaho	1.5
15	Illinois	1.7
21	Indiana	1.6
4	Iowa	2.0
21	Kansas	1.6
37	Kentucky	1.4
44	Louisiana	1.2
41	Maine	1.3
8	Maryland	1.8
46	Massachusetts	1.1
15	Michigan	1.7
4	Minnesota	2.0
48	Mississippi	1.0
30	Missouri	1.5
15	Montana	1.7
8	Nebraska	1.8
4	Nevada	2.0
44	New Hampshire	1.2
8	New Jersey	1.8
8	New Mexico	1.8
21	New York	1.6
30	North Carolina	1.5
37	North Dakota	1.4
21	Ohio	1.6
30	Oklahoma	1.5
46	Oregon	1.1
30	Pennsylvania	1.5
48	Rhode Island	1.0
41	South Carolina	1.3
30	South Dakota	1.5
37	Tennessee	1.4
8	Texas	1.8
1	Utah	2.8
21	Vermont	1.6
8	Virginia	1.8
21	Washington	1.6
37	West Virginia	1.4
15	Wisconsin	1.7
15	Wyoming	1.7

RANK ORDER

RANK	STATE	PERCENT
1	Utah	2.8
2	Colorado	2.2
3	Arizona	2.1
4	Iowa	2.0
4	Minnesota	2.0
4	Nevada	2.0
7	Florida	1.9
8	Hawaii	1.8
8	Maryland	1.8
8	Nebraska	1.8
8	New Jersey	1.8
8	New Mexico	1.8
8	Texas	1.8
8	Virginia	1.8
15	Alaska	1.7
15	Illinois	1.7
15	Michigan	1.7
15	Montana	1.7
15	Wisconsin	1.7
15	Wyoming	1.7
21	California	1.6
21	Connecticut	1.6
21	Georgia	1.6
21	Indiana	1.6
21	Kansas	1.6
21	New York	1.6
21	Ohio	1.6
21	Vermont	1.6
21	Washington	1.6
30	Delaware	1.5
30	Idaho	1.5
30	Missouri	1.5
30	North Carolina	1.5
30	Oklahoma	1.5
30	Pennsylvania	1.5
30	South Dakota	1.5
37	Kentucky	1.4
37	North Dakota	1.4
37	Tennessee	1.4
37	West Virginia	1.4
41	Alabama	1.3
41	Maine	1.3
41	South Carolina	1.3
44	Louisiana	1.2
44	New Hampshire	1.2
46	Massachusetts	1.1
46	Oregon	1.1
48	Mississippi	1.0
48	Rhode Island	1.0
50	Arkansas	0.9

District of Columbia   0.8

Source: Morgan Quitno Press using data from U.S. Dept of Health & Human Services, Health Care Financing Admin. "State Health Expenditure Accounts" (Health Care Financing Review, Fall 1995, Volume 17, Number 1)
*By state of provider. Includes eyeglasses, hearing aids, surgical appliances and supplies, bulk and cylinder oxygen and medical equipment rentals.

Per Capita Expenditures for Vision Products and Other Medical Durables in 1993

National Per Capita = $49*

ALPHA ORDER				RANK ORDER		
RANK	STATE	PER CAPITA		RANK	STATE	PER CAPITA
39	Alabama	$37		1	Florida	$64
30	Alaska	43		2	Colorado	63
7	Arizona	58		2	Utah	63
49	Arkansas	23		4	Minnesota	61
17	California	49		5	New York	60
2	Colorado	63		6	Connecticut	59
6	Connecticut	59		7	Arizona	58
15	Delaware	50		7	New Jersey	58
1	Florida	64		9	Hawaii	55
19	Georgia	48		9	Maryland	55
9	Hawaii	55		9	Nevada	55
46	Idaho	32		12	Illinois	52
12	Illinois	52		12	Iowa	52
23	Indiana	47		14	Pennsylvania	51
12	Iowa	52		15	Delaware	50
33	Kansas	42		15	Nebraska	50
39	Kentucky	37		17	California	49
39	Louisiana	37		17	Texas	49
39	Maine	37		19	Georgia	48
9	Maryland	55		19	Michigan	48
27	Massachusetts	45		19	Ohio	48
19	Michigan	48		19	Wisconsin	48
4	Minnesota	61		23	Indiana	47
49	Mississippi	23		23	Missouri	47
23	Missouri	47		25	Virginia	46
30	Montana	43		25	Washington	46
15	Nebraska	50		27	Massachusetts	45
9	Nevada	55		27	Tennessee	45
38	New Hampshire	38		29	North Dakota	44
7	New Jersey	58		30	Alaska	43
30	New Mexico	43		30	Montana	43
5	New York	60		30	New Mexico	43
37	North Carolina	39		33	Kansas	42
29	North Dakota	44		33	South Dakota	42
19	Ohio	48		33	Vermont	42
39	Oklahoma	37		36	West Virginia	41
48	Oregon	30		37	North Carolina	39
14	Pennsylvania	51		38	New Hampshire	38
45	Rhode Island	33		39	Alabama	37
46	South Carolina	32		39	Kentucky	37
33	South Dakota	42		39	Louisiana	37
27	Tennessee	45		39	Maine	37
17	Texas	49		39	Oklahoma	37
2	Utah	63		44	Wyoming	36
33	Vermont	42		45	Rhode Island	33
25	Virginia	46		46	Idaho	32
25	Washington	46		46	South Carolina	32
36	West Virginia	41		48	Oregon	30
19	Wisconsin	48		49	Arkansas	23
44	Wyoming	36		49	Mississippi	23
					District of Columbia	59

Source: Morgan Quitno Press using data from U.S. Dept of Health & Human Services, Health Care Financing Admin. "State Health Expenditure Accounts" (Health Care Financing Review, Fall 1995, Volume 17, Number 1)
By state of provider. Includes eyeglasses, hearing aids, surgical appliances and supplies, bulk and cylinder oxygen and medical equipment rentals.

Expenditures for Nursing Home Care in 1993

National Total = $66,201,000,000*

ALPHA ORDER

ALPHA ORDER

RANK ORDER

RANK	STATE	EXPENDITURES	% of USA		RANK	STATE	EXPENDITURES	% of USA
27	Alabama	$703,000,000	1.1%		1	New York	$9,106,000,000	13.8%
50	Alaska	56,000,000	0.1%		2	Pennsylvania	4,153,000,000	6.3%
31	Arizona	567,000,000	0.9%		3	California	4,103,000,000	6.2%
32	Arkansas	558,000,000	0.8%		4	Ohio	3,758,000,000	5.7%
3	California	4,103,000,000	6.2%		5	Illinois	3,148,000,000	4.8%
28	Colorado	661,000,000	1.0%		6	Texas	3,104,000,000	4.7%
14	Connecticut	1,749,000,000	2.6%		7	Florida	3,089,000,000	4.7%
41	Delaware	217,000,000	0.3%		8	Massachusetts	2,737,000,000	4.1%
7	Florida	3,089,000,000	4.7%		9	New Jersey	2,128,000,000	3.2%
21	Georgia	1,038,000,000	1.6%		10	Indiana	2,018,000,000	3.1%
45	Hawaii	181,000,000	0.3%		11	Minnesota	1,884,000,000	2.9%
44	Idaho	197,000,000	0.3%		12	Michigan	1,849,000,000	2.8%
5	Illinois	3,148,000,000	4.8%		13	Wisconsin	1,752,000,000	2.7%
10	Indiana	2,018,000,000	3.1%		14	Connecticut	1,749,000,000	2.6%
23	Iowa	927,000,000	1.4%		15	North Carolina	1,562,000,000	2.4%
26	Kansas	721,000,000	1.1%		16	Missouri	1,368,000,000	2.1%
24	Kentucky	850,000,000	1.3%		17	Washington	1,291,000,000	2.0%
18	Louisiana	1,186,000,000	1.8%		18	Louisiana	1,186,000,000	1.8%
36	Maine	453,000,000	0.7%		19	Maryland	1,185,000,000	1.8%
19	Maryland	1,185,000,000	1.8%		20	Tennessee	1,085,000,000	1.6%
8	Massachusetts	2,737,000,000	4.1%		21	Georgia	1,038,000,000	1.6%
12	Michigan	1,849,000,000	2.8%		22	Virginia	976,000,000	1.5%
11	Minnesota	1,884,000,000	2.9%		23	Iowa	927,000,000	1.4%
35	Mississippi	460,000,000	0.7%		24	Kentucky	850,000,000	1.3%
16	Missouri	1,368,000,000	2.1%		25	Oklahoma	748,000,000	1.1%
46	Montana	178,000,000	0.3%		26	Kansas	721,000,000	1.1%
34	Nebraska	482,000,000	0.7%		27	Alabama	703,000,000	1.1%
47	Nevada	164,000,000	0.3%		28	Colorado	661,000,000	1.0%
38	New Hampshire	268,000,000	0.4%		29	Oregon	656,000,000	1.0%
9	New Jersey	2,128,000,000	3.2%		30	South Carolina	638,000,000	1.0%
43	New Mexico	215,000,000	0.3%		31	Arizona	567,000,000	0.9%
1	New York	9,106,000,000	13.8%		32	Arkansas	558,000,000	0.8%
15	North Carolina	1,562,000,000	2.4%		33	Rhode Island	485,000,000	0.7%
40	North Dakota	246,000,000	0.4%		34	Nebraska	482,000,000	0.7%
4	Ohio	3,758,000,000	5.7%		35	Mississippi	460,000,000	0.7%
25	Oklahoma	748,000,000	1.1%		36	Maine	453,000,000	0.7%
29	Oregon	656,000,000	1.0%		37	West Virginia	365,000,000	0.6%
2	Pennsylvania	4,153,000,000	6.3%		38	New Hampshire	268,000,000	0.4%
33	Rhode Island	485,000,000	0.7%		39	Utah	260,000,000	0.4%
30	South Carolina	638,000,000	1.0%		40	North Dakota	246,000,000	0.4%
42	South Dakota	216,000,000	0.3%		41	Delaware	217,000,000	0.3%
20	Tennessee	1,085,000,000	1.6%		42	South Dakota	216,000,000	0.3%
6	Texas	3,104,000,000	4.7%		43	New Mexico	215,000,000	0.3%
39	Utah	260,000,000	0.4%		44	Idaho	197,000,000	0.3%
48	Vermont	148,000,000	0.2%		45	Hawaii	181,000,000	0.3%
22	Virginia	976,000,000	1.5%		46	Montana	178,000,000	0.3%
17	Washington	1,291,000,000	2.0%		47	Nevada	164,000,000	0.3%
37	West Virginia	365,000,000	0.6%		48	Vermont	148,000,000	0.2%
13	Wisconsin	1,752,000,000	2.7%		49	Wyoming	83,000,000	0.1%
49	Wyoming	83,000,000	0.1%		50	Alaska	56,000,000	0.1%
						District of Columbia	231,000,000	0.4%

Source: U.S. Department of Health and Human Services, Health Care Financing Administration
"State Health Expenditure Accounts" (Health Care Financing Review, Fall 1995, Volume 17, Number 1)
*By state of provider. Includes freestanding nursing and personal-care facilities. Includes Medicare- and Medicaid-certified skilled nursing and intermediate care facilities as well as facilities that are not certified. Excludes hospital-based facilities as they are counted in hospital care expenditures.

Percent of Total Personal Health Care Expenditures
Spent on Nursing Home Care in 1993
National Percent = 8.5%*

ALPHA ORDER				RANK ORDER		
RANK	STATE	PERCENT		RANK	STATE	PERCENT
43	Alabama	5.8		1	Connecticut	14.3
50	Alaska	3.6		2	Rhode Island	14.1
45	Arizona	5.3		3	New York	13.6
19	Arkansas	9.1		4	Minnesota	13.3
48	California	4.4		5	Maine	13.2
39	Colorado	6.6		6	Iowa	12.6
1	Connecticut	14.3		7	Indiana	12.3
17	Delaware	9.6		8	North Dakota	12.2
36	Florida	6.9		9	Wisconsin	12.1
46	Georgia	5.2		10	Massachusetts	11.7
46	Hawaii	5.2		11	Ohio	11.2
22	Idaho	8.7		12	South Dakota	11.1
19	Illinois	9.1		13	Nebraska	11.0
7	Indiana	12.3		14	Kansas	10.4
6	Iowa	12.6		15	Pennsylvania	10.0
14	Kansas	10.4		16	Vermont	9.9
29	Kentucky	8.2		17	Delaware	9.6
19	Louisiana	9.1		18	Oklahoma	9.3
5	Maine	13.2		19	Arkansas	9.1
31	Maryland	7.8		19	Illinois	9.1
10	Massachusetts	11.7		19	Louisiana	9.1
37	Michigan	6.8		22	Idaho	8.7
4	Minnesota	13.3		23	Missouri	8.6
33	Mississippi	7.4		23	North Carolina	8.6
23	Missouri	8.6		25	Montana	8.5
25	Montana	8.5		25	Washington	8.5
13	Nebraska	11.0		27	New Jersey	8.3
48	Nevada	4.4		27	Wyoming	8.3
31	New Hampshire	7.8		29	Kentucky	8.2
27	New Jersey	8.3		29	Oregon	8.2
44	New Mexico	5.5		31	Maryland	7.8
3	New York	13.6		31	New Hampshire	7.8
23	North Carolina	8.6		33	Mississippi	7.4
8	North Dakota	12.2		34	South Carolina	7.1
11	Ohio	11.2		35	West Virginia	7.0
18	Oklahoma	9.3		36	Florida	6.9
29	Oregon	8.2		37	Michigan	6.8
15	Pennsylvania	10.0		38	Tennessee	6.7
2	Rhode Island	14.1		39	Colorado	6.6
34	South Carolina	7.1		40	Utah	6.3
12	South Dakota	11.1		41	Texas	6.2
38	Tennessee	6.7		42	Virginia	5.9
41	Texas	6.2		43	Alabama	5.8
40	Utah	6.3		44	New Mexico	5.5
16	Vermont	9.9		45	Arizona	5.3
42	Virginia	5.9		46	Georgia	5.2
25	Washington	8.5		46	Hawaii	5.2
35	West Virginia	7.0		48	California	4.4
9	Wisconsin	12.1		48	Nevada	4.4
27	Wyoming	8.3		50	Alaska	3.6
				District of Columbia		5.4

Source: Morgan Quitno Press using data from U.S. Dept of Health & Human Services, Health Care Financing Admin. "State Health Expenditure Accounts" (Health Care Financing Review, Fall 1995, Volume 17, Number 1)
By state of provider. Includes freestanding nursing and personal-care facilities. Includes Medicare- and Medicaid-certified skilled nursing and intermediate care facilities as well as facilities that are not certified. Excludes hospital-based facilities as they are counted in hospital care expenditures.

Per Capita Expenditures for Nursing Home Care in 1993

National Per Capita = $257*

ALPHA ORDER				RANK ORDER		
RANK	STATE	PER CAPITA		RANK	STATE	PER CAPITA
41	Alabama	$168		1	Connecticut	$534
50	Alaska	94		2	New York	502
45	Arizona	144		3	Rhode Island	485
26	Arkansas	230		4	Massachusetts	455
48	California	131		5	Minnesota	416
35	Colorado	185		6	North Dakota	386
1	Connecticut	534		7	Maine	366
13	Delaware	310		8	Indiana	354
27	Florida	225		9	Wisconsin	347
44	Georgia	150		10	Pennsylvania	345
42	Hawaii	155		11	Ohio	340
36	Idaho	179		12	Iowa	328
19	Illinois	269		13	Delaware	310
8	Indiana	354		14	South Dakota	301
12	Iowa	328		15	Nebraska	299
16	Kansas	285		16	Kansas	285
29	Kentucky	224		17	Louisiana	277
17	Louisiana	277		18	New Jersey	271
7	Maine	366		19	Illinois	269
23	Maryland	239		20	Missouri	261
4	Massachusetts	455		21	Vermont	257
34	Michigan	196		22	Washington	246
5	Minnesota	416		23	Maryland	239
39	Mississippi	174		23	New Hampshire	239
20	Missouri	261		25	Oklahoma	231
32	Montana	212		26	Arkansas	230
15	Nebraska	299		27	Florida	225
49	Nevada	118		27	North Carolina	225
23	New Hampshire	239		29	Kentucky	224
18	New Jersey	271		30	Oregon	216
47	New Mexico	133		31	Tennessee	213
2	New York	502		32	Montana	212
27	North Carolina	225		33	West Virginia	201
6	North Dakota	386		34	Michigan	196
11	Ohio	340		35	Colorado	185
25	Oklahoma	231		36	Idaho	179
30	Oregon	216		37	Wyoming	177
10	Pennsylvania	345		38	South Carolina	176
3	Rhode Island	485		39	Mississippi	174
38	South Carolina	176		40	Texas	172
14	South Dakota	301		41	Alabama	168
31	Tennessee	213		42	Hawaii	155
40	Texas	172		43	Virginia	151
46	Utah	140		44	Georgia	150
21	Vermont	257		45	Arizona	144
43	Virginia	151		46	Utah	140
22	Washington	246		47	New Mexico	133
33	West Virginia	201		48	California	131
9	Wisconsin	347		49	Nevada	118
37	Wyoming	177		50	Alaska	94
					District of Columbia	400

Source: Morgan Quitno Press using data from U.S. Dept of Health & Human Services, Health Care Financing Admin. "State Health Expenditure Accounts" (Health Care Financing Review, Fall 1995, Volume 17, Number 1)
*By state of provider. Includes freestanding nursing and personal-care facilities. Includes Medicare- and Medicaid-certified skilled nursing and intermediate care facilities as well as facilities that are not certified. Excludes hospital-based facilities as they are counted in hospital care expenditures.

Persons Not Covered by Health Insurance in 1998

National Total = 44,050,000 Uninsured

ALPHA ORDER					RANK ORDER			
RANK	STATE	UNINSURED	% of USA		RANK	STATE	UNINSURED	% of USA
17	Alabama	740,000	1.7%		1	California	7,223,000	16.4%
45	Alaska	106,000	0.2%		2	Texas	4,830,000	11.0%
12	Arizona	1,129,000	2.6%		3	New York	3,142,000	7.1%
28	Arkansas	475,000	1.1%		4	Florida	2,609,000	5.9%
1	California	7,223,000	16.4%		5	Illinois	1,810,000	4.1%
23	Colorado	599,000	1.4%		6	Georgia	1,336,000	3.0%
31	Connecticut	412,000	0.9%		7	New Jersey	1,328,000	3.0%
44	Delaware	109,000	0.2%		8	Michigan	1,296,000	2.9%
4	Florida	2,609,000	5.9%		9	Pennsylvania	1,260,000	2.9%
6	Georgia	1,336,000	3.0%		10	Ohio	1,169,000	2.7%
43	Hawaii	119,000	0.3%		11	North Carolina	1,132,000	2.6%
38	Idaho	218,000	0.5%		12	Arizona	1,129,000	2.6%
5	Illinois	1,810,000	4.1%		13	Virginia	957,000	2.2%
15	Indiana	851,000	1.9%		14	Maryland	852,000	1.9%
37	Iowa	266,000	0.6%		15	Indiana	851,000	1.9%
36	Kansas	272,000	0.6%		16	Louisiana	829,000	1.9%
26	Kentucky	555,000	1.3%		17	Alabama	740,000	1.7%
16	Louisiana	829,000	1.9%		18	Tennessee	706,000	1.6%
40	Maine	158,000	0.4%		19	Washington	700,000	1.6%
14	Maryland	852,000	1.9%		20	Massachusetts	633,000	1.4%
20	Massachusetts	633,000	1.4%		21	Wisconsin	616,000	1.4%
8	Michigan	1,296,000	2.9%		22	Oklahoma	611,000	1.4%
30	Minnesota	440,000	1.0%		23	Colorado	599,000	1.4%
27	Mississippi	550,000	1.2%		24	South Carolina	591,000	1.3%
25	Missouri	571,000	1.3%		25	Missouri	571,000	1.3%
39	Montana	172,000	0.4%		26	Kentucky	555,000	1.3%
41	Nebraska	149,000	0.3%		27	Mississippi	550,000	1.2%
32	Nevada	370,000	0.8%		28	Arkansas	475,000	1.1%
42	New Hampshire	134,000	0.3%		29	Oregon	469,000	1.1%
7	New Jersey	1,328,000	3.0%		30	Minnesota	440,000	1.0%
33	New Mexico	366,000	0.8%		31	Connecticut	412,000	0.9%
3	New York	3,142,000	7.1%		32	Nevada	370,000	0.8%
11	North Carolina	1,132,000	2.6%		33	New Mexico	366,000	0.8%
48	North Dakota	91,000	0.2%		34	West Virginia	312,000	0.7%
10	Ohio	1,169,000	2.7%		35	Utah	292,000	0.7%
22	Oklahoma	611,000	1.4%		36	Kansas	272,000	0.6%
29	Oregon	469,000	1.1%		37	Iowa	266,000	0.6%
9	Pennsylvania	1,260,000	2.9%		38	Idaho	218,000	0.5%
47	Rhode Island	99,000	0.2%		39	Montana	172,000	0.4%
24	South Carolina	591,000	1.3%		40	Maine	158,000	0.4%
46	South Dakota	105,000	0.2%		41	Nebraska	149,000	0.3%
18	Tennessee	706,000	1.6%		42	New Hampshire	134,000	0.3%
2	Texas	4,830,000	11.0%		43	Hawaii	119,000	0.3%
35	Utah	292,000	0.7%		44	Delaware	109,000	0.2%
50	Vermont	58,000	0.1%		45	Alaska	106,000	0.2%
13	Virginia	957,000	2.2%		46	South Dakota	105,000	0.2%
19	Washington	700,000	1.6%		47	Rhode Island	99,000	0.2%
34	West Virginia	312,000	0.7%		48	North Dakota	91,000	0.2%
21	Wisconsin	616,000	1.4%		49	Wyoming	81,000	0.2%
49	Wyoming	81,000	0.2%		50	Vermont	58,000	0.1%
						District of Columbia	89,000	0.2%

Source: Morgan Quitno Press using data from U.S. Bureau of the Census
"Health Insurance Historical Table 4" (http://www.census.gov/hhes/hlthins/historic/hihistt4.html)

Percent of Population Not Covered by Health Insurance in 1998

National Percent = 16.3% Not Covered by Health Insurance

ALPHA ORDER

RANK	STATE	PERCENT
17	Alabama	17.0
14	Alaska	17.3
2	Arizona	24.2
9	Arkansas	18.7
3	California	22.1
22	Colorado	15.1
36	Connecticut	12.6
25	Delaware	14.7
12	Florida	17.5
12	Georgia	17.5
45	Hawaii	10.0
11	Idaho	17.7
23	Illinois	15.0
26	Indiana	14.4
48	Iowa	9.3
43	Kansas	10.3
30	Kentucky	14.1
8	Louisiana	19.0
35	Maine	12.7
19	Maryland	16.6
43	Massachusetts	10.3
33	Michigan	13.2
48	Minnesota	9.3
6	Mississippi	20.0
40	Missouri	10.5
7	Montana	19.6
50	Nebraska	9.0
4	Nevada	21.2
39	New Hampshire	11.3
20	New Jersey	16.4
5	New Mexico	21.1
14	New York	17.3
23	North Carolina	15.0
29	North Dakota	14.2
42	Ohio	10.4
10	Oklahoma	18.3
27	Oregon	14.3
40	Pennsylvania	10.5
45	Rhode Island	10.0
21	South Carolina	15.4
27	South Dakota	14.3
34	Tennessee	13.0
1	Texas	24.5
32	Utah	13.9
47	Vermont	9.9
30	Virginia	14.1
37	Washington	12.3
16	West Virginia	17.2
38	Wisconsin	11.8
18	Wyoming	16.9

RANK ORDER

RANK	STATE	PERCENT
1	Texas	24.5
2	Arizona	24.2
3	California	22.1
4	Nevada	21.2
5	New Mexico	21.1
6	Mississippi	20.0
7	Montana	19.6
8	Louisiana	19.0
9	Arkansas	18.7
10	Oklahoma	18.3
11	Idaho	17.7
12	Florida	17.5
12	Georgia	17.5
14	Alaska	17.3
14	New York	17.3
16	West Virginia	17.2
17	Alabama	17.0
18	Wyoming	16.9
19	Maryland	16.6
20	New Jersey	16.4
21	South Carolina	15.4
22	Colorado	15.1
23	Illinois	15.0
23	North Carolina	15.0
25	Delaware	14.7
26	Indiana	14.4
27	Oregon	14.3
27	South Dakota	14.3
29	North Dakota	14.2
30	Kentucky	14.1
30	Virginia	14.1
32	Utah	13.9
33	Michigan	13.2
34	Tennessee	13.0
35	Maine	12.7
36	Connecticut	12.6
37	Washington	12.3
38	Wisconsin	11.8
39	New Hampshire	11.3
40	Missouri	10.5
40	Pennsylvania	10.5
42	Ohio	10.4
43	Kansas	10.3
43	Massachusetts	10.3
45	Hawaii	10.0
45	Rhode Island	10.0
47	Vermont	9.9
48	Iowa	9.3
48	Minnesota	9.3
50	Nebraska	9.0
	District of Columbia	17.0

Source: Morgan Quitno Press using data from U.S. Bureau of the Census
"Health Insurance Historical Table 4" (http://www.census.gov/hhes/hlthins/historic/hihistt4.html)

Persons Covered by Health Insurance in 1998

National Total = 226,198,000 Insured

ALPHA ORDER

RANK	STATE	INSURED	% of USA
21	Alabama	3,611,000	1.6%
49	Alaska	509,000	0.2%
22	Arizona	3,538,000	1.6%
33	Arkansas	2,064,000	0.9%
1	California	25,460,000	11.3%
25	Colorado	3,370,000	1.5%
27	Connecticut	2,860,000	1.3%
45	Delaware	635,000	0.3%
4	Florida	12,299,000	5.4%
11	Georgia	6,300,000	2.8%
40	Hawaii	1,071,000	0.5%
42	Idaho	1,013,000	0.4%
6	Illinois	10,259,000	4.5%
14	Indiana	5,057,000	2.2%
30	Iowa	2,595,000	1.1%
31	Kansas	2,367,000	1.0%
24	Kentucky	3,380,000	1.5%
23	Louisiana	3,534,000	1.6%
39	Maine	1,089,000	0.5%
20	Maryland	4,278,000	1.9%
13	Massachusetts	5,512,000	2.4%
8	Michigan	8,524,000	3.8%
19	Minnesota	4,287,000	1.9%
32	Mississippi	2,201,000	1.0%
16	Missouri	4,867,000	2.2%
44	Montana	707,000	0.3%
35	Nebraska	1,511,000	0.7%
37	Nevada	1,374,000	0.6%
41	New Hampshire	1,052,000	0.5%
9	New Jersey	6,768,000	3.0%
38	New Mexico	1,368,000	0.6%
2	New York	15,018,000	6.6%
10	North Carolina	6,414,000	2.8%
47	North Dakota	547,000	0.2%
7	Ohio	10,069,000	4.5%
29	Oklahoma	2,728,000	1.2%
28	Oregon	2,813,000	1.2%
5	Pennsylvania	10,742,000	4.7%
43	Rhode Island	889,000	0.4%
26	South Carolina	3,248,000	1.4%
46	South Dakota	626,000	0.3%
17	Tennessee	4,726,000	2.1%
3	Texas	14,883,000	6.6%
34	Utah	1,809,000	0.8%
48	Vermont	532,000	0.2%
12	Virginia	5,832,000	2.6%
15	Washington	4,988,000	2.2%
36	West Virginia	1,500,000	0.7%
18	Wisconsin	4,606,000	2.0%
50	Wyoming	399,000	0.2%

RANK ORDER

RANK	STATE	INSURED	% of USA
1	California	25,460,000	11.3%
2	New York	15,018,000	6.6%
3	Texas	14,883,000	6.6%
4	Florida	12,299,000	5.4%
5	Pennsylvania	10,742,000	4.7%
6	Illinois	10,259,000	4.5%
7	Ohio	10,069,000	4.5%
8	Michigan	8,524,000	3.8%
9	New Jersey	6,768,000	3.0%
10	North Carolina	6,414,000	2.8%
11	Georgia	6,300,000	2.8%
12	Virginia	5,832,000	2.6%
13	Massachusetts	5,512,000	2.4%
14	Indiana	5,057,000	2.2%
15	Washington	4,988,000	2.2%
16	Missouri	4,867,000	2.2%
17	Tennessee	4,726,000	2.1%
18	Wisconsin	4,606,000	2.0%
19	Minnesota	4,287,000	1.9%
20	Maryland	4,278,000	1.9%
21	Alabama	3,611,000	1.6%
22	Arizona	3,538,000	1.6%
23	Louisiana	3,534,000	1.6%
24	Kentucky	3,380,000	1.5%
25	Colorado	3,370,000	1.5%
26	South Carolina	3,248,000	1.4%
27	Connecticut	2,860,000	1.3%
28	Oregon	2,813,000	1.2%
29	Oklahoma	2,728,000	1.2%
30	Iowa	2,595,000	1.1%
31	Kansas	2,367,000	1.0%
32	Mississippi	2,201,000	1.0%
33	Arkansas	2,064,000	0.9%
34	Utah	1,809,000	0.8%
35	Nebraska	1,511,000	0.7%
36	West Virginia	1,500,000	0.7%
37	Nevada	1,374,000	0.6%
38	New Mexico	1,368,000	0.6%
39	Maine	1,089,000	0.5%
40	Hawaii	1,071,000	0.5%
41	New Hampshire	1,052,000	0.5%
42	Idaho	1,013,000	0.4%
43	Rhode Island	889,000	0.4%
44	Montana	707,000	0.3%
45	Delaware	635,000	0.3%
46	South Dakota	626,000	0.3%
47	North Dakota	547,000	0.2%
48	Vermont	532,000	0.2%
49	Alaska	509,000	0.2%
50	Wyoming	399,000	0.2%
	District of Columbia	433,000	0.2%

Source: Morgan Quitno Press using data from U.S. Bureau of the Census
"Health Insurance Historical Table 4" (http://www.census.gov/hhes/hlthins/historic/hihistt4.html)

Percent of Population Covered by Health Insurance in 1998

National Percent = 83.7% of Population Covered by Health Insurance

ALPHA ORDER

RANK	STATE	PERCENT
34	Alabama	83.0
36	Alaska	82.7
49	Arizona	75.8
42	Arkansas	81.3
48	California	77.9
29	Colorado	84.9
15	Connecticut	87.4
26	Delaware	85.3
38	Florida	82.5
38	Georgia	82.5
5	Hawaii	90.0
40	Idaho	82.3
27	Illinois	85.0
25	Indiana	85.6
2	Iowa	90.7
7	Kansas	89.7
20	Kentucky	85.9
43	Louisiana	81.0
16	Maine	87.3
32	Maryland	83.4
7	Massachusetts	89.7
18	Michigan	86.8
2	Minnesota	90.7
45	Mississippi	80.0
10	Missouri	89.5
44	Montana	80.4
1	Nebraska	91.0
47	Nevada	78.8
12	New Hampshire	88.7
31	New Jersey	83.6
46	New Mexico	78.9
36	New York	82.7
27	North Carolina	85.0
22	North Dakota	85.8
9	Ohio	89.6
41	Oklahoma	81.7
23	Oregon	85.7
10	Pennsylvania	89.5
5	Rhode Island	90.0
30	South Carolina	84.6
23	South Dakota	85.7
17	Tennessee	87.0
50	Texas	75.5
19	Utah	86.1
4	Vermont	90.1
20	Virginia	85.9
14	Washington	87.7
35	West Virginia	82.8
13	Wisconsin	88.2
33	Wyoming	83.1

RANK ORDER

RANK	STATE	PERCENT
1	Nebraska	91.0
2	Iowa	90.7
2	Minnesota	90.7
4	Vermont	90.1
5	Hawaii	90.0
5	Rhode Island	90.0
7	Kansas	89.7
7	Massachusetts	89.7
9	Ohio	89.6
10	Missouri	89.5
10	Pennsylvania	89.5
12	New Hampshire	88.7
13	Wisconsin	88.2
14	Washington	87.7
15	Connecticut	87.4
16	Maine	87.3
17	Tennessee	87.0
18	Michigan	86.8
19	Utah	86.1
20	Kentucky	85.9
20	Virginia	85.9
22	North Dakota	85.8
23	Oregon	85.7
23	South Dakota	85.7
25	Indiana	85.6
26	Delaware	85.3
27	Illinois	85.0
27	North Carolina	85.0
29	Colorado	84.9
30	South Carolina	84.6
31	New Jersey	83.6
32	Maryland	83.4
33	Wyoming	83.1
34	Alabama	83.0
35	West Virginia	82.8
36	Alaska	82.7
36	New York	82.7
38	Florida	82.5
38	Georgia	82.5
40	Idaho	82.3
41	Oklahoma	81.7
42	Arkansas	81.3
43	Louisiana	81.0
44	Montana	80.4
45	Mississippi	80.0
46	New Mexico	78.9
47	Nevada	78.8
48	California	77.9
49	Arizona	75.8
50	Texas	75.5
	District of Columbia	83.0

Source: Morgan Quitno Press using data from U.S. Bureau of the Census
"Health Insurance Historical Table 4" (http://www.census.gov/hhes/hlthins/historic/hihistt4.html)

Persons Not Covered by Health Insurance in 1994

National Total = 39,570,000 Uninsured

RANK	STATE	UNINSURED	% of USA
14	Alabama	813,000	2.1%
46	Alaska	80,000	0.2%
12	Arizona	838,000	2.1%
29	Arkansas	426,000	1.1%
1	California	6,608,000	16.7%
27	Colorado	453,000	1.1%
32	Connecticut	340,000	0.9%
45	Delaware	96,000	0.2%
4	Florida	2,401,000	6.1%
8	Georgia	1,141,000	2.9%
44	Hawaii	108,000	0.3%
40	Idaho	159,000	0.4%
5	Illinois	1,346,000	3.4%
20	Indiana	603,000	1.5%
35	Iowa	272,000	0.7%
33	Kansas	331,000	0.8%
21	Kentucky	581,000	1.5%
13	Louisiana	827,000	2.1%
39	Maine	162,000	0.4%
19	Maryland	628,000	1.6%
16	Massachusetts	754,000	1.9%
9	Michigan	1,035,000	2.6%
28	Minnesota	434,000	1.1%
25	Mississippi	474,000	1.2%
18	Missouri	644,000	1.6%
42	Montana	116,000	0.3%
38	Nebraska	174,000	0.4%
36	Nevada	229,000	0.6%
41	New Hampshire	135,000	0.3%
10	New Jersey	1,029,000	2.6%
31	New Mexico	382,000	1.0%
3	New York	2,905,000	7.3%
11	North Carolina	939,000	2.4%
49	North Dakota	54,000	0.1%
7	Ohio	1,222,000	3.1%
22	Oklahoma	578,000	1.5%
30	Oregon	404,000	1.0%
6	Pennsylvania	1,277,000	3.2%
43	Rhode Island	114,000	0.3%
24	South Carolina	521,000	1.3%
48	South Dakota	72,000	0.2%
23	Tennessee	527,000	1.3%
2	Texas	4,438,000	11.2%
37	Utah	222,000	0.6%
50	Vermont	50,000	0.1%
15	Virginia	784,000	2.0%
17	Washington	678,000	1.7%
34	West Virginia	295,000	0.7%
26	Wisconsin	454,000	1.1%
47	Wyoming	73,000	0.2%

RANK	STATE	UNINSURED	% of USA
1	California	6,608,000	16.7%
2	Texas	4,438,000	11.2%
3	New York	2,905,000	7.3%
4	Florida	2,401,000	6.1%
5	Illinois	1,346,000	3.4%
6	Pennsylvania	1,277,000	3.2%
7	Ohio	1,222,000	3.1%
8	Georgia	1,141,000	2.9%
9	Michigan	1,035,000	2.6%
10	New Jersey	1,029,000	2.6%
11	North Carolina	939,000	2.4%
12	Arizona	838,000	2.1%
13	Louisiana	827,000	2.1%
14	Alabama	813,000	2.1%
15	Virginia	784,000	2.0%
16	Massachusetts	754,000	1.9%
17	Washington	678,000	1.7%
18	Missouri	644,000	1.6%
19	Maryland	628,000	1.6%
20	Indiana	603,000	1.5%
21	Kentucky	581,000	1.5%
22	Oklahoma	578,000	1.5%
23	Tennessee	527,000	1.3%
24	South Carolina	521,000	1.3%
25	Mississippi	474,000	1.2%
26	Wisconsin	454,000	1.1%
27	Colorado	453,000	1.1%
28	Minnesota	434,000	1.1%
29	Arkansas	426,000	1.1%
30	Oregon	404,000	1.0%
31	New Mexico	382,000	1.0%
32	Connecticut	340,000	0.9%
33	Kansas	331,000	0.8%
34	West Virginia	295,000	0.7%
35	Iowa	272,000	0.7%
36	Nevada	229,000	0.6%
37	Utah	222,000	0.6%
38	Nebraska	174,000	0.4%
39	Maine	162,000	0.4%
40	Idaho	159,000	0.4%
41	New Hampshire	135,000	0.3%
42	Montana	116,000	0.3%
43	Rhode Island	114,000	0.3%
44	Hawaii	108,000	0.3%
45	Delaware	96,000	0.2%
46	Alaska	80,000	0.2%
47	Wyoming	73,000	0.2%
48	South Dakota	72,000	0.2%
49	North Dakota	54,000	0.1%
50	Vermont	50,000	0.1%
	District of Columbia	93,000	0.2%

Source: Morgan Quitno Press using data from U.S. Bureau of the Census
"Health Insurance Historical Table 4" (http://www.census.gov/hhes/hlthins/historic/hihistt4.html)

Percent of Population Not Covered by Health Insurance in 1994

National Percent = 15.2% Not Covered by Health Insurance

ALPHA ORDER

RANK	STATE	PERCENT
5	Alabama	19.2
21	Alaska	13.3
4	Arizona	20.2
9	Arkansas	17.4
3	California	21.1
30	Colorado	12.4
42	Connecticut	10.4
20	Delaware	13.5
10	Florida	17.2
11	Georgia	16.2
47	Hawaii	9.2
18	Idaho	14.0
36	Illinois	11.4
41	Indiana	10.5
45	Iowa	9.6
26	Kansas	12.9
16	Kentucky	15.2
5	Louisiana	19.2
23	Maine	13.1
28	Maryland	12.6
29	Massachusetts	12.5
38	Michigan	10.8
46	Minnesota	9.5
7	Mississippi	17.8
31	Missouri	12.2
19	Montana	13.6
39	Nebraska	10.7
14	Nevada	15.7
33	New Hampshire	11.9
25	New Jersey	13.0
2	New Mexico	23.1
13	New York	16.0
21	North Carolina	13.3
50	North Dakota	8.4
37	Ohio	11.0
7	Oklahoma	17.8
23	Oregon	13.1
40	Pennsylvania	10.6
34	Rhode Island	11.5
17	South Carolina	14.2
44	South Dakota	10.0
43	Tennessee	10.2
1	Texas	24.2
34	Utah	11.5
49	Vermont	8.6
32	Virginia	12.0
27	Washington	12.7
11	West Virginia	16.2
48	Wisconsin	8.9
15	Wyoming	15.4

RANK ORDER

RANK	STATE	PERCENT
1	Texas	24.2
2	New Mexico	23.1
3	California	21.1
4	Arizona	20.2
5	Alabama	19.2
5	Louisiana	19.2
7	Mississippi	17.8
7	Oklahoma	17.8
9	Arkansas	17.4
10	Florida	17.2
11	Georgia	16.2
11	West Virginia	16.2
13	New York	16.0
14	Nevada	15.7
15	Wyoming	15.4
16	Kentucky	15.2
17	South Carolina	14.2
18	Idaho	14.0
19	Montana	13.6
20	Delaware	13.5
21	Alaska	13.3
21	North Carolina	13.3
23	Maine	13.1
23	Oregon	13.1
25	New Jersey	13.0
26	Kansas	12.9
27	Washington	12.7
28	Maryland	12.6
29	Massachusetts	12.5
30	Colorado	12.4
31	Missouri	12.2
32	Virginia	12.0
33	New Hampshire	11.9
34	Rhode Island	11.5
34	Utah	11.5
36	Illinois	11.4
37	Ohio	11.0
38	Michigan	10.8
39	Nebraska	10.7
40	Pennsylvania	10.6
41	Indiana	10.5
42	Connecticut	10.4
43	Tennessee	10.2
44	South Dakota	10.0
45	Iowa	9.6
46	Minnesota	9.5
47	Hawaii	9.2
48	Wisconsin	8.9
49	Vermont	8.6
50	North Dakota	8.4

District of Columbia 16.4

Source: Morgan Quitno Press using data from U.S. Bureau of the Census
"Health Insurance Historical Table 4" (http://www.census.gov/hhes/hlthins/historic/hihistt4.html)

Change in Number of Persons Uninsured: 1994 to 1998

National Change = 4,480,000 Increase

RANK	STATE	CHANGE
48	Alabama	(73,000)
29	Alaska	26,000
5	Arizona	291,000
25	Arkansas	49,000
1	California	615,000
16	Colorado	146,000
19	Connecticut	72,000
32	Delaware	13,000
10	Florida	208,000
11	Georgia	195,000
33	Hawaii	11,000
23	Idaho	59,000
2	Illinois	464,000
7	Indiana	248,000
40	Iowa	(6,000)
47	Kansas	(59,000)
45	Kentucky	(26,000)
37	Louisiana	2,000
39	Maine	(4,000)
9	Maryland	224,000
50	Massachusetts	(121,000)
6	Michigan	261,000
36	Minnesota	6,000
18	Mississippi	76,000
48	Missouri	(73,000)
24	Montana	56,000
44	Nebraska	(25,000)
17	Nevada	141,000
38	New Hampshire	(1,000)
4	New Jersey	299,000
42	New Mexico	(16,000)
8	New York	237,000
12	North Carolina	193,000
26	North Dakota	37,000
46	Ohio	(53,000)
27	Oklahoma	33,000
22	Oregon	65,000
43	Pennsylvania	(17,000)
41	Rhode Island	(15,000)
20	South Carolina	70,000
27	South Dakota	33,000
13	Tennessee	179,000
3	Texas	392,000
20	Utah	70,000
34	Vermont	8,000
14	Virginia	173,000
30	Washington	22,000
31	West Virginia	17,000
15	Wisconsin	162,000
34	Wyoming	8,000

RANK	STATE	CHANGE
1	California	615,000
2	Illinois	464,000
3	Texas	392,000
4	New Jersey	299,000
5	Arizona	291,000
6	Michigan	261,000
7	Indiana	248,000
8	New York	237,000
9	Maryland	224,000
10	Florida	208,000
11	Georgia	195,000
12	North Carolina	193,000
13	Tennessee	179,000
14	Virginia	173,000
15	Wisconsin	162,000
16	Colorado	146,000
17	Nevada	141,000
18	Mississippi	76,000
19	Connecticut	72,000
20	South Carolina	70,000
20	Utah	70,000
22	Oregon	65,000
23	Idaho	59,000
24	Montana	56,000
25	Arkansas	49,000
26	North Dakota	37,000
27	Oklahoma	33,000
27	South Dakota	33,000
29	Alaska	26,000
30	Washington	22,000
31	West Virginia	17,000
32	Delaware	13,000
33	Hawaii	11,000
34	Vermont	8,000
34	Wyoming	8,000
36	Minnesota	6,000
37	Louisiana	2,000
38	New Hampshire	(1,000)
39	Maine	(4,000)
40	Iowa	(6,000)
41	Rhode Island	(15,000)
42	New Mexico	(16,000)
43	Pennsylvania	(17,000)
44	Nebraska	(25,000)
45	Kentucky	(26,000)
46	Ohio	(53,000)
47	Kansas	(59,000)
48	Alabama	(73,000)
48	Missouri	(73,000)
50	Massachusetts	(121,000)

| | District of Columbia | (4,000) |

Source: Morgan Quitno Press using data from U.S. Bureau of the Census
"Health Insurance Historical Table 4" (http://www.census.gov/hhes/hlthins/historic/hihistt4.html)
Table HI-4: "Health Insurance Coverage Status and Type of Coverage by State - 1987 to 1997"

Percent Change in Number of Uninsured: 1994 to 1998

National Percent Change = 11.3% Increase

ALPHA ORDER

RANK ORDER

RANK	STATE	PERCENT CHANGE	RANK	STATE	PERCENT CHANGE
45	Alabama	(9.0)	1	North Dakota	68.5
12	Alaska	32.5	2	Nevada	61.6
9	Arizona	34.7	3	Montana	48.3
26	Arkansas	11.5	4	South Dakota	45.8
29	California	9.3	5	Indiana	41.1
13	Colorado	32.2	6	Idaho	37.1
18	Connecticut	21.2	7	Maryland	35.7
24	Delaware	13.5	7	Wisconsin	35.7
31	Florida	8.7	9	Arizona	34.7
20	Georgia	17.1	10	Illinois	34.5
28	Hawaii	10.2	11	Tennessee	34.0
6	Idaho	37.1	12	Alaska	32.5
10	Illinois	34.5	13	Colorado	32.2
5	Indiana	41.1	14	Utah	31.5
40	Iowa	(2.2)	15	New Jersey	29.1
50	Kansas	(17.8)	16	Michigan	25.2
44	Kentucky	(4.5)	17	Virginia	22.1
37	Louisiana	0.2	18	Connecticut	21.2
41	Maine	(2.5)	19	North Carolina	20.6
7	Maryland	35.7	20	Georgia	17.1
49	Massachusetts	(16.0)	21	Oregon	16.1
16	Michigan	25.2	22	Mississippi	16.0
36	Minnesota	1.4	22	Vermont	16.0
22	Mississippi	16.0	24	Delaware	13.5
46	Missouri	(11.3)	25	South Carolina	13.4
3	Montana	48.3	26	Arkansas	11.5
48	Nebraska	(14.4)	27	Wyoming	11.0
2	Nevada	61.6	28	Hawaii	10.2
38	New Hampshire	(0.7)	29	California	9.3
15	New Jersey	29.1	30	Texas	8.8
42	New Mexico	(4.2)	31	Florida	8.7
32	New York	8.2	32	New York	8.2
19	North Carolina	20.6	33	West Virginia	5.8
1	North Dakota	68.5	34	Oklahoma	5.7
43	Ohio	(4.3)	35	Washington	3.2
34	Oklahoma	5.7	36	Minnesota	1.4
21	Oregon	16.1	37	Louisiana	0.2
39	Pennsylvania	(1.3)	38	New Hampshire	(0.7)
47	Rhode Island	(13.2)	39	Pennsylvania	(1.3)
25	South Carolina	13.4	40	Iowa	(2.2)
4	South Dakota	45.8	41	Maine	(2.5)
11	Tennessee	34.0	42	New Mexico	(4.2)
30	Texas	8.8	43	Ohio	(4.3)
14	Utah	31.5	44	Kentucky	(4.5)
22	Vermont	16.0	45	Alabama	(9.0)
17	Virginia	22.1	46	Missouri	(11.3)
35	Washington	3.2	47	Rhode Island	(13.2)
33	West Virginia	5.8	48	Nebraska	(14.4)
7	Wisconsin	35.7	49	Massachusetts	(16.0)
27	Wyoming	11.0	50	Kansas	(17.8)

District of Columbia (4.3)

Source: Morgan Quitno Press using data from U.S. Bureau of the Census
"Health Insurance Historical Table 4" (http://www.census.gov/hhes/hlthins/historic/hihistt4.html)
Table HI-4: "Health Insurance Coverage Status and Type of Coverage by State - 1987 to 1997"

Change in Percent of Population Uninsured: 1994 to 1998

National Percent Change = 7.2% Increase

RANK	STATE	PERCENT CHANGE
45	Alabama	(11.5)
9	Alaska	30.1
17	Arizona	19.8
29	Arkansas	7.5
31	California	4.7
14	Colorado	21.8
15	Connecticut	21.2
24	Delaware	8.9
33	Florida	1.7
28	Georgia	8.0
25	Hawaii	8.7
11	Idaho	26.4
8	Illinois	31.6
4	Indiana	37.1
38	Iowa	(3.1)
50	Kansas	(20.2)
43	Kentucky	(7.2)
36	Louisiana	(1.0)
38	Maine	(3.1)
7	Maryland	31.7
49	Massachusetts	(17.6)
13	Michigan	22.2
37	Minnesota	(2.1)
21	Mississippi	12.4
47	Missouri	(13.9)
2	Montana	44.1
48	Nebraska	(15.9)
5	Nevada	35.0
41	New Hampshire	(5.0)
12	New Jersey	26.2
44	New Mexico	(8.7)
27	New York	8.1
20	North Carolina	12.8
1	North Dakota	69.0
42	Ohio	(5.5)
32	Oklahoma	2.8
23	Oregon	9.2
35	Pennsylvania	(0.9)
46	Rhode Island	(13.0)
26	South Carolina	8.5
3	South Dakota	43.0
10	Tennessee	27.5
34	Texas	1.2
16	Utah	20.9
19	Vermont	15.1
18	Virginia	17.5
38	Washington	(3.1)
30	West Virginia	6.2
6	Wisconsin	32.6
22	Wyoming	9.7

RANK	STATE	PERCENT CHANGE
1	North Dakota	69.0
2	Montana	44.1
3	South Dakota	43.0
4	Indiana	37.1
5	Nevada	35.0
6	Wisconsin	32.6
7	Maryland	31.7
8	Illinois	31.6
9	Alaska	30.1
10	Tennessee	27.5
11	Idaho	26.4
12	New Jersey	26.2
13	Michigan	22.2
14	Colorado	21.8
15	Connecticut	21.2
16	Utah	20.9
17	Arizona	19.8
18	Virginia	17.5
19	Vermont	15.1
20	North Carolina	12.8
21	Mississippi	12.4
22	Wyoming	9.7
23	Oregon	9.2
24	Delaware	8.9
25	Hawaii	8.7
26	South Carolina	8.5
27	New York	8.1
28	Georgia	8.0
29	Arkansas	7.5
30	West Virginia	6.2
31	California	4.7
32	Oklahoma	2.8
33	Florida	1.7
34	Texas	1.2
35	Pennsylvania	(0.9)
36	Louisiana	(1.0)
37	Minnesota	(2.1)
38	Iowa	(3.1)
38	Maine	(3.1)
38	Washington	(3.1)
41	New Hampshire	(5.0)
42	Ohio	(5.5)
43	Kentucky	(7.2)
44	New Mexico	(8.7)
45	Alabama	(11.5)
46	Rhode Island	(13.0)
47	Missouri	(13.9)
48	Nebraska	(15.9)
49	Massachusetts	(17.6)
50	Kansas	(20.2)

| | District of Columbia | 3.7 |

Source: Morgan Quitno Press using data from U.S. Bureau of the Census
"Health Insurance Historical Table 4" (http://www.census.gov/hhes/hlthins/historic/hihistt4.html)

Percent of Population Covered by Private Health Insurance in 1998

National Percent = 70.2% of Population

RANK	STATE (ALPHA ORDER)	PERCENT		RANK	STATE (RANK ORDER)	PERCENT
31	Alabama	71.5		1	Iowa	83.0
47	Alaska	62.5		2	Minnesota	81.1
48	Arizona	62.3		3	Nebraska	79.7
38	Arkansas	67.7		4	Wisconsin	78.7
50	California	61.3		5	Kansas	78.5
14	Colorado	76.0		6	Indiana	78.2
20	Connecticut	74.8		7	Utah	77.8
28	Delaware	72.8		8	Ohio	77.5
40	Florida	66.6		9	Missouri	77.3
36	Georgia	68.0		10	Pennsylvania	77.2
22	Hawaii	74.6		11	New Hampshire	76.9
26	Idaho	73.5		12	South Dakota	76.6
21	Illinois	74.7		13	Rhode Island	76.3
6	Indiana	78.2		14	Colorado	76.0
1	Iowa	83.0		15	North Dakota	75.9
5	Kansas	78.5		16	Maryland	75.3
29	Kentucky	72.7		17	Maine	75.2
44	Louisiana	63.9		18	Vermont	75.0
17	Maine	75.2		19	Michigan	74.9
16	Maryland	75.3		20	Connecticut	74.8
27	Massachusetts	73.0		21	Illinois	74.7
19	Michigan	74.9		22	Hawaii	74.6
2	Minnesota	81.1		22	Washington	74.6
43	Mississippi	64.3		24	Virginia	74.3
9	Missouri	77.3		25	New Jersey	74.0
37	Montana	67.8		26	Idaho	73.5
3	Nebraska	79.7		27	Massachusetts	73.0
34	Nevada	70.2		28	Delaware	72.8
11	New Hampshire	76.9		29	Kentucky	72.7
25	New Jersey	74.0		30	Oregon	72.0
49	New Mexico	61.5		31	Alabama	71.5
42	New York	64.8		32	South Carolina	71.0
33	North Carolina	70.9		33	North Carolina	70.9
15	North Dakota	75.9		34	Nevada	70.2
8	Ohio	77.5		35	Wyoming	69.7
38	Oklahoma	67.7		36	Georgia	68.0
30	Oregon	72.0		37	Montana	67.8
10	Pennsylvania	77.2		38	Arkansas	67.7
13	Rhode Island	76.3		38	Oklahoma	67.7
32	South Carolina	71.0		40	Florida	66.6
12	South Dakota	76.6		41	Tennessee	66.2
41	Tennessee	66.2		42	New York	64.8
46	Texas	63.0		43	Mississippi	64.3
7	Utah	77.8		44	Louisiana	63.9
18	Vermont	75.0		44	West Virginia	63.9
24	Virginia	74.3		46	Texas	63.0
22	Washington	74.6		47	Alaska	62.5
44	West Virginia	63.9		48	Arizona	62.3
4	Wisconsin	78.7		49	New Mexico	61.5
35	Wyoming	69.7		50	California	61.3
					District of Columbia	61.7

Source: U.S. Bureau of the Census
"Health Insurance Historical Table 4" (http://www.census.gov/hhes/hlthins/historic/hihistt4.html)

Percent of Population Covered by Government Health Insurance in 1998

National Percent = 26.7% of Population*

ALPHA ORDER

RANK	STATE	PERCENT
29	Alabama	26.6
13	Alaska	30.3
33	Arizona	25.8
4	Arkansas	32.2
25	California	27.0
50	Colorado	18.5
37	Connecticut	23.9
27	Delaware	26.8
7	Florida	32.1
22	Georgia	28.2
3	Hawaii	33.0
38	Idaho	23.5
44	Illinois	22.1
46	Indiana	19.4
40	Iowa	23.2
21	Kansas	28.3
11	Kentucky	30.7
4	Louisiana	32.2
10	Maine	30.8
45	Maryland	21.8
16	Massachusetts	28.8
35	Michigan	24.9
42	Minnesota	22.8
14	Mississippi	30.0
31	Missouri	26.4
24	Montana	27.8
22	Nebraska	28.2
46	Nevada	19.4
39	New Hampshire	23.3
48	New Jersey	18.9
8	New Mexico	31.5
9	New York	31.0
18	North Carolina	28.6
25	North Dakota	27.0
32	Ohio	26.2
4	Oklahoma	32.2
16	Oregon	28.8
29	Pennsylvania	26.6
18	Rhode Island	28.6
15	South Carolina	29.3
36	South Dakota	24.7
2	Tennessee	34.3
41	Texas	22.9
49	Utah	18.6
12	Vermont	30.4
27	Virginia	26.8
20	Washington	28.4
1	West Virginia	38.4
42	Wisconsin	22.8
34	Wyoming	25.4

RANK ORDER

RANK	STATE	PERCENT
1	West Virginia	38.4
2	Tennessee	34.3
3	Hawaii	33.0
4	Arkansas	32.2
4	Louisiana	32.2
4	Oklahoma	32.2
7	Florida	32.1
8	New Mexico	31.5
9	New York	31.0
10	Maine	30.8
11	Kentucky	30.7
12	Vermont	30.4
13	Alaska	30.3
14	Mississippi	30.0
15	South Carolina	29.3
16	Massachusetts	28.8
16	Oregon	28.8
18	North Carolina	28.6
18	Rhode Island	28.6
20	Washington	28.4
21	Kansas	28.3
22	Georgia	28.2
22	Nebraska	28.2
24	Montana	27.8
25	California	27.0
25	North Dakota	27.0
27	Delaware	26.8
27	Virginia	26.8
29	Alabama	26.6
29	Pennsylvania	26.6
31	Missouri	26.4
32	Ohio	26.2
33	Arizona	25.8
34	Wyoming	25.4
35	Michigan	24.9
36	South Dakota	24.7
37	Connecticut	23.9
38	Idaho	23.5
39	New Hampshire	23.3
40	Iowa	23.2
41	Texas	22.9
42	Minnesota	22.8
42	Wisconsin	22.8
44	Illinois	22.1
45	Maryland	21.8
46	Indiana	19.4
46	Nevada	19.4
48	New Jersey	18.9
49	Utah	18.6
50	Colorado	18.5
	District of Columbia	39.3

Source: Morgan Quitno Press using data from U.S. Bureau of the Census
"Health Insurance Historical Table 4" (http://www.census.gov/hhes/hlthins/historic/hihistt4.html)
*Includes Medicaid, Medicare and Military health care.

Percent of Population Covered by Military Health Insurance in 1998

National Percent = 3.1% of Population*

ALPHA ORDER				RANK ORDER		
RANK	STATE	PERCENT		RANK	STATE	PERCENT
46	Alabama	1.2		1	Alaska	22.8
1	Alaska	22.8		2	Hawaii	11.7
9	Arizona	5.7		3	Oklahoma	11.3
17	Arkansas	4.5		4	Virginia	10.1
29	California	2.6		5	Nebraska	7.2
10	Colorado	5.5		6	North Dakota	6.8
33	Connecticut	2.3		7	Washington	6.7
27	Delaware	2.7		8	North Carolina	5.9
23	Florida	3.3		9	Arizona	5.7
21	Georgia	3.6		10	Colorado	5.5
2	Hawaii	11.7		11	Kentucky	5.1
39	Idaho	1.9		12	Kansas	5.0
42	Illinois	1.6		12	Louisiana	5.0
50	Indiana	0.5		14	Maine	4.9
38	Iowa	2.0		15	Montana	4.8
12	Kansas	5.0		16	South Carolina	4.7
11	Kentucky	5.1		17	Arkansas	4.5
12	Louisiana	5.0		18	Tennessee	4.0
14	Maine	4.9		18	West Virginia	4.0
25	Maryland	3.2		20	Vermont	3.7
36	Massachusetts	2.1		21	Georgia	3.6
49	Michigan	0.6		22	Missouri	3.5
31	Minnesota	2.5		23	Florida	3.3
31	Mississippi	2.5		23	Wyoming	3.3
22	Missouri	3.5		25	Maryland	3.2
15	Montana	4.8		25	Utah	3.2
5	Nebraska	7.2		27	Delaware	2.7
35	Nevada	2.2		27	New Hampshire	2.7
27	New Hampshire	2.7		29	California	2.6
43	New Jersey	1.5		29	Ohio	2.6
33	New Mexico	2.3		31	Minnesota	2.5
43	New York	1.5		31	Mississippi	2.5
8	North Carolina	5.9		33	Connecticut	2.3
6	North Dakota	6.8		33	New Mexico	2.3
29	Ohio	2.6		35	Nevada	2.2
3	Oklahoma	11.3		36	Massachusetts	2.1
36	Oregon	2.1		36	Oregon	2.1
43	Pennsylvania	1.5		38	Iowa	2.0
48	Rhode Island	1.0		39	Idaho	1.9
16	South Carolina	4.7		39	South Dakota	1.9
39	South Dakota	1.9		39	Texas	1.9
18	Tennessee	4.0		42	Illinois	1.6
39	Texas	1.9		43	New Jersey	1.5
25	Utah	3.2		43	New York	1.5
20	Vermont	3.7		43	Pennsylvania	1.5
4	Virginia	10.1		46	Alabama	1.2
7	Washington	6.7		46	Wisconsin	1.2
18	West Virginia	4.0		48	Rhode Island	1.0
46	Wisconsin	1.2		49	Michigan	0.6
23	Wyoming	3.3		50	Indiana	0.5
					District of Columbia	1.8

Source: Morgan Quitno Press using data from U.S. Bureau of the Census
"Health Insurance Historical Table 4" (http://www.census.gov/hhes/hlthins/historic/hihistt4.html)
*Includes CHAMPUS (Comprehensive Health and Medical Plan for Uniformed Services)/Tricare, Veterans and military health care.

Percent of Children Not Covered by Health Insurance in 1998

National Percent = 15.4% of Children*

ALPHA ORDER

RANK	STATE	PERCENT
12	Alabama	17.9
25	Alaska	13.7
1	Arizona	26.3
9	Arkansas	19.0
6	California	20.4
29	Colorado	12.5
35	Connecticut	10.1
13	Delaware	17.6
11	Florida	18.0
8	Georgia	19.1
40	Hawaii	9.5
13	Idaho	17.6
22	Illinois	14.6
20	Indiana	15.2
45	Iowa	8.7
46	Kansas	8.0
23	Kentucky	14.0
10	Louisiana	18.4
34	Maine	10.4
15	Maryland	17.5
46	Massachusetts	8.0
32	Michigan	10.7
36	Minnesota	10.0
5	Mississippi	21.2
44	Missouri	8.9
7	Montana	19.8
50	Nebraska	5.5
3	Nevada	23.1
38	New Hampshire	9.6
26	New Jersey	13.4
16	New Mexico	17.1
24	New York	13.8
27	North Carolina	13.2
17	North Dakota	16.4
42	Ohio	9.1
4	Oklahoma	22.5
30	Oregon	11.8
42	Pennsylvania	9.1
48	Rhode Island	7.6
21	South Carolina	14.8
19	South Dakota	15.3
32	Tennessee	10.7
2	Texas	25.4
31	Utah	11.5
49	Vermont	6.3
28	Virginia	12.9
41	Washington	9.4
38	West Virginia	9.6
37	Wisconsin	9.7
17	Wyoming	16.4

RANK ORDER

RANK	STATE	PERCENT
1	Arizona	26.3
2	Texas	25.4
3	Nevada	23.1
4	Oklahoma	22.5
5	Mississippi	21.2
6	California	20.4
7	Montana	19.8
8	Georgia	19.1
9	Arkansas	19.0
10	Louisiana	18.4
11	Florida	18.0
12	Alabama	17.9
13	Delaware	17.6
13	Idaho	17.6
15	Maryland	17.5
16	New Mexico	17.1
17	North Dakota	16.4
17	Wyoming	16.4
19	South Dakota	15.3
20	Indiana	15.2
21	South Carolina	14.8
22	Illinois	14.6
23	Kentucky	14.0
24	New York	13.8
25	Alaska	13.7
26	New Jersey	13.4
27	North Carolina	13.2
28	Virginia	12.9
29	Colorado	12.5
30	Oregon	11.8
31	Utah	11.5
32	Michigan	10.7
32	Tennessee	10.7
34	Maine	10.4
35	Connecticut	10.1
36	Minnesota	10.0
37	Wisconsin	9.7
38	New Hampshire	9.6
38	West Virginia	9.6
40	Hawaii	9.5
41	Washington	9.4
42	Ohio	9.1
42	Pennsylvania	9.1
44	Missouri	8.9
45	Iowa	8.7
46	Kansas	8.0
46	Massachusetts	8.0
48	Rhode Island	7.6
49	Vermont	6.3
50	Nebraska	5.5
	District of Columbia	17.9

Source: Morgan Quitno Press using data from U.S. Bureau of the Census
    "Health Insurance Historical Table 5" (http://www.census.gov/hhes/hlthins/historic/hihistt5.html)
*Children under 18 years old.

State Children's Health Insurance Program Enrollment in 1999

National Total = 1,959,330 Children*

ALPHA ORDER

RANK	STATE	CHILDREN	% of USA
15	Alabama	38,980	2.0%
35	Alaska	8,033	0.4%
18	Arizona	26,807	1.4%
45	Arkansas	913	0.0%
2	California	222,351	11.3%
20	Colorado	24,116	1.2%
30	Connecticut	9,912	0.5%
42	Delaware	2,433	0.1%
3	Florida	154,594	7.9%
11	Georgia	47,581	2.4%
48	Hawaii	0	0.0%
34	Idaho	8,482	0.4%
13	Illinois	42,699	2.2%
16	Indiana	31,246	1.6%
31	Iowa	9,795	0.5%
25	Kansas	14,443	0.7%
22	Kentucky	18,579	0.9%
21	Louisiana	21,580	1.1%
26	Maine	13,657	0.7%
23	Maryland	18,072	0.9%
7	Massachusetts	67,852	3.5%
19	Michigan	26,652	1.4%
47	Minnesota	21	0.0%
27	Mississippi	13,218	0.7%
10	Missouri	49,529	2.5%
44	Montana	1,019	0.1%
33	Nebraska	9,713	0.5%
37	Nevada	7,802	0.4%
39	New Hampshire	4,554	0.2%
6	New Jersey	75,652	3.9%
40	New Mexico	4,500	0.2%
1	New York	521,301	26.6%
8	North Carolina	57,300	2.9%
46	North Dakota	266	0.0%
4	Ohio	83,688	4.3%
14	Oklahoma	40,196	2.1%
17	Oregon	27,285	1.4%
5	Pennsylvania	81,758	4.2%
38	Rhode Island	7,288	0.4%
12	South Carolina	45,737	2.3%
41	South Dakota	3,191	0.2%
32	Tennessee	9,732	0.5%
9	Texas	50,878	2.6%
28	Utah	13,040	0.7%
43	Vermont	2,055	0.1%
24	Virginia	16,895	0.9%
48	Washington	0	0.0%
36	West Virginia	7,957	0.4%
29	Wisconsin	12,949	0.7%
48	Wyoming	0	0.0%

RANK ORDER

RANK	STATE	CHILDREN	% of USA
1	New York	521,301	26.6%
2	California	222,351	11.3%
3	Florida	154,594	7.9%
4	Ohio	83,688	4.3%
5	Pennsylvania	81,758	4.2%
6	New Jersey	75,652	3.9%
7	Massachusetts	67,852	3.5%
8	North Carolina	57,300	2.9%
9	Texas	50,878	2.6%
10	Missouri	49,529	2.5%
11	Georgia	47,581	2.4%
12	South Carolina	45,737	2.3%
13	Illinois	42,699	2.2%
14	Oklahoma	40,196	2.1%
15	Alabama	38,980	2.0%
16	Indiana	31,246	1.6%
17	Oregon	27,285	1.4%
18	Arizona	26,807	1.4%
19	Michigan	26,652	1.4%
20	Colorado	24,116	1.2%
21	Louisiana	21,580	1.1%
22	Kentucky	18,579	0.9%
23	Maryland	18,072	0.9%
24	Virginia	16,895	0.9%
25	Kansas	14,443	0.7%
26	Maine	13,657	0.7%
27	Mississippi	13,218	0.7%
28	Utah	13,040	0.7%
29	Wisconsin	12,949	0.7%
30	Connecticut	9,912	0.5%
31	Iowa	9,795	0.5%
32	Tennessee	9,732	0.5%
33	Nebraska	9,713	0.5%
34	Idaho	8,482	0.4%
35	Alaska	8,033	0.4%
36	West Virginia	7,957	0.4%
37	Nevada	7,802	0.4%
38	Rhode Island	7,288	0.4%
39	New Hampshire	4,554	0.2%
40	New Mexico	4,500	0.2%
41	South Dakota	3,191	0.2%
42	Delaware	2,433	0.1%
43	Vermont	2,055	0.1%
44	Montana	1,019	0.1%
45	Arkansas	913	0.0%
46	North Dakota	266	0.0%
47	Minnesota	21	0.0%
48	Hawaii	0	0.0%
48	Washington	0	0.0%
48	Wyoming	0	0.0%
	District of Columbia	3,029	0.2%

Source: U.S. Department of Health and Human Services, Health Care Financing Administration
   "SCHIP Annual Enrollment Report" (FY 1999, January 11, 2000)
*The State Children's Health Insurance Program (SCHIP) was created in 1997 to help states expand health insurance to children whose families earn too much to qualify for Medicaid, yet not enough to afford private health insurance. National total does not include 2,120 enrollees in U.S. territories.

Preferred Provider Organizations (PPOs) in 1995

National Total = 1,023 PPOs*

RANK	STATE	PPOs	% of USA
15	Alabama	25	2.4%
45	Alaska	3	0.3%
11	Arizona	27	2.6%
36	Arkansas	8	0.8%
1	California	72	7.0%
10	Colorado	28	2.7%
31	Connecticut	11	1.1%
40	Delaware	5	0.5%
1	Florida	72	7.0%
7	Georgia	37	3.6%
40	Hawaii	5	0.5%
47	Idaho	1	0.1%
5	Illinois	46	4.5%
9	Indiana	30	2.9%
30	Iowa	13	1.3%
26	Kansas	17	1.7%
28	Kentucky	16	1.6%
13	Louisiana	26	2.5%
37	Maine	7	0.7%
23	Maryland	18	1.8%
21	Massachusetts	19	1.9%
11	Michigan	27	2.6%
28	Minnesota	16	1.6%
37	Mississippi	7	0.7%
15	Missouri	25	2.4%
49	Montana	0	0.0%
31	Nebraska	11	1.1%
17	Nevada	24	2.4%
42	New Hampshire	4	0.4%
21	New Jersey	19	1.9%
34	New Mexico	9	0.9%
19	New York	22	2.2%
18	North Carolina	23	2.3%
47	North Dakota	1	0.1%
6	Ohio	44	4.3%
23	Oklahoma	18	1.8%
33	Oregon	10	1.0%
4	Pennsylvania	54	5.3%
42	Rhode Island	4	0.4%
26	South Carolina	17	1.7%
42	South Dakota	4	0.4%
7	Tennessee	37	3.6%
3	Texas	71	6.9%
34	Utah	9	0.9%
46	Vermont	2	0.2%
23	Virginia	18	1.8%
20	Washington	21	2.1%
39	West Virginia	6	0.6%
13	Wisconsin	26	2.5%
49	Wyoming	0	0.0%

RANK	STATE	PPOs	% of USA
1	California	72	7.0%
1	Florida	72	7.0%
3	Texas	71	6.9%
4	Pennsylvania	54	5.3%
5	Illinois	46	4.5%
6	Ohio	44	4.3%
7	Georgia	37	3.6%
7	Tennessee	37	3.6%
9	Indiana	30	2.9%
10	Colorado	28	2.7%
11	Arizona	27	2.6%
11	Michigan	27	2.6%
13	Louisiana	26	2.5%
13	Wisconsin	26	2.5%
15	Alabama	25	2.4%
15	Missouri	25	2.4%
17	Nevada	24	2.4%
18	North Carolina	23	2.3%
19	New York	22	2.2%
20	Washington	21	2.1%
21	Massachusetts	19	1.9%
21	New Jersey	19	1.9%
23	Maryland	18	1.8%
23	Oklahoma	18	1.8%
23	Virginia	18	1.8%
26	Kansas	17	1.7%
26	South Carolina	17	1.7%
28	Kentucky	16	1.6%
28	Minnesota	16	1.6%
30	Iowa	13	1.3%
31	Connecticut	11	1.1%
31	Nebraska	11	1.1%
33	Oregon	10	1.0%
34	New Mexico	9	0.9%
34	Utah	9	0.9%
36	Arkansas	8	0.8%
37	Maine	7	0.7%
37	Mississippi	7	0.7%
39	West Virginia	6	0.6%
40	Delaware	5	0.5%
40	Hawaii	5	0.5%
42	New Hampshire	4	0.4%
42	Rhode Island	4	0.4%
42	South Dakota	4	0.4%
45	Alaska	3	0.3%
46	Vermont	2	0.2%
47	Idaho	1	0.1%
47	North Dakota	1	0.1%
49	Montana	0	0.0%
49	Wyoming	0	0.0%
	District of Columbia	6	0.6%

*Source: American Association of Health Plans (formerly American Managed Care and Review Association)
"1995-1996 Managed Health Care Overview"*

As of October 1995. Total does not include two PPOs in Puerto Rico. Health plans are allocated to states based upon their primary service areas. This means each plan is counted once. However, many plans serve more than one state.

Health Maintenance Organizations (HMOs) in 1999

National Total = 638 HMOs*

ALPHA ORDER

RANK	STATE	HMOs	% of USA
24	Alabama	10	1.6%
50	Alaska	0	0.0%
20	Arizona	11	1.7%
37	Arkansas	5	0.8%
3	California	36	5.6%
13	Colorado	17	2.7%
18	Connecticut	14	2.2%
33	Delaware	6	0.9%
4	Florida	35	5.5%
18	Georgia	14	2.2%
30	Hawaii	7	1.1%
43	Idaho	3	0.5%
6	Illinois	26	4.1%
13	Indiana	17	2.7%
43	Iowa	3	0.5%
24	Kansas	10	1.6%
20	Kentucky	11	1.7%
15	Louisiana	15	2.4%
37	Maine	5	0.8%
26	Maryland	9	1.4%
20	Massachusetts	11	1.7%
8	Michigan	22	3.4%
28	Minnesota	8	1.3%
30	Mississippi	7	1.1%
9	Missouri	21	3.3%
41	Montana	4	0.6%
30	Nebraska	7	1.1%
26	Nevada	9	1.4%
41	New Hampshire	4	0.6%
15	New Jersey	15	2.4%
37	New Mexico	5	0.8%
5	New York	34	5.3%
9	North Carolina	21	3.3%
46	North Dakota	2	0.3%
2	Ohio	39	6.1%
20	Oklahoma	11	1.7%
33	Oregon	6	0.9%
7	Pennsylvania	24	3.8%
46	Rhode Island	2	0.3%
33	South Carolina	6	0.9%
43	South Dakota	3	0.5%
12	Tennessee	20	3.1%
1	Texas	41	6.4%
28	Utah	8	1.3%
48	Vermont	1	0.2%
15	Virginia	15	2.4%
33	Washington	6	0.9%
37	West Virginia	5	0.8%
9	Wisconsin	21	3.3%
48	Wyoming	1	0.2%

RANK ORDER

RANK	STATE	HMOs	% of USA
1	Texas	41	6.4%
2	Ohio	39	6.1%
3	California	36	5.6%
4	Florida	35	5.5%
5	New York	34	5.3%
6	Illinois	26	4.1%
7	Pennsylvania	24	3.8%
8	Michigan	22	3.4%
9	Missouri	21	3.3%
9	North Carolina	21	3.3%
9	Wisconsin	21	3.3%
12	Tennessee	20	3.1%
13	Colorado	17	2.7%
13	Indiana	17	2.7%
15	Louisiana	15	2.4%
15	New Jersey	15	2.4%
15	Virginia	15	2.4%
18	Connecticut	14	2.2%
18	Georgia	14	2.2%
20	Arizona	11	1.7%
20	Kentucky	11	1.7%
20	Massachusetts	11	1.7%
20	Oklahoma	11	1.7%
24	Alabama	10	1.6%
24	Kansas	10	1.6%
26	Maryland	9	1.4%
26	Nevada	9	1.4%
28	Minnesota	8	1.3%
28	Utah	8	1.3%
30	Hawaii	7	1.1%
30	Mississippi	7	1.1%
30	Nebraska	7	1.1%
33	Delaware	6	0.9%
33	Oregon	6	0.9%
33	South Carolina	6	0.9%
33	Washington	6	0.9%
37	Arkansas	5	0.8%
37	Maine	5	0.8%
37	New Mexico	5	0.8%
37	West Virginia	5	0.8%
41	Montana	4	0.6%
41	New Hampshire	4	0.6%
43	Idaho	3	0.5%
43	Iowa	3	0.5%
43	South Dakota	3	0.5%
46	North Dakota	2	0.3%
46	Rhode Island	2	0.3%
48	Vermont	1	0.2%
48	Wyoming	1	0.2%
50	Alaska	0	0.0%
	District of Columbia	5	0.8%

Source: InterStudy Publications (Minneapolis, MN)
   "The Competitive Edge Industry Report 9.2" (Press Release, October 21, 1999)
*As of January 1, 1999. Total does not include two HMOs in Guam and three in Puerto Rico. Health plans are allocated to states based upon their primary service areas. This means each plan is counted once. However, many plans serve more than one state.

Enrollees in Health Maintenance Organizations (HMOs) in 1999

National Total = 79,886,260 Enrollees*

ALPHA ORDER

RANK	STATE	ENROLLEES	% of USA
31	Alabama	437,278	0.5%
50	Alaska	0	0.0%
16	Arizona	1,496,204	1.9%
38	Arkansas	312,304	0.4%
1	California	17,024,945	21.3%
15	Colorado	1,563,173	2.0%
22	Connecticut	1,271,687	1.6%
37	Delaware	339,769	0.4%
3	Florida	4,900,217	6.1%
23	Georgia	1,239,364	1.6%
34	Hawaii	402,147	0.5%
44	Idaho	78,728	0.1%
9	Illinois	2,505,830	3.1%
25	Indiana	777,028	1.0%
42	Iowa	139,082	0.2%
30	Kansas	441,857	0.6%
21	Kentucky	1,281,275	1.6%
26	Louisiana	775,263	1.0%
40	Maine	251,146	0.3%
11	Maryland	2,362,432	3.0%
6	Massachusetts	3,251,575	4.1%
8	Michigan	2,647,990	3.3%
17	Minnesota	1,436,513	1.8%
43	Mississippi	89,299	0.1%
13	Missouri	1,860,334	2.3%
45	Montana	58,217	0.1%
39	Nebraska	305,353	0.4%
33	Nevada	409,781	0.5%
32	New Hampshire	413,136	0.5%
10	New Jersey	2,391,180	3.0%
28	New Mexico	661,070	0.8%
2	New York	6,939,872	8.7%
19	North Carolina	1,415,916	1.8%
48	North Dakota	16,145	0.0%
7	Ohio	2,842,772	3.6%
29	Oklahoma	476,363	0.6%
18	Oregon	1,421,693	1.8%
4	Pennsylvania	4,036,097	5.1%
35	Rhode Island	400,476	0.5%
36	South Carolina	382,839	0.5%
46	South Dakota	45,278	0.1%
12	Tennessee	2,045,530	2.6%
5	Texas	3,675,949	4.6%
27	Utah	738,568	0.9%
47	Vermont	23,416	0.0%
20	Virginia**	1,331,518	1.7%
24	Washington	984,697	1.2%
41	West Virginia	189,282	0.2%
14	Wisconsin	1,613,776	2.0%
49	Wyoming	5,760	0.0%

RANK ORDER

RANK	STATE	ENROLLEES	% of USA
1	California	17,024,945	21.3%
2	New York	6,939,872	8.7%
3	Florida	4,900,217	6.1%
4	Pennsylvania	4,036,097	5.1%
5	Texas	3,675,949	4.6%
6	Massachusetts	3,251,575	4.1%
7	Ohio	2,842,772	3.6%
8	Michigan	2,647,990	3.3%
9	Illinois	2,505,830	3.1%
10	New Jersey	2,391,180	3.0%
11	Maryland	2,362,432	3.0%
12	Tennessee	2,045,530	2.6%
13	Missouri	1,860,334	2.3%
14	Wisconsin	1,613,776	2.0%
15	Colorado	1,563,173	2.0%
16	Arizona	1,496,204	1.9%
17	Minnesota	1,436,513	1.8%
18	Oregon	1,421,693	1.8%
19	North Carolina	1,415,916	1.8%
20	Virginia**	1,331,518	1.7%
21	Kentucky	1,281,275	1.6%
22	Connecticut	1,271,687	1.6%
23	Georgia	1,239,364	1.6%
24	Washington	984,697	1.2%
25	Indiana	777,028	1.0%
26	Louisiana	775,263	1.0%
27	Utah	738,568	0.9%
28	New Mexico	661,070	0.8%
29	Oklahoma	476,363	0.6%
30	Kansas	441,857	0.6%
31	Alabama	437,278	0.5%
32	New Hampshire	413,136	0.5%
33	Nevada	409,781	0.5%
34	Hawaii	402,147	0.5%
35	Rhode Island	400,476	0.5%
36	South Carolina	382,839	0.5%
37	Delaware	339,769	0.4%
38	Arkansas	312,304	0.4%
39	Nebraska	305,353	0.4%
40	Maine	251,146	0.3%
41	West Virginia	189,282	0.2%
42	Iowa	139,082	0.2%
43	Mississippi	89,299	0.1%
44	Idaho	78,728	0.1%
45	Montana	58,217	0.1%
46	South Dakota	45,278	0.1%
47	Vermont	23,416	0.0%
48	North Dakota	16,145	0.0%
49	Wyoming	5,760	0.0%
50	Alaska	0	0.0%
	District of Columbia	176,136	0.2%

Source: InterStudy Publications (Minneapolis, MN)
  "The Competitive Edge Industry Report 9.2" (Press Release, October 21, 1999)
*As of January 1, 1999. Total does not include 1,446,748 enrollees in U.S. territories.
**Virginia includes enrollment from two HMOs serving the Washington, DC metropolitan area.

Percent Change in Enrollees in Health Maintenance Organizations (HMOs): 1998 to 1999
National Percent Change = 6.5% Increase*

RANK	STATE	PERCENT CHANGE
45	Alabama	(6.7)
36	Alaska	0.0
17	Arizona	8.5
9	Arkansas	15.3
12	California	12.1
14	Colorado	10.2
47	Connecticut	(9.4)
41	Delaware	(3.5)
25	Florida	6.2
23	Georgia	6.8
30	Hawaii	3.4
10	Idaho	14.4
33	Illinois	1.3
43	Indiana	(5.4)
37	Iowa	(0.2)
6	Kansas	18.0
7	Kentucky	17.9
19	Louisiana	7.2
27	Maine	6.1
24	Maryland	6.5
38	Massachusetts	(1.9)
19	Michigan	7.2
44	Minnesota	(5.5)
48	Mississippi	(9.7)
21	Missouri	7.1
1	Montana	71.2
16	Nebraska	8.9
46	Nevada	(8.9)
28	New Hampshire	4.2
42	New Jersey	(5.2)
5	New Mexico	18.5
34	New York	1.2
13	North Carolina	11.6
11	North Dakota	12.4
17	Ohio	8.5
29	Oklahoma	4.1
40	Oregon	(3.2)
14	Pennsylvania	10.2
3	Rhode Island	36.2
31	South Carolina	3.0
4	South Dakota	21.2
21	Tennessee	7.1
25	Texas	6.2
35	Utah	0.9
NA	Vermont**	NA
8	Virginia	16.9
49	Washington	(33.2)
39	West Virginia	(2.3)
32	Wisconsin	1.5
2	Wyoming	63.9

RANK	STATE	PERCENT CHANGE
1	Montana	71.2
2	Wyoming	63.9
3	Rhode Island	36.2
4	South Dakota	21.2
5	New Mexico	18.5
6	Kansas	18.0
7	Kentucky	17.9
8	Virginia	16.9
9	Arkansas	15.3
10	Idaho	14.4
11	North Dakota	12.4
12	California	12.1
13	North Carolina	11.6
14	Colorado	10.2
14	Pennsylvania	10.2
16	Nebraska	8.9
17	Arizona	8.5
17	Ohio	8.5
19	Louisiana	7.2
19	Michigan	7.2
21	Missouri	7.1
21	Tennessee	7.1
23	Georgia	6.8
24	Maryland	6.5
25	Florida	6.2
25	Texas	6.2
27	Maine	6.1
28	New Hampshire	4.2
29	Oklahoma	4.1
30	Hawaii	3.4
31	South Carolina	3.0
32	Wisconsin	1.5
33	Illinois	1.3
34	New York	1.2
35	Utah	0.9
36	Alaska	0.0
37	Iowa	(0.2)
38	Massachusetts	(1.9)
39	West Virginia	(2.3)
40	Oregon	(3.2)
41	Delaware	(3.5)
42	New Jersey	(5.2)
43	Indiana	(5.4)
44	Minnesota	(5.5)
45	Alabama	(6.7)
46	Nevada	(8.9)
47	Connecticut	(9.4)
48	Mississippi	(9.7)
49	Washington	(33.2)
NA	Vermont**	NA
	District of Columbia	1.0

Source: InterStudy Publications (Minneapolis, MN)
"The Competitive Edge Industry Report 9.2" (Press Release, October 21, 1999)
*As of January 1, 1999. National rate includes enrollees in U.S. territories.
**Not applicable.

Percent of Population Enrolled in Health Maintenance Organizations (HMOs) in 1999
National Percent = 29.3% Enrolled in HMOs*

ALPHA ORDER

RANK	STATE	PERCENT
40	Alabama	10.0
50	Alaska	0.0
19	Arizona	31.3
38	Arkansas	12.2
2	California	51.4
8	Colorado	38.5
7	Connecticut	38.7
4	Delaware	45.1
17	Florida	32.4
35	Georgia	15.9
15	Hawaii	33.9
43	Idaho	6.3
26	Illinois	20.7
37	Indiana	13.1
45	Iowa	4.8
34	Kansas	16.6
18	Kentucky	32.3
32	Louisiana	17.7
27	Maine	20.0
3	Maryland	45.7
1	Massachusetts	52.7
23	Michigan	26.8
21	Minnesota	30.1
47	Mississippi	3.2
14	Missouri	34.0
42	Montana	6.6
30	Nebraska	18.3
25	Nevada	22.6
13	New Hampshire	34.4
22	New Jersey	29.4
10	New Mexico	38.0
9	New York	38.1
29	North Carolina	18.5
48	North Dakota	2.5
24	Ohio	25.3
36	Oklahoma	14.2
5	Oregon	42.9
16	Pennsylvania	33.7
6	Rhode Island	40.4
41	South Carolina	9.9
44	South Dakota	6.2
11	Tennessee	37.3
30	Texas	18.3
12	Utah	34.7
46	Vermont	3.9
28	Virginia	19.4
33	Washington	17.1
39	West Virginia	10.5
20	Wisconsin	30.7
49	Wyoming	1.2

RANK ORDER

RANK	STATE	PERCENT
1	Massachusetts	52.7
2	California	51.4
3	Maryland	45.7
4	Delaware	45.1
5	Oregon	42.9
6	Rhode Island	40.4
7	Connecticut	38.7
8	Colorado	38.5
9	New York	38.1
10	New Mexico	38.0
11	Tennessee	37.3
12	Utah	34.7
13	New Hampshire	34.4
14	Missouri	34.0
15	Hawaii	33.9
16	Pennsylvania	33.7
17	Florida	32.4
18	Kentucky	32.3
19	Arizona	31.3
20	Wisconsin	30.7
21	Minnesota	30.1
22	New Jersey	29.4
23	Michigan	26.8
24	Ohio	25.3
25	Nevada	22.6
26	Illinois	20.7
27	Maine	20.0
28	Virginia	19.4
29	North Carolina	18.5
30	Nebraska	18.3
30	Texas	18.3
32	Louisiana	17.7
33	Washington	17.1
34	Kansas	16.6
35	Georgia	15.9
36	Oklahoma	14.2
37	Indiana	13.1
38	Arkansas	12.2
39	West Virginia	10.5
40	Alabama	10.0
41	South Carolina	9.9
42	Montana	6.6
43	Idaho	6.3
44	South Dakota	6.2
45	Iowa	4.8
46	Vermont	3.9
47	Mississippi	3.2
48	North Dakota	2.5
49	Wyoming	1.2
50	Alaska	0.0
	District of Columbia	33.9

Source: Morgan Quitno Press using data from InterStudy Publications (Minneapolis, MN)
"The Competitive Edge Industry Report 9.2" (Press Release, October 21, 1999)
*As of January 1, 1999. National percent does not include enrollees or population in U.S. territories.

Percent of Insured Population Enrolled in
Health Maintenance Organizations (HMOs) in 1999
National Percent = 35.3% of Insured are Enrolled in HMOs*

ALPHA ORDER

RANK	STATE	PERCENT
40	Alabama	12.1
50	Alaska	0.0
12	Arizona	42.3
38	Arkansas	15.1
1	California	66.9
7	Colorado	46.4
10	Connecticut	44.5
4	Delaware	53.5
14	Florida	39.8
33	Georgia	19.7
19	Hawaii	37.5
43	Idaho	7.8
27	Illinois	24.4
37	Indiana	15.4
45	Iowa	5.4
35	Kansas	18.7
17	Kentucky	37.9
31	Louisiana	21.9
28	Maine	23.1
3	Maryland	55.2
2	Massachusetts	59.0
23	Michigan	31.1
22	Minnesota	33.5
47	Mississippi	4.1
16	Missouri	38.2
42	Montana	8.2
32	Nebraska	20.2
24	Nevada	29.8
15	New Hampshire	39.3
20	New Jersey	35.3
6	New Mexico	48.3
8	New York	46.2
30	North Carolina	22.1
48	North Dakota	3.0
25	Ohio	28.2
36	Oklahoma	17.5
5	Oregon	50.5
18	Pennsylvania	37.6
9	Rhode Island	45.0
41	South Carolina	11.8
44	South Dakota	7.2
11	Tennessee	43.3
26	Texas	24.7
13	Utah	40.8
46	Vermont	4.4
29	Virginia	22.8
33	Washington	19.7
39	West Virginia	12.6
21	Wisconsin	35.0
49	Wyoming	1.4

RANK ORDER

RANK	STATE	PERCENT
1	California	66.9
2	Massachusetts	59.0
3	Maryland	55.2
4	Delaware	53.5
5	Oregon	50.5
6	New Mexico	48.3
7	Colorado	46.4
8	New York	46.2
9	Rhode Island	45.0
10	Connecticut	44.5
11	Tennessee	43.3
12	Arizona	42.3
13	Utah	40.8
14	Florida	39.8
15	New Hampshire	39.3
16	Missouri	38.2
17	Kentucky	37.9
18	Pennsylvania	37.6
19	Hawaii	37.5
20	New Jersey	35.3
21	Wisconsin	35.0
22	Minnesota	33.5
23	Michigan	31.1
24	Nevada	29.8
25	Ohio	28.2
26	Texas	24.7
27	Illinois	24.4
28	Maine	23.1
29	Virginia	22.8
30	North Carolina	22.1
31	Louisiana	21.9
32	Nebraska	20.2
33	Georgia	19.7
33	Washington	19.7
35	Kansas	18.7
36	Oklahoma	17.5
37	Indiana	15.4
38	Arkansas	15.1
39	West Virginia	12.6
40	Alabama	12.1
41	South Carolina	11.8
42	Montana	8.2
43	Idaho	7.8
44	South Dakota	7.2
45	Iowa	5.4
46	Vermont	4.4
47	Mississippi	4.1
48	North Dakota	3.0
49	Wyoming	1.4
50	Alaska	0.0

District of Columbia 40.7

Source: Morgan Quitno Press using data from InterStudy Publications (Minneapolis, MN)
"The Competitive Edge Industry Report 9.2" (Press Release, October 21, 1999)
*As of January 1, 1999. Calculated using estimated number of insured as of 1998 from Census.

Medicare Benefit Payments in 1998

National Total = $210,101,815,777*

ALPHA ORDER

RANK	STATE	BENEFITS	% of USA
19	Alabama	$3,560,717,508	1.7%
50	Alaska	159,758,199	0.1%
22	Arizona	2,985,530,968	1.4%
30	Arkansas	1,928,749,334	0.9%
1	California	22,557,637,106	10.7%
28	Colorado	2,278,634,923	1.1%
21	Connecticut	3,128,330,518	1.5%
47	Delaware	405,179,514	0.2%
2	Florida	17,902,925,272	8.5%
15	Georgia	4,287,055,620	2.0%
42	Hawaii	638,739,135	0.3%
43	Idaho	600,569,407	0.3%
7	Illinois	8,490,218,565	4.0%
16	Indiana	4,263,103,328	2.0%
32	Iowa	1,809,851,994	0.9%
33	Kansas	1,808,698,803	0.9%
23	Kentucky	2,897,036,258	1.4%
14	Louisiana	4,293,485,495	2.0%
40	Maine	793,293,556	0.4%
18	Maryland	3,641,544,943	1.7%
10	Massachusetts	5,806,660,558	2.8%
8	Michigan	7,710,609,123	3.7%
25	Minnesota	2,798,007,301	1.3%
29	Mississippi	2,216,407,663	1.1%
13	Missouri	4,695,447,829	2.2%
44	Montana	534,258,341	0.3%
36	Nebraska	1,079,689,239	0.5%
35	Nevada	1,105,343,755	0.5%
41	New Hampshire	647,514,836	0.3%
9	New Jersey	6,907,721,916	3.3%
39	New Mexico	829,432,056	0.4%
3	New York	17,065,062,152	8.1%
11	North Carolina	5,295,680,613	2.5%
46	North Dakota	480,392,514	0.2%
6	Ohio	8,834,503,816	4.2%
27	Oklahoma	2,372,547,734	1.1%
31	Oregon	1,831,805,057	0.9%
5	Pennsylvania	13,183,135,104	6.3%
37	Rhode Island	1,022,126,351	0.5%
26	South Carolina	2,563,287,620	1.2%
45	South Dakota	503,514,478	0.2%
12	Tennessee	4,728,188,173	2.3%
4	Texas	14,666,114,703	7.0%
38	Utah	888,315,472	0.4%
48	Vermont	289,235,157	0.1%
17	Virginia	3,657,019,701	1.7%
24	Washington	2,883,183,663	1.4%
34	West Virginia	1,528,209,589	0.7%
20	Wisconsin	3,267,431,972	1.6%
49	Wyoming	218,451,250	0.1%

RANK ORDER

RANK	STATE	BENEFITS	% of USA
1	California	$22,557,637,106	10.7%
2	Florida	17,902,925,272	8.5%
3	New York	17,065,062,152	8.1%
4	Texas	14,666,114,703	7.0%
5	Pennsylvania	13,183,135,104	6.3%
6	Ohio	8,834,503,816	4.2%
7	Illinois	8,490,218,565	4.0%
8	Michigan	7,710,609,123	3.7%
9	New Jersey	6,907,721,916	3.3%
10	Massachusetts	5,806,660,558	2.8%
11	North Carolina	5,295,680,613	2.5%
12	Tennessee	4,728,188,173	2.3%
13	Missouri	4,695,447,829	2.2%
14	Louisiana	4,293,485,495	2.0%
15	Georgia	4,287,055,620	2.0%
16	Indiana	4,263,103,328	2.0%
17	Virginia	3,657,019,701	1.7%
18	Maryland	3,641,544,943	1.7%
19	Alabama	3,560,717,508	1.7%
20	Wisconsin	3,267,431,972	1.6%
21	Connecticut	3,128,330,518	1.5%
22	Arizona	2,985,530,968	1.4%
23	Kentucky	2,897,036,258	1.4%
24	Washington	2,883,183,663	1.4%
25	Minnesota	2,798,007,301	1.3%
26	South Carolina	2,563,287,620	1.2%
27	Oklahoma	2,372,547,734	1.1%
28	Colorado	2,278,634,923	1.1%
29	Mississippi	2,216,407,663	1.1%
30	Arkansas	1,928,749,334	0.9%
31	Oregon	1,831,805,057	0.9%
32	Iowa	1,809,851,994	0.9%
33	Kansas	1,808,698,803	0.9%
34	West Virginia	1,528,209,589	0.7%
35	Nevada	1,105,343,755	0.5%
36	Nebraska	1,079,689,239	0.5%
37	Rhode Island	1,022,126,351	0.5%
38	Utah	888,315,472	0.4%
39	New Mexico	829,432,056	0.4%
40	Maine	793,293,556	0.4%
41	New Hampshire	647,514,836	0.3%
42	Hawaii	638,739,135	0.3%
43	Idaho	600,569,407	0.3%
44	Montana	534,258,341	0.3%
45	South Dakota	503,514,478	0.2%
46	North Dakota	480,392,514	0.2%
47	Delaware	405,179,514	0.2%
48	Vermont	289,235,157	0.1%
49	Wyoming	218,451,250	0.1%
50	Alaska	159,758,199	0.1%
	District of Columbia	922,292,162	0.4%

*Source: U.S. Department of Health and Human Services, Health Care Financing Administration
   unpublished data*

For fiscal year 1998. Includes payments to aged and disabled enrollees. Total includes $1,085,621,690 in payments to enrollees in Puerto Rico and $53,543,743 to enrollees in "other outlying areas."

Medicare Enrollees in 1998

National Total = 38,444,739 Enrollees*

ALPHA ORDER

RANK	STATE	ENROLLEES	% of USA
19	Alabama	662,299	1.7%
50	Alaska	36,522	0.1%
21	Arizona	636,450	1.7%
31	Arkansas	431,020	1.1%
1	California	3,738,081	9.7%
30	Colorado	442,452	1.2%
26	Connecticut	507,927	1.3%
46	Delaware	105,693	0.3%
2	Florida	2,727,545	7.1%
12	Georgia	869,443	2.3%
42	Hawaii	156,103	0.4%
43	Idaho	155,810	0.4%
7	Illinois	1,622,181	4.2%
15	Indiana	835,183	2.2%
29	Iowa	475,786	1.2%
33	Kansas	387,589	1.0%
23	Kentucky	602,570	1.6%
24	Louisiana	592,543	1.5%
38	Maine	207,784	0.5%
22	Maryland	619,700	1.6%
11	Massachusetts	946,879	2.5%
8	Michigan	1,369,629	3.6%
20	Minnesota	639,293	1.7%
32	Mississippi	407,440	1.1%
14	Missouri	844,920	2.2%
44	Montana	133,089	0.3%
35	Nebraska	251,029	0.7%
37	Nevada	213,742	0.6%
41	New Hampshire	161,759	0.4%
9	New Jersey	1,182,204	3.1%
36	New Mexico	221,061	0.6%
3	New York	2,651,677	6.9%
10	North Carolina	1,073,564	2.8%
47	North Dakota	102,764	0.3%
6	Ohio	1,683,167	4.4%
27	Oklahoma	497,066	1.3%
28	Oregon	477,022	1.2%
5	Pennsylvania	2,084,565	5.4%
40	Rhode Island	169,359	0.4%
25	South Carolina	534,827	1.4%
45	South Dakota	117,931	0.3%
16	Tennessee	796,692	2.1%
4	Texas	2,162,917	5.6%
39	Utah	195,326	0.5%
48	Vermont	85,562	0.2%
13	Virginia	849,493	2.2%
18	Washington	708,607	1.8%
34	West Virginia	333,217	0.9%
17	Wisconsin	770,405	2.0%
49	Wyoming	62,654	0.2%

RANK ORDER

RANK	STATE	ENROLLEES	% of USA
1	California	3,738,081	9.7%
2	Florida	2,727,545	7.1%
3	New York	2,651,677	6.9%
4	Texas	2,162,917	5.6%
5	Pennsylvania	2,084,565	5.4%
6	Ohio	1,683,167	4.4%
7	Illinois	1,622,181	4.2%
8	Michigan	1,369,629	3.6%
9	New Jersey	1,182,204	3.1%
10	North Carolina	1,073,564	2.8%
11	Massachusetts	946,879	2.5%
12	Georgia	869,443	2.3%
13	Virginia	849,493	2.2%
14	Missouri	844,920	2.2%
15	Indiana	835,183	2.2%
16	Tennessee	796,692	2.1%
17	Wisconsin	770,405	2.0%
18	Washington	708,607	1.8%
19	Alabama	662,299	1.7%
20	Minnesota	639,293	1.7%
21	Arizona	636,450	1.7%
22	Maryland	619,700	1.6%
23	Kentucky	602,570	1.6%
24	Louisiana	592,543	1.5%
25	South Carolina	534,827	1.4%
26	Connecticut	507,927	1.3%
27	Oklahoma	497,066	1.3%
28	Oregon	477,022	1.2%
29	Iowa	475,786	1.2%
30	Colorado	442,452	1.2%
31	Arkansas	431,020	1.1%
32	Mississippi	407,440	1.1%
33	Kansas	387,589	1.0%
34	West Virginia	333,217	0.9%
35	Nebraska	251,029	0.7%
36	New Mexico	221,061	0.6%
37	Nevada	213,742	0.6%
38	Maine	207,784	0.5%
39	Utah	195,326	0.5%
40	Rhode Island	169,359	0.4%
41	New Hampshire	161,759	0.4%
42	Hawaii	156,103	0.4%
43	Idaho	155,810	0.4%
44	Montana	133,089	0.3%
45	South Dakota	117,931	0.3%
46	Delaware	105,693	0.3%
47	North Dakota	102,764	0.3%
48	Vermont	85,562	0.2%
49	Wyoming	62,654	0.2%
50	Alaska	36,522	0.1%
	District of Columbia	78,151	0.2%

Source: U.S. Department of Health and Human Services, Health Care Financing Administration
unpublished data

*For fiscal year 1998. Includes aged and disabled enrollees. Total includes 502,780 enrollees in Puerto Rico and 323,287 enrollees in "other outlying areas."

Medicare Payments per Enrollee in 1998

National Rate = $5,465*

ALPHA ORDER

RANK	STATE	PER ENROLLEE
16	Alabama	$5,376
34	Alaska	4,374
27	Arizona	4,691
32	Arkansas	4,475
8	California	6,035
20	Colorado	5,150
6	Connecticut	6,159
45	Delaware	3,834
3	Florida	6,564
23	Georgia	4,931
39	Hawaii	4,092
43	Idaho	3,854
18	Illinois	5,234
21	Indiana	5,104
47	Iowa	3,804
29	Kansas	4,667
24	Kentucky	4,808
1	Louisiana	7,246
46	Maine	3,818
11	Maryland	5,876
7	Massachusetts	6,132
13	Michigan	5,630
33	Minnesota	4,377
15	Mississippi	5,440
14	Missouri	5,557
41	Montana	4,014
36	Nebraska	4,301
19	Nevada	5,171
42	New Hampshire	4,003
12	New Jersey	5,843
48	New Mexico	3,752
4	New York	6,436
22	North Carolina	4,933
28	North Dakota	4,675
17	Ohio	5,249
26	Oklahoma	4,773
44	Oregon	3,840
5	Pennsylvania	6,324
8	Rhode Island	6,035
25	South Carolina	4,793
37	South Dakota	4,270
10	Tennessee	5,935
2	Texas	6,781
31	Utah	4,548
50	Vermont	3,380
35	Virginia	4,305
40	Washington	4,069
30	West Virginia	4,586
38	Wisconsin	4,241
49	Wyoming	3,487

RANK ORDER

RANK	STATE	PER ENROLLEE
1	Louisiana	$7,246
2	Texas	6,781
3	Florida	6,564
4	New York	6,436
5	Pennsylvania	6,324
6	Connecticut	6,159
7	Massachusetts	6,132
8	California	6,035
8	Rhode Island	6,035
10	Tennessee	5,935
11	Maryland	5,876
12	New Jersey	5,843
13	Michigan	5,630
14	Missouri	5,557
15	Mississippi	5,440
16	Alabama	5,376
17	Ohio	5,249
18	Illinois	5,234
19	Nevada	5,171
20	Colorado	5,150
21	Indiana	5,104
22	North Carolina	4,933
23	Georgia	4,931
24	Kentucky	4,808
25	South Carolina	4,793
26	Oklahoma	4,773
27	Arizona	4,691
28	North Dakota	4,675
29	Kansas	4,667
30	West Virginia	4,586
31	Utah	4,548
32	Arkansas	4,475
33	Minnesota	4,377
34	Alaska	4,374
35	Virginia	4,305
36	Nebraska	4,301
37	South Dakota	4,270
38	Wisconsin	4,241
39	Hawaii	4,092
40	Washington	4,069
41	Montana	4,014
42	New Hampshire	4,003
43	Idaho	3,854
44	Oregon	3,840
45	Delaware	3,834
46	Maine	3,818
47	Iowa	3,804
48	New Mexico	3,752
49	Wyoming	3,487
50	Vermont	3,380
	District of Columbia	11,801

*Source: U.S. Department of Health and Human Services, Health Care Financing Administration
unpublished data*

For fiscal year 1998. Includes aged and disabled enrollees. National rate includes payments to enrollees in Puerto Rico and in "other outlying areas."

Percent of Population Enrolled in Medicare in 1998

National Percent = 13.9% of Population*

RANK	STATE	RATE
14	Alabama	15.2
50	Alaska	5.9
32	Arizona	13.6
5	Arkansas	17.0
45	California	11.4
47	Colorado	11.1
10	Connecticut	15.5
27	Delaware	14.2
2	Florida	18.3
45	Georgia	11.4
37	Hawaii	13.1
39	Idaho	12.7
35	Illinois	13.5
27	Indiana	14.2
7	Iowa	16.6
20	Kansas	14.7
13	Kentucky	15.3
32	Louisiana	13.6
6	Maine	16.7
44	Maryland	12.1
12	Massachusetts	15.4
30	Michigan	14.0
35	Minnesota	13.5
19	Mississippi	14.8
10	Missouri	15.5
15	Montana	15.1
15	Nebraska	15.1
43	Nevada	12.2
32	New Hampshire	13.6
23	New Jersey	14.6
39	New Mexico	12.7
23	New York	14.6
27	North Carolina	14.2
8	North Dakota	16.1
17	Ohio	15.0
18	Oklahoma	14.9
25	Oregon	14.5
3	Pennsylvania	17.4
4	Rhode Island	17.1
31	South Carolina	13.9
9	South Dakota	16.0
20	Tennessee	14.7
48	Texas	10.9
49	Utah	9.3
25	Vermont	14.5
41	Virginia	12.5
41	Washington	12.5
1	West Virginia	18.4
20	Wisconsin	14.7
38	Wyoming	13.0

RANK	STATE	RATE
1	West Virginia	18.4
2	Florida	18.3
3	Pennsylvania	17.4
4	Rhode Island	17.1
5	Arkansas	17.0
6	Maine	16.7
7	Iowa	16.6
8	North Dakota	16.1
9	South Dakota	16.0
10	Connecticut	15.5
10	Missouri	15.5
12	Massachusetts	15.4
13	Kentucky	15.3
14	Alabama	15.2
15	Montana	15.1
15	Nebraska	15.1
17	Ohio	15.0
18	Oklahoma	14.9
19	Mississippi	14.8
20	Kansas	14.7
20	Tennessee	14.7
20	Wisconsin	14.7
23	New Jersey	14.6
23	New York	14.6
25	Oregon	14.5
25	Vermont	14.5
27	Delaware	14.2
27	Indiana	14.2
27	North Carolina	14.2
30	Michigan	14.0
31	South Carolina	13.9
32	Arizona	13.6
32	Louisiana	13.6
32	New Hampshire	13.6
35	Illinois	13.5
35	Minnesota	13.5
37	Hawaii	13.1
38	Wyoming	13.0
39	Idaho	12.7
39	New Mexico	12.7
41	Virginia	12.5
41	Washington	12.5
43	Nevada	12.2
44	Maryland	12.1
45	California	11.4
45	Georgia	11.4
47	Colorado	11.1
48	Texas	10.9
49	Utah	9.3
50	Alaska	5.9

| | District of Columbia | 14.9 |

Source: Morgan Quitno Press using data from U.S. Dept. of Health and Human Services, Health Care Financing Admn
  unpublished data

*For fiscal year 1998. Includes aged and disabled enrollees. National rate includes only residents of the 50 states
and the District of Columbia.

Medicare Managed Care Enrollees in 2000

National Total = 6,848,119 Enrollees*

ALPHA ORDER

RANK ORDER

RANK	STATE	ENROLLEES	% of USA		RANK	STATE	ENROLLEES	% of USA
23	Alabama	54,837	0.8%		1	California	1,579,568	23.1%
46	Alaska	0	0.0%		2	Florida	782,906	11.4%
6	Arizona	276,731	4.0%		3	Pennsylvania	574,186	8.4%
34	Arkansas	16,478	0.2%		4	New York	499,795	7.3%
1	California	1,579,568	23.1%		5	Texas	408,614	6.0%
14	Colorado	160,102	2.3%		6	Arizona	276,731	4.0%
15	Connecticut	104,840	1.5%		7	Ohio	238,539	3.5%
40	Delaware	3,681	0.1%		8	Massachusetts	225,190	3.3%
2	Florida	782,906	11.4%		9	Oregon	192,249	2.8%
22	Georgia	55,114	0.8%		10	Illinois	182,742	2.7%
24	Hawaii	53,648	0.8%		11	New Jersey	179,081	2.6%
35	Idaho	13,606	0.2%		12	Washington	166,917	2.4%
10	Illinois	182,742	2.7%		13	Missouri	166,189	2.4%
19	Indiana	81,884	1.2%		14	Colorado	160,102	2.3%
39	Iowa	7,746	0.1%		15	Connecticut	104,840	1.5%
38	Kansas	8,479	0.1%		16	Louisiana	99,122	1.4%
32	Kentucky	17,343	0.3%		17	Maryland	97,825	1.4%
16	Louisiana	99,122	1.4%		18	Minnesota	88,913	1.3%
43	Maine	1,376	0.0%		19	Indiana	81,884	1.2%
17	Maryland	97,825	1.4%		20	Michigan	73,739	1.1%
8	Massachusetts	225,190	3.3%		21	Rhode Island	68,301	1.0%
20	Michigan	73,739	1.1%		22	Georgia	55,114	0.8%
18	Minnesota	88,913	1.3%		23	Alabama	54,837	0.8%
41	Mississippi	3,171	0.0%		24	Hawaii	53,648	0.8%
13	Missouri	166,189	2.4%		25	New Mexico	50,550	0.7%
46	Montana	0	0.0%		26	Nevada	45,808	0.7%
36	Nebraska	10,310	0.2%		27	North Carolina	44,777	0.7%
26	Nevada	45,808	0.7%		28	Tennessee	42,839	0.6%
42	New Hampshire	1,510	0.0%		29	Wisconsin	38,963	0.6%
11	New Jersey	179,081	2.6%		30	Oklahoma	20,320	0.3%
25	New Mexico	50,550	0.7%		31	Utah	18,747	0.3%
4	New York	499,795	7.3%		32	Kentucky	17,343	0.3%
27	North Carolina	44,777	0.7%		33	Virginia	17,301	0.3%
44	North Dakota	680	0.0%		34	Arkansas	16,478	0.2%
7	Ohio	238,539	3.5%		35	Idaho	13,606	0.2%
30	Oklahoma	20,320	0.3%		36	Nebraska	10,310	0.2%
9	Oregon	192,249	2.8%		37	West Virginia	9,930	0.1%
3	Pennsylvania	574,186	8.4%		38	Kansas	8,479	0.1%
21	Rhode Island	68,301	1.0%		39	Iowa	7,746	0.1%
46	South Carolina	0	0.0%		40	Delaware	3,681	0.1%
45	South Dakota	42	0.0%		41	Mississippi	3,171	0.0%
28	Tennessee	42,839	0.6%		42	New Hampshire	1,510	0.0%
5	Texas	408,614	6.0%		43	Maine	1,376	0.0%
31	Utah	18,747	0.3%		44	North Dakota	680	0.0%
46	Vermont	0	0.0%		45	South Dakota	42	0.0%
33	Virginia	17,301	0.3%		46	Alaska	0	0.0%
12	Washington	166,917	2.4%		46	Montana	0	0.0%
37	West Virginia	9,930	0.1%		46	South Carolina	0	0.0%
29	Wisconsin	38,963	0.6%		46	Vermont	0	0.0%
46	Wyoming	0	0.0%		46	Wyoming	0	0.0%
						District of Columbia	922	0.0%

Source: U.S. Department of Health and Human Services, Health Care Financing Administration
"Medicare Managed Care Contract Report" (February 1, 2000, http://www.hcfa.gov/stats/mmcc0200.txt)
*As of February 1st. Includes TEFRA, Cost, and Health Care Prepayment Plans (HCPP) and other demo plans.
National total includes National total includes 62,508 enrollees in the United Mine Workers' plan not shown
separately by state.*

Percent of Medicare Enrollees in Managed Care Programs in 2000

National Percent = 18.2% of Medicare Enrollees*

ALPHA ORDER

RANK	STATE	PERCENT
26	Alabama	8.2
45	Alaska	0.0
1	Arizona	42.5
34	Arkansas	3.8
2	California	41.8
5	Colorado	35.5
12	Connecticut	20.6
35	Delaware	3.4
7	Florida	28.4
27	Georgia	6.2
6	Hawaii	33.7
25	Idaho	8.6
22	Illinois	11.2
23	Indiana	9.7
40	Iowa	1.6
38	Kansas	2.2
37	Kentucky	2.8
17	Louisiana	16.6
43	Maine	0.7
18	Maryland	15.6
9	Massachusetts	23.7
28	Michigan	5.3
21	Minnesota	13.8
42	Mississippi	0.8
14	Missouri	19.5
45	Montana	0.0
31	Nebraska	4.1
13	Nevada	20.5
41	New Hampshire	0.9
19	New Jersey	15.1
11	New Mexico	22.5
15	New York	18.7
31	North Carolina	4.1
43	North Dakota	0.7
20	Ohio	14.1
31	Oklahoma	4.1
4	Oregon	40.0
8	Pennsylvania	27.5
3	Rhode Island	40.2
45	South Carolina	0.0
45	South Dakota	0.0
28	Tennessee	5.3
16	Texas	18.6
24	Utah	9.5
45	Vermont	0.0
39	Virginia	2.0
10	Washington	23.2
36	West Virginia	3.0
30	Wisconsin	5.0
45	Wyoming	0.0

RANK ORDER

RANK	STATE	PERCENT
1	Arizona	42.5
2	California	41.8
3	Rhode Island	40.2
4	Oregon	40.0
5	Colorado	35.5
6	Hawaii	33.7
7	Florida	28.4
8	Pennsylvania	27.5
9	Massachusetts	23.7
10	Washington	23.2
11	New Mexico	22.5
12	Connecticut	20.6
13	Nevada	20.5
14	Missouri	19.5
15	New York	18.7
16	Texas	18.6
17	Louisiana	16.6
18	Maryland	15.6
19	New Jersey	15.1
20	Ohio	14.1
21	Minnesota	13.8
22	Illinois	11.2
23	Indiana	9.7
24	Utah	9.5
25	Idaho	8.6
26	Alabama	8.2
27	Georgia	6.2
28	Michigan	5.3
28	Tennessee	5.3
30	Wisconsin	5.0
31	Nebraska	4.1
31	North Carolina	4.1
31	Oklahoma	4.1
34	Arkansas	3.8
35	Delaware	3.4
36	West Virginia	3.0
37	Kentucky	2.8
38	Kansas	2.2
39	Virginia	2.0
40	Iowa	1.6
41	New Hampshire	0.9
42	Mississippi	0.8
43	Maine	0.7
43	North Dakota	0.7
45	Alaska	0.0
45	Montana	0.0
45	South Carolina	0.0
45	South Dakota	0.0
45	Vermont	0.0
45	Wyoming	0.0

District of Columbia — 1.2

Source: Morgan Quitno Press using data from U.S. Dept. of Health and Human Services, Health Care Financing Admin.
"Medicare Managed Care Contract Report" (February 1, 2000, http://www.hcfa.gov/stats/mmcc0200.txt)
*As of February 1st. Based on September 1998 Medicare enrollees. Includes aged and disabled enrollees.
National percent does not include enrollees in Puerto Rico and other outlying areas.

Medicare Physicians in 1998

National Total = 807,674 Physicians*

ALPHA ORDER

RANK	STATE	PHYSICIANS	% of USA
25	Alabama	9,685	1.2%
49	Alaska	1,412	0.2%
24	Arizona	11,127	1.4%
31	Arkansas	6,866	0.9%
1	California	96,634	12.0%
22	Colorado	12,619	1.6%
23	Connecticut	11,878	1.5%
45	Delaware	2,294	0.3%
5	Florida	41,483	5.1%
12	Georgia	18,489	2.3%
40	Hawaii**	3,871	0.5%
44	Idaho	2,451	0.3%
7	Illinois	31,869	3.9%
19	Indiana	15,293	1.9%
28	Iowa	8,492	1.1%
32	Kansas	6,793	0.8%
27	Kentucky	9,092	1.1%
21	Louisiana	13,156	1.6%
36	Maine	4,425	0.5%
11	Maryland	18,572	2.3%
9	Massachusetts	27,476	3.4%
8	Michigan	28,234	3.5%
18	Minnesota	15,367	1.9%
33	Mississippi	5,274	0.7%
16	Missouri	16,301	2.0%
43	Montana	2,571	0.3%
37	Nebraska	4,226	0.5%
41	Nevada	3,383	0.4%
38	New Hampshire	4,200	0.5%
10	New Jersey	27,448	3.4%
39	New Mexico	4,012	0.5%
2	New York	73,813	9.1%
13	North Carolina	17,615	2.2%
46	North Dakota	2,244	0.3%
6	Ohio	31,875	3.9%
30	Oklahoma	7,332	0.9%
26	Oregon	9,447	1.2%
3	Pennsylvania	50,141	6.2%
42	Rhode Island	3,340	0.4%
29	South Carolina	8,444	1.0%
47	South Dakota	2,173	0.3%
20	Tennessee	14,773	1.8%
4	Texas	48,958	6.1%
34	Utah	4,879	0.6%
48	Vermont	2,116	0.3%
14	Virginia	16,829	2.1%
15	Washington	16,407	2.0%
35	West Virginia	4,708	0.6%
17	Wisconsin	16,074	2.0%
50	Wyoming	1,238	0.2%

RANK ORDER

RANK	STATE	PHYSICIANS	% of USA
1	California	96,634	12.0%
2	New York	73,813	9.1%
3	Pennsylvania	50,141	6.2%
4	Texas	48,958	6.1%
5	Florida	41,483	5.1%
6	Ohio	31,875	3.9%
7	Illinois	31,869	3.9%
8	Michigan	28,234	3.5%
9	Massachusetts	27,476	3.4%
10	New Jersey	27,448	3.4%
11	Maryland	18,572	2.3%
12	Georgia	18,489	2.3%
13	North Carolina	17,615	2.2%
14	Virginia	16,829	2.1%
15	Washington	16,407	2.0%
16	Missouri	16,301	2.0%
17	Wisconsin	16,074	2.0%
18	Minnesota	15,367	1.9%
19	Indiana	15,293	1.9%
20	Tennessee	14,773	1.8%
21	Louisiana	13,156	1.6%
22	Colorado	12,619	1.6%
23	Connecticut	11,878	1.5%
24	Arizona	11,127	1.4%
25	Alabama	9,685	1.2%
26	Oregon	9,447	1.2%
27	Kentucky	9,092	1.1%
28	Iowa	8,492	1.1%
29	South Carolina	8,444	1.0%
30	Oklahoma	7,332	0.9%
31	Arkansas	6,866	0.9%
32	Kansas	6,793	0.8%
33	Mississippi	5,274	0.7%
34	Utah	4,879	0.6%
35	West Virginia	4,708	0.6%
36	Maine	4,425	0.5%
37	Nebraska	4,226	0.5%
38	New Hampshire	4,200	0.5%
39	New Mexico	4,012	0.5%
40	Hawaii**	3,871	0.5%
41	Nevada	3,383	0.4%
42	Rhode Island	3,340	0.4%
43	Montana	2,571	0.3%
44	Idaho	2,451	0.3%
45	Delaware	2,294	0.3%
46	North Dakota	2,244	0.3%
47	South Dakota	2,173	0.3%
48	Vermont	2,116	0.3%
49	Alaska	1,412	0.2%
50	Wyoming	1,238	0.2%
	District of Columbia	4,235	0.5%

Source: U.S. Department of Health and Human Services, Health Care Financing Administration "Medicare Physician Registry" (August 1998)

Medicare Part B. "Physicians" include MD, DO, DDM, DDS, DPM, OD and CH. National total includes 6,265 physicians in Puerto Rico and the Virgin Islands.
**Physicians for Guam are included in Hawaii's total.

Percent of Physicians Participating in Medicare in 1997

National Percent = 80.2% of Physicians Participate in Medicare*

ALPHA ORDER				RANK ORDER		
RANK	STATE	PERCENT		RANK	STATE	PERCENT
1	Alabama	93.5		1	Alabama	93.5
36	Alaska	79.0		2	North Dakota	93.2
17	Arizona	86.6		3	Ohio	92.7
37	Arkansas	78.9		4	Nevada	92.2
31	California	80.9		5	Kansas	91.8
30	Colorado	81.4		6	West Virginia	90.8
18	Connecticut	86.4		7	Utah	90.2
43	Delaware	74.4		8	Washington	89.9
44	Florida	73.9		9	Maryland	89.6
11	Georgia	88.6		10	Kentucky	88.7
23	Hawaii	84.0		11	Georgia	88.6
48	Idaho	67.6		12	Iowa	88.5
25	Illinois	83.3		13	Missouri	88.1
42	Indiana	76.8		14	Oregon	87.6
12	Iowa	88.5		15	Tennessee	87.5
5	Kansas	91.8		16	Nebraska	87.2
10	Kentucky	88.7		17	Arizona	86.6
49	Louisiana	64.6		18	Connecticut	86.4
32	Maine	79.9		19	Virginia	85.7
9	Maryland	89.6		20	South Carolina	85.5
41	Massachusetts	77.2		21	Wisconsin	85.2
27	Michigan	82.6		22	North Carolina	84.6
40	Minnesota	77.3		23	Hawaii	84.0
34	Mississippi	79.3		23	Oklahoma	84.0
13	Missouri	88.1		25	Illinois	83.3
38	Montana	78.7		25	Wyoming	83.3
16	Nebraska	87.2		27	Michigan	82.6
4	Nevada	92.2		28	Texas	82.1
33	New Hampshire	79.7		29	New Mexico	81.7
50	New Jersey	62.8		30	Colorado	81.4
29	New Mexico	81.7		31	California	80.9
46	New York	70.0		32	Maine	79.9
22	North Carolina	84.6		33	New Hampshire	79.7
2	North Dakota	93.2		34	Mississippi	79.3
3	Ohio	92.7		34	South Dakota	79.3
23	Oklahoma	84.0		36	Alaska	79.0
14	Oregon	87.6		37	Arkansas	78.9
45	Pennsylvania	72.0		38	Montana	78.7
47	Rhode Island	68.4		39	Vermont	78.6
20	South Carolina	85.5		40	Minnesota	77.3
34	South Dakota	79.3		41	Massachusetts	77.2
15	Tennessee	87.5		42	Indiana	76.8
28	Texas	82.1		43	Delaware	74.4
7	Utah	90.2		44	Florida	73.9
39	Vermont	78.6		45	Pennsylvania	72.0
19	Virginia	85.7		46	New York	70.0
8	Washington	89.9		47	Rhode Island	68.4
6	West Virginia	90.8		48	Idaho	67.6
21	Wisconsin	85.2		49	Louisiana	64.6
25	Wyoming	83.3		50	New Jersey	62.8
					District of Columbia	68.6

Source: U.S. Department of Health and Human Services, Health Care Financing Administration
  "Practitioner Enrollment in Medicare Program Increases for 1997" (Press Release, May 6, 1997)
*Medicare Part B. Physicians include MD's, DO's, limited license practitioners and non-physician practitioners.

Medicaid Payments in 1997

National Total = $124,429,756,495*

ALPHA ORDER

RANK	STATE	PAYMENTS	% of USA
24	Alabama	$1,571,203,741	1.3%
44	Alaska	320,829,650	0.3%
49	Arizona	245,821,514	0.2%
28	Arkansas	1,301,593,755	1.0%
2	California	11,433,311,901	9.2%
30	Colorado	1,123,843,562	0.9%
20	Connecticut	2,003,015,959	1.6%
48	Delaware	274,826,560	0.2%
6	Florida	4,884,588,899	3.9%
12	Georgia	3,090,016,213	2.5%
38	Hawaii	628,742,323	0.5%
40	Idaho	432,361,263	0.3%
5	Illinois	5,782,847,483	4.6%
14	Indiana	2,381,860,140	1.9%
31	Iowa	1,083,164,078	0.9%
33	Kansas	919,272,243	0.7%
17	Kentucky	2,268,938,421	1.8%
16	Louisiana	2,336,007,497	1.9%
35	Maine	779,569,232	0.6%
18	Maryland	2,200,668,586	1.8%
8	Massachusetts	3,855,391,508	3.1%
10	Michigan	3,591,221,336	2.9%
15	Minnesota	2,358,826,359	1.9%
26	Mississippi	1,424,219,167	1.1%
19	Missouri	2,097,275,522	1.7%
46	Montana	317,733,011	0.3%
37	Nebraska	696,226,804	0.6%
42	Nevada	372,877,260	0.3%
39	New Hampshire	553,935,895	0.4%
11	New Jersey	3,569,003,878	2.9%
34	New Mexico	822,360,613	0.7%
1	New York	21,339,566,488	17.1%
9	North Carolina	3,788,456,205	3.0%
43	North Dakota	328,362,994	0.3%
4	Ohio	5,847,639,671	4.7%
32	Oklahoma	1,038,028,999	0.8%
25	Oregon	1,474,863,025	1.2%
7	Pennsylvania	4,689,468,962	3.8%
36	Rhode Island	737,994,298	0.6%
23	South Carolina	1,607,427,848	1.3%
45	South Dakota	318,474,724	0.3%
13	Tennessee	2,936,393,617	2.4%
3	Texas	7,345,173,561	5.9%
41	Utah	423,724,395	0.3%
47	Vermont	308,611,188	0.2%
22	Virginia	1,857,931,916	1.5%
27	Washington	1,392,671,086	1.1%
29	West Virginia	1,256,997,370	1.0%
21	Wisconsin	1,878,572,907	1.5%
50	Wyoming	184,256,251	0.1%

RANK ORDER

RANK	STATE	PAYMENTS	% of USA
1	New York	$21,339,566,488	17.1%
2	California	11,433,311,901	9.2%
3	Texas	7,345,173,561	5.9%
4	Ohio	5,847,639,671	4.7%
5	Illinois	5,782,847,483	4.6%
6	Florida	4,884,588,899	3.9%
7	Pennsylvania	4,689,468,962	3.8%
8	Massachusetts	3,855,391,508	3.1%
9	North Carolina	3,788,456,205	3.0%
10	Michigan	3,591,221,336	2.9%
11	New Jersey	3,569,003,878	2.9%
12	Georgia	3,090,016,213	2.5%
13	Tennessee	2,936,393,617	2.4%
14	Indiana	2,381,860,140	1.9%
15	Minnesota	2,358,826,359	1.9%
16	Louisiana	2,336,007,497	1.9%
17	Kentucky	2,268,938,421	1.8%
18	Maryland	2,200,668,586	1.8%
19	Missouri	2,097,275,522	1.7%
20	Connecticut	2,003,015,959	1.6%
21	Wisconsin	1,878,572,907	1.5%
22	Virginia	1,857,931,916	1.5%
23	South Carolina	1,607,427,848	1.3%
24	Alabama	1,571,203,741	1.3%
25	Oregon	1,474,863,025	1.2%
26	Mississippi	1,424,219,167	1.1%
27	Washington	1,392,671,086	1.1%
28	Arkansas	1,301,593,755	1.0%
29	West Virginia	1,256,997,370	1.0%
30	Colorado	1,123,843,562	0.9%
31	Iowa	1,083,164,078	0.9%
32	Oklahoma	1,038,028,999	0.8%
33	Kansas	919,272,243	0.7%
34	New Mexico	822,360,613	0.7%
35	Maine	779,569,232	0.6%
36	Rhode Island	737,994,298	0.6%
37	Nebraska	696,226,804	0.6%
38	Hawaii	628,742,323	0.5%
39	New Hampshire	553,935,895	0.4%
40	Idaho	432,361,263	0.3%
41	Utah	423,724,395	0.3%
42	Nevada	372,877,260	0.3%
43	North Dakota	328,362,994	0.3%
44	Alaska	320,829,650	0.3%
45	South Dakota	318,474,724	0.3%
46	Montana	317,733,011	0.3%
47	Vermont	308,611,188	0.2%
48	Delaware	274,826,560	0.2%
49	Arizona	245,821,514	0.2%
50	Wyoming	184,256,251	0.1%
	District of Columbia	696,209,244	0.6%

Source: U.S. Department of Health and Human Services, Health Care Financing Administration
"Medicaid Medical Vendor Payments by Type of Service, Region and State: FY 1997" (HCFA-2082)
*Revised figures for fiscal year ending September 30, 1997. National total includes payments for the Virgin Islands.

Percent Change in Medicaid Payments: 1990 to 1997

National Percent Change = 91.8% Increase*

ALPHA ORDER

RANK	STATE	PERCENT CHANGE
9	Alabama	157.9
16	Alaska	130.6
NA	Arizona**	NA
21	Arkansas	117.2
35	California	75.7
20	Colorado	117.9
41	Connecticut	66.2
19	Delaware	123.1
23	Florida	106.9
47	Georgia	48.8
2	Hawaii	228.6
6	Idaho	166.6
13	Illinois	138.6
34	Indiana	77.4
36	Iowa	74.6
28	Kansas	87.4
15	Kentucky	132.3
33	Louisiana	77.7
31	Maine	80.5
24	Maryland	101.8
49	Massachusetts	41.2
42	Michigan	63.6
39	Minnesota	67.2
12	Mississippi	143.0
14	Missouri	133.7
30	Montana	86.3
18	Nebraska	125.1
11	Nevada	150.9
17	New Hampshire	127.9
44	New Jersey	55.3
4	New Mexico	198.8
32	New York	79.7
7	North Carolina	165.7
38	North Dakota	69.4
29	Ohio	86.7
45	Oklahoma	51.0
5	Oregon	184.3
43	Pennsylvania	62.7
40	Rhode Island	66.9
22	South Carolina	116.3
26	South Dakota	91.8
10	Tennessee	152.5
8	Texas	164.1
37	Utah	71.8
24	Vermont	101.8
27	Virginia	88.6
48	Washington	46.2
1	West Virginia	248.1
46	Wisconsin	50.5
3	Wyoming	212.7

RANK ORDER

RANK	STATE	PERCENT CHANGE
1	West Virginia	248.1
2	Hawaii	228.6
3	Wyoming	212.7
4	New Mexico	198.8
5	Oregon	184.3
6	Idaho	166.6
7	North Carolina	165.7
8	Texas	164.1
9	Alabama	157.9
10	Tennessee	152.5
11	Nevada	150.9
12	Mississippi	143.0
13	Illinois	138.6
14	Missouri	133.7
15	Kentucky	132.3
16	Alaska	130.6
17	New Hampshire	127.9
18	Nebraska	125.1
19	Delaware	123.1
20	Colorado	117.9
21	Arkansas	117.2
22	South Carolina	116.3
23	Florida	106.9
24	Maryland	101.8
24	Vermont	101.8
26	South Dakota	91.8
27	Virginia	88.6
28	Kansas	87.4
29	Ohio	86.7
30	Montana	86.3
31	Maine	80.5
32	New York	79.7
33	Louisiana	77.7
34	Indiana	77.4
35	California	75.7
36	Iowa	74.6
37	Utah	71.8
38	North Dakota	69.4
39	Minnesota	67.2
40	Rhode Island	66.9
41	Connecticut	66.2
42	Michigan	63.6
43	Pennsylvania	62.7
44	New Jersey	55.3
45	Oklahoma	51.0
46	Wisconsin	50.5
47	Georgia	48.8
48	Washington	46.2
49	Massachusetts	41.2
NA	Arizona**	NA

District of Columbia   183.3

Source: Morgan Quitno Press using data from U.S. Dept. of Health & Human Services, Health Care Financing Admin.
"Medicaid Recipients, Vendor Payments and Average Cost per Recipient by State: FY 1997" (HCFA-2082)
*Revised figures for fiscal year ending September 30, 1997.
**Not available.

Medicaid Recipients in 1997

National Total = 34,872,275 Recipients*

<u>ALPHA ORDER</u>

RANK	STATE	RECIPIENTS	% of USA
17	Alabama	546,140	1.6%
48	Alaska	73,050	0.2%
18	Arizona	540,785	1.6%
28	Arkansas	370,386	1.1%
1	California	4,854,546	13.9%
33	Colorado	251,423	0.7%
37	Connecticut	201,779	0.6%
46	Delaware	83,956	0.2%
4	Florida	1,597,461	4.6%
8	Georgia	1,208,445	3.5%
35	Hawaii	206,081	0.6%
41	Idaho	115,087	0.3%
6	Illinois	1,399,960	4.0%
23	Indiana	514,683	1.5%
32	Iowa	293,596	0.8%
34	Kansas	232,888	0.7%
14	Kentucky	664,454	1.9%
12	Louisiana	746,461	2.1%
38	Maine	167,221	0.5%
25	Maryland	402,002	1.2%
13	Massachusetts	723,472	2.1%
9	Michigan	1,132,783	3.2%
27	Minnesota	371,483	1.1%
24	Mississippi	504,017	1.4%
19	Missouri	540,487	1.5%
44	Montana	95,562	0.3%
36	Nebraska	203,340	0.6%
43	Nevada	105,588	0.3%
45	New Hampshire	95,215	0.3%
20	New Jersey	537,890	1.5%
30	New Mexico	320,223	0.9%
2	New York	3,151,837	9.0%
10	North Carolina	1,112,931	3.2%
49	North Dakota	61,117	0.2%
7	Ohio	1,395,540	4.0%
31	Oklahoma	315,801	0.9%
21	Oregon	531,242	1.5%
11	Pennsylvania	1,024,993	2.9%
40	Rhode Island	116,766	0.3%
22	South Carolina	519,875	1.5%
47	South Dakota	75,444	0.2%
5	Tennessee	1,415,612	4.1%
3	Texas	2,538,655	7.3%
39	Utah	144,749	0.4%
42	Vermont	109,283	0.3%
16	Virginia	595,234	1.7%
15	Washington	630,165	1.8%
29	West Virginia	359,091	1.0%
26	Wisconsin	392,223	1.1%
50	Wyoming	48,865	0.1%

<u>RANK ORDER</u>

RANK	STATE	RECIPIENTS	% of USA
1	California	4,854,546	13.9%
2	New York	3,151,837	9.0%
3	Texas	2,538,655	7.3%
4	Florida	1,597,461	4.6%
5	Tennessee	1,415,612	4.1%
6	Illinois	1,399,960	4.0%
7	Ohio	1,395,540	4.0%
8	Georgia	1,208,445	3.5%
9	Michigan	1,132,783	3.2%
10	North Carolina	1,112,931	3.2%
11	Pennsylvania	1,024,993	2.9%
12	Louisiana	746,461	2.1%
13	Massachusetts	723,472	2.1%
14	Kentucky	664,454	1.9%
15	Washington	630,165	1.8%
16	Virginia	595,234	1.7%
17	Alabama	546,140	1.6%
18	Arizona	540,785	1.6%
19	Missouri	540,487	1.5%
20	New Jersey	537,890	1.5%
21	Oregon	531,242	1.5%
22	South Carolina	519,875	1.5%
23	Indiana	514,683	1.5%
24	Mississippi	504,017	1.4%
25	Maryland	402,002	1.2%
26	Wisconsin	392,223	1.1%
27	Minnesota	371,483	1.1%
28	Arkansas	370,386	1.1%
29	West Virginia	359,091	1.0%
30	New Mexico	320,223	0.9%
31	Oklahoma	315,801	0.9%
32	Iowa	293,596	0.8%
33	Colorado	251,423	0.7%
34	Kansas	232,888	0.7%
35	Hawaii	206,081	0.6%
36	Nebraska	203,340	0.6%
37	Connecticut	201,779	0.6%
38	Maine	167,221	0.5%
39	Utah	144,749	0.4%
40	Rhode Island	116,766	0.3%
41	Idaho	115,087	0.3%
42	Vermont	109,283	0.3%
43	Nevada	105,588	0.3%
44	Montana	95,562	0.3%
45	New Hampshire	95,215	0.3%
46	Delaware	83,956	0.2%
47	South Dakota	75,444	0.2%
48	Alaska	73,050	0.2%
49	North Dakota	61,117	0.2%
50	Wyoming	48,865	0.1%
	District of Columbia	128,008	0.4%

Source: U.S. Department of Health and Human Services, Health Care Financing Administration
"Medicaid Recipients by Basis of Eligibility and by State: FY 1997" (HCFA-2082)
*Revised figures for fiscal year ending September 30, 1997. National total includes recipients in the Virgin Islands.

Percent Change in Number of Medicaid Recipients: 1990 to 1997

National Percent Change = 38.1% Increase*

ALPHA ORDER				RANK ORDER		
RANK	STATE	PERCENT CHANGE		RANK	STATE	PERCENT CHANGE
19	Alabama	55.2		1	New Mexico	146.6
10	Alaska	87.1		2	Hawaii	142.5
NA	Arizona**	NA		3	Oregon	133.8
26	Arkansas	40.1		4	Tennessee	130.8
28	California	33.9		5	Nevada	124.6
30	Colorado	31.9		6	New Hampshire	112.4
49	Connecticut	(19.2)		7	Idaho	111.0
8	Delaware	104.7		8	Delaware	104.7
20	Florida	53.8		9	North Carolina	97.6
11	Georgia	85.7		10	Alaska	87.1
2	Hawaii	142.5		11	Georgia	85.7
7	Idaho	111.0		12	Vermont	80.9
31	Illinois	31.1		13	Texas	76.0
22	Indiana	48.0		14	Nebraska	70.6
35	Iowa	22.5		15	Wyoming	68.8
39	Kansas	19.8		16	South Carolina	63.9
24	Kentucky	42.1		17	Virginia	56.9
32	Louisiana	27.6		18	Montana	56.5
33	Maine	25.7		19	Alabama	55.2
37	Maryland	21.7		20	Florida	53.8
35	Massachusetts	22.5		21	South Dakota	53.0
43	Michigan	8.1		22	Indiana	48.0
46	Minnesota	(2.3)		23	West Virginia	43.5
40	Mississippi	16.4		24	Kentucky	42.1
38	Missouri	20.6		25	Washington	40.8
18	Montana	56.5		26	Arkansas	40.1
14	Nebraska	70.6		27	New York	35.3
5	Nevada	124.6		28	California	33.9
6	New Hampshire	112.4		29	Utah	33.7
47	New Jersey	(5.1)		30	Colorado	31.9
1	New Mexico	146.6		31	Illinois	31.1
27	New York	35.3		32	Louisiana	27.6
9	North Carolina	97.6		33	Maine	25.7
34	North Dakota	24.7		34	North Dakota	24.7
42	Ohio	14.3		35	Iowa	22.5
41	Oklahoma	15.6		35	Massachusetts	22.5
3	Oregon	133.8		37	Maryland	21.7
48	Pennsylvania	(12.9)		38	Missouri	20.6
45	Rhode Island	(0.2)		39	Kansas	19.8
16	South Carolina	63.9		40	Mississippi	16.4
21	South Dakota	53.0		41	Oklahoma	15.6
4	Tennessee	130.8		42	Ohio	14.3
13	Texas	76.0		43	Michigan	8.1
29	Utah	33.7		44	Wisconsin	(0.1)
12	Vermont	80.9		45	Rhode Island	(0.2)
17	Virginia	56.9		46	Minnesota	(2.3)
25	Washington	40.8		47	New Jersey	(5.1)
23	West Virginia	43.5		48	Pennsylvania	(12.9)
44	Wisconsin	(0.1)		49	Connecticut	(19.2)
15	Wyoming	68.8		NA	Arizona**	NA
					District of Columbia	36.9

Source: Morgan Quitno Press using data from U.S. Dept. of Health & Human Services, Health Care Financing Admin. "HCFA-2082 Report" (FY97 and FY90)

*Revised figures for fiscal year ending September 30, 1997. National rate includes recipients Puerto Rico and the Virgin Islands.

**Not available.

Medicaid Payments per Recipient in 1997

National Rate = $3,568 per Recipient*

ALPHA ORDER

RANK	STATE	PER RECIPIENT
40	Alabama	$2,877
14	Alaska	4,392
49	Arizona	455
24	Arkansas	3,514
46	California	2,355
13	Colorado	4,470
NA	Connecticut**	NA
31	Delaware	3,273
36	Florida	3,058
45	Georgia	2,557
37	Hawaii	3,051
21	Idaho	3,757
17	Illinois	4,131
11	Indiana	4,628
22	Iowa	3,689
18	Kansas	3,947
27	Kentucky	3,415
33	Louisiana	3,129
10	Maine	4,662
6	Maryland	5,474
8	Massachusetts	5,329
32	Michigan	3,170
3	Minnesota	6,350
41	Mississippi	2,826
19	Missouri	3,880
29	Montana	3,325
26	Nebraska	3,424
23	Nevada	3,531
5	New Hampshire	5,818
2	New Jersey	6,635
44	New Mexico	2,568
1	New York	6,771
28	North Carolina	3,404
7	North Dakota	5,373
16	Ohio	4,190
30	Oklahoma	3,287
43	Oregon	2,776
12	Pennsylvania	4,575
4	Rhode Island	6,320
35	South Carolina	3,092
15	South Dakota	4,221
48	Tennessee	2,074
39	Texas	2,893
38	Utah	2,927
42	Vermont	2,824
34	Virginia	3,121
47	Washington	2,210
25	West Virginia	3,500
9	Wisconsin	4,790
20	Wyoming	3,771

RANK ORDER

RANK	STATE	PER RECIPIENT
1	New York	$6,771
2	New Jersey	6,635
3	Minnesota	6,350
4	Rhode Island	6,320
5	New Hampshire	5,818
6	Maryland	5,474
7	North Dakota	5,373
8	Massachusetts	5,329
9	Wisconsin	4,790
10	Maine	4,662
11	Indiana	4,628
12	Pennsylvania	4,575
13	Colorado	4,470
14	Alaska	4,392
15	South Dakota	4,221
16	Ohio	4,190
17	Illinois	4,131
18	Kansas	3,947
19	Missouri	3,880
20	Wyoming	3,771
21	Idaho	3,757
22	Iowa	3,689
23	Nevada	3,531
24	Arkansas	3,514
25	West Virginia	3,500
26	Nebraska	3,424
27	Kentucky	3,415
28	North Carolina	3,404
29	Montana	3,325
30	Oklahoma	3,287
31	Delaware	3,273
32	Michigan	3,170
33	Louisiana	3,129
34	Virginia	3,121
35	South Carolina	3,092
36	Florida	3,058
37	Hawaii	3,051
38	Utah	2,927
39	Texas	2,893
40	Alabama	2,877
41	Mississippi	2,826
42	Vermont	2,824
43	Oregon	2,776
44	New Mexico	2,568
45	Georgia	2,557
46	California	2,355
47	Washington	2,210
48	Tennessee	2,074
49	Arizona	455
NA	Connecticut**	NA
	District of Columbia	5,439

Source: Morgan Quitno Press using data from U.S. Dept. of Health & Human Services, Health Care Financing Admin.
    "HCFA-2082 Report: FY97" (www.hcfa.gov/medicaid/mstats.htm)
*Revised figures for fiscal year ending September 30, 1997.
**Not available.

Percent Change in Payments per Medicaid Recipient: 1990 to 1997

National Percent Change = 38.9% Increase*

<table>
<tr><td colspan="3">ALPHA ORDER</td><td colspan="3">RANK ORDER</td></tr>
<tr><td>RANK</td><td>STATE</td><td>PERCENT CHANGE</td><td>RANK</td><td>STATE</td><td>PERCENT CHANGE</td></tr>
<tr><td>9</td><td>Alabama</td><td>66.2</td><td>1</td><td>West Virginia</td><td>142.6</td></tr>
<tr><td>35</td><td>Alaska</td><td>23.3</td><td>2</td><td>Mississippi</td><td>108.7</td></tr>
<tr><td>NA</td><td>Arizona**</td><td>NA</td><td>3</td><td>Missouri</td><td>93.8</td></tr>
<tr><td>16</td><td>Arkansas</td><td>55.0</td><td>4</td><td>Pennsylvania</td><td>86.8</td></tr>
<tr><td>30</td><td>California</td><td>31.2</td><td>5</td><td>Wyoming</td><td>85.2</td></tr>
<tr><td>11</td><td>Colorado</td><td>65.2</td><td>6</td><td>Illinois</td><td>81.9</td></tr>
<tr><td>NA</td><td>Connecticut**</td><td>NA</td><td>7</td><td>Minnesota</td><td>71.2</td></tr>
<tr><td>45</td><td>Delaware</td><td>9.0</td><td>8</td><td>Rhode Island</td><td>67.3</td></tr>
<tr><td>25</td><td>Florida</td><td>34.5</td><td>9</td><td>Alabama</td><td>66.2</td></tr>
<tr><td>48</td><td>Georgia</td><td>(19.8)</td><td>10</td><td>Maryland</td><td>65.9</td></tr>
<tr><td>24</td><td>Hawaii</td><td>35.5</td><td>11</td><td>Colorado</td><td>65.2</td></tr>
<tr><td>33</td><td>Idaho</td><td>26.4</td><td>12</td><td>New Jersey</td><td>63.7</td></tr>
<tr><td>6</td><td>Illinois</td><td>81.9</td><td>13</td><td>Kentucky</td><td>63.5</td></tr>
<tr><td>39</td><td>Indiana</td><td>19.9</td><td>14</td><td>Ohio</td><td>63.3</td></tr>
<tr><td>21</td><td>Iowa</td><td>42.5</td><td>15</td><td>Kansas</td><td>56.4</td></tr>
<tr><td>15</td><td>Kansas</td><td>56.4</td><td>16</td><td>Arkansas</td><td>55.0</td></tr>
<tr><td>13</td><td>Kentucky</td><td>63.5</td><td>17</td><td>Michigan</td><td>51.4</td></tr>
<tr><td>22</td><td>Louisiana</td><td>39.3</td><td>18</td><td>Wisconsin</td><td>50.7</td></tr>
<tr><td>20</td><td>Maine</td><td>43.5</td><td>19</td><td>Texas</td><td>50.1</td></tr>
<tr><td>10</td><td>Maryland</td><td>65.9</td><td>20</td><td>Maine</td><td>43.5</td></tr>
<tr><td>41</td><td>Massachusetts</td><td>15.3</td><td>21</td><td>Iowa</td><td>42.5</td></tr>
<tr><td>17</td><td>Michigan</td><td>51.4</td><td>22</td><td>Louisiana</td><td>39.3</td></tr>
<tr><td>7</td><td>Minnesota</td><td>71.2</td><td>23</td><td>North Dakota</td><td>35.9</td></tr>
<tr><td>2</td><td>Mississippi</td><td>108.7</td><td>24</td><td>Hawaii</td><td>35.5</td></tr>
<tr><td>3</td><td>Missouri</td><td>93.8</td><td>25</td><td>Florida</td><td>34.5</td></tr>
<tr><td>40</td><td>Montana</td><td>19.0</td><td>25</td><td>North Carolina</td><td>34.5</td></tr>
<tr><td>29</td><td>Nebraska</td><td>31.9</td><td>27</td><td>New York</td><td>32.8</td></tr>
<tr><td>42</td><td>Nevada</td><td>11.7</td><td>28</td><td>South Carolina</td><td>32.0</td></tr>
<tr><td>46</td><td>New Hampshire</td><td>7.3</td><td>29</td><td>Nebraska</td><td>31.9</td></tr>
<tr><td>12</td><td>New Jersey</td><td>63.7</td><td>30</td><td>California</td><td>31.2</td></tr>
<tr><td>37</td><td>New Mexico</td><td>21.1</td><td>31</td><td>Oklahoma</td><td>30.6</td></tr>
<tr><td>27</td><td>New York</td><td>32.8</td><td>32</td><td>Utah</td><td>28.4</td></tr>
<tr><td>25</td><td>North Carolina</td><td>34.5</td><td>33</td><td>Idaho</td><td>26.4</td></tr>
<tr><td>23</td><td>North Dakota</td><td>35.9</td><td>34</td><td>South Dakota</td><td>25.3</td></tr>
<tr><td>14</td><td>Ohio</td><td>63.3</td><td>35</td><td>Alaska</td><td>23.3</td></tr>
<tr><td>31</td><td>Oklahoma</td><td>30.6</td><td>36</td><td>Oregon</td><td>21.6</td></tr>
<tr><td>36</td><td>Oregon</td><td>21.6</td><td>37</td><td>New Mexico</td><td>21.1</td></tr>
<tr><td>4</td><td>Pennsylvania</td><td>86.8</td><td>38</td><td>Virginia</td><td>20.2</td></tr>
<tr><td>8</td><td>Rhode Island</td><td>67.3</td><td>39</td><td>Indiana</td><td>19.9</td></tr>
<tr><td>28</td><td>South Carolina</td><td>32.0</td><td>40</td><td>Montana</td><td>19.0</td></tr>
<tr><td>34</td><td>South Dakota</td><td>25.3</td><td>41</td><td>Massachusetts</td><td>15.3</td></tr>
<tr><td>44</td><td>Tennessee</td><td>9.4</td><td>42</td><td>Nevada</td><td>11.7</td></tr>
<tr><td>19</td><td>Texas</td><td>50.1</td><td>43</td><td>Vermont</td><td>11.6</td></tr>
<tr><td>32</td><td>Utah</td><td>28.4</td><td>44</td><td>Tennessee</td><td>9.4</td></tr>
<tr><td>43</td><td>Vermont</td><td>11.6</td><td>45</td><td>Delaware</td><td>9.0</td></tr>
<tr><td>38</td><td>Virginia</td><td>20.2</td><td>46</td><td>New Hampshire</td><td>7.3</td></tr>
<tr><td>47</td><td>Washington</td><td>3.9</td><td>47</td><td>Washington</td><td>3.9</td></tr>
<tr><td>1</td><td>West Virginia</td><td>142.6</td><td>48</td><td>Georgia</td><td>(19.8)</td></tr>
<tr><td>18</td><td>Wisconsin</td><td>50.7</td><td>NA</td><td>Arizona**</td><td>NA</td></tr>
<tr><td>5</td><td>Wyoming</td><td>85.2</td><td>NA</td><td>Connecticut**</td><td>NA</td></tr>
<tr><td></td><td></td><td></td><td></td><td>District of Columbia</td><td>106.9</td></tr>
</table>

Source: Morgan Quitno Press using data from U.S. Dept. of Health & Human Services, Health Care Financing Admin. "Medicaid Recipients, Vendor Payments and Average Cost per Recipient by State: FY 1997" (HCFA-2082)
*Revised figures for fiscal year ending September 30, 1997.
**Not available.

Federal Medicaid Matching Fund Rate for 2000

National Average = 72.52% of States' Funds Matched by Federal Government*

ALPHA ORDER				RANK ORDER		
RANK	STATE	RATE		RANK	STATE	RATE
13	Alabama	78.70		1	Mississippi	83.76
29	Alaska	71.86		2	West Virginia	82.35
16	Arizona	76.14		3	New Mexico	81.32
4	Arkansas	80.99		4	Arkansas	80.99
37	California	66.17		5	Montana	80.61
41	Colorado	65.00		6	Utah	80.08
41	Connecticut	65.00		7	Oklahoma	79.76
41	Delaware	65.00		8	Kentucky	79.38
32	Florida	69.57		9	North Dakota	79.29
28	Georgia	71.91		10	Louisiana	79.22
40	Hawaii	65.71		11	Idaho	79.11
11	Idaho	79.11		12	South Carolina	78.96
41	Illinois	65.00		13	Alabama	78.70
22	Indiana	73.22		14	South Dakota	78.11
19	Iowa	74.14		15	Maine	76.36
26	Kansas	72.02		16	Arizona	76.14
8	Kentucky	79.38		17	Wyoming	74.83
10	Louisiana	79.22		18	Tennessee	74.17
15	Maine	76.36		19	Iowa	74.14
41	Maryland	65.00		20	North Carolina	73.74
41	Massachusetts	65.00		21	Vermont	73.57
33	Michigan	68.58		22	Indiana	73.22
39	Minnesota	66.04		23	Texas	72.95
1	Mississippi	83.76		24	Nebraska	72.62
25	Missouri	72.36		25	Missouri	72.36
5	Montana	80.61		26	Kansas	72.02
24	Nebraska	72.62		27	Oregon	71.97
41	Nevada	65.00		28	Georgia	71.91
41	New Hampshire	65.00		29	Alaska	71.86
41	New Jersey	65.00		30	Wisconsin	71.15
3	New Mexico	81.32		31	Ohio	71.07
41	New York	65.00		32	Florida	69.57
20	North Carolina	73.74		33	Michigan	68.58
9	North Dakota	79.29		34	Pennsylvania	67.67
31	Ohio	71.07		35	Rhode Island	67.64
7	Oklahoma	79.76		36	Washington	66.28
27	Oregon	71.97		37	California	66.17
34	Pennsylvania	67.67		37	Virginia	66.17
35	Rhode Island	67.64		39	Minnesota	66.04
12	South Carolina	78.96		40	Hawaii	65.71
14	South Dakota	78.11		41	Colorado	65.00
18	Tennessee	74.17		41	Connecticut	65.00
23	Texas	72.95		41	Delaware	65.00
6	Utah	80.08		41	Illinois	65.00
21	Vermont	73.57		41	Maryland	65.00
37	Virginia	66.17		41	Massachusetts	65.00
36	Washington	66.28		41	Nevada	65.00
2	West Virginia	82.35		41	New Hampshire	65.00
30	Wisconsin	71.15		41	New Jersey	65.00
17	Wyoming	74.83		41	New York	65.00
					District of Columbia	79.00

Source: U.S. Department of Health and Human Services, Health Care Financing Administration
   "Enhanced Federal Medical Assistance Percentages" (Federal Register, 1/12/99)
*For fiscal year 1999. These are "enhanced" matching rates established by the Children's Health Insurance Program, signed into law in August 1997. Sixty-five percent is the minimum. National average is a simple average of the 51 individual rates and is not weighted for population or funds.

Percent of Population Receiving Medicaid in 1998

National Percent = 11.1% of Population*

ALPHA ORDER

RANK ORDER

RANK	STATE	PERCENT
16	Alabama	11.7
25	Alaska	10.7
29	Arizona	9.3
12	Arkansas	13.1
5	California	15.0
49	Colorado	5.5
28	Connecticut	9.4
22	Delaware	10.9
27	Florida	9.5
17	Georgia	11.6
9	Hawaii	13.8
42	Idaho	7.2
23	Illinois	10.8
44	Indiana	6.8
42	Iowa	7.2
46	Kansas	6.5
11	Kentucky	13.2
3	Louisiana	17.3
13	Maine	12.3
34	Maryland	8.9
9	Massachusetts	13.8
19	Michigan	11.3
32	Minnesota	9.1
6	Mississippi	14.0
20	Missouri	11.2
38	Montana	7.7
32	Nebraska	9.1
50	Nevada	5.2
47	New Hampshire	6.2
37	New Jersey	7.9
6	New Mexico	14.0
15	New York	11.8
23	North Carolina	10.8
45	North Dakota	6.7
31	Ohio	9.2
29	Oklahoma	9.3
26	Oregon	10.3
21	Pennsylvania	11.0
14	Rhode Island	11.9
18	South Carolina	11.5
36	South Dakota	8.5
1	Tennessee	23.4
35	Texas	8.7
48	Utah	5.9
2	Vermont	18.3
41	Virginia	7.3
8	Washington	13.9
4	West Virginia	17.1
39	Wisconsin	7.6
40	Wyoming	7.4

RANK	STATE	PERCENT
1	Tennessee	23.4
2	Vermont	18.3
3	Louisiana	17.3
4	West Virginia	17.1
5	California	15.0
6	Mississippi	14.0
6	New Mexico	14.0
8	Washington	13.9
9	Hawaii	13.8
9	Massachusetts	13.8
11	Kentucky	13.2
12	Arkansas	13.1
13	Maine	12.3
14	Rhode Island	11.9
15	New York	11.8
16	Alabama	11.7
17	Georgia	11.6
18	South Carolina	11.5
19	Michigan	11.3
20	Missouri	11.2
21	Pennsylvania	11.0
22	Delaware	10.9
23	Illinois	10.8
23	North Carolina	10.8
25	Alaska	10.7
26	Oregon	10.3
27	Florida	9.5
28	Connecticut	9.4
29	Arizona	9.3
29	Oklahoma	9.3
31	Ohio	9.2
32	Minnesota	9.1
32	Nebraska	9.1
34	Maryland	8.9
35	Texas	8.7
36	South Dakota	8.5
37	New Jersey	7.9
38	Montana	7.7
39	Wisconsin	7.6
40	Wyoming	7.4
41	Virginia	7.3
42	Idaho	7.2
42	Iowa	7.2
44	Indiana	6.8
45	North Dakota	6.7
46	Kansas	6.5
47	New Hampshire	6.2
48	Utah	5.9
49	Colorado	5.5
50	Nevada	5.2

District of Columbia   21.6

Source: Morgan Quitno Press using data from US Dept. of Health & Human Services, Health Care Financing Admin.
    "Medicaid Managed Care State Enrollment" (http://www.hcfa.gov/medicaid/mcsten98.htm)
*As of June 30, 1998. National percent does not include recipients or population in Puerto Rico or the Virgin Islands.

Medicaid Managed Care Enrollment in 1998

National Total = 16,573,996 Medicaid Enrollees*

ALPHA ORDER

RANK	STATE	ENROLLEES	% of USA
14	Alabama	362,272	2.2%
49	Alaska	0	0.0%
13	Arizona	368,344	2.2%
28	Arkansas	186,215	1.1%
1	California	2,246,406	13.6%
24	Colorado	215,936	1.3%
23	Connecticut	220,803	1.3%
39	Delaware	62,010	0.4%
3	Florida	915,554	5.5%
7	Georgia	673,528	4.1%
32	Hawaii	131,761	0.8%
44	Idaho	30,866	0.2%
29	Illinois	175,649	1.1%
21	Indiana	233,065	1.4%
27	Iowa	190,692	1.2%
36	Kansas	84,437	0.5%
15	Kentucky	325,233	2.0%
42	Louisiana	40,729	0.2%
46	Maine	16,295	0.1%
16	Maryland	306,474	1.8%
10	Massachusetts	532,971	3.2%
5	Michigan	752,568	4.5%
22	Minnesota	225,498	1.4%
31	Mississippi	153,562	0.9%
20	Missouri	252,097	1.5%
38	Montana	66,331	0.4%
35	Nebraska	110,606	0.7%
43	Nevada	35,089	0.2%
48	New Hampshire	7,368	0.0%
12	New Jersey	376,839	2.3%
26	New Mexico	193,818	1.2%
8	New York	634,233	3.8%
9	North Carolina	559,035	3.4%
45	North Dakota	22,045	0.1%
19	Ohio	292,819	1.8%
30	Oklahoma	154,270	0.9%
17	Oregon	299,826	1.8%
4	Pennsylvania	904,701	5.5%
37	Rhode Island	74,446	0.4%
47	South Carolina	15,823	0.1%
41	South Dakota	43,834	0.3%
2	Tennessee	1,268,769	7.7%
11	Texas	437,898	2.6%
34	Utah	112,803	0.7%
40	Vermont	52,153	0.3%
18	Virginia	299,266	1.8%
6	Washington	718,023	4.3%
33	West Virginia	131,349	0.8%
25	Wisconsin	194,874	1.2%
49	Wyoming	0	0.0%

RANK ORDER

RANK	STATE	ENROLLEES	% of USA
1	California	2,246,406	13.6%
2	Tennessee	1,268,769	7.7%
3	Florida	915,554	5.5%
4	Pennsylvania	904,701	5.5%
5	Michigan	752,568	4.5%
6	Washington	718,023	4.3%
7	Georgia	673,528	4.1%
8	New York	634,233	3.8%
9	North Carolina	559,035	3.4%
10	Massachusetts	532,971	3.2%
11	Texas	437,898	2.6%
12	New Jersey	376,839	2.3%
13	Arizona	368,344	2.2%
14	Alabama	362,272	2.2%
15	Kentucky	325,233	2.0%
16	Maryland	306,474	1.8%
17	Oregon	299,826	1.8%
18	Virginia	299,266	1.8%
19	Ohio	292,819	1.8%
20	Missouri	252,097	1.5%
21	Indiana	233,065	1.4%
22	Minnesota	225,498	1.4%
23	Connecticut	220,803	1.3%
24	Colorado	215,936	1.3%
25	Wisconsin	194,874	1.2%
26	New Mexico	193,818	1.2%
27	Iowa	190,692	1.2%
28	Arkansas	186,215	1.1%
29	Illinois	175,649	1.1%
30	Oklahoma	154,270	0.9%
31	Mississippi	153,562	0.9%
32	Hawaii	131,761	0.8%
33	West Virginia	131,349	0.8%
34	Utah	112,803	0.7%
35	Nebraska	110,606	0.7%
36	Kansas	84,437	0.5%
37	Rhode Island	74,446	0.4%
38	Montana	66,331	0.4%
39	Delaware	62,010	0.4%
40	Vermont	52,153	0.3%
41	South Dakota	43,834	0.3%
42	Louisiana	40,729	0.2%
43	Nevada	35,089	0.2%
44	Idaho	30,866	0.2%
45	North Dakota	22,045	0.1%
46	Maine	16,295	0.1%
47	South Carolina	15,823	0.1%
48	New Hampshire	7,368	0.0%
49	Alaska	0	0.0%
49	Wyoming	0	0.0%
	District of Columbia	51,022	0.3%

Source: U.S. Department of Health and Human Services, Health Care Financing Administration
"Medicaid Managed Care State Enrollment" (http://www.hcfa.gov/medicaid/mcsten98.htm)
As of June 30, 1998. Enrollment in state health care reform programs that expand eligibility beyond traditional
Medicaid standards. National total includes 813,791 Medicaid enrollees in Puerto Rico.

Percent of Medicaid Enrollees in Managed Care in 1998

National Percent = 53.6% of Medicaid Enrollees*

ALPHA ORDER

RANK	STATE	PERCENT
15	Alabama	70.9
49	Alaska	0.0
8	Arizona	85.1
28	Arkansas	56.0
35	California	45.8
2	Colorado	99.0
14	Connecticut	71.9
11	Delaware	76.8
21	Florida	64.6
12	Georgia	76.3
9	Hawaii	80.5
40	Idaho	34.8
44	Illinois	13.4
27	Indiana	57.7
4	Iowa	92.1
32	Kansas	49.4
23	Kentucky	62.7
47	Louisiana	5.4
45	Maine	10.7
20	Maryland	67.1
23	Massachusetts	62.7
19	Michigan	68.0
29	Minnesota	52.6
38	Mississippi	40.0
37	Missouri	41.5
3	Montana	98.4
13	Nebraska	72.8
39	Nevada	38.7
46	New Hampshire	10.1
26	New Jersey	58.6
10	New Mexico	79.7
41	New York	29.6
17	North Carolina	68.6
30	North Dakota	51.9
42	Ohio	28.4
31	Oklahoma	49.7
7	Oregon	88.7
18	Pennsylvania	68.3
22	Rhode Island	63.2
48	South Carolina	3.6
16	South Dakota	70.6
1	Tennessee	100.0
43	Texas	25.5
5	Utah	91.3
34	Vermont	48.3
25	Virginia	60.0
6	Washington	91.0
36	West Virginia	42.5
33	Wisconsin	49.1
49	Wyoming	0.0

RANK ORDER

RANK	STATE	PERCENT
1	Tennessee	100.0
2	Colorado	99.0
3	Montana	98.4
4	Iowa	92.1
5	Utah	91.3
6	Washington	91.0
7	Oregon	88.7
8	Arizona	85.1
9	Hawaii	80.5
10	New Mexico	79.7
11	Delaware	76.8
12	Georgia	76.3
13	Nebraska	72.8
14	Connecticut	71.9
15	Alabama	70.9
16	South Dakota	70.6
17	North Carolina	68.6
18	Pennsylvania	68.3
19	Michigan	68.0
20	Maryland	67.1
21	Florida	64.6
22	Rhode Island	63.2
23	Kentucky	62.7
23	Massachusetts	62.7
25	Virginia	60.0
26	New Jersey	58.6
27	Indiana	57.7
28	Arkansas	56.0
29	Minnesota	52.6
30	North Dakota	51.9
31	Oklahoma	49.7
32	Kansas	49.4
33	Wisconsin	49.1
34	Vermont	48.3
35	California	45.8
36	West Virginia	42.5
37	Missouri	41.5
38	Mississippi	40.0
39	Nevada	38.7
40	Idaho	34.8
41	New York	29.6
42	Ohio	28.4
43	Texas	25.5
44	Illinois	13.4
45	Maine	10.7
46	New Hampshire	10.1
47	Louisiana	5.4
48	South Carolina	3.6
49	Alaska	0.0
49	Wyoming	0.0
	District of Columbia	45.3

Source: U.S. Department of Health and Human Services, Health Care Financing Administration
"Medicaid Managed Care State Enrollment" (http://www.hcfa.gov/medicaid/mcsten98.htm)
*As of June 30, 1998. Enrollment in state health care reform programs that expand eligibility beyond traditional Medicaid standards. National percent includes Medicaid enrollees in Puerto Rico and the Virgin Islands.

Estimated State Funds from the Tobacco Settlement Through 2025

National Total = $195,918,675,920*

ALPHA ORDER

ALPHA ORDER

RANK	STATE	FUNDS	% of USA
21	Alabama	$3,166,302,119	1.6%
45	Alaska	668,903,057	0.3%
22	Arizona	2,887,614,909	1.5%
30	Arkansas	1,622,336,126	0.8%
1	California	25,006,972,511	12.8%
23	Colorado	2,685,773,549	1.4%
19	Connecticut	3,637,303,382	1.9%
41	Delaware	774,798,677	0.4%
NA	Florida**	NA	NA
9	Georgia	4,808,740,669	2.5%
35	Hawaii	1,179,165,923	0.6%
43	Idaho	711,700,479	0.4%
5	Illinois	9,118,539,559	4.7%
18	Indiana	3,996,355,551	2.0%
28	Iowa	1,703,839,986	0.9%
29	Kansas	1,633,317,646	0.8%
20	Kentucky	3,450,438,586	1.8%
14	Louisiana	4,418,657,915	2.3%
31	Maine	1,507,301,276	0.8%
13	Maryland	4,428,657,384	2.3%
7	Massachusetts	7,913,114,213	4.0%
6	Michigan	8,526,278,034	4.4%
NA	Minnesota**	NA	NA
NA	Mississippi**	NA	NA
12	Missouri	4,456,368,286	2.3%
39	Montana	832,182,431	0.4%
37	Nebraska	1,165,683,457	0.6%
34	Nevada	1,194,976,855	0.6%
33	New Hampshire	1,304,689,150	0.7%
8	New Jersey	7,576,167,918	3.9%
36	New Mexico	1,168,438,809	0.6%
2	New York	25,003,202,243	12.8%
11	North Carolina	4,569,381,898	2.3%
42	North Dakota	717,089,369	0.4%
4	Ohio	9,869,422,449	5.0%
26	Oklahoma	2,029,985,862	1.0%
25	Oregon	2,248,476,833	1.1%
3	Pennsylvania	11,259,169,603	5.7%
32	Rhode Island	1,408,469,747	0.7%
24	South Carolina	2,304,693,120	1.2%
44	South Dakota	683,650,009	0.3%
10	Tennessee	4,782,168,127	2.4%
NA	Texas**	NA	NA
38	Utah	871,616,513	0.4%
40	Vermont	805,588,329	0.4%
17	Virginia	4,006,037,550	2.0%
16	Washington	4,022,716,267	2.1%
27	West Virginia	1,736,741,427	0.9%
15	Wisconsin	4,059,511,421	2.1%
46	Wyoming	486,553,976	0.2%

RANK ORDER

RANK	STATE	FUNDS	% of USA
1	California	$25,006,972,511	12.8%
2	New York	25,003,202,243	12.8%
3	Pennsylvania	11,259,169,603	5.7%
4	Ohio	9,869,422,449	5.0%
5	Illinois	9,118,539,559	4.7%
6	Michigan	8,526,278,034	4.4%
7	Massachusetts	7,913,114,213	4.0%
8	New Jersey	7,576,167,918	3.9%
9	Georgia	4,808,740,669	2.5%
10	Tennessee	4,782,168,127	2.4%
11	North Carolina	4,569,381,898	2.3%
12	Missouri	4,456,368,286	2.3%
13	Maryland	4,428,657,384	2.3%
14	Louisiana	4,418,657,915	2.3%
15	Wisconsin	4,059,511,421	2.1%
16	Washington	4,022,716,267	2.1%
17	Virginia	4,006,037,550	2.0%
18	Indiana	3,996,355,551	2.0%
19	Connecticut	3,637,303,382	1.9%
20	Kentucky	3,450,438,586	1.8%
21	Alabama	3,166,302,119	1.6%
22	Arizona	2,887,614,909	1.5%
23	Colorado	2,685,773,549	1.4%
24	South Carolina	2,304,693,120	1.2%
25	Oregon	2,248,476,833	1.1%
26	Oklahoma	2,029,985,862	1.0%
27	West Virginia	1,736,741,427	0.9%
28	Iowa	1,703,839,986	0.9%
29	Kansas	1,633,317,646	0.8%
30	Arkansas	1,622,336,126	0.8%
31	Maine	1,507,301,276	0.8%
32	Rhode Island	1,408,469,747	0.7%
33	New Hampshire	1,304,689,150	0.7%
34	Nevada	1,194,976,855	0.6%
35	Hawaii	1,179,165,923	0.6%
36	New Mexico	1,168,438,809	0.6%
37	Nebraska	1,165,683,457	0.6%
38	Utah	871,616,513	0.4%
39	Montana	832,182,431	0.4%
40	Vermont	805,588,329	0.4%
41	Delaware	774,798,677	0.4%
42	North Dakota	717,089,369	0.4%
43	Idaho	711,700,479	0.4%
44	South Dakota	683,650,009	0.3%
45	Alaska	668,903,057	0.3%
46	Wyoming	486,553,976	0.2%
NA	Florida**	NA	NA
NA	Minnesota**	NA	NA
NA	Mississippi**	NA	NA
NA	Texas**	NA	NA
	District of Columbia	1,189,458,106	0.6%

Source: National Association of Attorneys General
"Attorneys General Announce Tobacco Settlement Proposal" (News release, http://www.naag.org/tob2.htm)
This settlement was reached in November 1998. National total includes $4,640,249,229 for U.S. territories.
***Total does not include $40 billion in previous settlements with Florida, Minnesota, Mississippi and Texas.*

State Government Expenditures for Health Programs in 1997

National Total = $33,879,585,000*

<table>
<tr><td colspan="4">ALPHA ORDER</td><td colspan="4">RANK ORDER</td></tr>
<tr><th>RANK</th><th>STATE</th><th>EXPENDITURES</th><th>% of USA</th><th>RANK</th><th>STATE</th><th>EXPENDITURES</th><th>% of USA</th></tr>
<tr><td>18</td><td>Alabama</td><td>$566,651,000</td><td>1.7%</td><td>1</td><td>California</td><td>$6,083,766,000</td><td>18.0%</td></tr>
<tr><td>42</td><td>Alaska</td><td>159,454,000</td><td>0.5%</td><td>2</td><td>New York</td><td>2,147,669,000</td><td>6.3%</td></tr>
<tr><td>19</td><td>Arizona</td><td>558,780,000</td><td>1.6%</td><td>3</td><td>Michigan</td><td>2,046,674,000</td><td>6.0%</td></tr>
<tr><td>32</td><td>Arkansas</td><td>261,311,000</td><td>0.8%</td><td>4</td><td>Florida</td><td>1,850,393,000</td><td>5.5%</td></tr>
<tr><td>1</td><td>California</td><td>6,083,766,000</td><td>18.0%</td><td>5</td><td>Illinois</td><td>1,702,964,000</td><td>5.0%</td></tr>
<tr><td>35</td><td>Colorado</td><td>247,006,000</td><td>0.7%</td><td>6</td><td>Pennsylvania</td><td>1,379,050,000</td><td>4.1%</td></tr>
<tr><td>24</td><td>Connecticut</td><td>402,219,000</td><td>1.2%</td><td>7</td><td>Ohio</td><td>1,352,057,000</td><td>4.0%</td></tr>
<tr><td>40</td><td>Delaware</td><td>166,892,000</td><td>0.5%</td><td>8</td><td>Texas</td><td>1,331,742,000</td><td>3.9%</td></tr>
<tr><td>4</td><td>Florida</td><td>1,850,393,000</td><td>5.5%</td><td>9</td><td>Massachusetts</td><td>1,325,680,000</td><td>3.9%</td></tr>
<tr><td>15</td><td>Georgia</td><td>691,605,000</td><td>2.0%</td><td>10</td><td>Washington</td><td>1,009,328,000</td><td>3.0%</td></tr>
<tr><td>30</td><td>Hawaii</td><td>276,988,000</td><td>0.8%</td><td>11</td><td>North Carolina</td><td>899,998,000</td><td>2.7%</td></tr>
<tr><td>45</td><td>Idaho</td><td>92,562,000</td><td>0.3%</td><td>12</td><td>Maryland</td><td>779,238,000</td><td>2.3%</td></tr>
<tr><td>5</td><td>Illinois</td><td>1,702,964,000</td><td>5.0%</td><td>13</td><td>New Jersey</td><td>754,228,000</td><td>2.2%</td></tr>
<tr><td>23</td><td>Indiana</td><td>406,647,000</td><td>1.2%</td><td>14</td><td>South Carolina</td><td>703,186,000</td><td>2.1%</td></tr>
<tr><td>38</td><td>Iowa</td><td>185,579,000</td><td>0.5%</td><td>15</td><td>Georgia</td><td>691,605,000</td><td>2.0%</td></tr>
<tr><td>29</td><td>Kansas</td><td>301,760,000</td><td>0.9%</td><td>16</td><td>Tennessee</td><td>572,837,000</td><td>1.7%</td></tr>
<tr><td>28</td><td>Kentucky</td><td>302,747,000</td><td>0.9%</td><td>17</td><td>Missouri</td><td>569,282,000</td><td>1.7%</td></tr>
<tr><td>25</td><td>Louisiana</td><td>395,194,000</td><td>1.2%</td><td>18</td><td>Alabama</td><td>566,651,000</td><td>1.7%</td></tr>
<tr><td>37</td><td>Maine</td><td>207,689,000</td><td>0.6%</td><td>19</td><td>Arizona</td><td>558,780,000</td><td>1.6%</td></tr>
<tr><td>12</td><td>Maryland</td><td>779,238,000</td><td>2.3%</td><td>20</td><td>Virginia</td><td>540,595,000</td><td>1.6%</td></tr>
<tr><td>9</td><td>Massachusetts</td><td>1,325,680,000</td><td>3.9%</td><td>21</td><td>Minnesota</td><td>501,351,000</td><td>1.5%</td></tr>
<tr><td>3</td><td>Michigan</td><td>2,046,674,000</td><td>6.0%</td><td>22</td><td>Wisconsin</td><td>497,319,000</td><td>1.5%</td></tr>
<tr><td>21</td><td>Minnesota</td><td>501,351,000</td><td>1.5%</td><td>23</td><td>Indiana</td><td>406,647,000</td><td>1.2%</td></tr>
<tr><td>34</td><td>Mississippi</td><td>247,910,000</td><td>0.7%</td><td>24</td><td>Connecticut</td><td>402,219,000</td><td>1.2%</td></tr>
<tr><td>17</td><td>Missouri</td><td>569,282,000</td><td>1.7%</td><td>25</td><td>Louisiana</td><td>395,194,000</td><td>1.2%</td></tr>
<tr><td>41</td><td>Montana</td><td>162,858,000</td><td>0.5%</td><td>26</td><td>Oregon</td><td>366,493,000</td><td>1.1%</td></tr>
<tr><td>36</td><td>Nebraska</td><td>215,305,000</td><td>0.6%</td><td>27</td><td>Oklahoma</td><td>324,915,000</td><td>1.0%</td></tr>
<tr><td>46</td><td>Nevada</td><td>89,068,000</td><td>0.3%</td><td>28</td><td>Kentucky</td><td>302,747,000</td><td>0.9%</td></tr>
<tr><td>43</td><td>New Hampshire</td><td>138,275,000</td><td>0.4%</td><td>29</td><td>Kansas</td><td>301,760,000</td><td>0.9%</td></tr>
<tr><td>13</td><td>New Jersey</td><td>754,228,000</td><td>2.2%</td><td>30</td><td>Hawaii</td><td>276,988,000</td><td>0.8%</td></tr>
<tr><td>31</td><td>New Mexico</td><td>269,931,000</td><td>0.8%</td><td>31</td><td>New Mexico</td><td>269,931,000</td><td>0.8%</td></tr>
<tr><td>2</td><td>New York</td><td>2,147,669,000</td><td>6.3%</td><td>32</td><td>Arkansas</td><td>261,311,000</td><td>0.8%</td></tr>
<tr><td>11</td><td>North Carolina</td><td>899,998,000</td><td>2.7%</td><td>33</td><td>Rhode Island</td><td>248,079,000</td><td>0.7%</td></tr>
<tr><td>49</td><td>North Dakota</td><td>56,870,000</td><td>0.2%</td><td>34</td><td>Mississippi</td><td>247,910,000</td><td>0.7%</td></tr>
<tr><td>7</td><td>Ohio</td><td>1,352,057,000</td><td>4.0%</td><td>35</td><td>Colorado</td><td>247,006,000</td><td>0.7%</td></tr>
<tr><td>27</td><td>Oklahoma</td><td>324,915,000</td><td>1.0%</td><td>36</td><td>Nebraska</td><td>215,305,000</td><td>0.6%</td></tr>
<tr><td>26</td><td>Oregon</td><td>366,493,000</td><td>1.1%</td><td>37</td><td>Maine</td><td>207,689,000</td><td>0.6%</td></tr>
<tr><td>6</td><td>Pennsylvania</td><td>1,379,050,000</td><td>4.1%</td><td>38</td><td>Iowa</td><td>185,579,000</td><td>0.5%</td></tr>
<tr><td>33</td><td>Rhode Island</td><td>248,079,000</td><td>0.7%</td><td>39</td><td>Utah</td><td>172,481,000</td><td>0.5%</td></tr>
<tr><td>14</td><td>South Carolina</td><td>703,186,000</td><td>2.1%</td><td>40</td><td>Delaware</td><td>166,892,000</td><td>0.5%</td></tr>
<tr><td>48</td><td>South Dakota</td><td>58,861,000</td><td>0.2%</td><td>41</td><td>Montana</td><td>162,858,000</td><td>0.5%</td></tr>
<tr><td>16</td><td>Tennessee</td><td>572,837,000</td><td>1.7%</td><td>42</td><td>Alaska</td><td>159,454,000</td><td>0.5%</td></tr>
<tr><td>8</td><td>Texas</td><td>1,331,742,000</td><td>3.9%</td><td>43</td><td>New Hampshire</td><td>138,275,000</td><td>0.4%</td></tr>
<tr><td>39</td><td>Utah</td><td>172,481,000</td><td>0.5%</td><td>44</td><td>West Virginia</td><td>134,349,000</td><td>0.4%</td></tr>
<tr><td>50</td><td>Vermont</td><td>49,852,000</td><td>0.1%</td><td>45</td><td>Idaho</td><td>92,562,000</td><td>0.3%</td></tr>
<tr><td>20</td><td>Virginia</td><td>540,595,000</td><td>1.6%</td><td>46</td><td>Nevada</td><td>89,068,000</td><td>0.3%</td></tr>
<tr><td>10</td><td>Washington</td><td>1,009,328,000</td><td>3.0%</td><td>47</td><td>Wyoming</td><td>73,897,000</td><td>0.2%</td></tr>
<tr><td>44</td><td>West Virginia</td><td>134,349,000</td><td>0.4%</td><td>48</td><td>South Dakota</td><td>58,861,000</td><td>0.2%</td></tr>
<tr><td>22</td><td>Wisconsin</td><td>497,319,000</td><td>1.5%</td><td>49</td><td>North Dakota</td><td>56,870,000</td><td>0.2%</td></tr>
<tr><td>47</td><td>Wyoming</td><td>73,897,000</td><td>0.2%</td><td>50</td><td>Vermont</td><td>49,852,000</td><td>0.1%</td></tr>
<tr><td></td><td></td><td></td><td></td><td></td><td>District of Columbia**</td><td>NA</td><td>NA</td></tr>
</table>

Source: U.S. Bureau of the Census, Governments Division
"1997 State Government Finance Data" (http://www.census.gov/govs/www/st97.html)
*Includes outpatient health services other than hospital care, research and education, categorical health programs, treatment and immunization clinics, nursing and environmental health activities. Includes capital expenditures.
**Not applicable.

Per Capita State Government Expenditures for Health Programs in 1997

National Per Capita = $127*

ALPHA ORDER

RANK	STATE	PER CAPITA
16	Alabama	$131
1	Alaska	262
19	Arizona	123
31	Arkansas	104
7	California	189
49	Colorado	63
19	Connecticut	123
4	Delaware	227
18	Florida	126
35	Georgia	92
3	Hawaii	232
43	Idaho	77
15	Illinois	142
46	Indiana	69
48	Iowa	65
25	Kansas	116
43	Kentucky	77
36	Louisiana	91
11	Maine	167
14	Maryland	153
5	Massachusetts	217
6	Michigan	209
28	Minnesota	107
36	Mississippi	91
30	Missouri	105
9	Montana	185
17	Nebraska	130
50	Nevada	53
23	New Hampshire	118
34	New Jersey	94
12	New Mexico	157
23	New York	118
21	North Carolina	121
38	North Dakota	89
21	Ohio	121
32	Oklahoma	98
27	Oregon	113
26	Pennsylvania	115
2	Rhode Island	251
8	South Carolina	186
41	South Dakota	80
28	Tennessee	107
46	Texas	69
40	Utah	84
39	Vermont	85
41	Virginia	80
10	Washington	180
45	West Virginia	74
33	Wisconsin	96
13	Wyoming	154

RANK ORDER

RANK	STATE	PER CAPITA
1	Alaska	$262
2	Rhode Island	251
3	Hawaii	232
4	Delaware	227
5	Massachusetts	217
6	Michigan	209
7	California	189
8	South Carolina	186
9	Montana	185
10	Washington	180
11	Maine	167
12	New Mexico	157
13	Wyoming	154
14	Maryland	153
15	Illinois	142
16	Alabama	131
17	Nebraska	130
18	Florida	126
19	Arizona	123
19	Connecticut	123
21	North Carolina	121
21	Ohio	121
23	New Hampshire	118
23	New York	118
25	Kansas	116
26	Pennsylvania	115
27	Oregon	113
28	Minnesota	107
28	Tennessee	107
30	Missouri	105
31	Arkansas	104
32	Oklahoma	98
33	Wisconsin	96
34	New Jersey	94
35	Georgia	92
36	Louisiana	91
36	Mississippi	91
38	North Dakota	89
39	Vermont	85
40	Utah	84
41	South Dakota	80
41	Virginia	80
43	Idaho	77
43	Kentucky	77
45	West Virginia	74
46	Indiana	69
46	Texas	69
48	Iowa	65
49	Colorado	63
50	Nevada	53
	District of Columbia**	NA

Source: Morgan Quitno Press using data from U.S. Bureau of the Census, Governments Division
"1997 State Government Finance Data" (http://www.census.gov/govs/www/st97.html)
*Includes outpatient health services other than hospital care, research and education, categorical health programs, treatment and immunization clinics, nursing and environmental health activities. Includes capital expenditures.
**Not applicable.

State Government Expenditures for Hospitals in 1997

National Total = $29,313,344,000*

ALPHA ORDER

RANK	STATE	EXPENDITURES	% of USA
11	Alabama	$882,613,000	3.0%
49	Alaska	28,220,000	0.1%
41	Arizona	54,907,000	0.2%
27	Arkansas	362,721,000	1.2%
2	California	2,917,670,000	10.0%
36	Colorado	145,875,000	0.5%
8	Connecticut	977,504,000	3.3%
40	Delaware	60,422,000	0.2%
18	Florida	551,166,000	1.9%
15	Georgia	652,117,000	2.2%
34	Hawaii	237,641,000	0.8%
46	Idaho	37,764,000	0.1%
13	Illinois	846,042,000	2.9%
35	Indiana	227,424,000	0.8%
20	Iowa	493,587,000	1.7%
32	Kansas	303,263,000	1.0%
21	Kentucky	447,971,000	1.5%
7	Louisiana	1,063,310,000	3.6%
42	Maine	53,917,000	0.2%
31	Maryland	319,502,000	1.1%
10	Massachusetts	886,275,000	3.0%
5	Michigan	1,420,141,000	4.8%
25	Minnesota	428,811,000	1.5%
26	Mississippi	422,071,000	1.4%
23	Missouri	441,048,000	1.5%
47	Montana	28,715,000	0.1%
28	Nebraska	328,258,000	1.1%
39	Nevada	67,089,000	0.2%
44	New Hampshire	41,250,000	0.1%
9	New Jersey	974,484,000	3.3%
29	New Mexico	320,578,000	1.1%
1	New York	3,311,633,000	11.3%
14	North Carolina	781,710,000	2.7%
43	North Dakota	44,984,000	0.2%
12	Ohio	875,478,000	3.0%
33	Oklahoma	290,809,000	1.0%
24	Oregon	438,214,000	1.5%
4	Pennsylvania	1,697,003,000	5.8%
38	Rhode Island	79,877,000	0.3%
16	South Carolina	611,090,000	2.1%
45	South Dakota	39,703,000	0.1%
19	Tennessee	544,800,000	1.9%
3	Texas	1,961,616,000	6.7%
30	Utah	319,921,000	1.1%
50	Vermont	8,714,000	0.0%
6	Virginia	1,163,248,000	4.0%
17	Washington	564,674,000	1.9%
37	West Virginia	82,939,000	0.3%
22	Wisconsin	446,159,000	1.5%
48	Wyoming	28,416,000	0.1%

RANK ORDER

RANK	STATE	EXPENDITURES	% of USA
1	New York	$3,311,633,000	11.3%
2	California	2,917,670,000	10.0%
3	Texas	1,961,616,000	6.7%
4	Pennsylvania	1,697,003,000	5.8%
5	Michigan	1,420,141,000	4.8%
6	Virginia	1,163,248,000	4.0%
7	Louisiana	1,063,310,000	3.6%
8	Connecticut	977,504,000	3.3%
9	New Jersey	974,484,000	3.3%
10	Massachusetts	886,275,000	3.0%
11	Alabama	882,613,000	3.0%
12	Ohio	875,478,000	3.0%
13	Illinois	846,042,000	2.9%
14	North Carolina	781,710,000	2.7%
15	Georgia	652,117,000	2.2%
16	South Carolina	611,090,000	2.1%
17	Washington	564,674,000	1.9%
18	Florida	551,166,000	1.9%
19	Tennessee	544,800,000	1.9%
20	Iowa	493,587,000	1.7%
21	Kentucky	447,971,000	1.5%
22	Wisconsin	446,159,000	1.5%
23	Missouri	441,048,000	1.5%
24	Oregon	438,214,000	1.5%
25	Minnesota	428,811,000	1.5%
26	Mississippi	422,071,000	1.4%
27	Arkansas	362,721,000	1.2%
28	Nebraska	328,258,000	1.1%
29	New Mexico	320,578,000	1.1%
30	Utah	319,921,000	1.1%
31	Maryland	319,502,000	1.1%
32	Kansas	303,263,000	1.0%
33	Oklahoma	290,809,000	1.0%
34	Hawaii	237,641,000	0.8%
35	Indiana	227,424,000	0.8%
36	Colorado	145,875,000	0.5%
37	West Virginia	82,939,000	0.3%
38	Rhode Island	79,877,000	0.3%
39	Nevada	67,089,000	0.2%
40	Delaware	60,422,000	0.2%
41	Arizona	54,907,000	0.2%
42	Maine	53,917,000	0.2%
43	North Dakota	44,984,000	0.2%
44	New Hampshire	41,250,000	0.1%
45	South Dakota	39,703,000	0.1%
46	Idaho	37,764,000	0.1%
47	Montana	28,715,000	0.1%
48	Wyoming	28,416,000	0.1%
49	Alaska	28,220,000	0.1%
50	Vermont	8,714,000	0.0%
	District of Columbia**	NA	NA

Source: U.S. Bureau of the Census, Governments Division
   "1997 State Government Finance Data" (http://www.census.gov/govs/www/st97.html)
*Financing, construction, acquisition, maintenance or operation of hospital facilities, provision of hospital care and support of public or private hospitals.
**Not applicable.

Per Capita State Government Expenditures for Hospitals in 1997

National Per Capita = $109*

ALPHA ORDER				RANK ORDER		
RANK	STATE	PER CAPITA		RANK	STATE	PER CAPITA
3	Alabama	$204		1	Connecticut	$299
39	Alaska	46		2	Louisiana	244
50	Arizona	12		3	Alabama	204
15	Arkansas	144		4	Hawaii	199
25	California	91		5	Nebraska	198
45	Colorado	37		6	New Mexico	186
1	Connecticut	299		7	New York	182
30	Delaware	82		8	Iowa	173
44	Florida	38		8	Virginia	173
28	Georgia	87		10	South Carolina	161
4	Hawaii	199		11	Mississippi	155
48	Idaho	31		11	Utah	155
34	Illinois	71		13	Massachusetts	145
43	Indiana	39		13	Michigan	145
8	Iowa	173		15	Arkansas	144
19	Kansas	117		16	Pennsylvania	141
20	Kentucky	115		17	Oregon	135
2	Louisiana	244		18	New Jersey	121
41	Maine	43		19	Kansas	117
36	Maryland	63		20	Kentucky	115
13	Massachusetts	145		21	North Carolina	105
13	Michigan	145		22	Tennessee	101
25	Minnesota	91		22	Texas	101
11	Mississippi	155		22	Washington	101
30	Missouri	82		25	California	91
47	Montana	33		25	Minnesota	91
5	Nebraska	198		27	Oklahoma	88
42	Nevada	40		28	Georgia	87
46	New Hampshire	35		29	Wisconsin	86
18	New Jersey	121		30	Delaware	82
6	New Mexico	186		30	Missouri	82
7	New York	182		32	Rhode Island	81
21	North Carolina	105		33	Ohio	78
35	North Dakota	70		34	Illinois	71
33	Ohio	78		35	North Dakota	70
27	Oklahoma	88		36	Maryland	63
17	Oregon	135		37	Wyoming	59
16	Pennsylvania	141		38	South Dakota	54
32	Rhode Island	81		39	Alaska	46
10	South Carolina	161		39	West Virginia	46
38	South Dakota	54		41	Maine	43
22	Tennessee	101		42	Nevada	40
22	Texas	101		43	Indiana	39
11	Utah	155		44	Florida	38
49	Vermont	15		45	Colorado	37
8	Virginia	173		46	New Hampshire	35
22	Washington	101		47	Montana	33
39	West Virginia	46		48	Idaho	31
29	Wisconsin	86		49	Vermont	15
37	Wyoming	59		50	Arizona	12
				District of Columbia**		NA

Source: Morgan Quitno Press using data from U.S. Bureau of the Census, Governments Division
   "1997 State Government Finance Data" (http://www.census.gov/govs/www/st97.html)
*Financing, construction, acquisition, maintenance or operation of hospital facilities, provision of hospital care and support of public or private hospitals.
**Not applicable.

Payroll of Health Service Establishments in 1997

National Total = $378,205,694,000*

ALPHA ORDER

RANK	STATE	PAYROLL	% of USA
23	Alabama	$5,568,734,000	1.5%
48	Alaska	893,033,000	0.2%
24	Arizona	5,263,953,000	1.4%
33	Arkansas	3,038,789,000	0.8%
1	California	38,369,116,000	10.1%
26	Colorado	4,930,145,000	1.3%
21	Connecticut	6,496,024,000	1.7%
44	Delaware	1,188,715,000	0.3%
4	Florida	21,410,912,000	5.7%
12	Georgia	9,635,723,000	2.5%
42	Hawaii	1,617,690,000	0.4%
43	Idaho	1,227,414,000	0.3%
6	Illinois	16,792,361,000	4.4%
17	Indiana	7,736,720,000	2.0%
30	Iowa	3,966,111,000	1.0%
31	Kansas	3,588,875,000	0.9%
25	Kentucky	5,006,735,000	1.3%
22	Louisiana	5,967,380,000	1.6%
38	Maine	1,886,136,000	0.5%
20	Maryland	7,354,690,000	1.9%
10	Massachusetts	12,721,109,000	3.4%
8	Michigan	14,006,589,000	3.7%
16	Minnesota	7,839,331,000	2.1%
32	Mississippi	3,207,907,000	0.8%
14	Missouri	8,007,261,000	2.1%
47	Montana	1,031,703,000	0.3%
35	Nebraska	2,233,875,000	0.6%
39	Nevada	1,865,823,000	0.5%
41	New Hampshire	1,714,458,000	0.5%
9	New Jersey	12,742,883,000	3.4%
37	New Mexico	1,953,604,000	0.5%
2	New York	34,343,629,000	9.1%
11	North Carolina	9,866,432,000	2.6%
46	North Dakota	1,055,287,000	0.3%
7	Ohio	16,570,607,000	4.4%
28	Oklahoma	4,002,486,000	1.1%
29	Oregon	3,997,226,000	1.1%
5	Pennsylvania	19,855,425,000	5.2%
40	Rhode Island	1,779,702,000	0.5%
27	South Carolina	4,283,923,000	1.1%
45	South Dakota	1,167,627,000	0.3%
13	Tennessee	8,089,446,000	2.1%
3	Texas	23,082,750,000	6.1%
36	Utah	2,086,299,000	0.6%
49	Vermont	770,451,000	0.2%
15	Virginia	7,957,706,000	2.1%
19	Washington	7,430,081,000	2.0%
34	West Virginia	2,407,195,000	0.6%
18	Wisconsin	7,536,649,000	2.0%
50	Wyoming	530,840,000	0.1%

RANK ORDER

RANK	STATE	PAYROLL	% of USA
1	California	$38,369,116,000	10.1%
2	New York	34,343,629,000	9.1%
3	Texas	23,082,750,000	6.1%
4	Florida	21,410,912,000	5.7%
5	Pennsylvania	19,855,425,000	5.2%
6	Illinois	16,792,361,000	4.4%
7	Ohio	16,570,607,000	4.4%
8	Michigan	14,006,589,000	3.7%
9	New Jersey	12,742,883,000	3.4%
10	Massachusetts	12,721,109,000	3.4%
11	North Carolina	9,866,432,000	2.6%
12	Georgia	9,635,723,000	2.5%
13	Tennessee	8,089,446,000	2.1%
14	Missouri	8,007,261,000	2.1%
15	Virginia	7,957,706,000	2.1%
16	Minnesota	7,839,331,000	2.1%
17	Indiana	7,736,720,000	2.0%
18	Wisconsin	7,536,649,000	2.0%
19	Washington	7,430,081,000	2.0%
20	Maryland	7,354,690,000	1.9%
21	Connecticut	6,496,024,000	1.7%
22	Louisiana	5,967,380,000	1.6%
23	Alabama	5,568,734,000	1.5%
24	Arizona	5,263,953,000	1.4%
25	Kentucky	5,006,735,000	1.3%
26	Colorado	4,930,145,000	1.3%
27	South Carolina	4,283,923,000	1.1%
28	Oklahoma	4,002,486,000	1.1%
29	Oregon	3,997,226,000	1.1%
30	Iowa	3,966,111,000	1.0%
31	Kansas	3,588,875,000	0.9%
32	Mississippi	3,207,907,000	0.8%
33	Arkansas	3,038,789,000	0.8%
34	West Virginia	2,407,195,000	0.6%
35	Nebraska	2,233,875,000	0.6%
36	Utah	2,086,299,000	0.6%
37	New Mexico	1,953,604,000	0.5%
38	Maine	1,886,136,000	0.5%
39	Nevada	1,865,823,000	0.5%
40	Rhode Island	1,779,702,000	0.5%
41	New Hampshire	1,714,458,000	0.5%
42	Hawaii	1,617,690,000	0.4%
43	Idaho	1,227,414,000	0.3%
44	Delaware	1,188,715,000	0.3%
45	South Dakota	1,167,627,000	0.3%
46	North Dakota	1,055,287,000	0.3%
47	Montana	1,031,703,000	0.3%
48	Alaska	893,033,000	0.2%
49	Vermont	770,451,000	0.2%
50	Wyoming	530,840,000	0.1%
	District of Columbia	2,128,134,000	0.6%

Source: U.S. Bureau of the Census
 "1997 Economic Census, Health Care and Social Assistance" (EC97562A, October 1999)
*Includes establishments exempt from as well as subject to the federal income tax. Includes those establishments within the Standard Industry Classification (SIC) 8000. These include those primarily engaged in furnishing medical, surgical and other health services to persons. See Facilities Chapter for establishments.

Average Pay per Health Service Establishment Employee in 1997

National Average = $27,888 per Employee*

RANK	STATE	AVERAGE PAY		RANK	STATE	AVERAGE PAY
17	Alabama	$28,075		1	Hawaii	$34,010
2	Alaska	33,058		2	Alaska	33,058
14	Arizona	28,266		3	Nevada	32,930
45	Arkansas	23,923		4	New Jersey	31,845
5	California	30,672		5	California	30,672
19	Colorado	27,903		6	New York	30,476
7	Connecticut	30,394		7	Connecticut	30,394
8	Delaware	29,739		8	Delaware	29,739
9	Florida	28,881		9	Florida	28,881
10	Georgia	28,772		10	Georgia	28,772
1	Hawaii	34,010		11	Michigan	28,700
38	Idaho	24,986		12	Tennessee	28,414
20	Illinois	27,817		13	Massachusetts	28,277
32	Indiana	25,762		14	Arizona	28,266
49	Iowa	22,790		15	Maryland	28,260
43	Kansas	24,187		16	Washington	28,186
34	Kentucky	25,692		17	Alabama	28,075
40	Louisiana	24,800		18	Rhode Island	27,905
41	Maine	24,704		19	Colorado	27,903
15	Maryland	28,260		20	Illinois	27,817
13	Massachusetts	28,277		21	Virginia	27,755
11	Michigan	28,700		22	Pennsylvania	27,724
27	Minnesota	26,279		23	South Carolina	27,679
30	Mississippi	25,784		24	North Carolina	27,299
36	Missouri	25,369		25	Ohio	26,989
48	Montana	22,826		26	Oregon	26,506
39	Nebraska	24,821		27	Minnesota	26,279
3	Nevada	32,930		28	Wisconsin	26,014
33	New Hampshire	25,757		29	Texas	25,890
4	New Jersey	31,845		30	Mississippi	25,784
35	New Mexico	25,596		31	Utah	25,769
6	New York	30,476		32	Indiana	25,762
24	North Carolina	27,299		33	New Hampshire	25,757
50	North Dakota	22,569		34	Kentucky	25,692
25	Ohio	26,989		35	New Mexico	25,596
46	Oklahoma	23,718		36	Missouri	25,369
26	Oregon	26,506		37	West Virginia	25,144
22	Pennsylvania	27,724		38	Idaho	24,986
18	Rhode Island	27,905		39	Nebraska	24,821
23	South Carolina	27,679		40	Louisiana	24,800
42	South Dakota	24,326		41	Maine	24,704
12	Tennessee	28,414		42	South Dakota	24,326
29	Texas	25,890		43	Kansas	24,187
31	Utah	25,769		44	Vermont	23,943
44	Vermont	23,943		45	Arkansas	23,923
21	Virginia	27,755		46	Oklahoma	23,718
16	Washington	28,186		47	Wyoming	23,114
37	West Virginia	25,144		48	Montana	22,826
28	Wisconsin	26,014		49	Iowa	22,790
47	Wyoming	23,114		50	North Dakota	22,569
					District of Columbia	35,750

*Source: Morgan Quitno Press using data from U.S. Bureau of the Census
"1997 Economic Census, Health Care and Social Assistance" (EC97562A, October 1999)*
Includes establishments exempt from as well as subject to the federal income tax. Includes those establishments within the Standard Industry Classification (SIC) 8000. These include those primarily engaged in furnishing medical, surgical and other health services to persons. See Facilities Chapter for establishments.

Receipts of Health Services Establishments in 1997

National Total = $885,054,001,000*

ALPHA ORDER

RANK	STATE	RECEIPTS	% of USA
23	Alabama	$13,192,253,000	1.5%
48	Alaska	2,041,248,000	0.2%
24	Arizona	12,841,177,000	1.5%
33	Arkansas	7,297,065,000	0.8%
1	California	100,746,815,000	11.4%
26	Colorado	11,657,625,000	1.3%
22	Connecticut	13,907,989,000	1.6%
44	Delaware	2,631,828,000	0.3%
4	Florida	51,974,200,000	5.9%
11	Georgia	23,711,573,000	2.7%
41	Hawaii	3,975,313,000	0.4%
43	Idaho	2,835,543,000	0.3%
6	Illinois	39,775,490,000	4.5%
16	Indiana	18,042,945,000	2.0%
30	Iowa	8,765,614,000	1.0%
31	Kansas	8,198,279,000	0.9%
25	Kentucky	11,962,976,000	1.4%
21	Louisiana	14,444,944,000	1.6%
39	Maine	4,249,374,000	0.5%
17	Maryland	17,465,676,000	2.0%
10	Massachusetts	27,452,916,000	3.1%
8	Michigan	31,270,014,000	3.5%
18	Minnesota	16,829,464,000	1.9%
32	Mississippi	7,881,283,000	0.9%
15	Missouri	18,421,088,000	2.1%
46	Montana	2,368,999,000	0.3%
35	Nebraska	5,102,506,000	0.6%
37	Nevada	4,668,075,000	0.5%
40	New Hampshire	3,980,324,000	0.4%
9	New Jersey	28,531,121,000	3.2%
38	New Mexico	4,469,602,000	0.5%
2	New York	74,767,808,000	8.4%
12	North Carolina	23,109,073,000	2.6%
47	North Dakota	2,367,774,000	0.3%
7	Ohio	36,863,598,000	4.2%
28	Oklahoma	9,344,954,000	1.1%
29	Oregon	9,300,512,000	1.1%
5	Pennsylvania	45,253,553,000	5.1%
42	Rhode Island	3,902,244,000	0.4%
27	South Carolina	10,048,402,000	1.1%
45	South Dakota	2,528,389,000	0.3%
13	Tennessee	19,212,914,000	2.2%
3	Texas	56,758,770,000	6.4%
36	Utah	5,059,071,000	0.6%
49	Vermont	1,760,664,000	0.2%
14	Virginia	18,835,208,000	2.1%
19	Washington	16,779,905,000	1.9%
34	West Virginia	5,825,082,000	0.7%
20	Wisconsin	16,572,139,000	1.9%
50	Wyoming	1,189,498,000	0.1%

RANK ORDER

RANK	STATE	RECEIPTS	% of USA
1	California	$100,746,815,000	11.4%
2	New York	74,767,808,000	8.4%
3	Texas	56,758,770,000	6.4%
4	Florida	51,974,200,000	5.9%
5	Pennsylvania	45,253,553,000	5.1%
6	Illinois	39,775,490,000	4.5%
7	Ohio	36,863,598,000	4.2%
8	Michigan	31,270,014,000	3.5%
9	New Jersey	28,531,121,000	3.2%
10	Massachusetts	27,452,916,000	3.1%
11	Georgia	23,711,573,000	2.7%
12	North Carolina	23,109,073,000	2.6%
13	Tennessee	19,212,914,000	2.2%
14	Virginia	18,835,208,000	2.1%
15	Missouri	18,421,088,000	2.1%
16	Indiana	18,042,945,000	2.0%
17	Maryland	17,465,676,000	2.0%
18	Minnesota	16,829,464,000	1.9%
19	Washington	16,779,905,000	1.9%
20	Wisconsin	16,572,139,000	1.9%
21	Louisiana	14,444,944,000	1.6%
22	Connecticut	13,907,989,000	1.6%
23	Alabama	13,192,253,000	1.5%
24	Arizona	12,841,177,000	1.5%
25	Kentucky	11,962,976,000	1.4%
26	Colorado	11,657,625,000	1.3%
27	South Carolina	10,048,402,000	1.1%
28	Oklahoma	9,344,954,000	1.1%
29	Oregon	9,300,512,000	1.1%
30	Iowa	8,765,614,000	1.0%
31	Kansas	8,198,279,000	0.9%
32	Mississippi	7,881,283,000	0.9%
33	Arkansas	7,297,065,000	0.8%
34	West Virginia	5,825,082,000	0.7%
35	Nebraska	5,102,506,000	0.6%
36	Utah	5,059,071,000	0.6%
37	Nevada	4,668,075,000	0.5%
38	New Mexico	4,469,602,000	0.5%
39	Maine	4,249,374,000	0.5%
40	New Hampshire	3,980,324,000	0.4%
41	Hawaii	3,975,313,000	0.4%
42	Rhode Island	3,902,244,000	0.4%
43	Idaho	2,835,543,000	0.3%
44	Delaware	2,631,828,000	0.3%
45	South Dakota	2,528,389,000	0.3%
46	Montana	2,368,999,000	0.3%
47	North Dakota	2,367,774,000	0.3%
48	Alaska	2,041,248,000	0.2%
49	Vermont	1,760,664,000	0.2%
50	Wyoming	1,189,498,000	0.1%
	District of Columbia	4,881,124,000	0.6%

Source: Morgan Quitno Press using data from U.S. Bureau of the Census
"1997 Economic Census, Health Care and Social Assistance" (EC97562A, October 1999)
*Includes establishments exempt from as well as subject to the federal income tax. These include those primarily engaged in furnishing medical, surgical and other health services to persons. See Facilities Chapter for establishments.

Receipts per Health Service Establishment in 1997

National Rate = $1,370,364 per Establishment*

RANK	STATE	PER ESTABLISHMENT	RANK	STATE	PER ESTABLISHMENT
5	Alabama	$1,552,760	1	Massachusetts	$1,671,512
32	Alaska	1,300,158	2	New York	1,627,723
38	Arizona	1,220,528	3	Mississippi	1,580,683
35	Arkansas	1,263,342	4	Tennessee	1,562,915
36	California	1,250,395	5	Alabama	1,552,760
42	Colorado	1,129,615	6	Minnesota	1,535,255
10	Connecticut	1,488,600	7	Illinois	1,527,359
15	Delaware	1,438,157	8	North Dakota	1,525,628
28	Florida	1,307,922	9	North Carolina	1,502,931
11	Georgia	1,483,086	10	Connecticut	1,488,600
22	Hawaii	1,351,688	11	Georgia	1,483,086
48	Idaho	923,630	12	Ohio	1,464,119
7	Illinois	1,527,359	13	Rhode Island	1,456,061
19	Indiana	1,409,495	14	Missouri	1,439,935
39	Iowa	1,218,292	15	Delaware	1,438,157
34	Kansas	1,278,185	16	Pennsylvania	1,436,074
18	Kentucky	1,426,882	17	Louisiana	1,432,178
17	Louisiana	1,432,178	18	Kentucky	1,426,882
44	Maine	1,117,962	19	Indiana	1,409,495
23	Maryland	1,341,244	20	West Virginia	1,374,164
1	Massachusetts	1,671,512	21	Wisconsin	1,353,159
26	Michigan	1,323,486	22	Hawaii	1,351,688
6	Minnesota	1,535,255	23	Maryland	1,341,244
3	Mississippi	1,580,683	24	South Carolina	1,334,095
14	Missouri	1,439,935	25	Virginia	1,330,452
50	Montana	869,357	26	Michigan	1,323,486
33	Nebraska	1,284,942	27	New Jersey	1,318,017
31	Nevada	1,301,387	28	Florida	1,307,922
37	New Hampshire	1,241,136	29	South Dakota	1,305,312
27	New Jersey	1,318,017	30	Texas	1,304,200
40	New Mexico	1,207,674	31	Nevada	1,301,387
2	New York	1,627,723	32	Alaska	1,300,158
9	North Carolina	1,502,931	33	Nebraska	1,284,942
8	North Dakota	1,525,628	34	Kansas	1,278,185
12	Ohio	1,464,119	35	Arkansas	1,263,342
45	Oklahoma	1,105,388	36	California	1,250,395
46	Oregon	1,020,240	37	New Hampshire	1,241,136
16	Pennsylvania	1,436,074	38	Arizona	1,220,528
13	Rhode Island	1,456,061	39	Iowa	1,218,292
24	South Carolina	1,334,095	40	New Mexico	1,207,674
29	South Dakota	1,305,312	41	Utah	1,157,153
4	Tennessee	1,562,915	42	Colorado	1,129,615
30	Texas	1,304,200	43	Washington	1,127,303
41	Utah	1,157,153	44	Maine	1,117,962
47	Vermont	949,657	45	Oklahoma	1,105,388
25	Virginia	1,330,452	46	Oregon	1,020,240
43	Washington	1,127,303	47	Vermont	949,657
20	West Virginia	1,374,164	48	Idaho	923,630
21	Wisconsin	1,353,159	49	Wyoming	877,211
49	Wyoming	877,211	50	Montana	869,357

	District of Columbia	2,303,504

Source: Morgan Quitno Press using data from U.S. Bureau of the Census
"1997 Economic Census, Health Care and Social Assistance" (EC97562A, October 1999)
*Includes establishments exempt from as well as subject to the federal income tax. These include those primarily engaged in furnishing medical, surgical and other health services to persons. See Facilities Chapter for establishments.

Receipts of Offices and Clinics of Doctors of Medicine in 1997

National Total = $168,251,883,000*

ALPHA ORDER

RANK	STATE	RECEIPTS	% of USA
20	Alabama	$2,780,846,000	1.7%
48	Alaska	316,616,000	0.2%
22	Arizona	2,684,355,000	1.6%
32	Arkansas	1,402,756,000	0.8%
1	California	22,317,451,000	13.3%
26	Colorado	2,286,435,000	1.4%
23	Connecticut	2,616,269,000	1.6%
44	Delaware	500,577,000	0.3%
4	Florida	11,676,140,000	6.9%
10	Georgia	4,785,337,000	2.8%
38	Hawaii	720,675,000	0.4%
42	Idaho	600,721,000	0.4%
6	Illinois	7,233,092,000	4.3%
15	Indiana	3,475,948,000	2.1%
31	Iowa	1,465,067,000	0.9%
30	Kansas	1,566,643,000	0.9%
25	Kentucky	2,342,075,000	1.4%
21	Louisiana	2,741,786,000	1.6%
39	Maine	635,181,000	0.4%
16	Maryland	3,354,135,000	2.0%
14	Massachusetts	3,574,465,000	2.1%
9	Michigan	5,137,607,000	3.1%
24	Minnesota	2,367,336,000	1.4%
33	Mississippi	1,392,642,000	0.8%
17	Missouri	3,134,275,000	1.9%
45	Montana	438,816,000	0.3%
37	Nebraska	882,168,000	0.5%
34	Nevada	1,220,665,000	0.7%
41	New Hampshire	613,805,000	0.4%
8	New Jersey	6,087,711,000	3.6%
40	New Mexico	626,170,000	0.4%
3	New York	11,965,964,000	7.1%
11	North Carolina	4,271,873,000	2.5%
46	North Dakota	427,765,000	0.3%
7	Ohio	6,785,438,000	4.0%
29	Oklahoma	1,812,514,000	1.1%
28	Oregon	1,862,397,000	1.1%
5	Pennsylvania	7,594,668,000	4.5%
43	Rhode Island	525,592,000	0.3%
27	South Carolina	2,055,054,000	1.2%
47	South Dakota	424,223,000	0.3%
12	Tennessee	4,137,600,000	2.5%
2	Texas	12,439,354,000	7.4%
36	Utah	1,039,815,000	0.6%
49	Vermont	278,755,000	0.2%
13	Virginia	3,983,290,000	2.4%
19	Washington	2,818,141,000	1.7%
35	West Virginia	1,124,036,000	0.7%
18	Wisconsin	3,049,648,000	1.8%
50	Wyoming	215,604,000	0.1%

RANK ORDER

RANK	STATE	RECEIPTS	% of USA
1	California	$22,317,451,000	13.3%
2	Texas	12,439,354,000	7.4%
3	New York	11,965,964,000	7.1%
4	Florida	11,676,140,000	6.9%
5	Pennsylvania	7,594,668,000	4.5%
6	Illinois	7,233,092,000	4.3%
7	Ohio	6,785,438,000	4.0%
8	New Jersey	6,087,711,000	3.6%
9	Michigan	5,137,607,000	3.1%
10	Georgia	4,785,337,000	2.8%
11	North Carolina	4,271,873,000	2.5%
12	Tennessee	4,137,600,000	2.5%
13	Virginia	3,983,290,000	2.4%
14	Massachusetts	3,574,465,000	2.1%
15	Indiana	3,475,948,000	2.1%
16	Maryland	3,354,135,000	2.0%
17	Missouri	3,134,275,000	1.9%
18	Wisconsin	3,049,648,000	1.8%
19	Washington	2,818,141,000	1.7%
20	Alabama	2,780,846,000	1.7%
21	Louisiana	2,741,786,000	1.6%
22	Arizona	2,684,355,000	1.6%
23	Connecticut	2,616,269,000	1.6%
24	Minnesota	2,367,336,000	1.4%
25	Kentucky	2,342,075,000	1.4%
26	Colorado	2,286,435,000	1.4%
27	South Carolina	2,055,054,000	1.2%
28	Oregon	1,862,397,000	1.1%
29	Oklahoma	1,812,514,000	1.1%
30	Kansas	1,566,643,000	0.9%
31	Iowa	1,465,067,000	0.9%
32	Arkansas	1,402,756,000	0.8%
33	Mississippi	1,392,642,000	0.8%
34	Nevada	1,220,665,000	0.7%
35	West Virginia	1,124,036,000	0.7%
36	Utah	1,039,815,000	0.6%
37	Nebraska	882,168,000	0.5%
38	Hawaii	720,675,000	0.4%
39	Maine	635,181,000	0.4%
40	New Mexico	626,170,000	0.4%
41	New Hampshire	613,805,000	0.4%
42	Idaho	600,721,000	0.4%
43	Rhode Island	525,592,000	0.3%
44	Delaware	500,577,000	0.3%
45	Montana	438,816,000	0.3%
46	North Dakota	427,765,000	0.3%
47	South Dakota	424,223,000	0.3%
48	Alaska	316,616,000	0.2%
49	Vermont	278,755,000	0.2%
50	Wyoming	215,604,000	0.1%
	District of Columbia	462,387,000	0.3%

Source: U.S. Bureau of the Census
"1997 Economic Census, Health Care and Social Assistance" (EC97562A, October 1999)
*Includes only establishments subject to the federal income tax. See Facilities Chapter for establishments.

Receipts per Office or Clinic of Doctors of Medicine in 1997

National Rate = $909,008 per Establishment*

ALPHA ORDER

RANK ORDER

RANK	STATE	PER ESTABLISHMENT
10	Alabama	$1,032,237
28	Alaska	889,371
38	Arizona	821,155
33	Arkansas	852,739
21	California	926,843
30	Colorado	884,159
13	Connecticut	983,190
31	Delaware	875,135
34	Florida	847,079
16	Georgia	941,810
47	Hawaii	705,161
39	Idaho	798,831
14	Illinois	972,190
11	Indiana	1,026,262
7	Iowa	1,141,907
5	Kansas	1,145,207
15	Kentucky	946,675
26	Louisiana	898,652
45	Maine	757,973
44	Maryland	772,308
19	Massachusetts	929,882
37	Michigan	824,127
2	Minnesota	1,945,223
23	Mississippi	916,212
12	Missouri	991,859
46	Montana	748,833
8	Nebraska	1,139,752
24	Nevada	914,356
17	New Hampshire	935,678
40	New Jersey	796,404
49	New Mexico	665,430
42	New York	790,511
9	North Carolina	1,107,277
1	North Dakota	2,239,607
27	Ohio	896,004
36	Oklahoma	828,010
25	Oregon	912,940
35	Pennsylvania	836,601
48	Rhode Island	687,948
20	South Carolina	927,371
4	South Dakota	1,277,780
6	Tennessee	1,142,983
29	Texas	885,931
32	Utah	853,007
43	Vermont	774,319
18	Virginia	931,328
22	Washington	921,563
41	West Virginia	794,372
3	Wisconsin	1,387,465
50	Wyoming	624,939

RANK	STATE	PER ESTABLISHMENT
1	North Dakota	$2,239,607
2	Minnesota	1,945,223
3	Wisconsin	1,387,465
4	South Dakota	1,277,780
5	Kansas	1,145,207
6	Tennessee	1,142,983
7	Iowa	1,141,907
8	Nebraska	1,139,752
9	North Carolina	1,107,277
10	Alabama	1,032,237
11	Indiana	1,026,262
12	Missouri	991,859
13	Connecticut	983,190
14	Illinois	972,190
15	Kentucky	946,675
16	Georgia	941,810
17	New Hampshire	935,678
18	Virginia	931,328
19	Massachusetts	929,882
20	South Carolina	927,371
21	California	926,843
22	Washington	921,563
23	Mississippi	916,212
24	Nevada	914,356
25	Oregon	912,940
26	Louisiana	898,652
27	Ohio	896,004
28	Alaska	889,371
29	Texas	885,931
30	Colorado	884,159
31	Delaware	875,135
32	Utah	853,007
33	Arkansas	852,739
34	Florida	847,079
35	Pennsylvania	836,601
36	Oklahoma	828,010
37	Michigan	824,127
38	Arizona	821,155
39	Idaho	798,831
40	New Jersey	796,404
41	West Virginia	794,372
42	New York	790,511
43	Vermont	774,319
44	Maryland	772,308
45	Maine	757,973
46	Montana	748,833
47	Hawaii	705,161
48	Rhode Island	687,948
49	New Mexico	665,430
50	Wyoming	624,939
	District of Columbia	787,712

Source: Morgan Quitno Press using data from U.S. Bureau of the Census
  "1997 Economic Census, Health Care and Social Assistance" (EC97562A, October 1999)
*Includes only establishments subject to the federal income tax. See Facilities Chapter for establishments.

Receipts of Offices and Clinics of Dentists in 1997

National Total = $48,482,037,000*

ALPHA ORDER

RANK	STATE	RECEIPTS	% of USA
26	Alabama	$585,733,000	1.2%
44	Alaska	158,519,000	0.3%
24	Arizona	758,561,000	1.6%
33	Arkansas	348,004,000	0.7%
1	California	7,262,097,000	15.0%
19	Colorado	833,314,000	1.7%
20	Connecticut	826,385,000	1.7%
45	Delaware	142,256,000	0.3%
4	Florida	2,677,391,000	5.5%
12	Georgia	1,228,077,000	2.5%
36	Hawaii	267,597,000	0.6%
40	Idaho	226,822,000	0.5%
6	Illinois	2,032,882,000	4.2%
18	Indiana	902,891,000	1.9%
30	Iowa	430,789,000	0.9%
31	Kansas	428,608,000	0.9%
28	Kentucky	479,806,000	1.0%
25	Louisiana	642,671,000	1.3%
41	Maine	205,278,000	0.4%
16	Maryland	952,528,000	2.0%
11	Massachusetts	1,343,014,000	2.8%
7	Michigan	1,960,298,000	4.0%
17	Minnesota	942,837,000	1.9%
35	Mississippi	290,042,000	0.6%
23	Missouri	783,697,000	1.6%
46	Montana	138,694,000	0.3%
37	Nebraska	252,505,000	0.5%
34	Nevada	328,676,000	0.7%
38	New Hampshire	248,132,000	0.5%
8	New Jersey	1,803,107,000	3.7%
39	New Mexico	232,855,000	0.5%
2	New York	3,365,098,000	6.9%
13	North Carolina	1,171,773,000	2.4%
49	North Dakota	98,802,000	0.2%
9	Ohio	1,778,689,000	3.7%
29	Oklahoma	455,446,000	0.9%
22	Oregon	810,438,000	1.7%
5	Pennsylvania	2,040,175,000	4.2%
43	Rhode Island	193,380,000	0.4%
27	South Carolina	531,705,000	1.1%
48	South Dakota	109,481,000	0.2%
21	Tennessee	813,990,000	1.7%
3	Texas	2,811,112,000	5.8%
32	Utah	402,171,000	0.8%
47	Vermont	110,917,000	0.2%
14	Virginia	1,135,960,000	2.3%
10	Washington	1,554,248,000	3.2%
42	West Virginia	200,351,000	0.4%
15	Wisconsin	979,157,000	2.0%
50	Wyoming	69,332,000	0.1%

RANK ORDER

RANK	STATE	RECEIPTS	% of USA
1	California	$7,262,097,000	15.0%
2	New York	3,365,098,000	6.9%
3	Texas	2,811,112,000	5.8%
4	Florida	2,677,391,000	5.5%
5	Pennsylvania	2,040,175,000	4.2%
6	Illinois	2,032,882,000	4.2%
7	Michigan	1,960,298,000	4.0%
8	New Jersey	1,803,107,000	3.7%
9	Ohio	1,778,689,000	3.7%
10	Washington	1,554,248,000	3.2%
11	Massachusetts	1,343,014,000	2.8%
12	Georgia	1,228,077,000	2.5%
13	North Carolina	1,171,773,000	2.4%
14	Virginia	1,135,960,000	2.3%
15	Wisconsin	979,157,000	2.0%
16	Maryland	952,528,000	2.0%
17	Minnesota	942,837,000	1.9%
18	Indiana	902,891,000	1.9%
19	Colorado	833,314,000	1.7%
20	Connecticut	826,385,000	1.7%
21	Tennessee	813,990,000	1.7%
22	Oregon	810,438,000	1.7%
23	Missouri	783,697,000	1.6%
24	Arizona	758,561,000	1.6%
25	Louisiana	642,671,000	1.3%
26	Alabama	585,733,000	1.2%
27	South Carolina	531,705,000	1.1%
28	Kentucky	479,806,000	1.0%
29	Oklahoma	455,446,000	0.9%
30	Iowa	430,789,000	0.9%
31	Kansas	428,608,000	0.9%
32	Utah	402,171,000	0.8%
33	Arkansas	348,004,000	0.7%
34	Nevada	328,676,000	0.7%
35	Mississippi	290,042,000	0.6%
36	Hawaii	267,597,000	0.6%
37	Nebraska	252,505,000	0.5%
38	New Hampshire	248,132,000	0.5%
39	New Mexico	232,855,000	0.5%
40	Idaho	226,822,000	0.5%
41	Maine	205,278,000	0.4%
42	West Virginia	200,351,000	0.4%
43	Rhode Island	193,380,000	0.4%
44	Alaska	158,519,000	0.3%
45	Delaware	142,256,000	0.3%
46	Montana	138,694,000	0.3%
47	Vermont	110,917,000	0.2%
48	South Dakota	109,481,000	0.2%
49	North Dakota	98,802,000	0.2%
50	Wyoming	69,332,000	0.1%
	District of Columbia	135,746,000	0.3%

Source: U.S. Bureau of the Census
"1997 Economic Census, Health Care and Social Assistance" (EC97562A, October 1999)
*Includes only establishments subject to the federal income tax. See Facilities Chapter for establishments.

Receipts per Office or Clinic of Dentists in 1997

National Rate = $424,618 per Establishment*

ALPHA ORDER				RANK ORDER		
RANK	STATE	PER ESTABLISHMENT		RANK	STATE	PER ESTABLISHMENT
22	Alabama	$431,956		1	Delaware	$652,550
4	Alaska	542,873		2	Nevada	571,610
12	Arizona	462,255		3	Washington	549,787
37	Arkansas	387,532		4	Alaska	542,873
16	California	446,376		5	North Carolina	504,422
31	Colorado	408,087		6	Oregon	482,404
10	Connecticut	465,831		7	Georgia	477,108
1	Delaware	652,550		8	Rhode Island	471,659
21	Florida	433,095		9	Minnesota	470,948
7	Georgia	477,108		10	Connecticut	465,831
32	Hawaii	407,301		11	New Hampshire	465,538
14	Idaho	451,837		12	Arizona	462,255
41	Illinois	377,649		13	Massachusetts	458,523
30	Indiana	408,918		14	Idaho	451,837
39	Iowa	387,052		15	Michigan	450,436
24	Kansas	423,526		16	California	446,376
50	Kentucky	316,495		17	Wisconsin	444,465
28	Louisiana	417,048		18	Maine	444,325
18	Maine	444,325		19	South Carolina	437,257
33	Maryland	401,741		20	Vermont	433,270
13	Massachusetts	458,523		21	Florida	433,095
15	Michigan	450,436		22	Alabama	431,956
9	Minnesota	470,948		23	Virginia	429,474
43	Mississippi	371,849		24	Kansas	423,526
40	Missouri	381,919		25	New Jersey	422,076
49	Montana	331,012		26	Texas	420,133
47	Nebraska	334,887		27	New Mexico	418,052
2	Nevada	571,610		28	Louisiana	417,048
11	New Hampshire	465,538		29	South Dakota	410,041
25	New Jersey	422,076		30	Indiana	408,918
27	New Mexico	418,052		31	Colorado	408,087
38	New York	387,060		32	Hawaii	407,301
5	North Carolina	504,422		33	Maryland	401,741
34	North Dakota	401,634		34	North Dakota	401,634
36	Ohio	393,602		35	Tennessee	397,068
45	Oklahoma	359,185		36	Ohio	393,602
6	Oregon	482,404		37	Arkansas	387,532
42	Pennsylvania	375,515		38	New York	387,060
8	Rhode Island	471,659		39	Iowa	387,052
19	South Carolina	437,257		40	Missouri	381,919
29	South Dakota	410,041		41	Illinois	377,649
35	Tennessee	397,068		42	Pennsylvania	375,515
26	Texas	420,133		43	Mississippi	371,849
44	Utah	369,642		44	Utah	369,642
20	Vermont	433,270		45	Oklahoma	359,185
23	Virginia	429,474		46	West Virginia	340,733
3	Washington	549,787		47	Nebraska	334,887
46	West Virginia	340,733		48	Wyoming	331,732
17	Wisconsin	444,465		49	Montana	331,012
48	Wyoming	331,732		50	Kentucky	316,495
					District of Columbia	412,602

Source: Morgan Quitno Press using data from U.S. Bureau of the Census
   "1997 Economic Census, Health Care and Social Assistance" (EC97562A, October 1999)
*Includes only establishments subject to the federal income tax. See Facilities Chapter for establishments.

Receipts of Offices and Clinics of Doctors of Osteopathy in 1997

National Total = $3,377,296,000*

ALPHA ORDER				RANK ORDER			
RANK	STATE	RECEIPTS	% of USA	RANK	STATE	RECEIPTS	% of USA
22	Alabama	$45,430,000	1.3%	1	California	$425,716,000	12.6%
45	Alaska	4,601,000	0.1%	2	Texas	300,438,000	8.9%
26	Arizona	37,254,000	1.1%	3	New York	272,021,000	8.1%
29	Arkansas	29,570,000	0.9%	4	Florida	258,042,000	7.6%
1	California	425,716,000	12.6%	5	Illinois	179,870,000	5.3%
17	Colorado	60,383,000	1.8%	6	Pennsylvania	141,145,000	4.2%
16	Connecticut	68,752,000	2.0%	7	Ohio	125,958,000	3.7%
37	Delaware	12,654,000	0.4%	8	Georgia	117,068,000	3.5%
4	Florida	258,042,000	7.6%	9	Michigan	107,541,000	3.2%
8	Georgia	117,068,000	3.5%	10	New Jersey	102,862,000	3.0%
42	Hawaii	10,601,000	0.3%	11	Maryland	100,093,000	3.0%
38	Idaho	12,390,000	0.4%	12	Virginia	94,264,000	2.8%
5	Illinois	179,870,000	5.3%	13	Massachusetts	93,306,000	2.8%
25	Indiana	39,040,000	1.2%	14	Tennessee	81,762,000	2.4%
27	Iowa	31,950,000	0.9%	15	North Carolina	71,073,000	2.1%
31	Kansas	23,680,000	0.7%	16	Connecticut	68,752,000	2.0%
21	Kentucky	48,192,000	1.4%	17	Colorado	60,383,000	1.8%
20	Louisiana	48,382,000	1.4%	18	Missouri	57,368,000	1.7%
41	Maine	11,023,000	0.3%	19	Wisconsin	53,107,000	1.6%
11	Maryland	100,093,000	3.0%	20	Louisiana	48,382,000	1.4%
13	Massachusetts	93,306,000	2.8%	21	Kentucky	48,192,000	1.4%
9	Michigan	107,541,000	3.2%	22	Alabama	45,430,000	1.3%
23	Minnesota	44,516,000	1.3%	23	Minnesota	44,516,000	1.3%
32	Mississippi	21,876,000	0.6%	24	Washington	41,342,000	1.2%
18	Missouri	57,368,000	1.7%	25	Indiana	39,040,000	1.2%
47	Montana	4,334,000	0.1%	26	Arizona	37,254,000	1.1%
43	Nebraska	10,013,000	0.3%	27	Iowa	31,950,000	0.9%
39	Nevada	12,073,000	0.4%	28	South Carolina	31,153,000	0.9%
36	New Hampshire	14,638,000	0.4%	29	Arkansas	29,570,000	0.9%
10	New Jersey	102,862,000	3.0%	30	Oklahoma	27,037,000	0.8%
44	New Mexico	8,262,000	0.2%	31	Kansas	23,680,000	0.7%
3	New York	272,021,000	8.1%	32	Mississippi	21,876,000	0.6%
15	North Carolina	71,073,000	2.1%	33	Oregon	20,879,000	0.6%
49	North Dakota	3,029,000	0.1%	34	West Virginia	19,382,000	0.6%
7	Ohio	125,958,000	3.7%	35	Utah	14,765,000	0.4%
30	Oklahoma	27,037,000	0.8%	36	New Hampshire	14,638,000	0.4%
33	Oregon	20,879,000	0.6%	37	Delaware	12,654,000	0.4%
6	Pennsylvania	141,145,000	4.2%	38	Idaho	12,390,000	0.4%
40	Rhode Island	11,809,000	0.3%	39	Nevada	12,073,000	0.4%
28	South Carolina	31,153,000	0.9%	40	Rhode Island	11,809,000	0.3%
46	South Dakota	4,531,000	0.1%	41	Maine	11,023,000	0.3%
14	Tennessee	81,762,000	2.4%	42	Hawaii	10,601,000	0.3%
2	Texas	300,438,000	8.9%	43	Nebraska	10,013,000	0.3%
35	Utah	14,765,000	0.4%	44	New Mexico	8,262,000	0.2%
48	Vermont	3,421,000	0.1%	45	Alaska	4,601,000	0.1%
12	Virginia	94,264,000	2.8%	46	South Dakota	4,531,000	0.1%
24	Washington	41,342,000	1.2%	47	Montana	4,334,000	0.1%
34	West Virginia	19,382,000	0.6%	48	Vermont	3,421,000	0.1%
19	Wisconsin	53,107,000	1.6%	49	North Dakota	3,029,000	0.1%
50	Wyoming	1,761,000	0.1%	50	Wyoming	1,761,000	0.1%
					District of Columbia	16,939,000	0.5%

Source: U.S. Bureau of the Census
"1997 Economic Census, Health Care and Social Assistance" (EC97562A, October 1999)
*Includes only establishments subject to the federal income tax. See Facilities Chapter for establishments.

Receipts per Office or Clinic of Doctors of Osteopathy in 1997

National Rate = $326,151 per Establishment*

ALPHA ORDER

RANK	STATE	PER ESTABLISHMENT
6	Alabama	$441,068
17	Alaska	353,923
41	Arizona	260,517
5	Arkansas	441,343
35	California	292,387
29	Colorado	309,656
21	Connecticut	337,020
9	Delaware	395,438
24	Florida	325,400
15	Georgia	369,300
46	Hawaii	196,315
31	Idaho	302,195
14	Illinois	369,343
33	Indiana	298,015
1	Iowa	491,538
30	Kansas	303,590
8	Kentucky	398,281
32	Louisiana	300,509
25	Maine	324,206
20	Maryland	338,152
16	Massachusetts	358,869
27	Michigan	310,812
4	Minnesota	445,160
38	Mississippi	287,842
36	Missouri	291,208
43	Montana	240,778
44	Nebraska	227,568
23	Nevada	326,297
10	New Hampshire	385,211
34	New Jersey	297,289
50	New Mexico	162,000
28	New York	310,526
22	North Carolina	333,676
12	North Dakota	378,625
18	Ohio	351,838
42	Oklahoma	255,066
47	Oregon	186,420
19	Pennsylvania	338,477
37	Rhode Island	288,024
39	South Carolina	283,209
2	South Dakota	453,100
3	Tennessee	446,787
11	Texas	382,724
40	Utah	263,661
49	Vermont	162,905
26	Virginia	322,822
45	Washington	223,470
7	West Virginia	412,383
13	Wisconsin	376,645
48	Wyoming	176,100

RANK ORDER

RANK	STATE	PER ESTABLISHMENT
1	Iowa	$491,538
2	South Dakota	453,100
3	Tennessee	446,787
4	Minnesota	445,160
5	Arkansas	441,343
6	Alabama	441,068
7	West Virginia	412,383
8	Kentucky	398,281
9	Delaware	395,438
10	New Hampshire	385,211
11	Texas	382,724
12	North Dakota	378,625
13	Wisconsin	376,645
14	Illinois	369,343
15	Georgia	369,300
16	Massachusetts	358,869
17	Alaska	353,923
18	Ohio	351,838
19	Pennsylvania	338,477
20	Maryland	338,152
21	Connecticut	337,020
22	North Carolina	333,676
23	Nevada	326,297
24	Florida	325,400
25	Maine	324,206
26	Virginia	322,822
27	Michigan	310,812
28	New York	310,526
29	Colorado	309,656
30	Kansas	303,590
31	Idaho	302,195
32	Louisiana	300,509
33	Indiana	298,015
34	New Jersey	297,289
35	California	292,387
36	Missouri	291,208
37	Rhode Island	288,024
38	Mississippi	287,842
39	South Carolina	283,209
40	Utah	263,661
41	Arizona	260,517
42	Oklahoma	255,066
43	Montana	240,778
44	Nebraska	227,568
45	Washington	223,470
46	Hawaii	196,315
47	Oregon	186,420
48	Wyoming	176,100
49	Vermont	162,905
50	New Mexico	162,000

District of Columbia   211,738

Source: Morgan Quitno Press using data from U.S. Bureau of the Census
   "1997 Economic Census, Health Care and Social Assistance" (EC97562A, October 1999)
Includes only establishments subject to the federal income tax. See Facilities Chapter for establishments.

Receipts of Offices and Clinics of Chiropractors in 1997

National Total = $6,570,083,000*

ALPHA ORDER

RANK	STATE	RECEIPTS	% of USA
31	Alabama	$56,576,000	0.9%
43	Alaska	23,241,000	0.4%
16	Arizona	148,864,000	2.3%
33	Arkansas	44,148,000	0.7%
1	California	854,273,000	13.0%
17	Colorado	118,067,000	1.8%
20	Connecticut	105,246,000	1.6%
48	Delaware	15,814,000	0.2%
2	Florida	497,495,000	7.6%
14	Georgia	157,509,000	2.4%
44	Hawaii	20,149,000	0.3%
41	Idaho	26,072,000	0.4%
8	Illinois	276,850,000	4.2%
19	Indiana	105,465,000	1.6%
22	Iowa	92,270,000	1.4%
30	Kansas	65,115,000	1.0%
28	Kentucky	72,402,000	1.1%
27	Louisiana	73,450,000	1.1%
39	Maine	26,192,000	0.4%
26	Maryland	75,613,000	1.2%
13	Massachusetts	172,089,000	2.6%
9	Michigan	195,822,000	3.0%
10	Minnesota	194,611,000	3.0%
42	Mississippi	23,400,000	0.4%
21	Missouri	98,281,000	1.5%
45	Montana	20,021,000	0.3%
34	Nebraska	40,840,000	0.6%
32	Nevada	50,813,000	0.8%
38	New Hampshire	26,744,000	0.4%
3	New Jersey	382,180,000	5.8%
37	New Mexico	29,900,000	0.5%
5	New York	378,437,000	5.8%
15	North Carolina	148,949,000	2.3%
46	North Dakota	19,478,000	0.3%
7	Ohio	280,080,000	4.3%
29	Oklahoma	67,851,000	1.0%
24	Oregon	84,140,000	1.3%
6	Pennsylvania	338,472,000	5.2%
47	Rhode Island	18,171,000	0.3%
25	South Carolina	78,467,000	1.2%
40	South Dakota	26,158,000	0.4%
23	Tennessee	86,841,000	1.3%
4	Texas	381,230,000	5.8%
35	Utah	33,255,000	0.5%
49	Vermont	13,464,000	0.2%
18	Virginia	107,473,000	1.6%
12	Washington	179,123,000	2.7%
36	West Virginia	31,746,000	0.5%
11	Wisconsin	194,349,000	3.0%
50	Wyoming	8,897,000	0.1%

RANK ORDER

RANK	STATE	RECEIPTS	% of USA
1	California	$854,273,000	13.0%
2	Florida	497,495,000	7.6%
3	New Jersey	382,180,000	5.8%
4	Texas	381,230,000	5.8%
5	New York	378,437,000	5.8%
6	Pennsylvania	338,472,000	5.2%
7	Ohio	280,080,000	4.3%
8	Illinois	276,850,000	4.2%
9	Michigan	195,822,000	3.0%
10	Minnesota	194,611,000	3.0%
11	Wisconsin	194,349,000	3.0%
12	Washington	179,123,000	2.7%
13	Massachusetts	172,089,000	2.6%
14	Georgia	157,509,000	2.4%
15	North Carolina	148,949,000	2.3%
16	Arizona	148,864,000	2.3%
17	Colorado	118,067,000	1.8%
18	Virginia	107,473,000	1.6%
19	Indiana	105,465,000	1.6%
20	Connecticut	105,246,000	1.6%
21	Missouri	98,281,000	1.5%
22	Iowa	92,270,000	1.4%
23	Tennessee	86,841,000	1.3%
24	Oregon	84,140,000	1.3%
25	South Carolina	78,467,000	1.2%
26	Maryland	75,613,000	1.2%
27	Louisiana	73,450,000	1.1%
28	Kentucky	72,402,000	1.1%
29	Oklahoma	67,851,000	1.0%
30	Kansas	65,115,000	1.0%
31	Alabama	56,576,000	0.9%
32	Nevada	50,813,000	0.8%
33	Arkansas	44,148,000	0.7%
34	Nebraska	40,840,000	0.6%
35	Utah	33,255,000	0.5%
36	West Virginia	31,746,000	0.5%
37	New Mexico	29,900,000	0.5%
38	New Hampshire	26,744,000	0.4%
39	Maine	26,192,000	0.4%
40	South Dakota	26,158,000	0.4%
41	Idaho	26,072,000	0.4%
42	Mississippi	23,400,000	0.4%
43	Alaska	23,241,000	0.4%
44	Hawaii	20,149,000	0.3%
45	Montana	20,021,000	0.3%
46	North Dakota	19,478,000	0.3%
47	Rhode Island	18,171,000	0.3%
48	Delaware	15,814,000	0.2%
49	Vermont	13,464,000	0.2%
50	Wyoming	8,897,000	0.1%
	District of Columbia	3,990,000	0.1%

Source: U.S. Bureau of the Census
"1997 Economic Census, Health Care and Social Assistance" (EC97562A, October 1999)
*Includes only establishments subject to the federal income tax. See Facilities Chapter for establishments.

Receipts per Office or Clinic of Chiropractors in 1997

National Rate = $215,504 per Establishment*

ALPHA ORDER

RANK	STATE	PER ESTABLISHMENT
41	Alabama	$177,354
1	Alaska	286,926
26	Arizona	200,625
39	Arkansas	178,737
21	California	207,802
36	Colorado	186,226
3	Connecticut	274,078
6	Delaware	263,567
9	Florida	253,436
34	Georgia	189,999
19	Hawaii	212,095
48	Idaho	162,950
17	Illinois	217,137
23	Indiana	203,208
45	Iowa	169,303
42	Kansas	176,463
20	Kentucky	211,085
10	Louisiana	249,830
38	Maine	183,161
2	Maryland	276,971
5	Massachusetts	268,051
33	Michigan	192,928
15	Minnesota	219,899
40	Mississippi	178,626
49	Missouri	153,086
50	Montana	147,213
24	Nebraska	203,184
12	Nevada	247,868
22	New Hampshire	204,153
4	New Jersey	270,092
47	New Mexico	164,286
30	New York	197,617
11	North Carolina	249,496
35	North Dakota	187,288
7	Ohio	261,757
28	Oklahoma	198,977
43	Oregon	176,025
18	Pennsylvania	213,952
25	Rhode Island	201,900
27	South Carolina	200,171
31	South Dakota	196,677
29	Tennessee	198,721
14	Texas	223,595
46	Utah	168,807
37	Vermont	184,438
16	Virginia	218,886
32	Washington	194,488
8	West Virginia	253,968
13	Wisconsin	242,330
44	Wyoming	174,451

RANK ORDER

RANK	STATE	PER ESTABLISHMENT
1	Alaska	$286,926
2	Maryland	276,971
3	Connecticut	274,078
4	New Jersey	270,092
5	Massachusetts	268,051
6	Delaware	263,567
7	Ohio	261,757
8	West Virginia	253,968
9	Florida	253,436
10	Louisiana	249,830
11	North Carolina	249,496
12	Nevada	247,868
13	Wisconsin	242,330
14	Texas	223,595
15	Minnesota	219,899
16	Virginia	218,886
17	Illinois	217,137
18	Pennsylvania	213,952
19	Hawaii	212,095
20	Kentucky	211,085
21	California	207,802
22	New Hampshire	204,153
23	Indiana	203,208
24	Nebraska	203,184
25	Rhode Island	201,900
26	Arizona	200,625
27	South Carolina	200,171
28	Oklahoma	198,977
29	Tennessee	198,721
30	New York	197,617
31	South Dakota	196,677
32	Washington	194,488
33	Michigan	192,928
34	Georgia	189,999
35	North Dakota	187,288
36	Colorado	186,226
37	Vermont	184,438
38	Maine	183,161
39	Arkansas	178,737
40	Mississippi	178,626
41	Alabama	177,354
42	Kansas	176,463
43	Oregon	176,025
44	Wyoming	174,451
45	Iowa	169,303
46	Utah	168,807
47	New Mexico	164,286
48	Idaho	162,950
49	Missouri	153,086
50	Montana	147,213
	District of Columbia	332,500

Source: Morgan Quitno Press using data from U.S. Bureau of the Census
"1997 Economic Census, Health Care and Social Assistance" (EC97562A, October 1999)
*Includes only establishments subject to the federal income tax. See Facilities Chapter for establishments.

Receipts of Offices and Clinics of Optometrists in 1997

National Total = $6,361,839,000*

ALPHA ORDER

RANK	STATE	RECEIPTS	% of USA
28	Alabama	$75,889,000	1.2%
49	Alaska	17,253,000	0.3%
26	Arizona	83,773,000	1.3%
30	Arkansas	67,990,000	1.1%
1	California	893,973,000	14.1%
22	Colorado	98,375,000	1.5%
29	Connecticut	75,813,000	1.2%
48	Delaware	20,635,000	0.3%
4	Florida	296,073,000	4.7%
14	Georgia	130,195,000	2.0%
40	Hawaii	30,857,000	0.5%
39	Idaho	34,126,000	0.5%
7	Illinois	254,420,000	4.0%
11	Indiana	192,712,000	3.0%
19	Iowa	106,315,000	1.7%
20	Kansas	105,680,000	1.7%
25	Kentucky	94,522,000	1.5%
32	Louisiana	59,096,000	0.9%
37	Maine	43,619,000	0.7%
24	Maryland	96,038,000	1.5%
16	Massachusetts	122,845,000	1.9%
9	Michigan	242,108,000	3.8%
23	Minnesota	96,623,000	1.5%
36	Mississippi	46,681,000	0.7%
21	Missouri	100,441,000	1.6%
42	Montana	27,883,000	0.4%
33	Nebraska	51,730,000	0.8%
34	Nevada	48,890,000	0.8%
43	New Hampshire	27,205,000	0.4%
10	New Jersey	198,301,000	3.1%
38	New Mexico	42,399,000	0.7%
8	New York	248,108,000	3.9%
3	North Carolina	326,595,000	5.1%
46	North Dakota	22,845,000	0.4%
5	Ohio	290,100,000	4.6%
18	Oklahoma	106,835,000	1.7%
27	Oregon	77,475,000	1.2%
6	Pennsylvania	285,719,000	4.5%
45	Rhode Island	24,225,000	0.4%
31	South Carolina	63,838,000	1.0%
44	South Dakota	25,946,000	0.4%
13	Tennessee	139,531,000	2.2%
2	Texas	464,456,000	7.3%
41	Utah	28,150,000	0.4%
50	Vermont	13,498,000	0.2%
12	Virginia	140,232,000	2.2%
15	Washington	129,999,000	2.0%
35	West Virginia	48,545,000	0.8%
17	Wisconsin	116,916,000	1.8%
47	Wyoming	21,684,000	0.3%

RANK ORDER

RANK	STATE	RECEIPTS	% of USA
1	California	$893,973,000	14.1%
2	Texas	464,456,000	7.3%
3	North Carolina	326,595,000	5.1%
4	Florida	296,073,000	4.7%
5	Ohio	290,100,000	4.6%
6	Pennsylvania	285,719,000	4.5%
7	Illinois	254,420,000	4.0%
8	New York	248,108,000	3.9%
9	Michigan	242,108,000	3.8%
10	New Jersey	198,301,000	3.1%
11	Indiana	192,712,000	3.0%
12	Virginia	140,232,000	2.2%
13	Tennessee	139,531,000	2.2%
14	Georgia	130,195,000	2.0%
15	Washington	129,999,000	2.0%
16	Massachusetts	122,845,000	1.9%
17	Wisconsin	116,916,000	1.8%
18	Oklahoma	106,835,000	1.7%
19	Iowa	106,315,000	1.7%
20	Kansas	105,680,000	1.7%
21	Missouri	100,441,000	1.6%
22	Colorado	98,375,000	1.5%
23	Minnesota	96,623,000	1.5%
24	Maryland	96,038,000	1.5%
25	Kentucky	94,522,000	1.5%
26	Arizona	83,773,000	1.3%
27	Oregon	77,475,000	1.2%
28	Alabama	75,889,000	1.2%
29	Connecticut	75,813,000	1.2%
30	Arkansas	67,990,000	1.1%
31	South Carolina	63,838,000	1.0%
32	Louisiana	59,096,000	0.9%
33	Nebraska	51,730,000	0.8%
34	Nevada	48,890,000	0.8%
35	West Virginia	48,545,000	0.8%
36	Mississippi	46,681,000	0.7%
37	Maine	43,619,000	0.7%
38	New Mexico	42,399,000	0.7%
39	Idaho	34,126,000	0.5%
40	Hawaii	30,857,000	0.5%
41	Utah	28,150,000	0.4%
42	Montana	27,883,000	0.4%
43	New Hampshire	27,205,000	0.4%
44	South Dakota	25,946,000	0.4%
45	Rhode Island	24,225,000	0.4%
46	North Dakota	22,845,000	0.4%
47	Wyoming	21,684,000	0.3%
48	Delaware	20,635,000	0.3%
49	Alaska	17,253,000	0.3%
50	Vermont	13,498,000	0.2%
	District of Columbia	4,682,000	0.1%

Source: U.S. Bureau of the Census
"1997 Economic Census, Health Care and Social Assistance" (EC97562A, October 1999)
*Includes only establishments subject to the federal income tax. See Facilities Chapter for establishments.

Receipts per Office or Clinic of Optometrists in 1997

National Rate = $355,907 per Establishment*

ALPHA ORDER

RANK	STATE	PER ESTABLISHMENT
43	Alabama	$311,020
12	Alaska	375,065
5	Arizona	395,156
32	Arkansas	334,926
14	California	365,185
25	Colorado	345,175
26	Connecticut	343,045
2	Delaware	429,896
34	Florida	329,703
28	Georgia	339,049
48	Hawaii	277,991
49	Idaho	275,210
15	Illinois	363,977
10	Indiana	377,867
7	Iowa	383,809
4	Kansas	411,206
19	Kentucky	360,771
38	Louisiana	314,340
16	Maine	363,492
11	Maryland	376,620
37	Massachusetts	322,428
3	Michigan	413,860
17	Minnesota	361,884
42	Mississippi	311,207
29	Missouri	338,185
45	Montana	306,407
8	Nebraska	383,185
6	Nevada	394,274
21	New Hampshire	353,312
31	New Jersey	336,674
13	New Mexico	365,509
33	New York	330,811
1	North Carolina	553,551
23	North Dakota	351,462
30	Ohio	336,934
40	Oklahoma	312,383
36	Oregon	324,163
44	Pennsylvania	307,887
50	Rhode Island	269,167
41	South Carolina	311,405
24	South Dakota	350,622
20	Tennessee	355,946
9	Texas	379,148
39	Utah	312,778
47	Vermont	293,435
35	Virginia	329,183
27	Washington	343,005
46	West Virginia	301,522
22	Wisconsin	352,157
18	Wyoming	361,400

RANK ORDER

RANK	STATE	PER ESTABLISHMENT
1	North Carolina	$553,551
2	Delaware	429,896
3	Michigan	413,860
4	Kansas	411,206
5	Arizona	395,156
6	Nevada	394,274
7	Iowa	383,809
8	Nebraska	383,185
9	Texas	379,148
10	Indiana	377,867
11	Maryland	376,620
12	Alaska	375,065
13	New Mexico	365,509
14	California	365,185
15	Illinois	363,977
16	Maine	363,492
17	Minnesota	361,884
18	Wyoming	361,400
19	Kentucky	360,771
20	Tennessee	355,946
21	New Hampshire	353,312
22	Wisconsin	352,157
23	North Dakota	351,462
24	South Dakota	350,622
25	Colorado	345,175
26	Connecticut	343,045
27	Washington	343,005
28	Georgia	339,049
29	Missouri	338,185
30	Ohio	336,934
31	New Jersey	336,674
32	Arkansas	334,926
33	New York	330,811
34	Florida	329,703
35	Virginia	329,183
36	Oregon	324,163
37	Massachusetts	322,428
38	Louisiana	314,340
39	Utah	312,778
40	Oklahoma	312,383
41	South Carolina	311,405
42	Mississippi	311,207
43	Alabama	311,020
44	Pennsylvania	307,887
45	Montana	306,407
46	West Virginia	301,522
47	Vermont	293,435
48	Hawaii	277,991
49	Idaho	275,210
50	Rhode Island	269,167
	District of Columbia	292,625

Source: Morgan Quitno Press using data from U.S. Bureau of the Census
  "1997 Economic Census, Health Care and Social Assistance" (EC97562A, October 1999)
*Includes only establishments subject to the federal income tax. See Facilities Chapter for establishments.

Receipts of Offices and Clinics of Podiatrists in 1997

National Total = $2,393,443,000*

ALPHA ORDER

RANK	STATE	RECEIPTS	% of USA
23	Alabama	$22,060,000	0.9%
46	Alaska	3,379,000	0.1%
20	Arizona	31,824,000	1.3%
37	Arkansas	10,386,000	0.4%
2	California	213,960,000	8.9%
22	Colorado	26,935,000	1.1%
14	Connecticut	47,498,000	2.0%
41	Delaware	7,244,000	0.3%
3	Florida	185,375,000	7.7%
10	Georgia	71,030,000	3.0%
45	Hawaii	3,692,000	0.2%
43	Idaho	6,818,000	0.3%
6	Illinois	133,296,000	5.6%
15	Indiana	45,568,000	1.9%
24	Iowa	21,064,000	0.9%
32	Kansas	13,681,000	0.6%
25	Kentucky	19,430,000	0.8%
26	Louisiana	18,171,000	0.8%
38	Maine	9,370,000	0.4%
11	Maryland	61,283,000	2.6%
12	Massachusetts	60,843,000	2.5%
7	Michigan	133,001,000	5.6%
27	Minnesota	17,329,000	0.7%
42	Mississippi	7,154,000	0.3%
19	Missouri	32,837,000	1.4%
44	Montana	5,257,000	0.2%
36	Nebraska	10,541,000	0.4%
35	Nevada	10,625,000	0.4%
40	New Hampshire	8,820,000	0.4%
5	New Jersey	143,208,000	6.0%
34	New Mexico	10,968,000	0.5%
1	New York	286,531,000	12.0%
16	North Carolina	44,593,000	1.9%
49	North Dakota	1,754,000	0.1%
9	Ohio	124,970,000	5.2%
29	Oklahoma	16,008,000	0.7%
28	Oregon	16,788,000	0.7%
4	Pennsylvania	157,226,000	6.6%
31	Rhode Island	13,734,000	0.6%
30	South Carolina	15,268,000	0.6%
47	South Dakota	2,712,000	0.1%
21	Tennessee	30,476,000	1.3%
8	Texas	125,444,000	5.2%
33	Utah	12,282,000	0.5%
48	Vermont	2,241,000	0.1%
13	Virginia	54,177,000	2.3%
17	Washington	40,820,000	1.7%
39	West Virginia	8,960,000	0.4%
18	Wisconsin	37,187,000	1.6%
50	Wyoming	1,563,000	0.1%

RANK ORDER

RANK	STATE	RECEIPTS	% of USA
1	New York	$286,531,000	12.0%
2	California	213,960,000	8.9%
3	Florida	185,375,000	7.7%
4	Pennsylvania	157,226,000	6.6%
5	New Jersey	143,208,000	6.0%
6	Illinois	133,296,000	5.6%
7	Michigan	133,001,000	5.6%
8	Texas	125,444,000	5.2%
9	Ohio	124,970,000	5.2%
10	Georgia	71,030,000	3.0%
11	Maryland	61,283,000	2.6%
12	Massachusetts	60,843,000	2.5%
13	Virginia	54,177,000	2.3%
14	Connecticut	47,498,000	2.0%
15	Indiana	45,568,000	1.9%
16	North Carolina	44,593,000	1.9%
17	Washington	40,820,000	1.7%
18	Wisconsin	37,187,000	1.6%
19	Missouri	32,837,000	1.4%
20	Arizona	31,824,000	1.3%
21	Tennessee	30,476,000	1.3%
22	Colorado	26,935,000	1.1%
23	Alabama	22,060,000	0.9%
24	Iowa	21,064,000	0.9%
25	Kentucky	19,430,000	0.8%
26	Louisiana	18,171,000	0.8%
27	Minnesota	17,329,000	0.7%
28	Oregon	16,788,000	0.7%
29	Oklahoma	16,008,000	0.7%
30	South Carolina	15,268,000	0.6%
31	Rhode Island	13,734,000	0.6%
32	Kansas	13,681,000	0.6%
33	Utah	12,282,000	0.5%
34	New Mexico	10,968,000	0.5%
35	Nevada	10,625,000	0.4%
36	Nebraska	10,541,000	0.4%
37	Arkansas	10,386,000	0.4%
38	Maine	9,370,000	0.4%
39	West Virginia	8,960,000	0.4%
40	New Hampshire	8,820,000	0.4%
41	Delaware	7,244,000	0.3%
42	Mississippi	7,154,000	0.3%
43	Idaho	6,818,000	0.3%
44	Montana	5,257,000	0.2%
45	Hawaii	3,692,000	0.2%
46	Alaska	3,379,000	0.1%
47	South Dakota	2,712,000	0.1%
48	Vermont	2,241,000	0.1%
49	North Dakota	1,754,000	0.1%
50	Wyoming	1,563,000	0.1%
	District of Columbia	8,062,000	0.3%

Source: U.S. Bureau of the Census
"1997 Economic Census, Health Care and Social Assistance" (EC97562A, October 1999)
*Includes only establishments subject to the federal income tax. See Facilities Chapter for establishments.

Receipts per Office or Clinic of Podiatrists in 1997

National Rate = $276,315 per Establishment*

ALPHA ORDER

RANK	STATE	PER ESTABLISHMENT
3	Alabama	$361,639
1	Alaska	422,375
29	Arizona	269,695
4	Arkansas	358,138
37	California	259,345
19	Colorado	289,624
15	Connecticut	300,620
5	Delaware	344,952
14	Florida	302,406
2	Georgia	405,886
22	Hawaii	284,000
7	Idaho	340,900
27	Illinois	272,589
35	Indiana	261,885
36	Iowa	260,049
38	Kansas	253,352
11	Kentucky	313,387
6	Louisiana	342,849
46	Maine	223,095
26	Maryland	276,050
33	Massachusetts	264,535
10	Michigan	315,917
17	Minnesota	293,712
32	Mississippi	264,963
24	Missouri	280,658
48	Montana	210,280
40	Nebraska	250,976
12	Nevada	312,500
21	New Hampshire	284,516
29	New Jersey	269,695
42	New Mexico	243,733
34	New York	263,598
9	North Carolina	316,262
18	North Dakota	292,333
39	Ohio	252,465
23	Oklahoma	280,842
31	Oregon	266,476
44	Pennsylvania	237,143
20	Rhode Island	286,125
8	South Carolina	324,851
49	South Dakota	208,615
25	Tennessee	279,596
16	Texas	293,780
47	Utah	211,759
45	Vermont	224,100
28	Virginia	270,885
43	Washington	241,538
41	West Virginia	248,889
13	Wisconsin	307,331
50	Wyoming	195,375

RANK ORDER

RANK	STATE	PER ESTABLISHMENT
1	Alaska	$422,375
2	Georgia	405,886
3	Alabama	361,639
4	Arkansas	358,138
5	Delaware	344,952
6	Louisiana	342,849
7	Idaho	340,900
8	South Carolina	324,851
9	North Carolina	316,262
10	Michigan	315,917
11	Kentucky	313,387
12	Nevada	312,500
13	Wisconsin	307,331
14	Florida	302,406
15	Connecticut	300,620
16	Texas	293,780
17	Minnesota	293,712
18	North Dakota	292,333
19	Colorado	289,624
20	Rhode Island	286,125
21	New Hampshire	284,516
22	Hawaii	284,000
23	Oklahoma	280,842
24	Missouri	280,658
25	Tennessee	279,596
26	Maryland	276,050
27	Illinois	272,589
28	Virginia	270,885
29	Arizona	269,695
29	New Jersey	269,695
31	Oregon	266,476
32	Mississippi	264,963
33	Massachusetts	264,535
34	New York	263,598
35	Indiana	261,885
36	Iowa	260,049
37	California	259,345
38	Kansas	253,352
39	Ohio	252,465
40	Nebraska	250,976
41	West Virginia	248,889
42	New Mexico	243,733
43	Washington	241,538
44	Pennsylvania	237,143
45	Vermont	224,100
46	Maine	223,095
47	Utah	211,759
48	Montana	210,280
49	South Dakota	208,615
50	Wyoming	195,375
	District of Columbia	260,065

Source: Morgan Quitno Press using data from U.S. Bureau of the Census
   "1997 Economic Census, Health Care and Social Assistance" (EC97562A, October 1999)
*Includes only establishments subject to the federal income tax. See Facilities Chapter for establishments.

Receipts of Hospitals in 1997

National Total = $379,178,312,000*

ALPHA ORDER

RANK	STATE	RECEIPTS	% of USA
20	Alabama	$6,354,027,000	1.7%
48	Alaska	1,005,475,000	0.3%
26	Arizona	4,787,752,000	1.3%
31	Arkansas	3,531,991,000	0.9%
1	California	35,729,221,000	9.4%
27	Colorado	4,442,729,000	1.2%
25	Connecticut**	4,797,486,000	1.3%
45	Delaware**	1,157,237,000	0.3%
4	Florida	21,117,137,000	5.6%
12	Georgia	10,623,885,000	2.8%
41	Hawaii**	1,527,862,000	0.4%
44	Idaho	1,245,683,000	0.3%
6	Illinois	18,515,836,000	4.9%
16	Indiana	8,157,243,000	2.2%
30	Iowa**	4,052,045,000	1.1%
33	Kansas**	2,999,713,000	0.8%
23	Kentucky	5,603,713,000	1.5%
17	Louisiana	7,244,276,000	1.9%
40	Maine**	1,702,483,000	0.4%
18	Maryland	6,801,682,000	1.8%
10	Massachusetts	10,966,399,000	2.9%
8	Michigan	14,580,184,000	3.8%
22	Minnesota**	5,814,780,000	1.5%
28	Mississippi	4,292,837,000	1.1%
13	Missouri	9,013,034,000	2.4%
46	Montana**	1,100,902,000	0.3%
35	Nebraska**	2,346,897,000	0.6%
38	Nevada	1,882,577,000	0.5%
42	New Hampshire	1,527,161,000	0.4%
9	New Jersey	11,677,458,000	3.1%
37	New Mexico	2,030,749,000	0.5%
2	New York	33,493,372,000	8.8%
11	North Carolina	10,729,994,000	2.8%
47	North Dakota**	1,051,689,000	0.3%
7	Ohio	16,408,126,000	4.3%
29	Oklahoma	4,143,476,000	1.1%
32	Oregon	3,464,752,000	0.9%
5	Pennsylvania	20,306,035,000	5.4%
39	Rhode Island**	1,727,436,000	0.5%
24	South Carolina	5,057,641,000	1.3%
43	South Dakota	1,272,118,000	0.3%
14	Tennessee	8,623,439,000	2.3%
3	Texas	24,502,981,000	6.5%
36	Utah	2,211,878,000	0.6%
49	Vermont	689,929,000	0.2%
15	Virginia	8,373,942,000	2.2%
21	Washington	6,197,449,000	1.6%
34	West Virginia	2,961,078,000	0.8%
19	Wisconsin	6,623,633,000	1.7%
50	Wyoming	565,835,000	0.1%

RANK ORDER

RANK	STATE	RECEIPTS	% of USA
1	California	$35,729,221,000	9.4%
2	New York	33,493,372,000	8.8%
3	Texas	24,502,981,000	6.5%
4	Florida	21,117,137,000	5.6%
5	Pennsylvania	20,306,035,000	5.4%
6	Illinois	18,515,836,000	4.9%
7	Ohio	16,408,126,000	4.3%
8	Michigan	14,580,184,000	3.8%
9	New Jersey	11,677,458,000	3.1%
10	Massachusetts	10,966,399,000	2.9%
11	North Carolina	10,729,994,000	2.8%
12	Georgia	10,623,885,000	2.8%
13	Missouri	9,013,034,000	2.4%
14	Tennessee	8,623,439,000	2.3%
15	Virginia	8,373,942,000	2.2%
16	Indiana	8,157,243,000	2.2%
17	Louisiana	7,244,276,000	1.9%
18	Maryland	6,801,682,000	1.8%
19	Wisconsin	6,623,633,000	1.7%
20	Alabama	6,354,027,000	1.7%
21	Washington	6,197,449,000	1.6%
22	Minnesota**	5,814,780,000	1.5%
23	Kentucky	5,603,713,000	1.5%
24	South Carolina	5,057,641,000	1.3%
25	Connecticut**	4,797,486,000	1.3%
26	Arizona	4,787,752,000	1.3%
27	Colorado	4,442,729,000	1.2%
28	Mississippi	4,292,837,000	1.1%
29	Oklahoma	4,143,476,000	1.1%
30	Iowa**	4,052,045,000	1.1%
31	Arkansas	3,531,991,000	0.9%
32	Oregon	3,464,752,000	0.9%
33	Kansas**	2,999,713,000	0.8%
34	West Virginia	2,961,078,000	0.8%
35	Nebraska**	2,346,897,000	0.6%
36	Utah	2,211,878,000	0.6%
37	New Mexico	2,030,749,000	0.5%
38	Nevada	1,882,577,000	0.5%
39	Rhode Island**	1,727,436,000	0.5%
40	Maine**	1,702,483,000	0.4%
41	Hawaii**	1,527,862,000	0.4%
42	New Hampshire	1,527,161,000	0.4%
43	South Dakota	1,272,118,000	0.3%
44	Idaho	1,245,683,000	0.3%
45	Delaware**	1,157,237,000	0.3%
46	Montana**	1,100,902,000	0.3%
47	North Dakota**	1,051,689,000	0.3%
48	Alaska	1,005,475,000	0.3%
49	Vermont	689,929,000	0.2%
50	Wyoming	565,835,000	0.1%
	District of Columbia	2,978,620,000	0.8%

Source: Morgan Quitno Press using data from U.S. Bureau of the Census
"1997 Economic Census, Health Care and Social Assistance" (EC97562A, October 1999)
*Includes establishments exempt from as well as subject to the federal income tax. Includes general medical and surgical hospitals, psychiatric hospitals and other specialty hospitals. Includes government owned hospitals.
**Amounts shown for these states are only for establishments exempt from federal income tax.

Receipts per Hospital in 1997

National Rate = $56,720,765 per Hospital*

<table>
<tr><td colspan="3">ALPHA ORDER</td><td colspan="3">RANK ORDER</td></tr>
<tr><td>RANK</td><td>STATE</td><td>PER HOSPITAL</td><td>RANK</td><td>STATE</td><td>PER HOSPITAL</td></tr>
<tr><td>27</td><td>Alabama</td><td>$46,379,759</td><td>1</td><td>New York</td><td>$108,392,790</td></tr>
<tr><td>39</td><td>Alaska</td><td>37,239,815</td><td>2</td><td>Delaware**</td><td>96,436,417</td></tr>
<tr><td>22</td><td>Arizona</td><td>52,040,783</td><td>3</td><td>Connecticut**</td><td>95,949,720</td></tr>
<tr><td>40</td><td>Arkansas</td><td>36,040,724</td><td>4</td><td>New Jersey</td><td>91,948,488</td></tr>
<tr><td>13</td><td>California</td><td>66,287,980</td><td>5</td><td>Rhode Island**</td><td>90,917,684</td></tr>
<tr><td>23</td><td>Colorado</td><td>51,659,640</td><td>6</td><td>Maryland</td><td>79,089,326</td></tr>
<tr><td>3</td><td>Connecticut**</td><td>95,949,720</td><td>7</td><td>Massachusetts</td><td>76,688,105</td></tr>
<tr><td>2</td><td>Delaware**</td><td>96,436,417</td><td>8</td><td>Illinois</td><td>75,884,574</td></tr>
<tr><td>11</td><td>Florida</td><td>69,236,515</td><td>9</td><td>Ohio</td><td>73,910,477</td></tr>
<tr><td>24</td><td>Georgia</td><td>51,572,257</td><td>10</td><td>Michigan</td><td>71,471,490</td></tr>
<tr><td>20</td><td>Hawaii**</td><td>54,566,500</td><td>11</td><td>Florida</td><td>69,236,515</td></tr>
<tr><td>44</td><td>Idaho</td><td>23,503,453</td><td>12</td><td>Pennsylvania</td><td>68,141,057</td></tr>
<tr><td>8</td><td>Illinois</td><td>75,884,574</td><td>13</td><td>California</td><td>66,287,980</td></tr>
<tr><td>26</td><td>Indiana</td><td>49,140,018</td><td>14</td><td>North Carolina</td><td>65,828,184</td></tr>
<tr><td>42</td><td>Iowa**</td><td>31,905,866</td><td>15</td><td>Virginia</td><td>61,573,103</td></tr>
<tr><td>46</td><td>Kansas**</td><td>21,895,715</td><td>16</td><td>South Carolina</td><td>58,809,779</td></tr>
<tr><td>30</td><td>Kentucky</td><td>43,779,008</td><td>17</td><td>Missouri</td><td>56,331,463</td></tr>
<tr><td>36</td><td>Louisiana</td><td>38,533,383</td><td>18</td><td>Nevada</td><td>55,369,912</td></tr>
<tr><td>35</td><td>Maine**</td><td>40,535,310</td><td>19</td><td>Washington</td><td>54,844,681</td></tr>
<tr><td>6</td><td>Maryland</td><td>79,089,326</td><td>20</td><td>Hawaii**</td><td>54,566,500</td></tr>
<tr><td>7</td><td>Massachusetts</td><td>76,688,105</td><td>21</td><td>Tennessee</td><td>52,581,945</td></tr>
<tr><td>10</td><td>Michigan</td><td>71,471,490</td><td>22</td><td>Arizona</td><td>52,040,783</td></tr>
<tr><td>37</td><td>Minnesota**</td><td>37,758,312</td><td>23</td><td>Colorado</td><td>51,659,640</td></tr>
<tr><td>38</td><td>Mississippi</td><td>37,329,017</td><td>24</td><td>Georgia</td><td>51,572,257</td></tr>
<tr><td>17</td><td>Missouri</td><td>56,331,463</td><td>25</td><td>Oregon</td><td>50,952,235</td></tr>
<tr><td>49</td><td>Montana**</td><td>19,658,964</td><td>26</td><td>Indiana</td><td>49,140,018</td></tr>
<tr><td>45</td><td>Nebraska**</td><td>23,468,970</td><td>27</td><td>Alabama</td><td>46,379,759</td></tr>
<tr><td>18</td><td>Nevada</td><td>55,369,912</td><td>28</td><td>Wisconsin</td><td>46,319,112</td></tr>
<tr><td>31</td><td>New Hampshire</td><td>42,421,139</td><td>29</td><td>Texas</td><td>45,460,076</td></tr>
<tr><td>4</td><td>New Jersey</td><td>91,948,488</td><td>30</td><td>Kentucky</td><td>43,779,008</td></tr>
<tr><td>41</td><td>New Mexico</td><td>32,234,111</td><td>31</td><td>New Hampshire</td><td>42,421,139</td></tr>
<tr><td>1</td><td>New York</td><td>108,392,790</td><td>32</td><td>Utah</td><td>41,733,547</td></tr>
<tr><td>14</td><td>North Carolina</td><td>65,828,184</td><td>33</td><td>West Virginia</td><td>41,705,324</td></tr>
<tr><td>47</td><td>North Dakota**</td><td>21,463,041</td><td>34</td><td>Vermont</td><td>40,584,059</td></tr>
<tr><td>9</td><td>Ohio</td><td>73,910,477</td><td>35</td><td>Maine**</td><td>40,535,310</td></tr>
<tr><td>43</td><td>Oklahoma</td><td>28,186,912</td><td>36</td><td>Louisiana</td><td>38,533,383</td></tr>
<tr><td>25</td><td>Oregon</td><td>50,952,235</td><td>37</td><td>Minnesota**</td><td>37,758,312</td></tr>
<tr><td>12</td><td>Pennsylvania</td><td>68,141,057</td><td>38</td><td>Mississippi</td><td>37,329,017</td></tr>
<tr><td>5</td><td>Rhode Island**</td><td>90,917,684</td><td>39</td><td>Alaska</td><td>37,239,815</td></tr>
<tr><td>16</td><td>South Carolina</td><td>58,809,779</td><td>40</td><td>Arkansas</td><td>36,040,724</td></tr>
<tr><td>48</td><td>South Dakota</td><td>20,518,032</td><td>41</td><td>New Mexico</td><td>32,234,111</td></tr>
<tr><td>21</td><td>Tennessee</td><td>52,581,945</td><td>42</td><td>Iowa**</td><td>31,905,866</td></tr>
<tr><td>29</td><td>Texas</td><td>45,460,076</td><td>43</td><td>Oklahoma</td><td>28,186,912</td></tr>
<tr><td>32</td><td>Utah</td><td>41,733,547</td><td>44</td><td>Idaho</td><td>23,503,453</td></tr>
<tr><td>34</td><td>Vermont</td><td>40,584,059</td><td>45</td><td>Nebraska**</td><td>23,468,970</td></tr>
<tr><td>15</td><td>Virginia</td><td>61,573,103</td><td>46</td><td>Kansas**</td><td>21,895,715</td></tr>
<tr><td>19</td><td>Washington</td><td>54,844,681</td><td>47</td><td>North Dakota**</td><td>21,463,041</td></tr>
<tr><td>33</td><td>West Virginia</td><td>41,705,324</td><td>48</td><td>South Dakota</td><td>20,518,032</td></tr>
<tr><td>28</td><td>Wisconsin</td><td>46,319,112</td><td>49</td><td>Montana**</td><td>19,658,964</td></tr>
<tr><td>50</td><td>Wyoming</td><td>18,252,742</td><td>50</td><td>Wyoming</td><td>18,252,742</td></tr>
<tr><td></td><td></td><td></td><td></td><td>District of Columbia</td><td>165,478,889</td></tr>
</table>

Source: Morgan Quitno Press using data from U.S. Bureau of the Census
   "1997 Economic Census, Health Care and Social Assistance" (EC97562A, October 1999)
*Includes establishments exempt from as well as subject to the federal income tax. Includes general medical and surgical hospitals, psychiatric hospitals and other specialty hospitals. Includes government owned hospitals.
**Amounts shown for these states are only for establishments exempt from federal income tax.

V. INCIDENCE OF DISEASE

V. INCIDENCE OF DISEASE (Continued)

Estimated New Cancer Cases in 2000

National Estimated Total = 1,220,100 New Cases*

ALPHA ORDER

RANK	STATE	CASES	% of USA
20	Alabama	21,500	1.8%
50	Alaska	1,500	0.1%
23	Arizona	20,300	1.7%
30	Arkansas	13,700	1.1%
1	California	113,200	9.3%
31	Colorado	13,400	1.1%
28	Connecticut	15,400	1.3%
45	Delaware	3,900	0.3%
2	Florida	88,100	7.2%
12	Georgia	29,400	2.4%
43	Hawaii	4,300	0.4%
42	Idaho	4,700	0.4%
7	Illinois	55,100	4.5%
14	Indiana	27,900	2.3%
29	Iowa	14,200	1.2%
33	Kansas	11,900	1.0%
22	Kentucky	20,500	1.7%
21	Louisiana	20,800	1.7%
37	Maine	6,800	0.6%
19	Maryland	22,600	1.9%
11	Massachusetts	30,100	2.5%
8	Michigan	44,100	3.6%
24	Minnesota	19,900	1.6%
32	Mississippi	13,200	1.1%
16	Missouri	27,000	2.2%
44	Montana	4,100	0.3%
36	Nebraska	7,300	0.6%
35	Nevada	8,300	0.7%
39	New Hampshire	5,500	0.5%
9	New Jersey	40,000	3.3%
38	New Mexico	6,600	0.5%
3	New York	81,500	6.7%
10	North Carolina	35,700	2.9%
47	North Dakota	3,000	0.2%
6	Ohio	56,100	4.6%
26	Oklahoma	16,100	1.3%
27	Oregon	15,800	1.3%
5	Pennsylvania	66,600	5.5%
40	Rhode Island	5,400	0.4%
25	South Carolina	18,000	1.5%
46	South Dakota	3,500	0.3%
15	Tennessee	27,300	2.2%
4	Texas	76,100	6.2%
41	Utah	5,100	0.4%
48	Vermont	2,700	0.2%
13	Virginia	29,300	2.4%
17	Washington	23,600	1.9%
34	West Virginia	10,500	0.9%
17	Wisconsin	23,600	1.9%
49	Wyoming	2,000	0.2%

RANK ORDER

RANK	STATE	CASES	% of USA
1	California	113,200	9.3%
2	Florida	88,100	7.2%
3	New York	81,500	6.7%
4	Texas	76,100	6.2%
5	Pennsylvania	66,600	5.5%
6	Ohio	56,100	4.6%
7	Illinois	55,100	4.5%
8	Michigan	44,100	3.6%
9	New Jersey	40,000	3.3%
10	North Carolina	35,700	2.9%
11	Massachusetts	30,100	2.5%
12	Georgia	29,400	2.4%
13	Virginia	29,300	2.4%
14	Indiana	27,900	2.3%
15	Tennessee	27,300	2.2%
16	Missouri	27,000	2.2%
17	Washington	23,600	1.9%
17	Wisconsin	23,600	1.9%
19	Maryland	22,600	1.9%
20	Alabama	21,500	1.8%
21	Louisiana	20,800	1.7%
22	Kentucky	20,500	1.7%
23	Arizona	20,300	1.7%
24	Minnesota	19,900	1.6%
25	South Carolina	18,000	1.5%
26	Oklahoma	16,100	1.3%
27	Oregon	15,800	1.3%
28	Connecticut	15,400	1.3%
29	Iowa	14,200	1.2%
30	Arkansas	13,700	1.1%
31	Colorado	13,400	1.1%
32	Mississippi	13,200	1.1%
33	Kansas	11,900	1.0%
34	West Virginia	10,500	0.9%
35	Nevada	8,300	0.7%
36	Nebraska	7,300	0.6%
37	Maine	6,800	0.6%
38	New Mexico	6,600	0.5%
39	New Hampshire	5,500	0.5%
40	Rhode Island	5,400	0.4%
41	Utah	5,100	0.4%
42	Idaho	4,700	0.4%
43	Hawaii	4,300	0.4%
44	Montana	4,100	0.3%
45	Delaware	3,900	0.3%
46	South Dakota	3,500	0.3%
47	North Dakota	3,000	0.2%
48	Vermont	2,700	0.2%
49	Wyoming	2,000	0.2%
50	Alaska	1,500	0.1%
	District of Columbia	2,700	0.2%

Source: American Cancer Society
"Cancer Facts & Figures 2000" (Copyright 2000, Reprinted with permission from the American Cancer Society)
*These estimates are offered as a rough guide and should not be regarded as definitive. They are calculated according to the distribution of estimated 2000 cancer deaths by state. Totals do not include basal and squamous cell skin cancers or in situ carcinomas except urinary bladder.

Estimated Rate of New Cancer Cases in 2000

National Estimated Rate = 447.4 New Cases per 100,000 Population*

<u>ALPHA ORDER</u>

RANK	STATE	RATE
13	Alabama	492.0
49	Alaska	242.1
38	Arizona	424.8
6	Arkansas	537.0
47	California	341.5
48	Colorado	330.4
23	Connecticut	469.2
7	Delaware	517.6
1	Florida	583.0
44	Georgia	377.5
46	Hawaii	362.7
45	Idaho	375.5
30	Illinois	454.3
22	Indiana	469.5
11	Iowa	494.9
32	Kansas	448.4
7	Kentucky	517.6
20	Louisiana	475.8
5	Maine	542.7
36	Maryland	437.0
15	Massachusetts	487.4
34	Michigan	447.1
40	Minnesota	416.7
18	Mississippi	476.8
12	Missouri	493.8
25	Montana	464.4
35	Nebraska	438.2
27	Nevada	458.8
28	New Hampshire	457.9
14	New Jersey	491.2
43	New Mexico	379.3
33	New York	447.9
24	North Carolina	466.6
21	North Dakota	473.4
9	Ohio	498.4
16	Oklahoma	479.4
19	Oregon	476.5
3	Pennsylvania	555.3
4	Rhode Island	545.0
26	South Carolina	463.2
17	South Dakota	477.4
10	Tennessee	497.9
42	Texas	379.7
50	Utah	239.5
29	Vermont	454.7
37	Virginia	426.3
41	Washington	410.0
2	West Virginia	581.1
31	Wisconsin	449.5
39	Wyoming	417.0

<u>RANK ORDER</u>

RANK	STATE	RATE
1	Florida	583.0
2	West Virginia	581.1
3	Pennsylvania	555.3
4	Rhode Island	545.0
5	Maine	542.7
6	Arkansas	537.0
7	Delaware	517.6
7	Kentucky	517.6
9	Ohio	498.4
10	Tennessee	497.9
11	Iowa	494.9
12	Missouri	493.8
13	Alabama	492.0
14	New Jersey	491.2
15	Massachusetts	487.4
16	Oklahoma	479.4
17	South Dakota	477.4
18	Mississippi	476.8
19	Oregon	476.5
20	Louisiana	475.8
21	North Dakota	473.4
22	Indiana	469.5
23	Connecticut	469.2
24	North Carolina	466.6
25	Montana	464.4
26	South Carolina	463.2
27	Nevada	458.8
28	New Hampshire	457.9
29	Vermont	454.7
30	Illinois	454.3
31	Wisconsin	449.5
32	Kansas	448.4
33	New York	447.9
34	Michigan	447.1
35	Nebraska	438.2
36	Maryland	437.0
37	Virginia	426.3
38	Arizona	424.8
39	Wyoming	417.0
40	Minnesota	416.7
41	Washington	410.0
42	Texas	379.7
43	New Mexico	379.3
44	Georgia	377.5
45	Idaho	375.5
46	Hawaii	362.7
47	California	341.5
48	Colorado	330.4
49	Alaska	242.1
50	Utah	239.5
	District of Columbia	520.2

Source: Morgan Quitno Press using data from American Cancer Society
"Cancer Facts & Figures 2000" (Copyright 2000, Reprinted with permission from the American Cancer Society)
*These estimates are offered as a rough guide and should not be regarded as definitive. They are calculated according to the distribution of estimated 2000 cancer deaths by state. Totals do not include basal and squamous cell skin cancers or in situ carcinomas except urinary bladder. Rates calculated using 1999 Census resident population estimates.

Estimated New Cases of Bladder Cancer in 2000

National Estimated Total = 53,200 New Cases*

ALPHA ORDER

RANK	STATE	CASES	% of USA
22	Alabama	800	1.5%
45	Alaska	100	0.2%
20	Arizona	900	1.7%
31	Arkansas	500	0.9%
1	California	5,200	9.8%
28	Colorado	600	1.1%
22	Connecticut	800	1.5%
40	Delaware	200	0.4%
2	Florida	4,300	8.1%
16	Georgia	1,000	1.9%
45	Hawaii	100	0.2%
40	Idaho	200	0.4%
7	Illinois	2,400	4.5%
12	Indiana	1,200	2.3%
28	Iowa	600	1.1%
31	Kansas	500	0.9%
28	Kentucky	600	1.1%
25	Louisiana	700	1.3%
33	Maine	400	0.8%
16	Maryland	1,000	1.9%
10	Massachusetts	1,700	3.2%
8	Michigan	2,100	3.9%
16	Minnesota	1,000	1.9%
36	Mississippi	300	0.6%
14	Missouri	1,100	2.1%
40	Montana	200	0.4%
36	Nebraska	300	0.6%
33	Nevada	400	0.8%
36	New Hampshire	300	0.6%
8	New Jersey	2,100	3.9%
40	New Mexico	200	0.4%
3	New York	4,100	7.7%
11	North Carolina	1,400	2.6%
45	North Dakota	100	0.2%
6	Ohio	2,500	4.7%
25	Oklahoma	700	1.3%
25	Oregon	700	1.3%
4	Pennsylvania	3,100	5.8%
36	Rhode Island	300	0.6%
22	South Carolina	800	1.5%
45	South Dakota	100	0.2%
20	Tennessee	900	1.7%
5	Texas	2,800	5.3%
40	Utah	200	0.4%
45	Vermont	100	0.2%
14	Virginia	1,100	2.1%
16	Washington	1,000	1.9%
33	West Virginia	400	0.8%
12	Wisconsin	1,200	2.3%
NA	Wyoming**	NA	NA

RANK ORDER

RANK	STATE	CASES	% of USA
1	California	5,200	9.8%
2	Florida	4,300	8.1%
3	New York	4,100	7.7%
4	Pennsylvania	3,100	5.8%
5	Texas	2,800	5.3%
6	Ohio	2,500	4.7%
7	Illinois	2,400	4.5%
8	Michigan	2,100	3.9%
8	New Jersey	2,100	3.9%
10	Massachusetts	1,700	3.2%
11	North Carolina	1,400	2.6%
12	Indiana	1,200	2.3%
12	Wisconsin	1,200	2.3%
14	Missouri	1,100	2.1%
14	Virginia	1,100	2.1%
16	Georgia	1,000	1.9%
16	Maryland	1,000	1.9%
16	Minnesota	1,000	1.9%
16	Washington	1,000	1.9%
20	Arizona	900	1.7%
20	Tennessee	900	1.7%
22	Alabama	800	1.5%
22	Connecticut	800	1.5%
22	South Carolina	800	1.5%
25	Louisiana	700	1.3%
25	Oklahoma	700	1.3%
25	Oregon	700	1.3%
28	Colorado	600	1.1%
28	Iowa	600	1.1%
28	Kentucky	600	1.1%
31	Arkansas	500	0.9%
31	Kansas	500	0.9%
33	Maine	400	0.8%
33	Nevada	400	0.8%
33	West Virginia	400	0.8%
36	Mississippi	300	0.6%
36	Nebraska	300	0.6%
36	New Hampshire	300	0.6%
36	Rhode Island	300	0.6%
40	Delaware	200	0.4%
40	Idaho	200	0.4%
40	Montana	200	0.4%
40	New Mexico	200	0.4%
40	Utah	200	0.4%
45	Alaska	100	0.2%
45	Hawaii	100	0.2%
45	North Dakota	100	0.2%
45	South Dakota	100	0.2%
45	Vermont	100	0.2%
NA	Wyoming**	NA	NA
	District of Columbia	100	0.2%

Source: American Cancer Society
   "Cancer Facts & Figures 2000" (Copyright 2000, Reprinted with permission from the American Cancer Society)
*These estimates are offered as a rough guide and should be interpreted with caution. They are calculated according to the distribution of estimated 2000 cancer deaths by state.
**Fewer than 50 cases.

Estimated Rate of New Cases of Bladder Cancer in 2000

National Estimated Rate = 19.5 New Cases per 100,000 Population*

ALPHA ORDER

RANK	STATE	RATE
29	Alabama	18.3
35	Alaska	16.1
27	Arizona	18.8
25	Arkansas	19.6
40	California	15.7
42	Colorado	14.8
9	Connecticut	24.4
5	Delaware	26.5
3	Florida	28.5
45	Georgia	12.8
49	Hawaii	8.4
36	Idaho	16.0
24	Illinois	19.8
22	Indiana	20.2
18	Iowa	20.9
27	Kansas	18.8
41	Kentucky	15.1
36	Louisiana	16.0
1	Maine	31.9
26	Maryland	19.3
4	Massachusetts	27.5
16	Michigan	21.3
18	Minnesota	20.9
47	Mississippi	10.8
23	Missouri	20.1
11	Montana	22.7
31	Nebraska	18.0
14	Nevada	22.1
8	New Hampshire	25.0
6	New Jersey	25.8
46	New Mexico	11.5
12	New York	22.5
29	North Carolina	18.3
39	North Dakota	15.8
13	Ohio	22.2
20	Oklahoma	20.8
17	Oregon	21.1
6	Pennsylvania	25.8
2	Rhode Island	30.3
21	South Carolina	20.6
44	South Dakota	13.6
34	Tennessee	16.4
43	Texas	14.0
48	Utah	9.4
33	Vermont	16.8
36	Virginia	16.0
32	Washington	17.4
14	West Virginia	22.1
10	Wisconsin	22.9
NA	Wyoming**	NA

RANK ORDER

RANK	STATE	RATE
1	Maine	31.9
2	Rhode Island	30.3
3	Florida	28.5
4	Massachusetts	27.5
5	Delaware	26.5
6	New Jersey	25.8
6	Pennsylvania	25.8
8	New Hampshire	25.0
9	Connecticut	24.4
10	Wisconsin	22.9
11	Montana	22.7
12	New York	22.5
13	Ohio	22.2
14	Nevada	22.1
14	West Virginia	22.1
16	Michigan	21.3
17	Oregon	21.1
18	Iowa	20.9
18	Minnesota	20.9
20	Oklahoma	20.8
21	South Carolina	20.6
22	Indiana	20.2
23	Missouri	20.1
24	Illinois	19.8
25	Arkansas	19.6
26	Maryland	19.3
27	Arizona	18.8
27	Kansas	18.8
29	Alabama	18.3
29	North Carolina	18.3
31	Nebraska	18.0
32	Washington	17.4
33	Vermont	16.8
34	Tennessee	16.4
35	Alaska	16.1
36	Idaho	16.0
36	Louisiana	16.0
36	Virginia	16.0
39	North Dakota	15.8
40	California	15.7
41	Kentucky	15.1
42	Colorado	14.8
43	Texas	14.0
44	South Dakota	13.6
45	Georgia	12.8
46	New Mexico	11.5
47	Mississippi	10.8
48	Utah	9.4
49	Hawaii	8.4
NA	Wyoming**	NA
	District of Columbia	19.3

Source: Morgan Quitno Press using data from American Cancer Society
"Cancer Facts & Figures 2000" (Copyright 2000, Reprinted with permission from the American Cancer Society)
*These estimates are offered as a rough guide and should be interpreted with caution. They are calculated according to the distribution of estimated 2000 cancer deaths by state. Rates calculated using 1999 Census resident population estimates.
**Fewer than 50 cases.

Estimated New Female Breast Cancer Cases in 2000

National Estimated Total = 182,800 New Cases*

ALPHA ORDER

RANK	STATE	CASES	% of USA
23	Alabama	2,700	1.5%
50	Alaska	200	0.1%
21	Arizona	2,800	1.5%
32	Arkansas	1,900	1.0%
1	California	17,900	9.8%
30	Colorado	2,000	1.1%
27	Connecticut	2,300	1.3%
44	Delaware	500	0.3%
3	Florida	12,000	6.6%
11	Georgia	4,600	2.5%
44	Hawaii	500	0.3%
41	Idaho	700	0.4%
6	Illinois	8,900	4.9%
14	Indiana	4,200	2.3%
29	Iowa	2,100	1.1%
33	Kansas	1,600	0.9%
23	Kentucky	2,700	1.5%
20	Louisiana	3,200	1.8%
38	Maine	900	0.5%
16	Maryland	3,700	2.0%
13	Massachusetts	4,400	2.4%
8	Michigan	6,700	3.7%
21	Minnesota	2,800	1.5%
30	Mississippi	2,000	1.1%
16	Missouri	3,700	2.0%
43	Montana	600	0.3%
35	Nebraska	1,100	0.6%
36	Nevada	1,000	0.5%
41	New Hampshire	700	0.4%
9	New Jersey	6,400	3.5%
36	New Mexico	1,000	0.5%
2	New York	13,700	7.5%
10	North Carolina	5,200	2.8%
44	North Dakota	500	0.3%
7	Ohio	8,600	4.7%
26	Oklahoma	2,400	1.3%
28	Oregon	2,200	1.2%
5	Pennsylvania	10,500	5.7%
40	Rhode Island	800	0.4%
25	South Carolina	2,600	1.4%
47	South Dakota	400	0.2%
15	Tennessee	3,800	2.1%
4	Texas	11,500	6.3%
38	Utah	900	0.5%
47	Vermont	400	0.2%
12	Virginia	4,500	2.5%
18	Washington	3,500	1.9%
34	West Virginia	1,400	0.8%
19	Wisconsin	3,300	1.8%
49	Wyoming	300	0.2%

RANK ORDER

RANK	STATE	CASES	% of USA
1	California	17,900	9.8%
2	New York	13,700	7.5%
3	Florida	12,000	6.6%
4	Texas	11,500	6.3%
5	Pennsylvania	10,500	5.7%
6	Illinois	8,900	4.9%
7	Ohio	8,600	4.7%
8	Michigan	6,700	3.7%
9	New Jersey	6,400	3.5%
10	North Carolina	5,200	2.8%
11	Georgia	4,600	2.5%
12	Virginia	4,500	2.5%
13	Massachusetts	4,400	2.4%
14	Indiana	4,200	2.3%
15	Tennessee	3,800	2.1%
16	Maryland	3,700	2.0%
16	Missouri	3,700	2.0%
18	Washington	3,500	1.9%
19	Wisconsin	3,300	1.8%
20	Louisiana	3,200	1.8%
21	Arizona	2,800	1.5%
21	Minnesota	2,800	1.5%
23	Alabama	2,700	1.5%
23	Kentucky	2,700	1.5%
25	South Carolina	2,600	1.4%
26	Oklahoma	2,400	1.3%
27	Connecticut	2,300	1.3%
28	Oregon	2,200	1.2%
29	Iowa	2,100	1.1%
30	Colorado	2,000	1.1%
30	Mississippi	2,000	1.1%
32	Arkansas	1,900	1.0%
33	Kansas	1,600	0.9%
34	West Virginia	1,400	0.8%
35	Nebraska	1,100	0.6%
36	Nevada	1,000	0.5%
36	New Mexico	1,000	0.5%
38	Maine	900	0.5%
38	Utah	900	0.5%
40	Rhode Island	800	0.4%
41	Idaho	700	0.4%
41	New Hampshire	700	0.4%
43	Montana	600	0.3%
44	Delaware	500	0.3%
44	Hawaii	500	0.3%
44	North Dakota	500	0.3%
47	South Dakota	400	0.2%
47	Vermont	400	0.2%
49	Wyoming	300	0.2%
50	Alaska	200	0.1%
	District of Columbia	500	0.3%

Source: American Cancer Society

"Cancer Facts & Figures 2000" (Copyright 2000, Reprinted with permission from the American Cancer Society)
*These estimates are offered as a rough guide and should be interpreted with caution. They are calculated according to the distribution of estimated 2000 cancer deaths by state.

Estimated Rate of New Female Breast Cancer Cases in 2000

National Estimated Rate = 132.2 New Cases per 100,000 Female Population*

ALPHA ORDER

RANK	STATE	RATE
36	Alabama	119.3
50	Alaska	68.5
37	Arizona	118.7
9	Arkansas	144.8
45	California	109.5
47	Colorado	99.9
19	Connecticut	136.5
28	Delaware	130.9
2	Florida	156.3
38	Georgia	117.2
49	Hawaii	84.1
43	Idaho	113.7
10	Illinois	144.2
17	Indiana	138.7
11	Iowa	143.0
35	Kansas	119.7
23	Kentucky	133.3
12	Louisiana	141.1
12	Maine	141.1
14	Maryland	140.1
18	Massachusetts	138.2
25	Michigan	132.9
39	Minnesota	116.8
16	Mississippi	139.6
27	Missouri	131.9
20	Montana	135.5
30	Nebraska	129.5
40	Nevada	116.6
41	New Hampshire	116.3
5	New Jersey	153.0
44	New Mexico	113.3
8	New York	145.2
22	North Carolina	133.8
3	North Dakota	156.0
7	Ohio	148.5
14	Oklahoma	140.1
26	Oregon	132.4
1	Pennsylvania	168.5
4	Rhode Island	155.8
29	South Carolina	130.8
46	South Dakota	106.7
21	Tennessee	135.2
42	Texas	114.8
48	Utah	85.2
24	Vermont	133.2
30	Virginia	129.5
34	Washington	122.3
6	West Virginia	149.2
33	Wisconsin	124.2
32	Wyoming	125.4

RANK ORDER

RANK	STATE	RATE
1	Pennsylvania	168.5
2	Florida	156.3
3	North Dakota	156.0
4	Rhode Island	155.8
5	New Jersey	153.0
6	West Virginia	149.2
7	Ohio	148.5
8	New York	145.2
9	Arkansas	144.8
10	Illinois	144.2
11	Iowa	143.0
12	Louisiana	141.1
12	Maine	141.1
14	Maryland	140.1
14	Oklahoma	140.1
16	Mississippi	139.6
17	Indiana	138.7
18	Massachusetts	138.2
19	Connecticut	136.5
20	Montana	135.5
21	Tennessee	135.2
22	North Carolina	133.8
23	Kentucky	133.3
24	Vermont	133.2
25	Michigan	132.9
26	Oregon	132.4
27	Missouri	131.9
28	Delaware	130.9
29	South Carolina	130.8
30	Nebraska	129.5
30	Virginia	129.5
32	Wyoming	125.4
33	Wisconsin	124.2
34	Washington	122.3
35	Kansas	119.7
36	Alabama	119.3
37	Arizona	118.7
38	Georgia	117.2
39	Minnesota	116.8
40	Nevada	116.6
41	New Hampshire	116.3
42	Texas	114.8
43	Idaho	113.7
44	New Mexico	113.3
45	California	109.5
46	South Dakota	106.7
47	Colorado	99.9
48	Utah	85.2
49	Hawaii	84.1
50	Alaska	68.5

| | District of Columbia | 179.8 |

Source: Morgan Quitno Press using data from American Cancer Society
    "Cancer Facts & Figures 2000" (Copyright 2000, Reprinted with permission from the American Cancer Society)
*These estimates are offered as a rough guide and should be interpreted with caution. They are calculated
according to the distribution of estimated 2000 cancer deaths by state. Rates calculated using 1998 Census female
resident population estimates.

Percent of Women 40 and Older
Who Have Ever Had a Mammogram: 1998
National Percent = 84.7% of Women 40 and Older

<table>
<tr><td colspan="3">ALPHA ORDER</td><td colspan="3">RANK ORDER</td></tr>
<tr><td>RANK</td><td>STATE</td><td>PERCENT</td><td>RANK</td><td>STATE</td><td>PERCENT</td></tr>
<tr><td>17</td><td>Alabama</td><td>85.7</td><td>1</td><td>Massachusetts</td><td>91.6</td></tr>
<tr><td>3</td><td>Alaska</td><td>89.4</td><td>2</td><td>Delaware</td><td>90.1</td></tr>
<tr><td>42</td><td>Arizona</td><td>82.0</td><td>3</td><td>Alaska</td><td>89.4</td></tr>
<tr><td>40</td><td>Arkansas</td><td>82.5</td><td>4</td><td>Michigan</td><td>89.3</td></tr>
<tr><td>NA</td><td>California*</td><td>NA</td><td>5</td><td>Maryland</td><td>89.1</td></tr>
<tr><td>6</td><td>Colorado</td><td>89.0</td><td>6</td><td>Colorado</td><td>89.0</td></tr>
<tr><td>10</td><td>Connecticut</td><td>87.1</td><td>6</td><td>Washington</td><td>89.0</td></tr>
<tr><td>2</td><td>Delaware</td><td>90.1</td><td>8</td><td>Hawaii</td><td>88.9</td></tr>
<tr><td>11</td><td>Florida</td><td>87.0</td><td>9</td><td>Rhode Island</td><td>88.3</td></tr>
<tr><td>27</td><td>Georgia</td><td>84.4</td><td>10</td><td>Connecticut</td><td>87.1</td></tr>
<tr><td>8</td><td>Hawaii</td><td>88.9</td><td>11</td><td>Florida</td><td>87.0</td></tr>
<tr><td>44</td><td>Idaho</td><td>81.8</td><td>12</td><td>Maine</td><td>86.9</td></tr>
<tr><td>35</td><td>Illinois</td><td>83.5</td><td>13</td><td>New York</td><td>86.7</td></tr>
<tr><td>30</td><td>Indiana</td><td>84.1</td><td>14</td><td>Virginia</td><td>86.4</td></tr>
<tr><td>20</td><td>Iowa</td><td>85.1</td><td>15</td><td>Oregon</td><td>86.2</td></tr>
<tr><td>34</td><td>Kansas</td><td>83.9</td><td>16</td><td>Nevada</td><td>86.1</td></tr>
<tr><td>38</td><td>Kentucky</td><td>82.8</td><td>17</td><td>Alabama</td><td>85.7</td></tr>
<tr><td>46</td><td>Louisiana</td><td>80.6</td><td>18</td><td>North Dakota</td><td>85.4</td></tr>
<tr><td>12</td><td>Maine</td><td>86.9</td><td>18</td><td>Wisconsin</td><td>85.4</td></tr>
<tr><td>5</td><td>Maryland</td><td>89.1</td><td>20</td><td>Iowa</td><td>85.1</td></tr>
<tr><td>1</td><td>Massachusetts</td><td>91.6</td><td>21</td><td>Tennessee</td><td>85.0</td></tr>
<tr><td>4</td><td>Michigan</td><td>89.3</td><td>22</td><td>New Hampshire</td><td>84.9</td></tr>
<tr><td>49</td><td>Minnesota</td><td>72.5</td><td>23</td><td>North Carolina</td><td>84.8</td></tr>
<tr><td>47</td><td>Mississippi</td><td>80.5</td><td>23</td><td>Pennsylvania</td><td>84.8</td></tr>
<tr><td>25</td><td>Missouri</td><td>84.7</td><td>25</td><td>Missouri</td><td>84.7</td></tr>
<tr><td>39</td><td>Montana</td><td>82.7</td><td>26</td><td>Ohio</td><td>84.6</td></tr>
<tr><td>45</td><td>Nebraska</td><td>81.4</td><td>27</td><td>Georgia</td><td>84.4</td></tr>
<tr><td>16</td><td>Nevada</td><td>86.1</td><td>28</td><td>South Carolina</td><td>84.2</td></tr>
<tr><td>22</td><td>New Hampshire</td><td>84.9</td><td>28</td><td>Vermont</td><td>84.2</td></tr>
<tr><td>36</td><td>New Jersey</td><td>83.2</td><td>30</td><td>Indiana</td><td>84.1</td></tr>
<tr><td>33</td><td>New Mexico</td><td>84.0</td><td>30</td><td>South Dakota</td><td>84.1</td></tr>
<tr><td>13</td><td>New York</td><td>86.7</td><td>30</td><td>Utah</td><td>84.1</td></tr>
<tr><td>23</td><td>North Carolina</td><td>84.8</td><td>33</td><td>New Mexico</td><td>84.0</td></tr>
<tr><td>18</td><td>North Dakota</td><td>85.4</td><td>34</td><td>Kansas</td><td>83.9</td></tr>
<tr><td>26</td><td>Ohio</td><td>84.6</td><td>35</td><td>Illinois</td><td>83.5</td></tr>
<tr><td>48</td><td>Oklahoma</td><td>75.1</td><td>36</td><td>New Jersey</td><td>83.2</td></tr>
<tr><td>15</td><td>Oregon</td><td>86.2</td><td>37</td><td>West Virginia</td><td>83.0</td></tr>
<tr><td>23</td><td>Pennsylvania</td><td>84.8</td><td>38</td><td>Kentucky</td><td>82.8</td></tr>
<tr><td>9</td><td>Rhode Island</td><td>88.3</td><td>39</td><td>Montana</td><td>82.7</td></tr>
<tr><td>28</td><td>South Carolina</td><td>84.2</td><td>40</td><td>Arkansas</td><td>82.5</td></tr>
<tr><td>30</td><td>South Dakota</td><td>84.1</td><td>40</td><td>Wyoming</td><td>82.5</td></tr>
<tr><td>21</td><td>Tennessee</td><td>85.0</td><td>42</td><td>Arizona</td><td>82.0</td></tr>
<tr><td>43</td><td>Texas</td><td>81.9</td><td>43</td><td>Texas</td><td>81.9</td></tr>
<tr><td>30</td><td>Utah</td><td>84.1</td><td>44</td><td>Idaho</td><td>81.8</td></tr>
<tr><td>28</td><td>Vermont</td><td>84.2</td><td>45</td><td>Nebraska</td><td>81.4</td></tr>
<tr><td>14</td><td>Virginia</td><td>86.4</td><td>46</td><td>Louisiana</td><td>80.6</td></tr>
<tr><td>6</td><td>Washington</td><td>89.0</td><td>47</td><td>Mississippi</td><td>80.5</td></tr>
<tr><td>37</td><td>West Virginia</td><td>83.0</td><td>48</td><td>Oklahoma</td><td>75.1</td></tr>
<tr><td>18</td><td>Wisconsin</td><td>85.4</td><td>49</td><td>Minnesota</td><td>72.5</td></tr>
<tr><td>40</td><td>Wyoming</td><td>82.5</td><td>NA</td><td>California*</td><td>NA</td></tr>
<tr><td></td><td></td><td></td><td></td><td>District of Columbia</td><td>91.7</td></tr>
</table>

Source: U.S. Department of Health and Human Services, Centers for Disease Control and Prevention
"1998 Behavioral Risk Factor Surveillance Summary Prevalence Report" (June 18, 1999)
*Not available.

Estimated New Colon and Rectum Cancer Cases in 2000

National Estimated Total = 130,200 New Cases*

ALPHA ORDER

RANK	STATE	CASES	% of USA
26	Alabama	1,800	1.4%
50	Alaska	200	0.2%
22	Arizona	2,000	1.5%
31	Arkansas	1,300	1.0%
1	California	11,400	8.8%
30	Colorado	1,400	1.1%
29	Connecticut	1,500	1.2%
43	Delaware	400	0.3%
3	Florida	9,100	7.0%
16	Georgia	2,800	2.2%
43	Hawaii	400	0.3%
42	Idaho	500	0.4%
7	Illinois	6,000	4.6%
12	Indiana	3,100	2.4%
24	Iowa	1,900	1.5%
33	Kansas	1,200	0.9%
20	Kentucky	2,200	1.7%
20	Louisiana	2,200	1.7%
37	Maine	700	0.5%
17	Maryland	2,600	2.0%
11	Massachusetts	3,500	2.7%
8	Michigan	4,800	3.7%
22	Minnesota	2,000	1.5%
31	Mississippi	1,300	1.0%
13	Missouri	2,900	2.2%
43	Montana	400	0.3%
35	Nebraska	1,000	0.8%
36	Nevada	900	0.7%
39	New Hampshire	600	0.5%
9	New Jersey	4,600	3.5%
37	New Mexico	700	0.5%
2	New York	9,200	7.1%
10	North Carolina	3,700	2.8%
43	North Dakota	400	0.3%
6	Ohio	6,200	4.8%
27	Oklahoma	1,700	1.3%
28	Oregon	1,600	1.2%
5	Pennsylvania	7,800	6.0%
39	Rhode Island	600	0.5%
24	South Carolina	1,900	1.5%
43	South Dakota	400	0.3%
13	Tennessee	2,900	2.2%
4	Texas	8,300	6.4%
39	Utah	600	0.5%
43	Vermont	400	0.3%
13	Virginia	2,900	2.2%
19	Washington	2,300	1.8%
34	West Virginia	1,100	0.8%
18	Wisconsin	2,500	1.9%
49	Wyoming	300	0.2%

RANK ORDER

RANK	STATE	CASES	% of USA
1	California	11,400	8.8%
2	New York	9,200	7.1%
3	Florida	9,100	7.0%
4	Texas	8,300	6.4%
5	Pennsylvania	7,800	6.0%
6	Ohio	6,200	4.8%
7	Illinois	6,000	4.6%
8	Michigan	4,800	3.7%
9	New Jersey	4,600	3.5%
10	North Carolina	3,700	2.8%
11	Massachusetts	3,500	2.7%
12	Indiana	3,100	2.4%
13	Missouri	2,900	2.2%
13	Tennessee	2,900	2.2%
13	Virginia	2,900	2.2%
16	Georgia	2,800	2.2%
17	Maryland	2,600	2.0%
18	Wisconsin	2,500	1.9%
19	Washington	2,300	1.8%
20	Kentucky	2,200	1.7%
20	Louisiana	2,200	1.7%
22	Arizona	2,000	1.5%
22	Minnesota	2,000	1.5%
24	Iowa	1,900	1.5%
24	South Carolina	1,900	1.5%
26	Alabama	1,800	1.4%
27	Oklahoma	1,700	1.3%
28	Oregon	1,600	1.2%
29	Connecticut	1,500	1.2%
30	Colorado	1,400	1.1%
31	Arkansas	1,300	1.0%
31	Mississippi	1,300	1.0%
33	Kansas	1,200	0.9%
34	West Virginia	1,100	0.8%
35	Nebraska	1,000	0.8%
36	Nevada	900	0.7%
37	Maine	700	0.5%
37	New Mexico	700	0.5%
39	New Hampshire	600	0.5%
39	Rhode Island	600	0.5%
39	Utah	600	0.5%
42	Idaho	500	0.4%
43	Delaware	400	0.3%
43	Hawaii	400	0.3%
43	Montana	400	0.3%
43	North Dakota	400	0.3%
43	South Dakota	400	0.3%
43	Vermont	400	0.3%
49	Wyoming	300	0.2%
50	Alaska	200	0.2%
	District of Columbia	300	0.2%

Source: American Cancer Society

"Cancer Facts & Figures 2000" (Copyright 2000, Reprinted with permission from the American Cancer Society)
*These estimates are offered as a rough guide and should be interpreted with caution. They are calculated according to the distribution of estimated 2000 cancer deaths by state.

Estimated Rate of New Colon and Rectum Cancer Cases in 2000

National Estimated Rate = 47.7 New Cases per 100,000 Population*

ALPHA ORDER

RANK	STATE	RATE
41	Alabama	41.2
49	Alaska	32.3
38	Arizona	41.9
20	Arkansas	51.0
47	California	34.4
46	Colorado	34.5
34	Connecticut	45.7
16	Delaware	53.1
8	Florida	60.2
45	Georgia	36.0
48	Hawaii	33.7
44	Idaho	39.9
27	Illinois	49.5
19	Indiana	52.2
2	Iowa	66.2
36	Kansas	45.2
13	Kentucky	55.5
23	Louisiana	50.3
12	Maine	55.9
23	Maryland	50.3
10	Massachusetts	56.7
29	Michigan	48.7
38	Minnesota	41.9
33	Mississippi	47.0
17	Missouri	53.0
35	Montana	45.3
9	Nebraska	60.0
26	Nevada	49.7
25	New Hampshire	50.0
11	New Jersey	56.5
42	New Mexico	40.2
21	New York	50.6
30	North Carolina	48.4
4	North Dakota	63.1
14	Ohio	55.1
21	Oklahoma	50.6
31	Oregon	48.2
3	Pennsylvania	65.0
7	Rhode Island	60.6
28	South Carolina	48.9
15	South Dakota	54.6
18	Tennessee	52.9
40	Texas	41.4
50	Utah	28.2
1	Vermont	67.4
37	Virginia	42.2
43	Washington	40.0
6	West Virginia	60.9
32	Wisconsin	47.6
5	Wyoming	62.6

RANK ORDER

RANK	STATE	RATE
1	Vermont	67.4
2	Iowa	66.2
3	Pennsylvania	65.0
4	North Dakota	63.1
5	Wyoming	62.6
6	West Virginia	60.9
7	Rhode Island	60.6
8	Florida	60.2
9	Nebraska	60.0
10	Massachusetts	56.7
11	New Jersey	56.5
12	Maine	55.9
13	Kentucky	55.5
14	Ohio	55.1
15	South Dakota	54.6
16	Delaware	53.1
17	Missouri	53.0
18	Tennessee	52.9
19	Indiana	52.2
20	Arkansas	51.0
21	New York	50.6
21	Oklahoma	50.6
23	Louisiana	50.3
23	Maryland	50.3
25	New Hampshire	50.0
26	Nevada	49.7
27	Illinois	49.5
28	South Carolina	48.9
29	Michigan	48.7
30	North Carolina	48.4
31	Oregon	48.2
32	Wisconsin	47.6
33	Mississippi	47.0
34	Connecticut	45.7
35	Montana	45.3
36	Kansas	45.2
37	Virginia	42.2
38	Arizona	41.9
38	Minnesota	41.9
40	Texas	41.4
41	Alabama	41.2
42	New Mexico	40.2
43	Washington	40.0
44	Idaho	39.9
45	Georgia	36.0
46	Colorado	34.5
47	California	34.4
48	Hawaii	33.7
49	Alaska	32.3
50	Utah	28.2
	District of Columbia	57.8

Source: Morgan Quitno Press using data from American Cancer Society
  "Cancer Facts & Figures 2000" (Copyright 2000, Reprinted with permission from the American Cancer Society)
These estimates are offered as a rough guide and should be interpreted with caution. They are calculated according to the distribution of estimated 2000 cancer deaths by state. Rates calculated using 1999 Census resident population estimates.

Estimated New Cancer of the Kidney Cases in 2000

National Estimated Total = 31,200 New Cases*

ALPHA ORDER

RANK	STATE	CASES	% of USA
26	Alabama	400	1.3%
NA	Alaska**	NA	NA
22	Arizona	500	1.6%
26	Arkansas	400	1.3%
1	California	2,900	9.3%
26	Colorado	400	1.3%
26	Connecticut	400	1.3%
40	Delaware	100	0.3%
3	Florida	2,000	6.4%
12	Georgia	700	2.2%
40	Hawaii	100	0.3%
35	Idaho	200	0.6%
7	Illinois	1,400	4.5%
11	Indiana	800	2.6%
26	Iowa	400	1.3%
32	Kansas	300	1.0%
18	Kentucky	600	1.9%
18	Louisiana	600	1.9%
35	Maine	200	0.6%
22	Maryland	500	1.6%
12	Massachusetts	700	2.2%
8	Michigan	1,200	3.8%
18	Minnesota	600	1.9%
32	Mississippi	300	1.0%
12	Missouri	700	2.2%
40	Montana	100	0.3%
35	Nebraska	200	0.6%
35	Nevada	200	0.6%
40	New Hampshire	100	0.3%
9	New Jersey	1,000	3.2%
35	New Mexico	200	0.6%
4	New York	1,900	6.1%
10	North Carolina	900	2.9%
40	North Dakota	100	0.3%
6	Ohio	1,500	4.8%
22	Oklahoma	500	1.6%
26	Oregon	400	1.3%
5	Pennsylvania	1,700	5.4%
40	Rhode Island	100	0.3%
22	South Carolina	500	1.6%
40	South Dakota	100	0.3%
12	Tennessee	700	2.2%
2	Texas	2,200	7.1%
40	Utah	100	0.3%
40	Vermont	100	0.3%
12	Virginia	700	2.2%
18	Washington	600	1.9%
32	West Virginia	300	1.0%
12	Wisconsin	700	2.2%
40	Wyoming	100	0.3%

RANK ORDER

RANK	STATE	CASES	% of USA
1	California	2,900	9.3%
2	Texas	2,200	7.1%
3	Florida	2,000	6.4%
4	New York	1,900	6.1%
5	Pennsylvania	1,700	5.4%
6	Ohio	1,500	4.8%
7	Illinois	1,400	4.5%
8	Michigan	1,200	3.8%
9	New Jersey	1,000	3.2%
10	North Carolina	900	2.9%
11	Indiana	800	2.6%
12	Georgia	700	2.2%
12	Massachusetts	700	2.2%
12	Missouri	700	2.2%
12	Tennessee	700	2.2%
12	Virginia	700	2.2%
12	Wisconsin	700	2.2%
18	Kentucky	600	1.9%
18	Louisiana	600	1.9%
18	Minnesota	600	1.9%
18	Washington	600	1.9%
22	Arizona	500	1.6%
22	Maryland	500	1.6%
22	Oklahoma	500	1.6%
22	South Carolina	500	1.6%
26	Alabama	400	1.3%
26	Arkansas	400	1.3%
26	Colorado	400	1.3%
26	Connecticut	400	1.3%
26	Iowa	400	1.3%
26	Oregon	400	1.3%
32	Kansas	300	1.0%
32	Mississippi	300	1.0%
32	West Virginia	300	1.0%
35	Idaho	200	0.6%
35	Maine	200	0.6%
35	Nebraska	200	0.6%
35	Nevada	200	0.6%
35	New Mexico	200	0.6%
40	Delaware	100	0.3%
40	Hawaii	100	0.3%
40	Montana	100	0.3%
40	New Hampshire	100	0.3%
40	North Dakota	100	0.3%
40	Rhode Island	100	0.3%
40	South Dakota	100	0.3%
40	Utah	100	0.3%
40	Vermont	100	0.3%
40	Wyoming	100	0.3%
NA	Alaska**	NA	NA
	District of Columbia**	NA	NA

Source: American Cancer Society
"Cancer Facts & Figures 2000" (Copyright 2000, Reprinted with permission from the American Cancer Society)
*These estimates are offered as a rough guide and should be interpreted with caution. They are calculated according to the distribution of estimated 2000 cancer deaths by state.
**Fewer than 50 cases.

Estimated Rate of New Cancer of the Kidney Cases in 2000

National Estimated Rate = 11.4 New Cases per 100,000 Population*

ALPHA ORDER				RANK ORDER		
RANK	STATE	RATE		RANK	STATE	RATE
44	Alabama	9.2		1	Wyoming	20.9
NA	Alaska**	NA		2	Vermont	16.8
37	Arizona	10.5		3	West Virginia	16.6
7	Arkansas	15.7		4	Idaho	16.0
46	California	8.7		4	Maine	16.0
42	Colorado	9.9		6	North Dakota	15.8
24	Connecticut	12.2		7	Arkansas	15.7
15	Delaware	13.3		8	Kentucky	15.1
18	Florida	13.2		9	Oklahoma	14.9
45	Georgia	9.0		10	Pennsylvania	14.2
47	Hawaii	8.4		11	Iowa	13.9
4	Idaho	16.0		12	Louisiana	13.7
29	Illinois	11.5		13	South Dakota	13.6
14	Indiana	13.5		14	Indiana	13.5
11	Iowa	13.9		15	Delaware	13.3
31	Kansas	11.3		15	Ohio	13.3
8	Kentucky	15.1		15	Wisconsin	13.3
12	Louisiana	13.7		18	Florida	13.2
4	Maine	16.0		19	South Carolina	12.9
43	Maryland	9.7		20	Missouri	12.8
31	Massachusetts	11.3		20	Tennessee	12.8
24	Michigan	12.2		22	Minnesota	12.6
22	Minnesota	12.6		23	New Jersey	12.3
36	Mississippi	10.8		24	Connecticut	12.2
20	Missouri	12.8		24	Michigan	12.2
31	Montana	11.3		26	Oregon	12.1
27	Nebraska	12.0		27	Nebraska	12.0
34	Nevada	11.1		28	North Carolina	11.8
48	New Hampshire	8.3		29	Illinois	11.5
23	New Jersey	12.3		29	New Mexico	11.5
29	New Mexico	11.5		31	Kansas	11.3
38	New York	10.4		31	Massachusetts	11.3
28	North Carolina	11.8		31	Montana	11.3
6	North Dakota	15.8		34	Nevada	11.1
15	Ohio	13.3		35	Texas	11.0
9	Oklahoma	14.9		36	Mississippi	10.8
26	Oregon	12.1		37	Arizona	10.5
10	Pennsylvania	14.2		38	New York	10.4
41	Rhode Island	10.1		38	Washington	10.4
19	South Carolina	12.9		40	Virginia	10.2
13	South Dakota	13.6		41	Rhode Island	10.1
20	Tennessee	12.8		42	Colorado	9.9
35	Texas	11.0		43	Maryland	9.7
49	Utah	4.7		44	Alabama	9.2
2	Vermont	16.8		45	Georgia	9.0
40	Virginia	10.2		46	California	8.7
38	Washington	10.4		47	Hawaii	8.4
3	West Virginia	16.6		48	New Hampshire	8.3
15	Wisconsin	13.3		49	Utah	4.7
1	Wyoming	20.9		NA	Alaska**	NA
					District of Columbia**	NA

Source: Morgan Quitno Press using data from American Cancer Society
"Cancer Facts & Figures 2000" (Copyright 2000, Reprinted with permission from the American Cancer Society)
*These estimates are offered as a rough guide and should be interpreted with caution. They are calculated according to the distribution of estimated 2000 cancer deaths by state. Rates calculated using 1999 Census resident population estimates.
**Fewer than 50 cases.

Estimated New Lung Cancer Cases in 2000

National Estimated Total = 164,100 New Cases*

<table>
<tr><td colspan="4">ALPHA ORDER</td><td colspan="4">RANK ORDER</td></tr>
<tr><td>RANK</td><td>STATE</td><td>CASES</td><td>% of USA</td><td>RANK</td><td>STATE</td><td>CASES</td><td>% of USA</td></tr>
<tr><td>20</td><td>Alabama</td><td>3,000</td><td>1.8%</td><td>1</td><td>California</td><td>14,000</td><td>8.5%</td></tr>
<tr><td>49</td><td>Alaska</td><td>200</td><td>0.1%</td><td>2</td><td>Florida</td><td>12,600</td><td>7.7%</td></tr>
<tr><td>22</td><td>Arizona</td><td>2,800</td><td>1.7%</td><td>3</td><td>Texas</td><td>10,700</td><td>6.5%</td></tr>
<tr><td>27</td><td>Arkansas</td><td>2,200</td><td>1.3%</td><td>4</td><td>New York</td><td>9,800</td><td>6.0%</td></tr>
<tr><td>1</td><td>California</td><td>14,000</td><td>8.5%</td><td>5</td><td>Pennsylvania</td><td>8,600</td><td>5.2%</td></tr>
<tr><td>34</td><td>Colorado</td><td>1,500</td><td>0.9%</td><td>6</td><td>Ohio</td><td>7,800</td><td>4.8%</td></tr>
<tr><td>29</td><td>Connecticut</td><td>1,900</td><td>1.2%</td><td>7</td><td>Illinois</td><td>7,300</td><td>4.4%</td></tr>
<tr><td>41</td><td>Delaware</td><td>600</td><td>0.4%</td><td>8</td><td>Michigan</td><td>6,100</td><td>3.7%</td></tr>
<tr><td>2</td><td>Florida</td><td>12,600</td><td>7.7%</td><td>9</td><td>North Carolina</td><td>5,200</td><td>3.2%</td></tr>
<tr><td>11</td><td>Georgia</td><td>4,200</td><td>2.6%</td><td>10</td><td>New Jersey</td><td>4,800</td><td>2.9%</td></tr>
<tr><td>43</td><td>Hawaii</td><td>500</td><td>0.3%</td><td>11</td><td>Georgia</td><td>4,200</td><td>2.6%</td></tr>
<tr><td>41</td><td>Idaho</td><td>600</td><td>0.4%</td><td>11</td><td>Tennessee</td><td>4,200</td><td>2.6%</td></tr>
<tr><td>7</td><td>Illinois</td><td>7,300</td><td>4.4%</td><td>13</td><td>Indiana</td><td>4,000</td><td>2.4%</td></tr>
<tr><td>13</td><td>Indiana</td><td>4,000</td><td>2.4%</td><td>13</td><td>Missouri</td><td>4,000</td><td>2.4%</td></tr>
<tr><td>29</td><td>Iowa</td><td>1,900</td><td>1.2%</td><td>13</td><td>Virginia</td><td>4,000</td><td>2.4%</td></tr>
<tr><td>32</td><td>Kansas</td><td>1,600</td><td>1.0%</td><td>16</td><td>Massachusetts</td><td>3,900</td><td>2.4%</td></tr>
<tr><td>17</td><td>Kentucky</td><td>3,400</td><td>2.1%</td><td>17</td><td>Kentucky</td><td>3,400</td><td>2.1%</td></tr>
<tr><td>21</td><td>Louisiana</td><td>2,900</td><td>1.8%</td><td>18</td><td>Maryland</td><td>3,100</td><td>1.9%</td></tr>
<tr><td>36</td><td>Maine</td><td>1,000</td><td>0.6%</td><td>18</td><td>Washington</td><td>3,100</td><td>1.9%</td></tr>
<tr><td>18</td><td>Maryland</td><td>3,100</td><td>1.9%</td><td>20</td><td>Alabama</td><td>3,000</td><td>1.8%</td></tr>
<tr><td>16</td><td>Massachusetts</td><td>3,900</td><td>2.4%</td><td>21</td><td>Louisiana</td><td>2,900</td><td>1.8%</td></tr>
<tr><td>8</td><td>Michigan</td><td>6,100</td><td>3.7%</td><td>22</td><td>Arizona</td><td>2,800</td><td>1.7%</td></tr>
<tr><td>26</td><td>Minnesota</td><td>2,300</td><td>1.4%</td><td>22</td><td>Wisconsin</td><td>2,800</td><td>1.7%</td></tr>
<tr><td>29</td><td>Mississippi</td><td>1,900</td><td>1.2%</td><td>24</td><td>Oklahoma</td><td>2,500</td><td>1.5%</td></tr>
<tr><td>13</td><td>Missouri</td><td>4,000</td><td>2.4%</td><td>24</td><td>South Carolina</td><td>2,500</td><td>1.5%</td></tr>
<tr><td>43</td><td>Montana</td><td>500</td><td>0.3%</td><td>26</td><td>Minnesota</td><td>2,300</td><td>1.4%</td></tr>
<tr><td>37</td><td>Nebraska</td><td>900</td><td>0.5%</td><td>27</td><td>Arkansas</td><td>2,200</td><td>1.3%</td></tr>
<tr><td>35</td><td>Nevada</td><td>1,200</td><td>0.7%</td><td>27</td><td>Oregon</td><td>2,200</td><td>1.3%</td></tr>
<tr><td>39</td><td>New Hampshire</td><td>700</td><td>0.4%</td><td>29</td><td>Connecticut</td><td>1,900</td><td>1.2%</td></tr>
<tr><td>10</td><td>New Jersey</td><td>4,800</td><td>2.9%</td><td>29</td><td>Iowa</td><td>1,900</td><td>1.2%</td></tr>
<tr><td>39</td><td>New Mexico</td><td>700</td><td>0.4%</td><td>29</td><td>Mississippi</td><td>1,900</td><td>1.2%</td></tr>
<tr><td>4</td><td>New York</td><td>9,800</td><td>6.0%</td><td>32</td><td>Kansas</td><td>1,600</td><td>1.0%</td></tr>
<tr><td>9</td><td>North Carolina</td><td>5,200</td><td>3.2%</td><td>32</td><td>West Virginia</td><td>1,600</td><td>1.0%</td></tr>
<tr><td>48</td><td>North Dakota</td><td>300</td><td>0.2%</td><td>34</td><td>Colorado</td><td>1,500</td><td>0.9%</td></tr>
<tr><td>6</td><td>Ohio</td><td>7,800</td><td>4.8%</td><td>35</td><td>Nevada</td><td>1,200</td><td>0.7%</td></tr>
<tr><td>24</td><td>Oklahoma</td><td>2,500</td><td>1.5%</td><td>36</td><td>Maine</td><td>1,000</td><td>0.6%</td></tr>
<tr><td>27</td><td>Oregon</td><td>2,200</td><td>1.3%</td><td>37</td><td>Nebraska</td><td>900</td><td>0.5%</td></tr>
<tr><td>5</td><td>Pennsylvania</td><td>8,600</td><td>5.2%</td><td>38</td><td>Rhode Island</td><td>800</td><td>0.5%</td></tr>
<tr><td>38</td><td>Rhode Island</td><td>800</td><td>0.5%</td><td>39</td><td>New Hampshire</td><td>700</td><td>0.4%</td></tr>
<tr><td>24</td><td>South Carolina</td><td>2,500</td><td>1.5%</td><td>39</td><td>New Mexico</td><td>700</td><td>0.4%</td></tr>
<tr><td>45</td><td>South Dakota</td><td>400</td><td>0.2%</td><td>41</td><td>Delaware</td><td>600</td><td>0.4%</td></tr>
<tr><td>11</td><td>Tennessee</td><td>4,200</td><td>2.6%</td><td>41</td><td>Idaho</td><td>600</td><td>0.4%</td></tr>
<tr><td>3</td><td>Texas</td><td>10,700</td><td>6.5%</td><td>43</td><td>Hawaii</td><td>500</td><td>0.3%</td></tr>
<tr><td>45</td><td>Utah</td><td>400</td><td>0.2%</td><td>43</td><td>Montana</td><td>500</td><td>0.3%</td></tr>
<tr><td>45</td><td>Vermont</td><td>400</td><td>0.2%</td><td>45</td><td>South Dakota</td><td>400</td><td>0.2%</td></tr>
<tr><td>13</td><td>Virginia</td><td>4,000</td><td>2.4%</td><td>45</td><td>Utah</td><td>400</td><td>0.2%</td></tr>
<tr><td>18</td><td>Washington</td><td>3,100</td><td>1.9%</td><td>45</td><td>Vermont</td><td>400</td><td>0.2%</td></tr>
<tr><td>32</td><td>West Virginia</td><td>1,600</td><td>1.0%</td><td>48</td><td>North Dakota</td><td>300</td><td>0.2%</td></tr>
<tr><td>22</td><td>Wisconsin</td><td>2,800</td><td>1.7%</td><td>49</td><td>Alaska</td><td>200</td><td>0.1%</td></tr>
<tr><td>49</td><td>Wyoming</td><td>200</td><td>0.1%</td><td>49</td><td>Wyoming</td><td>200</td><td>0.1%</td></tr>
<tr><td></td><td></td><td></td><td></td><td></td><td>District of Columbia</td><td>300</td><td>0.2%</td></tr>
</table>

Source: American Cancer Society
   "Cancer Facts & Figures 2000" (Copyright 2000, Reprinted with permission from the American Cancer Society)
*These estimates are offered as a rough guide and should be interpreted with caution. They are calculated according to the distribution of estimated 2000 cancer deaths by state.

Estimated Rate of New Lung Cancer Cases in 2000

National Estimated Rate = 60.2 New Cases per 100,000 Population*

ALPHA ORDER

RANK	STATE	RATE
13	Alabama	68.7
49	Alaska	32.3
29	Arizona	58.6
2	Arkansas	86.2
44	California	42.2
48	Colorado	37.0
32	Connecticut	57.9
7	Delaware	79.6
4	Florida	83.4
36	Georgia	53.9
44	Hawaii	42.2
42	Idaho	47.9
26	Illinois	60.2
17	Indiana	67.3
21	Iowa	66.2
25	Kansas	60.3
3	Kentucky	85.8
18	Louisiana	66.3
6	Maine	79.8
27	Maryland	59.9
23	Massachusetts	63.2
24	Michigan	61.8
41	Minnesota	48.2
14	Mississippi	68.6
10	Missouri	73.1
33	Montana	56.6
35	Nebraska	54.0
18	Nevada	66.3
30	New Hampshire	58.3
28	New Jersey	58.9
47	New Mexico	40.2
36	New York	53.9
15	North Carolina	68.0
43	North Dakota	47.3
12	Ohio	69.3
9	Oklahoma	74.4
18	Oregon	66.3
11	Pennsylvania	71.7
5	Rhode Island	80.7
22	South Carolina	64.3
34	South Dakota	54.6
8	Tennessee	76.6
39	Texas	53.4
50	Utah	18.8
16	Vermont	67.4
31	Virginia	58.2
36	Washington	53.9
1	West Virginia	88.5
40	Wisconsin	53.3
46	Wyoming	41.7

RANK ORDER

RANK	STATE	RATE
1	West Virginia	88.5
2	Arkansas	86.2
3	Kentucky	85.8
4	Florida	83.4
5	Rhode Island	80.7
6	Maine	79.8
7	Delaware	79.6
8	Tennessee	76.6
9	Oklahoma	74.4
10	Missouri	73.1
11	Pennsylvania	71.7
12	Ohio	69.3
13	Alabama	68.7
14	Mississippi	68.6
15	North Carolina	68.0
16	Vermont	67.4
17	Indiana	67.3
18	Louisiana	66.3
18	Nevada	66.3
18	Oregon	66.3
21	Iowa	66.2
22	South Carolina	64.3
23	Massachusetts	63.2
24	Michigan	61.8
25	Kansas	60.3
26	Illinois	60.2
27	Maryland	59.9
28	New Jersey	58.9
29	Arizona	58.6
30	New Hampshire	58.3
31	Virginia	58.2
32	Connecticut	57.9
33	Montana	56.6
34	South Dakota	54.6
35	Nebraska	54.0
36	Georgia	53.9
36	New York	53.9
36	Washington	53.9
39	Texas	53.4
40	Wisconsin	53.3
41	Minnesota	48.2
42	Idaho	47.9
43	North Dakota	47.3
44	California	42.2
44	Hawaii	42.2
46	Wyoming	41.7
47	New Mexico	40.2
48	Colorado	37.0
49	Alaska	32.3
50	Utah	18.8
	District of Columbia	57.8

Source: Morgan Quitno Press using data from American Cancer Society
    "Cancer Facts & Figures 2000" (Copyright 2000, Reprinted with permission from the American Cancer Society)
*These estimates are offered as a rough guide and should be interpreted with caution. They are calculated
according to the distribution of estimated 2000 cancer deaths by state. Rates calculated using 1999 Census
resident population estimates.

Estimated New Non-Hodgkin's Lymphoma Cases in 2000

National Estimated Total = 54,900 New Cases*

ALPHA ORDER

RANK	STATE	CASES	% of USA
20	Alabama	900	1.6%
47	Alaska	100	0.2%
20	Arizona	900	1.6%
31	Arkansas	500	0.9%
1	California	5,300	9.7%
25	Colorado	700	1.3%
25	Connecticut	700	1.3%
42	Delaware	200	0.4%
2	Florida	4,000	7.3%
19	Georgia	1,000	1.8%
42	Hawaii	200	0.4%
42	Idaho	200	0.4%
7	Illinois	2,500	4.6%
12	Indiana	1,200	2.2%
25	Iowa	700	1.3%
31	Kansas	500	0.9%
23	Kentucky	800	1.5%
23	Louisiana	800	1.5%
35	Maine	300	0.5%
20	Maryland	900	1.6%
10	Massachusetts	1,400	2.6%
8	Michigan	2,100	3.8%
16	Minnesota	1,100	2.0%
31	Mississippi	500	0.9%
16	Missouri	1,100	2.0%
42	Montana	200	0.4%
35	Nebraska	300	0.5%
35	Nevada	300	0.5%
35	New Hampshire	300	0.5%
9	New Jersey	1,900	3.5%
35	New Mexico	300	0.5%
3	New York	3,800	6.9%
10	North Carolina	1,400	2.6%
47	North Dakota	100	0.2%
6	Ohio	2,700	4.9%
25	Oklahoma	700	1.3%
25	Oregon	700	1.3%
5	Pennsylvania	3,000	5.5%
35	Rhode Island	300	0.5%
25	South Carolina	700	1.3%
42	South Dakota	200	0.4%
12	Tennessee	1,200	2.2%
4	Texas	3,600	6.6%
35	Utah	300	0.5%
47	Vermont	100	0.2%
12	Virginia	1,200	2.2%
16	Washington	1,100	2.0%
34	West Virginia	400	0.7%
12	Wisconsin	1,200	2.2%
47	Wyoming	100	0.2%

RANK ORDER

RANK	STATE	CASES	% of USA
1	California	5,300	9.7%
2	Florida	4,000	7.3%
3	New York	3,800	6.9%
4	Texas	3,600	6.6%
5	Pennsylvania	3,000	5.5%
6	Ohio	2,700	4.9%
7	Illinois	2,500	4.6%
8	Michigan	2,100	3.8%
9	New Jersey	1,900	3.5%
10	Massachusetts	1,400	2.6%
10	North Carolina	1,400	2.6%
12	Indiana	1,200	2.2%
12	Tennessee	1,200	2.2%
12	Virginia	1,200	2.2%
12	Wisconsin	1,200	2.2%
16	Minnesota	1,100	2.0%
16	Missouri	1,100	2.0%
16	Washington	1,100	2.0%
19	Georgia	1,000	1.8%
20	Alabama	900	1.6%
20	Arizona	900	1.6%
20	Maryland	900	1.6%
23	Kentucky	800	1.5%
23	Louisiana	800	1.5%
25	Colorado	700	1.3%
25	Connecticut	700	1.3%
25	Iowa	700	1.3%
25	Oklahoma	700	1.3%
25	Oregon	700	1.3%
25	South Carolina	700	1.3%
31	Arkansas	500	0.9%
31	Kansas	500	0.9%
31	Mississippi	500	0.9%
34	West Virginia	400	0.7%
35	Maine	300	0.5%
35	Nebraska	300	0.5%
35	Nevada	300	0.5%
35	New Hampshire	300	0.5%
35	New Mexico	300	0.5%
35	Rhode Island	300	0.5%
35	Utah	300	0.5%
42	Delaware	200	0.4%
42	Hawaii	200	0.4%
42	Idaho	200	0.4%
42	Montana	200	0.4%
42	South Dakota	200	0.4%
47	Alaska	100	0.2%
47	North Dakota	100	0.2%
47	Vermont	100	0.2%
47	Wyoming	100	0.2%
	District of Columbia	100	0.2%

Source: American Cancer Society
"Cancer Facts & Figures 2000" (Copyright 2000, Reprinted with permission from the American Cancer Society)
*These estimates are offered as a rough guide and should be interpreted with caution. They are calculated according to the distribution of estimated 2000 cancer deaths by state.

Estimated Rate of New Non-Hodgkin's Lymphoma Cases in 2000

National Estimated Rate = 20.1 New Cases per 100,000 Population*

ALPHA ORDER

RANK	STATE	RATE
23	Alabama	20.6
45	Alaska	16.1
30	Arizona	18.8
28	Arkansas	19.6
46	California	16.0
40	Colorado	17.3
17	Connecticut	21.3
3	Delaware	26.5
3	Florida	26.5
50	Georgia	12.8
42	Hawaii	16.9
46	Idaho	16.0
23	Illinois	20.6
25	Indiana	20.2
7	Iowa	24.4
30	Kansas	18.8
25	Kentucky	20.2
32	Louisiana	18.3
9	Maine	23.9
39	Maryland	17.4
13	Massachusetts	22.7
17	Michigan	21.3
11	Minnesota	23.0
34	Mississippi	18.1
27	Missouri	20.1
13	Montana	22.7
35	Nebraska	18.0
44	Nevada	16.6
5	New Hampshire	25.0
10	New Jersey	23.3
41	New Mexico	17.2
20	New York	20.9
32	North Carolina	18.3
48	North Dakota	15.8
8	Ohio	24.0
22	Oklahoma	20.8
19	Oregon	21.1
5	Pennsylvania	25.0
1	Rhode Island	30.3
35	South Carolina	18.0
2	South Dakota	27.3
16	Tennessee	21.9
35	Texas	18.0
49	Utah	14.1
43	Vermont	16.8
38	Virginia	17.5
29	Washington	19.1
15	West Virginia	22.1
12	Wisconsin	22.9
20	Wyoming	20.9

RANK ORDER

RANK	STATE	RATE
1	Rhode Island	30.3
2	South Dakota	27.3
3	Delaware	26.5
3	Florida	26.5
5	New Hampshire	25.0
5	Pennsylvania	25.0
7	Iowa	24.4
8	Ohio	24.0
9	Maine	23.9
10	New Jersey	23.3
11	Minnesota	23.0
12	Wisconsin	22.9
13	Massachusetts	22.7
13	Montana	22.7
15	West Virginia	22.1
16	Tennessee	21.9
17	Connecticut	21.3
17	Michigan	21.3
19	Oregon	21.1
20	New York	20.9
20	Wyoming	20.9
22	Oklahoma	20.8
23	Alabama	20.6
23	Illinois	20.6
25	Indiana	20.2
25	Kentucky	20.2
27	Missouri	20.1
28	Arkansas	19.6
29	Washington	19.1
30	Arizona	18.8
30	Kansas	18.8
32	Louisiana	18.3
32	North Carolina	18.3
34	Mississippi	18.1
35	Nebraska	18.0
35	South Carolina	18.0
35	Texas	18.0
38	Virginia	17.5
39	Maryland	17.4
40	Colorado	17.3
41	New Mexico	17.2
42	Hawaii	16.9
43	Vermont	16.8
44	Nevada	16.6
45	Alaska	16.1
46	California	16.0
46	Idaho	16.0
48	North Dakota	15.8
49	Utah	14.1
50	Georgia	12.8

District of Columbia   19.3

Source: Morgan Quitno Press using data from American Cancer Society
"Cancer Facts & Figures 2000" (Copyright 2000, Reprinted with permission from the American Cancer Society)
*These estimates are offered as a rough guide and should be interpreted with caution. They are calculated according to the distribution of estimated 2000 cancer deaths by state. Rates calculated using 1999 Census resident population estimates.

Estimated New Prostate Cancer Cases in 2000

National Estimated Total = 180,400 New Cases*

ALPHA ORDER

RANK	STATE	CASES	% of USA
18	Alabama	3,500	1.9%
50	Alaska	100	0.1%
19	Arizona	3,300	1.8%
28	Arkansas	2,200	1.2%
1	California	16,400	9.1%
32	Colorado	1,800	1.0%
27	Connecticut	2,300	1.3%
45	Delaware	600	0.3%
2	Florida	13,700	7.6%
11	Georgia	4,400	2.4%
41	Hawaii	700	0.4%
40	Idaho	800	0.4%
6	Illinois	7,800	4.3%
14	Indiana	3,900	2.2%
28	Iowa	2,200	1.2%
32	Kansas	1,800	1.0%
26	Kentucky	2,600	1.4%
22	Louisiana	3,200	1.8%
39	Maine	900	0.5%
19	Maryland	3,300	1.8%
13	Massachusetts	4,200	2.3%
8	Michigan	6,600	3.7%
19	Minnesota	3,300	1.8%
28	Mississippi	2,200	1.2%
16	Missouri	3,600	2.0%
41	Montana	700	0.4%
38	Nebraska	1,000	0.6%
35	Nevada	1,200	0.7%
41	New Hampshire	700	0.4%
9	New Jersey	5,600	3.1%
35	New Mexico	1,200	0.7%
3	New York	11,800	6.5%
10	North Carolina	5,300	2.9%
47	North Dakota	500	0.3%
6	Ohio	7,800	4.3%
31	Oklahoma	2,100	1.2%
25	Oregon	2,700	1.5%
5	Pennsylvania	10,000	5.5%
41	Rhode Island	700	0.4%
24	South Carolina	2,900	1.6%
45	South Dakota	600	0.3%
16	Tennessee	3,600	2.0%
4	Texas	11,300	6.3%
35	Utah	1,200	0.7%
49	Vermont	300	0.2%
11	Virginia	4,400	2.4%
22	Washington	3,200	1.8%
34	West Virginia	1,300	0.7%
15	Wisconsin	3,800	2.1%
48	Wyoming	400	0.2%

RANK ORDER

RANK	STATE	CASES	% of USA
1	California	16,400	9.1%
2	Florida	13,700	7.6%
3	New York	11,800	6.5%
4	Texas	11,300	6.3%
5	Pennsylvania	10,000	5.5%
6	Illinois	7,800	4.3%
6	Ohio	7,800	4.3%
8	Michigan	6,600	3.7%
9	New Jersey	5,600	3.1%
10	North Carolina	5,300	2.9%
11	Georgia	4,400	2.4%
11	Virginia	4,400	2.4%
13	Massachusetts	4,200	2.3%
14	Indiana	3,900	2.2%
15	Wisconsin	3,800	2.1%
16	Missouri	3,600	2.0%
16	Tennessee	3,600	2.0%
18	Alabama	3,500	1.9%
19	Arizona	3,300	1.8%
19	Maryland	3,300	1.8%
19	Minnesota	3,300	1.8%
22	Louisiana	3,200	1.8%
22	Washington	3,200	1.8%
24	South Carolina	2,900	1.6%
25	Oregon	2,700	1.5%
26	Kentucky	2,600	1.4%
27	Connecticut	2,300	1.3%
28	Arkansas	2,200	1.2%
28	Iowa	2,200	1.2%
28	Mississippi	2,200	1.2%
31	Oklahoma	2,100	1.2%
32	Colorado	1,800	1.0%
32	Kansas	1,800	1.0%
34	West Virginia	1,300	0.7%
35	Nevada	1,200	0.7%
35	New Mexico	1,200	0.7%
35	Utah	1,200	0.7%
38	Nebraska	1,000	0.6%
39	Maine	900	0.5%
40	Idaho	800	0.4%
41	Hawaii	700	0.4%
41	Montana	700	0.4%
41	New Hampshire	700	0.4%
41	Rhode Island	700	0.4%
45	Delaware	600	0.3%
45	South Dakota	600	0.3%
47	North Dakota	500	0.3%
48	Wyoming	400	0.2%
49	Vermont	300	0.2%
50	Alaska	100	0.1%
	District of Columbia	600	0.3%

Source: American Cancer Society
"Cancer Facts & Figures 2000" (Copyright 2000, Reprinted with permission from the American Cancer Society)
*These estimates are offered as a rough guide and should be interpreted with caution. They are calculated according to the distribution of estimated 2000 cancer deaths by state.

Estimated Rate of New Prostate Cancer Cases in 2000

National Estimated Rate = 136.6 New Cases per 100,000 Male Population*

RANK	STATE	RATE		RANK	STATE	RATE
4	Alabama	167.6		1	Florida	189.3
50	Alaska	31.0		2	Arkansas	179.4
22	Arizona	142.9		3	Pennsylvania	173.3
2	Arkansas	179.4		4	Alabama	167.6
48	California	100.5		5	Mississippi	166.8
49	Colorado	91.5		6	Oregon	166.6
19	Connecticut	144.8		7	Delaware	165.9
7	Delaware	165.9		8	Wyoming	165.5
1	Florida	189.3		9	South Dakota	165.2
42	Georgia	118.3		10	Montana	159.9
43	Hawaii	117.0		11	Iowa	157.8
38	Idaho	130.5		12	North Dakota	157.4
35	Illinois	132.8		13	South Carolina	156.9
32	Indiana	135.9		14	Louisiana	152.3
11	Iowa	157.8		15	West Virginia	149.0
27	Kansas	139.3		16	Maine	148.4
31	Kentucky	136.1		17	Wisconsin	148.0
14	Louisiana	152.3		18	Rhode Island	147.3
16	Maine	148.4		19	Connecticut	144.8
37	Maryland	132.3		19	North Carolina	144.8
25	Massachusetts	141.7		21	Ohio	144.0
28	Michigan	138.2		22	Arizona	142.9
24	Minnesota	141.8		23	New Jersey	142.5
5	Mississippi	166.8		24	Minnesota	141.8
30	Missouri	136.7		25	Massachusetts	141.7
10	Montana	159.9		26	New Mexico	140.4
40	Nebraska	122.9		27	Kansas	139.3
33	Nevada	135.0		28	Michigan	138.2
41	New Hampshire	120.1		29	Tennessee	137.4
23	New Jersey	142.5		30	Missouri	136.7
26	New Mexico	140.4		31	Kentucky	136.1
33	New York	135.0		32	Indiana	135.9
19	North Carolina	144.8		33	Nevada	135.0
12	North Dakota	157.4		33	New York	135.0
21	Ohio	144.0		35	Illinois	132.8
39	Oklahoma	128.5		36	Virginia	132.7
6	Oregon	166.6		37	Maryland	132.3
3	Pennsylvania	173.3		38	Idaho	130.5
18	Rhode Island	147.3		39	Oklahoma	128.5
13	South Carolina	156.9		40	Nebraska	122.9
9	South Dakota	165.2		41	New Hampshire	120.1
29	Tennessee	137.4		42	Georgia	118.3
44	Texas	115.9		43	Hawaii	117.0
45	Utah	115.0		44	Texas	115.9
47	Vermont	103.3		45	Utah	115.0
36	Virginia	132.7		46	Washington	113.1
46	Washington	113.1		47	Vermont	103.3
15	West Virginia	149.0		48	California	100.5
17	Wisconsin	148.0		49	Colorado	91.5
8	Wyoming	165.5		50	Alaska	31.0
					District of Columbia	244.9

Source: Morgan Quitno Press using data from American Cancer Society
   "Cancer Facts & Figures 2000" (Copyright 2000, Reprinted with permission from the American Cancer Society)
*These estimates are offered as a rough guide and should be interpreted with caution. They are calculated
according to the distribution of estimated 2000 cancer deaths by state. Rates calculated using 1998 Census male
resident population estimates.

Estimated New Skin Melanoma Cases in 2000

National Estimated Total = 47,700 New Cases*

ALPHA ORDER

RANK	STATE	CASES	% of USA
20	Alabama	900	1.9%
45	Alaska	100	0.2%
16	Arizona	1,000	2.1%
32	Arkansas	400	0.8%
1	California	5,000	10.5%
23	Colorado	700	1.5%
28	Connecticut	600	1.3%
45	Delaware	100	0.2%
2	Florida	3,500	7.3%
16	Georgia	1,000	2.1%
45	Hawaii	100	0.2%
38	Idaho	200	0.4%
6	Illinois	1,900	4.0%
16	Indiana	1,000	2.1%
29	Iowa	500	1.0%
29	Kansas	500	1.0%
20	Kentucky	900	1.9%
23	Louisiana	700	1.5%
38	Maine	200	0.4%
22	Maryland	800	1.7%
10	Massachusetts	1,300	2.7%
9	Michigan	1,400	2.9%
23	Minnesota	700	1.5%
32	Mississippi	400	0.8%
14	Missouri	1,100	2.3%
45	Montana	100	0.2%
38	Nebraska	200	0.4%
32	Nevada	400	0.8%
38	New Hampshire	200	0.4%
8	New Jersey	1,700	3.6%
37	New Mexico	300	0.6%
4	New York	2,600	5.5%
10	North Carolina	1,300	2.7%
45	North Dakota	100	0.2%
6	Ohio	1,900	4.0%
23	Oklahoma	700	1.5%
23	Oregon	700	1.5%
5	Pennsylvania	2,400	5.0%
38	Rhode Island	200	0.4%
29	South Carolina	500	1.0%
38	South Dakota	200	0.4%
10	Tennessee	1,300	2.7%
3	Texas	3,400	7.1%
32	Utah	400	0.8%
38	Vermont	200	0.4%
13	Virginia	1,200	2.5%
14	Washington	1,100	2.3%
32	West Virginia	400	0.8%
16	Wisconsin	1,000	2.1%
45	Wyoming	100	0.2%

RANK ORDER

RANK	STATE	CASES	% of USA
1	California	5,000	10.5%
2	Florida	3,500	7.3%
3	Texas	3,400	7.1%
4	New York	2,600	5.5%
5	Pennsylvania	2,400	5.0%
6	Illinois	1,900	4.0%
6	Ohio	1,900	4.0%
8	New Jersey	1,700	3.6%
9	Michigan	1,400	2.9%
10	Massachusetts	1,300	2.7%
10	North Carolina	1,300	2.7%
10	Tennessee	1,300	2.7%
13	Virginia	1,200	2.5%
14	Missouri	1,100	2.3%
14	Washington	1,100	2.3%
16	Arizona	1,000	2.1%
16	Georgia	1,000	2.1%
16	Indiana	1,000	2.1%
16	Wisconsin	1,000	2.1%
20	Alabama	900	1.9%
20	Kentucky	900	1.9%
22	Maryland	800	1.7%
23	Colorado	700	1.5%
23	Louisiana	700	1.5%
23	Minnesota	700	1.5%
23	Oklahoma	700	1.5%
23	Oregon	700	1.5%
28	Connecticut	600	1.3%
29	Iowa	500	1.0%
29	Kansas	500	1.0%
29	South Carolina	500	1.0%
32	Arkansas	400	0.8%
32	Mississippi	400	0.8%
32	Nevada	400	0.8%
32	Utah	400	0.8%
32	West Virginia	400	0.8%
37	New Mexico	300	0.6%
38	Idaho	200	0.4%
38	Maine	200	0.4%
38	Nebraska	200	0.4%
38	New Hampshire	200	0.4%
38	Rhode Island	200	0.4%
38	South Dakota	200	0.4%
38	Vermont	200	0.4%
45	Alaska	100	0.2%
45	Delaware	100	0.2%
45	Hawaii	100	0.2%
45	Montana	100	0.2%
45	North Dakota	100	0.2%
45	Wyoming	100	0.2%
	District of Columbia**	NA	NA

Source: American Cancer Society
   "Cancer Facts & Figures 2000" (Copyright 2000, Reprinted with permission from the American Cancer Society)
*These estimates are offered as a rough guide and should be interpreted with caution. They are calculated according to the distribution of estimated 2000 cancer deaths by state.
**Fewer than 50 cases.

Estimated Rate of New Skin Melanoma Cases in 2000

National Estimated Rate = 17.5 New Cases per 100,000 Population*

ALPHA ORDER				RANK ORDER		
RANK	STATE	RATE		RANK	STATE	RATE
14	Alabama	20.6		1	Vermont	33.7
32	Alaska	16.1		2	South Dakota	27.3
10	Arizona	20.9		3	Tennessee	23.7
37	Arkansas	15.7		4	Florida	23.2
40	California	15.1		5	Kentucky	22.7
25	Colorado	17.3		6	Nevada	22.1
22	Connecticut	18.3		6	West Virginia	22.1
45	Delaware	13.3		8	Massachusetts	21.1
4	Florida	23.2		8	Oregon	21.1
47	Georgia	12.8		10	Arizona	20.9
50	Hawaii	8.4		10	New Jersey	20.9
33	Idaho	16.0		10	Wyoming	20.9
37	Illinois	15.7		13	Oklahoma	20.8
30	Indiana	16.8		14	Alabama	20.6
24	Iowa	17.4		15	Rhode Island	20.2
20	Kansas	18.8		16	Missouri	20.1
5	Kentucky	22.7		17	Pennsylvania	20.0
33	Louisiana	16.0		18	Washington	19.1
33	Maine	16.0		19	Wisconsin	19.0
39	Maryland	15.5		20	Kansas	18.8
8	Massachusetts	21.1		20	Utah	18.8
44	Michigan	14.2		22	Connecticut	18.3
41	Minnesota	14.7		23	Virginia	17.5
42	Mississippi	14.4		24	Iowa	17.4
16	Missouri	20.1		25	Colorado	17.3
49	Montana	11.3		26	New Mexico	17.2
48	Nebraska	12.0		27	North Carolina	17.0
6	Nevada	22.1		27	Texas	17.0
31	New Hampshire	16.7		29	Ohio	16.9
10	New Jersey	20.9		30	Indiana	16.8
26	New Mexico	17.2		31	New Hampshire	16.7
43	New York	14.3		32	Alaska	16.1
27	North Carolina	17.0		33	Idaho	16.0
36	North Dakota	15.8		33	Louisiana	16.0
29	Ohio	16.9		33	Maine	16.0
13	Oklahoma	20.8		36	North Dakota	15.8
8	Oregon	21.1		37	Arkansas	15.7
17	Pennsylvania	20.0		37	Illinois	15.7
15	Rhode Island	20.2		39	Maryland	15.5
46	South Carolina	12.9		40	California	15.1
2	South Dakota	27.3		41	Minnesota	14.7
3	Tennessee	23.7		42	Mississippi	14.4
27	Texas	17.0		43	New York	14.3
20	Utah	18.8		44	Michigan	14.2
1	Vermont	33.7		45	Delaware	13.3
23	Virginia	17.5		46	South Carolina	12.9
18	Washington	19.1		47	Georgia	12.8
6	West Virginia	22.1		48	Nebraska	12.0
19	Wisconsin	19.0		49	Montana	11.3
10	Wyoming	20.9		50	Hawaii	8.4
				District of Columbia**		NA

Source: Morgan Quitno Press using data from American Cancer Society
    "Cancer Facts & Figures 2000" (Copyright 2000, Reprinted with permission from the American Cancer Society)
*These estimates are offered as a rough guide and should be interpreted with caution. They are calculated according to the distribution of estimated 2000 cancer deaths by state. Rates calculated using 1999 Census resident population estimates.
**Fewer than 50 cases.

Estimated New Cancer of the Uterus (Cervix) Cases in 2000

National Estimated Total = 12,800 New Cases*

ALPHA ORDER

RANK	STATE	CASES	% of USA
19	Alabama	200	1.6%
NA	Alaska**	NA	NA
19	Arizona	200	1.6%
28	Arkansas	100	0.8%
1	California	1,300	10.2%
28	Colorado	100	0.8%
28	Connecticut	100	0.8%
28	Delaware	100	0.8%
4	Florida	900	7.0%
8	Georgia	400	3.1%
NA	Hawaii**	NA	NA
NA	Idaho**	NA	NA
5	Illinois	600	4.7%
13	Indiana	300	2.3%
28	Iowa	100	0.8%
28	Kansas	100	0.8%
13	Kentucky	300	2.3%
13	Louisiana	300	2.3%
28	Maine	100	0.8%
13	Maryland	300	2.3%
19	Massachusetts	200	1.6%
8	Michigan	400	3.1%
19	Minnesota	200	1.6%
19	Mississippi	200	1.6%
13	Missouri	300	2.3%
NA	Montana**	NA	NA
28	Nebraska	100	0.8%
28	Nevada	100	0.8%
NA	New Hampshire**	NA	NA
8	New Jersey	400	3.1%
28	New Mexico	100	0.8%
2	New York	1,000	7.8%
8	North Carolina	400	3.1%
NA	North Dakota**	NA	NA
5	Ohio	600	4.7%
19	Oklahoma	200	1.6%
28	Oregon	100	0.8%
5	Pennsylvania	600	4.7%
28	Rhode Island	100	0.8%
19	South Carolina	200	1.6%
NA	South Dakota**	NA	NA
8	Tennessee	400	3.1%
2	Texas	1,000	7.8%
28	Utah	100	0.8%
28	Vermont	100	0.8%
13	Virginia	300	2.3%
19	Washington	200	1.6%
28	West Virginia	100	0.8%
19	Wisconsin	200	1.6%
NA	Wyoming**	NA	NA

RANK ORDER

RANK	STATE	CASES	% of USA
1	California	1,300	10.2%
2	New York	1,000	7.8%
2	Texas	1,000	7.8%
4	Florida	900	7.0%
5	Illinois	600	4.7%
5	Ohio	600	4.7%
5	Pennsylvania	600	4.7%
8	Georgia	400	3.1%
8	Michigan	400	3.1%
8	New Jersey	400	3.1%
8	North Carolina	400	3.1%
8	Tennessee	400	3.1%
13	Indiana	300	2.3%
13	Kentucky	300	2.3%
13	Louisiana	300	2.3%
13	Maryland	300	2.3%
13	Missouri	300	2.3%
13	Virginia	300	2.3%
19	Alabama	200	1.6%
19	Arizona	200	1.6%
19	Massachusetts	200	1.6%
19	Minnesota	200	1.6%
19	Mississippi	200	1.6%
19	Oklahoma	200	1.6%
19	South Carolina	200	1.6%
19	Washington	200	1.6%
19	Wisconsin	200	1.6%
28	Arkansas	100	0.8%
28	Colorado	100	0.8%
28	Connecticut	100	0.8%
28	Delaware	100	0.8%
28	Iowa	100	0.8%
28	Kansas	100	0.8%
28	Maine	100	0.8%
28	Nebraska	100	0.8%
28	Nevada	100	0.8%
28	New Mexico	100	0.8%
28	Oregon	100	0.8%
28	Rhode Island	100	0.8%
28	Utah	100	0.8%
28	Vermont	100	0.8%
28	West Virginia	100	0.8%
NA	Alaska**	NA	NA
NA	Hawaii**	NA	NA
NA	Idaho**	NA	NA
NA	Montana**	NA	NA
NA	New Hampshire**	NA	NA
NA	North Dakota**	NA	NA
NA	South Dakota**	NA	NA
NA	Wyoming**	NA	NA
	District of Columbia**	NA	NA

Source: American Cancer Society

"Cancer Facts & Figures 2000" (Copyright 2000, Reprinted with permission from the American Cancer Society)
These estimates are offered as a rough guide and should be interpreted with caution. They are calculated according to the distribution of estimated 2000 cancer deaths by state.
**Fewer than 50 cases.*

Estimated Rate of New Cancer of the Uterus (Cervix) Cases in 2000

National Estimated Rate = 9.3 New Cases per 100,000 Female Population*

ALPHA ORDER

RANK	STATE	RATE
28	Alabama	8.8
NA	Alaska**	NA
30	Arizona	8.5
34	Arkansas	7.6
32	California	8.0
42	Colorado	5.0
41	Connecticut	5.9
2	Delaware	26.2
10	Florida	11.7
20	Georgia	10.2
NA	Hawaii**	NA
NA	Idaho**	NA
24	Illinois	9.7
23	Indiana	9.9
38	Iowa	6.8
35	Kansas	7.5
5	Kentucky	14.8
8	Louisiana	13.2
4	Maine	15.7
13	Maryland	11.4
39	Massachusetts	6.3
33	Michigan	7.9
31	Minnesota	8.3
7	Mississippi	14.0
15	Missouri	10.7
NA	Montana**	NA
9	Nebraska	11.8
10	Nevada	11.7
NA	New Hampshire**	NA
25	New Jersey	9.6
14	New Mexico	11.3
17	New York	10.6
19	North Carolina	10.3
NA	North Dakota**	NA
18	Ohio	10.4
10	Oklahoma	11.7
40	Oregon	6.0
25	Pennsylvania	9.6
3	Rhode Island	19.5
21	South Carolina	10.1
NA	South Dakota**	NA
6	Tennessee	14.2
22	Texas	10.0
27	Utah	9.5
1	Vermont	33.3
29	Virginia	8.6
37	Washington	7.0
15	West Virginia	10.7
35	Wisconsin	7.5
NA	Wyoming**	NA

RANK ORDER

RANK	STATE	RATE
1	Vermont	33.3
2	Delaware	26.2
3	Rhode Island	19.5
4	Maine	15.7
5	Kentucky	14.8
6	Tennessee	14.2
7	Mississippi	14.0
8	Louisiana	13.2
9	Nebraska	11.8
10	Florida	11.7
10	Nevada	11.7
10	Oklahoma	11.7
13	Maryland	11.4
14	New Mexico	11.3
15	Missouri	10.7
15	West Virginia	10.7
17	New York	10.6
18	Ohio	10.4
19	North Carolina	10.3
20	Georgia	10.2
21	South Carolina	10.1
22	Texas	10.0
23	Indiana	9.9
24	Illinois	9.7
25	New Jersey	9.6
25	Pennsylvania	9.6
27	Utah	9.5
28	Alabama	8.8
29	Virginia	8.6
30	Arizona	8.5
31	Minnesota	8.3
32	California	8.0
33	Michigan	7.9
34	Arkansas	7.6
35	Kansas	7.5
35	Wisconsin	7.5
37	Washington	7.0
38	Iowa	6.8
39	Massachusetts	6.3
40	Oregon	6.0
41	Connecticut	5.9
42	Colorado	5.0
NA	Alaska**	NA
NA	Hawaii**	NA
NA	Idaho**	NA
NA	Montana**	NA
NA	New Hampshire**	NA
NA	North Dakota**	NA
NA	South Dakota**	NA
NA	Wyoming**	NA
	District of Columbia**	NA

Source: Morgan Quitno Press using data from American Cancer Society
   "Cancer Facts & Figures 2000" (Copyright 2000, Reprinted with permission from the American Cancer Society)
*These estimates are offered as a rough guide and should be interpreted with caution. They are calculated according to the distribution of estimated 2000 cancer deaths by state. Rates calculated using 1998 Census female resident population estimates.
**Fewer than 50 cases.

Percent of Women 18 Years and Older
Who Had a Pap Smear Within the Past Three Years: 1998
National Median = 84.9% of Women 18 Years and Older*

ALPHA ORDER

RANK	STATE	PERCENT
19	Alabama	85.3
1	Alaska	89.5
42	Arizona	81.7
48	Arkansas	78.9
NA	California**	NA
7	Colorado	87.0
10	Connecticut	86.2
6	Delaware	87.1
14	Florida	85.9
11	Georgia	86.1
8	Hawaii	86.3
39	Idaho	82.5
28	Illinois	84.5
46	Indiana	80.9
28	Iowa	84.5
15	Kansas	85.6
31	Kentucky	84.3
26	Louisiana	84.8
22	Maine	85.0
2	Maryland	89.2
4	Massachusetts	87.7
3	Michigan	88.1
22	Minnesota	85.0
30	Mississippi	84.4
17	Missouri	85.4
47	Montana	80.6
40	Nebraska	82.4
21	Nevada	85.1
32	New Hampshire	84.2
44	New Jersey	81.4
38	New Mexico	82.6
34	New York	83.8
4	North Carolina	87.7
16	North Dakota	85.5
32	Ohio	84.2
26	Oklahoma	84.8
36	Oregon	83.7
34	Pennsylvania	83.8
20	Rhode Island	85.2
22	South Carolina	85.0
8	South Dakota	86.3
11	Tennessee	86.1
43	Texas	81.5
49	Utah	78.4
13	Vermont	86.0
25	Virginia	84.9
17	Washington	85.4
45	West Virginia	81.0
37	Wisconsin	83.4
41	Wyoming	82.0

RANK ORDER

RANK	STATE	PERCENT
1	Alaska	89.5
2	Maryland	89.2
3	Michigan	88.1
4	Massachusetts	87.7
4	North Carolina	87.7
6	Delaware	87.1
7	Colorado	87.0
8	Hawaii	86.3
8	South Dakota	86.3
10	Connecticut	86.2
11	Georgia	86.1
11	Tennessee	86.1
13	Vermont	86.0
14	Florida	85.9
15	Kansas	85.6
16	North Dakota	85.5
17	Missouri	85.4
17	Washington	85.4
19	Alabama	85.3
20	Rhode Island	85.2
21	Nevada	85.1
22	Maine	85.0
22	Minnesota	85.0
22	South Carolina	85.0
25	Virginia	84.9
26	Louisiana	84.8
26	Oklahoma	84.8
28	Illinois	84.5
28	Iowa	84.5
30	Mississippi	84.4
31	Kentucky	84.3
32	New Hampshire	84.2
32	Ohio	84.2
34	New York	83.8
34	Pennsylvania	83.8
36	Oregon	83.7
37	Wisconsin	83.4
38	New Mexico	82.6
39	Idaho	82.5
40	Nebraska	82.4
41	Wyoming	82.0
42	Arizona	81.7
43	Texas	81.5
44	New Jersey	81.4
45	West Virginia	81.0
46	Indiana	80.9
47	Montana	80.6
48	Arkansas	78.9
49	Utah	78.4
NA	California**	NA
	District of Columbia	93.9

Source: U.S. Department of Health and Human Services, Centers for Disease Control and Prevention
"1998 Behavioral Risk Factor Surveillance Summary Prevalence Report" (June 18, 1999)
*Of women with intact cervix. Pap smear is a test for cancer, especially of the female genital tract. Named after George Papanicolaou (1883-1962), American anatomist.
**Not available.

AIDS Cases Reported in 1999

National Total = 45,000 New AIDS Cases*

RANK	STATE	CASES	% of USA
21	Alabama	476	1.1%
47	Alaska	15	0.0%
13	Arizona	880	2.0%
29	Arkansas	194	0.4%
3	California	5,445	12.1%
25	Colorado	319	0.7%
18	Connecticut	585	1.3%
31	Delaware	186	0.4%
2	Florida	5,468	12.2%
7	Georgia	1,678	3.7%
37	Hawaii	100	0.2%
44	Idaho	25	0.1%
8	Illinois	1,557	3.5%
23	Indiana	363	0.8%
39	Iowa	87	0.2%
32	Kansas	171	0.4%
26	Kentucky	277	0.6%
14	Louisiana	854	1.9%
40	Maine	80	0.2%
9	Maryland	1,525	3.4%
10	Massachusetts	1,454	3.2%
17	Michigan	649	1.4%
30	Minnesota	190	0.4%
22	Mississippi	421	0.9%
20	Missouri	531	1.2%
49	Montana	13	0.0%
42	Nebraska	67	0.1%
27	Nevada	242	0.5%
43	New Hampshire	46	0.1%
5	New Jersey	2,043	4.5%
38	New Mexico	93	0.2%
1	New York	7,703	17.1%
15	North Carolina	794	1.8%
50	North Dakota	7	0.0%
19	Ohio	547	1.2%
35	Oklahoma	148	0.3%
28	Oregon	225	0.5%
6	Pennsylvania	1,967	4.4%
36	Rhode Island	108	0.2%
11	South Carolina	959	2.1%
46	South Dakota	16	0.0%
16	Tennessee	759	1.7%
4	Texas	3,181	7.1%
33	Utah	155	0.3%
45	Vermont	20	0.0%
12	Virginia	943	2.1%
24	Washington	360	0.8%
41	West Virginia	69	0.2%
34	Wisconsin	152	0.3%
47	Wyoming	15	0.0%

RANK	STATE	CASES	% of USA
1	New York	7,703	17.1%
2	Florida	5,468	12.2%
3	California	5,445	12.1%
4	Texas	3,181	7.1%
5	New Jersey	2,043	4.5%
6	Pennsylvania	1,967	4.4%
7	Georgia	1,678	3.7%
8	Illinois	1,557	3.5%
9	Maryland	1,525	3.4%
10	Massachusetts	1,454	3.2%
11	South Carolina	959	2.1%
12	Virginia	943	2.1%
13	Arizona	880	2.0%
14	Louisiana	854	1.9%
15	North Carolina	794	1.8%
16	Tennessee	759	1.7%
17	Michigan	649	1.4%
18	Connecticut	585	1.3%
19	Ohio	547	1.2%
20	Missouri	531	1.2%
21	Alabama	476	1.1%
22	Mississippi	421	0.9%
23	Indiana	363	0.8%
24	Washington	360	0.8%
25	Colorado	319	0.7%
26	Kentucky	277	0.6%
27	Nevada	242	0.5%
28	Oregon	225	0.5%
29	Arkansas	194	0.4%
30	Minnesota	190	0.4%
31	Delaware	186	0.4%
32	Kansas	171	0.4%
33	Utah	155	0.3%
34	Wisconsin	152	0.3%
35	Oklahoma	148	0.3%
36	Rhode Island	108	0.2%
37	Hawaii	100	0.2%
38	New Mexico	93	0.2%
39	Iowa	87	0.2%
40	Maine	80	0.2%
41	West Virginia	69	0.2%
42	Nebraska	67	0.1%
43	New Hampshire	46	0.1%
44	Idaho	25	0.1%
45	Vermont	20	0.0%
46	South Dakota	16	0.0%
47	Alaska	15	0.0%
47	Wyoming	15	0.0%
49	Montana	13	0.0%
50	North Dakota	7	0.0%
	District of Columbia	838	1.9%

Source: U.S. Department of Health and Human Services, National Center for Health Statistics
"Morbidity and Mortality Weekly Report" (January 7, 2000, Vol. 48, No. 51)
*Provisional data. AIDS is Acquired Immunodeficiency Syndrome. It is a specific group of diseases or conditions which are indicative of severe immunosuppression related to infection with the Human Immunodeficiency Virus (HIV). National total does not include 1,247 cases in Puerto Rico, 39 cases in the Virgin Islands or 10 cases in Guam.

AIDS Rate in 1999

National Rate = 16.5 New AIDS Cases Reported per 100,000 Population*

ALPHA ORDER			RANK ORDER		
RANK	STATE	RATE	RANK	STATE	RATE
20	Alabama	10.9	1	New York	42.3
46	Alaska	2.4	2	Florida	36.2
10	Arizona	18.4	3	Maryland	29.5
26	Arkansas	7.6	4	New Jersey	25.1
12	California	16.4	5	Delaware	24.7
25	Colorado	7.9	5	South Carolina	24.7
11	Connecticut	17.8	7	Massachusetts	23.5
5	Delaware	24.7	8	Georgia	21.5
2	Florida	36.2	9	Louisiana	19.5
8	Georgia	21.5	10	Arizona	18.4
24	Hawaii	8.4	11	Connecticut	17.8
48	Idaho	2.0	12	California	16.4
19	Illinois	12.8	12	Pennsylvania	16.4
34	Indiana	6.1	14	Texas	15.9
44	Iowa	3.0	15	Mississippi	15.2
31	Kansas	6.4	16	Tennessee	13.8
28	Kentucky	7.0	17	Virginia	13.7
9	Louisiana	19.5	18	Nevada	13.4
31	Maine	6.4	19	Illinois	12.8
3	Maryland	29.5	20	Alabama	10.9
7	Massachusetts	23.5	20	Rhode Island	10.9
30	Michigan	6.6	22	North Carolina	10.4
38	Minnesota	4.0	23	Missouri	9.7
15	Mississippi	15.2	24	Hawaii	8.4
23	Missouri	9.7	25	Colorado	7.9
49	Montana	1.5	26	Arkansas	7.6
38	Nebraska	4.0	27	Utah	7.3
18	Nevada	13.4	28	Kentucky	7.0
40	New Hampshire	3.8	29	Oregon	6.8
4	New Jersey	25.1	30	Michigan	6.6
35	New Mexico	5.3	31	Kansas	6.4
1	New York	42.3	31	Maine	6.4
22	North Carolina	10.4	33	Washington	6.3
50	North Dakota	1.1	34	Indiana	6.1
36	Ohio	4.9	35	New Mexico	5.3
37	Oklahoma	4.4	36	Ohio	4.9
29	Oregon	6.8	37	Oklahoma	4.4
12	Pennsylvania	16.4	38	Minnesota	4.0
20	Rhode Island	10.9	38	Nebraska	4.0
5	South Carolina	24.7	40	New Hampshire	3.8
47	South Dakota	2.2	40	West Virginia	3.8
16	Tennessee	13.8	42	Vermont	3.4
14	Texas	15.9	43	Wyoming	3.1
27	Utah	7.3	44	Iowa	3.0
42	Vermont	3.4	45	Wisconsin	2.9
17	Virginia	13.7	46	Alaska	2.4
33	Washington	6.3	47	South Dakota	2.2
40	West Virginia	3.8	48	Idaho	2.0
45	Wisconsin	2.9	49	Montana	1.5
43	Wyoming	3.1	50	North Dakota	1.1
				District of Columbia	161.5

Source: Morgan Quitno Press using data from U.S. Dept. of Health & Human Serv's, National Center for Health Statistics "Morbidity and Mortality Weekly Report" (January 7, 2000, Vol. 48, No. 51)

*Provisional data. AIDS is Acquired Immunodeficiency Syndrome. It is a specific group of diseases or conditions which are indicative of severe immunosuppression related to infection with the Human Immunodeficiency Virus (HIV). National rate does not include cases or population in Puerto Rico, the Virgin Islands or in Guam.

AIDS Cases Reported Through June 1999

National Total = 679,125 Reported AIDS Cases*

ALPHA ORDER

RANK	STATE	CASES	% of USA
24	Alabama	5,508	0.8%
45	Alaska	448	0.1%
22	Arizona	6,501	1.0%
32	Arkansas	2,644	0.4%
2	California	112,444	16.6%
21	Colorado	6,586	1.0%
13	Connecticut	10,518	1.5%
34	Delaware	2,238	0.3%
3	Florida	71,815	10.6%
8	Georgia	20,789	3.1%
33	Hawaii	2,280	0.3%
44	Idaho	459	0.1%
6	Illinois	22,102	3.3%
23	Indiana	5,573	0.8%
39	Iowa	1,185	0.2%
35	Kansas	2,165	0.3%
31	Kentucky	2,988	0.4%
11	Louisiana	11,466	1.7%
42	Maine	856	0.1%
9	Maryland	19,136	2.8%
10	Massachusetts	14,281	2.1%
15	Michigan	10,161	1.5%
28	Minnesota	3,450	0.5%
27	Mississippi	3,783	0.6%
18	Missouri	8,451	1.2%
47	Montana	298	0.0%
40	Nebraska	981	0.1%
26	Nevada	3,968	0.6%
43	New Hampshire	820	0.1%
5	New Jersey	38,614	5.7%
37	New Mexico	1,858	0.3%
1	New York	129,882	19.1%
16	North Carolina	9,226	1.4%
50	North Dakota	100	0.0%
14	Ohio	10,373	1.5%
29	Oklahoma	3,338	0.5%
25	Oregon	4,438	0.7%
7	Pennsylvania	21,757	3.2%
36	Rhode Island	1,890	0.3%
19	South Carolina	8,275	1.2%
49	South Dakota	151	0.0%
20	Tennessee	7,335	1.1%
4	Texas	49,795	7.3%
38	Utah	1,731	0.3%
46	Vermont	350	0.1%
12	Virginia	11,442	1.7%
17	Washington	8,798	1.3%
41	West Virginia	968	0.1%
30	Wisconsin	3,283	0.5%
48	Wyoming	159	0.0%

RANK ORDER

RANK	STATE	CASES	% of USA
1	New York	129,882	19.1%
2	California	112,444	16.6%
3	Florida	71,815	10.6%
4	Texas	49,795	7.3%
5	New Jersey	38,614	5.7%
6	Illinois	22,102	3.3%
7	Pennsylvania	21,757	3.2%
8	Georgia	20,789	3.1%
9	Maryland	19,136	2.8%
10	Massachusetts	14,281	2.1%
11	Louisiana	11,466	1.7%
12	Virginia	11,442	1.7%
13	Connecticut	10,518	1.5%
14	Ohio	10,373	1.5%
15	Michigan	10,161	1.5%
16	North Carolina	9,226	1.4%
17	Washington	8,798	1.3%
18	Missouri	8,451	1.2%
19	South Carolina	8,275	1.2%
20	Tennessee	7,335	1.1%
21	Colorado	6,586	1.0%
22	Arizona	6,501	1.0%
23	Indiana	5,573	0.8%
24	Alabama	5,508	0.8%
25	Oregon	4,438	0.7%
26	Nevada	3,968	0.6%
27	Mississippi	3,783	0.6%
28	Minnesota	3,450	0.5%
29	Oklahoma	3,338	0.5%
30	Wisconsin	3,283	0.5%
31	Kentucky	2,988	0.4%
32	Arkansas	2,644	0.4%
33	Hawaii	2,280	0.3%
34	Delaware	2,238	0.3%
35	Kansas	2,165	0.3%
36	Rhode Island	1,890	0.3%
37	New Mexico	1,858	0.3%
38	Utah	1,731	0.3%
39	Iowa	1,185	0.2%
40	Nebraska	981	0.1%
41	West Virginia	968	0.1%
42	Maine	856	0.1%
43	New Hampshire	820	0.1%
44	Idaho	459	0.1%
45	Alaska	448	0.1%
46	Vermont	350	0.1%
47	Montana	298	0.0%
48	Wyoming	159	0.0%
49	South Dakota	151	0.0%
50	North Dakota	100	0.0%
	District of Columbia	11,468	1.7%

Source: U.S. Department of Health and Human Services, Centers for Disease Control and Prevention
    "HIV/AIDS Surveillance Report, 1999" (Mid-year Edition, Vol. 11, No. 1)
*Cumulative through June 1999. AIDS is Acquired Immunodeficiency Syndrome. It is a specific group of diseases or conditions which are indicative of severe immunosuppression related to infection with the Human Immunodeficiency Virus (HIV). National total does not include 22,640 cases in Puerto Rico, 408 cases in the Virgin Islands and 30 cases in other U.S. territories.

AIDS Cases in Children 12 Years and Younger Through June 1999

National Total = 8,188 Juvenile AIDS Cases*

ALPHA ORDER				RANK ORDER			
RANK	STATE	CASES	% of USA	RANK	STATE	CASES	% of USA
18	Alabama	67	0.8%	1	New York	2,204	26.9%
44	Alaska	5	0.1%	2	Florida	1,353	16.5%
26	Arizona	27	0.3%	3	New Jersey	730	8.9%
22	Arkansas	38	0.5%	4	California	581	7.1%
4	California	581	7.1%	5	Texas	363	4.4%
25	Colorado	28	0.3%	6	Pennsylvania	300	3.7%
11	Connecticut	173	2.1%	7	Maryland	293	3.6%
32	Delaware	21	0.3%	8	Illinois	246	3.0%
2	Florida	1,353	16.5%	9	Massachusetts	202	2.5%
10	Georgia	194	2.4%	10	Georgia	194	2.4%
36	Hawaii	15	0.2%	11	Connecticut	173	2.1%
48	Idaho	2	0.0%	12	Virginia	161	2.0%
8	Illinois	246	3.0%	13	Ohio	119	1.5%
23	Indiana	37	0.5%	14	Louisiana	118	1.4%
38	Iowa	9	0.1%	15	North Carolina	113	1.4%
37	Kansas	11	0.1%	16	Michigan	106	1.3%
30	Kentucky	23	0.3%	17	South Carolina	77	0.9%
14	Louisiana	118	1.4%	18	Alabama	67	0.8%
38	Maine	9	0.1%	19	Missouri	56	0.7%
7	Maryland	293	3.6%	20	Mississippi	53	0.6%
9	Massachusetts	202	2.5%	21	Tennessee	48	0.6%
16	Michigan	106	1.3%	22	Arkansas	38	0.5%
31	Minnesota	22	0.3%	23	Indiana	37	0.5%
20	Mississippi	53	0.6%	24	Washington	33	0.4%
19	Missouri	56	0.7%	25	Colorado	28	0.3%
47	Montana	3	0.0%	26	Arizona	27	0.3%
38	Nebraska	9	0.1%	26	Nevada	27	0.3%
26	Nevada	27	0.3%	26	Wisconsin	27	0.3%
38	New Hampshire	9	0.1%	29	Oklahoma	26	0.3%
3	New Jersey	730	8.9%	30	Kentucky	23	0.3%
43	New Mexico	8	0.1%	31	Minnesota	22	0.3%
1	New York	2,204	26.9%	32	Delaware	21	0.3%
15	North Carolina	113	1.4%	32	Utah	21	0.3%
50	North Dakota	0	0.0%	34	Rhode Island	20	0.2%
13	Ohio	119	1.5%	35	Oregon	16	0.2%
29	Oklahoma	26	0.3%	36	Hawaii	15	0.2%
35	Oregon	16	0.2%	37	Kansas	11	0.1%
6	Pennsylvania	300	3.7%	38	Iowa	9	0.1%
34	Rhode Island	20	0.2%	38	Maine	9	0.1%
17	South Carolina	77	0.9%	38	Nebraska	9	0.1%
45	South Dakota	4	0.0%	38	New Hampshire	9	0.1%
21	Tennessee	48	0.6%	38	West Virginia	9	0.1%
5	Texas	363	4.4%	43	New Mexico	8	0.1%
32	Utah	21	0.3%	44	Alaska	5	0.1%
45	Vermont	4	0.0%	45	South Dakota	4	0.0%
12	Virginia	161	2.0%	45	Vermont	4	0.0%
24	Washington	33	0.4%	47	Montana	3	0.0%
38	West Virginia	9	0.1%	48	Idaho	2	0.0%
26	Wisconsin	27	0.3%	48	Wyoming	2	0.0%
48	Wyoming	2	0.0%	50	North Dakota	0	0.0%
					District of Columbia	166	2.0%

*Source: U.S. Department of Health and Human Services, Centers for Disease Control and Prevention
"HIV/AIDS Surveillance Report, 1999" (Mid-year Edition, Vol. 11, No. 1)*
Cumulative through June 1999. AIDS is Acquired Immunodeficiency Syndrome. It is a specific group of diseases or conditions which are indicative of severe immunosuppression related to infection with the Human Immunodeficiency Virus (HIV). National total does not include 387 cases in Puerto Rico and 16 cases in the Virgin Islands.

E-Coli Cases Reported in 1999

National Total = 5,959 Cases*

ALPHA ORDER

RANK	STATE	CASES	% of USA
33	Alabama	46	0.8%
50	Alaska	2	0.0%
28	Arizona	62	1.0%
44	Arkansas	23	0.4%
5	California	326	5.5%
9	Colorado	200	3.4%
13	Connecticut	171	2.9%
49	Delaware	9	0.2%
21	Florida	107	1.8%
34	Georgia	41	0.7%
45	Hawaii	22	0.4%
19	Idaho	121	2.0%
6	Illinois	308	5.2%
12	Indiana	181	3.0%
11	Iowa	191	3.2%
36	Kansas	37	0.6%
31	Kentucky	48	0.8%
41	Louisiana	27	0.5%
35	Maine	38	0.6%
31	Maryland	48	0.8%
3	Massachusetts	360	6.0%
10	Michigan	196	3.3%
2	Minnesota	423	7.1%
48	Mississippi	10	0.2%
17	Missouri	135	2.3%
43	Montana	25	0.4%
8	Nebraska	227	3.8%
45	Nevada	22	0.4%
26	New Hampshire	68	1.1%
23	New Jersey	97	1.6%
47	New Mexico	20	0.3%
7	New York	303	5.1%
18	North Carolina	126	2.1%
37	North Dakota	35	0.6%
1	Ohio	481	8.1%
26	Oklahoma	68	1.1%
15	Oregon	143	2.4%
40	Pennsylvania	29	0.5%
29	Rhode Island	53	0.9%
37	South Carolina	35	0.6%
20	South Dakota	109	1.8%
22	Tennessee	99	1.7%
14	Texas	150	2.5%
24	Utah	88	1.5%
29	Vermont	53	0.9%
16	Virginia	137	2.3%
4	Washington	331	5.6%
41	West Virginia	27	0.5%
25	Wisconsin	69	1.2%
39	Wyoming	31	0.5%

RANK ORDER

RANK	STATE	CASES	% of USA
1	Ohio	481	8.1%
2	Minnesota	423	7.1%
3	Massachusetts	360	6.0%
4	Washington	331	5.6%
5	California	326	5.5%
6	Illinois	308	5.2%
7	New York	303	5.1%
8	Nebraska	227	3.8%
9	Colorado	200	3.4%
10	Michigan	196	3.3%
11	Iowa	191	3.2%
12	Indiana	181	3.0%
13	Connecticut	171	2.9%
14	Texas	150	2.5%
15	Oregon	143	2.4%
16	Virginia	137	2.3%
17	Missouri	135	2.3%
18	North Carolina	126	2.1%
19	Idaho	121	2.0%
20	South Dakota	109	1.8%
21	Florida	107	1.8%
22	Tennessee	99	1.7%
23	New Jersey	97	1.6%
24	Utah	88	1.5%
25	Wisconsin	69	1.2%
26	New Hampshire	68	1.1%
26	Oklahoma	68	1.1%
28	Arizona	62	1.0%
29	Rhode Island	53	0.9%
29	Vermont	53	0.9%
31	Kentucky	48	0.8%
31	Maryland	48	0.8%
33	Alabama	46	0.8%
34	Georgia	41	0.7%
35	Maine	38	0.6%
36	Kansas	37	0.6%
37	North Dakota	35	0.6%
37	South Carolina	35	0.6%
39	Wyoming	31	0.5%
40	Pennsylvania	29	0.5%
41	Louisiana	27	0.5%
41	West Virginia	27	0.5%
43	Montana	25	0.4%
44	Arkansas	23	0.4%
45	Hawaii	22	0.4%
45	Nevada	22	0.4%
47	New Mexico	20	0.3%
48	Mississippi	10	0.2%
49	Delaware	9	0.2%
50	Alaska	2	0.0%
	District of Columbia	1	0.0%

Source: U.S. Department of Health and Human Services, National Center for Health Statistics
    "Morbidity and Mortality Weekly Report" (January 7, 2000, Vol. 48, No. 51)
*Individual cases may be reported through both the Public Health Laboratory Information System and the National Electronic Telecommunications System for Surveillance. Escherichia Coli is a common bacterium that normally inhabits the intestinal tracts of humans and animals but can cause infection in other parts of the body, especially the urinary tract. One strain, sometimes transmitted in hamburger meat, can cause serious infection resulting in sickness and death.

E-Coli Rate in 1999

National Rate = 2.2 Cases per 100,000 Population*

ALPHA ORDER

RANK	STATE	RATE
38	Alabama	1.1
49	Alaska	0.3
32	Arizona	1.3
41	Arkansas	0.9
40	California	1.0
14	Colorado	4.9
13	Connecticut	5.2
34	Delaware	1.2
44	Florida	0.7
47	Georgia	0.5
26	Hawaii	1.9
3	Idaho	9.7
21	Illinois	2.5
18	Indiana	3.0
6	Iowa	6.7
31	Kansas	1.4
34	Kentucky	1.2
46	Louisiana	0.6
18	Maine	3.0
41	Maryland	0.9
8	Massachusetts	5.8
23	Michigan	2.0
4	Minnesota	8.9
48	Mississippi	0.4
21	Missouri	2.5
20	Montana	2.8
2	Nebraska	13.6
34	Nevada	1.2
10	New Hampshire	5.7
34	New Jersey	1.2
38	New Mexico	1.1
28	New York	1.7
29	North Carolina	1.6
11	North Dakota	5.5
15	Ohio	4.3
23	Oklahoma	2.0
15	Oregon	4.3
50	Pennsylvania	0.2
12	Rhode Island	5.3
41	South Carolina	0.9
1	South Dakota	14.9
27	Tennessee	1.8
44	Texas	0.7
17	Utah	4.1
4	Vermont	8.9
23	Virginia	2.0
8	Washington	5.8
30	West Virginia	1.5
32	Wisconsin	1.3
7	Wyoming	6.5

RANK ORDER

RANK	STATE	RATE
1	South Dakota	14.9
2	Nebraska	13.6
3	Idaho	9.7
4	Minnesota	8.9
4	Vermont	8.9
6	Iowa	6.7
7	Wyoming	6.5
8	Massachusetts	5.8
8	Washington	5.8
10	New Hampshire	5.7
11	North Dakota	5.5
12	Rhode Island	5.3
13	Connecticut	5.2
14	Colorado	4.9
15	Ohio	4.3
15	Oregon	4.3
17	Utah	4.1
18	Indiana	3.0
18	Maine	3.0
20	Montana	2.8
21	Illinois	2.5
21	Missouri	2.5
23	Michigan	2.0
23	Oklahoma	2.0
23	Virginia	2.0
26	Hawaii	1.9
27	Tennessee	1.8
28	New York	1.7
29	North Carolina	1.6
30	West Virginia	1.5
31	Kansas	1.4
32	Arizona	1.3
32	Wisconsin	1.3
34	Delaware	1.2
34	Kentucky	1.2
34	Nevada	1.2
34	New Jersey	1.2
38	Alabama	1.1
38	New Mexico	1.1
40	California	1.0
41	Arkansas	0.9
41	Maryland	0.9
41	South Carolina	0.9
44	Florida	0.7
44	Texas	0.7
46	Louisiana	0.6
47	Georgia	0.5
48	Mississippi	0.4
49	Alaska	0.3
50	Pennsylvania	0.2

District of Columbia | 0.2

Source: Morgan Quitno Press using data from U.S. Dept. of Health & Human Serv's, National Center for Health Statistics "Morbidity and Mortality Weekly Report" (January 7, 2000, Vol. 48, No. 51)

*Individual cases may be reported through both the Public Health Laboratory Information System and the National Electronic Telecommunications System for Surveillance. Escherichia Coli is a common bacterium that normally inhabits the intestinal tracts of humans and animals but can cause infection in other parts of the body, especially the urinary tract. One strain, sometimes transmitted in hamburger meat, can cause serious infection resulting in sickness and death.

German Measles (Rubella) Cases Reported in 1999

National Total = 238 Cases*

RANK	STATE	CASES	% of USA
14	Alabama	1	0.4%
22	Alaska	0	0.0%
5	Arizona	13	5.5%
8	Arkansas	6	2.5%
9	California	5	2.1%
14	Colorado	1	0.4%
22	Connecticut	0	0.0%
22	Delaware	0	0.0%
14	Florida	1	0.4%
22	Georgia	0	0.0%
22	Hawaii	0	0.0%
22	Idaho	0	0.0%
14	Illinois	1	0.4%
14	Indiana	1	0.4%
3	Iowa	29	12.2%
22	Kansas	0	0.0%
22	Kentucky	0	0.0%
22	Louisiana	0	0.0%
22	Maine	0	0.0%
14	Maryland	1	0.4%
7	Massachusetts	7	2.9%
22	Michigan	0	0.0%
9	Minnesota	5	2.1%
22	Mississippi	0	0.0%
11	Missouri	3	1.3%
22	Montana	0	0.0%
1	Nebraska	90	37.8%
14	Nevada	1	0.4%
22	New Hampshire	0	0.0%
14	New Jersey	1	0.4%
22	New Mexico	0	0.0%
4	New York	21	8.8%
2	North Carolina	37	15.5%
22	North Dakota	0	0.0%
22	Ohio	0	0.0%
22	Oklahoma	0	0.0%
22	Oregon	0	0.0%
11	Pennsylvania	3	1.3%
22	Rhode Island	0	0.0%
22	South Carolina	0	0.0%
22	South Dakota	0	0.0%
22	Tennessee	0	0.0%
6	Texas	9	3.8%
13	Utah	2	0.8%
22	Vermont	0	0.0%
22	Virginia	0	0.0%
22	Washington	0	0.0%
22	West Virginia	0	0.0%
22	Wisconsin	0	0.0%
22	Wyoming	0	0.0%

RANK	STATE	CASES	% of USA
1	Nebraska	90	37.8%
2	North Carolina	37	15.5%
3	Iowa	29	12.2%
4	New York	21	8.8%
5	Arizona	13	5.5%
6	Texas	9	3.8%
7	Massachusetts	7	2.9%
8	Arkansas	6	2.5%
9	California	5	2.1%
9	Minnesota	5	2.1%
11	Missouri	3	1.3%
11	Pennsylvania	3	1.3%
13	Utah	2	0.8%
14	Alabama	1	0.4%
14	Colorado	1	0.4%
14	Florida	1	0.4%
14	Illinois	1	0.4%
14	Indiana	1	0.4%
14	Maryland	1	0.4%
14	Nevada	1	0.4%
14	New Jersey	1	0.4%
22	Alaska	0	0.0%
22	Connecticut	0	0.0%
22	Delaware	0	0.0%
22	Georgia	0	0.0%
22	Hawaii	0	0.0%
22	Idaho	0	0.0%
22	Kansas	0	0.0%
22	Kentucky	0	0.0%
22	Louisiana	0	0.0%
22	Maine	0	0.0%
22	Michigan	0	0.0%
22	Mississippi	0	0.0%
22	Montana	0	0.0%
22	New Hampshire	0	0.0%
22	New Mexico	0	0.0%
22	North Dakota	0	0.0%
22	Ohio	0	0.0%
22	Oklahoma	0	0.0%
22	Oregon	0	0.0%
22	Rhode Island	0	0.0%
22	South Carolina	0	0.0%
22	South Dakota	0	0.0%
22	Tennessee	0	0.0%
22	Vermont	0	0.0%
22	Virginia	0	0.0%
22	Washington	0	0.0%
22	West Virginia	0	0.0%
22	Wisconsin	0	0.0%
22	Wyoming	0	0.0%
	District of Columbia	0	0.0%

Source: U.S. Department of Health and Human Services, National Center for Health Statistics
"Morbidity and Mortality Weekly Report" (January 7, 2000, Vol. 48, No. 51)
*Provisional data. A mild, contagious, eruptive disease caused by a virus and capable of producing congenital defects in infants born to mothers infected during the first three months of pregnancy.

German Measles (Rubella) Rate in 1999

National Rate = 0.09 Cases per 100,000 Population*

RANK	STATE	RATE
14	Alabama	0.02
22	Alaska	0.00
4	Arizona	0.27
5	Arkansas	0.24
14	California	0.02
14	Colorado	0.02
22	Connecticut	0.00
22	Delaware	0.00
19	Florida	0.01
22	Georgia	0.00
22	Hawaii	0.00
22	Idaho	0.00
19	Illinois	0.01
14	Indiana	0.02
2	Iowa	1.01
22	Kansas	0.00
22	Kentucky	0.00
22	Louisiana	0.00
22	Maine	0.00
14	Maryland	0.02
7	Massachusetts	0.11
22	Michigan	0.00
8	Minnesota	0.10
22	Mississippi	0.00
11	Missouri	0.05
22	Montana	0.00
1	Nebraska	5.40
10	Nevada	0.06
22	New Hampshire	0.00
19	New Jersey	0.01
22	New Mexico	0.00
6	New York	0.12
3	North Carolina	0.48
22	North Dakota	0.00
22	Ohio	0.00
22	Oklahoma	0.00
22	Oregon	0.00
13	Pennsylvania	0.03
22	Rhode Island	0.00
22	South Carolina	0.00
22	South Dakota	0.00
22	Tennessee	0.00
12	Texas	0.04
9	Utah	0.09
22	Vermont	0.00
22	Virginia	0.00
22	Washington	0.00
22	West Virginia	0.00
22	Wisconsin	0.00
22	Wyoming	0.00

RANK	STATE	RATE
1	Nebraska	5.40
2	Iowa	1.01
3	North Carolina	0.48
4	Arizona	0.27
5	Arkansas	0.24
6	New York	0.12
7	Massachusetts	0.11
8	Minnesota	0.10
9	Utah	0.09
10	Nevada	0.06
11	Missouri	0.05
12	Texas	0.04
13	Pennsylvania	0.03
14	Alabama	0.02
14	California	0.02
14	Colorado	0.02
14	Indiana	0.02
14	Maryland	0.02
19	Florida	0.01
19	Illinois	0.01
19	New Jersey	0.01
22	Alaska	0.00
22	Connecticut	0.00
22	Delaware	0.00
22	Georgia	0.00
22	Hawaii	0.00
22	Idaho	0.00
22	Kansas	0.00
22	Kentucky	0.00
22	Louisiana	0.00
22	Maine	0.00
22	Michigan	0.00
22	Mississippi	0.00
22	Montana	0.00
22	New Hampshire	0.00
22	New Mexico	0.00
22	North Dakota	0.00
22	Ohio	0.00
22	Oklahoma	0.00
22	Oregon	0.00
22	Rhode Island	0.00
22	South Carolina	0.00
22	South Dakota	0.00
22	Tennessee	0.00
22	Vermont	0.00
22	Virginia	0.00
22	Washington	0.00
22	West Virginia	0.00
22	Wisconsin	0.00
22	Wyoming	0.00
	District of Columbia	0.00

Source: Morgan Quitno Press using data from U.S. Dept. of Health & Human Serv's, National Center for Health Statistics
"Morbidity and Mortality Weekly Report" (January 7, 2000, Vol. 48, No. 51)
*Provisional data. A mild, contagious, eruptive disease caused by a virus and capable of producing congenital defects in infants born to mothers infected during the first three months of pregnancy.

Hepatitis (Viral) Cases Reported in 1999

National Total = 23,414 Cases*

ALPHA ORDER

RANK ORDER

RANK	STATE	CASES	% of USA	RANK	STATE	CASES	% of USA
31	Alabama	138	0.6%	1	California	4,665	19.9%
44	Alaska	31	0.1%	2	Texas	3,564	15.2%
7	Arizona	888	3.8%	3	Michigan	1,771	7.6%
29	Arkansas	150	0.6%	4	Florida	1,205	5.1%
1	California	4,665	19.9%	5	New York	988	4.2%
19	Colorado	312	1.3%	6	Missouri	984	4.2%
30	Connecticut	142	0.6%	7	Arizona	888	3.8%
50	Delaware	3	0.0%	8	Ohio	753	3.2%
4	Florida	1,205	5.1%	9	Illinois	747	3.2%
11	Georgia	650	2.8%	10	Oklahoma	664	2.8%
41	Hawaii	35	0.1%	11	Georgia	650	2.8%
37	Idaho	77	0.3%	12	Washington	560	2.4%
9	Illinois	747	3.2%	13	Maryland	528	2.3%
27	Indiana	153	0.7%	14	Pennsylvania	401	1.7%
23	Iowa	191	0.8%	15	North Carolina	391	1.7%
38	Kansas	67	0.3%	16	Louisiana	371	1.6%
33	Kentucky	108	0.5%	17	Tennessee	354	1.5%
16	Louisiana	371	1.6%	18	Oregon	338	1.4%
47	Maine	15	0.1%	19	Colorado	312	1.3%
13	Maryland	528	2.3%	20	Virginia	279	1.2%
26	Massachusetts	165	0.7%	21	Mississippi	250	1.1%
3	Michigan	1,771	7.6%	22	New Mexico	241	1.0%
25	Minnesota	170	0.7%	23	Iowa	191	0.8%
21	Mississippi	250	1.1%	24	Nevada	179	0.8%
6	Missouri	984	4.2%	25	Minnesota	170	0.7%
43	Montana	34	0.1%	26	Massachusetts	165	0.7%
36	Nebraska	82	0.4%	27	Indiana	153	0.7%
24	Nevada	179	0.8%	27	New Jersey	153	0.7%
41	New Hampshire	35	0.1%	29	Arkansas	150	0.6%
27	New Jersey	153	0.7%	30	Connecticut	142	0.6%
22	New Mexico	241	1.0%	31	Alabama	138	0.6%
5	New York	988	4.2%	32	South Carolina	111	0.5%
15	North Carolina	391	1.7%	33	Kentucky	108	0.5%
49	North Dakota	5	0.0%	34	Utah	103	0.4%
8	Ohio	753	3.2%	35	Wisconsin	95	0.4%
10	Oklahoma	664	2.8%	36	Nebraska	82	0.4%
18	Oregon	338	1.4%	37	Idaho	77	0.3%
14	Pennsylvania	401	1.7%	38	Kansas	67	0.3%
40	Rhode Island	60	0.3%	38	West Virginia	67	0.3%
32	South Carolina	111	0.5%	40	Rhode Island	60	0.3%
48	South Dakota	10	0.0%	41	Hawaii	35	0.1%
17	Tennessee	354	1.5%	41	New Hampshire	35	0.1%
2	Texas	3,564	15.2%	43	Montana	34	0.1%
34	Utah	103	0.4%	44	Alaska	31	0.1%
45	Vermont	27	0.1%	45	Vermont	27	0.1%
20	Virginia	279	1.2%	46	Wyoming	21	0.1%
12	Washington	560	2.4%	47	Maine	15	0.1%
38	West Virginia	67	0.3%	48	South Dakota	10	0.0%
35	Wisconsin	95	0.4%	49	North Dakota	5	0.0%
46	Wyoming	21	0.1%	50	Delaware	3	0.0%
					District of Columbia	83	0.4%

Source: U.S. Department of Health and Human Services, National Center for Health Statistics
"Morbidity and Mortality Weekly Report" (January 7, 2000, Vol. 48, No. 51)
*Provisional data. An inflammation of the liver. Includes types A and B.

Hepatitis (Viral) Rate in 1999

National Rate = 8.6 Cases per 100,000 Population*

ALPHA ORDER			RANK ORDER		
RANK	STATE	RATE	RANK	STATE	RATE
37	Alabama	3.2	1	Oklahoma	19.8
26	Alaska	5.0	2	Arizona	18.6
2	Arizona	18.6	3	Michigan	18.0
23	Arkansas	5.9	3	Missouri	18.0
6	California	14.1	5	Texas	17.8
16	Colorado	7.7	6	California	14.1
31	Connecticut	4.3	7	New Mexico	13.9
50	Delaware	0.4	8	Maryland	10.2
15	Florida	8.0	8	Oregon	10.2
14	Georgia	8.3	10	Nevada	9.9
38	Hawaii	3.0	11	Washington	9.7
20	Idaho	6.2	12	Mississippi	9.0
20	Illinois	6.2	13	Louisiana	8.5
43	Indiana	2.6	14	Georgia	8.3
17	Iowa	6.7	15	Florida	8.0
44	Kansas	2.5	16	Colorado	7.7
41	Kentucky	2.7	17	Iowa	6.7
13	Louisiana	8.5	17	Ohio	6.7
48	Maine	1.2	19	Tennessee	6.5
8	Maryland	10.2	20	Idaho	6.2
41	Massachusetts	2.7	20	Illinois	6.2
3	Michigan	18.0	22	Rhode Island	6.1
35	Minnesota	3.6	23	Arkansas	5.9
12	Mississippi	9.0	24	New York	5.4
3	Missouri	18.0	25	North Carolina	5.1
33	Montana	3.9	26	Alaska	5.0
27	Nebraska	4.9	27	Nebraska	4.9
10	Nevada	9.9	28	Utah	4.8
39	New Hampshire	2.9	29	Vermont	4.5
45	New Jersey	1.9	30	Wyoming	4.4
7	New Mexico	13.9	31	Connecticut	4.3
24	New York	5.4	32	Virginia	4.1
25	North Carolina	5.1	33	Montana	3.9
49	North Dakota	0.8	34	West Virginia	3.7
17	Ohio	6.7	35	Minnesota	3.6
1	Oklahoma	19.8	36	Pennsylvania	3.3
8	Oregon	10.2	37	Alabama	3.2
36	Pennsylvania	3.3	38	Hawaii	3.0
22	Rhode Island	6.1	39	New Hampshire	2.9
39	South Carolina	2.9	39	South Carolina	2.9
47	South Dakota	1.4	41	Kentucky	2.7
19	Tennessee	6.5	41	Massachusetts	2.7
5	Texas	17.8	43	Indiana	2.6
28	Utah	4.8	44	Kansas	2.5
29	Vermont	4.5	45	New Jersey	1.9
32	Virginia	4.1	46	Wisconsin	1.8
11	Washington	9.7	47	South Dakota	1.4
34	West Virginia	3.7	48	Maine	1.2
46	Wisconsin	1.8	49	North Dakota	0.8
30	Wyoming	4.4	50	Delaware	0.4
				District of Columbia	16.0

Source: Morgan Quitno Press using data from U.S. Dept. of Health & Human Serv's, National Center for Health Statistics "Morbidity and Mortality Weekly Report" (January 7, 2000, Vol. 48, No. 51)
*Provisional data. An inflammation of the liver. Includes types A and B.

Legionellosis Cases Reported in 1999

National Total = 956 Cases*

ALPHA ORDER

RANK	STATE	CASES	% of USA
34	Alabama	4	0.4%
41	Alaska	1	0.1%
30	Arizona	7	0.7%
43	Arkansas	0	0.0%
4	California	64	6.7%
20	Colorado	15	1.6%
20	Connecticut	15	1.6%
20	Delaware	15	1.6%
11	Florida	28	2.9%
36	Georgia	3	0.3%
43	Hawaii	0	0.0%
36	Idaho	3	0.3%
12	Illinois	27	2.8%
6	Indiana	46	4.8%
20	Iowa	15	1.6%
43	Kansas	0	0.0%
13	Kentucky	22	2.3%
34	Louisiana	4	0.4%
36	Maine	3	0.3%
9	Maryland	34	3.6%
10	Massachusetts	31	3.2%
5	Michigan	60	6.3%
26	Minnesota	13	1.4%
43	Mississippi	0	0.0%
18	Missouri	17	1.8%
43	Montana	0	0.0%
30	Nebraska	7	0.7%
32	Nevada	6	0.6%
29	New Hampshire	8	0.8%
16	New Jersey	18	1.9%
41	New Mexico	1	0.1%
3	New York	72	7.5%
20	North Carolina	15	1.6%
40	North Dakota	2	0.2%
2	Ohio	85	8.9%
33	Oklahoma	5	0.5%
NA	Oregon**	NA	NA
1	Pennsylvania	101	10.6%
27	Rhode Island	12	1.3%
27	South Carolina	12	1.3%
36	South Dakota	3	0.3%
13	Tennessee	22	2.3%
16	Texas	18	1.9%
15	Utah	19	2.0%
20	Vermont	15	1.6%
8	Virginia	40	4.2%
18	Washington	17	1.8%
NA	West Virginia**	NA	NA
6	Wisconsin	46	4.8%
43	Wyoming	0	0.0%

RANK ORDER

RANK	STATE	CASES	% of USA
1	Pennsylvania	101	10.6%
2	Ohio	85	8.9%
3	New York	72	7.5%
4	California	64	6.7%
5	Michigan	60	6.3%
6	Indiana	46	4.8%
6	Wisconsin	46	4.8%
8	Virginia	40	4.2%
9	Maryland	34	3.6%
10	Massachusetts	31	3.2%
11	Florida	28	2.9%
12	Illinois	27	2.8%
13	Kentucky	22	2.3%
13	Tennessee	22	2.3%
15	Utah	19	2.0%
16	New Jersey	18	1.9%
16	Texas	18	1.9%
18	Missouri	17	1.8%
18	Washington	17	1.8%
20	Colorado	15	1.6%
20	Connecticut	15	1.6%
20	Delaware	15	1.6%
20	Iowa	15	1.6%
20	North Carolina	15	1.6%
20	Vermont	15	1.6%
26	Minnesota	13	1.4%
27	Rhode Island	12	1.3%
27	South Carolina	12	1.3%
29	New Hampshire	8	0.8%
30	Arizona	7	0.7%
30	Nebraska	7	0.7%
32	Nevada	6	0.6%
33	Oklahoma	5	0.5%
34	Alabama	4	0.4%
34	Louisiana	4	0.4%
36	Georgia	3	0.3%
36	Idaho	3	0.3%
36	Maine	3	0.3%
36	South Dakota	3	0.3%
40	North Dakota	2	0.2%
41	Alaska	1	0.1%
41	New Mexico	1	0.1%
43	Arkansas	0	0.0%
43	Hawaii	0	0.0%
43	Kansas	0	0.0%
43	Mississippi	0	0.0%
43	Montana	0	0.0%
43	Wyoming	0	0.0%
NA	Oregon**	NA	NA
NA	West Virginia**	NA	NA
	District of Columbia	5	0.5%

Source: U.S. Department of Health and Human Services, National Center for Health Statistics
   "Morbidity and Mortality Weekly Report" (January 7, 2000, Vol. 48, No. 51)
*Provisional data. A pneumonia-like disease (Legionnaire's Disease).
**Not notifiable.

Legionellosis Rate in 1999

National Rate = 0.4 Cases per 100,000 Population*

ALPHA ORDER

RANK	STATE	RATE
36	Alabama	0.1
28	Alaska	0.2
36	Arizona	0.1
42	Arkansas	0.0
28	California	0.2
17	Colorado	0.4
14	Connecticut	0.5
2	Delaware	2.0
28	Florida	0.2
42	Georgia	0.0
42	Hawaii	0.0
28	Idaho	0.2
28	Illinois	0.2
6	Indiana	0.8
14	Iowa	0.5
42	Kansas	0.0
11	Kentucky	0.6
36	Louisiana	0.1
28	Maine	0.2
9	Maryland	0.7
14	Massachusetts	0.5
11	Michigan	0.6
22	Minnesota	0.3
42	Mississippi	0.0
22	Missouri	0.3
42	Montana	0.0
17	Nebraska	0.4
22	Nevada	0.3
9	New Hampshire	0.7
28	New Jersey	0.2
36	New Mexico	0.1
17	New York	0.4
28	North Carolina	0.2
22	North Dakota	0.3
6	Ohio	0.8
36	Oklahoma	0.1
NA	Oregon**	NA
6	Pennsylvania	0.8
3	Rhode Island	1.2
22	South Carolina	0.3
17	South Dakota	0.4
17	Tennessee	0.4
36	Texas	0.1
4	Utah	0.9
1	Vermont	2.5
11	Virginia	0.6
22	Washington	0.3
NA	West Virginia**	NA
4	Wisconsin	0.9
42	Wyoming	0.0

RANK ORDER

RANK	STATE	RATE
1	Vermont	2.5
2	Delaware	2.0
3	Rhode Island	1.2
4	Utah	0.9
4	Wisconsin	0.9
6	Indiana	0.8
6	Ohio	0.8
6	Pennsylvania	0.8
9	Maryland	0.7
9	New Hampshire	0.7
11	Kentucky	0.6
11	Michigan	0.6
11	Virginia	0.6
14	Connecticut	0.5
14	Iowa	0.5
14	Massachusetts	0.5
17	Colorado	0.4
17	Nebraska	0.4
17	New York	0.4
17	South Dakota	0.4
17	Tennessee	0.4
22	Minnesota	0.3
22	Missouri	0.3
22	Nevada	0.3
22	North Dakota	0.3
22	South Carolina	0.3
22	Washington	0.3
28	Alaska	0.2
28	California	0.2
28	Florida	0.2
28	Idaho	0.2
28	Illinois	0.2
28	Maine	0.2
28	New Jersey	0.2
28	North Carolina	0.2
36	Alabama	0.1
36	Arizona	0.1
36	Louisiana	0.1
36	New Mexico	0.1
36	Oklahoma	0.1
36	Texas	0.1
42	Arkansas	0.0
42	Georgia	0.0
42	Hawaii	0.0
42	Kansas	0.0
42	Mississippi	0.0
42	Montana	0.0
42	Wyoming	0.0
NA	Oregon**	NA
NA	West Virginia**	NA

District of Columbia 1.0

Source: Morgan Quitno Press using data from U.S. Dept. of Health & Human Serv's, National Center for Health Statistics "Morbidity and Mortality Weekly Report" (January 7, 2000, Vol. 48, No. 51)

Provisional data. A pneumonia-like disease (Legionnaire's Disease).

**Not notifiable.*

Lyme Disease Cases in 1999

National Total = 13,306 Cases*

ALPHA ORDER

RANK	STATE	CASES	% of USA
24	Alabama	19	0.1%
45	Alaska	0	0.0%
40	Arizona	2	0.0%
35	Arkansas	7	0.1%
9	California	141	1.1%
45	Colorado	0	0.0%
3	Connecticut	2,302	17.3%
14	Delaware	64	0.5%
15	Florida	57	0.4%
45	Georgia	0	0.0%
NA	Hawaii**	NA	NA
37	Idaho	5	0.0%
29	Illinois	12	0.1%
23	Indiana	21	0.2%
22	Iowa	22	0.2%
29	Kansas	12	0.1%
24	Kentucky	19	0.1%
31	Louisiana	11	0.1%
17	Maine	41	0.3%
6	Maryland	826	6.2%
4	Massachusetts	999	7.5%
42	Michigan	1	0.0%
8	Minnesota	253	1.9%
28	Mississippi	13	0.1%
19	Missouri	28	0.2%
45	Montana	0	0.0%
31	Nebraska	11	0.1%
40	Nevada	2	0.0%
20	New Hampshire	26	0.2%
5	New Jersey	966	7.3%
42	New Mexico	1	0.0%
1	New York	4,091	30.7%
13	North Carolina	74	0.6%
42	North Dakota	1	0.0%
12	Ohio	78	0.6%
34	Oklahoma	8	0.1%
27	Oregon	14	0.1%
2	Pennsylvania	2,312	17.4%
7	Rhode Island	464	3.5%
35	South Carolina	7	0.1%
45	South Dakota	0	0.0%
15	Tennessee	57	0.4%
18	Texas	35	0.3%
37	Utah	5	0.0%
21	Vermont	24	0.2%
10	Virginia	119	0.9%
31	Washington	11	0.1%
24	West Virginia	19	0.1%
11	Wisconsin	117	0.9%
39	Wyoming	3	0.0%

RANK ORDER

RANK	STATE	CASES	% of USA
1	New York	4,091	30.7%
2	Pennsylvania	2,312	17.4%
3	Connecticut	2,302	17.3%
4	Massachusetts	999	7.5%
5	New Jersey	966	7.3%
6	Maryland	826	6.2%
7	Rhode Island	464	3.5%
8	Minnesota	253	1.9%
9	California	141	1.1%
10	Virginia	119	0.9%
11	Wisconsin	117	0.9%
12	Ohio	78	0.6%
13	North Carolina	74	0.6%
14	Delaware	64	0.5%
15	Florida	57	0.4%
15	Tennessee	57	0.4%
17	Maine	41	0.3%
18	Texas	35	0.3%
19	Missouri	28	0.2%
20	New Hampshire	26	0.2%
21	Vermont	24	0.2%
22	Iowa	22	0.2%
23	Indiana	21	0.2%
24	Alabama	19	0.1%
24	Kentucky	19	0.1%
24	West Virginia	19	0.1%
27	Oregon	14	0.1%
28	Mississippi	13	0.1%
29	Illinois	12	0.1%
29	Kansas	12	0.1%
31	Louisiana	11	0.1%
31	Nebraska	11	0.1%
31	Washington	11	0.1%
34	Oklahoma	8	0.1%
35	Arkansas	7	0.1%
35	South Carolina	7	0.1%
37	Idaho	5	0.0%
37	Utah	5	0.0%
39	Wyoming	3	0.0%
40	Arizona	2	0.0%
40	Nevada	2	0.0%
42	Michigan	1	0.0%
42	New Mexico	1	0.0%
42	North Dakota	1	0.0%
45	Alaska	0	0.0%
45	Colorado	0	0.0%
45	Georgia	0	0.0%
45	Montana	0	0.0%
45	South Dakota	0	0.0%
NA	Hawaii**	NA	NA
	District of Columbia	6	0.0%

Source: U.S. Department of Health and Human Services, National Center for Health Statistics
  "Morbidity and Mortality Weekly Report" (January 7, 2000, Vol. 48, No. 51)
*Provisional data. Caused by ticks-lesions, followed by arthritis of large joints, myalgia, malaise and neurologic and cardiac manifestations. Named after Old Lyme, CT, where the disease was first reported.
**Not notifiable.

Lyme Disease Rate in 1999

National Rate = 4.9 Cases per 100,000 Population*

ALPHA ORDER				RANK ORDER		
RANK	STATE	RATE		RANK	STATE	RATE
26	Alabama	0.4		1	Connecticut	70.1
43	Alaska	0.0		2	Rhode Island	46.8
43	Arizona	0.0		3	New York	22.5
32	Arkansas	0.3		4	Pennsylvania	19.3
26	California	0.4		5	Massachusetts	16.2
43	Colorado	0.0		6	Maryland	16.0
1	Connecticut	70.1		7	New Jersey	11.9
8	Delaware	8.5		8	Delaware	8.5
26	Florida	0.4		9	Minnesota	5.3
43	Georgia	0.0		10	Vermont	4.0
NA	Hawaii**	NA		11	Maine	3.3
26	Idaho	0.4		12	New Hampshire	2.2
40	Illinois	0.1		12	Wisconsin	2.2
26	Indiana	0.4		14	Virginia	1.7
18	Iowa	0.8		15	West Virginia	1.1
22	Kansas	0.5		16	North Carolina	1.0
22	Kentucky	0.5		16	Tennessee	1.0
32	Louisiana	0.3		18	Iowa	0.8
11	Maine	3.3		19	Nebraska	0.7
6	Maryland	16.0		19	Ohio	0.7
5	Massachusetts	16.2		21	Wyoming	0.6
43	Michigan	0.0		22	Kansas	0.5
9	Minnesota	5.3		22	Kentucky	0.5
22	Mississippi	0.5		22	Mississippi	0.5
22	Missouri	0.5		22	Missouri	0.5
43	Montana	0.0		26	Alabama	0.4
19	Nebraska	0.7		26	California	0.4
40	Nevada	0.1		26	Florida	0.4
12	New Hampshire	2.2		26	Idaho	0.4
7	New Jersey	11.9		26	Indiana	0.4
40	New Mexico	0.1		26	Oregon	0.4
3	New York	22.5		32	Arkansas	0.3
16	North Carolina	1.0		32	Louisiana	0.3
34	North Dakota	0.2		34	North Dakota	0.2
19	Ohio	0.7		34	Oklahoma	0.2
34	Oklahoma	0.2		34	South Carolina	0.2
26	Oregon	0.4		34	Texas	0.2
4	Pennsylvania	19.3		34	Utah	0.2
2	Rhode Island	46.8		34	Washington	0.2
34	South Carolina	0.2		40	Illinois	0.1
43	South Dakota	0.0		40	Nevada	0.1
16	Tennessee	1.0		40	New Mexico	0.1
34	Texas	0.2		43	Alaska	0.0
34	Utah	0.2		43	Arizona	0.0
10	Vermont	4.0		43	Colorado	0.0
14	Virginia	1.7		43	Georgia	0.0
34	Washington	0.2		43	Michigan	0.0
15	West Virginia	1.1		43	Montana	0.0
12	Wisconsin	2.2		43	South Dakota	0.0
21	Wyoming	0.6		NA	Hawaii**	NA

District of Columbia	1.2

Source: Morgan Quitno Press using data from U.S. Dept. of Health & Human Serv's, National Center for Health Statistics
"Morbidity and Mortality Weekly Report" (January 7, 2000, Vol. 48, No. 51)
*Provisional data. Caused by ticks-lesions, followed by arthritis of large joints, myalgia, malaise and neurologic and cardiac manifestations. Named after Old Lyme, CT, where the disease was first reported.
**Not notifiable.

Malaria Cases Reported in 1999

National Total = 1,354 Cases*

ALPHA ORDER

RANK	STATE	CASES	% of USA
28	Alabama	7	0.5%
44	Alaska	1	0.1%
26	Arizona	9	0.7%
38	Arkansas	3	0.2%
2	California	208	15.4%
19	Colorado	17	1.3%
14	Connecticut	28	2.1%
44	Delaware	1	0.1%
4	Florida	83	6.1%
13	Georgia	29	2.1%
23	Hawaii	12	0.9%
38	Idaho	3	0.2%
6	Illinois	61	4.5%
16	Indiana	21	1.6%
22	Iowa	13	1.0%
32	Kansas	4	0.3%
28	Kentucky	7	0.5%
25	Louisiana	11	0.8%
38	Maine	3	0.2%
3	Maryland	100	7.4%
15	Massachusetts	24	1.8%
9	Michigan	42	3.1%
8	Minnesota	47	3.5%
32	Mississippi	4	0.3%
21	Missouri	15	1.1%
32	Montana	4	0.3%
44	Nebraska	1	0.1%
32	Nevada	4	0.3%
41	New Hampshire	2	0.1%
7	New Jersey	48	3.5%
41	New Mexico	2	0.1%
1	New York	243	17.9%
11	North Carolina	36	2.7%
49	North Dakota	0	0.0%
18	Ohio	18	1.3%
41	Oklahoma	2	0.1%
16	Oregon	21	1.6%
10	Pennsylvania	38	2.8%
30	Rhode Island	5	0.4%
19	South Carolina	17	1.3%
49	South Dakota	0	0.0%
26	Tennessee	9	0.7%
44	Texas	1	0.1%
32	Utah	4	0.3%
30	Vermont	5	0.4%
5	Virginia	73	5.4%
12	Washington	33	2.4%
32	West Virginia	4	0.3%
23	Wisconsin	12	0.9%
44	Wyoming	1	0.1%

RANK ORDER

RANK	STATE	CASES	% of USA
1	New York	243	17.9%
2	California	208	15.4%
3	Maryland	100	7.4%
4	Florida	83	6.1%
5	Virginia	73	5.4%
6	Illinois	61	4.5%
7	New Jersey	48	3.5%
8	Minnesota	47	3.5%
9	Michigan	42	3.1%
10	Pennsylvania	38	2.8%
11	North Carolina	36	2.7%
12	Washington	33	2.4%
13	Georgia	29	2.1%
14	Connecticut	28	2.1%
15	Massachusetts	24	1.8%
16	Indiana	21	1.6%
16	Oregon	21	1.6%
18	Ohio	18	1.3%
19	Colorado	17	1.3%
19	South Carolina	17	1.3%
21	Missouri	15	1.1%
22	Iowa	13	1.0%
23	Hawaii	12	0.9%
23	Wisconsin	12	0.9%
25	Louisiana	11	0.8%
26	Arizona	9	0.7%
26	Tennessee	9	0.7%
28	Alabama	7	0.5%
28	Kentucky	7	0.5%
30	Rhode Island	5	0.4%
30	Vermont	5	0.4%
32	Kansas	4	0.3%
32	Mississippi	4	0.3%
32	Montana	4	0.3%
32	Nevada	4	0.3%
32	Utah	4	0.3%
32	West Virginia	4	0.3%
38	Arkansas	3	0.2%
38	Idaho	3	0.2%
38	Maine	3	0.2%
41	New Hampshire	2	0.1%
41	New Mexico	2	0.1%
41	Oklahoma	2	0.1%
44	Alaska	1	0.1%
44	Delaware	1	0.1%
44	Nebraska	1	0.1%
44	Texas	1	0.1%
44	Wyoming	1	0.1%
49	North Dakota	0	0.0%
49	South Dakota	0	0.0%
	District of Columbia	18	1.3%

Source: U.S. Department of Health and Human Services, National Center for Health Statistics
    "Morbidity and Mortality Weekly Report" (January 7, 2000, Vol. 48, No. 51)
*Provisional data. Infectious disease usually transmitted by bites of infected mosquitoes. Symptoms include high fever, shaking chills, sweating and anemia.

Malaria Rate in 1999

National Rate = 0.5 Cases per 100,000 Population*

ALPHA ORDER

RANK	STATE	RATE
27	Alabama	0.2
27	Alaska	0.2
27	Arizona	0.2
42	Arkansas	0.1
8	California	0.6
18	Colorado	0.4
6	Connecticut	0.9
42	Delaware	0.1
12	Florida	0.5
18	Georgia	0.4
4	Hawaii	1.0
27	Idaho	0.2
12	Illinois	0.5
18	Indiana	0.4
12	Iowa	0.5
27	Kansas	0.2
27	Kentucky	0.2
24	Louisiana	0.3
27	Maine	0.2
1	Maryland	1.9
18	Massachusetts	0.4
18	Michigan	0.4
4	Minnesota	1.0
42	Mississippi	0.1
24	Missouri	0.3
12	Montana	0.5
42	Nebraska	0.1
27	Nevada	0.2
27	New Hampshire	0.2
8	New Jersey	0.6
42	New Mexico	0.1
2	New York	1.3
12	North Carolina	0.5
48	North Dakota	0.0
27	Ohio	0.2
42	Oklahoma	0.1
8	Oregon	0.6
24	Pennsylvania	0.3
12	Rhode Island	0.5
18	South Carolina	0.4
48	South Dakota	0.0
27	Tennessee	0.2
48	Texas	0.0
27	Utah	0.2
7	Vermont	0.8
3	Virginia	1.1
8	Washington	0.6
27	West Virginia	0.2
27	Wisconsin	0.2
27	Wyoming	0.2

RANK ORDER

RANK	STATE	RATE
1	Maryland	1.9
2	New York	1.3
3	Virginia	1.1
4	Hawaii	1.0
4	Minnesota	1.0
6	Connecticut	0.9
7	Vermont	0.8
8	California	0.6
8	New Jersey	0.6
8	Oregon	0.6
8	Washington	0.6
12	Florida	0.5
12	Illinois	0.5
12	Iowa	0.5
12	Montana	0.5
12	North Carolina	0.5
12	Rhode Island	0.5
18	Colorado	0.4
18	Georgia	0.4
18	Indiana	0.4
18	Massachusetts	0.4
18	Michigan	0.4
18	South Carolina	0.4
24	Louisiana	0.3
24	Missouri	0.3
24	Pennsylvania	0.3
27	Alabama	0.2
27	Alaska	0.2
27	Arizona	0.2
27	Idaho	0.2
27	Kansas	0.2
27	Kentucky	0.2
27	Maine	0.2
27	Nevada	0.2
27	New Hampshire	0.2
27	Ohio	0.2
27	Tennessee	0.2
27	Utah	0.2
27	West Virginia	0.2
27	Wisconsin	0.2
27	Wyoming	0.2
42	Arkansas	0.1
42	Delaware	0.1
42	Mississippi	0.1
42	Nebraska	0.1
42	New Mexico	0.1
42	Oklahoma	0.1
48	North Dakota	0.0
48	South Dakota	0.0
48	Texas	0.0

District of Columbia   3.5

Source: Morgan Quitno Press using data from U.S. Dept. of Health & Human Serv's, National Center for Health Statistics
"Morbidity and Mortality Weekly Report" (January 7, 2000, Vol. 48, No. 51)
*Provisional data. Infectious disease usually transmitted by bites of infected mosquitoes. Symptoms include high fever, shaking chills, sweating and anemia.

Measles (Rubeola) Cases Reported in 1999

National Total = 87 Cases*

ALPHA ORDER

RANK ORDER

RANK	STATE	CASES	% of USA		RANK	STATE	CASES	% of USA
19	Alabama	0	0.0%		1	Virginia	18	20.7%
19	Alaska	0	0.0%		2	California	17	19.5%
15	Arizona	1	1.1%		3	Oregon	9	10.3%
6	Arkansas	5	5.7%		3	Texas	9	10.3%
2	California	17	19.5%		5	Massachusetts	8	9.2%
19	Colorado	0	0.0%		6	Arkansas	5	5.7%
8	Connecticut	2	2.3%		7	Michigan	3	3.4%
19	Delaware	0	0.0%		8	Connecticut	2	2.3%
8	Florida	2	2.3%		8	Florida	2	2.3%
19	Georgia	0	0.0%		8	Hawaii	2	2.3%
8	Hawaii	2	2.3%		8	Indiana	2	2.3%
19	Idaho	0	0.0%		8	Kentucky	2	2.3%
19	Illinois	0	0.0%		8	New York	2	2.3%
8	Indiana	2	2.3%		8	Utah	2	2.3%
19	Iowa	0	0.0%		15	Arizona	1	1.1%
19	Kansas	0	0.0%		15	Minnesota	1	1.1%
8	Kentucky	2	2.3%		15	Nevada	1	1.1%
19	Louisiana	0	0.0%		15	New Hampshire	1	1.1%
19	Maine	0	0.0%		19	Alabama	0	0.0%
19	Maryland	0	0.0%		19	Alaska	0	0.0%
5	Massachusetts	8	9.2%		19	Colorado	0	0.0%
7	Michigan	3	3.4%		19	Delaware	0	0.0%
15	Minnesota	1	1.1%		19	Georgia	0	0.0%
19	Mississippi	0	0.0%		19	Idaho	0	0.0%
19	Missouri	0	0.0%		19	Illinois	0	0.0%
19	Montana	0	0.0%		19	Iowa	0	0.0%
19	Nebraska	0	0.0%		19	Kansas	0	0.0%
15	Nevada	1	1.1%		19	Louisiana	0	0.0%
15	New Hampshire	1	1.1%		19	Maine	0	0.0%
19	New Jersey	0	0.0%		19	Maryland	0	0.0%
19	New Mexico	0	0.0%		19	Mississippi	0	0.0%
8	New York	2	2.3%		19	Missouri	0	0.0%
19	North Carolina	0	0.0%		19	Montana	0	0.0%
19	North Dakota	0	0.0%		19	Nebraska	0	0.0%
19	Ohio	0	0.0%		19	New Jersey	0	0.0%
19	Oklahoma	0	0.0%		19	New Mexico	0	0.0%
3	Oregon	9	10.3%		19	North Carolina	0	0.0%
19	Pennsylvania	0	0.0%		19	North Dakota	0	0.0%
19	Rhode Island	0	0.0%		19	Ohio	0	0.0%
19	South Carolina	0	0.0%		19	Oklahoma	0	0.0%
19	South Dakota	0	0.0%		19	Pennsylvania	0	0.0%
19	Tennessee	0	0.0%		19	Rhode Island	0	0.0%
3	Texas	9	10.3%		19	South Carolina	0	0.0%
8	Utah	2	2.3%		19	South Dakota	0	0.0%
19	Vermont	0	0.0%		19	Tennessee	0	0.0%
1	Virginia	18	20.7%		19	Vermont	0	0.0%
19	Washington	0	0.0%		19	Washington	0	0.0%
19	West Virginia	0	0.0%		19	West Virginia	0	0.0%
19	Wisconsin	0	0.0%		19	Wisconsin	0	0.0%
19	Wyoming	0	0.0%		19	Wyoming	0	0.0%
						District of Columbia	0	0.0%

Source: U.S. Department of Health and Human Services, National Center for Health Statistics
"Morbidity and Mortality Weekly Report" (January 7, 2000, Vol. 48, No. 51)
*Provisional data. Includes indigenous and imported cases.

Measles (Rubeola) Rate in 1999

National Rate = 0.03 Cases per 100,000 Population*

ALPHA ORDER				RANK ORDER		
RANK	STATE	RATE		RANK	STATE	RATE
19	Alabama	0.00		1	Oregon	0.27
19	Alaska	0.00		2	Virginia	0.26
15	Arizona	0.02		3	Arkansas	0.20
3	Arkansas	0.20		4	Hawaii	0.17
10	California	0.05		5	Massachusetts	0.13
19	Colorado	0.00		6	Utah	0.09
8	Connecticut	0.06		7	New Hampshire	0.08
19	Delaware	0.00		8	Connecticut	0.06
17	Florida	0.01		8	Nevada	0.06
19	Georgia	0.00		10	California	0.05
4	Hawaii	0.17		10	Kentucky	0.05
19	Idaho	0.00		12	Texas	0.04
19	Illinois	0.00		13	Indiana	0.03
13	Indiana	0.03		13	Michigan	0.03
19	Iowa	0.00		15	Arizona	0.02
19	Kansas	0.00		15	Minnesota	0.02
10	Kentucky	0.05		17	Florida	0.01
19	Louisiana	0.00		17	New York	0.01
19	Maine	0.00		19	Alabama	0.00
19	Maryland	0.00		19	Alaska	0.00
5	Massachusetts	0.13		19	Colorado	0.00
13	Michigan	0.03		19	Delaware	0.00
15	Minnesota	0.02		19	Georgia	0.00
19	Mississippi	0.00		19	Idaho	0.00
19	Missouri	0.00		19	Illinois	0.00
19	Montana	0.00		19	Iowa	0.00
19	Nebraska	0.00		19	Kansas	0.00
8	Nevada	0.06		19	Louisiana	0.00
7	New Hampshire	0.08		19	Maine	0.00
19	New Jersey	0.00		19	Maryland	0.00
19	New Mexico	0.00		19	Mississippi	0.00
17	New York	0.01		19	Missouri	0.00
19	North Carolina	0.00		19	Montana	0.00
19	North Dakota	0.00		19	Nebraska	0.00
19	Ohio	0.00		19	New Jersey	0.00
19	Oklahoma	0.00		19	New Mexico	0.00
1	Oregon	0.27		19	North Carolina	0.00
19	Pennsylvania	0.00		19	North Dakota	0.00
19	Rhode Island	0.00		19	Ohio	0.00
19	South Carolina	0.00		19	Oklahoma	0.00
19	South Dakota	0.00		19	Pennsylvania	0.00
19	Tennessee	0.00		19	Rhode Island	0.00
12	Texas	0.04		19	South Carolina	0.00
6	Utah	0.09		19	South Dakota	0.00
19	Vermont	0.00		19	Tennessee	0.00
2	Virginia	0.26		19	Vermont	0.00
19	Washington	0.00		19	Washington	0.00
19	West Virginia	0.00		19	West Virginia	0.00
19	Wisconsin	0.00		19	Wisconsin	0.00
19	Wyoming	0.00		19	Wyoming	0.00
					District of Columbia	0.00

Source: Morgan Quitno Press using data from U.S. Dept. of Health & Human Serv's, National Center for Health Statistics "Morbidity and Mortality Weekly Report" (January 7, 2000, Vol. 48, No. 51)
Provisional data. Includes indigenous and imported cases.

Meningococcal Infections Reported in 1999

National Total = 2,352 Cases*

<u>ALPHA ORDER</u>

RANK	STATE	CASES	% of USA
30	Alabama	32	1.4%
44	Alaska	7	0.3%
24	Arizona	43	1.8%
28	Arkansas	35	1.5%
1	California	287	12.2%
26	Colorado	39	1.7%
33	Connecticut	17	0.7%
42	Delaware	8	0.3%
2	Florida	137	5.8%
11	Georgia	66	2.8%
40	Hawaii	9	0.4%
36	Idaho	15	0.6%
6	Illinois	101	4.3%
10	Indiana	70	3.0%
22	Iowa	45	1.9%
32	Kansas	18	0.8%
29	Kentucky	34	1.4%
14	Louisiana	58	2.5%
46	Maine	5	0.2%
15	Maryland	57	2.4%
11	Massachusetts	66	2.8%
19	Michigan	47	2.0%
17	Minnesota	54	2.3%
31	Mississippi	24	1.0%
5	Missouri	103	4.4%
49	Montana	4	0.2%
37	Nebraska	13	0.6%
42	Nevada	8	0.3%
37	New Hampshire	13	0.6%
18	New Jersey	49	2.1%
34	New Mexico	16	0.7%
4	New York	121	5.1%
19	North Carolina	47	2.0%
49	North Dakota	4	0.2%
3	Ohio	132	5.6%
27	Oklahoma	36	1.5%
7	Oregon	77	3.3%
23	Pennsylvania	44	1.9%
44	Rhode Island	7	0.3%
21	South Carolina	46	2.0%
39	South Dakota	11	0.5%
13	Tennessee	64	2.7%
9	Texas	74	3.1%
34	Utah	16	0.7%
46	Vermont	5	0.2%
16	Virginia	56	2.4%
8	Washington	75	3.2%
40	West Virginia	9	0.4%
25	Wisconsin	41	1.7%
46	Wyoming	5	0.2%

<u>RANK ORDER</u>

RANK	STATE	CASES	% of USA
1	California	287	12.2%
2	Florida	137	5.8%
3	Ohio	132	5.6%
4	New York	121	5.1%
5	Missouri	103	4.4%
6	Illinois	101	4.3%
7	Oregon	77	3.3%
8	Washington	75	3.2%
9	Texas	74	3.1%
10	Indiana	70	3.0%
11	Georgia	66	2.8%
11	Massachusetts	66	2.8%
13	Tennessee	64	2.7%
14	Louisiana	58	2.5%
15	Maryland	57	2.4%
16	Virginia	56	2.4%
17	Minnesota	54	2.3%
18	New Jersey	49	2.1%
19	Michigan	47	2.0%
19	North Carolina	47	2.0%
21	South Carolina	46	2.0%
22	Iowa	45	1.9%
23	Pennsylvania	44	1.9%
24	Arizona	43	1.8%
25	Wisconsin	41	1.7%
26	Colorado	39	1.7%
27	Oklahoma	36	1.5%
28	Arkansas	35	1.5%
29	Kentucky	34	1.4%
30	Alabama	32	1.4%
31	Mississippi	24	1.0%
32	Kansas	18	0.8%
33	Connecticut	17	0.7%
34	New Mexico	16	0.7%
34	Utah	16	0.7%
36	Idaho	15	0.6%
37	Nebraska	13	0.6%
37	New Hampshire	13	0.6%
39	South Dakota	11	0.5%
40	Hawaii	9	0.4%
40	West Virginia	9	0.4%
42	Delaware	8	0.3%
42	Nevada	8	0.3%
44	Alaska	7	0.3%
44	Rhode Island	7	0.3%
46	Maine	5	0.2%
46	Vermont	5	0.2%
46	Wyoming	5	0.2%
49	Montana	4	0.2%
49	North Dakota	4	0.2%
	District of Columbia	2	0.1%

Source: U.S. Department of Health and Human Services, National Center for Health Statistics
"Morbidity and Mortality Weekly Report" (January 7, 2000, Vol. 48, No. 51)
*Provisional data. A bacterium (Neisseria meningitidis) that causes cerebrospinal meningitis.

Meningococcal Infection Rate in 1999

National Rate = 0.9 Cases per 100,000 Population*

ALPHA ORDER

RANK	STATE	RATE
36	Alabama	0.7
13	Alaska	1.1
22	Arizona	0.9
5	Arkansas	1.4
22	California	0.9
20	Colorado	1.0
43	Connecticut	0.5
13	Delaware	1.1
22	Florida	0.9
28	Georgia	0.8
28	Hawaii	0.8
8	Idaho	1.2
28	Illinois	0.8
8	Indiana	1.2
3	Iowa	1.6
36	Kansas	0.7
22	Kentucky	0.9
6	Louisiana	1.3
47	Maine	0.4
13	Maryland	1.1
13	Massachusetts	1.1
43	Michigan	0.5
13	Minnesota	1.1
22	Mississippi	0.9
2	Missouri	1.9
43	Montana	0.5
28	Nebraska	0.8
47	Nevada	0.4
13	New Hampshire	1.1
40	New Jersey	0.6
22	New Mexico	0.9
36	New York	0.7
40	North Carolina	0.6
40	North Dakota	0.6
8	Ohio	1.2
13	Oklahoma	1.1
1	Oregon	2.3
47	Pennsylvania	0.4
36	Rhode Island	0.7
8	South Carolina	1.2
4	South Dakota	1.5
8	Tennessee	1.2
47	Texas	0.4
28	Utah	0.8
28	Vermont	0.8
28	Virginia	0.8
6	Washington	1.3
43	West Virginia	0.5
28	Wisconsin	0.8
20	Wyoming	1.0

RANK ORDER

RANK	STATE	RATE
1	Oregon	2.3
2	Missouri	1.9
3	Iowa	1.6
4	South Dakota	1.5
5	Arkansas	1.4
6	Louisiana	1.3
6	Washington	1.3
8	Idaho	1.2
8	Indiana	1.2
8	Ohio	1.2
8	South Carolina	1.2
8	Tennessee	1.2
13	Alaska	1.1
13	Delaware	1.1
13	Maryland	1.1
13	Massachusetts	1.1
13	Minnesota	1.1
13	New Hampshire	1.1
13	Oklahoma	1.1
20	Colorado	1.0
20	Wyoming	1.0
22	Arizona	0.9
22	California	0.9
22	Florida	0.9
22	Kentucky	0.9
22	Mississippi	0.9
22	New Mexico	0.9
28	Georgia	0.8
28	Hawaii	0.8
28	Illinois	0.8
28	Nebraska	0.8
28	Utah	0.8
28	Vermont	0.8
28	Virginia	0.8
28	Wisconsin	0.8
36	Alabama	0.7
36	Kansas	0.7
36	New York	0.7
36	Rhode Island	0.7
40	New Jersey	0.6
40	North Carolina	0.6
40	North Dakota	0.6
43	Connecticut	0.5
43	Michigan	0.5
43	Montana	0.5
43	West Virginia	0.5
47	Maine	0.4
47	Nevada	0.4
47	Pennsylvania	0.4
47	Texas	0.4
	District of Columbia	0.4

Source: Morgan Quitno Press using data from U.S. Dept. of Health & Human Serv's, National Center for Health Statistics
"Morbidity and Mortality Weekly Report" (January 7, 2000, Vol. 48, No. 51)
*Provisional data. A bacterium (Neisseria meningitidis) that causes cerebrospinal meningitis.

Mumps Cases Reported in 1999

National Total = 352 Cases*

ALPHA ORDER				RANK ORDER			
RANK	STATE	CASES	% of USA	RANK	STATE	CASES	% of USA
9	Alabama	11	3.1%	1	California	90	25.6%
25	Alaska	3	0.9%	2	Texas	29	8.2%
13	Arizona	8	2.3%	3	Ohio	21	6.0%
37	Arkansas	0	0.0%	4	Pennsylvania	19	5.4%
1	California	90	25.6%	5	New York	17	4.8%
19	Colorado	5	1.4%	6	Florida	16	4.5%
37	Connecticut	0	0.0%	7	Hawaii	13	3.7%
37	Delaware	0	0.0%	7	Illinois	13	3.7%
6	Florida	16	4.5%	9	Alabama	11	3.1%
22	Georgia	4	1.1%	9	Louisiana	11	3.1%
7	Hawaii	13	3.7%	11	Virginia	10	2.8%
22	Idaho	4	1.1%	12	North Carolina	9	2.6%
7	Illinois	13	3.7%	13	Arizona	8	2.3%
19	Indiana	5	1.4%	13	Iowa	8	2.3%
13	Iowa	8	2.3%	15	Maryland	7	2.0%
25	Kansas	3	0.9%	15	Michigan	7	2.0%
37	Kentucky	0	0.0%	15	Utah	7	2.0%
9	Louisiana	11	3.1%	18	South Carolina	6	1.7%
37	Maine	0	0.0%	19	Colorado	5	1.4%
15	Maryland	7	2.0%	19	Indiana	5	1.4%
22	Massachusetts	4	1.1%	19	Nevada	5	1.4%
15	Michigan	7	2.0%	22	Georgia	4	1.1%
31	Minnesota	1	0.3%	22	Idaho	4	1.1%
25	Mississippi	3	0.9%	22	Massachusetts	4	1.1%
31	Missouri	1	0.3%	25	Alaska	3	0.9%
37	Montana	0	0.0%	25	Kansas	3	0.9%
37	Nebraska	0	0.0%	25	Mississippi	3	0.9%
19	Nevada	5	1.4%	28	Rhode Island	2	0.6%
31	New Hampshire	1	0.3%	28	Washington	2	0.6%
37	New Jersey	0	0.0%	28	Wisconsin	2	0.6%
NA	New Mexico**	NA	NA	31	Minnesota	1	0.3%
5	New York	17	4.8%	31	Missouri	1	0.3%
12	North Carolina	9	2.6%	31	New Hampshire	1	0.3%
31	North Dakota	1	0.3%	31	North Dakota	1	0.3%
3	Ohio	21	6.0%	31	Oklahoma	1	0.3%
31	Oklahoma	1	0.3%	31	Vermont	1	0.3%
NA	Oregon**	NA	NA	37	Arkansas	0	0.0%
4	Pennsylvania	19	5.4%	37	Connecticut	0	0.0%
28	Rhode Island	2	0.6%	37	Delaware	0	0.0%
18	South Carolina	6	1.7%	37	Kentucky	0	0.0%
37	South Dakota	0	0.0%	37	Maine	0	0.0%
37	Tennessee	0	0.0%	37	Montana	0	0.0%
2	Texas	29	8.2%	37	Nebraska	0	0.0%
15	Utah	7	2.0%	37	New Jersey	0	0.0%
31	Vermont	1	0.3%	37	South Dakota	0	0.0%
11	Virginia	10	2.8%	37	Tennessee	0	0.0%
28	Washington	2	0.6%	37	West Virginia	0	0.0%
37	West Virginia	0	0.0%	37	Wyoming	0	0.0%
28	Wisconsin	2	0.6%	NA	New Mexico**	NA	NA
37	Wyoming	0	0.0%	NA	Oregon**	NA	NA
					District of Columbia	2	0.6%

Source: U.S. Department of Health and Human Services, National Center for Health Statistics
  "Morbidity and Mortality Weekly Report" (January 7, 2000, Vol. 48, No. 51)
*Provisional data. An acute, inflammatory, contagious disease caused by a paramyxovirus and characterized by swelling of the salivary glands, especially the parotids, and sometimes of the pancreas, ovaries, or testes. This disease, mainly affecting children, can be prevented by vaccination.
**Mumps is not a notifiable disease in New Mexico or Oregon.

Mumps Rate in 1999

National Rate = 0.13 Cases per 100,000 Population*

RANK	STATE	RATE
8	Alabama	0.25
2	Alaska	0.48
12	Arizona	0.17
37	Arkansas	0.00
7	California	0.27
20	Colorado	0.12
37	Connecticut	0.00
37	Delaware	0.00
22	Florida	0.11
31	Georgia	0.05
1	Hawaii	1.10
4	Idaho	0.32
22	Illinois	0.11
27	Indiana	0.08
5	Iowa	0.28
22	Kansas	0.11
37	Kentucky	0.00
8	Louisiana	0.25
37	Maine	0.00
18	Maryland	0.14
30	Massachusetts	0.06
29	Michigan	0.07
35	Minnesota	0.02
22	Mississippi	0.11
35	Missouri	0.02
37	Montana	0.00
37	Nebraska	0.00
5	Nevada	0.28
27	New Hampshire	0.08
37	New Jersey	0.00
NA	New Mexico**	NA
26	New York	0.09
20	North Carolina	0.12
14	North Dakota	0.16
11	Ohio	0.19
33	Oklahoma	0.03
NA	Oregon**	NA
14	Pennsylvania	0.16
10	Rhode Island	0.20
16	South Carolina	0.15
37	South Dakota	0.00
37	Tennessee	0.00
18	Texas	0.14
3	Utah	0.33
12	Vermont	0.17
16	Virginia	0.15
33	Washington	0.03
37	West Virginia	0.00
32	Wisconsin	0.04
37	Wyoming	0.00

RANK	STATE	RATE
1	Hawaii	1.10
2	Alaska	0.48
3	Utah	0.33
4	Idaho	0.32
5	Iowa	0.28
5	Nevada	0.28
7	California	0.27
8	Alabama	0.25
8	Louisiana	0.25
10	Rhode Island	0.20
11	Ohio	0.19
12	Arizona	0.17
12	Vermont	0.17
14	North Dakota	0.16
14	Pennsylvania	0.16
16	South Carolina	0.15
16	Virginia	0.15
18	Maryland	0.14
18	Texas	0.14
20	Colorado	0.12
20	North Carolina	0.12
22	Florida	0.11
22	Illinois	0.11
22	Kansas	0.11
22	Mississippi	0.11
26	New York	0.09
27	Indiana	0.08
27	New Hampshire	0.08
29	Michigan	0.07
30	Massachusetts	0.06
31	Georgia	0.05
32	Wisconsin	0.04
33	Oklahoma	0.03
33	Washington	0.03
35	Minnesota	0.02
35	Missouri	0.02
37	Arkansas	0.00
37	Connecticut	0.00
37	Delaware	0.00
37	Kentucky	0.00
37	Maine	0.00
37	Montana	0.00
37	Nebraska	0.00
37	New Jersey	0.00
37	South Dakota	0.00
37	Tennessee	0.00
37	West Virginia	0.00
37	Wyoming	0.00
NA	New Mexico**	NA
NA	Oregon**	NA
	District of Columbia	0.39

Source: Morgan Quitno Press using data from U.S. Dept. of Health & Human Serv's, National Center for Health Statistics "Morbidity and Mortality Weekly Report" (January 7, 2000, Vol. 48, No. 51)

*Provisional data. An acute, inflammatory, contagious disease caused by a paramyxovirus and characterized by swelling of the salivary glands, especially the parotids, and sometimes of the pancreas, ovaries, or testes. This disease, mainly affecting children, can be prevented by vaccination.

**Mumps is not a notifiable disease in New Mexico or Oregon.

Rabies (Animal) Cases Reported in 1999

National Total = 5,844 Cases*

ALPHA ORDER

RANK	STATE	CASES	% of USA
17	Alabama	125	2.1%
39	Alaska	7	0.1%
26	Arizona	66	1.1%
34	Arkansas	14	0.2%
5	California	324	5.5%
44	Colorado	1	0.0%
6	Connecticut	253	4.3%
30	Delaware	43	0.7%
9	Florida	185	3.2%
7	Georgia	241	4.1%
46	Hawaii	0	0.0%
40	Idaho	5	0.1%
36	Illinois	10	0.2%
35	Indiana	13	0.2%
13	Iowa	162	2.8%
24	Kansas	87	1.5%
32	Kentucky	35	0.6%
46	Louisiana	0	0.0%
11	Maine	171	2.9%
4	Maryland	395	6.8%
8	Massachusetts	223	3.8%
24	Michigan	87	1.5%
18	Minnesota	115	2.0%
44	Mississippi	1	0.0%
33	Missouri	15	0.3%
27	Montana	59	1.0%
42	Nebraska	3	0.1%
40	Nevada	5	0.1%
28	New Hampshire	50	0.9%
10	New Jersey	173	3.0%
37	New Mexico	9	0.2%
1	New York	812	13.9%
3	North Carolina	413	7.1%
15	North Dakota	139	2.4%
31	Ohio	36	0.6%
22	Oklahoma	93	1.6%
43	Oregon	2	0.0%
14	Pennsylvania	152	2.6%
20	Rhode Island	95	1.6%
16	South Carolina	133	2.3%
12	South Dakota	163	2.8%
20	Tennessee	95	1.6%
46	Texas	0	0.0%
38	Utah	8	0.1%
23	Vermont	92	1.6%
2	Virginia	578	9.9%
46	Washington	0	0.0%
19	West Virginia	111	1.9%
46	Wisconsin	0	0.0%
29	Wyoming	45	0.8%

RANK ORDER

RANK	STATE	CASES	% of USA
1	New York	812	13.9%
2	Virginia	578	9.9%
3	North Carolina	413	7.1%
4	Maryland	395	6.8%
5	California	324	5.5%
6	Connecticut	253	4.3%
7	Georgia	241	4.1%
8	Massachusetts	223	3.8%
9	Florida	185	3.2%
10	New Jersey	173	3.0%
11	Maine	171	2.9%
12	South Dakota	163	2.8%
13	Iowa	162	2.8%
14	Pennsylvania	152	2.6%
15	North Dakota	139	2.4%
16	South Carolina	133	2.3%
17	Alabama	125	2.1%
18	Minnesota	115	2.0%
19	West Virginia	111	1.9%
20	Rhode Island	95	1.6%
20	Tennessee	95	1.6%
22	Oklahoma	93	1.6%
23	Vermont	92	1.6%
24	Kansas	87	1.5%
24	Michigan	87	1.5%
26	Arizona	66	1.1%
27	Montana	59	1.0%
28	New Hampshire	50	0.9%
29	Wyoming	45	0.8%
30	Delaware	43	0.7%
31	Ohio	36	0.6%
32	Kentucky	35	0.6%
33	Missouri	15	0.3%
34	Arkansas	14	0.2%
35	Indiana	13	0.2%
36	Illinois	10	0.2%
37	New Mexico	9	0.2%
38	Utah	8	0.1%
39	Alaska	7	0.1%
40	Idaho	5	0.1%
40	Nevada	5	0.1%
42	Nebraska	3	0.1%
43	Oregon	2	0.0%
44	Colorado	1	0.0%
44	Mississippi	1	0.0%
46	Hawaii	0	0.0%
46	Louisiana	0	0.0%
46	Texas	0	0.0%
46	Washington	0	0.0%
46	Wisconsin	0	0.0%
	District of Columbia	0	0.0%

Source: U.S. Department of Health and Human Services, National Center for Health Statistics
"Morbidity and Mortality Weekly Report" (January 7, 2000, Vol. 48, No. 51)
*Provisional data. An acute, infectious, often fatal viral disease of most warm-blooded animals, especially wolves, cats, and dogs, that attacks the central nervous system and is transmitted by the bite of infected animals.

Rabies (Animal) Rate in 1999

National Rate = 2.1 Cases per 100,000 Human Population*

ALPHA ORDER

RANK ORDER

RANK	STATE	RATE		RANK	STATE	RATE
21	Alabama	2.9		1	South Dakota	22.2
29	Alaska	1.1		2	North Dakota	21.9
26	Arizona	1.4		3	Vermont	15.5
33	Arkansas	0.5		4	Maine	13.6
30	California	1.0		5	Rhode Island	9.6
44	Colorado	0.0		6	Wyoming	9.4
8	Connecticut	7.7		7	Virginia	8.4
12	Delaware	5.7		8	Connecticut	7.7
28	Florida	1.2		9	Maryland	7.6
20	Georgia	3.1		10	Montana	6.7
44	Hawaii	0.0		11	West Virginia	6.1
35	Idaho	0.4		12	Delaware	5.7
42	Illinois	0.1		13	Iowa	5.6
40	Indiana	0.2		14	North Carolina	5.4
13	Iowa	5.6		15	New York	4.5
19	Kansas	3.3		16	New Hampshire	4.2
31	Kentucky	0.9		17	Massachusetts	3.6
44	Louisiana	0.0		18	South Carolina	3.4
4	Maine	13.6		19	Kansas	3.3
9	Maryland	7.6		20	Georgia	3.1
17	Massachusetts	3.6		21	Alabama	2.9
31	Michigan	0.9		22	Oklahoma	2.8
23	Minnesota	2.4		23	Minnesota	2.4
44	Mississippi	0.0		24	New Jersey	2.1
37	Missouri	0.3		25	Tennessee	1.7
10	Montana	6.7		26	Arizona	1.4
40	Nebraska	0.2		27	Pennsylvania	1.3
37	Nevada	0.3		28	Florida	1.2
16	New Hampshire	4.2		29	Alaska	1.1
24	New Jersey	2.1		30	California	1.0
33	New Mexico	0.5		31	Kentucky	0.9
15	New York	4.5		31	Michigan	0.9
14	North Carolina	5.4		33	Arkansas	0.5
2	North Dakota	21.9		33	New Mexico	0.5
37	Ohio	0.3		35	Idaho	0.4
22	Oklahoma	2.8		35	Utah	0.4
42	Oregon	0.1		37	Missouri	0.3
27	Pennsylvania	1.3		37	Nevada	0.3
5	Rhode Island	9.6		37	Ohio	0.3
18	South Carolina	3.4		40	Indiana	0.2
1	South Dakota	22.2		40	Nebraska	0.2
25	Tennessee	1.7		42	Illinois	0.1
44	Texas	0.0		42	Oregon	0.1
35	Utah	0.4		44	Colorado	0.0
3	Vermont	15.5		44	Hawaii	0.0
7	Virginia	8.4		44	Louisiana	0.0
44	Washington	0.0		44	Mississippi	0.0
11	West Virginia	6.1		44	Texas	0.0
44	Wisconsin	0.0		44	Washington	0.0
6	Wyoming	9.4		44	Wisconsin	0.0
					District of Columbia	0.0

Source: Morgan Quitno Press using data from U.S. Dept. of Health & Human Serv's, National Center for Health Statistics "Morbidity and Mortality Weekly Report" (January 7, 2000, Vol. 48, No. 51)
*Provisional data. An acute, infectious, often fatal viral disease of most warm-blooded animals, especially wolves, cats, and dogs, that attacks the central nervous system and is transmitted by the bite of infected animals.

Salmonellosis Cases Reported in 1999

National Total = 68,623 Cases*

ALPHA ORDER

RANK	STATE	CASES	% of USA
25	Alabama	1,086	1.6%
49	Alaska	85	0.1%
14	Arizona	1,785	2.6%
30	Arkansas	762	1.1%
1	California	7,095	10.3%
19	Colorado	1,413	2.1%
26	Connecticut	971	1.4%
38	Delaware	307	0.4%
4	Florida	3,284	4.8%
4	Georgia	3,284	4.8%
33	Hawaii	604	0.9%
44	Idaho	233	0.3%
11	Illinois	1,964	2.9%
27	Indiana	961	1.4%
34	Iowa	473	0.7%
35	Kansas	444	0.6%
36	Kentucky	413	0.6%
22	Louisiana	1,180	1.7%
43	Maine	236	0.3%
13	Maryland	1,875	2.7%
8	Massachusetts	2,365	3.4%
12	Michigan	1,878	2.7%
20	Minnesota	1,310	1.9%
31	Mississippi	671	1.0%
16	Missouri	1,656	2.4%
50	Montana	84	0.1%
40	Nebraska	290	0.4%
42	Nevada	238	0.3%
41	New Hampshire	279	0.4%
15	New Jersey	1,664	2.4%
32	New Mexico	619	0.9%
2	New York	5,337	7.8%
6	North Carolina	2,638	3.8%
48	North Dakota	112	0.2%
7	Ohio	2,410	3.5%
29	Oklahoma	793	1.2%
28	Oregon	924	1.3%
10	Pennsylvania	2,029	3.0%
39	Rhode Island	302	0.4%
21	South Carolina	1,190	1.7%
45	South Dakota	214	0.3%
23	Tennessee	1,158	1.7%
3	Texas	4,870	7.1%
24	Utah	1,150	1.7%
46	Vermont	183	0.3%
9	Virginia	2,244	3.3%
18	Washington	1,459	2.1%
37	West Virginia	328	0.5%
17	Wisconsin	1,587	2.3%
47	Wyoming	117	0.2%

RANK ORDER

RANK	STATE	CASES	% of USA
1	California	7,095	10.3%
2	New York	5,337	7.8%
3	Texas	4,870	7.1%
4	Florida	3,284	4.8%
4	Georgia	3,284	4.8%
6	North Carolina	2,638	3.8%
7	Ohio	2,410	3.5%
8	Massachusetts	2,365	3.4%
9	Virginia	2,244	3.3%
10	Pennsylvania	2,029	3.0%
11	Illinois	1,964	2.9%
12	Michigan	1,878	2.7%
13	Maryland	1,875	2.7%
14	Arizona	1,785	2.6%
15	New Jersey	1,664	2.4%
16	Missouri	1,656	2.4%
17	Wisconsin	1,587	2.3%
18	Washington	1,459	2.1%
19	Colorado	1,413	2.1%
20	Minnesota	1,310	1.9%
21	South Carolina	1,190	1.7%
22	Louisiana	1,180	1.7%
23	Tennessee	1,158	1.7%
24	Utah	1,150	1.7%
25	Alabama	1,086	1.6%
26	Connecticut	971	1.4%
27	Indiana	961	1.4%
28	Oregon	924	1.3%
29	Oklahoma	793	1.2%
30	Arkansas	762	1.1%
31	Mississippi	671	1.0%
32	New Mexico	619	0.9%
33	Hawaii	604	0.9%
34	Iowa	473	0.7%
35	Kansas	444	0.6%
36	Kentucky	413	0.6%
37	West Virginia	328	0.5%
38	Delaware	307	0.4%
39	Rhode Island	302	0.4%
40	Nebraska	290	0.4%
41	New Hampshire	279	0.4%
42	Nevada	238	0.3%
43	Maine	236	0.3%
44	Idaho	233	0.3%
45	South Dakota	214	0.3%
46	Vermont	183	0.3%
47	Wyoming	117	0.2%
48	North Dakota	112	0.2%
49	Alaska	85	0.1%
50	Montana	84	0.1%
	District of Columbia	69	0.1%

Source: U.S. Department of Health and Human Services, National Center for Health Statistics
 "Morbidity and Mortality Weekly Report" (January 7, 2000, Vol. 48, No. 51)
*Provisional data. Any disease caused by a salmonella infection, which may be manifested as food poisoning with acute gastroenteritis, vomiting and diarrhea.

Salmonellosis Rate in 1999

National Rate = 25.2 Cases per 100,000 Population*

ALPHA ORDER

RANK	STATE	RATE
25	Alabama	24.9
47	Alaska	13.7
6	Arizona	37.4
17	Arkansas	29.9
32	California	21.4
9	Colorado	34.8
18	Connecticut	29.6
4	Delaware	40.7
31	Florida	21.7
3	Georgia	42.2
2	Hawaii	50.9
38	Idaho	18.6
45	Illinois	16.2
45	Indiana	16.2
44	Iowa	16.5
43	Kansas	16.7
49	Kentucky	10.4
23	Louisiana	27.0
37	Maine	18.8
7	Maryland	36.3
5	Massachusetts	38.3
36	Michigan	19.0
22	Minnesota	27.4
28	Mississippi	24.2
15	Missouri	30.3
50	Montana	9.5
41	Nebraska	17.4
48	Nevada	13.2
30	New Hampshire	23.2
35	New Jersey	20.4
8	New Mexico	35.6
19	New York	29.3
10	North Carolina	34.5
40	North Dakota	17.7
32	Ohio	21.4
29	Oklahoma	23.6
21	Oregon	27.9
42	Pennsylvania	16.9
14	Rhode Island	30.5
13	South Carolina	30.6
20	South Dakota	29.2
34	Tennessee	21.1
27	Texas	24.3
1	Utah	54.0
12	Vermont	30.8
11	Virginia	32.6
24	Washington	25.3
39	West Virginia	18.2
16	Wisconsin	30.2
26	Wyoming	24.4

RANK ORDER

RANK	STATE	RATE
1	Utah	54.0
2	Hawaii	50.9
3	Georgia	42.2
4	Delaware	40.7
5	Massachusetts	38.3
6	Arizona	37.4
7	Maryland	36.3
8	New Mexico	35.6
9	Colorado	34.8
10	North Carolina	34.5
11	Virginia	32.6
12	Vermont	30.8
13	South Carolina	30.6
14	Rhode Island	30.5
15	Missouri	30.3
16	Wisconsin	30.2
17	Arkansas	29.9
18	Connecticut	29.6
19	New York	29.3
20	South Dakota	29.2
21	Oregon	27.9
22	Minnesota	27.4
23	Louisiana	27.0
24	Washington	25.3
25	Alabama	24.9
26	Wyoming	24.4
27	Texas	24.3
28	Mississippi	24.2
29	Oklahoma	23.6
30	New Hampshire	23.2
31	Florida	21.7
32	California	21.4
32	Ohio	21.4
34	Tennessee	21.1
35	New Jersey	20.4
36	Michigan	19.0
37	Maine	18.8
38	Idaho	18.6
39	West Virginia	18.2
40	North Dakota	17.7
41	Nebraska	17.4
42	Pennsylvania	16.9
43	Kansas	16.7
44	Iowa	16.5
45	Illinois	16.2
45	Indiana	16.2
47	Alaska	13.7
48	Nevada	13.2
49	Kentucky	10.4
50	Montana	9.5

| | District of Columbia | 13.3 |

Source: Morgan Quitno Press using data from U.S. Dept. of Health & Human Serv's, National Center for Health Statistics "Morbidity and Mortality Weekly Report" (January 7, 2000, Vol. 48, No. 51)
*Provisional data. Any disease caused by a salmonella infection, which may be manifested as food poisoning with acute gastroenteritis, vomiting and diarrhea.

Shigellosis Cases Reported in 1999

National Total = 23,915 Cases*

ALPHA ORDER

RANK	STATE	CASES	% of USA
29	Alabama	179	0.7%
47	Alaska	7	0.0%
7	Arizona	1,048	4.4%
35	Arkansas	98	0.4%
2	California	2,311	9.7%
16	Colorado	365	1.5%
33	Connecticut	131	0.5%
43	Delaware	22	0.1%
4	Florida	1,658	6.9%
19	Georgia	327	1.4%
38	Hawaii	62	0.3%
40	Idaho	41	0.2%
3	Illinois	1,726	7.2%
15	Indiana	449	1.9%
34	Iowa	123	0.5%
37	Kansas	91	0.4%
23	Kentucky	235	1.0%
20	Louisiana	318	1.3%
48	Maine	5	0.0%
25	Maryland	223	0.9%
5	Massachusetts	1,439	6.0%
9	Michigan	941	3.9%
14	Minnesota	505	2.1%
30	Mississippi	172	0.7%
8	Missouri	1,037	4.3%
46	Montana	10	0.0%
31	Nebraska	152	0.6%
36	Nevada	96	0.4%
41	New Hampshire	34	0.1%
17	New Jersey	352	1.5%
22	New Mexico	249	1.0%
10	New York	773	3.2%
21	North Carolina	301	1.3%
48	North Dakota	5	0.0%
13	Ohio	567	2.4%
12	Oklahoma	691	2.9%
28	Oregon	185	0.8%
18	Pennsylvania	338	1.4%
39	Rhode Island	59	0.2%
27	South Carolina	186	0.8%
42	South Dakota	28	0.1%
6	Tennessee	1,114	4.7%
1	Texas	3,919	16.4%
32	Utah	137	0.6%
45	Vermont	11	0.0%
26	Virginia	194	0.8%
24	Washington	233	1.0%
44	West Virginia	14	0.1%
11	Wisconsin	699	2.9%
50	Wyoming	4	0.0%

RANK ORDER

RANK	STATE	CASES	% of USA
1	Texas	3,919	16.4%
2	California	2,311	9.7%
3	Illinois	1,726	7.2%
4	Florida	1,658	6.9%
5	Massachusetts	1,439	6.0%
6	Tennessee	1,114	4.7%
7	Arizona	1,048	4.4%
8	Missouri	1,037	4.3%
9	Michigan	941	3.9%
10	New York	773	3.2%
11	Wisconsin	699	2.9%
12	Oklahoma	691	2.9%
13	Ohio	567	2.4%
14	Minnesota	505	2.1%
15	Indiana	449	1.9%
16	Colorado	365	1.5%
17	New Jersey	352	1.5%
18	Pennsylvania	338	1.4%
19	Georgia	327	1.4%
20	Louisiana	318	1.3%
21	North Carolina	301	1.3%
22	New Mexico	249	1.0%
23	Kentucky	235	1.0%
24	Washington	233	1.0%
25	Maryland	223	0.9%
26	Virginia	194	0.8%
27	South Carolina	186	0.8%
28	Oregon	185	0.8%
29	Alabama	179	0.7%
30	Mississippi	172	0.7%
31	Nebraska	152	0.6%
32	Utah	137	0.6%
33	Connecticut	131	0.5%
34	Iowa	123	0.5%
35	Arkansas	98	0.4%
36	Nevada	96	0.4%
37	Kansas	91	0.4%
38	Hawaii	62	0.3%
39	Rhode Island	59	0.2%
40	Idaho	41	0.2%
41	New Hampshire	34	0.1%
42	South Dakota	28	0.1%
43	Delaware	22	0.1%
44	West Virginia	14	0.1%
45	Vermont	11	0.0%
46	Montana	10	0.0%
47	Alaska	7	0.0%
48	Maine	5	0.0%
48	North Dakota	5	0.0%
50	Wyoming	4	0.0%
	District of Columbia	51	0.2%

Source: U.S. Department of Health and Human Services, National Center for Health Statistics
   "Morbidity and Mortality Weekly Report" (January 7, 2000, Vol. 48, No. 51)
*Provisional data. Dysentery caused by any of various species of shigellae, occurring most frequently in areas where poor sanitation and malnutrition are prevalent and commonly affecting children and infants.

Shigellosis Rate in 1999

National Rate = 8.8 Cases per 100,000 Population*

RANK	STATE	RATE
32	Alabama	4.1
45	Alaska	1.1
2	Arizona	21.9
36	Arkansas	3.8
17	California	7.0
14	Colorado	9.0
33	Connecticut	4.0
40	Delaware	2.9
10	Florida	11.0
30	Georgia	4.2
24	Hawaii	5.2
39	Idaho	3.3
8	Illinois	14.2
15	Indiana	7.6
27	Iowa	4.3
38	Kansas	3.4
21	Kentucky	5.9
16	Louisiana	7.3
50	Maine	0.4
27	Maryland	4.3
1	Massachusetts	23.3
12	Michigan	9.5
11	Minnesota	10.6
19	Mississippi	6.2
6	Missouri	19.0
45	Montana	1.1
13	Nebraska	9.1
23	Nevada	5.3
41	New Hampshire	2.8
27	New Jersey	4.3
7	New Mexico	14.3
30	New York	4.2
35	North Carolina	3.9
47	North Dakota	0.8
25	Ohio	5.0
3	Oklahoma	20.6
22	Oregon	5.6
41	Pennsylvania	2.8
20	Rhode Island	6.0
26	South Carolina	4.8
36	South Dakota	3.8
4	Tennessee	20.3
5	Texas	19.6
18	Utah	6.4
44	Vermont	1.9
41	Virginia	2.8
33	Washington	4.0
47	West Virginia	0.8
9	Wisconsin	13.3
47	Wyoming	0.8

RANK	STATE	RATE
1	Massachusetts	23.3
2	Arizona	21.9
3	Oklahoma	20.6
4	Tennessee	20.3
5	Texas	19.6
6	Missouri	19.0
7	New Mexico	14.3
8	Illinois	14.2
9	Wisconsin	13.3
10	Florida	11.0
11	Minnesota	10.6
12	Michigan	9.5
13	Nebraska	9.1
14	Colorado	9.0
15	Indiana	7.6
16	Louisiana	7.3
17	California	7.0
18	Utah	6.4
19	Mississippi	6.2
20	Rhode Island	6.0
21	Kentucky	5.9
22	Oregon	5.6
23	Nevada	5.3
24	Hawaii	5.2
25	Ohio	5.0
26	South Carolina	4.8
27	Iowa	4.3
27	Maryland	4.3
27	New Jersey	4.3
30	Georgia	4.2
30	New York	4.2
32	Alabama	4.1
33	Connecticut	4.0
33	Washington	4.0
35	North Carolina	3.9
36	Arkansas	3.8
36	South Dakota	3.8
38	Kansas	3.4
39	Idaho	3.3
40	Delaware	2.9
41	New Hampshire	2.8
41	Pennsylvania	2.8
41	Virginia	2.8
44	Vermont	1.9
45	Alaska	1.1
45	Montana	1.1
47	North Dakota	0.8
47	West Virginia	0.8
47	Wyoming	0.8
50	Maine	0.4

District of Columbia 9.8

Source: Morgan Quitno Press using data from U.S. Dept. of Health & Human Serv's, National Center for Health Statistics "Morbidity and Mortality Weekly Report" (January 7, 2000, Vol. 48, No. 51)

*Provisional data. Dysentery caused by any of various species of shigellae, occurring most frequently in areas where poor sanitation and malnutrition are prevalent and commonly affecting children and infants.

Tuberculosis Cases Reported in 1999

National Total = 13,996 Cases*

ALPHA ORDER

RANK	STATE	CASES	% of USA
11	Alabama	314	2.2%
32	Alaska	60	0.4%
17	Arizona	239	1.7%
23	Arkansas	167	1.2%
1	California	3,008	21.5%
NA	Colorado**	NA	NA
27	Connecticut	112	0.8%
44	Delaware	12	0.1%
4	Florida	1,007	7.2%
5	Georgia	575	4.1%
21	Hawaii	180	1.3%
42	Idaho	15	0.1%
6	Illinois	537	3.8%
26	Indiana	137	1.0%
33	Iowa	58	0.4%
39	Kansas	19	0.1%
24	Kentucky	166	1.2%
NA	Louisiana**	NA	NA
38	Maine	20	0.1%
14	Maryland	267	1.9%
15	Massachusetts	263	1.9%
12	Michigan	282	2.0%
20	Minnesota	189	1.4%
34	Mississippi	56	0.4%
22	Missouri	171	1.2%
43	Montana	13	0.1%
40	Nebraska	17	0.1%
30	Nevada	82	0.6%
45	New Hampshire	10	0.1%
7	New Jersey	517	3.7%
31	New Mexico	63	0.5%
2	New York	1,641	11.7%
8	North Carolina	430	3.1%
46	North Dakota	6	0.0%
16	Ohio	253	1.8%
25	Oklahoma	144	1.0%
28	Oregon	99	0.7%
9	Pennsylvania	381	2.7%
35	Rhode Island	42	0.3%
18	South Carolina	226	1.6%
40	South Dakota	17	0.1%
10	Tennessee	333	2.4%
3	Texas	1,179	8.4%
37	Utah	40	0.3%
48	Vermont	2	0.0%
13	Virginia	268	1.9%
19	Washington	190	1.4%
36	West Virginia	41	0.3%
29	Wisconsin	95	0.7%
47	Wyoming	3	0.0%

RANK ORDER

RANK	STATE	CASES	% of USA
1	California	3,008	21.5%
2	New York	1,641	11.7%
3	Texas	1,179	8.4%
4	Florida	1,007	7.2%
5	Georgia	575	4.1%
6	Illinois	537	3.8%
7	New Jersey	517	3.7%
8	North Carolina	430	3.1%
9	Pennsylvania	381	2.7%
10	Tennessee	333	2.4%
11	Alabama	314	2.2%
12	Michigan	282	2.0%
13	Virginia	268	1.9%
14	Maryland	267	1.9%
15	Massachusetts	263	1.9%
16	Ohio	253	1.8%
17	Arizona	239	1.7%
18	South Carolina	226	1.6%
19	Washington	190	1.4%
20	Minnesota	189	1.4%
21	Hawaii	180	1.3%
22	Missouri	171	1.2%
23	Arkansas	167	1.2%
24	Kentucky	166	1.2%
25	Oklahoma	144	1.0%
26	Indiana	137	1.0%
27	Connecticut	112	0.8%
28	Oregon	99	0.7%
29	Wisconsin	95	0.7%
30	Nevada	82	0.6%
31	New Mexico	63	0.5%
32	Alaska	60	0.4%
33	Iowa	58	0.4%
34	Mississippi	56	0.4%
35	Rhode Island	42	0.3%
36	West Virginia	41	0.3%
37	Utah	40	0.3%
38	Maine	20	0.1%
39	Kansas	19	0.1%
40	Nebraska	17	0.1%
40	South Dakota	17	0.1%
42	Idaho	15	0.1%
43	Montana	13	0.1%
44	Delaware	12	0.1%
45	New Hampshire	10	0.1%
46	North Dakota	6	0.0%
47	Wyoming	3	0.0%
48	Vermont	2	0.0%
NA	Colorado**	NA	NA
NA	Louisiana**	NA	NA
	District of Columbia	50	0.4%

Source: U.S. Department of Health and Human Services, National Center for Health Statistics
"Morbidity and Mortality Weekly Report" (January 7, 2000, Vol. 48, No. 51)
*Provisional data. An infectious disease caused by the tubercle bacillus and causing the formation of tubercles on the lungs and other tissues of the body, often developing long after the initial infection. Characterized by the coughing up of mucus and sputum, fever, weight loss, and chest pain.
**Not available.

Tuberculosis Rate in 1999

National Rate = 5.1 Cases per 100,000 Population*

ALPHA ORDER

RANK	STATE	RATE
6	Alabama	7.2
2	Alaska	9.7
15	Arizona	5.0
8	Arkansas	6.5
3	California	9.1
NA	Colorado**	NA
25	Connecticut	3.4
39	Delaware	1.6
7	Florida	6.7
5	Georgia	7.4
1	Hawaii	15.2
42	Idaho	1.2
17	Illinois	4.4
31	Indiana	2.3
35	Iowa	2.0
46	Kansas	0.7
20	Kentucky	4.2
NA	Louisiana**	NA
39	Maine	1.6
14	Maryland	5.2
18	Massachusetts	4.3
30	Michigan	2.9
22	Minnesota	4.0
35	Mississippi	2.0
28	Missouri	3.1
41	Montana	1.5
43	Nebraska	1.0
16	Nevada	4.5
45	New Hampshire	0.8
9	New Jersey	6.3
24	New Mexico	3.6
4	New York	9.0
13	North Carolina	5.6
44	North Dakota	0.9
34	Ohio	2.2
18	Oklahoma	4.3
29	Oregon	3.0
27	Pennsylvania	3.2
20	Rhode Island	4.2
12	South Carolina	5.8
31	South Dakota	2.3
10	Tennessee	6.1
11	Texas	5.9
37	Utah	1.9
48	Vermont	0.3
23	Virginia	3.9
26	Washington	3.3
31	West Virginia	2.3
38	Wisconsin	1.8
47	Wyoming	0.6

RANK ORDER

RANK	STATE	RATE
1	Hawaii	15.2
2	Alaska	9.7
3	California	9.1
4	New York	9.0
5	Georgia	7.4
6	Alabama	7.2
7	Florida	6.7
8	Arkansas	6.5
9	New Jersey	6.3
10	Tennessee	6.1
11	Texas	5.9
12	South Carolina	5.8
13	North Carolina	5.6
14	Maryland	5.2
15	Arizona	5.0
16	Nevada	4.5
17	Illinois	4.4
18	Massachusetts	4.3
18	Oklahoma	4.3
20	Kentucky	4.2
20	Rhode Island	4.2
22	Minnesota	4.0
23	Virginia	3.9
24	New Mexico	3.6
25	Connecticut	3.4
26	Washington	3.3
27	Pennsylvania	3.2
28	Missouri	3.1
29	Oregon	3.0
30	Michigan	2.9
31	Indiana	2.3
31	South Dakota	2.3
31	West Virginia	2.3
34	Ohio	2.2
35	Iowa	2.0
35	Mississippi	2.0
37	Utah	1.9
38	Wisconsin	1.8
39	Delaware	1.6
39	Maine	1.6
41	Montana	1.5
42	Idaho	1.2
43	Nebraska	1.0
44	North Dakota	0.9
45	New Hampshire	0.8
46	Kansas	0.7
47	Wyoming	0.6
48	Vermont	0.3
NA	Colorado**	NA
NA	Louisiana**	NA

District of Columbia   9.6

*Source: Morgan Quitno Press using data from U.S. Dept. of Health & Human Serv's, National Center for Health Statistics
"Morbidity and Mortality Weekly Report" (January 7, 2000, Vol. 48, No. 51)*
*Provisional data. An infectious disease caused by the tubercle bacillus and causing the formation of tubercles on the lungs and other tissues of the body, often developing long after the initial infection. Characterized by the coughing up of mucus and sputum, fever, weight loss, and chest pain.
**Not available.*

Whooping Cough (Pertussis) Cases Reported in 1999

National Total = 6,031 Cases*

ALPHA ORDER

RANK	STATE	CASES	% of USA
35	Alabama	21	0.3%
45	Alaska	5	0.1%
11	Arizona	128	2.1%
36	Arkansas	19	0.3%
1	California	936	15.5%
6	Colorado	245	4.1%
32	Connecticut	31	0.5%
42	Delaware	7	0.1%
14	Florida	102	1.7%
28	Georgia	40	0.7%
31	Hawaii	34	0.6%
10	Idaho	141	2.3%
14	Illinois	102	1.7%
20	Indiana	77	1.3%
18	Iowa	79	1.3%
30	Kansas	35	0.6%
33	Kentucky	29	0.5%
41	Louisiana	10	0.2%
50	Maine	0	0.0%
13	Maryland	107	1.8%
4	Massachusetts	527	8.7%
21	Michigan	70	1.2%
7	Minnesota	236	3.9%
47	Mississippi	2	0.0%
22	Missouri	65	1.1%
47	Montana	2	0.0%
44	Nebraska	6	0.1%
40	Nevada	11	0.2%
19	New Hampshire	78	1.3%
38	New Jersey	12	0.2%
8	New Mexico	221	3.7%
2	New York	817	13.5%
16	North Carolina	101	1.7%
37	North Dakota	18	0.3%
5	Ohio	329	5.5%
38	Oklahoma	12	0.2%
24	Oregon	58	1.0%
9	Pennsylvania	191	3.2%
29	Rhode Island	38	0.6%
33	South Carolina	29	0.5%
42	South Dakota	7	0.1%
27	Tennessee	45	0.7%
12	Texas	124	2.1%
23	Utah	61	1.0%
17	Vermont	88	1.5%
26	Virginia	51	0.8%
3	Washington	625	10.4%
46	West Virginia	4	0.1%
25	Wisconsin	52	0.9%
47	Wyoming	2	0.0%

RANK ORDER

RANK	STATE	CASES	% of USA
1	California	936	15.5%
2	New York	817	13.5%
3	Washington	625	10.4%
4	Massachusetts	527	8.7%
5	Ohio	329	5.5%
6	Colorado	245	4.1%
7	Minnesota	236	3.9%
8	New Mexico	221	3.7%
9	Pennsylvania	191	3.2%
10	Idaho	141	2.3%
11	Arizona	128	2.1%
12	Texas	124	2.1%
13	Maryland	107	1.8%
14	Florida	102	1.7%
14	Illinois	102	1.7%
16	North Carolina	101	1.7%
17	Vermont	88	1.5%
18	Iowa	79	1.3%
19	New Hampshire	78	1.3%
20	Indiana	77	1.3%
21	Michigan	70	1.2%
22	Missouri	65	1.1%
23	Utah	61	1.0%
24	Oregon	58	1.0%
25	Wisconsin	52	0.9%
26	Virginia	51	0.8%
27	Tennessee	45	0.7%
28	Georgia	40	0.7%
29	Rhode Island	38	0.6%
30	Kansas	35	0.6%
31	Hawaii	34	0.6%
32	Connecticut	31	0.5%
33	Kentucky	29	0.5%
33	South Carolina	29	0.5%
35	Alabama	21	0.3%
36	Arkansas	19	0.3%
37	North Dakota	18	0.3%
38	New Jersey	12	0.2%
38	Oklahoma	12	0.2%
40	Nevada	11	0.2%
41	Louisiana	10	0.2%
42	Delaware	7	0.1%
42	South Dakota	7	0.1%
44	Nebraska	6	0.1%
45	Alaska	5	0.1%
46	West Virginia	4	0.1%
47	Mississippi	2	0.0%
47	Montana	2	0.0%
47	Wyoming	2	0.0%
50	Maine	0	0.0%
	District of Columbia	1	0.0%

Source: U.S. Department of Health and Human Services, National Center for Health Statistics
    "Morbidity and Mortality Weekly Report" (January 7, 2000, Vol. 48, No. 51)
*Provisional data. Acute, highly contagious infection of respiratory tract.

Whooping Cough (Pertussis) Rate in 1999

National Rate = 2.2 Cases per 100,000 Population*

ALPHA ORDER

RANK	STATE	RATE
40	Alabama	0.5
29	Alaska	0.8
17	Arizona	2.7
32	Arkansas	0.7
14	California	2.8
7	Colorado	6.0
27	Connecticut	0.9
27	Delaware	0.9
32	Florida	0.7
40	Georgia	0.5
11	Hawaii	2.9
3	Idaho	11.3
29	Illinois	0.8
21	Indiana	1.3
14	Iowa	2.8
21	Kansas	1.3
32	Kentucky	0.7
45	Louisiana	0.2
50	Maine	0.0
18	Maryland	2.1
5	Massachusetts	8.5
32	Michigan	0.7
8	Minnesota	4.9
48	Mississippi	0.1
24	Missouri	1.2
45	Montana	0.2
42	Nebraska	0.4
38	Nevada	0.6
6	New Hampshire	6.5
48	New Jersey	0.1
2	New Mexico	12.7
9	New York	4.5
21	North Carolina	1.3
14	North Dakota	2.8
11	Ohio	2.9
42	Oklahoma	0.4
19	Oregon	1.7
20	Pennsylvania	1.6
10	Rhode Island	3.8
32	South Carolina	0.7
25	South Dakota	1.0
29	Tennessee	0.8
38	Texas	0.6
11	Utah	2.9
1	Vermont	14.8
32	Virginia	0.7
4	Washington	10.9
45	West Virginia	0.2
25	Wisconsin	1.0
42	Wyoming	0.4

RANK ORDER

RANK	STATE	RATE
1	Vermont	14.8
2	New Mexico	12.7
3	Idaho	11.3
4	Washington	10.9
5	Massachusetts	8.5
6	New Hampshire	6.5
7	Colorado	6.0
8	Minnesota	4.9
9	New York	4.5
10	Rhode Island	3.8
11	Hawaii	2.9
11	Ohio	2.9
11	Utah	2.9
14	California	2.8
14	Iowa	2.8
14	North Dakota	2.8
17	Arizona	2.7
18	Maryland	2.1
19	Oregon	1.7
20	Pennsylvania	1.6
21	Indiana	1.3
21	Kansas	1.3
21	North Carolina	1.3
24	Missouri	1.2
25	South Dakota	1.0
25	Wisconsin	1.0
27	Connecticut	0.9
27	Delaware	0.9
29	Alaska	0.8
29	Illinois	0.8
29	Tennessee	0.8
32	Arkansas	0.7
32	Florida	0.7
32	Kentucky	0.7
32	Michigan	0.7
32	South Carolina	0.7
32	Virginia	0.7
38	Nevada	0.6
38	Texas	0.6
40	Alabama	0.5
40	Georgia	0.5
42	Nebraska	0.4
42	Oklahoma	0.4
42	Wyoming	0.4
45	Louisiana	0.2
45	Montana	0.2
45	West Virginia	0.2
48	Mississippi	0.1
48	New Jersey	0.1
50	Maine	0.0
	District of Columbia	0.2

Source: Morgan Quitno Press using data from U.S. Dept. of Health & Human Serv's, National Center for Health Statistics
"Morbidity and Mortality Weekly Report" (January 7, 2000, Vol. 48, No. 51)
*Provisional data. Acute, highly contagious infection of respiratory tract.

Percent of Children Aged 19 to 35 Months Fully Immunized in 1997

National Percent = 76%*

ALPHA ORDER

RANK	STATE	PERCENT
21	Alabama	78
42	Alaska	72
47	Arizona	69
31	Arkansas	75
31	California	75
39	Colorado	73
1	Connecticut	88
19	Delaware	79
26	Florida	77
13	Georgia	80
13	Hawaii	80
50	Idaho	67
30	Illinois	76
45	Indiana	71
13	Iowa	80
26	Kansas	77
26	Kentucky	77
6	Louisiana	82
3	Maine	85
21	Maryland	78
2	Massachusetts	86
39	Michigan	73
5	Minnesota	83
10	Mississippi	81
36	Missouri	74
21	Montana	78
21	Nebraska	78
46	Nevada	70
6	New Hampshire	82
39	New Jersey	73
31	New Mexico	75
36	New York	74
13	North Carolina	80
13	North Dakota	80
31	Ohio	75
47	Oklahoma	69
42	Oregon	72
6	Pennsylvania	82
10	Rhode Island	81
6	South Carolina	82
26	South Dakota	77
21	Tennessee	78
42	Texas	72
49	Utah	68
4	Vermont	84
31	Virginia	75
10	Washington	81
13	West Virginia	80
19	Wisconsin	79
36	Wyoming	74

RANK ORDER

RANK	STATE	PERCENT
1	Connecticut	88
2	Massachusetts	86
3	Maine	85
4	Vermont	84
5	Minnesota	83
6	Louisiana	82
6	New Hampshire	82
6	Pennsylvania	82
6	South Carolina	82
10	Mississippi	81
10	Rhode Island	81
10	Washington	81
13	Georgia	80
13	Hawaii	80
13	Iowa	80
13	North Carolina	80
13	North Dakota	80
13	West Virginia	80
19	Delaware	79
19	Wisconsin	79
21	Alabama	78
21	Maryland	78
21	Montana	78
21	Nebraska	78
21	Tennessee	78
26	Florida	77
26	Kansas	77
26	Kentucky	77
26	South Dakota	77
30	Illinois	76
31	Arkansas	75
31	California	75
31	New Mexico	75
31	Ohio	75
31	Virginia	75
36	Missouri	74
36	New York	74
36	Wyoming	74
39	Colorado	73
39	Michigan	73
39	New Jersey	73
42	Alaska	72
42	Oregon	72
42	Texas	72
45	Indiana	71
46	Nevada	70
47	Arizona	69
47	Oklahoma	69
49	Utah	68
50	Idaho	67

District of Columbia**	NA

Source: U.S. Department of Health and Human Services, Centers for Disease Control and Prevention
    "State Vaccination Coverage Levels" (Morbidity and Mortality Weekly Report, Vol. 47, No. 6, 02/20/98)
*As of June 1997. Fully immunized children received four doses of DTP/DT (Diphtheria, Tetanus, Pertussis (Whooping Cough)), three doses of OPV (Poliovirus), one dose of MCV (Measles Containing Vaccine) and three doses of Hib (Haemophilus influenzae type b).
**Not available.

Sexually Transmitted Diseases in 1998

National Total = 970,426 Cases*

ALPHA ORDER					RANK ORDER			
RANK	STATE	CASES	% of USA		RANK	STATE	CASES	% of USA
15	Alabama	23,077	2.4%		1	California	96,319	9.9%
42	Alaska	2,239	0.2%		2	Texas	93,746	9.7%
22	Arizona	15,889	1.6%		3	Illinois	48,522	5.0%
31	Arkansas	8,191	0.8%		4	Georgia	46,251	4.8%
1	California	96,319	9.9%		5	Ohio	46,198	4.8%
25	Colorado	11,156	1.1%		6	New York	45,481	4.7%
28	Connecticut	10,182	1.0%		7	Florida	44,326	4.6%
36	Delaware	4,185	0.4%		8	North Carolina	42,159	4.3%
7	Florida	44,326	4.6%		9	Michigan	38,726	4.0%
4	Georgia	46,251	4.8%		10	Pennsylvania	36,446	3.8%
39	Hawaii	3,114	0.3%		11	South Carolina	30,375	3.1%
43	Idaho	2,219	0.2%		12	Louisiana	28,118	2.9%
3	Illinois	48,522	5.0%		13	Tennessee	26,124	2.7%
21	Indiana	17,324	1.8%		14	Maryland	24,999	2.6%
32	Iowa	6,795	0.7%		15	Alabama	23,077	2.4%
30	Kansas	8,224	0.8%		16	Virginia	22,982	2.4%
27	Kentucky	10,360	1.1%		17	Missouri	22,242	2.3%
12	Louisiana	28,118	2.9%		18	Mississippi	21,567	2.2%
46	Maine	1,141	0.1%		19	Wisconsin	20,291	2.1%
14	Maryland	24,999	2.6%		20	New Jersey	19,651	2.0%
26	Massachusetts	10,667	1.1%		21	Indiana	17,324	1.8%
9	Michigan	38,726	4.0%		22	Arizona	15,889	1.6%
29	Minnesota	9,687	1.0%		23	Oklahoma	14,734	1.5%
18	Mississippi	21,567	2.2%		24	Washington	12,991	1.3%
17	Missouri	22,242	2.3%		25	Colorado	11,156	1.1%
45	Montana	1,467	0.2%		26	Massachusetts	10,667	1.1%
37	Nebraska	4,123	0.4%		27	Kentucky	10,360	1.1%
34	Nevada	4,780	0.5%		28	Connecticut	10,182	1.0%
48	New Hampshire	1,053	0.1%		29	Minnesota	9,687	1.0%
20	New Jersey	19,651	2.0%		30	Kansas	8,224	0.8%
35	New Mexico	4,764	0.5%		31	Arkansas	8,191	0.8%
6	New York	45,481	4.7%		32	Iowa	6,795	0.7%
8	North Carolina	42,159	4.3%		33	Oregon	6,741	0.7%
47	North Dakota	1,116	0.1%		34	Nevada	4,780	0.5%
5	Ohio	46,198	4.8%		35	New Mexico	4,764	0.5%
23	Oklahoma	14,734	1.5%		36	Delaware	4,185	0.4%
33	Oregon	6,741	0.7%		37	Nebraska	4,123	0.4%
10	Pennsylvania	36,446	3.8%		38	West Virginia	3,714	0.4%
40	Rhode Island	2,738	0.3%		39	Hawaii	3,114	0.3%
11	South Carolina	30,375	3.1%		40	Rhode Island	2,738	0.3%
44	South Dakota	1,794	0.2%		41	Utah	2,449	0.3%
13	Tennessee	26,124	2.7%		42	Alaska	2,239	0.2%
2	Texas	93,746	9.7%		43	Idaho	2,219	0.2%
41	Utah	2,449	0.3%		44	South Dakota	1,794	0.2%
50	Vermont	455	0.0%		45	Montana	1,467	0.2%
16	Virginia	22,982	2.4%		46	Maine	1,141	0.1%
24	Washington	12,991	1.3%		47	North Dakota	1,116	0.1%
38	West Virginia	3,714	0.4%		48	New Hampshire	1,053	0.1%
19	Wisconsin	20,291	2.1%		49	Wyoming	763	0.1%
49	Wyoming	763	0.1%		50	Vermont	455	0.0%
						District of Columbia	7,771	0.8%

Source: Morgan Quitno Press using data from U.S. Dept. of Health and Human Services, Nat'l Center for Health Statistics "Sexually Transmitted Disease Surveillance 1998" (http://www.cdc.gov/nchstp/dstd/dstdp.html)
*Includes chancroid, chlamydia, gonorrhea and primary and secondary syphilis.

Sexually Transmitted Disease Rate in 1998

National Rate - 372.2 Cases per 100,000 Population*

ALPHA ORDER

RANK	STATE	RATE
7	Alabama	534.2
18	Alaska	367.5
19	Arizona	348.8
21	Arkansas	324.7
26	California	298.4
28	Colorado	286.6
23	Connecticut	311.5
5	Delaware	572.1
25	Florida	302.5
4	Georgia	617.8
33	Hawaii	262.4
42	Idaho	183.3
15	Illinois	407.9
27	Indiana	295.5
37	Iowa	238.3
22	Kansas	316.8
32	Kentucky	265.1
3	Louisiana	646.1
48	Maine	91.9
8	Maryland	490.7
43	Massachusetts	174.4
16	Michigan	396.3
40	Minnesota	206.8
2	Mississippi	789.9
14	Missouri	411.7
45	Montana	167.0
34	Nebraska	248.9
29	Nevada	285.1
49	New Hampshire	89.9
35	New Jersey	244.0
31	New Mexico	275.4
11	New York	463.4
6	North Carolina	567.7
44	North Dakota	174.2
13	Ohio	413.0
12	Oklahoma	444.3
39	Oregon	207.8
24	Pennsylvania	303.2
30	Rhode Island	277.2
1	South Carolina	807.8
36	South Dakota	243.0
9	Tennessee	486.7
10	Texas	482.3
47	Utah	119.0
50	Vermont	77.3
20	Virginia	341.3
38	Washington	231.5
41	West Virginia	204.6
17	Wisconsin	392.6
46	Wyoming	159.0

RANK ORDER

RANK	STATE	RATE
1	South Carolina	807.8
2	Mississippi	789.9
3	Louisiana	646.1
4	Georgia	617.8
5	Delaware	572.1
6	North Carolina	567.7
7	Alabama	534.2
8	Maryland	490.7
9	Tennessee	486.7
10	Texas	482.3
11	New York	463.4
12	Oklahoma	444.3
13	Ohio	413.0
14	Missouri	411.7
15	Illinois	407.9
16	Michigan	396.3
17	Wisconsin	392.6
18	Alaska	367.5
19	Arizona	348.8
20	Virginia	341.3
21	Arkansas	324.7
22	Kansas	316.8
23	Connecticut	311.5
24	Pennsylvania	303.2
25	Florida	302.5
26	California	298.4
27	Indiana	295.5
28	Colorado	286.6
29	Nevada	285.1
30	Rhode Island	277.2
31	New Mexico	275.4
32	Kentucky	265.1
33	Hawaii	262.4
34	Nebraska	248.9
35	New Jersey	244.0
36	South Dakota	243.0
37	Iowa	238.3
38	Washington	231.5
39	Oregon	207.8
40	Minnesota	206.8
41	West Virginia	204.6
42	Idaho	183.3
43	Massachusetts	174.4
44	North Dakota	174.2
45	Montana	167.0
46	Wyoming	159.0
47	Utah	119.0
48	Maine	91.9
49	New Hampshire	89.9
50	Vermont	77.3

District of Columbia 1,490.3

Source: Morgan Quitno Press using data from U.S. Dept. of Health and Human Services, Nat'l Center for Health Statistics "Sexually Transmitted Disease Surveillance 1998" (http://www.cdc.gov/nchstp/dstd/dstdp.html)
*Includes chancroid, chlamydia, gonorrhea and primary and secondary syphilis.

Chancroid Cases Reported in 1998

National Total = 189 Cases*

ALPHA ORDER

RANK	STATE	CASES	% of USA
15	Alabama	1	0.5%
21	Alaska	0	0.0%
11	Arizona	2	1.1%
6	Arkansas	7	3.7%
5	California	8	4.2%
21	Colorado	0	0.0%
11	Connecticut	2	1.1%
21	Delaware	0	0.0%
8	Florida	3	1.6%
11	Georgia	2	1.1%
21	Hawaii	0	0.0%
21	Idaho	0	0.0%
21	Illinois	0	0.0%
15	Indiana	1	0.5%
21	Iowa	0	0.0%
15	Kansas	1	0.5%
21	Kentucky	0	0.0%
15	Louisiana	1	0.5%
21	Maine	0	0.0%
21	Maryland	0	0.0%
21	Massachusetts	0	0.0%
21	Michigan	0	0.0%
21	Minnesota	0	0.0%
8	Mississippi	3	1.6%
21	Missouri	0	0.0%
21	Montana	0	0.0%
21	Nebraska	0	0.0%
21	Nevada	0	0.0%
21	New Hampshire	0	0.0%
21	New Jersey	0	0.0%
21	New Mexico	0	0.0%
1	New York	82	43.4%
4	North Carolina	9	4.8%
21	North Dakota	0	0.0%
8	Ohio	3	1.6%
21	Oklahoma	0	0.0%
21	Oregon	0	0.0%
21	Pennsylvania	0	0.0%
21	Rhode Island	0	0.0%
3	South Carolina	19	10.1%
21	South Dakota	0	0.0%
21	Tennessee	0	0.0%
2	Texas	34	18.0%
21	Utah	0	0.0%
21	Vermont	0	0.0%
6	Virginia	7	3.7%
15	Washington	1	0.5%
21	West Virginia	0	0.0%
11	Wisconsin	2	1.1%
15	Wyoming	1	0.5%

RANK ORDER

RANK	STATE	CASES	% of USA
1	New York	82	43.4%
2	Texas	34	18.0%
3	South Carolina	19	10.1%
4	North Carolina	9	4.8%
5	California	8	4.2%
6	Arkansas	7	3.7%
6	Virginia	7	3.7%
8	Florida	3	1.6%
8	Mississippi	3	1.6%
8	Ohio	3	1.6%
11	Arizona	2	1.1%
11	Connecticut	2	1.1%
11	Georgia	2	1.1%
11	Wisconsin	2	1.1%
15	Alabama	1	0.5%
15	Indiana	1	0.5%
15	Kansas	1	0.5%
15	Louisiana	1	0.5%
15	Washington	1	0.5%
15	Wyoming	1	0.5%
21	Alaska	0	0.0%
21	Colorado	0	0.0%
21	Delaware	0	0.0%
21	Hawaii	0	0.0%
21	Idaho	0	0.0%
21	Illinois	0	0.0%
21	Iowa	0	0.0%
21	Kentucky	0	0.0%
21	Maine	0	0.0%
21	Maryland	0	0.0%
21	Massachusetts	0	0.0%
21	Michigan	0	0.0%
21	Minnesota	0	0.0%
21	Missouri	0	0.0%
21	Montana	0	0.0%
21	Nebraska	0	0.0%
21	Nevada	0	0.0%
21	New Hampshire	0	0.0%
21	New Jersey	0	0.0%
21	New Mexico	0	0.0%
21	North Dakota	0	0.0%
21	Oklahoma	0	0.0%
21	Oregon	0	0.0%
21	Pennsylvania	0	0.0%
21	Rhode Island	0	0.0%
21	South Dakota	0	0.0%
21	Tennessee	0	0.0%
21	Utah	0	0.0%
21	Vermont	0	0.0%
21	West Virginia	0	0.0%
	District of Columbia	0	0.0%

Source: U.S. Department of Health and Human Services, National Center for Health Statistics
"Sexually Transmitted Disease Surveillance 1998" (http://www.cdc.gov/nchstp/dstd/dstdp.html)
*A soft, highly infectious, nonsyphilitic venereal ulcer of the genital region, caused by the bacillus Hemophilus ducreyi. Also called soft chancre.

Chancroid Rate in 1998

National Rate = 0.1 Cases per 100,000 Population*

ALPHA ORDER

RANK	STATE	RATE
10	Alabama	0.0
10	Alaska	0.0
10	Arizona	0.0
3	Arkansas	0.3
10	California	0.0
10	Colorado	0.0
6	Connecticut	0.1
10	Delaware	0.0
10	Florida	0.0
10	Georgia	0.0
10	Hawaii	0.0
10	Idaho	0.0
10	Illinois	0.0
10	Indiana	0.0
10	Iowa	0.0
10	Kansas	0.0
10	Kentucky	0.0
10	Louisiana	0.0
10	Maine	0.0
10	Maryland	0.0
10	Massachusetts	0.0
10	Michigan	0.0
10	Minnesota	0.0
6	Mississippi	0.1
10	Missouri	0.0
10	Montana	0.0
10	Nebraska	0.0
10	Nevada	0.0
10	New Hampshire	0.0
10	New Jersey	0.0
10	New Mexico	0.0
1	New York	0.5
6	North Carolina	0.1
10	North Dakota	0.0
10	Ohio	0.0
10	Oklahoma	0.0
10	Oregon	0.0
10	Pennsylvania	0.0
10	Rhode Island	0.0
1	South Carolina	0.5
10	South Dakota	0.0
10	Tennessee	0.0
4	Texas	0.2
10	Utah	0.0
10	Vermont	0.0
6	Virginia	0.1
10	Washington	0.0
10	West Virginia	0.0
10	Wisconsin	0.0
4	Wyoming	0.2

RANK ORDER

RANK	STATE	RATE
1	New York	0.5
1	South Carolina	0.5
3	Arkansas	0.3
4	Texas	0.2
4	Wyoming	0.2
6	Connecticut	0.1
6	Mississippi	0.1
6	North Carolina	0.1
6	Virginia	0.1
10	Alabama	0.0
10	Alaska	0.0
10	Arizona	0.0
10	California	0.0
10	Colorado	0.0
10	Delaware	0.0
10	Florida	0.0
10	Georgia	0.0
10	Hawaii	0.0
10	Idaho	0.0
10	Illinois	0.0
10	Indiana	0.0
10	Iowa	0.0
10	Kansas	0.0
10	Kentucky	0.0
10	Louisiana	0.0
10	Maine	0.0
10	Maryland	0.0
10	Massachusetts	0.0
10	Michigan	0.0
10	Minnesota	0.0
10	Missouri	0.0
10	Montana	0.0
10	Nebraska	0.0
10	Nevada	0.0
10	New Hampshire	0.0
10	New Jersey	0.0
10	New Mexico	0.0
10	North Dakota	0.0
10	Ohio	0.0
10	Oklahoma	0.0
10	Oregon	0.0
10	Pennsylvania	0.0
10	Rhode Island	0.0
10	South Dakota	0.0
10	Tennessee	0.0
10	Utah	0.0
10	Vermont	0.0
10	Washington	0.0
10	West Virginia	0.0
10	Wisconsin	0.0
	District of Columbia	0.0

Source: U.S. Department of Health and Human Services, National Center for Health Statistics
    "Sexually Transmitted Disease Surveillance 1998" (http://www.cdc.gov/nchstp/dstd/dstdp.html)
*A soft, highly infectious, nonsyphilitic venereal ulcer of the genital region, caused by the bacillus Hemophilus ducreyi. Also called soft chancre.

Chlamydia Cases Reported in 1998

National Total = 607,602 Cases*

ALPHA ORDER

RANK	STATE	CASES	% of USA
23	Alabama	10,065	1.7%
43	Alaska	1,907	0.3%
19	Arizona	11,489	1.9%
33	Arkansas	4,123	0.7%
1	California	76,490	12.6%
25	Colorado	9,113	1.5%
27	Connecticut	6,977	1.1%
38	Delaware	2,608	0.4%
7	Florida	24,949	4.1%
6	Georgia	25,250	4.2%
39	Hawaii	2,604	0.4%
42	Idaho	2,035	0.3%
4	Illinois	26,363	4.3%
21	Indiana	10,801	1.8%
32	Iowa	5,174	0.9%
31	Kansas	5,587	0.9%
29	Kentucky	6,441	1.1%
12	Louisiana	15,188	2.5%
46	Maine	1,073	0.2%
16	Maryland	13,097	2.2%
26	Massachusetts	8,363	1.4%
10	Michigan	22,156	3.6%
28	Minnesota	6,970	1.1%
22	Mississippi	10,614	1.7%
17	Missouri	12,670	2.1%
45	Montana	1,412	0.2%
36	Nebraska	2,911	0.5%
35	Nevada	3,320	0.5%
48	New Hampshire	960	0.2%
18	New Jersey	11,686	1.9%
34	New Mexico	3,793	0.6%
5	New York	26,218	4.3%
9	North Carolina	22,197	3.7%
47	North Dakota	1,036	0.2%
3	Ohio	27,786	4.6%
24	Oklahoma	9,393	1.5%
30	Oregon	5,855	1.0%
8	Pennsylvania	24,629	4.1%
40	Rhode Island	2,307	0.4%
11	South Carolina	18,510	3.0%
44	South Dakota	1,572	0.3%
14	Tennessee	13,717	2.3%
2	Texas	60,436	9.9%
41	Utah	2,209	0.4%
50	Vermont	413	0.1%
15	Virginia	13,561	2.2%
20	Washington	10,998	1.8%
37	West Virginia	2,791	0.5%
13	Wisconsin	13,878	2.3%
49	Wyoming	725	0.1%

RANK ORDER

RANK	STATE	CASES	% of USA
1	California	76,490	12.6%
2	Texas	60,436	9.9%
3	Ohio	27,786	4.6%
4	Illinois	26,363	4.3%
5	New York	26,218	4.3%
6	Georgia	25,250	4.2%
7	Florida	24,949	4.1%
8	Pennsylvania	24,629	4.1%
9	North Carolina	22,197	3.7%
10	Michigan	22,156	3.6%
11	South Carolina	18,510	3.0%
12	Louisiana	15,188	2.5%
13	Wisconsin	13,878	2.3%
14	Tennessee	13,717	2.3%
15	Virginia	13,561	2.2%
16	Maryland	13,097	2.2%
17	Missouri	12,670	2.1%
18	New Jersey	11,686	1.9%
19	Arizona	11,489	1.9%
20	Washington	10,998	1.8%
21	Indiana	10,801	1.8%
22	Mississippi	10,614	1.7%
23	Alabama	10,065	1.7%
24	Oklahoma	9,393	1.5%
25	Colorado	9,113	1.5%
26	Massachusetts	8,363	1.4%
27	Connecticut	6,977	1.1%
28	Minnesota	6,970	1.1%
29	Kentucky	6,441	1.1%
30	Oregon	5,855	1.0%
31	Kansas	5,587	0.9%
32	Iowa	5,174	0.9%
33	Arkansas	4,123	0.7%
34	New Mexico	3,793	0.6%
35	Nevada	3,320	0.5%
36	Nebraska	2,911	0.5%
37	West Virginia	2,791	0.5%
38	Delaware	2,608	0.4%
39	Hawaii	2,604	0.4%
40	Rhode Island	2,307	0.4%
41	Utah	2,209	0.4%
42	Idaho	2,035	0.3%
43	Alaska	1,907	0.3%
44	South Dakota	1,572	0.3%
45	Montana	1,412	0.2%
46	Maine	1,073	0.2%
47	North Dakota	1,036	0.2%
48	New Hampshire	960	0.2%
49	Wyoming	725	0.1%
50	Vermont	413	0.1%
	District of Columbia	3,182	0.5%

Source: U.S. Department of Health and Human Services, National Center for Health Statistics
"Sexually Transmitted Disease Surveillance 1998" (http://www.cdc.gov/nchstp/dstd/dstdp.html)
*Any of several common, often asymptomatic, sexually transmitted diseases caused by the microorganism Chlamydia trachomatis, including nonspecific urethritis in men.

Chlamydia Rate in 1998

National Rate = 236.6 Cases per 100,000 Population*

ALPHA ORDER				RANK ORDER		
RANK	STATE	RATE		RANK	STATE	RATE
20	Alabama	233.0		1	South Carolina	492.3
7	Alaska	313.0		2	Mississippi	388.7
14	Arizona	252.2		3	New York	357.1
39	Arkansas	163.4		4	Delaware	356.5
16	California	237.0		5	Louisiana	349.0
18	Colorado	234.1		6	Georgia	337.3
26	Connecticut	213.4		7	Alaska	313.0
4	Delaware	356.5		8	Texas	310.9
36	Florida	170.3		9	North Carolina	298.9
6	Georgia	337.3		10	Oklahoma	283.2
23	Hawaii	219.5		11	Wisconsin	268.5
37	Idaho	168.1		12	Maryland	257.1
22	Illinois	221.6		13	Tennessee	255.5
32	Indiana	184.2		14	Arizona	252.2
33	Iowa	181.4		15	Ohio	248.4
25	Kansas	215.3		16	California	237.0
38	Kentucky	164.8		17	Missouri	234.5
5	Louisiana	349.0		18	Colorado	234.1
48	Maine	86.4		19	Rhode Island	233.6
12	Maryland	257.1		20	Alabama	233.0
46	Massachusetts	136.7		21	Michigan	226.7
21	Michigan	226.7		22	Illinois	221.6
44	Minnesota	148.8		23	Hawaii	219.5
2	Mississippi	388.7		24	New Mexico	219.3
17	Missouri	234.5		25	Kansas	215.3
41	Montana	160.7		26	Connecticut	213.4
35	Nebraska	175.7		27	South Dakota	213.0
30	Nevada	198.0		28	Pennsylvania	204.9
49	New Hampshire	81.9		29	Virginia	201.4
45	New Jersey	145.1		30	Nevada	198.0
24	New Mexico	219.3		31	Washington	196.0
3	New York	357.1		32	Indiana	184.2
9	North Carolina	298.9		33	Iowa	181.4
40	North Dakota	161.7		34	Oregon	180.5
15	Ohio	248.4		35	Nebraska	175.7
10	Oklahoma	283.2		36	Florida	170.3
34	Oregon	180.5		37	Idaho	168.1
28	Pennsylvania	204.9		38	Kentucky	164.8
19	Rhode Island	233.6		39	Arkansas	163.4
1	South Carolina	492.3		40	North Dakota	161.7
27	South Dakota	213.0		41	Montana	160.7
13	Tennessee	255.5		42	West Virginia	153.7
8	Texas	310.9		43	Wyoming	151.1
47	Utah	107.3		44	Minnesota	148.8
50	Vermont	70.1		45	New Jersey	145.1
29	Virginia	201.4		46	Massachusetts	136.7
31	Washington	196.0		47	Utah	107.3
42	West Virginia	153.7		48	Maine	86.4
11	Wisconsin	268.5		49	New Hampshire	81.9
43	Wyoming	151.1		50	Vermont	70.1
					District of Columbia	610.2

Source: U.S. Department of Health and Human Services, National Center for Health Statistics
    "Sexually Transmitted Disease Surveillance 1998" (http://www.cdc.gov/nchstp/dstd/dstdp.html)
*Any of several common, often asymptomatic, sexually transmitted diseases caused by the microorganism Chlamydia trachomatis, including nonspecific urethritis in men.

Gonorrhea Cases Reported in 1998

National Total = 355,642 Cases*

ALPHA ORDER

RANK	STATE	CASES	% of USA
10	Alabama	12,737	3.6%
41	Alaska	331	0.1%
23	Arizona	4,213	1.2%
24	Arkansas	3,953	1.1%
4	California	19,518	5.5%
30	Colorado	2,033	0.6%
26	Connecticut	3,177	0.9%
33	Delaware	1,556	0.4%
6	Florida	19,080	5.4%
3	Georgia	20,666	5.8%
39	Hawaii	506	0.1%
44	Idaho	182	0.1%
2	Illinois	21,735	6.1%
21	Indiana	6,307	1.8%
32	Iowa	1,616	0.5%
28	Kansas	2,622	0.7%
25	Kentucky	3,813	1.1%
11	Louisiana	12,499	3.5%
47	Maine	67	0.0%
15	Maryland	11,254	3.2%
29	Massachusetts	2,258	0.6%
9	Michigan	16,359	4.6%
27	Minnesota	2,708	0.8%
16	Mississippi	10,689	3.0%
17	Missouri	9,463	2.7%
48	Montana	55	0.0%
35	Nebraska	1,204	0.3%
34	Nevada	1,445	0.4%
45	New Hampshire	91	0.0%
19	New Jersey	7,858	2.2%
36	New Mexico	957	0.3%
7	New York	19,062	5.4%
5	North Carolina	19,230	5.4%
46	North Dakota	80	0.0%
8	Ohio	18,275	5.1%
22	Oklahoma	5,243	1.5%
38	Oregon	880	0.2%
13	Pennsylvania	11,719	3.3%
40	Rhode Island	430	0.1%
14	South Carolina	11,575	3.3%
43	South Dakota	221	0.1%
12	Tennessee	11,840	3.3%
1	Texas	32,833	9.2%
42	Utah	236	0.1%
49	Vermont	38	0.0%
18	Virginia	9,265	2.6%
31	Washington	1,948	0.5%
37	West Virginia	920	0.3%
20	Wisconsin	6,351	1.8%
50	Wyoming	36	0.0%

RANK ORDER

RANK	STATE	CASES	% of USA
1	Texas	32,833	9.2%
2	Illinois	21,735	6.1%
3	Georgia	20,666	5.8%
4	California	19,518	5.5%
5	North Carolina	19,230	5.4%
6	Florida	19,080	5.4%
7	New York	19,062	5.4%
8	Ohio	18,275	5.1%
9	Michigan	16,359	4.6%
10	Alabama	12,737	3.6%
11	Louisiana	12,499	3.5%
12	Tennessee	11,840	3.3%
13	Pennsylvania	11,719	3.3%
14	South Carolina	11,575	3.3%
15	Maryland	11,254	3.2%
16	Mississippi	10,689	3.0%
17	Missouri	9,463	2.7%
18	Virginia	9,265	2.6%
19	New Jersey	7,858	2.2%
20	Wisconsin	6,351	1.8%
21	Indiana	6,307	1.8%
22	Oklahoma	5,243	1.5%
23	Arizona	4,213	1.2%
24	Arkansas	3,953	1.1%
25	Kentucky	3,813	1.1%
26	Connecticut	3,177	0.9%
27	Minnesota	2,708	0.8%
28	Kansas	2,622	0.7%
29	Massachusetts	2,258	0.6%
30	Colorado	2,033	0.6%
31	Washington	1,948	0.5%
32	Iowa	1,616	0.5%
33	Delaware	1,556	0.4%
34	Nevada	1,445	0.4%
35	Nebraska	1,204	0.3%
36	New Mexico	957	0.3%
37	West Virginia	920	0.3%
38	Oregon	880	0.2%
39	Hawaii	506	0.1%
40	Rhode Island	430	0.1%
41	Alaska	331	0.1%
42	Utah	236	0.1%
43	South Dakota	221	0.1%
44	Idaho	182	0.1%
45	New Hampshire	91	0.0%
46	North Dakota	80	0.0%
47	Maine	67	0.0%
48	Montana	55	0.0%
49	Vermont	38	0.0%
50	Wyoming	36	0.0%
	District of Columbia	4,508	1.3%

Source: U.S. Department of Health and Human Services, National Center for Health Statistics
"Sexually Transmitted Disease Surveillance 1998" (http://www.cdc.gov/nchstp/dstd/dstdp.html)
*Gonorrhea is a sexually transmitted disease caused by gonococcal bacteria that affects the mucous membrane chiefly of the genital and urinary tracts and is characterized by an acute purulent discharge and painful or difficult urination, though women often have no symptoms.

Gonorrhea Rate in 1998

National Rate = 132.9 Cases per 100,000 Population*

ALPHA ORDER				RANK ORDER		
RANK	STATE	RATE		RANK	STATE	RATE
3	Alabama	294.9		1	Mississippi	391.5
34	Alaska	54.3		2	South Carolina	307.8
27	Arizona	92.5		3	Alabama	294.9
16	Arkansas	156.7		4	Louisiana	287.2
30	California	60.5		5	Georgia	276.1
35	Colorado	52.2		6	North Carolina	259.0
26	Connecticut	97.2		7	Maryland	220.9
9	Delaware	212.7		8	Tennessee	220.6
18	Florida	130.2		9	Delaware	212.7
5	Georgia	276.1		10	Illinois	182.7
38	Hawaii	42.6		11	Missouri	175.2
43	Idaho	15.0		12	Texas	168.9
10	Illinois	182.7		13	Michigan	167.4
20	Indiana	107.6		14	Ohio	163.4
32	Iowa	56.7		15	Oklahoma	158.1
22	Kansas	101.0		16	Arkansas	156.7
23	Kentucky	97.6		17	Virginia	137.6
4	Louisiana	287.2		18	Florida	130.2
50	Maine	5.4		19	Wisconsin	122.9
7	Maryland	220.9		20	Indiana	107.6
39	Massachusetts	36.9		21	New York	105.1
13	Michigan	167.4		22	Kansas	101.0
31	Minnesota	57.8		23	Kentucky	97.6
1	Mississippi	391.5		23	New Jersey	97.6
11	Missouri	175.2		25	Pennsylvania	97.5
49	Montana	6.3		26	Connecticut	97.2
29	Nebraska	72.7		27	Arizona	92.5
28	Nevada	86.2		28	Nevada	86.2
46	New Hampshire	7.8		29	Nebraska	72.7
23	New Jersey	97.6		30	California	60.5
33	New Mexico	55.3		31	Minnesota	57.8
21	New York	105.1		32	Iowa	56.7
6	North Carolina	259.0		33	New Mexico	55.3
44	North Dakota	12.5		34	Alaska	54.3
14	Ohio	163.4		35	Colorado	52.2
15	Oklahoma	158.1		36	West Virginia	50.7
42	Oregon	27.1		37	Rhode Island	43.5
25	Pennsylvania	97.5		38	Hawaii	42.6
37	Rhode Island	43.5		39	Massachusetts	36.9
2	South Carolina	307.8		40	Washington	34.7
41	South Dakota	29.9		41	South Dakota	29.9
8	Tennessee	220.6		42	Oregon	27.1
12	Texas	168.9		43	Idaho	15.0
45	Utah	11.5		44	North Dakota	12.5
48	Vermont	6.5		45	Utah	11.5
17	Virginia	137.6		46	New Hampshire	7.8
40	Washington	34.7		47	Wyoming	7.5
36	West Virginia	50.7		48	Vermont	6.5
19	Wisconsin	122.9		49	Montana	6.3
47	Wyoming	7.5		50	Maine	5.4

District of Columbia 864.6

Source: U.S. Department of Health and Human Services, National Center for Health Statistics
    "Sexually Transmitted Disease Surveillance 1998" (http://www.cdc.gov/nchstp/dstd/dstdp.html)
*Gonorrhea is a sexually transmitted disease caused by gonococcal bacteria that affects the mucous membrane chiefly of the genital and urinary tracts and is characterized by an acute purulent discharge and painful or difficult urination, though women often have no symptoms.

Syphilis Cases Reported in 1998

National Total = 6,993 Cases*

ALPHA ORDER

RANK	STATE	CASES	% of USA
10	Alabama	274	3.9%
44	Alaska	1	0.0%
15	Arizona	185	2.6%
20	Arkansas	108	1.5%
8	California	303	4.3%
33	Colorado	10	0.1%
28	Connecticut	26	0.4%
29	Delaware	21	0.3%
9	Florida	294	4.2%
7	Georgia	333	4.8%
38	Hawaii	4	0.1%
42	Idaho	2	0.0%
6	Illinois	424	6.1%
13	Indiana	215	3.1%
37	Iowa	5	0.1%
31	Kansas	14	0.2%
22	Kentucky	106	1.5%
5	Louisiana	430	6.1%
44	Maine	1	0.0%
2	Maryland	648	9.3%
26	Massachusetts	46	0.7%
14	Michigan	211	3.0%
34	Minnesota	9	0.1%
12	Mississippi	261	3.7%
19	Missouri	109	1.6%
49	Montana	0	0.0%
35	Nebraska	8	0.1%
30	Nevada	15	0.2%
42	New Hampshire	2	0.0%
21	New Jersey	107	1.5%
31	New Mexico	14	0.2%
18	New York	119	1.7%
1	North Carolina	723	10.3%
49	North Dakota	0	0.0%
17	Ohio	134	1.9%
23	Oklahoma	98	1.4%
36	Oregon	6	0.1%
23	Pennsylvania	98	1.4%
44	Rhode Island	1	0.0%
11	South Carolina	271	3.9%
44	South Dakota	1	0.0%
3	Tennessee	567	8.1%
4	Texas	443	6.3%
38	Utah	4	0.1%
38	Vermont	4	0.1%
16	Virginia	149	2.1%
27	Washington	44	0.6%
41	West Virginia	3	0.0%
25	Wisconsin	60	0.9%
44	Wyoming	1	0.0%

RANK ORDER

RANK	STATE	CASES	% of USA
1	North Carolina	723	10.3%
2	Maryland	648	9.3%
3	Tennessee	567	8.1%
4	Texas	443	6.3%
5	Louisiana	430	6.1%
6	Illinois	424	6.1%
7	Georgia	333	4.8%
8	California	303	4.3%
9	Florida	294	4.2%
10	Alabama	274	3.9%
11	South Carolina	271	3.9%
12	Mississippi	261	3.7%
13	Indiana	215	3.1%
14	Michigan	211	3.0%
15	Arizona	185	2.6%
16	Virginia	149	2.1%
17	Ohio	134	1.9%
18	New York	119	1.7%
19	Missouri	109	1.6%
20	Arkansas	108	1.5%
21	New Jersey	107	1.5%
22	Kentucky	106	1.5%
23	Oklahoma	98	1.4%
23	Pennsylvania	98	1.4%
25	Wisconsin	60	0.9%
26	Massachusetts	46	0.7%
27	Washington	44	0.6%
28	Connecticut	26	0.4%
29	Delaware	21	0.3%
30	Nevada	15	0.2%
31	Kansas	14	0.2%
31	New Mexico	14	0.2%
33	Colorado	10	0.1%
34	Minnesota	9	0.1%
35	Nebraska	8	0.1%
36	Oregon	6	0.1%
37	Iowa	5	0.1%
38	Hawaii	4	0.1%
38	Utah	4	0.1%
38	Vermont	4	0.1%
41	West Virginia	3	0.0%
42	Idaho	2	0.0%
42	New Hampshire	2	0.0%
44	Alaska	1	0.0%
44	Maine	1	0.0%
44	Rhode Island	1	0.0%
44	South Dakota	1	0.0%
44	Wyoming	1	0.0%
49	Montana	0	0.0%
49	North Dakota	0	0.0%
	District of Columbia	81	1.2%

Source: U.S. Department of Health and Human Services, National Center for Health Statistics
"Sexually Transmitted Disease Surveillance 1998" (http://www.cdc.gov/nchstp/dstd/dstdp.html)
*Includes only primary and secondary cases. Does not include 30,984 cases in other stages. A chronic infectious disease caused by a spirochete (Treponema pallidum), either transmitted by direct contact, usually in sexual intercourse, or passed from mother to child in utero, and progressing through three stages characterized respectively by local formation of chancres, ulcerous skin eruptions, and systemic infection leading to general paresis.

Syphilis Rate in 1998

National Rate = 2.6 Cases per 100,000 Population*

ALPHA ORDER

RANK	STATE	RATE
7	Alabama	6.3
37	Alaska	0.2
10	Arizona	4.1
9	Arkansas	4.3
24	California	0.9
35	Colorado	0.3
26	Connecticut	0.8
14	Delaware	2.9
19	Florida	2.0
8	Georgia	4.4
35	Hawaii	0.3
37	Idaho	0.2
12	Illinois	3.6
11	Indiana	3.7
37	Iowa	0.2
33	Kansas	0.5
15	Kentucky	2.7
3	Louisiana	9.9
46	Maine	0.1
1	Maryland	12.7
26	Massachusetts	0.8
17	Michigan	2.2
37	Minnesota	0.2
5	Mississippi	9.6
19	Missouri	2.0
49	Montana	0.0
33	Nebraska	0.5
24	Nevada	0.9
37	New Hampshire	0.2
21	New Jersey	1.3
26	New Mexico	0.8
31	New York	0.7
4	North Carolina	9.7
49	North Dakota	0.0
22	Ohio	1.2
13	Oklahoma	3.0
37	Oregon	0.2
26	Pennsylvania	0.8
46	Rhode Island	0.1
6	South Carolina	7.2
46	South Dakota	0.1
2	Tennessee	10.6
16	Texas	2.3
37	Utah	0.2
31	Vermont	0.7
17	Virginia	2.2
26	Washington	0.8
37	West Virginia	0.2
22	Wisconsin	1.2
37	Wyoming	0.2

RANK ORDER

RANK	STATE	RATE
1	Maryland	12.7
2	Tennessee	10.6
3	Louisiana	9.9
4	North Carolina	9.7
5	Mississippi	9.6
6	South Carolina	7.2
7	Alabama	6.3
8	Georgia	4.4
9	Arkansas	4.3
10	Arizona	4.1
11	Indiana	3.7
12	Illinois	3.6
13	Oklahoma	3.0
14	Delaware	2.9
15	Kentucky	2.7
16	Texas	2.3
17	Michigan	2.2
17	Virginia	2.2
19	Florida	2.0
19	Missouri	2.0
21	New Jersey	1.3
22	Ohio	1.2
22	Wisconsin	1.2
24	California	0.9
24	Nevada	0.9
26	Connecticut	0.8
26	Massachusetts	0.8
26	New Mexico	0.8
26	Pennsylvania	0.8
26	Washington	0.8
31	New York	0.7
31	Vermont	0.7
33	Kansas	0.5
33	Nebraska	0.5
35	Colorado	0.3
35	Hawaii	0.3
37	Alaska	0.2
37	Idaho	0.2
37	Iowa	0.2
37	Minnesota	0.2
37	New Hampshire	0.2
37	Oregon	0.2
37	Utah	0.2
37	West Virginia	0.2
37	Wyoming	0.2
46	Maine	0.1
46	Rhode Island	0.1
46	South Dakota	0.1
49	Montana	0.0
49	North Dakota	0.0

District of Columbia 15.5

Source: U.S. Department of Health and Human Services, National Center for Health Statistics
"Sexually Transmitted Disease Surveillance 1998" (http://www.cdc.gov/nchstp/dstd/dstdp.html)
*Includes only primary and secondary cases. Does not include 30,984 cases in other stages. A chronic infectious disease caused by a spirochete (Treponema pallidum), either transmitted by direct contact, usually in sexual intercourse, or passed from mother to child in utero, and progressing through three stages characterized respectively by local formation of chancres, ulcerous skin eruptions, and systemic infection leading to general paresis.

VI. PROVIDERS

VI. PROVIDERS (continued)

Physicians in 1998

National Total = 765,922 Physicians*

ALPHA ORDER

RANK	STATE	PHYSICIANS	% of USA
25	Alabama	9,500	1.2%
49	Alaska	1,247	0.2%
23	Arizona	11,479	1.5%
32	Arkansas	5,464	0.7%
1	California	93,000	12.1%
24	Colorado	10,876	1.4%
20	Connecticut	12,859	1.7%
46	Delaware	1,972	0.3%
4	Florida	43,297	5.7%
14	Georgia	18,175	2.4%
38	Hawaii	3,774	0.5%
43	Idaho	2,232	0.3%
6	Illinois	34,375	4.5%
21	Indiana	12,769	1.7%
31	Iowa	5,745	0.8%
30	Kansas	6,205	0.8%
26	Kentucky	9,080	1.2%
22	Louisiana	11,728	1.5%
42	Maine	3,252	0.4%
11	Maryland	22,580	2.9%
8	Massachusetts	27,646	3.6%
10	Michigan	24,263	3.2%
18	Minnesota	13,290	1.7%
33	Mississippi	5,133	0.7%
17	Missouri	13,699	1.8%
45	Montana	2,009	0.3%
37	Nebraska	4,071	0.5%
40	Nevada	3,479	0.5%
41	New Hampshire	3,253	0.4%
9	New Jersey	26,135	3.4%
36	New Mexico	4,378	0.6%
2	New York	76,157	9.9%
12	North Carolina	19,795	2.6%
48	North Dakota	1,585	0.2%
7	Ohio	29,282	3.8%
29	Oklahoma	6,412	0.8%
28	Oregon	8,796	1.1%
5	Pennsylvania	38,609	5.0%
39	Rhode Island	3,673	0.5%
27	South Carolina	8,967	1.2%
47	South Dakota	1,592	0.2%
16	Tennessee	14,790	1.9%
3	Texas	44,560	5.8%
34	Utah	4,750	0.6%
44	Vermont	2,097	0.3%
13	Virginia	18,990	2.5%
15	Washington	15,834	2.1%
35	West Virginia	4,383	0.6%
19	Wisconsin	13,260	1.7%
50	Wyoming	986	0.1%

RANK ORDER

RANK	STATE	PHYSICIANS	% of USA
1	California	93,000	12.1%
2	New York	76,157	9.9%
3	Texas	44,560	5.8%
4	Florida	43,297	5.7%
5	Pennsylvania	38,609	5.0%
6	Illinois	34,375	4.5%
7	Ohio	29,282	3.8%
8	Massachusetts	27,646	3.6%
9	New Jersey	26,135	3.4%
10	Michigan	24,263	3.2%
11	Maryland	22,580	2.9%
12	North Carolina	19,795	2.6%
13	Virginia	18,990	2.5%
14	Georgia	18,175	2.4%
15	Washington	15,834	2.1%
16	Tennessee	14,790	1.9%
17	Missouri	13,699	1.8%
18	Minnesota	13,290	1.7%
19	Wisconsin	13,260	1.7%
20	Connecticut	12,859	1.7%
21	Indiana	12,769	1.7%
22	Louisiana	11,728	1.5%
23	Arizona	11,479	1.5%
24	Colorado	10,876	1.4%
25	Alabama	9,500	1.2%
26	Kentucky	9,080	1.2%
27	South Carolina	8,967	1.2%
28	Oregon	8,796	1.1%
29	Oklahoma	6,412	0.8%
30	Kansas	6,205	0.8%
31	Iowa	5,745	0.8%
32	Arkansas	5,464	0.7%
33	Mississippi	5,133	0.7%
34	Utah	4,750	0.6%
35	West Virginia	4,383	0.6%
36	New Mexico	4,378	0.6%
37	Nebraska	4,071	0.5%
38	Hawaii	3,774	0.5%
39	Rhode Island	3,673	0.5%
40	Nevada	3,479	0.5%
41	New Hampshire	3,253	0.4%
42	Maine	3,252	0.4%
43	Idaho	2,232	0.3%
44	Vermont	2,097	0.3%
45	Montana	2,009	0.3%
46	Delaware	1,972	0.3%
47	South Dakota	1,592	0.2%
48	North Dakota	1,585	0.2%
49	Alaska	1,247	0.2%
50	Wyoming	986	0.1%
	District of Columbia	4,439	0.6%

Source: American Medical Association (Chicago, Illinois)
    "Physician Characteristics and Distribution in the U.S." (2000-2001 Edition)
*As of December 31, 1998. Comprised of federal and nonfederal physicians. Total does not include 11,937
physicians in the U.S. territories and possessions, at APO's and FPO's and whose addresses are unknown.

Male Physicians in 1998

National Total = 591,992 Physicians*

ALPHA ORDER

RANK	STATE	PHYSICIANS	% of USA
25	Alabama	7,842	1.3%
49	Alaska	951	0.2%
23	Arizona	9,114	1.5%
32	Arkansas	4,535	0.8%
1	California	72,003	12.2%
24	Colorado	8,355	1.4%
21	Connecticut	9,804	1.7%
46	Delaware	1,506	0.3%
3	Florida	36,072	6.1%
14	Georgia	14,396	2.4%
38	Hawaii	2,951	0.5%
43	Idaho	1,935	0.3%
6	Illinois	25,134	4.2%
19	Indiana	10,269	1.7%
31	Iowa	4,704	0.8%
30	Kansas	4,925	0.8%
27	Kentucky	7,279	1.2%
22	Louisiana	9,320	1.6%
42	Maine	2,552	0.4%
11	Maryland	16,582	2.8%
8	Massachusetts	19,839	3.4%
10	Michigan	18,375	3.1%
20	Minnesota	10,243	1.7%
33	Mississippi	4,306	0.7%
17	Missouri	10,735	1.8%
44	Montana	1,708	0.3%
36	Nebraska	3,310	0.6%
39	Nevada	2,903	0.5%
41	New Hampshire	2,587	0.4%
9	New Jersey	19,298	3.3%
37	New Mexico	3,186	0.5%
2	New York	55,616	9.4%
12	North Carolina	15,559	2.6%
48	North Dakota	1,335	0.2%
7	Ohio	22,504	3.8%
29	Oklahoma	5,239	0.9%
28	Oregon	6,938	1.2%
5	Pennsylvania	29,445	5.0%
40	Rhode Island	2,722	0.5%
26	South Carolina	7,295	1.2%
47	South Dakota	1,339	0.2%
16	Tennessee	12,007	2.0%
4	Texas	35,060	5.9%
34	Utah	3,992	0.7%
45	Vermont	1,569	0.3%
13	Virginia	14,563	2.5%
15	Washington	12,272	2.1%
35	West Virginia	3,508	0.6%
18	Wisconsin	10,384	1.8%
50	Wyoming	835	0.1%

RANK ORDER

RANK	STATE	PHYSICIANS	% of USA
1	California	72,003	12.2%
2	New York	55,616	9.4%
3	Florida	36,072	6.1%
4	Texas	35,060	5.9%
5	Pennsylvania	29,445	5.0%
6	Illinois	25,134	4.2%
7	Ohio	22,504	3.8%
8	Massachusetts	19,839	3.4%
9	New Jersey	19,298	3.3%
10	Michigan	18,375	3.1%
11	Maryland	16,582	2.8%
12	North Carolina	15,559	2.6%
13	Virginia	14,563	2.5%
14	Georgia	14,396	2.4%
15	Washington	12,272	2.1%
16	Tennessee	12,007	2.0%
17	Missouri	10,735	1.8%
18	Wisconsin	10,384	1.8%
19	Indiana	10,269	1.7%
20	Minnesota	10,243	1.7%
21	Connecticut	9,804	1.7%
22	Louisiana	9,320	1.6%
23	Arizona	9,114	1.5%
24	Colorado	8,355	1.4%
25	Alabama	7,842	1.3%
26	South Carolina	7,295	1.2%
27	Kentucky	7,279	1.2%
28	Oregon	6,938	1.2%
29	Oklahoma	5,239	0.9%
30	Kansas	4,925	0.8%
31	Iowa	4,704	0.8%
32	Arkansas	4,535	0.8%
33	Mississippi	4,306	0.7%
34	Utah	3,992	0.7%
35	West Virginia	3,508	0.6%
36	Nebraska	3,310	0.6%
37	New Mexico	3,186	0.5%
38	Hawaii	2,951	0.5%
39	Nevada	2,903	0.5%
40	Rhode Island	2,722	0.5%
41	New Hampshire	2,587	0.4%
42	Maine	2,552	0.4%
43	Idaho	1,935	0.3%
44	Montana	1,708	0.3%
45	Vermont	1,569	0.3%
46	Delaware	1,506	0.3%
47	South Dakota	1,339	0.2%
48	North Dakota	1,335	0.2%
49	Alaska	951	0.2%
50	Wyoming	835	0.1%
	District of Columbia	3,091	0.5%

Source: American Medical Association (Chicago, Illinois)
    "Physician Characteristics and Distribution in the U.S." (2000-2001 Edition)
*As of December 31, 1998. Comprised of federal and nonfederal physicians. Total does not include 8,837 male physicians in the U.S. territories and possessions, at APO's and FPO's and whose addresses are unknown.

Female Physicians in 1998

National Total = 173,930 Physicians*

ALPHA ORDER

RANK	STATE	PHYSICIANS	% of USA
28	Alabama	1,658	1.0%
47	Alaska	296	0.2%
24	Arizona	2,365	1.4%
34	Arkansas	929	0.5%
1	California	20,997	12.1%
21	Colorado	2,521	1.4%
16	Connecticut	3,055	1.8%
44	Delaware	466	0.3%
7	Florida	7,225	4.2%
14	Georgia	3,779	2.2%
37	Hawaii	823	0.5%
46	Idaho	297	0.2%
4	Illinois	9,241	5.3%
22	Indiana	2,500	1.4%
32	Iowa	1,041	0.6%
29	Kansas	1,280	0.7%
26	Kentucky	1,801	1.0%
23	Louisiana	2,408	1.4%
40	Maine	700	0.4%
10	Maryland	5,998	3.4%
6	Massachusetts	7,807	4.5%
11	Michigan	5,888	3.4%
17	Minnesota	3,047	1.8%
36	Mississippi	827	0.5%
18	Missouri	2,964	1.7%
45	Montana	301	0.2%
38	Nebraska	761	0.4%
42	Nevada	576	0.3%
41	New Hampshire	666	0.4%
8	New Jersey	6,837	3.9%
30	New Mexico	1,192	0.7%
2	New York	20,541	11.8%
13	North Carolina	4,236	2.4%
49	North Dakota	250	0.1%
9	Ohio	6,778	3.9%
31	Oklahoma	1,173	0.7%
25	Oregon	1,858	1.1%
5	Pennsylvania	9,164	5.3%
33	Rhode Island	951	0.5%
27	South Carolina	1,672	1.0%
48	South Dakota	253	0.1%
20	Tennessee	2,783	1.6%
3	Texas	9,500	5.5%
39	Utah	758	0.4%
43	Vermont	528	0.3%
12	Virginia	4,427	2.5%
15	Washington	3,562	2.0%
35	West Virginia	875	0.5%
19	Wisconsin	2,876	1.7%
50	Wyoming	151	0.1%

RANK ORDER

RANK	STATE	PHYSICIANS	% of USA
1	California	20,997	12.1%
2	New York	20,541	11.8%
3	Texas	9,500	5.5%
4	Illinois	9,241	5.3%
5	Pennsylvania	9,164	5.3%
6	Massachusetts	7,807	4.5%
7	Florida	7,225	4.2%
8	New Jersey	6,837	3.9%
9	Ohio	6,778	3.9%
10	Maryland	5,998	3.4%
11	Michigan	5,888	3.4%
12	Virginia	4,427	2.5%
13	North Carolina	4,236	2.4%
14	Georgia	3,779	2.2%
15	Washington	3,562	2.0%
16	Connecticut	3,055	1.8%
17	Minnesota	3,047	1.8%
18	Missouri	2,964	1.7%
19	Wisconsin	2,876	1.7%
20	Tennessee	2,783	1.6%
21	Colorado	2,521	1.4%
22	Indiana	2,500	1.4%
23	Louisiana	2,408	1.4%
24	Arizona	2,365	1.4%
25	Oregon	1,858	1.1%
26	Kentucky	1,801	1.0%
27	South Carolina	1,672	1.0%
28	Alabama	1,658	1.0%
29	Kansas	1,280	0.7%
30	New Mexico	1,192	0.7%
31	Oklahoma	1,173	0.7%
32	Iowa	1,041	0.6%
33	Rhode Island	951	0.5%
34	Arkansas	929	0.5%
35	West Virginia	875	0.5%
36	Mississippi	827	0.5%
37	Hawaii	823	0.5%
38	Nebraska	761	0.4%
39	Utah	758	0.4%
40	Maine	700	0.4%
41	New Hampshire	666	0.4%
42	Nevada	576	0.3%
43	Vermont	528	0.3%
44	Delaware	466	0.3%
45	Montana	301	0.2%
46	Idaho	297	0.2%
47	Alaska	296	0.2%
48	South Dakota	253	0.1%
49	North Dakota	250	0.1%
50	Wyoming	151	0.1%
	District of Columbia	1,348	0.8%

Source: American Medical Association (Chicago, Illinois)
   "Physician Characteristics and Distribution in the U.S." (2000-2001 Edition)
*As of December 31, 1998. Comprised of federal and nonfederal physicians. Total does not include 3,100 female physicians in the U.S. territories and possessions, at APO's and FPO's and whose addresses are unknown.

Percent of Physicians Who Are Female: 1998

National Percent = 22.7% of Physicians*

ALPHA ORDER

RANK	STATE	PERCENT
40	Alabama	17.5
11	Alaska	23.7
28	Arizona	20.6
41	Arkansas	17.0
18	California	22.6
15	Colorado	23.2
10	Connecticut	23.8
13	Delaware	23.6
42	Florida	16.7
27	Georgia	20.8
20	Hawaii	21.8
50	Idaho	13.3
4	Illinois	26.9
34	Indiana	19.6
39	Iowa	18.1
28	Kansas	20.6
33	Kentucky	19.8
30	Louisiana	20.5
23	Maine	21.5
5	Maryland	26.6
1	Massachusetts	28.2
9	Michigan	24.3
17	Minnesota	22.9
44	Mississippi	16.1
22	Missouri	21.6
49	Montana	15.0
36	Nebraska	18.7
43	Nevada	16.6
30	New Hampshire	20.5
6	New Jersey	26.2
2	New Mexico	27.2
3	New York	27.0
24	North Carolina	21.4
47	North Dakota	15.8
16	Ohio	23.1
38	Oklahoma	18.3
26	Oregon	21.1
11	Pennsylvania	23.7
7	Rhode Island	25.9
37	South Carolina	18.6
46	South Dakota	15.9
35	Tennessee	18.8
25	Texas	21.3
45	Utah	16.0
8	Vermont	25.2
14	Virginia	23.3
19	Washington	22.5
32	West Virginia	20.0
21	Wisconsin	21.7
48	Wyoming	15.3

RANK ORDER

RANK	STATE	PERCENT
1	Massachusetts	28.2
2	New Mexico	27.2
3	New York	27.0
4	Illinois	26.9
5	Maryland	26.6
6	New Jersey	26.2
7	Rhode Island	25.9
8	Vermont	25.2
9	Michigan	24.3
10	Connecticut	23.8
11	Alaska	23.7
11	Pennsylvania	23.7
13	Delaware	23.6
14	Virginia	23.3
15	Colorado	23.2
16	Ohio	23.1
17	Minnesota	22.9
18	California	22.6
19	Washington	22.5
20	Hawaii	21.8
21	Wisconsin	21.7
22	Missouri	21.6
23	Maine	21.5
24	North Carolina	21.4
25	Texas	21.3
26	Oregon	21.1
27	Georgia	20.8
28	Arizona	20.6
28	Kansas	20.6
30	Louisiana	20.5
30	New Hampshire	20.5
32	West Virginia	20.0
33	Kentucky	19.8
34	Indiana	19.6
35	Tennessee	18.8
36	Nebraska	18.7
37	South Carolina	18.6
38	Oklahoma	18.3
39	Iowa	18.1
40	Alabama	17.5
41	Arkansas	17.0
42	Florida	16.7
43	Nevada	16.6
44	Mississippi	16.1
45	Utah	16.0
46	South Dakota	15.9
47	North Dakota	15.8
48	Wyoming	15.3
49	Montana	15.0
50	Idaho	13.3

	District of Columbia	30.4

Source: Morgan Quitno Press using data from American Medical Association (Chicago, Illinois)
    "Physician Characteristics and Distribution in the U.S." (2000-2001 Edition)
*As of December 31, 1998. Comprised of federal and nonfederal physicians. National percent does not include
physicians in the U.S. territories and possessions, at APO's and FPO's and whose addresses are unknown.

421

Physicians Under 35 Years Old in 1998

National Total = 133,929 Physicians*

ALPHA ORDER

RANK	STATE	PHYSICIANS	% of USA
24	Alabama	1,646	1.2%
48	Alaska	128	0.1%
26	Arizona	1,574	1.2%
33	Arkansas	873	0.7%
2	California	12,964	9.7%
25	Colorado	1,607	1.2%
20	Connecticut	2,176	1.6%
44	Delaware	319	0.2%
9	Florida	4,648	3.5%
14	Georgia	3,159	2.4%
39	Hawaii	487	0.4%
46	Idaho	231	0.2%
4	Illinois	7,771	5.8%
22	Indiana	2,034	1.5%
29	Iowa	1,028	0.8%
30	Kansas	1,023	0.8%
27	Kentucky	1,560	1.2%
17	Louisiana	2,511	1.9%
42	Maine	329	0.2%
10	Maryland	4,112	3.1%
7	Massachusetts	5,767	4.3%
8	Michigan	5,235	3.9%
18	Minnesota	2,438	1.8%
32	Mississippi	888	0.7%
15	Missouri	2,765	2.1%
50	Montana	107	0.1%
35	Nebraska	785	0.6%
41	Nevada	407	0.3%
40	New Hampshire	415	0.3%
11	New Jersey	3,989	3.0%
38	New Mexico	586	0.4%
1	New York	16,049	12.0%
12	North Carolina	3,906	2.9%
45	North Dakota	236	0.2%
6	Ohio	6,112	4.6%
31	Oklahoma	997	0.7%
28	Oregon	1,067	0.8%
5	Pennsylvania	7,517	5.6%
34	Rhode Island	803	0.6%
23	South Carolina	1,702	1.3%
47	South Dakota	183	0.1%
16	Tennessee	2,679	2.0%
3	Texas	8,568	6.4%
36	Utah	754	0.6%
43	Vermont	326	0.2%
13	Virginia	3,375	2.5%
21	Washington	2,039	1.5%
37	West Virginia	725	0.5%
19	Wisconsin	2,204	1.6%
49	Wyoming	124	0.1%

RANK ORDER

RANK	STATE	PHYSICIANS	% of USA
1	New York	16,049	12.0%
2	California	12,964	9.7%
3	Texas	8,568	6.4%
4	Illinois	7,771	5.8%
5	Pennsylvania	7,517	5.6%
6	Ohio	6,112	4.6%
7	Massachusetts	5,767	4.3%
8	Michigan	5,235	3.9%
9	Florida	4,648	3.5%
10	Maryland	4,112	3.1%
11	New Jersey	3,989	3.0%
12	North Carolina	3,906	2.9%
13	Virginia	3,375	2.5%
14	Georgia	3,159	2.4%
15	Missouri	2,765	2.1%
16	Tennessee	2,679	2.0%
17	Louisiana	2,511	1.9%
18	Minnesota	2,438	1.8%
19	Wisconsin	2,204	1.6%
20	Connecticut	2,176	1.6%
21	Washington	2,039	1.5%
22	Indiana	2,034	1.5%
23	South Carolina	1,702	1.3%
24	Alabama	1,646	1.2%
25	Colorado	1,607	1.2%
26	Arizona	1,574	1.2%
27	Kentucky	1,560	1.2%
28	Oregon	1,067	0.8%
29	Iowa	1,028	0.8%
30	Kansas	1,023	0.8%
31	Oklahoma	997	0.7%
32	Mississippi	888	0.7%
33	Arkansas	873	0.7%
34	Rhode Island	803	0.6%
35	Nebraska	785	0.6%
36	Utah	754	0.6%
37	West Virginia	725	0.5%
38	New Mexico	586	0.4%
39	Hawaii	487	0.4%
40	New Hampshire	415	0.3%
41	Nevada	407	0.3%
42	Maine	329	0.2%
43	Vermont	326	0.2%
44	Delaware	319	0.2%
45	North Dakota	236	0.2%
46	Idaho	231	0.2%
47	South Dakota	183	0.1%
48	Alaska	128	0.1%
49	Wyoming	124	0.1%
50	Montana	107	0.1%
	District of Columbia	1,001	0.7%

Source: American Medical Association (Chicago, Illinois)
    "Physician Characteristics and Distribution in the U.S." (2000-2001 Edition)
*As of December 31, 1998. Comprised of federal and nonfederal physicians. Total does not include 1,683 physicians in the U.S. territories and possessions, at APO's and FPO's and whose addresses are unknown.

Percent of Physicians Under 35 Years Old in 1998

National Percent = 17.5% of Physicians*

ALPHA ORDER

RANK	STATE	PERCENT
20	Alabama	17.3
47	Alaska	10.3
37	Arizona	13.7
28	Arkansas	16.0
36	California	13.9
35	Colorado	14.8
23	Connecticut	16.9
27	Delaware	16.2
46	Florida	10.7
19	Georgia	17.4
39	Hawaii	12.9
47	Idaho	10.3
1	Illinois	22.6
29	Indiana	15.9
17	Iowa	17.9
25	Kansas	16.5
22	Kentucky	17.2
4	Louisiana	21.4
49	Maine	10.1
15	Maryland	18.2
6	Massachusetts	20.9
3	Michigan	21.6
14	Minnesota	18.3
20	Mississippi	17.3
8	Missouri	20.2
50	Montana	5.3
11	Nebraska	19.3
44	Nevada	11.7
41	New Hampshire	12.8
33	New Jersey	15.3
38	New Mexico	13.4
5	New York	21.1
9	North Carolina	19.7
34	North Dakota	14.9
6	Ohio	20.9
31	Oklahoma	15.5
43	Oregon	12.1
10	Pennsylvania	19.5
2	Rhode Island	21.9
13	South Carolina	19.0
45	South Dakota	11.5
16	Tennessee	18.1
12	Texas	19.2
29	Utah	15.9
31	Vermont	15.5
18	Virginia	17.8
39	Washington	12.9
25	West Virginia	16.5
24	Wisconsin	16.6
42	Wyoming	12.6

RANK ORDER

RANK	STATE	PERCENT
1	Illinois	22.6
2	Rhode Island	21.9
3	Michigan	21.6
4	Louisiana	21.4
5	New York	21.1
6	Massachusetts	20.9
6	Ohio	20.9
8	Missouri	20.2
9	North Carolina	19.7
10	Pennsylvania	19.5
11	Nebraska	19.3
12	Texas	19.2
13	South Carolina	19.0
14	Minnesota	18.3
15	Maryland	18.2
16	Tennessee	18.1
17	Iowa	17.9
18	Virginia	17.8
19	Georgia	17.4
20	Alabama	17.3
20	Mississippi	17.3
22	Kentucky	17.2
23	Connecticut	16.9
24	Wisconsin	16.6
25	Kansas	16.5
25	West Virginia	16.5
27	Delaware	16.2
28	Arkansas	16.0
29	Indiana	15.9
29	Utah	15.9
31	Oklahoma	15.5
31	Vermont	15.5
33	New Jersey	15.3
34	North Dakota	14.9
35	Colorado	14.8
36	California	13.9
37	Arizona	13.7
38	New Mexico	13.4
39	Hawaii	12.9
39	Washington	12.9
41	New Hampshire	12.8
42	Wyoming	12.6
43	Oregon	12.1
44	Nevada	11.7
45	South Dakota	11.5
46	Florida	10.7
47	Alaska	10.3
47	Idaho	10.3
49	Maine	10.1
50	Montana	5.3
	District of Columbia	22.6

Source: Morgan Quitno Press using data from American Medical Association (Chicago, Illinois)
    "Physician Characteristics and Distribution in the U.S." (2000-2001 Edition)
*As of December 31, 1998. Comprised of federal and nonfederal physicians. National percent does not include physicians in the U.S. territories and possessions, at APO's and FPO's and whose addresses are unknown.

Physicians 35 to 44 Years Old in 1998

National Total = 210,945 Physicians*

ALPHA ORDER

RANK	STATE	PHYSICIANS	% of USA
25	Alabama	2,925	1.4%
49	Alaska	412	0.2%
23	Arizona	3,091	1.5%
32	Arkansas	1,620	0.8%
1	California	22,021	10.4%
24	Colorado	3,044	1.4%
21	Connecticut	3,560	1.7%
46	Delaware	554	0.3%
4	Florida	11,405	5.4%
13	Georgia	5,638	2.7%
38	Hawaii	1,048	0.5%
43	Idaho	635	0.3%
6	Illinois	9,298	4.4%
20	Indiana	3,779	1.8%
31	Iowa	1,630	0.8%
29	Kansas	1,726	0.8%
26	Kentucky	2,722	1.3%
22	Louisiana	3,189	1.5%
42	Maine	851	0.4%
11	Maryland	6,354	3.0%
8	Massachusetts	7,916	3.8%
10	Michigan	6,516	3.1%
19	Minnesota	3,931	1.9%
33	Mississippi	1,459	0.7%
18	Missouri	4,077	1.9%
44	Montana	563	0.3%
36	Nebraska	1,207	0.6%
40	Nevada	1,032	0.5%
41	New Hampshire	890	0.4%
9	New Jersey	7,308	3.5%
35	New Mexico	1,225	0.6%
2	New York	20,546	9.7%
12	North Carolina	6,039	2.9%
48	North Dakota	482	0.2%
7	Ohio	8,055	3.8%
30	Oklahoma	1,696	0.8%
28	Oregon	2,240	1.1%
5	Pennsylvania	10,797	5.1%
39	Rhode Island	1,041	0.5%
27	South Carolina	2,630	1.2%
47	South Dakota	501	0.2%
15	Tennessee	4,518	2.1%
3	Texas	12,810	6.1%
34	Utah	1,420	0.7%
45	Vermont	562	0.3%
14	Virginia	5,258	2.5%
16	Washington	4,301	2.0%
37	West Virginia	1,130	0.5%
17	Wisconsin	4,079	1.9%
50	Wyoming	237	0.1%

RANK ORDER

RANK	STATE	PHYSICIANS	% of USA
1	California	22,021	10.4%
2	New York	20,546	9.7%
3	Texas	12,810	6.1%
4	Florida	11,405	5.4%
5	Pennsylvania	10,797	5.1%
6	Illinois	9,298	4.4%
7	Ohio	8,055	3.8%
8	Massachusetts	7,916	3.8%
9	New Jersey	7,308	3.5%
10	Michigan	6,516	3.1%
11	Maryland	6,354	3.0%
12	North Carolina	6,039	2.9%
13	Georgia	5,638	2.7%
14	Virginia	5,258	2.5%
15	Tennessee	4,518	2.1%
16	Washington	4,301	2.0%
17	Wisconsin	4,079	1.9%
18	Missouri	4,077	1.9%
19	Minnesota	3,931	1.9%
20	Indiana	3,779	1.8%
21	Connecticut	3,560	1.7%
22	Louisiana	3,189	1.5%
23	Arizona	3,091	1.5%
24	Colorado	3,044	1.4%
25	Alabama	2,925	1.4%
26	Kentucky	2,722	1.3%
27	South Carolina	2,630	1.2%
28	Oregon	2,240	1.1%
29	Kansas	1,726	0.8%
30	Oklahoma	1,696	0.8%
31	Iowa	1,630	0.8%
32	Arkansas	1,620	0.8%
33	Mississippi	1,459	0.7%
34	Utah	1,420	0.7%
35	New Mexico	1,225	0.6%
36	Nebraska	1,207	0.6%
37	West Virginia	1,130	0.5%
38	Hawaii	1,048	0.5%
39	Rhode Island	1,041	0.5%
40	Nevada	1,032	0.5%
41	New Hampshire	890	0.4%
42	Maine	851	0.4%
43	Idaho	635	0.3%
44	Montana	563	0.3%
45	Vermont	562	0.3%
46	Delaware	554	0.3%
47	South Dakota	501	0.2%
48	North Dakota	482	0.2%
49	Alaska	412	0.2%
50	Wyoming	237	0.1%
	District of Columbia	977	0.5%

Source: American Medical Association (Chicago, Illinois)
    "Physician Characteristics and Distribution in the U.S." (2000-2001 Edition)
*As of December 31, 1998. Comprised of federal and nonfederal physicians. Total does not include 3,475 physicians in the U.S. territories and possessions, at APO's and FPO's and whose addresses are unknown.

Physicians 45 to 54 Years Old in 1998

National Total = 181,221 Physicians*

ALPHA ORDER

RANK	STATE	PHYSICIANS	% of USA
26	Alabama	2,285	1.3%
49	Alaska	368	0.2%
24	Arizona	2,643	1.5%
32	Arkansas	1,345	0.7%
1	California	23,750	13.1%
22	Colorado	2,847	1.6%
21	Connecticut	3,027	1.7%
47	Delaware	436	0.2%
4	Florida	9,822	5.4%
15	Georgia	4,293	2.4%
37	Hawaii	979	0.5%
43	Idaho	579	0.3%
6	Illinois	7,645	4.2%
18	Indiana	3,129	1.7%
31	Iowa	1,362	0.8%
30	Kansas	1,447	0.8%
27	Kentucky	2,179	1.2%
23	Louisiana	2,741	1.5%
39	Maine	887	0.5%
10	Maryland	5,435	3.0%
9	Massachusetts	6,358	3.5%
11	Michigan	5,399	3.0%
17	Minnesota	3,240	1.8%
35	Mississippi	1,175	0.6%
20	Missouri	3,099	1.7%
44	Montana	565	0.3%
38	Nebraska	951	0.5%
40	Nevada	875	0.5%
41	New Hampshire	840	0.5%
7	New Jersey	6,517	3.6%
34	New Mexico	1,193	0.7%
2	New York	16,387	9.0%
13	North Carolina	4,416	2.4%
48	North Dakota	421	0.2%
8	Ohio	6,423	3.5%
29	Oklahoma	1,633	0.9%
25	Oregon	2,414	1.3%
5	Pennsylvania	8,821	4.9%
42	Rhode Island	700	0.4%
28	South Carolina	2,025	1.1%
46	South Dakota	445	0.2%
16	Tennessee	3,591	2.0%
3	Texas	10,470	5.8%
33	Utah	1,230	0.7%
45	Vermont	510	0.3%
12	Virginia	4,581	2.5%
14	Washington	4,344	2.4%
36	West Virginia	1,092	0.6%
19	Wisconsin	3,119	1.7%
50	Wyoming	269	0.1%

RANK ORDER

RANK	STATE	PHYSICIANS	% of USA
1	California	23,750	13.1%
2	New York	16,387	9.0%
3	Texas	10,470	5.8%
4	Florida	9,822	5.4%
5	Pennsylvania	8,821	4.9%
6	Illinois	7,645	4.2%
7	New Jersey	6,517	3.6%
8	Ohio	6,423	3.5%
9	Massachusetts	6,358	3.5%
10	Maryland	5,435	3.0%
11	Michigan	5,399	3.0%
12	Virginia	4,581	2.5%
13	North Carolina	4,416	2.4%
14	Washington	4,344	2.4%
15	Georgia	4,293	2.4%
16	Tennessee	3,591	2.0%
17	Minnesota	3,240	1.8%
18	Indiana	3,129	1.7%
19	Wisconsin	3,119	1.7%
20	Missouri	3,099	1.7%
21	Connecticut	3,027	1.7%
22	Colorado	2,847	1.6%
23	Louisiana	2,741	1.5%
24	Arizona	2,643	1.5%
25	Oregon	2,414	1.3%
26	Alabama	2,285	1.3%
27	Kentucky	2,179	1.2%
28	South Carolina	2,025	1.1%
29	Oklahoma	1,633	0.9%
30	Kansas	1,447	0.8%
31	Iowa	1,362	0.8%
32	Arkansas	1,345	0.7%
33	Utah	1,230	0.7%
34	New Mexico	1,193	0.7%
35	Mississippi	1,175	0.6%
36	West Virginia	1,092	0.6%
37	Hawaii	979	0.5%
38	Nebraska	951	0.5%
39	Maine	887	0.5%
40	Nevada	875	0.5%
41	New Hampshire	840	0.5%
42	Rhode Island	700	0.4%
43	Idaho	579	0.3%
44	Montana	565	0.3%
45	Vermont	510	0.3%
46	South Dakota	445	0.2%
47	Delaware	436	0.2%
48	North Dakota	421	0.2%
49	Alaska	368	0.2%
50	Wyoming	269	0.1%
	District of Columbia	919	0.5%

Source: American Medical Association (Chicago, Illinois)
   "Physician Characteristics and Distribution in the U.S." (2000-2001 Edition)
*As of December 31, 1998. Comprised of federal and nonfederal physicians. Total does not include 2,594 physicians in the U.S. territories and possessions, at APO's and FPO's and whose addresses are unknown.

Physicians 55 to 64 Years Old in 1998

National Total = 107,751 Physicians*

ALPHA ORDER

RANK	STATE	PHYSICIANS	% of USA
27	Alabama	1,242	1.2%
49	Alaska	215	0.2%
21	Arizona	1,674	1.6%
31	Arkansas	779	0.7%
1	California	14,895	13.8%
23	Colorado	1,560	1.4%
18	Connecticut	1,808	1.7%
45	Delaware	300	0.3%
3	Florida	6,321	5.9%
13	Georgia	2,522	2.3%
37	Hawaii	537	0.5%
44	Idaho	348	0.3%
6	Illinois	4,836	4.5%
20	Indiana	1,681	1.6%
34	Iowa	735	0.7%
30	Kansas	880	0.8%
26	Kentucky	1,276	1.2%
24	Louisiana	1,550	1.4%
41	Maine	484	0.4%
11	Maryland	3,282	3.0%
9	Massachusetts	3,490	3.2%
10	Michigan	3,360	3.1%
22	Minnesota	1,639	1.5%
33	Mississippi	747	0.7%
17	Missouri	1,853	1.7%
43	Montana	353	0.3%
39	Nebraska	490	0.5%
38	Nevada	510	0.5%
42	New Hampshire	444	0.4%
7	New Jersey	4,029	3.7%
35	New Mexico	653	0.6%
2	New York	10,406	9.7%
14	North Carolina	2,385	2.2%
47	North Dakota	218	0.2%
8	Ohio	3,935	3.7%
29	Oklahoma	986	0.9%
25	Oregon	1,363	1.3%
5	Pennsylvania	4,931	4.6%
40	Rhode Island	487	0.5%
28	South Carolina	1,137	1.1%
48	South Dakota	217	0.2%
16	Tennessee	1,871	1.7%
4	Texas	6,041	5.6%
36	Utah	613	0.6%
46	Vermont	277	0.3%
12	Virginia	2,615	2.4%
15	Washington	2,297	2.1%
32	West Virginia	759	0.7%
19	Wisconsin	1,760	1.6%
50	Wyoming	161	0.1%

RANK ORDER

RANK	STATE	PHYSICIANS	% of USA
1	California	14,895	13.8%
2	New York	10,406	9.7%
3	Florida	6,321	5.9%
4	Texas	6,041	5.6%
5	Pennsylvania	4,931	4.6%
6	Illinois	4,836	4.5%
7	New Jersey	4,029	3.7%
8	Ohio	3,935	3.7%
9	Massachusetts	3,490	3.2%
10	Michigan	3,360	3.1%
11	Maryland	3,282	3.0%
12	Virginia	2,615	2.4%
13	Georgia	2,522	2.3%
14	North Carolina	2,385	2.2%
15	Washington	2,297	2.1%
16	Tennessee	1,871	1.7%
17	Missouri	1,853	1.7%
18	Connecticut	1,808	1.7%
19	Wisconsin	1,760	1.6%
20	Indiana	1,681	1.6%
21	Arizona	1,674	1.6%
22	Minnesota	1,639	1.5%
23	Colorado	1,560	1.4%
24	Louisiana	1,550	1.4%
25	Oregon	1,363	1.3%
26	Kentucky	1,276	1.2%
27	Alabama	1,242	1.2%
28	South Carolina	1,137	1.1%
29	Oklahoma	986	0.9%
30	Kansas	880	0.8%
31	Arkansas	779	0.7%
32	West Virginia	759	0.7%
33	Mississippi	747	0.7%
34	Iowa	735	0.7%
35	New Mexico	653	0.6%
36	Utah	613	0.6%
37	Hawaii	537	0.5%
38	Nevada	510	0.5%
39	Nebraska	490	0.5%
40	Rhode Island	487	0.5%
41	Maine	484	0.4%
42	New Hampshire	444	0.4%
43	Montana	353	0.3%
44	Idaho	348	0.3%
45	Delaware	300	0.3%
46	Vermont	277	0.3%
47	North Dakota	218	0.2%
48	South Dakota	217	0.2%
49	Alaska	215	0.2%
50	Wyoming	161	0.1%
	District of Columbia	799	0.7%

Source: American Medical Association (Chicago, Illinois)
    "Physician Characteristics and Distribution in the U.S." (2000-2001 Edition)
*As of December 31, 1998. Comprised of federal and nonfederal physicians. Total does not include 1,591 physicians in the U.S. territories and possessions, at APO's and FPO's and whose addresses are unknown.

Physicians 65 Years Old and Older in 1998

National Total = 132,076 Physicians*

ALPHA ORDER

RANK	STATE	PHYSICIANS	% of USA
27	Alabama	1,402	1.1%
50	Alaska	124	0.1%
16	Arizona	2,497	1.9%
33	Arkansas	847	0.6%
1	California	19,370	14.7%
23	Colorado	1,818	1.4%
17	Connecticut	2,288	1.7%
46	Delaware	363	0.3%
3	Florida	11,101	8.4%
15	Georgia	2,563	1.9%
35	Hawaii	723	0.5%
43	Idaho	439	0.3%
6	Illinois	4,825	3.7%
18	Indiana	2,146	1.6%
31	Iowa	990	0.7%
29	Kansas	1,129	0.9%
28	Kentucky	1,343	1.0%
24	Louisiana	1,737	1.3%
37	Maine	701	0.5%
11	Maryland	3,397	2.6%
9	Massachusetts	4,115	3.1%
10	Michigan	3,753	2.8%
21	Minnesota	2,042	1.5%
32	Mississippi	864	0.7%
22	Missouri	1,905	1.4%
45	Montana	421	0.3%
42	Nebraska	638	0.5%
40	Nevada	655	0.5%
39	New Hampshire	664	0.5%
8	New Jersey	4,292	3.2%
36	New Mexico	721	0.5%
2	New York	12,769	9.7%
13	North Carolina	3,049	2.3%
48	North Dakota	228	0.2%
7	Ohio	4,757	3.6%
30	Oklahoma	1,100	0.8%
25	Oregon	1,712	1.3%
5	Pennsylvania	6,543	5.0%
41	Rhode Island	642	0.5%
26	South Carolina	1,473	1.1%
47	South Dakota	246	0.2%
19	Tennessee	2,131	1.6%
4	Texas	6,671	5.1%
34	Utah	733	0.6%
44	Vermont	422	0.3%
12	Virginia	3,161	2.4%
14	Washington	2,853	2.2%
38	West Virginia	677	0.5%
20	Wisconsin	2,098	1.6%
49	Wyoming	195	0.1%

RANK ORDER

RANK	STATE	PHYSICIANS	% of USA
1	California	19,370	14.7%
2	New York	12,769	9.7%
3	Florida	11,101	8.4%
4	Texas	6,671	5.1%
5	Pennsylvania	6,543	5.0%
6	Illinois	4,825	3.7%
7	Ohio	4,757	3.6%
8	New Jersey	4,292	3.2%
9	Massachusetts	4,115	3.1%
10	Michigan	3,753	2.8%
11	Maryland	3,397	2.6%
12	Virginia	3,161	2.4%
13	North Carolina	3,049	2.3%
14	Washington	2,853	2.2%
15	Georgia	2,563	1.9%
16	Arizona	2,497	1.9%
17	Connecticut	2,288	1.7%
18	Indiana	2,146	1.6%
19	Tennessee	2,131	1.6%
20	Wisconsin	2,098	1.6%
21	Minnesota	2,042	1.5%
22	Missouri	1,905	1.4%
23	Colorado	1,818	1.4%
24	Louisiana	1,737	1.3%
25	Oregon	1,712	1.3%
26	South Carolina	1,473	1.1%
27	Alabama	1,402	1.1%
28	Kentucky	1,343	1.0%
29	Kansas	1,129	0.9%
30	Oklahoma	1,100	0.8%
31	Iowa	990	0.7%
32	Mississippi	864	0.7%
33	Arkansas	847	0.6%
34	Utah	733	0.6%
35	Hawaii	723	0.5%
36	New Mexico	721	0.5%
37	Maine	701	0.5%
38	West Virginia	677	0.5%
39	New Hampshire	664	0.5%
40	Nevada	655	0.5%
41	Rhode Island	642	0.5%
42	Nebraska	638	0.5%
43	Idaho	439	0.3%
44	Vermont	422	0.3%
45	Montana	421	0.3%
46	Delaware	363	0.3%
47	South Dakota	246	0.2%
48	North Dakota	228	0.2%
49	Wyoming	195	0.1%
50	Alaska	124	0.1%
	District of Columbia	743	0.6%

Source: American Medical Association (Chicago, Illinois)
"Physician Characteristics and Distribution in the U.S." (2000-2001 Edition)
*As of December 31, 1998. Comprised of federal and nonfederal physicians. Total does not include 2,594 physicians in the U.S. territories and possessions, at APO's and FPO's and whose addresses are unknown.

Percent of Physicians 65 Years Old and Older in 1998

National Percent = 17.2% of Physicians*

RANK	STATE	PERCENT
42	Alabama	14.8
50	Alaska	9.9
2	Arizona	21.8
32	Arkansas	15.5
5	California	20.8
24	Colorado	16.7
16	Connecticut	17.8
13	Delaware	18.4
1	Florida	25.6
47	Georgia	14.1
11	Hawaii	19.2
9	Idaho	19.7
48	Illinois	14.0
21	Indiana	16.8
18	Iowa	17.2
14	Kansas	18.2
42	Kentucky	14.8
42	Louisiana	14.8
3	Maine	21.6
39	Maryland	15.0
41	Massachusetts	14.9
32	Michigan	15.5
35	Minnesota	15.4
21	Mississippi	16.8
49	Missouri	13.9
4	Montana	21.0
31	Nebraska	15.7
12	Nevada	18.8
6	New Hampshire	20.4
27	New Jersey	16.4
26	New Mexico	16.5
21	New York	16.8
35	North Carolina	15.4
45	North Dakota	14.4
29	Ohio	16.2
18	Oklahoma	17.2
10	Oregon	19.5
20	Pennsylvania	16.9
17	Rhode Island	17.5
27	South Carolina	16.4
32	South Dakota	15.5
45	Tennessee	14.4
39	Texas	15.0
35	Utah	15.4
7	Vermont	20.1
25	Virginia	16.6
15	Washington	18.0
35	West Virginia	15.4
30	Wisconsin	15.8
8	Wyoming	19.8

RANK	STATE	PERCENT
1	Florida	25.6
2	Arizona	21.8
3	Maine	21.6
4	Montana	21.0
5	California	20.8
6	New Hampshire	20.4
7	Vermont	20.1
8	Wyoming	19.8
9	Idaho	19.7
10	Oregon	19.5
11	Hawaii	19.2
12	Nevada	18.8
13	Delaware	18.4
14	Kansas	18.2
15	Washington	18.0
16	Connecticut	17.8
17	Rhode Island	17.5
18	Iowa	17.2
18	Oklahoma	17.2
20	Pennsylvania	16.9
21	Indiana	16.8
21	Mississippi	16.8
21	New York	16.8
24	Colorado	16.7
25	Virginia	16.6
26	New Mexico	16.5
27	New Jersey	16.4
27	South Carolina	16.4
29	Ohio	16.2
30	Wisconsin	15.8
31	Nebraska	15.7
32	Arkansas	15.5
32	Michigan	15.5
32	South Dakota	15.5
35	Minnesota	15.4
35	North Carolina	15.4
35	Utah	15.4
35	West Virginia	15.4
39	Maryland	15.0
39	Texas	15.0
41	Massachusetts	14.9
42	Alabama	14.8
42	Kentucky	14.8
42	Louisiana	14.8
45	North Dakota	14.4
45	Tennessee	14.4
47	Georgia	14.1
48	Illinois	14.0
49	Missouri	13.9
50	Alaska	9.9
	District of Columbia	16.7

Source: Morgan Quitno Press using data from American Medical Association (Chicago, Illinois)
   "Physician Characteristics and Distribution in the U.S." (2000-2001 Edition)
*As of December 31, 1998. Comprised of federal and nonfederal physicians. National percent does not include physicians in the U.S. territories and possessions, at APO's and FPO's and whose addresses are unknown.

Federal Physicians in 1998

National Total = 18,945 Physicians*

ALPHA ORDER

RANK	STATE	PHYSICIANS	% of USA
26	Alabama	219	1.2%
33	Alaska	158	0.8%
13	Arizona	454	2.4%
33	Arkansas	158	0.8%
1	California	2,060	10.9%
16	Colorado	322	1.7%
32	Connecticut	166	0.9%
47	Delaware	55	0.3%
4	Florida	1,128	6.0%
7	Georgia	766	4.0%
26	Hawaii	219	1.2%
42	Idaho	68	0.4%
9	Illinois	572	3.0%
35	Indiana	149	0.8%
39	Iowa	102	0.5%
29	Kansas	181	1.0%
30	Kentucky	179	0.9%
23	Louisiana	238	1.3%
45	Maine	57	0.3%
2	Maryland	1,819	9.6%
14	Massachusetts	418	2.2%
19	Michigan	262	1.4%
21	Minnesota	243	1.3%
24	Mississippi	235	1.2%
18	Missouri	284	1.5%
45	Montana	57	0.3%
41	Nebraska	71	0.4%
38	Nevada	106	0.6%
44	New Hampshire	58	0.3%
17	New Jersey	305	1.6%
22	New Mexico	240	1.3%
5	New York	974	5.1%
11	North Carolina	488	2.6%
49	North Dakota	38	0.2%
12	Ohio	455	2.4%
28	Oklahoma	196	1.0%
25	Oregon	221	1.2%
10	Pennsylvania	529	2.8%
43	Rhode Island	67	0.4%
20	South Carolina	245	1.3%
40	South Dakota	91	0.5%
15	Tennessee	378	2.0%
3	Texas	1,528	8.1%
37	Utah	108	0.6%
50	Vermont	36	0.2%
6	Virginia	967	5.1%
8	Washington	580	3.1%
36	West Virginia	134	0.7%
31	Wisconsin	174	0.9%
48	Wyoming	43	0.2%

RANK ORDER

RANK	STATE	PHYSICIANS	% of USA
1	California	2,060	10.9%
2	Maryland	1,819	9.6%
3	Texas	1,528	8.1%
4	Florida	1,128	6.0%
5	New York	974	5.1%
6	Virginia	967	5.1%
7	Georgia	766	4.0%
8	Washington	580	3.1%
9	Illinois	572	3.0%
10	Pennsylvania	529	2.8%
11	North Carolina	488	2.6%
12	Ohio	455	2.4%
13	Arizona	454	2.4%
14	Massachusetts	418	2.2%
15	Tennessee	378	2.0%
16	Colorado	322	1.7%
17	New Jersey	305	1.6%
18	Missouri	284	1.5%
19	Michigan	262	1.4%
20	South Carolina	245	1.3%
21	Minnesota	243	1.3%
22	New Mexico	240	1.3%
23	Louisiana	238	1.3%
24	Mississippi	235	1.2%
25	Oregon	221	1.2%
26	Alabama	219	1.2%
26	Hawaii	219	1.2%
28	Oklahoma	196	1.0%
29	Kansas	181	1.0%
30	Kentucky	179	0.9%
31	Wisconsin	174	0.9%
32	Connecticut	166	0.9%
33	Alaska	158	0.8%
33	Arkansas	158	0.8%
35	Indiana	149	0.8%
36	West Virginia	134	0.7%
37	Utah	108	0.6%
38	Nevada	106	0.6%
39	Iowa	102	0.5%
40	South Dakota	91	0.5%
41	Nebraska	71	0.4%
42	Idaho	68	0.4%
43	Rhode Island	67	0.4%
44	New Hampshire	58	0.3%
45	Maine	57	0.3%
45	Montana	57	0.3%
47	Delaware	55	0.3%
48	Wyoming	43	0.2%
49	North Dakota	38	0.2%
50	Vermont	36	0.2%
	District of Columbia	344	1.8%

Source: American Medical Association (Chicago, Illinois)
   "Physician Characteristics and Distribution in the U.S." (2000-2001 Edition)
*As of December 31, 1998. Total does not include 1,049 physicians in U.S. territories and possessions.

Rate of Federal Physicians in 1998

National Rate = 7.0 Physicians per 100,000 Population*

ALPHA ORDER			RANK ORDER		
RANK	STATE	RATE	RANK	STATE	RATE
38	Alabama	5.0	1	Maryland	35.5
2	Alaska	25.7	2	Alaska	25.7
9	Arizona	9.7	3	Hawaii	18.4
26	Arkansas	6.2	4	Virginia	14.2
25	California	6.3	5	New Mexico	13.8
12	Colorado	8.1	6	South Dakota	12.5
35	Connecticut	5.1	7	Washington	10.2
15	Delaware	7.4	8	Georgia	10.0
14	Florida	7.6	9	Arizona	9.7
8	Georgia	10.0	10	Wyoming	9.0
3	Hawaii	18.4	11	Mississippi	8.5
31	Idaho	5.5	12	Colorado	8.1
40	Illinois	4.7	13	Texas	7.8
50	Indiana	2.5	14	Florida	7.6
47	Iowa	3.6	15	Delaware	7.4
18	Kansas	6.9	15	West Virginia	7.4
42	Kentucky	4.5	17	Tennessee	7.0
31	Louisiana	5.5	18	Kansas	6.9
41	Maine	4.6	19	Massachusetts	6.8
1	Maryland	35.5	19	Rhode Island	6.8
19	Massachusetts	6.8	21	Oregon	6.7
49	Michigan	2.7	22	Montana	6.5
35	Minnesota	5.1	22	North Carolina	6.5
11	Mississippi	8.5	24	South Carolina	6.4
34	Missouri	5.2	25	California	6.3
22	Montana	6.5	26	Arkansas	6.2
44	Nebraska	4.3	27	Nevada	6.1
27	Nevada	6.1	27	Vermont	6.1
39	New Hampshire	4.9	29	North Dakota	6.0
46	New Jersey	3.8	30	Oklahoma	5.9
5	New Mexico	13.8	31	Idaho	5.5
33	New York	5.4	31	Louisiana	5.5
22	North Carolina	6.5	33	New York	5.4
29	North Dakota	6.0	34	Missouri	5.2
45	Ohio	4.0	35	Connecticut	5.1
30	Oklahoma	5.9	35	Minnesota	5.1
21	Oregon	6.7	35	Utah	5.1
43	Pennsylvania	4.4	38	Alabama	5.0
19	Rhode Island	6.8	39	New Hampshire	4.9
24	South Carolina	6.4	40	Illinois	4.7
6	South Dakota	12.5	41	Maine	4.6
17	Tennessee	7.0	42	Kentucky	4.5
13	Texas	7.8	43	Pennsylvania	4.4
35	Utah	5.1	44	Nebraska	4.3
27	Vermont	6.1	45	Ohio	4.0
4	Virginia	14.2	46	New Jersey	3.8
7	Washington	10.2	47	Iowa	3.6
15	West Virginia	7.4	48	Wisconsin	3.3
48	Wisconsin	3.3	49	Michigan	2.7
10	Wyoming	9.0	50	Indiana	2.5
				District of Columbia	66.0

Source: Morgan Quitno Press using data from American Medical Association (Chicago, Illinois)
    "Physician Characteristics and Distribution in the U.S." (2000-2001 Edition)
*As of December 31, 1998. National rate does not include physicians in U.S. territories and possessions.

Nonfederal Physicians in 1998

National Total = 746,977 Physicians*

ALPHA ORDER

RANK	STATE	PHYSICIANS	% of USA
25	Alabama	9,281	1.2%
49	Alaska	1,089	0.1%
23	Arizona	11,025	1.5%
32	Arkansas	5,306	0.7%
1	California	90,940	12.2%
24	Colorado	10,554	1.4%
20	Connecticut	12,693	1.7%
46	Delaware	1,917	0.3%
4	Florida	42,169	5.6%
14	Georgia	17,409	2.3%
39	Hawaii	3,555	0.5%
43	Idaho	2,164	0.3%
6	Illinois	33,803	4.5%
21	Indiana	12,620	1.7%
31	Iowa	5,643	0.8%
30	Kansas	6,024	0.8%
26	Kentucky	8,901	1.2%
22	Louisiana	11,490	1.5%
41	Maine	3,195	0.4%
11	Maryland	20,761	2.8%
8	Massachusetts	27,228	3.6%
10	Michigan	24,001	3.2%
19	Minnesota	13,047	1.7%
33	Mississippi	4,898	0.7%
17	Missouri	13,415	1.8%
45	Montana	1,952	0.3%
37	Nebraska	4,000	0.5%
40	Nevada	3,373	0.5%
41	New Hampshire	3,195	0.4%
9	New Jersey	25,830	3.5%
36	New Mexico	4,138	0.6%
2	New York	75,183	10.1%
12	North Carolina	19,307	2.6%
47	North Dakota	1,547	0.2%
7	Ohio	28,827	3.9%
29	Oklahoma	6,216	0.8%
28	Oregon	8,575	1.1%
5	Pennsylvania	38,080	5.1%
38	Rhode Island	3,606	0.5%
27	South Carolina	8,722	1.2%
48	South Dakota	1,501	0.2%
16	Tennessee	14,412	1.9%
3	Texas	43,032	5.8%
34	Utah	4,642	0.6%
44	Vermont	2,061	0.3%
13	Virginia	18,023	2.4%
15	Washington	15,254	2.0%
35	West Virginia	4,249	0.6%
18	Wisconsin	13,086	1.8%
50	Wyoming	943	0.1%

RANK ORDER

RANK	STATE	PHYSICIANS	% of USA
1	California	90,940	12.2%
2	New York	75,183	10.1%
3	Texas	43,032	5.8%
4	Florida	42,169	5.6%
5	Pennsylvania	38,080	5.1%
6	Illinois	33,803	4.5%
7	Ohio	28,827	3.9%
8	Massachusetts	27,228	3.6%
9	New Jersey	25,830	3.5%
10	Michigan	24,001	3.2%
11	Maryland	20,761	2.8%
12	North Carolina	19,307	2.6%
13	Virginia	18,023	2.4%
14	Georgia	17,409	2.3%
15	Washington	15,254	2.0%
16	Tennessee	14,412	1.9%
17	Missouri	13,415	1.8%
18	Wisconsin	13,086	1.8%
19	Minnesota	13,047	1.7%
20	Connecticut	12,693	1.7%
21	Indiana	12,620	1.7%
22	Louisiana	11,490	1.5%
23	Arizona	11,025	1.5%
24	Colorado	10,554	1.4%
25	Alabama	9,281	1.2%
26	Kentucky	8,901	1.2%
27	South Carolina	8,722	1.2%
28	Oregon	8,575	1.1%
29	Oklahoma	6,216	0.8%
30	Kansas	6,024	0.8%
31	Iowa	5,643	0.8%
32	Arkansas	5,306	0.7%
33	Mississippi	4,898	0.7%
34	Utah	4,642	0.6%
35	West Virginia	4,249	0.6%
36	New Mexico	4,138	0.6%
37	Nebraska	4,000	0.5%
38	Rhode Island	3,606	0.5%
39	Hawaii	3,555	0.5%
40	Nevada	3,373	0.5%
41	Maine	3,195	0.4%
41	New Hampshire	3,195	0.4%
43	Idaho	2,164	0.3%
44	Vermont	2,061	0.3%
45	Montana	1,952	0.3%
46	Delaware	1,917	0.3%
47	North Dakota	1,547	0.2%
48	South Dakota	1,501	0.2%
49	Alaska	1,089	0.1%
50	Wyoming	943	0.1%
	District of Columbia	4,095	0.5%

Source: American Medical Association (Chicago, Illinois)
  "Physician Characteristics and Distribution in the U.S." (2000-2001 Edition)
*As of December 31, 1998. Total does not include 10,888 nonfederal physicians in U.S. territories and possessions.

Rate of Nonfederal Physicians in 1998

National Rate = 276 Physicians per 100,000 Population*

ALPHA ORDER

RANK	STATE	RATE
41	Alabama	213
49	Alaska	177
31	Arizona	236
42	Arkansas	209
12	California	278
16	Colorado	266
4	Connecticut	388
21	Delaware	258
10	Florida	283
33	Georgia	228
9	Hawaii	299
50	Idaho	176
11	Illinois	280
40	Indiana	214
44	Iowa	197
33	Kansas	228
36	Kentucky	226
19	Louisiana	263
23	Maine	256
3	Maryland	405
1	Massachusetts	443
27	Michigan	244
13	Minnesota	276
48	Mississippi	178
26	Missouri	247
37	Montana	222
29	Nebraska	241
46	Nevada	193
14	New Hampshire	269
7	New Jersey	319
30	New Mexico	239
2	New York	414
23	North Carolina	256
28	North Dakota	243
22	Ohio	257
47	Oklahoma	186
20	Oregon	261
8	Pennsylvania	317
5	Rhode Island	365
35	South Carolina	227
43	South Dakota	205
17	Tennessee	265
39	Texas	218
38	Utah	221
6	Vermont	349
17	Virginia	265
15	Washington	268
32	West Virginia	235
25	Wisconsin	251
45	Wyoming	196

RANK ORDER

RANK	STATE	RATE
1	Massachusetts	443
2	New York	414
3	Maryland	405
4	Connecticut	388
5	Rhode Island	365
6	Vermont	349
7	New Jersey	319
8	Pennsylvania	317
9	Hawaii	299
10	Florida	283
11	Illinois	280
12	California	278
13	Minnesota	276
14	New Hampshire	269
15	Washington	268
16	Colorado	266
17	Tennessee	265
17	Virginia	265
19	Louisiana	263
20	Oregon	261
21	Delaware	258
22	Ohio	257
23	Maine	256
23	North Carolina	256
25	Wisconsin	251
26	Missouri	247
27	Michigan	244
28	North Dakota	243
29	Nebraska	241
30	New Mexico	239
31	Arizona	236
32	West Virginia	235
33	Georgia	228
33	Kansas	228
35	South Carolina	227
36	Kentucky	226
37	Montana	222
38	Utah	221
39	Texas	218
40	Indiana	214
41	Alabama	213
42	Arkansas	209
43	South Dakota	205
44	Iowa	197
45	Wyoming	196
46	Nevada	193
47	Oklahoma	186
48	Mississippi	178
49	Alaska	177
50	Idaho	176
	District of Columbia	785

Source: Morgan Quitno Press using data from American Medical Association (Chicago, Illinois)
"Physician Characteristics and Distribution in the U.S." (2000-2001 Edition)
*As of December 31, 1998.

Nonfederal Physicians in Patient Care in 1998

National Total = 598,286 Physicians*

ALPHA ORDER

RANK	STATE	PHYSICIANS	% of USA
25	Alabama	7,745	1.3%
49	Alaska	933	0.2%
23	Arizona	8,418	1.4%
31	Arkansas	4,443	0.7%
1	California	70,408	11.8%
24	Colorado	8,406	1.4%
21	Connecticut	10,000	1.7%
46	Delaware	1,530	0.3%
4	Florida	32,051	5.4%
14	Georgia	14,405	2.4%
39	Hawaii	2,844	0.5%
43	Idaho	1,773	0.3%
6	Illinois	27,630	4.6%
20	Indiana	10,411	1.7%
32	Iowa	4,420	0.7%
30	Kansas	4,844	0.8%
26	Kentucky	7,485	1.3%
22	Louisiana	9,681	1.6%
42	Maine	2,494	0.4%
11	Maryland	16,090	2.7%
8	Massachusetts	21,033	3.5%
10	Michigan	19,427	3.2%
19	Minnesota	10,438	1.7%
33	Mississippi	4,107	0.7%
17	Missouri	11,023	1.8%
45	Montana	1,554	0.3%
36	Nebraska	3,277	0.5%
40	Nevada	2,766	0.5%
41	New Hampshire	2,556	0.4%
9	New Jersey	20,967	3.5%
37	New Mexico	3,227	0.5%
2	New York	60,202	10.1%
12	North Carolina	15,481	2.6%
47	North Dakota	1,300	0.2%
7	Ohio	23,540	3.9%
29	Oklahoma	5,110	0.9%
28	Oregon	6,624	1.1%
5	Pennsylvania	30,699	5.1%
38	Rhode Island	2,934	0.5%
27	South Carolina	7,153	1.2%
48	South Dakota	1,266	0.2%
15	Tennessee	12,019	2.0%
3	Texas	35,738	6.0%
34	Utah	3,725	0.6%
44	Vermont	1,583	0.3%
13	Virginia	14,673	2.5%
16	Washington	11,810	2.0%
35	West Virginia	3,496	0.6%
18	Wisconsin	10,692	1.8%
50	Wyoming	742	0.1%

RANK ORDER

RANK	STATE	PHYSICIANS	% of USA
1	California	70,408	11.8%
2	New York	60,202	10.1%
3	Texas	35,738	6.0%
4	Florida	32,051	5.4%
5	Pennsylvania	30,699	5.1%
6	Illinois	27,630	4.6%
7	Ohio	23,540	3.9%
8	Massachusetts	21,033	3.5%
9	New Jersey	20,967	3.5%
10	Michigan	19,427	3.2%
11	Maryland	16,090	2.7%
12	North Carolina	15,481	2.6%
13	Virginia	14,673	2.5%
14	Georgia	14,405	2.4%
15	Tennessee	12,019	2.0%
16	Washington	11,810	2.0%
17	Missouri	11,023	1.8%
18	Wisconsin	10,692	1.8%
19	Minnesota	10,438	1.7%
20	Indiana	10,411	1.7%
21	Connecticut	10,000	1.7%
22	Louisiana	9,681	1.6%
23	Arizona	8,418	1.4%
24	Colorado	8,406	1.4%
25	Alabama	7,745	1.3%
26	Kentucky	7,485	1.3%
27	South Carolina	7,153	1.2%
28	Oregon	6,624	1.1%
29	Oklahoma	5,110	0.9%
30	Kansas	4,844	0.8%
31	Arkansas	4,443	0.7%
32	Iowa	4,420	0.7%
33	Mississippi	4,107	0.7%
34	Utah	3,725	0.6%
35	West Virginia	3,496	0.6%
36	Nebraska	3,277	0.5%
37	New Mexico	3,227	0.5%
38	Rhode Island	2,934	0.5%
39	Hawaii	2,844	0.5%
40	Nevada	2,766	0.5%
41	New Hampshire	2,556	0.4%
42	Maine	2,494	0.4%
43	Idaho	1,773	0.3%
44	Vermont	1,583	0.3%
45	Montana	1,554	0.3%
46	Delaware	1,530	0.3%
47	North Dakota	1,300	0.2%
48	South Dakota	1,266	0.2%
49	Alaska	933	0.2%
50	Wyoming	742	0.1%
	District of Columbia	3,113	0.5%

Source: American Medical Association (Chicago, Illinois)
"Physician Characteristics and Distribution in the U.S." (2000-2001 Edition)
*As of December 31, 1998. Total does not include 8,139 physicians in U.S. territories and possessions.

Rate of Nonfederal Physicians in Patient Care in 1998

National Rate = 221 Physicians per 100,000 Population*

ALPHA ORDER

RANK	STATE	RATE
38	Alabama	178
48	Alaska	152
37	Arizona	180
42	Arkansas	175
16	California	215
18	Colorado	212
4	Connecticut	306
21	Delaware	206
16	Florida	215
32	Georgia	189
9	Hawaii	239
50	Idaho	144
10	Illinois	229
41	Indiana	176
46	Iowa	154
35	Kansas	184
31	Kentucky	190
11	Louisiana	222
27	Maine	200
3	Maryland	314
1	Massachusetts	342
28	Michigan	198
12	Minnesota	221
49	Mississippi	149
25	Missouri	203
39	Montana	177
29	Nebraska	197
44	Nevada	159
14	New Hampshire	216
7	New Jersey	259
33	New Mexico	186
2	New York	332
22	North Carolina	205
24	North Dakota	204
19	Ohio	209
47	Oklahoma	153
26	Oregon	202
8	Pennsylvania	256
5	Rhode Island	297
33	South Carolina	186
43	South Dakota	173
12	Tennessee	221
36	Texas	181
39	Utah	177
6	Vermont	268
14	Virginia	216
20	Washington	208
30	West Virginia	193
22	Wisconsin	205
45	Wyoming	155

RANK ORDER

RANK	STATE	RATE
1	Massachusetts	342
2	New York	332
3	Maryland	314
4	Connecticut	306
5	Rhode Island	297
6	Vermont	268
7	New Jersey	259
8	Pennsylvania	256
9	Hawaii	239
10	Illinois	229
11	Louisiana	222
12	Minnesota	221
12	Tennessee	221
14	New Hampshire	216
14	Virginia	216
16	California	215
16	Florida	215
18	Colorado	212
19	Ohio	209
20	Washington	208
21	Delaware	206
22	North Carolina	205
22	Wisconsin	205
24	North Dakota	204
25	Missouri	203
26	Oregon	202
27	Maine	200
28	Michigan	198
29	Nebraska	197
30	West Virginia	193
31	Kentucky	190
32	Georgia	189
33	New Mexico	186
33	South Carolina	186
35	Kansas	184
36	Texas	181
37	Arizona	180
38	Alabama	178
39	Montana	177
39	Utah	177
41	Indiana	176
42	Arkansas	175
43	South Dakota	173
44	Nevada	159
45	Wyoming	155
46	Iowa	154
47	Oklahoma	153
48	Alaska	152
49	Mississippi	149
50	Idaho	144
	District of Columbia	597

Source: Morgan Quitno Press using data from American Medical Association (Chicago, Illinois) "Physician Characteristics and Distribution in the U.S." (2000-2001 Edition)
As of December 31, 1998. National rate does not include physicians in U.S. territories and possessions.

Physicians in Primary Care in 1998

National Total = 259,316 Physicians*

ALPHA ORDER

RANK	STATE	PHYSICIANS	% of USA
25	Alabama	3,460	1.3%
49	Alaska	516	0.2%
24	Arizona	3,624	1.4%
31	Arkansas	2,022	0.8%
1	California	30,463	11.7%
23	Colorado	3,671	1.4%
21	Connecticut	4,155	1.6%
48	Delaware	619	0.2%
4	Florida	12,840	5.0%
14	Georgia	6,453	2.5%
38	Hawaii	1,364	0.5%
43	Idaho	804	0.3%
5	Illinois	12,839	5.0%
19	Indiana	4,552	1.8%
32	Iowa	2,006	0.8%
30	Kansas	2,244	0.9%
26	Kentucky	3,221	1.2%
22	Louisiana	3,923	1.5%
41	Maine	1,124	0.4%
11	Maryland	7,019	2.7%
10	Massachusetts	8,365	3.2%
9	Michigan	8,525	3.3%
17	Minnesota	4,911	1.9%
33	Mississippi	1,831	0.7%
20	Missouri	4,479	1.7%
45	Montana	669	0.3%
37	Nebraska	1,547	0.6%
40	Nevada	1,190	0.5%
42	New Hampshire	1,094	0.4%
8	New Jersey	9,163	3.5%
35	New Mexico	1,576	0.6%
2	New York	25,760	9.9%
12	North Carolina	6,721	2.6%
47	North Dakota	626	0.2%
7	Ohio	10,273	4.0%
29	Oklahoma	2,282	0.9%
28	Oregon	2,941	1.1%
6	Pennsylvania	12,596	4.9%
39	Rhode Island	1,306	0.5%
27	South Carolina	3,214	1.2%
46	South Dakota	643	0.2%
16	Tennessee	5,130	2.0%
3	Texas	15,121	5.8%
36	Utah	1,574	0.6%
44	Vermont	769	0.3%
13	Virginia	6,633	2.6%
15	Washington	5,366	2.1%
34	West Virginia	1,607	0.6%
18	Wisconsin	4,739	1.8%
50	Wyoming	407	0.2%

RANK ORDER

RANK	STATE	PHYSICIANS	% of USA
1	California	30,463	11.7%
2	New York	25,760	9.9%
3	Texas	15,121	5.8%
4	Florida	12,840	5.0%
5	Illinois	12,839	5.0%
6	Pennsylvania	12,596	4.9%
7	Ohio	10,273	4.0%
8	New Jersey	9,163	3.5%
9	Michigan	8,525	3.3%
10	Massachusetts	8,365	3.2%
11	Maryland	7,019	2.7%
12	North Carolina	6,721	2.6%
13	Virginia	6,633	2.6%
14	Georgia	6,453	2.5%
15	Washington	5,366	2.1%
16	Tennessee	5,130	2.0%
17	Minnesota	4,911	1.9%
18	Wisconsin	4,739	1.8%
19	Indiana	4,552	1.8%
20	Missouri	4,479	1.7%
21	Connecticut	4,155	1.6%
22	Louisiana	3,923	1.5%
23	Colorado	3,671	1.4%
24	Arizona	3,624	1.4%
25	Alabama	3,460	1.3%
26	Kentucky	3,221	1.2%
27	South Carolina	3,214	1.2%
28	Oregon	2,941	1.1%
29	Oklahoma	2,282	0.9%
30	Kansas	2,244	0.9%
31	Arkansas	2,022	0.8%
32	Iowa	2,006	0.8%
33	Mississippi	1,831	0.7%
34	West Virginia	1,607	0.6%
35	New Mexico	1,576	0.6%
36	Utah	1,574	0.6%
37	Nebraska	1,547	0.6%
38	Hawaii	1,364	0.5%
39	Rhode Island	1,306	0.5%
40	Nevada	1,190	0.5%
41	Maine	1,124	0.4%
42	New Hampshire	1,094	0.4%
43	Idaho	804	0.3%
44	Vermont	769	0.3%
45	Montana	669	0.3%
46	South Dakota	643	0.2%
47	North Dakota	626	0.2%
48	Delaware	619	0.2%
49	Alaska	516	0.2%
50	Wyoming	407	0.2%
	District of Columbia	1,339	0.5%

Source: American Medical Association (Chicago, Illinois)
   "Physician Characteristics and Distribution in the U.S." (2000-2001 Edition)
*Federal and nonfederal physicians as of December 31, 1998. National total does not include 4,861 physicians in U.S. territories and possessions. Primary Care Specialties include Family Practice, General Practice, Internal Medicine, Obstetrics/Gynecology and Pediatrics.

Rate of Physicians in Primary Care in 1998

National Rate = 96 Physicians per 100,000 Population*

ALPHA ORDER

RANK	STATE	RATE
39	Alabama	80
34	Alaska	84
41	Arizona	78
39	Arkansas	80
16	California	93
18	Colorado	92
6	Connecticut	127
36	Delaware	83
30	Florida	86
31	Georgia	85
7	Hawaii	115
50	Idaho	65
9	Illinois	106
42	Indiana	77
46	Iowa	70
31	Kansas	85
37	Kentucky	82
23	Louisiana	90
23	Maine	90
2	Maryland	137
3	Massachusetts	136
29	Michigan	87
11	Minnesota	104
49	Mississippi	67
37	Missouri	82
44	Montana	76
16	Nebraska	93
47	Nevada	68
18	New Hampshire	92
8	New Jersey	113
20	New Mexico	91
1	New York	142
26	North Carolina	89
12	North Dakota	98
20	Ohio	91
47	Oklahoma	68
23	Oregon	90
10	Pennsylvania	105
4	Rhode Island	132
34	South Carolina	84
28	South Dakota	88
14	Tennessee	94
42	Texas	77
45	Utah	75
5	Vermont	130
12	Virginia	98
14	Washington	94
26	West Virginia	89
20	Wisconsin	91
31	Wyoming	85

RANK ORDER

RANK	STATE	RATE
1	New York	142
2	Maryland	137
3	Massachusetts	136
4	Rhode Island	132
5	Vermont	130
6	Connecticut	127
7	Hawaii	115
8	New Jersey	113
9	Illinois	106
10	Pennsylvania	105
11	Minnesota	104
12	North Dakota	98
12	Virginia	98
14	Tennessee	94
14	Washington	94
16	California	93
16	Nebraska	93
18	Colorado	92
18	New Hampshire	92
20	New Mexico	91
20	Ohio	91
20	Wisconsin	91
23	Louisiana	90
23	Maine	90
23	Oregon	90
26	North Carolina	89
26	West Virginia	89
28	South Dakota	88
29	Michigan	87
30	Florida	86
31	Georgia	85
31	Kansas	85
31	Wyoming	85
34	Alaska	84
34	South Carolina	84
36	Delaware	83
37	Kentucky	82
37	Missouri	82
39	Alabama	80
39	Arkansas	80
41	Arizona	78
42	Indiana	77
42	Texas	77
44	Montana	76
45	Utah	75
46	Iowa	70
47	Nevada	68
47	Oklahoma	68
49	Mississippi	67
50	Idaho	65

	District of Columbia	257

Source: Morgan Quitno Press using data from American Medical Association (Chicago, Illinois)
     "Physician Characteristics and Distribution in the U.S." (2000-2001 Edition)
*Federal and nonfederal physicians as of January 1, 1998. National rate does not include physicians in U.S.
territories and possessions. Primary Care Specialties include Family Practice, General Practice, Internal Medicine,
Obstetrics/Gynecology and Pediatrics.*

Percent of Physicians in Primary Care in 1998

National Percent = 33.9% of Physicians*

ALPHA ORDER

RANK ORDER

RANK	STATE	PERCENT		RANK	STATE	PERCENT
11	Alabama	36.4		1	Alaska	41.4
1	Alaska	41.4		2	Wyoming	41.3
46	Arizona	31.6		3	South Dakota	40.4
7	Arkansas	37.0		4	North Dakota	39.5
42	California	32.8		5	Nebraska	38.0
35	Colorado	33.8		6	Illinois	37.3
45	Connecticut	32.3		7	Arkansas	37.0
47	Delaware	31.4		7	Minnesota	37.0
50	Florida	29.7		9	Vermont	36.7
22	Georgia	35.5		9	West Virginia	36.7
13	Hawaii	36.1		11	Alabama	36.4
14	Idaho	36.0		12	Kansas	36.2
6	Illinois	37.3		13	Hawaii	36.1
19	Indiana	35.6		14	Idaho	36.0
27	Iowa	34.9		14	New Mexico	36.0
12	Kansas	36.2		16	South Carolina	35.8
22	Kentucky	35.5		17	Mississippi	35.7
38	Louisiana	33.4		17	Wisconsin	35.7
30	Maine	34.6		19	Indiana	35.6
48	Maryland	31.1		19	Oklahoma	35.6
49	Massachusetts	30.3		19	Rhode Island	35.6
24	Michigan	35.1		22	Georgia	35.5
7	Minnesota	37.0		22	Kentucky	35.5
17	Mississippi	35.7		24	Michigan	35.1
43	Missouri	32.7		24	New Jersey	35.1
40	Montana	33.3		24	Ohio	35.1
5	Nebraska	38.0		27	Iowa	34.9
31	Nevada	34.2		27	Virginia	34.9
37	New Hampshire	33.6		29	Tennessee	34.7
24	New Jersey	35.1		30	Maine	34.6
14	New Mexico	36.0		31	Nevada	34.2
35	New York	33.8		32	North Carolina	34.0
32	North Carolina	34.0		33	Texas	33.9
4	North Dakota	39.5		33	Washington	33.9
24	Ohio	35.1		35	Colorado	33.8
19	Oklahoma	35.6		35	New York	33.8
38	Oregon	33.4		37	New Hampshire	33.6
44	Pennsylvania	32.6		38	Louisiana	33.4
19	Rhode Island	35.6		38	Oregon	33.4
16	South Carolina	35.8		40	Montana	33.3
3	South Dakota	40.4		41	Utah	33.1
29	Tennessee	34.7		42	California	32.8
33	Texas	33.9		43	Missouri	32.7
41	Utah	33.1		44	Pennsylvania	32.6
9	Vermont	36.7		45	Connecticut	32.3
27	Virginia	34.9		46	Arizona	31.6
33	Washington	33.9		47	Delaware	31.4
9	West Virginia	36.7		48	Maryland	31.1
17	Wisconsin	35.7		49	Massachusetts	30.3
2	Wyoming	41.3		50	Florida	29.7

District of Columbia 30.2

Source: Morgan Quitno Press using data from American Medical Association (Chicago, Illinois)
    "Physician Characteristics and Distribution in the U.S." (2000-2001 Edition)
*Federal and nonfederal physicians as of January 1, 1998. National rate does not include physicians in U.S.
territories and possessions. Primary Care Specialties include Family Practice, General Practice, Internal Medicine,
Obstetrics/Gynecology and Pediatrics.

Percent of Population Lacking Access to Primary Care in 1999

National Percent = 9.4% of Population*

ALPHA ORDER

RANK	STATE	PERCENT
3	Alabama	22.1
12	Alaska	14.4
31	Arizona	8.1
16	Arkansas	12.4
44	California	5.3
35	Colorado	7.8
40	Connecticut	6.8
47	Delaware	4.7
36	Florida	7.6
9	Georgia	15.0
50	Hawaii	3.0
5	Idaho	21.0
39	Illinois	6.9
24	Indiana	9.8
28	Iowa	9.3
30	Kansas	8.3
13	Kentucky	13.2
2	Louisiana	23.0
33	Maine	8.0
49	Maryland	4.0
42	Massachusetts	6.3
18	Michigan	11.9
43	Minnesota	5.5
1	Mississippi	26.7
11	Missouri	14.7
13	Montana	13.2
34	Nebraska	7.9
19	Nevada	11.7
44	New Hampshire	5.3
44	New Jersey	5.3
8	New Mexico	15.5
25	New York	9.7
22	North Carolina	10.3
10	North Dakota	14.8
37	Ohio	7.5
29	Oklahoma	9.2
26	Oregon	9.5
47	Pennsylvania	4.7
27	Rhode Island	9.4
13	South Carolina	13.2
6	South Dakota	20.4
21	Tennessee	10.7
20	Texas	11.3
4	Utah	21.9
38	Vermont	7.1
41	Virginia	6.4
31	Washington	8.1
17	West Virginia	12.2
23	Wisconsin	10.0
7	Wyoming	18.8

RANK ORDER

RANK	STATE	PERCENT
1	Mississippi	26.7
2	Louisiana	23.0
3	Alabama	22.1
4	Utah	21.9
5	Idaho	21.0
6	South Dakota	20.4
7	Wyoming	18.8
8	New Mexico	15.5
9	Georgia	15.0
10	North Dakota	14.8
11	Missouri	14.7
12	Alaska	14.4
13	Kentucky	13.2
13	Montana	13.2
13	South Carolina	13.2
16	Arkansas	12.4
17	West Virginia	12.2
18	Michigan	11.9
19	Nevada	11.7
20	Texas	11.3
21	Tennessee	10.7
22	North Carolina	10.3
23	Wisconsin	10.0
24	Indiana	9.8
25	New York	9.7
26	Oregon	9.5
27	Rhode Island	9.4
28	Iowa	9.3
29	Oklahoma	9.2
30	Kansas	8.3
31	Arizona	8.1
31	Washington	8.1
33	Maine	8.0
34	Nebraska	7.9
35	Colorado	7.8
36	Florida	7.6
37	Ohio	7.5
38	Vermont	7.1
39	Illinois	6.9
40	Connecticut	6.8
41	Virginia	6.4
42	Massachusetts	6.3
43	Minnesota	5.5
44	California	5.3
44	New Hampshire	5.3
44	New Jersey	5.3
47	Delaware	4.7
47	Pennsylvania	4.7
49	Maryland	4.0
50	Hawaii	3.0

| | District of Columbia | 21.5 |

Source: Morgan Quitno Press using data from U.S. Dept. of Health and Human Services, Div. of Shortage Designation "Selected Statistics on Health Manpower Shortage Areas, As of December 31, 1999"

*Percent of population considered under-served by primary medical practitioners (Family & General Practice doctors, Internists, Ob/Gyns and Pediatricians). An under-served population does not have primary medical care within reasonable economic and geographic bounds.

Nonfederal Physicians in General/Family Practice in 1998

National Total = 79,303 Physicians*

ALPHA ORDER

RANK ORDER

RANK	STATE	PHYSICIANS	% of USA
23	Alabama	1,194	1.5%
47	Alaska	226	0.3%
20	Arizona	1,266	1.6%
28	Arkansas	1,059	1.3%
1	California	9,626	12.1%
18	Colorado	1,464	1.8%
36	Connecticut	589	0.7%
50	Delaware	202	0.3%
3	Florida	4,273	5.4%
15	Georgia	1,893	2.4%
45	Hawaii	307	0.4%
39	Idaho	467	0.6%
6	Illinois	3,521	4.4%
13	Indiana	2,187	2.8%
27	Iowa	1,089	1.4%
29	Kansas	1,049	1.3%
21	Kentucky	1,261	1.6%
23	Louisiana	1,194	1.5%
38	Maine	475	0.6%
22	Maryland	1,222	1.5%
26	Massachusetts	1,119	1.4%
8	Michigan	2,460	3.1%
10	Minnesota	2,325	2.9%
33	Mississippi	708	0.9%
25	Missouri	1,165	1.5%
44	Montana	328	0.4%
32	Nebraska	810	1.0%
40	Nevada	392	0.5%
41	New Hampshire	371	0.5%
17	New Jersey	1,544	1.9%
35	New Mexico	604	0.8%
5	New York	3,719	4.7%
11	North Carolina	2,287	2.9%
43	North Dakota	336	0.4%
7	Ohio	3,238	4.1%
31	Oklahoma	969	1.2%
30	Oregon	1,027	1.3%
4	Pennsylvania	3,866	4.9%
49	Rhode Island	211	0.3%
19	South Carolina	1,341	1.7%
42	South Dakota	346	0.4%
16	Tennessee	1,667	2.1%
2	Texas	5,396	6.8%
37	Utah	586	0.7%
46	Vermont	249	0.3%
12	Virginia	2,194	2.8%
9	Washington	2,413	3.0%
34	West Virginia	653	0.8%
14	Wisconsin	2,046	2.6%
48	Wyoming	217	0.3%

RANK	STATE	PHYSICIANS	% of USA
1	California	9,626	12.1%
2	Texas	5,396	6.8%
3	Florida	4,273	5.4%
4	Pennsylvania	3,866	4.9%
5	New York	3,719	4.7%
6	Illinois	3,521	4.4%
7	Ohio	3,238	4.1%
8	Michigan	2,460	3.1%
9	Washington	2,413	3.0%
10	Minnesota	2,325	2.9%
11	North Carolina	2,287	2.9%
12	Virginia	2,194	2.8%
13	Indiana	2,187	2.8%
14	Wisconsin	2,046	2.6%
15	Georgia	1,893	2.4%
16	Tennessee	1,667	2.1%
17	New Jersey	1,544	1.9%
18	Colorado	1,464	1.8%
19	South Carolina	1,341	1.7%
20	Arizona	1,266	1.6%
21	Kentucky	1,261	1.6%
22	Maryland	1,222	1.5%
23	Alabama	1,194	1.5%
23	Louisiana	1,194	1.5%
25	Missouri	1,165	1.5%
26	Massachusetts	1,119	1.4%
27	Iowa	1,089	1.4%
28	Arkansas	1,059	1.3%
29	Kansas	1,049	1.3%
30	Oregon	1,027	1.3%
31	Oklahoma	969	1.2%
32	Nebraska	810	1.0%
33	Mississippi	708	0.9%
34	West Virginia	653	0.8%
35	New Mexico	604	0.8%
36	Connecticut	589	0.7%
37	Utah	586	0.7%
38	Maine	475	0.6%
39	Idaho	467	0.6%
40	Nevada	392	0.5%
41	New Hampshire	371	0.5%
42	South Dakota	346	0.4%
43	North Dakota	336	0.4%
44	Montana	328	0.4%
45	Hawaii	307	0.4%
46	Vermont	249	0.3%
47	Alaska	226	0.3%
48	Wyoming	217	0.3%
49	Rhode Island	211	0.3%
50	Delaware	202	0.3%
	District of Columbia	152	0.2%

Source: American Medical Association (Chicago, Illinois)
  "Physician Characteristics and Distribution in the U.S." (2000-2001 Edition)
*As of December 31, 1998. Total does not include 2,033 nonfederal physicians in U.S. territories and possessions.

Rate of Nonfederal Physicians in General/Family Practice in 1998

National Rate = 29 Physicians per 100,000 Population*

ALPHA ORDER

RANK	STATE	RATE
34	Alabama	27
14	Alaska	37
34	Arizona	27
6	Arkansas	42
28	California	29
14	Colorado	37
49	Connecticut	18
34	Delaware	27
28	Florida	29
41	Georgia	25
39	Hawaii	26
11	Idaho	38
28	Illinois	29
14	Indiana	37
11	Iowa	38
9	Kansas	40
21	Kentucky	32
34	Louisiana	27
11	Maine	38
43	Maryland	24
49	Massachusetts	18
41	Michigan	25
2	Minnesota	49
39	Mississippi	26
45	Missouri	21
14	Montana	37
2	Nebraska	49
44	Nevada	22
24	New Hampshire	31
48	New Jersey	19
19	New Mexico	35
47	New York	20
27	North Carolina	30
1	North Dakota	53
28	Ohio	29
28	Oklahoma	29
24	Oregon	31
21	Pennsylvania	32
45	Rhode Island	21
19	South Carolina	35
4	South Dakota	47
24	Tennessee	31
34	Texas	27
33	Utah	28
6	Vermont	42
21	Virginia	32
6	Washington	42
18	West Virginia	36
10	Wisconsin	39
5	Wyoming	45

RANK ORDER

RANK	STATE	RATE
1	North Dakota	53
2	Minnesota	49
2	Nebraska	49
4	South Dakota	47
5	Wyoming	45
6	Arkansas	42
6	Vermont	42
6	Washington	42
9	Kansas	40
10	Wisconsin	39
11	Idaho	38
11	Iowa	38
11	Maine	38
14	Alaska	37
14	Colorado	37
14	Indiana	37
14	Montana	37
18	West Virginia	36
19	New Mexico	35
19	South Carolina	35
21	Kentucky	32
21	Pennsylvania	32
21	Virginia	32
24	New Hampshire	31
24	Oregon	31
24	Tennessee	31
27	North Carolina	30
28	California	29
28	Florida	29
28	Illinois	29
28	Ohio	29
28	Oklahoma	29
33	Utah	28
34	Alabama	27
34	Arizona	27
34	Delaware	27
34	Louisiana	27
34	Texas	27
39	Hawaii	26
39	Mississippi	26
41	Georgia	25
41	Michigan	25
43	Maryland	24
44	Nevada	22
45	Missouri	21
45	Rhode Island	21
47	New York	20
48	New Jersey	19
49	Connecticut	18
49	Massachusetts	18
	District of Columbia	29

Source: Morgan Quitno Press using data from American Medical Association (Chicago, Illinois)
"Physician Characteristics and Distribution in the U.S." (2000-2001 Edition)
*As of December 31, 1998. National rate does not include physicians in U.S. territories and possessions.

Percent of Family Physicians Who Practice Pediatrics in 1998

National Percent = 87.9% of Family Physicians*

RANK	STATE	PERCENT
37	Alabama	86.7
33	Alaska	87.5
38	Arizona	86.4
33	Arkansas	87.5
42	California	85.8
5	Colorado	93.1
36	Connecticut	87.1
22	Delaware	89.7
50	Florida	76.5
38	Georgia	86.4
21	Hawaii	89.8
11	Idaho	91.9
32	Illinois	87.6
12	Indiana	91.8
13	Iowa	91.6
15	Kansas	91.3
26	Kentucky	89.0
41	Louisiana	86.0
16	Maine	90.7
49	Maryland	82.1
9	Massachusetts	92.1
26	Michigan	89.0
8	Minnesota	92.2
35	Mississippi	87.3
30	Missouri	87.8
9	Montana	92.1
2	Nebraska	95.2
28	Nevada	88.8
4	New Hampshire	93.5
43	New Jersey	85.6
18	New Mexico	90.1
45	New York	83.5
29	North Carolina	87.9
30	North Dakota	87.8
25	Ohio	89.1
19	Oklahoma	90.0
20	Oregon	89.9
23	Pennsylvania	89.4
16	Rhode Island	90.7
43	South Carolina	85.6
1	South Dakota	97.1
38	Tennessee	86.4
47	Texas	82.5
5	Utah	93.1
14	Vermont	91.4
24	Virginia	89.3
7	Washington	92.8
46	West Virginia	82.6
3	Wisconsin	93.8
47	Wyoming	82.5

RANK	STATE	PERCENT
1	South Dakota	97.1
2	Nebraska	95.2
3	Wisconsin	93.8
4	New Hampshire	93.5
5	Colorado	93.1
5	Utah	93.1
7	Washington	92.8
8	Minnesota	92.2
9	Massachusetts	92.1
9	Montana	92.1
11	Idaho	91.9
12	Indiana	91.8
13	Iowa	91.6
14	Vermont	91.4
15	Kansas	91.3
16	Maine	90.7
16	Rhode Island	90.7
18	New Mexico	90.1
19	Oklahoma	90.0
20	Oregon	89.9
21	Hawaii	89.8
22	Delaware	89.7
23	Pennsylvania	89.4
24	Virginia	89.3
25	Ohio	89.1
26	Kentucky	89.0
26	Michigan	89.0
28	Nevada	88.8
29	North Carolina	87.9
30	Missouri	87.8
30	North Dakota	87.8
32	Illinois	87.6
33	Alaska	87.5
33	Arkansas	87.5
35	Mississippi	87.3
36	Connecticut	87.1
37	Alabama	86.7
38	Arizona	86.4
38	Georgia	86.4
38	Tennessee	86.4
41	Louisiana	86.0
42	California	85.8
43	New Jersey	85.6
43	South Carolina	85.6
45	New York	83.5
46	West Virginia	82.6
47	Texas	82.5
47	Wyoming	82.5
49	Maryland	82.1
50	Florida	76.5
	District of Columbia	80.0

Source: The American Academy of Family Physicians
  "Facts About Family Practice 1998"
*As of January 1, 1998. Includes members of the Academy who are in direct patient care and who practice pediatrics "in some fashion".

Percent of Family Physicians Who Practice Obstetrics in 1998

National Percent = 30.4% of Family Physicians*

ALPHA ORDER

RANK	STATE	PERCENT
44	Alabama	12.9
3	Alaska	59.7
26	Arizona	26.0
30	Arkansas	23.0
30	California	23.0
14	Colorado	45.5
42	Connecticut	14.7
40	Delaware	15.5
50	Florida	6.3
36	Georgia	17.3
29	Hawaii	25.4
7	Idaho	53.7
23	Illinois	31.1
15	Indiana	44.0
11	Iowa	49.6
9	Kansas	51.9
47	Kentucky	12.6
38	Louisiana	16.3
18	Maine	39.8
46	Maryland	12.7
25	Massachusetts	28.1
19	Michigan	38.7
5	Minnesota	58.8
49	Mississippi	11.3
28	Missouri	25.7
8	Montana	52.5
4	Nebraska	59.4
48	Nevada	12.5
21	New Hampshire	34.1
41	New Jersey	14.8
22	New Mexico	33.8
26	New York	26.0
34	North Carolina	20.2
2	North Dakota	63.3
35	Ohio	18.1
16	Oklahoma	42.5
17	Oregon	42.0
39	Pennsylvania	16.1
24	Rhode Island	30.2
37	South Carolina	16.7
1	South Dakota	71.4
32	Tennessee	21.7
33	Texas	20.3
13	Utah	45.8
20	Vermont	37.0
44	Virginia	12.9
10	Washington	51.6
43	West Virginia	13.9
6	Wisconsin	58.4
12	Wyoming	49.2

RANK ORDER

RANK	STATE	PERCENT
1	South Dakota	71.4
2	North Dakota	63.3
3	Alaska	59.7
4	Nebraska	59.4
5	Minnesota	58.8
6	Wisconsin	58.4
7	Idaho	53.7
8	Montana	52.5
9	Kansas	51.9
10	Washington	51.6
11	Iowa	49.6
12	Wyoming	49.2
13	Utah	45.8
14	Colorado	45.5
15	Indiana	44.0
16	Oklahoma	42.5
17	Oregon	42.0
18	Maine	39.8
19	Michigan	38.7
20	Vermont	37.0
21	New Hampshire	34.1
22	New Mexico	33.8
23	Illinois	31.1
24	Rhode Island	30.2
25	Massachusetts	28.1
26	Arizona	26.0
26	New York	26.0
28	Missouri	25.7
29	Hawaii	25.4
30	Arkansas	23.0
30	California	23.0
32	Tennessee	21.7
33	Texas	20.3
34	North Carolina	20.2
35	Ohio	18.1
36	Georgia	17.3
37	South Carolina	16.7
38	Louisiana	16.3
39	Pennsylvania	16.1
40	Delaware	15.5
41	New Jersey	14.8
42	Connecticut	14.7
43	West Virginia	13.9
44	Alabama	12.9
44	Virginia	12.9
46	Maryland	12.7
47	Kentucky	12.6
48	Nevada	12.5
49	Mississippi	11.3
50	Florida	6.3
	District of Columbia	20.0

Source: The American Academy of Family Physicians
    "Facts About Family Practice 1998"

As of January 1, 1998. Includes members of the Academy who are in direct patient care and who practice obstetrics "in some fashion".

Percent of Nonfederal Physicians Who Are Specialists in 1998

National Percent = 75.0% of Physicians*

ALPHA ORDER

RANK	STATE	PERCENT
16	Alabama	75.3
38	Alaska	68.4
36	Arizona	69.5
41	Arkansas	67.6
26	California	72.3
28	Colorado	71.5
2	Connecticut	81.6
18	Delaware	74.7
34	Florida	69.8
10	Georgia	76.8
13	Hawaii	76.1
49	Idaho	62.4
11	Illinois	76.7
33	Indiana	69.9
47	Iowa	64.5
42	Kansas	67.4
21	Kentucky	74.0
8	Louisiana	78.4
39	Maine	68.1
6	Maryland	80.3
4	Massachusetts	81.3
13	Michigan	76.1
40	Minnesota	67.7
25	Mississippi	72.7
7	Missouri	79.2
45	Montana	65.7
44	Nebraska	66.4
22	Nevada	73.9
24	New Hampshire	72.8
5	New Jersey	80.8
37	New Mexico	69.3
3	New York	81.5
19	North Carolina	74.1
46	North Dakota	65.5
16	Ohio	75.3
30	Oklahoma	71.2
35	Oregon	69.7
9	Pennsylvania	76.9
1	Rhode Island	81.7
30	South Carolina	71.2
48	South Dakota	63.7
12	Tennessee	76.6
15	Texas	75.5
23	Utah	73.7
27	Vermont	71.6
19	Virginia	74.1
43	Washington	67.3
29	West Virginia	71.4
32	Wisconsin	71.1
50	Wyoming	59.9

RANK ORDER

RANK	STATE	PERCENT
1	Rhode Island	81.7
2	Connecticut	81.6
3	New York	81.5
4	Massachusetts	81.3
5	New Jersey	80.8
6	Maryland	80.3
7	Missouri	79.2
8	Louisiana	78.4
9	Pennsylvania	76.9
10	Georgia	76.8
11	Illinois	76.7
12	Tennessee	76.6
13	Hawaii	76.1
13	Michigan	76.1
15	Texas	75.5
16	Alabama	75.3
16	Ohio	75.3
18	Delaware	74.7
19	North Carolina	74.1
19	Virginia	74.1
21	Kentucky	74.0
22	Nevada	73.9
23	Utah	73.7
24	New Hampshire	72.8
25	Mississippi	72.7
26	California	72.3
27	Vermont	71.6
28	Colorado	71.5
29	West Virginia	71.4
30	Oklahoma	71.2
30	South Carolina	71.2
32	Wisconsin	71.1
33	Indiana	69.9
34	Florida	69.8
35	Oregon	69.7
36	Arizona	69.5
37	New Mexico	69.3
38	Alaska	68.4
39	Maine	68.1
40	Minnesota	67.7
41	Arkansas	67.6
42	Kansas	67.4
43	Washington	67.3
44	Nebraska	66.4
45	Montana	65.7
46	North Dakota	65.5
47	Iowa	64.5
48	South Dakota	63.7
49	Idaho	62.4
50	Wyoming	59.9
	District of Columbia	83.1

Source: Morgan Quitno Press using data from American Medical Association (Chicago, Illinois)
"Physician Characteristics and Distribution in the U.S." (2000 2001 Edition)
*As of December 31, 1998. National rate does not include physicians in U.S. territories and possessions. Includes physicians in medical, surgical and other specialties.

Nonfederal Physicians in Medical Specialties in 1998

National Total = 226,930 Physicians*

RANK	STATE	PHYSICIANS	% of USA
24	Alabama	2,808	1.2%
49	Alaska	231	0.1%
23	Arizona	2,870	1.3%
32	Arkansas	1,283	0.6%
2	California	26,038	11.5%
25	Colorado	2,753	1.2%
15	Connecticut	4,540	2.0%
44	Delaware	537	0.2%
4	Florida	11,890	5.2%
14	Georgia	5,111	2.3%
37	Hawaii	1,094	0.5%
46	Idaho	392	0.2%
6	Illinois	11,221	4.9%
22	Indiana	3,201	1.4%
33	Iowa	1,280	0.6%
30	Kansas	1,445	0.6%
26	Kentucky	2,459	1.1%
21	Louisiana	3,441	1.5%
42	Maine	802	0.4%
11	Maryland	7,170	3.2%
7	Massachusetts	9,937	4.4%
10	Michigan	7,464	3.3%
19	Minnesota	3,553	1.6%
34	Mississippi	1,264	0.6%
16	Missouri	4,414	1.9%
45	Montana	403	0.2%
39	Nebraska	972	0.4%
40	Nevada	947	0.4%
41	New Hampshire	847	0.4%
8	New Jersey	9,739	4.3%
38	New Mexico	1,077	0.5%
1	New York	27,992	12.3%
12	North Carolina	5,546	2.4%
47	North Dakota	357	0.2%
9	Ohio	8,821	3.9%
29	Oklahoma	1,630	0.7%
27	Oregon	2,243	1.0%
5	Pennsylvania	11,762	5.2%
31	Rhode Island	1,371	0.6%
28	South Carolina	2,194	1.0%
48	South Dakota	338	0.1%
17	Tennessee	4,381	1.9%
3	Texas	12,167	5.4%
35	Utah	1,223	0.5%
43	Vermont	578	0.3%
13	Virginia	5,203	2.3%
18	Washington	3,694	1.6%
36	West Virginia	1,128	0.5%
20	Wisconsin	3,508	1.5%
50	Wyoming	163	0.1%

RANK	STATE	PHYSICIANS	% of USA
1	New York	27,992	12.3%
2	California	26,038	11.5%
3	Texas	12,167	5.4%
4	Florida	11,890	5.2%
5	Pennsylvania	11,762	5.2%
6	Illinois	11,221	4.9%
7	Massachusetts	9,937	4.4%
8	New Jersey	9,739	4.3%
9	Ohio	8,821	3.9%
10	Michigan	7,464	3.3%
11	Maryland	7,170	3.2%
12	North Carolina	5,546	2.4%
13	Virginia	5,203	2.3%
14	Georgia	5,111	2.3%
15	Connecticut	4,540	2.0%
16	Missouri	4,414	1.9%
17	Tennessee	4,381	1.9%
18	Washington	3,694	1.6%
19	Minnesota	3,553	1.6%
20	Wisconsin	3,508	1.5%
21	Louisiana	3,441	1.5%
22	Indiana	3,201	1.4%
23	Arizona	2,870	1.3%
24	Alabama	2,808	1.2%
25	Colorado	2,753	1.2%
26	Kentucky	2,459	1.1%
27	Oregon	2,243	1.0%
28	South Carolina	2,194	1.0%
29	Oklahoma	1,630	0.7%
30	Kansas	1,445	0.6%
31	Rhode Island	1,371	0.6%
32	Arkansas	1,283	0.6%
33	Iowa	1,280	0.6%
34	Mississippi	1,264	0.6%
35	Utah	1,223	0.5%
36	West Virginia	1,128	0.5%
37	Hawaii	1,094	0.5%
38	New Mexico	1,077	0.5%
39	Nebraska	972	0.4%
40	Nevada	947	0.4%
41	New Hampshire	847	0.4%
42	Maine	802	0.4%
43	Vermont	578	0.3%
44	Delaware	537	0.2%
45	Montana	403	0.2%
46	Idaho	392	0.2%
47	North Dakota	357	0.2%
48	South Dakota	338	0.1%
49	Alaska	231	0.1%
50	Wyoming	163	0.1%
	District of Columbia	1,448	0.6%

Source: American Medical Association (Chicago, Illinois)
"Physician Characteristics and Distribution in the U.S." (2000-2001 Edition)

As of December 31, 1998. Total does not include 2,721 physicians in U.S. territories and possessions. Medical Specialties are Allergy/Immunology, Cardiovascular Diseases, Dermatology, Gastroenterology, Internal Medicine, Pediatrics, Pediatric Cardiology and Pulmonary Diseases.

Rate of Nonfederal Physicians in Medical Specialties in 1998

National Rate = 84 Physicians per 100,000 Population*

ALPHA ORDER				RANK ORDER		
RANK	**STATE**	**RATE**		**RANK**	**STATE**	**RATE**
27	Alabama	65		1	Massachusetts	162
48	Alaska	38		2	New York	154
34	Arizona	61		3	Maryland	140
42	Arkansas	51		4	Connecticut	139
13	California	80		4	Rhode Island	139
23	Colorado	69		6	New Jersey	120
4	Connecticut	139		7	Pennsylvania	98
21	Delaware	72		7	Vermont	98
13	Florida	80		9	Illinois	93
25	Georgia	67		10	Hawaii	92
10	Hawaii	92		11	Missouri	81
50	Idaho	32		11	Tennessee	81
9	Illinois	93		13	California	80
40	Indiana	54		13	Florida	80
47	Iowa	45		15	Louisiana	79
39	Kansas	55		16	Ohio	78
30	Kentucky	63		17	Virginia	77
15	Louisiana	79		18	Michigan	76
29	Maine	64		19	Minnesota	75
3	Maryland	140		20	North Carolina	73
1	Massachusetts	162		21	Delaware	72
18	Michigan	76		22	New Hampshire	71
19	Minnesota	75		23	Colorado	69
44	Mississippi	46		24	Oregon	68
11	Missouri	81		25	Georgia	67
44	Montana	46		25	Wisconsin	67
35	Nebraska	59		27	Alabama	65
40	Nevada	54		27	Washington	65
22	New Hampshire	71		29	Maine	64
6	New Jersey	120		30	Kentucky	63
31	New Mexico	62		31	New Mexico	62
2	New York	154		31	Texas	62
20	North Carolina	73		31	West Virginia	62
38	North Dakota	56		34	Arizona	61
16	Ohio	78		35	Nebraska	59
43	Oklahoma	49		36	Utah	58
24	Oregon	68		37	South Carolina	57
7	Pennsylvania	98		38	North Dakota	56
4	Rhode Island	139		39	Kansas	55
37	South Carolina	57		40	Indiana	54
44	South Dakota	46		40	Nevada	54
11	Tennessee	81		42	Arkansas	51
31	Texas	62		43	Oklahoma	49
36	Utah	58		44	Mississippi	46
7	Vermont	98		44	Montana	46
17	Virginia	77		44	South Dakota	46
27	Washington	65		47	Iowa	45
31	West Virginia	62		48	Alaska	38
25	Wisconsin	67		49	Wyoming	34
49	Wyoming	34		50	Idaho	32
					District of Columbia	278

Source: Morgan Quitno Press using data from American Medical Association (Chicago, Illinois)
   "Physician Characteristics and Distribution in the U.S." (2000-2001 Edition)
*As of December 31, 1998. National rate does not include physicians in U.S. territories and possessions. Medical
Specialties are Allergy/Immunology, Cardiovascular Diseases, Dermatology, Gastroenterology, Internal Medicine,
Pediatrics, Pediatric Cardiology and Pulmonary Diseases.

Nonfederal Physicians in Internal Medicine in 1998

National Total = 122,959 Physicians*

<table>
<tr><td colspan="4">ALPHA ORDER</td><td colspan="4">RANK ORDER</td></tr>
<tr><th>RANK</th><th>STATE</th><th>PHYSICIANS</th><th>% of USA</th><th>RANK</th><th>STATE</th><th>PHYSICIANS</th><th>% of USA</th></tr>
<tr><td>23</td><td>Alabama</td><td>1,518</td><td>1.2%</td><td>1</td><td>New York</td><td>16,388</td><td>13.3%</td></tr>
<tr><td>49</td><td>Alaska</td><td>112</td><td>0.1%</td><td>2</td><td>California</td><td>13,611</td><td>11.1%</td></tr>
<tr><td>25</td><td>Arizona</td><td>1,394</td><td>1.1%</td><td>3</td><td>Pennsylvania</td><td>6,663</td><td>5.4%</td></tr>
<tr><td>36</td><td>Arkansas</td><td>575</td><td>0.5%</td><td>4</td><td>Illinois</td><td>6,550</td><td>5.3%</td></tr>
<tr><td>2</td><td>California</td><td>13,611</td><td>11.1%</td><td>5</td><td>Massachusetts</td><td>5,947</td><td>4.8%</td></tr>
<tr><td>24</td><td>Colorado</td><td>1,417</td><td>1.2%</td><td>6</td><td>Texas</td><td>5,943</td><td>4.8%</td></tr>
<tr><td>15</td><td>Connecticut</td><td>2,647</td><td>2.2%</td><td>7</td><td>Florida</td><td>5,793</td><td>4.7%</td></tr>
<tr><td>44</td><td>Delaware</td><td>253</td><td>0.2%</td><td>8</td><td>New Jersey</td><td>5,230</td><td>4.3%</td></tr>
<tr><td>7</td><td>Florida</td><td>5,793</td><td>4.7%</td><td>9</td><td>Ohio</td><td>4,700</td><td>3.8%</td></tr>
<tr><td>13</td><td>Georgia</td><td>2,725</td><td>2.2%</td><td>10</td><td>Michigan</td><td>4,290</td><td>3.5%</td></tr>
<tr><td>35</td><td>Hawaii</td><td>615</td><td>0.5%</td><td>11</td><td>Maryland</td><td>4,042</td><td>3.3%</td></tr>
<tr><td>47</td><td>Idaho</td><td>197</td><td>0.2%</td><td>12</td><td>North Carolina</td><td>2,821</td><td>2.3%</td></tr>
<tr><td>4</td><td>Illinois</td><td>6,550</td><td>5.3%</td><td>13</td><td>Georgia</td><td>2,725</td><td>2.2%</td></tr>
<tr><td>22</td><td>Indiana</td><td>1,639</td><td>1.3%</td><td>14</td><td>Virginia</td><td>2,700</td><td>2.2%</td></tr>
<tr><td>34</td><td>Iowa</td><td>618</td><td>0.5%</td><td>15</td><td>Connecticut</td><td>2,647</td><td>2.2%</td></tr>
<tr><td>31</td><td>Kansas</td><td>793</td><td>0.6%</td><td>16</td><td>Missouri</td><td>2,399</td><td>2.0%</td></tr>
<tr><td>27</td><td>Kentucky</td><td>1,241</td><td>1.0%</td><td>17</td><td>Tennessee</td><td>2,313</td><td>1.9%</td></tr>
<tr><td>21</td><td>Louisiana</td><td>1,716</td><td>1.4%</td><td>18</td><td>Washington</td><td>1,996</td><td>1.6%</td></tr>
<tr><td>42</td><td>Maine</td><td>446</td><td>0.4%</td><td>19</td><td>Minnesota</td><td>1,974</td><td>1.6%</td></tr>
<tr><td>11</td><td>Maryland</td><td>4,042</td><td>3.3%</td><td>20</td><td>Wisconsin</td><td>1,911</td><td>1.6%</td></tr>
<tr><td>5</td><td>Massachusetts</td><td>5,947</td><td>4.8%</td><td>21</td><td>Louisiana</td><td>1,716</td><td>1.4%</td></tr>
<tr><td>10</td><td>Michigan</td><td>4,290</td><td>3.5%</td><td>22</td><td>Indiana</td><td>1,639</td><td>1.3%</td></tr>
<tr><td>19</td><td>Minnesota</td><td>1,974</td><td>1.6%</td><td>23</td><td>Alabama</td><td>1,518</td><td>1.2%</td></tr>
<tr><td>32</td><td>Mississippi</td><td>655</td><td>0.5%</td><td>24</td><td>Colorado</td><td>1,417</td><td>1.2%</td></tr>
<tr><td>16</td><td>Missouri</td><td>2,399</td><td>2.0%</td><td>25</td><td>Arizona</td><td>1,394</td><td>1.1%</td></tr>
<tr><td>46</td><td>Montana</td><td>212</td><td>0.2%</td><td>26</td><td>Oregon</td><td>1,349</td><td>1.1%</td></tr>
<tr><td>40</td><td>Nebraska</td><td>483</td><td>0.4%</td><td>27</td><td>Kentucky</td><td>1,241</td><td>1.0%</td></tr>
<tr><td>39</td><td>Nevada</td><td>529</td><td>0.4%</td><td>28</td><td>South Carolina</td><td>1,093</td><td>0.9%</td></tr>
<tr><td>41</td><td>New Hampshire</td><td>449</td><td>0.4%</td><td>29</td><td>Oklahoma</td><td>823</td><td>0.7%</td></tr>
<tr><td>8</td><td>New Jersey</td><td>5,230</td><td>4.3%</td><td>30</td><td>Rhode Island</td><td>795</td><td>0.6%</td></tr>
<tr><td>37</td><td>New Mexico</td><td>567</td><td>0.5%</td><td>31</td><td>Kansas</td><td>793</td><td>0.6%</td></tr>
<tr><td>1</td><td>New York</td><td>16,388</td><td>13.3%</td><td>32</td><td>Mississippi</td><td>655</td><td>0.5%</td></tr>
<tr><td>12</td><td>North Carolina</td><td>2,821</td><td>2.3%</td><td>33</td><td>West Virginia</td><td>627</td><td>0.5%</td></tr>
<tr><td>45</td><td>North Dakota</td><td>220</td><td>0.2%</td><td>34</td><td>Iowa</td><td>618</td><td>0.5%</td></tr>
<tr><td>9</td><td>Ohio</td><td>4,700</td><td>3.8%</td><td>35</td><td>Hawaii</td><td>615</td><td>0.5%</td></tr>
<tr><td>29</td><td>Oklahoma</td><td>823</td><td>0.7%</td><td>36</td><td>Arkansas</td><td>575</td><td>0.5%</td></tr>
<tr><td>26</td><td>Oregon</td><td>1,349</td><td>1.1%</td><td>37</td><td>New Mexico</td><td>567</td><td>0.5%</td></tr>
<tr><td>3</td><td>Pennsylvania</td><td>6,663</td><td>5.4%</td><td>38</td><td>Utah</td><td>542</td><td>0.4%</td></tr>
<tr><td>30</td><td>Rhode Island</td><td>795</td><td>0.6%</td><td>39</td><td>Nevada</td><td>529</td><td>0.4%</td></tr>
<tr><td>28</td><td>South Carolina</td><td>1,093</td><td>0.9%</td><td>40</td><td>Nebraska</td><td>483</td><td>0.4%</td></tr>
<tr><td>48</td><td>South Dakota</td><td>191</td><td>0.2%</td><td>41</td><td>New Hampshire</td><td>449</td><td>0.4%</td></tr>
<tr><td>17</td><td>Tennessee</td><td>2,313</td><td>1.9%</td><td>42</td><td>Maine</td><td>446</td><td>0.4%</td></tr>
<tr><td>6</td><td>Texas</td><td>5,943</td><td>4.8%</td><td>43</td><td>Vermont</td><td>340</td><td>0.3%</td></tr>
<tr><td>38</td><td>Utah</td><td>542</td><td>0.4%</td><td>44</td><td>Delaware</td><td>253</td><td>0.2%</td></tr>
<tr><td>43</td><td>Vermont</td><td>340</td><td>0.3%</td><td>45</td><td>North Dakota</td><td>220</td><td>0.2%</td></tr>
<tr><td>14</td><td>Virginia</td><td>2,700</td><td>2.2%</td><td>46</td><td>Montana</td><td>212</td><td>0.2%</td></tr>
<tr><td>18</td><td>Washington</td><td>1,996</td><td>1.6%</td><td>47</td><td>Idaho</td><td>197</td><td>0.2%</td></tr>
<tr><td>33</td><td>West Virginia</td><td>627</td><td>0.5%</td><td>48</td><td>South Dakota</td><td>191</td><td>0.2%</td></tr>
<tr><td>20</td><td>Wisconsin</td><td>1,911</td><td>1.6%</td><td>49</td><td>Alaska</td><td>112</td><td>0.1%</td></tr>
<tr><td>50</td><td>Wyoming</td><td>84</td><td>0.1%</td><td>50</td><td>Wyoming</td><td>84</td><td>0.1%</td></tr>
<tr><td></td><td></td><td></td><td></td><td></td><td>District of Columbia</td><td>823</td><td>0.7%</td></tr>
</table>

Source: American Medical Association (Chicago, Illinois)
  "Physician Characteristics and Distribution in the U.S." (2000-2001 Edition)
*As of December 31, 1998. Total does not include 1,247 physicians in U.S. territories and possessions. Internal Medicine includes Diabetes, Endocrinology, Geriatrics, Hematology, Infectious Diseases, Nephrology, Nutrition, Medical Oncology and Rheumatology.

Rate of Nonfederal Physicians in Internal Medicine in 1998

National Rate = 45 Physicians per 100,000 Population*

ALPHA ORDER

RANK	STATE	RATE
27	Alabama	35
48	Alaska	18
34	Arizona	30
46	Arkansas	23
14	California	42
24	Colorado	36
3	Connecticut	81
30	Delaware	34
19	Florida	39
24	Georgia	36
10	Hawaii	52
50	Idaho	16
9	Illinois	54
39	Indiana	28
47	Iowa	22
34	Kansas	30
33	Kentucky	32
19	Louisiana	39
24	Maine	36
5	Maryland	79
1	Massachusetts	97
11	Michigan	44
14	Minnesota	42
44	Mississippi	24
11	Missouri	44
44	Montana	24
38	Nebraska	29
34	Nevada	30
21	New Hampshire	38
6	New Jersey	65
32	New Mexico	33
2	New York	90
22	North Carolina	37
30	North Dakota	34
14	Ohio	42
43	Oklahoma	25
17	Oregon	41
8	Pennsylvania	56
4	Rhode Island	80
39	South Carolina	28
41	South Dakota	26
13	Tennessee	43
34	Texas	30
41	Utah	26
7	Vermont	58
18	Virginia	40
27	Washington	35
27	West Virginia	35
22	Wisconsin	37
49	Wyoming	17

RANK ORDER

RANK	STATE	RATE
1	Massachusetts	97
2	New York	90
3	Connecticut	81
4	Rhode Island	80
5	Maryland	79
6	New Jersey	65
7	Vermont	58
8	Pennsylvania	56
9	Illinois	54
10	Hawaii	52
11	Michigan	44
11	Missouri	44
13	Tennessee	43
14	California	42
14	Minnesota	42
14	Ohio	42
17	Oregon	41
18	Virginia	40
19	Florida	39
19	Louisiana	39
21	New Hampshire	38
22	North Carolina	37
22	Wisconsin	37
24	Colorado	36
24	Georgia	36
24	Maine	36
27	Alabama	35
27	Washington	35
27	West Virginia	35
30	Delaware	34
30	North Dakota	34
32	New Mexico	33
33	Kentucky	32
34	Arizona	30
34	Kansas	30
34	Nevada	30
34	Texas	30
38	Nebraska	29
39	Indiana	28
39	South Carolina	28
41	South Dakota	26
41	Utah	26
43	Oklahoma	25
44	Mississippi	24
44	Montana	24
46	Arkansas	23
47	Iowa	22
48	Alaska	18
49	Wyoming	17
50	Idaho	16

District of Columbia 158

*As of December 31, 1998. National rate does not include physicians in U.S. territories and possessions. Internal Medicine includes Diabetes, Endocrinology, Geriatrics, Hematology, Infectious Diseases, Nephrology, Nutrition, Medical Oncology and Rheumatology.

Nonfederal Physicians in Pediatrics in 1998

National Total = 55,157 Physicians*

ALPHA ORDER					RANK ORDER			
RANK	STATE	PHYSICIANS	% of USA		RANK	STATE	PHYSICIANS	% of USA
26	Alabama	657	1.2%		1	California	6,648	12.1%
47	Alaska	76	0.1%		2	New York	6,533	11.8%
23	Arizona	742	1.3%		3	Texas	3,392	6.1%
31	Arkansas	376	0.7%		4	Florida	2,784	5.0%
1	California	6,648	12.1%		5	Illinois	2,597	4.7%
24	Colorado	707	1.3%		6	New Jersey	2,458	4.5%
17	Connecticut	975	1.8%		7	Pennsylvania	2,397	4.3%
43	Delaware	171	0.3%		8	Ohio	2,314	4.2%
4	Florida	2,784	5.0%		9	Massachusetts	2,091	3.8%
14	Georgia	1,293	2.3%		10	Michigan	1,757	3.2%
36	Hawaii	299	0.5%		11	Maryland	1,724	3.1%
46	Idaho	79	0.1%		12	North Carolina	1,445	2.6%
5	Illinois	2,597	4.7%		13	Virginia	1,368	2.5%
22	Indiana	759	1.4%		14	Georgia	1,293	2.3%
35	Iowa	313	0.6%		15	Tennessee	1,125	2.0%
32	Kansas	339	0.6%		16	Missouri	1,021	1.9%
25	Kentucky	663	1.2%		17	Connecticut	975	1.8%
18	Louisiana	921	1.7%		18	Louisiana	921	1.7%
41	Maine	192	0.3%		19	Washington	903	1.6%
11	Maryland	1,724	3.1%		20	Wisconsin	835	1.5%
9	Massachusetts	2,091	3.8%		21	Minnesota	791	1.4%
10	Michigan	1,757	3.2%		22	Indiana	759	1.4%
21	Minnesota	791	1.4%		23	Arizona	742	1.3%
33	Mississippi	322	0.6%		24	Colorado	707	1.3%
16	Missouri	1,021	1.9%		25	Kentucky	663	1.2%
45	Montana	82	0.1%		26	Alabama	657	1.2%
39	Nebraska	253	0.5%		27	South Carolina	571	1.0%
42	Nevada	172	0.3%		28	Oregon	446	0.8%
40	New Hampshire	213	0.4%		29	Oklahoma	402	0.7%
6	New Jersey	2,458	4.5%		30	Utah	381	0.7%
37	New Mexico	286	0.5%		31	Arkansas	376	0.7%
2	New York	6,533	11.8%		32	Kansas	339	0.6%
12	North Carolina	1,445	2.6%		33	Mississippi	322	0.6%
48	North Dakota	64	0.1%		34	Rhode Island	317	0.6%
8	Ohio	2,314	4.2%		35	Iowa	313	0.6%
29	Oklahoma	402	0.7%		36	Hawaii	299	0.5%
28	Oregon	446	0.8%		37	New Mexico	286	0.5%
7	Pennsylvania	2,397	4.3%		38	West Virginia	270	0.5%
34	Rhode Island	317	0.6%		39	Nebraska	253	0.5%
27	South Carolina	571	1.0%		40	New Hampshire	213	0.4%
49	South Dakota	61	0.1%		41	Maine	192	0.3%
15	Tennessee	1,125	2.0%		42	Nevada	172	0.3%
3	Texas	3,392	6.1%		43	Delaware	171	0.3%
30	Utah	381	0.7%		44	Vermont	156	0.3%
44	Vermont	156	0.3%		45	Montana	82	0.1%
13	Virginia	1,368	2.5%		46	Idaho	79	0.1%
19	Washington	903	1.6%		47	Alaska	76	0.1%
38	West Virginia	270	0.5%		48	North Dakota	64	0.1%
20	Wisconsin	835	1.5%		49	South Dakota	61	0.1%
50	Wyoming	46	0.1%		50	Wyoming	46	0.1%
						District of Columbia	370	0.7%

Source: American Medical Association (Chicago, Illinois)
 "Physician Characteristics and Distribution in the U.S." (2000-2001 Edition)
*As of December 31, 1998. Total does not include 1,002 physicians in U.S. territories and possessions. Pediatrics includes Adolescent Medicine, Neonatal-Perinatal, Pediatric Allergy, Pediatric Endocrinology, Pediatric Pulmonology, Pediatric Hematology-Oncology and Pediatric Nephrology.

Rate of Nonfederal Physicians in Pediatrics in 1998

National Rate = 79 Physicians per 100,000 Population 17 Years and Younger*

ALPHA ORDER

RANK	STATE	RATE
29	Alabama	61
44	Alaska	40
33	Arizona	59
34	Arkansas	58
17	California	75
22	Colorado	68
5	Connecticut	123
9	Delaware	95
15	Florida	79
26	Georgia	64
8	Hawaii	100
50	Idaho	22
13	Illinois	81
39	Indiana	50
42	Iowa	43
40	Kansas	49
23	Kentucky	67
16	Louisiana	77
25	Maine	66
3	Maryland	134
2	Massachusetts	143
21	Michigan	69
27	Minnesota	63
42	Mississippi	43
19	Missouri	73
46	Montana	37
35	Nebraska	57
46	Nevada	37
20	New Hampshire	71
5	New Jersey	123
35	New Mexico	57
1	New York	145
17	North Carolina	75
45	North Dakota	39
13	Ohio	81
41	Oklahoma	46
37	Oregon	54
10	Pennsylvania	84
4	Rhode Island	133
31	South Carolina	60
49	South Dakota	30
10	Tennessee	84
31	Texas	60
37	Utah	54
7	Vermont	110
12	Virginia	83
29	Washington	61
23	West Virginia	67
28	Wisconsin	62
48	Wyoming	36

RANK ORDER

RANK	STATE	RATE
1	New York	145
2	Massachusetts	143
3	Maryland	134
4	Rhode Island	133
5	Connecticut	123
5	New Jersey	123
7	Vermont	110
8	Hawaii	100
9	Delaware	95
10	Pennsylvania	84
10	Tennessee	84
12	Virginia	83
13	Illinois	81
13	Ohio	81
15	Florida	79
16	Louisiana	77
17	California	75
17	North Carolina	75
19	Missouri	73
20	New Hampshire	71
21	Michigan	69
22	Colorado	68
23	Kentucky	67
23	West Virginia	67
25	Maine	66
26	Georgia	64
27	Minnesota	63
28	Wisconsin	62
29	Alabama	61
29	Washington	61
31	South Carolina	60
31	Texas	60
33	Arizona	59
34	Arkansas	58
35	Nebraska	57
35	New Mexico	57
37	Oregon	54
37	Utah	54
39	Indiana	50
40	Kansas	49
41	Oklahoma	46
42	Iowa	43
42	Mississippi	43
44	Alaska	40
45	North Dakota	39
46	Montana	37
46	Nevada	37
48	Wyoming	36
49	South Dakota	30
50	Idaho	22
	District of Columbia	359

Source: Morgan Quitno Press using data from American Medical Association (Chicago, Illinois)
   "Physician Characteristics and Distribution in the U.S." (2000-2001 Edition)
*As of December 31, 1998. National rate does not include physicians in U.S. territories and possessions. Pediatrics includes Adolescent Medicine, Neonatal-Perinatal, Pediatric Allergy, Pediatric Endocrinology, Pediatric Pulmonology, Pediatric Hematology-Oncology and Pediatric Nephrology.

Nonfederal Physicians in Surgical Specialties in 1998

National Total = 148,883 Physicians*

ALPHA ORDER

RANK	STATE	PHYSICIANS	% of USA
23	Alabama	2,157	1.4%
49	Alaska	241	0.2%
24	Arizona	2,108	1.4%
33	Arkansas	1,093	0.7%
1	California	17,105	11.5%
25	Colorado	2,089	1.4%
19	Connecticut	2,495	1.7%
45	Delaware	391	0.3%
4	Florida	8,329	5.6%
12	Georgia	3,995	2.7%
39	Hawaii	719	0.5%
43	Idaho	508	0.3%
6	Illinois	6,434	4.3%
21	Indiana	2,453	1.6%
32	Iowa	1,146	0.8%
31	Kansas	1,159	0.8%
26	Kentucky	1,935	1.3%
17	Louisiana	2,775	1.9%
42	Maine	594	0.4%
13	Maryland	3,932	2.6%
10	Massachusetts	4,526	3.0%
9	Michigan	4,837	3.2%
22	Minnesota	2,316	1.6%
30	Mississippi	1,194	0.8%
16	Missouri	2,928	2.0%
44	Montana	421	0.3%
36	Nebraska	817	0.5%
38	Nevada	722	0.5%
41	New Hampshire	658	0.4%
8	New Jersey	5,106	3.4%
37	New Mexico	753	0.5%
2	New York	14,061	9.4%
11	North Carolina	4,128	2.8%
48	North Dakota	307	0.2%
7	Ohio	5,987	4.0%
29	Oklahoma	1,304	0.9%
28	Oregon	1,667	1.1%
5	Pennsylvania	7,551	5.1%
40	Rhode Island	707	0.5%
27	South Carolina	1,931	1.3%
47	South Dakota	320	0.2%
15	Tennessee	3,215	2.2%
3	Texas	9,435	6.3%
34	Utah	1,015	0.7%
46	Vermont	368	0.2%
14	Virginia	3,796	2.5%
18	Washington	2,745	1.8%
35	West Virginia	906	0.6%
20	Wisconsin	2,483	1.7%
50	Wyoming	196	0.1%

RANK ORDER

RANK	STATE	PHYSICIANS	% of USA
1	California	17,105	11.5%
2	New York	14,061	9.4%
3	Texas	9,435	6.3%
4	Florida	8,329	5.6%
5	Pennsylvania	7,551	5.1%
6	Illinois	6,434	4.3%
7	Ohio	5,987	4.0%
8	New Jersey	5,106	3.4%
9	Michigan	4,837	3.2%
10	Massachusetts	4,526	3.0%
11	North Carolina	4,128	2.8%
12	Georgia	3,995	2.7%
13	Maryland	3,932	2.6%
14	Virginia	3,796	2.5%
15	Tennessee	3,215	2.2%
16	Missouri	2,928	2.0%
17	Louisiana	2,775	1.9%
18	Washington	2,745	1.8%
19	Connecticut	2,495	1.7%
20	Wisconsin	2,483	1.7%
21	Indiana	2,453	1.6%
22	Minnesota	2,316	1.6%
23	Alabama	2,157	1.4%
24	Arizona	2,108	1.4%
25	Colorado	2,089	1.4%
26	Kentucky	1,935	1.3%
27	South Carolina	1,931	1.3%
28	Oregon	1,667	1.1%
29	Oklahoma	1,304	0.9%
30	Mississippi	1,194	0.8%
31	Kansas	1,159	0.8%
32	Iowa	1,146	0.8%
33	Arkansas	1,093	0.7%
34	Utah	1,015	0.7%
35	West Virginia	906	0.6%
36	Nebraska	817	0.5%
37	New Mexico	753	0.5%
38	Nevada	722	0.5%
39	Hawaii	719	0.5%
40	Rhode Island	707	0.5%
41	New Hampshire	658	0.4%
42	Maine	594	0.4%
43	Idaho	508	0.3%
44	Montana	421	0.3%
45	Delaware	391	0.3%
46	Vermont	368	0.2%
47	South Dakota	320	0.2%
48	North Dakota	307	0.2%
49	Alaska	241	0.2%
50	Wyoming	196	0.1%
	District of Columbia	825	0.6%

Source: American Medical Association (Chicago, Illinois)
  "Physician Characteristics and Distribution in the U.S." (2000-2001 Edition)
*As of December 31, 1998. Total does not include 1,520 physicians in U.S. territories and possessions. Surgical Specialties include Colon and Rectal, General, Neurological, Obstetrics & Gynecology, Ophthalmology, Orthopedic, Otolaryngology, Plastic, Thoracic and Urological Surgeries.

Rate of Nonfederal Physicians in Surgical Specialties in 1998

National Rate = 55 Physicians per 100,000 Population*

ALPHA ORDER

RANK	STATE	RATE
24	Alabama	50
49	Alaska	39
38	Arizona	45
41	Arkansas	43
21	California	52
17	Colorado	53
3	Connecticut	76
17	Delaware	53
12	Florida	56
21	Georgia	52
10	Hawaii	60
45	Idaho	41
17	Illinois	53
44	Indiana	42
48	Iowa	40
39	Kansas	44
27	Kentucky	49
6	Louisiana	64
31	Maine	48
1	Maryland	77
4	Massachusetts	74
27	Michigan	49
27	Minnesota	49
41	Mississippi	43
16	Missouri	54
31	Montana	48
27	Nebraska	49
45	Nevada	41
14	New Hampshire	55
7	New Jersey	63
41	New Mexico	43
1	New York	77
14	North Carolina	55
31	North Dakota	48
17	Ohio	53
49	Oklahoma	39
23	Oregon	51
7	Pennsylvania	63
5	Rhode Island	72
24	South Carolina	50
39	South Dakota	44
11	Tennessee	59
31	Texas	48
31	Utah	48
9	Vermont	62
12	Virginia	56
31	Washington	48
24	West Virginia	50
31	Wisconsin	48
45	Wyoming	41

RANK ORDER

RANK	STATE	RATE
1	Maryland	77
1	New York	77
3	Connecticut	76
4	Massachusetts	74
5	Rhode Island	72
6	Louisiana	64
7	New Jersey	63
7	Pennsylvania	63
9	Vermont	62
10	Hawaii	60
11	Tennessee	59
12	Florida	56
12	Virginia	56
14	New Hampshire	55
14	North Carolina	55
16	Missouri	54
17	Colorado	53
17	Delaware	53
17	Illinois	53
17	Ohio	53
21	California	52
21	Georgia	52
23	Oregon	51
24	Alabama	50
24	South Carolina	50
24	West Virginia	50
27	Kentucky	49
27	Michigan	49
27	Minnesota	49
27	Nebraska	49
31	Maine	48
31	Montana	48
31	North Dakota	48
31	Texas	48
31	Utah	48
31	Washington	48
31	Wisconsin	48
38	Arizona	45
39	Kansas	44
39	South Dakota	44
41	Arkansas	43
41	Mississippi	43
41	New Mexico	43
44	Indiana	42
45	Idaho	41
45	Nevada	41
45	Wyoming	41
48	Iowa	40
49	Alaska	39
49	Oklahoma	39

| | District of Columbia | 158 |

Source: Morgan Quitno Press using data from American Medical Association (Chicago, Illinois)
    "Physician Characteristics and Distribution in the U.S." (2000-2001 Edition)
*As of December 31, 1998. National rate does not include physicians in U.S. territories and possessions. Surgical Specialties include Colon and Rectal, General, Neurological, Obstetrics & Gynecology, Ophthalmology, Orthopedic, Otolaryngology, Plastic, Thoracic and Urological Surgeries.

Nonfederal Physicians in General Surgery in 1998

National Total = 38,974 Physicians*

ALPHA ORDER

RANK	STATE	PHYSICIANS	% of USA
23	Alabama	582	1.5%
49	Alaska	57	0.1%
25	Arizona	511	1.3%
34	Arkansas	290	0.7%
1	California	4,023	10.3%
26	Colorado	509	1.3%
19	Connecticut	646	1.7%
44	Delaware	114	0.3%
5	Florida	1,960	5.0%
12	Georgia	1,022	2.6%
42	Hawaii	174	0.4%
43	Idaho	120	0.3%
6	Illinois	1,702	4.4%
21	Indiana	624	1.6%
30	Iowa	328	0.8%
29	Kansas	334	0.9%
24	Kentucky	580	1.5%
17	Louisiana	726	1.9%
41	Maine	175	0.4%
13	Maryland	1,007	2.6%
10	Massachusetts	1,329	3.4%
9	Michigan	1,337	3.4%
22	Minnesota	594	1.5%
32	Mississippi	316	0.8%
16	Missouri	770	2.0%
45	Montana	107	0.3%
35	Nebraska	239	0.6%
39	Nevada	182	0.5%
40	New Hampshire	178	0.5%
8	New Jersey	1,340	3.4%
37	New Mexico	198	0.5%
2	New York	4,005	10.3%
11	North Carolina	1,027	2.6%
47	North Dakota	92	0.2%
7	Ohio	1,685	4.3%
31	Oklahoma	317	0.8%
28	Oregon	401	1.0%
4	Pennsylvania	2,234	5.7%
38	Rhode Island	196	0.5%
27	South Carolina	499	1.3%
47	South Dakota	92	0.2%
15	Tennessee	894	2.3%
3	Texas	2,349	6.0%
36	Utah	210	0.5%
46	Vermont	102	0.3%
14	Virginia	923	2.4%
18	Washington	651	1.7%
33	West Virginia	296	0.8%
20	Wisconsin	626	1.6%
50	Wyoming	47	0.1%

RANK ORDER

RANK	STATE	PHYSICIANS	% of USA
1	California	4,023	10.3%
2	New York	4,005	10.3%
3	Texas	2,349	6.0%
4	Pennsylvania	2,234	5.7%
5	Florida	1,960	5.0%
6	Illinois	1,702	4.4%
7	Ohio	1,685	4.3%
8	New Jersey	1,340	3.4%
9	Michigan	1,337	3.4%
10	Massachusetts	1,329	3.4%
11	North Carolina	1,027	2.6%
12	Georgia	1,022	2.6%
13	Maryland	1,007	2.6%
14	Virginia	923	2.4%
15	Tennessee	894	2.3%
16	Missouri	770	2.0%
17	Louisiana	726	1.9%
18	Washington	651	1.7%
19	Connecticut	646	1.7%
20	Wisconsin	626	1.6%
21	Indiana	624	1.6%
22	Minnesota	594	1.5%
23	Alabama	582	1.5%
24	Kentucky	580	1.5%
25	Arizona	511	1.3%
26	Colorado	509	1.3%
27	South Carolina	499	1.3%
28	Oregon	401	1.0%
29	Kansas	334	0.9%
30	Iowa	328	0.8%
31	Oklahoma	317	0.8%
32	Mississippi	316	0.8%
33	West Virginia	296	0.8%
34	Arkansas	290	0.7%
35	Nebraska	239	0.6%
36	Utah	210	0.5%
37	New Mexico	198	0.5%
38	Rhode Island	196	0.5%
39	Nevada	182	0.5%
40	New Hampshire	178	0.5%
41	Maine	175	0.4%
42	Hawaii	174	0.4%
43	Idaho	120	0.3%
44	Delaware	114	0.3%
45	Montana	107	0.3%
46	Vermont	102	0.3%
47	North Dakota	92	0.2%
47	South Dakota	92	0.2%
49	Alaska	57	0.1%
50	Wyoming	47	0.1%
	District of Columbia	254	0.7%

Source: American Medical Association (Chicago, Illinois)
"Physician Characteristics and Distribution in the U.S." (2000-2001 Edition)

*As of December 31, 1998. Total does not include 407 physicians in U.S. territories and possessions. General Surgery includes Abdominal, Cardiovascular, Hand, Head and Neck, Pediatric, Traumatic and Vascular Surgeries.

Rate of Nonfederal Physicians in General Surgery in 1998

National Rate = 14.4 Physicians per 100,000 Population*

ALPHA ORDER

RANK	STATE	RATE
25	Alabama	13.4
50	Alaska	9.3
43	Arizona	10.9
40	Arkansas	11.4
33	California	12.3
29	Colorado	12.8
4	Connecticut	19.7
12	Delaware	15.3
27	Florida	13.1
25	Georgia	13.4
16	Hawaii	14.6
48	Idaho	9.7
20	Illinois	14.1
44	Indiana	10.6
38	Iowa	11.5
30	Kansas	12.7
15	Kentucky	14.7
8	Louisiana	16.6
21	Maine	14.0
5	Maryland	19.6
2	Massachusetts	21.6
22	Michigan	13.6
31	Minnesota	12.6
38	Mississippi	11.5
19	Missouri	14.2
34	Montana	12.2
17	Nebraska	14.4
45	Nevada	10.4
13	New Hampshire	15.0
8	New Jersey	16.6
40	New Mexico	11.4
1	New York	22.1
22	North Carolina	13.6
17	North Dakota	14.4
13	Ohio	15.0
49	Oklahoma	9.5
34	Oregon	12.2
6	Pennsylvania	18.6
3	Rhode Island	19.8
28	South Carolina	13.0
31	South Dakota	12.6
10	Tennessee	16.5
37	Texas	11.9
46	Utah	10.0
7	Vermont	17.3
22	Virginia	13.6
40	Washington	11.4
11	West Virginia	16.3
36	Wisconsin	12.0
47	Wyoming	9.8

RANK ORDER

RANK	STATE	RATE
1	New York	22.1
2	Massachusetts	21.6
3	Rhode Island	19.8
4	Connecticut	19.7
5	Maryland	19.6
6	Pennsylvania	18.6
7	Vermont	17.3
8	Louisiana	16.6
8	New Jersey	16.6
10	Tennessee	16.5
11	West Virginia	16.3
12	Delaware	15.3
13	New Hampshire	15.0
13	Ohio	15.0
15	Kentucky	14.7
16	Hawaii	14.6
17	Nebraska	14.4
17	North Dakota	14.4
19	Missouri	14.2
20	Illinois	14.1
21	Maine	14.0
22	Michigan	13.6
22	North Carolina	13.6
22	Virginia	13.6
25	Alabama	13.4
25	Georgia	13.4
27	Florida	13.1
28	South Carolina	13.0
29	Colorado	12.8
30	Kansas	12.7
31	Minnesota	12.6
31	South Dakota	12.6
33	California	12.3
34	Montana	12.2
34	Oregon	12.2
36	Wisconsin	12.0
37	Texas	11.9
38	Iowa	11.5
38	Mississippi	11.5
40	Arkansas	11.4
40	New Mexico	11.4
40	Washington	11.4
43	Arizona	10.9
44	Indiana	10.6
45	Nevada	10.4
46	Utah	10.0
47	Wyoming	9.8
48	Idaho	9.7
49	Oklahoma	9.5
50	Alaska	9.3

| District of Columbia | 48.7 |

Source: Morgan Quitno Press using data from American Medical Association (Chicago, Illinois)
     "Physician Characteristics and Distribution in the U.S." (2000-2001 Edition)
*As of December 31, 1998. National rate does not include physicians in U.S. territories and possessions. General Surgery includes Abdominal, Cardiovascular, Hand, Head and Neck, Pediatric, Traumatic and Vascular Surgeries.

Nonfederal Physicians in Obstetrics and Gynecology in 1998

National Total = 38,482 Physicians*

ALPHA ORDER

RANK	STATE	PHYSICIANS	% of USA
24	Alabama	529	1.4%
48	Alaska	60	0.2%
21	Arizona	571	1.5%
33	Arkansas	236	0.6%
1	California	4,473	11.6%
23	Colorado	539	1.4%
18	Connecticut	695	1.8%
45	Delaware	94	0.2%
4	Florida	1,998	5.2%
10	Georgia	1,182	3.1%
34	Hawaii	226	0.6%
43	Idaho	106	0.3%
5	Illinois	1,864	4.8%
20	Indiana	603	1.6%
35	Iowa	218	0.6%
31	Kansas	266	0.7%
27	Kentucky	459	1.2%
17	Louisiana	706	1.8%
42	Maine	130	0.3%
13	Maryland	1,101	2.9%
12	Massachusetts	1,111	2.9%
9	Michigan	1,354	3.5%
26	Minnesota	496	1.3%
30	Mississippi	299	0.8%
16	Missouri	729	1.9%
46	Montana	83	0.2%
40	Nebraska	169	0.4%
37	Nevada	214	0.6%
41	New Hampshire	168	0.4%
8	New Jersey	1,462	3.8%
38	New Mexico	193	0.5%
2	New York	3,680	9.6%
11	North Carolina	1,125	2.9%
49	North Dakota	57	0.1%
7	Ohio	1,537	4.0%
29	Oklahoma	311	0.8%
28	Oregon	391	1.0%
6	Pennsylvania	1,791	4.7%
39	Rhode Island	186	0.5%
25	South Carolina	519	1.3%
47	South Dakota	65	0.2%
15	Tennessee	808	2.1%
3	Texas	2,551	6.6%
32	Utah	258	0.7%
44	Vermont	96	0.2%
14	Virginia	1,072	2.8%
19	Washington	653	1.7%
36	West Virginia	215	0.6%
22	Wisconsin	545	1.4%
50	Wyoming	52	0.1%

RANK ORDER

RANK	STATE	PHYSICIANS	% of USA
1	California	4,473	11.6%
2	New York	3,680	9.6%
3	Texas	2,551	6.6%
4	Florida	1,998	5.2%
5	Illinois	1,864	4.8%
6	Pennsylvania	1,791	4.7%
7	Ohio	1,537	4.0%
8	New Jersey	1,462	3.8%
9	Michigan	1,354	3.5%
10	Georgia	1,182	3.1%
11	North Carolina	1,125	2.9%
12	Massachusetts	1,111	2.9%
13	Maryland	1,101	2.9%
14	Virginia	1,072	2.8%
15	Tennessee	808	2.1%
16	Missouri	729	1.9%
17	Louisiana	706	1.8%
18	Connecticut	695	1.8%
19	Washington	653	1.7%
20	Indiana	603	1.6%
21	Arizona	571	1.5%
22	Wisconsin	545	1.4%
23	Colorado	539	1.4%
24	Alabama	529	1.4%
25	South Carolina	519	1.3%
26	Minnesota	496	1.3%
27	Kentucky	459	1.2%
28	Oregon	391	1.0%
29	Oklahoma	311	0.8%
30	Mississippi	299	0.8%
31	Kansas	266	0.7%
32	Utah	258	0.7%
33	Arkansas	236	0.6%
34	Hawaii	226	0.6%
35	Iowa	218	0.6%
36	West Virginia	215	0.6%
37	Nevada	214	0.6%
38	New Mexico	193	0.5%
39	Rhode Island	186	0.5%
40	Nebraska	169	0.4%
41	New Hampshire	168	0.4%
42	Maine	130	0.3%
43	Idaho	106	0.3%
44	Vermont	96	0.2%
45	Delaware	94	0.2%
46	Montana	83	0.2%
47	South Dakota	65	0.2%
48	Alaska	60	0.2%
49	North Dakota	57	0.1%
50	Wyoming	52	0.1%
	District of Columbia	236	0.6%

Source: American Medical Association (Chicago, Illinois)
   "Physician Characteristics and Distribution in the U.S." (2000-2001 Edition)
*As of December 31, 1998. Total does not include 546 physicians in U.S. territories and possessions. Obstetrics and Gynecology includes Gynecology and Oncology, Maternal and Fetal Medicine and Reproductive Endocrinology.

Rate of Nonfederal Physicians in Obstetrics and Gynecology in 1998

National Rate = 28 Physicians per 100,000 Female Population*

ALPHA ORDER

RANK	STATE	RATE
30	Alabama	23
36	Alaska	21
27	Arizona	24
45	Arkansas	18
17	California	27
17	Colorado	27
2	Connecticut	41
24	Delaware	25
21	Florida	26
11	Georgia	30
4	Hawaii	38
48	Idaho	17
11	Illinois	30
40	Indiana	20
50	Iowa	15
40	Kansas	20
30	Kentucky	23
9	Louisiana	31
40	Maine	20
1	Maryland	42
6	Massachusetts	35
17	Michigan	27
36	Minnesota	21
36	Mississippi	21
21	Missouri	26
44	Montana	19
40	Nebraska	20
24	Nevada	25
16	New Hampshire	28
6	New Jersey	35
34	New Mexico	22
3	New York	39
13	North Carolina	29
45	North Dakota	18
17	Ohio	27
45	Oklahoma	18
27	Oregon	24
13	Pennsylvania	29
5	Rhode Island	36
21	South Carolina	26
48	South Dakota	17
13	Tennessee	29
24	Texas	25
27	Utah	24
8	Vermont	32
9	Virginia	31
30	Washington	23
30	West Virginia	23
36	Wisconsin	21
34	Wyoming	22

RANK ORDER

RANK	STATE	RATE
1	Maryland	42
2	Connecticut	41
3	New York	39
4	Hawaii	38
5	Rhode Island	36
6	Massachusetts	35
6	New Jersey	35
8	Vermont	32
9	Louisiana	31
9	Virginia	31
11	Georgia	30
11	Illinois	30
13	North Carolina	29
13	Pennsylvania	29
13	Tennessee	29
16	New Hampshire	28
17	California	27
17	Colorado	27
17	Michigan	27
17	Ohio	27
21	Florida	26
21	Missouri	26
21	South Carolina	26
24	Delaware	25
24	Nevada	25
24	Texas	25
27	Arizona	24
27	Oregon	24
27	Utah	24
30	Alabama	23
30	Kentucky	23
30	Washington	23
30	West Virginia	23
34	New Mexico	22
34	Wyoming	22
36	Alaska	21
36	Minnesota	21
36	Mississippi	21
36	Wisconsin	21
40	Indiana	20
40	Kansas	20
40	Maine	20
40	Nebraska	20
44	Montana	19
45	Arkansas	18
45	North Dakota	18
45	Oklahoma	18
48	Idaho	17
48	South Dakota	17
50	Iowa	15

| | District of Columbia | 85 |

Source: Morgan Quitno Press using data from American Medical Association (Chicago, Illinois)
    "Physician Characteristics and Distribution in the U.S." (2000-2001 Edition)
*As of December 31, 1998. National rate does not include physicians in U.S. territories and possessions. Obstetrics and Gynecology includes Gynecology and Oncology, Maternal and Fetal Medicine and Reproductive Endocrinology.

Nonfederal Physicians in Ophthalmology in 1998

National Total = 17,581 Physicians*

ALPHA ORDER

RANK	STATE	PHYSICIANS	% of USA
28	Alabama	199	1.1%
49	Alaska	28	0.2%
23	Arizona	257	1.5%
32	Arkansas	140	0.8%
1	California	2,105	12.0%
24	Colorado	254	1.4%
21	Connecticut	298	1.7%
45	Delaware	45	0.3%
3	Florida	1,116	6.3%
14	Georgia	400	2.3%
36	Hawaii	92	0.5%
43	Idaho	62	0.4%
6	Illinois	712	4.0%
22	Indiana	276	1.6%
29	Iowa	155	0.9%
29	Kansas	155	0.9%
27	Kentucky	207	1.2%
17	Louisiana	332	1.9%
40	Maine	71	0.4%
11	Maryland	506	2.9%
10	Massachusetts	542	3.1%
9	Michigan	577	3.3%
20	Minnesota	303	1.7%
32	Mississippi	140	0.8%
15	Missouri	340	1.9%
44	Montana	48	0.3%
37	Nebraska	91	0.5%
39	Nevada	75	0.4%
42	New Hampshire	66	0.4%
8	New Jersey	631	3.6%
38	New Mexico	79	0.4%
2	New York	1,793	10.2%
12	North Carolina	419	2.4%
47	North Dakota	38	0.2%
7	Ohio	651	3.7%
31	Oklahoma	144	0.8%
26	Oregon	209	1.2%
5	Pennsylvania	900	5.1%
40	Rhode Island	71	0.4%
25	South Carolina	231	1.3%
48	South Dakota	35	0.2%
18	Tennessee	331	1.9%
4	Texas	1,042	5.9%
34	Utah	115	0.7%
46	Vermont	43	0.2%
13	Virginia	402	2.3%
19	Washington	313	1.8%
35	West Virginia	95	0.5%
15	Wisconsin	340	1.9%
50	Wyoming	17	0.1%

RANK ORDER

RANK	STATE	PHYSICIANS	% of USA
1	California	2,105	12.0%
2	New York	1,793	10.2%
3	Florida	1,116	6.3%
4	Texas	1,042	5.9%
5	Pennsylvania	900	5.1%
6	Illinois	712	4.0%
7	Ohio	651	3.7%
8	New Jersey	631	3.6%
9	Michigan	577	3.3%
10	Massachusetts	542	3.1%
11	Maryland	506	2.9%
12	North Carolina	419	2.4%
13	Virginia	402	2.3%
14	Georgia	400	2.3%
15	Missouri	340	1.9%
15	Wisconsin	340	1.9%
17	Louisiana	332	1.9%
18	Tennessee	331	1.9%
19	Washington	313	1.8%
20	Minnesota	303	1.7%
21	Connecticut	298	1.7%
22	Indiana	276	1.6%
23	Arizona	257	1.5%
24	Colorado	254	1.4%
25	South Carolina	231	1.3%
26	Oregon	209	1.2%
27	Kentucky	207	1.2%
28	Alabama	199	1.1%
29	Iowa	155	0.9%
29	Kansas	155	0.9%
31	Oklahoma	144	0.8%
32	Arkansas	140	0.8%
32	Mississippi	140	0.8%
34	Utah	115	0.7%
35	West Virginia	95	0.5%
36	Hawaii	92	0.5%
37	Nebraska	91	0.5%
38	New Mexico	79	0.4%
39	Nevada	75	0.4%
40	Maine	71	0.4%
40	Rhode Island	71	0.4%
42	New Hampshire	66	0.4%
43	Idaho	62	0.4%
44	Montana	48	0.3%
45	Delaware	45	0.3%
46	Vermont	43	0.2%
47	North Dakota	38	0.2%
48	South Dakota	35	0.2%
49	Alaska	28	0.2%
50	Wyoming	17	0.1%
	District of Columbia	90	0.5%

Source: American Medical Association (Chicago, Illinois)
   "Physician Characteristics and Distribution in the U.S." (2000-2001 Edition)
*As of December 31, 1998. Total does not include 183 physicians in U.S. territories and possessions.
Ophthalmology is the branch of medicine dealing with the anatomy, functions and diseases of the eye.

Rate of Nonfederal Physicians in Ophthalmology in 1998

National Rate = 6.5 Physicians per 100,000 Population*

ALPHA ORDER

RANK ORDER

RANK	STATE	RATE
45	Alabama	4.6
45	Alaska	4.6
30	Arizona	5.5
30	Arkansas	5.5
13	California	6.4
13	Colorado	6.4
3	Connecticut	9.1
19	Delaware	6.0
8	Florida	7.5
39	Georgia	5.2
6	Hawaii	7.7
42	Idaho	5.0
22	Illinois	5.9
44	Indiana	4.7
36	Iowa	5.4
22	Kansas	5.9
37	Kentucky	5.3
7	Louisiana	7.6
27	Maine	5.7
1	Maryland	9.9
4	Massachusetts	8.8
22	Michigan	5.9
13	Minnesota	6.4
41	Mississippi	5.1
17	Missouri	6.3
30	Montana	5.5
30	Nebraska	5.5
48	Nevada	4.3
28	New Hampshire	5.6
5	New Jersey	7.8
45	New Mexico	4.6
1	New York	9.9
28	North Carolina	5.6
19	North Dakota	6.0
26	Ohio	5.8
48	Oklahoma	4.3
13	Oregon	6.4
8	Pennsylvania	7.5
11	Rhode Island	7.2
19	South Carolina	6.0
43	South Dakota	4.8
18	Tennessee	6.1
37	Texas	5.3
30	Utah	5.5
10	Vermont	7.3
22	Virginia	5.9
30	Washington	5.5
39	West Virginia	5.2
12	Wisconsin	6.5
50	Wyoming	3.5

RANK	STATE	RATE
1	Maryland	9.9
1	New York	9.9
3	Connecticut	9.1
4	Massachusetts	8.8
5	New Jersey	7.8
6	Hawaii	7.7
7	Louisiana	7.6
8	Florida	7.5
8	Pennsylvania	7.5
10	Vermont	7.3
11	Rhode Island	7.2
12	Wisconsin	6.5
13	California	6.4
13	Colorado	6.4
13	Minnesota	6.4
13	Oregon	6.4
17	Missouri	6.3
18	Tennessee	6.1
19	Delaware	6.0
19	North Dakota	6.0
19	South Carolina	6.0
22	Illinois	5.9
22	Kansas	5.9
22	Michigan	5.9
22	Virginia	5.9
26	Ohio	5.8
27	Maine	5.7
28	New Hampshire	5.6
28	North Carolina	5.6
30	Arizona	5.5
30	Arkansas	5.5
30	Montana	5.5
30	Nebraska	5.5
30	Utah	5.5
30	Washington	5.5
36	Iowa	5.4
37	Kentucky	5.3
37	Texas	5.3
39	Georgia	5.2
39	West Virginia	5.2
41	Mississippi	5.1
42	Idaho	5.0
43	South Dakota	4.8
44	Indiana	4.7
45	Alabama	4.6
45	Alaska	4.6
45	New Mexico	4.6
48	Nevada	4.3
48	Oklahoma	4.3
50	Wyoming	3.5

	District of Columbia	17.3

Source: Morgan Quitno Press using data from American Medical Association (Chicago, Illinois)
    "Physician Characteristics and Distribution in the U.S." (2000-2001 Edition)
*As of December 31, 1998. National rate does not include physicians in U.S. territories and possessions.
Ophthalmology is the branch of medicine dealing with the anatomy, functions and diseases of the eye.

Nonfederal Physicians in Orthopedic Surgery in 1998

National Total = 22,677 Physicians*

<table>
<tr><td colspan="4">ALPHA ORDER</td><td colspan="4">RANK ORDER</td></tr>
<tr><td>RANK</td><td>STATE</td><td>PHYSICIANS</td><td>% of USA</td><td>RANK</td><td>STATE</td><td>PHYSICIANS</td><td>% of USA</td></tr>
<tr><td>25</td><td>Alabama</td><td>342</td><td>1.5%</td><td>1</td><td>California</td><td>2,832</td><td>12.5%</td></tr>
<tr><td>48</td><td>Alaska</td><td>50</td><td>0.2%</td><td>2</td><td>New York</td><td>1,804</td><td>8.0%</td></tr>
<tr><td>24</td><td>Arizona</td><td>346</td><td>1.5%</td><td>3</td><td>Texas</td><td>1,408</td><td>6.2%</td></tr>
<tr><td>33</td><td>Arkansas</td><td>184</td><td>0.8%</td><td>4</td><td>Florida</td><td>1,272</td><td>5.6%</td></tr>
<tr><td>1</td><td>California</td><td>2,832</td><td>12.5%</td><td>5</td><td>Pennsylvania</td><td>1,091</td><td>4.8%</td></tr>
<tr><td>22</td><td>Colorado</td><td>374</td><td>1.6%</td><td>6</td><td>Ohio</td><td>919</td><td>4.1%</td></tr>
<tr><td>23</td><td>Connecticut</td><td>371</td><td>1.6%</td><td>7</td><td>Illinois</td><td>892</td><td>3.9%</td></tr>
<tr><td>47</td><td>Delaware</td><td>57</td><td>0.3%</td><td>8</td><td>New Jersey</td><td>722</td><td>3.2%</td></tr>
<tr><td>4</td><td>Florida</td><td>1,272</td><td>5.6%</td><td>9</td><td>Massachusetts</td><td>691</td><td>3.0%</td></tr>
<tr><td>12</td><td>Georgia</td><td>580</td><td>2.6%</td><td>10</td><td>North Carolina</td><td>638</td><td>2.8%</td></tr>
<tr><td>43</td><td>Hawaii</td><td>93</td><td>0.4%</td><td>11</td><td>Michigan</td><td>632</td><td>2.8%</td></tr>
<tr><td>41</td><td>Idaho</td><td>105</td><td>0.5%</td><td>12</td><td>Georgia</td><td>580</td><td>2.6%</td></tr>
<tr><td>7</td><td>Illinois</td><td>892</td><td>3.9%</td><td>13</td><td>Virginia</td><td>575</td><td>2.5%</td></tr>
<tr><td>21</td><td>Indiana</td><td>408</td><td>1.8%</td><td>14</td><td>Maryland</td><td>530</td><td>2.3%</td></tr>
<tr><td>30</td><td>Iowa</td><td>187</td><td>0.8%</td><td>15</td><td>Washington</td><td>510</td><td>2.2%</td></tr>
<tr><td>31</td><td>Kansas</td><td>186</td><td>0.8%</td><td>16</td><td>Tennessee</td><td>478</td><td>2.1%</td></tr>
<tr><td>28</td><td>Kentucky</td><td>280</td><td>1.2%</td><td>17</td><td>Wisconsin</td><td>450</td><td>2.0%</td></tr>
<tr><td>20</td><td>Louisiana</td><td>410</td><td>1.8%</td><td>18</td><td>Missouri</td><td>435</td><td>1.9%</td></tr>
<tr><td>38</td><td>Maine</td><td>118</td><td>0.5%</td><td>19</td><td>Minnesota</td><td>426</td><td>1.9%</td></tr>
<tr><td>14</td><td>Maryland</td><td>530</td><td>2.3%</td><td>20</td><td>Louisiana</td><td>410</td><td>1.8%</td></tr>
<tr><td>9</td><td>Massachusetts</td><td>691</td><td>3.0%</td><td>21</td><td>Indiana</td><td>408</td><td>1.8%</td></tr>
<tr><td>11</td><td>Michigan</td><td>632</td><td>2.8%</td><td>22</td><td>Colorado</td><td>374</td><td>1.6%</td></tr>
<tr><td>19</td><td>Minnesota</td><td>426</td><td>1.9%</td><td>23</td><td>Connecticut</td><td>371</td><td>1.6%</td></tr>
<tr><td>34</td><td>Mississippi</td><td>168</td><td>0.7%</td><td>24</td><td>Arizona</td><td>346</td><td>1.5%</td></tr>
<tr><td>18</td><td>Missouri</td><td>435</td><td>1.9%</td><td>25</td><td>Alabama</td><td>342</td><td>1.5%</td></tr>
<tr><td>44</td><td>Montana</td><td>90</td><td>0.4%</td><td>26</td><td>South Carolina</td><td>298</td><td>1.3%</td></tr>
<tr><td>36</td><td>Nebraska</td><td>140</td><td>0.6%</td><td>27</td><td>Oregon</td><td>282</td><td>1.2%</td></tr>
<tr><td>42</td><td>Nevada</td><td>99</td><td>0.4%</td><td>28</td><td>Kentucky</td><td>280</td><td>1.2%</td></tr>
<tr><td>37</td><td>New Hampshire</td><td>123</td><td>0.5%</td><td>29</td><td>Oklahoma</td><td>220</td><td>1.0%</td></tr>
<tr><td>8</td><td>New Jersey</td><td>722</td><td>3.2%</td><td>30</td><td>Iowa</td><td>187</td><td>0.8%</td></tr>
<tr><td>35</td><td>New Mexico</td><td>151</td><td>0.7%</td><td>31</td><td>Kansas</td><td>186</td><td>0.8%</td></tr>
<tr><td>2</td><td>New York</td><td>1,804</td><td>8.0%</td><td>32</td><td>Utah</td><td>185</td><td>0.8%</td></tr>
<tr><td>10</td><td>North Carolina</td><td>638</td><td>2.8%</td><td>33</td><td>Arkansas</td><td>184</td><td>0.8%</td></tr>
<tr><td>50</td><td>North Dakota</td><td>45</td><td>0.2%</td><td>34</td><td>Mississippi</td><td>168</td><td>0.7%</td></tr>
<tr><td>6</td><td>Ohio</td><td>919</td><td>4.1%</td><td>35</td><td>New Mexico</td><td>151</td><td>0.7%</td></tr>
<tr><td>29</td><td>Oklahoma</td><td>220</td><td>1.0%</td><td>36</td><td>Nebraska</td><td>140</td><td>0.6%</td></tr>
<tr><td>27</td><td>Oregon</td><td>282</td><td>1.2%</td><td>37</td><td>New Hampshire</td><td>123</td><td>0.5%</td></tr>
<tr><td>5</td><td>Pennsylvania</td><td>1,091</td><td>4.8%</td><td>38</td><td>Maine</td><td>118</td><td>0.5%</td></tr>
<tr><td>40</td><td>Rhode Island</td><td>113</td><td>0.5%</td><td>39</td><td>West Virginia</td><td>114</td><td>0.5%</td></tr>
<tr><td>26</td><td>South Carolina</td><td>298</td><td>1.3%</td><td>40</td><td>Rhode Island</td><td>113</td><td>0.5%</td></tr>
<tr><td>46</td><td>South Dakota</td><td>58</td><td>0.3%</td><td>41</td><td>Idaho</td><td>105</td><td>0.5%</td></tr>
<tr><td>16</td><td>Tennessee</td><td>478</td><td>2.1%</td><td>42</td><td>Nevada</td><td>99</td><td>0.4%</td></tr>
<tr><td>3</td><td>Texas</td><td>1,408</td><td>6.2%</td><td>43</td><td>Hawaii</td><td>93</td><td>0.4%</td></tr>
<tr><td>32</td><td>Utah</td><td>185</td><td>0.8%</td><td>44</td><td>Montana</td><td>90</td><td>0.4%</td></tr>
<tr><td>45</td><td>Vermont</td><td>65</td><td>0.3%</td><td>45</td><td>Vermont</td><td>65</td><td>0.3%</td></tr>
<tr><td>13</td><td>Virginia</td><td>575</td><td>2.5%</td><td>46</td><td>South Dakota</td><td>58</td><td>0.3%</td></tr>
<tr><td>15</td><td>Washington</td><td>510</td><td>2.2%</td><td>47</td><td>Delaware</td><td>57</td><td>0.3%</td></tr>
<tr><td>39</td><td>West Virginia</td><td>114</td><td>0.5%</td><td>48</td><td>Alaska</td><td>50</td><td>0.2%</td></tr>
<tr><td>17</td><td>Wisconsin</td><td>450</td><td>2.0%</td><td>49</td><td>Wyoming</td><td>46</td><td>0.2%</td></tr>
<tr><td>49</td><td>Wyoming</td><td>46</td><td>0.2%</td><td>50</td><td>North Dakota</td><td>45</td><td>0.2%</td></tr>
<tr><td></td><td></td><td></td><td></td><td></td><td>District of Columbia</td><td>84</td><td>0.4%</td></tr>
</table>

Source: American Medical Association (Chicago, Illinois)
   "Physician Characteristics and Distribution in the U.S." (2000-2001 Edition)
*As of December 31, 1998. Total does not include 122 physicians in U.S. territories and possessions.
Orthopedics is the branch of medicine dealing with the skeletal system.

Rate of Nonfederal Physicians in Orthopedic Surgery in 1998

National Rate = 8.4 Physicians per 100,000 Population*

ALPHA ORDER

RANK	STATE	RATE
31	Alabama	7.9
29	Alaska	8.1
37	Arizona	7.4
39	Arkansas	7.2
19	California	8.7
11	Colorado	9.4
2	Connecticut	11.3
35	Delaware	7.7
23	Florida	8.5
36	Georgia	7.6
33	Hawaii	7.8
23	Idaho	8.5
37	Illinois	7.4
44	Indiana	6.9
46	Iowa	6.5
43	Kansas	7.0
40	Kentucky	7.1
11	Louisiana	9.4
10	Maine	9.5
6	Maryland	10.3
3	Massachusetts	11.2
47	Michigan	6.4
14	Minnesota	9.0
49	Mississippi	6.1
30	Missouri	8.0
7	Montana	10.2
27	Nebraska	8.4
50	Nevada	5.7
5	New Hampshire	10.4
16	New Jersey	8.9
19	New Mexico	8.7
8	New York	9.9
23	North Carolina	8.5
40	North Dakota	7.1
28	Ohio	8.2
45	Oklahoma	6.6
21	Oregon	8.6
13	Pennsylvania	9.1
1	Rhode Island	11.4
33	South Carolina	7.8
31	South Dakota	7.9
17	Tennessee	8.8
40	Texas	7.1
17	Utah	8.8
4	Vermont	11.0
23	Virginia	8.5
14	Washington	9.0
48	West Virginia	6.3
21	Wisconsin	8.6
9	Wyoming	9.6

RANK ORDER

RANK	STATE	RATE
1	Rhode Island	11.4
2	Connecticut	11.3
3	Massachusetts	11.2
4	Vermont	11.0
5	New Hampshire	10.4
6	Maryland	10.3
7	Montana	10.2
8	New York	9.9
9	Wyoming	9.6
10	Maine	9.5
11	Colorado	9.4
11	Louisiana	9.4
13	Pennsylvania	9.1
14	Minnesota	9.0
14	Washington	9.0
16	New Jersey	8.9
17	Tennessee	8.8
17	Utah	8.8
19	California	8.7
19	New Mexico	8.7
21	Oregon	8.6
21	Wisconsin	8.6
23	Florida	8.5
23	Idaho	8.5
23	North Carolina	8.5
23	Virginia	8.5
27	Nebraska	8.4
28	Ohio	8.2
29	Alaska	8.1
30	Missouri	8.0
31	Alabama	7.9
31	South Dakota	7.9
33	Hawaii	7.8
33	South Carolina	7.8
35	Delaware	7.7
36	Georgia	7.6
37	Arizona	7.4
37	Illinois	7.4
39	Arkansas	7.2
40	Kentucky	7.1
40	North Dakota	7.1
40	Texas	7.1
43	Kansas	7.0
44	Indiana	6.9
45	Oklahoma	6.6
46	Iowa	6.5
47	Michigan	6.4
48	West Virginia	6.3
49	Mississippi	6.1
50	Nevada	5.7

District of Columbia   16.1

Source: Morgan Quitno Press using data from American Medical Association (Chicago, Illinois)
"Physician Characteristics and Distribution in the U.S." (2000-2001 Edition)
*As of December 31, 1998. National rate does not include physicians in U.S. territories and possessions.
Orthopedics is the branch of medicine dealing with the skeletal system.

Nonfederal Physicians in Plastic Surgery in 1998

National Total = 6,002 Physicians*

ALPHA ORDER

RANK	STATE	PHYSICIANS	% of USA
21	Alabama	84	1.4%
47	Alaska	8	0.1%
17	Arizona	117	1.9%
35	Arkansas	32	0.5%
1	California	901	15.0%
19	Colorado	93	1.5%
20	Connecticut	87	1.4%
44	Delaware	17	0.3%
3	Florida	467	7.8%
14	Georgia	143	2.4%
34	Hawaii	33	0.5%
41	Idaho	21	0.3%
6	Illinois	214	3.6%
22	Indiana	83	1.4%
37	Iowa	26	0.4%
31	Kansas	48	0.8%
25	Kentucky	75	1.2%
24	Louisiana	82	1.4%
45	Maine	15	0.2%
11	Maryland	152	2.5%
10	Massachusetts	154	2.6%
9	Michigan	176	2.9%
26	Minnesota	71	1.2%
33	Mississippi	34	0.6%
16	Missouri	128	2.1%
43	Montana	18	0.3%
36	Nebraska	29	0.5%
32	Nevada	39	0.6%
42	New Hampshire	19	0.3%
8	New Jersey	188	3.1%
38	New Mexico	25	0.4%
2	New York	573	9.5%
13	North Carolina	144	2.4%
46	North Dakota	13	0.2%
7	Ohio	211	3.5%
30	Oklahoma	49	0.8%
28	Oregon	62	1.0%
5	Pennsylvania	245	4.1%
38	Rhode Island	25	0.4%
29	South Carolina	61	1.0%
48	South Dakota	7	0.1%
15	Tennessee	138	2.3%
4	Texas	441	7.3%
27	Utah	63	1.0%
48	Vermont	7	0.1%
12	Virginia	145	2.4%
18	Washington	104	1.7%
40	West Virginia	24	0.4%
22	Wisconsin	83	1.4%
50	Wyoming	3	0.0%

RANK ORDER

RANK	STATE	PHYSICIANS	% of USA
1	California	901	15.0%
2	New York	573	9.5%
3	Florida	467	7.8%
4	Texas	441	7.3%
5	Pennsylvania	245	4.1%
6	Illinois	214	3.6%
7	Ohio	211	3.5%
8	New Jersey	188	3.1%
9	Michigan	176	2.9%
10	Massachusetts	154	2.6%
11	Maryland	152	2.5%
12	Virginia	145	2.4%
13	North Carolina	144	2.4%
14	Georgia	143	2.4%
15	Tennessee	138	2.3%
16	Missouri	128	2.1%
17	Arizona	117	1.9%
18	Washington	104	1.7%
19	Colorado	93	1.5%
20	Connecticut	87	1.4%
21	Alabama	84	1.4%
22	Indiana	83	1.4%
22	Wisconsin	83	1.4%
24	Louisiana	82	1.4%
25	Kentucky	75	1.2%
26	Minnesota	71	1.2%
27	Utah	63	1.0%
28	Oregon	62	1.0%
29	South Carolina	61	1.0%
30	Oklahoma	49	0.8%
31	Kansas	48	0.8%
32	Nevada	39	0.6%
33	Mississippi	34	0.6%
34	Hawaii	33	0.5%
35	Arkansas	32	0.5%
36	Nebraska	29	0.5%
37	Iowa	26	0.4%
38	New Mexico	25	0.4%
38	Rhode Island	25	0.4%
40	West Virginia	24	0.4%
41	Idaho	21	0.3%
42	New Hampshire	19	0.3%
43	Montana	18	0.3%
44	Delaware	17	0.3%
45	Maine	15	0.2%
46	North Dakota	13	0.2%
47	Alaska	8	0.1%
48	South Dakota	7	0.1%
48	Vermont	7	0.1%
50	Wyoming	3	0.0%
	District of Columbia	25	0.4%

Source: American Medical Association (Chicago, Illinois)
   "Physician Characteristics and Distribution in the U.S." (2000-2001 Edition)
*As of December 31, 1998. Total does not include 33 physicians in U.S. territories and possessions.

Rate of Nonfederal Physicians in Plastic Surgery in 1998

National Rate = 2.2 Physicians per 100,000 Population*

ALPHA ORDER

RANK	STATE	RATE
22	Alabama	1.9
42	Alaska	1.3
8	Arizona	2.5
42	Arkansas	1.3
5	California	2.8
13	Colorado	2.3
7	Connecticut	2.7
13	Delaware	2.3
2	Florida	3.1
22	Georgia	1.9
5	Hawaii	2.8
33	Idaho	1.7
29	Illinois	1.8
40	Indiana	1.4
49	Iowa	0.9
29	Kansas	1.8
22	Kentucky	1.9
22	Louisiana	1.9
45	Maine	1.2
3	Maryland	3.0
8	Massachusetts	2.5
29	Michigan	1.8
38	Minnesota	1.5
45	Mississippi	1.2
12	Missouri	2.4
19	Montana	2.0
33	Nebraska	1.7
16	Nevada	2.2
35	New Hampshire	1.6
13	New Jersey	2.3
40	New Mexico	1.4
1	New York	3.2
22	North Carolina	1.9
19	North Dakota	2.0
22	Ohio	1.9
38	Oklahoma	1.5
22	Oregon	1.9
19	Pennsylvania	2.0
8	Rhode Island	2.5
35	South Carolina	1.6
48	South Dakota	1.0
8	Tennessee	2.5
16	Texas	2.2
3	Utah	3.0
45	Vermont	1.2
18	Virginia	2.1
29	Washington	1.8
42	West Virginia	1.3
35	Wisconsin	1.6
50	Wyoming	0.6

RANK ORDER

RANK	STATE	RATE
1	New York	3.2
2	Florida	3.1
3	Maryland	3.0
3	Utah	3.0
5	California	2.8
5	Hawaii	2.8
7	Connecticut	2.7
8	Arizona	2.5
8	Massachusetts	2.5
8	Rhode Island	2.5
8	Tennessee	2.5
12	Missouri	2.4
13	Colorado	2.3
13	Delaware	2.3
13	New Jersey	2.3
16	Nevada	2.2
16	Texas	2.2
18	Virginia	2.1
19	Montana	2.0
19	North Dakota	2.0
19	Pennsylvania	2.0
22	Alabama	1.9
22	Georgia	1.9
22	Kentucky	1.9
22	Louisiana	1.9
22	North Carolina	1.9
22	Ohio	1.9
22	Oregon	1.9
29	Illinois	1.8
29	Kansas	1.8
29	Michigan	1.8
29	Washington	1.8
33	Idaho	1.7
33	Nebraska	1.7
35	New Hampshire	1.6
35	South Carolina	1.6
35	Wisconsin	1.6
38	Minnesota	1.5
38	Oklahoma	1.5
40	Indiana	1.4
40	New Mexico	1.4
42	Alaska	1.3
42	Arkansas	1.3
42	West Virginia	1.3
45	Maine	1.2
45	Mississippi	1.2
45	Vermont	1.2
48	South Dakota	1.0
49	Iowa	0.9
50	Wyoming	0.6

District of Columbia 4.8

Source: Morgan Quitno Press using data from American Medical Association (Chicago, Illinois)
"Physician Characteristics and Distribution in the U.S." (2000-2001 Edition)
*As of December 31, 1998. National rate does not include physicians in U.S. territories and possessions.

Nonfederal Physicians in Other Specialties in 1998

National Total = 184,350 Physicians*

ALPHA ORDER

RANK	STATE	PHYSICIANS	% of USA
28	Alabama	2,022	1.1%
49	Alaska	273	0.1%
24	Arizona	2,680	1.5%
32	Arkansas	1,210	0.7%
1	California	22,602	12.3%
23	Colorado	2,709	1.5%
17	Connecticut	3,326	1.8%
44	Delaware	504	0.3%
5	Florida	9,219	5.0%
14	Georgia	4,266	2.3%
37	Hawaii	892	0.5%
46	Idaho	451	0.2%
6	Illinois	8,262	4.5%
20	Indiana	3,163	1.7%
31	Iowa	1,214	0.7%
30	Kansas	1,458	0.8%
25	Kentucky	2,189	1.2%
22	Louisiana	2,790	1.5%
42	Maine	780	0.4%
11	Maryland	5,575	3.0%
7	Massachusetts	7,682	4.2%
10	Michigan	5,962	3.2%
21	Minnesota	2,968	1.6%
34	Mississippi	1,105	0.6%
19	Missouri	3,288	1.8%
45	Montana	459	0.2%
38	Nebraska	867	0.5%
40	Nevada	822	0.4%
41	New Hampshire	820	0.4%
9	New Jersey	6,018	3.3%
35	New Mexico	1,037	0.6%
2	New York	19,227	10.4%
12	North Carolina	4,635	2.5%
47	North Dakota	349	0.2%
8	Ohio	6,904	3.7%
29	Oklahoma	1,493	0.8%
27	Oregon	2,064	1.1%
4	Pennsylvania	9,966	5.4%
38	Rhode Island	867	0.5%
26	South Carolina	2,085	1.1%
48	South Dakota	298	0.2%
16	Tennessee	3,439	1.9%
3	Texas	10,877	5.9%
33	Utah	1,183	0.6%
43	Vermont	529	0.3%
13	Virginia	4,348	2.4%
15	Washington	3,830	2.1%
36	West Virginia	999	0.5%
18	Wisconsin	3,310	1.8%
50	Wyoming	206	0.1%

RANK ORDER

RANK	STATE	PHYSICIANS	% of USA
1	California	22,602	12.3%
2	New York	19,227	10.4%
3	Texas	10,877	5.9%
4	Pennsylvania	9,966	5.4%
5	Florida	9,219	5.0%
6	Illinois	8,262	4.5%
7	Massachusetts	7,682	4.2%
8	Ohio	6,904	3.7%
9	New Jersey	6,018	3.3%
10	Michigan	5,962	3.2%
11	Maryland	5,575	3.0%
12	North Carolina	4,635	2.5%
13	Virginia	4,348	2.4%
14	Georgia	4,266	2.3%
15	Washington	3,830	2.1%
16	Tennessee	3,439	1.9%
17	Connecticut	3,326	1.8%
18	Wisconsin	3,310	1.8%
19	Missouri	3,288	1.8%
20	Indiana	3,163	1.7%
21	Minnesota	2,968	1.6%
22	Louisiana	2,790	1.5%
23	Colorado	2,709	1.5%
24	Arizona	2,680	1.5%
25	Kentucky	2,189	1.2%
26	South Carolina	2,085	1.1%
27	Oregon	2,064	1.1%
28	Alabama	2,022	1.1%
29	Oklahoma	1,493	0.8%
30	Kansas	1,458	0.8%
31	Iowa	1,214	0.7%
32	Arkansas	1,210	0.7%
33	Utah	1,183	0.6%
34	Mississippi	1,105	0.6%
35	New Mexico	1,037	0.6%
36	West Virginia	999	0.5%
37	Hawaii	892	0.5%
38	Nebraska	867	0.5%
38	Rhode Island	867	0.5%
40	Nevada	822	0.4%
41	New Hampshire	820	0.4%
42	Maine	780	0.4%
43	Vermont	529	0.3%
44	Delaware	504	0.3%
45	Montana	459	0.2%
46	Idaho	451	0.2%
47	North Dakota	349	0.2%
48	South Dakota	298	0.2%
49	Alaska	273	0.1%
50	Wyoming	206	0.1%
	District of Columbia	1,128	0.6%

Source: American Medical Association (Chicago, Illinois)
"Physician Characteristics and Distribution in the U.S." (2000-2001 Edition)

*As of December 31, 1998. Total does not include 2,269 physicians in U.S. territories and possessions. Other Specialties include Aerospace Medicine, Anesthesiology, Child Psychiatry, Diagnostic Radiology, Emergency Medicine, Forensic Pathology, Nuclear Medicine, Occupational Medicine, Neurology, Psychiatry, Public Health, Anatomic/Clinical Pathology, Radiology, Radiation Oncology and other specialties.

462

Rate of Nonfederal Physicians in Other Specialties in 1998

National Rate = 68 Physicians per 100,000 Population*

ALPHA ORDER

RANK	STATE	RATE
43	Alabama	46
45	Alaska	44
29	Arizona	57
41	Arkansas	48
10	California	69
12	Colorado	68
4	Connecticut	102
12	Delaware	68
23	Florida	62
30	Georgia	56
8	Hawaii	75
50	Idaho	37
12	Illinois	68
37	Indiana	54
47	Iowa	42
33	Kansas	55
30	Kentucky	56
16	Louisiana	64
18	Maine	63
2	Maryland	109
1	Massachusetts	125
24	Michigan	61
18	Minnesota	63
49	Mississippi	40
27	Missouri	60
39	Montana	52
39	Nebraska	52
42	Nevada	47
10	New Hampshire	69
9	New Jersey	74
27	New Mexico	60
3	New York	106
24	North Carolina	61
33	North Dakota	55
24	Ohio	61
44	Oklahoma	45
18	Oregon	63
7	Pennsylvania	83
6	Rhode Island	88
37	South Carolina	54
48	South Dakota	41
18	Tennessee	63
33	Texas	55
30	Utah	56
5	Vermont	90
16	Virginia	64
15	Washington	67
33	West Virginia	55
18	Wisconsin	63
46	Wyoming	43

RANK ORDER

RANK	STATE	RATE
1	Massachusetts	125
2	Maryland	109
3	New York	106
4	Connecticut	102
5	Vermont	90
6	Rhode Island	88
7	Pennsylvania	83
8	Hawaii	75
9	New Jersey	74
10	California	69
10	New Hampshire	69
12	Colorado	68
12	Delaware	68
12	Illinois	68
15	Washington	67
16	Louisiana	64
16	Virginia	64
18	Maine	63
18	Minnesota	63
18	Oregon	63
18	Tennessee	63
18	Wisconsin	63
23	Florida	62
24	Michigan	61
24	North Carolina	61
24	Ohio	61
27	Missouri	60
27	New Mexico	60
29	Arizona	57
30	Georgia	56
30	Kentucky	56
30	Utah	56
33	Kansas	55
33	North Dakota	55
33	Texas	55
33	West Virginia	55
37	Indiana	54
37	South Carolina	54
39	Montana	52
39	Nebraska	52
41	Arkansas	48
42	Nevada	47
43	Alabama	46
44	Oklahoma	45
45	Alaska	44
46	Wyoming	43
47	Iowa	42
48	South Dakota	41
49	Mississippi	40
50	Idaho	37
	District of Columbia	216

Source: Morgan Quitno Press using data from American Medical Association (Chicago, Illinois) "Physician Characteristics and Distribution in the U.S." (2000-2001 Edition)
As of December 31, 1998. National rate does not include physicians in U.S. territories and possessions. Other Specialties include Aerospace Medicine, Anesthesiology, Child Psychiatry, Diagnostic Radiology, Emergency Medicine, Forensic Pathology, Nuclear Medicine, Occupational Medicine, Neurology, Psychiatry, Public Health, Anatomic/Clinical Pathology, Radiology, Radiation Oncology and other specialties.

Nonfederal Physicians in Anesthesiology in 1998

National Total = 33,105 Physicians*

ALPHA ORDER					RANK ORDER			
RANK	STATE	PHYSICIANS	% of USA		RANK	STATE	PHYSICIANS	% of USA
27	Alabama	400	1.2%		1	California	4,087	12.3%
47	Alaska	53	0.2%		2	New York	3,031	9.2%
19	Arizona	597	1.8%		3	Texas	2,465	7.4%
32	Arkansas	241	0.7%		4	Florida	1,971	6.0%
1	California	4,087	12.3%		5	Illinois	1,582	4.8%
22	Colorado	478	1.4%		6	Pennsylvania	1,574	4.8%
21	Connecticut	502	1.5%		7	Ohio	1,284	3.9%
45	Delaware	64	0.2%		8	New Jersey	1,192	3.6%
4	Florida	1,971	6.0%		9	Massachusetts	1,191	3.6%
13	Georgia	759	2.3%		10	Maryland	865	2.6%
40	Hawaii	129	0.4%		11	Michigan	818	2.5%
44	Idaho	76	0.2%		12	Washington	805	2.4%
5	Illinois	1,582	4.8%		13	Georgia	759	2.3%
14	Indiana	733	2.2%		14	Indiana	733	2.2%
31	Iowa	248	0.7%		15	North Carolina	731	2.2%
32	Kansas	241	0.7%		16	Virginia	717	2.2%
23	Kentucky	451	1.4%		17	Tennessee	685	2.1%
24	Louisiana	448	1.4%		18	Wisconsin	649	2.0%
39	Maine	137	0.4%		19	Arizona	597	1.8%
10	Maryland	865	2.6%		20	Missouri	575	1.7%
9	Massachusetts	1,191	3.6%		21	Connecticut	502	1.5%
11	Michigan	818	2.5%		22	Colorado	478	1.4%
25	Minnesota	444	1.3%		23	Kentucky	451	1.4%
34	Mississippi	230	0.7%		24	Louisiana	448	1.4%
20	Missouri	575	1.7%		25	Minnesota	444	1.3%
42	Montana	104	0.3%		26	Oregon	407	1.2%
36	Nebraska	175	0.5%		27	Alabama	400	1.2%
35	Nevada	203	0.6%		28	South Carolina	357	1.1%
40	New Hampshire	129	0.4%		29	Oklahoma	296	0.9%
8	New Jersey	1,192	3.6%		30	Utah	265	0.8%
37	New Mexico	173	0.5%		31	Iowa	248	0.7%
2	New York	3,031	9.2%		32	Arkansas	241	0.7%
15	North Carolina	731	2.2%		32	Kansas	241	0.7%
49	North Dakota	46	0.1%		34	Mississippi	230	0.7%
7	Ohio	1,284	3.9%		35	Nevada	203	0.6%
29	Oklahoma	296	0.9%		36	Nebraska	175	0.5%
26	Oregon	407	1.2%		37	New Mexico	173	0.5%
6	Pennsylvania	1,574	4.8%		38	West Virginia	155	0.5%
43	Rhode Island	99	0.3%		39	Maine	137	0.4%
28	South Carolina	357	1.1%		40	Hawaii	129	0.4%
48	South Dakota	47	0.1%		40	New Hampshire	129	0.4%
17	Tennessee	685	2.1%		42	Montana	104	0.3%
3	Texas	2,465	7.4%		43	Rhode Island	99	0.3%
30	Utah	265	0.8%		44	Idaho	76	0.2%
46	Vermont	60	0.2%		45	Delaware	64	0.2%
16	Virginia	717	2.2%		46	Vermont	60	0.2%
12	Washington	805	2.4%		47	Alaska	53	0.2%
38	West Virginia	155	0.5%		48	South Dakota	47	0.1%
18	Wisconsin	649	2.0%		49	North Dakota	46	0.1%
50	Wyoming	41	0.1%		50	Wyoming	41	0.1%
						District of Columbia	95	0.3%

Source: American Medical Association (Chicago, Illinois)
    "Physician Characteristics and Distribution in the U.S." (2000-2001 Edition)
*As of December 31, 1998. Total does not include 211 physicians in U.S. territories and possessions.

Rate of Nonfederal Physicians in Anesthesiology in 1998

National Rate = 12.2 Physicians per 100,000 Population*

ALPHA ORDER

RANK ORDER

RANK	STATE	RATE
38	Alabama	9.2
42	Alaska	8.6
10	Arizona	12.8
35	Arkansas	9.5
13	California	12.5
18	Colorado	12.0
4	Connecticut	15.3
42	Delaware	8.6
7	Florida	13.2
33	Georgia	9.9
25	Hawaii	10.8
50	Idaho	6.2
8	Illinois	13.1
15	Indiana	12.4
41	Iowa	8.7
39	Kansas	9.1
21	Kentucky	11.5
29	Louisiana	10.3
23	Maine	11.0
2	Maryland	16.9
1	Massachusetts	19.4
47	Michigan	8.3
36	Minnesota	9.4
46	Mississippi	8.4
26	Missouri	10.6
19	Montana	11.8
28	Nebraska	10.5
20	Nevada	11.6
24	New Hampshire	10.9
5	New Jersey	14.7
31	New Mexico	10.0
3	New York	16.7
34	North Carolina	9.7
48	North Dakota	7.2
22	Ohio	11.4
40	Oklahoma	8.9
15	Oregon	12.4
8	Pennsylvania	13.1
31	Rhode Island	10.0
37	South Carolina	9.3
49	South Dakota	6.4
11	Tennessee	12.6
13	Texas	12.5
11	Utah	12.6
30	Vermont	10.2
26	Virginia	10.6
6	Washington	14.2
42	West Virginia	8.6
15	Wisconsin	12.4
45	Wyoming	8.5

RANK	STATE	RATE
1	Massachusetts	19.4
2	Maryland	16.9
3	New York	16.7
4	Connecticut	15.3
5	New Jersey	14.7
6	Washington	14.2
7	Florida	13.2
8	Illinois	13.1
8	Pennsylvania	13.1
10	Arizona	12.8
11	Tennessee	12.6
11	Utah	12.6
13	California	12.5
13	Texas	12.5
15	Indiana	12.4
15	Oregon	12.4
15	Wisconsin	12.4
18	Colorado	12.0
19	Montana	11.8
20	Nevada	11.6
21	Kentucky	11.5
22	Ohio	11.4
23	Maine	11.0
24	New Hampshire	10.9
25	Hawaii	10.8
26	Missouri	10.6
26	Virginia	10.6
28	Nebraska	10.5
29	Louisiana	10.3
30	Vermont	10.2
31	New Mexico	10.0
31	Rhode Island	10.0
33	Georgia	9.9
34	North Carolina	9.7
35	Arkansas	9.5
36	Minnesota	9.4
37	South Carolina	9.3
38	Alabama	9.2
39	Kansas	9.1
40	Oklahoma	8.9
41	Iowa	8.7
42	Alaska	8.6
42	Delaware	8.6
42	West Virginia	8.6
45	Wyoming	8.5
46	Mississippi	8.4
47	Michigan	8.3
48	North Dakota	7.2
49	South Dakota	6.4
50	Idaho	6.2

	District of Columbia	18.2

Source: Morgan Quitno Press using data from American Medical Association (Chicago, Illinois)
"Physician Characteristics and Distribution in the U.S." (2000-2001 Edition)
*As of December 31, 1998. National rate does not include physicians in U.S. territories and possessions.

Nonfederal Physicians in Psychiatry in 1998

National Total = 37,128 Physicians*

ALPHA ORDER

RANK	STATE	PHYSICIANS	% of USA
29	Alabama	287	0.8%
48	Alaska	57	0.2%
23	Arizona	469	1.3%
33	Arkansas	191	0.5%
2	California	5,013	13.5%
17	Colorado	550	1.5%
13	Connecticut	882	2.4%
44	Delaware	92	0.2%
6	Florida	1,558	4.2%
15	Georgia	794	2.1%
33	Hawaii	191	0.5%
46	Idaho	65	0.2%
7	Illinois	1,530	4.1%
24	Indiana	434	1.2%
36	Iowa	181	0.5%
28	Kansas	323	0.9%
27	Kentucky	365	1.0%
21	Louisiana	512	1.4%
37	Maine	175	0.5%
9	Maryland	1,252	3.4%
3	Massachusetts	1,943	5.2%
11	Michigan	1,064	2.9%
22	Minnesota	489	1.3%
39	Mississippi	159	0.4%
19	Missouri	533	1.4%
47	Montana	64	0.2%
42	Nebraska	144	0.4%
43	Nevada	114	0.3%
35	New Hampshire	190	0.5%
8	New Jersey	1,312	3.5%
31	New Mexico	219	0.6%
1	New York	5,534	14.9%
12	North Carolina	887	2.4%
45	North Dakota	67	0.2%
10	Ohio	1,119	3.0%
30	Oklahoma	261	0.7%
26	Oregon	382	1.0%
4	Pennsylvania	1,931	5.2%
32	Rhode Island	195	0.5%
25	South Carolina	418	1.1%
48	South Dakota	57	0.2%
20	Tennessee	518	1.4%
5	Texas	1,690	4.6%
38	Utah	165	0.4%
41	Vermont	148	0.4%
14	Virginia	849	2.3%
16	Washington	668	1.8%
40	West Virginia	158	0.4%
17	Wisconsin	550	1.5%
50	Wyoming	34	0.1%

RANK ORDER

RANK	STATE	PHYSICIANS	% of USA
1	New York	5,534	14.9%
2	California	5,013	13.5%
3	Massachusetts	1,943	5.2%
4	Pennsylvania	1,931	5.2%
5	Texas	1,690	4.6%
6	Florida	1,558	4.2%
7	Illinois	1,530	4.1%
8	New Jersey	1,312	3.5%
9	Maryland	1,252	3.4%
10	Ohio	1,119	3.0%
11	Michigan	1,064	2.9%
12	North Carolina	887	2.4%
13	Connecticut	882	2.4%
14	Virginia	849	2.3%
15	Georgia	794	2.1%
16	Washington	668	1.8%
17	Colorado	550	1.5%
17	Wisconsin	550	1.5%
19	Missouri	533	1.4%
20	Tennessee	518	1.4%
21	Louisiana	512	1.4%
22	Minnesota	489	1.3%
23	Arizona	469	1.3%
24	Indiana	434	1.2%
25	South Carolina	418	1.1%
26	Oregon	382	1.0%
27	Kentucky	365	1.0%
28	Kansas	323	0.9%
29	Alabama	287	0.8%
30	Oklahoma	261	0.7%
31	New Mexico	219	0.6%
32	Rhode Island	195	0.5%
33	Arkansas	191	0.5%
33	Hawaii	191	0.5%
35	New Hampshire	190	0.5%
36	Iowa	181	0.5%
37	Maine	175	0.5%
38	Utah	165	0.4%
39	Mississippi	159	0.4%
40	West Virginia	158	0.4%
41	Vermont	148	0.4%
42	Nebraska	144	0.4%
43	Nevada	114	0.3%
44	Delaware	92	0.2%
45	North Dakota	67	0.2%
46	Idaho	65	0.2%
47	Montana	64	0.2%
48	Alaska	57	0.2%
48	South Dakota	57	0.2%
50	Wyoming	34	0.1%
	District of Columbia	345	0.9%

Source: American Medical Association (Chicago, Illinois)
   "Physician Characteristics and Distribution in the U.S." (2000-2001 Edition)
*As of December 31, 1998. Total does not include 345 physicians in U.S. territories and possessions. Psychiatry includes psychoanalysis.

Rate of Nonfederal Physicians in Psychiatry in 1998

National Rate = 13.7 Physicians per 100,000 Population*

ALPHA ORDER

RANK	STATE	RATE
46	Alabama	6.6
34	Alaska	9.3
30	Arizona	10.0
42	Arkansas	7.5
11	California	15.3
13	Colorado	13.9
3	Connecticut	27.0
17	Delaware	12.4
25	Florida	10.5
28	Georgia	10.4
9	Hawaii	16.0
50	Idaho	5.3
14	Illinois	12.7
43	Indiana	7.3
48	Iowa	6.3
18	Kansas	12.2
34	Kentucky	9.3
20	Louisiana	11.7
12	Maine	14.0
5	Maryland	24.4
1	Massachusetts	31.6
24	Michigan	10.8
29	Minnesota	10.3
49	Mississippi	5.8
32	Missouri	9.8
43	Montana	7.3
36	Nebraska	8.7
47	Nevada	6.5
9	New Hampshire	16.0
7	New Jersey	16.2
15	New Mexico	12.6
2	New York	30.5
19	North Carolina	11.8
25	North Dakota	10.5
30	Ohio	10.0
40	Oklahoma	7.8
22	Oregon	11.6
8	Pennsylvania	16.1
6	Rhode Island	19.7
23	South Carolina	10.9
40	South Dakota	7.8
33	Tennessee	9.5
38	Texas	8.6
39	Utah	7.9
4	Vermont	25.1
16	Virginia	12.5
20	Washington	11.7
36	West Virginia	8.7
25	Wisconsin	10.5
45	Wyoming	7.1

RANK ORDER

RANK	STATE	RATE
1	Massachusetts	31.6
2	New York	30.5
3	Connecticut	27.0
4	Vermont	25.1
5	Maryland	24.4
6	Rhode Island	19.7
7	New Jersey	16.2
8	Pennsylvania	16.1
9	Hawaii	16.0
9	New Hampshire	16.0
11	California	15.3
12	Maine	14.0
13	Colorado	13.9
14	Illinois	12.7
15	New Mexico	12.6
16	Virginia	12.5
17	Delaware	12.4
18	Kansas	12.2
19	North Carolina	11.8
20	Louisiana	11.7
20	Washington	11.7
22	Oregon	11.6
23	South Carolina	10.9
24	Michigan	10.8
25	Florida	10.5
25	North Dakota	10.5
25	Wisconsin	10.5
28	Georgia	10.4
29	Minnesota	10.3
30	Arizona	10.0
30	Ohio	10.0
32	Missouri	9.8
33	Tennessee	9.5
34	Alaska	9.3
34	Kentucky	9.3
36	Nebraska	8.7
36	West Virginia	8.7
38	Texas	8.6
39	Utah	7.9
40	Oklahoma	7.8
40	South Dakota	7.8
42	Arkansas	7.5
43	Indiana	7.3
43	Montana	7.3
45	Wyoming	7.1
46	Alabama	6.6
47	Nevada	6.5
48	Iowa	6.3
49	Mississippi	5.8
50	Idaho	5.3

District of Columbia 66.2

Source: Morgan Quitno Press using data from American Medical Association (Chicago, Illinois)
"Physician Characteristics and Distribution in the U.S." (2000-2001 Edition)
*As of December 31, 1998. National rate does not include physicians in U.S. territories and possessions.
Psychiatry includes psychoanalysis.

Percent of Population Lacking Access to Mental Health Care in 1999

National Percent = 11.5% of Population*

ALPHA ORDER

ALPHA ORDER

RANK	STATE	PERCENT
2	Alabama	47.8
39	Alaska	2.7
26	Arizona	11.6
3	Arkansas	44.0
41	California	1.7
47	Colorado	0.0
45	Connecticut	0.5
47	Delaware	0.0
37	Florida	3.1
21	Georgia	17.2
38	Hawaii	2.8
4	Idaho	38.2
33	Illinois	4.9
35	Indiana	4.5
8	Iowa	32.2
11	Kansas	30.0
18	Kentucky	18.8
20	Louisiana	17.3
29	Maine	9.1
43	Maryland	0.7
42	Massachusetts	0.8
24	Michigan	15.9
25	Minnesota	12.9
17	Mississippi	19.8
12	Missouri	27.7
7	Montana	34.3
10	Nebraska	30.6
33	Nevada	4.9
31	New Hampshire	6.5
40	New Jersey	1.8
5	New Mexico	36.6
32	New York	5.7
27	North Carolina	9.8
6	North Dakota	35.3
36	Ohio	3.5
16	Oklahoma	20.1
22	Oregon	16.5
30	Pennsylvania	8.0
47	Rhode Island	0.0
9	South Carolina	32.1
46	South Dakota	0.3
19	Tennessee	17.7
13	Texas	22.7
23	Utah	16.1
47	Vermont	0.0
43	Virginia	0.7
28	Washington	9.7
15	West Virginia	20.9
14	Wisconsin	22.6
1	Wyoming	86.1

RANK ORDER

RANK	STATE	PERCENT
1	Wyoming	86.1
2	Alabama	47.8
3	Arkansas	44.0
4	Idaho	38.2
5	New Mexico	36.6
6	North Dakota	35.3
7	Montana	34.3
8	Iowa	32.2
9	South Carolina	32.1
10	Nebraska	30.6
11	Kansas	30.0
12	Missouri	27.7
13	Texas	22.7
14	Wisconsin	22.6
15	West Virginia	20.9
16	Oklahoma	20.1
17	Mississippi	19.8
18	Kentucky	18.8
19	Tennessee	17.7
20	Louisiana	17.3
21	Georgia	17.2
22	Oregon	16.5
23	Utah	16.1
24	Michigan	15.9
25	Minnesota	12.9
26	Arizona	11.6
27	North Carolina	9.8
28	Washington	9.7
29	Maine	9.1
30	Pennsylvania	8.0
31	New Hampshire	6.5
32	New York	5.7
33	Illinois	4.9
33	Nevada	4.9
35	Indiana	4.5
36	Ohio	3.5
37	Florida	3.1
38	Hawaii	2.8
39	Alaska	2.7
40	New Jersey	1.8
41	California	1.7
42	Massachusetts	0.8
43	Maryland	0.7
43	Virginia	0.7
45	Connecticut	0.5
46	South Dakota	0.3
47	Colorado	0.0
47	Delaware	0.0
47	Rhode Island	0.0
47	Vermont	0.0

District of Columbia   12.9

Source: Morgan Quitno Press using data from U.S. Dept. of Health and Human Services, Div. of Shortage Designation "Selected Statistics on Health Manpower Shortage Areas, As of December 31, 1999"
*Percent of population considered under-served by mental health practitioners. An under-served population does not have primary medical care within reasonable economic and geographic bounds.

International Medical School Graduates Practicing in the U.S. in 1998

National Total = 175,469 Nonfederal Physicians*

ALPHA ORDER

RANK	STATE	PHYSICIANS	% of USA
26	Alabama	1,214	0.7%
48	Alaska	67	0.0%
20	Arizona	1,753	1.0%
35	Arkansas	537	0.3%
2	California	19,401	11.1%
33	Colorado	615	0.4%
13	Connecticut	3,361	1.9%
37	Delaware	524	0.3%
3	Florida	14,142	8.1%
14	Georgia	2,744	1.6%
36	Hawaii	532	0.3%
49	Idaho	62	0.0%
5	Illinois	11,495	6.6%
16	Indiana	2,173	1.2%
30	Iowa	850	0.5%
27	Kansas	990	0.6%
22	Kentucky	1,647	0.9%
21	Louisiana	1,679	1.0%
42	Maine	371	0.2%
10	Maryland	5,714	3.3%
11	Massachusetts	5,384	3.1%
9	Michigan	7,445	4.2%
23	Minnesota	1,512	0.9%
39	Mississippi	482	0.3%
15	Missouri	2,676	1.5%
47	Montana	76	0.0%
40	Nebraska	400	0.2%
32	Nevada	685	0.4%
41	New Hampshire	383	0.2%
4	New Jersey	11,500	6.6%
38	New Mexico	504	0.3%
1	New York	31,730	18.1%
18	North Carolina	1,972	1.1%
43	North Dakota	302	0.2%
8	Ohio	7,520	4.3%
28	Oklahoma	989	0.6%
34	Oregon	561	0.3%
7	Pennsylvania	8,638	4.9%
29	Rhode Island	950	0.5%
31	South Carolina	835	0.5%
46	South Dakota	156	0.1%
19	Tennessee	1,934	1.1%
6	Texas	9,325	5.3%
44	Utah	261	0.1%
45	Vermont	161	0.1%
12	Virginia	3,504	2.0%
25	Washington	1,405	0.8%
24	West Virginia	1,453	0.8%
17	Wisconsin	2,029	1.2%
50	Wyoming	45	0.0%

RANK ORDER

RANK	STATE	PHYSICIANS	% of USA
1	New York	31,730	18.1%
2	California	19,401	11.1%
3	Florida	14,142	8.1%
4	New Jersey	11,500	6.6%
5	Illinois	11,495	6.6%
6	Texas	9,325	5.3%
7	Pennsylvania	8,638	4.9%
8	Ohio	7,520	4.3%
9	Michigan	7,445	4.2%
10	Maryland	5,714	3.3%
11	Massachusetts	5,384	3.1%
12	Virginia	3,504	2.0%
13	Connecticut	3,361	1.9%
14	Georgia	2,744	1.6%
15	Missouri	2,676	1.5%
16	Indiana	2,173	1.2%
17	Wisconsin	2,029	1.2%
18	North Carolina	1,972	1.1%
19	Tennessee	1,934	1.1%
20	Arizona	1,753	1.0%
21	Louisiana	1,679	1.0%
22	Kentucky	1,647	0.9%
23	Minnesota	1,512	0.9%
24	West Virginia	1,453	0.8%
25	Washington	1,405	0.8%
26	Alabama	1,214	0.7%
27	Kansas	990	0.6%
28	Oklahoma	989	0.6%
29	Rhode Island	950	0.5%
30	Iowa	850	0.5%
31	South Carolina	835	0.5%
32	Nevada	685	0.4%
33	Colorado	615	0.4%
34	Oregon	561	0.3%
35	Arkansas	537	0.3%
36	Hawaii	532	0.3%
37	Delaware	524	0.3%
38	New Mexico	504	0.3%
39	Mississippi	482	0.3%
40	Nebraska	400	0.2%
41	New Hampshire	383	0.2%
42	Maine	371	0.2%
43	North Dakota	302	0.2%
44	Utah	261	0.1%
45	Vermont	161	0.1%
46	South Dakota	156	0.1%
47	Montana	76	0.0%
48	Alaska	67	0.0%
49	Idaho	62	0.0%
50	Wyoming	45	0.0%
	District of Columbia	781	0.4%

Source: American Medical Association (Chicago, Illinois)
"Physician Characteristics and Distribution in the U.S." (2000-2001 Edition)
*As of December 31, 1998. Total does not include 5,275 physicians in U.S. territories and possessions.

Rate of International Medical School Graduates Practicing in the U.S. in 1998

National Rate = 65 Nonfederal Physicians per 100,000 Population*

ALPHA ORDER

RANK	STATE	RATE
35	Alabama	28
47	Alaska	11
23	Arizona	38
41	Arkansas	21
14	California	59
45	Colorado	15
4	Connecticut	103
12	Delaware	70
6	Florida	95
27	Georgia	36
19	Hawaii	45
50	Idaho	5
6	Illinois	95
26	Indiana	37
31	Iowa	30
23	Kansas	38
20	Kentucky	42
23	Louisiana	38
31	Maine	30
3	Maryland	111
8	Massachusetts	88
10	Michigan	76
29	Minnesota	32
43	Mississippi	18
16	Missouri	49
48	Montana	9
39	Nebraska	24
21	Nevada	39
29	New Hampshire	32
2	New Jersey	142
34	New Mexico	29
1	New York	175
37	North Carolina	26
17	North Dakota	47
13	Ohio	67
31	Oklahoma	30
44	Oregon	17
11	Pennsylvania	72
5	Rhode Island	96
40	South Carolina	22
41	South Dakota	21
27	Tennessee	36
17	Texas	47
46	Utah	12
36	Vermont	27
15	Virginia	52
38	Washington	25
9	West Virginia	80
21	Wisconsin	39
48	Wyoming	9

RANK ORDER

RANK	STATE	RATE
1	New York	175
2	New Jersey	142
3	Maryland	111
4	Connecticut	103
5	Rhode Island	96
6	Florida	95
6	Illinois	95
8	Massachusetts	88
9	West Virginia	80
10	Michigan	76
11	Pennsylvania	72
12	Delaware	70
13	Ohio	67
14	California	59
15	Virginia	52
16	Missouri	49
17	North Dakota	47
17	Texas	47
19	Hawaii	45
20	Kentucky	42
21	Nevada	39
21	Wisconsin	39
23	Arizona	38
23	Kansas	38
23	Louisiana	38
26	Indiana	37
27	Georgia	36
27	Tennessee	36
29	Minnesota	32
29	New Hampshire	32
31	Iowa	30
31	Maine	30
31	Oklahoma	30
34	New Mexico	29
35	Alabama	28
36	Vermont	27
37	North Carolina	26
38	Washington	25
39	Nebraska	24
40	South Carolina	22
41	Arkansas	21
41	South Dakota	21
43	Mississippi	18
44	Oregon	17
45	Colorado	15
46	Utah	12
47	Alaska	11
48	Montana	9
48	Wyoming	9
50	Idaho	5
	District of Columbia	150

Source: Morgan Quitno Press using data from American Medical Association (Chicago, Illinois)
"Physician Characteristics and Distribution in the U.S." (2000-2001 Edition)
*As of December 31, 1998. National rate does not include physicians in U.S. territories and possessions.

International Medical School Graduates
As a Percent of Nonfederal Physicians in 1998
National Percent = 23.5% of Nonfederal Physicians*

ALPHA ORDER

RANK	STATE	PERCENT
31	Alabama	13.1
45	Alaska	6.2
23	Arizona	15.9
38	Arkansas	10.1
14	California	21.3
46	Colorado	5.8
9	Connecticut	26.5
8	Delaware	27.3
5	Florida	33.5
25	Georgia	15.8
28	Hawaii	15.0
50	Idaho	2.9
4	Illinois	34.0
21	Indiana	17.2
27	Iowa	15.1
22	Kansas	16.4
20	Kentucky	18.5
29	Louisiana	14.6
34	Maine	11.6
7	Maryland	27.5
17	Massachusetts	19.8
6	Michigan	31.0
34	Minnesota	11.6
40	Mississippi	9.8
16	Missouri	19.9
49	Montana	3.9
39	Nebraska	10.0
15	Nevada	20.3
33	New Hampshire	12.0
1	New Jersey	44.5
32	New Mexico	12.2
2	New York	42.2
37	North Carolina	10.2
18	North Dakota	19.5
11	Ohio	26.1
23	Oklahoma	15.9
44	Oregon	6.5
12	Pennsylvania	22.7
10	Rhode Island	26.3
41	South Carolina	9.6
36	South Dakota	10.4
30	Tennessee	13.4
13	Texas	21.7
47	Utah	5.6
43	Vermont	7.8
19	Virginia	19.4
42	Washington	9.2
3	West Virginia	34.2
26	Wisconsin	15.5
48	Wyoming	4.8

RANK ORDER

RANK	STATE	PERCENT
1	New Jersey	44.5
2	New York	42.2
3	West Virginia	34.2
4	Illinois	34.0
5	Florida	33.5
6	Michigan	31.0
7	Maryland	27.5
8	Delaware	27.3
9	Connecticut	26.5
10	Rhode Island	26.3
11	Ohio	26.1
12	Pennsylvania	22.7
13	Texas	21.7
14	California	21.3
15	Nevada	20.3
16	Missouri	19.9
17	Massachusetts	19.8
18	North Dakota	19.5
19	Virginia	19.4
20	Kentucky	18.5
21	Indiana	17.2
22	Kansas	16.4
23	Arizona	15.9
23	Oklahoma	15.9
25	Georgia	15.8
26	Wisconsin	15.5
27	Iowa	15.1
28	Hawaii	15.0
29	Louisiana	14.6
30	Tennessee	13.4
31	Alabama	13.1
32	New Mexico	12.2
33	New Hampshire	12.0
34	Maine	11.6
34	Minnesota	11.6
36	South Dakota	10.4
37	North Carolina	10.2
38	Arkansas	10.1
39	Nebraska	10.0
40	Mississippi	9.8
41	South Carolina	9.6
42	Washington	9.2
43	Vermont	7.8
44	Oregon	6.5
45	Alaska	6.2
46	Colorado	5.8
47	Utah	5.6
48	Wyoming	4.8
49	Montana	3.9
50	Idaho	2.9
	District of Columbia	19.1

Source: Morgan Quitno Press using data from American Medical Association (Chicago, Illinois)
"Physician Characteristics and Distribution in the U.S." (2000-2001 Edition)
As of December 31, 1998. National rate does not include physicians in U.S. territories and possessions.

Osteopathic Physicians in 1999

National Total = 42,324 Osteopathic Physicians*

ALPHA ORDER					RANK ORDER			
RANK	STATE	OSTEOPATHS	% of USA		RANK	STATE	OSTEOPATHS	% of USA
29	Alabama	260	0.6%		1	Michigan	4,982	11.8%
47	Alaska	64	0.2%		2	Pennsylvania	4,939	11.7%
12	Arizona	1,189	2.8%		3	Ohio	3,336	7.9%
38	Arkansas	169	0.4%		4	Florida	3,017	7.1%
8	California	1,982	4.7%		5	Texas	2,595	6.1%
14	Colorado	688	1.6%		6	New Jersey	2,532	6.0%
33	Connecticut	196	0.5%		7	New York	2,428	5.7%
36	Delaware	181	0.4%		8	California	1,982	4.7%
4	Florida	3,017	7.1%		9	Missouri	1,793	4.2%
18	Georgia	535	1.3%		10	Illinois	1,713	4.0%
40	Hawaii	105	0.2%		11	Oklahoma	1,220	2.9%
41	Idaho	103	0.2%		12	Arizona	1,189	2.8%
10	Illinois	1,713	4.0%		13	Iowa	956	2.3%
15	Indiana	606	1.4%		14	Colorado	688	1.6%
13	Iowa	956	2.3%		15	Indiana	606	1.4%
16	Kansas	557	1.3%		16	Kansas	557	1.3%
31	Kentucky	210	0.5%		17	Washington	536	1.3%
43	Louisiana	98	0.2%		18	Georgia	535	1.3%
21	Maine	450	1.1%		19	West Virginia	476	1.1%
26	Maryland	317	0.7%		20	Wisconsin	457	1.1%
24	Massachusetts	384	0.9%		21	Maine	450	1.1%
1	Michigan	4,982	11.8%		22	Oregon	408	1.0%
30	Minnesota	224	0.5%		23	Virginia	391	0.9%
33	Mississippi	196	0.5%		24	Massachusetts	384	0.9%
9	Missouri	1,793	4.2%		25	Tennessee	325	0.8%
44	Montana	83	0.2%		26	Maryland	317	0.7%
45	Nebraska	68	0.2%		27	Nevada	273	0.6%
27	Nevada	273	0.6%		28	North Carolina	270	0.6%
42	New Hampshire	100	0.2%		29	Alabama	260	0.6%
6	New Jersey	2,532	6.0%		30	Minnesota	224	0.5%
32	New Mexico	208	0.5%		31	Kentucky	210	0.5%
7	New York	2,428	5.7%		32	New Mexico	208	0.5%
28	North Carolina	270	0.6%		33	Connecticut	196	0.5%
49	North Dakota	51	0.1%		33	Mississippi	196	0.5%
3	Ohio	3,336	7.9%		35	South Carolina	182	0.4%
11	Oklahoma	1,220	2.9%		36	Delaware	181	0.4%
22	Oregon	408	1.0%		37	Rhode Island	176	0.4%
2	Pennsylvania	4,939	11.7%		38	Arkansas	169	0.4%
37	Rhode Island	176	0.4%		39	Utah	107	0.3%
35	South Carolina	182	0.4%		40	Hawaii	105	0.2%
46	South Dakota	67	0.2%		41	Idaho	103	0.2%
25	Tennessee	325	0.8%		42	New Hampshire	100	0.2%
5	Texas	2,595	6.1%		43	Louisiana	98	0.2%
39	Utah	107	0.3%		44	Montana	83	0.2%
48	Vermont	54	0.1%		45	Nebraska	68	0.2%
23	Virginia	391	0.9%		46	South Dakota	67	0.2%
17	Washington	536	1.3%		47	Alaska	64	0.2%
19	West Virginia	476	1.1%		48	Vermont	54	0.1%
20	Wisconsin	457	1.1%		49	North Dakota	51	0.1%
50	Wyoming	36	0.1%		50	Wyoming	36	0.1%
						District of Columbia	31	0.1%

Source: American Osteopathic Association
   "AOA Yearbook and Directory of Osteopathic Physicians 1999"
*Excludes retired, disabled, foreign and federal osteopaths. Osteopaths practice a system of medicine based on the theory that disturbances in the musculoskeletal system affect other body parts, causing many disorders that can be corrected by various manipulative techniques in conjunction with conventional medical, surgical, pharmacological, and other therapeutic procedures.

Rate of Osteopathic Physicians in 1999

National Rate = 16 Osteopaths per 100,000 Population*

ALPHA ORDER

RANK ORDER

RANK	STATE	RATE		RANK	STATE	RATE
37	Alabama	6		1	Michigan	51
22	Alaska	10		2	Pennsylvania	41
10	Arizona	25		3	Maine	36
34	Arkansas	7		3	Oklahoma	36
37	California	6		5	Iowa	33
15	Colorado	17		5	Missouri	33
37	Connecticut	6		7	New Jersey	31
11	Delaware	24		8	Ohio	30
13	Florida	20		9	West Virginia	26
34	Georgia	7		10	Arizona	25
24	Hawaii	9		11	Delaware	24
30	Idaho	8		12	Kansas	21
17	Illinois	14		13	Florida	20
22	Indiana	10		14	Rhode Island	18
5	Iowa	33		15	Colorado	17
12	Kansas	21		16	Nevada	15
44	Kentucky	5		17	Illinois	14
50	Louisiana	2		18	New York	13
3	Maine	36		18	Texas	13
37	Maryland	6		20	New Mexico	12
37	Massachusetts	6		20	Oregon	12
1	Michigan	51		22	Alaska	10
44	Minnesota	5		22	Indiana	10
34	Mississippi	7		24	Hawaii	9
5	Missouri	33		24	Montana	9
24	Montana	9		24	South Dakota	9
48	Nebraska	4		24	Vermont	9
16	Nevada	15		24	Washington	9
30	New Hampshire	8		24	Wisconsin	9
7	New Jersey	31		30	Idaho	8
20	New Mexico	12		30	New Hampshire	8
18	New York	13		30	North Dakota	8
48	North Carolina	4		30	Wyoming	8
30	North Dakota	8		34	Arkansas	7
8	Ohio	30		34	Georgia	7
3	Oklahoma	36		34	Mississippi	7
20	Oregon	12		37	Alabama	6
2	Pennsylvania	41		37	California	6
14	Rhode Island	18		37	Connecticut	6
44	South Carolina	5		37	Maryland	6
24	South Dakota	9		37	Massachusetts	6
37	Tennessee	6		37	Tennessee	6
18	Texas	13		37	Virginia	6
44	Utah	5		44	Kentucky	5
24	Vermont	9		44	Minnesota	5
37	Virginia	6		44	South Carolina	5
24	Washington	9		44	Utah	5
9	West Virginia	26		48	Nebraska	4
24	Wisconsin	9		48	North Carolina	4
30	Wyoming	8		50	Louisiana	2
					District of Columbia	6

Source: Morgan Quitno Press using data from American Osteopathic Association
"AOA Yearbook and Directory of Osteopathic Physicians 1999"
*Excludes retired, disabled, foreign and federal osteopaths. Osteopaths practice a system of medicine based on the theory that disturbances in the musculoskeletal system affect other body parts, causing many disorders that can be corrected by various manipulative techniques in conjunction with conventional medical, surgical, pharmacological, and other therapeutic procedures.

Podiatric Physicians in 1999

National Total = 13,318 Podiatric Physicians*

ALPHA ORDER

RANK	STATE	PODIATRISTS	% of USA
27	Alabama	97	0.7%
46	Alaska	24	0.2%
17	Arizona	198	1.5%
38	Arkansas	55	0.4%
2	California	1,522	11.4%
24	Colorado	128	1.0%
12	Connecticut	269	2.0%
43	Delaware	36	0.3%
4	Florida	914	6.9%
14	Georgia	241	1.8%
47	Hawaii	22	0.2%
42	Idaho	39	0.3%
5	Illinois	863	6.5%
14	Indiana	241	1.8%
21	Iowa	152	1.1%
28	Kansas	90	0.7%
30	Kentucky	82	0.6%
26	Louisiana	103	0.8%
36	Maine	59	0.4%
11	Maryland	290	2.2%
10	Massachusetts	439	3.3%
9	Michigan	530	4.0%
22	Minnesota	134	1.0%
43	Mississippi	36	0.3%
20	Missouri	171	1.3%
41	Montana	41	0.3%
35	Nebraska	60	0.5%
38	Nevada	55	0.4%
40	New Hampshire	54	0.4%
6	New Jersey	744	5.6%
36	New Mexico	59	0.4%
1	New York	1,602	12.0%
18	North Carolina	195	1.5%
47	North Dakota	22	0.2%
7	Ohio	688	5.2%
31	Oklahoma	81	0.6%
29	Oregon	85	0.6%
3	Pennsylvania	1,120	8.4%
32	Rhode Island	77	0.6%
33	South Carolina	66	0.5%
45	South Dakota	27	0.2%
22	Tennessee	134	1.0%
8	Texas	569	4.3%
25	Utah	113	0.8%
49	Vermont	16	0.1%
13	Virginia	248	1.9%
19	Washington	192	1.4%
34	West Virginia	65	0.5%
16	Wisconsin	201	1.5%
50	Wyoming	11	0.1%

RANK ORDER

RANK	STATE	PODIATRISTS	% of USA
1	New York	1,602	12.0%
2	California	1,522	11.4%
3	Pennsylvania	1,120	8.4%
4	Florida	914	6.9%
5	Illinois	863	6.5%
6	New Jersey	744	5.6%
7	Ohio	688	5.2%
8	Texas	569	4.3%
9	Michigan	530	4.0%
10	Massachusetts	439	3.3%
11	Maryland	290	2.2%
12	Connecticut	269	2.0%
13	Virginia	248	1.9%
14	Georgia	241	1.8%
14	Indiana	241	1.8%
16	Wisconsin	201	1.5%
17	Arizona	198	1.5%
18	North Carolina	195	1.5%
19	Washington	192	1.4%
20	Missouri	171	1.3%
21	Iowa	152	1.1%
22	Minnesota	134	1.0%
22	Tennessee	134	1.0%
24	Colorado	128	1.0%
25	Utah	113	0.8%
26	Louisiana	103	0.8%
27	Alabama	97	0.7%
28	Kansas	90	0.7%
29	Oregon	85	0.6%
30	Kentucky	82	0.6%
31	Oklahoma	81	0.6%
32	Rhode Island	77	0.6%
33	South Carolina	66	0.5%
34	West Virginia	65	0.5%
35	Nebraska	60	0.5%
36	Maine	59	0.4%
36	New Mexico	59	0.4%
38	Arkansas	55	0.4%
38	Nevada	55	0.4%
40	New Hampshire	54	0.4%
41	Montana	41	0.3%
42	Idaho	39	0.3%
43	Delaware	36	0.3%
43	Mississippi	36	0.3%
45	South Dakota	27	0.2%
46	Alaska	24	0.2%
47	Hawaii	22	0.2%
47	North Dakota	22	0.2%
49	Vermont	16	0.1%
50	Wyoming	11	0.1%
	District of Columbia	58	0.4%

Source: American Podiatric Medical Association, Inc.
    "Podiatric Physicians in Active Practice"
*As of Fall 1999. Includes only Podiatric physicians considered in "active practice." Podiatry deals with the diagnosis, treatment, and prevention of diseases of the human foot. National total does not include four podiatrists in Puerto Rico.

Rate of Podiatric Physicians in 1999

National Rate = 4.9 Podiatrists per 100,000 Population*

ALPHA ORDER

RANK	STATE	RATE
45	Alabama	2.2
21	Alaska	3.9
19	Arizona	4.1
45	Arkansas	2.2
16	California	4.6
31	Colorado	3.2
4	Connecticut	8.2
14	Delaware	4.8
9	Florida	6.0
32	Georgia	3.1
48	Hawaii	1.9
32	Idaho	3.1
6	Illinois	7.1
19	Indiana	4.1
12	Iowa	5.3
28	Kansas	3.4
47	Kentucky	2.1
41	Louisiana	2.4
15	Maine	4.7
10	Maryland	5.6
6	Massachusetts	7.1
11	Michigan	5.4
36	Minnesota	2.8
50	Mississippi	1.3
32	Missouri	3.1
16	Montana	4.6
24	Nebraska	3.6
35	Nevada	3.0
18	New Hampshire	4.5
2	New Jersey	9.1
28	New Mexico	3.4
3	New York	8.8
40	North Carolina	2.5
27	North Dakota	3.5
8	Ohio	6.1
41	Oklahoma	2.4
39	Oregon	2.6
1	Pennsylvania	9.3
5	Rhode Island	7.8
49	South Carolina	1.7
23	South Dakota	3.7
41	Tennessee	2.4
36	Texas	2.8
12	Utah	5.3
38	Vermont	2.7
24	Virginia	3.6
30	Washington	3.3
24	West Virginia	3.6
22	Wisconsin	3.8
44	Wyoming	2.3

RANK ORDER

RANK	STATE	RATE
1	Pennsylvania	9.3
2	New Jersey	9.1
3	New York	8.8
4	Connecticut	8.2
5	Rhode Island	7.8
6	Illinois	7.1
6	Massachusetts	7.1
8	Ohio	6.1
9	Florida	6.0
10	Maryland	5.6
11	Michigan	5.4
12	Iowa	5.3
12	Utah	5.3
14	Delaware	4.8
15	Maine	4.7
16	California	4.6
16	Montana	4.6
18	New Hampshire	4.5
19	Arizona	4.1
19	Indiana	4.1
21	Alaska	3.9
22	Wisconsin	3.8
23	South Dakota	3.7
24	Nebraska	3.6
24	Virginia	3.6
24	West Virginia	3.6
27	North Dakota	3.5
28	Kansas	3.4
28	New Mexico	3.4
30	Washington	3.3
31	Colorado	3.2
32	Georgia	3.1
32	Idaho	3.1
32	Missouri	3.1
35	Nevada	3.0
36	Minnesota	2.8
36	Texas	2.8
38	Vermont	2.7
39	Oregon	2.6
40	North Carolina	2.5
41	Louisiana	2.4
41	Oklahoma	2.4
41	Tennessee	2.4
44	Wyoming	2.3
45	Alabama	2.2
45	Arkansas	2.2
47	Kentucky	2.1
48	Hawaii	1.9
49	South Carolina	1.7
50	Mississippi	1.3
	District of Columbia	11.2

Source: Morgan Quitno Press using data from American Podiatric Medical Association, Inc.
     "Podiatric Physicians in Active Practice"
*Includes only Podiatric physicians considered in "active practice." Podiatry deals with the diagnosis, treatment, and prevention of diseases of the human foot. National rate does not include podiatrists in Puerto Rico.

Doctors of Chiropractic in 1998

National Total = 79,674 Chiropractors*

ALPHA ORDER

RANK	STATE	CHIROPRACTORS	% of USA
28	Alabama	764	1.0%
50	Alaska	166	0.2%
10	Arizona	2,514	3.2%
33	Arkansas	542	0.7%
1	California	12,732	16.0%
12	Colorado	1,916	2.4%
26	Connecticut	884	1.1%
47	Delaware	195	0.2%
4	Florida	4,153	5.2%
5	Georgia	3,482	4.4%
34	Hawaii	522	0.7%
39	Idaho	339	0.4%
8	Illinois	3,260	4.1%
25	Indiana	964	1.2%
21	Iowa	1,367	1.7%
29	Kansas	675	0.8%
23	Kentucky	1,090	1.4%
35	Louisiana	515	0.6%
38	Maine	360	0.5%
31	Maryland	602	0.8%
16	Massachusetts	1,813	2.3%
9	Michigan	2,568	3.2%
15	Minnesota	1,823	2.3%
41	Mississippi	311	0.4%
14	Missouri	1,871	2.3%
43	Montana	277	0.3%
42	Nebraska	310	0.4%
37	Nevada	385	0.5%
36	New Hampshire	435	0.5%
7	New Jersey	3,387	4.3%
32	New Mexico	553	0.7%
2	New York	5,524	6.9%
19	North Carolina	1,490	1.9%
45	North Dakota	252	0.3%
13	Ohio	1,877	2.4%
24	Oklahoma	1,062	1.3%
20	Oregon	1,410	1.8%
6	Pennsylvania	3,434	4.3%
49	Rhode Island	170	0.2%
22	South Carolina	1,165	1.5%
40	South Dakota	317	0.4%
27	Tennessee	802	1.0%
3	Texas	4,240	5.3%
30	Utah	639	0.8%
46	Vermont	206	0.3%
11	Virginia	2,308	2.9%
17	Washington	1,809	2.3%
44	West Virginia	262	0.3%
18	Wisconsin	1,710	2.1%
48	Wyoming	177	0.2%

RANK ORDER

RANK	STATE	CHIROPRACTORS	% of USA
1	California	12,732	16.0%
2	New York	5,524	6.9%
3	Texas	4,240	5.3%
4	Florida	4,153	5.2%
5	Georgia	3,482	4.4%
6	Pennsylvania	3,434	4.3%
7	New Jersey	3,387	4.3%
8	Illinois	3,260	4.1%
9	Michigan	2,568	3.2%
10	Arizona	2,514	3.2%
11	Virginia	2,308	2.9%
12	Colorado	1,916	2.4%
13	Ohio	1,877	2.4%
14	Missouri	1,871	2.3%
15	Minnesota	1,823	2.3%
16	Massachusetts	1,813	2.3%
17	Washington	1,809	2.3%
18	Wisconsin	1,710	2.1%
19	North Carolina	1,490	1.9%
20	Oregon	1,410	1.8%
21	Iowa	1,367	1.7%
22	South Carolina	1,165	1.5%
23	Kentucky	1,090	1.4%
24	Oklahoma	1,062	1.3%
25	Indiana	964	1.2%
26	Connecticut	884	1.1%
27	Tennessee	802	1.0%
28	Alabama	764	1.0%
29	Kansas	675	0.8%
30	Utah	639	0.8%
31	Maryland	602	0.8%
32	New Mexico	553	0.7%
33	Arkansas	542	0.7%
34	Hawaii	522	0.7%
35	Louisiana	515	0.6%
36	New Hampshire	435	0.5%
37	Nevada	385	0.5%
38	Maine	360	0.5%
39	Idaho	339	0.4%
40	South Dakota	317	0.4%
41	Mississippi	311	0.4%
42	Nebraska	310	0.4%
43	Montana	277	0.3%
44	West Virginia	262	0.3%
45	North Dakota	252	0.3%
46	Vermont	206	0.3%
47	Delaware	195	0.2%
48	Wyoming	177	0.2%
49	Rhode Island	170	0.2%
50	Alaska	166	0.2%
	District of Columbia	45	0.1%

Source: Federation of Chiropractic Licensing Boards
"1999-2000 Official Directory"
As of December 1998. Licensed active doctors. There is some duplication as some doctors are licensed in more than one state.

Rate of Doctors of Chiropractic in 1998

National Rate = 29 Chiropractors per 100,000 Population*

ALPHA ORDER

RANK	STATE	RATE
42	Alabama	18
31	Alaska	27
1	Arizona	54
39	Arkansas	21
10	California	39
2	Colorado	48
31	Connecticut	27
34	Delaware	26
28	Florida	28
4	Georgia	46
5	Hawaii	44
28	Idaho	28
31	Illinois	27
45	Indiana	16
2	Iowa	48
34	Kansas	26
28	Kentucky	28
48	Louisiana	12
26	Maine	29
48	Maryland	12
22	Massachusetts	30
34	Michigan	26
10	Minnesota	39
50	Mississippi	11
15	Missouri	34
21	Montana	31
41	Nebraska	19
37	Nevada	22
12	New Hampshire	37
8	New Jersey	42
18	New Mexico	32
22	New York	30
40	North Carolina	20
9	North Dakota	40
43	Ohio	17
18	Oklahoma	32
6	Oregon	43
26	Pennsylvania	29
43	Rhode Island	17
22	South Carolina	30
6	South Dakota	43
46	Tennessee	15
37	Texas	22
22	Utah	30
14	Vermont	35
15	Virginia	34
18	Washington	32
47	West Virginia	14
17	Wisconsin	33
12	Wyoming	37

RANK ORDER

RANK	STATE	RATE
1	Arizona	54
2	Colorado	48
2	Iowa	48
4	Georgia	46
5	Hawaii	44
6	Oregon	43
6	South Dakota	43
8	New Jersey	42
9	North Dakota	40
10	California	39
10	Minnesota	39
12	New Hampshire	37
12	Wyoming	37
14	Vermont	35
15	Missouri	34
15	Virginia	34
17	Wisconsin	33
18	New Mexico	32
18	Oklahoma	32
18	Washington	32
21	Montana	31
22	Massachusetts	30
22	New York	30
22	South Carolina	30
22	Utah	30
26	Maine	29
26	Pennsylvania	29
28	Florida	28
28	Idaho	28
28	Kentucky	28
31	Alaska	27
31	Connecticut	27
31	Illinois	27
34	Delaware	26
34	Kansas	26
34	Michigan	26
37	Nevada	22
37	Texas	22
39	Arkansas	21
40	North Carolina	20
41	Nebraska	19
42	Alabama	18
43	Ohio	17
43	Rhode Island	17
45	Indiana	16
46	Tennessee	15
47	West Virginia	14
48	Louisiana	12
48	Maryland	12
50	Mississippi	11
	District of Columbia	9

Source: Morgan Quitno Press using data from Federation of Chiropractic Licensing Boards
"1999-2000 Official Directory"
*As of December 1998. Licensed active doctors. There is some duplication as some doctors are licensed in more than one state.

Physician Assistants in Clinical Practice in 2000

National Total = 36,141 Physician Assistants*

ALPHA ORDER

RANK	STATE	PA'S	% of USA
36	Alabama	238	0.7%
34	Alaska	253	0.7%
17	Arizona	645	1.8%
49	Arkansas	51	0.1%
2	California	3,488	9.7%
12	Colorado	813	2.2%
15	Connecticut	744	2.1%
47	Delaware	86	0.2%
6	Florida	1,898	5.3%
8	Georgia	1,232	3.4%
48	Hawaii	84	0.2%
42	Idaho	177	0.5%
14	Illinois	795	2.2%
36	Indiana	238	0.7%
21	Iowa	480	1.3%
26	Kansas	436	1.2%
22	Kentucky	453	1.3%
35	Louisiana	245	0.7%
28	Maine	377	1.0%
11	Maryland	1,064	2.9%
13	Massachusetts	802	2.2%
7	Michigan	1,524	4.2%
20	Minnesota	536	1.5%
50	Mississippi	37	0.1%
33	Missouri	256	0.7%
43	Montana	160	0.4%
27	Nebraska	415	1.1%
40	Nevada	184	0.5%
41	New Hampshire	179	0.5%
25	New Jersey	438	1.2%
29	New Mexico	352	1.0%
1	New York	4,470	12.4%
5	North Carolina	1,900	5.3%
39	North Dakota	192	0.5%
10	Ohio	1,067	3.0%
19	Oklahoma	549	1.5%
30	Oregon	318	0.9%
4	Pennsylvania	1,974	5.5%
45	Rhode Island	119	0.3%
32	South Carolina	296	0.8%
38	South Dakota	236	0.7%
22	Tennessee	453	1.3%
3	Texas	2,317	6.4%
31	Utah	308	0.9%
44	Vermont	124	0.3%
18	Virginia	593	1.6%
9	Washington	1,114	3.1%
24	West Virginia	441	1.2%
15	Wisconsin	744	2.1%
46	Wyoming	99	0.3%

RANK ORDER

RANK	STATE	PA'S	% of USA
1	New York	4,470	12.4%
2	California	3,488	9.7%
3	Texas	2,317	6.4%
4	Pennsylvania	1,974	5.5%
5	North Carolina	1,900	5.3%
6	Florida	1,898	5.3%
7	Michigan	1,524	4.2%
8	Georgia	1,232	3.4%
9	Washington	1,114	3.1%
10	Ohio	1,067	3.0%
11	Maryland	1,064	2.9%
12	Colorado	813	2.2%
13	Massachusetts	802	2.2%
14	Illinois	795	2.2%
15	Connecticut	744	2.1%
15	Wisconsin	744	2.1%
17	Arizona	645	1.8%
18	Virginia	593	1.6%
19	Oklahoma	549	1.5%
20	Minnesota	536	1.5%
21	Iowa	480	1.3%
22	Kentucky	453	1.3%
22	Tennessee	453	1.3%
24	West Virginia	441	1.2%
25	New Jersey	438	1.2%
26	Kansas	436	1.2%
27	Nebraska	415	1.1%
28	Maine	377	1.0%
29	New Mexico	352	1.0%
30	Oregon	318	0.9%
31	Utah	308	0.9%
32	South Carolina	296	0.8%
33	Missouri	256	0.7%
34	Alaska	253	0.7%
35	Louisiana	245	0.7%
36	Alabama	238	0.7%
36	Indiana	238	0.7%
38	South Dakota	236	0.7%
39	North Dakota	192	0.5%
40	Nevada	184	0.5%
41	New Hampshire	179	0.5%
42	Idaho	177	0.5%
43	Montana	160	0.4%
44	Vermont	124	0.3%
45	Rhode Island	119	0.3%
46	Wyoming	99	0.3%
47	Delaware	86	0.2%
48	Hawaii	84	0.2%
49	Arkansas	51	0.1%
50	Mississippi	37	0.1%
	District of Columbia	147	0.4%

Source: The American Academy of Physician Assistants
   "Projected Number of PAs in Clinical Practice as of January 1, 2000" (Information Update, October 8, 1999)
*Projected.

Rate of Physician Assistants in Clinical Practice in 2000

National Rate = 13.3 PA's per 100,000 Population*

ALPHA ORDER

RANK	STATE	RATE
45	Alabama	5.4
1	Alaska	40.8
27	Arizona	13.5
49	Arkansas	2.0
35	California	10.5
14	Colorado	20.0
9	Connecticut	22.7
32	Delaware	11.4
29	Florida	12.6
21	Georgia	15.8
42	Hawaii	7.1
26	Idaho	14.1
43	Illinois	6.6
48	Indiana	4.0
17	Iowa	16.7
19	Kansas	16.4
32	Kentucky	11.4
44	Louisiana	5.6
4	Maine	30.1
11	Maryland	20.6
28	Massachusetts	13.0
22	Michigan	15.5
34	Minnesota	11.2
50	Mississippi	1.3
47	Missouri	4.7
16	Montana	18.1
5	Nebraska	24.9
36	Nevada	10.2
23	New Hampshire	14.9
45	New Jersey	5.4
13	New Mexico	20.2
7	New York	24.6
6	North Carolina	24.8
3	North Dakota	30.3
38	Ohio	9.5
20	Oklahoma	16.3
37	Oregon	9.6
18	Pennsylvania	16.5
30	Rhode Island	12.0
41	South Carolina	7.6
2	South Dakota	32.2
40	Tennessee	8.3
31	Texas	11.6
24	Utah	14.5
10	Vermont	20.9
39	Virginia	8.6
15	Washington	19.4
8	West Virginia	24.4
25	Wisconsin	14.2
11	Wyoming	20.6

RANK ORDER

RANK	STATE	RATE
1	Alaska	40.8
2	South Dakota	32.2
3	North Dakota	30.3
4	Maine	30.1
5	Nebraska	24.9
6	North Carolina	24.8
7	New York	24.6
8	West Virginia	24.4
9	Connecticut	22.7
10	Vermont	20.9
11	Maryland	20.6
11	Wyoming	20.6
13	New Mexico	20.2
14	Colorado	20.0
15	Washington	19.4
16	Montana	18.1
17	Iowa	16.7
18	Pennsylvania	16.5
19	Kansas	16.4
20	Oklahoma	16.3
21	Georgia	15.8
22	Michigan	15.5
23	New Hampshire	14.9
24	Utah	14.5
25	Wisconsin	14.2
26	Idaho	14.1
27	Arizona	13.5
28	Massachusetts	13.0
29	Florida	12.6
30	Rhode Island	12.0
31	Texas	11.6
32	Delaware	11.4
32	Kentucky	11.4
34	Minnesota	11.2
35	California	10.5
36	Nevada	10.2
37	Oregon	9.6
38	Ohio	9.5
39	Virginia	8.6
40	Tennessee	8.3
41	South Carolina	7.6
42	Hawaii	7.1
43	Illinois	6.6
44	Louisiana	5.6
45	Alabama	5.4
45	New Jersey	5.4
47	Missouri	4.7
48	Indiana	4.0
49	Arkansas	2.0
50	Mississippi	1.3
	District of Columbia	28.3

Source: Morgan Quitno Press using data from The American Academy of Physician Assistants
"Projected Number of PAs in Clinical Practice as of January 1, 2000" (Information Update, October 8, 1999)
*Projected. Rates calculated using 1999 Census population estimates.

Registered Nurses in 1996

National Total = 2,161,700 Registered Nurses*

<u>ALPHA ORDER</u>

RANK	STATE	NURSES	% of USA
23	Alabama	32,800	1.5%
48	Alaska	6,300	0.3%
22	Arizona	33,200	1.5%
33	Arkansas	17,900	0.8%
1	California	179,700	8.3%
25	Colorado	30,900	1.4%
21	Connecticut	33,400	1.5%
43	Delaware	7,700	0.4%
5	Florida	119,300	5.5%
13	Georgia	53,600	2.5%
42	Hawaii	8,900	0.4%
45	Idaho	7,100	0.3%
6	Illinois	104,700	4.8%
15	Indiana	46,900	2.2%
27	Iowa	29,100	1.3%
30	Kansas	21,600	1.0%
26	Kentucky	30,400	1.4%
24	Louisiana	32,400	1.5%
36	Maine	13,300	0.6%
20	Maryland	43,000	2.0%
9	Massachusetts	73,300	3.4%
8	Michigan	79,600	3.7%
17	Minnesota	46,200	2.1%
31	Mississippi	19,900	0.9%
14	Missouri	51,200	2.4%
45	Montana	7,100	0.3%
34	Nebraska	15,200	0.7%
41	Nevada	9,900	0.5%
40	New Hampshire	11,200	0.5%
10	New Jersey	67,100	3.1%
38	New Mexico	11,700	0.5%
2	New York	167,600	7.8%
11	North Carolina	62,000	2.9%
47	North Dakota	7,000	0.3%
7	Ohio	101,200	4.7%
32	Oklahoma	19,600	0.9%
29	Oregon	26,500	1.2%
3	Pennsylvania	126,300	5.8%
39	Rhode Island	11,400	0.5%
28	South Carolina	27,400	1.3%
43	South Dakota	7,700	0.4%
16	Tennessee	46,400	2.1%
4	Texas	124,200	5.7%
37	Utah	13,000	0.6%
49	Vermont	5,300	0.2%
12	Virginia	54,400	2.5%
19	Washington	43,500	2.0%
35	West Virginia	15,000	0.7%
18	Wisconsin	45,600	2.1%
50	Wyoming	4,200	0.2%

<u>RANK ORDER</u>

RANK	STATE	NURSES	% of USA
1	California	179,700	8.3%
2	New York	167,600	7.8%
3	Pennsylvania	126,300	5.8%
4	Texas	124,200	5.7%
5	Florida	119,300	5.5%
6	Illinois	104,700	4.8%
7	Ohio	101,200	4.7%
8	Michigan	79,600	3.7%
9	Massachusetts	73,300	3.4%
10	New Jersey	67,100	3.1%
11	North Carolina	62,000	2.9%
12	Virginia	54,400	2.5%
13	Georgia	53,600	2.5%
14	Missouri	51,200	2.4%
15	Indiana	46,900	2.2%
16	Tennessee	46,400	2.1%
17	Minnesota	46,200	2.1%
18	Wisconsin	45,600	2.1%
19	Washington	43,500	2.0%
20	Maryland	43,000	2.0%
21	Connecticut	33,400	1.5%
22	Arizona	33,200	1.5%
23	Alabama	32,800	1.5%
24	Louisiana	32,400	1.5%
25	Colorado	30,900	1.4%
26	Kentucky	30,400	1.4%
27	Iowa	29,100	1.3%
28	South Carolina	27,400	1.3%
29	Oregon	26,500	1.2%
30	Kansas	21,600	1.0%
31	Mississippi	19,900	0.9%
32	Oklahoma	19,600	0.9%
33	Arkansas	17,900	0.8%
34	Nebraska	15,200	0.7%
35	West Virginia	15,000	0.7%
36	Maine	13,300	0.6%
37	Utah	13,000	0.6%
38	New Mexico	11,700	0.5%
39	Rhode Island	11,400	0.5%
40	New Hampshire	11,200	0.5%
41	Nevada	9,900	0.5%
42	Hawaii	8,900	0.4%
43	Delaware	7,700	0.4%
43	South Dakota	7,700	0.4%
45	Idaho	7,100	0.3%
45	Montana	7,100	0.3%
47	North Dakota	7,000	0.3%
48	Alaska	6,300	0.3%
49	Vermont	5,300	0.2%
50	Wyoming	4,200	0.2%
	District of Columbia	8,900	0.4%

Source: U.S. Department of Health and Human Services, Health Resources and Services Administration unpublished data

*As of December 1996.

Rate of Registered Nurses in 1996

National Rate = 815 Nurses per 100,000 Population*

ALPHA ORDER

RANK	STATE	RATE
36	Alabama	764
8	Alaska	1,041
38	Arizona	749
43	Arkansas	715
50	California	566
31	Colorado	810
9	Connecticut	1,023
5	Delaware	1,059
27	Florida	827
42	Georgia	731
37	Hawaii	750
48	Idaho	599
19	Illinois	877
33	Indiana	805
10	Iowa	1,022
25	Kansas	836
35	Kentucky	783
39	Louisiana	747
4	Maine	1,074
22	Maryland	850
1	Massachusetts	1,205
29	Michigan	818
11	Minnesota	994
40	Mississippi	734
13	Missouri	954
31	Montana	810
15	Nebraska	922
47	Nevada	619
12	New Hampshire	966
24	New Jersey	838
44	New Mexico	685
14	New York	924
23	North Carolina	848
3	North Dakota	1,089
16	Ohio	906
49	Oklahoma	595
26	Oregon	829
6	Pennsylvania	1,050
2	Rhode Island	1,154
41	South Carolina	733
7	South Dakota	1,044
21	Tennessee	874
45	Texas	653
46	Utah	643
17	Vermont	904
30	Virginia	816
34	Washington	788
28	West Virginia	824
18	Wisconsin	881
20	Wyoming	875

RANK ORDER

RANK	STATE	RATE
1	Massachusetts	1,205
2	Rhode Island	1,154
3	North Dakota	1,089
4	Maine	1,074
5	Delaware	1,059
6	Pennsylvania	1,050
7	South Dakota	1,044
8	Alaska	1,041
9	Connecticut	1,023
10	Iowa	1,022
11	Minnesota	994
12	New Hampshire	966
13	Missouri	954
14	New York	924
15	Nebraska	922
16	Ohio	906
17	Vermont	904
18	Wisconsin	881
19	Illinois	877
20	Wyoming	875
21	Tennessee	874
22	Maryland	850
23	North Carolina	848
24	New Jersey	838
25	Kansas	836
26	Oregon	829
27	Florida	827
28	West Virginia	824
29	Michigan	818
30	Virginia	816
31	Colorado	810
31	Montana	810
33	Indiana	805
34	Washington	788
35	Kentucky	783
36	Alabama	764
37	Hawaii	750
38	Arizona	749
39	Louisiana	747
40	Mississippi	734
41	South Carolina	733
42	Georgia	731
43	Arkansas	715
44	New Mexico	685
45	Texas	653
46	Utah	643
47	Nevada	619
48	Idaho	599
49	Oklahoma	595
50	California	566
	District of Columbia	1,649

Source: Morgan Quitno Press using data from U.S. Dept. of Health & Human Services, Health Resources/Services Admn. unpublished data

*As of December 1996. Calculated with updated Census population estimates for July 1, 1996.

Dentists in 1997

National Total = 160,529 Dentists*

ALPHA ORDER

RANK	STATE	DENTISTS	% of USA
27	Alabama	1,697	1.1%
45	Alaska	338	0.2%
26	Arizona	1,878	1.2%
34	Arkansas	995	0.6%
1	California	20,676	12.9%
19	Colorado	2,501	1.6%
22	Connecticut	2,378	1.5%
48	Delaware	301	0.2%
6	Florida	6,740	4.2%
14	Georgia	3,024	1.9%
36	Hawaii	902	0.6%
40	Idaho	612	0.4%
4	Illinois	7,559	4.7%
18	Indiana	2,683	1.7%
30	Iowa	1,424	0.9%
32	Kansas	1,204	0.8%
25	Kentucky	1,912	1.2%
24	Louisiana	1,920	1.2%
41	Maine	586	0.4%
13	Maryland	3,136	2.0%
10	Massachusetts	4,462	2.8%
8	Michigan	5,736	3.6%
17	Minnesota	2,787	1.7%
35	Mississippi	986	0.6%
21	Missouri	2,461	1.5%
44	Montana	449	0.3%
33	Nebraska	997	0.6%
41	Nevada	586	0.4%
38	New Hampshire	664	0.4%
7	New Jersey	5,826	3.6%
39	New Mexico	645	0.4%
2	New York	12,864	8.0%
16	North Carolina	2,815	1.8%
49	North Dakota	285	0.2%
9	Ohio	5,662	3.5%
28	Oklahoma	1,483	0.9%
23	Oregon	2,049	1.3%
5	Pennsylvania	7,259	4.5%
43	Rhode Island	544	0.3%
29	South Carolina	1,459	0.9%
47	South Dakota	310	0.2%
20	Tennessee	2,492	1.6%
3	Texas	8,078	5.0%
31	Utah	1,237	0.8%
46	Vermont	328	0.2%
11	Virginia	3,330	2.1%
12	Washington	3,263	2.0%
37	West Virginia	765	0.5%
15	Wisconsin	2,889	1.8%
50	Wyoming	235	0.2%

RANK ORDER

RANK	STATE	DENTISTS	% of USA
1	California	20,676	12.9%
2	New York	12,864	8.0%
3	Texas	8,078	5.0%
4	Illinois	7,559	4.7%
5	Pennsylvania	7,259	4.5%
6	Florida	6,740	4.2%
7	New Jersey	5,826	3.6%
8	Michigan	5,736	3.6%
9	Ohio	5,662	3.5%
10	Massachusetts	4,462	2.8%
11	Virginia	3,330	2.1%
12	Washington	3,263	2.0%
13	Maryland	3,136	2.0%
14	Georgia	3,024	1.9%
15	Wisconsin	2,889	1.8%
16	North Carolina	2,815	1.8%
17	Minnesota	2,787	1.7%
18	Indiana	2,683	1.7%
19	Colorado	2,501	1.6%
20	Tennessee	2,492	1.6%
21	Missouri	2,461	1.5%
22	Connecticut	2,378	1.5%
23	Oregon	2,049	1.3%
24	Louisiana	1,920	1.2%
25	Kentucky	1,912	1.2%
26	Arizona	1,878	1.2%
27	Alabama	1,697	1.1%
28	Oklahoma	1,483	0.9%
29	South Carolina	1,459	0.9%
30	Iowa	1,424	0.9%
31	Utah	1,237	0.8%
32	Kansas	1,204	0.8%
33	Nebraska	997	0.6%
34	Arkansas	995	0.6%
35	Mississippi	986	0.6%
36	Hawaii	902	0.6%
37	West Virginia	765	0.5%
38	New Hampshire	664	0.4%
39	New Mexico	645	0.4%
40	Idaho	612	0.4%
41	Maine	586	0.4%
41	Nevada	586	0.4%
43	Rhode Island	544	0.3%
44	Montana	449	0.3%
45	Alaska	338	0.2%
46	Vermont	328	0.2%
47	South Dakota	310	0.2%
48	Delaware	301	0.2%
49	North Dakota	285	0.2%
50	Wyoming	235	0.2%
	District of Columbia	583	0.4%

Source: American Dental Association
   "1997 ADA Dentist Masterfile"
*National total includes 14,534 dentists working for the military, Public Health Service or whose address is unknown. These are not distributed among the states. Does not include 4,411 dental graduate students.

Rate of Dentists in 1997

National Rate = 60 Dentists per 100,000 Population*

ALPHA ORDER

RANK ORDER

RANK	STATE	RATE
44	Alabama	39
20	Alaska	55
41	Arizona	41
44	Arkansas	39
6	California	64
6	Colorado	64
2	Connecticut	73
41	Delaware	41
30	Florida	46
43	Georgia	40
1	Hawaii	76
22	Idaho	51
6	Illinois	64
30	Indiana	46
25	Iowa	50
30	Kansas	46
26	Kentucky	49
36	Louisiana	44
29	Maine	47
10	Maryland	62
2	Massachusetts	73
14	Michigan	59
14	Minnesota	59
49	Mississippi	36
30	Missouri	46
22	Montana	51
11	Nebraska	60
50	Nevada	35
17	New Hampshire	57
4	New Jersey	72
48	New Mexico	37
5	New York	71
47	North Carolina	38
36	North Dakota	44
22	Ohio	51
35	Oklahoma	45
9	Oregon	63
11	Pennsylvania	60
20	Rhode Island	55
44	South Carolina	39
38	South Dakota	42
30	Tennessee	46
38	Texas	42
11	Utah	60
18	Vermont	56
26	Virginia	49
16	Washington	58
38	West Virginia	42
18	Wisconsin	56
26	Wyoming	49

RANK	STATE	RATE
1	Hawaii	76
2	Connecticut	73
2	Massachusetts	73
4	New Jersey	72
5	New York	71
6	California	64
6	Colorado	64
6	Illinois	64
9	Oregon	63
10	Maryland	62
11	Nebraska	60
11	Pennsylvania	60
11	Utah	60
14	Michigan	59
14	Minnesota	59
16	Washington	58
17	New Hampshire	57
18	Vermont	56
18	Wisconsin	56
20	Alaska	55
20	Rhode Island	55
22	Idaho	51
22	Montana	51
22	Ohio	51
25	Iowa	50
26	Kentucky	49
26	Virginia	49
26	Wyoming	49
29	Maine	47
30	Florida	46
30	Indiana	46
30	Kansas	46
30	Missouri	46
30	Tennessee	46
35	Oklahoma	45
36	Louisiana	44
36	North Dakota	44
38	South Dakota	42
38	Texas	42
38	West Virginia	42
41	Arizona	41
41	Delaware	41
43	Georgia	40
44	Alabama	39
44	Arkansas	39
44	South Carolina	39
47	North Carolina	38
48	New Mexico	37
49	Mississippi	36
50	Nevada	35

District of Columbia 110

Source: Morgan Quitno Press using data from American Dental Association
    "1997 ADA Dentist Masterfile"
*National total includes dentists working for the military, Public Health Service or whose address is unknown.
These are not distributed among the states. Does not include dental graduate students.

Percent of Population Lacking Access to Dental Care in 1999

National Percent = 5.3% of Population*

ALPHA ORDER			RANK ORDER		
RANK	STATE	PERCENT	RANK	STATE	PERCENT
10	Alabama	9.2	1	Tennessee	21.4
50	Alaska	0.0	2	New Mexico	17.8
35	Arizona	2.8	3	Oregon	15.6
20	Arkansas	5.0	4	Nevada	15.1
40	California	2.0	5	Idaho	13.9
25	Colorado	4.4	6	Michigan	12.6
29	Connecticut	3.6	7	Mississippi	12.3
8	Delaware	11.9	8	Delaware	11.9
19	Florida	5.3	9	Maine	9.7
22	Georgia	4.8	10	Alabama	9.2
33	Hawaii	3.1	11	Utah	8.9
5	Idaho	13.9	12	Rhode Island	8.7
37	Illinois	2.6	12	Texas	8.7
33	Indiana	3.1	14	Washington	8.2
44	Iowa	1.2	15	South Dakota	7.7
24	Kansas	4.5	16	Louisiana	6.2
28	Kentucky	4.1	17	New York	6.0
16	Louisiana	6.2	18	North Dakota	5.4
9	Maine	9.7	19	Florida	5.3
41	Maryland	1.7	20	Arkansas	5.0
42	Massachusetts	1.6	21	South Carolina	4.9
6	Michigan	12.6	22	Georgia	4.8
49	Minnesota	0.4	22	North Carolina	4.8
7	Mississippi	12.3	24	Kansas	4.5
32	Missouri	3.3	25	Colorado	4.4
45	Montana	1.0	26	Oklahoma	4.2
36	Nebraska	2.7	26	Pennsylvania	4.2
4	Nevada	15.1	28	Kentucky	4.1
46	New Hampshire	0.7	29	Connecticut	3.6
43	New Jersey	1.4	29	Wisconsin	3.6
2	New Mexico	17.8	31	Ohio	3.4
17	New York	6.0	32	Missouri	3.3
22	North Carolina	4.8	33	Hawaii	3.1
18	North Dakota	5.4	33	Indiana	3.1
31	Ohio	3.4	35	Arizona	2.8
26	Oklahoma	4.2	36	Nebraska	2.7
3	Oregon	15.6	37	Illinois	2.6
26	Pennsylvania	4.2	38	Virginia	2.3
12	Rhode Island	8.7	39	West Virginia	2.2
21	South Carolina	4.9	40	California	2.0
15	South Dakota	7.7	41	Maryland	1.7
1	Tennessee	21.4	42	Massachusetts	1.6
12	Texas	8.7	43	New Jersey	1.4
11	Utah	8.9	44	Iowa	1.2
46	Vermont	0.7	45	Montana	1.0
38	Virginia	2.3	46	New Hampshire	0.7
14	Washington	8.2	46	Vermont	0.7
39	West Virginia	2.2	48	Wyoming	0.5
29	Wisconsin	3.6	49	Minnesota	0.4
48	Wyoming	0.5	50	Alaska	0.0
				District of Columbia	1.2

Source: Morgan Quitno Press using data from U.S. Dept. of Health and Human Services, Div. of Shortage Designation
"Selected Statistics on Health Manpower Shortage Areas, As of December 31, 1999"
*Percent of population considered under-served by dental practitioners. An under-served population does not have primary medical care within reasonable economic and geographic bounds.

Employment in Health Services Industries in 1997

National Total = 13,561,576 Employees*

ALPHA ORDER

RANK	STATE	EMPLOYEES	% of USA
23	Alabama	198,350	1.5%
49	Alaska	27,014	0.2%
25	Arizona	186,232	1.4%
32	Arkansas	127,025	0.9%
1	California	1,250,953	9.2%
26	Colorado	176,689	1.3%
22	Connecticut	213,729	1.6%
47	Delaware	39,971	0.3%
4	Florida	741,357	5.5%
12	Georgia	334,895	2.5%
44	Hawaii	47,565	0.4%
42	Idaho	49,125	0.4%
7	Illinois	603,680	4.5%
14	Indiana	300,310	2.2%
27	Iowa	174,032	1.3%
31	Kansas	148,380	1.1%
24	Kentucky	194,876	1.4%
21	Louisiana	240,622	1.8%
37	Maine	76,348	0.6%
20	Maryland	260,249	1.9%
9	Massachusetts	449,870	3.3%
8	Michigan	488,032	3.6%
15	Minnesota	298,312	2.2%
33	Mississippi	124,415	0.9%
13	Missouri	315,628	2.3%
46	Montana	45,199	0.3%
35	Nebraska	89,998	0.7%
41	Nevada	56,661	0.4%
39	New Hampshire	66,563	0.5%
10	New Jersey	400,157	3.0%
38	New Mexico	76,325	0.6%
2	New York	1,126,910	8.3%
11	North Carolina	361,421	2.7%
45	North Dakota	46,759	0.3%
6	Ohio	613,974	4.5%
28	Oklahoma	168,752	1.2%
30	Oregon	150,802	1.1%
5	Pennsylvania	716,182	5.3%
40	Rhode Island	63,777	0.5%
29	South Carolina	154,769	1.1%
43	South Dakota	48,000	0.4%
18	Tennessee	284,695	2.1%
3	Texas	891,570	6.6%
36	Utah	80,962	0.6%
48	Vermont	32,178	0.2%
17	Virginia	286,714	2.1%
19	Washington	263,605	1.9%
34	West Virginia	95,738	0.7%
16	Wisconsin	289,714	2.1%
50	Wyoming	22,966	0.2%

RANK ORDER

RANK	STATE	EMPLOYEES	% of USA
1	California	1,250,953	9.2%
2	New York	1,126,910	8.3%
3	Texas	891,570	6.6%
4	Florida	741,357	5.5%
5	Pennsylvania	716,182	5.3%
6	Ohio	613,974	4.5%
7	Illinois	603,680	4.5%
8	Michigan	488,032	3.6%
9	Massachusetts	449,870	3.3%
10	New Jersey	400,157	3.0%
11	North Carolina	361,421	2.7%
12	Georgia	334,895	2.5%
13	Missouri	315,628	2.3%
14	Indiana	300,310	2.2%
15	Minnesota	298,312	2.2%
16	Wisconsin	289,714	2.1%
17	Virginia	286,714	2.1%
18	Tennessee	284,695	2.1%
19	Washington	263,605	1.9%
20	Maryland	260,249	1.9%
21	Louisiana	240,622	1.8%
22	Connecticut	213,729	1.6%
23	Alabama	198,350	1.5%
24	Kentucky	194,876	1.4%
25	Arizona	186,232	1.4%
26	Colorado	176,689	1.3%
27	Iowa	174,032	1.3%
28	Oklahoma	168,752	1.2%
29	South Carolina	154,769	1.1%
30	Oregon	150,802	1.1%
31	Kansas	148,380	1.1%
32	Arkansas	127,025	0.9%
33	Mississippi	124,415	0.9%
34	West Virginia	95,738	0.7%
35	Nebraska	89,998	0.7%
36	Utah	80,962	0.6%
37	Maine	76,348	0.6%
38	New Mexico	76,325	0.6%
39	New Hampshire	66,563	0.5%
40	Rhode Island	63,777	0.5%
41	Nevada	56,661	0.4%
42	Idaho	49,125	0.4%
43	South Dakota	48,000	0.4%
44	Hawaii	47,565	0.4%
45	North Dakota	46,759	0.3%
46	Montana	45,199	0.3%
47	Delaware	39,971	0.3%
48	Vermont	32,178	0.2%
49	Alaska	27,014	0.2%
50	Wyoming	22,966	0.2%
	District of Columbia	59,529	0.4%

Source: U.S. Bureau of the Census
"1997 Economic Census, Health Care and Social Assistance" (EC97562A, October 1999)
*Total of employment in 1997. An establishment is a single physical location at which business is conducted or where services or industrial operations are performed. It is not necessarily identical with a company or enterprise, which may consist of one establishment or more.

485

VII. PHYSICAL FITNESS

Users of Exercise Equipment in 1998

National Total = 46,145,000 Users

ALPHA ORDER

RANK	STATE	USERS	% of USA
23	Alabama	789,000	1.7%
NA	Alaska*	NA	NA
20	Arizona	895,000	1.9%
32	Arkansas	357,000	0.8%
1	California	5,891,000	12.8%
17	Colorado	1,005,000	2.2%
27	Connecticut	647,000	1.4%
48	Delaware	84,000	0.2%
6	Florida	1,941,000	4.2%
13	Georgia	1,230,000	2.7%
NA	Hawaii*	NA	NA
37	Idaho	283,000	0.6%
5	Illinois	1,951,000	4.2%
21	Indiana	835,000	1.8%
30	Iowa	511,000	1.1%
33	Kansas	326,000	0.7%
28	Kentucky	592,000	1.3%
15	Louisiana	1,056,000	2.3%
39	Maine	256,000	0.6%
12	Maryland	1,234,000	2.7%
18	Massachusetts	975,000	2.1%
8	Michigan	1,653,000	3.6%
25	Minnesota	737,000	1.6%
35	Mississippi	295,000	0.6%
14	Missouri	1,083,000	2.3%
43	Montana	132,000	0.3%
34	Nebraska	303,000	0.7%
41	Nevada	195,000	0.4%
40	New Hampshire	238,000	0.5%
11	New Jersey	1,331,000	2.9%
38	New Mexico	262,000	0.6%
3	New York	2,988,000	6.5%
9	North Carolina	1,382,000	3.0%
45	North Dakota	105,000	0.2%
4	Ohio	1,994,000	4.3%
31	Oklahoma	442,000	1.0%
24	Oregon	774,000	1.7%
7	Pennsylvania	1,940,000	4.2%
44	Rhode Island	114,000	0.2%
29	South Carolina	589,000	1.3%
46	South Dakota	104,000	0.2%
26	Tennessee	720,000	1.6%
2	Texas	3,169,000	6.9%
22	Utah	801,000	1.7%
47	Vermont	87,000	0.2%
10	Virginia	1,336,000	2.9%
19	Washington	941,000	2.0%
35	West Virginia	295,000	0.6%
16	Wisconsin	1,022,000	2.2%
42	Wyoming	151,000	0.3%

RANK ORDER

RANK	STATE	USERS	% of USA
1	California	5,891,000	12.8%
2	Texas	3,169,000	6.9%
3	New York	2,988,000	6.5%
4	Ohio	1,994,000	4.3%
5	Illinois	1,951,000	4.2%
6	Florida	1,941,000	4.2%
7	Pennsylvania	1,940,000	4.2%
8	Michigan	1,653,000	3.6%
9	North Carolina	1,382,000	3.0%
10	Virginia	1,336,000	2.9%
11	New Jersey	1,331,000	2.9%
12	Maryland	1,234,000	2.7%
13	Georgia	1,230,000	2.7%
14	Missouri	1,083,000	2.3%
15	Louisiana	1,056,000	2.3%
16	Wisconsin	1,022,000	2.2%
17	Colorado	1,005,000	2.2%
18	Massachusetts	975,000	2.1%
19	Washington	941,000	2.0%
20	Arizona	895,000	1.9%
21	Indiana	835,000	1.8%
22	Utah	801,000	1.7%
23	Alabama	789,000	1.7%
24	Oregon	774,000	1.7%
25	Minnesota	737,000	1.6%
26	Tennessee	720,000	1.6%
27	Connecticut	647,000	1.4%
28	Kentucky	592,000	1.3%
29	South Carolina	589,000	1.3%
30	Iowa	511,000	1.1%
31	Oklahoma	442,000	1.0%
32	Arkansas	357,000	0.8%
33	Kansas	326,000	0.7%
34	Nebraska	303,000	0.7%
35	Mississippi	295,000	0.6%
35	West Virginia	295,000	0.6%
37	Idaho	283,000	0.6%
38	New Mexico	262,000	0.6%
39	Maine	256,000	0.6%
40	New Hampshire	238,000	0.5%
41	Nevada	195,000	0.4%
42	Wyoming	151,000	0.3%
43	Montana	132,000	0.3%
44	Rhode Island	114,000	0.2%
45	North Dakota	105,000	0.2%
46	South Dakota	104,000	0.2%
47	Vermont	87,000	0.2%
48	Delaware	84,000	0.2%
NA	Alaska*	NA	NA
NA	Hawaii*	NA	NA
	District of Columbia*	NA	NA

Source: The National Sporting Goods Association
"NSGA Sports Participation Survey, January-December 1998 (Copyright 1999, reprinted with permission)
*Not available.

Participants in Golf in 1998

National Total = 27,496,000 Golfers

ALPHA ORDER

RANK ORDER

RANK	STATE	GOLFERS	% of USA	RANK	STATE	GOLFERS	% of USA
24	Alabama	404,000	1.5%	1	California	2,625,000	9.5%
NA	Alaska*	NA	NA	2	Illinois	1,701,000	6.2%
25	Arizona	390,000	1.4%	3	Florida	1,635,000	5.9%
33	Arkansas	228,000	0.8%	4	Ohio	1,632,000	5.9%
1	California	2,625,000	9.5%	5	Texas	1,502,000	5.5%
23	Colorado	421,000	1.5%	6	New York	1,413,000	5.1%
28	Connecticut	380,000	1.4%	7	Pennsylvania	1,276,000	4.6%
48	Delaware	36,000	0.1%	8	Michigan	1,187,000	4.3%
3	Florida	1,635,000	5.9%	9	North Carolina	1,031,000	3.7%
11	Georgia	803,000	2.9%	10	Wisconsin	914,000	3.3%
NA	Hawaii*	NA	NA	11	Georgia	803,000	2.9%
37	Idaho	184,000	0.7%	12	Washington	679,000	2.5%
2	Illinois	1,701,000	6.2%	13	Indiana	657,000	2.4%
13	Indiana	657,000	2.4%	14	Massachusetts	611,000	2.2%
21	Iowa	443,000	1.6%	15	New Jersey	607,000	2.2%
33	Kansas	228,000	0.8%	16	South Carolina	599,000	2.2%
21	Kentucky	443,000	1.6%	17	Minnesota	576,000	2.1%
30	Louisiana	330,000	1.2%	18	Missouri	549,000	2.0%
45	Maine	51,000	0.2%	19	Oregon	499,000	1.8%
27	Maryland	385,000	1.4%	20	Virginia	477,000	1.7%
14	Massachusetts	611,000	2.2%	21	Iowa	443,000	1.6%
8	Michigan	1,187,000	4.3%	21	Kentucky	443,000	1.6%
17	Minnesota	576,000	2.1%	23	Colorado	421,000	1.5%
35	Mississippi	226,000	0.8%	24	Alabama	404,000	1.5%
18	Missouri	549,000	2.0%	25	Arizona	390,000	1.4%
43	Montana	80,000	0.3%	26	Oklahoma	387,000	1.4%
32	Nebraska	266,000	1.0%	27	Maryland	385,000	1.4%
39	Nevada	143,000	0.5%	28	Connecticut	380,000	1.4%
47	New Hampshire	47,000	0.2%	29	Tennessee	372,000	1.4%
15	New Jersey	607,000	2.2%	30	Louisiana	330,000	1.2%
38	New Mexico	152,000	0.6%	31	Utah	293,000	1.1%
6	New York	1,413,000	5.1%	32	Nebraska	266,000	1.0%
9	North Carolina	1,031,000	3.7%	33	Arkansas	228,000	0.8%
41	North Dakota	96,000	0.3%	33	Kansas	228,000	0.8%
4	Ohio	1,632,000	5.9%	35	Mississippi	226,000	0.8%
26	Oklahoma	387,000	1.4%	36	West Virginia	214,000	0.8%
19	Oregon	499,000	1.8%	37	Idaho	184,000	0.7%
7	Pennsylvania	1,276,000	4.6%	38	New Mexico	152,000	0.6%
40	Rhode Island	111,000	0.4%	39	Nevada	143,000	0.5%
16	South Carolina	599,000	2.2%	40	Rhode Island	111,000	0.4%
42	South Dakota	81,000	0.3%	41	North Dakota	96,000	0.3%
29	Tennessee	372,000	1.4%	42	South Dakota	81,000	0.3%
5	Texas	1,502,000	5.5%	43	Montana	80,000	0.3%
31	Utah	293,000	1.1%	44	Vermont	62,000	0.2%
44	Vermont	62,000	0.2%	45	Maine	51,000	0.2%
20	Virginia	477,000	1.7%	46	Wyoming	50,000	0.2%
12	Washington	679,000	2.5%	47	New Hampshire	47,000	0.2%
36	West Virginia	214,000	0.8%	48	Delaware	36,000	0.1%
10	Wisconsin	914,000	3.3%	NA	Alaska*	NA	NA
46	Wyoming	50,000	0.2%	NA	Hawaii*	NA	NA
					District of Columbia*	NA	NA

Source: The National Sporting Goods Association
"NSGA Sports Participation Survey, January-December 1998 (Copyright 1999, reprinted with permission)
*Not available.

Participants in Running/Jogging in 1998

National Total = 22,525,000 Runners/Joggers

<table>
<tr><td colspan="4">ALPHA ORDER</td><td colspan="4">RANK ORDER</td></tr>
<tr><td>RANK</td><td>STATE</td><td>RUNNERS</td><td>% of USA</td><td>RANK</td><td>STATE</td><td>RUNNERS</td><td>% of USA</td></tr>
<tr><td>16</td><td>Alabama</td><td>475,000</td><td>2.1%</td><td>1</td><td>California</td><td>3,186,000</td><td>14.1%</td></tr>
<tr><td>NA</td><td>Alaska*</td><td>NA</td><td>NA</td><td>2</td><td>Texas</td><td>2,024,000</td><td>9.0%</td></tr>
<tr><td>15</td><td>Arizona</td><td>518,000</td><td>2.3%</td><td>3</td><td>New York</td><td>1,323,000</td><td>5.9%</td></tr>
<tr><td>27</td><td>Arkansas</td><td>285,000</td><td>1.3%</td><td>4</td><td>Ohio</td><td>962,000</td><td>4.3%</td></tr>
<tr><td>1</td><td>California</td><td>3,186,000</td><td>14.1%</td><td>5</td><td>Illinois</td><td>893,000</td><td>4.0%</td></tr>
<tr><td>16</td><td>Colorado</td><td>475,000</td><td>2.1%</td><td>6</td><td>Florida</td><td>876,000</td><td>3.9%</td></tr>
<tr><td>35</td><td>Connecticut</td><td>168,000</td><td>0.7%</td><td>7</td><td>Virginia</td><td>766,000</td><td>3.4%</td></tr>
<tr><td>46</td><td>Delaware</td><td>45,000</td><td>0.2%</td><td>8</td><td>Michigan</td><td>740,000</td><td>3.3%</td></tr>
<tr><td>6</td><td>Florida</td><td>876,000</td><td>3.9%</td><td>9</td><td>New Jersey</td><td>701,000</td><td>3.1%</td></tr>
<tr><td>11</td><td>Georgia</td><td>664,000</td><td>2.9%</td><td>10</td><td>Pennsylvania</td><td>680,000</td><td>3.0%</td></tr>
<tr><td>NA</td><td>Hawaii*</td><td>NA</td><td>NA</td><td>11</td><td>Georgia</td><td>664,000</td><td>2.9%</td></tr>
<tr><td>33</td><td>Idaho</td><td>183,000</td><td>0.8%</td><td>12</td><td>North Carolina</td><td>655,000</td><td>2.9%</td></tr>
<tr><td>5</td><td>Illinois</td><td>893,000</td><td>4.0%</td><td>13</td><td>Missouri</td><td>604,000</td><td>2.7%</td></tr>
<tr><td>19</td><td>Indiana</td><td>429,000</td><td>1.9%</td><td>14</td><td>Maryland</td><td>593,000</td><td>2.6%</td></tr>
<tr><td>35</td><td>Iowa</td><td>168,000</td><td>0.7%</td><td>15</td><td>Arizona</td><td>518,000</td><td>2.3%</td></tr>
<tr><td>29</td><td>Kansas</td><td>215,000</td><td>1.0%</td><td>16</td><td>Alabama</td><td>475,000</td><td>2.1%</td></tr>
<tr><td>31</td><td>Kentucky</td><td>201,000</td><td>0.9%</td><td>16</td><td>Colorado</td><td>475,000</td><td>2.1%</td></tr>
<tr><td>21</td><td>Louisiana</td><td>391,000</td><td>1.7%</td><td>18</td><td>Tennessee</td><td>474,000</td><td>2.1%</td></tr>
<tr><td>42</td><td>Maine</td><td>69,000</td><td>0.3%</td><td>19</td><td>Indiana</td><td>429,000</td><td>1.9%</td></tr>
<tr><td>14</td><td>Maryland</td><td>593,000</td><td>2.6%</td><td>20</td><td>Massachusetts</td><td>396,000</td><td>1.8%</td></tr>
<tr><td>20</td><td>Massachusetts</td><td>396,000</td><td>1.8%</td><td>21</td><td>Louisiana</td><td>391,000</td><td>1.7%</td></tr>
<tr><td>8</td><td>Michigan</td><td>740,000</td><td>3.3%</td><td>22</td><td>Utah</td><td>369,000</td><td>1.6%</td></tr>
<tr><td>28</td><td>Minnesota</td><td>248,000</td><td>1.1%</td><td>23</td><td>Wisconsin</td><td>347,000</td><td>1.5%</td></tr>
<tr><td>29</td><td>Mississippi</td><td>215,000</td><td>1.0%</td><td>24</td><td>Oregon</td><td>345,000</td><td>1.5%</td></tr>
<tr><td>13</td><td>Missouri</td><td>604,000</td><td>2.7%</td><td>25</td><td>Washington</td><td>304,000</td><td>1.3%</td></tr>
<tr><td>41</td><td>Montana</td><td>71,000</td><td>0.3%</td><td>26</td><td>South Carolina</td><td>294,000</td><td>1.3%</td></tr>
<tr><td>32</td><td>Nebraska</td><td>186,000</td><td>0.8%</td><td>27</td><td>Arkansas</td><td>285,000</td><td>1.3%</td></tr>
<tr><td>40</td><td>Nevada</td><td>72,000</td><td>0.3%</td><td>28</td><td>Minnesota</td><td>248,000</td><td>1.1%</td></tr>
<tr><td>38</td><td>New Hampshire</td><td>126,000</td><td>0.6%</td><td>29</td><td>Kansas</td><td>215,000</td><td>1.0%</td></tr>
<tr><td>9</td><td>New Jersey</td><td>701,000</td><td>3.1%</td><td>29</td><td>Mississippi</td><td>215,000</td><td>1.0%</td></tr>
<tr><td>39</td><td>New Mexico</td><td>120,000</td><td>0.5%</td><td>31</td><td>Kentucky</td><td>201,000</td><td>0.9%</td></tr>
<tr><td>3</td><td>New York</td><td>1,323,000</td><td>5.9%</td><td>32</td><td>Nebraska</td><td>186,000</td><td>0.8%</td></tr>
<tr><td>12</td><td>North Carolina</td><td>655,000</td><td>2.9%</td><td>33</td><td>Idaho</td><td>183,000</td><td>0.8%</td></tr>
<tr><td>46</td><td>North Dakota</td><td>45,000</td><td>0.2%</td><td>34</td><td>West Virginia</td><td>175,000</td><td>0.8%</td></tr>
<tr><td>4</td><td>Ohio</td><td>962,000</td><td>4.3%</td><td>35</td><td>Connecticut</td><td>168,000</td><td>0.7%</td></tr>
<tr><td>37</td><td>Oklahoma</td><td>165,000</td><td>0.7%</td><td>35</td><td>Iowa</td><td>168,000</td><td>0.7%</td></tr>
<tr><td>24</td><td>Oregon</td><td>345,000</td><td>1.5%</td><td>37</td><td>Oklahoma</td><td>165,000</td><td>0.7%</td></tr>
<tr><td>10</td><td>Pennsylvania</td><td>680,000</td><td>3.0%</td><td>38</td><td>New Hampshire</td><td>126,000</td><td>0.6%</td></tr>
<tr><td>45</td><td>Rhode Island</td><td>53,000</td><td>0.2%</td><td>39</td><td>New Mexico</td><td>120,000</td><td>0.5%</td></tr>
<tr><td>26</td><td>South Carolina</td><td>294,000</td><td>1.3%</td><td>40</td><td>Nevada</td><td>72,000</td><td>0.3%</td></tr>
<tr><td>43</td><td>South Dakota</td><td>59,000</td><td>0.3%</td><td>41</td><td>Montana</td><td>71,000</td><td>0.3%</td></tr>
<tr><td>18</td><td>Tennessee</td><td>474,000</td><td>2.1%</td><td>42</td><td>Maine</td><td>69,000</td><td>0.3%</td></tr>
<tr><td>2</td><td>Texas</td><td>2,024,000</td><td>9.0%</td><td>43</td><td>South Dakota</td><td>59,000</td><td>0.3%</td></tr>
<tr><td>22</td><td>Utah</td><td>369,000</td><td>1.6%</td><td>43</td><td>Vermont</td><td>59,000</td><td>0.3%</td></tr>
<tr><td>43</td><td>Vermont</td><td>59,000</td><td>0.3%</td><td>45</td><td>Rhode Island</td><td>53,000</td><td>0.2%</td></tr>
<tr><td>7</td><td>Virginia</td><td>766,000</td><td>3.4%</td><td>46</td><td>Delaware</td><td>45,000</td><td>0.2%</td></tr>
<tr><td>25</td><td>Washington</td><td>304,000</td><td>1.3%</td><td>46</td><td>North Dakota</td><td>45,000</td><td>0.2%</td></tr>
<tr><td>34</td><td>West Virginia</td><td>175,000</td><td>0.8%</td><td>48</td><td>Wyoming</td><td>36,000</td><td>0.2%</td></tr>
<tr><td>23</td><td>Wisconsin</td><td>347,000</td><td>1.5%</td><td>NA</td><td>Alaska*</td><td>NA</td><td>NA</td></tr>
<tr><td>48</td><td>Wyoming</td><td>36,000</td><td>0.2%</td><td>NA</td><td>Hawaii*</td><td>NA</td><td>NA</td></tr>
<tr><td></td><td></td><td></td><td></td><td colspan="2">District of Columbia*</td><td>NA</td><td>NA</td></tr>
</table>

Source: The National Sporting Goods Association
"NSGA Sports Participation Survey, January-December 1998 (Copyright 1999, reprinted with permission)
Not available.

Participants in Soccer in 1998

National Total = 13,167,000 Soccer Players

ALPHA ORDER					RANK ORDER			

RANK	STATE	PARTICIPANTS	% of USA		RANK	STATE	PARTICIPANTS	% of USA
20	Alabama	246,000	1.9%		1	California	1,707,000	13.0%
NA	Alaska*	NA	NA		2	New York	1,012,000	7.7%
12	Arizona	342,000	2.6%		3	Texas	751,000	5.7%
35	Arkansas	104,000	0.8%		4	Pennsylvania	711,000	5.4%
1	California	1,707,000	13.0%		5	Michigan	507,000	3.9%
14	Colorado	334,000	2.5%		6	Ohio	492,000	3.7%
32	Connecticut	112,000	0.9%		7	Wisconsin	479,000	3.6%
46	Delaware	25,000	0.2%		8	Washington	445,000	3.4%
15	Florida	293,000	2.2%		9	New Jersey	425,000	3.2%
22	Georgia	230,000	1.7%		10	Maryland	361,000	2.7%
NA	Hawaii*	NA	NA		11	Illinois	358,000	2.7%
44	Idaho	27,000	0.2%		12	Arizona	342,000	2.6%
11	Illinois	358,000	2.7%		13	North Carolina	337,000	2.6%
19	Indiana	249,000	1.9%		14	Colorado	334,000	2.5%
28	Iowa	169,000	1.3%		15	Florida	293,000	2.2%
31	Kansas	119,000	0.9%		16	Missouri	289,000	2.2%
24	Kentucky	214,000	1.6%		17	Oregon	288,000	2.2%
23	Louisiana	220,000	1.7%		18	Minnesota	259,000	2.0%
33	Maine	109,000	0.8%		19	Indiana	249,000	1.9%
10	Maryland	361,000	2.7%		20	Alabama	246,000	1.9%
29	Massachusetts	161,000	1.2%		21	New Hampshire	233,000	1.8%
5	Michigan	507,000	3.9%		22	Georgia	230,000	1.7%
18	Minnesota	259,000	2.0%		23	Louisiana	220,000	1.7%
47	Mississippi	24,000	0.2%		24	Kentucky	214,000	1.6%
16	Missouri	289,000	2.2%		25	Oklahoma	211,000	1.6%
40	Montana	78,000	0.6%		26	Utah	210,000	1.6%
41	Nebraska	67,000	0.5%		27	Virginia	207,000	1.6%
NA	Nevada*	NA	NA		28	Iowa	169,000	1.3%
21	New Hampshire	233,000	1.8%		29	Massachusetts	161,000	1.2%
9	New Jersey	425,000	3.2%		30	Tennessee	149,000	1.1%
34	New Mexico	105,000	0.8%		31	Kansas	119,000	0.9%
2	New York	1,012,000	7.7%		32	Connecticut	112,000	0.9%
13	North Carolina	337,000	2.6%		33	Maine	109,000	0.8%
42	North Dakota	58,000	0.4%		34	New Mexico	105,000	0.8%
6	Ohio	492,000	3.7%		35	Arkansas	104,000	0.8%
25	Oklahoma	211,000	1.6%		36	South Carolina	96,000	0.7%
17	Oregon	288,000	2.2%		37	West Virginia	88,000	0.7%
4	Pennsylvania	711,000	5.4%		38	Rhode Island	86,000	0.7%
38	Rhode Island	86,000	0.7%		39	Wyoming	79,000	0.6%
36	South Carolina	96,000	0.7%		40	Montana	78,000	0.6%
45	South Dakota	26,000	0.2%		41	Nebraska	67,000	0.5%
30	Tennessee	149,000	1.1%		42	North Dakota	58,000	0.4%
3	Texas	751,000	5.7%		43	Vermont	44,000	0.3%
26	Utah	210,000	1.6%		44	Idaho	27,000	0.2%
43	Vermont	44,000	0.3%		45	South Dakota	26,000	0.2%
27	Virginia	207,000	1.6%		46	Delaware	25,000	0.2%
8	Washington	445,000	3.4%		47	Mississippi	24,000	0.2%
37	West Virginia	88,000	0.7%		NA	Alaska*	NA	NA
7	Wisconsin	479,000	3.6%		NA	Hawaii*	NA	NA
39	Wyoming	79,000	0.6%		NA	Nevada*	NA	NA
						District of Columbia*	NA	NA

Source: The National Sporting Goods Association
"NSGA Sports Participation Survey, January-December 1998 (Copyright 1999, reprinted with permission)
*Not available.

Participants in Swimming in 1998

National Total = 58,249,000 Swimmers

RANK	STATE	SWIMMERS	% of USA
22	Alabama	990,000	1.7%
NA	Alaska*	NA	NA
18	Arizona	1,276,000	2.2%
31	Arkansas	501,000	0.9%
1	California	6,705,000	11.5%
29	Colorado	634,000	1.1%
24	Connecticut	876,000	1.5%
48	Delaware	7,000	0.0%
4	Florida	3,521,000	6.0%
12	Georgia	1,362,000	2.3%
NA	Hawaii*	NA	NA
39	Idaho	301,000	0.5%
6	Illinois	2,595,000	4.5%
11	Indiana	1,454,000	2.5%
27	Iowa	749,000	1.3%
32	Kansas	476,000	0.8%
23	Kentucky	896,000	1.5%
20	Louisiana	1,206,000	2.1%
38	Maine	350,000	0.6%
15	Maryland	1,338,000	2.3%
17	Massachusetts	1,305,000	2.2%
9	Michigan	1,829,000	3.1%
28	Minnesota	652,000	1.1%
34	Mississippi	426,000	0.7%
10	Missouri	1,502,000	2.6%
44	Montana	138,000	0.2%
36	Nebraska	390,000	0.7%
40	Nevada	298,000	0.5%
36	New Hampshire	390,000	0.7%
7	New Jersey	2,316,000	4.0%
41	New Mexico	282,000	0.5%
3	New York	4,165,000	7.2%
14	North Carolina	1,345,000	2.3%
47	North Dakota	63,000	0.1%
8	Ohio	1,991,000	3.4%
30	Oklahoma	552,000	0.9%
25	Oregon	850,000	1.5%
5	Pennsylvania	2,757,000	4.7%
43	Rhode Island	150,000	0.3%
26	South Carolina	798,000	1.4%
46	South Dakota	107,000	0.2%
19	Tennessee	1,240,000	2.1%
2	Texas	4,448,000	7.6%
33	Utah	447,000	0.8%
44	Vermont	138,000	0.2%
16	Virginia	1,317,000	2.3%
21	Washington	1,104,000	1.9%
35	West Virginia	410,000	0.7%
13	Wisconsin	1,355,000	2.3%
42	Wyoming	183,000	0.3%

RANK	STATE	SWIMMERS	% of USA
1	California	6,705,000	11.5%
2	Texas	4,448,000	7.6%
3	New York	4,165,000	7.2%
4	Florida	3,521,000	6.0%
5	Pennsylvania	2,757,000	4.7%
6	Illinois	2,595,000	4.5%
7	New Jersey	2,316,000	4.0%
8	Ohio	1,991,000	3.4%
9	Michigan	1,829,000	3.1%
10	Missouri	1,502,000	2.6%
11	Indiana	1,454,000	2.5%
12	Georgia	1,362,000	2.3%
13	Wisconsin	1,355,000	2.3%
14	North Carolina	1,345,000	2.3%
15	Maryland	1,338,000	2.3%
16	Virginia	1,317,000	2.3%
17	Massachusetts	1,305,000	2.2%
18	Arizona	1,276,000	2.2%
19	Tennessee	1,240,000	2.1%
20	Louisiana	1,206,000	2.1%
21	Washington	1,104,000	1.9%
22	Alabama	990,000	1.7%
23	Kentucky	896,000	1.5%
24	Connecticut	876,000	1.5%
25	Oregon	850,000	1.5%
26	South Carolina	798,000	1.4%
27	Iowa	749,000	1.3%
28	Minnesota	652,000	1.1%
29	Colorado	634,000	1.1%
30	Oklahoma	552,000	0.9%
31	Arkansas	501,000	0.9%
32	Kansas	476,000	0.8%
33	Utah	447,000	0.8%
34	Mississippi	426,000	0.7%
35	West Virginia	410,000	0.7%
36	Nebraska	390,000	0.7%
36	New Hampshire	390,000	0.7%
38	Maine	350,000	0.6%
39	Idaho	301,000	0.5%
40	Nevada	298,000	0.5%
41	New Mexico	282,000	0.5%
42	Wyoming	183,000	0.3%
43	Rhode Island	150,000	0.3%
44	Montana	138,000	0.2%
44	Vermont	138,000	0.2%
46	South Dakota	107,000	0.2%
47	North Dakota	63,000	0.1%
48	Delaware	7,000	0.0%
NA	Alaska*	NA	NA
NA	Hawaii*	NA	NA
	District of Columbia*	NA	NA

Source: The National Sporting Goods Association
"NSGA Sports Participation Survey, January-December 1998 (Copyright 1999, reprinted with permission)
Not available.

Participants in Tennis in 1998

National Total = 11,227,000 Tennis Players

ALPHA ORDER				RANK ORDER			
RANK	STATE	PLAYERS	% of USA	RANK	STATE	PLAYERS	% of USA
19	Alabama	198,000	1.8%	1	California	2,034,000	18.1%
NA	Alaska*	NA	NA	2	Texas	742,000	6.6%
26	Arizona	146,000	1.3%	3	New York	626,000	5.6%
32	Arkansas	82,000	0.7%	4	Pennsylvania	610,000	5.4%
1	California	2,034,000	18.1%	5	Florida	557,000	5.0%
29	Colorado	118,000	1.1%	6	Ohio	542,000	4.8%
24	Connecticut	156,000	1.4%	7	Illinois	529,000	4.7%
43	Delaware	15,000	0.1%	8	Georgia	339,000	3.0%
5	Florida	557,000	5.0%	9	North Carolina	334,000	3.0%
8	Georgia	339,000	3.0%	10	Michigan	319,000	2.8%
NA	Hawaii*	NA	NA	10	New Jersey	319,000	2.8%
36	Idaho	46,000	0.4%	12	Maryland	300,000	2.7%
7	Illinois	529,000	4.7%	13	Virginia	272,000	2.4%
30	Indiana	112,000	1.0%	14	Utah	254,000	2.3%
20	Iowa	187,000	1.7%	15	Massachusetts	249,000	2.2%
33	Kansas	77,000	0.7%	16	Tennessee	240,000	2.1%
25	Kentucky	153,000	1.4%	17	South Carolina	228,000	2.0%
31	Louisiana	100,000	0.9%	18	Missouri	201,000	1.8%
44	Maine	14,000	0.1%	19	Alabama	198,000	1.8%
12	Maryland	300,000	2.7%	20	Iowa	187,000	1.7%
15	Massachusetts	249,000	2.2%	21	Wisconsin	172,000	1.5%
10	Michigan	319,000	2.8%	22	West Virginia	167,000	1.5%
28	Minnesota	134,000	1.2%	23	Oregon	165,000	1.5%
38	Mississippi	39,000	0.3%	24	Connecticut	156,000	1.4%
18	Missouri	201,000	1.8%	25	Kentucky	153,000	1.4%
44	Montana	14,000	0.1%	26	Arizona	146,000	1.3%
34	Nebraska	67,000	0.6%	27	Washington	137,000	1.2%
41	Nevada	20,000	0.2%	28	Minnesota	134,000	1.2%
37	New Hampshire	42,000	0.4%	29	Colorado	118,000	1.1%
10	New Jersey	319,000	2.8%	30	Indiana	112,000	1.0%
42	New Mexico	17,000	0.2%	31	Louisiana	100,000	0.9%
3	New York	626,000	5.6%	32	Arkansas	82,000	0.7%
9	North Carolina	334,000	3.0%	33	Kansas	77,000	0.7%
46	North Dakota	10,000	0.1%	34	Nebraska	67,000	0.6%
6	Ohio	542,000	4.8%	35	Oklahoma	59,000	0.5%
35	Oklahoma	59,000	0.5%	36	Idaho	46,000	0.4%
23	Oregon	165,000	1.5%	37	New Hampshire	42,000	0.4%
4	Pennsylvania	610,000	5.4%	38	Mississippi	39,000	0.3%
40	Rhode Island	27,000	0.2%	39	Vermont	35,000	0.3%
17	South Carolina	228,000	2.0%	40	Rhode Island	27,000	0.2%
46	South Dakota	10,000	0.1%	41	Nevada	20,000	0.2%
16	Tennessee	240,000	2.1%	42	New Mexico	17,000	0.2%
2	Texas	742,000	6.6%	43	Delaware	15,000	0.1%
14	Utah	254,000	2.3%	44	Maine	14,000	0.1%
39	Vermont	35,000	0.3%	44	Montana	14,000	0.1%
13	Virginia	272,000	2.4%	46	North Dakota	10,000	0.1%
27	Washington	137,000	1.2%	46	South Dakota	10,000	0.1%
22	West Virginia	167,000	1.5%	NA	Alaska*	NA	NA
21	Wisconsin	172,000	1.5%	NA	Hawaii*	NA	NA
NA	Wyoming*	NA	NA	NA	Wyoming*	NA	NA
					District of Columbia*	NA	NA

Source: The National Sporting Goods Association
    "NSGA Sports Participation Survey, January-December 1998 (Copyright 1999, reprinted with permission)
*Not available.

Alcohol Consumption in 1997

National Total = 465,680,000 Gallons*

ALPHA ORDER

RANK	STATE	GALLONS	% of USA
25	Alabama	6,339,000	1.4%
48	Alaska	1,191,000	0.3%
17	Arizona	9,177,000	2.0%
35	Arkansas	3,570,000	0.8%
1	California	56,492,000	12.1%
23	Colorado	7,995,000	1.7%
27	Connecticut	5,864,000	1.3%
45	Delaware	1,705,000	0.4%
3	Florida	31,229,000	6.7%
10	Georgia	13,056,000	2.8%
40	Hawaii	2,230,000	0.5%
42	Idaho	1,919,000	0.4%
5	Illinois	21,841,000	4.7%
18	Indiana	9,054,000	1.9%
32	Iowa	4,340,000	0.9%
34	Kansas	3,587,000	0.8%
28	Kentucky	5,485,000	1.2%
21	Louisiana	8,476,000	1.8%
39	Maine	2,236,000	0.5%
20	Maryland	8,514,000	1.8%
11	Massachusetts	12,075,000	2.6%
8	Michigan	16,051,000	3.4%
19	Minnesota	8,857,000	1.9%
30	Mississippi	4,530,000	1.0%
16	Missouri	9,426,000	2.0%
44	Montana	1,730,000	0.4%
37	Nebraska	2,815,000	0.6%
29	Nevada	5,245,000	1.1%
33	New Hampshire	3,854,000	0.8%
9	New Jersey	14,193,000	3.0%
36	New Mexico	3,184,000	0.7%
4	New York	28,095,000	6.0%
12	North Carolina	11,712,000	2.5%
47	North Dakota	1,204,000	0.3%
7	Ohio	17,321,000	3.7%
31	Oklahoma	4,435,000	1.0%
26	Oregon	5,969,000	1.3%
6	Pennsylvania	18,323,000	3.9%
42	Rhode Island	1,919,000	0.4%
24	South Carolina	7,109,000	1.5%
46	South Dakota	1,285,000	0.3%
22	Tennessee	8,099,000	1.7%
2	Texas	33,993,000	7.3%
41	Utah	1,981,000	0.4%
49	Vermont	1,123,000	0.2%
14	Virginia	10,465,000	2.2%
15	Washington	9,813,000	2.1%
38	West Virginia	2,419,000	0.5%
13	Wisconsin	11,477,000	2.5%
50	Wyoming	911,000	0.2%

RANK ORDER

RANK	STATE	GALLONS	% of USA
1	California	56,492,000	12.1%
2	Texas	33,993,000	7.3%
3	Florida	31,229,000	6.7%
4	New York	28,095,000	6.0%
5	Illinois	21,841,000	4.7%
6	Pennsylvania	18,323,000	3.9%
7	Ohio	17,321,000	3.7%
8	Michigan	16,051,000	3.4%
9	New Jersey	14,193,000	3.0%
10	Georgia	13,056,000	2.8%
11	Massachusetts	12,075,000	2.6%
12	North Carolina	11,712,000	2.5%
13	Wisconsin	11,477,000	2.5%
14	Virginia	10,465,000	2.2%
15	Washington	9,813,000	2.1%
16	Missouri	9,426,000	2.0%
17	Arizona	9,177,000	2.0%
18	Indiana	9,054,000	1.9%
19	Minnesota	8,857,000	1.9%
20	Maryland	8,514,000	1.8%
21	Louisiana	8,476,000	1.8%
22	Tennessee	8,099,000	1.7%
23	Colorado	7,995,000	1.7%
24	South Carolina	7,109,000	1.5%
25	Alabama	6,339,000	1.4%
26	Oregon	5,969,000	1.3%
27	Connecticut	5,864,000	1.3%
28	Kentucky	5,485,000	1.2%
29	Nevada	5,245,000	1.1%
30	Mississippi	4,530,000	1.0%
31	Oklahoma	4,435,000	1.0%
32	Iowa	4,340,000	0.9%
33	New Hampshire	3,854,000	0.8%
34	Kansas	3,587,000	0.8%
35	Arkansas	3,570,000	0.8%
36	New Mexico	3,184,000	0.7%
37	Nebraska	2,815,000	0.6%
38	West Virginia	2,419,000	0.5%
39	Maine	2,236,000	0.5%
40	Hawaii	2,230,000	0.5%
41	Utah	1,981,000	0.4%
42	Idaho	1,919,000	0.4%
42	Rhode Island	1,919,000	0.4%
44	Montana	1,730,000	0.4%
45	Delaware	1,705,000	0.4%
46	South Dakota	1,285,000	0.3%
47	North Dakota	1,204,000	0.3%
48	Alaska	1,191,000	0.3%
49	Vermont	1,123,000	0.2%
50	Wyoming	911,000	0.2%
	District of Columbia	1,767,000	0.4%

Source: U.S. Department of Health and Human Services, National Institute on Alcohol Abuse and Alcoholism
"Volume Beverage and Ethanol Consumption for States" (http://silk.nih.gov/silk/niaaa1/database/consum02.txt)
*This is apparent consumption of actual alcohol, not entire volume of an alcoholic beverage (e.g. wine is roughly 11% absolute alcohol content). Apparent consumption is based on several sources which together approximate sales but do not actually measure consumption. Accordingly, figures for some states may be skewed by purchases by nonresidents.

Adult Per Capita Alcohol Consumption in 1997

National Per Capita = 2.5 Gallons Consumed per Adult Age 21 & Older*

ALPHA ORDER

RANK	STATE	PER CAPITA
42	Alabama	2.1
5	Alaska	3.1
7	Arizona	2.9
45	Arkansas	2.0
20	California	2.6
6	Colorado	3.0
25	Connecticut	2.5
3	Delaware	3.2
7	Florida	2.9
25	Georgia	2.5
13	Hawaii	2.7
33	Idaho	2.4
20	Illinois	2.6
36	Indiana	2.2
36	Iowa	2.2
45	Kansas	2.0
45	Kentucky	2.0
7	Louisiana	2.9
25	Maine	2.5
35	Maryland	2.3
13	Massachusetts	2.7
33	Michigan	2.4
13	Minnesota	2.7
25	Mississippi	2.5
25	Missouri	2.5
10	Montana	2.8
25	Nebraska	2.5
2	Nevada	4.5
1	New Hampshire	4.6
25	New Jersey	2.5
10	New Mexico	2.8
36	New York	2.2
36	North Carolina	2.2
13	North Dakota	2.7
36	Ohio	2.2
48	Oklahoma	1.9
20	Oregon	2.6
42	Pennsylvania	2.1
13	Rhode Island	2.7
13	South Carolina	2.7
20	South Dakota	2.6
42	Tennessee	2.1
20	Texas	2.6
50	Utah	1.6
13	Vermont	2.7
36	Virginia	2.2
25	Washington	2.5
49	West Virginia	1.8
3	Wisconsin	3.2
10	Wyoming	2.8

RANK ORDER

RANK	STATE	PER CAPITA
1	New Hampshire	4.6
2	Nevada	4.5
3	Delaware	3.2
3	Wisconsin	3.2
5	Alaska	3.1
6	Colorado	3.0
7	Arizona	2.9
7	Florida	2.9
7	Louisiana	2.9
10	Montana	2.8
10	New Mexico	2.8
10	Wyoming	2.8
13	Hawaii	2.7
13	Massachusetts	2.7
13	Minnesota	2.7
13	North Dakota	2.7
13	Rhode Island	2.7
13	South Carolina	2.7
13	Vermont	2.7
20	California	2.6
20	Illinois	2.6
20	Oregon	2.6
20	South Dakota	2.6
20	Texas	2.6
25	Connecticut	2.5
25	Georgia	2.5
25	Maine	2.5
25	Mississippi	2.5
25	Missouri	2.5
25	Nebraska	2.5
25	New Jersey	2.5
25	Washington	2.5
33	Idaho	2.4
33	Michigan	2.4
35	Maryland	2.3
36	Indiana	2.2
36	Iowa	2.2
36	New York	2.2
36	North Carolina	2.2
36	Ohio	2.2
36	Virginia	2.2
42	Alabama	2.1
42	Pennsylvania	2.1
42	Tennessee	2.1
45	Arkansas	2.0
45	Kansas	2.0
45	Kentucky	2.0
48	Oklahoma	1.9
49	West Virginia	1.8
50	Utah	1.6

	District of Columbia	4.3

Source: Morgan Quitno Press using data from U.S. Department of Health and Human Services, National Institute on Alcohol Abuse and Alcoholism "Volume Beverage and Ethanol Consumption for States"
*This is apparent consumption of actual alcohol, not entire volume of an alcoholic beverage (e.g. wine is roughly 11% absolute alcohol content). Apparent consumption is based on several sources which together approximate sales but do not actually measure consumption. Accordingly, figures for some states may be skewed by purchases by nonresidents.

Percent of Adults Who Abstain from Drinking Alcohol: 1997

National Percent = 50.1% of Adults*

ALPHA ORDER

RANK	STATE	PERCENT
9	Alabama	63.2
33	Alaska	44.8
12	Arizona	58.9
3	Arkansas	69.4
45	California	38.6
46	Colorado	38.0
47	Connecticut	37.9
29	Delaware	45.8
31	Florida	45.2
15	Georgia	55.4
22	Hawaii	48.9
16	Idaho	52.4
30	Illinois	45.3
17	Indiana	51.5
28	Iowa	46.1
13	Kansas	58.7
6	Kentucky	66.3
21	Louisiana	49.4
34	Maine	44.6
14	Maryland	55.6
49	Massachusetts	35.2
38	Michigan	42.6
24	Minnesota	46.5
8	Mississippi	64.9
18	Missouri	50.8
37	Montana	42.8
39	Nebraska	42.0
48	Nevada	37.1
44	New Hampshire	38.7
40	New Jersey	41.7
26	New Mexico	46.4
24	New York	46.5
10	North Carolina	62.4
27	North Dakota	46.3
6	Ohio	66.3
5	Oklahoma	67.2
36	Oregon	43.3
19	Pennsylvania	50.7
41	Rhode Island	40.6
11	South Carolina	60.3
35	South Dakota	44.5
2	Tennessee	71.3
20	Texas	50.6
1	Utah	71.7
42	Vermont	39.8
32	Virginia	45.1
43	Washington	39.6
4	West Virginia	69.0
50	Wisconsin	29.8
23	Wyoming	47.4

RANK ORDER

RANK	STATE	PERCENT
1	Utah	71.7
2	Tennessee	71.3
3	Arkansas	69.4
4	West Virginia	69.0
5	Oklahoma	67.2
6	Kentucky	66.3
6	Ohio	66.3
8	Mississippi	64.9
9	Alabama	63.2
10	North Carolina	62.4
11	South Carolina	60.3
12	Arizona	58.9
13	Kansas	58.7
14	Maryland	55.6
15	Georgia	55.4
16	Idaho	52.4
17	Indiana	51.5
18	Missouri	50.8
19	Pennsylvania	50.7
20	Texas	50.6
21	Louisiana	49.4
22	Hawaii	48.9
23	Wyoming	47.4
24	Minnesota	46.5
24	New York	46.5
26	New Mexico	46.4
27	North Dakota	46.3
28	Iowa	46.1
29	Delaware	45.8
30	Illinois	45.3
31	Florida	45.2
32	Virginia	45.1
33	Alaska	44.8
34	Maine	44.6
35	South Dakota	44.5
36	Oregon	43.3
37	Montana	42.8
38	Michigan	42.6
39	Nebraska	42.0
40	New Jersey	41.7
41	Rhode Island	40.6
42	Vermont	39.8
43	Washington	39.6
44	New Hampshire	38.7
45	California	38.6
46	Colorado	38.0
47	Connecticut	37.9
48	Nevada	37.1
49	Massachusetts	35.2
50	Wisconsin	29.8
	District of Columbia	56.3

Source: U.S. Department of Heath and Human Services, National Institute on Alcohol Abuse and Alcoholism
"Per Capita and Per Drinker Ethanol Consumption for Selected States, 1986-97"
(http://silk.nih.gov/silk/niaaa1/database/consum04.txt)
National average is a simple average of all states.

Apparent Beer Consumption in 1997

National Total = 5,879,132,000 Gallons of Beer Consumed*

ALPHA ORDER

RANK	STATE	GALLONS	% of USA
25	Alabama	88,807,000	1.5%
48	Alaska	13,569,000	0.2%
16	Arizona	121,315,000	2.1%
34	Arkansas	49,949,000	0.8%
1	California	627,850,000	10.7%
24	Colorado	93,210,000	1.6%
32	Connecticut	57,055,000	1.0%
45	Delaware	18,439,000	0.3%
3	Florida	369,357,000	6.3%
9	Georgia	161,788,000	2.8%
39	Hawaii	29,513,000	0.5%
42	Idaho	24,322,000	0.4%
5	Illinois	270,769,000	4.6%
17	Indiana	119,194,000	2.0%
28	Iowa	66,865,000	1.1%
33	Kansas	50,997,000	0.9%
26	Kentucky	75,226,000	1.3%
18	Louisiana	116,143,000	2.0%
41	Maine	26,134,000	0.4%
23	Maryland	95,792,000	1.6%
14	Massachusetts	127,402,000	2.2%
8	Michigan	202,667,000	3.4%
21	Minnesota	104,045,000	1.8%
29	Mississippi	66,745,000	1.1%
15	Missouri	127,040,000	2.2%
43	Montana	23,761,000	0.4%
36	Nebraska	40,276,000	0.7%
31	Nevada	57,686,000	1.0%
38	New Hampshire	36,662,000	0.6%
12	New Jersey	144,225,000	2.5%
35	New Mexico	45,963,000	0.8%
4	New York	312,992,000	5.3%
10	North Carolina	158,271,000	2.7%
47	North Dakota	16,280,000	0.3%
7	Ohio	257,204,000	4.4%
30	Oklahoma	65,561,000	1.1%
27	Oregon	70,741,000	1.2%
6	Pennsylvania	265,867,000	4.5%
44	Rhode Island	22,599,000	0.4%
22	South Carolina	96,207,000	1.6%
46	South Dakota	17,776,000	0.3%
19	Tennessee	114,549,000	1.9%
2	Texas	525,261,000	8.9%
40	Utah	26,707,000	0.5%
49	Vermont	13,238,000	0.2%
13	Virginia	138,220,000	2.4%
20	Washington	112,384,000	1.9%
37	West Virginia	38,145,000	0.6%
11	Wisconsin	147,860,000	2.5%
50	Wyoming	11,800,000	0.2%

RANK ORDER

RANK	STATE	GALLONS	% of USA
1	California	627,850,000	10.7%
2	Texas	525,261,000	8.9%
3	Florida	369,357,000	6.3%
4	New York	312,992,000	5.3%
5	Illinois	270,769,000	4.6%
6	Pennsylvania	265,867,000	4.5%
7	Ohio	257,204,000	4.4%
8	Michigan	202,667,000	3.4%
9	Georgia	161,788,000	2.8%
10	North Carolina	158,271,000	2.7%
11	Wisconsin	147,860,000	2.5%
12	New Jersey	144,225,000	2.5%
13	Virginia	138,220,000	2.4%
14	Massachusetts	127,402,000	2.2%
15	Missouri	127,040,000	2.2%
16	Arizona	121,315,000	2.1%
17	Indiana	119,194,000	2.0%
18	Louisiana	116,143,000	2.0%
19	Tennessee	114,549,000	1.9%
20	Washington	112,384,000	1.9%
21	Minnesota	104,045,000	1.8%
22	South Carolina	96,207,000	1.6%
23	Maryland	95,792,000	1.6%
24	Colorado	93,210,000	1.6%
25	Alabama	88,807,000	1.5%
26	Kentucky	75,226,000	1.3%
27	Oregon	70,741,000	1.2%
28	Iowa	66,865,000	1.1%
29	Mississippi	66,745,000	1.1%
30	Oklahoma	65,561,000	1.1%
31	Nevada	57,686,000	1.0%
32	Connecticut	57,055,000	1.0%
33	Kansas	50,997,000	0.9%
34	Arkansas	49,949,000	0.8%
35	New Mexico	45,963,000	0.8%
36	Nebraska	40,276,000	0.7%
37	West Virginia	38,145,000	0.6%
38	New Hampshire	36,662,000	0.6%
39	Hawaii	29,513,000	0.5%
40	Utah	26,707,000	0.5%
41	Maine	26,134,000	0.4%
42	Idaho	24,322,000	0.4%
43	Montana	23,761,000	0.4%
44	Rhode Island	22,599,000	0.4%
45	Delaware	18,439,000	0.3%
46	South Dakota	17,776,000	0.3%
47	North Dakota	16,280,000	0.3%
48	Alaska	13,569,000	0.2%
49	Vermont	13,238,000	0.2%
50	Wyoming	11,800,000	0.2%
	District of Columbia	14,703,000	0.3%

Source: U.S. Department of Health and Human Services, National Institute on Alcohol Abuse and Alcoholism
"Volume Beverage and Ethanol Consumption for States" (http://silk.nih.gov/silk/niaaa1/database/consum02.txt)
*This is apparent consumption and is based on several sources which together approximate sales but do not actually measure consumption. Reported state volumes reflect only in-state purchases. Accordingly, figures for some states may be skewed by purchases by nonresidents.

Adult Per Capita Beer Consumption in 1997

National Per Capita = 31.5 Gallons Consumed per Adult 21 Years and Older*

ALPHA ORDER

RANK	STATE	PER CAPITA
34	Alabama	29.2
17	Alaska	34.9
8	Arizona	38.9
43	Arkansas	28.5
40	California	28.6
19	Colorado	34.4
49	Connecticut	24.1
16	Delaware	35.0
18	Florida	34.6
27	Georgia	31.3
15	Hawaii	35.2
29	Idaho	30.6
23	Illinois	32.6
36	Indiana	29.1
21	Iowa	33.4
43	Kansas	28.5
45	Kentucky	27.4
6	Louisiana	39.7
34	Maine	29.2
46	Maryland	26.4
40	Massachusetts	28.6
33	Michigan	29.7
24	Minnesota	32.2
10	Mississippi	36.4
20	Missouri	33.7
7	Montana	39.0
14	Nebraska	35.4
1	Nevada	49.1
2	New Hampshire	44.0
47	New Jersey	25.0
5	New Mexico	40.3
48	New York	24.2
31	North Carolina	30.2
9	North Dakota	36.6
22	Ohio	32.7
40	Oklahoma	28.6
28	Oregon	30.9
29	Pennsylvania	30.6
25	Rhode Island	31.7
12	South Carolina	36.1
13	South Dakota	35.6
32	Tennessee	30.0
4	Texas	40.6
50	Utah	21.6
26	Vermont	31.4
38	Virginia	28.7
38	Washington	28.7
37	West Virginia	29.0
3	Wisconsin	40.8
10	Wyoming	36.4

RANK ORDER

RANK	STATE	PER CAPITA
1	Nevada	49.1
2	New Hampshire	44.0
3	Wisconsin	40.8
4	Texas	40.6
5	New Mexico	40.3
6	Louisiana	39.7
7	Montana	39.0
8	Arizona	38.9
9	North Dakota	36.6
10	Mississippi	36.4
10	Wyoming	36.4
12	South Carolina	36.1
13	South Dakota	35.6
14	Nebraska	35.4
15	Hawaii	35.2
16	Delaware	35.0
17	Alaska	34.9
18	Florida	34.6
19	Colorado	34.4
20	Missouri	33.7
21	Iowa	33.4
22	Ohio	32.7
23	Illinois	32.6
24	Minnesota	32.2
25	Rhode Island	31.7
26	Vermont	31.4
27	Georgia	31.3
28	Oregon	30.9
29	Idaho	30.6
29	Pennsylvania	30.6
31	North Carolina	30.2
32	Tennessee	30.0
33	Michigan	29.7
34	Alabama	29.2
34	Maine	29.2
36	Indiana	29.1
37	West Virginia	29.0
38	Virginia	28.7
38	Washington	28.7
40	California	28.6
40	Massachusetts	28.6
40	Oklahoma	28.6
43	Arkansas	28.5
43	Kansas	28.5
45	Kentucky	27.4
46	Maryland	26.4
47	New Jersey	25.0
48	New York	24.2
49	Connecticut	24.1
50	Utah	21.6

	District of Columbia	36.2

Source: Morgan Quitno Press using data from U.S. Department of Health and Human Services, National Institute on Alcohol Abuse and Alcoholism "Volume Beverage and Ethanol Consumption for States"
*This is apparent consumption and is based on several sources which together approximate sales but do not actually measure consumption. Reported state volumes reflect only in-state purchases. Accordingly, figures for some states may be skewed by purchases by nonresidents.

Wine Consumption in 1997

National Total = 508,042,000 Gallons of Wine Consumed*

ALPHA ORDER

RANK	STATE	GALLONS	% of USA
29	Alabama	4,057,000	0.8%
45	Alaska	1,307,000	0.3%
19	Arizona	9,021,000	1.8%
40	Arkansas	1,908,000	0.4%
1	California	97,352,000	19.2%
16	Colorado	9,320,000	1.8%
15	Connecticut	10,144,000	2.0%
38	Delaware	2,154,000	0.4%
3	Florida	35,956,000	7.1%
13	Georgia	11,692,000	2.3%
32	Hawaii	2,818,000	0.6%
33	Idaho	2,662,000	0.5%
4	Illinois	25,720,000	5.1%
23	Indiana	6,915,000	1.4%
39	Iowa	2,142,000	0.4%
37	Kansas	2,254,000	0.4%
30	Kentucky	3,192,000	0.6%
25	Louisiana	6,069,000	1.2%
34	Maine	2,585,000	0.5%
17	Maryland	9,199,000	1.8%
7	Massachusetts	19,337,000	3.8%
10	Michigan	13,538,000	2.7%
21	Minnesota	7,832,000	1.5%
44	Mississippi	1,514,000	0.3%
22	Missouri	7,445,000	1.5%
43	Montana	1,603,000	0.3%
41	Nebraska	1,890,000	0.4%
24	Nevada	6,331,000	1.2%
28	New Hampshire	4,059,000	0.8%
6	New Jersey	21,679,000	4.3%
36	New Mexico	2,461,000	0.5%
2	New York	42,931,000	8.5%
14	North Carolina	10,869,000	2.1%
49	North Dakota	519,000	0.1%
12	Ohio	12,443,000	2.4%
35	Oklahoma	2,553,000	0.5%
18	Oregon	9,139,000	1.8%
8	Pennsylvania	14,989,000	3.0%
31	Rhode Island	2,865,000	0.6%
27	South Carolina	4,522,000	0.9%
48	South Dakota	599,000	0.1%
26	Tennessee	5,540,000	1.1%
5	Texas	23,979,000	4.7%
46	Utah	1,285,000	0.3%
42	Vermont	1,736,000	0.3%
11	Virginia	12,497,000	2.5%
9	Washington	14,883,000	2.9%
47	West Virginia	1,112,000	0.2%
20	Wisconsin	8,223,000	1.6%
50	Wyoming	505,000	0.1%

RANK ORDER

RANK	STATE	GALLONS	% of USA
1	California	97,352,000	19.2%
2	New York	42,931,000	8.5%
3	Florida	35,956,000	7.1%
4	Illinois	25,720,000	5.1%
5	Texas	23,979,000	4.7%
6	New Jersey	21,679,000	4.3%
7	Massachusetts	19,337,000	3.8%
8	Pennsylvania	14,989,000	3.0%
9	Washington	14,883,000	2.9%
10	Michigan	13,538,000	2.7%
11	Virginia	12,497,000	2.5%
12	Ohio	12,443,000	2.4%
13	Georgia	11,692,000	2.3%
14	North Carolina	10,869,000	2.1%
15	Connecticut	10,144,000	2.0%
16	Colorado	9,320,000	1.8%
17	Maryland	9,199,000	1.8%
18	Oregon	9,139,000	1.8%
19	Arizona	9,021,000	1.8%
20	Wisconsin	8,223,000	1.6%
21	Minnesota	7,832,000	1.5%
22	Missouri	7,445,000	1.5%
23	Indiana	6,915,000	1.4%
24	Nevada	6,331,000	1.2%
25	Louisiana	6,069,000	1.2%
26	Tennessee	5,540,000	1.1%
27	South Carolina	4,522,000	0.9%
28	New Hampshire	4,059,000	0.8%
29	Alabama	4,057,000	0.8%
30	Kentucky	3,192,000	0.6%
31	Rhode Island	2,865,000	0.6%
32	Hawaii	2,818,000	0.6%
33	Idaho	2,662,000	0.5%
34	Maine	2,585,000	0.5%
35	Oklahoma	2,553,000	0.5%
36	New Mexico	2,461,000	0.5%
37	Kansas	2,254,000	0.4%
38	Delaware	2,154,000	0.4%
39	Iowa	2,142,000	0.4%
40	Arkansas	1,908,000	0.4%
41	Nebraska	1,890,000	0.4%
42	Vermont	1,736,000	0.3%
43	Montana	1,603,000	0.3%
44	Mississippi	1,514,000	0.3%
45	Alaska	1,307,000	0.3%
46	Utah	1,285,000	0.3%
47	West Virginia	1,112,000	0.2%
48	South Dakota	599,000	0.1%
49	North Dakota	519,000	0.1%
50	Wyoming	505,000	0.1%
	District of Columbia	2,696,000	0.5%

Source: U.S. Department of Health and Human Services, National Institute on Alcohol Abuse and Alcoholism
   "Volume Beverage and Ethanol Consumption for States" (http://sllk.nlh.gov/silk/niaaa1/database/consum02.txt)
*This is apparent consumption and is based on several sources which together approximate sales but do not actually measure consumption. Reported state volumes reflect only in-state purchases. Accordingly, figures for some states may be skewed by purchases by nonresidents.

Adult Per Capita Wine Consumption in 1997

National Per Capita = 2.7 Gallons Consumed per Adult Age 21 Years and Older*

ALPHA ORDER

RANK	STATE	PER CAPITA
40	Alabama	1.3
12	Alaska	3.4
19	Arizona	2.9
45	Arkansas	1.1
3	California	4.4
12	Colorado	3.4
4	Connecticut	4.3
6	Delaware	4.1
12	Florida	3.4
25	Georgia	2.3
12	Hawaii	3.4
12	Idaho	3.4
18	Illinois	3.1
33	Indiana	1.7
45	Iowa	1.1
40	Kansas	1.3
42	Kentucky	1.2
28	Louisiana	2.1
19	Maine	2.9
23	Maryland	2.5
4	Massachusetts	4.3
30	Michigan	2.0
24	Minnesota	2.4
49	Mississippi	0.8
30	Missouri	2.0
21	Montana	2.6
33	Nebraska	1.7
1	Nevada	5.4
2	New Hampshire	4.9
10	New Jersey	3.8
27	New Mexico	2.2
17	New York	3.3
28	North Carolina	2.1
42	North Dakota	1.2
37	Ohio	1.6
45	Oklahoma	1.1
8	Oregon	4.0
33	Pennsylvania	1.7
8	Rhode Island	4.0
33	South Carolina	1.7
42	South Dakota	1.2
39	Tennessee	1.5
32	Texas	1.9
48	Utah	1.0
6	Vermont	4.1
21	Virginia	2.6
10	Washington	3.8
49	West Virginia	0.8
25	Wisconsin	2.3
37	Wyoming	1.6

RANK ORDER

RANK	STATE	PER CAPITA
1	Nevada	5.4
2	New Hampshire	4.9
3	California	4.4
4	Connecticut	4.3
4	Massachusetts	4.3
6	Delaware	4.1
6	Vermont	4.1
8	Oregon	4.0
8	Rhode Island	4.0
10	New Jersey	3.8
10	Washington	3.8
12	Alaska	3.4
12	Colorado	3.4
12	Florida	3.4
12	Hawaii	3.4
12	Idaho	3.4
17	New York	3.3
18	Illinois	3.1
19	Arizona	2.9
19	Maine	2.9
21	Montana	2.6
21	Virginia	2.6
23	Maryland	2.5
24	Minnesota	2.4
25	Georgia	2.3
25	Wisconsin	2.3
27	New Mexico	2.2
28	Louisiana	2.1
28	North Carolina	2.1
30	Michigan	2.0
30	Missouri	2.0
32	Texas	1.9
33	Indiana	1.7
33	Nebraska	1.7
33	Pennsylvania	1.7
33	South Carolina	1.7
37	Ohio	1.6
37	Wyoming	1.6
39	Tennessee	1.5
40	Alabama	1.3
40	Kansas	1.3
42	Kentucky	1.2
42	North Dakota	1.2
42	South Dakota	1.2
45	Arkansas	1.1
45	Iowa	1.1
45	Oklahoma	1.1
48	Utah	1.0
49	Mississippi	0.8
49	West Virginia	0.8

| | District of Columbia | 6.6 |

Source: Morgan Quitno Press using data from U.S. Department of Health and Human Services, National Institute on Alcohol Abuse and Alcoholism "Volume Beverage and Ethanol Consumption for States"

*This is apparent consumption and is based on several sources which together approximate sales but do not actually measure consumption. Reported state volumes reflect only in-state purchases. Accordingly, figures for some states may be skewed by purchases by nonresidents.

Distilled Spirits Consumption in 1997

National Total = 329,882,000 Gallons of Distilled Spirits Consumed*

ALPHA ORDER

RANK	STATE	GALLONS	% of USA
27	Alabama	4,427,000	1.3%
46	Alaska	1,002,000	0.3%
21	Arizona	6,214,000	1.9%
33	Arkansas	2,619,000	0.8%
1	California	38,152,000	11.6%
20	Colorado	6,321,000	1.9%
25	Connecticut	4,837,000	1.5%
40	Delaware	1,453,000	0.4%
2	Florida	24,258,000	7.4%
9	Georgia	10,382,000	3.1%
42	Hawaii	1,310,000	0.4%
44	Idaho	1,171,000	0.4%
5	Illinois	15,423,000	4.7%
17	Indiana	6,808,000	2.1%
34	Iowa	2,567,000	0.8%
35	Kansas	2,436,000	0.7%
28	Kentucky	4,108,000	1.2%
22	Louisiana	6,002,000	1.8%
38	Maine	1,767,000	0.5%
15	Maryland	7,341,000	2.2%
11	Massachusetts	9,360,000	2.8%
6	Michigan	12,614,000	3.8%
14	Minnesota	7,701,000	2.3%
31	Mississippi	3,238,000	1.0%
18	Missouri	6,688,000	2.0%
45	Montana	1,104,000	0.3%
37	Nebraska	1,847,000	0.6%
26	Nevada	4,459,000	1.4%
29	New Hampshire	4,088,000	1.2%
7	New Jersey	11,937,000	3.6%
36	New Mexico	1,941,000	0.6%
3	New York	20,614,000	6.2%
13	North Carolina	7,755,000	2.4%
48	North Dakota	985,000	0.3%
10	Ohio	10,076,000	3.1%
32	Oklahoma	2,812,000	0.9%
30	Oregon	3,909,000	1.2%
8	Pennsylvania	10,768,000	3.3%
43	Rhode Island	1,296,000	0.4%
24	South Carolina	5,344,000	1.6%
47	South Dakota	993,000	0.3%
23	Tennessee	5,424,000	1.6%
4	Texas	17,672,000	5.4%
39	Utah	1,492,000	0.5%
50	Vermont	737,000	0.2%
19	Virginia	6,407,000	1.9%
16	Washington	6,899,000	2.1%
41	West Virginia	1,360,000	0.4%
12	Wisconsin	9,155,000	2.8%
49	Wyoming	766,000	0.2%

RANK ORDER

RANK	STATE	GALLONS	% of USA
1	California	38,152,000	11.6%
2	Florida	24,258,000	7.4%
3	New York	20,614,000	6.2%
4	Texas	17,672,000	5.4%
5	Illinois	15,423,000	4.7%
6	Michigan	12,614,000	3.8%
7	New Jersey	11,937,000	3.6%
8	Pennsylvania	10,768,000	3.3%
9	Georgia	10,382,000	3.1%
10	Ohio	10,076,000	3.1%
11	Massachusetts	9,360,000	2.8%
12	Wisconsin	9,155,000	2.8%
13	North Carolina	7,755,000	2.4%
14	Minnesota	7,701,000	2.3%
15	Maryland	7,341,000	2.2%
16	Washington	6,899,000	2.1%
17	Indiana	6,808,000	2.1%
18	Missouri	6,688,000	2.0%
19	Virginia	6,407,000	1.9%
20	Colorado	6,321,000	1.9%
21	Arizona	6,214,000	1.9%
22	Louisiana	6,002,000	1.8%
23	Tennessee	5,424,000	1.6%
24	South Carolina	5,344,000	1.6%
25	Connecticut	4,837,000	1.5%
26	Nevada	4,459,000	1.4%
27	Alabama	4,427,000	1.3%
28	Kentucky	4,108,000	1.2%
29	New Hampshire	4,088,000	1.2%
30	Oregon	3,909,000	1.2%
31	Mississippi	3,238,000	1.0%
32	Oklahoma	2,812,000	0.9%
33	Arkansas	2,619,000	0.8%
34	Iowa	2,567,000	0.8%
35	Kansas	2,436,000	0.7%
36	New Mexico	1,941,000	0.6%
37	Nebraska	1,847,000	0.6%
38	Maine	1,767,000	0.5%
39	Utah	1,492,000	0.5%
40	Delaware	1,453,000	0.4%
41	West Virginia	1,360,000	0.4%
42	Hawaii	1,310,000	0.4%
43	Rhode Island	1,296,000	0.4%
44	Idaho	1,171,000	0.4%
45	Montana	1,104,000	0.3%
46	Alaska	1,002,000	0.3%
47	South Dakota	993,000	0.3%
48	North Dakota	985,000	0.3%
49	Wyoming	766,000	0.2%
50	Vermont	737,000	0.2%
	District of Columbia	1,843,000	0.6%

Source: U.S. Department of Health and Human Services, National Institute on Alcohol Abuse and Alcoholism
"Volume Beverage and Ethanol Consumption for States" (http://silk.nih.gov/silk/niaaa1/database/consum02.txt)
*This is apparent consumption and is based on several sources which together approximate sales but do not actually measure consumption. Reported state volumes reflect only in-state purchases. Accordingly, figures for some states may be skewed by purchases by nonresidents.

Adult Per Capita Apparent Distilled Spirits Consumption in 1997

National Per Capita = 1.8 Gallons Consumed per Adult 21 Years and Older*

ALPHA ORDER

RANK ORDER

RANK	STATE	PER CAPITA
36	Alabama	1.5
4	Alaska	2.6
14	Arizona	2.0
36	Arkansas	1.5
28	California	1.7
8	Colorado	2.3
14	Connecticut	2.0
3	Delaware	2.8
8	Florida	2.3
14	Georgia	2.0
33	Hawaii	1.6
36	Idaho	1.5
21	Illinois	1.9
28	Indiana	1.7
44	Iowa	1.3
41	Kansas	1.4
36	Kentucky	1.5
11	Louisiana	2.1
14	Maine	2.0
14	Maryland	2.0
11	Massachusetts	2.1
21	Michigan	1.9
6	Minnesota	2.4
23	Mississippi	1.8
23	Missouri	1.8
23	Montana	1.8
33	Nebraska	1.6
2	Nevada	3.8
1	New Hampshire	4.9
11	New Jersey	2.1
28	New Mexico	1.7
33	New York	1.6
36	North Carolina	1.5
10	North Dakota	2.2
44	Ohio	1.3
47	Oklahoma	1.2
28	Oregon	1.7
47	Pennsylvania	1.2
23	Rhode Island	1.8
14	South Carolina	2.0
14	South Dakota	2.0
41	Tennessee	1.4
41	Texas	1.4
47	Utah	1.2
28	Vermont	1.7
44	Virginia	1.3
23	Washington	1.8
50	West Virginia	1.0
5	Wisconsin	2.5
6	Wyoming	2.4

RANK	STATE	PER CAPITA
1	New Hampshire	4.9
2	Nevada	3.8
3	Delaware	2.8
4	Alaska	2.6
5	Wisconsin	2.5
6	Minnesota	2.4
6	Wyoming	2.4
8	Colorado	2.3
8	Florida	2.3
10	North Dakota	2.2
11	Louisiana	2.1
11	Massachusetts	2.1
11	New Jersey	2.1
14	Arizona	2.0
14	Connecticut	2.0
14	Georgia	2.0
14	Maine	2.0
14	Maryland	2.0
14	South Carolina	2.0
14	South Dakota	2.0
21	Illinois	1.9
21	Michigan	1.9
23	Mississippi	1.8
23	Missouri	1.8
23	Montana	1.8
23	Rhode Island	1.8
23	Washington	1.8
28	California	1.7
28	Indiana	1.7
28	New Mexico	1.7
28	Oregon	1.7
28	Vermont	1.7
33	Hawaii	1.6
33	Nebraska	1.6
33	New York	1.6
36	Alabama	1.5
36	Arkansas	1.5
36	Idaho	1.5
36	Kentucky	1.5
36	North Carolina	1.5
41	Kansas	1.4
41	Tennessee	1.4
41	Texas	1.4
44	Iowa	1.3
44	Ohio	1.3
44	Virginia	1.3
47	Oklahoma	1.2
47	Pennsylvania	1.2
47	Utah	1.2
50	West Virginia	1.0

| | District of Columbia | 4.5 |

Source: Morgan Quitno Press using data from U.S. Department of Health and Human Services, National Institute on Alcohol Abuse and Alcoholism "Volume Beverage and Ethanol Consumption for States"
*This is apparent consumption and is based on several sources which together approximate sales but do not actually measure consumption. Reported state volumes reflect only in-state purchases. Accordingly, figures for some states may be skewed by purchases by nonresidents.

Percent of Adults Who Are Binge Drinkers: 1997

National Median = 14.5% of Adults*

ALPHA ORDER				RANK ORDER		
RANK	STATE	PERCENT		RANK	STATE	PERCENT
36	Alabama	11.4		1	Wisconsin	23.3
10	Alaska	16.5		2	South Dakota	20.9
44	Arizona	8.8		3	Nevada	19.2
41	Arkansas	9.2		4	Michigan	18.9
19	California	15.2		5	North Dakota	18.4
18	Colorado	15.3		6	Iowa	17.9
15	Connecticut	15.6		6	Massachusetts	17.9
35	Delaware	11.9		8	Texas	17.4
32	Florida	13.1		9	Hawaii	17.1
39	Georgia	9.4		10	Alaska	16.5
9	Hawaii	17.1		11	Illinois	16.3
22	Idaho	14.9		11	Nebraska	16.3
11	Illinois	16.3		13	New Hampshire	16.1
34	Indiana	12.6		13	Vermont	16.1
6	Iowa	17.9		15	Connecticut	15.6
31	Kansas	13.3		15	Minnesota	15.6
39	Kentucky	9.4		17	Wyoming	15.4
19	Louisiana	15.2		18	Colorado	15.3
30	Maine	13.8		19	California	15.2
50	Maryland	6.3		19	Louisiana	15.2
6	Massachusetts	17.9		21	Missouri	15.1
4	Michigan	18.9		22	Idaho	14.9
15	Minnesota	15.6		22	Rhode Island	14.9
38	Mississippi	9.5		24	New Mexico	14.6
21	Missouri	15.1		24	Pennsylvania	14.6
29	Montana	14.0		26	Virginia	14.5
11	Nebraska	16.3		26	Washington	14.5
3	Nevada	19.2		28	Oregon	14.3
13	New Hampshire	16.1		29	Montana	14.0
32	New Jersey	13.1		30	Maine	13.8
24	New Mexico	14.6		31	Kansas	13.3
41	New York	9.2		32	Florida	13.1
43	North Carolina	9.0		32	New Jersey	13.1
5	North Dakota	18.4		34	Indiana	12.6
46	Ohio	8.7		35	Delaware	11.9
44	Oklahoma	8.8		36	Alabama	11.4
28	Oregon	14.3		37	South Carolina	9.7
24	Pennsylvania	14.6		38	Mississippi	9.5
22	Rhode Island	14.9		39	Georgia	9.4
37	South Carolina	9.7		39	Kentucky	9.4
2	South Dakota	20.9		41	Arkansas	9.2
49	Tennessee	7.2		41	New York	9.2
8	Texas	17.4		43	North Carolina	9.0
48	Utah	7.7		44	Arizona	8.8
13	Vermont	16.1		44	Oklahoma	8.8
26	Virginia	14.5		46	Ohio	8.7
26	Washington	14.5		47	West Virginia	8.4
47	West Virginia	8.4		48	Utah	7.7
1	Wisconsin	23.3		49	Tennessee	7.2
17	Wyoming	15.4		50	Maryland	6.3
					District of Columbia	12.1

Source: U.S. Department of Health and Human Services, Centers for Disease Control and Prevention
"1997 Behavioral Risk Factor Surveillance Summary Prevalence Report" (August 17, 1998)
Persons 18 and older reporting consumption of five or more alcoholic drinks on one or more occasions during the previous month.

Percent of Adults Who Smoke: 1998

National Percent = 22.9% of Adults*

RANK	STATE	PERCENT
14	Alabama	24.6
7	Alaska	26.1
36	Arizona	21.9
11	Arkansas	25.9
47	California	19.2
27	Colorado	22.8
40	Connecticut	21.2
16	Delaware	24.4
34	Florida	22.0
21	Georgia	23.6
46	Hawaii	19.5
44	Idaho	20.3
25	Illinois	23.1
10	Indiana	26.0
22	Iowa	23.4
41	Kansas	21.1
1	Kentucky	30.8
12	Louisiana	25.5
31	Maine	22.4
31	Maryland	22.4
43	Massachusetts	20.9
4	Michigan	27.4
49	Minnesota	18.0
17	Mississippi	24.1
6	Missouri	26.4
38	Montana	21.5
34	Nebraska	22.0
2	Nevada	30.4
24	New Hampshire	23.3
48	New Jersey	19.1
29	New Mexico	22.6
17	New York	24.1
14	North Carolina	24.6
45	North Dakota	20.0
7	Ohio	26.1
19	Oklahoma	23.9
41	Oregon	21.1
20	Pennsylvania	23.8
29	Rhode Island	22.6
13	South Carolina	24.7
5	South Dakota	27.2
7	Tennessee	26.1
36	Texas	21.9
50	Utah	14.2
33	Vermont	22.3
26	Virginia	22.9
39	Washington	21.4
3	West Virginia	27.9
22	Wisconsin	23.4
27	Wyoming	22.8

RANK	STATE	PERCENT
1	Kentucky	30.8
2	Nevada	30.4
3	West Virginia	27.9
4	Michigan	27.4
5	South Dakota	27.2
6	Missouri	26.4
7	Alaska	26.1
7	Ohio	26.1
7	Tennessee	26.1
10	Indiana	26.0
11	Arkansas	25.9
12	Louisiana	25.5
13	South Carolina	24.7
14	Alabama	24.6
14	North Carolina	24.6
16	Delaware	24.4
17	Mississippi	24.1
17	New York	24.1
19	Oklahoma	23.9
20	Pennsylvania	23.8
21	Georgia	23.6
22	Iowa	23.4
22	Wisconsin	23.4
24	New Hampshire	23.3
25	Illinois	23.1
26	Virginia	22.9
27	Colorado	22.8
27	Wyoming	22.8
29	New Mexico	22.6
29	Rhode Island	22.6
31	Maine	22.4
31	Maryland	22.4
33	Vermont	22.3
34	Florida	22.0
34	Nebraska	22.0
36	Arizona	21.9
36	Texas	21.9
38	Montana	21.5
39	Washington	21.4
40	Connecticut	21.2
41	Kansas	21.1
41	Oregon	21.1
43	Massachusetts	20.9
44	Idaho	20.3
45	North Dakota	20.0
46	Hawaii	19.5
47	California	19.2
48	New Jersey	19.1
49	Minnesota	18.0
50	Utah	14.2
	District of Columbia	21.6

Source: U.S. Department of Health and Human Services, Centers for Disease Control and Prevention "1998 Behavioral Risk Factor Surveillance Summary Prevalence Report" (June 18, 1999)
*Persons 18 and older who have ever smoked 100 cigarettes and currently smoke.

Percent of Men Who Smoke: 1998

National Median = 25.3% of Men*

RANK	STATE	PERCENT		RANK	STATE	PERCENT
17	Alabama	27.2		1	South Dakota	36.5
12	Alaska	28.3		2	Kentucky	33.4
29	Arizona	24.6		3	Nevada	32.6
11	Arkansas	28.5		4	Michigan	30.3
42	California	21.9		5	Tennessee	30.2
20	Colorado	26.4		6	South Carolina	29.8
41	Connecticut	22.1		7	Ohio	29.7
16	Delaware	27.3		7	West Virginia	29.7
36	Florida	23.4		9	Indiana	29.6
14	Georgia	28.0		10	Missouri	29.4
40	Hawaii	22.2		11	Arkansas	28.5
42	Idaho	21.9		12	Alaska	28.3
21	Illinois	25.9		13	Louisiana	28.2
9	Indiana	29.6		14	Georgia	28.0
21	Iowa	25.9		15	North Carolina	27.4
37	Kansas	23.0		16	Delaware	27.3
2	Kentucky	33.4		17	Alabama	27.2
13	Louisiana	28.2		18	Mississippi	26.9
47	Maine	21.2		19	Oklahoma	26.7
30	Maryland	24.3		20	Colorado	26.4
38	Massachusetts	22.5		21	Illinois	25.9
4	Michigan	30.3		21	Iowa	25.9
49	Minnesota	19.7		23	Virginia	25.8
18	Mississippi	26.9		24	New Hampshire	25.7
10	Missouri	29.4		25	New York	25.6
46	Montana	21.5		26	Nebraska	25.3
26	Nebraska	25.3		26	Texas	25.3
3	Nevada	32.6		28	New Mexico	25.1
24	New Hampshire	25.7		29	Arizona	24.6
48	New Jersey	20.9		30	Maryland	24.3
28	New Mexico	25.1		31	Pennsylvania	24.1
25	New York	25.6		32	Rhode Island	24.0
15	North Carolina	27.4		32	Wisconsin	24.0
44	North Dakota	21.8		34	Wyoming	23.9
7	Ohio	29.7		35	Vermont	23.7
19	Oklahoma	26.7		36	Florida	23.4
45	Oregon	21.6		37	Kansas	23.0
31	Pennsylvania	24.1		38	Massachusetts	22.5
32	Rhode Island	24.0		39	Washington	22.4
6	South Carolina	29.8		40	Hawaii	22.2
1	South Dakota	36.5		41	Connecticut	22.1
5	Tennessee	30.2		42	California	21.9
26	Texas	25.3		42	Idaho	21.9
50	Utah	16.0		44	North Dakota	21.8
35	Vermont	23.7		45	Oregon	21.6
23	Virginia	25.8		46	Montana	21.5
39	Washington	22.4		47	Maine	21.2
7	West Virginia	29.7		48	New Jersey	20.9
32	Wisconsin	24.0		49	Minnesota	19.7
34	Wyoming	23.9		50	Utah	16.0
					District of Columbia	24.4

Source: U.S. Department of Health and Human Services, Centers for Disease Control and Prevention "1998 Behavioral Risk Factor Surveillance Summary Prevalence Report" (June 18, 1999)
Persons 18 and older who have ever smoked 100 cigarettes and currently smoke.

Percent of Women Who Smoke: 1998

National Percent = 20.8% of Women*

RANK	STATE	PERCENT
15	Alabama	22.3
5	Alaska	23.7
40	Arizona	19.2
5	Arkansas	23.7
48	California	16.6
38	Colorado	19.4
31	Connecticut	20.4
18	Delaware	21.8
28	Florida	20.6
36	Georgia	19.7
47	Hawaii	16.7
43	Idaho	18.7
28	Illinois	20.6
14	Indiana	22.7
24	Iowa	21.1
38	Kansas	19.4
1	Kentucky	28.5
10	Louisiana	23.1
8	Maine	23.5
27	Maryland	20.7
37	Massachusetts	19.5
4	Michigan	24.8
49	Minnesota	16.4
20	Mississippi	21.6
7	Missouri	23.6
21	Montana	21.4
41	Nebraska	19.1
2	Nevada	28.0
25	New Hampshire	21.0
46	New Jersey	17.4
33	New Mexico	20.2
11	New York	22.8
17	North Carolina	22.2
45	North Dakota	18.3
11	Ohio	22.8
23	Oklahoma	21.2
30	Oregon	20.5
8	Pennsylvania	23.5
22	Rhode Island	21.3
35	South Carolina	20.1
44	South Dakota	18.4
15	Tennessee	22.3
42	Texas	18.8
50	Utah	12.6
25	Vermont	21.0
33	Virginia	20.2
31	Washington	20.4
3	West Virginia	26.4
11	Wisconsin	22.8
18	Wyoming	21.8

RANK	STATE	PERCENT
1	Kentucky	28.5
2	Nevada	28.0
3	West Virginia	26.4
4	Michigan	24.8
5	Alaska	23.7
5	Arkansas	23.7
7	Missouri	23.6
8	Maine	23.5
8	Pennsylvania	23.5
10	Louisiana	23.1
11	New York	22.8
11	Ohio	22.8
11	Wisconsin	22.8
14	Indiana	22.7
15	Alabama	22.3
15	Tennessee	22.3
17	North Carolina	22.2
18	Delaware	21.8
18	Wyoming	21.8
20	Mississippi	21.6
21	Montana	21.4
22	Rhode Island	21.3
23	Oklahoma	21.2
24	Iowa	21.1
25	New Hampshire	21.0
25	Vermont	21.0
27	Maryland	20.7
28	Florida	20.6
28	Illinois	20.6
30	Oregon	20.5
31	Connecticut	20.4
31	Washington	20.4
33	New Mexico	20.2
33	Virginia	20.2
35	South Carolina	20.1
36	Georgia	19.7
37	Massachusetts	19.5
38	Colorado	19.4
38	Kansas	19.4
40	Arizona	19.2
41	Nebraska	19.1
42	Texas	18.8
43	Idaho	18.7
44	South Dakota	18.4
45	North Dakota	18.3
46	New Jersey	17.4
47	Hawaii	16.7
48	California	16.6
49	Minnesota	16.4
50	Utah	12.6
	District of Columbia	19.3

Source: U.S. Department of Health and Human Services, Centers for Disease Control and Prevention
"1998 Behavioral Risk Factor Surveillance Summary Prevalence Report" (June 18, 1999)
Persons 18 and older who have ever smoked 100 cigarettes and currently smoke.

Percent of Adults Who Smoke Cigars: 1998

National Median = 5.2% of Adults*

RANK	STATE	PERCENT
8	Alabama	6.3
12	Alaska	6.1
50	Arizona	1.4
22	Arkansas	5.4
13	California	5.9
35	Colorado	4.4
23	Connecticut	5.2
31	Delaware	4.9
9	Florida	6.2
13	Georgia	5.9
45	Hawaii	3.7
36	Idaho	4.3
3	Illinois	7.1
2	Indiana	7.3
23	Iowa	5.2
47	Kansas	2.8
20	Kentucky	5.5
39	Louisiana	4.1
39	Maine	4.1
29	Maryland	5.0
13	Massachusetts	5.9
4	Michigan	6.9
36	Minnesota	4.3
29	Mississippi	5.0
9	Missouri	6.2
39	Montana	4.1
23	Nebraska	5.2
1	Nevada	7.4
13	New Hampshire	5.9
5	New Jersey	6.6
38	New Mexico	4.2
9	New York	6.2
33	North Carolina	4.5
42	North Dakota	4.0
17	Ohio	5.7
49	Oklahoma	2.3
32	Oregon	4.8
6	Pennsylvania	6.5
20	Rhode Island	5.5
19	South Carolina	5.6
23	South Dakota	5.2
43	Tennessee	3.9
33	Texas	4.5
48	Utah	2.5
27	Vermont	5.1
17	Virginia	5.7
27	Washington	5.1
44	West Virginia	3.8
6	Wisconsin	6.5
46	Wyoming	3.5

RANK	STATE	PERCENT
1	Nevada	7.4
2	Indiana	7.3
3	Illinois	7.1
4	Michigan	6.9
5	New Jersey	6.6
6	Pennsylvania	6.5
6	Wisconsin	6.5
8	Alabama	6.3
9	Florida	6.2
9	Missouri	6.2
9	New York	6.2
12	Alaska	6.1
13	California	5.9
13	Georgia	5.9
13	Massachusetts	5.9
13	New Hampshire	5.9
17	Ohio	5.7
17	Virginia	5.7
19	South Carolina	5.6
20	Kentucky	5.5
20	Rhode Island	5.5
22	Arkansas	5.4
23	Connecticut	5.2
23	Iowa	5.2
23	Nebraska	5.2
23	South Dakota	5.2
27	Vermont	5.1
27	Washington	5.1
29	Maryland	5.0
29	Mississippi	5.0
31	Delaware	4.9
32	Oregon	4.8
33	North Carolina	4.5
33	Texas	4.5
35	Colorado	4.4
36	Idaho	4.3
36	Minnesota	4.3
38	New Mexico	4.2
39	Louisiana	4.1
39	Maine	4.1
39	Montana	4.1
42	North Dakota	4.0
43	Tennessee	3.9
44	West Virginia	3.8
45	Hawaii	3.7
46	Wyoming	3.5
47	Kansas	2.8
48	Utah	2.5
49	Oklahoma	2.3
50	Arizona	1.4

	District of Columbia	3.8

Source: U.S. Department of Health and Human Services, Centers for Disease Control and Prevention
"State-Specific Prevalence of Current Cigarette and Cigar Smoking Among Adults"
(Morbidity Mortality Weekly Report, Vol. 48, No. 45, November 19, 1999)
*By state of residence. Persons 18 and older who reported smoking a cigar within the previous month.

Percent of Adults Overweight: 1998

National Percent = 32.4% of Adults*

ALPHA ORDER

RANK	STATE	PERCENT
5	Alabama	35.8
3	Alaska	36.2
50	Arizona	22.5
19	Arkansas	33.4
33	California	31.0
47	Colorado	27.2
45	Connecticut	27.4
21	Delaware	32.8
27	Florida	32.3
20	Georgia	33.3
44	Hawaii	27.8
36	Idaho	29.9
17	Illinois	33.5
13	Indiana	34.5
10	Iowa	34.6
31	Kansas	31.7
5	Kentucky	35.8
4	Louisiana	36.1
32	Maine	31.2
13	Maryland	34.5
49	Massachusetts	26.9
10	Michigan	34.6
24	Minnesota	32.5
2	Mississippi	37.5
7	Missouri	35.6
39	Montana	29.1
27	Nebraska	32.3
48	Nevada	27.0
41	New Hampshire	28.7
38	New Jersey	29.7
36	New Mexico	29.9
42	New York	28.6
23	North Carolina	32.7
17	North Dakota	33.5
16	Ohio	33.6
25	Oklahoma	32.4
21	Oregon	32.8
9	Pennsylvania	34.8
35	Rhode Island	30.3
10	South Carolina	34.6
34	South Dakota	30.5
25	Tennessee	32.4
8	Texas	34.9
40	Utah	28.8
45	Vermont	27.4
30	Virginia	31.8
27	Washington	32.3
1	West Virginia	37.8
15	Wisconsin	34.0
43	Wyoming	28.1

RANK ORDER

RANK	STATE	PERCENT
1	West Virginia	37.8
2	Mississippi	37.5
3	Alaska	36.2
4	Louisiana	36.1
5	Alabama	35.8
5	Kentucky	35.8
7	Missouri	35.6
8	Texas	34.9
9	Pennsylvania	34.8
10	Iowa	34.6
10	Michigan	34.6
10	South Carolina	34.6
13	Indiana	34.5
13	Maryland	34.5
15	Wisconsin	34.0
16	Ohio	33.6
17	Illinois	33.5
17	North Dakota	33.5
19	Arkansas	33.4
20	Georgia	33.3
21	Delaware	32.8
21	Oregon	32.8
23	North Carolina	32.7
24	Minnesota	32.5
25	Oklahoma	32.4
25	Tennessee	32.4
27	Florida	32.3
27	Nebraska	32.3
27	Washington	32.3
30	Virginia	31.8
31	Kansas	31.7
32	Maine	31.2
33	California	31.0
34	South Dakota	30.5
35	Rhode Island	30.3
36	Idaho	29.9
36	New Mexico	29.9
38	New Jersey	29.7
39	Montana	29.1
40	Utah	28.8
41	New Hampshire	28.7
42	New York	28.6
43	Wyoming	28.1
44	Hawaii	27.8
45	Connecticut	27.4
45	Vermont	27.4
47	Colorado	27.2
48	Nevada	27.0
49	Massachusetts	26.9
50	Arizona	22.5
	District of Columbia	31.8

Source: U.S. Department of Health and Human Services, Centers for Disease Control and Prevention
"1998 Behavioral Risk Factor Surveillance Summary Prevalence Report" (June 18, 1999)
*Persons 18 and older. Overweight is defined as men with a Body Mass Index (BMI) of 27.8 or greater and women with an index of 27.3 or greater. BMI is a ratio of height to weight. As an example, a person 5' 8" and weighing 185 pounds has a BMI of 28. See http://www.mealformation.com/bmassidx.htm.

506

Number of Days in Past Month When Physical Health was "Not Good": 1998

National Median = 3.1 Days*

<table>
<tr><td colspan="3">ALPHA ORDER</td><td colspan="3">RANK ORDER</td></tr>
<tr><td>RANK</td><td>STATE</td><td>DAYS</td><td>RANK</td><td>STATE</td><td>DAYS</td></tr>
<tr><td>1</td><td>Alabama</td><td>4.2</td><td>1</td><td>Alabama</td><td>4.2</td></tr>
<tr><td>40</td><td>Alaska</td><td>2.8</td><td>2</td><td>Michigan</td><td>3.7</td></tr>
<tr><td>50</td><td>Arizona</td><td>1.1</td><td>2</td><td>Mississippi</td><td>3.7</td></tr>
<tr><td>5</td><td>Arkansas</td><td>3.6</td><td>2</td><td>North Carolina</td><td>3.7</td></tr>
<tr><td>23</td><td>California</td><td>3.1</td><td>5</td><td>Arkansas</td><td>3.6</td></tr>
<tr><td>35</td><td>Colorado</td><td>2.9</td><td>5</td><td>Kentucky</td><td>3.6</td></tr>
<tr><td>35</td><td>Connecticut</td><td>2.9</td><td>7</td><td>New Mexico</td><td>3.5</td></tr>
<tr><td>19</td><td>Delaware</td><td>3.2</td><td>8</td><td>Florida</td><td>3.4</td></tr>
<tr><td>8</td><td>Florida</td><td>3.4</td><td>8</td><td>Missouri</td><td>3.4</td></tr>
<tr><td>30</td><td>Georgia</td><td>3.0</td><td>8</td><td>Rhode Island</td><td>3.4</td></tr>
<tr><td>49</td><td>Hawaii</td><td>2.2</td><td>8</td><td>Utah</td><td>3.4</td></tr>
<tr><td>23</td><td>Idaho</td><td>3.1</td><td>8</td><td>West Virginia</td><td>3.4</td></tr>
<tr><td>40</td><td>Illinois</td><td>2.8</td><td>13</td><td>Indiana</td><td>3.3</td></tr>
<tr><td>13</td><td>Indiana</td><td>3.3</td><td>13</td><td>Maine</td><td>3.3</td></tr>
<tr><td>35</td><td>Iowa</td><td>2.9</td><td>13</td><td>Oregon</td><td>3.3</td></tr>
<tr><td>40</td><td>Kansas</td><td>2.8</td><td>13</td><td>Pennsylvania</td><td>3.3</td></tr>
<tr><td>5</td><td>Kentucky</td><td>3.6</td><td>13</td><td>Tennessee</td><td>3.3</td></tr>
<tr><td>30</td><td>Louisiana</td><td>3.0</td><td>13</td><td>Texas</td><td>3.3</td></tr>
<tr><td>13</td><td>Maine</td><td>3.3</td><td>19</td><td>Delaware</td><td>3.2</td></tr>
<tr><td>30</td><td>Maryland</td><td>3.0</td><td>19</td><td>Minnesota</td><td>3.2</td></tr>
<tr><td>40</td><td>Massachusetts</td><td>2.8</td><td>19</td><td>Nevada</td><td>3.2</td></tr>
<tr><td>2</td><td>Michigan</td><td>3.7</td><td>19</td><td>New York</td><td>3.2</td></tr>
<tr><td>19</td><td>Minnesota</td><td>3.2</td><td>23</td><td>California</td><td>3.1</td></tr>
<tr><td>2</td><td>Mississippi</td><td>3.7</td><td>23</td><td>Idaho</td><td>3.1</td></tr>
<tr><td>8</td><td>Missouri</td><td>3.4</td><td>23</td><td>Nebraska</td><td>3.1</td></tr>
<tr><td>30</td><td>Montana</td><td>3.0</td><td>23</td><td>Ohio</td><td>3.1</td></tr>
<tr><td>23</td><td>Nebraska</td><td>3.1</td><td>23</td><td>South Carolina</td><td>3.1</td></tr>
<tr><td>19</td><td>Nevada</td><td>3.2</td><td>23</td><td>Vermont</td><td>3.1</td></tr>
<tr><td>30</td><td>New Hampshire</td><td>3.0</td><td>23</td><td>Washington</td><td>3.1</td></tr>
<tr><td>40</td><td>New Jersey</td><td>2.8</td><td>30</td><td>Georgia</td><td>3.0</td></tr>
<tr><td>7</td><td>New Mexico</td><td>3.5</td><td>30</td><td>Louisiana</td><td>3.0</td></tr>
<tr><td>19</td><td>New York</td><td>3.2</td><td>30</td><td>Maryland</td><td>3.0</td></tr>
<tr><td>2</td><td>North Carolina</td><td>3.7</td><td>30</td><td>Montana</td><td>3.0</td></tr>
<tr><td>46</td><td>North Dakota</td><td>2.7</td><td>30</td><td>New Hampshire</td><td>3.0</td></tr>
<tr><td>23</td><td>Ohio</td><td>3.1</td><td>35</td><td>Colorado</td><td>2.9</td></tr>
<tr><td>47</td><td>Oklahoma</td><td>2.6</td><td>35</td><td>Connecticut</td><td>2.9</td></tr>
<tr><td>13</td><td>Oregon</td><td>3.3</td><td>35</td><td>Iowa</td><td>2.9</td></tr>
<tr><td>13</td><td>Pennsylvania</td><td>3.3</td><td>35</td><td>Wisconsin</td><td>2.9</td></tr>
<tr><td>8</td><td>Rhode Island</td><td>3.4</td><td>35</td><td>Wyoming</td><td>2.9</td></tr>
<tr><td>23</td><td>South Carolina</td><td>3.1</td><td>40</td><td>Alaska</td><td>2.8</td></tr>
<tr><td>47</td><td>South Dakota</td><td>2.6</td><td>40</td><td>Illinois</td><td>2.8</td></tr>
<tr><td>13</td><td>Tennessee</td><td>3.3</td><td>40</td><td>Kansas</td><td>2.8</td></tr>
<tr><td>13</td><td>Texas</td><td>3.3</td><td>40</td><td>Massachusetts</td><td>2.8</td></tr>
<tr><td>8</td><td>Utah</td><td>3.4</td><td>40</td><td>New Jersey</td><td>2.8</td></tr>
<tr><td>23</td><td>Vermont</td><td>3.1</td><td>40</td><td>Virginia</td><td>2.8</td></tr>
<tr><td>40</td><td>Virginia</td><td>2.8</td><td>46</td><td>North Dakota</td><td>2.7</td></tr>
<tr><td>23</td><td>Washington</td><td>3.1</td><td>47</td><td>Oklahoma</td><td>2.6</td></tr>
<tr><td>8</td><td>West Virginia</td><td>3.4</td><td>47</td><td>South Dakota</td><td>2.6</td></tr>
<tr><td>35</td><td>Wisconsin</td><td>2.9</td><td>49</td><td>Hawaii</td><td>2.2</td></tr>
<tr><td>35</td><td>Wyoming</td><td>2.9</td><td>50</td><td>Arizona</td><td>1.1</td></tr>
<tr><td></td><td></td><td></td><td></td><td>District of Columbia</td><td>2.2</td></tr>
</table>

Source: U.S. Department of Health and Human Services, Centers for Disease Control and Prevention
 "1998 Behavioral Risk Factor Surveillance Summary Prevalence Report" (June 18, 1999)
*Persons 18 and older.

Average Number of Days in the Past Month
When Mental Health was "Not Good": 1998
National Median = 3.0 Days*

ALPHA ORDER

RANK	STATE	DAYS
2	Alabama	3.7
46	Alaska	2.3
50	Arizona	0.8
4	Arkansas	3.6
20	California	3.0
20	Colorado	3.0
33	Connecticut	2.8
16	Delaware	3.1
20	Florida	3.0
9	Georgia	3.4
48	Hawaii	2.2
33	Idaho	2.8
33	Illinois	2.8
14	Indiana	3.2
20	Iowa	3.0
39	Kansas	2.7
1	Kentucky	4.5
33	Louisiana	2.8
39	Maine	2.7
9	Maryland	3.4
33	Massachusetts	2.8
4	Michigan	3.6
14	Minnesota	3.2
11	Mississippi	3.3
16	Missouri	3.1
43	Montana	2.6
20	Nebraska	3.0
6	Nevada	3.5
20	New Hampshire	3.0
39	New Jersey	2.7
11	New Mexico	3.3
20	New York	3.0
39	North Carolina	2.7
44	North Dakota	2.5
30	Ohio	2.9
49	Oklahoma	1.9
11	Oregon	3.3
30	Pennsylvania	2.9
20	Rhode Island	3.0
20	South Carolina	3.0
44	South Dakota	2.5
6	Tennessee	3.5
6	Texas	3.5
2	Utah	3.7
33	Vermont	2.8
20	Virginia	3.0
16	Washington	3.1
46	West Virginia	2.3
30	Wisconsin	2.9
16	Wyoming	3.1

RANK ORDER

RANK	STATE	DAYS
1	Kentucky	4.5
2	Alabama	3.7
2	Utah	3.7
4	Arkansas	3.6
4	Michigan	3.6
6	Nevada	3.5
6	Tennessee	3.5
6	Texas	3.5
9	Georgia	3.4
9	Maryland	3.4
11	Mississippi	3.3
11	New Mexico	3.3
11	Oregon	3.3
14	Indiana	3.2
14	Minnesota	3.2
16	Delaware	3.1
16	Missouri	3.1
16	Washington	3.1
16	Wyoming	3.1
20	California	3.0
20	Colorado	3.0
20	Florida	3.0
20	Iowa	3.0
20	Nebraska	3.0
20	New Hampshire	3.0
20	New York	3.0
20	Rhode Island	3.0
20	South Carolina	3.0
20	Virginia	3.0
30	Ohio	2.9
30	Pennsylvania	2.9
30	Wisconsin	2.9
33	Connecticut	2.8
33	Idaho	2.8
33	Illinois	2.8
33	Louisiana	2.8
33	Massachusetts	2.8
33	Vermont	2.8
39	Kansas	2.7
39	Maine	2.7
39	New Jersey	2.7
39	North Carolina	2.7
43	Montana	2.6
44	North Dakota	2.5
44	South Dakota	2.5
46	Alaska	2.3
46	West Virginia	2.3
48	Hawaii	2.2
49	Oklahoma	1.9
50	Arizona	0.8
	District of Columbia	2.2

Source: U.S. Department of Health and Human Services, Centers for Disease Control and Prevention
    "1998 Behavioral Risk Factor Surveillance Summary Prevalence Report" (June 18, 1999)
Persons 18 and older.

Percent of Adults Who Have Not Been Tested in Past Year for HIV: 1998

National Percent = 61.1% Have Not Been Tested in Past Year*

<table>
<thead>
<tr><th colspan="3">ALPHA ORDER</th><th colspan="3">RANK ORDER</th></tr>
<tr><th>RANK</th><th>STATE</th><th>PERCENT</th><th>RANK</th><th>STATE</th><th>PERCENT</th></tr>
</thead>
<tbody>
<tr><td>39</td><td>Alabama</td><td>56.4</td><td>1</td><td>North Dakota</td><td>70.7</td></tr>
<tr><td>31</td><td>Alaska</td><td>58.8</td><td>2</td><td>Arizona</td><td>69.4</td></tr>
<tr><td>2</td><td>Arizona</td><td>69.4</td><td>3</td><td>Utah</td><td>69.0</td></tr>
<tr><td>24</td><td>Arkansas</td><td>61.2</td><td>4</td><td>Colorado</td><td>68.4</td></tr>
<tr><td>NA</td><td>California**</td><td>NA</td><td>5</td><td>Wyoming</td><td>67.3</td></tr>
<tr><td>4</td><td>Colorado</td><td>68.4</td><td>6</td><td>Ohio</td><td>66.4</td></tr>
<tr><td>30</td><td>Connecticut</td><td>59.1</td><td>7</td><td>Illinois</td><td>66.2</td></tr>
<tr><td>36</td><td>Delaware</td><td>57.0</td><td>8</td><td>Iowa</td><td>66.1</td></tr>
<tr><td>39</td><td>Florida</td><td>56.4</td><td>9</td><td>Massachusetts</td><td>64.7</td></tr>
<tr><td>47</td><td>Georgia</td><td>51.2</td><td>10</td><td>Idaho</td><td>64.5</td></tr>
<tr><td>49</td><td>Hawaii</td><td>45.4</td><td>11</td><td>Vermont</td><td>63.9</td></tr>
<tr><td>10</td><td>Idaho</td><td>64.5</td><td>12</td><td>Washington</td><td>63.6</td></tr>
<tr><td>7</td><td>Illinois</td><td>66.2</td><td>12</td><td>Wisconsin</td><td>63.6</td></tr>
<tr><td>23</td><td>Indiana</td><td>61.6</td><td>14</td><td>Michigan</td><td>63.2</td></tr>
<tr><td>8</td><td>Iowa</td><td>66.1</td><td>14</td><td>New Jersey</td><td>63.2</td></tr>
<tr><td>43</td><td>Kansas</td><td>53.7</td><td>16</td><td>Nebraska</td><td>63.1</td></tr>
<tr><td>21</td><td>Kentucky</td><td>61.8</td><td>17</td><td>New Mexico</td><td>63.0</td></tr>
<tr><td>45</td><td>Louisiana</td><td>53.3</td><td>18</td><td>Rhode Island</td><td>62.7</td></tr>
<tr><td>20</td><td>Maine</td><td>62.2</td><td>19</td><td>Missouri</td><td>62.5</td></tr>
<tr><td>35</td><td>Maryland</td><td>57.1</td><td>20</td><td>Maine</td><td>62.2</td></tr>
<tr><td>9</td><td>Massachusetts</td><td>64.7</td><td>21</td><td>Kentucky</td><td>61.8</td></tr>
<tr><td>14</td><td>Michigan</td><td>63.2</td><td>21</td><td>Oregon</td><td>61.8</td></tr>
<tr><td>26</td><td>Minnesota</td><td>61.1</td><td>23</td><td>Indiana</td><td>61.6</td></tr>
<tr><td>48</td><td>Mississippi</td><td>49.8</td><td>24</td><td>Arkansas</td><td>61.2</td></tr>
<tr><td>19</td><td>Missouri</td><td>62.5</td><td>24</td><td>New Hampshire</td><td>61.2</td></tr>
<tr><td>27</td><td>Montana</td><td>59.9</td><td>26</td><td>Minnesota</td><td>61.1</td></tr>
<tr><td>16</td><td>Nebraska</td><td>63.1</td><td>27</td><td>Montana</td><td>59.9</td></tr>
<tr><td>28</td><td>Nevada</td><td>59.5</td><td>28</td><td>Nevada</td><td>59.5</td></tr>
<tr><td>24</td><td>New Hampshire</td><td>61.2</td><td>29</td><td>Texas</td><td>59.4</td></tr>
<tr><td>14</td><td>New Jersey</td><td>63.2</td><td>30</td><td>Connecticut</td><td>59.1</td></tr>
<tr><td>17</td><td>New Mexico</td><td>63.0</td><td>31</td><td>Alaska</td><td>58.8</td></tr>
<tr><td>34</td><td>New York</td><td>57.2</td><td>32</td><td>South Carolina</td><td>58.7</td></tr>
<tr><td>44</td><td>North Carolina</td><td>53.6</td><td>33</td><td>Oklahoma</td><td>58.4</td></tr>
<tr><td>1</td><td>North Dakota</td><td>70.7</td><td>34</td><td>New York</td><td>57.2</td></tr>
<tr><td>6</td><td>Ohio</td><td>66.4</td><td>35</td><td>Maryland</td><td>57.1</td></tr>
<tr><td>33</td><td>Oklahoma</td><td>58.4</td><td>36</td><td>Delaware</td><td>57.0</td></tr>
<tr><td>21</td><td>Oregon</td><td>61.8</td><td>37</td><td>Pennsylvania</td><td>56.8</td></tr>
<tr><td>37</td><td>Pennsylvania</td><td>56.8</td><td>38</td><td>South Dakota</td><td>56.7</td></tr>
<tr><td>18</td><td>Rhode Island</td><td>62.7</td><td>39</td><td>Alabama</td><td>56.4</td></tr>
<tr><td>32</td><td>South Carolina</td><td>58.7</td><td>39</td><td>Florida</td><td>56.4</td></tr>
<tr><td>38</td><td>South Dakota</td><td>56.7</td><td>39</td><td>Virginia</td><td>56.4</td></tr>
<tr><td>42</td><td>Tennessee</td><td>55.7</td><td>42</td><td>Tennessee</td><td>55.7</td></tr>
<tr><td>29</td><td>Texas</td><td>59.4</td><td>43</td><td>Kansas</td><td>53.7</td></tr>
<tr><td>3</td><td>Utah</td><td>69.0</td><td>44</td><td>North Carolina</td><td>53.6</td></tr>
<tr><td>11</td><td>Vermont</td><td>63.9</td><td>45</td><td>Louisiana</td><td>53.3</td></tr>
<tr><td>39</td><td>Virginia</td><td>56.4</td><td>46</td><td>West Virginia</td><td>51.9</td></tr>
<tr><td>12</td><td>Washington</td><td>63.6</td><td>47</td><td>Georgia</td><td>51.2</td></tr>
<tr><td>46</td><td>West Virginia</td><td>51.9</td><td>48</td><td>Mississippi</td><td>49.8</td></tr>
<tr><td>12</td><td>Wisconsin</td><td>63.6</td><td>49</td><td>Hawaii</td><td>45.4</td></tr>
<tr><td>5</td><td>Wyoming</td><td>67.3</td><td>NA</td><td>California**</td><td>NA</td></tr>
<tr><td></td><td></td><td></td><td></td><td>District of Columbia</td><td>58.8</td></tr>
</tbody>
</table>

Source: U.S. Department of Health and Human Services, Centers for Disease Control and Prevention
"1998 Behavioral Risk Factor Surveillance Summary Prevalence Report" (June 18, 1999)
*Persons 18 to 64 years old.
**Not available.

Percent of Adults Who Believe They Have a Chance of Getting HIV: 1998

National Percent = 6.2% of Adults*

RANK	STATE	PERCENT
26	Alabama	6.1
34	Alaska	5.6
49	Arizona	1.9
36	Arkansas	5.5
NA	California**	NA
24	Colorado	6.2
15	Connecticut	6.7
43	Delaware	4.7
26	Florida	6.1
33	Georgia	5.7
5	Hawaii	7.7
12	Idaho	6.9
15	Illinois	6.7
20	Indiana	6.5
38	Iowa	5.4
41	Kansas	5.0
40	Kentucky	5.2
8	Louisiana	7.3
32	Maine	5.8
28	Maryland	6.0
8	Massachusetts	7.3
46	Michigan	4.1
3	Minnesota	9.3
4	Mississippi	7.8
20	Missouri	6.5
47	Montana	3.8
5	Nebraska	7.7
20	Nevada	6.5
45	New Hampshire	4.2
7	New Jersey	7.4
36	New Mexico	5.5
8	New York	7.3
18	North Carolina	6.6
43	North Dakota	4.7
28	Ohio	6.0
24	Oklahoma	6.2
30	Oregon	5.9
18	Pennsylvania	6.6
13	Rhode Island	6.8
13	South Carolina	6.8
2	South Dakota	11.0
15	Tennessee	6.7
11	Texas	7.0
42	Utah	4.8
39	Vermont	5.3
30	Virginia	5.9
47	Washington	3.8
1	West Virginia	11.4
34	Wisconsin	5.6
23	Wyoming	6.3

RANK	STATE	PERCENT
1	West Virginia	11.4
2	South Dakota	11.0
3	Minnesota	9.3
4	Mississippi	7.8
5	Hawaii	7.7
5	Nebraska	7.7
7	New Jersey	7.4
8	Louisiana	7.3
8	Massachusetts	7.3
8	New York	7.3
11	Texas	7.0
12	Idaho	6.9
13	Rhode Island	6.8
13	South Carolina	6.8
15	Connecticut	6.7
15	Illinois	6.7
15	Tennessee	6.7
18	North Carolina	6.6
18	Pennsylvania	6.6
20	Indiana	6.5
20	Missouri	6.5
20	Nevada	6.5
23	Wyoming	6.3
24	Colorado	6.2
24	Oklahoma	6.2
26	Alabama	6.1
26	Florida	6.1
28	Maryland	6.0
28	Ohio	6.0
30	Oregon	5.9
30	Virginia	5.9
32	Maine	5.8
33	Georgia	5.7
34	Alaska	5.6
34	Wisconsin	5.6
36	Arkansas	5.5
36	New Mexico	5.5
38	Iowa	5.4
39	Vermont	5.3
40	Kentucky	5.2
41	Kansas	5.0
42	Utah	4.8
43	Delaware	4.7
43	North Dakota	4.7
45	New Hampshire	4.2
46	Michigan	4.1
47	Montana	3.8
47	Washington	3.8
49	Arizona	1.9
NA	California**	NA

District of Columbia	8.5

Source: U.S. Department of Health and Human Services, Centers for Disease Control and Prevention
  "1998 Behavioral Risk Factor Surveillance Summary Prevalence Report" (June 18, 1999)
For persons 18 to 64 years old who believe their chances of getting HIV are "medium" or "high."
**Not available.*

Safety Belt Usage Rate in 1999

National Rate = 65.0% Use Safety Belts*

ALPHA ORDER

RANK	STATE	PERCENT
46	Alabama	52.0
40	Alaska	57.0
30	Arizona	61.5
45	Arkansas	52.6
1	California	88.6
19	Colorado	66.0
15	Connecticut	70.1
27	Delaware	62.3
39	Florida	57.2
12	Georgia	73.6
5	Hawaii	80.5
38	Idaho	57.3
23	Illinois	64.5
29	Indiana	61.8
7	Iowa	76.9
34	Kansas	58.7
44	Kentucky	54.3
20	Louisiana	65.6
31	Maine	61.3
2	Maryland	82.6
47	Massachusetts	51.0
16	Michigan	69.9
24	Minnesota	64.2
37	Mississippi	58.0
33	Missouri	60.4
14	Montana	73.1
21	Nebraska	65.1
9	Nevada	76.2
34	New Hampshire	58.7
25	New Jersey	63.0
2	New Mexico	82.6
10	New York	75.3
8	North Carolina	76.7
50	North Dakota	40.0
32	Ohio	60.6
43	Oklahoma	56.0
2	Oregon	82.6
17	Pennsylvania	67.8
36	Rhode Island	58.6
22	South Carolina	64.8
49	South Dakota	45.7
41	Tennessee	56.7
11	Texas	74.4
18	Utah	66.7
26	Vermont	62.7
12	Virginia	73.6
6	Washington	79.1
42	West Virginia	56.5
28	Wisconsin	61.9
48	Wyoming	50.1

RANK ORDER

RANK	STATE	PERCENT
1	California	88.6
2	Maryland	82.6
2	New Mexico	82.6
2	Oregon	82.6
5	Hawaii	80.5
6	Washington	79.1
7	Iowa	76.9
8	North Carolina	76.7
9	Nevada	76.2
10	New York	75.3
11	Texas	74.4
12	Georgia	73.6
12	Virginia	73.6
14	Montana	73.1
15	Connecticut	70.1
16	Michigan	69.9
17	Pennsylvania	67.8
18	Utah	66.7
19	Colorado	66.0
20	Louisiana	65.6
21	Nebraska	65.1
22	South Carolina	64.8
23	Illinois	64.5
24	Minnesota	64.2
25	New Jersey	63.0
26	Vermont	62.7
27	Delaware	62.3
28	Wisconsin	61.9
29	Indiana	61.8
30	Arizona	61.5
31	Maine	61.3
32	Ohio	60.6
33	Missouri	60.4
34	Kansas	58.7
34	New Hampshire	58.7
36	Rhode Island	58.6
37	Mississippi	58.0
38	Idaho	57.3
39	Florida	57.2
40	Alaska	57.0
41	Tennessee	56.7
42	West Virginia	56.5
43	Oklahoma	56.0
44	Kentucky	54.3
45	Arkansas	52.6
46	Alabama	52.0
47	Massachusetts	51.0
48	Wyoming	50.1
49	South Dakota	45.7
50	North Dakota	40.0
	District of Columbia	79.6

Source: U.S. Department of Transportation, National Highway Safety Traffic Safety Administration
     "Key Provisions of Safety Belt Use" (October 1999)
*As of March 1999. National average is a simple average of reporting states' rates.
**Not reported.

Percent of Adults Whose Children Use a Car Safety Seat: 1997

National Median = 94.4% of Adults*

<table>
<tr><td colspan="3">ALPHA ORDER</td><td colspan="3">RANK ORDER</td></tr>
<tr><th>RANK</th><th>STATE</th><th>PERCENT</th><th>RANK</th><th>STATE</th><th>PERCENT</th></tr>
<tr><td>28</td><td>Alabama</td><td>93.9</td><td>1</td><td>Maine</td><td>99.6</td></tr>
<tr><td>38</td><td>Alaska</td><td>92.8</td><td>2</td><td>Georgia</td><td>99.3</td></tr>
<tr><td>12</td><td>Arizona</td><td>96.7</td><td>3</td><td>Vermont</td><td>98.3</td></tr>
<tr><td>49</td><td>Arkansas</td><td>85.9</td><td>4</td><td>Kentucky</td><td>98.1</td></tr>
<tr><td>35</td><td>California</td><td>93.3</td><td>5</td><td>Delaware</td><td>97.7</td></tr>
<tr><td>21</td><td>Colorado</td><td>94.9</td><td>5</td><td>Missouri</td><td>97.7</td></tr>
<tr><td>13</td><td>Connecticut</td><td>96.3</td><td>7</td><td>New Hampshire</td><td>97.6</td></tr>
<tr><td>5</td><td>Delaware</td><td>97.7</td><td>8</td><td>Tennessee</td><td>97.5</td></tr>
<tr><td>15</td><td>Florida</td><td>96.2</td><td>9</td><td>South Carolina</td><td>97.4</td></tr>
<tr><td>2</td><td>Georgia</td><td>99.3</td><td>10</td><td>Maryland</td><td>97.1</td></tr>
<tr><td>45</td><td>Hawaii</td><td>90.6</td><td>11</td><td>North Dakota</td><td>96.8</td></tr>
<tr><td>47</td><td>Idaho</td><td>88.8</td><td>12</td><td>Arizona</td><td>96.7</td></tr>
<tr><td>19</td><td>Illinois</td><td>95.7</td><td>13</td><td>Connecticut</td><td>96.3</td></tr>
<tr><td>42</td><td>Indiana</td><td>91.2</td><td>13</td><td>West Virginia</td><td>96.3</td></tr>
<tr><td>40</td><td>Iowa</td><td>91.9</td><td>15</td><td>Florida</td><td>96.2</td></tr>
<tr><td>20</td><td>Kansas</td><td>95.2</td><td>16</td><td>Virginia</td><td>96.1</td></tr>
<tr><td>4</td><td>Kentucky</td><td>98.1</td><td>17</td><td>New Jersey</td><td>96.0</td></tr>
<tr><td>30</td><td>Louisiana</td><td>93.8</td><td>18</td><td>Rhode Island</td><td>95.8</td></tr>
<tr><td>1</td><td>Maine</td><td>99.6</td><td>19</td><td>Illinois</td><td>95.7</td></tr>
<tr><td>10</td><td>Maryland</td><td>97.1</td><td>20</td><td>Kansas</td><td>95.2</td></tr>
<tr><td>23</td><td>Massachusetts</td><td>94.7</td><td>21</td><td>Colorado</td><td>94.9</td></tr>
<tr><td>45</td><td>Michigan</td><td>90.6</td><td>21</td><td>Pennsylvania</td><td>94.9</td></tr>
<tr><td>28</td><td>Minnesota</td><td>93.9</td><td>23</td><td>Massachusetts</td><td>94.7</td></tr>
<tr><td>30</td><td>Mississippi</td><td>93.8</td><td>23</td><td>Nevada</td><td>94.7</td></tr>
<tr><td>5</td><td>Missouri</td><td>97.7</td><td>25</td><td>New York</td><td>94.6</td></tr>
<tr><td>39</td><td>Montana</td><td>92.0</td><td>26</td><td>Nebraska</td><td>94.4</td></tr>
<tr><td>26</td><td>Nebraska</td><td>94.4</td><td>27</td><td>Ohio</td><td>94.3</td></tr>
<tr><td>23</td><td>Nevada</td><td>94.7</td><td>28</td><td>Alabama</td><td>93.9</td></tr>
<tr><td>7</td><td>New Hampshire</td><td>97.6</td><td>28</td><td>Minnesota</td><td>93.9</td></tr>
<tr><td>17</td><td>New Jersey</td><td>96.0</td><td>30</td><td>Louisiana</td><td>93.8</td></tr>
<tr><td>30</td><td>New Mexico</td><td>93.8</td><td>30</td><td>Mississippi</td><td>93.8</td></tr>
<tr><td>25</td><td>New York</td><td>94.6</td><td>30</td><td>New Mexico</td><td>93.8</td></tr>
<tr><td>34</td><td>North Carolina</td><td>93.5</td><td>33</td><td>Wisconsin</td><td>93.6</td></tr>
<tr><td>11</td><td>North Dakota</td><td>96.8</td><td>34</td><td>North Carolina</td><td>93.5</td></tr>
<tr><td>27</td><td>Ohio</td><td>94.3</td><td>35</td><td>California</td><td>93.3</td></tr>
<tr><td>35</td><td>Oklahoma</td><td>93.3</td><td>35</td><td>Oklahoma</td><td>93.3</td></tr>
<tr><td>37</td><td>Oregon</td><td>93.0</td><td>37</td><td>Oregon</td><td>93.0</td></tr>
<tr><td>21</td><td>Pennsylvania</td><td>94.9</td><td>38</td><td>Alaska</td><td>92.8</td></tr>
<tr><td>18</td><td>Rhode Island</td><td>95.8</td><td>39</td><td>Montana</td><td>92.0</td></tr>
<tr><td>9</td><td>South Carolina</td><td>97.4</td><td>40</td><td>Iowa</td><td>91.9</td></tr>
<tr><td>43</td><td>South Dakota</td><td>91.0</td><td>41</td><td>Wyoming</td><td>91.5</td></tr>
<tr><td>8</td><td>Tennessee</td><td>97.5</td><td>42</td><td>Indiana</td><td>91.2</td></tr>
<tr><td>49</td><td>Texas</td><td>85.9</td><td>43</td><td>South Dakota</td><td>91.0</td></tr>
<tr><td>44</td><td>Utah</td><td>90.7</td><td>44</td><td>Utah</td><td>90.7</td></tr>
<tr><td>3</td><td>Vermont</td><td>98.3</td><td>45</td><td>Hawaii</td><td>90.6</td></tr>
<tr><td>16</td><td>Virginia</td><td>96.1</td><td>45</td><td>Michigan</td><td>90.6</td></tr>
<tr><td>48</td><td>Washington</td><td>87.3</td><td>47</td><td>Idaho</td><td>88.8</td></tr>
<tr><td>13</td><td>West Virginia</td><td>96.3</td><td>48</td><td>Washington</td><td>87.3</td></tr>
<tr><td>33</td><td>Wisconsin</td><td>93.6</td><td>49</td><td>Arkansas</td><td>85.9</td></tr>
<tr><td>41</td><td>Wyoming</td><td>91.5</td><td>49</td><td>Texas</td><td>85.9</td></tr>
<tr><td></td><td></td><td></td><td></td><td>District of Columbia</td><td>85.0</td></tr>
</table>

Source: U.S. Department of Health and Human Services, Centers for Disease Control and Prevention
"1997 Behavioral Risk Factor Surveillance Summary Prevalence Report" (August 17, 1998)
*Persons whose children under 5 years old "always or nearly always use a safety seat".

VIII. APPENDIX

Population Charts

Population in 1999

National Total = 272,690,813*

ALPHA ORDER

RANK	STATE	POPULATION	% of USA
23	Alabama	4,369,862	1.6%
48	Alaska	619,500	0.2%
20	Arizona	4,778,332	1.8%
33	Arkansas	2,551,373	0.9%
1	California	33,145,121	12.2%
24	Colorado	4,056,133	1.5%
29	Connecticut	3,282,031	1.2%
45	Delaware	753,538	0.3%
4	Florida	15,111,244	5.5%
10	Georgia	7,788,240	2.9%
42	Hawaii	1,185,497	0.4%
40	Idaho	1,251,700	0.5%
5	Illinois	12,128,370	4.4%
14	Indiana	5,942,901	2.2%
30	Iowa	2,869,413	1.1%
32	Kansas	2,654,052	1.0%
25	Kentucky	3,960,825	1.5%
22	Louisiana	4,372,035	1.6%
39	Maine	1,253,040	0.5%
19	Maryland	5,171,634	1.9%
13	Massachusetts	6,175,169	2.3%
8	Michigan	9,863,775	3.6%
21	Minnesota	4,775,508	1.8%
31	Mississippi	2,768,619	1.0%
17	Missouri	5,468,338	2.0%
44	Montana	882,779	0.3%
38	Nebraska	1,666,028	0.6%
35	Nevada	1,809,253	0.7%
41	New Hampshire	1,201,134	0.4%
9	New Jersey	8,143,412	3.0%
37	New Mexico	1,739,844	0.6%
3	New York	18,196,601	6.7%
11	North Carolina	7,650,789	2.8%
47	North Dakota	633,666	0.2%
7	Ohio	11,256,654	4.1%
27	Oklahoma	3,358,044	1.2%
28	Oregon	3,316,154	1.2%
6	Pennsylvania	11,994,016	4.4%
43	Rhode Island	990,819	0.4%
26	South Carolina	3,885,736	1.4%
46	South Dakota	733,133	0.3%
16	Tennessee	5,483,535	2.0%
2	Texas	20,044,141	7.4%
34	Utah	2,129,836	0.8%
49	Vermont	593,740	0.2%
12	Virginia	6,872,912	2.5%
15	Washington	5,756,361	2.1%
36	West Virginia	1,806,928	0.7%
18	Wisconsin	5,250,446	1.9%
50	Wyoming	479,602	0.2%

RANK ORDER

RANK	STATE	POPULATION	% of USA
1	California	33,145,121	12.2%
2	Texas	20,044,141	7.4%
3	New York	18,196,601	6.7%
4	Florida	15,111,244	5.5%
5	Illinois	12,128,370	4.4%
6	Pennsylvania	11,994,016	4.4%
7	Ohio	11,256,654	4.1%
8	Michigan	9,863,775	3.6%
9	New Jersey	8,143,412	3.0%
10	Georgia	7,788,240	2.9%
11	North Carolina	7,650,789	2.8%
12	Virginia	6,872,912	2.5%
13	Massachusetts	6,175,169	2.3%
14	Indiana	5,942,901	2.2%
15	Washington	5,756,361	2.1%
16	Tennessee	5,483,535	2.0%
17	Missouri	5,468,338	2.0%
18	Wisconsin	5,250,446	1.9%
19	Maryland	5,171,634	1.9%
20	Arizona	4,778,332	1.8%
21	Minnesota	4,775,508	1.8%
22	Louisiana	4,372,035	1.6%
23	Alabama	4,369,862	1.6%
24	Colorado	4,056,133	1.5%
25	Kentucky	3,960,825	1.5%
26	South Carolina	3,885,736	1.4%
27	Oklahoma	3,358,044	1.2%
28	Oregon	3,316,154	1.2%
29	Connecticut	3,282,031	1.2%
30	Iowa	2,869,413	1.1%
31	Mississippi	2,768,619	1.0%
32	Kansas	2,654,052	1.0%
33	Arkansas	2,551,373	0.9%
34	Utah	2,129,836	0.8%
35	Nevada	1,809,253	0.7%
36	West Virginia	1,806,928	0.7%
37	New Mexico	1,739,844	0.6%
38	Nebraska	1,666,028	0.6%
39	Maine	1,253,040	0.5%
40	Idaho	1,251,700	0.5%
41	New Hampshire	1,201,134	0.4%
42	Hawaii	1,185,497	0.4%
43	Rhode Island	990,819	0.4%
44	Montana	882,779	0.3%
45	Delaware	753,538	0.3%
46	South Dakota	733,133	0.3%
47	North Dakota	633,666	0.2%
48	Alaska	619,500	0.2%
49	Vermont	593,740	0.2%
50	Wyoming	479,602	0.2%
	District of Columbia	519,000	0.2%

Source: U.S. Bureau of the Census
"State Population Estimates" (December 29, 1999, http://www.census.gov/population/estimates/state/st-99-3.txt)
Includes armed forces residing in each state.

Population in 1998

National Total = 270,248,003*

ALPHA ORDER

RANK	STATE	POPULATION	% of USA
23	Alabama	4,351,037	1.6%
48	Alaska	615,205	0.2%
21	Arizona	4,667,277	1.7%
33	Arkansas	2,538,202	0.9%
1	California	32,682,794	12.1%
24	Colorado	3,968,967	1.5%
29	Connecticut	3,272,563	1.2%
45	Delaware	744,066	0.3%
4	Florida	14,908,230	5.5%
10	Georgia	7,636,522	2.8%
41	Hawaii	1,190,472	0.4%
40	Idaho	1,230,923	0.5%
5	Illinois	12,069,774	4.5%
14	Indiana	5,907,617	2.2%
30	Iowa	2,861,025	1.1%
32	Kansas	2,638,667	1.0%
25	Kentucky	3,934,310	1.5%
22	Louisiana	4,362,758	1.6%
39	Maine	1,247,554	0.5%
19	Maryland	5,130,072	1.9%
13	Massachusetts	6,144,407	2.3%
8	Michigan	9,820,231	3.6%
20	Minnesota	4,726,411	1.7%
31	Mississippi	2,751,335	1.0%
16	Missouri	5,437,562	2.0%
44	Montana	879,533	0.3%
38	Nebraska	1,660,772	0.6%
36	Nevada	1,743,772	0.6%
42	New Hampshire	1,185,823	0.4%
9	New Jersey	8,095,542	3.0%
37	New Mexico	1,733,535	0.6%
3	New York	18,159,175	6.7%
11	North Carolina	7,545,828	2.8%
47	North Dakota	637,808	0.2%
7	Ohio	11,237,752	4.2%
27	Oklahoma	3,339,478	1.2%
28	Oregon	3,282,055	1.2%
6	Pennsylvania	12,002,329	4.4%
43	Rhode Island	987,704	0.4%
26	South Carolina	3,839,578	1.4%
46	South Dakota	730,789	0.3%
17	Tennessee	5,432,679	2.0%
2	Texas	19,712,389	7.3%
34	Utah	2,100,562	0.8%
49	Vermont	590,579	0.2%
12	Virginia	6,789,225	2.5%
15	Washington	5,687,832	2.1%
35	West Virginia	1,811,688	0.7%
18	Wisconsin	5,222,124	1.9%
50	Wyoming	480,045	0.2%

RANK ORDER

RANK	STATE	POPULATION	% of USA
1	California	32,682,794	12.1%
2	Texas	19,712,389	7.3%
3	New York	18,159,175	6.7%
4	Florida	14,908,230	5.5%
5	Illinois	12,069,774	4.5%
6	Pennsylvania	12,002,329	4.4%
7	Ohio	11,237,752	4.2%
8	Michigan	9,820,231	3.6%
9	New Jersey	8,095,542	3.0%
10	Georgia	7,636,522	2.8%
11	North Carolina	7,545,828	2.8%
12	Virginia	6,789,225	2.5%
13	Massachusetts	6,144,407	2.3%
14	Indiana	5,907,617	2.2%
15	Washington	5,687,832	2.1%
16	Missouri	5,437,562	2.0%
17	Tennessee	5,432,679	2.0%
18	Wisconsin	5,222,124	1.9%
19	Maryland	5,130,072	1.9%
20	Minnesota	4,726,411	1.7%
21	Arizona	4,667,277	1.7%
22	Louisiana	4,362,758	1.6%
23	Alabama	4,351,037	1.6%
24	Colorado	3,968,967	1.5%
25	Kentucky	3,934,310	1.5%
26	South Carolina	3,839,578	1.4%
27	Oklahoma	3,339,478	1.2%
28	Oregon	3,282,055	1.2%
29	Connecticut	3,272,563	1.2%
30	Iowa	2,861,025	1.1%
31	Mississippi	2,751,335	1.0%
32	Kansas	2,638,667	1.0%
33	Arkansas	2,538,202	0.9%
34	Utah	2,100,562	0.8%
35	West Virginia	1,811,688	0.7%
36	Nevada	1,743,772	0.6%
37	New Mexico	1,733,535	0.6%
38	Nebraska	1,660,772	0.6%
39	Maine	1,247,554	0.5%
40	Idaho	1,230,923	0.5%
41	Hawaii	1,190,472	0.4%
42	New Hampshire	1,185,823	0.4%
43	Rhode Island	987,704	0.4%
44	Montana	879,533	0.3%
45	Delaware	744,066	0.3%
46	South Dakota	730,789	0.3%
47	North Dakota	637,808	0.2%
48	Alaska	615,205	0.2%
49	Vermont	590,579	0.2%
50	Wyoming	480,045	0.2%
	District of Columbia	521,426	0.2%

Source: U.S. Bureau of the Census
"State Population Estimates" (December 29, 1999, http://www.census.gov/population/estimates/state/st-99-3.txt)
*Includes armed forces residing in each state. This updates earlier 1998 population estimates.

Male Population in 1998

National Total = 132,046,327 Males

ALPHA ORDER

RANK	STATE	MALES	% of USA
23	Alabama	2,087,920	1.6%
47	Alaska	322,224	0.2%
21	Arizona	2,308,970	1.7%
33	Arkansas	1,226,076	0.9%
1	California	16,322,534	12.4%
24	Colorado	1,968,174	1.5%
29	Connecticut	1,588,607	1.2%
46	Delaware	361,616	0.3%
4	Florida	7,237,561	5.5%
10	Georgia	3,718,346	2.8%
41	Hawaii	598,147	0.5%
39	Idaho	613,087	0.5%
5	Illinois	5,873,187	4.4%
14	Indiana	2,870,506	2.2%
30	Iowa	1,393,733	1.1%
32	Kansas	1,292,344	1.0%
25	Kentucky	1,910,252	1.4%
22	Louisiana	2,100,755	1.6%
40	Maine	606,595	0.5%
19	Maryland	2,494,656	1.9%
13	Massachusetts	2,963,722	2.2%
8	Michigan	4,776,586	3.6%
20	Minnesota	2,327,908	1.8%
31	Mississippi	1,318,940	1.0%
16	Missouri	2,633,300	2.0%
44	Montana	437,662	0.3%
38	Nebraska	813,421	0.6%
35	Nevada	889,114	0.7%
42	New Hampshire	582,969	0.4%
9	New Jersey	3,930,864	3.0%
37	New Mexico	854,549	0.6%
3	New York	8,742,890	6.6%
11	North Carolina	3,660,352	2.8%
48	North Dakota	317,656	0.2%
7	Ohio	5,417,572	4.1%
27	Oklahoma	1,634,259	1.2%
28	Oregon	1,620,801	1.2%
6	Pennsylvania	5,769,552	4.4%
43	Rhode Island	475,121	0.4%
26	South Carolina	1,848,646	1.4%
45	South Dakota	363,134	0.3%
17	Tennessee	2,620,557	2.0%
2	Texas	9,745,965	7.4%
34	Utah	1,043,442	0.8%
49	Vermont	290,540	0.2%
12	Virginia	3,316,764	2.5%
15	Washington	2,828,525	2.1%
36	West Virginia	872,716	0.7%
18	Wisconsin	2,566,723	1.9%
50	Wyoming	241,740	0.2%

RANK ORDER

RANK	STATE	MALES	% of USA
1	California	16,322,534	12.4%
2	Texas	9,745,965	7.4%
3	New York	8,742,890	6.6%
4	Florida	7,237,561	5.5%
5	Illinois	5,873,187	4.4%
6	Pennsylvania	5,769,552	4.4%
7	Ohio	5,417,572	4.1%
8	Michigan	4,776,586	3.6%
9	New Jersey	3,930,864	3.0%
10	Georgia	3,718,346	2.8%
11	North Carolina	3,660,352	2.8%
12	Virginia	3,316,764	2.5%
13	Massachusetts	2,963,722	2.2%
14	Indiana	2,870,506	2.2%
15	Washington	2,828,525	2.1%
16	Missouri	2,633,300	2.0%
17	Tennessee	2,620,557	2.0%
18	Wisconsin	2,566,723	1.9%
19	Maryland	2,494,656	1.9%
20	Minnesota	2,327,908	1.8%
21	Arizona	2,308,970	1.7%
22	Louisiana	2,100,755	1.6%
23	Alabama	2,087,920	1.6%
24	Colorado	1,968,174	1.5%
25	Kentucky	1,910,252	1.4%
26	South Carolina	1,848,646	1.4%
27	Oklahoma	1,634,259	1.2%
28	Oregon	1,620,801	1.2%
29	Connecticut	1,588,607	1.2%
30	Iowa	1,393,733	1.1%
31	Mississippi	1,318,940	1.0%
32	Kansas	1,292,344	1.0%
33	Arkansas	1,226,076	0.9%
34	Utah	1,043,442	0.8%
35	Nevada	889,114	0.7%
36	West Virginia	872,716	0.7%
37	New Mexico	854,549	0.6%
38	Nebraska	813,421	0.6%
39	Idaho	613,087	0.5%
40	Maine	606,595	0.5%
41	Hawaii	598,147	0.5%
42	New Hampshire	582,969	0.4%
43	Rhode Island	475,121	0.4%
44	Montana	437,662	0.3%
45	South Dakota	363,134	0.3%
46	Delaware	361,616	0.3%
47	Alaska	322,224	0.2%
48	North Dakota	317,656	0.2%
49	Vermont	290,540	0.2%
50	Wyoming	241,740	0.2%
	District of Columbia	245,047	0.2%

Source: U.S. Bureau of the Census
"Population Estimates for the U.S. and States by Single Year of Age and Sex" (ST-98-10, June 15, 1999)
(http://www.census.gov/population/estimates/state/stats/ag9898.txt)

Female Population in 1998

National Total = 138,252,197 Females

ALPHA ORDER				RANK ORDER			
RANK	STATE	FEMALES	% of USA	RANK	STATE	FEMALES	% of USA
23	Alabama	2,264,079	1.6%	1	California	16,344,016	11.8%
49	Alaska	291,786	0.2%	2	Texas	10,013,649	7.2%
21	Arizona	2,359,661	1.7%	3	New York	9,432,411	6.8%
33	Arkansas	1,312,227	0.9%	4	Florida	7,678,419	5.6%
1	California	16,344,016	11.8%	5	Pennsylvania	6,231,899	4.5%
25	Colorado	2,002,797	1.4%	6	Illinois	6,172,139	4.5%
28	Connecticut	1,685,462	1.2%	7	Ohio	5,791,921	4.2%
45	Delaware	381,987	0.3%	8	Michigan	5,040,656	3.6%
4	Florida	7,678,419	5.6%	9	New Jersey	4,184,147	3.0%
10	Georgia	3,923,861	2.8%	10	Georgia	3,923,861	2.8%
42	Hawaii	594,854	0.4%	11	North Carolina	3,886,141	2.8%
40	Idaho	615,597	0.4%	12	Virginia	3,474,581	2.5%
6	Illinois	6,172,139	4.5%	13	Massachusetts	3,183,410	2.3%
14	Indiana	3,028,689	2.2%	14	Indiana	3,028,689	2.2%
30	Iowa	1,468,714	1.1%	15	Washington	2,860,738	2.1%
32	Kansas	1,336,723	1.0%	16	Tennessee	2,810,064	2.0%
24	Kentucky	2,026,247	1.5%	17	Missouri	2,805,259	2.0%
22	Louisiana	2,268,212	1.6%	18	Wisconsin	2,656,777	1.9%
39	Maine	637,655	0.5%	19	Maryland	2,640,152	1.9%
19	Maryland	2,640,152	1.9%	20	Minnesota	2,397,511	1.7%
13	Massachusetts	3,183,410	2.3%	21	Arizona	2,359,661	1.7%
8	Michigan	5,040,656	3.6%	22	Louisiana	2,268,212	1.6%
20	Minnesota	2,397,511	1.7%	23	Alabama	2,264,079	1.6%
31	Mississippi	1,433,152	1.0%	24	Kentucky	2,026,247	1.5%
17	Missouri	2,805,259	2.0%	25	Colorado	2,002,797	1.4%
44	Montana	442,791	0.3%	26	South Carolina	1,987,316	1.4%
38	Nebraska	849,298	0.6%	27	Oklahoma	1,712,454	1.2%
37	Nevada	857,784	0.6%	28	Connecticut	1,685,462	1.2%
41	New Hampshire	602,079	0.4%	29	Oregon	1,661,173	1.2%
9	New Jersey	4,184,147	3.0%	30	Iowa	1,468,714	1.1%
36	New Mexico	882,382	0.6%	31	Mississippi	1,433,152	1.0%
3	New York	9,432,411	6.8%	32	Kansas	1,336,723	1.0%
11	North Carolina	3,886,141	2.8%	33	Arkansas	1,312,227	0.9%
47	North Dakota	320,588	0.2%	34	Utah	1,056,316	0.8%
7	Ohio	5,791,921	4.2%	35	West Virginia	938,440	0.7%
27	Oklahoma	1,712,454	1.2%	36	New Mexico	882,382	0.6%
29	Oregon	1,661,173	1.2%	37	Nevada	857,784	0.6%
5	Pennsylvania	6,231,899	4.5%	38	Nebraska	849,298	0.6%
43	Rhode Island	513,359	0.4%	39	Maine	637,655	0.5%
26	South Carolina	1,987,316	1.4%	40	Idaho	615,597	0.4%
46	South Dakota	375,037	0.3%	41	New Hampshire	602,079	0.4%
16	Tennessee	2,810,064	2.0%	42	Hawaii	594,854	0.4%
2	Texas	10,013,649	7.2%	43	Rhode Island	513,359	0.4%
34	Utah	1,056,316	0.8%	44	Montana	442,791	0.3%
48	Vermont	300,343	0.2%	45	Delaware	381,987	0.3%
12	Virginia	3,474,581	2.5%	46	South Dakota	375,037	0.3%
15	Washington	2,860,738	2.1%	47	North Dakota	320,588	0.2%
35	West Virginia	938,440	0.7%	48	Vermont	300,343	0.2%
18	Wisconsin	2,656,777	1.9%	49	Alaska	291,786	0.2%
50	Wyoming	239,167	0.2%	50	Wyoming	239,167	0.2%
					District of Columbia	278,077	0.2%

Source: U.S. Bureau of the Census
"Population Estimates for the U.S. and States by Single Year of Age and Sex" (ST-98-10, June 15, 1999)
(http://www.census.gov/population/estimates/state/stats/ag9898.txt)

Population in 1993

National Total = 257,782,608*

ALPHA ORDER

RANK	STATE	POPULATION	% of USA
22	Alabama	4,193,114	1.6%
48	Alaska	596,993	0.2%
23	Arizona	3,993,390	1.5%
33	Arkansas	2,423,743	0.9%
1	California	31,147,208	12.1%
26	Colorado	3,560,884	1.4%
27	Connecticut	3,272,325	1.3%
46	Delaware	699,475	0.3%
4	Florida	13,713,593	5.3%
11	Georgia	6,894,092	2.7%
40	Hawaii	1,161,508	0.5%
42	Idaho	1,101,204	0.4%
6	Illinois	11,725,984	4.5%
14	Indiana	5,701,965	2.2%
30	Iowa	2,820,525	1.1%
32	Kansas	2,547,605	1.0%
24	Kentucky	3,792,288	1.5%
21	Louisiana	4,284,749	1.7%
39	Maine	1,238,256	0.5%
19	Maryland	4,942,504	1.9%
13	Massachusetts	6,010,884	2.3%
8	Michigan	9,529,240	3.7%
20	Minnesota	4,521,709	1.8%
31	Mississippi	2,635,574	1.0%
16	Missouri	5,237,757	2.0%
44	Montana	839,876	0.3%
37	Nebraska	1,612,149	0.6%
38	Nevada	1,380,197	0.5%
41	New Hampshire	1,122,191	0.4%
9	New Jersey	7,874,891	3.1%
36	New Mexico	1,614,937	0.6%
2	New York	18,140,894	7.0%
10	North Carolina	6,947,412	2.7%
47	North Dakota	637,229	0.2%
7	Ohio	11,070,385	4.3%
28	Oklahoma	3,228,829	1.3%
29	Oregon	3,034,490	1.2%
5	Pennsylvania	12,022,128	4.7%
43	Rhode Island	997,852	0.4%
25	South Carolina	3,634,507	1.4%
45	South Dakota	716,258	0.3%
17	Tennessee	5,085,666	2.0%
3	Texas	17,996,764	7.0%
34	Utah	1,875,993	0.7%
49	Vermont	574,004	0.2%
12	Virginia	6,464,795	2.5%
15	Washington	5,247,704	2.0%
35	West Virginia	1,816,179	0.7%
18	Wisconsin	5,055,318	2.0%
50	Wyoming	469,033	0.2%

RANK ORDER

RANK	STATE	POPULATION	% of USA
1	California	31,147,208	12.1%
2	New York	18,140,894	7.0%
3	Texas	17,996,764	7.0%
4	Florida	13,713,593	5.3%
5	Pennsylvania	12,022,128	4.7%
6	Illinois	11,725,984	4.5%
7	Ohio	11,070,385	4.3%
8	Michigan	9,529,240	3.7%
9	New Jersey	7,874,891	3.1%
10	North Carolina	6,947,412	2.7%
11	Georgia	6,894,092	2.7%
12	Virginia	6,464,795	2.5%
13	Massachusetts	6,010,884	2.3%
14	Indiana	5,701,965	2.2%
15	Washington	5,247,704	2.0%
16	Missouri	5,237,757	2.0%
17	Tennessee	5,085,666	2.0%
18	Wisconsin	5,055,318	2.0%
19	Maryland	4,942,504	1.9%
20	Minnesota	4,521,709	1.8%
21	Louisiana	4,284,749	1.7%
22	Alabama	4,193,114	1.6%
23	Arizona	3,993,390	1.5%
24	Kentucky	3,792,288	1.5%
25	South Carolina	3,634,507	1.4%
26	Colorado	3,560,884	1.4%
27	Connecticut	3,272,325	1.3%
28	Oklahoma	3,228,829	1.3%
29	Oregon	3,034,490	1.2%
30	Iowa	2,820,525	1.1%
31	Mississippi	2,635,574	1.0%
32	Kansas	2,547,605	1.0%
33	Arkansas	2,423,743	0.9%
34	Utah	1,875,993	0.7%
35	West Virginia	1,816,179	0.7%
36	New Mexico	1,614,937	0.6%
37	Nebraska	1,612,149	0.6%
38	Nevada	1,380,197	0.5%
39	Maine	1,238,256	0.5%
40	Hawaii	1,161,508	0.5%
41	New Hampshire	1,122,191	0.4%
42	Idaho	1,101,204	0.4%
43	Rhode Island	997,852	0.4%
44	Montana	839,876	0.3%
45	South Dakota	716,258	0.3%
46	Delaware	699,475	0.3%
47	North Dakota	637,229	0.2%
48	Alaska	596,993	0.2%
49	Vermont	574,004	0.2%
50	Wyoming	469,033	0.2%
	District of Columbia	576,358	0.2%

Source: U.S. Bureau of the Census
"State Population Estimates" (December 29, 1999, http://www.census.gov/population/estimates/state/st-99-3.txt)
*Includes armed forces residing in each state. This updates earlier 1993 population estimates.

IX. SOURCES

American Academy of Family Physicians
11400 Tomahawk Creek Parkway
Leawood, KS 66211-2672
913-906-6000
Internet: www.aafp.org

American Academy of Physicians Assistants
950 North Washington Street
Alexandria, VA 22314-1552
703-836-2272
Internet: www.aapa.org

American Cancer Society, Inc.
1599 Clifton Road, NE.
Atlanta, GA 30329-4251
800-227-2345
Internet: http://www.cancer.org

American Dental Association
211 E. Chicago Ave.
Chicago, IL 60611
312-440-2500
Internet: www.ada.org

American Hospital Association
One North Franklin
Chicago, IL 60606-3401
312-422-3000
Internet: www.aha.org

American Medical Association
515 North State Street
Chicago, IL 60610
312-464-5000
Internet: http://www.ama-assn.org

American Osteopathic Association
142 East Ontario Street
Chicago, IL 60611
312-202-8000
Internet: www.am-osteo-assn.org

American Podiatric Medical Association
9312 Old Georgetown Road
Bethesda, MD 20814-1698
301-571-9200
Internet: www.apma.org

Bureau of Labor Statistics
Census of Fatal Occupational Injuries
2 Massachusetts Ave., NE
Washington, DC 20212
202-691-7828
Internet: http://stats.bls.gov/oshhome.htm

Census Bureau
3 Silver Hill and Suitland Roads
Suitland, MD 20746
301-457-2794
Internet: http://www.census.gov

Centers for Disease Control and Prevention
1600 Clifton Road, NE.
Atlanta, GA 30333
404-639-3535 (Public Affairs)
800-458-5231 (AIDS Clearinghouse)
Internet: http://www.cdc.gov

Federation of Chiropractic Licensing Boards
901 54th Ave., Ste. 101
Greeley, CO 80634
970-356-3500
Internet: www.fclb.org

Health Care Financing Administration
U.S. Department of Health and Human Services
7500 Security Boulevard
Baltimore, MD 21244
410-786-3000
Internet: http://www.hcfa.gov

InterStudy
P.O. Box 4366
St. Paul, MN 55104
800-844-3351
Internet: www.hmodata.com

National Center for Health Statistics
U.S. Department of Health and Human Services
6525 Belcrest Road
Hyattsville, MD 20782-2003
301-436-8951 (vital statistics division)
Internet: http://www.cdc.gov/nchswww/

**National Institute on Alcohol Abuse
and Alcoholism**
National Institutes of Health
6000 Executive Boulevard
Bethesda, MD 20892-7003
301-443-9970
Internet: www.niaaa.nih.gov/

National Highway Traffic Safety Admin.
400 Seventh Street, SW
Washington, DC 20590
202-366-9550
Internet: www.nhtsa.dot.gov

National Sporting Goods Association
1699 Wall Street, Suite 700
Mt. Prospect, IL 60056-5780
847-439-4000
Internet: www.nsga.org

Smoking and Health Office
Centers for Disease Control and Prevention
4770 Buford Hwy, NE., Mail Stop K-50
Atlanta, GA 30341-3724
770-488-5705
www.cdc.gov/nccdphp/osh/oshresfa.htm

X. INDEX

X. INDEX (continued)

X. INDEX (continued)

Births and Reproductive Health

Deaths

Facilities

Finance

Incidence of Disease

Providers

Physical Fitness

CHAPTER INDEX

HOW TO USE THIS INDEX

Place left thumb on the outer edge of this page. To locate the desired entry, fold back the remaining page edges and align the index edge mark with the appropriate page edge mark.

Other books by Morgan Quitno Press:

- *State Statistical Trends (monthly journal)*
- *State Rankings 2000 ($52.95)*
- *Crime State Rankings 2000 ($52.95)*
- *City Crime Rankings, 6th Edition ($39.95)*

Call toll free: 1-800-457-0742 or
visit us at www.morganquitno.com